T0188931

More information about this series at http://www.springer.com/series/7412

# Lecture Notes in Computer Science     9906

Commenced Publication in 1973
Founding and Former Series Editors:
Gerhard Goos, Juris Hartmanis, and Jan van Leeuwen

Bastian Leibe · Jiri Matas
Nicu Sebe · Max Welling (Eds.)

# Computer Vision – ECCV 2016

14th European Conference
Amsterdam, The Netherlands, October 11–14, 2016
Proceedings, Part II

 Springer

*Editors*

Bastian Leibe
RWTH Aachen
Aachen
Germany

Jiri Matas
Czech Technical University
Prague 2
Czech Republic

Nicu Sebe
University of Trento
Povo - Trento
Italy

Max Welling
University of Amsterdam
Amsterdam
The Netherlands

ISSN 0302-9743            ISSN 1611-3349   (electronic)
Lecture Notes in Computer Science
ISBN 978-3-319-46474-9        ISBN 978-3-319-46475-6   (eBook)
DOI 10.1007/978-3-319-46475-6

Library of Congress Control Number: 2016951693

LNCS Sublibrary: SL6 – Image Processing, Computer Vision, Pattern Recognition, and Graphics

Printed on acid-free paper

This Springer imprint is published by Springer Nature
The registered company is Springer International Publishing AG
The registered company address is: Gewerbestrasse 11, 6330 Cham, Switzerland

# Foreword

Welcome to the proceedings of the 2016 edition of the European Conference on Computer Vision held in Amsterdam! It is safe to say that the European Conference on Computer Vision is one of the top conferences in computer vision. It is good to reiterate the history of the conference to see the broad base the conference has built in its 13 editions. First held in 1990 in Antibes (France), it was followed by subsequent conferences in Santa Margherita Ligure (Italy) in 1992, Stockholm (Sweden) in 1994, Cambridge (UK) in 1996, Freiburg (Germany) in 1998, Dublin (Ireland) in 2000, Copenhagen (Denmark) in 2002, Prague (Czech Republic) in 2004, Graz (Austria) in 2006, Marseille (France) in 2008, Heraklion (Greece) in 2010, Florence (Italy) in 2012, and Zürich (Switzerland) in 2014.

For the 14th edition, many people worked hard to provide attendees with a most warm welcome while enjoying the best science. The Program Committee, Bastian Leibe, Jiri Matas, Nicu Sebe, and Max Welling, did an excellent job. Apart from the scientific program, the workshops were selected and handled by Hervé Jégou and Gang Hua, and the tutorials by Jacob Verbeek and Rita Cucchiara. Thanks for the great job. The coordination with the subsequent ACM Multimedia offered an opportunity to expand the tutorials with an additional invited session, offered by the University of Amsterdam and organized together with the help of ACM Multimedia.

Of the many people who worked hard as local organizers, we would like to single out Martine de Wit of the UvA Conference Office, who delicately and efficiently organized the main body. Also the local organizers Hamdi Dibeklioglu, Efstratios Gavves, Jan van Gemert, Thomas Mensink, and Mihir Jain had their hands full. As a venue, we chose the Royal Theatre Carré located on the canals of the Amstel River in downtown Amsterdam. Space in Amsterdam is sparse, so it was a little tighter than usual. The university lent us their downtown campuses for the tutorials and the workshops. A relatively new thing was the industry and the sponsors for which Ronald Poppe and Peter de With did a great job, while Andy Bagdanov and John Schavemaker arranged the demos. Michael Wilkinson took care to make Yom Kippur as comfortable as possible for those for whom it is an important day. We thank Marc Pollefeys, Alberto del Bimbo, and Virginie Mes for their advice and help behind the scenes. We thank all the anonymous volunteers for their hard and precise work. We also thank our generous sponsors. Their support is an essential part of the program. It is good to see such a level of industrial interest in what our community is doing!

Amsterdam does not need any introduction. Please emerge yourself but do not drown in it, have a nice time.

October 2016

Theo Gevers
Arnold Smeulders

# Preface

Welcome to the proceedings of the 2016 European Conference on Computer Vision (ECCV 2016) held in Amsterdam, The Netherlands. We are delighted to present this volume reflecting a strong and exciting program, the result of an extensive review process. In total, we received 1,561 paper submissions. Of these, 81 violated the ECCV submission guidelines or did not pass the plagiarism test and were rejected without review. We employed the iThenticate software (www.ithenticate.com) for plagiarism detection. Of the remaining papers, 415 were accepted (26.6 %): 342 as posters (22.6 %), 45 as spotlights (2.9 %), and 28 as oral presentations (1.8 %). The spotlights – short, five-minute podium presentations – are novel to ECCV and were introduced after their success at the CVPR 2016 conference. All orals and spotlights are presented as posters as well. The selection process was a combined effort of four program co-chairs (PCs), 74 area chairs (ACs), 1,086 Program Committee members, and 77 additional reviewers.

As PCs, we were primarily responsible for the design and execution of the review process. Beyond administrative rejections, we were involved in acceptance decisions only in the very few cases where the ACs were not able to agree on a decision. PCs, as is customary in the field, were not allowed to co-author a submission. General co-chairs and other co-organizers played no role in the review process, were permitted to submit papers, and were treated as any other author.

Acceptance decisions were made by two independent ACs. There were 74 ACs, selected by the PCs according to their technical expertise, experience, and geographical diversity (41 from European, five from Asian, two from Australian, and 26 from North American institutions). The ACs were aided by 1,086 Program Committee members to whom papers were assigned for reviewing. There were 77 additional reviewers, each supervised by a Program Committee member. The Program Committee was selected from committees of previous ECCV, ICCV, and CVPR conferences and was extended on the basis of suggestions from the ACs and the PCs. Having a large pool of Program Committee members for reviewing allowed us to match expertise while bounding reviewer loads. Typically five papers, but never more than eight, were assigned to a Program Committee member. Graduate students had a maximum of four papers to review.

The ECCV 2016 review process was in principle double-blind. Authors did not know reviewer identities, nor the ACs handling their paper(s). However, anonymity becomes difficult to maintain as more and more submissions appear concurrently on arXiv.org. This was not against the ECCV 2016 double submission rules, which followed the practice of other major computer vision conferences in the recent past. The existence of arXiv publications, mostly not peer-reviewed, raises difficult problems with the assessment of unpublished, concurrent, and prior art, content overlap, plagiarism, and self-plagiarism. Moreover, it undermines the anonymity of submissions. We found that not all cases can be covered by a simple set of rules. Almost all controversies during the review process were related to the arXiv issue. Most of the reviewer inquiries were resolved by giving the benefit of the doubt to ECCV authors. However, the problem will have to be discussed by the community so that consensus is found on how to handle the issues brought by publishing on arXiv.

Particular attention was paid to handling conflicts of interest. Conflicts of interest between ACs, Program Committee members, and papers were identified based on the authorship of ECCV 2016 submissions, on the home institutions, and on previous collaborations of all researchers involved. To find institutional conflicts, all authors, Program Committee members, and ACs were asked to list the Internet domains of their current institutions. To find collaborators, the Researcher.cc database (http://researcher.cc/), funded by the Computer Vision Foundation, was used to find any co-authored papers in the period 2012–2016. We pre-assigned approximately 100 papers to each AC, based on affinity scores from the Toronto Paper Matching System. ACs then bid on these, indicating their level of expertise. Based on these bids, and conflicts of interest, approximately 40 papers were assigned to each AC. The ACs then suggested seven reviewers from the pool of Program Committee members for each paper, in ranked order, from which three were chosen automatically by CMT (Microsofts Academic Conference Management Service), taking load balancing and conflicts of interest into account.

The initial reviewing period was five weeks long, after which reviewers provided reviews with preliminary recommendations. With the generous help of several last-minute reviewers, each paper received three reviews. Submissions with all three reviews suggesting rejection were independently checked by two ACs and if they agreed, the manuscript was rejected at this stage ("early rejects"). In total, 334 manuscripts (22.5 %) were early-rejected, reducing the average AC load to about 30.

Authors of the remaining submissions were then given the opportunity to rebut the reviews, primarily to identify factual errors. Following this, reviewers and ACs discussed papers at length, after which reviewers finalized their reviews and gave a final recommendation to the ACs. Each manuscript was evaluated independently by two ACs who were not aware of each others, identities. In most of the cases, after extensive discussions, the two ACs arrived at a common decision, which was always adhered to by the PCs. In the very few borderline cases where an agreement was not reached, the PCs acted as tie-breakers. Owing to the rapid expansion of the field, which led to an unexpectedly large increase in the number of submissions, the size of the venue became a limiting factor and a hard upper bound on the number of accepted papers had to be imposed. We were able to increase the limit by replacing one oral session by a poster session. Nevertheless, this forced the PCs to reject some borderline papers that could otherwise have been accepted.

We want to thank everyone involved in making the ECCV 2016 possible. First and foremost, the success of ECCV 2016 depended on the quality of papers submitted by the authors, and on the very hard work of the ACs, the Program Committee members, and the additional reviewers. We are particularly grateful to Rene Vidal for his continuous support and sharing experience from organizing ICCV 2015, to Laurent Charlin for the use of the Toronto Paper Matching System, to Ari Kobren for the use of the Researcher.cc tools, to the Computer Vision Foundation (CVF) for facilitating the use of the iThenticate plagiarism detection software, and to Gloria Zen and Radu-Laurentiu Vieriu for setting up CMT and managing the various tools involved. We also owe a debt of gratitude for the support of the Amsterdam local organizers, especially Hamdi Dibeklioglu for keeping the website always up to date. Finally, the preparation of these proceedings would not have been possible without the diligent effort of the publication chairs, Albert Ali Salah and Robby Tan, and of Anna Kramer from Springer.

October 2016

Bastian Leibe
Jiri Matas
Nicu Sebe
Max Welling

# Organization

## General Chairs

| | |
|---|---|
| Theo Gevers | University of Amsterdam, The Netherlands |
| Arnold Smeulders | University of Amsterdam, The Netherlands |

## Program Committee Co-chairs

| | |
|---|---|
| Bastian Leibe | RWTH Aachen, Germany |
| Jiri Matas | Czech Technical University, Czech Republic |
| Nicu Sebe | University of Trento, Italy |
| Max Welling | University of Amsterdam, The Netherlands |

## Honorary Chair

| | |
|---|---|
| Jan Koenderink | Delft University of Technology, The Netherlands and KU Leuven, Belgium |

## Advisory Program Chair

| | |
|---|---|
| Luc van Gool | ETH Zurich, Switzerland |

## Advisory Workshop Chair

| | |
|---|---|
| Josef Kittler | University of Surrey, UK |

## Advisory Conference Chair

| | |
|---|---|
| Alberto del Bimbo | University of Florence, Italy |

## Local Arrangements Chairs

| | |
|---|---|
| Hamdi Dibeklioglu | Delft University of Technology, The Netherlands |
| Efstratios Gavves | University of Amsterdam, The Netherlands |
| Jan van Gemert | Delft University of Technology, The Netherlands |
| Thomas Mensink | University of Amsterdam, The Netherlands |
| Michael Wilkinson | University of Groningen, The Netherlands |

## Workshop Chairs

Hervé Jégou                Facebook AI Research, USA
Gang Hua                   Microsoft Research Asia, China

## Tutorial Chairs

Jacob Verbeek             Inria Grenoble, France
Rita Cucchiara            University of Modena and Reggio Emilia, Italy

## Poster Chairs

Jasper Uijlings           University of Edinburgh, UK
Roberto Valenti           Sightcorp, The Netherlands

## Publication Chairs

Albert Ali Salah          Boğaziçi University, Turkey
Robby T. Tan              Yale-NUS College and National University
                            of Singapore, Singapore

## Video Chair

Mihir Jain                University of Amsterdam, The Netherlands

## Demo Chairs

John Schavemaker          Twnkls, The Netherlands
Andy Bagdanov             University of Florence, Italy

## Social Media Chair

Efstratios Gavves         University of Amsterdam, The Netherlands

## Industrial Liaison Chairs

Ronald Poppe              Utrecht University, The Netherlands
Peter de With             Eindhoven University of Technology, The Netherlands

## Conference Coordinator, Accommodation, and Finance

Conference Office
Martine de Wit            University of Amsterdam, The Netherlands
Melanie Venverloo         University of Amsterdam, The Netherlands
Niels Klein               University of Amsterdam, The Netherlands

# Area Chairs

| | |
|---|---|
| Radhakrishna Achanta | Ecole Polytechnique Fédérale de Lausanne, Switzerland |
| Antonis Argyros | FORTH and University of Crete, Greece |
| Michael Bronstein | Universitá della Svizzera Italiana, Switzerland |
| Gabriel Brostow | University College London, UK |
| Thomas Brox | University of Freiburg, Germany |
| Barbara Caputo | Sapienza University of Rome, Italy |
| Miguel Carreira-Perpinan | University of California, Merced, USA |
| Ondra Chum | Czech Technical University, Czech Republic |
| Daniel Cremers | Technical University of Munich, Germany |
| Rita Cucchiara | University of Modena and Reggio Emilia, Italy |
| Trevor Darrell | University of California, Berkeley, USA |
| Andrew Davison | Imperial College London, UK |
| Fernando de la Torre | Carnegie Mellon University, USA |
| Piotr Dollar | Facebook AI Research, USA |
| Vittorio Ferrari | University of Edinburgh, UK |
| Charless Fowlkes | University of California, Irvine, USA |
| Jan-Michael Frahm | University of North Carolina at Chapel Hill, USA |
| Mario Fritz | Max Planck Institute, Germany |
| Pascal Fua | Ecole Polytechnique Fédérale de Lausanne, Switzerland |
| Juergen Gall | University of Bonn, Germany |
| Peter Gehler | University of Tübingen — Max Planck Institute, Germany |
| Andreas Geiger | Max Planck Institute, Germany |
| Ross Girshick | Facebook AI Research, USA |
| Kristen Grauman | University of Texas at Austin, USA |
| Abhinav Gupta | Carnegie Mellon University, USA |
| Hervé Jégou | Facebook AI Research, USA |
| Fredrik Kahl | Lund University, Sweden |
| Iasonas Kokkinos | Ecole Centrale Paris, France |
| Philipp Krähenbühl | University of California, Berkeley, USA |
| Pawan Kumar | University of Oxford, UK |
| Christoph Lampert | Institute of Science and Technology Austria, Austria |
| Hugo Larochelle | Université de Sherbrooke, Canada |
| Neil Lawrence | University of Sheffield, UK |
| Svetlana Lazebnik | University of Illinois at Urbana-Champaign, USA |
| Honglak Lee | Stanford University, USA |
| Kyoung Mu Lee | Seoul National University, Republic of Korea |
| Vincent Lepetit | Graz University of Technology, Austria |
| Hongdong Li | Australian National University, Australia |
| Julien Mairal | Inria, France |
| Yasuyuki Matsushita | Osaka University, Japan |
| Nassir Navab | Technical University of Munich, Germany |

| | |
|---|---|
| Sebastian Nowozin | Microsoft Research, Cambridge, UK |
| Tomas Pajdla | Czech Technical University, Czech Republic |
| Maja Pantic | Imperial College London, UK |
| Devi Parikh | Virginia Tech, USA |
| Thomas Pock | Graz University of Technology, Austria |
| Elisa Ricci | FBK Technologies of Vision, Italy |
| Bodo Rosenhahn | Leibniz-University of Hannover, Germany |
| Stefan Roth | Technical University of Darmstadt, Germany |
| Carsten Rother | Technical University of Dresden, Germany |
| Silvio Savarese | Stanford University, USA |
| Bernt Schiele | Max Planck Institute, Germany |
| Konrad Schindler | ETH Zürich, Switzerland |
| Cordelia Schmid | Inria, France |
| Cristian Sminchisescu | Lund University, Sweden |
| Noah Snavely | Cornell University, USA |
| Sabine Süsstrunk | Ecole Polytechnique Fédérale de Lausanne, Switzerland |
| Qi Tian | University of Texas at San Antonio, USA |
| Antonio Torralba | Massachusetts Institute of Technology, USA |
| Zhuowen Tu | University of California, San Diego, USA |
| Raquel Urtasun | University of Toronto, Canada |
| Joost van de Weijer | Universitat Autònoma de Barcelona, Spain |
| Laurens van der Maaten | Facebook AI Research, USA |
| Nuno Vasconcelos | University of California, San Diego, USA |
| Andrea Vedaldi | University of Oxford, UK |
| Xiaogang Wang | Chinese University of Hong Kong, Hong Kong, SAR China |
| Jingdong Wang | Microsoft Research Asia, China |
| Lior Wolf | Tel Aviv University, Israel |
| Ying Wu | Northwestern University, USA |
| Dong Xu | University of Sydney, Australia |
| Shuicheng Yan | National University of Singapore, Singapore |
| MingHsuan Yang | University of California, Merced, USA |
| Ramin Zabih | Cornell NYC Tech, USA |
| Larry Zitnick | Facebook AI Research, USA |

## Technical Program Committee

| | | |
|---|---|---|
| Austin Abrams | Pulkit Agrawal | Andrea Albarelli |
| Supreeth Achar | Jorgen Ahlberg | Alexandra Albu |
| Tameem Adel | Haizhou Ai | Saad Ali |
| Khurrum Aftab | Zeynep Akata | Daniel Aliaga |
| Lourdes Agapito | Ijaz Akhter | Marina Alterman |
| Sameer Agarwal | Karteek Alahari | Hani Altwaijry |
| Aishwarya Agrawal | Xavier Alameda-Pineda | Jose M. Alvarez |

Mitsuru Ambai
Mohamed Amer
Senjian An
Cosmin Ancuti
Juan Andrade-Cetto
Marco Andreetto
Elli Angelopoulou
Relja Arandjelovic
Helder Araujo
Pablo Arbelaez
Chetan Arora
Carlos Arteta
Kalle Astroem
Nikolay Atanasov
Vassilis Athitsos
Mathieu Aubry
Yannis Avrithis
Hossein Azizpour
Artem Babenko
Andrew Bagdanov
Yuval Bahat
Xiang Bai
Lamberto Ballan
Arunava Banerjee
Adrian Barbu
Nick Barnes
Peter Barnum
Jonathan Barron
Adrien Bartoli
Dhruv Batra
Eduardo
    Bayro-Corrochano
Jean-Charles Bazin
Paul Beardsley
Vasileios Belagiannis
Ismail Ben Ayed
Boulbaba Benamor
Abhijit Bendale
Rodrigo Benenson
Fabian Benitez-Quiroz
Ohad Ben-Shahar
Dana Berman
Lucas Beyer
Subhabrata Bhattacharya
Binod Bhattarai
Arnav Bhavsar

Simone Bianco
Hakan Bilen
Horst Bischof
Tom Bishop
Arijit Biswas
Soma Biswas
Marten Bjoerkman
Volker Blanz
Federica Bogo
Xavier Boix
Piotr Bojanowski
Terrance Boult
Katie Bouman
Thierry Bouwmans
Edmond Boyer
Yuri Boykov
Hakan Boyraz
Steven Branson
Mathieu Bredif
Francois Bremond
Stefan Breuers
Michael Brown
Marcus Brubaker
Luc Brun
Andrei Bursuc
Zoya Bylinskii
Daniel Cabrini Hauagge
Deng Cai
Jianfei Cai
Simone Calderara
Neill Campbell
Octavia Camps
Liangliang Cao
Xiaochun Cao
Xun Cao
Gustavo Carneiro
Dan Casas
Tom Cashman
Umberto Castellani
Carlos Castillo
Andrea Cavallaro
Jan Cech
Ayan Chakrabarti
Rudrasis Chakraborty
Krzysztof Chalupka
Tat-Jen Cham

Antoni Chan
Manmohan Chandraker
Sharat Chandran
Hong Chang
Hyun Sung Chang
Jason Chang
Ju Yong Chang
Xiaojun Chang
Yu-Wei Chao
Visesh Chari
Rizwan Chaudhry
Rama Chellappa
Bo Chen
Chao Chen
Chao-Yeh Chen
Chu-Song Chen
Hwann-Tzong Chen
Lin Chen
Mei Chen
Terrence Chen
Xilin Chen
Yunjin Chen
Guang Chen
Qifeng Chen
Xinlei Chen
Jian Cheng
Ming-Ming Cheng
Anoop Cherian
Guilhem Cheron
Dmitry Chetverikov
Liang-Tien Chia
Naoki Chiba
Tat-Jun Chin
Margarita Chli
Minsu Cho
Sunghyun Cho
TaeEun Choe
Jongmoo Choi
Seungjin Choi
Wongun Choi
Wen-Sheng Chu
Yung-Yu Chuang
Albert Chung
Gokberk Cinbis
Arridhana Ciptadi
Javier Civera

James Clark
Brian Clipp
Michael Cogswell
Taco Cohen
Toby Collins
John Collomosse
Camille Couprie
David Crandall
Marco Cristani
James Crowley
Jinshi Cui
Yin Cui
Jifeng Dai
Qieyun Dai
Shengyang Dai
Yuchao Dai
Zhenwen Dai
Dima Damen
Kristin Dana
Kostas Danilidiis
Mohamed Daoudi
Larry Davis
Teofilo de Campos
Marleen de Bruijne
Koichiro Deguchi
Alessio Del Bue
Luca del Pero
Antoine Deleforge
Hervé Delingette
David Demirdjian
Jia Deng
Joachim Denzler
Konstantinos Derpanis
Frederic Devernay
Hamdi Dibeklioglu
Santosh Kumar Divvala
Carl Doersch
Weisheng Dong
Jian Dong
Gianfranco Doretto
Alexey Dosovitskiy
Matthijs Douze
Bruce Draper
Tom Drummond
Shichuan Du
Jean-Luc Dugelay

Enrique Dunn
Zoran Duric
Pinar Duygulu
Alexei Efros
Carl Henrik Ek
Jan-Olof Eklundh
Jayan Eledath
Ehsan Elhamifar
Ian Endres
Aykut Erdem
Anders Eriksson
Sergio Escalera
Victor Escorcia
Francisco Estrada
Bin Fan
Quanfu Fan
Chen Fang
Tian Fang
Masoud Faraki
Ali Farhadi
Giovanni Farinella
Ryan Farrell
Raanan Fattal
Michael Felsberg
Jiashi Feng
Michele Fenzi
Andras Ferencz
Basura Fernando
Sanja Fidler
Mario Figueiredo
Michael Firman
Robert Fisher
John Fisher III
Alexander Fix
Boris Flach
Matt Flagg
Francois Fleuret
Wolfgang Foerstner
David Fofi
Gianluca Foresti
Per-Erik Forssen
David Fouhey
Jean-Sebastien Franco
Friedrich Fraundorfer
Oren Freifeld
Simone Frintrop

Huazhu Fu
Yun Fu
Jan Funke
Brian Funt
Ryo Furukawa
Yasutaka Furukawa
Andrea Fusiello
David Gallup
Chuang Gan
Junbin Gao
Jochen Gast
Stratis Gavves
Xin Geng
Bogdan Georgescu
David Geronimo
Bernard Ghanem
Riccardo Gherardi
Golnaz Ghiasi
Soumya Ghosh
Andrew Gilbert
Ioannis Gkioulekas
Georgia Gkioxari
Guy Godin
Roland Goecke
Boqing Gong
Shaogang Gong
Yunchao Gong
German Gonzalez
Jordi Gonzalez
Paulo Gotardo
Stephen Gould
Venu M. Govindu
Helmut Grabner
Etienne Grossmann
Chunhui Gu
David Gu
Sergio Guadarrama
Li Guan
Matthieu Guillaumin
Jean-Yves Guillemaut
Guodong Guo
Ruiqi Guo
Yanwen Guo
Saurabh Gupta
Pierre Gurdjos
Diego Gutierrez

Abner Guzman Rivera
Christian Haene
Niels Haering
Ralf Haeusler
David Hall
Peter Hall
Onur Hamsici
Dongfeng Han
Mei Han
Xufeng Han
Yahong Han
Ankur Handa
Kenji Hara
Tatsuya Harada
Mehrtash Harandi
Bharath Hariharan
Tal Hassner
Soren Hauberg
Michal Havlena
Tamir Hazan
Junfeng He
Kaiming He
Lei He
Ran He
Xuming He
Zhihai He
Felix Heide
Janne Heikkila
Jared Heinly
Mattias Heinrich
Pierre Hellier
Stephane Herbin
Isabelle Herlin
Alexander Hermans
Anders Heyden
Adrian Hilton
Vaclav Hlavac
Minh Hoai
Judy Hoffman
Steven Hoi
Derek Hoiem
Seunghoon Hong
Byung-Woo Hong
Anthony Hoogs
Yedid Hoshen
Winston Hsu

Changbo Hu
Wenze Hu
Zhe Hu
Gang Hua
Dong Huang
Gary Huang
Heng Huang
Jia-Bin Huang
Kaiqi Huang
Qingming Huang
Rui Huang
Xinyu Huang
Weilin Huang
Zhiwu Huang
Ahmad Humayun
Mohamed Hussein
Wonjun Hwang
Juan Iglesias
Nazli Ikizler-Cinbis
Evren Imre
Eldar Insafutdinov
Catalin Ionescu
Go Irie
Hossam Isack
Phillip Isola
Hamid Izadinia
Nathan Jacobs
Varadarajan Jagannadan
Aastha Jain
Suyog Jain
Varun Jampani
Jeremy Jancsary
C.V. Jawahar
Dinesh Jayaraman
Ian Jermyn
Hueihan Jhuang
Hui Ji
Qiang Ji
Jiaya Jia
Kui Jia
Yangqing Jia
Hao Jiang
Tingting Jiang
Yu-Gang Jiang
Zhuolin Jiang
Alexis Joly

Shantanu Joshi
Frederic Jurie
Achuta Kadambi
Samuel Kadoury
Yannis Kalantidis
Amit Kale
Sebastian Kaltwang
Joni-Kristian Kamarainen
George Kamberov
Chandra Kambhamettu
Martin Kampel
Kenichi Kanatani
Atul Kanaujia
Melih Kandemir
Zhuoliang Kang
Mohan Kankanhalli
Abhishek Kar
Leonid Karlinsky
Andrej Karpathy
Zoltan Kato
Rei Kawakami
Kristian Kersting
Margret Keuper
Nima Khademi Kalantari
Sameh Khamis
Fahad Khan
Aditya Khosla
Hadi Kiapour
Edward Kim
Gunhee Kim
Hansung Kim
Jae-Hak Kim
Kihwan Kim
Seon Joo Kim
Tae Hyun Kim
Tae-Kyun Kim
Vladimir Kim
Benjamin Kimia
Akisato Kimura
Durk Kingma
Thomas Kipf
Kris Kitani
Martin Kleinsteuber
Laurent Kneip
Kevin Koeser
Effrosyni Kokiopoulou

Piotr Koniusz
Theodora Kontogianni
Sanjeev Koppal
Dimitrios Kosmopoulos
Adriana Kovashka
Adarsh Kowdle
Michael Kramp
Josip Krapac
Jonathan Krause
Pavel Krsek
Hilde Kuehne
Shiro Kumano
Avinash Kumar
Sebastian Kurtek
Kyros Kutulakos
Suha Kwak
In So Kweon
Roland Kwitt
Junghyun Kwon
Junseok Kwon
Jan Kybic
Jorma Laaksonen
Alexander Ladikos
Florent Lafarge
Pierre-Yves Laffont
Wei-Sheng Lai
Jean-Francois Lalonde
Michael Langer
Oswald Lanz
Agata Lapedriza
Ivan Laptev
Diane Larlus
Christoph Lassner
Olivier Le Meur
Laura Leal-Taixé
Joon-Young Lee
Seungkyu Lee
Chen-Yu Lee
Andreas Lehrmann
Ido Leichter
Frank Lenzen
Matt Leotta
Stefan Leutenegger
Baoxin Li
Chunming Li
Dingzeyu Li

Fuxin Li
Hao Li
Houqiang Li
Qi Li
Stan Li
Wu-Jun Li
Xirong Li
Xuelong Li
Yi Li
Yongjie Li
Wei Li
Wen Li
Yeqing Li
Yujia Li
Wang Liang
Shengcai Liao
Jongwoo Lim
Joseph Lim
Di Lin
Weiyao Lin
Yen-Yu Lin
Min Lin
Liang Lin
Haibin Ling
Jim Little
Buyu Liu
Miaomiao Liu
Risheng Liu
Si Liu
Wanquan Liu
Yebin Liu
Ziwei Liu
Zhen Liu
Sifei Liu
Marcus Liwicki
Roberto Lopez-Sastre
Javier Lorenzo
Christos Louizos
Manolis Lourakis
Brian Lovell
Chen-Change Loy
Cewu Lu
Huchuan Lu
Jiwen Lu
Le Lu
Yijuan Lu

Canyi Lu
Jiebo Luo
Ping Luo
Siwei Lyu
Zhigang Ma
Chao Ma
Oisin Mac Aodha
John MacCormick
Vijay Mahadevan
Dhruv Mahajan
Aravindh Mahendran
Mohammed Mahoor
Michael Maire
Subhransu Maji
Aditi Majumder
Atsuto Maki
Yasushi Makihara
Alexandros Makris
Mateusz Malinowski
Clement Mallet
Arun Mallya
Dixit Mandar
Junhua Mao
Dmitrii Marin
Elisabeta Marinoiu
Renaud Marlet
Ricardo Martin
Aleix Martinez
Jonathan Masci
David Masip
Diana Mateus
Markus Mathias
Iain Matthews
Kevin Matzen
Bruce Maxwell
Stephen Maybank
Scott McCloskey
Ted Meeds
Christopher Mei
Tao Mei
Xue Mei
Jason Meltzer
Heydi Mendez
Thomas Mensink
Michele Merler
Domingo Mery

Ajmal Mian
Tomer Michaeli
Ondrej Miksik
Anton Milan
Erik Miller
Gregor Miller
Majid Mirmehdi
Ishan Misra
Anurag Mittal
Daisuke Miyazaki
Hossein Mobahi
Pascal Monasse
Sandino Morales
Vlad Morariu
Philippos Mordohai
Francesc Moreno-Noguer
Greg Mori
Bryan Morse
Roozbeh Mottaghi
Yadong Mu
Yasuhiro Mukaigawa
Lopamudra Mukherjee
Joseph Mundy
Mario Munich
Ana Murillo
Vittorio Murino
Naila Murray
Damien Muselet
Sobhan Naderi Parizi
Hajime Nagahara
Nikhil Naik
P.J. Narayanan
Fabian Nater
Jan Neumann
Ram Nevatia
Shawn Newsam
Bingbing Ni
Juan Carlos Niebles
Jifeng Ning
Ko Nishino
Masashi Nishiyama
Shohei Nobuhara
Ifeoma Nwogu
Peter Ochs
Jean-Marc Odobez
Francesca Odone

Iason Oikonomidis
Takeshi Oishi
Takahiro Okabe
Takayuki Okatani
Carl Olsson
Vicente Ordonez
Ivan Oseledets
Magnus Oskarsson
Martin R. Oswald
Matthew O'Toole
Wanli Ouyang
Andrew Owens
Mustafa Ozuysal
Jason Pacheco
Manohar Paluri
Gang Pan
Jinshan Pan
Yannis Panagakis
Sharath Pankanti
George Papandreou
Hyun Soo Park
In Kyu Park
Jaesik Park
Seyoung Park
Omkar Parkhi
Ioannis Patras
Viorica Patraucean
Genevieve Patterson
Vladimir Pavlovic
Kim Pedersen
Robert Peharz
Shmuel Peleg
Marcello Pelillo
Otavio Penatti
Xavier Pennec
Federico Pernici
Adrian Peter
Stavros Petridis
Vladimir Petrovic
Tomas Pfister
Justus Piater
Pedro Pinheiro
Bernardo Pires
Fiora Pirri
Leonid Pishchulin
Daniel Pizarro

Robert Pless
Tobias Pltz
Yair Poleg
Gerard Pons-Moll
Jordi Pont-Tuset
Ronald Poppe
Andrea Prati
Jan Prokaj
Daniel Prusa
Nicolas Pugeault
Guido Pusiol
Guo-Jun Qi
Gang Qian
Yu Qiao
Novi Quadrianto
Julian Quiroga
Andrew Rabinovich
Rahul Raguram
Srikumar Ramalingam
Deva Ramanan
Narayanan Ramanathan
Vignesh Ramanathan
Sebastian Ramos
Rene Ranftl
Anand Rangarajan
Avinash Ravichandran
Ramin Raziperchikolaei
Carlo Regazzoni
Christian Reinbacher
Michal Reinstein
Emonet Remi
Fabio Remondino
Shaoqing Ren
Zhile Ren
Jerome Revaud
Hayko Riemenschneider
Tobias Ritschel
Mariano Rivera
Patrick Rives
Antonio Robles-Kelly
Jason Rock
Erik Rodner
Emanuele Rodola
Mikel Rodriguez
Antonio
   Rodriguez Sanchez

Gregory Rogez
Marcus Rohrbach
Javier Romero
Matteo Ronchi
German Ros
Charles Rosenberg
Guy Rosman
Arun Ross
Paolo Rota
Samuel Rota Bulò
Peter Roth
Volker Roth
Brandon Rothrock
Anastasios Roussos
Amit Roy-Chowdhury
Ognjen Rudovic
Daniel Rueckert
Christian Rupprecht
Olga Russakovsky
Bryan Russell
Emmanuel Sabu
Fereshteh Sadeghi
Hideo Saito
Babak Saleh
Mathieu Salzmann
Dimitris Samaras
Conrad Sanderson
Enver Sangineto
Aswin Sankaranarayanan
Imari Sato
Yoichi Sato
Shin'ichi Satoh
Torsten Sattler
Bogdan Savchynskyy
Yann Savoye
Arman Savran
Harpreet Sawhney
Davide Scaramuzza
Walter Scheirer
Frank Schmidt
Uwe Schmidt
Dirk Schnieders
Johannes Schönberger
Florian Schroff
Samuel Schulter
William Schwartz

Alexander Schwing
Stan Sclaroff
Nicu Sebe
Ari Seff
Anita Sellent
Giuseppe Serra
Laura Sevilla-Lara
Shishir Shah
Greg Shakhnarovich
Qi Shan
Shiguang Shan
Jing Shao
Ling Shao
Xiaowei Shao
Roman Shapovalov
Nataliya Shapovalova
Ali Sharif Razavian
Gaurav Sharma
Pramod Sharma
Viktoriia Sharmanska
Eli Shechtman
Alexander Shekhovtsov
Evan Shelhamer
Chunhua Shen
Jianbing Shen
Li Shen
Xiaoyong Shen
Wei Shen
Yu Sheng
Jianping Shi
Qinfeng Shi
Yonggang Shi
Baoguang Shi
Kevin Shih
Nobutaka Shimada
Ilan Shimshoni
Koichi Shinoda
Takaaki Shiratori
Jamie Shotton
Matthew Shreve
Abhinav Shrivastava
Nitesh Shroff
Leonid Sigal
Nathan Silberman
Tomas Simon
Edgar Simo-Serra

Dheeraj Singaraju
Gautam Singh
Maneesh Singh
Richa Singh
Saurabh Singh
Vikas Singh
Sudipta Sinha
Josef Sivic
Greg Slabaugh
William Smith
Patrick Snape
Jan Sochman
Kihyuk Sohn
Hyun Oh Song
Jingkuan Song
Qi Song
Shuran Song
Xuan Song
Yale Song
Yi-Zhe Song
Alexander
    Sorkine Hornung
Humberto Sossa
Aristeidis Sotiras
Richard Souvenir
Anuj Srivastava
Nitish Srivastava
Michael Stark
Bjorn Stenger
Rainer Stiefelhagen
Martin Storath
Joerg Stueckler
Hang Su
Hao Su
Jingyong Su
Shuochen Su
Yu Su
Ramanathan Subramanian
Yusuke Sugano
Akihiro Sugimoto
Libin Sun
Min Sun
Qing Sun
Yi Sun
Chen Sun
Deqing Sun

Ganesh Sundaramoorthi
Jinli Suo
Supasorn Suwajanakorn
Tomas Svoboda
Chris Sweeney
Paul Swoboda
Raza Syed Hussain
Christian Szegedy
Yuichi Taguchi
Yu-Wing Tai
Hugues Talbot
Toru Tamaki
Mingkui Tan
Robby Tan
Xiaoyang Tan
Masayuki Tanaka
Meng Tang
Siyu Tang
Ran Tao
Dacheng Tao
Makarand Tapaswi
Jean-Philippe Tarel
Camillo Taylor
Christian Theobalt
Diego Thomas
Rajat Thomas
Xinmei Tian
Yonglong Tian
YingLi Tian
Yonghong Tian
Kinh Tieu
Joseph Tighe
Radu Timofte
Massimo Tistarelli
Sinisa Todorovic
Giorgos Tolias
Federico Tombari
Akihiko Torii
Andrea Torsello
Du Tran
Quoc-Huy Tran
Rudolph Triebel
Roberto Tron
Leonardo Trujillo
Eduard Trulls
Tomasz Trzcinski

Yi-Hsuan Tsai
Gavriil Tsechpenakis
Chourmouzios Tsiotsios
Stavros Tsogkas
Kewei Tu
Shubham Tulsiani
Tony Tung
Pavan Turaga
Matthew Turk
Tinne Tuytelaars
Oncel Tuzel
Georgios Tzimiropoulos
Norimichi Ukita
Osman Ulusoy
Martin Urschler
Arash Vahdat
Michel Valstar
Ernest Valveny
Jan van Gemert
Kiran Varanasi
Mayank Vatsa
Javier Vazquez-Corral
Ramakrishna Vedantam
Ashok Veeraraghavan
Olga Veksler
Jakob Verbeek
Francisco Vicente
Rene Vidal
Jordi Vitria
Max Vladymyrov
Christoph Vogel
Carl Vondrick
Sven Wachsmuth
Toshikazu Wada
Catherine Wah
Jacob Walker
Xiaolong Wang
Wei Wang
Limin Wang
Liang Wang
Hua Wang
Lijun Wang
Naiyan Wang
Xinggang Wang
Yining Wang
Baoyuan Wang

Chaohui Wang
Gang Wang
Heng Wang
Lei Wang
Linwei Wang
Liwei Wang
Ping Wang
Qi Wang
Qian Wang
Shenlong Wang
Song Wang
Tao Wang
Yang Wang
Yu-Chiang Frank Wang
Zhaowen Wang
Simon Warfield
Yichen Wei
Philippe Weinzaepfel
Longyin Wen
Tomas Werner
Aaron Wetzler
Yonatan Wexler
Michael Wilber
Kyle Wilson
Thomas Windheuser
David Wipf
Paul Wohlhart
Christian Wolf
Kwan-Yee Kenneth Wong
John Wright
Jiajun Wu
Jianxin Wu
Tianfu Wu
Yang Wu
Yi Wu
Zheng Wu
Stefanie Wuhrer
Jonas Wulff
Rolf Wurtz
Lu Xia
Tao Xiang
Yu Xiang
Lei Xiao
Yang Xiao
Tong Xiao
Wenxuan Xie

Lingxi Xie
Pengtao Xie
Saining Xie
Yuchen Xie
Junliang Xing
Bo Xiong
Fei Xiong
Jia Xu
Yong Xu
Tianfan Xue
Toshihiko Yamasaki
Takayoshi Yamashita
Junjie Yan
Rong Yan
Yan Yan
Keiji Yanai
Jian Yang
Jianchao Yang
Jiaolong Yang
Jie Yang
Jimei Yang
Michael Ying Yang
Ming Yang
Ruiduo Yang
Yi Yang
Angela Yao
Cong Yao
Jian Yao
Jianhua Yao
Jinwei Ye
Shuai Yi
Alper Yilmaz
Lijun Yin
Zhaozheng Yin

Xianghua Ying
Kuk-Jin Yoon
Chong You
Aron Yu
Felix Yu
Fisher Yu
Lap-Fai Yu
Stella Yu
Jing Yuan
Junsong Yuan
Lu Yuan
Xiao-Tong Yuan
Alan Yuille
Xenophon Zabulis
Stefanos Zafeiriou
Sergey Zagoruyko
Amir Zamir
Andrei Zanfir
Mihai Zanfir
Lihi Zelnik-Manor
Xingyu Zeng
Josiane Zerubia
Changshui Zhang
Cheng Zhang
Guofeng Zhang
Jianguo Zhang
Junping Zhang
Ning Zhang
Quanshi Zhang
Shaoting Zhang
Tianzhu Zhang
Xiaoqun Zhang
Yinda Zhang
Yu Zhang

Shiliang Zhang
Lei Zhang
Xiaoqin Zhang
Shanshan Zhang
Ting Zhang
Bin Zhao
Rui Zhao
Yibiao Zhao
Enliang Zheng
Wenming Zheng
Yinqiang Zheng
Yuanjie Zheng
Yin Zheng
Wei-Shi Zheng
Liang Zheng
Dingfu Zhou
Wengang Zhou
Tinghui Zhou
Bolei Zhou
Feng Zhou
Huiyu Zhou
Jun Zhou
Kevin Zhou
Kun Zhou
Xiaowei Zhou
Zihan Zhou
Jun Zhu
Jun-Yan Zhu
Zhenyao Zhu
Zeeshan Zia
Henning Zimmer
Karel Zimmermann
Wangmeng Zuo

## Additional Reviewers

Felix Achilles
Sarah Adel Bargal
Hessam Bagherinezhad
Qinxun Bai
Gedas Bertasius
Michal Busta
Erik Bylow
Marinella Cadoni

Dan Andrei Calian
Lilian Calvet
Federico Camposeco
Olivier Canevet
Anirban Chakraborty
Yu-Wei Chao
Sotirios Chatzis
Tatjana Chavdarova

Jimmy Chen
Melissa Cote
Berkan Demirel
Zhiwei Deng
Guy Gilboa
Albert Gordo
Daniel Gordon
Ankur Gupta

Kun He
Yang He
Daniel Holtmann-Rice
Xun Huang
Liang Hui
Drew Jaegle
Cijo Jose
Marco Karrer
Mehran Khodabandeh
Anna Khoreva
Hyo-Jin Kim
Theodora Kontogianni
Pengpeng Liang
Shugao Ma
Ludovic Magerand
Francesco Malapelle
Julio Marco
Vlad Morariu

Rajitha Navarathna
Junhyuk Oh
Federico Perazzi
Marcel Piotraschke
Srivignesh Rajendran
Joe Redmon
Helge Rhodin
Anna Rohrbach
Beatrice Rossi
Wolfgang Roth
Pietro Salvagnini
Hosnieh Sattar
Ana Serrano
Zhixin Shu
Sven Sickert
Jakub Simanek
Ramprakash Srinivasan
Oren Tadmor

Xin Tao
Lucas Teixeira
Mårten Wädenback
Qing Wang
Yaser Yacoob
Takayoshi Yamashita
Huiyuan Yang
Ryo Yonetani
Sejong Yoon
Shaodi You
Xu Zhan
Jianming Zhang
Richard Zhang
Xiaoqun Zhang
Xu Zhang
Zheng Zhang

# Contents – Part II

**Optimization**

**Poster Session 3**

# Poster Session 2

# The Curious Robot: Learning Visual Representations via Physical Interactions

Lerrel Pinto[✉], Dhiraj Gandhi, Yuanfeng Han, Yong-Lae Park,
and Abhinav Gupta

The Robotics Institute, Carnegie Mellon University, Pittsburgh, USA
lerrel.pinto@gmail.com

**Abstract.** What is the right supervisory signal to train visual representations? Current approaches in computer vision use category labels from datasets such as ImageNet to train ConvNets. However, in case of biological agents, visual representation learning does not require millions of semantic labels. We argue that biological agents use physical interactions with the world to learn visual representations unlike current vision systems which just use passive observations (images and videos downloaded from web). For example, babies push objects, poke them, put them in their mouth and throw them to learn representations. Towards this goal, we build one of the first systems on a Baxter platform that pushes, pokes, grasps and observes objects in a tabletop environment. It uses four different types of physical interactions to collect more than 130K datapoints, with each datapoint providing supervision to a shared ConvNet architecture allowing us to learn visual representations. We show the quality of learned representations by observing neuron activations and performing nearest neighbor retrieval on this learned representation. Quantitatively, we evaluate our learned ConvNet on image classification tasks and show improvements compared to learning without external data. Finally, on the task of instance retrieval, our network outperforms the ImageNet network on recall@1 by 3 %.

## 1 Introduction

Recently most computer vision systems have moved from using hand-designed features to feature learning paradigm. Much of the visual feature learning is done in a completely supervised manner using category labels. However, in case of biological agents, visual learning typically does not require categorical labels and happens in a "unsupervised" manner[1].

Recently there has been a strong push to learn visual representations without using any category labels. Examples include using context from images [1], different viewpoints from videos [2], ego-motion from videos [3] and generative models of images and videos [4–7]. However, all these approaches still observe

---

[1] By "unsupervised" we mean no supervision from other agents but supervision can come from other modalities or from time.

© Springer International Publishing AG 2016
B. Leibe et al. (Eds.): ECCV 2016, Part II, LNCS 9906, pp. 3–18, 2016.
DOI: 10.1007/978-3-319-46475-6_1

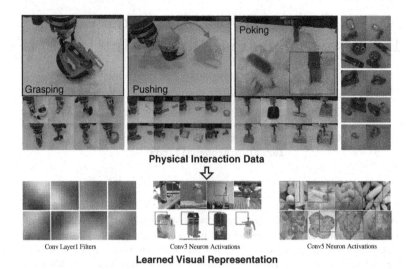

**Physical Interaction Data**

⇩

Conv Layer1 Filters          Conv3 Neuron Activations          Conv5 Neuron Activations

**Learned Visual Representation**

**Fig. 1.** Learning ConvNets from Physical Interactions: We propose a framework for training ConvNet using physical interaction data from robots. We first use a Baxter robot to grasp, push, poke and observe objects, with each interaction providing a training datapoint. We collect more than 130K datapoints to train a ConvNet. To the best of our knowledge, ours is one of the first system which trains visual representation using physical interactions.

the visual world passively without any physical interaction with the world. On the other hand, we argue visual learning in humans (or any biological agent) require physical exploration of the world. Our babies play with objects: They push them, grasp them, put them in their mouth, throw them etc. and with every interaction they develop a better visual representation.

In this paper, we break the traditional paradigm of visual learning from passive observation of data: images and videos on the web. We argue that the next step in visual learning requires signal/supervision from physical exploration of our world. We build a physical system (on a Baxter robot) with a parallel jaw gripper and a tactile skin-sensor which interacts with the world and develops a representation for visual understanding. Specifically, the robot tries to grasp objects, push objects, observe haptic data by touching them and also observe different viewpoints of objects. While there has been significant work in the vision and robotics community to develop vision algorithms for performing robotic tasks such as grasping, to the best of our knowledge this is the first effort that reverses the pipeline and uses robotic tasks for learning visual representations.

We also propose a shared-ConvNet architecture where the first few convolutional layers are shared across different tasks, followed by 1–2 separate convolutional and fully connected layers for each task. Since our architecture is shared, every interaction creates a data point to train this ConvNet architecture. This ConvNet architecture then forms the learned visual representation. Our physical exploration data includes 40,287 grasps, 5,472 pushes, 1372 tactile sensing observations and 84,430 pairs of different viewpoints of the same object.

# 2    Related Work

Our work touches two threads: how do you learn a representation in an unsupervised way, and how do you interact with the world for learning.

## 2.1    Unsupervised Learning

Unsupervised learning of visual representations is one of the most challenging problems in computer vision. There are two common approaches to unsupervised learning: generative and discriminative. Early work in generative learning focused on learning visual representations that (a) can reconstruct images and (b) are sparse. This idea was extended by Hinton and Salakhutdinov [8] to train a deep belief network in an unsupervised manner via stacking RBMs. Similar to this, Bengio et al. [9] investigated stacking of both RBMs and autoencoders. Recently, there has also been a lot of success in the ability to generate realistic images. Some examples include the generative adversarial network (GAN) [5] framework and its variant including Laplacian GAN (LAPGAN) [6], DCGAN [7] and $S^2$-GAN [10].

The discriminative approach to unsupervised learning is training a network on an auxiliary task where ground-truth is obtained automatically (or via sensors). For example, Doersch et al. [1] presented an approach to train networks via supervision from context. Other approaches such as [3,11,12] have tried to use videos and ego-motion to learn the underlying network. In an another work, [2] tracks patches in the video and uses the patches sampled from a track as different viewpoints of the same object instance and trains an embedding network. Finally, our approach is also related to other efforts which train deep networks using supervision from other sensors such as Kinect [13,14] or motion information such as optical flow [15].

However, all the above approaches still only observe passive data. We believe that the ability to physically interact with elements of the scene, is a key requirement for training visual representations. In fact, this has been supported by several psychological behavior experiments as well [16].

## 2.2    Robotic Tasks

We note that most work in this domain has been in using vision to solve a task. Here, we use these tasks to learn good visual representations. We design our experiments in which our robot interacts with objects with four different types of interactions.

**Grasping.** Grasping is probably the oldest problem in the field of robotics. A comprehensive literature review of this area can be found in [17,18]. Recently, data-driven learning-based approaches have started to appear, with initial work focused on using human annotators [19]. However, in this work we are more interested in building a self-supervision system [20–24]. For the purpose of this work we use the dataset provided in [23].

**Pushing.** The second task our system explores is the task of pushing objects. The origins of pushing as a manipulation task can be traced to the task of aligning objects to reduce pose uncertainty [25–27] and as a preceding realignment step before object manipulation [28–30]. The implementation of pushing strategies in the mentioned work requires physics based models to simulate and predict the actions required to achieve a specific object goal state given an object start state. However, similar to grasping, in this work we are interested in self-learning systems which perform push interactions and use the sensor readings from robots as supervision.

**Tactile Sensing.** The third task we explore is tactile sensing: that is, a robot with a skin sensor touches/pokes the objects followed by storing skin sensor readings. We then try to use the sensor reading to provide supervision to train the visual representations. Highly sensitive tactile optical sensors have been used for robot exoskeletal finger feedback control [31]. While there have been approaches that have attempted to combine tactile sensing with computer vision for object detection [32], this is the first paper that explores the idea of learning visual representation from tactile data.

**Identity Vision.** The final task we use our physical system for is to get multiple images of the same object from different viewpoints. This is similar to the idea of active vision [33,34]. However, in most of these approaches the next best view is chosen after inference [34]. In this work, we sample thousands of such pairs to provide training examples for learning ConvNets.

**Vision and Deep Learning for Robotics.** There has been a recent trend to use deep networks in robotics systems for grasp regression [23,35,36] or learning policies for a variety of tasks [37–39]. In this paper, we explore the idea of using robotic tasks to train ConvNets as visual representation. We then explore the effectiveness of these for tasks such as object classification and retrieval.

## 3   Approach

We now describe the formulation of the four tasks: planar grasping, planar pushing, poking (tactile sensing) and identity vision for different viewpoints of the objects.

### 3.1   Planar Grasps

We use the grasp dataset described in our earlier work [23] for our experiments on the grasping task. Here, the grasp configuration lies in 3 dimensions, $(x, y)$: position of grasp point on the surface of table and $\theta$: angle of grasp. The training dataset contains around 37K failed grasp interactions and around 3K successful grasp interactions as the training set. For testing, around 2.8K failed and 0.2K successful grasps on novel objects are provided. Some of the positive and negative grasp examples are shown in Fig. 2.

Successful grasps                   Unsuccessful grasps

**Fig. 2.** Examples of successful (left) and unsuccesful grasps (right). We use a patch based representation: given an input patch we predict 18-dim vector which represents whether the center location of the patch is graspable at $0°, 10°, \ldots 170°$.

**Grasp Prediction Formulation:** The grasp prediction problem can be formulated as finding a successful grasp configuration $(x_S, y_S, \theta_S)$ given an image of an object $I$. However, as mentioned in [23], this formulation is problematic due to the presence of multiple grasp locations for each object and that ConvNets are significantly better at classification than regression to a structured output space. Given an image patch, we output an 18-dimensional likelihood vector where each dimension represent the likelihood of whether the center of the patch is graspable at $0°, 10°, \ldots 170°$. Therefore, the grasping problem can be thought of as 18 binary classification problems. Hence the evaluation criterion is binary classification i.e. given a patch and executed grasp angle in the test set, predict whether the object was grasped or not.

### 3.2 Planar Push

We use a Baxter robot to collect push data as described in Fig. 3. Given an object placed on the robot's table and the model of the table, we perform background subtraction to determine the position of the object. After detecting an object using image $I_{begin}$, we sample two points on the workspace: the first point is the start point $X_{begin} = (x_{begin}, y_{begin}, z_{begin})$ from where the robot hand starts accelerating and gaining velocity. This start point is sampled from a Von Mises distribution to push the object towards the center of the robot's workspace. We also sample another 3D point, $X_{final} = (x_{final}, y_{final}, z_{final})$. This point defines the location at which the robot hand stops accelerating. Note that: (a) $z_{begin} = z_{final}$ since we are dealing with planar pushing; (b) $X_{final}$ and $X_{begin}$ define both the direction and velocity/force with which the object is hit by the robot. Therefore, in this work, we parametrize push actions with 5 parameters: $(x_{start}, y_{start}, x_{final}, y_{final}, z_{pushHeight})$.

An off-the-shelf planner plans and executes the push action $X_{begin} \rightarrow X_{final}$. The arm then retracts back, and $I_{final}$ is recorded. We collect 5K push actions on 70 objects using the above described method. Some of these push actions are visualized in Fig. 4.

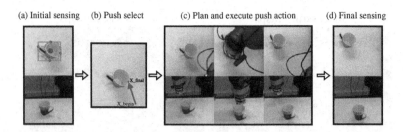

(a) Initial sensing    (b) Push select          (c) Plan and execute push action          (d) Final sensing

**Fig. 3.** We detect an object and apply planar push. Our push action is parameterized in terms of two 3D points: $X_{begin}$ and $X_{final}$.

Objects and push action pairs

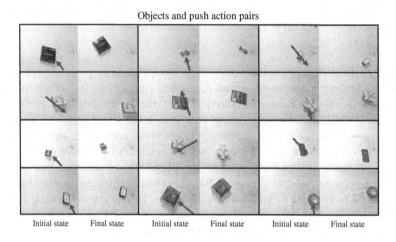

Initial state       Final state        Initial state       Final state        Initial state       Final state

**Fig. 4.** Examples of initial state and final state images taken for the push action. The arrows demonstrate the direction and magnitude of the push action.

**Push Prediction Formulation:** For incorporating learning from push, we build a siamese network (weights shared). One tower of siamese network takes $I_{begin}$ as input and the other tower takes $I_{end}$ as input. The output features of the two towers are then combined using fully connected layer to regress to what action caused this transformation. The push-action is parametrized by $\{X_{begin}, X_{final}\}$ and mean squared error is used as the regression loss. This action formulation captures the relevant magnitude as well as the localization and direction of the push.

### 3.3 Poking: Tactile Sensing

In this task, the robot pushes the object vertically into the table until the pressure applied on the object exceeds a limit threshold (Fig. 5). A random point is sampled inside the object as the poke location. This pressure is sensed by robust tactile sensors attached on the finger of the robot and is continuously recorded. On reaching the limit threshold, the arm pulls away from the object and repeats

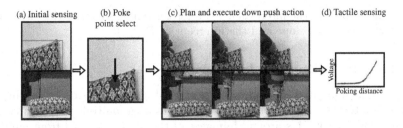

**Fig. 5.** The figure shows how the poke data with tactile sensing is collected. The profile of the tactile graph provides cues about material with which the object is made.

the motion for around 10 times per object. A total of 1K pushes are collected on 100 diverse objects.

The tactile skin-sensor used in this work increases its electrical resistance monotonically on the application of pressure. Hence an increase in pressure correlates to an increase in resistance which then correlates to an increase in voltage drop across the sensor. This voltage drop $\mathbf{p}_{do}$ is sensed via an Arduino and logged with appropriate time stamps.

During poking, the pressure voltage data stream $\mathbf{p}_{do}$ while pushing into the object is recorded. Some of this data are visualized in Fig. 6. It can be noted how soft objects like the plush toy have a more gradual force response than harder objects like the hardcover book.

**Tactile Prediction Formulation:** The poke tactile prediction problem is formulated as a regression of the polynomial parametrization $\mathcal{P}(\mathbf{p}_{do})$ of the poke action. Since a line parametrization works well to describe the poke response (Fig. 6), we use a linear parametrization making the problem a regression to two

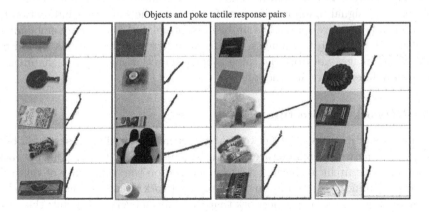

**Fig. 6.** Examples of the data collected by the poking action. On the left we show the object poked, and on the right we show force profiles as observed by the tactile sensor.

values (the slope and the intercept). Therefore, given an image of the object our ConvNet predicts the slope and the intercept of $\mathcal{P}(\mathbf{p}_{do})$.

### 3.4  Identity Vision: Pose Invariance

Given the grasping and pushing tasks described above, pairs of images in any one task's interaction contains images of objects with multiple viewpoints. The grasping dataset contains around 5 images of the object grasped from multiple viewpoints in every successful grasp interaction, while the planar push dataset contains 2 images of the object pushed in every push interaction. Figure 7 shows some examples of the pair of images of objects in different poses. In total, we use around 42K positive pairs of images and 42K negative pairs (images from different interactions).

**Fig. 7.** Examples of objects in different poses provided to the embedding network.

**Pose Invariance Formulation.** The pose invariance task is meant to serve as a supervisory signal to enforce images of objects in the same task interaction to be closer in fc7 feature space. The problem is formulated as a feature embedding problem, where, given two images, the distance between the features should be small if the images are from the same robot interaction and large if the images are from different robot interactions.

### 3.5  Network Architecture

We now describe our shared network architecture for the four tasks described above. The network architecture used is summarized in Fig. 8. The network exploits the hierarchical sharing of features based on the complexity of the task to learn a common representation at the root network. Hence our network architecture can be seen as a root network that learns from every datapoint; this root network is augmented with specialized task networks emanating from various levels. This is based on the insight that tasks which require simpler representations like the push action prediction should be predicted lower in the network

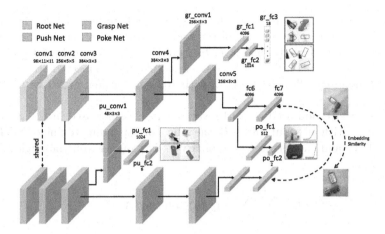

**Fig. 8.** Our shared convolutional architecture for four different tasks. (Color figure online)

than more complex tasks like object embedding. Specifically, push action needs pose-variance. However, more complex tasks like object embedding require the learning of pose invariant feature representations, which are usually learnt in the higher layers.

The tasks we deal with in this work require either one image as input (like the grasp prediction task and the poke tactile task) or two images (like the push action prediction task, the action invariance task). We however would like to learn a single root network for all these tasks. For this purpose the root network in both the streams share parameters and are updated simultaneously. The gray blocks in Fig. 8 show the root network which updates its parameters using loss gradients backpropagated from every task.

**Root Network:** The root network follows the architecture of layer scheme of AlexNet [40] and can be seen as the gray network in Fig. 8. The first convolutional layer (conv1) consists of 96 kernels with kernel size of $11 \times 11$. This convolutional layer and all the succeeding layers use a non linear Rectified Linear Unit (ReLU) as the transfer function. Local response normalization (LRN) is used and is followed by a spatial Max-Pooling (MP) of kernel size $3 \times 3$. This is followed by the second convolutional layer (conv2) that has 256 kernels of $5 \times 5$ kernel size and is followed by a LRN and a MP of $3 \times 3$. The third convolutional layer (conv3) has 386 $3 \times 3$ kernels which is followed by the fourth convolutional layer (conv4) with 384 $3 \times 3$ kernels. The fifth convolutional layer (conv5), with 256 $3 \times 3$ kernels, is followed by a MP with a $3 \times 3$ kernel. The convolutional layers are followed by two fully connected layers (fc6 and fc7) that have 4096 neurons each and are each followed by a ReLU. Since some tasks require two images as input, a clone of the root network is maintained with shared weights.

**Grasp Network:** The input to the grasp network (orange blocks in Fig. 8) emanates from the conv4 output of the root network. This network passes the input through one convolutional layer (gr_conv1) with 256 kernels of $3 \times 3$ kernel size followed by a $3 \times 3$ MP. This then passes into a fully connected layer (gr_fc1) with 4096 neurons followed by gr_fc2 with 1024 and a final gr_fc3 with $18 \times 2$ neurons.

The error criterion used is the 18-way binary classifier used in [23]. Given a batch size $B$, with an input image $I_i$, the label corresponding to angle $\theta_i$ defined by $l_i \in \{0, 1\}$ and the forward pass binary activations $A_{ji}$ on the angle bin $j$ the loss $L$ is:

$$L = \sum_{i=1}^{B} \sum_{j=1}^{N=18} \delta(j, \theta_i) \cdot \text{softmax}(A_{ji}, l_i) \qquad (1)$$

After an input training image $I_i$ is passed into the root network, the conv4 output is input into the grasp network that generates the classification loss that is backpropagated all through the chain. The weight update for the grasp network uses standard RMSprop, however the gradients for the root network are stored in memory and waits to be aggregated with the gradients from the other tasks.

**Push Network:** The input to the push network (blue blocks in Fig. 8) emanates from the conv3 output of the root network. This network consists of one convolutional layer (pu_conv1) with 48 kernels of $3 \times 3$ kernel size, a fully connected layer (pu_fc1) with 1024 neurons and a final fully connected layer (pu_fc2) with 5 neurons corresponding to the size of the action prediction. Since the input for the push task is two images, the outputs from the pu_conv1 for both the images are concatenated to result in a 96 dimensional feature map that is fed into pu_fc1. A mean squared error (MSE) criterion is used as this task's loss.

Given input images $I_{begin}$ and $I_{final}$, $I_{begin}$ is passed in the root network while $I_{final}$ is passed through the clone of the root network. The conv3 outputs from both the networks pass through two copies of pu_conv1 which is then concatenated and passed through the push network to generate MSE regression loss. The loss is backpropagated through the chain, with the weights in the push network getting updated in the batch using RMSprop while the gradients in the root network are stored in memory to be aggregated later. For the weights in pu_conv1, the gradients are accumulated and mean-aggregated before an update.

**Poke Network:** The input to the poke network (green in Fig. 8) emanates from the fc6 of the root network. The poke network then passes the input into a fully connected layer po_fc1 with 512 neurons followed by po_fc2 with 2 neurons as the tactile prediction. The MSE criterion is used to provide the regression loss for this task.

Given an input training image, it is first passed through the root network. The fc6 output is then fed as an input to the poke network that makes a tactile prediction. The loss from the MSE criterion is backpropagated through the chain.

**Identity Similarity Embedding:** Feature embedding is done via a cosine embedding loss on the fc7 feature output. Given a pair of images, one is passed through the root network while the other is passed through a clone of the root network. The cosine embedding loss on the fc7 feature representations are then backpropagated through the chain and the gradients for the two copies are accumulated and mean aggregated.

**Training Details:** We follow a two-step training procedure for the network. In the first stage, we first initialize the root network (upto conv4) and the grasp network with Gaussian initialization. We train only the grasp network and the lower root network for 20K iterations on the grasp data.

In the second stage, we create the full architecture with first conv4 copied from the grasp learning. Then, batches with size of 128 are prepared for each of the 4 tasks and are sequentially input into the network. Weights for the grasp, push and poke networks are updated during their respective backward propagation cycles, while the gradients for the root and the clone network are accumulated until one batch for each of the tasks is complete. After one cycle of the 4 task batches, the accumulated gradients for the root and clone network are mean aggregated and a weight update step is taken.

# 4   Results

We now demonstrate the effectiveness of learning visual representations via physical interactions. First, we analyze the learned network in terms of what it has learned and how effective the feature space is. Next, we evaluate the learned representations for tasks like image classification and image retrieval. Finally we analyze the importance of each task in the learnt representations using a task ablation analysis.

## 4.1   Analyzing the ConvNet

As a first experiment, we visualize the maximum activations of neurons in layer 4 and layer 5 of the network. Specifically, we run our learned network on 2500 ImageNet images corresponding to household items and find the images that maximally activates different neurons. We show these maximally activated images along with the receptive fields for some conv5 and conv4 neurons of our root network in Fig. 9. Notice that conv5 is able to correlate strong shape attributes like the spherical objects in row 4, the cereal bowls in row 5 and the circular biscuits in row 3. This is quite intuitive since tasks such as pushing, grasping etc. are functions of the object shapes.

As a next experiment, we analyze the learned network without fine tuning for the task of nearest neighbor. We use 25 household objects as query images and 2500 ImageNet images as the training dataset. We use the root network's conv5 feature space to perform nearest neighbors (See Fig. 10). Again, as expected, the nearest neighbors seem to be based on shape attributes.

## 4.2   Classification

For analyzing the effectiveness of our learned visual representation, we would like to analyze the root network of our learnt robot task model on ImageNet [41]

14      L. Pinto et al.

conv5                              conv4

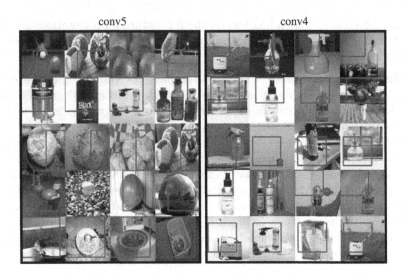

**Fig. 9.** The maximally activating images for the conv5 and conv4 neurons of our root network is shown here.

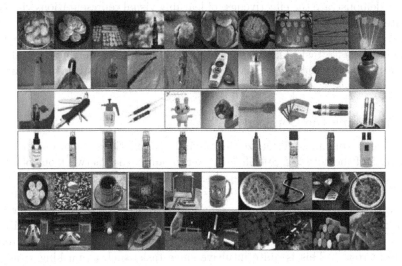

**Fig. 10.** The first column corresponds to query image and rest show the retrieval. Note how the network learns that cups and bowls are similar (row 5).

categories. However ImageNet image categories are of a wide variety while the image data the robot sees is mostly of objects on a tabletop setting. Hence for a more reasonable study we report results on a dataset containing 25 object synsets: atomizer, ball, biscuit, bomb, bottle, bowl, box, chalk, cup, device, hook, marker, pen, plush, rod, shaker, sharpener, sponge, spoons, spray, stapler, swatter, tool, toys and vegetable. Since some of these synsets contain very few images,

100 images from each of these are accumulated to make a 2500 ImageNet household dataset. We further evaluate classification on the UW RGBD dataset [42], and the Caltech-256 dataset. Results of classification accuracy on these dataset can be found in Table 1. We also report the performance of the network trained only on identity data and an auto-encoder trained on all the data.

**Table 1.** Classification accuracy on ImageNet Household, UW RGBD and Caltech-256

|  | Household | UW RGBD | Caltech-256 |
|---|---|---|---|
| Root network with random init | 0.250 | 0.468 | 0.242 |
| Root network trained on robot tasks (**ours**) | 0.354 | 0.693 | 0.317 |
| AlexNet trained on ImageNet | 0.625 | 0.820 | 0.656 |
| Root network trained on identity data | 0.315 | 0.660 | 0.252 |
| Auto-encoder trained on all robot data | 0.296 | 0.657 | 0.280 |

It is noteworthy that our network, finetuned on the ImageNet household 25 class dataset, gives around 35.4 % accuracy which is 10.4 % higher than training from scratch. This means that our network learns some features from the robot task training data that helps it perform better on the ImageNet task. This is quite encouraging since the correlation between robot tasks and semantic classification tasks have been assumed for decades but never been demonstrated. On the UW dataset, using leave one-out methodology, we report an accuracy of 69.3 %, which is about 22.5 % higher than learning from a scratch network. Similarly on the Caltech-256 dataset, our network has a performance of 31.7 % which is 7.5 % higher than learning from a scratch network.

Similar to an unsupervised baseline [2], we train a network using 150K rotation and viewpoint data (identity data). Note that we use more datapoints than our multi task network in the paper. Yet, this performs worse than the network trained with robot tasks. Similarly, an auto-encoder trained on all the robot data perform worse than our network.

### 4.3   Image Retrieval on UW RGBD Dataset

On the RGBD dataset [42] using fc7 features as visual representation, we perform and evaluate image retrieval. Our network's performance on instance level recall@k with k=1 and using cosine distance is 72 % which is higher than imageNet (69 %) and randomNet (6 %). On category level image retrieval ourNet's recall@1 is at 83 % a little lower than imageNet at 85 %. Table 2 shows more recall@k analysis.

### 4.4   Task Ablation Analysis

To understand the contribution of each task to classification performance, we perform ablation analysis where we train our network excluding 1 out of 4 tasks

**Table 2.** Image retrieval with Recall@k metric

|  | Instance level | | | | Category level | | | |
|---|---|---|---|---|---|---|---|---|
|  | k = 1 | k = 5 | k = 10 | k = 20 | k = 1 | k = 5 | k = 10 | k = 20 |
| Random network | 0.062 | 0.219 | 0.331 | 0.475 | 0.150 | 0.466 | 0.652 | 0.800 |
| Our network | 0.720 | 0.831 | 0.875 | 0.909 | 0.833 | 0.918 | 0.946 | 0.966 |
| AlexNet | 0.686 | 0.857 | 0.903 | 0.941 | 0.854 | 0.953 | 0.969 | 0.982 |

(Table 3). On all the three datasets, excluding Grasp data leads to the largest drop of performance which indicates that grasp task may be the most important among our tasks.

**Table 3.** Task ablation analysis on classification tasks

|  | Household | UW RGB-D | Caltech-256 |
|---|---|---|---|
| All robot tasks | 0.354 | 0.693 | 0.317 |
| Except grasp | 0.309 | 0.632 | 0.263 |
| Except push | 0.356 | 0.710 | 0.279 |
| Except poke | 0.342 | 0.684 | 0.289 |
| Except identity | 0.324 | 0.711 | 0.297 |

# 5   Conclusion

We present a method of learning visual representation using only robot interactions with the physical world. By experiencing over 130K physical interaction data points, our deep network is shown to have learnt a meaningful visual representation. We visualize the learned network, perform classification and retrieval tasks to validate our hypothesis. We note that this is just a small step in starting to integrate robotics and vision closely together.

**Acknowledgement.** This work was supported by ONR MURI N000141612007, NSF IIS-1320083 and gift from Google. The authors would like to thank Yahoo! and Nvidia for the compute cluster and GPU donations respectively. The authors would also like to thank Xiaolong Wang for helpful discussions and code.

# References

1. Doersch, C., Gupta, A., Efros, A.A.: Unsupervised visual representation learning by context prediction. In: Proceedings of the IEEE International Conference on Computer Vision, pp. 1422–1430 (2015)
2. Wang, X., Gupta, A.: Unsupervised learning of visual representations using videos. In: Proceedings of the IEEE International Conference on Computer Vision, pp. 2794–2802 (2015)

3. Jayaraman, D., Grauman, K.: Learning image representations tied to ego-motion. In: Proceedings of the IEEE International Conference on Computer Vision, pp. 1413–1421 (2015)
4. Kingma, D.P., Welling, M.: Auto-encoding variational bayes (2013). arXiv preprint arXiv:1312.6114
5. Goodfellow, I., Pouget-Abadie, J., Mirza, M., Xu, B., Warde-Farley, D., Ozair, S., Courville, A., Bengio, Y.: Generative adversarial nets. In: Advances in Neural Information Processing Systems, pp. 2672–2680 (2014)
6. Denton, E.L., Chintala, S., Fergus, R., et al.: Deep generative image models using Laplacian pyramid of adversarial networks. In: Advances in Neural Information Processing Systems, pp. 1486–1494 (2015)
7. Radford, A., Metz, L., Chintala, S.: Unsupervised representation learning with deep convolutional generative adversarial networks (2015). arXiv preprint arXiv:1511.06434
8. Salakhutdinov, R., Hinton, G.E.: Deep Boltzmann machines. In: International Conference on Artificial Intelligence and Statistics, pp. 448–455 (2009)
9. Bengio, Y., Lamblin, P., Popovici, D., Larochelle, H., et al.: Greedy layer-wise training of deep networks. Adv. Neural Inf. Process. Syst. **19**, 153 (2007)
10. Wang, X., Gupta, A.: Generative image modeling using style and structure adversarial networks. In: ECCV (2016)
11. Agrawal, P., Carreira, J., Malik, J.: Learning to see by moving. In: Proceedings of the IEEE International Conference on Computer Vision, pp. 37–45 (2015)
12. Mobahi, H., Collobert, R., Weston, J.: Deep learning from temporal coherence in video. In: Proceedings of the 26th Annual International Conference on Machine Learning, pp. 737–744. ACM (2009)
13. Eigen, D., Puhrsch, C., Fergus, R.: Depth map prediction from a single image using a multi-scale deep network. In: Advances in neural information processing systems, pp. 2366–2374 (2014)
14. Wang, X., Fouhey, D., Gupta, A.: Designing deep networks for surface normal estimation. In: Proceedings of the IEEE Conference on Computer Vision and Pattern Recognition, pp. 539–547 (2015)
15. Walker, J., Gupta, A., Hebert, M.: Dense optical flow prediction from a static image. In: Proceedings of the IEEE International Conference on Computer Vision, pp. 2443–2451 (2015)
16. Held, R., Hein, A.: Movement-produced stimulation in the development of visually guided behavior. J. Comp. Physiol. Psychol. **56**(5), 872 (1963)
17. Bicchi, A., Kumar, V.: Robotic grasping and contact: a review. In: ICRA, pp. 348–353, Citeseer (2000)
18. Bohg, J., Morales, A., Asfour, T., Kragic, D.: Data-driven grasp synthesis a survey. IEEE Trans. Robot. **30**(2), 289–309 (2014)
19. Lenz, I., Lee, H., Saxena, A.: Deep learning for detecting robotic grasps (2013). arXiv preprint arXiv:1301.3592
20. Morales, A., Chinellato, E., Fagg, A.H., Del Pobil, A.P.: Using experience for assessing grasp reliability. In: IJRR
21. Detry, R., Baseski, E., Popovic, M., Touati, Y., Kruger, N., Kroemer, O., Peters, J., Piater, J.: Learning object-specific grasp affordance densities. In: ICDL (2009)
22. Paolini, R., Rodriguez, A., Srinivasa, S., Mason, M.T.: A data-driven statistical framework for post-grasp manipulation. IJRR **33**(4), 600–615 (2014)
23. Pinto, L., Gupta, A.: Supersizing self-supervision: learning to grasp from 50k tries and 700 robot hours (2015). arXiv preprint arXiv:1509.06825

24. Levine, S., Pastor, P., Krizhevsky, A., Quillen, D.: Learning hand-eye coordination for robotic grasping with deep learning and large-scale data collection (2016). arXiv preprint arXiv:1603.02199

25. Balorda, Z.: Reducing uncertainty of objects by robot pushing. In: Proceedings of 1990 IEEE International Conference on Robotics and Automation, pp. 1051–1056. IEEE (1990)

26. Balorda, Z.: Automatic planning of robot pushing operations. In: Proceedings of 1993 IEEE International Conference on Robotics and Automation, pp. 732–737. IEEE (1993)

27. Lynch, K.M., Mason, M.T.: Stable pushing: mechanics, controllability, and planning. Int. J. Robot. Res. **15**(6), 533–556 (1996)

28. Dogar, M., Srinivasa, S.: A framework for push-grasping in clutter. In: Robotics: Science and Systems VII (2011)

29. Yun, X.: Object handling using two arms without grasping. Int. J. Robot. Res. **12**(1), 99–106 (1993)

30. Zhou, J., Paolini, R., Bagnell, J.A., Mason, M.T.: A convex polynomial force-motion model for planar sliding: Identification and application (2016)

31. Park, Y.L., Ryu, S.C., Black, R.J., Chau, K.K., Moslehi, B., Cutkosky, M.R.: Exoskeletal force-sensing end-effectors with embedded optical fiber-bragg-grating sensors. IEEE Trans. Robot. **25**(6), 1319–1331 (2009)

32. Schneider, A., Sturm, J., Stachniss, C., Reisert, M., Burkhardt, H., Burgard, W.: Object identification with tactile sensors using bag-of-features. In: IEEE/RSJ International Conference on Intelligent Robots and Systems, IROS 2009, pp. 243–248. IEEE (2009)

33. Aloimonos, J., Weiss, I., Bandyopadhyay, A.: Active vision. Int. J. Comput. Vis. **1**(4), 333–356 (1988)

34. Wu, Z., Song, S., Khosla, A., Yu, F., Zhang, L., Tang, X., Xiao, J.: 3D shapenets: a deep representation for volumetric shapes. In: Proceedings of the IEEE Conference on Computer Vision and Pattern Recognition, pp. 1912–1920 (2015)

35. Mahler, J., Pokorny, F.T., Hou, B., Roderick, M., Laskey, M., Aubry, M., Kohlhoff, K., Kroeger, T., Kuffner, J., Goldberg, K.: Dex-Net 1.0: a cloud-based network of 3D objects for robust grasp planning using a multi-armed bandit model with correlated rewards

36. Redmon, J., Angelova, A.: Real-time grasp detection using convolutional neural networks (2014). arXiv preprint arXiv:1412.3128

37. Levine, S., Wagener, N., Abbeel, P.: Learning contact-rich manipulation skills with guided policy search (2015). arXiv preprint arXiv:1501.05611

38. Tzeng, E., Devin, C., Hoffman, J., Finn, C., Peng, X., Levine, S., Saenko, K., Darrell, T.: Towards adapting deep visuomotor representations from simulated to real environments (2015). arXiv preprint arXiv:1511.07111

39. Finn, C., Tan, X.Y., Duan, Y., Darrell, T., Levine, S., Abbeel, P.: Deep spatial autoencoders for visuomotor learning. Reconstruction **117**(117), 240 (2015)

40. Krizhevsky, A., Sutskever, I., Hinton, G.E.: Imagenet classification with deep convolutional neural networks. In: NIPS, pp. 1097–1105 (2012)

41. Deng, J., Dong, W., Socher, R., Li, L.J., Li, K., Fei-Fei, L.: Imagenet: a large-scale hierarchical image database. In: CVPR 2009, pp. 248–255. IEEE (2009)

42. Lai, K., Bo, L., Ren, X., Fox, D.: A large-scale hierarchical multi-view RGB-D object dataset. In: 2011 IEEE International Conference on Robotics and Automation (ICRA), pp. 1817–1824. IEEE (2011)

# Image Co-localization by Mimicking a Good Detector's Confidence Score Distribution

Yao Li, Lingqiao Liu, Chunhua Shen$^{(\boxtimes)}$, and Anton van den Hengel

School of Computer Science, The University of Adelaide, Adelaide, Australia
`chunhua.shen@adelaide.edu.au`

**Abstract.** Given a set of images containing objects from the same category, the task of image co-localization is to identify and localize each instance. This paper shows that this problem can be solved by a simple but intriguing idea, that is, a common object detector can be learnt by making its detection confidence scores distributed like those of a strongly supervised detector. More specifically, we observe that given a set of object proposals extracted from an image that contains the object of interest, an accurate strongly supervised object detector should give high scores to only a small minority of proposals, and low scores to most of them. Thus, we devise an entropy-based objective function to enforce the above property when learning the common object detector. Once the detector is learnt, we resort to a segmentation approach to refine the localization. We show that despite its simplicity, our approach outperforms state-of-the-arts.

**Keywords:** Image co-localization · Unsupervised object discovery

## 1 Introduction

There has been an explosion of images available on the Internet in recent years, largely due to the popularity of photo sharing sites like Facebook and Flicker. However, most of these images are either unlabeled or weakly-labeled. One way of accessing these images is finding images depicting the same object, for instance, Google Image Search will return images containing a common object described by the user input keyword. In this paper, we aim to localize the common object in this scenario (without using any other forms of supervision, *e.g.*, manually-labeled negative samples). This task is known as the image co-localization task in literature [4,17,30].

Image co-localization is a particularly challenging task, and thus there exist a limited number of comparable methods [4,17,30]. These methods address this problem from various perspectives. The work in [30] introduces binary latent variables to indicate the presence of the common object and formulates the co-localization via latent variable inference. The work of [4], in contrast, localizes the common object by matching common object parts. Our work differs from

---

First two authors contributed equally.

© Springer International Publishing AG 2016
B. Leibe et al. (Eds.): ECCV 2016, Part II, LNCS 9906, pp. 19–34, 2016.
DOI: 10.1007/978-3-319-46475-6_2

previous approaches in that it directly learns the common object detector by modeling its detection confidence score distribution on each image, and achieves the localization with the learned detector.

The key insight of our method is that although we do not have sufficient supervision to learn a strongly supervised object detector, it is still possible to learn an "artificial" detector by modeling its detection confidence score distribution on object proposals [31,34]. The intuition is inspired from the behaviour of an accurate strongly supervised object detector, that is, when applied to object proposals extracted from an image contains the object of interest, only a small minority of proposals will be given high detection confidence scores while most of them are associated with low scores. Motivated the above observation, in this paper we design a novel Shannon-entropy-based objective function to promote the scarcity of high detection confidence scores within an image while avoiding the trivial solution of producing low scores for all proposals. In other words, by optimizing the proposed objective, our approach will encourage the existence of a few high response proposals in each image as the common object while suppressing responses in the remainder proposals which will be deemed as background.

To generate the final co-localization results, we have also devised a method for improving the bounding box estimate. Inspired by detection-by-segmentation approaches (e.g., [22]), we use the final detection heat map and color information to define a CRF-based segmentation algorithm, the output of which indicates the instances of the common object.

Through an extensive evaluation on several benchmark datasets, including the PASCAL VOC 2007 and 2012 [8], and also some subsets of the ImageNet [6], we demonstrate that our approach outperforms the state-of-the-arts for the image co-localization task.

## 2   Related Work

Image co-localization shares some similarities with image co-segmentation [3,16, 26] in the sense that both problems require a set of images containing objects from a common category as input. Instead of generating a precise segmentation of the related objects in each image, co-localization algorithms [4,17,30] aim to draw a tight bounding box around the object. Image co-localization is also related to works on weakly supervised object localization (WSOL) [1,5,7,24,28, 29,32,33] as both try to localize objects of the same type within an image set, the key difference is WSOL requires manually-labeled negative images whereas co-localization does not.

Tang et al. [30] formulate co-localization as a boolean constrained quadratic program which can be relaxed to a convex problem, which is further accelerated by the Frank-Wolfe Algorithm [17]. Recently, Cho et al. [4] propose a Probabilistic Hough Matching algorithm to match object proposals across images and then dominant objects are localized by selecting proposals based on matching scores. There are also approaches address the problem of co-localization in video [17,21,23]. Notably, Prest et al. [23] select spatio-temporal tubes which are likely to contain the common object, and Joulin *et al.* [17], in contrast, extend [30] by incorporating temporal consistency.

However, in this paper, we tackle the co-localization problem from a new perspective, that is, learning the common object detector by modeling its detection confidence score distribution, and thus get rid of the need of manually-labeled negative images. An advantage of the proposed approach for learning common object detectors is that it provides an explicit mechanism by which to exploit the relationship between localization and detection. The benefits of exploiting this relationship have been identified before in WSOL. For example, in [7], objects are localized by minimizing a Conditional Random Field (CRF) energy function which incorporates class-specific information, and the class-specific information is learned from the localized objects. Cinbis *et al.* [5] propose a multi-fold training procedure for Multiple Instance Learning whereby, at each iteration, positive instances in each fold are localized by a detector trained from other folds in the previous iteration. The approach that we propose here, however, is the first to systematically leverage the idea of jointly performing object detection and localization for co-localizing common objects in images.

## 3   Approach

We give an overview of our image co-localization framework in Fig. 1. The input to our framework is a set of $N$ images $\mathcal{I} = \{I_1, I_2, \ldots, I_N\}$ contains one common object (*e.g.*, aeroplane), and we aim to annotate the location of common object

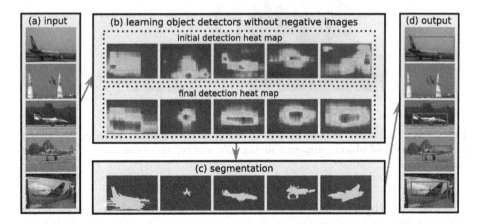

**Fig. 1.** An overview of our image co-localization framework. (a) The input of our system is a set of images contains a common object category (here, aeroplane). (b) The common object detector is learnt by modeling the distribution of detection confidence scores. (c) Detection heat maps generated by the learnt detector are used as the unary potential for graph-cuts segmentation. (d) The output for each image is the smallest rectangle which covers the corresponding segmentation.

instances in each image. Inspired by the behaviour of an accurate strongly supervised object detector (Sect. 3.1), the core of our framework is the procedure of learning the common object detector by modeling its detection confidence score distribution (Sect. 3.2). We further formulate object localization as a segmentation problem (Sect. 3.3), which involves using the detection heat map to define unary potentials of a binary energy function and solving it efficiently by standard graph-cuts.

### 3.1 The Behaviour of an Accurate Strongly Supervised Detector

Object proposals [31,34], which are image regions that are likely to contain objects, have been widely used in recent object detection approaches [10–12]. In this section we are interested in the statistics of proposal detection confidence scores on an image generated by a strongly supervised detector. The observation here motivates our formulation for learning common object detectors in Sect. 3.2.

More specifically, we apply one state-of-the-art strongly supervised object detector Fast R-CNN [10] (trained on PASCAL VOC 2007 trainval set [8]) to a PASCAL VOC 2007 test image which contains the object of interest (Fig. 2(a)). After obtaining the detection confidence scores of the more than 2000 object proposals [31] extracted from this image, we calculate the normalized histogram of detection confidence scores of all proposals (Fig. 2(b)).

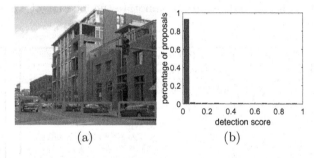

(a)                                    (b)

**Fig. 2.** (a) Predicted objects by Fast R-CNN [10]. (b) Normalized detection confidence score histogram of object proposals in (a). We observe the same statistics for most images.

From Fig. 2(b) it is clear that, although there are multiple instances of the object of interest ("car" in this case), more than 90 % of object proposals have a very low detection confidence score (less the 0.05), which indicates that a dominantly large portion of proposals are likely to cover image regions that do not cover the object of interest tightly. This is understandable as object proposal generation is a pre-processing step in object detection systems, where recall rate much more important than precision (not missing any objects of interest is more important than generating less false positives).

## 3.2   Learning Detectors by Modeling Detection Score Distribution

In the setting of image co-localization, although all we know is that there exists a common object category across images, we still aim to learn the common object detector. This is possible by modeling the distribution of proposals detection confidence scores. More specifically, in our method the common object detector will be learned by enforcing its the distribution of detection confidence scores to mimic that of an accurate strongly supervised detector (Sect. 3.1).

Formally, for each image $I_i \in \mathcal{I}$, we first extract a set of object proposals $\mathcal{B}_i = \{B_{i,1}, B_{i,2}, \ldots, B_{i,M_i}\}$ using EdgeBox [34], which shows good performance in a recent review [14]. Let $\phi(B_{i,j}) \in \mathbb{R}^K$ denote the feature representation of proposal $B_{i,j} \in \mathcal{B}_i$. The particular detection confidence scores that we use are formulated as follows

$$s_{i,j} = f(\mathbf{w}^T \phi(B_{i,j}) + b), \tag{1}$$

where $\mathbf{w} \in \mathbb{R}^K$, $b \in \mathbb{R}^1$ denote weight and bias terms of the detector respectively, and $f(\cdot)$ is the softplus function which has the form $f(x) = \ln(1 + \exp(x))$.

Irrespective of the form of the detector, we can construct the set of detection confidence scores $\mathcal{S}_i = \{s_{i,1}, s_{i,2}, \ldots, s_{i,M_i}\}$ over all the proposals $\mathcal{B}_i$, and normalize them as $p_{i,j} = \frac{s_{i,j}+\epsilon}{\sum_j (s_{i,j}+\epsilon)}$, where the parameter $\epsilon$ is a small constant. If the detector in Eq. (1) is trained with strong supervision, according to the observation in Sect. 3.1, most of its detection confidence scores in $\mathcal{S}_i$ should have near-zero values which means that the score vector $\mathbf{s}_i = [s_{i,1}, s_{i,2}, \cdots, s_{i,M_i}]^T$ and its normalized version $\mathbf{p}_i = [p_{i,1}, p_{i,2}, \cdots, p_{i,M_i}]^T$ should be sparse vectors. Note that when all proposals have zero detection confidence scores, $\mathbf{s}_i$ will be sparse but $\mathbf{p}_i$ will be dense due to the effect of the constant $\epsilon$. Thus, our method will be based on $\mathbf{p}_i$ because enforcing its sparsity will be equivalent to requiring the detector to have few high detection confidence scores and many low (zero) detection confidence scores, in other words, the detection confidence score distribution will mimic that of an accurate strongly supervised detector.

**Objective Function.** To measure the sparsity of the normalized detection confidence score vector $\mathbf{p}_i$, we opt for the Shannon entropy in this work, that is,

$$\mathcal{L}(\mathbf{p}_i) = -\sum_{j=1}^{M_i} p_{i,j} \log p_{i,j}, \tag{2}$$

and the objective for learning the common object detector is formulated as follows:

$$\min_{\mathbf{w},b} \frac{1}{N} \sum_{i=1}^{N} \mathcal{L}(\mathbf{p}_i) + \lambda \|\mathbf{w}\|_2^2, \tag{3}$$

where we use the square of the $L_2$-norm of $\mathbf{w}$ as a regularizer on the weight vector.

So the optimal value of the weight and bias of the detector is given by:

$$\mathbf{w}^*, b^* = \underset{\mathbf{w},b}{\operatorname{argmin}} -\frac{1}{N} \sum_{i=1}^{N} \sum_{j=1}^{M} p_{i,j} \log p_{i,j} + \lambda \|\mathbf{w}\|_2^2. \tag{4}$$

Note that Eq. (4) does not involve a set of manually-labeled negative samples which do not contain the object of interest, but rather describes the desired form of the detection confidence score distribution of object proposals. The learning process also implicitly takes advantage of the chicken-and-egg relationship between object localization and detection: precisely localized object instances are critical for training a good object detector, and objects can be localized more precisely by a well-trained detector.

**Optimization.** As our objective function in Eq. (4) is non-convex, we minimize it using stochastic gradient descent (SGD). Similar to the approach used in training a Convolutional Neural Network [19], we divide all data (*i.e.*, object proposals) into mini-batches. We initialize the weight vector $\mathbf{w}$ from a zero-mean Gaussian distribution, while the bias term $b$ is set to zero initially. During training we divide the learning rate (which is set to 0.1 initially) by 10 after each 10 epochs. We stop learning after 20 epochs when the objective function converges.

**Modification.** After minimizing Eq. (4), when we visualize the proposal with the maximal detection confidence score for each image (Fig. 3), it is interesting to note that the learnt detector may not fire at the common object but some common visual patterns (*e.g.*, common object parts, common object with some context) instead. Also, the discovered common visual patterns can be very different if the initialization of our detector varies (different local minimums). However in this work, as we aim to co-localize the common object, we reformulate Eq. (1) by incorporating the "objectness" score $o_{i,j}$ (outputs of Edgebox) of each proposal $B_{i,j}$ as a weight to favour proposals with high objectness score (which more likely to cover a whole object tightly)

$$s_{i,j} = o_{i,j} f(\mathbf{w}^T \phi(B_{i,j}) + b). \tag{5}$$

We experimentally find that minimizing Eq. (4) using $s_{i,j}$ defined in Eq. (5) gives a stable solution regardless of initialization.

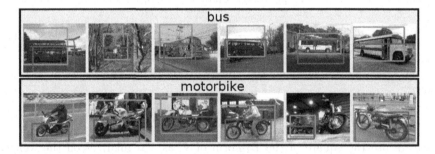

**Fig. 3.** Our detectors fire at different common visual patterns (denoted by red and green bounding boxes) by minimizing Eq. (4) with different random initializations. Although these common visual patterns may not be suitable for the co-localization task, they may be useful for other computer vision tasks, such as discovering common object parts for fine-grained image classification [18]. (Color figure online)

**Localizing the Common Object.** The optimal $\mathbf{w}$ and $b$, inserted into Eq. (1), lead to a mechanism for determining the detection confidence scores for all object proposals. The nature of the co-localization problem means that the maximal score for each image indicates the desired detection. This method is used as a baseline in the Experiments section (Sect. 4.1).

**Discussion.** Theoretically, other sparsity measures could be employed to replace the Shannon entropy. Note that the commonly used $L_1$ norm cannot be applied here because $\|\mathbf{p}_i\|_1 = 1$. One possible way to use $L_1$ norm is to redefine the normalization score $p_{i,j} = \frac{s_{i,j}+\epsilon}{\sqrt{\sum_j (s_{i,j}+\epsilon)^2}}$.

### 3.3  Refining the Bounding Box Estimate

The quality of the detections generated through the above described process depends entirely on the quality of object proposals. To overcome this dependency, and enable better final bounding box estimates to be achieved, we have developed a bounding box refinement process as follows.

Given the optimal $\mathbf{w}^*$ and $b^*$ identified by minimizing Eq. (4), we generate the detection heat map as follows. For each pixel in the image, we add up the weighted detection confidence score $s_{i,j}$ from Eq. (5) for all proposals $B_{i,j}$ that cover this pixel (zero for pixels not covered by any proposals). The values are then normalized to the interval $[0, 1]$. This gives rise to a set of detection heat maps $\mathcal{H} = \{H_1, H_2, \ldots, H_n\}$. Some examples are illustrated in Fig. 4.

**Fig. 4.** Examples of our co-localization process. From top to bottom: input images (predicted boxes in red), detection heat maps, segmentation results. (Color figure online)

Given the set of detection heat maps $\mathcal{H}$, we aim to produce a segmentation of the entire object. This approach is inspired by previous work which casts localization as a segmentation problem (*e.g.*, [22]).

Formally, we formulate the segmentation problem as a standard graph-cut problem. We first extract superpixels [9] to construct the vertex set $\{m\}$ and aim to label each superpixel as foreground ($y_m = 1$) or background ($y_m = 0$). Mathematically, the energy function is given by

$$E(\mathbf{y}) = \sum_m u_m(y_m) + \sum_{(m,n)\in\mathcal{E}} v_{mn}(y_m, y_n), \tag{6}$$

where $u_m$ and $v_{mn}$ are the unary and pairwise potential respectively. $\mathcal{E}$ is the set of edges connecting superpixels[1].

**Unary Potential** $u_m$. Inspired by [20], the unary potential is the novel part of our segmentation framework, which carries information from the detection heat map $H$:

$$u_p(y_m) = -\log A_m(y_m), \tag{7}$$

where $A_m$ is the prior information from the detection heat map $H$:

$$\begin{aligned} A_p(y_m = 1) &= H(m), \\ A_p(y_m = 0) &= 1 - H(m), \end{aligned} \tag{8}$$

where $H(m)$ is the mean of values inside superpixel $m$ on map $H$.

**Pairwise Potential** $v_{mn}$. Our pairwise potential is defined as follows.

$$v_{mn}(y_m, y_n) = [y_m \neq y_n]e^{-\beta||C(m)-C(n)||_2^2}, \tag{9}$$

where $C(m)$ is the color histogram feature. As in [20,25], this potential penalizes superpixels with different colors taking the same label.

As our pairwise potential in Eq. (9) is submodular, the optimal label $\mathbf{y}^*$ can be found efficiently by the graph-cuts [2]. As shown in Fig. 4, the segmentation derived through this approach is accurate. The final bounding box estimate is then calculated as the smallest rectangle which covers the segmentation.

## 4    Experiments

**Datasets.** We evaluate our approach on three datasets, including VOC 2007 and 2012 [8] datasets, six subsets of the ImageNet dataset [6] which have not been used in the ILSVRC [27][2]. For VOC datasets, following previous works in co-localization and weakly supervised object localization [1,4,5,33], we use all images on the *trainval* set discarding images that only contain object instances marked as "difficult" or "truncate".

**Evaluation Metric.** We use two metrics to evaluate our approach. Firstly, for comparison with state-of-the-art approaches, we use the CorLoc metric [7],

---

[1] In our case two superpixels are connected if the distance between their centroids is smaller than the sum of their major axis length.

[2] The six categories are chipmunk, rhino, stoat, racoon, rake and wheelchair. Note that ground-truth bounding box annotations are available for these categories, thus enable quantitative evaluation.

which is defined as the percentage of images that are correctly localized. An image is considered as correctly localized if the Intersection-over-Union (IoU) score between the predicted bounding box and any ground-truth bounding boxes of the object of interest exceeds 50 %.

**Implementation Details.** We use Edgebox [34] to extract object proposals with a maximum of 2000 proposals extracted from each image. We represent each Edgebox proposal as a 4096-dimensional CNN feature from the $fc6$ layer (after ReLU) from the *BVLC Reference CaffeNet* model [15]. We use a fixed value of 1 for $\lambda$ in Eq. (4) which controls the tradeoff between the loss function and regularizer. The value of $\beta$ in Eq. (9) is set to 10.

### 4.1   Ablation Study

**Baselines.** To investigate the impact of the various elements of our approach, we consider the following two baseline methods:

– "obj-sel": the predicted bounding box for an image is simply the proposal with maximum objectness score.
– "obj-seg": for each image, objectness scores of all proposals are treated as detection confidence scores to generate a fake detection heat map, which is then sent to our segmentation model in Sect. 3.3.

The two methods proposed in our work are:

– "our-sel": given the learnt detector (Sect. 3.2), we simply select the object proposal which has the maximum detection confidence score $p_{i,j}$ *i.e.*, $B_i^* = \mathrm{argmax}_{B_{i,j} \in \mathcal{B}_i} s_{i,j}$.
– "our-seg": combination of detector training (Sect. 3.2) and segmentation refinement (Sect. 3.3).

Corloc scores for the above four methods on the VOC 2007 dataset are illustrated in Fig. 5.

As shown in Fig. 5, the simplest baseline "obj-sel" does not work well (19.8 % CorLoc). This is because the objectness measure of Edgebox [34] is heuristically defined based on only edge information, which does not exploit the common object assumption.

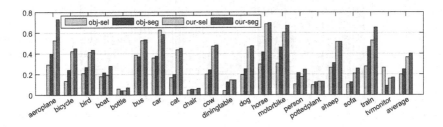

**Fig. 5.** CorLoc scores of our approaches, and baselines, on the VOC 2007 dataset.

However, the "obj-seg" baseline in which we use objectness scores to generate a detection heat map for each image, performs quite well, with CorLoc increasing to 24.7%. Surprisingly, this performance is on the par with one state-of-the-art image co-localization approach [17] (24.7% vs. 24.6%), even though there is no common object assumption. This phenomenon indicates that our segmentation model is quite effective.

Thanks to our common object detector learning procedure in Sect. 3.2, "our-sel" achieves a performance of 36.5%, outperforming "obj-sel" and "obj-seg" by over 16% and 11% respectively. This verifies the effectiveness of this procedure, and particularly that, although we do not have annotated image labels nor bounding boxes, the detector still captures the appearance of the common object, which improves co-localization significantly.

Combing the advantages of the common object detector learning procedure (Sect. 3.2) and segmentation refinement (Sect. 3.3), we observe another 3.5% boost in the case of "our-seg", reaching 40.0% Corloc. Thus we use "our-seg" to compare with state-of-the-art approaches.

**Number of Candidate Proposals.** To evaluate the robustness of our approach under different number of candidate object proposals, we test three settings— 500, 1000 and 2000, which results in 39.2%, 39.6% and 40.0% CorLoc respectively. This indicates that our approach is quite insensitive to the changes in the number of candidate proposals.

### 4.2   Diagnosing the Localization Error

In order to better understand the localization errors, following [5,13], each predicted bounding box predicted by our approach is categorized into the following five cases: (1) correct: IoU score exceeds 50%, (2) g.t. in hypothesis: ground-truth completely inside prediction, (3) hypothesis in g.t.: prediction completely inside ground-truth, (4) no overlap: IoU score equals zero, (5) low overlap: none of the above four cases. In Fig. 6 we show the error modes of our approach across all categories on the VOC 2007 dataset.

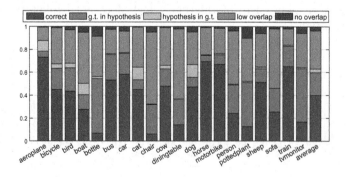

**Fig. 6.** An illustration of error types for our approach on the VOC 2007 dataset.

As shown in Fig. 6, the fraction of "no overlap" cases is quite small (3.5 %) across all categories, which means our approach can localize common objects to some extent in most cases. Comparing "g.t. in hypothesis" to its "hypothesis in g.t.", it is clear that the former appears more frequently (19.9 % *v.s.* 3.1 %), which means our approach tends to localize objects with some context details. In terms of correct localization, the three categories with lowest CorLoc values are *bottle* (6.8 %), *chair* (6.2 %) and *pottedplant* (12.8 %). Objects in these categories are always in very clustered environments with occlusion (*e.g.*, chair is often occluded by table) which makes the task quite challenging.

### 4.3  Comparison to State-of-the-Art Approaches

**Comparison to Image Co-localization Approaches.** We now compare the results of our approach to the state-of-the-art image co-localization approaches of Joulin *et al.* [17] and Cho *et al.* [4] on the VOC 2007 dataset (Table 1). The performance of our approach exceeds that of Joulin *et al.* [17] significantly in most categories, with an improvement of over 15 % in mean CorLoc. The recent approach of Cho *et al.* [4] relies on matching object parts by Hough Transform with the predicted bounding box is selected by a heuristic standout score. Candidate regions are object proposals represented by whitened HOG features. However, we found that this whitening process, whose mean vector and covariance matrix are estimated from the random sampled images from the same dataset (inevitably using images from other categories), is crucial for the performance of their algorithm. Our performance bypasses that of [4] by a reasonable margin of 3.4 %.

**Table 1.** Comparison to image co-localization approaches on the VOC 2007 dataset in terms of CorLoc metric [7].

| VOC | Aero | Bike | Bird | Boat | Bottle | Bus | Car | Cat | Chair | Cow | Table | Dog | Horse | Mbike | Person | Plant | Sheep | Sofa | Train | Tv | Mean |
|---|---|---|---|---|---|---|---|---|---|---|---|---|---|---|---|---|---|---|---|---|---|
| [17] | 32.8 | 17.3 | 20.9 | 18.2 | 4.5 | 26.9 | 32.7 | 41.0 | 5.8 | 29.1 | **34.5** | 31.6 | 26.1 | 40.4 | 17.9 | 11.8 | 25.0 | 27.5 | 35.6 | 12.1 | 24.6 |
| [4] | 50.3 | 42.8 | 30.0 | 18.5 | 4.0 | **62.3** | **64.5** | 42.5 | **8.6** | **49.0** | 12.2 | 44.0 | **64.1** | 57.2 | 15.3 | 9.4 | 30.9 | **34.0** | 61.6 | **31.5** | 36.6 |
| Ours | **73.1** | **45.0** | **43.4** | **27.7** | **6.8** | 53.3 | 58.3 | **45.0** | 6.2 | 48.0 | 14.3 | **47.3** | 69.4 | **66.8** | **24.3** | **12.8** | **51.5** | 25.5 | **65.2** | 16.8 | **40.0** |

To further verify the effectiveness of our approach, we now present an evaluation on the VOC 2012 dataset [8] which has twice the number of images of VOC 2007. Table 2 shows our performance along with that of Cho *et al.* [4] which we evaluated using their publicly available code. It is clear that on average our approach outperforms that of Cho *et al.* [4] by 2 %.

**Table 2.** Comparison to image co-localization approaches on the VOC 2012 dataset in terms of CorLoc metric [7].

| VOC | Aero | Bike | Bird | Boat | Bottle | Bus | Car | Cat | Chair | Cow | Table | Dog | Horse | Mbike | Person | Plant | Sheep | Sofa | Train | Tv | Mean |
|---|---|---|---|---|---|---|---|---|---|---|---|---|---|---|---|---|---|---|---|---|---|
| [4] | 57.0 | 41.2 | 36.0 | 26.9 | 5.0 | **81.1** | **54.6** | **50.9** | **18.2** | 54.0 | **31.2** | 44.9 | 61.8 | 48.0 | 13.0 | 11.7 | 51.4 | **45.3** | 64.6 | **39.2** | 41.8 |
| Ours | **65.7** | **57.8** | **47.9** | **28.9** | **6.0** | 74.9 | 48.4 | 48.4 | 14.6 | **54.4** | 23.9 | **50.2** | **69.9** | **68.4** | **24.0** | **14.2** | **52.7** | 30.9 | **72.4** | 21.6 | **43.8** |

**Comparison to Weakly Supervised Object Localization Approaches.**
We also compare our approach with some state-of-the-art approaches on weakly supervised object localization. Table 3 illustrates the comparison of several recent works and our approach on VOC 2007 dataset. In particular, our performance (40.0 %) is comparable to that of a very recent work [33] (40.2 %) which also uses CNN features and Edgebox proposals. As shown in Table 3, though we do not have any negative images, we still outperforms WSOL approaches on 3 of 20 categories.

**Table 3.** Comparison to weakly supervised object localization approaches on the VOC 2007 dataset in terms of CorLoc metric [7]. Note that these comparators require access to a negative image set, whereas our approach does not.

| VOC | Aero | Bike | Bird | Boat | Bottle | Bus | Car | Cat | Chair | Cow | Table | Dog | Horse | Mbike | Person | Plant | Sheep | Sofa | Train | Tv | Mean |
|---|---|---|---|---|---|---|---|---|---|---|---|---|---|---|---|---|---|---|---|---|---|
| [29] | 42.4 | 46.5 | 18.2 | 8.8 | 2.9 | 40.9 | 73.2 | 44.8 | 5.4 | 30.5 | 19.0 | 34.0 | 48.8 | 65.3 | 8.2 | 9.4 | 16.7 | 32.3 | 54.8 | 5.5 | 30.4 |
| [28] | 67.3 | 54.4 | 34.3 | 17.8 | 1.3 | 46.6 | 60.7 | **68.9** | 2.5 | 32.4 | 16.2 | **58.9** | 51.5 | 64.6 | 18.2 | 3.1 | 20.9 | 34.7 | 63.4 | 5.9 | 36.2 |
| [5] | 56.6 | 58.3 | 28.4 | 20.7 | 6.8 | 54.9 | 69.1 | 20.8 | 9.2 | 50.5 | 10.2 | 29.0 | 58.0 | 64.9 | 36.7 | 18.7 | 56.5 | 13.2 | 54.9 | 59.4 | 38.8 |
| [33] | 37.7 | 58.8 | 39.0 | 4.7 | 4.0 | 48.4 | 70.0 | 63.7 | 9.0 | 54.2 | **33.3** | 37.4 | 61.6 | 57.6 | 30.1 | 31.7 | 32.4 | **52.8** | 49.0 | 27.8 | 40.2 |
| [1] | 66.4 | 59.3 | 42.7 | 20.4 | **21.3** | **63.4** | **74.3** | 59.6 | 21.1 | 58.2 | 14.0 | 38.5 | 49.5 | 60.0 | 19.8 | 39.2 | 41.7 | 30.1 | 50.2 | 44.1 | 43.7 |
| [24] | 79.2 | 56.9 | 46.0 | 12.2 | 15.7 | 58.4 | 71.4 | 48.6 | 7.2 | **69.9** | 16.7 | 47.4 | 44.2 | **75.5** | **41.2** | **39.6** | 47.4 | 32.2 | 49.8 | 18.6 | 43.9 |
| [32] | **80.1** | **63.9** | **51.5** | 14.9 | 21.0 | 55.7 | 74.2 | 43.5 | **26.2** | 53.4 | 16.3 | 56.7 | 58.3 | 69.5 | 14.1 | 38.3 | **58.8** | 47.2 | 49.1 | **60.9** | **48.5** |
| Ours | 73.1 | 45.0 | 43.4 | **27.7** | 6.8 | 53.3 | 58.3 | 45.0 | 6.2 | 48.0 | 14.3 | 47.3 | **69.4** | 66.8 | 24.3 | 12.8 | 51.5 | 25.5 | **65.2** | 16.8 | 40.0 |

We have also conducted an object detection experiment on VOC 2007. Specifically, for each category, we treated predicted bounding boxes of our co-localization algorithm on trainval set as ground-truth annotations and sampled proposals from other categories or have a overlap ratio less than 0.1 against our localized bounding boxes as negative samples. The fc6 feature from the CaffeNet are extracted and hard negative mining is performed to train the detector. We achieve a mAP of 16.7 % on the testset when using a nms threshold of 0.5. Although our performance is lower than some WSOL approachs, it is understandable as we do not use negative data for co-localization. Moreover, we can easily extend our formulation (Eq. 4) to handle negative data and thus perform WSOL.

**Visualization.** In Fig. 7, we provide a set of successful co-localization results along with the corresponding detection heat maps for some categories of the VOC 2007 dataset. It demonstrates that detection heat maps successfully predict the correct location of the common object regardless of changes in scale, appearance and viewpoint. This provides a strong indication that, although trained without annotated positive or negative examples, our approach is able to discriminate the common object from other objects in the scene.

## 4.4   ImageNet Subsets

We note that the CNN model used for extracting features is pre-trained in the ILSVRC [27], whose training set may have some overlapping categories with the VOC datasets. In order to justify our approach is insensitive to the object

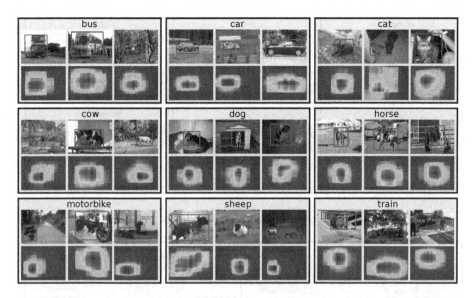

**Fig. 7.** Examples of successful co-localization results for the VOC 2007 dataset. For each category, the top row depicts predicted bounding boxes on the original image, the bottom row shows corresponding detection heat maps.

category, we randomly selected six subsets of the ImageNet [6] which have not been used in the ILSVRC (thus "unseen" by the CNN model) for evaluation.

Table 4 shows our co-localization result along with that of the current state-of-the-art work of Cho *et al.* [4]. Clearly, our approach outperforms [4] by a reasonable margin on all categories except the *rhino* category, whose images tend to have relatively large common instances and less cluttered background. Some successfully co-localization samples are depicted in Fig. 8.

**Table 4.** Comparison to image co-localization approaches on the ImageNet subsets in terms of CorLoc metric [7]. Note that these categories have not been used for pre-training the CNN model, which is used as a feature extractor in this work.

| ImageNet | Chipmunk | Rhino | Stoat | Racoon | Rake | Wheelchair | Mean |
|---|---|---|---|---|---|---|---|
| Cho *et al.* [4] | 26.6 | **81.8** | 44.2 | 30.1 | 8.3 | 35.3 | 37.7 |
| Ours | **44.9** | **81.8** | **67.3** | **41.8** | **14.5** | **39.3** | **48.3** |

We also visualize some failure cases of the two categories our approach performed worst—*rake* and *wheelchair* (Fig. 9). Interestingly, these failure cases are quite understandable. For example, a large portion of images in the *rake* category contains both people and rakes, thus our approach tends to capture this combination as the "common object". A similar phenomenon is also observed in the *wheelchair* category in which people occur along with wheelchairs.

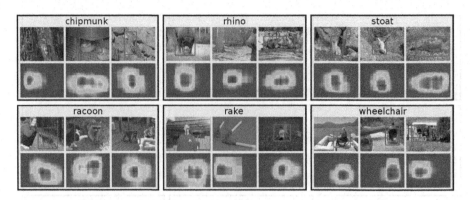

**Fig. 8.** Examples of successful co-localization results for the ImageNet subsets.

**Fig. 9.** Examples of failure cases of *rake* and *wheelchair* (ground truth in megenta and predicted boxes in yellow). (Color figure online)

## 5   Conclusion

We have addressed the image co-localization problem by directly learning a common object detector. The key discovery made in this paper is that this detector can be learned with the objective of making its detection score distribution mimic an accurate strongly supervised object detector. Also, we have illustrated that it is profitable to use a CRF model to refine the co-localization result, which has not been explored in recent works on co-localization.

**Acknowledgements.** This work was in part supported by the Data to Decisions CRC Centre. C. Shen's participation was in part supported by ARC Future Fellowship No. FT120100969.

## References

1. Bilen, H., Pedersoli, M., Tuytelaars, T.: Weakly supervised object detection with convex clustering. In: Proceedings of the IEEE Conference on Computer Vision and Pattern Recognition, pp. 1081–1089 (2015)
2. Boykov, Y., Veksler, O., Zabih, R.: Fast approximate energy minimization via graph cuts. IEEE Trans. Pattern Anal. Mach. Intell. **23**(11), 1222–1239 (2001)

3. Chen, X., Shrivastava, A., Gupta, A.: Enriching visual knowledge bases via object discovery and segmentation. In: Proceedings of the IEEE Conference on Computer Vision and Pattern Recognition, pp. 2035–2042 (2014)
4. Cho, M., Kwak, S., Schmid, C., Ponce, J.: Unsupervised object discovery and localization in the wild: part-based matching with bottom-up region proposals. In: Proceedings of the IEEE Conference on Computer Vision and Pattern Recognition, pp. 1201–1210 (2015)
5. Cinbis, R.G., Verbeek, J.J., Schmid, C.: Multi-fold MIL training for weakly supervised object localization. In: Proceedings of the IEEE Conference on Computer Vision and Pattern Recognition, pp. 2409–2416 (2014)
6. Deng, J., Dong, W., Socher, R., Li, L., Li, K., Li, F.: ImageNet: a large-scale hierarchical image database. In: Proceedings of the IEEE Conference on Computer Vision and Pattern Recognition, pp. 248–255 (2009)
7. Deselaers, T., Alexe, B., Ferrari, V.: Weakly supervised localization and learning with generic knowledge. Int. J. Comput. Vis. $100(3)$, 275–293 (2012)
8. Everingham, M., Eslami, S.M.A., Gool, L.V., Williams, C.K.I., Winn, J.M., Zisserman, A.: The PASCAL visual object classes challenge: a retrospective. Int. J. Comput. Vis. $111(1)$, 98–136 (2015)
9. Felzenszwalb, P.F., Huttenlocher, D.P.: Efficient graph-based image segmentation. Int. J. Comput. Vis. $59(2)$, 167–181 (2004)
10. Girshick, R.: Fast R-CNN. In: Proceedings of the IEEE International Conference on Computer Vision, pp. 1440–1448 (2015)
11. Girshick, R., Donahue, J., Darrell, T., Malik, J.: Region-based convolutional networks for accurate object detection and segmentation. IEEE Trans. Pattern Anal. Mach. Intell. $38(1)$, 142–158 (2016)
12. He, K., Zhang, X., Ren, S., Sun, J.: Spatial pyramid pooling in deep convolutional networks for visual recognition. IEEE Trans. Pattern Anal. Mach. Intell. $37(9)$, 1904–1916 (2015)
13. Hoiem, D., Chodpathumwan, Y., Dai, Q.: Diagnosing error in object detectors. In: Fitzgibbon, A., Lazebnik, S., Perona, P., Sato, Y., Schmid, C. (eds.) ECCV 2012, Part III. LNCS, vol. 7574, pp. 340–353. Springer, Heidelberg (2012)
14. Hosang, J.H., Benenson, R., Dollár, P., Schiele, B.: What makes for effective detection proposals? IEEE Trans. Pattern Anal. Mach. Intell. $38(4)$, 814–830 (2016)
15. Jia, Y., Shelhamer, E., Donahue, J., Karayev, S., Long, J., Girshick, R., Guadarrama, S., Darrell, T.: Caffe: convolutional architecture for fast feature embedding. arXiv preprint arXiv:1408.5093 (2014)
16. Joulin, A., Bach, F.R., Ponce, J.: Discriminative clustering for image cosegmentation. In: Proceedings of the IEEE Conference Computer Vision and Pattern Recognition, pp. 1943–1950 (2010)
17. Joulin, A., Tang, K., Fei-Fei, L.: Efficient image and video co-localization with Frank-Wolfe algorithm. In: Fleet, D., Pajdla, T., Schiele, B., Tuytelaars, T. (eds.) ECCV 2014, Part VI. LNCS, vol. 8694, pp. 253–268. Springer, Heidelberg (2014)
18. Krause, J., Jin, H., Yang, J., Li, F.: Fine-grained recognition without part annotations. In: Proceedings of the IEEE Conference on Computer Vision and Pattern Recognition, pp. 5546–5555 (2015)
19. Krizhevsky, A., Sutskever, I., Hinton, G.E.: ImageNet classification with deep convolutional neural networks. In: Proceedings of the Advances in Neural Information Processing Systems, pp. 1106–1114 (2012)
20. Küttel, D., Ferrari, V.: Figure-ground segmentation by transferring window masks. In: Proceedings of the EEE Conference on Computer Vision and Pattern Recognition, pp. 558–565 (2012)

21. Kwak, S., Cho, M., Ponce, J., Schmid, C., Laptev, I.: Unsupervised object discovery and tracking in video collections. In: Proceedings of the IEEE International Conference on Computer Vision, pp. 3173–3181 (2015)
22. Parkhi, O.M., Vedaldi, A., Jawahar, C.V., Zisserman, A.: The truth about cats and dogs. In: Proceedings of the IEEE International Conference on Computer Vision, pp. 1427–1434 (2011)
23. Prest, A., Leistner, C., Civera, J., Schmid, C., Ferrari, V.: Learning object class detectors from weakly annotated video. In: Proceedings of the IEEE Conference on Computer Vision and Pattern Recognition, pp. 3282–3289 (2012)
24. Ren, W., Huang, K., Tao, D., Tan, T.: Weakly supervised large scale object localization with multiple instance learning and bag splitting. IEEE Trans. Pattern Anal. Mach. Intell. $38(2)$, 405–416 (2016)
25. Rother, C., Kolmogorov, V., Blake, A.: GrabCut: interactive foreground extraction using iterated graph cuts. ACM Trans. Graph. $23(3)$, 309–314 (2004)
26. Rubinstein, M., Joulin, A., Kopf, J., Liu, C.: Unsupervised joint object discovery and segmentation in internet images. In: Proceedings of the IEEE Conference on Computer Vision and Pattern Recognition, pp. 1939–1946 (2013)
27. Russakovsky, O., Deng, J., Su, H., Krause, J., Satheesh, S., Ma, S., Huang, Z., Karpathy, A., Khosla, A., Bernstein, M.S., Berg, A.C., Li, F.: ImageNet large scale visual recognition challenge. Int. J. Comput. Vis. $115(3)$, 211–252 (2015)
28. Shi, Z., Hospedales, T.M., Xiang, T.: Bayesian joint topic modelling for weakly supervised object localisation. In: Proceedings of the IEEE International Conference on Computer Vision, pp. 2984–2991 (2013)
29. Siva, P., Xiang, T.: Weakly supervised object detector learning with model drift detection. In: Proceedings of the IEEE International Conference on Computer Vision, pp. 343–350 (2011)
30. Tang, K., Joulin, A., Li, L., Li, F.: Co-localization in real-world images. In: Proceedings of the IEEE Conference on Computer Vision and Pattern Recognition, pp. 1464–1471 (2014)
31. Uijlings, J.R.R., van de Sande, K.E.A., Gevers, T., Smeulders, A.W.M.: Selective search for object recognition. Int. J. Comput. Vis. $104(2)$, 154–171 (2013)
32. Galleguillos, C., Babenko, B., Rabinovich, A., Belongie, S., Wang, C., Ren, W., Huang, K., Tan, T.: Weakly supervised object localization with latent category learning. In: Fleet, D., Pajdla, T., Schiele, B., Tuytelaars, T. (eds.) ECCV 2014, Part VI. LNCS, vol. 8694, pp. 431–445. Springer, Heidelberg (2014)
33. Wang, X., Zhu, Z., Yao, C., Bai, X.: Relaxed multiple-instance SVM with application to object discovery. In: Proceedings of the IEEE International Conference on Computer Vision, pp. 1224–1232 (2015)
34. Zitnick, C.L., Dollár, P.: Edge boxes: locating object proposals from edges. In: Fleet, D., Pajdla, T., Schiele, B., Tuytelaars, T. (eds.) ECCV 2014, Part V. LNCS, vol. 8693, pp. 391–405. Springer, Heidelberg (2014)

# Facilitating and Exploring Planar Homogeneous Texture for Indoor Scene Understanding

Shahzor Ahmad$^{(\boxtimes)}$ and Loong-Fah Cheong

Department of ECE, National University of Singapore, Singapore, Singapore
shahzor.ahmad@gmail.com, eleclf@nus.edu.sg

**Abstract.** Indoor scenes tend to be abundant with planar homogeneous texture, manifesting as regularly repeating scene elements along a plane. In this work, we propose to exploit such structure to facilitate high-level scene understanding. By robustly fitting a texture projection model to optimal dominant frequency estimates in image patches, we arrive at a projective-invariant method to localize such semantically meaningful regions in multi-planar scenes. The recovered projective parameters also allow an affine-ambiguous rectification in real-world images marred with outliers, room clutter, and photometric severities. Qualitative and quantitative results show our method outperforms existing representative work for both rectification and detection. We then explore the potential of homogeneous texture for two indoor scene understanding tasks. In scenes where vanishing points cannot be reliably detected, or the Manhattan assumption is not satisfied, homogeneous texture detected by the proposed approach provides alternative cues to obtain an indoor scene geometric layout. Second, low-level feature descriptors extracted upon affine rectification of detected texture are found to be not only class-discriminative but also complementary to features without rectification, improving recognition performance on the MIT Indoor67 benchmark.

**Keywords:** Homogeneous texture · Shape from texture · Planar rectification · Invariant detection · Indoor scene understanding · Geometric layout · Scene classification

## 1 Introduction

Man-made environments abound with varied manifestation of planar homogeneous texture, i.e., regularly repeating structure or motifs aligned along planes. Figure 1 depicts such "texture" from various indoor scenes in the MIT Indoor67 dataset [1] — repeating objects defining scene content (stacked laundry machines, bookshelves, wine barrels, theater seating, etc.), architectural and

**Electronic supplementary material** The online version of this chapter (doi:10.1007/978-3-319-46475-6_3) contains supplementary material, which is available to authorized users.

© Springer International Publishing AG 2016
B. Leibe et al. (Eds.): ECCV 2016, Part II, LNCS 9906, pp. 35–51, 2016.
DOI: 10.1007/978-3-319-46475-6_3

**Fig. 1.** Abundantly present and variedly manifested, homogeneous texture in indoor scenes can serve as useful mid-level features for recognition. Rectification of such texture can mitigate in-class variation arising out of perspective projection.

structural elements (brickwork, frameworks, repeating beams and columns), carpets printed or engraved with uniform patterns, tilings, ceiling fixtures, and even shadows (provided the light source is sufficiently far away, and the blocking objects uniformly spaced)! Such ubiquitous textures must have great potential for favorably influencing high-level scene understanding. Yet, the tools currently at our disposal are woefully inadequate to the purpose of detecting and analyzing textured regions "in the wild", key for realizing the aforementioned potential. In this paper, we examine the technical challenges in detecting these textured regions, develop the machinery necessary to overcome these challenges, and then exploit these textured regions for scene understanding.

Even though invariant texture description and recognition have received regular attention for decades in computer vision, these low-level vision tasks have not been actively pursued as a means to solve high-level vision problems. The reasons are manifold. Firstly, it is difficult to secure a precise definition for texture [2], its optimal representation often necessitating a variety of different mechanisms (such as reaction-diffusion model, grey-level co-occurrence, transform methods, etc.) depending on the circumstances. The same texture can also look significantly different at different scales. When we want to detect and analyze textures in the wild (that is, the textured regions have not been segmented or cropped), the task is complicated by another order of magnitude. Figure 2 illustrates, using some MIT Indoor67 images, the **challenges** involved in localizing such patterns. The texture of interest is often interleaved with other scene content, and such outliers can often occupy large spatial extent — e.g. aisles separating seating sections, beams or arches interfering with repeating columns, visible backdrop through a colonnade, or music stands cluttering patterned woodwork on a concert stage. Photometric severities may be present, such as reflections blocking out under-water pool lanes, low image contrast or varying illumination over a given texture due to insufficient lighting in underground cellars. Finally, texture projected to the image plane inevitably exhibits perspective distortion. Existing region extractors [3] only afford affine invariance, detecting low-level features such as blobs and edges, and cannot localize potentially large patches depicting meaningful texture. In this regard, **our first contribution** is the **projective-invariant detection** of homogeneous textured planar patches in real-world images, as well as their **affine rectification**. In Fig. 2, our approach

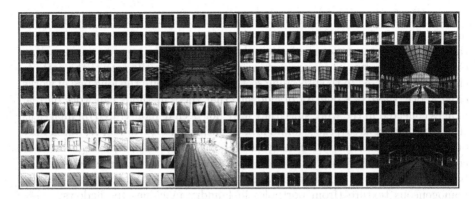

**Fig. 2.** Detection in the wild: the proposed method can detect and rectify meaningful planar homogeneous texture in indoor scenes, despite outliers with large spatial support, photometric severities and significant perspective distortion. Clockwise: `concert hall`, `train station`, `wine cellar`, `swimming pool`.

is seen to successfully overcome the aforementioned challenges, commonplace in real images. We also present **quantitative evaluations** of our method, outperforming existing work on the tasks of detection and rectification.

**Our second contribution** is to show how detected homogeneous texture, and their recovered projective parameters, can be used to obtain **indoor geometric layouts** in multi-planar textured scenes. In doing so, we sidestep the error-prone, ill-posed computation of vanishing points in order to establish room orientation, and eschew the simplistic Manhattan or box layout assumption [4]. This also contrasts with existing work [5] that employs machine learning to localize room faces in space and scale.

As seen in Fig. 1, semantically similar image patches can exhibit significant viewpoint differences. Since gradient based low-level image descriptors used in recognition such as SIFT or HOG are not invariant to projective transforms, this can adversely affect classification performance. **Our third contribution** is to demonstrate that plane projective rectification can potentially benefit a recognition pipeline by mitigating this geometric in-class variation. We report improved classification on the MIT Indoor67 [1] benchmark when densely extracted descriptors from affine-rectified texture are included in the image representation, suggesting the feasibility of employing texture cues to achieve rectification in realistic scenes, which, in turn, expectedly improves recognition performance.

## 2   Related Work

**Textured patch detection and rectification** are often performed together since by rectifying the perspective effect, the repeating patterns or symmetries are more easily detected. This can be done by exploiting recurring instances of low-level features [6–12], leveraging on different classes of symmetries detected in the images [13,14], or by rank minimization of the intensity matrix [15]. However, most of these works require restrictive assumptions, e.g. specific symmetries, that the repeating elements form a lattice, that the symmetry type or the repeating element is given, etc. These are serious qualifications in the face of the real-life challenges discussed in the preceding section. Thus, despite the long line of works cited above, there is a paucity of evidence that these methods can work on real images collected in the wild, since they have not been demonstrated on images as rich and complex as say, those found in the benchmark MIT Indoor67, but mainly on limited textures such as building facades, text, or even just pre-segmented or cropped patterns. Different from these approaches, we have adopted a frequency based approach [16] in this paper, as it is capable of describing any generic homogeneous texture (from portholes in laundry machines to shadows — see Fig. 1), not necessarily composed of texels that can be sensed by a given feature detector (lines, blobs, edges, etc.). While the TILT algorithm of [15] also does not involve feature detection, it is, however, applicable to a very limited class of texture — that which upon rectification gives a low-rank matrix. Homogeneity, on the other hand, is a more general assumption.

**Shape-From-Texture (SFT).** Our work is also related to classical shape-from-texture (SFT) theory — in particular the class of methods that work with planar homogeneous texture [16–18]. However, unlike SFT, our goal is not to recover surface normal, but to perform planar rectification. We therefore re-parameterize the local change in dominant texture frequency [16,19,20] as a function of the plane projective homography instead of the surface slant and tilt. The resulting formulation circumvents the need to define and relate coordinate systems and, more importantly, does not require knowledge of focal length, hence has wider applicability. [21] have previously performed SFT without a calibrated camera, jointly recovering surface normal and focal length, but assume the fronto-parallel appearance of the texture is known a priori. On the other hand, we only make the weak assumption of texture homogeneity. Criminsi and Zisserman [22] also recover vanishing lines from projected homogeneous texture, but their approach involves a computationally expensive search for the direction of maximum variance of a similarity measure, seems to be susceptible to such parameters as the size of image patch to compute the measure over, and has only been demonstrated on cropped texture exhibiting a grid structure.

**Scene Layout.** Automatic detection of dominant rectangular planar structure has been previously presented in limited, simplistic, and non-cluttered man-made indoor [23] or urban [24] environments. [5] have demonstrated the localization of primary indoor room faces (walls, ceiling, floor) by employing sophisticated machine learning, while [25] have detected depth-ordered planes. However, *all* these approaches assume the scene is aligned with a triplet of principal directions defining the coordinate frame (Manhattan layout), and that these directions can be reliably recovered in a scene. On the other hand, our method detects homogeneous texture to recover geometric layout in multi-planar indoor scenes that do not necessarily conform to the above assumptions.

**Indoor Scene Recognition.** Since indoor scenes can be well described by the objects and components they contain, their recognition has often been approached through the detection of class-discriminative, mid-level visual features or parts that preserve semantics and spatial information [1]. Automatic part learning from images labeled only with the scene category has received wide attention [26–29]. However, already an ill-posed problem — since both the appearance models of parts and their instances in given images are unknown — it is exacerbated by the large viewpoint variation inherent in scenes. Instead, we employ a generic hand-crafted texture projection model to perform appearance and projective invariant detection of a wide range of meaningful textured scene regions.

Finally, our work is fundamentally different from that on **invariant texture description or recognition** based on hand-crafted descriptors [30] or by training classifiers for semantic or material properties of texture [31]. Where that line of work is focused on recognizing a wide range of *generic* texture from *cropped* images, we aim to *detect* a *specified* form of texture in indoor scenes, identify and address the challenges therein, and to explore how it helps high-level scene understanding tasks. We also differ from work that aims to learn to predict the presence or absence of generic material attributes in scenes [32].

## 3 Main Framework

### 3.1 Texture Frequency Projection Model

Shape-from-texture relates texture surface coordinates to corresponding camera coordinates in terms of the slant and tilt of the tangent plane at a point [16,33], or in terms of the plane gradients or normal [19,21,34]. Surface coordinates (expressed in camera reference frame) are then projected to the image plane via scaled orthographic or perspective projection, assuming the camera focal length is known. Since we are interested in planar rectification, we can relate the surface and image points via a planar homography. This does not require the focal length, but the downside, as we shall see shortly, is that the rectification is only up to an affine ambiguity. Let us represent the projective transform from the image plane to the textured surface plane as a 3×3 homography $H$, i.e., $\mathbf{x'_s} = H\mathbf{x_i}$ (see Fig. 3). $H$ can be decomposed to separate the contributions of the affine part and the projective part [35]:

$$H = H_A H_P = \begin{pmatrix} a_{11} & a_{12} & a_{13} \\ a_{21} & a_{22} & a_{23} \\ 0 & 0 & 1 \end{pmatrix} \begin{pmatrix} 1 & 0 & 0 \\ 0 & 1 & 0 \\ h_7 & h_8 & 1 \end{pmatrix} \quad (1)$$

That is, the image coordinates $\mathbf{x_i}$ are first transformed by the "purely" projective homography (i.e. what is left in the projective group after removing the affine group) to some intermediate plane coordinates $\mathbf{x_s} = (x_s \ y_s)^T$, followed by the affine transform $H_A$ to obtain the world (fronto-parallel) plane coordinates

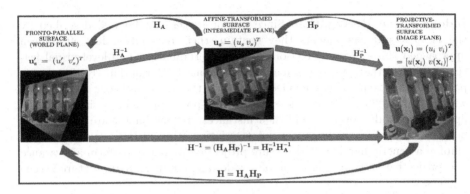

**Fig. 3.** Assorted hats along the bottom clutter this MIT Indoor67 `clothingstore` image (right), yet the *texture* is correctly affine-rectified by the proposed approach (center). For illustration, metric rectification (left) was manually performed, removing any rotation or anisotropic scaling.

$\mathbf{x'_s} = (x'_s \ y'_s)^T$. Note that the last row of $H_P$ is the same as the last row of $H$. We consider the role of $H_A$ first, which provides the transformation:

$$x'_s = a_{11}x_s + a_{12}y_s + a_{13}, \qquad y'_s = a_{21}x_s + a_{22}y_s + a_{23} \tag{2}$$

The transpose of the Jacobian of $H_A$, given as:

$$\mathbf{J_A^T} = \begin{pmatrix} \frac{\partial x'_s}{\partial x_s} & \frac{\partial y'_s}{\partial x_s} \\ \frac{\partial x'_s}{\partial y_s} & \frac{\partial y'_s}{\partial y_s} \end{pmatrix} = \begin{pmatrix} a_{11} & a_{21} \\ a_{12} & a_{22} \end{pmatrix} \tag{3}$$

transforms a world plane spatial frequency $\mathbf{u'_s} = (u'_s \ v'_s)^T$ — which is constant over the entire plane, since we have assumed homogeneity of texture on the surface — into the frequency $\mathbf{u_s} = (u_s \ v_s)^T = \mathbf{J_A^T}\mathbf{u'_s}$ on our intermediate plane (c.f., [16]). Clearly, frequency $\mathbf{u_s}$ on the intermediate plane, albeit different from world plane frequency $\mathbf{u'_s}$, is also constant, i.e., does not vary spatially. In other words, homogeneous texture upon affine transform remains homogeneous, as also observed in [22]. A similar analysis for $H_P$, which transforms image points $\mathbf{x_i} = (x_i \ y_i)^T$ into points $\mathbf{x_s} = (x_s \ y_s)^T$ on our intermediate plane, gives:

$$\mathbf{J_P^T} = \begin{pmatrix} \frac{\partial x_s}{\partial x_i} & \frac{\partial y_s}{\partial x_i} \\ \frac{\partial x_s}{\partial y_i} & \frac{\partial y_s}{\partial y_i} \end{pmatrix} = \frac{1}{(h_7x_i + h_8y_i + 1)^2} \begin{pmatrix} h_8y_i + 1 & -h_7y_i \\ -h_8x_i & h_7x_i + 1 \end{pmatrix} \tag{4}$$

$\mathbf{J_P^T}$ transforms the intermediate plane constant frequency $\mathbf{u_s} = (u_s \ v_s)^T$ to image plane variable frequency $\mathbf{u(x_i)} = (u_i \ v_i)^T = [u(\mathbf{x_i}) \ v(\mathbf{x_i})]^T = \mathbf{J_P^T}\mathbf{u_s}$. While the above analysis is applicable to *any* spatial frequency component, in Sect. 3.2 we shall obtain a robust instantaneous estimate of the *dominant* spatial frequency component in a given image patch depicting real-world texture, which inevitably contains multiple frequency components. Denote this estimate as $\tilde{\mathbf{u}}(\mathbf{x_i}) = (\tilde{u}_i \ \tilde{v}_i)' = [\tilde{u}(\mathbf{x_i}) \ \tilde{v}(\mathbf{x_i})]'$. We then arrive at a method to recover $H_P$ by minimizing the following **re-projection error** $E_{RP}(h_7, h_8, u_s, v_s)$ over the projective parameters $h_7$, $h_8$ and the intermediate plane frequency $u_s$, $v_s$:

$$E_{RP} = \sum_{x_i} \sum_{y_i} \left( \frac{(h_8 y_i + 1) u_s - h_7 y_i v_s}{(h_7 x_i + h_8 y_i + 1)^2} - \tilde{u}_i \right)^2 + \left( \frac{(h_7 x_i + 1) v_s - h_8 x_i u_s}{(h_7 x_i + h_8 y_i + 1)^2} - \tilde{v}_i \right)^2 \quad (5)$$

Optimizing Eq. 5 is a nonlinear least squares problem, and we solve it using the Levenberg-Marquardt algorithm. Observe that our method allows the recovery of $H_P$ and not $H_A$. This is because $\mathbf{J}_A^T$ maps the fronto-parallel plane frequency $\mathbf{u}_s' = (u_s' \ v_s')^T$ to a different but still constant frequency $\mathbf{u_s} = (u_s \ v_s)^T$. As such, a planar rectification only to within an ambiguous affine transform $H_A^{-1}$ of the fronto-parallel plane may be obtained.

### 3.2   Optimal Estimation of Dominant Frequency in Projected Homogeneous Texture

A Gabor filter $h(\mathbf{u}; \mathbf{x})$ with center frequency $\mathbf{u} = (u, v)$ can be convolved with an image $f(\mathbf{x})$ to give its frequency content near $\mathbf{u}$ at point $\mathbf{x} = (x, y)$:

$$A(\mathbf{u}; \mathbf{x}) = |f(\mathbf{x}) * h(\mathbf{u}; \mathbf{x})| \quad (6)$$

Since a given texture may exhibit multiple frequencies, which may also be oriented differently, one must discern the component that can be reliably tracked over the image, so as to be able to use the projection model developed in Sect. 3.1. In this regard, Super and Bovik [16] have previously demonstrated estimation of the *dominant* texture frequency — a distinct peak at any given point, around which most of the energy is concentrated in a narrow band — employing a frequency demodulation model (**DEMOD**) from [20]. Briefly, denote the horizontal and vertical partial derivatives of Gabor filter $h(\mathbf{u}; \mathbf{x})$ by $h_x(\mathbf{u}; \mathbf{x})$ and $h_y(\mathbf{u}; \mathbf{x})$, respectively, and the corresponding amplitude response (Eq. 6) by $B(\mathbf{u}; \mathbf{x})$ and $C(\mathbf{u}; \mathbf{x})$, respectively. Then, an *unsigned* instantaneous estimate $|\tilde{\mathbf{u}}(\mathbf{x})|$ of the *dominant* frequency component may be computed for the filter $h$ that maximizes the response $A(\mathbf{u}; \mathbf{x})$ at each point as:

$$|\tilde{u}(\mathbf{x})| = \frac{B(\mathbf{u}; \mathbf{x})}{2\pi A(\mathbf{u}; \mathbf{x})}, \qquad |\tilde{v}(\mathbf{x})| = \frac{C(\mathbf{u}; \mathbf{x})}{2\pi A(\mathbf{u}; \mathbf{x})} \quad (7)$$

The sign at each pixel is defined by the frequency plane quadrant wherefrom the maximizing Gabor is sampled. Only quadrants I or IV are used, since the Fourier spectrum is symmetric.

**Frequency Drift.** For the MIT Indoor67 `airport_inside` image patch shown in Fig. 4(a), DEMOD [16] provides a rather poor estimate of the dominant frequency, resulting in poor rectification using the model from Sect. 3.1. This is not

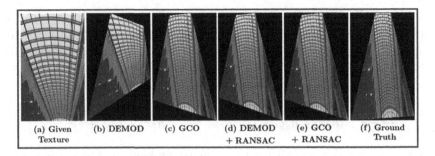

**Fig. 4.** Affine rectification of texture (a) via the model developed in Sect. 3.1, applied to non-optimal frequency estimate by DEMOD [16] is prone to drift (b); optimal frequency estimation via GCO improves performance (c).

surprising given the grim challenges we outlined in Sect. 1. Figure 5 examines the dominant frequency estimates in detail. Since the given texture does not extend to the lower left and lower right regions in the image patch, the maximizing Gabor *drifts* in *both* the center frequency (Fig. 5(a)) and orientation (Fig. 5(c)) in these regions (brighter pixels depict numerically larger values). A 1D plot along the dotted line (Fig. 5(b)) shows the center frequency deviates in these regions from an otherwise increasing pattern. The orientation plot (Fig. 5(d)) reveals that the Gabors pre-dominantly fire strongly at the horizontal bars in the image (18°, 0°, −18° as one moves from left to right). However, in the lower region, it is the vertical bars (−72°, 90°) that define the "dominant" Gabors. Figures 5(e) and (f), respectively, show the resulting horizontal and vertical estimates obtained via Eqs. 7. Corresponding surface plots are depicted in Figs. 5(f) and (h), showing large discontinuities. We propose to resolve drift by enforcing smoothness via the following regularized graph cut problem [36]:

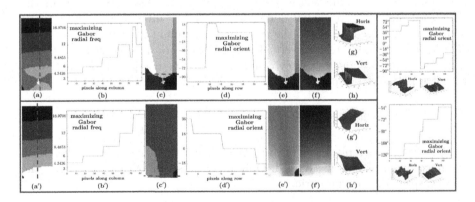

**Fig. 5. TOP:** Closer look at drift in dominant instantaneous frequency estimate via DEMOD [16]. **BOT:** GCO resolves drift in both center radial frequency and orientation. **Right:** GCO also resolves quadrant ambiguity, if any.

$$E(f) = \sum_{p \in \mathcal{P}} D_p(f_p) + \sum_{\{p,q\} \in \mathcal{N}} V_{p,q}(f_p, f_q) \tag{8}$$

where $\mathcal{P}$ is the set of sites $p$ to be labeled (pixels), and $\mathcal{N}$ is the 8-neighbourhood system. Our set of labels $\mathcal{L}$ is the Gabor filter bank. The unary term is defined as $D_p(f_p) = \alpha/A(f_p; p)$, where $A(\mathbf{u}; \mathbf{x})$ is as dictated by Eq. 6, $\alpha = 1$ and $f_p = (\Omega_p, \theta_p) \in \mathcal{L}$ gives the filter with center frequency $\mathbf{u} = (\Omega_p sin\theta_p, \Omega_p cos\theta_p)$ at $\mathbf{x} = p$. The pairwise term $V_{p,q}(f_p, f_q) = V(f_p, f_q)$ forces the center radial frequency $\Omega_p$ and orientation $\theta_p$ to be smooth:

$$V(f_p, f_q) = \beta(\Omega_p - \Omega_q)^2 + \gamma\{(sin\theta_p - sin\theta_q)^2 + (cos\theta_p - cos\theta_q)^2\} \tag{9}$$

Demodulation (Eqs. 7) is then performed *after* solving Eq. 8 for the optimal labeling $f$. We call this scheme Graph Cut Optimization (GCO), solved via $\alpha$-expansion [36]. As seen in Fig. 5(bottom) it yields a smooth, monotonically increasing frequency and orientation profile, consequently providing an improved rectification (Fig. 4(c)) compared to the non-optimal case (Fig. 4(b)).

A workaround to drift is to perform a robust parameter estimation via RANSAC [37]. While this can seemingly handle drift (see Fig. 4(d)), the %outliers is significantly higher compared to when GCO is also used in conjunction with RANSAC (Table 1). Later in Sect. 4.2, we employ the %outliers as a metric to "detect" homogeneous texture, and since GCO renders %outliers a more adequate measure, it is indispensable if we wish to reliably differentiate between non-textured surfaces from textured surfaces perturbed by other scene elements.

**Table 1.** Recovered projective parameters and % outliers for the example texture in Fig. 4(a) via DEMOD, GCO, DEMOD+RANSAC and GCO+RANSAC

|            | DEMOD   | GCO     | DEMOD+RANSAC | GCO+RANSAC | GT      |
|------------|---------|---------|--------------|------------|---------|
| h7         | 0.2940  | −0.0736 | −0.0750      | −0.0733    | 0.0089  |
| h8         | −0.2650 | −0.4923 | −0.5267      | −0.4962    | −0.6035 |
| % outliers | N/A     | N/A     | 10.36 %      | 3.63 %     | N/A     |

**Quadrant Ambiguity.** DEMOD [16] also fails on, e.g., the subway patch in Fig. 6(o), because it can only measure the frequency orientations modulo-$\pi$ (frequency estimates from opposite quadrants have the *same* magnitude). This wrapped orientation may result in sharp discontinuity between neighboring frequency estimates. As explained in Fig. 5(top right), the orientation of the rails increases as one moves from left to right ($36°$, $54°$, $72°$), and wraps around back to $-90°$. We extend our set of labels $\mathcal{L}$ to include filters sampled at orientations from *all* the four quadrants, and rely on the smoothness constraint between neighboring pixels to resolve the quadrant ambiguity. As seen in Fig. 5(lower right), the optimal orientations recovered by GCO are those sampled from quadrant III and not I, thereby ensuring a smoother transition into quadrant IV with respect to both the demodulated horizontal and vertical frequency.

44    S. Ahmad and L.-F. Cheong

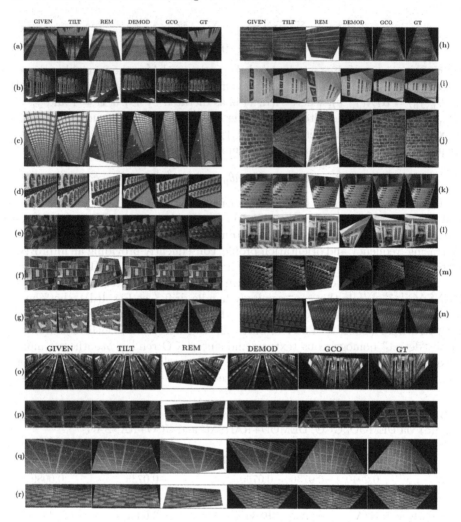

**Fig. 6.** Affine rectification of homogeneous texture: Given, TILT [15], REM [6], DEMOD [16] with our model in Sect. 3.1, Proposed (GCO) and Ground Truth.

## 4   Experiments

### 4.1   Affine Rectification

The proposed affine rectification is evaluated on $N = 30$ patches, cropped from various images in MIT Indoor67, depicting some homogeneous texture under perspective projection. We compare with TILT (Transform-Invariant Low-rank Texture) [15] using publicly available code, with REM (Repetition Maximization) [6] using their command-line tool, and our implementation of DEMOD [16] in conjunction with our model from Sect. 3.1, thereby encompassing techniques based on low-rankness, recurring elements and frequency. Following TILT and REM, a multi-scale approach is also implemented for the proposed GCO scheme (see supple. material). We define the **mean estimation error** as $\sum_{i=1}^{N} \sqrt{(\tilde{h}_{7i} - h_{7i})^2 + (\tilde{h}_{8i} - h_{8i})^2}$, where $\tilde{h}_{7i}$, $\tilde{h}_{8i}$ are the parameters returned by an algorithm, and $h_7$, $h_8$ are the ground truth parameters obtained by manual annotation of vanishing points. The various algorithms fare as follows: TILT: 0.496, DEMOD: 0.386, and GCO: **0.186**. REM does not return the estimated parameters, hence its performance is not quantified. Our proposed GCO has substantially improved upon the pure DEMOD. TILT performs even worse than DEMOD, but of that, more later.

Figure 6 presents some qualitative results. REM — which has only been demonstrated for properly cropped, printed patterns in [6] — seems to only perform in the infrequent cases where it can detect some regular lattice structure (e.g., k, l), but usually either produces a partial rectification (c, n), or fails altogether. TILT, in general, also performs well only on a few cases, where the underlying texture is low-rank (a, b), but breaks down when this assumption is violated — e.g., port-holes (d), or barrels (e), where the gradients are isotropic in all directions. On the other hand, our robustified frequency based scheme (GCO) is seen to handle such texture very well, corroborating our intuition that homogeneity is a more general assumption than low-rankness. TILT and REM also seem to fail on cases exhibiting large perspective distortion — e.g., the textured ceilings in cases (p, q) — and when illumination changes over the texture (m, o, r). On the other hand, use of Gabor filters allows our frequency based scheme to perform remarkably well in these challenging cases. Provided the scale of texture is small (i.e., texture contains higher frequencies) relative to the scale of the surface it covers, a frequency based representation is resilient to slow-varying (low-frequency) photometric changes [16].

## 4.2 Detection in the Wild

Overlapping patches ($80 \times 80$ pixels) are sampled over a multi-scale image pyramid (details in supple. material) to decide if they are textured planar patches or not. GCO and robust parameter estimation via RANSAC (with outlier threshold fixed at 0.01) is performed on each patch individually. Our error measure (Eq. 5) is not affine invariant, so we employ the following heuristic normalization. First, the dynamic range of the optimal radial frequency ($\tilde{\mathbf{u}}_{\mathbf{i}} = \tilde{\mathbf{u}}(\mathbf{x}_i) = \sqrt{\tilde{u_i}^2 + \tilde{v_i}^2}$) of RANSAC inliers is computed as $\mathcal{DR} = \max_{i \in inliers}(\tilde{\mathbf{u}}_{\mathbf{i}}) - \min_{i \in inliers}(\tilde{\mathbf{u}}_{\mathbf{i}})$. A normalized residual error is then computed for all pixels (i.e., inliers and outliers) as $\mathcal{E}(\mathbf{x}_i) = \{\tilde{\mathbf{u}}(\mathbf{x}_i) - \mathbf{J}_{\mathbf{P}}^{\mathbf{T}}(\mathbf{x}_i)\mathbf{u}_{\mathbf{s}}\}/\mathcal{DR}$, followed by re-evaluating %outliers (which serves as the decision score).

A quantitative evaluation is performed on 300 images sampled from the MIT Indoor67 (with at least 3 from each scene category) that have been manually annotated with quadrilaterals indicating the homogeneous textured regions, their plane projective parameters, and their semantic class IDs (left/right wall, ceiling, floor). We define true positives (TP), false positives (FP) and false negatives

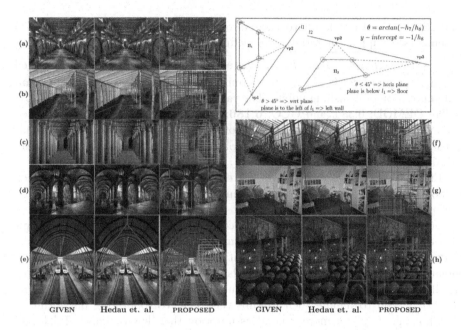

**Fig. 7.** Scene layout estimation by homogeneous texture detections, and associated vanishing lines. Scene with vanishing point clusters (left), box layouts [5] (center), proposed (right). Left wall = red, right wall = yellow, ceiling = blue, floor = green. **Best viewed in color.** (Color figure online)

(FN) as follows.[1] For **precision** [TP/(TP+FP)], TP is the number of candidate patches whose estimated semantic class (see Sect. 4.3) matches with an annotated region, with 50 % intersection-over-detection (i.e., at least 50 % of the candidate's area should cover the annotation), while FP is the number of candidates that fail this criterion. For **recall** [TP/(TP+FN)], TP is the number of annotated regions that are "fired on" by one or more candidates (with the correct semantic class), such that its area beyond a certain threshold is covered (we evaluated at both coverage >= 50 % and >= 80 %), while FN is the number of our annotated regions that fail this criterion. Note that for recall, TP + FN = 1367, which is the total number of annotated regions, similar to object detection [38].

Figure 8 presents precision-recall curves, and recall vs. # proposals curves for our method, as well as for TILT [15] (using ratio of final to initial rank as a decision score). One can observe a considerably superior performance by our method, with an **average precision = 0.53**, compared to 0.15 by TILT. Both methods improve in recall with increasing #proposals, but ours is seen to maintain a larger recall for the same #proposals from the outset. Some qualitative results are presented in Fig. 2 (and many more in supple. material).

---

[1] Since our detector is not "trained" to produce an exact bounding box, we somewhat differ in our definitions of these parameters from object detection [38]. Object detection methodology considers any more than one detection for a given ground truth as FPs, but all such detections are considered TPs in our scenario.

## 4.3  Indoor Scene Geometric Layout Estimation

Hedau et al. [5] have previously demonstrated the estimation of indoor scene geometric layout by using orthogonal vanishing points [39] to establish room orientation, and then using machine learning with rich feature sets [40] to localize room faces (i.e., ceiling, walls, floor) in space and scale. Figure 7 identifies the shortcomings of such an approach, using MIT Indoor67 images. Presence of more than three dominant planar directions (b, f, g), absence of straight lines in a certain direction (c), forked layout (d), and non-Manhattan structure (commonplace in real-world scenes) (e) are scenarios where such a scheme is apt to provide incorrect room orientation, while face localization is also prone to error (a, h) owing to the limitations of a learning based system, such as non-exhaustive training data.

Our detections and the recovered projective parameters provide an alternative scheme to estimate indoor geometric layout in textured scenes (Fig. 7), that requires neither vanishing points nor machine learning. A given detection may be classified as a vertical/horizontal surface depending on the slope of the vanishing line, and as left/right wall or ceiling/floor depending on the position of this line with respect to the patch center (see top right of Fig. 7 for details). The top 150 detections (sorted by % of RANSAC outliers) are then subjected to non-max suppression (NMS) performed *across* semantic classes (i.e., an incoming detection is not admitted if at least 50 % of its area is already occupied by *any* previously admitted and thus higher-ranked patch that is *not* from the same class). Of course, the proposed scheme requires the scene faces to be textured. For e.g., Fig. 7(g) shows a scenario where the non-textured ceiling or walls cannot be correctly assigned a semantic face category.

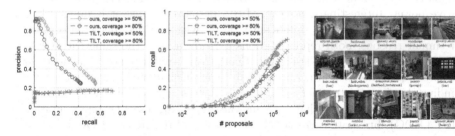

**Fig. 8.** Precision-recall and recall vs. # proposals.

**Fig. 9.** Sample correct classifications.

## 4.4  Indoor Scene Classification

Table 2 quantitatively demonstrates that affine rectification of textured patches detected (with decision threshold fixed at 50 % RANSAC outliers) via the proposed approach can improve scene classification performance. Best practices for dense local feature based classification as suggested in [41] are followed (details in supple. material), using Fisher Encoding with sum pooling [42], Hellinger

**Table 2. L**: MIT Indoor67 classification improvement with fisher encoding of dense descriptors (CENTRIST [44], LBP [45], SIFT [46,47], HOG2 × 2 [48,49]) extracted from affine-rectified texture patches. **R**: State of the art performance — *all* (except SIFT [28]) involve learning-based feature extraction, unlike ours

| Representation (Ours) | % Accuracy | Single Rep.(State of Art) | % Accuracy |
|---|---|---|---|
| LBP_u2(16,2) | 37.10% | OPM [50] | 51.45% |
| LBP_u2_Rect(16,2) | **40.84%** | Mode Seeking [29] | **64.03%** |
| LBP_u2 + LBP_u2_Rect | **41.28%** | SIFT [28] | 60.77% |
| CEN | 46.44% | BoP [28] | 46.10% |
| CEN_Rect | 46.30% | DSFL [51] | 52.24% |
| CEN + CEN_Rect | **50.22%** | DeCAF [51] (deep learn.) | 58.52% |
| | | MOP-CNN [52] (deep learn.) | **68.88%** |
| SIFT | 59.14% | **Combined Rep.(State of Art)** | **% Accuracy** |
| SIFT_Rect | 57.98% | | |
| SIFT + SIFT_Rect | **61.00%** | BoP + SIFT [28] | 63.10% |
| HOG | 57.69% | OMP + SPM [50] | 63.48% |
| HOG_Rect | 56.65% | Mode Seeking + SIFT [29] | 66.87% |
| HOG + HOG_Rect | **60.42%** | ISPR + SIFT [53] | **68.5%** |
| CEN + SIFT + HOG | 61.66% | SIFT + DeCAF [51] (deep learn.) | 70.51% |
| SIFT_Rect + HOG_Rect | 60.88% | DSFL + DeCAF [51] (deep learn.) | **76.23%** |
| CEN + SIFT + HOG + SIFT_Rect + HOG_Rect | **64.54%** | | |

Kernel mapping, one-vs-all linear SVMs [43], and various gradient and thresholding based descriptors. Both regular, as well as rectified representations (wherein dense descriptors are extracted from affine-rectified patches) are computed, and then combined via the score fusion scheme of [26].

In general, our rectification based representations, on their own, perform slightly lower than regular ones since descriptors are extracted only from *detected* textured regions, which, more often than not, span the image only in some spatial regions and at certain scales, and not exhaustively, therein losing some discriminative power. Interestingly, however, LBP, perhaps because it is inherently a *texture* descriptor, performs significantly better with rectified, detected texture. For similar reasons, both representations perform almost the same with CENTRIST — again, a texture descriptor. Finally, our results suggest that features extracted upon planar rectification are also complementary to regular features, a finding that is consistent across all the descriptors experimented with. Figure 9 shows some sample images that were mis-classified using a regular representation (SIFT+HOG), but were correctly classified using (SIFT_Rect +HOG_Rect). A notable property among most of them is the presence of large perspective distortion, as well as high-frequency homogeneous texture.

# 5   Conclusion

This paper has demonstrated a projective-invariant method to detect homogeneous texture, as well as to perform its affine rectification in challenging, real-world indoor scenes, outperforming existing representative work. Homogeneous texture is seen to provide cues for indoor geometric layout estimation in scenes where vanishing points cannot be reliably computed or the Manhattan assumption is violated. Rectified homogeneous texture also facilitates improved indoor scene recognition on the MIT Indoor67 benchmark, demonstrating that plane projective rectification can push performance in a recognition system.

# References

1. Quattoni, A., Torralba, A.: Recognizing indoor scenes. In: CVPR (2009)
2. Picard, R.W.: A society of models for video and image libraries. IBM Syst. J. **35**(3.4), 292–312 (2010)
3. Mikolajczyk, K., Tuytelaars, T., Schmid, C., Zisserman, A., Matas, J., Schaffalitzky, F., Kadir, T., Gool, L.V.: A comparison of affine region detectors. IJCV **65**(1–2), 43–72 (2005)
4. Coughlan, J.M., Yuille, A.L.: Manhattan world: compass direction from a single image by Bayesian inference. In: ICCV (1999)
5. Hedau, V., Hoiem, D., Forsyth, D.: Recovering the spatial layout of cluttered rooms. In: ICCV (2009)
6. Aiger, D., Cohen-Or, D., Mitra, N.J.: Repetition maximization based texture rectification. EUROGRAPHICS **31**(2pt2), 439–448 (2012)
7. Chum, O., Matas, J.: Planar affine rectification from change of scale. In: Kimmel, R., Klette, R., Sugimoto, A. (eds.) ACCV 2010, Part IV. LNCS, vol. 6495, pp. 347–360. Springer, Heidelberg (2011)
8. Leung, T., Malik, J.: Detecting, localizing and grouping repeated scene elements from an image. In: Buxton, B., Cipolla, R. (eds.) Computer Vision — ECCV 1996. LNCS, vol. 1064, pp. 546–555. Springer, Heidelberg (1996)
9. Pritts, J., Chum, O., Matas, J.: Detection, rectification and segmentation of coplanar repeated patterns. In: CVPR (2014)
10. Schaffalitzky, F., Zisserman, A.: Geometric grouping of repeated elements within images. In: BMVC (1998)
11. Wu, C., Frahm, J.-M., Pollefeys, M.: Detecting large repetitive structures with salient boundaries. In: Daniilidis, K., Maragos, P., Paragios, N. (eds.) ECCV 2010, Part II. LNCS, vol. 6312, pp. 142–155. Springer, Heidelberg (2010)
12. Wu, C., Frahm, J.M., Pollefeys, M.: Repetition-based dense single-view reconstruction. In: CVPR (2011)
13. Hong, W., Yang, A.Y., Huang, K., Ma, Y.: On symmetry and multiple-view geometry: Structure, pose, and calibration from a single image. IJCV **60**(3), 241–265 (2004)
14. Tuytelaars, T., Turina, A., Gool, L.V.: Noncombinatorial detection of regular repetitions under perspective skew. TPAMI **25**(4), 418–432 (2003)
15. Zhang, Z., Liang, X., Ganesh, A., Ma, Y.: TILT: transform invariant low-rank textures. In: Kimmel, R., Klette, R., Sugimoto, A. (eds.) ACCV 2010, Part III. LNCS, vol. 6494, pp. 314–328. Springer, Heidelberg (2010)
16. Super, B.J., Bovik, A.C.: Planar surface orientation from texture spatial frequencies. Pattern Recogn. **28**(5), 729–743 (1995)
17. Rosenholtz, R., Malik, J.: Surface orientation from texture: isotropy or homogeneity (or both)? Vis. Res. **37**(16), 2283–2293 (1997)
18. Ribeiro, E., Hancock, E.R.: Estimating the 3D orientation of texture planes using local spectral analysis. Image Vis. Comput. **18**(8), 619–631 (2000)

19. Super, B.J., Bovik, A.C.: Three-dimensional orientation from texture using gabor wavelets. In: Proceedings of the SPIE Visual Communications and Image Processing 1991: Image Processing (1991)
20. Havlicek, J.P., Bovik, A.C., Maragos, P.: Modulation models for image processing and wavelet-based image demodulation. In: Proceedings of the Asilomar Conference on Signals, Systems and Computers (1992)
21. Collins, T., Durou, J., Gurdjos, P., Bartoli, A.: Single-view perspective shape-from-texture with focal length estimation: a piecewise affine approach. In: Proceedings of the 3D Data Processing, Visualization and Transmission (3DPVT) (2010)
22. Criminsi, A., Zisserman, A.: Shape from texture: homogeneity revisited. In: BMVC (2000)
23. Shaw, D., Barnes, N.: Perspective rectangle detection. In: European Conference on Computer Vision Workshop on Applications of Computer Vision (2006)
24. Kosecka, J., Zhang, W.: Extraction, matching and pose recovery based on dominant rectangular structures. In: First IEEE International Workshop on Higher-Level Knowledge in 3D Modeling and Motion Analysis, 2003 (2003)
25. Stella, X.Y., Zhang, H., Malik, J.: Inferring spatial layout from a single image via depth-ordered grouping. In: CVPR Workshop (2008)
26. Pandey, M., Lazebnik, S.: Scene recognition and weakly supervised object localization with deformable part-based models. In: ICCV (2011)
27. Singh, S., Gupta, A., Efros, A.A.: Unsupervised discovery of mid-level discriminative patches. In: Fitzgibbon, A., Lazebnik, S., Perona, P., Sato, Y., Schmid, C. (eds.) ECCV 2012, Part II. LNCS, vol. 7573, pp. 73–86. Springer, Heidelberg (2012)
28. Juneja, M., Vedaldi, A., Jawahar, C.V., Zisserman, A.: Blocks that shout: distinctive parts for scene classification. In: CVPR (2013)
29. Doersch, C., Gupta, A., Efros, A.A.: Mid-level visual element discovery as discriminative mode seeking. In: Proceedings of the Neural Information Processing Systems (2013)
30. Zhang, J., Marszaek, M., Lazebnik, S., Schmid, C.: Local features and kernels for classification of texture and object categories: a comprehensive study. IJCV **73**(2), 213–238 (2007)
31. Cimpoi, M., Maji, S., Kokkinos, I., Mohamed, S., Vedaldi, A.: Describing textures in the wild. In: CVPR (2014)
32. Patterson, G., Xu, C., Su, H., Hays, J.: The SUN attribute database: beyond categories for deeper scene understanding. IJCV **108**(1), 59–81 (2014)
33. Super, B.J., Bovik, A.C.: Shape from texture using local spectral moments. TPAMI **17**(4), 333–343 (1995)
34. Krumm, J., Shafer, S.: Shape from periodic texture using the spectrogram. In: CVPR (1992)
35. Hartley, R.I., Zisserman, A.: Multiple View Geometry in Computer Vision, 2nd edn. Cambridge University Press, Cambridge (2004). ISBN 0521540518
36. Boykov, Y., Veksler, O., Zabih, R.: Fast approximate energy minimization via graph cuts. TPAMI **23**(11), 1222–1239 (2001)
37. Fischler, M.A., Bolles, R.C.: Random sample consensus: a paradigm for model fitting with applications to image analysis and automated cartography. Commun. ACM **24**(6), 381–395 (1981)
38. Everingham, M., Eslami, S.M.A., Gool, L.V., Williams, C.K.I., Winn, J., Zisserman, A.: The PASCAL visual object classes challenge: a retrospective. IJCV **111**(1), 98–136 (2014)

39. Rother, C.: A new approach for vanishing point detection in architectural environments. In: BMVC (2000)
40. Hoiem, D., Efros, A.A., Hebert, M.: Recovering surface layout from an image. IJCV **75**(1), 151–172 (2007)
41. Chatfield, K., Lempitsky, V., Vedaldi, A., Zisserman, A.: The devil is in the details: an evaluation of recent feature encoding methods. In: BMVC (2011)
42. Vedaldi, A., Fulkerson, B.: VLFeat: an open and portable library of computer vision algorithms (2008). http://www.vlfeat.org/
43. Chang, C.C., Lin, C.J.: LIBSVM: a library for support vector machines. ACM TILT **2**, 27:1–27:27 (2011). http://www.csie.ntu.edu.tw/cjlin/libsvm
44. Wu, J., Rehg, J.M.: CENTRIST: a visual descriptor for scene categorization. TPAMI **33**(8), 1489–1501 (2011)
45. Ojala, T., Pietikinen, M., Menp, T.: Multiresolution gray-scale and rotation invariant texture classification with local binary patterns. TPAMI **24**(7), 971–987 (2002)
46. Lowe, D.G.: Distinctive image features from scale-invariant keypoints. IJCV **60**(2), 91–110 (2004)
47. Lazebnik, S., Schmid, C., Ponce, J.: Beyond bags of features: spatial pyramid matching for recognizing natural scene categories. In: CVPR (2006)
48. Dalal, N., Triggs, B.: Histograms of oriented gradients for human detection. In: ICCV (2005)
49. Felzenszwalb, P.F., Girshick, R.B., McAllester, D., Ramanan, D.: Object detection with discriminatively trained part-based models. TPAMI **32**(9), 1627–1645 (2010)
50. Xie, L., Wang, J., Guo, B., Zhang, B., Tian, Q.: Orientational pyramid matching for recognizing indoor scenes. In: CVPR (2014)
51. Zuo, Z., Wang, G., Shuai, B., Zhao, L., Yang, Q., Jiang, X.: Learning discriminative and shareable features for scene classification. In: Fleet, D., Pajdla, T., Schiele, B., Tuytelaars, T. (eds.) ECCV 2014, Part I. LNCS, vol. 8689, pp. 552–568. Springer, Heidelberg (2014)
52. Gong, Y., Wang, L., Guo, R., Lazebnik, S.: Multi-scale orderless pooling of deep convolutional activation features. In: Fleet, D., Pajdla, T., Schiele, B., Tuytelaars, T. (eds.) ECCV 2014, Part VII. LNCS, vol. 8695, pp. 392–407. Springer, Heidelberg (2014)
53. Lin, D., Lu, C., Liao, R., Jia, J.: Learning important spatial pooling regions for scene classification. In: CVPR (2014)

# An Empirical Study and Analysis of Generalized Zero-Shot Learning for Object Recognition in the Wild

Wei-Lun Chao[1]($\boxtimes$), Soravit Changpinyo[1], Boqing Gong[2], and Fei Sha[3]

[1] Department of Computer Science, University of Southern California,
Los Angeles, USA
{weilunc,schangpi}@usc.edu
[2] Center for Research in Computer Vision, University of Central Florida,
Orlando, USA
bgong@crcv.ucf.edu
[3] Department of Computer Science, University of California,
Los Angeles, USA
feisha@cs.ucla.edu

**Abstract.** We investigate the problem of *generalized zero-shot learning* (GZSL). GZSL relaxes the unrealistic assumption in *conventional zero-shot learning* (ZSL) that test data belong only to unseen novel classes. In GZSL, test data might also come from seen classes and the labeling space is the union of both types of classes. We show empirically that a straightforward application of classifiers provided by existing ZSL approaches does not perform well in the setting of GZSL. Motivated by this, we propose a surprisingly simple but effective method to adapt ZSL approaches for GZSL. The main idea is to introduce a calibration factor to calibrate the classifiers for both seen and unseen classes so as to balance two conflicting forces: recognizing data from seen classes and those from unseen ones. We develop a new performance metric called the Area Under Seen-Unseen accuracy Curve to characterize this trade-off. We demonstrate the utility of this metric by analyzing existing ZSL approaches applied to the generalized setting. Extensive empirical studies reveal strengths and weaknesses of those approaches on three well-studied benchmark datasets, including the large-scale ImageNet with more than 20,000 unseen categories. We complement our comparative studies in learning methods by further establishing an upper bound on the performance limit of GZSL. In particular, our idea is to use class-representative visual features as the *idealized* semantic embeddings. We show that there is a large gap between the performance of existing approaches and the performance limit, suggesting that improving the quality of class semantic embeddings is vital to improving ZSL.

---

W.-L. Chao and S. Changpinyo—Equal contribution.

**Electronic supplementary material** The online version of this chapter (doi:10. 1007/978-3-319-46475-6_4) contains supplementary material, which is available to authorized users.

© Springer International Publishing AG 2016
B. Leibe et al. (Eds.): ECCV 2016, Part II, LNCS 9906, pp. 52–68, 2016.
DOI: 10.1007/978-3-319-46475-6_4

# 1   Introduction

The availability of large-scale labeled training images is one of the key factors that contribute to recent successes in visual object recognition and classification. It is well-known, however, that object frequencies in natural images follow long-tailed distributions [1–3]. For example, some animal or plant species are simply rare by nature — it is uncommon to find alpacas wandering around the streets. Furthermore, brand new categories could just emerge with zero or little labeled images; newly defined visual concepts or products are introduced everyday. In this *real-world* setting, it would be desirable for computer vision systems to be able to recognize instances of those rare classes, while demanding minimum human efforts and labeled examples.

Zero-shot learning (ZSL) has long been believed to hold the key to the above problem of recognition in the wild. ZSL differentiates two types of classes: *seen* and *unseen*, where labeled examples are available for seen classes only. Without labeled data, models for unseen classes are learned by relating them to seen ones. This is often achieved by embedding both seen and unseen classes into a common semantic space, such as visual attributes [4–6] or WORD2VEC representations of the class names [7–9]. This common semantic space enables transferring models for the seen classes to those for the unseen ones [10].

The setup for ZSL is that once models for unseen classes are learned, they are judged based on their ability to discriminate among unseen classes, assuming the absence of seen objects during the test phase. Originally proposed in the seminal work of Lampert et al. [4], this setting has almost always been adopted for evaluating ZSL methods [8,10–28].

But, *does this problem setting truly reflect what recognition in the wild entails?* While the ability to learn novel concepts is by all means a trait that any zero-shot learning systems should possess, it is merely one side of the coin. The other important — yet so far under-studied — trait is the ability to *remember* past experiences, i.e., the *seen* classes.

*Why is this trait desirable?* Consider how data are distributed in the real world. The seen classes are often more common than the unseen ones; it is therefore unrealistic to assume that we will never encounter them during the test stage. For models generated by ZSL to be truly useful, they should not only accurately discriminate among either seen *or* unseen classes themselves but also accurately discriminate between the seen *and* unseen ones.

Thus, to understand better how existing ZSL approaches will perform in the real world, we advocate evaluating them in the setting of *generalized zero-shot learning* (GZSL), where test data are from both seen and unseen classes and we need to classify them into the joint labeling space of both types of classes. Previous work in this direction is scarce. See related work for more details.

Our contributions include an extensive empirical study of several existing ZSL approaches in this new setting. We show that a straightforward application of classifiers constructed by those approaches performs poorly. In particular, test data from unseen classes are almost always classified as a class from the seen ones. We propose a surprisingly simple yet very effective method called *calibrated stacking* to address this problem. This method is mindful of the two conflicting forces: recognizing data from seen classes and recognizing data from unseen ones. We introduce a new performance metric called Area Under Seen-Unseen accuracy Curve (AUSUC) that can evaluate ZSL approaches on how well they can trade off between the two. We demonstrate the utility of this metric by evaluating several representative ZSL approaches under this metric on three benchmark datasets, including the full ImageNet Fall 2011 release dataset [29] that contains approximately 21,000 unseen categories.

We complement our comparative studies in learning methods by further establishing an upper bound on the performance limit of ZSL. In particular, our idea is to use class-representative visual features as the *idealized* semantic embeddings to construct ZSL classifiers. We show that there is a large gap between existing approaches and this ideal performance limit, suggesting that improving class semantic embeddings is vital to achieve GZSL.

The rest of the paper is organized as follows. Section 2 reviews relevant literature. We define GZSL formally and shed lights on its difficulty in Sect. 3. In Sect. 4, we propose a method to remedy the observed issues in the previous section and compare it to related approaches. Experimental results, detailed analysis, and discussions are provided in Sects. 5, 6, and 7, respectively.

## 2    Related Work

There has been very little work on generalized zero-shot learning. [8,17,30,31] allow the label space of their classifiers to include seen classes but they only test on the data from the unseen classes. [9] proposes a two-stage approach that first determines whether a test data point is from a seen or unseen class, and then apply the corresponding classifiers. However, their experiments are limited to only 2 or 6 unseen classes. We describe and compare to their methods in Sects. 4.3, 5, and the Supplementary Material. In the domain of action recognition, [32] investigates the generalized setting with only up to 3 seen classes. [33,34] focus on training a zero-shot binary classifier for *each* unseen class (against seen ones) — it is not clear how to distinguish multiple unseen classes from the seen ones. Finally, open set recognition [35–37] considers testing on both types of classes, but treating the unseen ones as a single outlier class.

## 3    Generalized Zero-Shot Learning

In this section, we describe formally the setting of *generalized zero-shot learning*. We then present empirical evidence to illustrate the difficulty of this problem.

### 3.1    Conventional and Generalized Zero-Shot Learning

Suppose we are given the training data $\mathcal{D} = \{(\boldsymbol{x}_n \in \mathbb{R}^D, y_n)\}_{n=1}^N$ with the labels $y_n$ from the label space of *seen* classes $\mathcal{S} = \{1, 2, \cdots, S\}$. Denote by

$\mathcal{U} = \{S + 1, \cdots, S + U\}$ the label space of *unseen* classes. We use $\mathcal{T} = \mathcal{S} \cup \mathcal{U}$ to represent the union of the two sets of classes.

In the (conventional) zero-shot learning (ZSL) setting, the main goal is to classify test data into the *unseen* classes, assuming the absence of the seen classes in the test phase. In other words, each test data point is assumed to come from and will be assigned to one of the labels in $\mathcal{U}$.

Existing research on ZSL has been almost entirely focusing on this setting [4, 8,10–28]. However, in real applications, the assumption of encountering data only from the unseen classes is hardly realistic. The seen classes are often the most common objects we see in the real world. Thus, the objective in the conventional ZSL does not truly reflect how the classifiers will perform recognition in the wild.

Motivated by this shortcoming of the conventional ZSL, we advocate studying the more general setting of *generalized zero-shot learning (GZSL)*, where we no longer limit the possible class memberships of test data — each of them belongs to one of the classes in $\mathcal{T}$.

## 3.2   Classifiers

Without the loss of generality, we assume that for each class $c \in \mathcal{T}$, we have a discriminant scoring function $f_c(\boldsymbol{x})$, from which we would be able to derive the label for $\boldsymbol{x}$. For instance, for an unseen class $u$, the method of synthesized classifiers [28] defines $f_u(\boldsymbol{x}) = \boldsymbol{w}_u^{\mathrm{T}} \boldsymbol{x}$, where $\boldsymbol{w}_u$ is the model parameter vector for the class $u$, constructed from its semantic embedding $\boldsymbol{a}_u$ (such as its attribute vector or the word vector associated with the name of the class). In ConSE [17], $f_u(\boldsymbol{x}) = \cos(s(\boldsymbol{x}), \boldsymbol{a}_u)$, where $s(\boldsymbol{x})$ is the predicted embedding of the data sample $\boldsymbol{x}$. In DAP/IAP [38], $f_u(\boldsymbol{x})$ is a probabilistic model of attribute vectors. We assume that similar discriminant functions for seen classes can be constructed in the same manner given their corresponding semantic embeddings.

How to assess an algorithm for GZSL? We define and differentiate the following performance metrics: $A_{\mathcal{U} \to \mathcal{U}}$ the accuracy of classifying test data from $\mathcal{U}$ into $\mathcal{U}$, $A_{\mathcal{S} \to \mathcal{S}}$ the accuracy of classifying test data from $\mathcal{S}$ into $\mathcal{S}$, and finally $A_{\mathcal{S} \to \mathcal{T}}$ and $A_{\mathcal{U} \to \mathcal{T}}$ the accuracies of classifying test data from either seen or unseen classes into the joint labeling space. Note that $A_{\mathcal{U} \to \mathcal{U}}$ is the standard performance metric used for conventional ZSL and $A_{\mathcal{S} \to \mathcal{S}}$ is the standard metric for multi-class classification. Furthermore, note that we do not report $A_{\mathcal{T} \to \mathcal{T}}$ as simply averaging $A_{\mathcal{S} \to \mathcal{T}}$ and $A_{\mathcal{U} \to \mathcal{S}}$ to compute $A_{\mathcal{T} \to \mathcal{T}}$ might be misleading when the two metrics are not balanced, as shown below.

## 3.3   Generalized ZSL is Hard

To demonstrate the difficulty of GZSL, we report the empirical results of using a simple but intuitive algorithm for GZSL. Given the discriminant functions, we adopt the following classification rule

$$\hat{y} = \arg\max_{c \in \mathcal{T}} \quad f_c(\boldsymbol{x}) \tag{1}$$

which we refer to as *direct stacking*.

We use the rule on "stacking" classifiers from the following zero-shot learning approaches: DAP and IAP [38], ConSE [17], and Synthesized Classifiers (SynC) [28]. We tune the hyper-parameters for each approach based on class-wise cross validation [26,28,33]. We test GZSL on two datasets **AwA** [38] and **CUB** [39] — details about those datasets can be found in Sect. 5.

**Table 1.** Classification accuracies (%) on conventional ZSL ($A_{\mathcal{U}\to\mathcal{U}}$), multi-class classification for seen classes ($A_{\mathcal{S}\to\mathcal{S}}$), and GZSL ($A_{\mathcal{S}\to\mathcal{T}}$ and $A_{\mathcal{U}\to\mathcal{T}}$), on **AwA** and **CUB**. Significant drops are observed from $A_{\mathcal{U}\to\mathcal{U}}$ to $A_{\mathcal{U}\to\mathcal{T}}$.

| Method | AwA | | | | CUB | | | |
|---|---|---|---|---|---|---|---|---|
| | $A_{\mathcal{U}\to\mathcal{U}}$ | $A_{\mathcal{S}\to\mathcal{S}}$ | $A_{\mathcal{U}\to\mathcal{T}}$ | $A_{\mathcal{S}\to\mathcal{T}}$ | $A_{\mathcal{U}\to\mathcal{U}}$ | $A_{\mathcal{S}\to\mathcal{S}}$ | $A_{\mathcal{U}\to\mathcal{T}}$ | $A_{\mathcal{S}\to\mathcal{T}}$ |
| DAP [38] | 51.1 | 78.5 | 2.4 | 77.9 | 38.8 | 56.0 | 4.0 | 55.1 |
| IAP [38] | 56.3 | 77.3 | 1.7 | 76.8 | 36.5 | 69.6 | 1.0 | 69.4 |
| ConSE [17] | 63.7 | 76.9 | 9.5 | 75.9 | 35.8 | 70.5 | 1.8 | 69.9 |
| SynC$^{\text{o-vs-o}}$ [28] | 70.1 | 67.3 | 0.3 | 67.3 | 53.0 | 67.2 | 8.4 | 66.5 |
| SynC$^{\text{struct}}$ [28] | 73.4 | 81.0 | 0.4 | 81.0 | 54.4 | 73.0 | 13.2 | 72.0 |

Table 1 reports experimental results based on the 4 performance metrics we have described previously. Our goal here is *not* to compare between methods. Instead, we examine the impact of relaxing the assumption of *the prior knowledge of* whether data are from seen or unseen classes.

We observe that, in this setting of GZSL, the classification performance for unseen classes ($A_{\mathcal{U}\to\mathcal{T}}$) drops significantly from the performance in conventional ZSL ($A_{\mathcal{U}\to\mathcal{U}}$), while that of seen ones ($A_{\mathcal{S}\to\mathcal{T}}$) remains roughly the same as in the multi-class task ($A_{\mathcal{S}\to\mathcal{S}}$). That is, *nearly all test data from unseen classes are misclassified into the seen classes*. This unusual degradation in performance highlights the challenges of GZSL; as we only see labeled data from seen classes during training, the scoring functions of seen classes tend to dominate those of unseen classes, leading to biased predictions in GZSL and aggressively classifying a new data point into the label space of $\mathcal{S}$ because classifiers for the seen classes do not get trained on "negative" examples from the unseen classes.

## 4   Approach for GZSL

The previous example shows that the classifiers for unseen classes constructed by conventional ZSL methods should not be naively combined with models for seen classes to expand the labeling space required by GZSL.

In what follows, we propose a simple variant to the naive approach of *direct stacking* to curb such a problem. We also develop a metric that measures the performance of GZSL, by acknowledging that there is an inherent trade-off between recognizing seen classes and recognizing unseen classes. This metric, referred to as the Area Under Seen-Unseen accuracy Curve (AUSUC), balances the two conflicting forces. We conclude this section by describing two related approaches: despite their sophistication, they do not perform well empirically.

## 4.1  Calibrated Stacking

Our approach stems from the observation that the scores of the discriminant functions for the seen classes are often greater than the scores for the unseen classes. Thus, intuitively, we would like to reduce the scores for the seen classes. This leads to the following classification rule:

$$\hat{y} = \arg\max_{c \in \mathcal{T}} \quad f_c(\boldsymbol{x}) - \gamma \mathbb{I}[c \in \mathcal{S}], \tag{2}$$

where the indicator $\mathbb{I}[\cdot] \in \{0,1\}$ indicates whether or not $c$ is a seen class and $\gamma$ is a calibration factor. We term this adjustable rule as *calibrated stacking*.

Another way to interpret $\gamma$ is to regard it as the prior likelihood of a data point coming from unseen classes. When $\gamma = 0$, the calibrated stacking rule reverts back to the direct stacking rule, described previously.

It is also instructive to consider the two extreme cases of $\gamma$. When $\gamma \to +\infty$, the classification rule will ignore all seen classes and classify all data points into one of the unseen classes. When there is no new data point coming from seen classes, this classification rule essentially implements what one would do in the setting of conventional ZSL. On the other hand, when $\gamma \to -\infty$, the classification rule only considers the label space of seen classes as in standard multi-way classification. The calibrated stacking rule thus represents a middle ground between aggressively classifying every data point into seen classes and conservatively classifying every data point into unseen classes. Adjusting this hyperparameter thus gives a trade-off, which we exploit to define a new performance metric.

## 4.2  Area Under Seen-Unseen Accuracy Curve (AUSUC)

Varying the calibration factor $\gamma$, we can compute a series of classification accuracies $(A_{\mathcal{U} \to \mathcal{T}}, A_{\mathcal{S} \to \mathcal{T}})$. Figure 1 plots those points for the dataset **AwA** using the classifiers generated by the method in [28] based on class-wise cross validation. We call such a plot the *Seen-Unseen accuracy Curve (SUC)*.

On the curve, $\gamma = 0$ corresponds to direct stacking, denoted by a cross. The curve is similar to many familiar curves for representing conflicting goals, such as the Precision-Recall (PR) curve and the Receiving Operator Characteristic (ROC) curve, with two ends for the extreme cases ($\gamma \to -\infty$ and $\gamma \to +\infty$).

A convenient way to summarize the plot with one number is to use the Area Under SUC (AUSUC)[1]. The higher the area is, the better an algorithm is able to balance $A_{\mathcal{U} \to \mathcal{T}}$ and $A_{\mathcal{S} \to \mathcal{T}}$. In Sects. 5, 6, and the Supplementary Material, we evaluate the performance of existing zero-shot learning methods under this metric, as well as provide further insights and analyses.

---

[1] If a single $\gamma$ is desired, the "F-score" that balances $A_{\mathcal{U} \to \mathcal{T}}$ and $A_{\mathcal{S} \to \mathcal{T}}$ can be used.

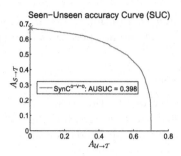

**Fig. 1.** The Seen-Unseen accuracy Curve (SUC) obtained by varying $\gamma$ in the calibrated stacking classification rule Eq. (2). The AUSUC summarizes the curve by computing the area under it. We use the method SynC$^{o\text{-}vs\text{-}o}$ on the **AwA** dataset, and tune hyperparameters as in Table 1. The red cross denotes the accuracies by direct stacking CoW.

An immediate and important use of the metric AUSUC is for model selection. Many ZSL learning methods require tuning hyperparameters — previous work tune them based on the accuracy $A_{\mathcal{U} \to \mathcal{U}}$. The selected model, however, does not necessarily balance optimally between $A_{\mathcal{U} \to \mathcal{T}}$ and $A_{\mathcal{S} \to \mathcal{T}}$. Instead, we advocate using AUSUC for model selection and hyperparamter tuning. Models with higher values of AUSUC are likely to perform in balance for the task of GZSL. For detailed discussions, see the Supplementary Material.

### 4.3   Alternative Approaches

Socher et al. [9] propose a two-stage zero-shot learning approach that first predicts whether an image is of seen or unseen classes and then accordingly applies the corresponding classifiers. The first stage is based on the idea of novelty detection and assigns a high novelty score if it is unlikely for the data point to come from seen classes. They experiment with two novelty detection strategies: Gaussian and LoOP models [40]. We briefly describe and contrast them to our approach below. The details are in the Supplementary Material.

***Novelty Detection.*** The main idea is to assign a novelty score $N(\boldsymbol{x})$ to each sample $\boldsymbol{x}$. With this novelty score, the final prediction rule becomes

$$\hat{y} = \begin{cases} \arg\max_{c \in \mathcal{S}} & f_c(\boldsymbol{x}), \quad \text{if } N(\boldsymbol{x}) \leq -\gamma. \\ \arg\max_{c \in \mathcal{U}} & f_c(\boldsymbol{x}), \quad \text{if } N(\boldsymbol{x}) > -\gamma. \end{cases} \tag{3}$$

where $-\gamma$ is the novelty threshold. The scores above this threshold indicate belonging to unseen classes. To estimate $N(\boldsymbol{x})$, for the Gaussian model, data points in seen classes are first modeled with a Gaussian mixture model. The novelty score of a data point is then its negative log probability value under this mixture model. Alternatively, the novelty score can be estimated using the Local Outlier Probabilities (LoOP) model [40]. The idea there is to compute the distances of $\boldsymbol{x}$ to its nearest seen classes. Such distances are then converted to an outlier probability, interpreted as the likelihood of $\boldsymbol{x}$ being from unseen classes.

**Relation to Calibrated Stacking.** If we define a new form of novelty score $N(\boldsymbol{x}) = \max_{u \in \mathcal{U}} f_u(\boldsymbol{x}) - \max_{s \in \mathcal{S}} f_s(\boldsymbol{x})$ in Eq. (3), we recover the prediction rule in Eq. (2). However, this relation holds only if we are interested in predicting one label $\hat{y}$. When we are interested in predicting a set of labels (for example, hoping that the correct labels are in the top $K$ predicted labels, (i.e., the Flat hit@K metric, cf. Sect. 5), the two prediction rules will give different results.

# 5 Experimental Results

## 5.1 Setup

**Datasets.** We mainly use three benchmark datasets: the **Animals with Attributes (AwA)** [38], **CUB-200-2011 Birds (CUB)** [39], and **ImageNet** (with full 21,841 classes) [41]. Table 2 summarizes their key characteristics.

**Table 2.** Key characteristics of the studied datasets.

| Dataset name | Number of seen classes | Number of unseen classes | Total number of images |
|---|---|---|---|
| AwA[†] | 40 | 10 | $30,475$ |
| CUB[‡] | 150 | 50 | $11,788$ |
| ImageNet[§] | 1000 | 20,842 | $14,197,122$ |

[†]: following the split in [38].
[‡]: following [28] to report the average over 4 random splits.
[§]: seen and unseen classes from ImageNet ILSVRC 2012 1K [41] and Fall 2011 release [29], respectively.

**Semantic Spaces.** For the classes in **AwA** and **CUB**, we use 85-dimensional and 312-dimensional binary or continuous-valued attributes, respectively [38,39]. For **ImageNet**, we use 500-dimensional word vectors (WORD2VEC) trained by the skip-gram model [7,42] provided by Changpinyo et al. [28]. We ignore classes without word vectors, resulting in 20,345 (out of 20,842) unseen classes. We follow [28] to normalize all but binary embeddings to have unit $\ell_2$ norms.

**Visual Features.** We use the GoogLeNet deep features [43] pre-trained on ILSVRC 2012 1K [41] for all datasets (all extracted with the Caffe package [44]). Extracted features come from the 1,024-dimensional activations of the pooling units, as in [20,28].

**Zero-Shot Learning Methods.** We examine several representative conventional zero-shot learning approaches, described briefly below. Direct Attribute Prediction (DAP) and Indirect Attribute Prediction (IAP) [38] are probabilistic models that perform attribute predictions as an intermediate step and then use them to compute MAP predictions of unseen class labels. ConSE [17] makes use of pre-trained classifiers for seen classes and their probabilitic outputs to infer the semantic embeddings of each test example, and then classifies it into the unseen class with the most similar semantic embedding. SynC [28] is a recently proposed multi-task learning approach that synthesizes a novel classifier based on semantic embeddings and base classifiers that are learned with labeled data from the seen classes. Two versions of this approach — SynC$^{\text{o-v-o}}$ and SynC$^{\text{struct}}$ — use one-versus-other and Crammer-Singer style [45] loss functions to train classifiers. We use binary attributes for DAP and IAP, and continuous attributes and WORD2VEC for ConSE and SynC, following [17,28,38].

***Generalized Zero-Shot Learning Tasks.*** There are no previously established benchmark tasks for GZSL. We thus define a set of tasks that reflects more closely how data are distributed in real-world applications.

We construct the GZSL tasks by composing test data as a combination of images from both seen and unseen classes. We follow existing splits of the datasets for the conventional ZSL to separate seen and unseen classes. Moreover, for the datasets **AwA** and **CUB**, we hold out 20 % of the data points from the seen classes (previously, all of them are used for training in the conventional zero-shot setting) and merge them with the data from the unseen classes to form the test set; for **ImageNet**, we combine its validation set (having the same classes as its training set) and the 21 K classes that are not in the ILSVRC 2012 1 K dataset.

***Evaluation Metrics.*** While we will primarily report the performance of ZSL approaches under the metric Area Under Seen-Unseen accuracy Curve (AUSUC) developed in Sect. 4.1, we explain how its two accuracy components $A_{\mathcal{S} \to \mathcal{T}}$ and $A_{\mathcal{U} \to \mathcal{T}}$ are computed below.

For **AwA** and **CUB**, seen and unseen accuracies correspond to (normalized-by-class-size) multi-way classification accuracy, where the seen accuracy is computed on the 20 % images from the seen classes and the unseen accuracy is computed on images from unseen classes.

For **ImageNet**, seen and unseen accuracies correspond to Flat hit@K (F@K), defined as the percentage of test images for which the model returns the true label in its top K predictions. Note that, F@1 is the unnormalized multi-way classification accuracy. Moreover, following the procedure in [8,17,28], we evaluate on three scenarios of increasing difficulty: (1) *2-hop* contains 1,509 unseen classes that are within two tree hops of the 1 K seen classes according to the ImageNet label hierarchy[2]. (2) *3-hop* contains 7,678 unseen classes that are within three tree hops of the seen classes. (3) *All* contains all 20,345 unseen classes.

## 5.2   Which Method to Use to Perform GZSL?

Table 3 provides an experimental comparison between several methods utilizing seen and unseen classifiers for generalized ZSL, with hyperparameters cross-validated to maximize AUSUC. Empirical results on additional datasets and ZSL methods are in the Supplementary Material.

---

[2] http://www.image-net.org/api/xml/structure_released.xml.

**Table 3.** Performances measured in AUSUC of several methods for Generalized Zero-Shot Learning on **AwA** and **CUB**. The higher the better (the upper bound is 1).

| Method | AwA | | | CUB | | |
|---|---|---|---|---|---|---|
| | Novelty detection [9] | | Calibrated stacking | Novelty detection [9] | | Calibrated stacking |
| | Gaussian | LoOP | | Gaussian | LoOP | |
| DAP | 0.302 | 0.272 | 0.366 | 0.122 | 0.137 | 0.194 |
| IAP | 0.307 | 0.287 | 0.394 | 0.129 | 0.145 | 0.199 |
| ConSE | 0.342 | 0.300 | 0.428 | 0.130 | 0.136 | 0.212 |
| SynC$^{\text{o-vs-o}}$ | 0.420 | 0.378 | 0.568 | 0.191 | 0.209 | 0.336 |
| SynC$^{\text{struct}}$ | 0.424 | 0.373 | 0.583 | 0.199 | 0.224 | 0.356 |

The results show that, irrespective of which ZSL methods are used to generate models for seen and unseen classes, our method of *calibrated stacking* for generalized ZSL outperforms other methods. In particular, despite their probabilistic justification, the two novelty detection methods do not perform well. We believe that this is because most existing zero-shot learning methods are discriminative and optimized to take full advantage of class labels and semantic information. In contrast, either Gaussian or LoOP approach models all the seen classes as a whole, possibly at the cost of modeling inter-class differences.

### 5.3 Which Zero-Shot Learning Approach is More Robust to GZSL?

Figure 2 contrasts in detail several ZSL approaches when tested on the task of GZSL, using the method of *calibrated stacking*. Clearly, the SynC method dominates all other methods in the whole ranges. The crosses on the plots mark the results of *direct stacking* (Sect. 3).

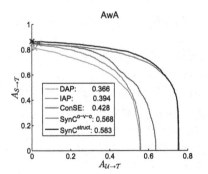 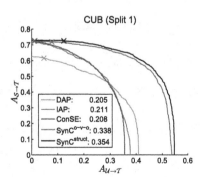

**Fig. 2.** Comparison between several ZSL approaches on the task of GZSL for **AwA** and **CUB**.

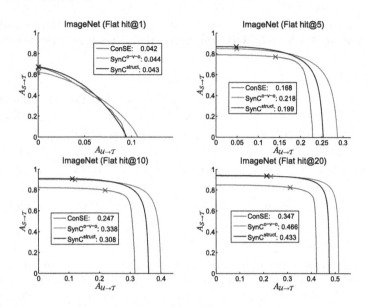

**Fig. 3.** Comparison between ConSE and SynC of their performances on the task of GZSL for **ImageNet** where the unseen classes are within 2 tree-hops from seen classes.

Figure 3 contrasts in detail ConSE to SynC, the two known methods for large-scale ZSL. When the accuracies measured in Flat hit@1 (i.e., multi-class classification accuracy), neither method dominates the other, suggesting the different trade-offs by the two methods. However, when we measure hit rates in the top $K > 1$, SynC dominates ConSE. Table 4 gives summarized comparison in AUSUC between the two methods on the **ImageNet** dataset. We observe that

**Table 4.** Performances measured in AUSUC by different zero-shot learning approaches on GZSL on **ImageNet**, using our method of *calibrated stacking*.

| Unseen classes | Method | Flat hit@K | | | |
|---|---|---|---|---|---|
| | | 1 | 5 | 10 | 20 |
| *2-hop* | ConSE | 0.042 | 0.168 | 0.247 | 0.347 |
| | $SynC^{o\text{-}vs\text{-}o}$ | 0.044 | 0.218 | 0.338 | 0.466 |
| | $SynC^{struct}$ | 0.043 | 0.199 | 0.308 | 0.433 |
| *3-hop* | ConSE | 0.013 | 0.057 | 0.090 | 0.135 |
| | $SynC^{o\text{-}vs\text{-}o}$ | 0.012 | 0.070 | 0.119 | 0.186 |
| | $SynC^{struct}$ | 0.013 | 0.066 | 0.110 | 0.170 |
| *All* | ConSE | 0.007 | 0.030 | 0.048 | 0.073 |
| | $SynC^{o\text{-}vs\text{-}o}$ | 0.006 | 0.034 | 0.059 | 0.097 |
| | $SynC^{struct}$ | 0.007 | 0.033 | 0.056 | 0.090 |

SynC in general outperforms ConSE except when Flat hit@1 is used, in which case the two methods' performances are nearly indistinguishable. Additional plots can be found in the Supplementary Material.

# 6  Analysis on (Generalized) Zero-Shot Learning

Zero-shot learning, either in conventional setting or generalized setting, is a challenging problem as there is no labeled data for the unseen classes. The performance of ZSL methods depends on at least two factors: (1) how seen and unseen classes are related; (2) how effectively the relation can be exploited by learning algorithms to generate models for the unseen classes. For generalized zero-shot learning, the performance further depends on how classifiers for seen and unseen classes are combined to classify new data into the joint label space.

Despite extensive study in ZSL, several questions remain understudied. For example, given a dataset and a split of seen and unseen classes, what is the best possible performance of any ZSL method? How far are we from there? What is the most crucial component we can improve in order to reduce the gap between the state-of-the-art and the ideal performances?

In this section, we empirically analyze ZSL methods in detail and shed light on some of those questions.

***Setup.*** As ZSL methods do not use labeled data from unseen classes for training classifiers, one reasonable estimate of their best possible performance is to measure the performance on a multi-class classification task where annotated data on the unseen classes are provided.

Concretely, to construct the multi-class classification task, on **AwA** and **CUB**, we randomly select 80 % of the data along with their labels from all classes (seen and unseen) to train classifiers. The remaining 20 % will be used to assess both the multi-class classifiers and the classifiers from ZSL. Note that, for ZSL, only the seen classes from the 80 % are used for training — the portion belonging to the unseen classes are not used.

On **ImageNet**, to reduce the computational cost (of constructing multi-class classifiers which would involve 20,345-way classification), we subsample another 1,000 unseen classes from its original 20,345 unseen classes. We call this new dataset **ImageNet-2K** (including the 1 K seen classes from **ImageNet**). The subsampling procedure is described in the Supplementary Material and the main goal is to keep the proportions of difficult unseen classes unchanged. Out of those 1,000 unseen classes, we randomly select 50 samples per class and reserve them for testing and use the remaining examples (along with their labels) to train 2000-way classifiers.

For ZSL methods, we use either attribute vectors or word vectors (WORD2VEC) as semantic embeddings. Since $SynC^{o\text{-}vs\text{-}o}$ [28] performs well on a range of datasets and settings, we focus on this method. For multi-class classification, we train one-versus-others SVMs. Once we obtain the classifiers for both seen and unseen classes, we use the *calibrated stacking* decision rule to

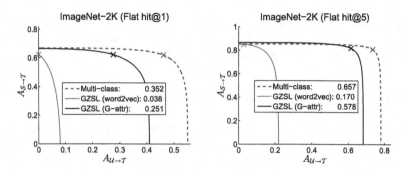

**Fig. 4.** We contrast the performances of GZSL to multi-class classifiers trained with labeled data from both seen and unseen classes on the dataset **ImageNet-2K**. GZSL uses WORD2VECTOR (in red color) and the idealized visual features (G-attr) as semantic embeddings (in black color). (Color figure online)

combine (as in generalized ZSL) and vary the calibration factor $\gamma$ to obtain the Seen-Unseen accuracy Curve, exemplified in Fig. 1.

**How Far Are We From the Ideal Performance?** Figure 4 displays the Seen-Unseen accuracy Curves for **ImageNet-2K** — additional plots on **ImageNet-2K** and similar ones on **AwA** and **CUB** are in the Supplementary Material. Clearly, there is a large gap between the performances of GZSL using the default WORD2VEC semantic embeddings and the ideal performance indicated by the multi-class classifiers. Note that the cross marks indicate the results of *direct stacking*. The multi-class classifiers not only dominate GZSL in the whole ranges (thus, with very high AUSUCs) but also are capable of learning classifiers that are well-balanced (such that *direct stacking* works well).

**How Much Can Idealized Semantic Embeddings Help?** We hypothesize that a large portion of the gap between GZSL and multi-class classification can be attributed to the weak semantic embeddings used by the GZSL approach.

We investigate this by using a form of *idealized* semantic embeddings. As the success of zero-shot learning relies heavily on how accurate semantic embeddings represent visual similarity among classes, we examine the idea of *visual features as semantic embeddings*. Concretely, for each class, semantic embeddings can be obtained by averaging visual features of images belonging to that class. We call them **G-attr** as we derive the visual features from GoogLeNet. Note that, for unseen classes, we only use the reserved training examples to derive the semantic embeddings; we do not use their labels to train classifiers.

Figure 4 shows the performance of GZSL using **G-attr** — the gaps to the multi-class classification performances are significantly reduced from those made by GZSL using WORD2VEC. In some cases (see the Supplementary Material for more comprehensive experiments), GZSL can almost match the performance of multi-class classifiers without using any labels from the unseen classes!

**Table 5.** Comparison of performances measured in AUSUC between GZSL (using WORD2VEC and **G-attr**) and multi-class classification on **ImageNet-2K**. Few-shot results are averaged over 100 rounds. GZSL with **G-attr** improves upon GZSL with WORD2VEC significantly and quickly approaches multi-class classification performance.

| Method | | Flat hit@K | | | |
|---|---|---|---|---|---|
| | | 1 | 5 | 10 | 20 |
| GZSL | WORD2VEC | 0.04 | 0.17 | 0.27 | 0.38 |
| | G-attr from 1 image | $0.08 \pm 0.003$ | $0.25 \pm 0.005$ | $0.33 \pm 0.005$ | $0.42 \pm 0.005$ |
| | G-attr from 10 images | $0.20 \pm 0.002$ | $0.50 \pm 0.002$ | $0.62 \pm 0.002$ | $0.72 \pm 0.002$ |
| | G-attr from 100 images | $0.25 \pm 0.001$ | $0.57 \pm 0.001$ | $0.69 \pm 0.001$ | $0.78 \pm 0.001$ |
| | G-attr from all images | 0.25 | 0.58 | 0.69 | 0.79 |
| Multi-class classification | | 0.35 | 0.66 | 0.75 | 0.82 |

***How Much Labeled Data Do We Need to Improve GZSL's Performance?*** Imagine we are given a budget to label data from unseen classes, how much those labels can improve GZSL's performance?

Table 5 contrasts the AUSUCs obtained by GZSL to those from mutli-class classification on **ImageNet-2K**, where GZSL is allowed to use visual features as embeddings — those features can be computed from a few labeled images from the unseen classes, a scenario we can refer to as "few-shot" learning. Using about (randomly sampled) 100 labeled images per class, GZSL can quickly approach the performance of multi-class classifiers, which use about 1,000 labeled images per class. Moreover, those G-attr visual features as semantic embeddings improve upon WORD2VEC more significantly under Flat hit@K = 1 than when K > 1.

We further examine on the whole **ImageNet** with 20,345 unseen classes in Table 6, where we keep 80 % of the unseen classes' examples to derive **G-attr** and test on the rest, and observe similar trends. Specifically on Flat hit@1, the performance of G-attr from merely 1 image is boosted **threefold** of that

**Table 6.** Comparison of performances measured in AUSUC between GZSL with WORD2VEC and GZSL with **G-attr** on the full **ImageNet** with 21,000 unseen classes. Few-shot results are averaged over 20 rounds.

| Method | Flat hit@K | | | |
|---|---|---|---|---|
| | 1 | 5 | 10 | 20 |
| WORD2VEC | 0.006 | 0.034 | 0.059 | 0.096 |
| G-attr from 1 image | $0.018 \pm 0.0002$ | $0.071 \pm 0.0007$ | $0.106 \pm 0.0009$ | $0.150 \pm 0.0011$ |
| G-attr from 10 images | $0.050 \pm 0.0002$ | $0.184 \pm 0.0003$ | $0.263 \pm 0.0004$ | $0.352 \pm 0.0005$ |
| G-attr from 100 images | $0.065 \pm 0.0001$ | $0.230 \pm 0.0002$ | $0.322 \pm 0.0002$ | $0.421 \pm 0.0002$ |
| G-attr from all images | 0.067 | 0.236 | 0.329 | 0.429 |

by WORD2VEC, while G-attr from 100 images achieves over tenfold. See the Supplementary Material for details, including results on **AwA** and **CUB**.

# 7   Discussion

Zero-shot learning (ZSL) methods have been studied in the unrealistic setting where the test data are assumed to come from unseen classes only. In contrast, we advocate studying the problem of Generalized ZSL where test data's class memberships are unconstrained. Naively using the classifiers constructed by ZSL approaches, however, does not perform well in this generalized setting. Instead, we propose a simple but effective method that can be used to balance two conflicting forces: recognizing data from seen classes versus unseen ones. We develop a performance metric to characterize the tradeoff and examine the utility of this metric in evaluating various ZSL approaches. Our analysis also leads us to investigate the best possible performance of any ZSL methods. We show that there is a large gap between existing approaches and the best possible. Moreover, we show that this gap can be reduced significantly if idealized semantic embeddings are used. Thus, an important direction for future research is to improve the quality of semantic embeddings of seen and unseen classes.

**Acknowledgements.** B.G. is partially supported by NSF IIS-1566511. Others are partially supported by USC Graduate Fellowship, NSF IIS-1065243, 1451412, 1513966, 1208500, CCF-1139148, a Google Research Award, an Alfred. P. Sloan Research Fellowship and ARO# W911NF-12-1-0241 and W911NF-15-1-0484.

# References

1. Sudderth, E.B., Jordan, M.I.: Shared segmentation of natural scenes using dependent Pitman-Yor processes. In: NIPS (2008)
2. Salakhutdinov, R., Torralba, A., Tenenbaum, J.: Learning to share visual appearance for multiclass object detection. In: CVPR (2011)
3. Zhu, X., Anguelov, D., Ramanan, D.: Capturing long-tail distributions of object subcategories. In: CVPR (2014)
4. Lampert, C.H., Nickisch, H., Harmeling, S.: Learning to detect unseen object classes by between-class attribute transfer. In: CVPR (2009)
5. Farhadi, A., Endres, I., Hoiem, D., Forsyth, D.: Describing objects by their attributes. In: CVPR (2009)
6. Parikh, D., Grauman, K.: Relative attributes. In: ICCV (2011)
7. Mikolov, T., Chen, K., Corrado, G.S., Dean, J.: Efficient estimation of word representations in vector space. In: ICLR Workshops (2013)
8. Frome, A., Corrado, G.S., Shlens, J., Bengio, S., Dean, J., Ranzato, M., Mikolov, T.: Devise: a deep visual-semantic embedding model. In: NIPS (2013)
9. Socher, R., Ganjoo, M., Manning, C.D., Ng, A.: Zero-shot learning through cross-modal transfer. In: NIPS (2013)
10. Palatucci, M., Pomerleau, D., Hinton, G.E., Mitchell, T.M.: Zero-shot learning with semantic output codes. In: NIPS (2009)

11. Yu, X., Aloimonos, Y.: Attribute-based transfer learning for object categorization with zero/one training example. In: Maragos, P., Paragios, N., Daniilidis, K. (eds.) ECCV 2010, Part V. LNCS, vol. 6315, pp. 127–140. Springer, Heidelberg (2010)
12. Rohrbach, M., Stark, M., Schiele, B.: Evaluating knowledge transfer and zero-shot learning in a large-scale setting. In: CVPR (2011)
13. Kankuekul, P., Kawewong, A., Tangruamsub, S., Hasegawa, O.: Online incremental attribute-based zero-shot learning. In: CVPR (2012)
14. Akata, Z., Perronnin, F., Harchaoui, Z., Schmid, C.: Label-embedding for attribute-based classification. In: CVPR (2013)
15. Yu, F.X., Cao, L., Feris, R.S., Smith, J.R., Chang, S.F.: Designing category-level attributes for discriminative visual recognition. In: CVPR (2013)
16. Mensink, T., Gavves, E., Snoek, C.G.: Costa: co-occurrence statistics for zero-shot classification. In: CVPR (2014)
17. Norouzi, M., Mikolov, T., Bengio, S., Singer, Y., Shlens, J., Frome, A., Corrado, G.S., Dean, J.: Zero-shot learning by convex combination of semantic embeddings. In: ICLR (2014)
18. Jayaraman, D., Grauman, K.: Zero-shot recognition with unreliable attributes. In: NIPS (2014)
19. Al-Halah, Z., Stiefelhagen, R.: How to transfer? Zero-shot object recognition via hierarchical transfer of semantic attributes. In: WACV (2015)
20. Akata, Z., Reed, S., Walter, D., Lee, H., Schiele, B.: Evaluation of output embeddings for fine-grained image classification. In: CVPR (2015)
21. Fu, Y., Hospedales, T.M., Xiang, T., Gong, S.: Transductive multi-view zero-shot learning. TPAMI 37, 2332–2345 (2015)
22. Fu, Z., Xiang, T., Kodirov, E., Gong, S.: Zero-shot object recognition by semantic manifold distance. In: CVPR (2015)
23. Li, X., Guo, Y., Schuurmans, D.: Semi-supervised zero-shot classification with label representation learning. In: ICCV (2015)
24. Romera-Paredes, B., Torr, P.H.S.: An embarrassingly simple approach to zero-shot learning. In: ICML (2015)
25. Kodirov, E., Xiang, T., Fu, Z., Gong, S.: Unsupervised domain adaptation for zero-shot learning. In: ICCV (2015)
26. Zhang, Z., Saligrama, V.: Zero-shot learning via semantic similarity embedding. In: ICCV (2015)
27. Zhang, Z., Saligrama, V.: Zero-shot learning via joint latent similarity embedding. In: CVPR (2016)
28. Changpinyo, S., Chao, W.L., Gong, B., Sha, F.: Synthesized classifiers for zero-shot learning. In: CVPR (2016)
29. Deng, J., Dong, W., Socher, R., Li, L.J., Li, K., Fei-Fei, L.: Imagenet: a large-scale hierarchical image database. In: CVPR (2009)
30. Mensink, T., Verbeek, J., Perronnin, F., Csurka, G.: Metric learning for large scale image classification: generalizing to new classes at near-zero cost. In: Fitzgibbon, A., Lazebnik, S., Perona, P., Sato, Y., Schmid, C. (eds.) ECCV 2012, Part II. LNCS, vol. 7573, pp. 488–501. Springer, Heidelberg (2012)
31. Tang, K.D., Tappen, M.F., Sukthankar, R., Lampert, C.H.: Optimizing one-shot recognition with micro-set learning. In: CVPR (2010)
32. Gan, C., Yang, Y., Zhu, L., Zhao, D., Zhuang, Y.: Recognizing an action using its name: a knowledge-based approach. IJCV 120, 1–17 (2016)
33. Elhoseiny, M., Saleh, B., Elgammal, A.: Write a classifier: zero-shot learning using purely textual descriptions. In: ICCV (2013)

34. Lei Ba, J., Swersky, K., Fidler, S., Salakhutdinov, R.: Predicting deep zero-shot convolutional neural networks using textual descriptions. In: ICCV (2015)
35. Scheirer, W.J., de Rezende Rocha, A., Sapkota, A., Boult, T.E.: Toward open set recognition. TPAMI **35**(7), 1757–1772 (2013)
36. Scheirer, W.J., Jain, L.P., Boult, T.E.: Probability models for open set recognition. TPAMI **36**(11), 2317–2324 (2014)
37. Jain, L.P., Scheirer, W.J., Boult, T.E.: Multi-class open set recognition using probability of inclusion. In: Fleet, D., Pajdla, T., Schiele, B., Tuytelaars, T. (eds.) ECCV 2014, Part III. LNCS, vol. 8691, pp. 393–409. Springer, Heidelberg (2014)
38. Lampert, C.H., Nickisch, H., Harmeling, S.: Attribute-based classification for zero-shot visual object categorization. TPAMI **36**(3), 453–465 (2014)
39. Wah, C., Branson, S., Welinder, P., Perona, P., Belongie, S.: The Caltech-UCSD Birds-200-2011 dataset. Technical report CNS-TR-2011-001, California Institute of Technology (2011)
40. Kriegel, H.P., Kröger, P., Schubert, E., Zimek, A.: LoOP: local outlier probabilities. In: CIKM (2009)
41. Russakovsky, O., Deng, J., Su, H., Krause, J., Satheesh, S., Ma, S., Huang, Z., Karpathy, A., Khosla, A., Bernstein, M., Berg, A.C., Fei-Fei, L.: ImageNet large scale visual recognition challenge. IJCV **115**(3), 211–252 (2015)
42. Mikolov, T., Sutskever, I., Chen, K., Corrado, G.S., Dean, J.: Distributed representations of words and phrases and their compositionality. In: NIPS (2013)
43. Szegedy, C., Liu, W., Jia, Y., Sermanet, P., Reed, S., Anguelov, D., Erhan, D., Vanhoucke, V., Rabinovich, A.: Going deeper with convolutions. In: CVPR (2015)
44. Jia, Y., Shelhamer, E., Donahue, J., Karayev, S., Long, J., Girshick, R., Guadarrama, S., Darrell, T.: Caffe: convolutional architecture for fast feature embedding. In: ACM Multimedia (2014)
45. Crammer, K., Singer, Y.: On the algorithmic implementation of multiclass kernel-based vector machines. JMLR **2**, 265–292 (2002)

# Modeling Context in Referring Expressions

Licheng Yu$^{(\boxtimes)}$, Patrick Poirson, Shan Yang, Alexander C. Berg, and Tamara L. Berg

Department of Computer Science, University of North Carolina at Chapel Hill, Chapel Hill, USA
{licheng,poirson,alexyang,aberg,tlberg}@cs.unc.edu

**Abstract.** Humans refer to objects in their environments all the time, especially in dialogue with other people. We explore generating and comprehending natural language referring expressions for objects in images. In particular, we focus on incorporating better measures of visual context into referring expression models and find that visual comparison to other objects within an image helps improve performance significantly. We also develop methods to tie the language generation process together, so that we generate expressions for all objects of a particular category jointly. Evaluation on three recent datasets - RefCOCO, RefCOCO+, and RefCOCOg (Datasets and toolbox can be downloaded from https://github.com/lichengunc/refer), shows the advantages of our methods for both referring expression generation and comprehension.

**Keywords:** Language · Language and vision · Generation · Referring expression generation

## 1 Introduction

In this paper, we look at the dual-tasks of generating and comprehending natural language expressions referring to particular objects within an image. Referring to objects is a natural and common experience. For example, one often uses referring expressions in everyday speech to indicate a particular person or object to a co-observer, e.g., "the man in the red hat" or "the book on the table". Computational models to generate and comprehend such expressions would have applicability to human-computer interactions, especially for agents such as robots, interacting with humans in the physical world.

Successful models will have to connect both recognition of visual attributes of objects and effective natural language generation to compose useful expressions for dialogue. A broader version of this latter goal was considered in 1975 by Paul Grice who introduced maxims describing cooperative conversation between people [9]. These maxims, called the Gricean Maxims, describe a set of rational

**Electronic supplementary material** The online version of this chapter (doi:10. 1007/978-3-319-46475-6_5) contains supplementary material, which is available to authorized users.

© Springer International Publishing AG 2016
B. Leibe et al. (Eds.): ECCV 2016, Part II, LNCS 9906, pp. 69–85, 2016.
DOI: 10.1007/978-3-319-46475-6_5

principles for natural language dialogue interactions. The 4 maxims are: quality (try to be truthful), quantity (make your contribution as informative as you can, giving as much information as is needed but no more), relevance (be relevant and pertinent to the discussion), and manner (be as clear, brief, and orderly as possible, avoiding obscurity and ambiguity).

For the purpose of referring to objects in complex real world scenes these maxims suggest that a well formed expression should be informative, succinct, and unambiguous. The last point is especially necessary for referring to objects in the real world since we often find multiple objects of a particular category situated together in a scene. For example, consider the image in Fig. 1 which contains three giraffes. We should not refer to the target (outlined in green) as "the spotted giraffe" since all of the giraffes are spotted and this would create an ambiguous reference. More reasonably we should refer to the target as "the giraffe with lowered head" to differentiate this giraffe from the other two.

RefCOCO:
1. giraffe on left
2. first giraffe on left

RefCOCO+:
1. giraffe with lowered head
2. giraffe head down

RefCOCOg:
1. an adult giraffe scratching its back with its horn
2. giraffe hugging another giraffe

**Fig. 1.** Example referring expressions for the giraffe outlined in green from three referring expression datasets (described in Sect. 4). (Color figure online)

The task of referring expression generation (REG) has been studied since the 1970s [5,18,25,34], with most work focused on studying particular aspects of the problem in some relatively constrained datasets. Recent approaches have pushed this work toward more realistic scenarios. Kazemzadeh et al. [15] introduced the first large-scale dataset of referring expressions for objects in real-world natural images, collected in a two-player game. This dataset was originally collected on top of the 20,000 image ImageCleft dataset, but has recently been extended to images from the MSCOCO collection. We make use of the RefCOCO and RefCOCO+ datasets in our work along with another recently collected referring expression dataset, released by Google, denoted in our paper as RefCOCOg [21].

The most relevant work to ours is Mao et al. [21] which introduced the first deep learning approach to REG. In this model, the authors use a Convolutional Neural Network (CNN) [30] model pre-trained on ImageNet [28] to extract visual features from a bounding box around the target object and from the entire image. They use these features plus 5 features encoding the target object location and size as input to a Long Short-term Memory (LSTM) [8] network that generates expressions. Additionally, they apply the same model to the inverse problem of referring expression comprehension where the input is a natural language expression and the goal is to localize the referred object in the image.

Similar to these recent methods, we also take a deep learning approach to referring expression generation and comprehension. However, while they use a generic model for object context – CNN features for the entire image containing the target object – we take a more focused approach to encode object comparisons. These object comparisons are critical for producing an unambiguous referring expression since one must consider visual characteristics of similar objects during generation in order to select the most distinct aspects for description. This mimics the process that a human would use to compose a good referring expression for an object, e.g. look at the object, look at other relevant objects, and generate an expression that could be used by a co-observer to unambiguously pick out the target object.

In addition, for the referring expression generation task, we introduce a method to tie the language generation process together for all depicted objects of the same type. This helps generate a good set of expressions such that the expressions differentiate between objects but are also complementary. For example, we never want to generate the exact same expression for two objects in an image. Alternatively, if we call one object "the red ball" then we may desire the expression for the other object to follow the same generation pattern, i.e., "the blue ball". Our experimental evaluations show that these visual and linguistic comparisons improve performance over previous state of the art.

In the rest of our paper, we first describe related work (Sect. 2). We then describe our improvements to models for referring expression generation and comprehension (Sect. 3), describe 3 referring expression datasets (Sect. 4), and perform experimental evaluations on several model variations (Sect. 5). Finally we present our conclusions (Sect. 6).

## 2   Related Work

Referring expressions are closely related to the more general problem of modeling the connection between images and descriptive language. In recent years, this has been studied in the **image captioning** task [4,10,19,26,31]. There, the aim is to condition the generation of language on the visual information from an image. The wide range of aspects of an image that could be described, and the variety of words that could be chosen for a particular description complicate studying image captioning. Our study of referring expressions is partially motivated by focusing on description for a specific, and more easily evaluated, communication goal. Although our task is somewhat different, we borrow machinery from state of the art caption generation [2,3,14,17,22,33,35] using LSTM to generate captions based on CNN features computed on an input image. Three recent approaches for referring expression generation [21] and comprehension [11,27] also take a deep learning approach. However, we add visual object comparisons and tie together language generation for multiple objects.

**Referring expression generation** has been studied for many years [18, 25,34] in linguistics and natural language processing. These works were limited by data collection and insufficient computer vision algorithms. Together Amazon Mechanical Turk and CNNs have somewhat mitigated these limitations, allowing us to revisit these ideas on large-scale datasets. We still use such work to motivate the architecture of our pipeline. For instance, Mitchell and Jordan et al. [13,25] show the importance of using attributes, Funakoshi et al. [6] show the importance of relative relations between objects in the same perceptual group, and Kelleher et al. [16] show the importance of spatial relationships. These provide motivation for our modeling choices: when considering a referring expression for an object, the model takes into account the relative spatial location of other objects of the same type and visual comparisons to objects in the same perceptual group.

**The REG datasets** of the past were sometimes limited to using computer generated images [32], or relatively small collections of natural objects [5,23,24]. Recently, a large-scale referring expression dataset was collected by Kazemzadeh et al. [15] featuring natural objects in the real world. Since then, another three REG datasets based on the object labels in MSCOCO have been collected [15, 21]. The availability of large-scale referring expression datasets allows us to train deep learning models. Additionally, our analysis of these datasets motivates our incorporation of visual comparisons between same-type objects, and the need to tie together choices for referring expression generation between objects.

## 3      Models

We implement several model variations for referring expression generation and comprehension. The first set of models are recent state of the art deep learning approaches from Mao et al. [21]. We use these as our baselines (Sect. 3.1). Next, we investigate incorporating better visual context features into the models (Sect. 3.2). Finally, we explore methods to jointly produce an entire set of referring expressions for all depicted objects of the same category (Sect. 3.3).

### 3.1      Baselines

For comparison, we implement both the baseline and strong model of Mao et al. [21]. Both models utilize a pre-trained CNN network to model the target object and its context within the image, and then use a LSTM for generation. In particular, object and context are modeled as features from a CNN trained to recognize 1,000 object categories [30] from ImageNet [28]. Specifically, the visual representation is composed of:

- Target object representation, $o_i$. The object is modeled as features extracted from the VGG-fc7 layer by forwarding its bounding box through the network.
- Global context representation, $g_i$. Context is modeled as features extracted from the VGG-fc7 layer for the entire image.

– Location/size representation, $l_i$, for the target object. Location and size are modeled as a 5-d vector encoding the x and y locations of the top left and bottom right corners of the target object bounding box, as well as the bounding box size with respect to the image, i.e., $l_i = [\frac{x_{tl}}{W}, \frac{y_{tl}}{H}, \frac{x_{br}}{W}, \frac{y_{br}}{H}, \frac{w \cdot h}{W \cdot H}]$.

Language generation is handled by a long short-term memory network (LSTM) [8] where inputs are the above visual features and the network is trained to generate natural language referring expressions. In Mao et al.'s baseline [21], the model uses maximum likelihood training and outputs the most likely referring expression given the target object, context, and location/size features. In addition, they also propose a stronger model that uses maximum mutual information (MMI) training to consider whether a listener would interpret a referring expression unambiguously. They impose this by penalizing the model if a generated referring expression could also be generated by some other object within the image. We implement both their original model and MMI model in our experiments. We subsequently refer to these two models as Baseline and MMI, respectively.

## 3.2   Visual Comparison

Previous works [1, 25] have shown that objects in an image, of the same type as the target object, are most important for influencing what attributes people use to describe the target. One drawback of considering a general feature over the entire image to encode context (as in the baseline models) is that it may not specifically focus on visual comparisons to the most relevant objects – the other objects of the same object category within the image.

In this paper, we propose a more explicit encoding of the visual difference between objects of the same category within an image. This helps for generating referring expressions which best discriminate the target object from the surrounding objects. For example, in an image with three cars, two blue and one red, visual appearance comparisons could help generate "the red car" as an expression for the latter object.

Given the referred object and its surrounding objects, we compute two types of features for visual comparison. The first type encodes the similarities and differences in *visual appearance* between the target object and other objects of the same cateogry depicted in the image. Inspired by Sadeghi et al. [29], we compute the difference in visual CNN features as our representation of relative appearance. Because there may be many surrounding objects of the same type in the image, and not every object will provide useful information about how to describe the target object, we need to first select which objects to compare and aggregate their visual differences. In Sect. 5, we experiment with selecting different subsets of comparison objects: objects of the same category, objects of different category, or all other depicted objects. For each selected comparison object, we compute the appearance difference as the subtraction of the target object and comparison object CNN representations. We experiment with three different strategies for computing an aggregate vector to represent the visual difference between the target object and the surrounding objects: minimum, maximum, and average over each feature dimension. In our experiments, pooling the average difference between the target object and surrounding objects seems to work best. Therefore, we use this pooling in all experiments.

- Visual appearance difference representation, $\delta v_i = \frac{1}{n} \sum_{j \neq i} \frac{o_i - o_j}{\|o_i - o_j\|}$, where $n$ is the number of objects chosen for comparisons and we use average pooling to aggregate the differences.

The second type of comparison feature encodes the *relative location and size* differences between the target object and surrounding objects of the same object category. People often use comparative size or location terms in referring expressions, e.g. "the second giraffe from the left" or "the smaller monkey" [32]. To address the dynamic number of nearby objects, we choose up to five comparison objects of the same category as the target object, sorted by distance to the target. When fewer than five objects of the same category are depicted, this 25-d vector (5-d x 5 surrounding objects) is padded with zeros.

- Location difference representation, $\delta l_i$, where each 5-d difference is computed as $\delta l_{ij} = [\frac{[\triangle x_{tl}]_{ij}}{w_i}, \frac{[\triangle y_{tl}]_{ij}}{h_i}, \frac{[\triangle x_{br}]_{ij}}{w_i}, \frac{[\triangle y_{br}]_{ij}}{h_i}, \frac{w_j h_j}{w_i h_i}]$.

In summary, our final visual representation for a target object is:

$$r_i = W_m[o_i, g_i, l_i, \delta v_i, \delta l_i] + b_m \qquad (1)$$

where $o_i$, $g_i$, $l_i$ are the target object, global context, and location/size features from the baseline model, $\delta v_i$ and $\delta l_i$ encodes visual appearance difference and location difference. $W_m$ and $b_m$ project the concatenation of the five types of features to be the final representation.

### 3.3   Joint Language Generation

For the referring expression generation task, rather than generating sentences for each object in an image separately [12,21], we consider tying the generation process together into a single task to jointly generate expressions for all objects of the same object category depicted in an image. This makes sense intuitively – when a person attempts to generate a referring expression for an object in an image they inherently compose that expression while keeping in mind expressions for the other objects in the picture. This can be observed in the fact that the expressions people generate for objects in an image tend to share similar patterns of expression. If you say "the man on the left" for one object then you tend to say "the man on the right" for the other object. We would like our algorithms to mimic these behaviors. Additionally, the algorithm should also be able to push generated expressions away from each other to create less ambiguous references. For example, if we use the word "red" to describe one object, then we probably shouldn't use the same word to describe another object.

To model this joint generation process, we model generation using an LSTM model where in addition to the usual connections between time steps within

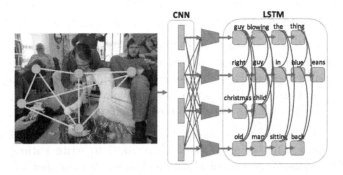

**Fig. 2.** Framework: we extract VGG-fc7 and location features for each object of the same type, then compute visual differences. These features and differences are then fed into LSTM. For sentence generation, the LSTMs are tied together, incorporating the hidden output difference as additional information for predicting words.

an expression we also add connections between expressions for different objects. This architecture is illustrated in Fig. 2.

Specifically, we use LSTM to generate multiple referring expressions, $\{r_i\}$, given depicted objects of the same type, $\{o_j\}$.

$$
\begin{aligned}
P(R|O) &= \prod_i P(r_i|o_i, \{o_{j \neq i}\}, \{r_{j \neq i}\}), \\
&= \prod_i \prod_t P(w_{i_t}|w_{i_{t-1}}, ..., w_{i_1}, v_i, \{h_{j_t, j \neq i}\})
\end{aligned}
\tag{2}
$$

where $w_{i_t}$ are words at time $t$, $v_i$ visual representations, and $h_{j_t}$ is the hidden output of j-th object at time step t that encodes the visual and sentence information for the j-th object. As visual comparison, we aggregate the difference of hidden outputs to push away ambiguous information. $h_{dif_{i_t}} = \frac{1}{n} \sum_{j \neq i} \frac{h_{i_t} - h_{j_t}}{\|h_{i_t} - h_{j_t}\|}$. There, $n$ is the the number of other objects of the same type. The hidden difference is jointly embedded with the target object's hidden output, and forwarded to the softmax layer for predicting the word.

$$
P(w_{i_t}|w_{i_{t-1}}, ..., w_{i_1}, v_i, \{h_{j_t, j \neq i}\}) = \text{softmax}(W_h[h_{i_t}, h_{dif_{i_t}}] + b_h)
\tag{3}
$$

## 4   Data

We make use of 3 referring expression datasets in our work, all collected on top of the Microsoft COCO image collection [20]. One dataset, RefCOCOg [21] is collected in a non-interactive setting, while the other two datasets, RefCOCO and RefCOCO+, are collected interactively in a two-player game [15]. In the following, we describe each dataset and provide some analysis of their similarities and differences, and then discuss splits of the datasets used in our experiments.

## 4.1   Datasets and Analysis

Images for each dataset were selected to contain multiple objects of the same category (object categories depicted cover the 80 common objects from MSCOCO with ground-truth segmentation). These images provide useful cases for referring expression generation since the referrer needs to compose a referring expression that uniquely singles out one object from other relevant objects.

**RefCOCOg:** This dataset was collected on Amazon Mechanical Turk in a non-interactive setting. One set of workers were asked to write natural language referring expressions for objects in MSCOCO images then another set of workers were asked to click on the indicated object given a referring expression. If the click overlapped with the correct object then the referring expression was considered valid and added to the dataset. If not, another referring expression was collected for the object. This dataset consists of 85,474 referring expressions for 54,822 objects in 26,711 images. Images were selected to contain between 2 and 4 objects of the same object category.

**RefCOCO & RefCOCO+:** These datasets were collected using the ReferitGame [15]. In this two-player game, the first player is shown an image with a segmented target object and asked to write a natural language expression referring to the target object. The second player is shown only the image and the referring expression and asked to click on the corresponding object. If the players do their job correctly, they receive points and swap roles. If not, they are presented with a new object and image for description. Images in these collections were selected to contain two or more objects of the same object category. In the RefCOCO dataset, no restrictions are placed on the type of language used in the referring expressions while in the RefCOCO+ dataset players are disallowed from using location words in their referring expressions by adding "taboo" words to the ReferItGame. This dataset was collected to obtain a referring expression dataset focsed on purely appearance based description, e.g., "the man in the yellow polka-dotted shirt" rather than "the second man from the left", which tend to be more interesting from a computer vision based perspective and are independent of viewer perspective. RefCOCO consists of 142,209 refer expressions for 50,000 objects in 19,994 images, and RefCOCO+ has 141,564 expressions for 49,856 objects in 19,992 images.

**Dataset Comparisons:** As shown in Fig. 1, the languages used in RefCOCO and RefCOCO+ datasets tend to be more concise and less flowery than the languages used in the RefCOCOg. RefCOCO expressions have an average length of 3.61 while RefCOCO+ have an average length of 3.53, and RefCOCOg contain an average of 8.43 words. This is most likely due to the differences in collection strategy. RefCOCO and RefCOCO+ were collected in a game scenario where players are trying to efficiently provide enough information to indicate the correct object to the other player. RefCOCOg was collected in independent rounds of Mechanical Turk without any interactive time constraints and therefore tend to provide more complex expressions, often entire sentences rather than phrases.

In addition, RefCOCO and RefCOCO+ do not limit the number of objects of the same type to 4 and thus contain some images with many objects of the same type. Both RefCOCO and RefCOCO+ contain an average of 3.9 same-type objects per image, while RefCOCOg contains an average of 1.63 same-type objects per image. The large number of same-type objects per image in RefCOCO and RefCOCO+ suggests that incorporating visual comparisons to same-type objecs will be useful.

**Dataset Splits:** There are two types of splits of the data into train/test sets: a per-object split and a people-vs-objects split.

The first type is **per-object split**. In this split, the dataset is divided by randomly partitioning objects into training and testing sets. This means that each object will only appear either in training or testing set, but that one object from an image may appear in the training set while another object from the same image may appear in the test set. We use this split for RefCOCOg since same division was used in the previous state-of-the-art approach [21].

The second type is **people-vs-objects splits**. One thing we observe from analyzing the datasets is that about half of the referred objects are people. Therefore, we create a split for RefCOCO and RefCOCO+ datasets that evaluates images containing multiple people (testA) vs images containing multiple instances of all other objects (testB). In this split all objects from an image will appear either in the training or testing sets, but not both. This split creates a more meaningfully separated division between training and testing, allowing us to evaluate the usefulness of context more fairly.

## 5   Experiments

We first perform some experiments to analyze the use of context in referring expressions (Sect. 5.1). Given these findings, we then perform experiments evaluating the usefulness of our proposed visual and language innovations on the comprehension (Sect. 5.2) and generation tasks (Sect. 5.3).

In experiments for the referring expression comprehension task, we use the same evaluation as Mao et al. [21], namely we first predict the region referred by the given expression, then we compute the intersection over union (IOU) ratio between the true and predicted bounding box. If the IOU is larger than 0.5 we count it as a true positive. Otherwise, we count it as a false positive. We average this score over all images. For the referring expression generation task we use automatic evaluation metrics, BLEU, ROUGE, and METEOR developed for evaluating machine translation results, commonly used to evaluate language generation results [3,14,19,22,33,35]. We further perform human evaluations, and propose a new metric evaluating the duplicate rate of generated expressions. For both tasks, we compare our models with "Baseline" and "MMI" [21]. Specifically, we denote "visdif" as our visual comparison model, and "tie" as the LSTM tying model. We also perform an ablation study, evaluating the combinations.

## 5.1  Analysis Experiments

**Context Representation:** As previously discussed, we suggest that the approaches proposed in recent referring expression works [11,21] make use of relatively weak contextual information, by only considering a single global image context for all objects. To verify this intuition, we implemented both the base-line and strong MMI models from Mao et al. [21], and compare the results for referring expression comprehension task with and without global context on RefCOCO and Refcoco+ in Table 1. Surprisingly we find that the global context does not improve the performance of the model. In fact, adding context even decreases performance slightly. This may be due to the fact that the global con-text for each object in an image would be the same, introducing some ambiguity into the referring expression comprehension task. Given these findings, we imple-mented a simple modification to the global context, computing the same visual representation, but on a somewhat scaled window centered around the target object. We found this to improve performance, suggesting room for improving the visual context feature. This motivate our development of a better context feature.

**Table 1.** Expression comprehension accuracies on RefCOCO and RefCOCO+ of the Baseline model with differenct context source. Scale $n$ indicates the size of the cropped window centered by the target object.

|  | RefCOCO | | RefCOCO+ | |
|---|---|---|---|---|
|  | Test A | Test B | Test A | Test B |
| No context | 63.91 % | 66.31 % | 50.09 % | 45.05 % |
| Global context | 63.15 % | 64.21 % | 48.73 % | 42.13 % |
| Scale 2 | 65.57 % | 67.13 % | 50.38 % | 44.89 % |
| Scale 3 | 66.14 % | 68.07 % | 50.25 % | 45.40 % |
| Scale 4 | **66.68 %** | **68.56 %** | **50.34 %** | **45.48 %** |

**Visual Comparison:** For our visual appearance comparison feature, we have some choice regarding which objects from the image should be compared to the target object. We experiment with three sets of reference objects: (a) objects of the same-category, (b) objects of different categories, and (c) all objects appear-ing in the image. We refer the readers to the supplementary file for details. The results show that visual appearance comparisons to objects of the same category are most useful for comprehension task. Therefore, we use this subset of objects for visual comparisons in all of the remaining experiments.

## 5.2  Referring Expression Comprehension

We evaluate performance on the referring expression comprehension task on Ref-COCO, RefCOCO+ and RefCOCOg datasets. For RefCOCO and RefCOCO+, we evaluate on the two subsets of people (testA) and all other objects (testB). For RefCOCOg, we evaluate on the per-object split as previous work [21]. Since the authors haven't released their testing set, we show the performance on their validation set only, using the optimized hyper-parameters on RefCOCO. Table 2 shows the comprehension accuracies. We observe that our implementation of Mao et al. [21] achieves comparable performance to the numbers reported in their paper. We also find that adding visual comparison features to the Baseline model improves performance across all datasets and splits. Similar improvements are also observed on top of the MMI model.

**Table 2.** Referring expression comprehension results on the RefCOCO, RefCOCO+, and RefCOCOg datasets. Rows of "method(det)" are the results of automatic system built on Fast-RCNN detections.

|  | RefCOCO | | RefCOCO+ | | RefCOCOg |
|---|---|---|---|---|---|
|  | Test A | Test B | Test A | Test B | Validation |
| Baseline [21] | 63.15% | 64.21% | 48.73% | 42.13% | 55.16% |
| visdif | 67.57% | 71.19% | 52.44% | 47.51% | 59.25% |
| MMI [21] | 71.72% | 71.09% | 58.42% | 51.23% | 62.14% |
| visdif+MMI | **73.98%** | **76.59%** | **59.17%** | **55.62%** | **64.02%** |
| Baseline(det) [21] | 58.32% | 48.48% | 46.86% | 34.04% | 40.75% |
| visdif(det) | 62.50% | 50.80% | 50.10% | 37.48% | 41.85% |
| MMI(det) [21] | 64.90% | 54.51% | 54.03% | 42.81% | 45.85% |
| visdif+MMI(det) | **67.64%** | **55.16%** | **55.81%** | **43.43%** | **46.86%** |

In order to make a fully automatic referring system, we also train a Fast-RCNN [7] detector and build our system on top of the detections[1]. Results on shown in the bottom half of Table 2. Although all comprehension accuracies drop due to imperfect detections, the improvements of our models over Baseline and MMI are still observed. One weakness of our automatic system is that it highly depends on detection performance, especially for general objects (testB). Note, our detector was trained on MSCOCO validation only, thus we believe such weakness may be alleviated with more training data and stronger detection techniques. Some examples for referring expression comprehension are shown in Fig. 3, where top 2 rows show correct comprehensions (object correctly localized) and bottom two rows show incorrect comprehensions (wrong object localized).

---

[1] We train Fast-RCNN on the validation portion only as the RefCOCO and Ref-COCO+ are collected using MSCOCO training data. For RefCOCOg, we use the detection results provided by [21].

**Fig. 3.** Some examples showing comprehension results of visdif+MMI based on detection. The blue and red bounding boxes are correct and incorrect comprehension respectively, while the green boxes indicate the ground-truth regions. (Color figure online)

## 5.3   Referring Expression Generation

For the referring expression generation task, we evaluate the usefulness of our visual comparison features as well as our joint language generation model. These serve to tie the generation process together so that the model considers other objects of the same type both visually and linguistically during generation. On the visual side, comparisons are used to judge similarity of the target object to other objects of the same type in terms of appearance, size and location. On the language side, the joint LSTM model serves to both differentiate and mimic language patterns in the referring expressions for the entire set of depicted objects. Figure 4 shows some comparison between our model with other methods.

Our full results are shown in Table 3. We find that incorporating our visual comparison features into the Baseline model improves generation quality (compare row "Baseline" to row "visdif"). It also improves the performance of MMI model (compare row "MMI" to row "visdif+MMI"). We also observe that tying the language generation together across all objects consistently improves the performance (compare the bottom three "+tie" rows with the above). Especially for

RefCOCO testA

RefCOCO testB

Baseline: woman
MMI: woman
visdif: woman
visdif+tie: woman on left

Baseline: pizza on the right
MMI: pizza on right
visdif: pizza in middle
visdif+tie: middle pizza

Baseline: front bike
MMI: bottom row third left
visdif: front bike
visdif+tie: second bottom bike

Baseline: red laptop
MMI: red book
visdff: black laptop
visdif+tie: laptop in back

RefCOCO+ testA

RefCOCO+ testB

Baseline: blue shirt
MMI: black shirt
visdif: person in stripped shirt
visdif+tie: arm with stripped shirt

Baseline: tennis player
MMI: girl
visdif: woman in white
visdif+tie: tennis player

Baseline: donut at 3
MMI: glazed donut
visdif: donut with hole
visdif+tie: donut with hole

Baseline: car with red roof
MMI: car
visdif: car with headlights
visdif+tie: car with headlights

**Fig. 4.** Referring expression generation by different methods.

**Table 3.** Referring expression generation results: Bleu, Rouge, Meteor evaluations for RefCOCO, RefCOCO+ and RefCOCOg.

RefCOCO

| | Test A | | | | Test B | | | |
|---|---|---|---|---|---|---|---|---|
| | Bleu 1 | Bleu 2 | Rouge | Meteor | Bleu 1 | Bleu 2 | Rouge | Meteor |
| Baseline [21] | 0.477 | 0.290 | 0.413 | 0.173 | 0.553 | 0.343 | 0.499 | 0.228 |
| MMI [21] | 0.478 | 0.295 | 0.418 | 0.175 | 0.547 | 0.341 | 0.497 | 0.228 |
| visdif | 0.505 | **0.322** | 0.441 | 0.184 | 0.583 | 0.382 | 0.530 | 0.245 |
| visdif+MMI | 0.494 | 0.307 | 0.441 | 0.185 | 0.578 | 0.375 | 0.531 | 0.247 |
| Baseline+tie | 0.490 | 0.308 | 0.431 | 0.181 | 0.561 | 0.352 | 0.505 | 0.234 |
| visdif+tie | **0.510** | 0.318 | **0.446** | **0.189** | **0.593** | **0.386** | **0.533** | **0.249** |
| visdif+MMI+tie | 0.506 | 0.312 | 0.445 | 0.188 | 0.579 | 0.370 | 0.525 | 0.246 |

RefCOCO+

| | Test A | | | | Test B | | | |
|---|---|---|---|---|---|---|---|---|
| | Bleu 1 | Bleu 2 | Rouge | Meteor | Bleu 1 | Bleu 2 | Rouge | Meteor |
| Baseline [21] | 0.391 | 0.218 | 0.356 | 0.140 | 0.331 | 0.174 | 0.322 | 0.135 |
| MMI [21] | 0.370 | 0.203 | 0.346 | 0.136 | 0.324 | 0.167 | 0.320 | 0.133 |
| visdif | 0.407 | 0.235 | 0.363 | 0.145 | 0.339 | 0.177 | 0.325 | 0.145 |
| visdif+MMI | 0.386 | 0.221 | 0.360 | 0.142 | 0.327 | 0.172 | 0.325 | 0.135 |
| Baseline+tie | 0.392 | 0.219 | 0.361 | 0.143 | 0.336 | 0.177 | 0.325 | 0.140 |
| visdif+tie | **0.409** | **0.232** | **0.372** | **0.150** | **0.340** | **0.178** | **0.328** | **0.143** |
| visdif+MMI+tie | 0.393 | 0.220 | 0.360 | 0.142 | 0.327 | 0.175 | 0.321 | 0.137 |

RefCOCOg

| | validation | | | |
|---|---|---|---|---|
| | Bleu 1 | Bleu 2 | Rouge | Meteor |
| Baseline [21] | 0.437 | 0.273 | 0.363 | 0.149 |
| MMI [21] | 0.428 | 0.263 | 0.354 | 0.144 |
| visdif | **0.442** | **0.277** | **0.370** | **0.151** |
| visdif+MMI | 0.430 | 0.262 | 0.356 | 0.145 |

method "visdif+tie", it achieves the highest score under almost every measurement. We do not perform language tying on RefCOCOg since here some objects from an image may appear in training while others may appear in testing.

We observe in Table 3 that models incoporating "+MMI" are worse than without "+MMI" under the automatic scoring metrics. To verify whether these metrics really reflect performance, we performed human evaluations on the expression generation task. Three Turkers were asked to click on the referred object given the image and the generated expression. If more than two clicked on the true target object, we consider this expression to be correct. Table 4 shows the human evaluation results, indicating that models with "+MMI" are consistently higher performance. We also find "+tie" methods perform the best, indicating that tying language together is able to produce less ambiguous referring expressions. Figure 5 shows examples of tied generations.

**Table 4.** Human evaluations on referring expression generation.

|  | RefCOCO | | RefCOCO+ | |
|---|---|---|---|---|
|  | Test A | Test B | Test A | Test B |
| Baseline [21] | 62.42 % | 64.99 % | 49.18 % | 42.03 % |
| MMI | 65.76 % | 68.25 % | 49.84 % | 45.38 % |
| visdif | 68.27 % | 74.92 % | 55.20 % | 43.65 % |
| visdif+MMI | 70.25 % | 75.47 % | 53.56 % | 47.58 % |
| Baseline+tie | 64.51 % | 68.34 % | 52.06 % | 43.53 % |
| visdif+tie | **71.40 %** | 76.14 % | **57.17 %** | 47.92 % |
| visdif+MMI+tie | 70.01 % | **76.31 %** | 55.64 % | **48.04%** |

**Fig. 5.** Joint referring expression generation using the tied language model of "visdif+MMI+tie".

Finally, we introduce another evaluation metric which measures the fraction of images for which an algorithm produces the same generated referring expression for multiple objects within the image. Obviously, a good referring expression generator should never produce the same expressions for two objects within the same image. Thus we would like this number to be as small as possible. The

**Table 5.** Fraction of images for which the algorithm generates the same referring expression for multiple objects. Smaller is better.

| | RefCOCO | | RefCOCO+ | |
|---|---|---|---|---|
| | Test A | Test B | Test A | Test B |
| Baseline [21] | 15.60 % | 16.40 % | 28.67 % | 46.27 % |
| MMI | 11.60 % | 11.73 % | 21.07 % | 26.40 % |
| visdif | 9.20 % | 8.80 % | 19.60 % | 31.07 % |
| visdif+MMI | 5.07 % | 6.13 % | 12.13 % | 16.00 % |
| Baseline+tie | 11.20 % | 14.93 % | 22.00 % | 32.13 % |
| visdif+tie | **4.27 %** | 5.33 % | 11.73 % | 16.27 % |
| visdif+MMI+tie | 6.53 % | **4.53 %** | **10.13 %** | **13.33 %** |

evaluation results under such metric are shown in Table 5. We find "+MMI" produces smaller number of duplicated expressions on both RefCOCO and Ref-COCO+, while "+tie" helps generating even more different expressions. Our combined model "visdif+MMI+tie" performs the best under this metric.

## 6  Conclusion

In this paper, we have developed a new model for incorporating detailed context into referring expression models. With this visual comparison based context we have improved performance over previous state of the art for referring expression generation and comprehension. In addition, for the referring expression generation task, we explore methods for joint generation over all relevant objects. Experiments verify that this joint generation improves results over previous attempts to reduce ambiguity during generation.

## References

1. Brown-Schmidt, S., Tanenhaus, M.K.: Watching the eyes when talking about size: an investigation of message formulation and utterance planning. J. Mem. Lang. **54**(4), 592–609 (2006)
2. Donahue, J., Anne Hendricks, L., Guadarrama, S., Rohrbach, M., Venugopalan, S., Saenko, K., Darrell, T.: Long-term recurrent convolutional networks for visual recognition and description. In: CVPR (2015)
3. Fang, H., Gupta, S., Iandola, F., Srivastava, R.K., Deng, L., Dollár, P., Gao, J., He, X., Mitchell, M., Platt, J.C., et al.: From captions to visual concepts and back. In: CVPR (2015)
4. Farhadi, A., Hejrati, M., Sadeghi, M.A., Young, P., Rashtchian, C., Hockenmaier, J., Forsyth, D.: Every picture tells a story: generating sentences from images. In: Daniilidis, K., Maragos, P., Paragios, N. (eds.) ECCV 2010. LNCS, vol. 6314, pp. 15–29. Springer, Heidelberg (2010). doi:10.1007/978-3-642-15561-1_2

5. FitzGerald, N., Artzi, Y., Zettlemoyer, L.S.: Learning distributions over logical forms for referring expression generation. In: EMNLP, pp. 1914–1925 (2013)
6. Funakoshi, K., Watanabe, S., Kuriyama, N., Tokunaga, T.: Generating referring expressions using perceptual groups. In: Belz, A., Evans, R., Piwek, P. (eds.) INLG 2004. LNCS, vol. 3123, pp. 51–60. Springer, Heidelberg (2004)
7. Girshick, R.: Fast R-CNN. In: Proceedings of the IEEE International Conference on Computer Vision, pp. 1440–1448 (2015)
8. Greff, K., Srivastava, R.K., Koutník, J., Steunebrink, B.R., Schmidhuber, J.: LSTM: a search space odyssey (2015). arXiv preprint arXiv:1503.04069
9. Grice, H.P.: Logic and conversation. In: Cole, P., Morgan, J.L. (eds.) Syntax and Semantics: Speech Acts, vol. 3, pp. 41–58. Academic Press, San Diego (1975)
10. Hodosh, M., Young, P., Hockenmaier, J.: Framing image description as a ranking task: data, models and evaluation metrics. J. Artif. Intell. Res. **47**, 853–899 (2013)
11. Hu, R., Xu, H., Rohrbach, M., Feng, J., Saenko, K., Darrell, T.: Natural language object retrieval. In: CVPR (2016)
12. Johnson, J., Karpathy, A., Fei-Fei, L.: Densecap: fully convolutional localization networks for dense captioning (2015). arXiv preprint arXiv:1511.07571
13. Jordan, P., Walker, M.: Learning attribute selections for non-pronominal expressions. In: ACL (2000)
14. Karpathy, A., Fei-Fei, L.: Deep visual-semantic alignments for generating image descriptions. In: CVPR (2015)
15. Kazemzadeh, S., Ordonez, V., Matten, M., Berg, T.L.: ReferitGame: referring to objects in photographs of natural scenes. In: EMNLP, pp. 787–798 (2014)
16. Kelleher, J.D., Kruijff, G.J.M.: Incremental generation of spatial referring expressions in situated dialog. In: ACL (2006)
17. Kiros, R., Salakhutdinov, R., Zemel, R.S.: Unifying visual-semantic embeddings with multimodal neural language models. In: TACL (2015)
18. Krahmer, E., Van Deemter, K.: Computational generation of referring expressions: a survey. Comput. Linguist. **38**(1), 173–218 (2012)
19. Kulkarni, G., Premraj, V., Ordonez, V., Dhar, S., Li, S., Choi, Y., Berg, A.C., Berg, T.: Babytalk: understanding and generating simple image descriptions. IEEE Trans. Pattern Anal. Mach. Intell. **35**, 2891–2903 (2013)
20. Lin, T.-Y., Maire, M., Belongie, S., Hays, J., Perona, P., Ramanan, D., Dollár, P., Zitnick, C.L.: Microsoft COCO: common objects in context. In: Fleet, D., Pajdla, T., Schiele, B., Tuytelaars, T. (eds.) ECCV 2014. LNCS, vol. 8693, pp. 740–755. Springer, Heidelberg (2014). doi:10.1007/978-3-319-10602-1_48
21. Mao, J., Huang, J., Toshev, A., Camburu, O., Yuille, A., Murphy, K.: Generation and comprehension of unambiguous object descriptions. In: CVPR (2016)
22. Mao, J., Xu, W., Yang, Y., Wang, J., Huang, Z., Yuille, A.: Deep captioning with multimodal recurrent neural networks (m-RNN). In: ICLR (2015)
23. Mitchell, M., van Deemter, K., Reiter, E.: Natural reference to objects in a visual domain. In: Proceedings of the 6th International Natural Language Generation Conference, pp. 95–104. Association for Computational Linguistics (2010)
24. Mitchell, M., Reiter, E., van Deemter, K.: Typicality and object reference. Cognitive Science (CogSci) (2013)
25. Mitchell, M., Van Deemter, K., Reiter, E.: Generating expressions that refer to visible objects. In: HLT-NAACL, pp. 1174–1184 (2013)
26. Ordonez, V., Kulkarni, G., Berg, T.L.: Im2Text: describing images using 1 million captioned photographs. In: Advances in Neural Information Processing Systems (2011)

27. Rohrbach, A., Rohrbach, M., Hu, R., Darrell, T., Schiele, B.: Grounding of textual phrases in images by reconstruction (2015). arXiv preprint arXiv:1511.03745
28. Russakovsky, O., Deng, J., Su, H., Krause, J., Satheesh, S., Ma, S., Huang, Z., Karpathy, A., Khosla, A., Bernstein, M., et al.: Imagenet large scale visual recognition challenge. Int. J. Comput. Vis. **115**(3), 211–252 (2015)
29. Sadeghi, F., Zitnick, C.L., Farhadi, A.: Visalogy: answering visual analogy questions. In: NIPS (2015)
30. Simonyan, K., Zisserman, A.: Very deep convolutional networks for large-scale image recognition (2014). arXiv preprint arXiv:1409.1556
31. Socher, R., Karpathy, A., Le, Q.V., Manning, C.D., Ng, A.Y.: Grounded compositional semantics for finding and describing images with sentences. Trans. Assoc. Comput. Linguist. **2**, 207–218 (2014)
32. Viethen, J., Dale, R.: The use of spatial relations in referring expression generation. In: Proceedings of the Fifth International Natural Language Generation Conference, pp. 59–67. Association for Computational Linguistics (2008)
33. Vinyals, O., Toshev, A., Bengio, S., Erhan, D.: Show and tell: a neural image caption generator. In: CVPR (2015)
34. Winograd, T.: Understanding natural language. Cogn. Psychol. **3**(1), 1–191 (1972)
35. Xu, K., Ba, J., Kiros, R., Courville, A., Salakhutdinov, R., Zemel, R., Bengio, Y.: Show, attend and tell: neural image caption generation with visual attention. In: ICML (2015)

# Taxonomy-Regularized Semantic Deep Convolutional Neural Networks

Wonjoon Goo[1], Juyong Kim[1], Gunhee Kim[1], and Sung Ju Hwang[2(✉)]

[1] Computer Science and Engineering, Seoul National University, Seoul, Korea
{wonjoon,gem0521,gunhee}@snu.ac.kr
[2] School of Electrical and Computer Engineering, UNIST, Ulsan, South Korea
sjhwang@unist.ac.kr
https://github.com/hiwonjoon/eccv16-taxonomy

**Abstract.** We propose a novel convolutional network architecture that abstracts and differentiates the categories based on a given class hierarchy. We exploit grouped and discriminative information provided by the taxonomy, by focusing on the general and specific components that comprise each category, through the min- and difference-pooling operations. Without using any additional parameters or substantial increase in time complexity, our model is able to learn the features that are discriminative for classifying often confused sub-classes belonging to the same superclass, and thus improve the overall classification performance. We validate our method on CIFAR-100, Places-205, and ImageNet Animal datasets, on which our model obtains significant improvements over the base convolutional networks.

**Keywords:** Deep learning · Object categorization · Taxonomy · Ontology

## 1 Introduction

Deep convolutional neural networks (CNNs) [12–14,18] have received much attention in recent years, due to its success on object categorization and many other visual recognition tasks. They have achieved the state-of-the-art performances for challenging categorization datasets such as ImageNet [3], owing to their ability to learn compositional representations for the target tasks, through multiple levels of non-linear transformations. This multi-layer learning is biologically inspired by the human visual system that also processes the visual stimuli through a similar hierarchical cascade.

However, while the deep CNNs closely resemble such low-level human visual processing systems, they pay less attention to the high-level reasoning employed for categorization. When performing categorization, humans do not treat each category as an independent entity that is different from everything else. Rather, they understand each object category in relation to others, performing generalization and specialization focusing on their commonalities and differences, either through observations or by the learned knowledge.

**Electronic supplementary material** The online version of this chapter (doi:10.1007/978-3-319-46475-6_6) contains supplementary material, which is available to authorized users.

© Springer International Publishing AG 2016
B. Leibe et al. (Eds.): ECCV 2016, Part II, LNCS 9906, pp. 86–101, 2016.
DOI: 10.1007/978-3-319-46475-6_6

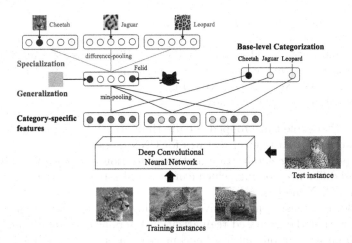

**Fig. 1. Concept:** Our taxonomy-regularized deep CNN learns grouped and discriminative features at multiple semantic levels, by introducing additional regularization layers that abstract and differentiate object categories based on a given class hierarchy. (1) At the generalization step, our network finds the commonalities between similar object categories that help recognize the supercategory, by finding the common components between per-category features. (2) At the specialization step, our network learns subcategory features as different as possible from the supercategory features, to discover unique features that help discriminate between sibling subcategories. These generalization and specialization layers work as regularizers that help the original network learn the features focusing on those commonalities and differences.

For example, consider the images of animals at the bottom of Fig. 1. Each image shows a different animal species (*e.g. cheetah, jaguar, leopard*). How can we tell them apart? We first notice that all these three animals have distinctive feline features, and have spots (*i.e.* discovery of commonalities). Then, since those common properties are no longer useful to discriminate between the animals, we start focusing on the properties that are specific to each animal, which are disjoint from the common properties that are shared among all the three animals. For example, we notice that they have different shapes of spots, and the leftmost animal has a distinctive tear mark. This fine-grained discrimination is not directly achieved by the low-level visual processing, and requires deliberate observations and reasoning.

How can we then construct a CNN such that it can mimic such high-level human reasoning process? Our idea is to implement the generalization/specialization process as additional regularization layers of the CNN, leveraging the class structure provided by a given taxonomy. Specifically, we add in multiple superclass layers on top of the CNN, which are implemented as channel-wise pooling layers that focus on the components shared by multiple subcategories, which we refer to as *min-pooling*. After this generalization process, our network performs specialization for each subcategory through *difference-pooling* between it and its superclass. It enforces the network to learn unique discriminative features for each object category (See Fig. 1).

These two pooling layers can be readily integrated into any conventional CNN models, to function as regularizers. We validate our taxonomy-regularized CNN on multiple datasets, including CIFAR-100 [11], Places-205 [25], and ImageNet Animal datasets [22], and obtain significant performance gain over the base CNN models such as AlexNet [12] and NIN [14].

Our contributions are threefold:

1. We show that exploiting grouped and discriminative information in a semantic taxonomy helps learn better features for CNN models.
2. We propose novel generalization and specialization layers implemented with min- and difference-pooling, which can be seamlessly integrated into any conventional CNN models.
3. We perform extensive quantitative and qualitative evaluation of our method, and show that the proposed regularization layers achieve significant classification improvement on multiple benchmark datasets such as CIFAR-100 [11], Places-205 [25], and ImageNet Animal datasets [22].

## 2    Related Work

**Using Semantic Taxonomies for Object Categorization.** Semantic taxonom-ies have been extensively explored for object categorization. Most existing work [1,5,15] exploits the tree structure for efficient branch-and-bound training and prediction, while a few use taxonomies as sources of relational knowledge between categories [2,6,9,24]. Our method shares the same goal with the latter group of work, and especially focuses on the parent-child and sibling-sibling relations.

**Deep Convolutional Neural Networks.** Deep CNNs [13] have recently gained enormous popularity for their impressive performance on a number of visual recognition tasks. Since Krizhevsky *et al.* [12] won the ImageNet ILSVRC challenge 2012 [3], many variants of this model have been proposed. GoogLeNet [21], and VGGNet [18] focus on increasing the network depth by adding more convolutional layers to the original model. Lin et al. [14], propose a model structure called *Network In Network* (NIN) to train non-linear filters with micro neural networks in convolutional layers, and replace the fully connected layers by global average pooling on per-category feature maps. Our model benefits from these recent advances in deep CNNs, as it can leverage any one of these deep networks as the base model.

Some existing work has explored the tree structure among tasks to regularize the learning of deep neural networks. Salakhutdinov *et al.* [17] propose to learn hierarchical Dirichlet process prior over the top-level features of a deep Boltzmann machine, which enables the model to generalize well even with few training examples. Srivastava and Salakhutdinov [19] further extend this idea to the discriminatively learned CNN, with both predefined and automatically-constructed tree hierarchies using Chinese Restaurant Process. However, these models only work as priors and do not exploit discriminative information in a class hierarchy that our model aims to learn. Recently, Yan *et al.* [23] propose a two-staged CNN architecture named HD-CNN, which leverages the taxonomy to separate the categories into easy coarse-grained ones and confusing fine-grained ones, trained in separate networks. However, such separate learning of coarse and fine grained categories results in larger memory footprints, while our model seamlessly integrates the two with minimal increase in memory usage. The main novelties of our approach in this line of research are twofold. First, we propose a generic regularization layers that can be merged into any types of CNNs. Second and more importantly, we exploit the tree structure to learn discriminative properties not only between supercategories, but also between sibling subcategories belonging to the same parents.

**Discriminative Feature Learning by Promoting Competition.** Some recent work in multitask learning focuses on promoting competitions among tasks to learn discriminative features per each task. Zhou *et al.* [27] introduce an exclusive lasso that regularizes the original least square objective with a $\ell_2$-norm over $\ell_1$-norm on parameters, which encourages competition for the features among different tasks. The orthogonal transfer proposed in [26] leverages the intuition that the classifiers in parent and child nodes of a taxonomy should be different, by minimizing the inner product of the parameters of a parent and a child classifier. A similar idea is explored in [7] in the context of metric learning, but the approach of [7] selects disjoint features instead of simply making the parameters to be different. This idea is further extended to the case of multiple taxonomies [8], where each taxonomy captures different sets of semantically discriminative features, which are combined in the multiple kernel learning framework. A recent work [9] also proposes a similar constraint, to relate the category embeddings learned for both the parent and child, and the sibling classes. Our idea shares a similar goal for learning unique and discriminative features for each class, but it is implemented with a much simpler means of pooling, which fits well into the CNN framework unlike all the other previous frameworks.

## 3   Architecture

Our goal is to exploit the class hierarchy information to learn grouped and discriminative features of categories in a deep convolutional neural network (CNN). We tackle this problem by augmenting the base CNN architecture with two additional generalization and specialization layers, which regularize the learning of the network to focus on the general and specific visual properties between similar visual object classes.

Figure 2 illustrates the overview of our network. We assume that a taxonomy of object categories is given as side information, which is either human-defined or constructed from data, and the base network is able to generate a feature map (or a vector) for each category. We will further discuss the details of base models in Sect. 3.1. Then, leveraging the class structure in the given taxonomy, our model imposes additional layers on top of these per-category feature maps (or vectors), to regularize the learning of the original network.

The first set of layers are generalization layers, which have the same structure with the given hierarchy $\mathcal{T}$. They mimic the human generalization process that learns increasingly more general and abstract classes by identifying the commonalities among the classes. Specifically, our network learns the feature maps of generalization layers by recursively applying the channel-wise *min-pooling* operation to grouped subclass feature maps guided by the taxonomy $\mathcal{T}$. Thus, each superclass feature map can identify the common activations among its child subclass feature maps. The generalization layers are learned to minimize the loss of superclass classification (*i.e.* classifying each superclass from all the other superclasses on the same level) (Sect. 3.2).

On top of the generalization layers are the specialization layers, which have the inverse structure of generalization layers (See Fig. 2). The specialization layers uniquely identify each object class as a specialization of a more generic object class. These layers learn a unique feature map for each subclass that is not explained by the feature map of its parent through *difference-pooling*, which computes the difference between each subclass feature map and its parent feature map. The specialization layers are learned to minimize the loss of subclass classification (Sect. 3.3).

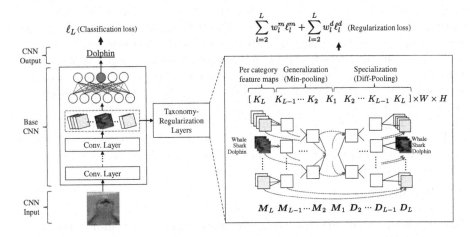

**Fig. 2.** Overview of our taxonomy-regularized CNN. Our network computes per category feature maps (in green dotted boxes) from the base CNN, and feed them into the taxonomy-regularization layers. Then, the regularization sub-network that is organized by the structure of the given taxonomy first learns supercategory feature maps that capture shared features among the grouped classes through min-pooling (generalization), and then learn exclusive feature maps for each child class that are disjoint from its parent class through difference-pooling (specialization). Rectangles indicate feature maps; red and blue arrows denote min- and difference-pooling respectively. (Color figure online)

Throughout the paper, we use $l = 1, \cdots, L$ to denote the level of taxonomy hierarchy ($L$ for the leaf and 1 for the root), $K_l$ for the number of nodes at level $l$, $n_l^k$ for the $k$-th node of the tree at level $l$, and $c_l^k$ for children nodes of $n_l^k$.

## 3.1 Base Network Models

We can use any types of CNN models as our base network. However, instead of directly using it, we make a small modification to the last convolutional layer, where we learn a per-class feature map $M_L^k \in \mathbb{R}^{h \times w}$ for each class $k \in \{1, \cdots, C\}$, where $h$ and $w$ are the height and width of the feature map, and $L$ in the subscript denotes that this feature map is for a base-level class. Note that the per-class features are not required to be two-dimensional maps, but can be one-dimensional vectors ($h = 1$). However, for generality we assume that the features are 2D maps, since this assumption is necessary for some CNN architectures (*e.g. Network in Network* (NIN) [14]). For architectures such as *AlexNet* that do not generate per-category feature maps, we can easily get such a network by simply adding convolutional layer having them to the last convolutional layer.

The feature map of each class is linked to the softmax loss layer through a *global average pooling* layer [14], which simply computes a single average value of all entries of an input feature map $M$ (*i.e.* $\frac{1}{h \times w} \sum M(i,j)$). The main role of the global average pooling is to learn the network such that each category-specific feature map produces high response for the input images of that category.

## 3.2 Min-Pooling for Superclasses

We learn the feature map for each superclass by exploiting the commonalities among the subclasses that belong to it (*e.g.* superclass *big cat* for subclasses *tiger, lion,* and *jaguar*). This is implemented by the min-pooling operation across subclass feature maps. The min-pooling simply computes the element-wise minimum over all input siblings' feature maps. Equation 1 and Fig. 3(a) describe the min-pooling:

$$M_{l-1}^k(i,j) = \min\{M_l^{k'}(i,j)\}_{k' \in \mathcal{C}_l^k} \tag{1}$$

where $M_l^k(i,j)$ is the $(i,j)$-th element of feature map for class node $n_l^k$, and $\mathcal{C}_l^k$ is the set of its children.

This operation captures features that are common across all children subclasses, but not unique to any of them, which can be captured by difference-pooling in next section. For example, in Fig. 1, using min-pooling on the feature maps captures only feline-features, such as the shape of the face and light brown color of their fur, but not their distinctive spots.

We attach the global-average pooling layer and then the softmax layer on top of the min-pooled superclass feature maps. Next we minimize the superclass loss, which learns the superclass feature maps to focus on the common properties of its children, which in turn propagate to lower layers.

**Min- vs. Max-Pooling.** Max-pooling is a more widely used downsampling method for object recognition using deep CNNs (*e.g.* [12]). However, it is not

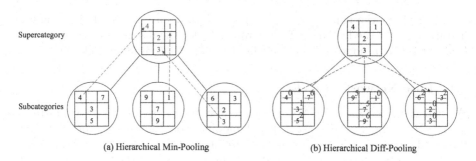

(a) Hierarchical Min-Pooling        (b) Hierarchical Diff-Pooling

**Fig. 3.** Illustration of min- and difference-pooling. (a) The *min-pooling* operation computes the elementwise minimums across multiple subcategory feature maps. (b) The *difference-pooling* computes the elementwise differences between the feature maps of each subcategory and its parent.

useful in our case where we aim to find general components across multiple object categories. For example, applying max-pooling on the category maps of the three animals in Fig. 1, would capture unique spot patterns for each animal as well as the general feline features. This helps recognize the superclass *big cat* better, but does not help discriminate between the subclass categories, since the model does not know which are common and which are unique.

### 3.3  Difference-Pooling Between Parent and Child Classes

Between each subcategory and its parent, we focus on finding the features that are as different as possible. Since the feature map of the parent captures the commonality between siblings, its activations may not be so useful for inter-subcategory discrimination. Thus we apply the difference-pooling between the response maps of the parent and its child subcategories. It retrieves the subcategory-specific entries that are not used in its parent response map.

Equation 2 and Fig. 3(b) describe the difference-pooling between a parent and its children. The feature map $D_l^k(i,j)$ for node $n_l^k$ of the difference-pooling layer between a parent and a child is defined as

$$D_l^k(i,j) = M_l^k(i,j) - M_{l-1}^{k'}(i,j), \text{ s.t. } k \in \mathcal{C}_{l-1}^{k'}. \tag{2}$$

The difference-pooling reduces the effect of supercategory-specific features, and thus makes the subcategory discrimination less dependent on supercategory-specific features. It in turn promotes learning the features that are required for fine-grained categorization at lower layers of the CNN.[1] As with the superclass

---

[1] We also test XOR-pooling that assign 0 to the elements of the children feature maps that are also selected at the parent feature map. However, in our experiments, the XOR-pooling results in a worse performance than diff-pooling, perhaps due to excessive sparsity.

feature maps, we attach the global average pooling and multinomial classification loss layers to the diff-pooling layers. This enforces the network to learn discriminative features that uniquely identifies each object category.

### 3.4 Unsupervised Construction of a Taxonomy

While the taxonomies for most generic object categories can be obtained from semantic taxonomies such as WordNet [16], such predefined taxonomies may be unavailable for domain-specific data. Furthermore, the semantic taxonomies do not always accurately reflect the feature distributions in the training set. Therefore, we propose a simple taxonomy construction method by examining the activations of the feature maps in the base network. Note that we do not declare this method as our major contribution, but as will be shown in experiments, it performs successfully when no taxonomy is available.

The key idea is to group the classes that have the similar activations of feature maps, because those are the confusing classes that we want to discriminate. First, we learn a base network using the original category labels, as done in normal image classification. We then define activation vector $g^k$ for each category $k$ by averaging the feature response maps for its training images. Next we perform agglomerative clustering on $\{g^k\}_{k=1}^{C}$ using $l_2$ distance metric and Ward's linkage criteria. Once we obtain the dendrogram between categories, we can cluster them for any given $K$ number of clusters, which become the superclasses and their members become subclasses. A single application of such agglomerative clustering can generate a two-level taxonomy. We can recursively apply this operation to obtain a multi-level taxonomy.

### 3.5 Training

We attach a softmax loss layer to every level of min- and diff- pooled layers via global average pooling layers (See Fig. 2). With the superclass classification loss, the feature maps generated by min-pooling is learned to preserve spatially consistent information across subclasses that belong to the same superclass. That is, the activations on those feature maps are unique to the group of subclasses, and not possessed by other superclass groups. However, the superclass loss can at the same time hamper the network from learning the representation that discriminates between the subclasses that belong to the same group. Thus we add in an additional loss layer on top of the diff-pooling layer, which is the classification loss over the classes in same level.

The resulting network has multiple loss layers including the loss layers for the base-level classes, subclasses, and superclasses. However, since we are mostly interested in improving on the base-level categorization accuracy, we balance the contribution of each loss by giving different weights so that the additional losses for min-pooled and diff-pooled layers act as regularizers. The combined loss term is described as follows:

$$\ell = \ell_L + \sum_{l=2}^{L} w_l^m \ell_l^m + \sum_{l=2}^{L} w_l^d \ell_l^d. \tag{3}$$

where $\ell_L$ is the original base-level categorization loss, $\ell_l^m$ are the losses from min-pooled layers for superclasses, $\ell_l^d$ are the losses from diff-pooled layers for subclasses, and $w_l^m, w_l^d$ are weights for each loss term.[2]

We implement the min- and diff-pooling layers on top of the publicly available Caffe [10] package. Note that the added pooling layers do not introduce any new parameters and the only additional computational burden is on computing the min- and diff-pooling; thus the increase in memory and computational complexity is minor compared to the original model. The increase in space and time complexity depends on an employed tree structure, specifically on the number of internal nodes. If the number of classes at all levels is $C$ and the memory usage of per class feature maps is $U$, then the increase in the space complexity will be $O(CU)$, where the worst case happens if the given tree is a full binary tree.

In our experiments, the increase in memory usage is less than 3 % and the increase in training time is 15 % at maximum, compared to those of the base networks. The HD-CNN [23], which is a similar approach that makes use of hierarchical class information, on the other hand, increases the memory usage and the training time by about 50 % and 150 % each. Thus, our model is more scalable with a much larger number of classes, with a large and complex class hierarchy. Also further speed-up can be achieved with a parallel implementation of the additional layers, although our current implementation does not fully exploit the parallelism on the problem.

## 4  Experiment

We evaluate the multiclass classification performance of our approach on multiple image datasets. Our main focus is to demonstrate that the taxonomy-based generalization and specialization layers improve the performance of base CNN models, by learning the discriminative features at multiple semantic granularity.

### 4.1  Dataset

**CIFAR-100.** The CIFAR-100 [11] consists of 100 generic object categories (*e.g. tiger, bed, palm,* and *bus*), and has been extensively used for the evaluation of deep neural networks.[3] It consists of 600 images per category (*i.e.* 60,000 images in total) with a size of 32×32, where 500 images are used for training and the remaining 100 images are for testing. We pre-process the images with global contrast normalization and ZCA whitening as done in [14,23]. For taxonomy, we use the trees provided in [11], [19], and another one discovered using our tree construction method in Sect. 3.4.

---

[2] Our experiments reveal that the network is not sensitive to these balancing parameters, as long as the base-level categorization loss has a higher weight than others. That is, $w_l^m, w_l^d < 1$.

[3] http://rodrigob.github.io/are_we_there_yet/build/classification_datasets_results.html

**Places-205.** The Places dataset [25] contains $2,448,873$ images from 205 scene categories. The set of scene classes includes both indoor scenes (*e.g. romantic bedroom, stylish kitchen*) and outdoor scenes (*e.g. rocky coast*, and *wintering forest path*). We use the provided training and test splits by [25] for our experiments. For taxonomy, we use the discovered class hierarchy using our tree construction method since no predefined one exists for this dataset.

**ImageNet Animal.** ImageNet 1K/22K Animal datasets, suggested in [22], are subsets of the widely-used ImageNet dataset [3]. For ImageNet 1K Animal dataset, we select all 398 animal classes out of the ImageNet 1 K and split the images into 501 K training images and 18 K test images. For ImageNet 22K Animal dataset, we collect 2,266 animal classes out of all ImageNet 22 K classes; we only consider the classes that have more than 100 images and are at leaf nodes of ImageNet hierarchy. The dataset consists of 1.6M training images and 282 K test images. Our ImageNet 22K Animal dataset has slightly different number of classes from [22] (2,282 classes), but the difference is less than 1 %. For taxonomy, we use the generated class hierarchy instead of the existing ImageNet hierarchy since the ImageNet class hierarchy is largely imbalanced and overly deep.

As for tree depth in automatic hierarchy construction, we experimentally found that the optimal value is around $\log_{10} k$, where $k$ is the number of classes; we used 2-level trees for CIFAR-100 and Places-205, and a 3-level tree for ImageNet 22K-Animals that comes with 2 K classes.

### 4.2   Quantitative Evaluation

**Results on CIFAR-100.** Figure 4 shows the classification results of our method and the baselines on the CIFAR-100 dataset. As our base model, we use the

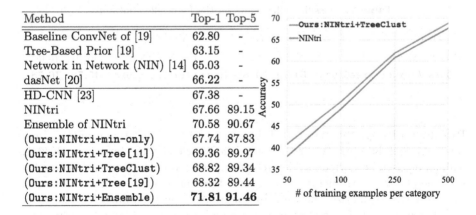

| Method | Top-1 | Top-5 |
|---|---|---|
| Baseline ConvNet of [19] | 62.80 | - |
| Tree-Based Prior [19] | 63.15 | - |
| Network in Network (NIN) [14] | 65.03 | - |
| dasNet [20] | 66.22 | - |
| HD-CNN [23] | 67.38 | - |
| NINtri | 67.66 | 89.15 |
| Ensemble of NINtri | 70.58 | 90.67 |
| (Ours:NINtri+min-only) | 67.74 | 87.83 |
| (Ours:NINtri+Tree[11]) | 69.36 | 89.97 |
| (Ours:NINtri+TreeClust) | 68.82 | 89.34 |
| (Ours:NINtri+Tree[19]) | 68.32 | 89.44 |
| (Ours:NINtri+Ensemble) | **71.81** | **91.46** |

**Fig. 4. Left:** The classification results on the CIFAR-100 dataset. We report top-1 and top-5 accuracy in percentage. **Right:** The classification accuracy with different number of training images per label.

Network-in-Network-triple denoted by (NINtri), which is the same as the original Network-in-Network model in [14], except that it has three times of the number of filters in the original network. This network is also used as a baseline in [23], in which the HD-CNN results in a lower accuracy than the NIN-triple, perhaps due to the difference in the number of learning parameters. We report the performance of our NIN-triple model regularized with different taxonomies. We use three different class hierarchies from [11], [19], and our tree construction method (denoted by a suffix +TreeClust). The performance varies depending on which taxonomy we use, but all of our models outperform the base NIN-triple. We obtain the best result using the class hierarchy in [11], which outperforms NIN-triple by 1.7 %p. This increase is larger than 0.35 %p reported in [19], and we attribute such larger enhancement to the exploitation of discriminative information from the taxonomy, through the proposed two pooling methods.

The performance can be further improved by ensemble learning with multiple taxonomies. We obtain a bagging predictor by simply averaging out the predictions of the models with the three taxonomies, and this ensemble model denoted by (Ours:NINtri+Ensemble) achieves 71.81 % of accuracy, which is significantly higher than the base network NIN-triple by 4.15 %p.

**Results on Places-205.** Table 1 shows the classification results on the Places dataset. As base networks, we test the NIN [14] and the AlexNet [12] trained on ILSVRC2012 dataset. Since no pre-trained model is publicly available for the Places dataset, we fine-tune those base models on the Places dataset, which we report as Places-Alexnet and Places-NIN. We generate the tree hierarchy using the method in Sect. 3.4, and then fine-tune each base network with the proposed generalization and specialization layers. Our tree-regularized networks outperform the base networks by 1.10 %p (Ours:Alexnet) and 2.32 %p (Ours:NIN), which are significant improvements.

**Table 1.** Classification results on the Places-205 dataset.

| Method | Top-1 | Top-5 | Method | Top-1 | Top-5 |
|---|---|---|---|---|---|
| Places-AlexNet [25] | 50.04 | 81.10 | Places-NIN | 43.46 | 75.00 |
| (Ours:AlexNet+TreeClust) | **51.14** | **81.85** | (Ours:NIN+TreeClust) | **45.78** | **76.78** |

**Results on ImageNet Animal.** Table 2 shows the classification results on ImageNet Animal datasets. We first pretrain the AlexNet on the ImageNet 1K/22K Animal datasets, reported as AlexNet-pretrained. From the learned base model, we generate the class hierarchy using our tree construction method. We then learn our tree-regularized network by fine-tuning the pretrained base AlexNet with the hierarchy. The resulting network outperforms [22] by 4.33 %p in ImageNet 1K Animal, and by 0.43 %p in ImageNet 22K Animal dataset. Also our network increases the performance of the base AlexNet model more than 1 % in the both datasets.

**Table 2.** Classification results on the ImageNet 1K/22K animal dataset.

| Dataset/method | Xiao *et al.* [22] | AlexNet-pretrained | (Ours) |
|---|---|---|---|
| Imagenet 1K Animal | 63.2 | 66.46 | **67.53** |
| Imagenet 22K Animal | 51.48 | 50.82 | **51.91** |

On all datasets, our method achieves larger improvements in top-1 accuracy rather than in top-5 accuracy, which suggest that the key improvement come from the correct category recognition at the fine-grained level. This may be due to our model's ability to learn features that are useful for fine-grained discrimination from class hierarchy, through min- and diff-pooling.

**Accuracy as a Function of Training Examples.** One can expect that our taxonomy-based regularization might be more effective with fewer training examples; to validate this point, we experiment with different number of training examples per class on CIFAR-100 dataset. We learn our model using 50, 100, 250, and 500 training examples, and plot the accuracy as a function of number of examples in Fig. 4 (right). The plot shows that our model becomes increasingly more effective than the base network when using less number of training examples. The largest relative performance gain using our model occurs when using as few as 50 training examples, outperforming the baseline by around 3 %p.

**Semantic Prediction Performance Using hp@k.** To validate that our tree-regularized network can obtain semantically meaningful predictions, we also evaluate with the hierarchical precision@k (hp@k) introduced in [4], which is a measure of semantic relevance between the predicted label and the groundtruth label. It is computed as a fraction of the top-$k$ predictions that are in the correct set, when considering the $k$ nearest classes based on the tree distance. For detailed description of the hp@k measure, please refer to [4]. Table 3 shows the results on the CIFAR-100 dataset.

We observe that our taxonomy-regularized network obtains high hierarchical precisions, outperforming the base network by more than 7 %p, using the

**Table 3.** Hierarchical precision@k results on the CIFAR-100 dataset.

| Method | hp@1 | hp@2 | hp@5 |
|---|---|---|---|
| Network in Network-triple (NINtri) [23] | 67.66 | 56.64 | 71.31 |
| Ensemble of NINtri [23] | 70.58 | 55.06 | 64.82 |
| (Ours:NINtri+min-only) | 67.74 | 60.34 | 79.19 |
| (Ours:NINtri+Tree[11]) | 69.36 | **62.33** | **79.71** |
| (Ours:NINtri+TreeClust) | 68.82 | 59.15 | 78.18 |
| (Ours:NINtri+Tree[19]) | 68.32 | 61.05 | 77.99 |
| (Ours:NINtri+Ensemble) | **71.81** | 57.85 | 67.44 |

semantic taxonomy from [11]. The improvement is less when using the constructed tree, but our network still outperforms the non-regularized base network. This performance gain in the semantic prediction mostly comes from the use of min-pooling, which groups the relevant classes together, with the diff-pooling also contributing to some degree with accurate discrimination of fine-grained categories. This point is clearly observed by comparing with the result of min-pooling only with the result of the full model (*i.e.* the third and fourth rows of Table 3).

### 4.3   Qualitative Analysis

Figure 5 shows selected examples of class prediction made using our model and the baseline NIN [14] network on the CIFAR-100 and the Places dataset. We observe that in many cases, our network predicts more semantically relevant categories in the top-5 predictions (See Fig. 5(a-d)). This is even true for the failure case of Fig. 5(e), where the top-5 classes predicted by our model (*i.e.* *woman, girl, man, boy,* and *baby*) are all semantically relevant to the correct class *girl*. On the other hand, the results of the base network include semantically irrelevant categories such as *skunk* and *flatfish* in the top-5 predictions. Also, our model is less likely to confuse between similar classes, while the base network is more prone to misclassification between them. Hence, the base network that often lists correct categories in the top-5 predictions still fails to predict the correct top-1 category (See Fig. 5(a-d)).

To further analyze where the improvement in classification performance comes from, we examine the response maps for the subcategories that share the same parent categories, in Fig. 6. From ImageNet 22 K animal dataset, we select one supercategory, *moth*, for which we select three subcategories. Note that the original feature maps do not represent discriminative activations, but diff-pooled activations clearly capture *discriminative* local properties for each subcategory. For example, in the *moth* subclasses, we can see that the diff-pooled activation maps exclusively focus on the wing patterns which are important for distinguishing different moth species. This example confirms that the hierarchical regularization layers can indeed capture discriminative traits for the subclasses, thus significantly eliminating confusions between subcategories.

We also compare between the feature maps learned by the base model NIN and our approach on the CIFAR-100 dataset, in Fig. 7. Since the base network NIN has only convolution layers except for the last classification loss layer, the forward pass can preserve the spatial information. Therefore, we can segment an image by using activations of the feature map on the image. We show segmentation results in Fig. 7. The segmentations by our method are qualitatively better, as they focus more on the target objects compared to the base network, which often generates loose and inaccurate segmentations. These results assure our taxonomy-based model's ability to learn unique features for each category, rather than learning features that are generic across all the categories.

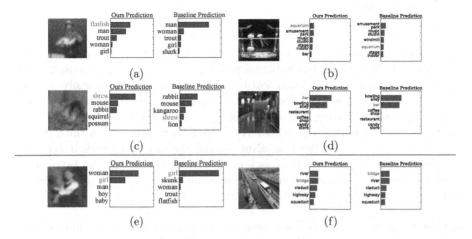

**Fig. 5.** Example predictions for the CIFAR-100 dataset (left column) and the Places-205 dataset (right column). For each image, we show the top-5 prediction result using our model and the base network (NIN). The last row shows failure cases.

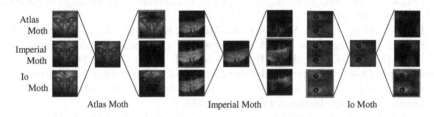

**Fig. 6.** Response maps for the subclasses that belong to the same superclasses in the ImageNet 22K Animal dataset for a given test instance. We superimpose the per-category, min-pooled, and diff-pooled response maps of these sibling classes on top of each input image. The correct feature map for each input image is highlighted in red. (Color figure online)

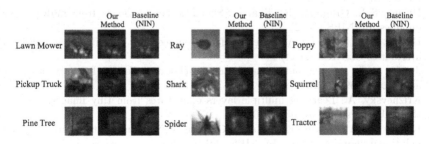

**Fig. 7.** Image segmentation results on the CIFAR-100 test images. Our network generates tighter segmentation boundaries compared to the base network.

## 5   Conclusion

We propose a regularization method that exploits hierarchical task relations to improve the categorization performance of deep convolutional neural networks. We focus on the task relations between the prediction of a parent and child classes in a taxonomy, and learn features common across semantically related classes through min-pooling, then learn discriminative feature maps for each object class by performing difference-pooling between the feature maps of each child class and its parent superclass. We validate our approach on the CIFAR-100, the Places-205, and the ImageNet Animal datasets, on which it achieves significant improvement over the baselines. We further show that our taxonomy-regularized network makes semantically meaningful predictions, and could be more useful when the training data is scarce.

**Acknowledgement.** This work was supported by Samsung Research Funding Center of Samsung Electronics under Project Number SRFC-IT1502-03.

## References

1. Bengio, S., Weston, J., Grangier, D.: Label embedding trees for large multi-class task. In: NIPS (2010)
2. Deng, J., Ding, N., Jia, Y., Frome, A., Murphy, K., Bengio, S., Li, Y., Neven, H., Adam, H.: Large-scale object classification using label relation graphs. In: Fleet, D., Pajdla, T., Schiele, B., Tuytelaars, T. (eds.) ECCV 2014. LNCS, vol. 8689, pp. 48–64. Springer, Heidelberg (2014). doi:10.1007/978-3-319-10590-1_4
3. Deng, J., Dong, W., Socher, R., Li, L.J., Li, K., Fei-Fei, L.: ImageNet: a large-scale hierarchical image database. In: CVPR (2009)
4. Frome, A., Corrado, G., Shlens, J., Bengio, S., Dean, J., Ranzato, M., Mikolov, T.: Devise: a deep visual-semantic embedding model. In: NIPS (2013)
5. Gao, T., Koller, D.: Discriminative learning of relaxed hierarchy for large-scale visual recognition. In: ICCV (2011)
6. Hwang, S.J.: Discriminative object categorization with external semantic knowledge. Ph.D. dissertation, The University of Texas at Austin (2013)
7. Hwang, S.J., Grauman, K., Sha, F.: Learning a tree of metrics with disjoint visual features. In: NIPS (2011)
8. Hwang, S.J., Grauman, K., Sha, F.: Semantic kernel forests from multiple taxonomies. In: NIPS (2012)
9. Hwang, S.J., Sigal, L.: A unified semantic embedding: relating taxonomies and attributes. In: NIPS (2014)
10. Jia, Y.: Caffe: an open source convolutional architecture for fast feature embedding. arXiv:1408.5093 (2013)
11. Krizhevsky, A.: Learning multiple layers of features from tiny images. Master's thesis, University of Toronto (2009)
12. Krizhevsky, A., Sutskever, I., Hinton, G.E.: ImageNet classification with deep convolutional neural networks. In: NIPS (2012)
13. Lecun, Y., Bottou, L., Bengio, Y., Haffner, P.: Gradient-based learning applied to document recognition. Proc. IEEE **86**(11), 2278–2324 (1998)
14. Lin, M., Chen, Q., Yan, S.: Network in network. In: ICLR (2014)

15. Marszałek, M., Schmid, C.: Constructing category hierarchies for visual recognition. In: Forsyth, D., Torr, P., Zisserman, A. (eds.) ECCV 2008. LNCS, vol. 5305, pp. 479–491. Springer, Heidelberg (2008). doi:10.1007/978-3-540-88693-8_35
16. Miller, G.A., Beckwith, R., Fellbaum, C.D., Gross, D., Miller, K.: WordNet: an online lexical database. Int. J. Lexicograph 3(4), 235–244 (1990)
17. Salakhutdinov, R.R., Tenenbaum, J.B., Torralba, A.: Learning to learn with compound HD models. In: NIPS (2011)
18. Simonyan, K., Zisserman, A.: Imagenet classification with deep convolutional neural networks. In: ICLR (2015)
19. Srivastava, N., Salakhutdinov, R.R.: Discriminative transfer learning with tree-based priors. In: NIPS (2013)
20. Stollenga, M.F., Masci, J., Gomez, F., Schmidhuber, J.: Deep networks with internal selective attention through feedback connections. In: NIPS (2014)
21. Szegedy, C., Liu, W., Jia, Y., Sermanet, P., Reed, S., Anguelov, D., Erhan, D., Vanhoucke, V., Rabinovich, A.: Going deeper with convolutions. In: CVPR (2015)
22. Xiao, T., Zhang, J., Yang, K., Peng, Y., Zhang, Z.: Error-driven incremental learning in deep convolutional neural network for large-scale image classification. In: ACM MM (2014)
23. Yan, Z., Zhang, H., Jagadeesh, V., DeCoste, D., Di, W., Yu, Y.: HD-CNN: hierarchical deep convolutional neural network for image classification. In: ICCV (2015)
24. Zhao, B., Fei-Fei, L., Xing, E.P.: Large-scale category structure aware image categorization. In: NIPS (2011)
25. Zhou, B., Lapedriza, A., Xiao, J., Torralba, A., Oliva, A.: Learning deep features for scene recognition using places database. In: NIPS (2014)
26. Zhou, D., Xiao, L., Wu, M.: Hierarchical classification via orthogonal transfer. In: ICML (2011)
27. Zhou, Y., Jin, R., Hoi, S.C.H.: Exclusive lasso for multi-task feature selection. JMLR 9, 988–995 (2010)

# Playing for Data: Ground Truth from Computer Games

Stephan R. Richter[1]([✉]), Vibhav Vineet[2], Stefan Roth[1], and Vladlen Koltun[2]

[1] TU Darmstadt, Darmstadt, Germany
`stephan.richter@visinf.tu-darmstadt.de`
[2] Intel Labs, Santa Clara, USA

**Abstract.** Recent progress in computer vision has been driven by high-capacity models trained on large datasets. Unfortunately, creating large datasets with pixel-level labels has been extremely costly due to the amount of human effort required. In this paper, we present an approach to rapidly creating pixel-accurate semantic label maps for images extracted from modern computer games. Although the source code and the internal operation of commercial games are inaccessible, we show that associations between image patches can be reconstructed from the communication between the game and the graphics hardware. This enables rapid propagation of semantic labels within and across images synthesized by the game, with no access to the source code or the content. We validate the presented approach by producing dense pixel-level semantic annotations for 25 thousand images synthesized by a photorealistic open-world computer game. Experiments on semantic segmentation datasets show that using the acquired data to supplement real-world images significantly increases accuracy and that the acquired data enables reducing the amount of hand-labeled real-world data: models trained with game data and just $\frac{1}{3}$ of the CamVid training set outperform models trained on the complete CamVid training set.

## 1 Introduction

Recent progress in computer vision has been driven by high-capacity models trained on large datasets. Image classification datasets with millions of labeled images support training deep and highly expressive models [24]. Following their success in image classification, these models have recently been adapted for detailed scene understanding tasks such as semantic segmentation [28]. Such semantic segmentation models are initially trained for image classification, for which large datasets are available, and then fine-tuned on semantic segmentation datasets, which have fewer images.

We are therefore interested in creating very large datasets with pixel-accurate semantic labels. Such datasets may enable the design of more diverse model

---

S.R. Richter and V. Vineet—Authors contributed equally.

B. Leibe et al. (Eds.): ECCV 2016, Part II, LNCS 9906, pp. 102–118, 2016.
DOI: 10.1007/978-3-319-46475-6_7

architectures that are not constrained by mandatory pre-training on image classification. They may also substantially increase the accuracy of semantic segmentation models, which at present appear to be limited by data rather than capacity. (For example, the top-performing semantic segmentation models on the PASCAL VOC leaderboard all use additional external sources of pixelwise labeled data for training.)

Creating large datasets with pixelwise semantic labels is known to be very challenging due to the amount of human effort required to trace accurate object boundaries. High-quality semantic labeling was reported to require 60 min per image for the CamVid dataset [8] and 90 min per image for the Cityscapes dataset [11]. Due to the substantial manual effort involved in producing pixel-accurate annotations, semantic segmentation datasets with precise and comprehensive label maps are orders of magnitude smaller than image classification datasets. This has been referred to as the "curse of dataset annotation" [50]: the more detailed the semantic labeling, the smaller the datasets.

In this work, we explore the use of commercial video games for creating large-scale pixel-accurate ground truth data for training semantic segmentation systems. Modern open-world games such as Grand Theft Auto, Watch Dogs, and Hitman feature extensive and highly realistic worlds. Their realism is not only in the high fidelity of material appearance and light transport simulation. It is also in the content of the game worlds: the layout of objects and environments, the realistic textures, the motion of vehicles and autonomous characters, the presence of small objects that add detail, and the interaction between the player and the environment.

The scale, appearance, and behavior of these game worlds are significant advantages over open-source sandboxes that lack this extensive content. However, detailed semantic annotation of images from off-the-shelf games is a challenge because the internal operation and content of the game are largely inaccessible. We show that this can be overcome by a technique known as detouring [19]. We inject a wrapper between the game and the operating system, allowing us to record, modify, and reproduce rendering commands. By hashing distinct rendering resources – such as geometry, textures, and shaders – communicated by the game to the graphics hardware, we generate object signatures that persist across scenes and across gameplay sessions. This allows us to create pixel-accurate object labels without tracing boundaries. Crucially, it also enables propagating object labels across time and across instances that share distinctive resources.

Using the presented approach, we have created pixel-level semantic segmentation ground truth for 25 thousand images extracted from the game Grand Theft Auto V. The labeling process was completed in only 49 h. Our labeling speed was thus roughly three orders of magnitude faster than for other semantic segmentation datasets with similar annotation density. The pixel-accurate propagation of label assignments through time and across instances led to a rapid acceleration of the labeling process: average annotation time per image decreased sharply during the process because new object labels were propagated across images. This is in contrast to prior labeling interfaces, in which annotation speed does not change significantly during the labeling process, and total labeling costs scale linearly with dataset size. Annotating the presented dataset with the approach used for CamVid or Cityscapes [8,11] would have taken at least 12 person-years. Three of the images we have labeled are shown in Fig. 1.

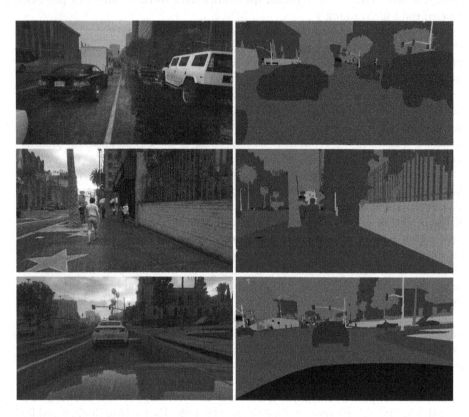

**Fig. 1.** Images and ground-truth semantic label maps produced by the presented approach. Left: images extracted from the game Grand Theft Auto V. Right: semantic label maps. The color coding is defined in Fig. 4. (Color figure online)

To evaluate the utility of using game data for training semantic segmentation systems, we used label definitions compatible with other datasets for urban scene understanding [8,11,13,50]. We conducted extensive experiments to evaluate the effectiveness of models trained with the acquired data. The experimental results show that using the acquired data to supplement the CamVid and KITTI training sets significantly increases accuracy on the respective datasets. In addition, the experiments demonstrate that the acquired data can reduce the need for expensive labeling of real-world images: models trained with game data and just $\frac{1}{3}$ of the CamVid training set outperform models trained on the complete CamVid training set.

## 2   Related Work

Synthetic data has been used for decades to benchmark the performance of computer vision algorithms. The use of synthetic data has been particularly significant in evaluating optical flow estimation due to the difficulty of obtaining accurate ground-truth flow measurements for real-world scenes [6,7,18,32]. Most recently, the MPI-Sintel dataset has become a standard benchmark for optical flow algorithms [9] and has additionally yielded ground-truth data for depth estimation and bottom-up segmentation. Synthetic scenes have been used for evaluating the robustness of image features [21] and for benchmarking the accuracy of visual odometry [16]. Renderings of object models have been used to analyze the sensitivity of convolutional network features [5]. In contrast to this line of work, we use synthetic data not for benchmarking but for training a vision system, and tackle the challenging problem of semantic segmentation.

Rendered depth maps of parametric models have been used prominently in training leading systems for human pose estimation and hand tracking [41, 42]. 3D object models are also increasingly used for training representations for object detection and object pose estimation [4,26,30,34,35,44]. Renderings of 3D object models have been used to train shape-from-shading algorithms [37] and convolutional networks for optical flow estimation [12]. Renderings of entire synthetic environments have been proposed for training convolutional networks for stereo disparity and scene flow estimation [31]. Our work is different in two ways. First, we tackle the problem of semantic segmentation, which involves both recognition and perceptual grouping [17,23,28,43]. Second, we obtain data not by rendering 3D object models or stylized environments, but by extracting photorealistic imagery from a modern open-world computer game with high-fidelity content.

Computer games – and associated tools such as game engines and level editors – have been used a number of times in computer vision research. Development tools accompanying the game Half Life 2 were used for evaluating visual surveillance systems [46]. These tools were subsequently used for creating an environment for training high-performing pedestrian detectors [29,49,51]. And an open-source driving simulator was used to learn mid-level cues for autonomous driving [10]. In contrast to these works, we deal with the problem of semantic image segmentation and demonstrate that data extracted from an unmodified off-the-shelf computer game with no access to the source code or the content can be used to substantially improve the performance of semantic segmentation systems.

Somewhat orthogonal to our work is the use of indoor scene models to train deep networks for semantic understanding of indoor environments from depth images [15,33]. These approaches compose synthetic indoor scenes from object models and synthesize depth maps with associated semantic labels. The training data synthesized in these works provides depth information but no appearance cues. The trained models are thus limited to analyzing depth maps. In contrast, we show that modern computer games can be used to increase the accuracy of state-of-the-art semantic segmentation models on challenging real-world benchmarks given regular color images only. Very recent concurrent work [53,54] demonstrates the heightened interest in using virtual worlds to train algorithms for scene understanding.

# 3    Breaking the Curse of Dataset Annotation

Extracting images and metadata from a game is easy if the source code and content are available [10,14]. Open-source games, however, lack the extensive, detailed, and realistic content of commercial productions. In this section, we show that rapid semantic labeling can be performed on images generated by off-the-shelf games, without access to their source code or content. We then demonstrate the presented approach by producing pixel-accurate semantic annotations for 25 thousand images from the game Grand Theft Auto V. (The publisher of Grand Theft Auto V allows non-commercial use of footage from the game as long as certain conditions are met, such as not distributing spoilers [38].)

## 3.1    Data Acquisition

**A Brief Introduction to Real-Time Rendering.** To present our approach to data acquisition, we first need to review some relevant aspects of the rendering pipeline used in modern computer games [2]. Modern real-time rendering systems are commonly based on deferred shading. Geometric resources are communicated to the GPU to create a depth buffer and a normal buffer. Maps that specify the diffuse and specular components of surface reflectance are communicated to create the diffuse and specular buffers. Buffers that collect such intermediate products of the rendering pipeline are called G-buffers. Illumination is applied to these G-buffers, rather than to the original scene components [40]. This decoupled processing of geometry, reflectance properties, and illumination significantly accelerates the rendering process. First, shading does not need to be performed on elements that are subsequently culled by the geometry pipeline. Second, shading can be performed much more efficiently on G-buffers than on an unstructured stream of objects. For these reasons, deferred shading has been widely adopted in high-performance game engines.

**Extracting Information from the Rendering Pipeline.** How can this pipeline be employed in creating ground-truth semantic labels if we don't have access to the game's code or content? The key lies in the game's communication with the graphics hardware. This communication is structured. Specifically, the game communicates resources of different types, including geometric meshes, texture maps, and shaders. The game then specifies how these resources should be combined to compose the scene. The content of these resources persists through time and across gameplay sessions. By tracking the application of resources to different scene elements, we can establish associations between these scene elements.

Our basic approach is to intercept the communication between the game and the graphics hardware. Games communicate with the hardware through

APIs such as OpenGL, Direct3D, or Vulkan, which are provided via dynamically loaded libraries. To initiate the use of the hardware, a game loads the library into its application memory. By posing as the graphics library during this loading process, a wrapper to the library can be injected and all subsequent communication between the game and the graphics API can be monitored and modified. This injection method is known as detouring [19] and is commonly used for patching software binaries and achieving program interoperability. It is also used by screen-capturing programs and off-the-shelf graphics debugging tools such as RenderDoc [22] and Intel Graphics Performance Analyzers [20]. To perform detouring, a wrapper needs to implement all relevant interfaces and forward calls to the original library. We implemented a wrapper for the DirectX 9 API and used RenderDoc for wrapping Direct3D 11. We successfully tested these two implementations on three different rendering engines used in AAA computer games. By intercepting all communication with the graphics hardware, we are able to monitor the creation, modification, and deletion of resources used to specify the scene and synthesize an image.

We now focus on the application of our approach to the game Grand Theft Auto V (GTA5), although much of the discussion applies more broadly. To collect data, we used RenderDoc to record every 40$^{th}$ frame during GTA5 gameplay. Being a debugger for applications, RenderDoc can be configured to record all calls of an application to the graphics API with their respective arguments and allows detailed inspection of the arguments. Since RenderDoc is scriptable and its source code is available as well, we modified it to automatically transform recorded data into a format that is suitable for annotation.

Specifically, the wrapper saves all information needed to reproduce a frame. The frames are then processed in batch after a gameplay session to extract all information needed for annotation. (This separate processing requires about 30 s per frame.) Annotation of large batches of collected and processed frames is performed later in an interactive interface that uses the extracted information to support highly efficient annotation (Fig. 3). In the following paragraphs, we discuss several challenges that had to be addressed:

1. Identify function calls that are relevant for rendering objects into the set of G-buffers that we are interested in.
2. Create persistent identities for resources that link their use across frames and across gameplay sessions.
3. Organize and store resource identities to support rapid annotation in a separate interactive interface.

**Identifying Relevant Function Calls.** To identify rendering passes, Render-Doc groups function calls into common rendering passes based on predefined heuristics. We found that strictly grouping the calls by the G-buffers that are assigned as render targets works more reliably. That way, we identify the main pass that processes the scene geometry and updates the albedo, surface normal, stencil, and depth buffers as well as the rendering passes that draw the head-up display on top of the scene image. GTA5 applies post-processing effects such as camera distortion to the rendered image before displaying it. To preserve the association of object information extracted from the main pass with pixels in the final image and to bypass drawing the head-up display (HUD), we omit the camera distortion and subsequent HUD passes.

**Identifying Resources.** To propagate labels across images, we need to reliably identify resources used to specify different scene elements. When the same mesh is used in two different frames to specify the shape of a scene element, we want to reliably recognize that it is the same mesh. During a single gameplay session, a resource can be recognized by its location in memory or by the ID used by the application to address this resource. However, the next time the game is launched, memory locations and IDs associated with resources will be different. To recognize resources across different gameplay sessions, we instead hash the associated memory content. We use a non-cryptographic hash function [3] to create a 128-bit key for the content of the memory occupied by the resource. This key is stored and is used to identify the resource in different frames. Thus, for each recorded frame, we create a lookup table to map the volatile resource IDs to persistent hash keys.

**Formatting for Annotation.** Although we can now identify and associate resources that are being used to create different frames, we have not yet associated these resources with pixels in the rendered images. We want to associate each mesh, texture, and shader with their footprint in each rendered image. One way to do this would be to step through the rendering calls and perform pixel-level comparisons of the content of each G-buffer before and after each call. However, this is unreliable and computationally expensive. Instead, we perform two complete rendering passes instead of one and produce two distinct images. The first rendering pass produces the color image and the associated buffers as described above: this is the conventional rendering pass performed by the game. The second rendering pass is used to encode IDs into pixels, such that after this pass each pixel stores the resource IDs for the mesh, texture, and shader that specify the scene element imaged at that pixel. For this second rendering pass, we replace all the shaders with our own custom shader that encodes the resource IDs of textures, meshes, and original shaders into colors and writes them into four render targets. Four render targets with three 8-bit color channels each provide us with 96 bits per pixel, which we use to store three 32-bit resource IDs: one for the mesh, one for the texture, one for the shader. In a subsequent processing stage, we read off these 32-bit IDs, which do not persist across frames, and map them to the persistent 128-bit hash keys created earlier.

## 3.2    Semantic Labeling

For each image extracted from the game, the pipeline described in Sect. 3.1 produces a corresponding resource ID map. For each pixel, this ID map identifies the mesh, texture, and shader that were used by the surface imaged at that pixel. These IDs are persistent: the same resource is identified by the same ID in different frames. This is the data used by the annotation process.

**Patch Decomposition.** We begin by automatically decomposing each image into patches of pixels that share a common ⟨mesh, texture, shader⟩ combination (henceforth, MTS). Figure 2 shows an image from the game and the resulting patches. The patches are fine-grained and each object is typically decomposed into multiple patches. Furthermore, a given patch is likely to be contained within a single object. A given mesh may contain multiple objects (a building and an adjacent sidewalk), a texture may be used on objects from different semantic classes (car and truck), and a shader may likewise be applied on semantically distinct objects, but an MTS combination is almost always used within a single object type.

**Fig. 2.** Illustration of the patches used as atomic units during the annotation process. Top left: one of the images in our dataset. Top right: patches constructed by grouping pixels that share a common MTS combination. Different patches are filled with different colors for illustration. Bottom row: partial magnifications of the top images. (Color figure online)

The identified patches are thus akin to superpixels [36], but have significant advantages over superpixels generated by a bottom-up segmentation algorithm. First, they are associated with the underlying surfaces in the scene, and patches that depict the same surface in different images are linked. Second, boundaries of semantic classes in an image coincide with patch boundaries. There is no need for a human annotator to delineate object boundaries: pixel-accurate label maps can be created simply by grouping patches. Third, as we shall see next, the metadata associated with each patch can be used to propagate labels even across object instances that do not share the same MTS.

**Association Rule Mining.** So far we have required that two patches share a complete MTS combination to be linked. However, requiring that the mesh, texture, and shader all be identical is sometimes too conservative: there are many cases in which just one or two resources are sufficient to uniquely identify the semantic class of a patch. For example, a car mesh is highly unlikely to be used for anything but a car. Instead of specifying such cases by hand, we discover them automatically during the labeling process via association rule mining [1].

During the annotation process, statistical regularities in associations between resources and semantic labels are detected. When sufficient evidence is available for a clear association between a resource and a semantic class, a rule is automatically created that labels other patches that use this resource by the associated class. This further speeds up annotation by propagating labels not just to observations of the same surface in the scene at different times, but also across different objects that use a distinctive resource that clearly identifies their semantic class.

**Annotation Process.** We use a simple interactive interface that supports labeling patches by clicking. The interface is shown in Fig. 3. Labeled areas are tinted by the color of their semantic class. (The color definitions are shown in Fig. 4.) The annotator selects a semantic class and then clicks on a patch that has not yet been labeled. In Fig. 3(left), four patches are unlabeled: part of a sidewalk, a fire hydrant, and two patches on the building. They are labeled in 14s to yield the complete label map shown in Fig. 3(right).

**Fig. 3.** Annotation interface. Labeled patches are tinted by the color of their semantic class. The annotator selects a semantic class and applies it to a patch with a single click. Left: an intermediate state with four patches yet unlabeled. Right: a complete labeling produced 14s later. (Color figure online)

Labeling the very first image still takes time due to the granularity of the patches. However, the annotation tool automatically propagates labels to all patches that share the same MTS in all images, as well as other patches that are linked by distinctive resources identified by association rule mining. As the annotation progresses, more and more patches in all images are pre-labeled. The annotation time per image decreases during the process: the more images have been annotated, the faster the labeling of each new image is. Our annotation tool only presents an image for annotation if more than 3 % of the image area has not been pre-labeled automatically by propagating labels from other frames. In this way, only a fraction of the images has to be explicitly handled by the annotator.

Labeling each pixel in every image directly would be difficult even with our single-click interface because distant or heavily occluded objects are often hard to recognize. The label propagation ensures that even if a patch is left unlabeled in a given image because it is small or far away, it will likely be labeled eventually when the underlying surface is seen more closely and its assigned label is propagated back.

## 3.3   Dataset and Analysis

We extracted 24,966 frames from GTA5. Each frame has a resolution of 1914×1052 pixels. The frames were then semantically labeled using the interface described in Sect. 3.2. The labeling process was completed in 49 h. In this time, 98.3 % of the pixel area of the extracted images was labeled with corresponding semantic classes. Classes were defined to be compatible with other semantic segmentation datasets for outdoor scenes [8,11,39,50]. The distribution of classes in our dataset is shown in Fig. 4.

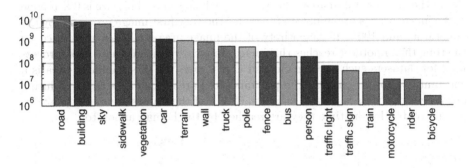

**Fig. 4.** Number of annotated pixels per class in our dataset. Note the logarithmic scale. (Color figure online)

General statistics for the dataset are summarized in Table 1. Our dataset is roughly two orders of magnitude larger than CamVid [8] and three orders of magnitude larger than semantic annotations created for the KITTI dataset [13,39]. The average annotation time for our dataset was 7 s per image: 514 times faster than the per-image annotation time reported for CamVid [8] and 771 times faster than the per-image annotation time for Cityscapes [11].

**Label Propagation.** The label propagation mechanisms significantly accelerated annotation time. Specific MTS combinations labeled during the process cover 73 % of the cumulative pixel area in the dataset. Only a fraction of that area was directly labeled by the annotator; most labels were propagated from other images. Patches covered by learned association rules account for 43 % of the dataset. During the annotation process, 2,295 association rules were automatically constructed. The union of the areas covered by labeled MTS combinations and learned association rules accounts for the 98.3 % annotation density of our dataset.

**Table 1.** Comparison of densely labeled semantic segmentation datasets for outdoor scenes. We achieve a three order of magnitude speed-up in annotation time, enabling us to densely label tens of thousands of high-resolution images.

|  | #Pixels $[10^9]$ | Annotation density [%] | Annotation time [sec/image] | Annotation speed [pixels/sec] |
|---|---|---|---|---|
| GTA5 | 50.15 | 98.3 | 7 | 279,540 |
| Cityscapes (fine) [11] | 9.43 | 97.1 | 5400 | 349 |
| Cityscapes (coarse) [11] | 26.0 | 67.5 | 420 | 3095 |
| CamVid [8] | 0.62 | 96.2 | 3,600 | 246 |
| KITTI [39] | 0.07 | 98.4 | N/A | N/A |

Define the pre-annotated area of an image to be the set of patches that are pre-labeled before the annotator reaches that image. The patches in the pre-annotated area are pre-labeled by label propagation across patches that share the same MTS and via learned association rules. For each image, we can measure the size of the pre-annotated area relative to the whole frame. This size is 0 % if none of the image area is pre-annotated (e.g., for the very first image processed by the annotator) and 100 % if the entirety of the image area is already annotated by the time the annotator reaches this image. In a conventional annotation process used for datasets such as CamVid and Cityscapes, the pre-annotated area is a constant 0 % for all images. The pre-annotated area for images handled during our labeling process is plotted in Fig. 5. 98.7 % of the frames are more than 90 % pre-annotated by the time they are reached by the human annotator.

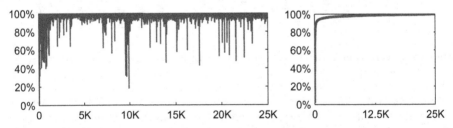

**Fig. 5.** Effect of label propagation. For each frame, the plots show the fraction of image area that is pre-annotated by the time the human annotator reaches that frame. On the left, the frames are arranged in the order they are processed; on the right, the frames are sorted by magnitude of pre-annotated area. Only 333 frames (1.3 % of the total) are less than 90 % pre-annotated by the time they are reached by the human annotator.

**Diversity of the Collected Data.** We also analyze the diversity of the images extracted from the game world. The effectiveness of label propagation may suggest that the collected images are visually uniform. This is not the case. Figure 6 shows the distribution of the number of frames in which MTS combinations in the dataset occur. As shown in the figure, 26.5 % of the MTS combinations only occur in a single image in the collected dataset. That is, more than a quarter of the MTS combinations observed in the 25 thousand collected images are only observed in a single image each. The median number of frames in which an MTS occurs is 4: that is, most of the MTS combinations are only seen in 4 images or less out of the 25 thousand collected images. This indicates the high degree of variability in the collected dataset.

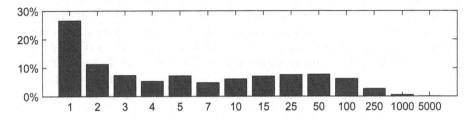

**Fig. 6.** Distribution of the number of frames in which an MTS combination occurs. 26.5 % of the MTS combinations only occur in a single image each and most of the MTS combinations are only seen in 4 images or less.

In addition, Fig. 7 shows 20 randomly sampled images from our dataset. As the figure demonstrates, the images in the collected dataset are highly variable in their content and layout.

**Fig. 7.** Randomly sampled images from the collected dataset, illustrating its diversity.

# 4    Semantic Segmentation

We now evaluate the effectiveness of using the acquired data for training semantic segmentation models. We evaluate on two datasets for semantic segmentation
of outdoor scenes: CamVid [8] and KITTI [13,39]. As our semantic segmentation model, we use the front-end prediction module of Yu and Koltun [52]. Our
training procedure consists of two stages. In the first stage, we jointly train on
real and synthetic data using mini-batch stochastic gradient descent with mini-
batches of 8 images: 4 real and 4 synthetic. 50 K iterations are performed with
a learning rate of $10^{-4}$ and momentum 0.99. The crop size is $628 \times 628$ and
the receptive field is $373 \times 373$ pixels. In the second stage, we fine-tune for 4 K
iterations on real data only, using the same parameters as in the first stage.

## 4.1    CamVid Dataset

We begin with experiments on the CamVid dataset. For ease of comparison to
prior work, we adopted the training and test setup of Sturgess et al. [45], which
has become standard for the CamVid dataset. This setup has 11 semantic classes
and a split of the dataset into 367 training, 100 validation, and 233 test images.

The main results are summarized in Table 2. The table shows that using
the synthetic data during training increases the mean IoU by 3.9 % points. In
addition, we used the full set of synthetic images and varied the proportion
of real images in the training set. The results show that when we train on $\frac{1}{3}$
of the CamVid training set along with the game data, we surpass the accuracy
achieved when training on the full CamVid training set without game data. This
suggests that the presented approach to acquiring and labeling synthetic data
can significantly reduce the amount of hand-labeled real-world images required
for training semantic segmentation models.

**Table 2.** Controlled experiments on the CamVid dataset. Training with the full
CamVid training set augmented by the synthetic images increases the mean IoU by
3.9 % points. Synthetic images also allow reducing the amount of labeled real-world
training data by a factor of 3.

| Real images | 100 % | - | 25 % | 33 % | 50 % | 100 % |
|---|---|---|---|---|---|---|
| Synthetic images (all) | - | 100 % | ✓ | ✓ | ✓ | ✓ |
| Mean IoU | 65.0 | 43.6 | 63.9 | 65.2 | 66.5 | **68.9** |

Table 3 provides a comparison of our results to prior work on semantic segmentation on the CamVid dataset. Our strongest baseline is the state-of-the-art
system of Kundu et al. [25], which used a bigger ConvNet and analyzed whole
video sequences. By using synthetic data during training, we outperform this
baseline by 2.8 % points, while considering individual frames only.

**Table 3.** Comparison to prior work on the CamVid dataset. We outperform the state-of-the-art system of Kundu et al. by 2.8 % points without utilizing temporal cues.

| Method | Building | Tree | Sky | Car | Sign | Road | Pedestrian | Fence | Pole | Sidewalk | Bicyclist | Mean IoU |
|---|---|---|---|---|---|---|---|---|---|---|---|---|
| SuperParsing [47] | 70.4 | 54.8 | 83.5 | 43.3 | 25.4 | 83.4 | 11.6 | 18.3 | 5.2 | 57.4 | 8.9 | 42.03 |
| Liu and He [27] | 66.8 | 66.6 | 90.1 | 62.9 | 21.4 | 85.8 | 28 | 17.8 | 8.3 | 63.5 | 8.5 | 47.2 |
| Tripathi et al. [48] | 74.2 | 67.9 | 91 | 66.5 | 23.6 | 90.7 | 26.2 | 28.5 | 16.3 | 71.9 | 28.2 | 53.18 |
| Yu and Koltun [52] | 82.6 | 76.2 | 89.9 | 84.0 | 46.9 | 92.2 | 56.3 | 35.8 | 23.4 | 75.3 | 55.5 | 65.3 |
| Kundu et al. [25] | **84** | **77.2** | **91.3** | **85.6** | 49.9 | 92.5 | **59.1** | 37.6 | 16.9 | 76.0 | 57.2 | 66.1 |
| Our result | **84.4** | **77.5** | 91.1 | 84.9 | 51.3 | 94.5 | 59 | **44.9** | **29.5** | 82 | **58.4** | **68.9** |

## 4.2 KITTI Dataset

We have also performed an evaluation on the KITTI semantic segmentation dataset. The results are reported in Table 4. We use the split of Ros et al. [39], which consists of 100 training images and 46 test images. We compare against several baselines for which the authors have either provided results on this dataset or released their code. The model trained with game data outperforms the model trained without game data by 2.6 % points.

**Table 4.** Results on the KITTI dataset. Training with game data yields a 2.6 % point improvement over training without game data.

| Method | Building | Tree | Sky | Car | Sign | Road | Pedestrian | Fence | Pole | Sidewalk | Bicyclist | Mean IoU |
|---|---|---|---|---|---|---|---|---|---|---|---|---|
| Ros et al. [39] | 71.8 | 69.5 | **84.4** | 51.2 | 4.2 | 72.4 | 1.7 | 32.4 | 2.6 | 45.3 | 3.2 | 39.9 |
| Tripathi et al. [48] | 75.1 | 74.0 | **84.4** | 61.8 | 0 | 75.4 | 0 | 1.0 | 2.2 | 37.9 | 0 | 37.4 |
| Yu and Koltun [52] | 84.6 | **81.1** | 83 | 81.4 | 41.8 | **92.9** | 4.6 | **47.1** | 35.2 | 73.1 | 26.4 | 59.2 |
| Ours (real only) | 84 | **81** | 83 | 80.2 | **43.2** | 92.4 | 1.0 | 46.0 | 35.4 | 74.8 | **27.9** | 59 |
| Ours (real+synth) | **85.7** | 80.3 | **85.2** | **83.2** | 40.5 | **92.7** | **29.7** | 42.8 | **38** | **75.9** | 22.6 | **61.6** |

## 5    Discussion

We presented an approach to rapidly producing pixel-accurate semantic label maps for images synthesized by modern computer games. We have demonstrated the approach by creating dense pixel-level semantic annotations for 25 thousand images extracted from a realistic open-world game. Our experiments have shown that data created with the presented approach can increase the performance of semantic segmentation models on real-world images and can reduce the need for expensive conventional labeling.

There are many extensions that would be interesting. First, the presented ideas can be extended to produce continuous video streams in which each frame is densely annotated. Second, the presented approach can be applied to produce ground-truth data for many dense prediction problems, including optical flow, scene flow, depth estimation, boundary detection, stereo reconstruction, intrinsic image decomposition, visual odometry, and more. Third, our ideas can be extended to produce instance-level – rather than class-level – segmentations. There are many other exciting opportunities and we believe that modern game worlds can play a significant role in training artificial vision systems.

**Acknowledgements.** SRR was supported in part by the German Research Foundation (DFG) within the GRK 1362. Additionally, SRR and SR were supported in part by the European Research Council under the European Union's Seventh Framework Programme (FP/2007-2013) / ERC Grant Agreement No. 307942. Work on this project was conducted in part while SRR was an intern at Intel Labs.

# References

1. Agrawal, R., Srikant, R.: Fast algorithms for mining association rules in large databases. In: VLDB (1994)
2. Akenine-Möller, T., Haines, E., Hoffman, N.: Real-Time Rendering, 3rd edn. A K Peters, Natick (2008)
3. Appleby, A.: Murmurhash. https://github.com/aappleby/smhasher
4. Aubry, M., Maturana, D., Efros, A.A., Russell, B.C., Sivic, J.: Seeing 3D chairs: exemplar part-based 2D–3D alignment using a large dataset of CAD models. In: CVPR (2014)
5. Aubry, M., Russell, B.C.: Understanding deep features with computer-generated imagery. In: ICCV (2015)
6. Baker, S., Scharstein, D., Lewis, J.P., Roth, S., Black, M.J., Szeliski, R.: A database and evaluation methodology for optical flow. IJCV **92**(1), 1–31 (2011)
7. Barron, J.L., Fleet, D.J., Beauchemin, S.S.: Performance of optical flow techniques. IJCV **12**(1), 43–77 (1994)
8. Brostow, G.J., Fauqueur, J., Cipolla, R.: Semantic object classes in video: a high-definition ground truth database. Pattern Recogn. Lett. **30**(2), 88–97 (2009)
9. Butler, D.J., Wulff, J., Stanley, G.B., Black, M.J.: A naturalistic open source movie for optical flow evaluation. In: Fitzgibbon, A., Lazebnik, S., Perona, P., Sato, Y., Schmid, C. (eds.) ECCV 2012. LNCS, vol. 7577, pp. 611–625. Springer, Heidelberg (2012). doi:10.1007/978-3-642-33783-3_44
10. Chen, C., Seff, A., Kornhauser, A.L., Xiao, J.: DeepDriving: learning affordance for direct perception in autonomous driving. In: ICCV (2015)
11. Cordts, M., Omran, M., Ramos, S., Rehfeld, T., Enzweiler, M., Benenson, R., Franke, U., Roth, S., Schiele, B.: The cityscapes dataset for semantic urban scene understanding. In: CVPR (2016)
12. Dosovitskiy, A., Fischer, P., Ilg, E., Häusser, P., Hazirbas, C., Golkov, V., van der Smagt, P., Cremers, D., Brox, T.: FlowNet: learning optical flow with convolutional networks. In: ICCV (2015)
13. Geiger, A., Lenz, P., Stiller, C., Urtasun, R.: Vision meets robotics: the KITTI dataset. Int. J. Rob. Res. **32**(11), 1231–1237 (2013)

14. Haltakov, V., Unger, C., Ilic, S.: Framework for generation of synthetic ground truth data for driver assistance applications. In: Weickert, J., Hein, M., Schiele, B. (eds.) GCPR 2013. LNCS, vol. 8142, pp. 323–332. Springer, Heidelberg (2013). doi:10.1007/978-3-642-40602-7_35
15. Handa, A., Pătrăucean, V., Badrinarayanan, V., Stent, S., Cipolla, R.: Understanding real world indoor scenes with synthetic data. In: CVPR (2016)
16. Handa, A., Whelan, T., McDonald, J., Davison, A.J.: A benchmark for RGB-D visual odometry, 3D reconstruction and SLAM. In: ICRA (2014)
17. He, X., Zemel, R.S., Carreira-Perpiñán, M.: Multiscale conditional random fields for image labeling. In: CVPR (2004)
18. Horn, B.K.P., Schunck, B.G.: Determining optical flow. Artif. Intell. 17(1–3), 185–203 (1981)
19. Hunt, G., Brubacher, D.: Detours: binary interception of Win32 functions. In: 3rd USENIX Windows NT Symposium (1999)
20. Intel: Intel Graphics Performance Analyzers. https://software.intel.com/en-us/gpa
21. Kaneva, B., Torralba, A., Freeman, W.T.: Evaluation of image features using a photorealistic virtual world. In: ICCV (2011)
22. Karlsson, B.: RenderDoc. https://renderdoc.org
23. Krähenbühl, P., Koltun, V.: Efficient inference in fully connected CRFs with Gaussian edge potentials. In: NIPS (2011)
24. Krizhevsky, A., Sutskever, I., Hinton, G.E.: ImageNet classification with deep convolutional neural networks. In: NIPS (2012)
25. Kundu, A., Vineet, V., Koltun, V.: Feature space optimization for semantic video segmentation. In: CVPR (2016)
26. Liebelt, J., Schmid, C., Schertler, K.: Viewpoint-independent object class detection using 3D feature maps. In: CVPR (2008)
27. Liu, B., He, X.: Multiclass semantic video segmentation with object-level active inference. In: CVPR (2015)
28. Long, J., Shelhamer, E., Darrell, T.: Fully convolutional networks for semantic segmentation. In: CVPR (2015)
29. Marín, J., Vázquez, D., Gerónimo, D., López, A.M.: Learning appearance in virtual scenarios for pedestrian detection. In: CVPR (2010)
30. Massa, F., Russell, B.C., Aubry, M.: Deep exemplar 2D–3D detection by adapting from real to rendered views. In: CVPR (2016)
31. Mayer, N., Ilg, E., Häusser, P., Fischer, P., Cremers, D., Dosovitskiy, A., Brox, T.: A large dataset to train convolutional networks for disparity, optical flow, and scene flow estimation. In: CVPR (2016)
32. McCane, B., Novins, K., Crannitch, D., Galvin, B.: On benchmarking optical flow. CVIU 84(1), 126–143 (2001)
33. Papon, J., Schoeler, M.: Semantic pose using deep networks trained on synthetic RGB-D. In: ICCV (2015)
34. Peng, X., Sun, B., Ali, K., Saenko, K.: Learning deep object detectors from 3D models. In: ICCV (2015)
35. Pepik, B., Stark, M., Gehler, P.V., Schiele, B.: Multi-view and 3D deformable part models. PAMI 37(11), 2232–2245 (2015)
36. Ren, X., Malik, J.: Learning a classification model for segmentation. In: ICCV (2003)
37. Richter, S.R., Roth, S.: Discriminative shape from shading in uncalibrated illumination. In: CVPR (2015)
38. Rockstar Games: Policy on posting copyrighted Rockstar Games material. http://tinyurl.com/pjfoqo5

39. Ros, G., Ramos, S., Granados, M., Bakhtiary, A., Vázquez, D., López, A.M.: Vision-based offline-online perception paradigm for autonomous driving. In: WACV (2015)
40. Saito, T., Takahashi, T.: Comprehensible rendering of 3-D shapes. In: SIGGRAPH (1990)
41. Sharp, T., Keskin, C., Robertson, D.P., Taylor, J., Shotton, J., Kim, D., Rhemann, C., Leichter, I., Vinnikov, A., Wei, Y., Freedman, D., Kohli, P., Krupka, E., Fitzgibbon, A.W., Izadi, S.: Accurate, robust, and flexible real-time hand tracking. In: CHI (2015)
42. Shotton, J., Girshick, R.B., Fitzgibbon, A.W., Sharp, T., Cook, M., Finocchio, M., Moore, R., Kohli, P., Criminisi, A., Kipman, A., Blake, A.: Efficient human pose estimation from single depth images. PAMI $35(12)$, 2821–2840 (2013)
43. Shotton, J., Winn, J.M., Rother, C., Criminisi, A.: Textonboost for image understanding: multi-class object recognition and segmentation by jointly modeling texture, layout, and context. IJCV $81(1)$, 2–23 (2009)
44. Stark, M., Goesele, M., Schiele, B.: Back to the future: learning shape models from 3D CAD data. In: BMVC (2010)
45. Sturgess, P., Alahari, K., Ladicky, L., Torr, P.H.S.: Combining appearance and structure from motion features for road scene understanding. In: BMVC (2009)
46. Taylor, G.R., Chosak, A.J., Brewer, P.C.: OVVV: using virtual worlds to design and evaluate surveillance systems. In: CVPR (2007)
47. Tighe, J., Lazebnik, S.: Superparsing – scalable nonparametric image parsing with superpixels. IJCV $101(2)$, 329–349 (2013)
48. Tripathi, S., Belongie, S., Hwang, Y., Nguyen, T.Q.: Semantic video segmentation: exploring inference efficiency. In: ISOCC (2015)
49. Vázquez, D., López, A.M., Marín, J., Ponsa, D., Gomez, D.G.: Virtual and real world adaptation for pedestrian detection. PAMI $36(4)$, 797–809 (2014)
50. Xie, J., Kiefel, M., Sun, M.T., Geiger, A.: Semantic instance annotation of street scenes by 3D to 2D label transfer. In: CVPR (2016)
51. Xu, J., Vázquez, D., López, A.M., Marín, J., Ponsa, D.: Learning a part-based pedestrian detector in a virtual world. IEEE Trans. Intell. Transp. Syst. $15(5)$, 2121–2131 (2014)
52. Yu, F., Koltun, V.: Multi-scale context aggregation by dilated convolutions. In: ICLR (2016)
53. Veeravasarapu, V.S.R., Rothkopf, C., Ramesh, V.: Model-driven simulations for deep convolutional neural networks (2016). arXiv preprint arXiv:1605.09582
54. Shafaei, A., Little, J.J., Schmidt, M.: Play and learn: using video Games to train computer vision models. In: BMVC (2016)

# Human Re-identification in Crowd Videos Using Personal, Social and Environmental Constraints

Shayan Modiri Assari$^{(\boxtimes)}$, Haroon Idrees, and Mubarak Shah

Center for Research in Computer Vision,
University of Central Florida, Orlando, USA
{smodiri,haroon,shah}@cs.ucf.edu

**Abstract.** This paper addresses the problem of human re-identification in videos of dense crowds. Re-identification in crowded scenes is a challenging problem due to large number of people and frequent occlusions, coupled with changes in their appearance due to different properties and exposure of cameras. To solve this problem, we model multiple Personal, Social and Environmental (PSE) constraints on human motion across cameras in crowded scenes. The personal constraints include appearance and preferred speed of each individual, while the social influences are modeled by grouping and collision avoidance. Finally, the environmental constraints model the transition probabilities between gates (entrances/exits). We incorporate these constraints into an energy minimization for solving human re-identification. Assigning 1–1 correspondence while modeling PSE constraints is NP-hard. We optimize using a greedy local neighborhood search algorithm to restrict the search space of hypotheses. We evaluated the proposed approach on several thousand frames of PRID and Grand Central datasets, and obtained significantly better results compared to existing methods.

**Keywords:** Video surveillance · Re-identification · Dense crowds · Social constraints · Multiple cameras · Human tracking

## 1 Introduction

Human re-identification is a fundamental and crucial problem for multi-camera surveillance systems [17,49]. It involves re-identifying individuals after they leave field-of-view (FOV) of one camera and appear in FOV of another camera (see Fig. 1(a)). The investigation process of the Boston Marathon bombing serves to highlight the importance of re-identification in crowded scenes. Authorities had to sift through a mountain of footage from government surveillance cameras, private security cameras and imagery shot by bystanders on smart phones [22]. Therefore, automatic re-identification in dense crowds will allow successful monitoring and analysis of crowded events.

Dense crowds are the most challenging scenario for human re-identification. For large number of people, appearance alone provides a weak cue. Often, people in crowds wear similar clothes that makes re-identification even harder (Fig. 1c).

© Springer International Publishing AG 2016
B. Leibe et al. (Eds.): ECCV 2016, Part II, LNCS 9906, pp. 119–136, 2016.
DOI: 10.1007/978-3-319-46475-6_8

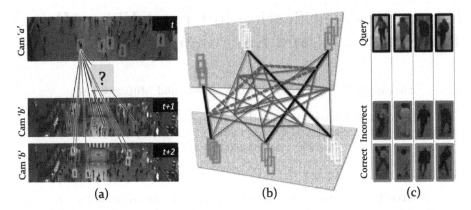

**Fig. 1.** (a) Our goal is to re-identify people leaving camera $a$ at time $t$ (top row) to when they appear in camera $b$ at some time $t+1, t+2, \ldots$ in the future. The invisible region between the cameras is not closed, which means people can leave one camera and never appear in the other camera. (b) We construct a graph *between individuals* in the two cameras, as shown with black lines. Some of the constraints are linear in nature (appearance, speed, destination) while others are quadratic (spatial and social grouping, collision avoidance). The quadratic constraints are shown in red and capture relationships *between matches*. In (c), the people in black boxes are from camera $a$, while the other two rows shows people with similar appearance from camera $b$. The red boxes indicate the best matches (using appearance) which are incorrect, and green boxes show the low-scoring correct matches. This highlights that crowded scenes make human re-identification across cameras significantly difficult. (Color figure online)

Unlike regular surveillance scenarios previously tackled in literature, we address this problem for thousands of people where at any 30 s interval, hundreds of people concurrently enter a single camera.

Traditionally, re-identification has been primarily concerned with matching static snapshots of people from multiple cameras. Although there have been few works that modeled social effects for re-identification such as grouping behavior [4,5,58], they mostly deal with static images. In this paper, we study the use of time and video information for this task, and propose to consider the dynamic spatio-temporal context of individuals and the environment to improve the performance of human re-identification. We complement appearance with multiple personal, social and environmental (PSE) constraints, many of which are applicable without knowledge of camera topology. The PSE constraints include *preferred speed and destination*, as well as *social grouping* and *collision avoidance*. The environmental constraints are modeled by learning the repetitive patterns that occur in surveillance networks, as individuals exiting camera from a particular location (gate) are likely to enter another camera from another specific location. These happen both as soft (*spatial grouping*) and hard constraints (*transition probabilities*). The PSE constraints that are linear in nature, i.e. occur between objects, are shown with black lines in Fig. 1(b), while quadratic ones occur between matching hypotheses, i.e., pairs of objects, are shown with red lines in Fig. 1(b). Thus, if there are $N_a$ and $N_b$ number of people in two cameras, then the total number of possible matching hypotheses is $N_a N_b$, and there are $(N_a N_b)^2$ possible quadratic hypotheses. The time limits naturally reduce some of the hypotheses, nonetheless for large number of people these can be overwhelming. Since the proposed PSE constraints are both linear and quadratic in nature, we employ a greedy local neighborhood search algorithm to optimize the resulting objective function simultaneously for all people. Thus, in addition to producing rankings for different queries, our method also outputs the more useful 1–1 correspondences for individuals.

To the best of our knowledge, this is the first paper to address human re-identification using personal, social and environmental constraints in dense crowds. The evaluation is performed on two datasets, PRID [19] and the challenging Grand Central dataset [53] which depicts dense crowds[1]. The rest of the paper is organized as follows. We discuss related work in Sect. 2, and present the proposed approach in Sect. 3. The results of our experiments are reported in Sect. 4, and we conclude with some directions for future research in Sect. 5.

## 2   Related Work

Our approach is at the crossroads of human re-identification in videos, dense crowd analysis and social force models. Next, we provide a brief literature review of each of these areas.

**Person Re-identification** is an active area of research in computer vision, with some of the recent works including [1,7,27–29,37,54,55,57] applicable to static images. In videos, several methods have been developed for handing over objects across cameras [6,10,20,45,49]. Most of them focus on non-crowd surveillance scenarios with emphasis on modeling color distortion and learning brightness transfer functions that relate different cameras [16,21,39,40], others relate objects by developing illumination-tolerant representations [31] or comparing possible matches to a reference set [9]. Similarly, Kuo *et al.* [24] used Multiple Instance Learning to combine complementary appearance descriptors.

The spatio-temporal relationships across cameras [32,46,47] or prior knowledge about topology has been used for human re-identification. Chen *et al.* [8] make use of prior knowledge about camera topology to adaptively learn appearance and spatio-temporal relationships between cameras, while Mazzon *et al.* [34] use prior knowledge about relative locations of cameras to limit potential paths people can follow. Javed *et al.* [20] presented a two-phase approach where transition times and exit/entrance relationships are learned first, which are later used to improve object correspondences. Fleuret *et al.* [14] predicted occlusions with a generative model and a probabilistic occupancy map. Dick and Brooks [11] used a stochastic transition matrix to model patterns of motion within and across cameras. These methods have been evaluated on non-crowd scenarios, where observations are sparse and appearance is distinctive.

---

[1] Data and ground truth available at: http://crcv.ucf.edu/projects/Crowd-Reidentification.

In crowded scenes, hundreds of people enter a camera simultaneously within a small window of few seconds, which makes learning transition times during an unsupervised training period virtually impossible. Furthermore, our approach is applicable whether or not the information about camera topology is available.

**Dense Crowds** studies [3,59,60] have shown that walking behavior of individuals in crowds is influenced by several constraints such as entrances, exits, boundaries, obstacles; as well as preferred speed and destination, along with interactions with other pedestrians whether moving [15,35] or stationary [53]. Wu *et al.* [51] proposed a two-stage network-flow framework for linking tracks interrupted by occlusions. Alahi *et al.* [2] identify origin-destination (OD) pairs using trajectory data of commuters which is similar to grouping. In contrast, we employ several PSE constraints besides social grouping.

**Social Force Models** have been used for improving tracking performance [25, 38,52]. Pellegrini *et al.* [38] were the first to use social force models for tracking. They modeled collision avoidance, desired speed and destination and showed its application for tracking. Yamaguchi *et al.* [52] proposed a similar approach using a more sophisticated model that tries to predict destinations and groups based on features and classifiers trained on annotated sequences. Both methods use agent-based models and predict future locations using techniques similar to crowd simulations. They are not applicable to re-identification, as our goal is not to predict but to associate hypotheses. Therefore, we use social and contextual constraints for re-identification in an offline manner. Furthermore, both these methods require observations to be in metric coordinates, which for many real scenarios might be impractical.

For re-identification in static images, group context was used by Zheng *et al.* [17,58], who proposed ratio-occurrence descriptors to capture groups. Cai *et al.* [5] use covariance descriptor to match groups of people, as it is invariant to illumination changes and rotations to a certain degree. For re-identifying players in group sports, Bialkowski *et al.* [4] aid appearance with group context where each person is assigned a role or position within the group structure of a team. In videos, Qin *et al.* [41] use grouping in non-crowded scenes to perform hand over of objects across cameras. They optimize track assignment and group detection in an alternative fashion. On the other hand, we refrain from optimizing over group detection, and use multiple PSE constraints (speed, destination, social grouping etc.) for hand over. We additionally use group context in space, i.e., objects that take the same amount of time between two gates are assigned a cost similar to grouping, when in reality they may not be traveling together in time. Mazzon and Cavallaro [33] presented a modified social force multi-camera tracker where individuals are attracted towards their goals, and repulsed by walls and barriers. They require a surveillance site model beforehand and do not use appearance. In contrast, our formulation avoids such assumptions and restrictions.

In summary, our approach does not require any prior knowledge about the scene nor any training phase to learn patterns of motion. Ours is the first work to incorporate multiple personal, social and environmental constraints simultaneously for the task of human re-identification in crowd videos.

## 3    Framework for Human Re-identification in Crowds

In this section, we present our approach to re-identify people using PSE constraints. Since transition probabilities between gates are not known a priori, we estimate correspondences and transition probabilities in an alternative fashion.

Let $O_{i_a}$ represent an observation of an object $i$ in camera $a$. Its trajectory is given by a set of points $[\mathbf{p}_{i_a}(t_{i_a}^{\eta}), \ldots, \mathbf{p}_{i_a}(t_{i_a}^{\chi})]$, where $t_{i_a}^{\eta}$ and $t_{i_a}^{\chi}$ represent the time it entered and exited the camera $a$, respectively. Given another observation of an object $j$ in camera $b$, $O_{j_b}$, a possible match between the two is denoted by $M_{i_a}^{j_b} = \langle O_{i_a}, O_{j_b} \rangle$. To simplify notation, we drop the symbol for time $t$ and use it only when necessary, thus, $\mathbf{p}_{i_a}^{\chi} \equiv \mathbf{p}_{i_a}(t_{i_a}^{\chi})$ and $\mathbf{p}_{j_b}^{\eta} \equiv \mathbf{p}_{j_b}(t_{j_b}^{\eta})$.

The entrances and exits in each camera are divided into multiple gates. For the case of two cameras $a$ and $b$, the gates (locations) are given by $\mathbf{G}_{1_a}, \ldots, \mathbf{G}_{U_a}$ and $\mathbf{G}_{1_b}, \ldots, \mathbf{G}_{U_b}$, where $U_a$ and $U_b$ are the total number of gates in both cameras, respectively. Furthermore, we define a function $g(\mathbf{p}(t))$, which returns the nearest gate when given a point in the camera. For instance, for a person $i_a$, $g(\mathbf{p}_{i_a}^{\chi})$ returns the gate from which the person $i$ exited camera $a$, by computing the distance of $\mathbf{p}_{i_a}^{\chi}$ to each gate. Mathematically, this is given by:

$$g(\mathbf{p}_{i_a}^{\chi}) = \arg\min_{\mathbf{G}_{u_a}} \|\mathbf{G}_{u_a} - \mathbf{p}_{i_a}^{\chi}\|^2, \ \forall u_a = 1, \ldots, U_a. \tag{1}$$

To compute appearance similarity, $\phi_{\mathrm{app}}(O_{i_a}, O_{j_b})$, between observations $O_{i_a}$ and $O_{j_b}$, we use features from Convolutional Neural Networks [44]. In particular, we extract features from Relu6 and Fc7 layers, followed by homogenous kernel mapping [48] and linear kernel as the the similarity metric. Next, we describe the costs for different PSE constraints, $\phi(.)$, employed in our framework for re-identification. Since all costs have their respective ranges, we use a sigmoid function, $\hat{\phi}(.) = (1 + \exp(-\beta\phi(.))^{-1}$, to balance them. Most of the constraints do not require knowledge about camera topology, and are described below.

### 3.1    PSE Constraints Without Camera Topology

**Preferred Speed:** The walking speed of individuals has been estimated to be around $1.3\,\mathrm{m/s}$ [42]. Since, we do not assume the availability of metric rectification information, we cannot use this fact directly in our formulation. However, a consequence of this observation is that we can assume the walking speed of individuals, *on average*, in different cameras is constant. We assume a Normal distribution, $\mathcal{N}(.)$, on observed speeds in each camera. The variation in walking speeds of different individuals is captured by the variance of the Normal distribution. Let $\mathcal{N}(\mu_a, \sigma_a)$ and $\mathcal{N}(\mu_b, \sigma_b)$ denote the distribution modeled in the two cameras. Since a particular person is being assumed to walk with the same speed in different cameras, the cost for preferred speed using the exit speed of person $i_a$, $\dot{\mathbf{p}}_{i_a}^{\chi}$, and the entrance speed of person $j_b$, $\dot{\mathbf{p}}_{j_b}^{\eta}$ is given by:

$$\dot{\mathbf{p}}_{i_a}^\chi = \sigma_a^{-1}(\|\mathbf{p}_{i_a}^\chi - \mathbf{p}_{i_a}^{\chi-1}\| - \mu_a), \quad \dot{\mathbf{p}}_{j_b}^\eta = \sigma_b^{-1}(\|\mathbf{p}_{j_b}^{\eta+1} - \mathbf{p}_{j_b}^\eta\| - \mu_b), \qquad (2)$$

$$\phi_{\mathrm{spd}}(O_{i_a}, O_{j_b}) = |\dot{\mathbf{p}}_{i_a}^\chi - \dot{\mathbf{p}}_{j_b}^\eta|. \qquad (3)$$

**Destination:** For re-identification in multiple cameras, the knowledge about destination gives a prior for an individual's location in another camera. Since individuals cannot be observed between cameras, we capture the common and frequent patterns of movement between gates in different cameras by modeling the transition probabilities between gates in those cameras. Assuming we have a set of putative matches $\{M_{i_a}^{j_b}\}$, we estimate the probability of transition between exit gate $G_{u_a}$ and entrance gate $G_{u_b}$ as:

$$p(G_{u_a}, G_{u_b}) = \frac{|g(\mathbf{p}_{i_a}^\chi) = G_{u_a} \wedge g(\mathbf{p}_{j_b}^\eta) = G_{u_b}|}{|g(\mathbf{p}_{i_a}^\chi) = G_{u_a} \wedge \sum_{u_b', j_b'} g(\mathbf{p}_{j_b'}^\eta) = G_{u_b'}|}. \qquad (4)$$

Thus, the cost for transition between gates for the match $\langle O_{i_a}, O_{j_b} \rangle$ is given by:

$$\phi_{\mathrm{tr}}(O_{i_a}, O_{j_b}) = 1 - p\big(g(\mathbf{p}_{i_a}^\chi), g(\mathbf{p}_{j_b}^\eta)\big). \qquad (5)$$

**Spatial Grouping:** The distance traveled by different individuals between two points (or gates) across cameras should be the same. Since the camera topology is not available in this case, the distance can be implicitly computed as a product of velocity and time. This is a quadratic cost computed between every two possible matches, $M_{i_a}^{j_b}$ and $M_{i_a'}^{j_b'}$, given by:

$$\varphi_{\mathrm{spt}}(M_{i_a}^{j_b}, M_{i_a'}^{j_b'}) = \exp(-|\mathbf{p}_{i_a}^\chi - \mathbf{p}_{i_a'}^\chi|) \cdot \exp(-|\mathbf{p}_{j_b}^\eta - \mathbf{p}_{j_b'}^\eta|)$$
$$\cdot |(\dot{\mathbf{p}}_{i_a}^\chi + \dot{\mathbf{p}}_{j_b}^\eta)(t_{j_b}^\eta - t_{i_a}^\chi) - (\dot{\mathbf{p}}_{i_a'}^\chi + \dot{\mathbf{p}}_{j_b'}^\eta)(t_{j_b'}^\eta - t_{i_a'}^\chi)|. \quad (6)$$

Effectively, if the exit and entrance locations are nearby (the first two terms in Eq. 6), then we compute the distance traveled by each match in the pair using the product of mean velocity and time required to travel between those locations (the third term). It is evident from Eq. 6 that the exponentiation in first two terms will allow this cost to take effect only when the entrance and exit locations are both proximal. If so, the third term will then measure the difference in distance traveled by the two possible matches (tracks), and penalize using that difference. If the distance is similar, the cost will be low suggesting both matches (tracks) should be included in the final solution. If the difference is distance is high, then at least one or both of the matches are incorrect.

**Social Grouping:** People tend to walk in groups. In our formulation, we reward individuals in a *social group* that exit and enter together from the same locations at the same times,

$$\varphi_{\mathrm{grp}}(M_{i_a}^{j_b}, M_{i_a'}^{j_b'}) = \exp(-|\mathbf{p}_{i_a}^\chi - \mathbf{p}_{i_a'}^\chi| - |\mathbf{p}_{j_b}^\eta - \mathbf{p}_{j_b'}^\eta| - |t_{j_b}^\eta - t_{j_b'}^\eta| - |t_{i_a}^\chi - t_{i_a'}^\chi|). \quad (7)$$

Here, the first two terms capture the difference in exit and entrance locations, respectively, and the third and fourth terms capture the difference in exit and entrance times, respectively.

## 3.2   Optimization with PSE Constraints

In this subsection, we present the optimization technique which uses the afore-mentioned constraints. Let $z_{i_a}^{j_b}$ be the variable corresponding to a possible match $M_{i_a}^{j_b}$. Our goal is to optimize the following loss function over all possible matches, which is the weighted sum of linear and quadratic terms:

$$
L = \sum_{i_a, j_b} z_{i_a}^{j_b} \underbrace{\left( \hat{\phi}_{\text{app}}(M_{i_a}^{j_b}) + \alpha_{\text{spd}}\hat{\phi}_{\text{spd}}(M_{i_a}^{j_b}) + \alpha_{\text{tr}}\hat{\phi}_{\text{tr}}(M_{i_a}^{j_b}) \right)}_{\text{Linear Terms}}
$$
$$
+ \sum_{\substack{i_a, j_b \\ i_a', j_b'}} z_{i_a}^{j_b} z_{i_a'}^{j_b'} \underbrace{\left( \alpha_{\text{spt}}\hat{\varphi}_{\text{spt}}(M_{i_a}^{j_b}, M_{i_a'}^{j_b'}) + \alpha_{\text{grp}}\hat{\varphi}_{\text{grp}}(M_{i_a}^{j_b}, M_{i_a'}^{j_b'}) \right)}_{\text{Quadratic Terms}}, \tag{8}
$$

subject to the following conditions:

$$
\sum_{i_a} z_{i_a}^{j_b} \leq 1, \forall j_b, \sum_{j_b} z_{i_a}^{j_b} \leq 1, \forall i_a, z_{i_a}^{j_b} \in \{0,1\}. \tag{9}
$$

---

**Algorithm 1.** Algorithm to find 1–1 correspondence between persons observed in different cameras using both linear and quadratic constraints.

**Input:** $O_{i_a}, O_{j_b}$  $\forall i_a, j_b, R$ (# steps)
**Output:** $L^*, \mathbf{z}^*$;   $0 \leq |t_{j_b}^{\eta} - t_{i_a}^{\chi}| \leq \tau, \forall z_{i_a}^{j_b}$

---

1: **procedure** RE-IDENTIFY()
2:      Initialize $[L^*, \mathbf{z}^*]$ for Linear Constraints with MUNKRES [36]    ▷ Initial solution
3:      **while** $L^*$ improves **do**
4:          **for** $r = 0$ to $R$ **do**
5:              $[L^-, \mathbf{z}^-] = $ REMOVEMAT$(L^*, \mathbf{z}^*, r)$          ▷ Probabilistically remove $r$ matches
6:              $L' = L^-, \mathbf{z}' = \mathbf{z}^-$          ▷ Consider it the new solution
7:              **for** $s = r + 1$ to 1 **do**
8:                  $[L^+, \mathbf{z}^+] = $ ADDMAT$(L', \mathbf{z}', s)$ ▷ Add $s$ new matches to the solution
9:                  **if** $L' > L^+$ **then**          ▷ Is the solution after adding new matches better?
10:                      $L' = L^+, \mathbf{z}' = \mathbf{z}^+$          ▷ If so, update it as the new solution
11:                  **end if**
12:              **end for**
13:              **if** $L^* > L'$ **then** ▷ Is the new solution better the best solution so far?
14:                  $L^* = L', \mathbf{z}^* = \mathbf{z}'$          ▷ If so, update it as the best solution
15:              **end if**
16:          **end for**
17:      **end while**
18: **end procedure**

Since the transition probabilities in Eq. 4 are not known in advance, we propose to use an EM-like approach that iterates between solving 1–1 correspondences using the linear and quadratic constraints, and estimating transition information using those correspondences. Furthermore, due to the binary nature of variables, the problem of finding 1–1 correspondences using PSE constraints is NP-hard. We use a local neighborhood search algorithm presented in Algorithm 1 which optimizes Eq. 8 subject to the conditions in Eq. 9. The solution is initialized for linear constraints with Munkres [36]. The subprocedure $\text{REMOVEMAT}(L, \mathbf{z}, r)$ removes $r$ hypotheses from the solution as well as their respective linear and quadratic costs by assigning probabilities (using respective costs) for each node in the current $z$. In contrast, the sub-procedure $\text{ADDMAT}(L, \mathbf{z}, s)$ adds new hypotheses to the solution using the following steps:

- Populate a list of matches for which $z_{i_a}^{j_b}$ can be 1 such that Eq. 9 is satisfied.
- Make combinations of $s$-lets using the list.
- Remove combinations which dissatisfy Eq. 9.
- Compute new $L$ in Eq. 8 for each combination. This is efficiently done by adding $|\mathbf{z}| * s$ quadratic values and $s$ linear values.
- Pick the combination with lowest loss $L$. Add $s$-let to $\mathbf{z}$ and return.

Algorithm 1 updates the solution when there is a decrease in the loss function in Eq. 8, as can be seen from Line 13. Once the change in loss is negligible, the algorithm stops and returns the best solution obtained. Figure 2 shows the results quantified for our approach using Algorithm 1. The $x$-axis is the step number, whereas the left $y$-axis shows the value of loss function in Eq. 8 (blue curve), and the right $y$-axis shows the F-Score in terms of correct matches (orange curve). We

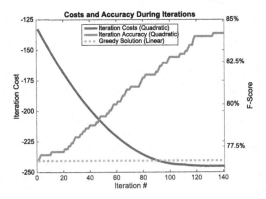

**Fig. 2.** The graph shows the performance of Algorithm 1 using both linear and quadratic constraints, compared against Hungarian Algorithm [36] using only the linear costs shown with orange dotted line. The loss function in Eq. 8 is shown in blue, whereas the accuracy is shown in red. Quadratic PSE constraints in conjunction with Algorithm 1 yield an improvement of $\sim 8\,\%$ over linear constraints. (Color figure online)

also show results of Hungarian Algorithm (Munkres) [36] in dotted orange line using linear constraints, which include appearance and speed similarity. These curves show that Algorithm 1 simultaneously improves the loss function in Eq. 8 and the accuracy of the matches as the number of steps increases.

## 3.3  PSE Constraints with Camera Topology

The PSE constraints presented in the previous section are applicable when the spatial relations between the cameras are not known. However, if the inter-camera topology is available, then it can be used to infer the motion of people as they travel in the invisible or unobserved regions between the cameras. The quality of paths in the invisible region can be subject to constraints such as *preferred speed* or *direction of movement*, which can be quantified and introduced into the framework. Furthermore, collision avoidance is another social constraint that can only be applied when inter-camera topology is known.

Given two objects in cameras $a$ and $b$, $O_{i_a}$ and $O_{i_b}$, in the same reference of time, we predict the possible path between the objects. This is obtained by fitting a spline, given by $\gamma_{i_a}^{j_b}$, in both $x$ and $y$ directions using cubic interpolation between the points $\mathbf{p}_{i_a}$ and $\mathbf{p}_{j_b}$ parameterized with their respective time stamps.

**Collision Avoidance:** Let the point of closest approach between two paths be given by:

$$d(\gamma_{i_a}^{j_b}, \gamma_{i'_a}^{j'}) = \min_{\max(t_{i_a}^{x}, t_{i'_a}^{x}), \dots, \min(t_{j_b}^{\eta}, t_{j'_b}^{\eta})} \|\gamma_{i_a}^{j_b}(t) - \gamma_{i'_a}^{j'}(t)\|, \tag{10}$$

we quantify the collision avoidance as a quadratic cost between pairs of possible matches:

$$\phi_{\text{invColl}}(M_{i_a}^{j_b}, M_{i'_a}^{j'}) = \left(1 - \varphi_{\text{grp}}(M_{i_a}^{j_b}, M_{i'_a}^{j'})\right) \cdot \exp\left(-d(\gamma_{i_a}^{j_b}, \gamma_{i'_a}^{j'})\right). \tag{11}$$

Since people avoid collisions with others and change their paths, this is only applicable to trajectories of people who are not traveling in a group, i.e., the cost will be high if two people not walking in a group come very close to each other when traveling through the invisible region between the cameras.

**Speed in Invisible Region:** The second constraint we compute is an improved version of the *preferred speed* - a linear constraint which now also takes into account the direction is addition to speed of the person in the invisible region. If the velocity of a person within visible region in cameras and while traveling through the invisible region is similar, this cost would be low. However, for an incorrect match, the difference between speed in visible and invisible regions will be high. Let $\dot{\gamma}$ denote the velocity at respective points in the path, both in the visible and invisible regions. Then, the difference of maximum and minimum speeds in the entire trajectory quantifies the quality of a match, given by,

$$\phi_{\text{invSpd}}(O_{i_a}, O_{j_b}) = |\max_{t_{i_a}^{\eta} \dots t_{j_b}^{x}} \dot{\gamma}_{i_a}^{j_b}(t) - \min_{t_{i_a}^{\eta} \dots t_{j_b}^{x}} \dot{\gamma}_{i_a}^{j_b}(t)|. \tag{12}$$

When the inter-camera topology is available, these constraints are added to the Eq. 8 and the method described in the Sect. 3.2 is used to re-identify people across cameras.

# 4   Experiments

Since PSE constraints depend on time and motion information in the videos, many commonly evaluated datasets such as VIPeR [18] and ETHZ [12] cannot be used for computing PSE constraints. We evaluate the proposed approach on the PRID dataset [19] and the challenging Grand Central Dataset [53]. First, we introduce the datasets and the ground truth that was generated for evaluation, followed by detailed analysis of our approach as well as contribution of different personal, social and environmental (PSE) constraints to the overall performance.

## 4.1   Datasets and Experimental Setup

**PRID 2011** is a camera network re-identification dataset containing 385 pedestrians in camera '$a$' and 749 pedestrians in camera '$b$'. The first 200 pedestrians from each camera form the ground truth pairs while the rest appear in one camera only. The most common evaluation method on this dataset is to match people from cam '$a$' to the ones in cam '$b$'. We used the video sequences and the bounding boxes provided by the authors of [19] so we can use the PSE constraints in our evaluation. Since the topology of the scene is unknown, we have used the constraints which do not need any prior knowledge about the camera locations. We evaluated on the entire one hour sequences and extract visual features in addition to various PSE constraints. In accordance with previous methods, we evaluate our approach by matching the 200 people in cam '$a$' to 749 people in cam '$b$' and quantify the ranking quality of matchings.

**Grand Central** is a dense crowd dataset that is particularly challenging for the task of human re-identification. The dataset contains 120,000 frames, with a resolution of 1920 × 1080 pixels. Recently, Yi *et al.* [53] used a portion of the dataset for detecting stationary crowd groups. They released annotations for trajectories of 12,684 individuals for 6,000 frames at 1.5 fps. We rectified the perspective distortion from the camera and put bounding boxes at correct scales using the trajectories provided by [53]. However, location of annotated points were not consistent for any single person, or across different people. Consequently, we manually adjusted the bounding boxes for 1,500 frames at 1.5 fps, resulting in ground truth for 17 min of video data.

We divide the scene into three horizontal sections, where two of them become separate cameras and the middle section is treated as invisible or unobserved region. The locations of people in each camera are in independent coordinate systems. The choice of dividing the scene in this way is meaningful, as both cameras have different illuminations due to external lighting effects, and the size of individuals is different due to perspective effects. Furthermore, due to the wide field of view in the scene, there are multiple entrances and exits in each camera, so that a person exiting the first camera at a particular location has the choice of entering from multiple different locations. Figure 1(c) shows real examples of individuals from the two cameras and elucidates the fact that due to the low resolution, change in brightness and scale, the incorrect nearest neighbors matches using the appearance features often rank much better than the correct ones for this dataset.

**Parameters:** Since there are multiple points/zones of entrances and exits, we divide the boundaries in each camera into $U_a = U_b = 11$ gates. The weights used in Eq. 8 are approximated using grid search on a separate set and then used for both datasets. They are $\alpha_{spt} = \alpha_{invColl} = .2$, $\alpha_{tr} = 1$, and $\alpha_{spd} = \alpha_{invSpd} = -\alpha_{grp} = 5$. Note that, social grouping is rewarded in our formulation, i.e. people who enter and exit together in space and time are more likely to be correct matches when re-identifying people across cameras.

## 4.2   Evaluation Measures

Cumulative Matching Characteristic (CMC) curves are typically used evaluating performance of re-identification methods. For each person, all the putative matches are ranked according to similarity scores, i.e. for each person $O_{i_a}$, the cost of assignment $M_{i_a}^{j_b} = \langle O_{i_a}, O_{j_b} \rangle$ is calculated for every possible match to $O_{j_b}$. Then, the accuracy over all the queries is computed for each rank. Area Under the Curve (AUC) for CMC gives a single quantified value over different ranks and an evaluation for overall performance. The advantage of CMC is that it does not require 1–1 correspondence between matches, and is the optimal choice for evaluating different cost functions or similarity measures.

The CMC curves are meaningful only for linear constraints. Unlike linear constraints which penalize or reward matches (pair of objects), quadratic constraints penalize or reward pairs of matches. Figure 3 illustrates the idea of quantifying both linear and quadratic costs through CMC, since this measure quantifies quality of costs independent of optimization. Given three objects $O_{1_a}, O_{2_a}, O_{3_a}$ and $O_{1_b}, O_{2_b}, O_{3_b}$ in cameras $a$ and $b$, respectively, the black lines in Fig. 3 (a) show linear constraints/matchings. Let us assume we intend to evaluate quadratic constraints for the match between $O_{1_a}$ and $O_{2_b}$. For this, we assume that all other matches are correct (red lines), and proceed with adding relevant quadratic (Fig. 3) and linear costs. For evaluating match between $O_{1_a}$ and $O_{2_b}$, we add linear costs between them, as well as quadratic costs between other matches (shown with red circles in Fig. 3(b)), and pair-wise costs of the match under consideration with all other matches (shown with orange circles). This is repeated for all possible matches. Later, the matches are sorted and evaluated similar to standard CMC. Note that, this approach gives an optimization-independent method of evaluating quadratic constraints. Nonetheless, the explicit use of ground truth during evaluation of quadratic constraints makes them only comparable to other quadratic constraints.

To evaluate 1–1 correspondence between matches, we use F-score which is defined as $2 \times (\mathsf{precision} \times \mathsf{recall})/(\mathsf{precision} + \mathsf{recall})$ on the output of optimization.

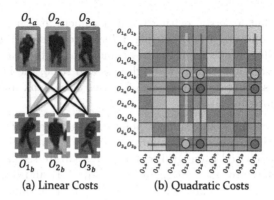

(a) Linear Costs          (b) Quadratic Costs

**Fig. 3.** This figure illustrates the CMC evaluation procedure with quadratic constraints. Given object tracks in the two cameras $O_{1_a}, O_{2_a}, O_{3_a}$ and $O_{1_b}, O_{2_b}, O_{3_b}$, (a) the linear constraints are computed between objects, and (b) quadratic constraints between each possible pair of matches. Adding a new match (shown with amber) requires adding one linear value and number of quadratic values equal to the size of current solution. (Color figure online)

We used Hungarian Algorithm (Munkres) [36] for comparison as it provides a globally optimal solution for linear costs. For the proposed PSE constraints, we use Algorithm 1 since we use both linear and quadratic costs.

### 4.3   Results and Comparison

In Table 1, we present the results on Grand Central dataset of our approach using PSE constraints and optimization in Algorithm 1 with several baselines. We report accuracy (number of correct matches), values of Cumulative Matching Characteristic curves at ranks 1, 5, 10, 20 and 50, as well as Area Under the Curve (AUC) for CMC between ranks 1 and 100. The values of CMC are computed before any optimization. The last column shows the F-Score of 1–1 assignments post optimization. In Table 1, the first row shows the results of random assignment, whereas next seven rows show results using several re-identification methods. These include LOMO-XQDA [28], SDALF [13], SAM [2], eSDC-knn [56], Manifold Learning [30] - normalized (Ln) and unnormalized (Lu), as well as CNN features [44] which use VGG-19 deep network. Finally, the last two rows show the results of our approach both for the case when camera topology is not known and when it is known. These results show that PSE constraints - both linear and quadratic - significantly improve the performance of human re-identification especially in challenging scenarios such as dense crowds.

Next, we present results on PRID dataset in Table 2. The first three rows show Reranking [26] on KissME [23], LMNN [50], and Mahalanobis distance learning [43] for re-identification. Next two rows show the performance of non-linear Metric Learning [37] and Descriptive & Discriminative features [19]. The last row shows the performance of our method which is better than existing unsupervised

**Table 1.** This table presents the quantitative results of the proposed approach and other methods on the **Grand Central Dataset.**

| Method | CMC | | | | | | F-Score |
|---|---|---|---|---|---|---|---|
| | Rank-1 | Rank-5 | Rank-10 | Rank-20 | Rank-50 | AUC (1:100) | (1–1) |
| Random | 1.83 % | 5.48 % | 11.36 % | 21.91 % | 54.36 % | 51.00 % | 6.90 % |
| LOMO-XQDA [28] | 4.06 % | 12.37 % | 21.91 % | 39.76 % | 71.40 % | 63.81 % | 11.16 % |
| SDALF [13] | 6.09 % | 16.23 % | 23.12 % | 40.16 % | 68.56 % | 63.01 % | 20.69 % |
| SAM [2] | 6.09 % | 27.18 % | 42.60 % | 51.72 % | 74.44 % | 69.60 % | 26.98 % |
| eSDC-knn [56] | 11.36 % | 27.38 % | 38.34 % | 50.71 % | 74.44 % | 69.49 % | 30.43 % |
| Manifold learning (Ln) [30] | 7.71 % | 24.54 % | 36.71 % | 54.97 % | 78.09 % | 72.11 % | 30.83 % |
| Manifold learning (Lu) [30] | 10.55 % | 34.08 % | 48.68 % | 66.53 % | 87.83 % | 80.50 % | 32.66 % |
| CNN features [44] | 12.98 % | 32.45 % | 44.62 % | 62.07 % | 83.77 % | 77.79 % | 41.99 % |
| **CrowdPSE (w/o topology)** | **25.56 %** | **81.54 %** | **93.31 %** | **97.57 %** | **98.38 %** | **95.80 %** | **67.94 %** |
| **CrowdPSE (w/topology)** | **49.29 %** | **95.13 %** | **98.17 %** | **98.17 %** | **98.17 %** | **97.31 %** | **84.19 %** |

**Table 2.** This table presents the quantitative results of the proposed approach and other methods on the **PRID Dataset.** We report accuracy (number of correct matches), values of Cumulative Matching Characteristic curves at ranks $1, 5, 10, 20$ and $50$. As can be seen, the proposed approach outperforms existing methods.

| Method | CMC | | | | |
|---|---|---|---|---|---|
| | Rank-1 | Rank-5 | Rank-10 | Rank-20 | Rank-50 |
| KissME [23] + Reranking [26] | 8.00 % | 19.00 % | 30.00 % | 41.00 % | 57.00 % |
| LMNN [50] + Reranking [26] | 10.00 % | 24.00 % | 34.00 % | 44.00 % | 61.00 % |
| Mahalanobis [43] + Reranking [26] | 11.00 % | 29.00 % | 37.00 % | 46.00 % | 60.00 % |
| Non-linear ML [37] | 17.90 % | 39.50 % | 50.00 % | 61.50 % | - |
| Desc + Disc [19] | 19.18 % | 41.44 % | 52.10 % | 66.56 % | 84.51 % |
| **CrowdPSE (w/o topology)** | **21.11 %** | **46.65 %** | **59.98 %** | **76.63 %** | **98.81 %** |

approaches for human re-identification. For this dataset, the spatial grouping did not improve the results since the dataset captures a straight sidewalk and does not involve decision makings and different travel times between different gates.

## 4.4  Contribution of Different PSE Constraints

We performed several experiments to gauge the performance of different PSE constraints and components of the proposed approach on Grand Central dataset. The comparison of different constraints using Cumulative Matching Characteristics (CMC) is shown in Fig. 4. In this figure, the $x$-axis is the rank, while $y$-axis is accuracy with corresponding rank on $x$-axis. First, we show the results of randomly assigning objects between cameras (blue curve). Then, we use appearance features (Convolutional Neural Network) for re-identification and do not use any personal, social or environmental constraints (shown with orange curve), which we also use to compute the appearance similarity for our method. The low

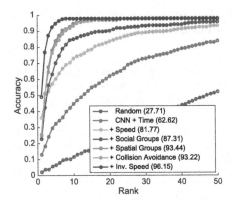

**Fig. 4.** This graph shows the CMC for different PSE constraints proposed in this paper on Grand Central Dataset. The results of random assignment are shown with blue curve, while appearance features with time limits yield the orange curve. Incorporating personal constraint such as preferred speed (amber), and social constraints such as social and spatial grouping (purple and green, respectively) further improve the performance. Given the topology, we can additionally incorporate collision avoidance (light blue) and preferred speed in the invisible region (maroon), which gives the best performance. (Color figure online)

performance highlights the difficult nature of this problem in crowded scenes. Next, we introduce linear constraint of preferred speed shown with amber curve which gives an improvement of ∼19 % in terms of Area under the Curve of CMC between ranks 1 and 50. Then, we add quadratic constraints of grouping, both of which make an improvement to matching performance, with social grouping contributing about ∼6 % while spatial grouping adding another ∼6 %. Remember that both these quadratic constraints are antipodal in the sense that former rewards while latter penalizes the loss function. The last two curves show the performance using constraints computable if camera topology is known. Given topology, we employ collision avoidance shown in light blue, whereas the constraint capturing the desire of people to walk with preferred speed between cameras is shown in maroon, which gives the maximum AUC of 96.15 % in conjunction with other PSE constraints.

This study shows that except for collision avoidance, all PSE constraints contribute significantly to the performance of human re-identification. We provide real examples of collision avoidance and social grouping in Fig. 5(a) and (b), respectively. In Fig. 5, the bounding boxes are color-coded with time using colormap shown on left. White-to-Yellow indicate earlier time stamps while Red-to-Black indicate later ones. The person under consideration is shown with dashed white line, while the track of two other people in each image are color-coded with costs using colormap on the right. Here, blue indicates low cost whereas red means high cost.

Collision avoidance which has been shown to work for tracking in non-crowded scenes [38] deteriorates the results slightly in crowded scenes.

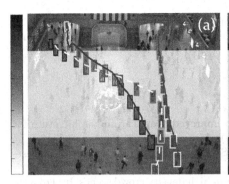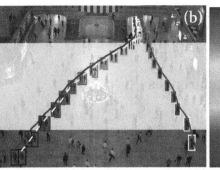

**Fig. 5.** This figure shows two examples of quadratic constraints. The color of bounding boxes indicates time using colorbar on the left, with white signifying start time and black representing end time. The person under consideration is shown with white trajectory, while the other two trajectories have the color of the cost for (a) collision avoidance and (b) grouping, color-coded with bar on the right. That is, blue and red trajectories indicate low and high costs, respectively. In (a), collision avoidance unnecessarily assigns high cost to a correct match, but not to a colliding person. On the other hand, grouping helps in re-identifying people who walk together by assigning a low cost between them. (Color figure online)

Figure 5(a) shows a case where collision avoidance constraint assigns a high cost to a pair of correct matches. Due to limitation in space in dense crowds, people do not change their path significantly. Furthermore, any slight change in path between cameras is unlikely to have any effect on matching for re-identification. On the other hand, the grouping constraint yields a strong increase in performance (~12 %) as also seen in Fig. 5(b). This is despite the fact that the Grand Central dataset depicts dense crowd of commuters in a busy subway station, many of whom walk alone.

## 5  Conclusion

This paper addressed the problem of re-identifying people across non-overlapping cameras in crowded scenes. Due to the difficult nature of the problem, the appearance similarity alone gives poor performance. We employed several personal, social and environmental constraints in the form of *preferred speed, destination probability* and *spatial and social grouping*. These constraints do not require knowledge about camera topology, however if available, it can be incorporated into our formulation. Since the problem with PSE constraints is NP-hard, we used a greedy local neighborhood search algorithm that can handle both quadratic and linear constraints. The crowd dataset used in the paper brings to light the difficulty and challenges of re-identifying and associating people across cameras in crowds. For future work, we plan to use discriminative appearance models independently trained on individuals, and inference of topology in an unsupervised manner for crowded scenes.

**Acknowledgment.** This material is based upon work supported in part by, the U.S. Army Research Laboratory, the U.S. Army Research Office under contract/grant number W911NF-14-1-0294.

# References

1. Ahmed, E., Jones, M., Marks, T.K.: An improved deep learning architecture for person re-identification. In: CVPR (2015)
2. Alahi, A., Ramanathan, V., Fei-Fei, L.: Socially-aware large-scale crowd forecasting. In: CVPR (2014)
3. Ali, S., Shah, M.: Floor fields for tracking in high density crowd scenes. In: Forsyth, D., Torr, P., Zisserman, A. (eds.) ECCV 2008, Part II. LNCS, vol. 5303, pp. 1–14. Springer, Heidelberg (2008)
4. Bialkowski, A., Lucey, P., Wei, X., Sridharan, S.: Person re-identification using group information. In: DICTA (2013)
5. Cai, Y., Takala, V., Pietikäinen, M.: Matching groups of people by covariance descriptor. In: ICPR (2010)
6. Chakraborty, A., Das, A., Roy-Chowdhury, A.: Network consistent data association (2014). http://ieeexplore.ieee.org/document/7299668/?arnumber=7299668&tag=1
7. Chen, D., Yuan, Z., Hua, G., Zheng, N., Wang, J.: Similarity learning on an explicit polynomial kernel feature map for person re-identification. In: CVPR (2015)
8. Chen, K.W., Lai, C.C., Hung, Y.P., Chen, C.S.: An adaptive learning method for target tracking across multiple cameras. In: CVPR (2008)
9. Chen, X., An, L., Bhanu, B.: Multitarget tracking in nonoverlapping cameras using a reference set. IEEE Sens. J. 15(5), 2692–2704 (2015)
10. Das, A., Chakraborty, A., Roy-Chowdhury, A.K.: Consistent re-identification in a camera network. In: Fleet, D., Pajdla, T., Schiele, B., Tuytelaars, T. (eds.) ECCV 2014, Part II. LNCS, vol. 8690, pp. 330–345. Springer, Heidelberg (2014)
11. Dick, A.R., Brooks, M.J.: A stochastic approach to tracking objects across multiple cameras. In: Webb, G.I., Yu, X. (eds.) AI 2004. LNCS (LNAI), vol. 3339, pp. 160–170. Springer, Heidelberg (2004)
12. Ess, A., Leibe, B., Schindler, K., Gool, L.V.: A mobile vision system for robust multi-person tracking. In: CVPR (2008)
13. Farenzena, M., Bazzani, L., Perina, A., Murino, V., Cristani, M.: Person re-identification by symmetry-driven accumulation of local features. In: CVPR (2010)
14. Fleuret, F., Berclaz, J., Lengagne, R., Fua, P.: Multicamera people tracking with a probabilistic occupancy map. IEEE TPAMI 30(2), 267–282 (2008)
15. Ge, W., Collins, R.T., Ruback, R.B.: Vision-based analysis of small groups in pedestrian crowds. IEEE TPAMI 34(5), 1003–1016 (2012)
16. Gilbert, A., Bowden, R.: Tracking objects across cameras by incrementally learning inter-camera colour calibration and patterns of activity. In: Leonardis, A., Bischof, H., Pinz, A. (eds.) ECCV 2006. LNCS, vol. 3952, pp. 125–136. Springer, Heidelberg (2006)
17. Gong, S., Cristani, M., Yan, S., Loy, C.C.: Person re-identification 1 (2014)
18. Gray, D., Tao, H.: Viewpoint invariant pedestrian recognition with an ensemble of localized features. In: Forsyth, D., Torr, P., Zisserman, A. (eds.) ECCV 2008, Part I. LNCS, vol. 5302, pp. 262–275. Springer, Heidelberg (2008)

19. Hirzer, M., Beleznai, C., Roth, P.M., Bischof, H.: Person re-identification by descriptive and discriminative classification. In: Scandinavian Conference on Image Analysis (2011)
20. Javed, O., Shafique, K., Rasheed, Z., Shah, M.: Modeling inter-camera space-time and appearance relationships for tracking across non-overlapping views. CVIU **109**(2), 146–162 (2008)
21. Javed, O., Shafique, K., Shah, M.: Appearance modeling for tracking in multiple non-overlapping cameras. CVPR **2**, 26–33 (2005)
22. Kelly, H.: After boston: the pros and cons of surveillance cameras. In: CNN, 26 April 2013. http://www.cnn.com/2013/04/26/tech/innovation/security-cameras-boston-bombings/. Accessed 1 Oct 2015
23. Koestinger, M., Hirzer, M., Wohlhart, P., Roth, P.M., Bischof, H.: Large scale metric learning from equivalence constraints. In: CVPR (2012)
24. Kuo, C.-H., Huang, C., Nevatia, R.: Inter-camera association of multi-target tracks by on-line learned appearance affinity models. In: Daniilidis, K., Maragos, P., Paragios, N. (eds.) ECCV 2010, Part I. LNCS, vol. 6311, pp. 383–396. Springer, Heidelberg (2010)
25. Leal-Taixé, L., Pons-Moll, G., Rosenhahn, B.: Everybody needs somebody: modeling social and grouping behavior on a linear programming multiple people tracker. In: ICCV Workshops (2011)
26. Leng, Q., Hu, R., Liang, C., Wang, Y., Chen, J.: Person re-identification with content and context re-ranking. Multimedia Tools Appl. **74**(17), 6989–7014 (2015)
27. Li, W., Zhao, R., Xiao, T., Wang, X.: DeepReID: deep filter pairing neural network for person re-identification. In: CVPR (2014)
28. Liao, S., Hu, Y., Zhu, X., Li, S.Z.: Person re-identification by local maximal occurrence representation and metric learning. In: CVPR (2015)
29. Lisanti, G., Masi, I., Bagdanov, A.D., Del Bimbo, A.: Person re-identification by iterative re-weighted sparse ranking. IEEE Trans. Pattern Anal. Mach. Intell. **37**(8), 1629–1642 (2015)
30. Loy, C.C., Liu, C., Gong, S.: Person re-identification by manifold ranking. In: ICIP (2013)
31. Madden, C., Cheng, E.D., Piccardi, M.: Tracking people across disjoint camera views by an illumination-tolerant appearance representation. MVA **18**(3–4), 233–247 (2007)
32. Makris, D., Ellis, T., Black, J.: Bridging the gaps between cameras. In: CVPR (2004)
33. Mazzon, R., Cavallaro, A.: Multi-camera tracking using a multi-goal social force model. Neurocomputing **100**, 41–50 (2013)
34. Mazzon, R., Tahir, S.F., Cavallaro, A.: Person re-identification in crowd. Pattern Recogn. Lett. **33**(14), 1828–1837 (2012)
35. Mehran, R., Oyama, A., Shah, M.: Abnormal crowd behavior detection using social force model. In: CVPR (2009)
36. Munkres, J.: Algorithms for the assignment and transportation problems. J. Soc. Indus. Appl. Math. **5**(1), 32–38 (1957)
37. Paisitkriangkrai, S., Shen, C., van den Hengel, A.: Learning to rank in person re-identification with metric ensembles. In: CVPR (2015)
38. Pellegrini, S., Ess, A., Schindler, K., Van Gool, L.: You'll never walk alone: modeling social behavior for multi-target tracking. In: ICCV (2009)
39. Porikli, F.: Inter-camera color calibration by correlation model function. In: ICIP, vol. 2 (2003)

40. Prosser, B., Gong, S., Xiang, T.: Multi-camera matching using bi-directional cumulative brightness transfer functions. In: BMVC (2008)
41. Qin, Z., Shelton, C.R., Chai, L.: Social grouping for target handover in multi-view video. In: ICME (2013)
42. Robin, T., Antonini, G., Bierlaire, M., Cruz, J.: Specification, estimation and validation of a pedestrian walking behavior model. Transp. Res. Part B: Methodol. **43**(1), 36–56 (2009)
43. Roth, P.M., Hirzer, M., Köstinger, M., Beleznai, C., Bischof, H.: Mahalanobis distance learning for person re-identification. In: Gong, S., Cristani, M., Yan, S., Loy, C.C. (eds.) Person Re-Identification. Advances in Computer Vision and Patttern Recognition, pp. 247–267. Springer, London (2014)
44. Simonyan, K., Zisserman, A.: Very deep convolutional networks for large-scale image recognition. arXiv preprint (2014). arXiv:1409.1556
45. Song, B., Roy-Chowdhury, A.K.: Robust tracking in a camera network: a multiobjective optimization framework. IEEE Sel. Top. Sign. Process. **2**(4), 582–596 (2008)
46. Stauffer, C.: Learning to track objects through unobserved regions. In: WACV/MOTIONS Volume 1, vol. 2 (2005)
47. Tieu, K., Dalley, G., Grimson, W.E.L.: Inference of non-overlapping camera network topology by measuring statistical dependence. In: ICCV, vol. 2 (2005)
48. Vedaldi, A., Zisserman, A.: Efficient additive kernels via explicit feature maps. IEEE Trans. Pattern Anal. Mach. Intell. **34**(3), 480–492 (2012)
49. Wang, X.: Intelligent multi-camera video surveillance: a review. Pattern Recogn. Lett. **34**(1), 3–19 (2013)
50. Weinberger, K.Q., Saul, L.K.: Fast solvers and efficient implementations for distance metric learning. In: ICML (2008)
51. Wu, Z., Kunz, T.H., Betke, M.: Efficient track linking methods for track graphs using network-flow and set-cover techniques. In: CVPR (2011)
52. Yamaguchi, K., Berg, A.C., Ortiz, L.E., Berg, T.L.: Who are you with and where are you going? In: CVPR (2011)
53. Yi, S., Li, H., Wang, X.: Understanding pedestrian behaviors from stationary crowd groups. In: CVPR (2015)
54. Zhang, N., Paluri, M., Taigman, Y., Fergus, R., Bourdev, L.: Beyond frontal faces: improving person recognition using multiple cues. In: CVPR (2015)
55. Zhang, Z., Chen, Y., Saligrama, V.: Group membership prediction. In: ICCV (2015)
56. Zhao, R., Ouyang, W., Wang, X.: Unsupervised salience learning for person re-identification. In: CVPR (2013)
57. Zheng, L., Shen, L., Tian, L., Wang, S., Wang, J., Tian, Q.: Scalable person re-identification: a benchmark. In: ICCV (2015)
58. Zheng, W.S., Gong, S., Xiang, T.: Associating groups of people. In: BMVC (2009)
59. Zhou, B., Tang, X., Wang, X.: Learning collective crowd behaviors with dynamic pedestrian-agents. IJCV **111**(1), 50–68 (2015)
60. Zhou, B., Wang, X., Tang, X.: Understanding collective crowd behaviors: Learning a mixture model of dynamic pedestrian-agents. In: CVPR (2012)

# Revisiting Additive Quantization

Julieta Martinez$^{(\boxtimes)}$, Joris Clement, Holger H. Hoos, and James J. Little

University of British Columbia, Vancouver, Canada
{julm,jclement,hoos,little}@cs.ubc.ca

**Abstract.** We revisit Additive Quantization (AQ), an approach to vector quantization that uses multiple, full-dimensional, and non-orthogonal codebooks. Despite its elegant and simple formulation, AQ has failed to achieve state-of-the-art performance on standard retrieval benchmarks, because the encoding problem, which amounts to MAP inference in multiple fully-connected Markov Random Fields (MRFs), has proven to be hard to solve. We demonstrate that the performance of AQ can be improved to surpass the state of the art by leveraging iterated local search, a stochastic local search approach known to work well for a range of NP-hard combinatorial problems. We further show a direct application of our approach to a recent formulation of vector quantization that enforces sparsity of the codebooks. Unlike previous work, which required specialized optimization techniques, our formulation can be plugged directly into state-of-the-art lasso optimizers. This results in a conceptually simple, easily implemented method that outperforms the previous state of the art in solving sparse vector quantization. Our implementation is publicly available (https://github.com/jltmtz/local-search-quantization).

## 1 Introduction

Computer vision applications often involve computing the similarity of many high-dimensional, real-valued image representations, in a process known as feature matching. When large databases of images are used, this results in significant computational bottlenecks. For example, in structure from motion [1], it is common to estimate the relative viewpoint of each image in large collections of photographs by computing the pairwise similarity of several million SIFT [2] descriptors; it is also now common for retrieval and classification datasets to comprise millions of images [3,4].

In practice, the large-scale retrieval problem often translates into large-scale approximate nearest neighbour (ANN) search and has traditionally been addressed with hashing [5,6]. However, a family of methods based on vector quantization has recently demonstrated superior performance and scalability, sparking interest from the machine learning, computer vision and multimedia retrieval communities [7–12]. These methods are all based on multi-codebook quantization (MCQ), a generalization of $k$-means clustering with cluster centres arising from the sum of entries in multiple codebooks. Other applications

© Springer International Publishing AG 2016
B. Leibe et al. (Eds.): ECCV 2016, Part II, LNCS 9906, pp. 137–153, 2016.
DOI: 10.1007/978-3-319-46475-6_9

of MCQ include large-scale maximum inner product search (MIPS) [13,14], and
the compression of deep neural networks for mobile devices [15].

Like $k$-means clustering, MCQ is posed as the search for a set of codes and
codebooks that best approximate a given dataset. While early approaches to
MCQ were designed enforcing codebook orthogonality [9,10], more recent methods make use of non-orthogonal, often full-dimensional codebooks [7,8,11]. A
problem faced by these methods is that encoding, in general, becomes NP-hard.
Moreover, encoding is to be performed on large databases and must therefore
often be carried out under very tight time constraints.

We note that the combinatorial optimization community has been dealing
with similar problems for many years, and competitions to solve NP-hard problems as efficiently as possible (*e.g.* the SAT competition series [16]) have driven
research on fast combinatorial optimization methods such as stochastic local
search [17] (SLS) and portfolio-based solvers [18]. Inspired by the combinatorial
optimization literature, our main contribution is the introduction of an SLS-
based algorithm that achieves low quantization error and high encoding speed
in MCQ. We also discuss a series of implementation details that make our algorithm fast in practice and demonstrate an application of our approach that
incorporates sparsity constraints in the codebooks.

## 2   Related Work

First, we introduce some notation, following mostly Norouzi and Fleet [19]. Formally, we denote the set to quantize as $X \in \mathbb{R}^{d \times n}$, having $n$ data points with $d$
dimensions each; MCQ is the problem of finding $m$ codebooks $C_i \in \mathbb{R}^{d \times h}$ and
the corresponding codes $B_i$ that minimize quantization error, *i.e.*, to determine

$$\min_{C_i, B_i} \|X - [C_1, C_2, \ldots, C_m] \begin{bmatrix} B_1 \\ B_2 \\ \vdots \\ B_m \end{bmatrix} \|_2^2, \tag{1}$$

where $B_i = [\mathbf{b}_{i1}, \mathbf{b}_{i2}, \ldots, \mathbf{b}_{in}] \in \{0,1\}^{h \times n}$, and each subcode $\mathbf{b}_i$ is limited to hav-
ing only one non-zero entry: $\|\mathbf{b}_i\|_0 = 1$, $\|\mathbf{b}_i\|_1 = 1$. Letting $C = [C_1, C_2, \ldots, C_m]$
and $B = [B_1, B_2, \ldots, B_m]^\top$, we can rewrite Expression 1 more succinctly as

$$\min_{C,B} \|X - CB\|_2^2. \tag{2}$$

Early work in MCQ can be traced back to the 1980s, when quantization was
heavily studied in the context of compressing signals before transmission [20].
Interest in the field was renewed in 2010, when Jégou *et al.* [10] introduced
product quantization (PQ), noticing that quantization could be effectively used
to search for nearest neighbours in high-dimensional spaces. PQ made a codebook orthogonality assumption that has the advantage of requiring only $m$ table
lookups to compute the approximate distance between a query and a compressed

database element. Moreover, optimal encoding is easily achieved by solving $m$ $d/m$-dimensional nearest neighbour problems in small sets of $h$ elements (typically, $h = 256$). It was later shown [9,19], that a global rotation of the data can also be easily learned, yielding lower quantization error. This approach is often called optimized product quantization (OPQ).

More recently, Babenko and Lempitsky proposed additive quantization (AQ) [7], which drops the orthogonality assumption of PQ and uses full-dimensional codebooks. This formulation corresponds to Expression 2 without further constraints and provides the basis for our work. In spite of achieving superior performance to PQ and OPQ, the authors quickly noticed two main disadvantages of their approach: first, that encoding (finding $B$) can be expressed as a large number of hard combinatorial problems and becomes a major computational bottleneck of the system; second, that distance computation requires $O(m^2)$ (as opposed to $m$) table lookups, increasing query time significantly with respect to PQ [7].

In a parallel line of research, Zhang *et al.* proposed composite quantization (CQ) [11], which also relaxes the orthogonality constraint of PQ and optimizes for codebooks with constant inner products: $\langle C_i^\top, C_j \rangle = \xi, \forall i,j \neq i \in \{1,2,\ldots,m\}$ (notice that, in PQ, $\xi = 0$). A crucial advantage of this formulation is that distance computation requires only $m$ table lookups and thus is directly comparable to PQ. As a side effect, the constraint renders the encoding problem easier to solve, and the authors note that using iterated conditional modes (ICM) with 3 iterations obtains "satisfactory results" [11].

**The Encoding Problem in AQ.** Our work focuses on improving the encoding time and performance of the AQ formulation – that is, given the data $X$ and codebooks $C$, we search for a method to find the codes $B$ that minimize Expression 2. Formally, the encoding problem amounts to MAP inference[1] in $n$ fully-connected MRFs with $m$ nodes each, which in the general case is NP-hard. In these MRFs, the minimum energy is achieved by finding the subcodes $\mathbf{b}_i$ that minimize the squared distance between the vector to encode $\mathbf{x}$, and its approximation $\hat{\mathbf{x}}$:

$$\|\mathbf{x} - \hat{\mathbf{x}}\|_2^2 = \|\mathbf{x} - \sum_i^m C_i \mathbf{b}_i\|_2^2 = \|\mathbf{x}\|_2^2 - 2 \cdot \sum_i^m \langle \mathbf{x}, C_i \mathbf{b}_i \rangle + \|\sum_i^m C_i \mathbf{b}_i\|_2^2 \quad (3)$$

where the norm of the approximation $\|\hat{\mathbf{x}}\|_2^2 = \|\sum_i^m C_i \mathbf{b}_i\|_2^2$ can be expanded as

$$\|\sum_i^m C_i \mathbf{b}_i\|_2^2 = \sum_i^m \|C_i \mathbf{b}_i\|_2^2 + \sum_i^m \sum_{j \neq i}^m \langle C_i \mathbf{b}_i, C_j \mathbf{b}_j \rangle. \quad (4)$$

Posed as an MRF with $m$ nodes, the $\|\mathbf{x}\|_2^2$ term in (3) can be discarded because it is a constant with respect to $\mathbf{b}_i$; the $-2 \cdot \sum_i^m \langle \mathbf{x}, C_i \mathbf{b}_i \rangle$ and $\sum_i^m \|C_i \mathbf{b}_i\|_2^2$

---

[1] Unfortunately enough, MAP inference is often called *decoding* due to its historical use in the receiving end of error-correcting codes [20].

terms are summed up and become the unary terms, and $\sum_i^m \sum_{j \neq i}^m \langle C_i \mathbf{b}_i, C_j \mathbf{b}_j \rangle$ becomes the pairwise terms. Since each code $\mathbf{b}_i$ may take any value between 1 and $h$, there are $h^m$ possible configurations for each MRF (typically, $m = \{8, 16\}$, and $h = 256$), which renders the problem inherently combinatorial and, in general, NP-hard [21].

Solving these MRFs is known to be challenging; in fact, the authors of AQ noted that "LBP and ICM, and [...] other algorithms from the MRF optimization library [22] perform poorly" [7]. This has led researchers to resort to expensive construction search methods such as beam search [7] and has since motivated the search for codebook structures where exact encoding is efficient [8, 11].

**Reducing Query Time in AQ.** As mentioned before, AQ involves major computational overhead during query time. This occurs when a new query $\mathbf{q}$ is received and the distance to the encoded vectors $\hat{\mathbf{x}}_i$ has to be estimated. This amounts to evaluating Eq. 3: $\|\mathbf{q} - \hat{\mathbf{x}}\|_2^2$, which, as we have seen, requires $O(m^2)$ table lookups for evaluating the norm of the encoded vector $\|\hat{\mathbf{x}}\|_2^2$. Babenko and Lempitsky [7] proposed a simple solution to this problem: use $m - 1$ codebooks to quantize $\mathbf{x}$, and use an extra byte to quantize the norm of the approximation $\|\hat{\mathbf{x}}\|_2^2$. The approximation of the norm is likely to be very good, as we are then using $h = 256$ centroids to quantize a scalar. The downside is that the beam search proposed in AQ becomes very expensive, so in [7], preference was given to a hybrid approach called Additive Product Quantization (APQ). APQ, although more tractable in encoding, still incurs considerable overhead at query time. Promising results for AQ were shown for 64 bit codes on SIFT1M (see AQ-7 in Fig. 5 of [7]) but have since been surpassed by CQ [11]. Our work starts from this idea and then focuses on improving the encoding process to improve the performance of AQ beyond the state of the art.

**Stochastic Local Search (SLS) Algorithms.** Top-performing methods for solving many NP-hard problems have been, at several points in time, variations of stochastic local search (SLS), and continue to define the state of the art for solving prominent NP-hard problems, such as the TSP [23]. Given a candidate solution to a given problem instance, SLS methods iteratively examine and move to neighbouring solutions. A formal treatment of the subject involves defining neighbourhood functions, characterizing problem instances and formally defining local search procedures; while this is beyond the scope of this work, we direct interested readers to [17].

Iterated local search (ILS) algorithms, which form the basis for the algorithm we propose in this work, alternate between perturbing the current solution $s$ (with the goal of escaping local minima) and performing local search starting from the perturbed solution, leading to a new candidate solution, $s'$. At the end of each local search phase, a so-called acceptance criterion is used to decide whether to continue the search process from $s$ or $s'$. In many applications of ILS, including ours described in the following, the acceptance criterion simply selects the better of $s$ and $s'$.

A downside of SLS algorithms (and many other heuristic methods that perform well in practice) is that their theoretical performance has historically proven hard to analyze. Similar to prominent deep learning techniques, SLS methods often perform far better than theory predicts, and thus, research in the area is heavily based on empirical analysis. An attempt to achieve a theoretical breakthrough for our method would be out of the scope of this work, so instead, we focus on the thorough empirical evaluation of its performance on a number of benchmarks with varying sizes, protocols and descriptor types to show the strength of our approach.

## 3    Iterated Local Search for AQ Encoding

We now introduce our ILS algorithm to optimize $B$ in Expression 2. In addition to the acceptance criterion stated above, our algorithm is defined by (a) a local search procedure, (b) a perturbation method to escape local minima, and (c) an initialization method to create the first solution; we next explain our design choices for these components.

### 3.1    Local Search Procedure

As our local search procedure we choose ICM. Although ICM was dismissed in [7] as poorly performant for the encoding problem, the algorithm has been successfully used (for solving an admittedly simpler problem) in CQ [11]. ICM offers two key advantages over other local search algorithms: (i) on the theoretical side, it exhibits very good speed, and, (ii) in practice, it can be implemented in a way that is amenable to caching and vectorization. We discuss both advantages in more detail below.

**Complexity Analysis of ICM.** ICM *iterates* over all the nodes in the given MRF, *conditioning* the current node on the assignments of other nodes, and minimizing (finding the *mode* of) the resulting univariate distribution. In a fully-connected MRF, such as the one in our problem, each node represents a subcode $b_i$. Thus, ICM cycles through $m$ subcodes, and conditions its value on the other $m - 1$ subcodes, adding $h$ terms for each conditioning. This results in a complexity of $O(m^2h)$. Comparing to the beam search procedure of AQ, which has a complexity of $O(mh^2(m + \log mh))$ [8], we can see that for typical values of $m \in \{8, 16\}$ and $h = 256$, a single ICM cycle is much faster than beam search. This suggests that we can afford to run several rounds of ICM, which is necessary for ILS, while keeping the overall encoding time low. In practice, our implementation is 30–50× faster than beam search in AQ[2].

---

[2] https://github.com/arbabenko/Quantizations.

**Cache Hits and Vectorization of ICM.** While this is not true in general, in our special case of interest ICM has a second crucial advantage: it can be programmed in a way that is cache-friendly and easy to vectorize.

In practice, the computational bottleneck of ICM arises in the conditioning step, when the algorithm looks at all the neighbours of the $i$th node and adds the assignments in those nodes to the current one. A naïve implementation, such as that available from off-the-shelf MRF libraries [22], encodes each data point sequentially, looking up the pairwise terms from $O(m^2)$ different tables of size $h \times h$. This results in a large number of cache-misses, as different tables are loaded into cache for each conditioning.

Our key observation from Eq. 3 is that only the unary term $-2\sum_i^m \langle \mathbf{x}, C_i \mathbf{b}_i \rangle$ depends on the vector to encode $\mathbf{x}$. Equivalently, it can be seen that the pairwise terms $\sum_i^m \sum_{j \neq i}^m \langle C_i \mathbf{b}_i, C_j \mathbf{b}_j \rangle$ are the same for all the MRFs that arise in the encoding problem. This means that, during the conditioning step, we can condition all the $i$th subcodes in the database w.r.t. the $j$th subcode, loading only one $h \times h$ pairwise lookup table into cache at a time. This results in better cache performance, is easily vectorized, and dramatically speeds up ICM in our case. In practice, this is accomplished by switching the order of the for loops in ICM over the entire (or a large portion of the) database. We call this implementation "batched ICM". Our code is publicly available to facilitate the understanding of these details.

## 3.2  ILS Perturbation

In each incumbent solution $s$, we choose $k$ codes to perturb by sampling without replacement from the discrete uniform distribution from 1 to $m$: $i_k \sim \mathcal{U}\{1, m\}$. We then perturb each selected code uniformly at random by setting it to a value between 1 and $h$: $\mathbf{b}_{i_k} \sim \mathcal{U}\{1, h\}$. This perturbed solution $s'$ is then used as the starting point for the subsequent local search phase, i.e., invocation of ICM. While simple, this perturbation method is commonly used in the SLS literature [17]. We note that our approach generalizes previous work where ICM was used but no perturbations were applied [7,11], which corresponds to setting $k = 0$. This method is both effective and very fast in practice: compared to ICM, the time spent in this step is negligible.

## 3.3  ILS Initialization

We use a simple initialization method, setting all the codes to values between 1 and $h$ uniformly at random: $\mathbf{b}_i \sim \mathcal{U}\{1, h\} \ \forall i \in \{1, 2, \ldots, m\}$. We also experimented with other initialization approaches, such as using FLANN [24] to copy the codes of the nearest neighbour in the training dataset, or using the code that minimizes the binary terms (which are expected to dominate the unary terms for large $m$). However, we did not observe significant improvements over our random initialization after a few rounds of ILS optimization.

Like AQ, we initialize our $C$ and $B$ by running OPQ, followed by a method similar to OTQ [8], but simplified to assume that the dimension assignments are given by a natural partition of adjacent dimensions.

## 4    The Advantages of a Simple Formulation: Easy Sparse Codebooks

Our approach, building on top of AQ, benefits from using a simple formulation with no extra constraints (Expression 2). The advantages of a simple formulation are not merely aesthetic; in practice, they result in a straightforward optimization procedure and less overhead for the programmer. Furthermore, a more standard formulation might render the problem more amenable to being solved using state-of-the-art optimizers. We now demonstrate one such use case, by implementing a recent MCQ formulation that enforces sparsity on the codebooks [12].

**Motivation for Sparse Codebooks.** Zhang *et al.* [12] motivate the use of sparse codebooks in the context of very large-scale applications, which deal with billions of data-points and are better suited for search with an inverted-index [25–27]. In this case, the time spent computing the lookup tables becomes non-negligible, which is specially true for methods that use full-dimensional codebooks, such as CQ [11], AQ [7] and, by extension, ours. For example, Zhang *et al.* have demonstrated that enforcing sparsity in the codebooks can lead up to 30 % speedups with a state-of-the-art inverted index [27] on the SIFT1B dataset (see Table 2 in [12]). This method is called Sparse CQ (SCQ).

There is a second use case for sparse codebooks. Recently, André *et al.* [28] have demonstrated that PQ scan and other lookup-based sums, such as those in our approach, can take advantage of vectorization. The authors have shown up to 6× speedups on distance computation, thus emphasizing further the time spent computing distance tables even for datasets with a few million data points, where linear scanning is the preferred search procedure.

**Solving the Sparsity Constraint.** Formally, the sparsity constraint on the codebooks amounts to determining

$$\min_{C,B}\|X - CB\|_2^2 \quad \text{s.t.} \quad \|C\|_0 \leq S. \tag{5}$$

Unfortunately, minimizing a squared function with an $\ell_0$ constraint is non-convex and, in general, hard to solve directly. Thus, the problem is often relaxed the minimize the convex $\ell_1$ norm. Our objective then becomes to determine

$$\min_{C,B}\|X - CB\|_2^2 \quad \text{s.t.} \quad \|C\|_1 \leq \lambda. \tag{6}$$

In SCQ [12], the problem becomes even harder, because on top of sparsity, the codebook elements are forced to have constant products. For this reason,

SCQ uses an ad-hoc soft-thresholding algorithm to solve for $C$. Our problem is simpler, because we do not have to satisfy the inter-codebook constraint and can be posed as an $\ell_1$-regularized least-squares problem. To achieve this, we rewrite Expression 6 as

$$\min_{C,B}\|B^\top C^\top - X^\top\|_2^2 \quad \text{s.t.} \quad \|C\|_1 \le \lambda, \tag{7}$$

and it becomes apparent that the approximation of the $i$th column of $X^\top$ depends only on product of $B^\top$ and the $i$th column of $C^\top$. Thus, we can rewrite Expression 7 as

$$\min_{C,B}\|\hat{B}\hat{\mathbf{c}} - \hat{\mathbf{x}}\|_2^2 \quad \text{s.t.} \quad \|\hat{\mathbf{c}}\|_1 \le \lambda, \tag{8}$$

where

$$\hat{B} = \begin{bmatrix} B_{(1)}^\top & 0 & \cdots & 0 \\ 0 & B_{(2)}^\top & \cdots & 0 \\ \vdots & & \ddots & \vdots \\ 0 & 0 & \cdots & B_{(d)}^\top \end{bmatrix}, \hat{\mathbf{c}} = \begin{bmatrix} \mathbf{c}_1^\top \\ \mathbf{c}_2^\top \\ \vdots \\ \mathbf{c}_d^\top \end{bmatrix}, \text{ and } \hat{\mathbf{x}} = \begin{bmatrix} \mathbf{x}_1^\top \\ \mathbf{x}_2^\top \\ \vdots \\ \mathbf{x}_d^\top \end{bmatrix}. \tag{9}$$

Here, $B_{(i)}^\top$ is the $i$th copy of $B^\top$, $\mathbf{c}_i$ is the $i$th row of $C$, and $\mathbf{x}_i$ is the $i$th row of $X$. This formulation corresponds to the well-known lasso. Nearly two decades of research in the lasso have produced many robust and scalable off-the-shelf optimization routines for this problem. Our approach, as opposed to previous work, lacks extra constraints and thus can directly take advantage of such procedures with little overhead to the programmer. For example, it took us less than an hour to integrate the SPGL1 solver by van den Berg and Friedlander [29] into our pipeline. This solver has the additional advantage of not requiring an explicit representation of $\hat{B}$, but can instead be given a function that evaluates to $\hat{B}\hat{\mathbf{c}}$ – this can be implemented as a `for` loop, so we only need to store one copy of the codes $B^\top$ in memory. Note that SPGL1 is only used to find the codebooks $C$; finding the codes $B$ is still done using our previously described ILS procedure.

## 5    Experimental Setup

**Evaluation Protocol.** We follow previous work and evaluate the performance of our system with recall@N [7–11]. Recall@N produces a monotonically increasing curve from 1 to N representing the empirical probability, computed over the query set, that the N estimated nearest neighbours include the actual nearest neighbour in the database. The goal is obtain the highest possible recall for given N. In information retrieval, recall@1 is considered the most important number on this curve. Also in line with previous work [7–12], in all our experiments, the codebooks have $h = 256$ elements, and we show results using 64 and 128 bits for code length.

We compute approximate squared Euclidean distances applying the expansion of Eq. 3, and we use only 7 and 15 codebooks to store codebook indices, while the last 8 bits are dedicated to quantize the (scalar) squared norm of each database entry. In all our experiments, we run our method for 100 iterations and use asymmetric distance, *i.e.*, the distance tables are computed for each query, as in all our baselines.

**Baselines.** We compare our approach to previous work, controlling for two critical factors in large-scale retrieval: code length and query time. To control for code length, we use subcodebooks with $h = 256$ entries and produce final codes of 64 and 128 bits. To control for query time, we restrict our comparison to methods that require $m = \{8, 16\}$ table lookups to compute approximate distances. Thus, we compare against PQ [10], OPQ [9] and CQ [11], as well as the AQ-7 method presented in [7] (*i.e.*, the original formulation of AQ that we are building on). For PQ and OPQ, we use the publicly available code of Mohammad Norouzi[3], and we reproduce the results reported on the original papers introducing CQ [11] and AQ [7]. We compare our sparse extension against SCQ [12], which is to our knowledge the only paper on the subject.

Another baseline that we could compare against is the recently introduced Optimized Tree Quantization (OTQ) [8]. OTQ learns a tree structure of the codebooks where encoding can be performed exactly using dynamic programming, and has demonstrated competitive results on SIFT1M. The method, however, requires $2m - 1$ table lookups to compute approximate distances during query time, so it does not fit the query time criterion that we are controlling for in our experiments.

**Datasets.** We tested our method on 6 datasets. Three of these, SIFT1M, SIFT10M and SIFT1B [10], consist of 128-dimensional gradient-based, hand-crafted SIFT features. We also collected a dataset of 128-dimensional deep features using the CNN-M-128 network provided by Chatfield *et al.* [30], computing the features from a central $224 \times 224$ crop of the 1.3M images of the ILSRVC-2012 dataset and then subsampling uniformly at random from all classes. It is known that deep features can be effectively used as descriptors for image retrieval [31,32], and Chatfield *et al.* have shown that this intra-net compression results in a minimal loss of performance [30]. SIFT1M and Convnet1M both have 100 000 training vectors, 10 000 query vectors and 1 million database vectors. SIFT1B has 100 million vectors for training, and 1 billion vectors for base, as well as 10 000 queries. On SIFT1B, we followed previous work [9,11] and used only the first 1 million vectors for training. Better results on SIFT1B can be obtained using an inverted index, but we did not implement this data structure as we focus on improving encoding performance. This also has the added benefit of making our results directly comparable to those shown in CQ [11] and OPQ [19]. With SIFT10M, we followed the same protocol, but only the 10 million first vectors of SIFT1B as base.

We also use 2 datasets where CQ, our closest competitor, was benchmarked: MNIST and LabelMe22K [33]. MNIST is 784-dimensional, and has 10 000 vectors for query and 60 000 vectors for base. LabelMe22K is 512-dimensional and has 2 000 vectors for query and 20 019 vectors for base.

---

[3] https://github.com/norouzi/ckmeans.

Different datasets have different partitions, and this leads to important differences in the way learning and encoding are performed. The classical datasets SIFT1M, SIFT10M and SIFT1B [10], as well as our Convnet1M dataset have three partitions: train, query and database. In this case, the protocol is to first learn the codebooks using only the train set, then use the learned codebooks to encode the database, and finally evaluate recall@N of the queries w.r.t. the database. We refer to this partition as train/query/base.

However, several earlier studies used only two partitions of the data: query and database. In this case, the iterative codebook learning procedure is run directly on the database, and recall@N is evaluated on the queries w.r.t. the database thereafter. For example, Locally Optimized PQ [34] was evaluated using this partition on SIFT1B by simply ignoring the training set, and CQ was evaluated on MNIST and LabelMe22K using the train/test partitions that the datasets provide for classification [11]. It has also been argued that this partition is better suited for learning inverted indices on very large-scale datasets (see the last paragraph of [27]). We refer to this partition as query/base.

**Parameter Settings.** Our approach needs to set the number of ILS iterations (*i.e.*, the number of times a solution is perturbed and local search is done). At the same time, ICM may cycle through the nodes a number of times, which we call *ICM iterations*. Finally $k$, the number of elements to perturb, also needs to be defined.

We chose our parameters using a held-out subset of the training set of SIFT1M, keeping the values that minimize quantization error. Figure 1 shows the results of our parameter search on 10 000 SIFT descriptors. We note that, given the same amount of ICM cycles, using 4 ICM iterations and perturbing $k = 4$ code elements results in good performance. We observed similar results on other descriptor types, so we used these values in all our experiments. As shown in Fig. 1, the performance of our system depends on the number of ILS iterations used, trading-off computation for recall. We evaluated our method using 16 and 32 ILS iterations on the base set of train/query/base datasets, and refer to these methods as LSQ-{16, 32}. During training, we used only 8 ILS iterations.

**Implementation Details and Reproducible Research.** We implemented all our code in Julia [35], a recent high-level language for scientific computing, making use of the @inbounds and @simd macros in performance-critical parts of the code. All reported running times were measured using a single core on a computer with 64 GB of RAM and an Intel i7-3930K CPU, which runs at 3.2 GHz and has 12 MB of cache. To render our results reproducible, all our code and data are publicly available.

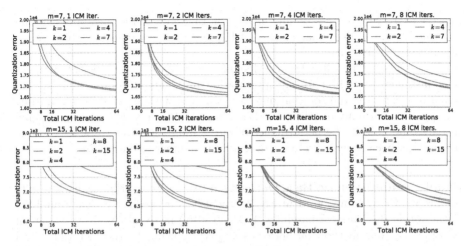

**Fig. 1.** Quantization error as a function of ILS iterations, ICM iterations and number of codes perturbed $k$ on $10\,000$ vectors of the SIFT1M train dataset after random initialization. The number of ICM iterations increases in 1, 2, 4, and 8 to the right, and we plot the quantization error for 64 ICM iterations in total – thus, the plots are comparable in amount of computation. Using 4 perturbations and 4 ICM iterations gives good results in all cases, so we use those parameters in all our experiments. Using no perturbations ($k = 0$), as done in previous work [7,11,12], leads to values that are above all the plots that we are showing, and stagnates after about 3 ICM iterations.

**Table 1.** Detailed recall@N values for our method on the SIFT1M dataset.

| | SIFT1M – 64 bits | | | | SIFT1M – 128 bits | | |
|---|---|---|---|---|---|---|---|
| | R@1 | R@10 | R@100 | | R@1 | R@2 | R@5 |
| PQ | $22.53 \pm 0.31$ | $60.14 \pm 0.41$ | $91.99 \pm 0.17$ | PQ | $44.62 \pm 0.47$ | $60.54 \pm 0.61$ | $78.88 \pm 0.30$ |
| OPQ | $24.34 \pm 0.52$ | $63.89 \pm 0.30$ | $94.04 \pm 0.08$ | OPQ | $46.05 \pm 0.25$ | $62.05 \pm 0.21$ | $80.59 \pm 0.31$ |
| AQ-7 [7] | 26 | 70 | 95 | AQ-15 [7] | – | – | – |
| CQ [11] | 29 | 71 | 96 | CQ [11] | 54 | 71 | 88 |
| LSQ-16 | $\underline{29.37} \pm 0.18$ | $\underline{72.54} \pm 0.26$ | $\underline{97.27} \pm 0.14$ | LSQ-16 | $\underline{54.47} \pm 0.37$ | $\underline{71.74} \pm 0.33$ | $\underline{88.21} \pm 0.48$ |
| LSQ-32 | $\mathbf{29.79} \pm 0.26$ | $\mathbf{73.12} \pm 0.20$ | $\mathbf{97.49} \pm 0.09$ | LSQ-32 | $\mathbf{55.28} \pm 0.21$ | $\mathbf{72.26} \pm 0.36$ | $\mathbf{88.93} \pm 0.14$ |

## 6    Results

Since our method relies heavily on randomness for encoding, it is natural to think that the final performance of the system could exhibit large variance. To quantify this effect, we ran our method 5 times on each dataset, and report the mean and standard deviation in recall@N achieved by our method. To see how this compares to previous work, we ran PQ and OPQ[4] 5 times (as for our method), and report their mean and standard deviation in recall@N as well. We

---

[4] PQ has randomness in the k-means initialization, and the OPQ code by Norouzi & Fleet chooses a random initial set of cluster centers.

observe that LSQ, despite relying heavily on randomness for encoding, exhibits a variability in recall similar to that of PQ and OPQ (and presumably that of other baselines as well).

This is consistent with the fact that LSQ solves a large number of independent instances of combinatorial optimisation problems of similar difficulty; in situations like this, the solution qualities achieved within a fixed running time are typically normally distributed ([17], Chap. 4). In other words, despite being heavily randomized, the performance of our system turns out to be very stable in practice, because it is averaged over a large number of data points.

**Small Training/Query/Base Datasets.** First, we report the recall@N results for SIFT1M and Convnet1M in Fig. 2, where it is immediately clear that LSQ outperforms the classical baselines, PQ and OPQ in recall@N for all values of N. Similarly, our method outperforms CQ when using 16 ILS iterations, and the gap is widened when using 32 iterations. As we will see, analogous effects are observed throughout our results. In Table 2 we show our results in more detail, providing mean recall@N values and standard deviations for the SIFT1M dataset.

On Convnet1M, the advantage of LSQ over PQ/OPQ is more pronounced. When using 64 bits, our method achieves a recall of 18.64, more than double that of PQ at 7.13, and with an 81 % improvement over OPQ at 10.28. These results

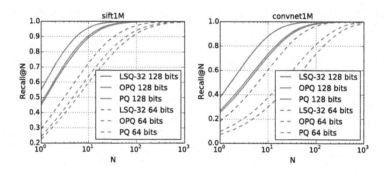

**Fig. 2.** Recall@N curves for (left) the SIFT1M, and (right) Convnet1M datasets.

**Table 2.** Detailed recall@N values for our method on the MNIST and LabelMe22K datasets.

| | MNIST – 64 bits | | | | LabelMe22K – 64 bits | | |
|---|---|---|---|---|---|---|---|
| | R@1 | R@2 | R@5 | | R@1 | R@2 | R@5 |
| PQ | 30.39 ± 0.28 | 45.70 ± 0.39 | 67.79 ± 0.46 | PQ | 17.05 ± 0.53 | 24.90 ± 0.48 | 38.78 ± 1.19 |
| OPQ | 37.81 ± 0.63 | 55.23 ± 0.44 | 78.10 ± 0.46 | OPQ | 32.96 ± 0.51 | 46.29 ± 0.68 | 66.80 ± 0.55 |
| CQ [11] | <u>44</u> | <u>63</u> | <u>84</u> | CQ [11] | <u>35</u> | 51 | <u>71</u> |
| LSQ-4 | **45.13** ± 0.50 | **63.98** ± 0.70 | **85.58** ± 0.40 | LSQ-4 | **35.69** ± 1.10 | <u>50.32</u> ± 1.46 | **71.05** ± 1.31 |

show an increased advantage of our method over orthogonal approaches like PQ/OPQ in deep-learned features, which are expected to dominate computer vision applications in coming years.

**Query/Base Datasets.** In Fig. 3, we report results on datasets with query/base partitions: MNIST and LabelMe22K. Despite requiring less computation in these datasets (only 4 ILS iterations, instead of 16–32), our method still outperforms the state of the art on MNIST, and performs on pair with CQ on LabelMe22K.

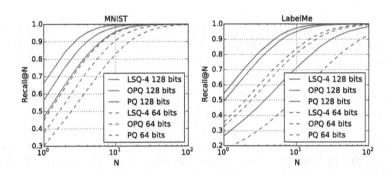

**Fig. 3.** Recall@N curves for (left) the MNIST, and (right) LabelMe22K datasets.

**Very Large-Scale Training/Query/Base Datasets.** Finally, we report results on two very large-scale datasets: SIFT10M and SIFT1B in Fig. 4, with detailed results in Table 3. Interestingly, the performance gap between our method and our baselines is more pronounced in these datasets, suggesting that the performance advantage of LSQ increases for larger datasets (as opposed to OPQ, whose gap over PQ consistently shrinks when more data is available). On SIFT1B with 64 bits, LSQ-32 shows a relative improvement of 13 % in recall@1

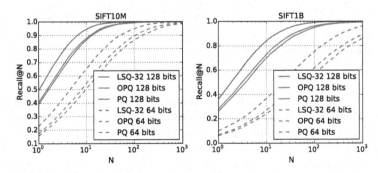

**Fig. 4.** Recall@N curves for very large-scale datasets: (left) the SIFT10M, and (right) SIFT1B.

**Table 3.** Detailed recall@N values for our method on large-scale datasets: SIFT10M and SIFT1B.

| | SIFT10M – 64 bits | | | SIFT10M – 128 bits | | | | SIFT1B – 64 bits | | | SIFT1B – 128 bits | | |
|---|---|---|---|---|---|---|---|---|---|---|---|---|---|
| | R@1 | R@10 | R@100 | R@1 | R@2 | R@5 | | R@1 | R@10 | R@100 | R@1 | R@2 | R@5 |
| PQ | 15.79 | 50.86 | 86.57 | 39.31 | 54.74 | 74.89 | PQ | 06.34 | 24.41 | 56.92 | 26.38 | 38.57 | 56.45 |
| OPQ | 17.49 | 54.92 | 89.41 | 40.80 | 56.73 | 77.15 | OPQ | 07.02 | 27.34 | 61.89 | 28.43 | 40.80 | 59.53 |
| CQ [11] | 21 | 63 | 93 | 47 | 64 | 84 | CQ [11] | 09 | 33 | 70 | 34 | 48 | 68 |
| LSQ-16 | 22.51 | 64.62 | 94.67 | 49.26 | 66.75 | 85.36 | LSQ-16 | 09.73 | 35.82 | 73.84 | 35.32 | 50.84 | 70.66 |
| LSQ-32 | **22.94** | **65.20** | **94.85** | **49.50** | **67.31** | **86.33** | LSQ-32 | **10.18** | **36.96** | **75.31** | **36.35** | **51.99** | **72.13** |

over CQ, our closest competitor, and consistently obtains between 2 and 3 points of advantage in recall over CQ in other cases. These are, to the best of our knowledge, the best results reported on SIFT1B using exhaustive search so far.

**Sparse Extension.** Following Zhang *et al.* [12], we evaluated the sparse version of our method using 2 different levels of sparsity: SLSQ1, with $\|C\|_0 \leq S = h \cdot d$, which has a query time comparable to PQ, and SLSQ2, with $\|C\|_0 \leq S = h \cdot d + d^2$, which has a query time comparable to OPQ. We compare against SCQ1 and SCQ2 from [12], which have the same levels of sparsity. We focus on SIFT1M; as noted in Sect. 4, substantial speedups can be obtained on small datasets by using sparse codebooks (Table 4).

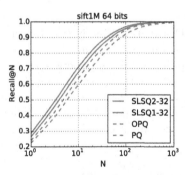

**Fig. 5.** Recall@N curves for our sparse methods SLSQ1 and SLSQ2 on SIFT1M.

**Table 4.** Recall@N values for the sparse extension of our method on SIFT1M using 64 bits.

| | SIFT1M – 64 bits | | |
|---|---|---|---|
| | R@1 | R@10 | R@100 |
| PQ | 22.53 ± 0.31 | 60.14 ± 0.41 | 91.99 ± 0.17 |
| SCQ1 [12] | 25 | 67 | 95 |
| SLSQ1-16 | 25.88 ± 0.31 | 66.69 ± 0.38 | 95.26 ± 0.14 |
| SLSQ1-32 | **26.36** ± 0.20 | **67.61** ± 0.08 | **95.66** ± 0.07 |
| OPQ | 24.34 ± 0.52 | 63.89 ± 0.30 | 94.04 ± 0.08 |
| SCQ2 [12] | 27 | 68 | 96 |
| SLSQ2-16 | 28.04 ± 0.40 | 70.10 ± 0.25 | 96.56 ± 0.08 |
| SLSQ2-32 | **28.72** ± 0.16 | **70.94** ± 0.32 | **96.81** ± 0.08 |

Again, in this scenario we observed improved performance compared to our baselines. While when using dense codebooks our method achieved a small gain of 0.79 in recall@1 over CQ, in this case the improvement jumps to 1.36 and 1.72 over SCQ. This is comparable to the 1.80 gain that OPQ achieves over PQ, and virtually equalizes the performance of CQ at 29: compared to CQ, our SLSQ2-32 method only loses 0.28 points in recall when using sparse codebooks (and thus having lower query time).

**Table 5.** Time spent per vector during encoding in our approach. "Sequential" refers to an LSQ implementation where ICM encodes each point sequentially (*i.e.*, does not take advantage of the shared pairwise terms). "Batched" is our LSQ implementation, which performs conditioning of shared pairwise terms among several data points.

| Method | Sequential | Batched | Method | GPU (batched) | | Method | Exhaustive NN | |
|---|---|---|---|---|---|---|---|---|
| codebooks ($m$) | 7 | 15 | 7 | 15 | codebooks ($m$) | 7 | 15 | codebooks ($m$) | 8 | 16 |
| LSQ-16 (ms.) | 1.52 | 7.02 | 0.53 | 2.01 | LSQ-16 ($\mu s$) | 17.9 | 67.2 | PQ ($\mu s$) | 42.6 | 77.9 |
| LSQ-32 (ms.) | 3.01 | 13.93 | 1.05 | 4.03 | LSQ-32 ($\mu s$) | 35.7 | 134.3 | OPQ ($\mu s$) | 49.2 | 90.3 |

**Encoding Speed and Comparison to CQ.** In Table 5 we show the speed advantage that sharing the pairwise terms gives to LSQ over a naïve implementation that encodes each point sequentially. The table shows that our method, implemented in a high-level language, remains fast when using up to 32 ILS iterations, handily achieving speeds faster than real-time (we believe that even better performance could be achieved with a C implementation). We also implemented a version of our method using an Nvidia GTX Titan X GPU. It took a novice CUDA developer about 2 days to complete this implementation, which again highlights the simplicity of our method (and suggests that better speeds are possible). Using this implementation, it is possible to encode SIFT1B using 128 bits and 32 ILS iterations in around 1.5 days.

Looking at our results, it is clear that our main competitor is CQ [11]. Our method has demonstrated higher recall on all datasets and benefits from a simpler formulation. Being free of additional constraints, our method is also better suited to make use of state-of-the-art L1 optimizers in the sparse codebook case, where we have also demonstrated state-of-the-art performance. Perhaps the most obvious downside of our method is encoding time. While CQ mentions using 3 ICM iterations, our method uses either 16, 64 or 128 iterations. In query/base partitions, we use 16 ICM iterations in total, which is not too large an overhead over the 3 iterations of CQ. Importantly, this protocol has been suggested as the most suitable for very large-scale datasets with inverted indices [27,34]. Regarding training/query/base partitions, the 64 and 128 ICM iterations of our method may appear to be a large overhead over CQ. However, we note that unlike CQ, our method does not require dataset-specific hyperparameter optimization. The authors of CQ have optimized the penalty parameter of L-BFGS for recall [11,12], which means the the method is actually run several times to find the best parameter value. In contrast, our method uses the same parameter settings for all datasets and only focuses on minimizing quantization error. CQ tries out ~10 different values of its hyperparameter[5], and thus ICM is run ~30 times. In that case, our method has only a 2–4× overhead over CQ in training/query/base partitions, and is overall faster in query/base datasets. In any

---

[5] Personal communication.

case, in a practical application one may always resort to our GPU implementation to offset the one-time cost of database encoding.

## 7 Conclusion

We have introduced a new method for solving the encoding problem in AQ based on stochastic local search (SLS). The high encoding performance of our method demonstrates that the elegant formulation introduced by AQ can be leveraged to achieve an improvement over the current state of the art in multi-codebook quantization. We have also shown that our method can be easily extended to accommodate sparsity constraints in the codebooks, which results in another conceptually simple method that also outperforms its competitors.

**Acknowledgements.** We thank NVIDIA for the donation of some of the GPUs used in this project. Joris Clement was supported by DAAD while doing an internship at the University of British Columbia. This research was supported in part by NSERC.

## References

1. Snavely, N., Seitz, S.M., Szeliski, R.: Photo tourism: exploring photo collections in 3D. In: TOG, vol. 25, no. 3 (2006)
2. Lowe, D.G.: Distinctive image features from scale-invariant keypoints. In: IJCV, vol. 60, no. 2 (2004)
3. Deng, J., Dong, W., Socher, R., Li, L.J., Li, K., Fei-Fei, L.: Imagenet: a large-scale hierarchical image database. In: CVPR (2009)
4. Torralba, A., Fergus, R., Freeman, W.T.: 80 million tiny images: a large data set for nonparametric object and scene recognition. In: TPAMI, vol. 30, no. 11 (2008)
5. Gong, Y., Lazebnik, S.: Iterative quantization: a procrustean approach to learning binary codes. In: CVPR (2011)
6. Weiss, Y., Torralba, A., Fergus, R.: Spectral hashing. In: NIPS (2009)
7. Babenko, A., Lempitsky, V.: Additive quantization for extreme vector compression. In: CVPR (2014)
8. Babenko, A., Lempitsky, V.: Tree quantization for large-scale similarity search and classification. In: CVPR (2015)
9. Ge, T., He, K., Ke, Q., Sun, J.: Optimized product quantization. In: TPAMI, vol. 36, no. 4 (2014)
10. Jégou, H., Douze, M., Schmid, C.: Product quantization for nearest neighbor search. In: TPAMI, vol. 33, no. 1 (2011)
11. Zhang, T., Du, C., Wang, J.: Composite quantization for approximate nearest neighbor search. In: ICML (2014)
12. Zhang, T., Qi, G.J., Tang, J., Wang, J.: Sparse composite quantization. In: CVPR (2015)
13. Guo, R., Kumar, S., Choromanski, K., Simcha, D.: Quantization based fast inner product search (2016)
14. Shrivastava, A., Li, P.: Asymmetric LSH (ALSH) for sublinear time maximum inner product search (MIPS). In: NIPS (2014)
15. Jiaxiang, W., Cong Leng, Y., Cheng, J.: Quantized convolutional neural networks for mobile devices. In: CVPR (2016)

16. Järvisalo, M., Le Berre, D., Roussel, O., Simon, L.: The international SAT solver competitions. AI Mag. **33**(1), 89–92 (2012)
17. Hoos, H.H., Stützle, T.: Stochastic Local Search: Foundations & Applications. Elsevier, Amsterdam (2004)
18. Xu, L., Hutter, F., Hoos, H.H., Leyton-Brown, K.: SATzilla: portfolio-based algorithm selection for SAT. J. Artif. Intell. Res. **32**, 565–606 (2008)
19. Norouzi, M., Fleet, D.J.: Cartesian k-means. In: CVPR (2013)
20. Gersho, A., Gray, R.M.: Vector Quantization and Signal Compression. Kluwer Academic Publishers, Berlin (1992)
21. Cooper, G.F.: The computational complexity of probabilistic inference using Bayesian belief networks. AI **42**(2), 393–405 (1990)
22. Kappes, J.H., Andres, B., Hamprecht, F., Schnorr, C., Nowozin, S., Batra, D., Kim, S., Kausler, B.X., Lellmann, J., Komodakis, N., et al.: A comparative study of modern inference techniques for discrete energy minimization problems. In: CVPR, pp. 1328–1335 (2013)
23. Nagata, Y., Kobayashi, S.: A powerful genetic algorithm using edge assembly crossover for the traveling salesman problem. INFORMS J. Comput. **25**(2), 346–363 (2013)
24. Muja, M., Lowe, D.G.: Fast approximate nearest neighbors with automatic algorithm configuration. In: VISAPP, no. 1 (2009)
25. Babenko, A., Lempitsky, V.: The inverted multi-index. In: CVPR (2012)
26. Xia, Y., He, K., Wen, F., Sun, J.: Joint inverted indexing. In: ICCV (2013)
27. Babenko, A., Lempitsky, V.: Improving bilayer product quantization for billion-scale approximate nearest neighbors in high dimensions (2014). arXiv preprint arXiv:1404.1831
28. André, F., Kermarrec, A.M., Le Scouarnec, N.: Cache locality is not enough: high-performance nearest neighbor search with product quantization fast scan. Proc. VLDB Endow. **9**(4), 288–299 (2015)
29. Van Den Berg, E., Friedlander, M.P.: Probing the pareto frontier for basis pursuit solutions. SIAM J. Sci. Comput. **31**(2), 890–912 (2008)
30. Chatfield, K., Simonyan, K., Vedaldi, A., Zisserman, A.: Return of the devil in the details: delving deep into convolutional nets. In: BMVC (2014)
31. Babenko, A., Slesarev, A., Chigorin, A., Lempitsky, V.: Neural codes for image retrieval. In: Fleet, D., Pajdla, T., Schiele, B., Tuytelaars, T. (eds.) ECCV 2014. LNCS, vol. 8689, pp. 584–599. Springer, Heidelberg (2014). doi:10.1007/978-3-319-10590-1_38
32. Razavian, A.S., Azizpour, H., Sullivan, J., Carlsson, S.: CNN features off-the-shelf: an astounding baseline for recognition. In: 2014 IEEE Conference on Computer Vision and Pattern Recognition Workshops (CVPRW), pp. 512–519. IEEE (2014)
33. Norouzi, M., Fleet, D.J.: Minimal loss hashing for compact binary codes. In: ICML (2011)
34. Kalantidis, Y., Avrithis, Y.: Locally optimized product quantization for approximate nearest neighbor search. In: CVPR (2014)
35. Bezanson, J., Edelman, A., Karpinski, S., Shah, V.B.: Julia: a fresh approach to numerical computing (2014). arXiv preprint arXiv:1411.1607

# Single Image Dehazing via Multi-scale Convolutional Neural Networks

Wenqi Ren[1,3], Si Liu[2], Hua Zhang[2], Jinshan Pan[3], Xiaochun Cao[1(✉)], and Ming-Hsuan Yang[3]

[1] Tianjin University, Tianjin, China
rwq.renwenqi@gmail.com, caoxiaochun@iie.ac.cn
[2] IIE, CAS, Beijing, China
{liusi,zhanghua}@iie.ac.cn
[3] University of California, Merced, Merced, USA
{jpan24,mhyang}@ucmerced.edu

**Abstract.** The performance of existing image dehazing methods is limited by hand-designed features, such as the dark channel, color disparity and maximum contrast, with complex fusion schemes. In this paper, we propose a multi-scale deep neural network for single-image dehazing by learning the mapping between hazy images and their corresponding transmission maps. The proposed algorithm consists of a coarse-scale net which predicts a holistic transmission map based on the entire image, and a fine-scale net which refines results locally. To train the multi-scale deep network, we synthesize a dataset comprised of hazy images and corresponding transmission maps based on the NYU Depth dataset. Extensive experiments demonstrate that the proposed algorithm performs favorably against the state-of-the-art methods on both synthetic and real-world images in terms of quality and speed.

**Keywords:** Image dehazing · Defogging · Convolutional neural network

## 1 Introduction

Image dehazing, which aims to recover a clear image from one single noisy frame caused by haze, fog or smoke, as shown in Fig. 1, is a classical problem in computer vision. The formulation of a hazy image can be modeled as

$$I(x) = J(x)t(x) + A(1 - t(x)), \qquad (1)$$

where $I(x)$ and $J(x)$ are the observed hazy image and the clear scene radiance, $A$ is the global atmospheric light, and $t(x)$ is the scene transmission describing the portion of light that is not scattered and reaches the camera sensors. Assuming that the haze is homogenous, we can express $t(x) = e^{-\beta d(x)}$, where $\beta$ is the medium extinction coefficient and $d(x)$ is the scene depth. As multiple solutions exist for a given hazy image, this problem is highly ill-posed.

**Electronic supplementary material** The online version of this chapter (doi:10.1007/978-3-319-46475-6_10) contains supplementary material, which is available to authorized users.

© Springer International Publishing AG 2016
B. Leibe et al. (Eds.): ECCV 2016, Part II, LNCS 9906, pp. 154–169, 2016.
DOI: 10.1007/978-3-319-46475-6_10

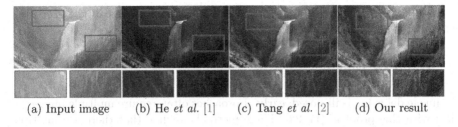

(a) Input image      (b) He *et al.* [1]     (c) Tang *et al.* [2]     (d) Our result

**Fig. 1.** Sample image dehazed results on a real input. The recovered image in (d) has rich details and vivid color information. (Color figure online)

Numerous haze removal methods have been proposed [3–8] in recent years with significant advancements. Most dehazing methods use a variety of visual cues to capture deterministic and statistical properties of hazy images [1,9–11]. The extracted features model chromatic [1], textural and contrast [10] properties of hazy images to determine the transmission in the scenes. Although these feature representations are useful, the assumptions in these aforementioned methods do not hold in all cases. For example, He *et al.* [1] assume that the values of dark channel in clear images are close to zero. This assumption is not true when the scene objects are similar to the atmospheric light. As the main goal of image dehazing is to estimate the transmission map from an input image, we propose a multi-scale convolutional neural network (CNN) to learn effective feature representations for this task. Recently, CNNs have shown an explosive popularity [12–15]. The features learned by the proposed algorithm do not depend on statistical priors of the scene images or haze-relevant properties. Since the learned features are based on a data-driven approach, they are able to describe the intrinsic properties of haze formation and help estimate transmission maps. To learn these features, we directly regress on the transmission maps using a neural network with two modules: the coarse-scale network first estimates the holistic structure of the scene transmission, and then a fine-scale network refines it using local information and the output from the coarse-scale module. This removes spurious pixel transmission estimates and encourages neighboring pixels to have the same labels. Based on this premise, we evaluate the proposed algorithm against the state-of-the-art methods on numerous datasets comprised of synthetic and real-world hazy images.

The contributions of this work are summarized as follows. First, we propose a multi-scale CNN to learn effective features from hazy images for the estimation of scene transmission map. The scene transmission map is first estimated by a coarse-scale network and then refined by a fine-scale network. Second, to learn the network, we develop a benchmark dataset consisting of hazy images and their transmission maps by synthesizing clean images and ground truth depth maps from the NYU Depth database [16]. Although the network is trained with the synthetic dataset, we show the learned multi-scale CNN is able to dehaze real-world hazy images well. Third, we analyze the differences between traditional hand-crafted features and the features learned by the proposed multi-scale CNN model. Finally, we show that the proposed algorithm is significantly faster than existing image dehazing methods.

## 2    Related Work

As image dehazing is ill-posed, early approaches often require multiple images to deal with this problem [17–22]. These methods assume that there are multiple images from the same scene. However, in most cases there only exists one image for a specified scene. Another line of research work is based on physical properties of hazy images. For example, Fattal [23] proposes a refined image formation model for surface shading and scene transmission. Based on this model, a hazy image can be separated into regions of constant albedo, and then the scene transmission can be inferred. Based on a similar model, Tan [10] proposes to enhance the visibility of hazy images by maximizing their local contrast, but the restored images often contain distorted colors and significant halos.

Numerous dehazing methods based on the dark channel prior [1] have been developed [24–27]. The dark channel prior has been shown to be effective for image dehazing. However, it is computationally expensive [28–30] and less effective for the scenes where the color of objects are inherently similar to the atmospheric light. A variety of multi-scale haze-relevant features are analyzed by Tang et al. [2] in a regression framework based on random forests. Nevertheless, this feature fusion approach relies largely on the dark channel features. Despite significant advances in this field, the state-of-the-art dehazing methods [2, 11, 29] are developed based on hand-crafted features.

## 3    Multi-scale CNN for Transmission Maps

Given a single hazy input, we aim to recover the latent clean image by estimating the scene transmission map. The main steps of the proposed algorithm are shown in Fig. 2(a). We first describe how to estimate the scene transmission map $t(x)$.

For each scene, we propose to estimate the scene transmission map $t(x)$ based on a multi-scale CNN. The coarse structure of the scene transmission map for each image is obtained from the coarse-scale network, and then refined by the fine-scale network. Both coarse and fine scale networks are applied to the original input hazy image. In addition, the output of the coarse network is passed to the fine network as additional information. Thus, the fine-scale network can refine the coarse prediction with details. The architecture of the proposed multi-scale CNN for learning haze-relevant features is shown in Fig. 2(b).

### 3.1    Coarse-Scale Network

The task of the coarse-scale network is to predict a holistic transmission map of the scene. The coarse-scale network (in the top half of Fig. 2(b)) consists of four operations: convolution, max-pooling, up-sampling and linear combination.

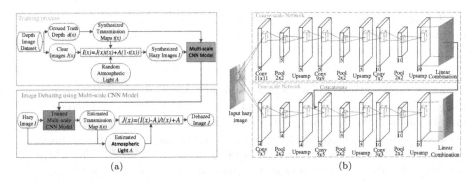

(a)                         (b)

**Fig. 2.** (a) Main steps of the proposed single-image dehazing algorithm. For training the multi-scale network, we synthesize hazy images and the corresponding transmission maps based on depth image dataset. In the test stage, we estimate the transmission map of the input hazy image based on the trained model, and then generate the dehazed image using the estimated atmospheric light and computed transmission map. (b) Proposed multi-scale convolutional neural network. Given a hazy image, the coarse-scale network (the green dashed rectangle) predicts a holistic transmission map and feeds it to the fine-scale network (the orange dashed rectangle) in order to generate a refined transmission map. (Color figure online)

**Convolution Layers:** This network takes an RGB image as input. The convolution layers consist of filter banks which are convolved with the input feature maps. The response of each convolution layer is given by $f_m^{l+1} = \sigma(\sum_m(f_m^l * k_{m,n}^{l+1}) + b^{l+1})$, where $f_n^l$ and $f_m^{l+1}$ are the feature maps of the current layer $l$ and the next layer $l+1$, respectively. In addition, $k$ is the convolution kernel, indices $(m,n)$ show the mapping from the current layer $m^{th}$ feature map to the next layer $n^{th}$, and $*$ denotes the convolution operator. The function $\sigma(\cdot)$ denotes the Rectified Linear Unit (ReLU) on the filter responses and $b$ is the bias.

**Max-Pooling:** We use max-pooling layers with a down-sampling factor of 2 after each convolution layer.

**Up-Sampling:** In our framework, the size of the ground truth transmission map is the same as the input image. However, the size of feature maps is reduced to half after max-pooling layers. Therefore, we add an up-sampling layer [31] to ensure that the sizes of output transmission maps and input hazy images are equal. Although we can alternatively remove the max-pooling and up-sampling layers to achieve the same goal, this method would reduce the non-linearity of the network [31], which is less effective (See Sect. 6.3). The up-sampling layer follows the pooling layer and restores the size of sub-sampled features while retaining the non-linearity of the network. The response of each up-sampling layer is defined as $f_n^{l+1}(2x-1:2x, 2y-1:2y) = f_n^l(x,y)$. This function copies a pixel value at location $(x,y)$ from the max-pooled features to a $2 \times 2$ block in the following up-sampling layer. Since each block in the up-sampling layer consists of the same value, the back-propagation rule of this layer is simply the average-pooling layer in the reverse direction, with a scale of 2, $f_n^l(x,y) = \frac{1}{4}\sum_{2\times 2} f_n^{l+1}(2x - 1 : 2x, 2y - 1 : 2y)$.

**Linear Combination:** In our coarse-scale convolution network, the features in the penultimate layer before the output have multiple channels. Therefore, we need to combine the feature channels from the last up-sampling layer through a linear combination [31]. A sigmoid activation function is then applied to produce the final output and the response is given by $t_c = s(\sum_n w_n f_n^p + b)$, where $t_c$ denotes the output scene transmission map in the coarse-scale network, $n$ is the feature map channel index, $s(\cdot)$ is a sigmoid function, and $f_n^p$ denotes the penultimate feature maps before the output transmission map. In addition, $w$ and $b$ are weights and bias of the linear combination, respectively.

### 3.2   Fine-Scale Network

After considering an entire image to predict the rough scene transmission map, we make refinements using a fine-scale network. The architecture of the fine-scale network stack is similar to the coarse-scale network except the first and second convolution layers. The structure of our fine-scale network is shown in the bottom half of Fig. 2(b) where the coarse output transmission map is used as an additional feature map. By design, the size of the coarse prediction is the same as the output of the first up-sampling layer. We concatenate these two together and use the predicted coarse transmission map combined with the learned feature maps in the fine-scale network to refine the transmission map.

### 3.3   Training

Learning the mapping between hazy images and corresponding transmission maps is achieved by minimizing the loss between the reconstructed transmission $t_i(x)$ and the corresponding ground truth map $t_i^*(x)$,

$$L(t_i(x), t_i^*(x)) = \frac{1}{q}\sum_{i=1}^{q} ||t_i(x) - t_i^*(x)||^2, \tag{2}$$

where $q$ is the number of hazy images in the training set. We minimize the loss using the stochastic gradient descent method with the backpropagation learning rule [12,32,33]. We first train the coarse network, and then use the coarse-scale output transmission maps to train the fine-scale network. The training loss (2) is used in both coarse- and fine-scale networks.

## 4   Dehazing with the Multi-scale Network

**Atmospheric Light Estimation:** In addition to scene transmission map $t(x)$, we need to estimate the atmospheric light $A$ in order to recover the clear image.

From the hazy image formation model (1), we derive $I(x) = A$ when $t(x) \to 0$. As the objects that appear in outdoor images can be far from the observers, the range of depth $d(x)$ is $[0, +\infty)$, and we have $t(x) = 0$ when $d(x) \to \infty$. Thus we estimate the atmosphere light $A$ by selecting 0.1 % darkest pixels in a transmission map $t(x)$. Among these pixels, the one with the highest intensity in the corresponding hazy image $I$ is selected as the atmospheric light.

**Haze Removal:** After $A$ and $t(x)$ are estimated by the proposed algorithm, we recover the haze-free image using (1). However, the direct attenuation term $J(x)t(x)$ may be close to zero when the transmission t(x) is close to zero [1]. Therefore, the final scene radiance $J(x)$ is recovered by

$$J(x) = \frac{I(x) - A}{\max\{0.1, t(x)\}} + A. \tag{3}$$

## 5    Experimental Results

We quantitatively evaluate the proposed algorithm on two synthetic datasets and real-world hazy photographs, with comparisons to the state-of-the-art methods in terms of accuracy and run time. The MATLAB code is available at https://sites.google.com/site/renwenqi888/research/dehazing/mscnndehazing.

### 5.1    Experimental Settings

We use 3 convolution layers for both coarse-scale and fine-scale networks in our experiments. In the coarse-scale network, the first two layers consist of 5 filters of size $11 \times 11$ and $9 \times 9$, respectively. The last layer consists of 10 filters with size $7 \times 7$. In the fine-scale network, the first convolution layer consists of 4 filters of size $7 \times 7$. We then concatenate these four feature maps with the output from the coarse-scale network together to generate the five feature maps. The last two layers consist of 5 and 10 filters with size $5 \times 5$ and $3 \times 3$, respectively.

Both the coarse and fine scale networks are trained by the stochastic gradient descent method with 0.9 momentum. We use a batch size of 100 images ($320 \times 240$ pixels), the initial learning rate is 0.001 and decreased by 0.1 after every 20 epochs and the epoch is set to be 70. The weight decay parameter is $5 \times 10^{-4}$ and the training time is approximately 8 h on a desktop computer with a 2.8 GHz CPU and an Nvidia K10 GPU.

### 5.2    Training Data

To train the multi-scale network, we generate a dataset with synthesized hazy images and their corresponding transmission maps. We randomly sample 6,000 clean images and the corresponding depth maps from the NYU Depth dataset [16] to construct the training set. In addition, we generate a validation set of 50 synthesized hazy images using the Middlebury stereo database [34–36].

160     W. Ren et al.

Given a clear image $J(x)$ and the ground truth depth $d(x)$, we synthesize a hazy image using the physical model (1). We generate the random atmospheric light $A = [k, k, k]$, where $k \in [0.7, 1.0]$, and sample three random $\beta \in [0.5, 1.5]$ for every image. We do not use small $\beta \in (0, 0.5)$ because it would lead to thin haze and boost noise [1]. On the other hand, we do not use large $\beta \in (1.5, \infty)$ as the resulting transmission maps are close to zero. Therefore, we have 18,000 hazy images and transmission maps (6,000 images × 3 medium extinction coefficients $\beta$) in the training set. All the training images are resized to the canonical size of 320 × 240 pixels.

### 5.3   Quantitative Evaluation on Benchmark Dataset

We compare the proposed algorithm with the state-of-the-art dehazing methods [1,2,27,28] using the Peak Signal-to-Noise Ratio (PSNR) and Structural Similarity (SSIM) metrics. We use five examples: *Bowling, Aloe, Baby, Monopoly* and *Books* for illustration. Figure 3(a) shows the input hazy images which are synthesized from the haze-free images with known depth maps [34]. As the method by He *et al.* [1] assumes that the dark channel values of clear images are zeros, it tends to overestimate the haze thickness and results in darker results as shown in Fig. 3(b). We note that the dehazed images generated by Meng *et al.* [27] and Tarel and Hautiere [28] tend to have some color distortions. For example, the colors of the *Books* dehazed image become darker as shown in Fig. 3(c) and (d). Although the dehazed results by Tang *et al.* [2] are better than those by [1,27,28],

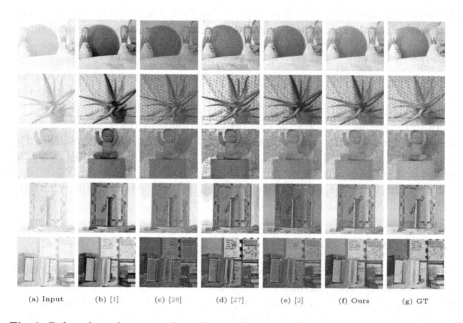

(a) Input     (b) [1]     (c) [28]     (d) [27]     (e) [2]     (f) Ours     (g) GT

**Fig. 3.** Dehazed results on synthetic hazy images using stereo images: *Bowling, Aloe, Baby, Monopoly* and *Books*. (Color figure online)

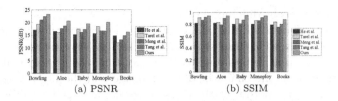

(a) PSNR                    (b) SSIM

**Fig. 4.** Quantitative comparisons of the dehazed images shown in Fig. 3.

the colors are still darker than the ground truth. In contrast, the dehazed results by the proposed algorithm in Fig. 3(e) are close to the ground truth haze-free images, which indicates that better transmission maps are estimated. Figure 4 shows that the proposed algorithm performs well on each image against the state-of-the-art dehazing methods [1,2,27,28] in terms of PSNR and SSIM.

**New Synthetic Dataset:** For quantitative performance evaluation, we construct a new dataset of synthesized hazy images. We select 40 images and their depth maps from the NYU Depth dataset [16] (different from those that used for training) to synthesize 40 transmission maps and hazy images. Figure 5 shows

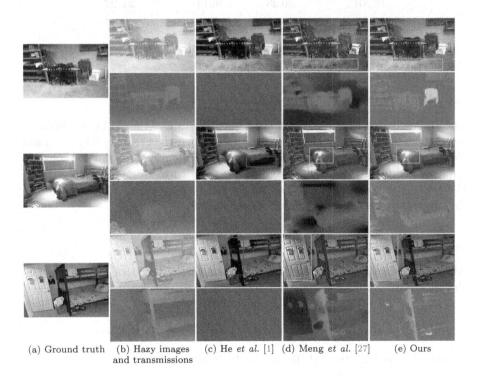

(a) Ground truth    (b) Hazy images    (c) He *et al.* [1]    (d) Meng *et al.* [27]    (e) Ours
                    and transmissions

**Fig. 5.** Dehazed results on our synthetic images. The red and yellow rectangles are for comparison of our method with [1] and [27] respectively. (Color figure online)

some dehazed images by different methods. The estimated transmission maps by He *et al.* [1] are uniform and the values almost do not vary with scene depth, and thus the haze thickness in some slight hazy regions is overestimated. This indicates that the dehazed results tend to be darker than the ground truth images in some regions, e.g., the chairs in the first image and the beds in the second and third images. We note that the dehazed results are similar to those by He *et al.* [1] in Fig. 3(b). Although the estimated transmission maps by Meng *et al.* [27] in Fig. 5(d) vary with scene depth, the final dehazed images contain some color distortions, e.g., the floor color is changed from gray to blue in the first image. The regions that contain color distortions in the dehazed images correspond to the darker areas in the estimated transmission maps. Figure 5(e) shows the estimated transmission maps and the final recovered images by the proposed algorithm. Overall, the dehazed results by the proposed algorithm have higher visual quality and less color distortions. The qualitative results are also reflected by the quantitative PSNR and SSIM metrics shown in Table 1.

**Table 1.** Average PSNR and SSIM of dehazed results on the new synthetic dataset.

| Average metrics | He *et al.* [1] | Meng *et al.* [27] | Ours |
|---|---|---|---|
| PSNR | 20.28 | 16.79 | **21.27** |
| SSIM | 0.80 | 0.41 | **0.85** |

### 5.4   Run Time

The proposed algorithm is more efficient than the state-of-the-art image dehazing methods [1,11,23,25,27] in terms of run time. We use the five images in Fig. 3 and the 40 images in the new synthetic dataset for evaluation. All the methods are implemented in MATLAB, and we evaluate them on the same machine without GPU acceleration (Intel CPU 3.40 GHz and 16 GB memory). The average run time using two image resolutions is shown in Table 2.

### 5.5   Real Images

Although our multi-scale network is trained on synthetic indoor images, we note that it can be applied for outdoor images as well. We evaluate the proposed

**Table 2.** Average run time (in seconds) on test images.

| Image size | Fattal [23] | He *et al.* [1] | Tarel *et al.* [25] | Meng *et al.* [27] | Zhu *et al.* [11] | Ours |
|---|---|---|---|---|---|---|
| 427 × 370 | 25.68 | 13.15 | 2.02 | 2.29 | 1.13 | **0.36** |
| 640 × 480 | 63.09 | 26.90 | 7.02 | 3.23 | 2.51 | **0.61** |

algorithm against the state-of-the-art single image dehazing methods [1, 2, 10, 23, 27, 28] using six challenging real images as shown in Figs. 6 and 7. More results can be found in the supplementary material. In Fig. 6, the dehazed *Yosemite* image by Tan [10] and the dehazed *Canyon* image by Fattal [23] have significant color distortions and miss most details as shown in (b) and (c). The dehazing method of He *et al.* [1] tend to overestimate the thickness of the haze and produce dark results. The method by Meng *et al.* [27] can augment the image details and enhance the image visibility. However, the colors in the recovered images still have color distortions. For example, the rock color is changed from gray to yellow in the *Yosemite* image in (e). In Fig. 7, the dehazing methods of Tarel *et al.* [28] and Tang *et al.* [2] overestimate the thickness of the haze and generate darker images than others. The results by Meng *et al.* [27] have some remaining haze as shown in the first line in Fig. 7(c). In contrast, the dehazed results by the

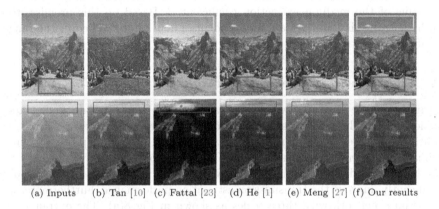

(a) Inputs    (b) Tan [10]    (c) Fattal [23]    (d) He [1]    (e) Meng [27]    (f) Our results

**Fig. 6.** Visual comparison for real image dehazing. (Color figure online)

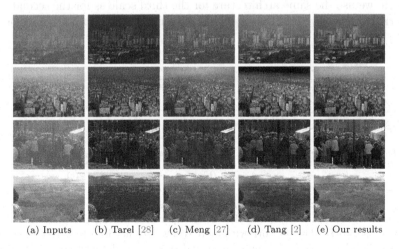

(a) Inputs    (b) Tarel [28]    (c) Meng [27]    (d) Tang [2]    (e) Our results

**Fig. 7.** Visual comparison for real image dehazing. (Color figure online)

proposed algorithm are visually more pleasing in dense haze regions without color distortions or artifacts.

# 6   Analysis and Discussions

## 6.1   Generalization Capability

As shown in Sect. 5.5, the proposed multi-scale network generalizes well for outdoor scenes. In the following, we explain why indoor scenes help for outdoor image dehazing.

The key observation is that image content is independent of scene depth and medium transmission [2], i.e., the same image (or patch) content can appear at different depths in different images. Therefore, although the training images have relatively shallow depths, we could increase the haze concentration by adjusting the value of the medium extinction coefficient $\beta$. Based on this premise, the synthetic transmission maps are independent of depth $d(x)$ and cover the range of values in real transmission maps.

## 6.2   Effectiveness of Fine-Scale Network

In this section we analyze how the fine-scale network helps estimate scene transmission maps. The transmission map from the coarse-scale network serves as additional features in the fine-scale network, which greatly improve the final estimation of scene transmission map. The validation cost convergence curves (the blue and red lines) in Fig. 8(b) show that using a fine-scale network could significantly improve the transmission estimation performance. Furthermore, we also train a network with three scales as shown in Fig. 8(a). The output from the second scale also serves as additional features in the third scale network. In addition, we use the same architecture for the third scale as for the second scale network. However, we find that networks with more scales do not help generate

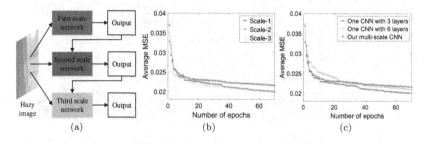

(a)                          (b)                          (c)

**Fig. 8.** (a) A multi-scale network with three scales. The output of each scale serves as an additional feature in next scale. (b) Comparisons among the first, second and third scale networks. The network with more scales does not lead to better results. (c) Comparisons of one CNN with more layers and the proposed multi-scale CNN. (Color figure online)

better results as shown in Fig. 8(b). The results also show that the proposed network architecture is compact and robust for image dehazing.

To better understand how the fine-scale network affects our method, we conduct a deeper architecture by adding more layers in the single scale network. Figure 8(c) shows that the CNN with more layers does not perform well compared to the proposed multi-scale CNN. This can be explained by that the output from the coarse-scale network provides sufficiently important features as the input for the fine-scale network. We note that similar observations have been reported in SRCNN [37], which indicates that the effectiveness of deeper structures for low-level tasks is not as apparent as that shown in high-level tasks (e.g., image classification). We also show an example of dehazed results with and without the fine-scale network in Fig. 9. Without the fine-scale network, the estimated transmission map lacks fine details and the edges of rock do not match with the input hazy image, which accordingly lead to the dehazed results containing halo artifacts around the rock edge. In contrast, the transmission map generated with fine-scale network is more informative and thus results in a clearer image.

## 6.3   Effectiveness of Up-Sampling Layers

For image dehazing, the size of the ground truth transmission map is the same as that of the input image. To maintain identical sizes, we can (i) set the strides to 1 in all convolutional and pooling layers, (ii) remove the max-pooling layers, or (iii) add the up-sampling layers to keep the size of input and output the same. However, it requires much more memory and longer training time when the stride is set to 1. On the other hand, the non-linearity of the network is reduced if the max-pooling layers are removed. Thus, we add the up-sampling layers in the

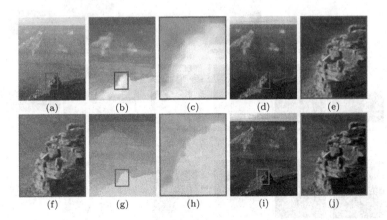

**Fig. 9.** Effectiveness of the proposed fine-scale network.(a) Hazy image. (b) and (d) are the transmission map and dehazed result without the fine-scale network. (g) and (i) denote transmission map and dehazed result with the fine-scale network. (f), (c), (e), (h), and (j) are the zoom-in views in (a), (b), (d), (g), and (i), respectively.

|     |     |     |     |
| :-: | :-: | :-: | :-: |
| (a) | (b) | (c) | (d) |

**Fig. 10.** Effect of up-sampling layers.(a) Input hazy image. (b) Dehazed result with stride of 1 for all layers. (c) Dehazed result without pooling layers.(d) Our result.

proposed network model as show in Fig. 2. Figure 10 shows the dehazed images using these three trained networks. As shown in Fig. 10, the dehazed image from the network with up-sampling layers is visually more pleasing than the others. Although the dehazed result in Fig. 10(b) is close to the one in (d), setting stride to 1 slows down the training process and requires much more memory compared with the proposed network using the up-sampling layers.

### 6.4  Effects of Different Features

In this section, we analyze the differences between the traditional hand-crafted features and the features learned by the proposed multi-scale CNN model. Traditional methods [1,2,10,38] focus on designing hand-crafted features while our method learns the effective haze-relevant features automatically.

Figure 11(a) shows an input hazy image. The dehazed result only using dark channel feature (b) is shown in (c). In the recent work, Tang *et al.* [2] propose a learning based dehazing model. However, this work involves a considerable

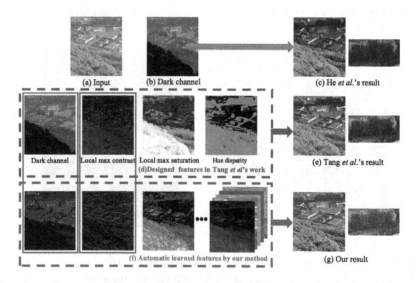

**Fig. 11.** Effectiveness of learned features. With these diverse features (f) automatically learned from the proposed algorithm, our dehazed result is sharper and visually more pleasing than others. (Color figure online)

amount of effort in the design of hand-crafted features including dark channel, local max contrast, local max saturation and hue disparity features as show in (d). By fusing all these features in a regression framework based on random forests, the dehazed result is shown in (e). In contrast, our data-driven framework automatically learns the effective features. Figure 11(f) show some features automatically learned by the multi-scale network for the input image. These features are randomly selected from the intermediate layers of the multi-scale CNN model. As shown in Fig. 11(f), the learned features include various kinds of information for the input, including luminance map, intensity map, edge information and amount of haze, and so on. More interestingly, some features learned by the proposed algorithm are similar to the dark channel and local max contrast as shown in the two red rectangles in Fig. 11(f), which indicates that the dark channel and local max contrast priors are useful for dehazing as demonstrated by prior studies. With these diverse features learned from the proposed algorithm, the dehazed image shown in Fig. 11(g) is sharper and visually more pleasing.

### 6.5 Failure Case

Our multi-scale CNN model is trained on the synthetic dataset which is created based on the hazy model (1). As the hazy model (1) usually does not hold for the nighttime hazy images [39,40], our method is less effective for such images. One failure example is shown in Fig. 12. In future work we will address this problem by developing an end-to-end network to simultaneously estimate the transmission map and atmospheric light for the input hazy image.

(a) Input          (b) Nighttime dehazing [39]          (c) Our result

**Fig. 12.** Failure case for nighttime hazy image.

## 7  Conclusions

In this paper, we address the image dehazing problem via a multi-scale deep network which learns effective features to estimate the scene transmission of a single hazy image. Compared to previous methods which require carefully designed features and combination strategies, the proposed feature learning method is easy to implement and reproduce. In the proposed multi-scale model, we first use a coarse-scale network to learn a holistic estimation of the scene transmission, and then use a fine-scale network to refine it using local information and the output from the coarse-scale network. Experimental results on synthetic and real images demonstrate the effectiveness of the proposed algorithm. In addition, we show that our multi-scale network generalizes and performs well for real scenes.

**Acknowledgements.** This work is supported by National High-tech R&D Program of China (2014BAK11B03), National Basic Research Program of China (2013CB329305), National Natural Science Foundation of China (No. 61422213), "Strategic Priority Research Program" of the Chinese Academy of Sciences (XDA06010701), and National Program for Support of Top-notch Young Professionals. W. Ren is supported by a scholarship from China Scholarship Council. M.-H. Yang is supported in part by the NSF CAREER grant #1149783, and gifts from Adobe and Nvidia.

# References

1. He, K., Sun, J., Tang, X.: Single image haze removal using dark channel prior. TPAMI **33**(12), 2341–2353 (2011)
2. Tang, K., Yang, J., Wang, J.: Investigating haze-relevant features in a learning framework for image dehazing. In: CVPR (2014)
3. Tan, R.T., Pettersson, N., Petersson, L.: Visibility enhancement for roads with foggy or hazy scenes. In: Intelligent Vehicles Symposium (2007)
4. Hautière, N., Tarel, J.P., Aubert, D.: Towards fog-free in-vehicle vision systems through contrast restoration. In: CVPR (2007)
5. Caraffa, L., Tarel, J.P.: Markov random field model for single image defogging. In: Intelligent Vehicles Symposium (2013)
6. Fattal, R.: Dehazing using color-lines. TOG **34**(1), 13 (2014)
7. Li, Z., Tan, P., Tan, R.T., Zou, D., Zhou, S.Z., Cheong, L.F.: Simultaneous video defogging and stereo reconstruction. In: CVPR (2015)
8. Pei, S.C., Lee, T.Y.: Nighttime haze removal using color transfer pre-processing and dark channel prior. In: ICIP (2012)
9. Ancuti, C.O., Ancuti, C.: Single image dehazing by multi-scale fusion. TIP **22**(8), 3271–3282 (2013)
10. Tan, R.T.: Visibility in bad weather from a single image. In: CVPR (2008)
11. Zhu, Q., Mai, J., Shao, L.: A fast single image haze removal algorithm using color attenuation prior. TIP **24**(11), 3522–3533 (2015)
12. Eigen, D., Puhrsch, C., Fergus, R.: Depth map prediction from a single image using a multi-scale deep network. In: NIPS (2014)
13. Liu, S., Liang, X., Liu, L., Shen, X., Yang, J., Xu, C., Lin, L., Cao, X., Yan, S.: Matching-CNN meets KNN: quasi-parametric human parsing. In: CVPR, pp. 1419–1427 (2015)
14. Liang, X., Liu, S., Shen, X., Yang, J., Liu, L., Dong, J., Lin, L., Yan, S.: Deep human parsing with active template regression. PAMI **37**(12), 2402–2414 (2015)
15. Zhang, H., Liu, S., Zhang, C., Ren, W., Wang, R., Cao, X.: SketchNet: sketch classification with web images. In: CVPR (2016)
16. Silberman, N., Hoiem, D., Kohli, P., Fergus, R.: Indoor segmentation and support inference from RGBD images. In: Fitzgibbon, A., Lazebnik, S., Perona, P., Sato, Y., Schmid, C. (eds.) ECCV 2012. LNCS, vol. 7576, pp. 746–760. Springer, Heidelberg (2012). doi:10.1007/978-3-642-33715-4_54

17. Kopf, J., Neubert, B., Chen, B., Cohen, M., Cohen-Or, D., Deussen, O., Uyttendaele, M., Lischinski, D.: Deep photo: model-based photograph enhancement and viewing. In: SIGGRAPH Asia (2008)
18. Treibitz, T., Schechner, Y.Y.: Polarization: beneficial for visibility enhancement? In: CVPR (2009)
19. Narasimhan, S.G., Nayar, S.K.: Contrast restoration of weather degraded images. TPAMI 25(6), 713–724 (2003)
20. Narasimhan, S.G., Nayar, S.K.: Chromatic framework for vision in bad weather. In: CVPR (2000)
21. Schechner, Y.Y., Narasimhan, S.G., Nayar, S.K.: Instant dehazing of images using polarization. In: CVPR (2001)
22. Shwartz, S., Namer, E., Schechner, Y.Y.: Blind haze separation. In: CVPR (2006)
23. Fattal, R.: Single image dehazing. In: SIGGRAPH (2008)
24. Kratz, L., Nishino, K.: Factorizing scene albedo and depth from a single foggy image. In: ICCV (2009)
25. Tarel, J.P., Hautière, N., Caraffa, L., Cord, A., Halmaoui, H., Gruyer, D.: Vision enhancement in homogeneous and heterogeneous fog. Intell. Transp. Syst. Mag. 4(2), 6–20 (2012)
26. Nishino, K., Kratz, L., Lombardi, S.: Bayesian defogging. IJCV 98(3), 263–278 (2012)
27. Meng, G., Wang, Y., Duan, J., Xiang, S., Pan, C.: Efficient image dehazing with boundary constraint and contextual regularization. In: ICCV (2013)
28. Tarel, J.P., Hautiere, N.: Fast visibility restoration from a single color or gray level image. In: ICCV (2009)
29. Gibson, K.B., Vo, D.T., Nguyen, T.Q.: An investigation of dehazing effects on image and video coding. TIP 21(2), 662–673 (2012)
30. He, K., Sun, J., Tang, X.: Guided image filtering. TPAMI 35(6), 1397–1409 (2013)
31. Yuan, J., Ni, B., Kassim, A.A.: Half-CNN: a general framework for whole-image regression (2014). arXiv preprint: arXiv:1412.6885
32. LeCun, Y., Bottou, L., Bengio, Y., Haffner, P.: Gradient-based learning applied to document recognition. Proc. IEEE 86(11), 2278–2324 (1998)
33. Khan, S.H., Bennamoun, M., Sohel, F., Togneri, R.: Automatic feature learning for robust shadow detection. In: CVPR (2014)
34. Scharstein, D., Szeliski, R.: A taxonomy and evaluation of dense two-frame stereo correspondence algorithms. IJCV 47(1–3), 7–42 (2002)
35. Scharstein, D., Szeliski, R.: High-accuracy stereo depth maps using structured light. In: CVPR (2003)
36. Hirschmüller, H., Scharstein, D.: Evaluation of cost functions for stereo matching. In: CVPR (2007)
37. Dong, C., Loy, C.C., He, K., Tang, X.: Learning a deep convolutional network for image super-resolution. In: Fleet, D., Pajdla, T., Schiele, B., Tuytelaars, T. (eds.) ECCV 2014. LNCS, vol. 8692, pp. 184–199. Springer, Heidelberg (2014). doi:10.1007/978-3-319-10593-2_13
38. Ancuti, C.O., Ancuti, C., Hermans, C., Bekaert, P.: A fast semi-inverse approach to detect and remove the haze from a single image. In: Kimmel, R., Klette, R., Sugimoto, A. (eds.) ACCV 2010. LNCS, vol. 6493, pp. 501–514. Springer, Heidelberg (2011). doi:10.1007/978-3-642-19309-5_39
39. Li, Y., Tan, R.T., Brown, M.S.: Nighttime haze removal with glow and multiple light colors. In: ICCV (2015)
40. Zhang, J., Cao, Y., Wang, Z.: Nighttime haze removal based on a new imaging model. In: ICIP (2014)

# Photometric Stereo Under Non-uniform Light Intensities and Exposures

Donghyeon Cho[1]([⊠]), Yasuyuki Matsushita[2], Yu-Wing Tai[3], and Inso Kweon[1]

[1] KAIST, Daejeon, South Korea
cdh12242@gmail.com, iskweon@kaist.ac.kr
[2] Osaka University, Suita, Japan
yasumat@ist.osaka-u.ac.jp
[3] SenseTime Group Limited, Beijing, China
yuwing@gmail.com

**Abstract.** This paper studies the effects of non-uniform light intensities and sensor exposures across observed images in photometric stereo. While conventional photometric stereo methods typically assume that light intensities are identical and sensor exposure is constant across observed images taken under varying lightings, these assumptions easily break down in practical settings due to individual light bulb's characteristics and limited control over sensors. Our method explicitly models these non-uniformities and develops a method for accurately determining surface normal without affected by these factors. In addition, we show that our method is advantageous for general photometric stereo settings, where auto-exposure control is desirable. We compare our method with conventional least-squares and robust photometric stereo methods, and the experimental result shows superior accuracy of our method in this practical circumstance.

**Keywords:** Photometric stereo · Shape estimation · Unknown light intensity and exposure · Surface normal

## 1 Introduction

Non-uniform light intensities and exposures across observed images are a practical and common circumstance in data acquisition for photometric stereo that uses multiple images under distinct light directions. For example, different light bulbs with different intensity characteristics may be used for illuminating a scene. Even with identical light bulbs, due to that scene radiance is determined by surface normal and light directions, auto-adjusted sensor exposure is desirable depending on the light directions to avoid over-/under-exposures, which results in non-uniform exposures (equivalently, non-uniform light intensities). Therefore, the capability of properly handling varying and unknown light intensities and exposures across observed images is an important feature for making photometric stereo practical.

---

Part of this work was done while the first author was an intern at Microsoft Research Asia.

© Springer International Publishing AG 2016
B. Leibe et al. (Eds.): ECCV 2016, Part II, LNCS 9906, pp. 170–186, 2016.
DOI: 10.1007/978-3-319-46475-6_11

The setting can be regarded as a "semi-calibrated" photometric stereo, where the light directions are known but their intensities are unknown. We argue that accurate light intensity calibration is practically a hard task to perform due to that the light bulb's luminous efficiency varies over time and quantization error in the measurement even with high-dynamic range imaging. This paper provides a way to bypass the difficult intensity calibration in photometric stereo.

In the Lambertian image formation model, a measured intensity $m$ is written as

$$m_{i,j} = E_i \rho_j \mathbf{n}_j^\top \mathbf{l}_i, \tag{1}$$

where $i$ and $j$ are indices of light direction and pixel location, $\mathbf{l}_i, \mathbf{n}_j \in \mathbb{R}^{3 \times 1}$ are unit vectors of light direction and surface normal, $\rho_j \in \mathbb{R}$ is a Lambertian diffuse albedo, and $E_i \in \mathbb{R}$ is a light source intensity. In a matrix form for representing all pixels and light directions at a time, it can be written as

$$\mathbf{M} = \mathbf{ELN}^\top \mathbf{P}, \tag{2}$$

where $\mathbf{M} \in \mathbb{R}^{f \times p}$ is an observation matrix, $\mathbf{E}$ is an $f \times f$ diagonal light intensity matrix, $\mathbf{L} \in \mathbb{R}^{f \times 3}$ is a light direction matrix, $\mathbf{N} \in \mathbb{R}^{p \times 3}$ is a surface normal matrix, $\mathbf{P}$ is a $p \times p$ diagonal diffuse albedo matrix, and $f$ and $p$ are the number of images and pixels, respectively. Conventional photometric stereo [1] assumes that light source intensities are identical across images, where the matrix $\mathbf{E}$ becomes a scaled identity matrix ($\mathbf{E} = e\mathbf{I}$), and computes albedo-scaled surface normal $\mathbf{B}(= \mathbf{P}^\top \mathbf{N})$ by

$$e\mathbf{B}^{*\top} = \mathbf{L}^\dagger \mathbf{M}, \tag{3}$$

up to a scale ambiguity $e$, where the superscript $^\dagger$ indicates a generalized inverse when $f \geq 3$.

Clearly, when the light source intensities are non-uniform or camera exposures vary across images, the assumption $\mathbf{E} = e\mathbf{I}$ does not hold, but instead its diagonal elements have individual scales. When this non-uniformity is present, the surface normal estimates by Eq. (2) naturally becomes biased by greater scales as illustrated in Fig. 1. While there are recently various robust estimation techniques used for photometric stereo [2–6], because the effect of non-uniform $\mathbf{E}$ neither increases the rank of the observation matrix nor sparsifies outliers, robust techniques such as rank minimization or $\ell_0$-norm minimization techniques cannot resolve this issue. In the rest of the paper, we collectively call this problem setting, non-uniform light intensities and exposures across images, a *varying light intensity condition*, because they are both considered intensity scaling on individual images.

This paper considers a method to effectively deal with the non-uniform light intensities and exposures. The problem that we deal with in this paper is a bilinear problem written as following.

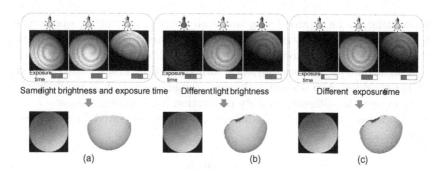

**Fig. 1.** (a) Conventional photometric stereo setting where constant light intensities and exposures are used, (b)(c): varying lighting intensity/exposure conditions. Estimated surface normal are biased toward brighter light source or images captured with longer exposures with a conventional solution method.

**Problem (Photometric Stereo Under Varying Light Intensity Condition).** *Given observations* $\mathbf{M}$ *and light directions* $\mathbf{L}$, *estimate a diagonal light intensity matrix* $\mathbf{E}$ *and an albedo-scaled surface normal matrix* $\mathbf{B}$ *from the following relationship:*

$$\mathbf{M} = \mathbf{ELB}^{\top}. \tag{4}$$

We first show that there exists a linear closed-form solution method, which simultaneously estimates scales of light intensities (or exposures) $\mathbf{E}$ and albedo-scaled surface normal $\mathbf{B}$. We call this method a linear joint estimation method. This method is straightforward to implement; however, inefficient in terms of computation time and memory consumption. We then introduce a factorization based method for determining only surface normal $\mathbf{B}$ in Eq. (4) without being affected by $\mathbf{E}$. It bypasses the estimation of $\mathbf{E}$ using algebraic distance minimization (or, cross product minimization) by making the problem independent of vector magnitudes. Finally, we show that this bilinear problem can be efficiently solved by an alternating minimization technique that determines $\mathbf{E}$ and $\mathbf{B}$ in each step. We discuss details and characteristics of each method later in this paper.

We further show that our method is advantageous in improving signal-to-quantization-noise ratio (SQNR) in comparison to a standard photometric stereo method when an auto-exposure control is used, and as a result more accurate surface normal estimates can be obtained. Experimental results show the effectiveness of the proposed method in practical settings. In this paper, we assumes a directional light setting where radiance from a light source to a scene is constant except for shadowing, *i.e.*, spatially varying incident radiance within a scene is not assumed.

## 2    Related Works

Photometric stereo was first introduced by Woodham [1] in 1980's for determining surface normal from images taken under known and varying light directions with a Lambertian reflectance assumption. After Woodham's work, there have been various techniques proposed for making photometric stereo more practical.

Their main focuses are to relax the assumptions of (1) calibrated light sources and (2) Lambertian image formation model.

The first class of the methods, called uncalibrated photometric stereo, tries to eliminate the need for calibrating light directions. When the light directions are unknown, it is understood that the solution can be obtained up to a $3 \times 3$ linear ambiguity [7]. If the integrability [8] of the surface is assumed, it has been shown that the linear ambiguity can be reduced to a generalized bas-relief (GBR) ambiguity [9], which only has three parameters. To fully resolve these ambiguities, various types of external clues have been used. For example, there are methods that use the entropy of albedo distributions [10], specular observations [11], shadows [12], and groups of color and intensity profiles [13]. Our problem setting has a similarity to the uncalibrated photometric stereo scenario in that we relax the assumptions of known light intensities and *constant light intensity* across varying light directions. And there has not been uncalibrated PS works that derive disambiguated solution without external assumptions such as albedo entropy [10] and pixel profiles [13].

The second class of the methods tries to make photometric stereo applicable to non-Lambertian scenes. There are methods that use more sophisticated reflectance models than Lambertian reflectance model, such as the works that use Torrance-Sparrow [14,15], Cook-Torrance [16], Phong [17], Blinn-Phong [18]. More recently, Shi *et al.* [19] propose a bi-polynomial reflectance model that produces successful results for non-Lambertian diffusive scenes.

There are approaches that use robust estimation techniques by treating non-Lambertian reflectances and shadows as outliers. In [2], the robustness against outliers is achieved by capturing hundreds of input images coupled with Markov Random Field (MRF) to maintain neighborhood smoothness. Verbiest and Van Gool [3] use a confidence approach to reject outliers in input images of photometric stereo. Wu *et al.* [4] proposed a robust method based on low-rank matrix factorization. Oh *et al.* [5] introduced a partial sum of singular values for rank minimization, and showed good performance in photometric stereo. Ikehata *et al.* [20] used a sparse Bayesian regression for effectively neglecting sparse outliers (specularities and shadows). While these techniques are effective, they are built upon the assumption of *constant light intensity*, and cannot directly address the issue of varying light intensities and exposures.

## 3  Photometric Stereo Under Varying Light Intensity Conditions

As discussed in Eq. (4), we are interested in determining albedo-scaled surface normal $\mathbf{B}$ with unknown non-uniform scalings of light intensities or exposures $\mathbf{E}$. In a least-squares framework, the problem can be written as

$$\{\mathbf{E}^*, \mathbf{B}^*\} = \underset{\mathbf{E}, \mathbf{B}}{\operatorname{argmin}} \|\mathbf{M} - \mathbf{E}\mathbf{L}\mathbf{B}^\top\|_F^2 \tag{5}$$

given the observations $\mathbf{M}$ and light directions $\mathbf{L}$.

We first present a linear estimation method that simultaneously estimates $\mathbf{B}$ and $\mathbf{E}$ in Sect. 3.1. We then describe a factorization based method in Sect. 3.2, which bypasses the estimation of unknown scalings $\mathbf{E}$. Finally, we describe an efficient alternating minimization method in Sect. 3.3.

## 3.1 Linear Joint Estimation Method

The original form $\mathbf{M} = \mathbf{ELB}^{\top}$ can be re-written as $\mathbf{E}^{-1}\mathbf{M} = \mathbf{LB}^{\top}$, because $\mathbf{E}$ is always invertible as it is a positive diagonal matrix. Given known $\mathbf{M}$ and $\mathbf{L}$, it can be viewed as a variant of a Sylvester equation [21]:

$$\mathbf{E}^{-1}\mathbf{M} - \mathbf{LB}^{\top} = \mathbf{0}. \tag{6}$$

By vectorizing unknown variables $\mathbf{E}^{-1}$ and $\mathbf{B}^{\top}$, Eq. (6) can be written as

$$\mathrm{diag}(\mathbf{m}_1)| \cdots |\mathrm{diag}(\mathbf{m}_p)^{\top}\mathbf{E}^{-1}\mathbf{1} - (\mathbf{I}_p \otimes \mathbf{L})\mathrm{vec}(\mathbf{B}^{\top}) = \mathbf{0}, \tag{7}$$

where $\mathrm{diag}(\cdot)$, $\mathrm{vec}(\cdot)$ and $\otimes$ are diagonalization, vectorization, and Kronecker product operators, respectively. $\mathbf{I}_p$ is a $p \times p$ identity matrix, and $\mathbf{1}$ indicates a vector whose elements are all one. By concatenating matrices and vectors in Eq. (7), a homogeneous equation can be obtained:

$$\underbrace{\left[-\mathbf{I}_p \otimes \mathbf{L}\middle| \left[\mathrm{diag}(\mathbf{m}_1)| \cdots |\mathrm{diag}(\mathbf{m}_p)\right]^{\top}\right]}_{\mathbf{D}} \underbrace{\begin{bmatrix} \mathrm{vec}(\mathbf{B}^{\top}) \\ \mathbf{E}^{-1}\mathbf{1} \end{bmatrix}}_{\mathbf{y}} = \mathbf{0}, \tag{8}$$

where $\mathbf{D} \in \mathbb{R}^{pf \times (3p+f)}$ is a sparse design matrix and $\mathbf{y} \in \mathbb{R}^{(3p+f) \times 1}$ is an unknown vector. The homogeneous system always has a trivial solution $\mathbf{y} = \mathbf{0}$. To have a unique (up to scale) non-trivial solution, the matrix $\mathbf{D}$ should have a one dimensional null space, i.e., when rank of $\mathbf{D}$ is $(3p+f-1)$, a unique solution can be obtained via singular value decomposition (SVD). The minimum condition to have a unique solution up to scale is $f \geq 5$ and $p \geq 3$, or $f = 4$ and $p \geq 2$. Unlike conventional photometric stereo, increasing the number of light directions does not necessarily make the problem easier in this setting, because it also increases the unknowns about light intensities.

## 3.2 Factorization Based Method

Although the linear joint estimation method is simple to implement, it has practical limitations in terms of its computational time and memory requirement when the sparse matrix $\mathbf{D}$ is large; not only constructing $\mathbf{D}$ but also computing SVD of $\mathbf{D}$. This limitation can be relaxed by dividing the observation matrix into small groups and deriving solutions for each group. However, this grouping should be performed carefully to avoid the condition numbers of divided submatrices to be high. The condition number increases when observations within each divided group are similar to each other, and as a result, the numerical error becomes greater. To avoid these issues, we develop a factorization based method described in this section.

Like solution methods of uncalibrated photometric stereo, light directions and surface normal can be solved directly via matrix factorization:

$$\mathbf{M} = \hat{\mathbf{S}}\hat{\mathbf{B}}^\top, \tag{9}$$

where $\hat{\mathbf{S}}$ and $\hat{\mathbf{B}}$ are *biased* intensity-scaled light direction and albedo-scaled surface normal, respectively. With an arbitrary $3 \times 3$ non-singular matrix $\mathbf{H}$, Eq. (9) can be re-written as

$$\mathbf{M} = (\hat{\mathbf{S}}\mathbf{H})(\mathbf{H}^{-1}\hat{\mathbf{B}}^\top). \tag{10}$$

In our setting, since we know the light directions $\mathbf{L}$, we can find an appropriate non-singular matrix $\mathbf{H}$ for resolving the biases. Regardless of the effect of light intensities, direction of $\hat{\mathbf{S}}\mathbf{H}$ should be the same with $\mathbf{L}$. Thus, we can use this constraint, $(\hat{\mathbf{S}}\mathbf{H}) \times \mathbf{L} = \mathbf{0}$ where $\times$ indicates a cross product, for determining $\mathbf{H}$ as

$$\begin{bmatrix} 0 & -l_{i,3}\hat{\mathbf{s}}_i & l_{i,2}\hat{\mathbf{s}}_i \\ l_{i,3}\hat{\mathbf{s}}_i & 0 & -l_{i,1}\hat{\mathbf{s}}_i \end{bmatrix} \begin{bmatrix} \mathbf{h_1}^\top \\ \mathbf{h_2}^\top \\ \mathbf{h_3}^\top \end{bmatrix} = \mathbf{0}, \tag{11}$$

where $\mathbf{H} = [\mathbf{h_1}|\mathbf{h_2}|\mathbf{h_3}]$, $l_{i,*}$ and $\hat{\mathbf{s}}_i$ are the $i$-th row of $\mathbf{L}$ and $\hat{\mathbf{S}}$, respectively. The solution of Eq. (11) is unique up to scale when there are more than 4 distinct light directions. Using estimated $\hat{\mathbf{H}}$, we can compute unbiased albedo-scaled surface normal $\mathbf{H}^{-1}\hat{\mathbf{B}}^\top$. Interestingly, this factorization based method can naturally bypass the light intensity estimation; thus, it is suitable for our setting. Compared to the linear joint estimation method, the computational cost of the factorization based method is lower, even without dividing observations $\mathbf{M}$ into small groups.

### 3.3 Alternating Minimization Method

While the previous two methods are effective in ideal settings, they are prone to large errors due to un-modelled observations, such as shadows and pixel saturations. To avoid this problem, we develop a robust method that is based on alternating minimization for solving Eq. (5).

Our method computes albedo-scaled surface normal $\mathbf{B}^{(t)}$ and non-uniform scalings $\mathbf{E}^{(t)}$ in an alternating manner using their intermediate estimates from the previous iteration. Using $\mathbf{E}^{(t)}$ from the previous iteration and by fixing it, albedo-scaled surface normal $\mathbf{B}^{(t+1)}$ is updated by

$$\mathbf{B}^{(t+1)} = \underset{\mathbf{B}}{\operatorname{argmin}} \left\| \mathbf{M} - \mathbf{E}^{(t)}\mathbf{L}\mathbf{B}^\top \right\|_F^2. \tag{12}$$

The above problem is a linear problem with respect to $\mathbf{B}$ and can be solved efficiently. Once matrix $\mathbf{B}^{(t+1)}$ is determined, $\mathbf{E}^{(t+1)}$ is then updated by solving

$$\mathbf{E}^{(t+1)} = \underset{\mathbf{E}}{\operatorname{argmin}} \left\| \mathbf{M} - \mathbf{ELB}^{(t+1)^{\top}} \right\|_{F}^{2}. \tag{13}$$

Since matrix $\mathbf{E}$ is diagonal, each element $E_i^{(t+1)}$ is simply determined by

$$E_i^{(t+1)} = \frac{\sum_j m_{i,j}(\mathbf{l}_i^{\top}\mathbf{b}_j^{(t+1)})^{\top}}{\sum_j (\mathbf{l}_i^{\top}\mathbf{b}_j^{(t+1)})(\mathbf{l}_i^{\top}\mathbf{b}_j^{(t+1)})^{\top}}. \tag{14}$$

The initial scaling matrix $\mathbf{E}^{(0)}$ is set to an identity matrix, and the convergence criteria is defined by the magnitude of variation of matrix $\mathbf{B}$, i.e., $\|\mathbf{B}^{(t+1)} - \mathbf{B}^{(t)}\|_F < \epsilon$, where $\epsilon$ is set to a small value (in our implementation, $\epsilon = 1.0\text{e-}8$).

If we consider $\mathbf{E}$ as weights, this alternating minimization is similar to iteratively re-weighted least squares (IRLS) [22] except that weights are defined row-wise (each image has same weight). We show how the alternating method operates in the following. Let us consider updating $\mathbf{B}^{(t+1)}$ with fixing $\mathbf{E}^{(t)}$, then Eq. (12) becomes

$$\mathbf{B}^{(t+1)} = \underset{\mathbf{B}}{\operatorname{argmin}} \left\| \mathbf{M} - \mathbf{E}^{(t)}\mathbf{LB}^{\top} \right\|_{F}^{2} \tag{15}$$
$$= \underset{\mathbf{B}}{\operatorname{argmin}} \left\| \mathbf{M} - \mathbf{E}^{*}\mathbf{LB}^{\top} - \mathbf{E}^{r}\mathbf{LB}^{\top} \right\|_{F}^{2},$$

where $\mathbf{E}^{(t)} = \mathbf{E}^{*} + \mathbf{E}^{r}$, $\mathbf{E}^{*}$ is the ground truth (that we do not know), and $\mathbf{E}^{r}$ is the error from $t$-th iteration. It shows that the smaller the scaling error $\mathbf{E}^{r}$ is, the smaller objective cost becomes. The elements of $\mathbf{E}^{(t)}$ can also be written as

$$E_i^{(t)} = \frac{\sum_j m_{i,j}(\mathbf{l}_i^{\top}\mathbf{b}_j^{(t)})^{\top}}{\sum_j (\mathbf{l}_i^{\top}\mathbf{b}_j^{(t)})(\mathbf{l}_i^{\top}\mathbf{b}_j^{(t)})^{\top}}$$
$$= \frac{\sum_j m_{i,j}\mathbf{l}_i^{\top}\mathbf{b}_j^{*\top} + \sum_j m_{i,j}\mathbf{l}_i^{\top}\mathbf{b}_j^{r\top}}{\sum_j (\mathbf{l}_i^{\top}(\mathbf{b}_j^{*} + \mathbf{b}_j^{r})^{\top})(\mathbf{l}_i^{\top}(\mathbf{b}_j^{*} + \mathbf{b}_j^{r})^{\top})}, \tag{16}$$

where $\mathbf{b}^{(t+1)} = \mathbf{b}^{*} + \mathbf{b}^{r}$, $\mathbf{b}^{*}$ is the ground truth, and $\mathbf{b}^{r}$ is the error from $t$-th iteration. Since the denominator is fixed for all images, and the left-hand side of the numerator is proportional to the ground truth scaling $\mathbf{E}^{*}$, the smaller the error $\mathbf{b}^{r}$ becomes, the better scaling elements $E$ becomes. To summarize, if the current estimate of albedo-scaled surface normal $\mathbf{B}^{(t)}$ is better than the previous one, $\mathbf{E}^{(t)}$ is better updated. In our experiments, above improvements are always observed since updated $\mathbf{E}^{(1)}$ becomes closer to the ground truth than $\mathbf{E}^{(0)}$. Then, $\mathbf{B}^{(t)}$ and $\mathbf{E}^{(t)}$ are alternately updated. The minimum condition for obtaining a stable solution is experimentally found to be $f \geq 5$ and $p \geq 3$.

## 4    Signal-to-Quantization-Noise Ratio Analysis

One of the important benefits of our method is its compatibility to the sensor's auto-exposure function that makes non-uniform scaling of observations. With auto-exposure, SQNR of observations is effectively increased by avoiding over-/under-exposures. As a result, the surface normal estimates are less suffered from quantization noise, and thus, a greater accuracy can be obtained. Based on the previous study of quantization noise [23], SQNR is written as

$$\text{SQNR} = \frac{\text{signal}}{\text{noise}} \propto \frac{C\mu}{\frac{CR}{Q}} = \frac{Q\mu}{R} = \frac{Q\mu}{(V_h - V_l)}, \tag{17}$$

where $\mu$ is the expectation of the signal, $Q$ is the number of quantization levels, and $C$ is a scaling factor representing the amount of exposure. Also, $R = V_h - V_l$, where $V_l$ and $V_h$ are the minimum and maximum scene irradiance. Thus, $R$ and $\mu$ are both the functions of exposure time. From Eq. (17), we can observe that SQNR without saturation is dependent of the number of quantization levels $Q$; thus, better exposed signals produce higher SQNR.

When the signals are over-exposed, the SQNR expression becomes more complicated due to saturation, as

$$\text{SQNR} = \frac{\text{signal}}{\text{noise}} \propto \frac{C_o\mu - \alpha}{\frac{(\lambda - C_o V_l)}{Q} + \alpha}, \tag{18}$$

where $\lambda$, $\alpha$, and $C_o$ are saturation threshold, expectation of error within saturation sub-interval, and scaling factor of the over-exposure case, respectively. Here, $C_o V_h$ is replaced by $\lambda$ due to saturation.

Let us assume that not all signals are saturated. Then, the condition that the well-exposed case has a greater SQNR than the over-exposed case is following:

$$\frac{Q\mu}{(V_h - V_l)} \geq \frac{C_o\mu - \alpha}{\frac{(\lambda - C_o V_l)}{Q} + \alpha} = \frac{C_o Q\mu - Q\alpha}{\lambda - C_o V_l + Q\alpha}. \tag{19}$$

Above can be simplified by some algebraic operations into:

$$\frac{Q\mu}{(V_h - V_l)} \geq \frac{Q\alpha}{(C_o V_h - \lambda) - Q\alpha}. \tag{20}$$

The condition to satisfy Eq. (19) with respect to $Q$ is

$$Q \leq \frac{(C_o V_h - \lambda)}{\alpha} - \frac{(V_h - V_l)}{\mu}, Q > \frac{(C_o V_h - \lambda)}{\alpha}, \tag{21}$$

where $(C_o V_h - \lambda)$ is the maximum error. Mathematically, over-exposed case can produce a higher SQNR than the well-exposed case. However, in general situations, SQNR of well-exposed case is better than over-exposed case because the number of quantization levels $Q$ is usually larger enough than maximum error $(C_o V_h - \lambda)$ over expectation error $\alpha$. Therefore, well-exposed signals have higher SQNR than over- or under-exposure cases in terms of quantization if the number of quantization levels is sufficient. Our method is beneficial with auto-exposure to increase SQNR since it can effectively handle non-uniformity caused by auto-exposure.

If there are quantization noise in the images, the observation matrix $\mathbf{M}$ becomes

$$\mathbf{M} = \mathbf{M}^* + \zeta = \mathbf{ELB}^\top + \zeta, \tag{22}$$

where $\mathbf{M}^*$ and $\zeta$ are the ideal observation and quantization noise, respectively. Using the noisy input in Eq. (22) , the objective function in Eq. (5) becomes

$$\{\mathbf{E}^*, \mathbf{B}^*\} = \underset{\mathbf{E},\mathbf{B}}{\mathrm{argmin}}\, \|\zeta\|_F^2, \quad \text{s.t.} \quad \zeta = \mathbf{M} - \mathbf{ELB}^\top. \tag{23}$$

Therefore, in the cases of high SQNR data, we can compute surface normal and intensities by optimizing Eq. (23) without biases since $\zeta$ is close to zero ($\mathbf{M} \approx \mathbf{M}^*$). However, in low SQNR inputs, minimizing Eq. (23) can produce biased results because $\zeta$ is not small anymore ($\mathbf{M} \neq \mathbf{M}^*$). As a result, auto-exposure can help to estimate surface normal by increasing SQNR of images, and our method is suitable for dealing with the exposure variations.

## 5    Light Intensity Calibration Analysis

One may consider that light intensity calibration is an easy task, but it actually requires both careful control over the environment and explicit knowledge about the reflectance of a calibration target. To show this, we perform light intensity calibration using a diffuse sphere[1]. Assuming a Lambertian reflectance model and known surface normal $\mathbf{N}$, the scaled light matrix $\mathbf{S}$ can be estimated from a set of measurements $\mathbf{M}$ as

$$\mathbf{S}^* = \underset{\mathbf{S}}{\mathrm{argmin}} \left\| \pi_{\Omega^c}(\mathbf{M}) - \pi_{\Omega^c}(\mathbf{SN}^\top) \right\|_F^2, \tag{24}$$

where $\Omega$ denotes the locations of shadowed entries in the observation $\mathbf{M}$, and $\pi_{\Omega^c}$ represents an operator that extracts entries that are not shadowed ($\Omega^c$). Since $\mathbf{S} = \mathbf{EL}$, with known light directions $\mathbf{L}$, we can determine the light intensities by

$$\mathbf{E} = \mathbf{S}^* \mathbf{L}^\dagger. \tag{25}$$

We recorded images of a diffuse sphere by changing the light directions of an identical light source with retaining its distance to the target object approximately the same. The camera response function is linear and uncompressed RAW images are used. Exposure times are kept constant with making sure that there is no under- or over-exposures. In addition, to neglect the perspective effect, a

---

[1] Due to the presence of saturations, a chrome sphere with specular highlights is not a proper calibration object for this task.

camera is placed far enough from the target object so that we can assume an orthographic projection model. Figure 2 shows some of the recorded images, and the light intensity matrix **E** is obtained by Eqs. (24) and (25).

As summarized in the numbers in Fig. 2, the estimated light intensities have variations while they are supposed to be uniform under this setting. The variations may be caused due to that (1) although the sphere is carefully selected, it still deviates from the Lambertian assumption, and (2) the assumed surface normal directions may be different from the truth due to errors of circle fitting. As such, even with a careful procedure, the light source intensity calibration is not a straightforward task. And in our setting, it had a non-negligible spread of estimated intensities (maximum 0.052 when the intensities are normalized to one, corresponding to 5 % error). Therefore, it is needed to directly model the variations of light intensities in the photometric stereo formulation.

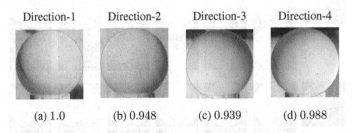

| Direction-1 | Direction-2 | Direction-3 | Direction-4 |
|:-----------:|:-----------:|:-----------:|:-----------:|
| (a) 1.0 | (b) 0.948 | (c) 0.939 | (d) 0.988 |

**Fig. 2.** Light intensity calibration. A diffuse sphere is illuminated under different light directions by moving an identical light source. The red point indicates the lighting direction, and a blue circle is a circle fitting to the image of a sphere. The numbers under photographs are the estimated light source intensities, that are relative to that of Direction 1. (Color figure online)

## 6    Experiments

We evaluate the proposed methods, linear joint estimation, factorization based, and alternating minimization (AM) methods, using synthetic (Sect. 6.1) and real-world (Sect. 6.2) scenes in the setting of non-uniform intensities and exposures. Although none of the previous techniques are designed for the non-uniform intensity setting, as previous methods to compare, we use standard Frobenius-norm minimization [1], robust L1-norm minimization used as a baseline method in [24], and the state-of-the-art photometric stereo method based on constrained bivariate regression (CBR) [24].

### 6.1    Synthetic Data

We first test our methods using synthetic examples that are textured and rendered with a Lambertian reflectance model with shadows. For qualitative and quantitative comparisons, we analyze the effects of non-uniform light intensities and auto-exposure.

**Non-uniform Light Intensities:** We first test the setting of non-uniform light intensities. The scenes are rendered under 20 varying light directions with their intensity variance 0.05. The qualitative visualization of surface normal estimates and error maps are summarized in Fig. 3 with comparison to other previous methods, *i.e.*, Frobenius-norm, L1-norm, CBR. Our methods, namely, linear joint, Factorization, and AM methods correspond to the ones described in Sects. 3.1, 3.2 and 3.3, respectively. Our proposed methods produce results close to the ground truth compared to other techniques that do not explicitly consider the non-uniform light intensities. The quantitative results are reported under each error map. The superior performance is consistently observed under varying numbers of images and light intensity variances as shown in Fig. 4.

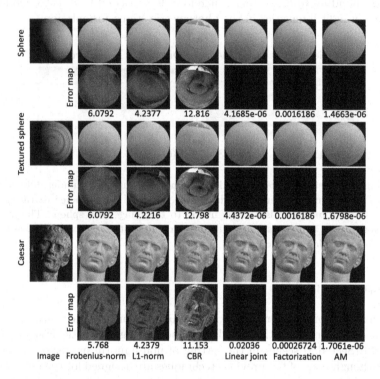

**Fig. 3.** Photometric stereo experiment under non-uniform light intensities. The scenes are rendered under 20 distinct light directions with their intensity variance 0.05. Our methods (linear joint, factorization and AM) effectively handle the condition of non-uniform light intensities. Error maps are scaled by 4. The numbers indicate the mean angular errors in degree.

**Auto-Exposure Case:** Auto-exposure allows us to obtain measurements with a higher Signal-to-Quantization-Noise ratio (SQNR). To assess the benefit of auto-exposure in photometric stereo and effectiveness of our methods in this setting, we render two datasets; one with auto-exposure and the other with fixed-exposure. In the auto-exposure dataset, the sensor irradiances are stretched to

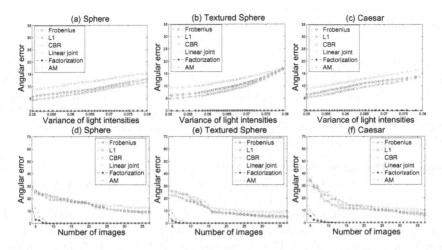

**Fig. 4.** Variations of mean angular errors of surface normal estimates over variance of light intensities (top row) and the number of images (bottom row) for the three datasets. (a, d) Sphere, (b, e) Textured Sphere, (c, f) Caesar. Our methods consistently yield favorable results across these variations.

properly include the most of dynamic range before quantization. For the fixed-exposure dataset, sensor irradiances are quantized without stretching. From the two types of dataset, we apply the same set of photometric stereo methods for performance evaluation. The results are summarized in Table 1. While the fixed-exposure setting suffers from a low SQNR (which leads to lower accuracy of surface normal estimates), the auto-exposure retains a higher SQNR. And with our methods, this setting is properly handled and accurate surface normal estimates are obtained.

**Table 1.** Comparison under auto-exposure (Auto) and fixed-exposure (Fixed) settings. SQNR and the mean angular errors of surface normal estimates in degree are shown.

| SQNR | Sphere | | Textured | | Caesar | |
|---|---|---|---|---|---|---|
| | Fixed | Auto | Fixed | Auto | Fixed | Auto |
| | 42.52 | 129.8 | 33.68 | 135.6 | 33.56 | 133.3 |
| Frobenius | 2.383 | 24.35 | 27.93 | 23.61 | 8.415 | 23.86 |
| L1 | 2.507 | 23.85 | 28.05 | 23.41 | 8.320 | 21.03 |
| CBR [24] | 21.47 | 14.54 | 47.15 | 16.53 | 33.02 | 21.49 |
| Linear joint | 20.49 | 0.886 | 59.63 | 1.561 | 43.72 | 1.725 |
| Factorization | 6.569 | 0.715 | 42.12 | 1.381 | 26.16 | 1.504 |
| AM | 3.970 | **0.256** | 29.74 | **0.565** | 9.684 | **0.564** |

## 6.2   Real Data

We design three different settings for the real-world experiment; (A) non-uniform light source intensities across images, (B) with auto-exposures under identical light intensities (by moving the same light source), and (C) use of an uncontrolled mobile phone camera for imaging where auto-exposure is turned on under varying light source intensities. For all real-world examples, we use a shiny sphere to calibrate the light directions. To suppress other un-modelled factors, our experiments are carried out in a dark room.

**Non-uniform Light Source Intensities:** To record images under different light intensities and directions, we use controllable light sources whose brightnesses can be manually controlled by the gain of power supply. The camera setting, such as shutter speed and aperture, are all fixed in this experiment, and a linear sensor response is used. In this experimental setting, we recorded 20 images for each static scene. The results are summarized in Fig. 5, in which the estimated surface normal and their 3D reconstruction using [25] are presented. As shown in the figures, our methods properly handle the varying light source intensities compared to Frobenius-norm, L1-norm and CBR methods, with which severe distortions are observed in their reconstructed surfaces.

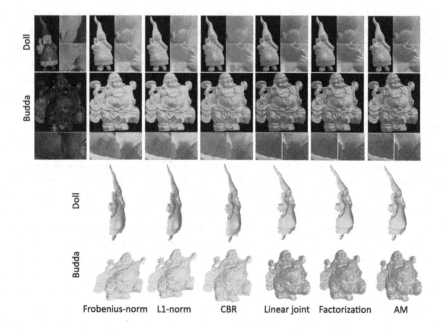

**Fig. 5.** Result of varying light source intensities case. From left to right, one of input images, results from Frobenius-norm, L1-norm, CBR [24], linear joint estimation, factorization and alternating minimization (AM) methods are shown.

**Auto-exposure:** When auto-exposure is used, the shutter speed and/or aperture size of a camera is automatically adjusted to record well-exposed images according to the amount of incoming light. While it increases SQNR, it results in the non-uniform intensity setting.

For this experiment, we recorded 20 images of each static scene with auto-exposure. Figure 6 shows the comparative result. As shown in the figure, our methods consistently yield higher quality outputs than the other methods because our method explicitly accounts for the non-uniform exposures.

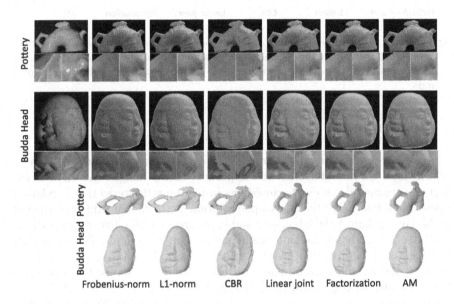

**Fig. 6.** Result of auto-exposure case. From left to right, one of input images, results from Frobenius-norm, L1-norm, CBR [24], linear joint estimation, factorization and alternating minimization (AM) methods are shown.

**Mobile Phone Cameras:** Our method is suitable for uncontrollable cameras like many of mobile phone cameras, where we cannot turn off the auto-exposure setting. With such cameras, recorded images are in the condition of non-uniform exposures across images. From recorded images from a mobile phone camera, we linearize the intensity observations using the method of [26] as preprocessing. Figure 7 shows the surface normal estimates and their 3D reconstructions. While the 3D reconstructions of conventional methods are severely deformed, our methods show better reconstructions in general. The linear joint estimation method suffered from the outliers in this case, but that is not observed in factorization based and AM methods.

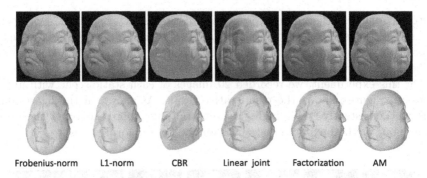

Fig. 7. Result using a mobile phone camera. Top: estimated surface normal, bottom: 3D reconstruction. Our methods (linear joint estimation, factorization, and alternating minimization (AM) methods) produce more faithful results than the conventional methods.

## 7    Conclusion

This paper described photometric stereo methods that can handle the non-uniform light source intensities and exposures across images. We showed the effect of *varying light intensity conditions* in photometric stereo that is relevant in practical settings. We then developed solution methods that explicitly account for the non-uniform light intensities and exposures; namely, linear joint estimation, factorization based, and alternating minimization methods. The linear joint estimation and factorization based methods are simple and easy to implement, they occasionally suffer from numerical instability due to un-modelled observations. The alternating minimization method showed a greater robustness over these techniques, while retaining the efficiency in computation. They are all effective in the non-uniform intensities setting compared to methods that neglect the effect of the setting. We further illustrate that our proposed methods can benefit from auto-exposure, with which measurements with a greater SQNR can be obtained. Our experiments on synthetic and real-world examples show the importance of properly handling varying light intensities and exposures.

**Acknowledgement.** This work is partly supported by JSPS KAKENHI Grant Number JP16H01732 and the Ministry of Trade, Industry & Energy and the Korea Evaluation Institute of Industrial Technology (KEIT) with the program number of 10060110.

## References

1. Woodham, R.J.: Photometric method for determining surface orientation from multiple images. Opt. Eng. **19**(1), 139–144 (1980)
2. Wu, T., Tang, K., Tang, C., Wong, T.: Dense photometric stereo: a Markov random field approach. IEEE Trans. Pattern Anal. Mach. Intell. (TPAMI) **28**(11), 1830–1846 (2006)

3. Verbiest, F., Van Gool, L.: Photometric stereo with coherent outlier handling and confidence estimation. In: Proceedings of Computer Vision and Pattern Recognition (CVPR), pp. 2886–2893 (2008)
4. Wu, L., Ganesh, A., Shi, B., Matsushita, Y., Wang, Y., Ma, Y.: Robust photometric stereo via low-rank matrix completion and recovery. In: Kimmel, R., Klette, R., Sugimoto, A. (eds.) ACCV 2010. LNCS, vol. 6494, pp. 703–717. Springer, Heidelberg (2011). doi:10.1007/978-3-642-19318-7_55
5. Oh, T.H., Kim, H., Tai, Y.W., Bazin, J.C., Kweon, I.S.: Partial sum minimization of singular values in RPCA for low-level vision. In: Proceedings of International Conference on Computer Vision (ICCV), pp. 145–152 (2013)
6. Zhang, Y., Mu, C., Kuo, H.W., Wright, J.: Toward guaranteed illumination models for non-covex objects. In: Proceedings of International Conference on Computer Vision (ICCV), pp. 937–944 (2013)
7. Hayakawa, H.: Photometric stereo under a light-source with arbitrary motion. J. Opt. Soc. Am. (JOSA) 11(11), 3078–3089 (1994)
8. Yuille, A.L., Snow, D.: Shape and albedo from multiple images using integrability. In: Proceedings of Computer Vision and Pattern Recognition (CVPR), pp. 158–164 (1997)
9. Belhumeur, P.N., Kriegman, D.J., Yuille, A.L.: The bas-relief ambiguity. Int. J. Comput. Vis. (IJCV) 35(1), 33–44 (1999)
10. Alldrin, N.G., Mallick, S.P., Kriegman, D.J.: Resolving the generalized bas-relief ambiguity by entropy minimization. In: Proceedings of Computer Vision and Pattern Recognition (CVPR), pp. 1–7 (2007)
11. Drbohlav, O., Chantler, M.: Can two specular pixels calibrate photometric stereo? In: Proceedings of International Conference on Computer Vision (ICCV), pp. 1850–1857 (2005)
12. Sunkavalli, K., Zickler, T., Pfister, H.: Visibility subspaces: uncalibrated photometric stereo with shadows. In: Daniilidis, K., Maragos, P., Paragios, N. (eds.) ECCV 2010. LNCS, vol. 6312, pp. 251–264. Springer, Heidelberg (2010). doi:10.1007/978-3-642-15552-9_19
13. Shi, B., Matsushita, Y., Wei, Y., Xu, C., Tan, P.: Self-calibrating photometric stereo. In: Proceedings of Computer Vision and Pattern Recognition (CVPR), pp. 1118–1125 (2010)
14. Solomon, F., Ikeuchi, K.: Extracting the shape and roughness of specular lobe objects using four light photometric stereo. IEEE Trans. Pattern Anal. Mach. Intell. (TPAMI) 18(4), 449–454 (1996)
15. Georghiades, A.: Incorporating the torrance and sparrow model of reflectance in uncalibrated photometric stereo. In: Proceedings of International Conference on Computer Vision (ICCV), pp. 816–823 (2003)
16. Lin, S., Lee, S.W.: Estimation of diffuse and specular appearance. In: Proceedings of International Conference on Computer Vision (ICCV), pp. 855–860 (1999)
17. Iwahori, Y., Woodham, R.J., H.T., Ishii, N.: Neural network to reconstruct specular surface shape from its three shading images. In: Proceedings of International Joint Conference on Neural Networks, pp. 1181–1184 (1993)
18. Malzbender, T., Wilburn, B., Gelb, D., Ambrisco, B.: Surface enhancement using real-time photometric stereo and reflectance transformation. In: Proceedings of the Eurographics Symposium on Rendering Techniques, pp. 245–250 (2006)
19. Shi, B., Tan, P., Matsushita, Y., Ikeuchi, K.: Bi-polynomial modeling of low-frequency reflectances. IEEE Trans. Pattern Anal. Mach. Intell. (TPAMI) 36(6), 1078–1091 (2014)

20. Ikehata, S., Wipf, D.P., Matsushita, Y., Aizawa, K.: Photometric stereo using sparse Bayesian regression for general diffuse surfaces. IEEE Trans. Pattern Anal. Mach. Intell. (TPAMI) **36**(9), 1816–1831 (2014)
21. Sylvester, J.: Sur lequations en matrices px = xq. C. R. Acad. Sci. Paris **99**(2), 67–71,115–116 (1884)
22. Holland, P.W., Welsch, R.E.: Robust regression using iteratively reweighted least-squares. Commun. Stat. Theor. Methods **6**(9), 813–827 (1977)
23. Kamgar-Parsi, B., Kamgar-Parsi, B.: Evaluation of quantization error in computer vision. IEEE Trans. Pattern Anal. Mach. Intell. (TPAMI) **11**(9), 929–940 (1989)
24. Ikehata, S., Aizawa, K.: Photometric stereo using constrained bivariate regression for general isotropic surfaces. In: Proceedings of Computer Vision and Pattern Recognition (CVPR), pp. 2187–2194 (2014)
25. Xie, W., Zhang, Y., Wang, C.C.L., Chung, R.C.K.: Surface-from-gradients: an approach based on discrete geometry processing. In: Proceedings of Computer Vision and Pattern Recognition (CVPR), pp. 2203–2210 (2014)
26. Lee, J.Y., Matsushita, Y., Shi, B., Kweon, I.S., Ikeuchi, K.: Radiometric calibration by rank minimization. IEEE Trans. Pattern Anal. Mach. Intell. (TPAMI) **35**(1), 144–156 (2013)

# Visual Motif Discovery via First-Person Vision

Ryo Yonetani[1(✉)], Kris M. Kitani[2], and Yoichi Sato[1]

[1] The University of Tokyo, Tokyo, Japan
{yonetani,ysato}@iis.u-tokyo.ac.jp
[2] Carnegie Mellon University, Pittsburgh, PA, USA
kkitani@cs.cmu.edu

**Abstract.** *Visual motifs* are images of visual experiences that are significant and shared across many people, such as an image of an informative sign viewed by many people and that of a familiar social situation such as when interacting with a clerk at a store. The goal of this study is to discover visual motifs from a collection of first-person videos recorded by a wearable camera. To achieve this goal, we develop a commonality clustering method that leverages three important aspects: inter-video similarity, intra-video sparseness, and people's visual attention. The problem is posed as normalized spectral clustering, and is solved efficiently using a weighted covariance matrix. Experimental results suggest the effectiveness of our method over several state-of-the-art methods in terms of both accuracy and efficiency of visual motif discovery.

**Keywords:** Commonality discovery · First-person video

## 1 Introduction

We are interested in understanding from a data-driven perspective, what images from a person's visual experience are common among the majority. By developing algorithms for automatically extracting such shared visual experiences, we aim to understand what parts of the physical world are meaningful to people. We denote these shared visual experiences that have significance across many people as *visual motifs*. While visual motifs can include images of physical objects like signs and historic buildings, they can also be images of social situations or observed human activities. Examples of visual motifs are illustrated in Fig. 1.

From a practical perspective, the ability to extract perceptually important images can be useful for such tasks as life-logging, video summarization, scene understanding, and assistive technologies for the blind. Automatically extracting important visual motifs can be helpful for identifying meaningful images for life-logging or summarization. By associating visual motifs to localized regions of the environment, we can inform scene understanding by identifying what parts of the scene are visual 'hot-spots.' The extraction of important visual information in the environment can also be helpful for assistive technologies, by conveying to blind people the information embedded in the visual world [1–3].

© Springer International Publishing AG 2016
B. Leibe et al. (Eds.): ECCV 2016, Part II, LNCS 9906, pp. 187–203, 2016.
DOI: 10.1007/978-3-319-46475-6_12

**Fig. 1.** Examples of visual motif discovery. Two signs annotated with colored rectangles are discovered as visual motifs from first-person videos. (Color figure online)

In this work, we automatically discover visual motifs using wearable cameras (*e.g.*, Google Glass), which we term *visual motif discovery*. Wearable cameras, especially when mounted on people's heads, can capture what people see clearly in the form of first-person point-of-view (POV) videos. This unique viewing perspective of wearable cameras has made it the platform of choice for understanding fine-grained human activities [4–9] and video summarization [10–15].

While it is intuitive that people will share meaningful visual experiences, it is not clear how these visual motifs can be extracted automatically from large first-person video collections. A common approach to discover visual motifs is to use *inter-video similarity*. Typically, a clustering algorithm is used to find cluster centroids corresponding to frequently occurring visual signatures shared across multiple images (*e.g.*, [16,17]). This is particularly problematic for first-person videos that tend to contain many mundane actions such as walking down a bare corridor or looking down at the ground. A straightforward application of clustering produces large clusters of mundane actions. This suggests that we need to discover visual commonalities while weighing them according to their significance. However, this raises the question of how to quantify significance.

To address this fundamental question of significance, we leverage visual cues unique to large collections of first-person videos taken in the same environment. As stated earlier, a large portion of the egocentric visual experience is *frequently* filled with mundane moments. Conversely, important visual motifs are typically distributed *sparsely* through our visual experience. This implies that *intra-video sparseness* is an important characteristic of meaningful visual motifs.

Another important feature of first-person videos is that they capture a person's focus of attention. Here we make the simple observation that when a person needs to acquire important visual information from a scene, she often stops and stays in the same position. Such an action can be observed clearly in the form of ego-motion of first-person videos. This implies that *egocentric attention* measured via camera ego-motion is a salient cue for discovering meaningful motifs.

We integrate the requirements of (1) inter-video similarity, (2) intra-video sparseness, and (3) egocentric attention into a constrained optimization problem to discover visual motifs across a large first-person video collection. In the proposed method, the problem can be formulated as normalized spectral clustering constrained by an intra-video sparseness prior and cues from the ego-centric attention, and is solved efficiently using a weighted covariance matrix. We empirically show that our method can discover meaningful visual motifs while processing a million first-person POV image frames in 90 s.

To the best of our knowledge, this work is the first to introduce the task of discovering visual motifs via first-person vision – significant first-person POV visual experiences shared across many people. The proposed method is tailored to discover visual motifs from a large collection of first-person videos using the constraints of intra-video sparseness and egocentric attention cues. Empirical validation shows that our method outperforms state-of-the-art commonality discovery methods [18,19] on first-person video datasets.

**Related Work.** The method of discovering commonalities in multiple images is adopted in many computer vision tasks such as common object discovery (co-segmentation or co-localization) [16–18,20–25], co-summarization [26], co-person detection [27], temporal commonality discovery [19], and popularity estimation [28]. They often generate candidates of commonalities (*e.g.*, superpixels, bounding-box proposals, video shots), in which the significance of each candidate is evaluated based on objectness or saliency. Significance measurements are also essential in automatic video summarization. Each video shot is evaluated for its significance using the presence of important persons and objects [10] or interestingness [12]. In contrast to previous work, we take advantage of using first-person videos by leveraging egocentric attention cues as a more natural feature for measuring the subjective significance of a visual experience. Although we limit our study to the use of a single wearable camera, the additional use of an eye tracker could help us to further understand visual attention [15].

In the field of first-person vision, recent studies proposed the use of multiple wearable cameras recording at the same time to estimate the joint focus of attention [29–31]. Accurate poses and positions of wearable cameras enabled by geometric information of the environment are used to find intersections of people's attention directions. In contrast, we focus on discovering shared visual experiences across many individuals without the use of temporal synchronization or assumption of interactive scenarios.

## 2  Discovering Visual Motifs from First-Person Videos

Suppose that we are given a collection of first-person videos recorded by many people in a certain environment (*e.g.*, a university campus). The goal of this work is to discover visual motifs specific to the environment: significant visual experiences shared across multiple people such as an image of an informative sign viewed by many people or that of a familiar social situation such as when interacting with a clerk at the university bookstore.

To discover visual motifs, we propose a method based on an unsupervised commonality clustering framework. We accept a collection of videos (a sequence of image frames) as input and output a cluster of images corresponding to visual motifs. In Sect. 2.1, we describe how image frames observed across multiple videos are analyzed using the clustering framework to discover visual motifs while taking into account inter-video similarity and intra-video sparseness. Then in Sect. 2.2, we outline a method for detecting pauses in visual attention as an egocentric attention cue, and describe how that information can be used to inform the proposed method of significant image frames. We further present a technique for increasing the computational efficiency of our method through the use of weighted covariance matrix for clustering in Sect. 2.3. Finally, we describe an incremental framework for discovering multiple visual motifs from a large video collection in Sect. 2.4.

## 2.1   Discovering Common Scenes

We first describe a general commonality clustering framework (*e.g.*, [18,20,23–26]) for discovering common scenes from multiple videos. This framework integrates the concepts of inter-video similarity and intra-video sparseness.

Let $\boldsymbol{f}_t^{(i)} \in \mathbb{R}^V$ be a $V$-dimensional feature vector describing a scene of the $t$-th image frame in the $i$-th video. We denote a sequence of scene features extracted from the $i$-th video as $F^{(i)} = [\boldsymbol{f}_1^{(i)}, \ldots, \boldsymbol{f}_{T^{(i)}}^{(i)}]^\top \in \mathbb{R}^{T^{(i)} \times V}$, where $T^{(i)}$ is the number of image frames. The moments when a common scene is observed in the $i$-th video are described by an indicator vector $\boldsymbol{x}^{(i)} = [x_1^{(i)}, \ldots, x_{T^{(i)}}^{(i)}]^\top \in \{0,1\}^{T^{(i)}}$ where $x_t^{(i)}$ takes 1 if the $t$-th image frame includes the common scene.

Our goal is to estimate the indicator vector $\boldsymbol{x}^{(i)}$ for $N$ given videos. To this end, we define the inter-video similarity by an affinity matrix, $W_{ij} \in \mathbb{R}^{T^{(i)} \times T^{(j)}}$, where the $(t, t')$-th entry of $W_{ij}$ is given by an affinity function $\sigma(\boldsymbol{f}_t^{(i)}, \boldsymbol{f}_{t'}^{(j)}) \in \mathbb{R}$ (*e.g.*, a dot product or a radial basis function). We also introduce a degree matrix $D_i = \text{diag}(d_1^{(i)} \ldots, d_{T^{(i)}}^{(i)})$ where $d_t^{(i)} = \sum_{t'=0}^{T^{(i)}} \max(\sigma(\boldsymbol{f}_t^{(i)}, \boldsymbol{f}_{t'}^{(i)}), 0)$. This degree matrix describes the inverse of intra-video sparseness; $d_t^{(i)}$ will increase when the $t$-th image frame of the $i$-th video is similar to the other frames in the same $i$-th video. The inter-video similarity $W_{ij}$ and the inverted intra-video sparseness $D_i$ are further combined across all combinations of $N$ videos:

$$W = \begin{bmatrix} W_{11} & \cdots & W_{1N} \\ \vdots & \ddots & \vdots \\ W_{N1} & \cdots & W_{NN} \end{bmatrix} \in \mathbb{R}^{T_{\text{all}} \times T_{\text{all}}}, \quad D = \begin{bmatrix} D_1 & 0 & 0 \\ 0 & \ddots & 0 \\ 0 & 0 & D_N \end{bmatrix} \in \mathbb{R}^{T_{\text{all}} \times T_{\text{all}}}, \quad (1)$$

where $T_{\text{all}} = \sum_i T^{(i)}$ is the total number of image frames. Likewise, we stack $\boldsymbol{x}^{(i)}$ to summarize the indicators across multiple videos:

$$\boldsymbol{x} = [(\boldsymbol{x}^{(1)})^\top, \ldots, (\boldsymbol{x}^{(N)})^\top]^\top \in \{0,1\}^{T_{\text{all}}}. \quad (2)$$

By maximizing the sum of inter-video similarities $\boldsymbol{x}^\top W \boldsymbol{x}$ with respect to $\boldsymbol{x}$, we can find a scene frequently observed across multiple videos. At the same time, the scenes sparsely distributed in each video can be found by minimizing the inverse of intra-video sparseness $x^\top D x$ on $x$. These two requirements can be satisfied simultaneously by solving the following maximization problem.

$$x = \arg\max_x \frac{x^\top W x}{x^\top D x} \text{ s.t. } x \in \{0,1\}^{T_{all}}. \tag{3}$$

Equation (3) can be solved via normalized spectral clustering [32,33] with two-clusters or normalized cuts [34]. We first compute two eigenvectors $Y = [y_1, y_2] \in \mathbb{R}^{T_{all} \times 2}$ of the matrix $L = D^{-\frac{1}{2}} W D^{-\frac{1}{2}}$ for the two largest eigenvalues[1]. Each row of the eigenvectors $Y$ is then divided into common-scene and non-common-scene clusters via k-means clustering, where the centroid of the common-scene cluster is more distant from the origin. Cluster assignments are finally used for $x$ such that $x_t^{(i)} = 1$ if and only if the corresponding elements of $Y$ belong to the common-scene cluster. Importantly, the eigenvalue problem on $L$ can be solved efficiently using various sparse eigensolvers (e.g., the Lanczos method) since $L$ is typically sparse and only two eigenvectors are required [34].

## 2.2 Learning to Detect Egocentric Attention Cues

The framework described above discovers common scenes that are not always significant to people, such as a hallway to reach a visual motif. In order to identify significant parts of visual experiences in videos, we focus on a specific but yet commonly occurring moment when people pause to acquire important visual information from a scene (e.g., looking at maps or purchasing something from vending machines). We can detect such pausing actions taken by camera wearers by observing ego-motion of first-person videos. Detection results can then be used as an *egocentric attention* cue to constrain the clustering process.

Formally, the egocentric attention cue is given for each frame by a score $p_t^{(i)} \in [0,1]$ that increases if a camera wearer is more likely to take a pausing action at the $t$-th frame of the $i$-th video. Similar to $D$ in Eq. (1), this egocentric attention cue is extended to handle multiple videos: $P = \text{diag}(P_1, \ldots, P_N)$ where $P_i = \text{diag}(p_1^{(i)}, \ldots, p_{T^{(i)}}^{(i)})$. We then constrain the clustering process by solving the eigenvalue problem on the following matrix $L'$:

$$L' = (D^{-\frac{1}{2}} P^{\frac{1}{2}}) W (D^{-\frac{1}{2}} P^{\frac{1}{2}}) = AWA. \tag{4}$$

The indicator $x$ obtained from $L'$ can maximize not only the inter-video similarity and intra-video sparseness, but also the sum of egocentric attention cues.

Pausing actions are detected as follows. We observe that people's heads can remain stable for a long period when people stay in the same locations and move quickly for a short period when actively scanning visual information. As illustrated in Fig. 2, these trends are observed clearly in the ego-motion of first-person videos. As shown in the left of the figure, we compute motion vectors on a $10 \times 5$ grid following [7]. By smoothing these motion vectors over time using a set

---

[1] Similar to [33], we compute the eigenvectors for the largest eigenvalues of $L$ instead of the smallest eigenvalues of $I - L$.

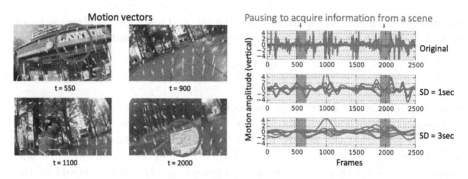

**Fig. 2.** Left: motion vectors computed on a $10 \times 5$ grid for several image frames where visual motifs are annotated with red circles. Right: amplitudes of motion vectors along the vertical direction smoothed over time with a set of Gaussian filters. (Color figure online)

of Gaussian filters with several standard deviations, we can see smaller motion amplitudes for larger deviations when people are pausing to acquire information from a scene (the right of the figure). The proposed method learns a pausing-action detector from these motion vectors. In a learning step, we apply the set of Gaussian filters independently to the horizontal and vertical elements as well as the magnitude of the motion vectors. A set of smoothed vectors and the original vectors for each frame are then aggregated to serve as a feature vector, and are learned using a binary classifier. Note that learning of the detector needs to be carried out only once and is not necessary for each environment or person.

In a testing step, the decision score of the detector obtained for each image frame is fed to the following postprocessing pipeline to generate egocentric attention cue $P$. A Gaussian filter is first applied to a sequence of decision scores to ensure its temporal smoothness. We then adopt a power normalization (*i.e.*, $\text{sgn}(p')\sqrt{\text{abs}(p')}$ for a smoothed score $p'$) to encourage small decision peaks and a sigmoid function to suppress extremely strong ones. Finally, we scale the sequence into $[0, 1]$ to use it as the diagonal entries of $P$.

### 2.3   Efficient Clustering Using Weighted Covariance Matrix

The clustering process in Sect. 2.1 should be conducted efficiently since a large collection of first-person videos is often required for visual motif discovery. Reliable motifs that are not just attractive to a limited number of people can be obtained from a video collection containing as many recordings as possible. In addition, each video can have a large number of frames when a camera wearer keeps recording everyday life (*e.g.*, [35]). As a result, the number of total frames $T_{\text{all}}$ will inevitably become huge. While the eigenvalue problem on $L'$ in Eq. (4) can be solved in linear time to $T_{\text{all}}$ by using sparse eigensolvers, there is a critical bottleneck in computing an affinity matrix $W$; the time complexity of computing $W$ is $\mathcal{O}(T_{\text{all}}^2 V)$. This computation is required for most cases when one tries to cluster commonalities based on pairwise affinities [18,20,23–26].

To address this problem, we use a compact weighted covariance matrix instead of the large $L'$. The only requirement to use this technique is to define an affinity function by a dot-product, $i.e.$, $\sigma(\boldsymbol{f}_t^{(i)}, \boldsymbol{f}_{t'}^{(j)}) \triangleq (\boldsymbol{f}_t^{(i)})^\top \boldsymbol{f}_{t'}^{(j)}$. Let us introduce a data matrix stacking all feature vectors: $F = [(F^{(1)})^\top, \ldots, (F^{(N)})^\top]^\top \in \mathbb{R}^{T_{\text{all}} \times V}$. We define $W$ by $W = FF^\top$. Then, $L'$ is rewritten as follows:

$$L' = AWA = (AF)(AF)^\top \in \mathbb{R}^{T_{\text{all}} \times T_{\text{all}}}. \tag{5}$$

Now we introduce a covariance matrix of $F$ weighted by $A$:

$$C = (AF)^\top (AF) \in \mathbb{R}^{V \times V}. \tag{6}$$

Crucially, the eigenvectors of $L'$ needed for spectral clustering can be obtained from those of the weighted covariance matrix $C$ [36,37]. Given $z_i \in \mathbb{R}^V$ as an eigenvector of $C$ for the $i$-th largest eigenvalue, the corresponding eigenvector $y_i \in \mathbb{R}^{T_{\text{all}}}$ of $L'$ can be reconstructed by $y_i \propto AFz_i$. The time complexity to compute $C$ is $\mathcal{O}(V^2 T_{\text{all}})$, which is much smaller than that of $L'$ when $V \ll T_{\text{all}}$. When $F$ is designed such that each feature dimension is less correlated, $C$ is sparse and the eigenvalue problem on $C$ can be solved efficiently. One limitation in using the weighted covariance matrix is that visual motifs should be linearly separable from other scenes in a feature space because we do not introduce any nonlinearity in the affinity function $\sigma$. We therefore use a high-level feature tailored to linear classifiers such as the Fisher vector [38] in $F$.

## 2.4   Discovering Multiple Visual Motifs

We have so far described how to discover a single visual motif from videos. Our method can be further extended to an incremental framework that allows videos to have multiple motifs. Specifically, we iteratively discover the most probable motif while updating $C$ based on the discovery result.

Suppose that a visual motif is discovered in the form of $\boldsymbol{x}_k \in \{0,1\}^{T_{\text{all}}}$ at the current $k$-th step. Here we denote the $i$-th row of matrix $AF$ and vector $\boldsymbol{x}$ as $AF[i]$ and $\boldsymbol{x}[i]$, respectively. Then, the degree of how the $k$-th motif biases the original $C$ is explained by $C_k = \sum_{i \in \{j | \boldsymbol{x}_k[j]=1\}} (AF[i])^\top (AF[i])$. Other motifs can therefore be discovered in the subsequent $k+1$-th step by updating $C \leftarrow C - C_k$. We also deflate $A$ of selected frames to zero ($i.e.$, $A \leftarrow A \cdot \text{diag}(\boldsymbol{1} - \boldsymbol{x}_k)$) so that they will not be selected again.

One important problem for discovering multiple motifs is the termination of iterative discovery, $i.e.$, how to estimate the number of motifs in a video collection. Some studies on spectral clustering proposed to observe eigenvalues to determine the number of clusters [32,39]. Intuitively, eigenvalues are large as long as the number of clusters is below that of actual groups. In our method, the eigenvalues will become small when no more common scenes remain in videos. We also observe that egocentric attention cue $P$ can indicate the number of motifs. If the attention cue of selected frames is small, these frames are not likely to be a visual motif but a scene incidentally observed across multiple videos.

**Algorithm 1.** Discovering multiple visual motifs

---

**Require:** Feature $F$, degree matrix $D$, egocentric attention cue $P$, threshold $e_{\min}$.
**Ensure:** Set of indicator vectors $x_1, x_2, \ldots$.

  1: Compute $A = D^{-\frac{1}{2}} P^{\frac{1}{2}}$.
  2: Compute $C = (AF)^\top (AF)$.
  3: Set $k = 0$
  4: **repeat**
  5:     Find two eigenvectors of $C$ for the two largest eigenvalues, $Z = [z_1, z_2]$.
  6:     Compute $Y = AFZ$.
  7:     Conduct two-clusters k-means clustering on $Y$ to obtain $x_k$.
  8:     Compute $e = \lambda \frac{x_k^\top P x_k}{x_k^\top x_k}$, where $\lambda$ is the largest eigenvalue in Step 5.
  9:     Compute $C_k = \sum_{i \in \{j \mid x_k[j]=1\}} (AF[i])^\top (AF[i])$
10:     Update $C \leftarrow C - C_k$.
11:     Update $A \leftarrow A \cdot \operatorname{diag}(1 - x_k)$.
12:     Update $k \leftarrow k + 1$.
13: **until** $e < e_{\min}$

---

To incorporate these two criteria, we define a *confidence score* for the $k$-th motif by $e = \lambda \frac{x_k^\top P x_k}{x_k^\top x_k}$, where $\lambda$ is the largest eigenvalue obtained in the eigenvalue problem of the $k$-th step. We discover visual motifs iteratively as long as $e$ is above a pre-defined threshold $e_{\min}$. A complete algorithm to discover multiple visual motifs is described in Algorithm 1. After running the algorithm, we finally refine the results (a sequence of indicator vectors $x_1, x_2, \ldots$) by omitting some indicator vectors that only select the image frames from a single video.

## 3  Experiments

To evaluate the effectiveness of the proposed method, we constructed a dataset composed of multiple first-person videos during a navigation task in several different environments. We also tested our method on a dataset recorded by people during social interactions [40]. The experimental results show that the proposed method successfully improves upon both accuracy and efficiency of visual motif discovery compared to several state-of-the-art methods [18,19].

### 3.1  Navigation Dataset

Because many prior studies on first-person vision focused on how their method could be generalized to a variety of environments (*e.g.*, GeorgiaTech Egocentric Activities [4], JPL First-Person Interaction [6], CMU Social Saliency [29]), there are few datasets of first-person videos that have been recorded many times in one environment. One prospective dataset that we will test in Sect. 3.5 is First-Person Social Interactions [40]. However, the number of visual motifs is not sufficient for quantitatively evaluating the accuracy of visual motif discovery.

We therefore introduce a new **Navigation** dataset that contains multiple recordings of 21 visual motifs. First-person videos were taken in six different

environments, where three to four subjects were assigned to each of the environments. Subjects joined in on a navigation task as follows. They visited several
pre-defined places with attractive physical objects such as map signs, vending
machines, and the entrance of a store. They were asked to look at what was
described on these objects (*e.g.*, reading a map sign). They were able to take
arbitrary positions, poses, and head motions when looking at the objects. This
made the appearance of motifs sufficiently variable for each recording. We only
instructed the subjects to look at objects from a reasonable distance to restrain
them from acquiring information in an extremely unusual way, such as reading signs from an extremely long (or short) distance. They were also allowed to
visit other places that were not pre-defined. In total, 44 first-person videos were
recorded at 30 fps. The time of each recording was 90 to 180 s and the total number of image frames for each environment was on average 27784.0. To complete
the feature extraction steps in a reasonable time, each video was resized to a
resolution of $320 \times 180$.

Ground truth labels of visual motifs were given as follows. We first annotated
the time intervals when image frames captured pre-defined objects roughly at
the center. Then, we refined the intervals so that the acceleration of head motion
was locally minimum and maximum at the beginning and end of the intervals,
respectively. The average time when subjects were judged as looking at the
objects was 5.8 s. These annotations were also used for learning a detector for
egocentric attention cues. Note that we confirmed by manual inspection that our
dataset did not contain other visual motifs (*i.e.*, images of other physical objects
seen by the majority of subjects) that were not in the pre-defined set.

## 3.2 Implementations

One important implementation of our method is the design of scene features. As
we stated in Sect. 2.3, the features should have the potential of linearly separating
visual motifs from other unimportant scenes to use a weighted covariance matrix.
In the experiments, the following two types of features were used:

**SIFT + Fisher vector (FV).** RootSIFT descriptors [41] were sparsely sampled from each image frame. They were then fed to the principal component analysis (PCA) with 64 components and the Fisher vector [38] with the
128-component Gaussian mixture model (GMM) followed by power and L2
normalizations. As the features were rather high dimensionally (16384 dimensions), we adopted the sparse random projection [42] to project the features
onto a 1024-dimensional feature space. We trained the PCA and GMM components for each environment independently.

**CNN feature (CNN).** A convolutional neural network (CNN) trained with
the MIT Places database [43] was used as a feature descriptor. To investigate
how the pre-trained CNN can be used to extract high-level features that
could cope with the variability of motif appearances, we utilized the *fc6* layer
outputs of the pre-trained network as a 4096-dimensional feature.

Note that both features were scaled for each environment so that each feature dimension had zero-mean and unit-variance. Based on these features, we implemented two variants of the proposed method: **Ours (FV)** and **Ours (CNN)**. For both methods, we set $e_{th} = 0.5$ which empirically worked well.

To enable an egocentric attention cue, we trained a linear support vector machine. Specifically, we split our dataset into two subsets based on environment IDs (videos of three environments recorded by three subjects and those of the other three environments by four subjects) and trained a pausing-action detector with one subset to test the other. Note that subjects and environments did not overlap between training and testing subsets. The standard deviations used for a set of Gaussian filters were 1 and 3 s in feature extraction, and 1 second in postprocessing. The impact of using the egocentric attention cue was validated with the following two degraded versions of our method: (1) **SC**, which uses a covariance matrix $C = (D^{-\frac{1}{2}}F)^\top(D^{-\frac{1}{2}}F)$ and a confidence score $e = \lambda$ to remove the effect of egocentric attention cue $P$ in Algorithm 1, and is equivalent to standard normalized spectral clustering; and (2) **EgoCue**, which directly uses $p_t^{(i)}$ as a confidence score for each frame, which can be regarded as a simple supervised learning method to detect visual motifs.

**Baselines.** Two state-of-the-art methods on commonality discovery served as baselines. One is the temporal commonality discovery method (**TCD**) [19][2]. Given a pair of videos, **TCD** discovers a pair of temporal intervals that include similar feature patterns. In the experiments, **TCD** was applied to all combinations of videos in a collection. Each image frame was then given a confidence score of visual motifs based on how many times the frame was discovered as a visual motif. We also took into account the egocentric attention cue of discovered frames, $p_t^{(i)}$, as follows. If the $t$-th frame of the $i$-th video was discovered by the combinations of $K$ other videos, the frame obtained a confidence score of $Kp_t^{(i)}$.

The other baseline is the object co-localization method (**COLOC**) [18][3]. This method discovers a single common object observed across multiple images by selecting one of the object proposals generated per image. Each proposal has a prior score given by objectness, and objects are discovered with a confidence score. Instead of the object proposals per image, we used image frames of a given video as a proposal. The prior score of each frame proposal was then given by $p_t^{(i)}$ instead of the objectness used in [18]. Importantly, our implementation of **COLOC** discovered, as a visual motif, only a single image frame for each video. However, visual motifs were observed for consecutive frames of a certain length. We therefore found the consecutive frames around the discovered frame via temporal dilation, where the dilation size was learned from training subsets.

---

[2] http://humansensing.cs.cmu.edu/wschu/project_tcd.html.
[3] http://ai.stanford.edu/~kdtang/.

## 3.3    Detecting Visual Motifs

We first compared how well the methods could detect *any* visual motifs. To evaluate detection performance, we extended the confidence score $e$ defined originally *per visual motif* in **Ours (FV)**, **Ours (CNN)**, **SC**, and **COLOC** to that defined *per frame* such as that given in **EgoCue** and **TCD**. Specifically, video frames discovered as a certain visual motif were given the confidence score of that motif; otherwise, they were given 0. These per-frame confidence scores were used to calculate precision-recall curves and average precision scores.

Since it was difficult to run the two baselines on **Navigation** in a reasonable time, we also constructed a smaller dataset, **Navigation-1**, which was cropped from **Navigation** to include a single visual motif per video. For each video, we cropped a shot including the time interval of visual motifs with a margin of 10 s (*i.e.*, 300 frames) before and after the interval. As a result, 21 collections of videos were generated. On **Navigation-1**, we detected a single motif with each method. We then tested the proposed method as well as its degraded versions on **Navigation**, where multiple motifs were discovered for evaluation.

Table 1 lists the average precision scores for all methods. Note that for **SC**, **TCD**, and **COLOC**, we describe the results using the **FV** feature, which were better than those using the **CNN** feature. The left of Fig. 3 also depicts precision-recall curves. Overall, the proposed method clearly outperformed the two baselines on **Navigation-1**. We also confirmed that this was achieved given the combination of common scene discovery and egocentric attention cue because the performance of **SC** and **EgoCue** was quite limited. The **FV** feature worked comparably to **CNN** on **Navigation-1** and the best on **Navigation**. The number of visual motifs pre-defined in **Navigation** and discovered with **Ours (FV)** are compared in Table 2. For most cases, our method could estimate the number of visual motifs accurately.

We also evaluated the computation times of each method, as shown on the right of Fig. 3. We generated videos of various numbers of frames simply by

**Table 1.** Average precision scores. **Navigation-1**: 21 video collections each of which includes single motif. **Navigation**: six video collections all including multiple motifs.

|  | Ours (FV) | Ours (CNN) | SC | EgoCue | TCD [19] | COLOC [18] |
|---|---|---|---|---|---|---|
| Navigation-1 | 0.77 | **0.79** | 0.64 | 0.67 | 0.63 | 0.63 |
| Navigation | **0.77** | 0.70 | 0.60 | 0.60 | - | - |

**Table 2.** Number of visual motifs pre-defined per environment on **Navigation** (top) and that discovered with **Ours (FV)** (bottom).

|  | Env 1 | Env 2 | Env 3 | Env 4 | Env 5 | Env 6 |
|---|---|---|---|---|---|---|
| # motifs | 4 | 4 | 4 | 3 | 3 | 3 |
| # discovered | 4 | 4 | 5 | 3 | 3 | 4 |

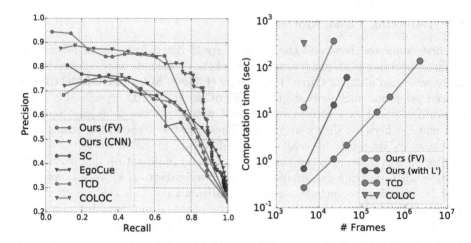

**Fig. 3.** Left: Precision-recall curves of methods on **Navigation-1**. Right: Computation times. For both **TCD** and **COLOC** we used codes available on authors' websites. **Ours (FV)** and **Ours (with L)** were implemented in Python. All methods were tested on MacPro with 2.7-GHz 12-Core Intel Xeon E5.

concatenating our videos multiple times. To show the impact of using a weighted covariance matrix, we also tested a variant of the proposed method that relied on $L'$ in Eq. (5) instead of $C$ in Eq. (6), which we referred to as **Ours (with L')** in the figure. Since the time complexity to compute the weighted covariance is linearly proportional to the number of image frames, the proposed method is an order-of-magnitude faster than the others. Note that high framerate videos are necessary only when computing ego-motion. Once egocentric attention cues are given, the clustering process can work under much lower framerates. If all videos are downsampled to 1 fps, our method can find visual motifs from 10 h of recording in 1 s.

### 3.4 Distinguishing Multiple Motifs

Next, we show how our method can distinguish multiple visual motifs. In Fig. 4, we describe confusion matrices and average accuracies of **Ours (FV)** and **SC** for each environment. To obtain the confusion matrices, we assigned pre-defined (*i.e.*, ground-truth) motifs to discovered (predicted) ones via linear assignment. By using an egocentric attention cue, we successfully classified visual motifs for many environments. As shown in Fig. 5, visual motifs were matched regardless of the points-of-view or parts of pre-defined objects that could be observed. Examples 3 and 6 also suggest that our method works well even when people are interacting with others and making frequent head and hand motions.

Figure 6 presents other examples of visual motifs. The use of high-level features such as **FV** allows us to match motifs even when a few changes were made in their appearance. Most failure cases were due to undiscovered instances (*i.e.*, incorrectly classified as unimportant background scenes). We found that these

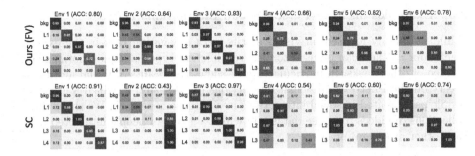

**Fig. 4.** Confusion matrices and average accuracies for multiple visual motif discovery on the six environments (Env 1, ..., Env 6) in **Navigation**. Annotated labels **L1** to **L4** indicate ID of visual motifs while **bkg** denotes other background scenes.

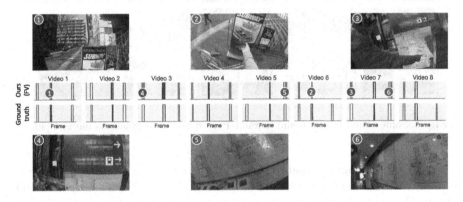

**Fig. 5.** Example of multiple visual motif discovery (on Env 4). Three motifs were discovered in timeline (colored plots in the middle) for each of eight videos in a video collection. Some discovered image frames are depicted at top and bottom. (Color figure online)

failures occurred when pre-defined objects were observed at different locations (the menu board in the fourth column of Fig. 6) or when they were not salient (the navigation sign in the fifth column).

**Fig. 6.** Examples of successfully-discovered and non-discovered motifs. Videos in each row were recorded on different days and times.

## 3.5    Examples on First-Person Social Interactions Dataset

While we mainly focused on visual motifs for a navigation task in the experiments, our method can be used to discover different types of visual motifs given a video of other tasks. In particular, Fig. 7 shows the results of visual motif discovery on the First-Person Social Interactions dataset [40], in which a group of people participated in social interactions in an amusement park. We chose three collections of videos from the dataset in which a group of people interacted with each other at several places.

**Fig. 7.** Some visual motifs found in First-Person Social Interactions dataset [40].

At a cafeteria, our method discovered a situation in which camera wearers were (1) waiting in line, (2) interacting with a clerk, and (3) preparing a dish on a table. Our method also found at an entrance, a situation of (4) waiting in line and (5) interacting with others. Interestingly, the method was able to find (6) a photographer jointly looked at by multiple camera wearers, which was similar to co-person detection [27]. All these situations correspond to the shared visual experiences across multiple camera wearers, while they are quite different from those found in the navigation tasks mentioned in previous sections.

## 4    Conclusions

We introduced a new task of visual motif discovery from a large collection of first-person videos and developed an efficient method tailored to the task. The proposed method can discover visual motifs more accurately and an order-of-magnitude faster than other state-of-the-art methods.

There are several possible extensions leading to interesting directions for future work. While we focused on a specific class of visual motifs observed when people paused to acquire information, there are other significant moments shared across people such as when carrying important belongings by hand, meeting with friends, *etc.* First-person videos can be used to recognize many types of actions, *e.g.*, not only pausing but using hands [4,5,8,9] and conversing with others [40], which are all informative for recognizing a variety of visual motifs. In addition, by combining geometric information enabled by visual simultaneous localization and mapping or GPS, our method will be able to distinguish visual motifs that are visually the same but observed at different locations (*e.g.*, the same signs placed at different entrance gates). Another interesting direction for future work is to extend our visual motif discovery method to work in an online manner. This allows us to handle extremely long recordings and makes it possible to extract a variety of visual motifs that we observe in everyday life.

**Acknowledgments.** This research was supported by CREST, JST and Kayamori Foundation of Informational Science Advancement.

# References

1. Leung, T.S., Medioni, G.: Visual navigation aid for the blind in dynamic environments. In: Proceedings of IEEE Conference on Computer Vision and Pattern Recognition Workshops (CVPRW), pp. 153–158 (2014)
2. Tang, T.J.J., Li, W.H.: An assistive eyewear prototype that interactively converts 3D object locations into spatial audio. In: Proceedings of ACM International Symposium on Wearable Computers (ISWC), pp. 119–126 (2014)
3. Templeman, R., Korayem, M., Crandall, D., Kapadia, A.: Placeavoider: steering first-person cameras away from sensitive spaces. In: Proceedings of Annual Network and Distributed System Security Symposium (NDSS) (2014)
4. Fathi, A., Li, Y., Rehg, J.M.: Learning to recognize daily actions using gaze. In: Fitzgibbon, A., Lazebnik, S., Perona, P., Sato, Y., Schmid, C. (eds.) ECCV 2012. LNCS, vol. 7572, pp. 314–327. Springer, Heidelberg (2012). doi:10.1007/978-3-642-33718-5_23
5. Pirsiavash, H., Ramanan, D.: Detecting activities of daily living in first-person camera views. In: Proceedings of IEEE Conference on Computer Vision and Pattern Recognition (CVPR), pp. 2847–2854 (2012)
6. Ryoo, M.S., Matthies, L.: First-person activity recognition: what are they doing to me? In: Proceedings of IEEE Conference on Computer Vision and Pattern Recognition (CVPR), pp. 2730–2737 (2013)
7. Poleg, Y., Arora, C., Peleg, S.: Temporal segmentation of egocentric videos. In: Proceedings of IEEE Conference on Computer Vision and Pattern Recognition (CVPR), pp. 2537–2544 (2014)
8. Saran, A., Teney, D., Kitani, K.M.: Hand parsing for fine-grained recognition of human grasps in monocular images. In: Proceedings of IEEE/RSJ International Conference on Intelligent Robots and Systems (IROS), pp. 1–7 (2015)
9. Cai, M., Kitani, K.M., Sato, Y.: A scalable approach for understanding the visual structures of hand grasps. In: Proceedings of IEEE International Conference on Robotics and Automation (ICRA), pp. 1360–1366 (2015)
10. Lee, Y.J., Ghosh, J., Grauman, K.: Discovering important people and objects for egocentric video summarization. In: Proceedings of IEEE Conference on Computer Vision and Pattern Recognition (CVPR), pp. 1346–1353 (2012)
11. Lu, Z., Grauman, K.: Story-driven summarization for egocentric video. In: Proceedings of IEEE Conference on Computer Vision and Pattern Recognition (CVPR), pp. 2714–2721 (2013)

12. Gygli, M., Grabner, H., Riemenschneider, H., Gool, L.: Creating summaries from user videos. In: Fleet, D., Pajdla, T., Schiele, B., Tuytelaars, T. (eds.) ECCV 2014. LNCS, vol. 8695, pp. 505–520. Springer, Heidelberg (2014). doi:10.1007/978-3-319-10584-0_33

13. Arev, I., Park, H.S., Sheikh, Y., Hodgins, J., Shamir, A.: Automatic editing of footage from multiple social cameras. ACM Trans. Graph. **33**(4), 81:1–81:11 (2014)

14. Xiong, B., Kim, G., Sigal, L.: Storyline representation of egocentric videos with an applications to story-based search. In: Proceedings of IEEE International Conference on Computer Vision (ICCV), pp. 4525–4533 (2015)

15. Xu, J., Mukherjee, L., Li, Y., Warner, J., Rehg, J.M., Singh, V.: Gaze-enabled egocentric video summarization via constrained submodular maximization. In: Proceedings of IEEE Conference on Computer Vision and Pattern Recognition (CVPR), pp. 2235–2244 (2015)

16. Joulin, A., Bach, F., Ponce, J.: Discriminative clustering for image co-segmentation. In: Proceedings of IEEE Conference on Computer Vision and Pattern Recognition (CVPR), pp. 1943–1950 (2010)

17. Zhou, F., De la Torre Frade, F., Hodgins, J.K.: Hierarchical aligned cluster analysis for temporal clustering of human motion. IEEE Trans. Pattern Anal. Mach. Intell. (PAMI) **35**(3), 582–596 (2013)

18. Tang, K., Joulin, A., Li, L.J., Fei-Fei, L.: Co-localization in real-world images. In: Proceedings of IEEE Conference on Computer Vision and Pattern Recognition (CVPR), pp. 1464–1471 (2014)

19. Chu, W.-S., Zhou, F., Torre, F.: Unsupervised temporal commonality discovery. In: Fitzgibbon, A., Lazebnik, S., Perona, P., Sato, Y., Schmid, C. (eds.) ECCV 2012. LNCS, vol. 7575, pp. 373–387. Springer, Heidelberg (2012). doi:10.1007/978-3-642-33765-9_27

20. Joulin, A., Tang, K., Fei-Fei, L.: Efficient image and video co-localization with Frank-Wolfe algorithm. In: Fleet, D., Pajdla, T., Schiele, B., Tuytelaars, T. (eds.) ECCV 2014. LNCS, vol. 8694, pp. 253–268. Springer, Heidelberg (2014). doi:10.1007/978-3-319-10599-4_17

21. Rother, C., Minka, T., Blake, A., Kolmogorov, V.: Cosegmentation of image pairs by histogram matching - incorporating a global constraint into mrfs. In: Proceedings of IEEE Conference on Computer Vision and Pattern Recognition (CVPR), pp. 993–1000 (2006)

22. Vicente, S., Rother, C., Kolmogorov, V.: Object cosegmentation. In: Proceedings of IEEE Conference on Computer Vision and Pattern Recognition (CVPR), pp. 2217–2224 (2011)

23. Zhang, D., Javed, O., Shah, M.: Video object co-segmentation by regulated maximum weight cliques. In: Fleet, D., Pajdla, T., Schiele, B., Tuytelaars, T. (eds.) ECCV 2014. LNCS, vol. 8695, pp. 551–566. Springer, Heidelberg (2014). doi:10.1007/978-3-319-10584-0_36

24. Fu, H., Xu, D., Zhang, B., Lin, S.: Object-based multiple foreground video co-segmentation. In: Proceedings of IEEE Conference on Computer Vision and Pattern Recognition (CVPR), pp. 3166–3173 (2014)

25. Wang, L., Hua, G., Sukthankar, R., Xue, J., Zheng, N.: Video object discovery and co-segmentation with extremely weak supervision. In: Fleet, D., Pajdla, T., Schiele, B., Tuytelaars, T. (eds.) ECCV 2014. LNCS, vol. 8692, pp. 640–655. Springer, Heidelberg (2014). doi:10.1007/978-3-319-10593-2_42

26. Chu, W.S., Song, Y., Jaimes, A.: Video co-summarization: video summarization by visual co-occurrence. In: Proceedings of IEEE Conference on Computer Vision and Pattern Recognition (CVPR), pp. 3584–3592 (2015)

27. Lin, Y., Abdelfatah, K., Zhou, Y., Fan, X., Yu, H., Qian, H., Wang, S.: Co-interest person detection from multiple wearable camera videos. In: Proceedings of International Conference on Computer Vision (ICCV), pp. 4426–4434 (2015)

28. Ortis, A., Farinella, G.M., D'amico, V., Addesso, L., Torrisi, G., Battiato, S.: Recfusion: automatic video curation driven by visual content popularity. In: Proceedings of ACM International Conference on Multimedia (MM), pp. 1179–1182 (2015)

29. Park, H.S., Jain, E., Sheikh, Y.: 3D social saliency from head-mounted cameras. In: Proceedings of Advances in Neural Information Processing Systems (NIPS), pp. 1–9 (2012)

30. Park, H.S., Jain, E., Sheikh, Y.: Predicting primary gaze behavior using social saliency fields. In: Proceedings of IEEE International Conference on Computer Vision (ICCV), pp. 3503–3510 (2013)

31. Park, H.S., Shi, J.: Social saliency prediction. In: Proceedings of IEEE Conference on Computer Vision and Pattern Recognition (CVPR), pp. 4777–4785 (2015)

32. Luxburg, U.: A tutorial on spectral clustering. Stat. Comput. **17**(4), 395–416 (2007)

33. Ng, A.Y., Jordan, M.I., Weiss, Y.: On spectral clustering: analysis and an algorithm. In: Proceedings of Advances in Neural Information Processing Systems (NIPS), pp. 849–856 (2001)

34. Shi, J., Malik, J.: Normalized cuts and image segmentation. IEEE Trans. Pattern Anal. Mach. Intell. (TPAMI) **22**(8), 888–905 (2000)

35. Singh, K.K., Fatahalian, K., Efros, A.A.: Krishnacam: using a longitudinal, single-person, egocentric dataset for scene understanding tasks. In: Proceedings of IEEE Winter Conference on Applications of Computer Vision (WACV), pp. 1–9 (2016)

36. Ghodsi, A.: Dimensionality Reduction a Short Tutorial. Department of Statistics and Actuarial Science, University of Waterloo, Ontario (2006)

37. Murakami, H., Kumar, B.: Efficient calculation of primary images from a set of images. IEEE Trans. Pattern Anal. Mach. Intell. (TPAMI) **PAMI–4**(5), 511–515 (1982)

38. Perronnin, F., Sánchez, J., Mensink, T.: Improving the Fisher kernel for large-scale image classification. In: Daniilidis, K., Maragos, P., Paragios, N. (eds.) ECCV 2010. LNCS, vol. 6314, pp. 143–156. Springer, Heidelberg (2010). doi:10.1007/978-3-642-15561-1_11

39. Zelnik-manor, L., Perona, P.: Self-tuning spectral clustering. In: Proceedings of Advances in Neural Information Processing Systems (NIPS), pp. 1601–1608 (2004)

40. Fathi, A., Hodgins, J.K., Rehg, J.M.: Social interactions: a first-person perspective. In: Proceedings of IEEE Conference on Computer Vision and Pattern Recognition (CVPR), pp. 1226–1233 (2012)

41. Arandjelovic, R., Zisserman, A.: Three things everyone should know to improve object retrieval. In: Proceedings of IEEE Conference on Computer Vision and Pattern Recognition (CVPR), pp. 2911–2918 (2012)

42. Li, P., Hastie, T.J., Church, K.W.: Very sparse random projections. In: Proceedings of ACM SIGKDD International Conference on Knowledge Discovery and Data Mining (KDD), pp. 287–296 (2006)

43. Zhou, B., Lapedriza, A., Xiao, J., Torralba, A., Oliva, A.: Learning deep features for scene recognition using places database. In: Proceedings of Advances in Neural Information Processing Systems (NIPS), pp. 487–495 (2014)

# A Cluster Sampling Method for Image Matting via Sparse Coding

Xiaoxue Feng, Xiaohui Liang$^{(\boxtimes)}$, and Zili Zhang

State Key Laboratory of Virtual Reality Technology and Systems,
Beihang University, Beijing, China
{feng_xiaoxue,liang_xiaohui,zhangzili}@buaa.edu.cn

**Abstract.** In this paper, we present a new image matting algorithm which solves two major problems encountered by previous sampling-based algorithms. The first is that existing sampling-based approaches typically rely on certain spatial assumptions in collecting samples from known regions, and thus their performance deteriorates if the underlying assumptions are not satisfied. Here, we propose a method that a more representative set of samples is collected so as not to miss out true samples. This is accomplished by clustering the foreground and background pixels and collecting samples from each of the clusters. The second problem is that the quality of matting result is determined by the goodness of a single sample pair which causes errors when sampling-based methods fail to select the best pairs. In this paper, we derive a new objective function for directly obtaining the estimation of the alpha matte from a bunch of samples. Comparison on a standard benchmark dataset demonstrates that the proposed approach generates more robust and accurate alpha matte than state-of-the-art methods.

**Keywords:** Image matting · Sampling · Clustering · Sparse coding · Foreground extraction

## 1 Introduction

Estimation of foreground and background layers of an image is fundamental in image and video editing. In the computer vision literatures, this problem is known as image matting or alpha matting. Mathematically, the process is modeled in [1] by considering the observed color of a pixel as a combination of foreground color and background color:

$$I_z = \alpha_z F_z + (1 - \alpha_z B_z) \tag{1}$$

where $F_z$ and $B_z$ are the foreground and background colors of pixel $z$, $\alpha_z$ represents the opacity of a pixel and takes values in the range [0,1] with $\alpha_z = 1$ for foreground pixels and $\alpha_z = 0$ for background pixels. This is a highly ill-posed problem since we have to estimate seven unknowns from three composition equations for each pixel - one for each color channel. Typically, matting approaches

© Springer International Publishing AG 2016
B. Leibe et al. (Eds.): ECCV 2016, Part II, LNCS 9906, pp. 204–219, 2016.
DOI: 10.1007/978-3-319-46475-6_13

rely on constraints such as assumption on image statistics [2,3] or user interactions such as a trimap to reduce the solution space. A trimap [4] partitions an image into three regions - known foreground, known background and unknown regions that consist of a mixture of foreground and background colors.

From the aspect of assumptions on image statistics, existing natural image matting methods fall into three categories: (1) propagation-based [2,5–10]; (2) color sampling-based [11–18]; (3) combination of sampling-based and propagation-based [19–22] methods. Propagation-based methods assume that neighboring pixels are correlated under some image statistics and use their affinities to propagate alpha values of known regions toward unknown ones. Sampling-based methods assume that the foreground and background colors of an unknown pixel can be explicitly estimated by examining nearby pixels. Thus, these methods collect sets of known foreground and background samples to estimate alpha values of unknown pixels. Early parametric sampling-based methods usually fit parametric statistical models to known foreground and background samples and then estimate alpha values by considering the distances of unknown pixels to known foreground and background distributions. However, it will generate large fitting errors when the color distribution could not significantly fit a statistical model. Recently, non-parametric sampling-based methods simply collect sets of known foreground and background samples and select best $(F, B)$ pairs via an objective function combining spatial, photometric and probabilistic characteristics of an image to estimate alphas value of unknown pixels. Once the best $(F, B)$ pair is selected, the alpha value is computed as

$$\alpha_z = \frac{(I_z - B) \cdot (F - B)}{\| F - B \|^2} \tag{2}$$

Combined methods [19–22] cast matting as an optimization problem and combine the color sampling component and the alpha propagation component in an energy function; solving for alpha matte becomes an energy minimization task. By the combination, more accurate and robust matting solutions can be expected. For a more comprehensive review on image matting methods, we refer the reader to [21,23].

The matting method proposed in this paper belongs to the group of sampling-based approaches. As we will discuss in next section in detail, these approaches suffer from the fact that the quality of the extracted matte highly depends on the selected samples and the performance degrades when the true foreground and background colors (true samples) of unknown pixels are not in the sample sets. Existing sampling-based methods sample foreground and background colors based on their spatial closeness to the unknown pixels only (sample around the boundaries of the known regions [8,13,21] or expand the sampling range for pixels farther from the foreground and background boundaries [16]) which lead to the missing out true samples problem, especially when the trimaps are coarse. To overcome this problem, we build a large set of representative samples that covers all the color clusters in the image to avoid the loss of true samples, and then select a set of candidate samples for each unknown pixel from these representative

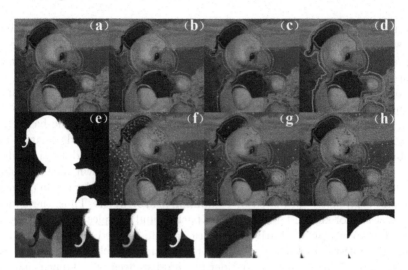

**Fig. 1.** Sampling-based matting approaches. Top and middle row: (a) An Original image with foreground and background boundaries marked as red and blue line respectively, (e) the ground truth alpha matte, sampling strategies of (b) Robust [21], (c) Shared [13], (d) Global [14], (f) Comprehensive [16], (g) KL-Divergence [18] and (h) proposed matting approaches. Bottom row: Comparison of the estimated alpha mattes by the proposed approach with Comprehensive sampling method [16] and KL-Divergence based sparse sampling method [18] (from left to right are zoomed area and corresponding alpha mattes estimated by [16,18] and the proposed, respectively) (Color figure online)

samples via an objective function that takes advantage of spatial as well as color statistics of the samples. The samples selected by proposed method are shown in Fig. 1(h).

The second disadvantage of current non-parametric sampling-based approaches is that they choose the best $(F, B)$ pair from candidate samples through optimization and use that pair to estimate $\alpha_z$ via Eq. (2). This implies that $\alpha_z$ is determined by a single $(F, B)$ pair and the goodness of that pair depends on how well the optimization is done. Thus if the optimization process fails to find the best pair, the extracted matte will not be accurate. Inspired by sparse coding matting [17], a new objective function is proposed which gives the estimation of alpha value directly from a bunch of candidate foreground and background samples for a given pixel instead of estimating it from a single best pair. This objective function contains measures of chromatic distortion and spatial statistics in the image, which is the main difference from the original sparse coding matting [17] which contains the chromatic distortion only.

This paper is organized as follows. We review sampling-based matting methods and their limitations in Sect. 2 followed by description of the proposed approach in Sect. 3. Experimental results are discussed in Sect. 4 and we conclude the paper in Sect. 5.

## 2    Related Work

Sampling-based image matting methods mainly differ from each other in (1) how they collect the candidate foreground and background samples for unknown pixels, and (2) how they estimate the alpha matte from the candidate samples.

**Samples Collection:** Early sampling-based methods simply collect foreground and background samples that are spatially close to the unknown pixel, either from a local window containing the unknown pixel [11] or along the boundaries of known regions [12,21] based on local smooth assumptions. This will cause large fitting errors when the assumptions do not hold.

Shared sampling matting [13] shots rays in different directions from unknown pixels that divide the image plane into disjoint sectors containing equal planar angles and collects samples on the rays. Fore each ray, it collects at most one background and at most one foreground sample - the ones closer to the unknown pixel along the ray as shown in Fig. 1(c). Global sampling matting [14] proposes a approach that takes all available samples into consideration. Their foreground (background) sample set consists of all known foreground (background) pixels on the boundaries of unknown regions as shown in Fig. 1(d).

The aforementioned sampling-based methods generally collect samples only around the boundaries of the known regions which may miss out true samples. Comprehensive sampling matting [16] builds a more comprehensive and representative set of known samples by expanding the sampling range farther from the foreground and background boundary and sampling from all color distributions in the sample regions as shown in Fig. 1(f). This approach gives better results than the previous sampling-based approaches. However, there is still a possibility of missing out true samples since the sampling strategy depends on spatial closeness. KL-Divergence sampling matting [18] formulates sampling as a row-sparsity regularized trace minimization problem and picks a small set of candidate samples that best explain the unknown pixels based on pairwise dissimilarities between known and unknown pixels as shown in Fig. 1(g). This method gathers a uniform sparse set of samples for all unknown pixels which might also miss out true samples. A visual comparison of the alpha mattes estimated by the proposed method with comprehensive [16] and KL-Divergence sampling methods [18] is shown in the last row of Fig. 1.

**Alpha Matte Estimation:** Classical parametric sampling-based image matting algorithms focus on how to model the relations between the samples and the alpha parameter. The *Knockout* method [12] adopts a weighted sum of candidate samples to estimate foreground and background colors of unknown pixels and uses them to estimate the alpha value in each channel. The final alpha value is estimated as a weighted sum of the values in all channels. Bayesian matting [11] models foreground and background colors as mixtures of Gaussians and the matting problem is formulated in a well-defined Bayesian framework, then the matte is solved with a maximum-likelihood criterion.

Due to the improperness of estimating alpha values with the statistical model in parametric sampling-based methods, recent non-parametric sampling-based approaches focus on selecting a best foreground and background sample pair $(F, B)$ from candidate samples and using the best pair to estimate alpha value via Eq. (2), as suggested in [13–16, 18, 21]. They use an objective function containing different image characteristics to find the best $(F, B)$ pair. These methods differ from each other in what image characteristics they use.

In non-parametric sampling-based methods, the alpha values are determined by a single $(F, B)$ pair, thus when the designed objective function fails to find the best sample pair, inaccurate alpha matte will be generated. To overcome this limitation, sparse coding matting [17] cast image matting as a sparse coding problem and generates alpha values from a bunch of foreground and background samples instead of choosing a single best $(F, B)$ pair. This approach gives visually superior matte than previous non-parametric sampling-based approaches.

## 3   Proposed Method

In this section, we first describe our clustering-based sampling method which collects a representative set of samples for all known pixels. Next, a simple objective function is proposed to select a set of candidate foreground and background samples for each unknown pixel from the previous collected representative set of samples. Then, we elaborate how an objective function containing both chromatic distortion and spatial statistics is proposed that gives the estimation of alpha values directly from a bunch of foreground and background samples. Finally, we describe how the pre and post-processing are used to refine the matting performance.

### 3.1   Gathering Samples Using K-means Clustering

The goal of sampling is to gather a representative set of foreground and background samples that covers a large range of diverse color clusters in the image so as not to miss out true samples. This is accomplished by clustering the foreground and background pixels respectively via a two-level hierarchical k-means clustering framework considering the spatial statistics as well as the color statistics in the image. This is motivated by the observation that the foreground and background colors in an image could be represented by a sparse set of pixels.

For the foreground region defined by a trimap, we first cluster the pixels into $K$ clusters. We defined the feature vector $q(z)$ at a given pixel $z$ as a 5-D vector $[R_z \ G_z \ B_z \ x_z \ y_z]^T$ consisting of the concatenation of $RGB$ color and spatial position in the image coordinates. Then, we create a matrix $Q$ such that each column corresponds to a feature vector of one known foreground pixel. Thus, we can treat $Q$ as the data matrix in the k-means clustering algorithm [24]. After the first level of clustering, the same clustering process is applied on pixels in each cluster but with respect to color statistics only. The numbers of clusters in the second level clustering are determined by the sum color variances of three color channels in each cluster obtained in the first level. The mean color values in each cluster at the second level constitutes the representative set of foreground samples. Using exactly the same method, a representative set of background samples could be obtained.

## 3.2  Selecting Candidate Samples

In the k-means clustering sample gathering step, we collect two large set of foreground and background samples that covers various color clusters in the image for all the unknown pixels. To reduce the number of legal hypotheses to be tested in the estimation of alpha matte, for each unknown pixel $z$ , we choose a set of candidate samples that could better represent the true foreground and background colors of the pixel from that representative sample sets. Hence, a simple objective function $O_z$ adopting previously suggested measures of chromatic distortion $C_z$ and spatial statistics $S_z$ in [8,15,16,18] is proposed:

$$O_z(F_i, B_j) = C_z(F_i, B_j) \times S_z(F_i, B_j) \qquad (3)$$

$C_z$ quantifies how well the estimated alpha value $\alpha_z$ of pixel $z$ obtained using Eq. (2) from a sample pair $(F_i, B_j)$ fits the linear model of composition Eq. (1), and is given by:

$$C_z(F_i, B_j) = exp(- \parallel I_z - (\alpha_z F_i + (1 - \alpha_z B_j)) \parallel) \qquad (4)$$

where $I_z$ denotes the observed color of unknown pixel $z$. It has a high value for $(F, B)$ pair whose estimated alpha could well fit the linear composite equation.

The term $S_z$ quantifies the closeness between the unknown pixel $z$ and the sample pair$(F, B)$ in the spatial coordinates domain. It is formulated as:

$$S_z(F_i, B_j) = exp(-\frac{\parallel z - F_i^s \parallel}{Z^F}) \times exp(-\frac{\parallel z - B_j^s \parallel}{Z^B}) \qquad (5)$$

where $F_i^s$ denotes the spatial coordinates of foreground sample $F_i$ and $B_j^s$ denotes the spatial coordinates of $B_j$. $Z^F = \frac{1}{|S^F|}\sum_{F_k \in S^F} \parallel z - F_k^s \parallel$ and $Z^B = \frac{1}{|S^B|}\sum_{B_k \in S^B} \parallel z - B_k^s \parallel$ correspond to the mean spatial distances from the unknown pixel $z$ to all the foreground samples $S^F$ with $|S^F|$ elements and background samples $S^B$ with $|S^B|$ elements respectively which are used as scaling factors. Hence, it tends to select samples that are spatially close to the unknown pixel.

Finally, for each pixel $z$, we select a number of $N$ foreground and background pairs with the highest values for the objective function (3). The corresponding foreground samples and background samples of the $N$ pairs constitutes the foreground sample set $S_z^F$ and background sample set $S_z^B$ of the unknown pixel $z$.

Figure 2 shows the sampling process of the proposed method. The original image is shown in Fig. 2(a) whose trimap consists of background, unknown and foreground regions labeled as black, gray and white respectively as shown in Fig. 2(b). The foreground and background clusters obtained by a two-level k-means clustering framework are shown in Fig. 2(c), with clusters represented by different colors. Figure 2(d) shows the selected candidate samples (with red and blue points representing foreground and background samples, respectively) for pixel $p$ (yellow point). As it can be seen, the proposed sampling strategy selects foreground and background samples from known regions for each pixel meanwhile avoids missing out true samples.

(a)Input Image    (b) Trimap    (c) Clusters    (d) Candidate Samples    (e) Output Matte

**Fig. 2.** Cluster-based sampling and candidate samples choosing. (a) Original image. (b) Trimap. (c) Foreground and background clusters via two-level k-means clustering. (d) Candidate samples for pixel $p$. (e) The generated alpha matte (Color figure online)

### 3.3   Estimating $\alpha$ via Sparse Coding

As mentioned in Sect. 2, previous non-parametric sampling-based methods generally select the best foreground and background pair $(F, B)$ for each pixel from the candidate sample through an optimization process and use it to estimate alpha value by Eq. (2). The main drawback of these methods is that the alpha value is determined by a single best pair thus that they would generate incorrect alpha matte if the optimization fails to find the best pairs. To overcome this limitation, inspired by [17], the proposed method capitalizes on the sparse coding to establish an objective function for generating alpha values directly from a bunch of candidate foreground and background samples.

In [17], the authors form a dictionary $\mathcal{D}$ for each unknown pixel $z$ using the collected foreground and background samples. The word vector used for constituting the dictionary is a 6-D vector $[R\ G\ B\ L\ a\ b]^T$ consisting of the concatenation of the $RGB$ and $Lab$ color spaces, and is normalized to unit length. $\mathcal{D}$ is a matrix with each column corresponding to a word vector with respect to the candidate sample. Then, the alpha value of pixel $z$ is determined by sparse coding as

$$\beta = \underset{\beta}{argmin} \parallel v_z - \mathcal{D}\beta \parallel^2 \qquad s.t. \quad \parallel \beta \parallel_1 \leq 1;\ \beta \geq 0 \qquad (6)$$

where $v_z$ is the single vector at pixel $z$ composed of $(R_z, G_z, B_z, L_z, a_z, b_z)$. The sparse codes $\beta$ corresponding to words in the dictionary that belong to foreground sample set are added to form the alpha value for the unknown pixel.

$$\alpha_z = \sum_{p \in F_z} \beta_p \qquad (7)$$

where $F_z$ is the set of foreground samples of pixel $z$. Since the non-zero values in $\beta$ indicate the ratios of the corresponding sample colors in composing the color of unknown pixel, the sparse codes directly provide the alpha value.

The proposed method also takes advantage of the sparse coding to directly generate $\alpha$ from a bunch of candidate samples. Moreover, we take extra characteristics of the samples into consideration while sparse coding. The extra characteristics we use are spatial distances of the samples to the unknown pixel and the color variances of the clusters which generate the sample colors. The alpha value is determined by an objective function derived from a weighted sparse coding as

$$\beta = \underset{\beta}{argmin} \parallel v_z - \mathcal{D}\beta \parallel_2^2 + \lambda \parallel diag(\boldsymbol{w})\beta \parallel_1$$

$$s.t. \quad \parallel \beta \parallel_1 \leq 1; \quad \beta \geq 0$$

(8)

where $v_z$ and $\mathcal{D}$ have the same meaning as that in Eq. (6). $\lambda$ is a weighting parameter balancing the weights of the chromatic distortion and spatial statistics. $diag(\boldsymbol{w})$ is a diagonal matrix corresponding to vector $\boldsymbol{w}$ and indicates the weights of the words in the dictionary with respect to the characteristics of the corresponding samples, thus it is formulated as:

$$w_p = 1 - T_z(Y_p) \times U_z(Y_p)$$

(9)

where $T$ represents the spatial statistics of the image and $U$ indicates the color variances of the clusters.

The term $T_z$ measures the spatial distance of the sample $Y_p$ to the unknown pixel $z$ and is given by:

$$T_z(Y_p) = \begin{cases} exp(-\dfrac{\parallel z - Y_p^s \parallel}{Z_z^F}), & Y_p \in \mathcal{S}_z^F \\ exp(-\dfrac{\parallel z - Y_p^s \parallel}{Z_z^B}), & Y_p \in \mathcal{S}_z^B \end{cases} \quad p = 1, 2, \cdots, P \quad (10)$$

where $P$ is the size of the dictionary $\mathcal{D}$. $Z_z^F$ and $Z_z^B$ represent the mean spatial distances from the unknown pixel $z$ to all the candidate foreground and background samples of that pixel, respectively. Hence, the sparse codes tend to have high values for the words in $\mathcal{D}$ that are computed by spatially close samples to the unknown pixel.

The term $U_z$ forces the sparse codes be biased towards those samples that come from clusters with low color variances and is formulated as:

$$U_z(Y_p) = \begin{cases} exp(-(1 + \dfrac{\log_{10} Y_p^r}{M_F})), & Y_p \in \mathcal{S}_z^F \\ exp(-(1 + \dfrac{\log_{10} Y_p^r}{M_B})), & Y_p \in \mathcal{S}_z^B \end{cases} \quad p = 1, 2, \cdots, P \quad (11)$$

where $Y_p^r$ is the sum variances of each color channel in the cluster the sample $Y_p$ comes from. The scalars $M_F = max_{F_k \in \mathcal{S}_z^F}(|\log_{10} F_k^r|)$ and $M_B = max_{B_k \in B_z^F}(|\log_{10} B_k^r|)$ are used as scaling factors, which correspond to the maximum absolute logarithm of the sum variances in three color channels in clusters forming the foreground sample set and background sample set, respectively.

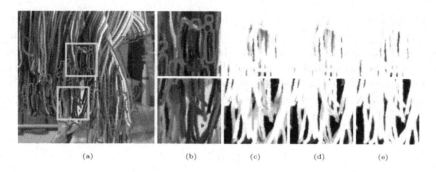

**Fig. 3.** Effect of spatial statistics and color variances. (a) Original image. (b) Zoomed areas. Estimated matte with (c) $\lambda = 0$ and (d) $\lambda = 0.0025$. (e) Ground truth mattes (Color figure online)

The optimization of Eq. (8) can be solved as quadratic programming problem. We use a variant of active-set algorithm [25] that can benefit from the sparsity solution [26] to solve the optimization problem. Once the codes $\beta$ are generated, the alpha value of pixel $z$ could be obtained using Eq. (7).

Figure 3 shows the effect of taking spatial statistics and color variances into consideration while estimating alpha matte. The original image is shown in Fig. 3(a) with corresponding foreground and background boundaries. Zoomed areas are shown in Fig. 3(b). Figure 3(c) shows the alpha mattes of zoomed areas obtained with $\lambda = 0$ and (d) with $\lambda = 0.0025$ in Eq. (8). The ground truth mattes of zoomed areas are shown in Fig. 3(e). As it can be seen, combining chromatic distortion, spatial statistics and color variances into a weighted spare coding framework provides more accurate alpha matte than just using chromatic distortion [17].

### 3.4   Pre and Post-processing

Akin to recent sampling-based matting approaches [16–18], we adopt some pre- and post-processing steps on the proposed method.

**Expansion of Known Regions:** To obtain a more refined trimap, the proposed method uses a pre-processing step to extrapolate known foreground and known background regions into the unknown regions based on certain chromatic and spatial thresholds. An unknown pixel $z$ is considered as foreground if, there exists a pixel $r \in F$ satisfying

$$(\| z - r \| < E_{thr}) \wedge (\| I_z - I_r \| \le C_{thr} - \| z - r \|)) \tag{12}$$

where $E_{thr}$ and $C_{thr}$ are threshold in spatial and color spaces, respectively. A similar formulation is applied to expand the background regions.

**Local Smoothing:** As a post-processing, we perform local smoothing on the initial alpha matte estimated by weighted sparse coding to obtain a smooth matte using a modified version of the Laplacian matting model [2] adopted in [13]. Hence, the final alpha matte is optimized with a cost function consisting of the data term $\hat{\alpha}$ and a confidence value $f$ together with a local smoothness term expressed by matting Laplacian given by:

$$\alpha = \underset{\alpha}{argmin}\, \alpha^T L \alpha + (\alpha - \hat{\alpha})^T (\varepsilon \Sigma + \gamma \Gamma)(\alpha - \hat{\alpha}) \tag{13}$$

where $\hat{\alpha}$ is the initial alpha matte generated using Eq. (7). $L$ is the matting Laplacian defined in [2]. $\varepsilon$ is a large weighting parameter penalizing the divergence of the alpha values of the known pixels and $\gamma$ is a constant value denoting the relative importance of the data and smoothness terms. The data term imposes the final alpha matte to be close to the initial alpha matte $\hat{\alpha}$ and the matting Laplacian enforce local smoothing. $\Sigma$ is a diagonal matrix with values 1 for known foreground and background pixels and 0 for unknown pixels, while the diagonal matrix $\Gamma$ has values 0 for known pixels and $f$ for unknown pixels. The confidence value $f_z$ at a given pixel $z$ is computed by:

$$f_z = R_z \times C_z \tag{14}$$

$$R_z = exp(- \parallel v_z - \mathcal{D}\beta \parallel) \tag{15}$$

where $R_z$ measures the deviation in reconstructing the input single vector based on sparse coefficients; $C_z$ measures the distortion between estimated color and observed color which has been explained in Eq. (4).

## 4 Experimental Results

In this section, we first assess the effect of $\lambda$ in Eq. (8). Then the performance of the proposed matting method is evaluated on a benchmark dataset [27]. It consists of 27 training images and 8 testing images. The training images have two types of trimaps: small and large while the testing images have three types of trimaps: small, large and user defined which are available at www.alphamatting. com. The ground-truth alpha mattes for the training set are publicly available and hidden from the public for testing images. An independent quantitative evaluation is provided in terms of the mean squared error (MSE), the sum of absolute difference (SAD), the gradient error and the connectivity error. Finally, we evaluate the effectiveness of the proposed sampling method in dealing with missing out true samples problem.

### 4.1 Effect of Parameter $\lambda$

To verify the effectiveness of our weighted sparse coding in generating alpha value in a quantitative manner, we evaluate the average MSE values over all the training images with all trimaps on the benchmark dataset with different

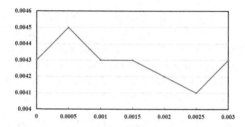

**Fig. 4.** Effect of $\lambda$ on the performance. Plot shows average MSE values over all training images and all trimaps

values of $\lambda$, and is shown in Fig. 4. When $\lambda = 0$, the objective function used to estimate alpha matte becomes the same to that in [17]. As it can be seen in Fig. 4, our objective function considers both chromatic distortion and spatial statistics performs better than that in [17] which only considers chromatic distortion when $\lambda$ is set properly. In the experiments, $\lambda$ is set to 0.0025 as it provides the minimum MSE value for the training set.

## 4.2 Evaluation on Benchmark Dataset

Table 1 shows the quantitative evaluation of the proposed matting approach compared with current matting methods via the alpha matting website [27]. Only ten best preforming methods are shown in the table. We report the average rankings over the 8 testing images according to SAD, MSE and gradient error metrics. "Average small/large/user ranks" represent the average ranks over images for each of the three types of trimaps. The overall rank is the average over all the

**Table 1.** Evaluation of matting methods on the benchmark dataset [27] with three trimaps with respect to SAD, MSE and Gradient error metrics

| Sum of Absolute Difference | | | | | Mean Square Error | | | | | Gradient Error | | | | |
|---|---|---|---|---|---|---|---|---|---|---|---|---|---|---|
| Method | overall rank | avg. small rank | avg. large rank | avg. user rank | Method | overall rank | avg. small rank | avg. large rank | avg. user rank | Method | overall rank | avg. small rank | avg. large rank | avg. user rank |
| 1.Proposed | 10.2 | 14 | **6.3** | **10.4** | 1.LNSP | 8.8 | **6.3** | **8.1** | 12.1 | 1.KL-D | 10.5 | 9.1 | 8.4 | 14.1 |
| 2.LNSP | 10.5 | **7** | 10 | 14.5 | 2.KL-D | 11.9 | 11.5 | 10.3 | 13.9 | 2.LNSP | 10.7 | **8.3** | 10 | 13.8 |
| 3.KL-D | 11.8 | 11.3 | 10.6 | 13.6 | 3.CCM | 12.2 | 15.3 | 12.1 | **9.1** | 3.Compre | 11.8 | 12.1 | 11 | 12.4 |
| 4.Compre | 13.5 | 11.3 | 13.5 | 15.8 | 4.Compre | 13.3 | 12.3 | 13 | 14.5 | 4.CCM | 13.8 | 16.5 | 13.5 | **11.5** |
| 5.IT | 13.9 | 15.4 | 13.1 | 13.1 | 5.SVR | 13.5 | 17.5 | 11.9 | 11.1 | 5.SVR | 14 | 16.6 | 15.1 | 10.3 |
| 6.CWCT | 14.3 | 14.8 | 14.8 | 13.3 | 6.CWCT | 14.6 | 14.5 | 15.4 | 13.9 | 6.SparseCoded | 14 | 16 | 12.8 | 13.4 |
| 7.SVR | 14.4 | 17.1 | 14 | 12 | 7.Proposed | 15.8 | 19.4 | 9.5 | 18.4 | 7.Global | 15 | 14.9 | 16.8 | 13.4 |
| 8.SparseCoded | 14.8 | 18.1 | 15.3 | 11.1 | 8.WCT | 17.1 | 15.9 | 18.4 | 17.1 | 8.ImprovedC | 15.3 | 16.9 | 16.8 | 12.3 |
| 9.WCT | 16.6 | 14.5 | 18.3 | 17 | 9.SparseCoded | 17.2 | 19.4 | 18.3 | 13.9 | 9.Shared | 15.5 | 15.8 | 17 | 13.8 |
| 10.CCM | 16.7 | 19.5 | 16.4 | 14.3 | 10.Global | 17.8 | 13.4 | 21.6 | 18.5 | 10.Proposed | 16.2 | 19 | **7.3** | 22.4 |

testing images for all types of trimaps. The proposed method ranks first with respect to SAD with a overall rank of 10.2. We achieve the best ranking among all the methods with respect to SAD and gradient error on the large trimap and ranks second with respect to MSE (the first is LNSP [22]). The proposed method also ranks first on the user trimap with respect to SAD error. This implies that the proposed method are more robust to the fineness of the trimap than previous sampling-based methods since it weakens the spatial assumptions while sampling for unknown pixels.

Figure 5 shows the visual comparison of our approach with the recent matting methods [16–18, 22] on the *doll*, *plant* and *pineapple* images from the benchmark dataset. Original images and zoomed areas are shown in Fig. 5(a) and (b) respectively. The estimated mattes for zoomed areas by recent matting methods of LNSP [22], Comprehensive sampling [16], Sparse coding matting [17], KL-Divergence based sparse sampling [18] and ours are shown in Fig. 5(c–g). The *doll* (first and second rows) is placed in front of a highly textured background which makes it hard for sampling-based approaches to discriminate between foreground and background as shown in Fig. 5(c,d,f). Sparse coding matting [17] which employs the success of sparse coding proposes a better matte as shown in Fig. 5(e). The same problem happens on the first zoomed area of *plant* (third row) where some characters of the background are considered as foreground as

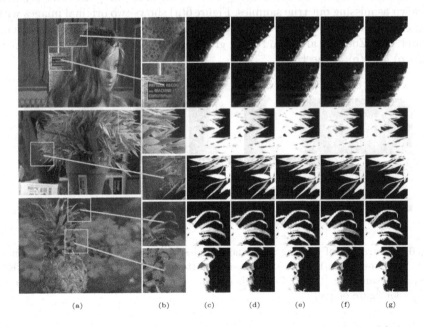

(a)          (b)     (c)     (d)     (e)     (f)     (g)

**Fig. 5.** Visual Comparison of our approach with other matting methods. (a) Original image, (b) Zoomed areas. (c) LNSP [22], (d) Comprehensive sampling [16], (e) Sparse coding matting [17], (f) KL-Divergence based sparse sampling [18] and (g) proposed approach (Color figure online)

shown in Fig. 5(c,d,f). Sampling-based methods typically rely on certain spatial assumptions while collecting samples from known regions which might lead to missing out true foreground and background colors for some unknown pixels such as *pineapple* and the second zoomed area in *plant* (last three rows) as shown in Fig. 5(d). Although KL-Divergence sampling approach formulates sampling as a sparse subset selection problem, it collects the same set of samples for all the unknown pixels which also leads to missing out true samples as seen in Fig. 5(f).

The proposed method builds a representative sample set for all unknown pixels to cover all true samples, and then selects a set of candidate samples for each unknown pixel via an objective function. Moreover, inspired by sparse coding matting [17], we use a weighted sparse coding to generate alpha value directly from a bunch of foreground and background samples which avoids the limitation that the quality of the alpha matte is highly rely on the goodness of a single simple pair. These two characteristics make the proposed approach extract out a visually superior matte in these ambiguous areas as shown in Fig. 5(g).

### 4.3    Missing True Samples

Previous sampling-based image matting methods typically rely on spatial closeness while collecting samples which would fail to generate accurate alpha matte when the true samples are not spatially close to the unknown pixels, this problem is known as missing out true samples. Figure 6(a) shows two original images with their corresponding foreground and background boundaries from the benchmark dataset [27]. Zoomed areas and their ground truth alpha mattes are shown in Fig. 6(b) and (c), respectively.

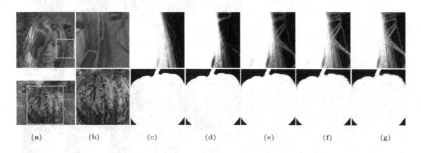

**Fig. 6.** Illustration of missing out true samples. (a) Original images. (b) Zoomed areas. (c) Ground truth mattes. Estimated mattes by (d) Proposed method, (e) KL-Divergence sampling [18] (f) Comprehensive sampling [16] and (g) Global Sampling [14] (Color figure online)

In the zoomed area of *doll girl* image (first row), the true background colors of the gray pixels in the unknown region are far away from the them, thus the set of background samples by comprehensive and global sampling methods do no contain the gray colors. They wrongly estimate these pixels as foreground as shown in the first row of Fig. 6(f) and (g). The *pumpkin* image (second row) has a complex foreground and the distribution of the true foreground samples do not satisfy the spatial closeness assumption, thus are missed out in the foreground sample set collected by comprehensive and global sampling methods for some parts of the pumpkin. They are mistakenly estimated as background as shown in the second row of Fig. 6(f) and (g). KL-Divergence sampling select a sparse set of foreground and background samples which might also miss out true samples as shown in Fig. 6(e). The proposed method collects a relatively large and representative set of samples from all the known regions and selects a candidate set of samples for each unknown pixels based on both color and spatial statistics to solve the problem of missing out true samples. The visual comparison between ground truth mattes and estimated ones by proposed method is shown in Fig. 6(c) and (d), demonstrating that the sampling strategy proposed in this paper could well solve the missing out true samples problem.

## 5  Conclusions

A robust sampling-based image matting approach is proposed that applies a new sampling strategy to build a representative set of samples from known regions. Rather than collecting samples according to spatial assumptions or selecting a uniform sample set for all unknown pixels, we select samples for each unknown pixel based on both color and spatial statistic to solve the problem of missing out true samples. Moreover, based on weighted sparse coding, we adopt a new objective function to generate alpha values from a bunch of candidate samples directly to remove the restriction of a single (F,B) pair in determining the alpha value. Finally, the quality of the estimated matte is refined using a local smooth priors. Experimental results show that the proposed method achieves more robust performance than state-of-the-art approaches evaluated on a benchmark dataset.

**Acknowledgements.** This work is supported by the funds of National Natural Science Foundation of China (No. 61572058) and National High Technology Research and Development Program of China (No. 2015AA016402). The authors would like to thank the anonymous reviewers for their insightful comments and suggestions on this work.

## References

1. Porter, T., Duff, T.: Compositing digital images. In: Proceedings of 11th Annual Conference on Computer Graphics and Interactive Techniques, SIGGRAPH 1984, pp. 253–259. ACM, New York (1984)
2. Levin, A., Lischinski, D., Weiss, Y.: A closed form solution to natural image matting. In: Proceedings of 2006 IEEE Conference on Computer Vision and Pattern Recognition, vol. 1, pp. 61–68, June 2006
3. Levin, A., Rav-Acha, A., Lischinski, D.: Spectral matting. In: 2007 IEEE Conference on Computer Vision and Pattern Recognition, pp. 1–8, June 2007

4. Juan, O., Keriven, R.: Trimap segmentation for fast and user-friendly alpha matting. In: Paragios, N., Faugeras, O., Chan, T., Schnörr, C. (eds.) VLSM 2005. LNCS, vol. 3752, pp. 186–197. Springer, Heidelberg (2005). doi:10.1007/11567646_16

5. Sun, J., Jia, J., Tang, C.K., Shum, H.Y.: Poisson matting. ACM Trans. Graph. 23(3), 315–321 (2004)

6. Bai, X., Sapiro, G.: A geodesic framework for fast interactive image and video segmentation and matting. In: IEEE 11th International Conference on Computer Vision, pp. 1–8, October 2007

7. Singaraju, D., Rother, C., Rhemann, C.: New appearance models for natural image matting. In: Proceedings of 2009 IEEE Conference on Computer Vision and Pattern Recognition, pp. 659–666, June 2009

8. He, K., Sun, J., Tang, X.: Fast matting using large kernel matting Laplacian matrices. In: Proceedings of 2010 IEEE Conference on Computer Vision and Pattern Recognition, pp. 2165–2172, June 2010

9. Rhemann, C., Rother, C., Rav-Acha, A., Sharp, T.: High resolution matting via interactive trimap segmentation. In: Proceedings of 2008 IEEE Conference on Computer Vision and Pattern Recognition, pp. 1–8, June 2008

10. Chen, Q., Li, D., Tang, C.K.: KNN matting. In: Proceedings of 2012 IEEE Conference on Computer Vision and Pattern Recognition, pp. 869–876, June 2012

11. Chuang, Y.Y., Curless, B., Salesin, D., Szeliski, R.: A Bayesian approach to digital matting. In: Proceedings of 2001 IEEE Conference on Computer Vision and Pattern Recognition, vol. 2, pp. 264–271 (2001)

12. Berman, A., Dadourian, A., Vlahos, P.: Method for removing from an image the background surrounding a selected object. US Patent 6134346 (2000)

13. Gastal, E.S.L., Oliveira, M.M.: Shared sampling for real-time alpha matting. Comput. Graph. Forum 29(2), 575–584 (2010)

14. He, K., Rhemann, C., Rother, C., Tang, X., Sun, J.: A global sampling method for alpha matting. In: Proceedings of 2011 IEEE Conference on Computer Vision and Pattern Recognition, pp. 2049–2056, June 2011

15. Shahrian, E., Rajan, D.: Weighted color and texture sample selection for image matting. In: Proceedings of 2012 IEEE Conference on Computer Vision and Pattern Recognition, pp. 718–725, June 2012

16. Shahrian, E., Rajan, D., Price, B., Cohen, S.: Improving image matting using comprehensive sampling sets. In: Proceedings of 2013 IEEE Conference on Computer Vision and Pattern Recognition, pp. 636–643, June 2013

17. Johnson, J., Rajan, D., Cholakkal, H.: Sparse codes as alpha matte. In: Proceedings of British Machine Vision Conference. BMVA Press (2014)

18. Karacan, L., Erdem, A., Erdem, E.: Image matting with KL-divergence based sparse sampling. In: IEEE 15th International Conference on Computer Vision, pp. 424–432 (2015)

19. Wang, J., Cohen, M.: An iterative optimization approach for unified image segmentation and matting. In: IEEE 10th International Conference on Computer Vision, vol. 2, pp. 936–943, October 2005

20. Guan, Y., Chen, W., Liang, X., Ding, Z., Peng, Q.: Easy matting - a stroke based approach for continuous image matting. Comput. Graph. Forum 25, 567–576 (2006)

21. Wang, J., Cohen, M.: Optimized color sampling for robust matting. In: Proceedings of 2007 IEEE Conference on Computer Vision and Pattern Recognition, pp. 1–8, June 2007

22. Chen, X., Zou, D., Zhou, S., Zhao, Q., Tan, P.: Image matting with local and nonlocal smooth priors. In: Proceedings of 2013 IEEE Conference on Computer Vision and Pattern Recognition, pp. 1902–1907, June 2013

23. Zhu, Q., Shao, L., Li, X., Wang, L.: Targeting accurate object extraction from an image: a comprehensive study of natural image matting. IEEE Trans. Neural Netw. Learn. Syst. **26**(2), 185–207 (2015)

24. Hartigan, J.A., Wong, M.A.: A k-means clustering algorithm. Appl. Stat. **28**(1), 100–108 (1979)

25. Chen, Y., Mairal, J., Harchaoui, Z.: Fast and robust archetypal analysis for representation learning. CoRR abs/1405.6472 (2014)

26. Bach, F., Jenatton, R., Mairal, J., Obozinski, G.: Optimization with sparsity-inducing penalties. Found. Trends Mach. Learn. **4**(1), 1–106 (2012)

27. Rhemann, C., Rother, C., Wang, J., Gelautz, M., Kohli, P., Rott, P.: A perceptually motivated online benchmark for image matting. In: Proceedings of 2009 IEEE Conference on Computer Vision and Pattern Recognition, pp. 1826–1833, June 2009

# Fundamental Matrices from Moving Objects Using Line Motion Barcodes

Yoni Kasten$^{(\boxtimes)}$, Gil Ben-Artzi, Shmuel Peleg, and Michael Werman

School of Computer Science and Engineering,
The Hebrew University of Jerusalem, Jerusalem, Israel
yonikasten@cs.huji.ac.il

**Abstract.** Computing the epipolar geometry between cameras with very different viewpoints is often very difficult. The appearance of objects can vary greatly, and it is difficult to find corresponding feature points. Prior methods searched for corresponding epipolar lines using points on the convex hull of the silhouette of a single moving object. These methods fail when the scene includes multiple moving objects. This paper extends previous work to scenes having multiple moving objects by using the "Motion Barcodes", a temporal signature of lines. Corresponding epipolar lines have similar motion barcodes, and candidate pairs of corresponding epipoar lines are found by the similarity of their motion barcodes. As in previous methods we assume that cameras are relatively stationary and that moving objects have already been extracted using background subtraction.

**Keywords:** Fundamental matrix · Epipolar geometry · Motion barcodes · Epipolar lines · Multi-camera calibration

## 1 Introduction

### 1.1 Related Work

Calibrating a network of cameras is typically carried out by finding corresponding points between views. Finding such correspondences often fails when the cameras have very different viewpoints, since objects and background do not look similar across these views. Previous approaches to solve this problem utilized points on convex hull of the silhouette of a moving foreground object.

Sinha and Pollefeys [1] used silhouettes to calibrate a network of cameras, assuming a single moving silhouette in a video. Each RANSAC iteration takes a different frame and samples two pairs of corresponding tangent lines to the convex hull of the silhouette [2]. The intersection of each pair of lines proposes an epipole.

Ben-Artzi et al. [3] proposed an efficient way to accelerate Sinha's method. Generalizing the concept of Motion Barcodes [4] to lines, they proposed using the best pair of matching tangent lines between the two views from each frame.

© Springer International Publishing AG 2016
B. Leibe et al. (Eds.): ECCV 2016, Part II, LNCS 9906, pp. 220–228, 2016.
DOI: 10.1007/978-3-319-46475-6_14

The quality of line correspondence was determined by the normalized cross correlation of the Motion Barcodes of the lines.

Both methods above [1,3] fail when there are multiple moving objects in the scene, as they are based on the convex hull of all the moving objects in the image. In the example shown in Fig. 1, objects that appear only in one of the cameras have a destructive effect on the convex hull. Our current paper presents an approach that does not use the convex hull, and can be used with videos having multiple moving objects.

Camera A                Camera B

**Fig. 1.** Using the convex hull of moving objects fails in scenes with multiple objects. In this case the convex hull (*red polygon*) is very different on these two corresponding views, as different objects are visible from the cameras. (Color figure online)

In other related work, Meingast et al. [5] computed essential matrices between each pair of cameras from image trajectories of moving objects. They used the image centroids of the objects as corresponding points. However, since for most objects and most different views the centroids do not represent the same 3D point, this computation is error prone.

Other methods assumed that the objects are moving on a plane [6], or assume that the objects are people walking on a plane, for both single camera calibration [7,8] and two camera calibration [9].

### 1.2   Motion Barcodes of Lines

We address the case of synchronized stationary cameras viewing a scene with moving objects. Following background subtraction [10] we obtain a binary video, where "0" represents static background and "1" moving objects.

Given a video of $N$ binary frames, the Motion Barcode of a given image line $l$ [3] is a binary vector $b_l$ in $\{0,1\}^N$. $b_l(i) = 1$ iff a silhouette, pixel with value 1, of a foreground object is incident to line $l$ in the $i^{th}$ frame. An example of a Motion Barcode is shown in Fig. 2.

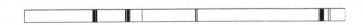

**Fig. 2.** A motion barcode $b$ of a line $l$ is a vector in $\{0,1\}^N$. The value of $b_l(i)$ is "1" when a moving object intersects the line in frame $i$ (*black entries*) and "0" otherwise (*white entries*).

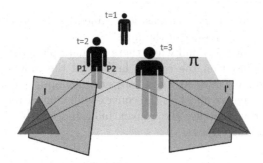

**Fig. 3.** Illustration of a scene with a moving object viewed by two video cameras. The lines $l$ and $l'$ are corresponding epipolar lines, and $\pi$ is the 3D epipolar plane that projects to $l$ and $l'$. At time $t = 1$ the object does not intersect the plane $\pi$, and thus does not intersect $l$ or $l'$ in the video. At times $t = 2, 3$ the object intersects the plane $\pi$, so the projections of this object on the cameras does intersect the epipolar lines $l$ and $l'$. The motion barcodes of both $l$ and $l'$ is $(0, 1, 1)$

The case of a moving object seen by two cameras is illustrated in Fig. 3. If the object intersects the epipolar plane $\pi$ at frame $i$, and does not intersect the plane $\pi$ at frame $j$, both Motion Barcodes of lines $l$ and $l'$ will be $1, 0$ at frames $i, j$ respectively. Corresponding epipolar lines therefore have highly correlated Motion Barcodes.

### 1.3    Similarity Score Between Two Motion Barcodes

It was suggested in [4] that a good similarity measure between motion barcodes $b$ and $b'$ is their normalized cross correlation.

$$corr(b, b') = \sum_{i=1}^{N} \frac{(b(i) - mean(b)) \cdot (b'(i) - mean(b'))}{\|b - mean(b)\|_2 \|b' - mean(b')\|_2} \tag{1}$$

### 1.4    Overall Structure of the Paper

Our camera calibration approach includes two steps. The first step, described in Sect. 2, finds candidates for corresponding epipolar lines between two cameras. The second step, Sect. 3, describes how a fundamental matrix between these two cameras is computed from those candidates. Section 4 presents our experiments.

## 2    Corresponding Epipolar Lines Candidates

Given 2 synchronized videos recorded by a pair of stationary cameras, $A$ and $B$, we want to compute their Fundamental Matrix $F$. The Fundamental Matrix $F$ satisfies for each pair of corresponding points, $x \in A$ and $x' \in B$:

$$x'^T F x = 0. \tag{2}$$

The $F$ matrix maps each point $x \in A$ to an epipolar line $l' = Fx$ in $B$ so that the point $x'$ is on the line $l'$. Any point in image $B$ that lies on the line $l'$ including $x'$ is transformed to a line $l = F^T x'$ such that $x$ is on the line $l$. $l$ and $l'$ are corresponding epipolar lines. $F$ can be computed from points correspondences or from epipolar line correspondences [11].

In previous methods [1,3] the convex hull of the silhouette of a moving object was used to search for corresponding epipolar lines.

Our proposed process to find candidates for corresponding epipolar lines does not use the silhouette of a moving object, and can therefore be applied also in cases of multiple moving objects.

Given a video, lines are selected by sampling pairs of points on the border of the image and connecting them. For each line, the Motion Barcode is computed. We continue only with informative lines, i.e. lines having enough zeros and ones in their motion barcode.

Given two cameras A and B, Motion Barcodes are generated for all selected lines in each camera, resulting $n_1$ vectors in $\{0,1\}^N$ for Camera A, and $n_2$ vectors in $\{0,1\}^N$ for Camera B, where $N$ is the number of frames in the video.

The $n_1 \times n_2$ correlation matrix of the barcodes of the lines selected from Camera A with the lines selected from Camera B is computed using Eq. 1. The goal is to find corresponding line pairs from Camera A and Camera B. 1, 000 line pairs are selected using the correlation matrix as follows. For visual results see Fig. 4.

- If the correlation of a pair of lines is in the mutual top 3 of each other, i.e. top 3 in both row and column, it is considered a candidate.
- The 1,000 candidate pairs with the highest correlations are taken as corresponding epipolar lines candidates.

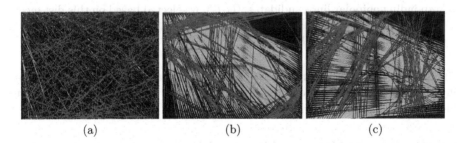

(a)                    (b)                    (c)

Fig. 4. An example of the effect of filtering candidate pairs using motion barcode similarity. Most datasets are very similar. (a) Initial candidate lines in Camera A are randomly distributed. (b) Candidate lines in Camera A having a similar motion barcode to lines in Camera B, as described in Sect. 2. Most mismatches were removed, and correct epipolar lines dominate. (c) Same as (b), showing lines in Camera B.

## 3  Fundamental Matrix from Corresponding Lines

Given a set of candidate corresponding pairs of epipolar lines between cameras $A$ and $B$, our goal is to find the fundamental matrix $F$ between the cameras.

Experimentally, of the 1000 candidates for corresponding epipolar lines described in Sect. 2, about half are correct. As not all of our candidates are real correspondences the algorithm continues using a RANSAC approach.

In each RANSAC trial, two pairs of candidate corresponding epipolar lines are selected. This gives two candidates for epipolar lines in each camera, and the epipole candidate for this camera is the intersection of these two epipolar lines. Next, an additional pair of corresponding epipolar lines is found from lines incident to these epipoles. The homography $H$ between corresponding epipolar lines is computed from these three pairs of epipolar lines. This is described in detail in Sect. 3.1.

The proposed homography $H$ gets a consistency score depending on the number of inliers that $H$ transformed successfully as described in Sect. 3.2.

Given the homography $H$, and the epipole $e'$ in $B$, the fundamental matrix $F$ is [11]:

$$F = [e']_x H^{-T} \tag{3}$$

### 3.1  Computing the Epipolar Line Homography

We compute the Epipolar Line Homography using RANSAC. We sample pairs of corresponding epipolar line candidates with a probability proportional to the correlation of their Motion Barcodes as in Eq. 1. Given 2 sampled pairs $(l_1, l_1')$ and $(l_2, l_2')$, corresponding epipole candidates are computed by: $e = l_1 \times l_2$ in Camera A, and $e' = l_1' \times l_2'$ in Camera B. Given $e$ and $e'$, the distances from these epipoles of each of the 1,000 candidate pairs is computed. A third pair of corresponding epipolar line candidates, $(l_3, l_3')$, is selected based on this distance:

$$(l_3, l_3') = \operatorname*{arg\,min}_{(l_i, l_i') \in \{candidates\} \setminus \{(l_1, l_1'), (l_2, l_2')\}} d(l_i, e) + d(l_i', e') \tag{4}$$

The homography $H$ between the epipolar pencils is calculated by the homography DLT algorithm [11], using the 3 proposed pairs of corresponding epipolar lines.

### 3.2  Consistency Measure of Proposed Homography

Given the homography $H$, a consistency measure with all epipolar line candidates is calculated. This is done for each corresponding candidate pair $(l, l')$ by comparing the similarity between $l'$ and $\tilde{l}' = Hl$. A perfect consistency should give $l' \cong \tilde{l}'$.

Each candidate line $l$ in $A$ is transformed to $B$ using the homography $H$ giving $\tilde{l}' = Hl$. We measure the similarity in $B$ between $l'$ and $\tilde{l}'$ as the area between the lines (illustrated in Fig. 5).

The candidate pair $(l, l')$ is considered an inlier relative to the homography $H$ if the area between $l'$ and $\tilde{l}'$ is smaller than a predefined threshold. In the experiments in Sect. 4 this threshold was taken to be 3 pixels times the width of the image. The consistency score of $H$ is the number of inliers among all candidate lines.

**Fig. 5.** Illustration of our distance measure between two lines. The distance measure between line 1 (*green line*) and line 2 (*blue line*) is the image area enclosed between the two lines (*yellow area*). (Color figure online)

## 4   Experiments

We tested our method on both synthetic and real video sequences. We created two synthetic datasets: *cubes* and *thin cubes*, using the Model Renderer that was developed by Assif and Hassner and was used in [12]. Each Cube dataset contains multiple views of a synthetic scene with flying cubes, while *thin cubes* dataset has smaller cubes. Background subtraction is done automatically using the tool. As a real dataset we used PETS2009 [13], using [10] for background subtraction. All datasets have 800 synchronized video frames, recorded by multiple cameras.

These datasets cannot be calibrated using matching of image features (e.g. SIFT), since there is no overlapping background between views. The datasets cannot be calibrated by [1,3] since they have multiple objects, causing problems with the convex hull. The cubes datasets can not be calibrated by [6–9] since the assumption of planar motion does not hold.

The approach described in Sect. 2 was applied to each pair of cameras from each dataset. Initial lines were generated by uniformly sampling two points on the border of Cameras A and B, where Every two points sampled define a line passing through the image.

### 4.1   Consistency of the Epipolar Line Pairs Candidates

Using the algorithm from Sect. 2, 1,000 pairs of corresponding epipolar lines candidates were generated.

The simplest distance measure between a candidate line to a true epipolar line is the distance of the candidate line from the true epipole. But this distance does not take into account the distance of the epipole from the image, and is inappropriate for epipoles that are far from the image. Instead, we measure the image area between the candidate line and a true epipolar line: the epipolar line going through the midpoint of the candidate line. This distance measure is illustrated in Fig. 5.

If this area is smaller than 3 times image length then the candidate line is considered a true positive. We call a pair of corresponding epipolar lines true if both lines are true. For each pair of cameras in each dataset we measured the true positives rate from all the 1,000 candidates, after removing the lines of motion (Sect. 4.2). The average rate of true positives from each dataset is as follows: *thin cubes*: 67.8 %, *cubes*: 71.67 % and *pets2009*: 37.81 %.

## 4.2   Multiple Objects Moving Same Straight Path

In some cases, e.g. busy roads, many objects in the scene may move in the same straight line. The projection of those lines on the video frames are straight lines. This may result in a high correspondence between two non epipolar lines, as both will have similar Motion Barcodes. To overcome this problem, we create a motion heat map by summing all binary motion frames of each video to a single image. Candidate epipolar lines pairs, where both substantially overlap lines with heavy traffic in their corresponding images, are removed from consideration. See Fig. 6.

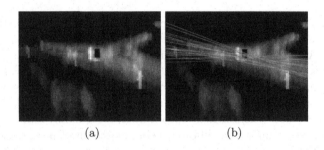

(a)                                   (b)

**Fig. 6.** Detection of motion along lines for Camera 1 of Pets2009 dataset. (a) Heat map obtained by summing the segmented frames over time. (b) Line detection on the heat map gives motion along lines. Lines close to these lines will not be used as epipolar lines.

## 4.3   Finding Fundamental Matrices

After completing the procedure in Sect. 2, we have 1,000 candidates for corresponding epipolar lines for each pair of cameras. Erroneous candidate lines, created by multiple objects moving in straight lines, are filtered out using the procedure in Sect. 4.2.

Given the candidates for corresponding epipolar lines, we perform up to 10,000 RANSAC iterations to compute the fundamental matrix according to Sect. 3. The quality of a generated fundamental matrix is determined by the number of inliers among all candidate pairs (See Sect. 3.2). We used the inlier threshold of 3 times the length of the image for all the datasets.

We checked our method on the 3 datasets which contains 37 pairs of cameras. Except for one camera pair in Pets2009 dataset, all fundamental matrices were found with high accuracy. One fundamental matrix for pair of cameras in Pets2009 could not be reproduced using our method. The reason is that all people in the scene are moving along one straight line which happens to be projected to the corresponding epipolar lines in the images of the cameras. Although we get a high correlation between lines that are close to one of the epipolar lines, since the objects barely cross the epipolar lines, there is no pencil of corresponding true epipolar lines in the image, essentially there is only one epipolar line pair which doesn't allow finding the true fundamental matrix.

For each resulting $F$ we checked its accuracy compared to the ground truth $F_{truth}$. The accuracy was measured using Symmetric Epipolar Distance [11]. By generating ground truth corresponding points using $F_{truth}$, the Symmetric Epipolar error of the resulting $F$, is measured on those points. Table 1 shows the results for the datasets that were tested. The table shows for each dataset, the average symmetric epipolar distance of all camera pairs, and how many camera pairs converged.

**Table 1.** Average symmetric epipolar distances for each dataset

| Dataset | Average error | Number of good pairs | |
|---------|---------------|----------------------|---|
| Cubes | 0.31 | 10/10 | |
| Thin Cubes | 0.79 | 21/21 | |
| Pets 2009 | 1.69 | 5/6 | |

## 5    Conclusions

A method has been presented to calibrate two cameras having a very different viewpoints. The method has the following steps:

- Given two pairs of corresponding points, they are used to efficiently find candidates pairs of corresponding epipolar lines.

- Using a RANSAC process, three corresponding pairs of epipolar lines are selected, and the fundamental matrix is computed.
- A method to evaluate the quality of the fundamental matrix has also been proposed.

The proposed method is very accurate.

This method can be applied to cases where other methods fail, such as two cameras with very different viewpoints observing a scene with multiple moving objects. (i) Point matching will fail as the appearance can be very different from very different viewpoints. (ii) Silhouette methods will work on very different viewpoints, but only if they include a single object.

**Acknowledgment.** This research was supported by Google, by Intel ICRI-CI, by DFG, and by the Israel Science Foundation.

# References

1. Sinha, S.N., Pollefeys, M.: Camera network calibration and synchronization from silhouettes in archived video. IJCV **87**(3), 266–283 (2010)
2. Cipolla, R., Giblin, P.: Visual Motion of Curves and Surfaces. Cambridge University Press, Cambridge (2000)
3. Ben-Artzi, G., Kasten, Y., Peleg, S., Werman, M.: Camera calibration from dynamic silhouettes using motion barcodes (2015). arXiv preprint arXiv:1506.07866
4. Ben-Artzi, G., Werman, M., Peleg, S.: Event retrieval using motion barcodes. In: 2015 IEEE International Conference on Image Processing (ICIP), pp. 2621–2625. IEEE (2015)
5. Meingast, M., Oh, S., Sastry, S.: Automatic camera network localization using object image tracks. In: 2007 IEEE 11th International Conference on Computer Vision, ICCV 2007, pp. 1–8. IEEE (2007)
6. Stein, G.P.: Tracking from multiple view points: self-calibration of space and time. In: 1999 IEEE Computer Society Conference on Computer Vision and Pattern Recognition, vol. 1. IEEE (1999)
7. Krahnstoever, N., Mendonca, P.R.: Bayesian autocalibration for surveillance. In: 2005 Tenth IEEE International Conference on Computer Vision, ICCV 2005, vol. 2, pp. 1858–1865. IEEE (2005)
8. Lv, F., Zhao, T., Nevatia, R.: Camera calibration from video of a walking human. IEEE Trans. Pattern Anal. Mach. Intell. **9**, 1513–1518 (2006)
9. Chen, T., Bimbo, A.D., Pernici, F., Serra, G.: Accurate self-calibration of two cameras by observations of a moving person on a ground plane. In: 2007 IEEE Conference on Advanced Video and Signal Based Surveillance, AVSS 2007, pp. 129–134. IEEE (2007)
10. Cucchiara, R., Grana, C., Piccardi, M., Prati, A.: Detecting moving objects, ghosts, and shadows in video streams. IEEE Trans. Pattern Anal. Mach. Intell. **25**(10), 1337–1342 (2003)
11. Hartley, R., Zisserman, A.: Multiple view geometry in computer vision (2003)
12. Hassner, T.: Viewing real-world faces in 3D. In: Proceedings of the IEEE International Conference on Computer Vision, pp. 3607–3614 (2013)
13. Pets-2009: Data set (2009). http://www.cvg.reading.ac.uk/pets2009/a.html

# Fashion Landmark Detection in the Wild

Ziwei Liu[1], Sijie Yan[1], Ping Luo[1,2(✉)], Xiaogang Wang[1,2], and Xiaoou Tang[1,2]

[1] Department of Information Engineering, The Chinese University of Hong Kong,
Hong Kong, China
{lz013,siyan,pluo,xtang}@ie.cuhk.edu.hk, xgwang@ee.cuhk.edu.hk
[2] Shenzhen Key Laboratory for Computer Vision and Pattern Recognition,
Shenzhen Institutes of Advanced Technology, CAS, Shenzhen, China

**Abstract.** Visual fashion analysis has attracted many attentions in the
recent years. Previous work represented clothing regions by either bounding boxes or human joints. This work presents fashion landmark detection or fashion alignment, which is to predict the positions of functional
key points defined on the fashion items, such as the corners of neckline,
hemline, and cuff. To encourage future studies, we introduce a fashion
landmark dataset (The dataset is available at http://mmlab.ie.cuhk.edu.
hk/projects/DeepFashion/LandmarkDetection.html.) with over 120K
images, where each image is labeled with eight landmarks. With this
dataset, we study fashion alignment by cascading multiple convolutional
neural networks in three stages. These stages gradually improve the accuracies of landmark predictions. Extensive experiments demonstrate the
effectiveness of the proposed method, as well as its generalization ability to pose estimation. Fashion landmark is also compared to clothing
bounding boxes and human joints in two applications, fashion attribute
prediction and clothes retrieval, showing that fashion landmark is a more
discriminative representation to understand fashion images.

**Keywords:** Clothes landmark detection · Cascaded deep convolutional
neural networks · Attribute prediction · Clothes retrieval

## 1 Introduction

Visual fashion analysis has drawn lots of attentions recently, due to its wide
spectrum of applications such as clothes recognition [1–3], retrieval [3–5], and
recommendation [6,7]. It is a challenging task because of the large variations
presented in the clothing items, such as the changes of poses, scales, and appearances. To reduce these variations, existing works tackled the problem by looking
for informative regions, *i.e.* detecting the clothes bounding boxes [1,2] or the
human joints [8,9]. We go beyond the above by studying a more discriminative
representation, fashion landmark, which is the key-point located at the functional region of clothes, for example the neckline and the cuff.

---

The first two authors contribute equally and share first authorship.

© Springer International Publishing AG 2016
B. Leibe et al. (Eds.): ECCV 2016, Part II, LNCS 9906, pp. 229–245, 2016.
DOI: 10.1007/978-3-319-46475-6_15

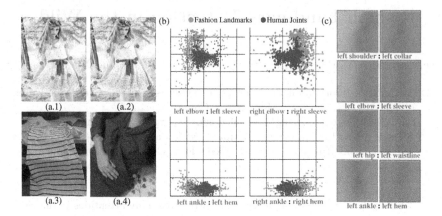

**Fig. 1.** Comparisons of fashion landmarks and human joints: (a.1) sample annotations for human joints, (a.2) sample annotations for fashion landmarks (a.3–4) typical deformation and scale variations present in clothing items, (b) spatial variances of human joints (in blue) and fashion landmarks (in green) and (c) appearance variances of human joints (in blue) and fashion landmarks (in green). (Color figure online)

This work addresses fashion landmark detection or fashion alignment in the wild. Different from human pose estimation, which detects human joints such as neck and elbows as shown in Fig. 1(a.1), fashion alignment localizes fashion landmarks as shown in (a.2). These landmarks facilitate fashion analysis in the sense that they not only implicitly capture bounding boxes of clothes, but also indicate their functional regions, which can better distinguish design/pattern/category of the clothes. Therefore, features extracted from these landmarks are more discriminative than those extracted from human joints. For example, when search for a dress with 'V-neck and fringed-hem', it is more desirable to extract features from collar and hemline.

To fully benchmark the task of fashion landmark detection, we select a large subset of images from the DeepFashion database [3] to constitute a fashion landmark dataset (FLD). These images have large pose and scale variations. With FLD, we show that fashion landmark detection in clothes images is a more challenging task than human joint detection in three aspects. First, clothes undergo *non-rigid deformations* or *scale variations* as shown in Fig. 1(a.3–4), while rigid deformations are usually presented in human joints. Second, fashion landmarks exhibit much larger *spatial variances* than human joints, as illustrated in Fig. 1(b), where we plot the positions of the landmarks and the relative human joints in the test set of the FLD dataset. For instance, the positions of 'left sleeve' are more diverse than those of the 'left elbow' in both the vertical and horizontal directions. Third, the local regions of fashion landmarks also have larger *appearance variances* than those of human joints. As shown in Fig. 1(c), we average the patches centered at the fashion landmarks and human joints respectively, resulting in several visual comparisons. The patterns of the mean patches of human joints are still recognizable, but those of the mean patches of fashion landmarks are not.

To tackle the above challenges, we propose a deep fashion alignment (DFA) framework, which cascades three deep convolutional networks (CNNs) for landmark estimation. It has three appealing properties. First, to ensure the CNNs have high discriminative powers, unlike existing works [10–14] that only estimated the landmarks' positions, we train the cascaded CNNs to predict both the landmarks' positions and the pseudo-labels, which encode the similarities between training samples to boost the estimation accuracy. In each stage of the network cascade, the scheme of pseudo-label is carefully designed to reduce different variations presented in the fashion images. Second, instead of training multiple networks for each body part as previous work did [10,15], the DFA framework trains CNNs using the full image as input to significantly reduce computations. Third, in the DFA framework, an auto-routing strategy is introduced to partition the challenging and easy samples, such that different samples can be handled by different branches of CNNs.

Extensive experiments demonstrate the effectiveness of the proposed method, as well as its generalization ability to pose estimation. Fashion landmark is also compared to clothing bounding boxes and human joints in two applications, fashion attribute prediction and clothes retrieval, showing that fashion landmark is a more discriminative representation to understand fashion images.

## 1.1   Related Work

**Visual Fashion Understanding.** Visual fashion understanding has been a long-pursuing topic due to the many human-centric applications it enables. Recent advances include predicting semantic attributes [3,8,9,16,17], clothes recognition and retrieval [2–4,18–20] and fashion trends discovery [6,7,21]. To better capture discriminative information in fashion items, previous works have explored the usage of full image [2], general object proposals [2], bounding boxes [9,17] and even masks [18,22–24]. However, these representations either lack sufficient discriminative ability or are too expensive to obtain. To overcome these drawbacks, we introduce the problem of clothes alignment in this work, which is a necessary step toward robust fashion recognition.

**Human Pose Estimation.** We further convert the problem of clothes alignment into fashion landmark estimation. Though there are no prior work in fashion landmarks, approaches from similar fields (*e.g.* human pose estimation [10,11,25–28]) serve as good candidates to explore. Recently, deep learning [10–12,29] has shown great advantages in locating human joints and there are generally two directions here. The first direction [10,13,30] utilizes the power of cascading for iterative error correction. DeepPose [10] employs devide-and-conquer strategy and designs a cascaded deep regression framework on part level while Iterative Error Feedback [13] emphasizes more on the target scheduling in each stage. The second direction [11,12,31,32], on the other hand, focuses on the explicit modeling of landmark relationships using graphical models. Chen *et al.* [11] proposed the combination of CNN and structural SVM [33] to model the tree-like relationships among landmarks while Thompson *et al.* [12] plugged Markov Random Field (MRF) [34] into CNN for joint training. Here, our framework attempts to absorb the advantages of both directions. The cascading and auto-routing mechanisms enable both stage-wise and branch-wise variation reductions while pseudo-labels encode multi-level sample relationships which depict typical global and local landmark configurations.

## 2   Fashion Landmark Dataset (FLD)

To benchmark fashion landmark detection, we select a subset of images with large pose and scale variations from DeepFashion database [3], to constitute FLD. We label and refine landmark annotations in FLD to make sure each image is correctly labeled with 8 fashion landmarks along with their visibility[1]. Overall, FLD contains more than $120K$ images. Sample images and annotations are shown in Fig. 2(a). To characterize the properties of FLD, we divide the images into five subsets according to the positions and visibility of their ground truth landmarks, including the subsets of normal/medium/large poses and medium/large zoom-ins. The 'normal' subset represents images with frontal

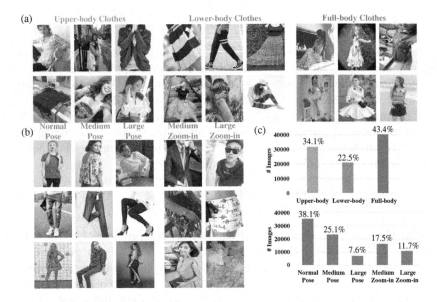

**Fig. 2.** Illustration of the Fashion Landmark Dataset (FLD): (a) sample images and annotations for different types of clothing items, including upper/lower/full-body clothes, (b) sample images and annotations for different subsets, including normal/medium/large poses and medium/large scales, (c) quantitative data distributions.

---

[1] Three states of visibility are defined for each landmark, including visible (located inside of the image and visible), invisible (inside of the image but occluded), and truncated/cut-off (outside of the image).

pose and no cut-off landmarks. The subsets of 'medium' and 'large' poses contain images with side or back views, while the subsets of 'medium' and 'large' zoom-ins contain clothing items with more than one or three cut-off landmarks, respectively. Sample images of the five subsets are illustrated in Fig. 2(b) and their statistics are demonstrated in Fig. 2(c), which shows that FLD contains substantial percentages of images with large poses/scales.

## 3  Our Approach

Fashion landmark exhibits large variations in both spatial and appearance domain (see Fig. 1(b, c)). Figure 2(c) further shows that more than 30 % images have large pose and zoom-in variations. To account for these challenges, we propose a deep fashion alignment (DFA) framework as shown in Fig. 3(a), which consists of three stages, where each stage subsequently refines previous predictions. Unlike the existing representative model for human joints prediction, such as DeepPose [10] as shown in (b), which trained multiple networks for all localized parts in each stage, the proposed DFA framework that functions on full image is able to achieve superior performance with much lower computations.

**Framework Overview.** As shown in Fig. 3(a), DFA has three stages. In each stage, VGG-16 [35] is employed as network architecture. In the first stage, DFA takes the raw image $I$ as input and predicts rough landmark positions, denoted as $\hat{l}^1$, as well as pseudo-labels, denoted as $\hat{f}^1$, which represent landmark configurations such as clothing categories and poses. In the second stage, both the input image $I$ and the predictions of stage-1, $\hat{l}^1$, are fed in. The whole network is

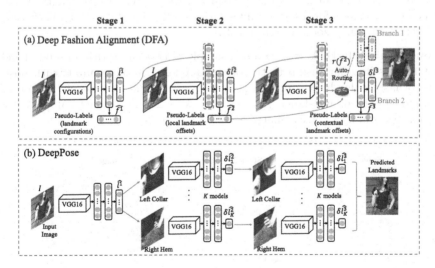

**Fig. 3.** Pipeline of (a) Deep Fashion Alignment (DFA) and (b) DeepPose [10]. DFA leverages pseudo-labels and auto-routing mechanism to reduce the large variations presented in fashion images with much less computational costs.

required to predict landmark offsets, signified as $\hat{\delta l}^2$, and pseudo-labels $\hat{f}^2$ that represent local landmark offsets. The landmark prediction of stage-2 is computed as $\hat{l}^2 = \hat{l}^1 + \hat{\delta l}^2$. The third stage has two CNNs as two branches, which have identical input and output. Similar to the second stage, each CNN employs image $I$ as input and learns to estimate landmark offsets $\hat{\delta l}^3$ and pseudo-labels $\hat{f}^3$, which contains information about contextual landmark offsets. In stage-3, each image is passed through one of these two branches. The selection of branch is determined by the predicted pseudo-labels $\hat{f}^2$ in stage-2. The final prediction is computed as $\hat{l}^3 = \hat{l}^2 + \hat{\delta l}^3$.

**Network Cascade.** Cascade [36] has been proven an effective technique for reducing variations sequentially in pose estimation [10]. Here, we build the DFA system by cascading three CNNs. The first CNN directly regresses landmark positions and visibility from input images, aided by pseudo-labels in the space of landmark configuration. These pseudo-labels are achieved by clustering absolute landmark positions, indicating different clothing categories and poses, as shown in Fig. 4 stage 1. For example, cluster 1 and 4 represents 'short T-shirt in front view' and 'long coat in side view', respectively. The second CNN takes both the input image and the predictions from stage-1 as input, and estimates the offsets that should be made to correct the predictions of the first stage. In this case, we are learning in the space of landmark offset. Thus, the pseudo-labels generated here represent typical error patterns and their magnitudes, as shown in Fig. 4 stage 2. For instance, cluster 1 represents the corrections should be made along upside and downside, while cluster 2 suggests left/right-direction corrections. In stage-3, we partition data into two subsets, according to the error patterns predicted in the second stage as shown in Fig. 4 stage 3, where branch one deals with 'easy' samples such as frontal T-shirt with different sleeve length, while branch two accounts for 'hard' samples such as selfie pose (cluster 1), back view (cluster 2) and large zoom-in (cluster 3).

**Pseudo-Label.** In DFA, each training sample is associated with a pseudo-label that reflects its relationship to the other samples. Let the ground truth positions of fashion landmarks denote as $l$, where $l_i$ specifies the pixel location of landmark $i$. The pseudo-label, $f(k) \in \mathbb{R}^{k \times 1}, k = 1 \ldots K$, of each sample $i$ is a $K$-dim vector and can be calculated as

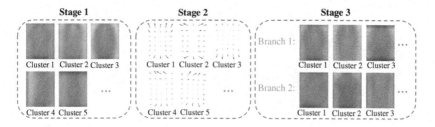

**Fig. 4.** Visualization of pseudo-labels obtained for each stage. Pseudo-labels in stage-1 indicate clothing categories and poses; pseudo-labels in stage-2 represent typical error patterns; pseudo-labels in stage-3 partition within 'easy' and 'hard' samples.

$$f(k) = \exp\left(-\frac{dist(i, C)}{T}\right), \tag{1}$$

where $dist(\cdot)$ is a distance measure. $C_k$ is a set of $k$ cluster centers, obtaining by k-means algorithm on the spaces of landmark coordinates (stage-1) or offsets (stage-2 and 3). $T$ is the temperature parameter to soften pseudo-labels. We adopt $K = 20$ for all three stages.

Here we explain the pseudo-label in each of the three stages. Cluster centers $C_k^1$ in stage-1 are obtained in landmark configuration space $l_i$, where $l_i$ is the ground truth landmark positions for sample $i$. Then pseudo-label $f_i^1$ of sample $i$ in stage-1 can be written as $f_i^1(k) = \exp\left(-\frac{\|l_i - C_k^1\|_2}{T}\right)$. We now have a landmark estimation $\hat{l}_i^1$ from stage-1 for sample $i$. In stage-2, we first define the landmark offset $\delta l_i^2 = \hat{l}_i^1 - l_i$, which is the correction should be made on stage-1 estimation. Cluster centers $C_k^2$ in stage-2 are obtained in landmark offset space $\delta l_i^2$. Similarly, pseudo-label $f_i^2$ of sample $i$ in stage-2 can be written as $f_i^2(k) = \exp\left(-\frac{\|\delta l_i^2 - C_k^2\|_2}{T}\right)$. Since outer product $\otimes$ of two offsets contains the correlations between different fashion landmarks (*e.g.* 'left collar' v.s. 'left sleeve'), we further include these contextual information into the pseudo-labels of stage-3 $f^3$. To make the results of outer product comparable, we convert them into vectors by stacking columns, which is denoted as $lin()$. The landmark offset of stage-3 is defined as $\delta l_i^3 = \hat{l}_i^2 - l_i$, where $\hat{l}_i^2 = \hat{l}_i^2 + \delta \hat{l}_i^2$ is the estimation made by stage-2. Thus, cluster centers $C_k^3$ in stage-3 are obtained in contextual offset space $\delta_{context} l_i^3 = lin\left(\delta l_i^3 \otimes \delta l_i^3\right)$. Similarly, pseudo-label $f_i^3$ of sample $i$ in stage-3 can be written as $f_i^3(k) = \exp\left(-\frac{\|\delta_{context} l_i^3 - C_k^3\|_2}{T}\right)$. The pseudo-labels used in each stage are summarized in Table 1.

**Table 1.** Summary of pseudo-labels used in each stage. $l_i$ is the ground truth landmark positions. $\hat{l}_i^1$ and $\hat{l}_i^2$ are the landmark estimations from stage-1 and 2, respectively. $\otimes$ is the outer product and $lin(\cdot)$ is the linearize operation.

| Stage | Clustering space | Indication | Dimension |
|---|---|---|---|
| 1 | $l_i$ | Landmark configuration | 20 |
| 2 | $\delta l_i^2 = \hat{l}_i^1 - l_i$ | Landmark offset | 20 |
| 3 | $\delta_{context} l_i^3 = lin\left(\delta l_i^3 \otimes \delta l_i^3\right)$ $\delta l_i^3 = \hat{l}_i^2 - l_i$ | Contextual offset | 20 |

**Auto-Routing.** Another important building block of DFA is the auto-routing mechanism. It is built upon the fact that the estimated pseudo-labels in stage-2 $f^2$ reflects the error patterns for each sample. We first associate each cluster center with an average error magnitude $e\left(C_k^2\right), k = 1 \ldots K$. This can be done by averaging the errors of training samples in each cluster. Then, we define the error function

$G\left(\cdot\right)$ within pseudo-label $\hat{f}_i^2$ for sample $i$ in stage-2: $G\left(\hat{f}_i^2\right) = \sum_{k=1}^{K} e\left(C_k^2\right) \cdot \hat{f}_i^2\left(k\right)$. Therefore, the routing function $r_i$ for sample $i$ is formulated as

$$r_i = \mathbf{1}\left(G\left(\hat{f}_i^2\right) < \epsilon\right), \tag{2}$$

where $\mathbf{1}\left(\cdot\right)$ is the indicator function and $\epsilon$ is the error threshold for auto-routing. We set $\epsilon = 0.3$ empirically. If $r_i = 1$ indicates sample $i$ will go through branch 1 in stage-3, and $r_i = 0$ indicates otherwise.

**Training.** Each stage of DFA is trained with multiple loss functions, including landmark estimation $L_{positions}$, visibility prediction $L_{visibility}$, and pseudo-label approximation $L_{labels}$. The overall loss function $L_{overall}$ is

$$L_{overall} = L_{positions}(l, \hat{l}) + \alpha(t)L_{visibility}(v, \hat{v}) + \beta(t)L_{labels}(f, \hat{f}), \tag{3}$$

where $\hat{l}$, $\hat{v}$ and $\hat{f}$ are the predicted landmark positions, visibility, and pseudo-labels respectively. We employ the Euclidean loss for $L_{positions}$ and $L_{labels}$, and the multinomial logistic loss is adopted for $L_{visibility}$. $\alpha\left(t\right)$ and $\beta\left(t\right)$ are the balancing weights between them. All the VGG-16 networks are pre-trained using ImageNet [37] and the entire DFA cascaded network is fine-tuned by stochastic gradient decent with back-propagation.

The proper scheduling of $\alpha\left(t\right)$ and $\beta\left(t\right)$ is very important for network performance. If they are too large, it disturbs the training of landmark positions. If they are too small, the training procedure cannot benefit from these auxiliary information. Similar to [38], we design a piecewise adjustment strategy for $\alpha\left(t\right)$ and $\beta\left(t\right)$ during training process,

$$\alpha\left(t\right) = \begin{cases} \alpha & t < t_1, \\ \frac{t-t_1}{t_2-t_1}\alpha & t_1 \le t < t_2, \\ 0 & t_2 \le t, \end{cases} \tag{4}$$

where $t_1 = 2000$ iterations and $t_2 = 4000$ iterations in our implementation. The adjustment for $\beta\left(t\right)$ takes a similar form.

**Computations.** For a three stage cascade to predict 8 fashion landmarks, Deep-Pose is required to train 17 VGG-16 models in total, while only three VGG-16 models need to be trained for DFA. Thus, our proposed approach at least saved 5 times computational costs.

## 4    Experiments

This section presents evaluation and analytical results of fashion landmark detection, as well as two applications including clothing attribute prediction and clothes retrieval.

**Experimental Settings.** For each clothing category, we randomly select $5K$ images for validation and another $5K$ images for test. The remaining $30K{\sim}40K$ images are used for training. We employ two metrics to evaluate fashion landmark detection, normalized error (NE) and the percentage of detected landmarks (PDL) [10]. NE is defined as the $\ell_2$ distance between predicted landmarks and ground truth landmarks in the normalized coordinate space (*i.e.* divided by the width/height of the image), while PDL is calculated as the percentage of detected landmarks under certain overlapping criterion. Typically, smaller values of NE or higher values of PDL indicate better results.

**Competing Methods.** Since this work is the first study of fashion landmark detection, it is difficult to find direct comparisons. Nevertheless, to fully demonstrate the effectiveness of DFA, we compare it with two deep models, including DeepPose [10] and Image Dependent Pairwise Relations (IDPR) [11], which achieved best-performing results in human pose estimation. They are two representative methods that explored network cascade and graphical model to handle human pose. Specifically, DeepPose designed a cascaded deep regression framework on human body parts, while IDPR combined CNN and structural SVM [33] to model the relations among landmarks. To have a fair comparison, we replace the backbone networks in DeepPose and IDPR with VGG-16 and carefully train them using the same data and protocol as DFA did.

### 4.1 Ablation Study

We demonstrate the merits of each component in DFA.

**Effectiveness of Network Cascade.** Table 2 lists the performance of NE among three stages, where we have two observations. First, as shown in stage one, training DFA with both landmark position and visibility, denoted as 'direct regression', outperforms training DFA with only landmark position, denoted as '-visibility', showing that visibility helps landmark detection because it indicates variations of pose and scale (*e.g.* zoom-in). Second, cascade networks gradually reduce localization errors on all fashion landmarks from stage one to stage three. By predicting the corrections over previous stage, DFA decomposes a complex mapping problem into several subspace regression. For example, Fig. 8(e–g) demonstrates the quantitative stage-wise landmark detection results of DFA on different clothing items. In these cases, stage-1 gives rough predictions with shape constraints, while stage-2 and stage-3 refine results by referring to local and contextual correction patterns.

**Effectiveness of Different Pseudo-Labels.** Within each stage, choices of different pseudo-labels are explored. We design pseudo-labels representing landmark configurations, local landmark offsets and contextual landmark offsets for three stages respectively. Table 3 shows that pseudo-labels lead to substantial gains beyond direction regression, especially for the first stage. Next, we further

**Table 2.** Ablation study of DFA on different fashion landmarks. The normalized error (NE) is used here. 'abs.' indicates pseudo-labels obtained from absolute landmark positions. 'offset' indicates pseudo-labels obtained from local landmark offsets. 'c. offset' indicates pseudo-labels obtained from contextual landmark offsets. Intuitively, for the image size of $224 \times 224$, the best prediction is achieved in stage-3 using contextual offset as pseudo-labels, whose errors in pixels are $0.048 \times 224 = 10.752, 10.752, 20.384, 19.936, 15.904$, and $16.128$ respectively. '$T = 20$' is found empirically in the experiments.

| Stage | Component | L. Collar | R. Collar | L. Sleeve | R. Sleeve | L. Hem | R. Hem | Avg. |
|---|---|---|---|---|---|---|---|---|
| 1 | Direct regression | .071 | .071 | .134 | .130 | .103 | .102 | .102 |
| | − visibility | .104 | .102 | .213 | .212 | .141 | .143 | .153 |
| | + p.-labels($T = 1$) | .065 | .065 | .113 | .112 | .094 | .095 | .091 |
| | + p.-labels($T = 20$) | **.057** | **.058** | **.106** | **.104** | **.088** | **.089** | **.084** |
| 2 | Direct regression | .051 | .051 | .098 | .096 | .082 | .080 | .078 |
| | + p.-labels(abs.) | .050 | .051 | .097 | .096 | .080 | .079 | .076 |
| | + p.-labels(offset) | **.049** | **.050** | **.095** | **.093** | **.077** | **.078** | **.074** |
| 3 | Direct regression | .049 | .049 | .094 | .093 | .074 | .076 | .073 |
| | + two-branch | **.048** | .049 | .094 | .093 | .073 | .075 | .072 |
| | + auto-routing | **.048** | .049 | .092 | .091 | **.071** | .073 | .070 |
| | + p.-labels(offset) | **.048** | **.048** | **.091** | .090 | **.071** | .073 | .069 |
| | + p.-labels(c. offset) | **.048** | **.048** | **.091** | **.089** | **.071** | **.072** | **.068** |

**Table 3.** Ablation study of DFA on different evaluation subsets. NE is used here.

| Stage | Component | N. Pose | M. Pose | L. Pose | M. Zoom-in | L. Zoom-in |
|---|---|---|---|---|---|---|
| 1 | Direct regression | .079 | .100 | .111 | .151 | .193 |
| | + p.-label($T = 20$) | **.064** | **.077** | **.085** | **.120** | **.156** |
| 2 | Direct regression | .055 | .072 | .081 | .104 | .151 |
| | + p.-label(offset) | **.053** | **.069** | **.078** | **.102** | **.148** |
| 3 | Direct regression | .052 | .069 | .078 | .096 | .148 |
| | + auto-routing | .051 | .067 | .077 | .093 | .146 |
| | + p.-label(c. offset) | **.050** | **.066** | **.075** | **.091** | **.144** |

justify the forms of different pseudo-labels adopted for each stage. In stage-1, we find that using soft label, denoted as '$+p.$ $labels$ $(T = 20)$', instead of hard label, denoted as '$+p.$ $labels$ $(T = 1)$', results in better performance, because soft label is more informative in identifying landmark configuration of samples. In stage-2, pseudo-label generated from offset landmark positions is superior to that generated from absolute landmark positions since landmark offsets can provide more guidance on the local corrections to be predicted. In stage-3, including contextual landmark offsets help achieve further gains, due to the fact that landmark corrections to be made are generally correlated.

**Effectiveness of Auto-Routing.** Finally, we show that auto-routing is an effective way to tackle data with different correction difficulties. From Table 2 stage-3, we can see that auto-routing (denoted as '+auto-routing') provides more benefits when compared with averaging the predictions from two branches trained using all data (denoted as '+two-branch'). By further inspecting the stage-wise performance on each evaluation set, which is shown in Table 3, we can observe that auto-routing mechanism improves the performance of medium/large zoom-in subsets, showing that the routing function makes one of the branch in stage-3 focus on difficult samples.

## 4.2   Benchmarking

To illustrate the effectiveness of DFA, we compare it with state-of-the-art human pose estimation methods like DeepPose [10] and IDPR [11]. We also analyze the strengths and weaknesses of each method on fashion landmark detection.

**Landmark Types.** Figure 5 (the first row) shows the percentage of detection rates on different fashion landmarks, where we have three observations. First, on landmark 'hem', DeepPose performs better when distance threshold is small, while IDPR catches up when the threshold is large, because DeepPose is a part-based method which can locally refines the results for easy cases. Second, collars are the easiest landmarks to be detected while sleeves are the hardest. Third, DFA consistently outperforms both DeepPose and IDPR or shows comparable results on all fashion landmarks, showing that the pseudo-labels and auto-routing mechanisms enable robust fashion landmark detection.

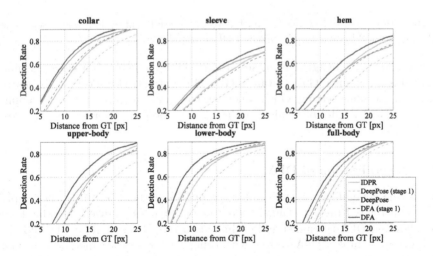

**Fig. 5.** Performance of fashion landmark detection on different fashion landmarks (the first row) and different clothing types (the second row). [px] represents pixels. The percentage of detected landmarks (PDL) is used here.

**Clothing Types.** Figure 5 (the second row) shows the percentage of detection rates on different clothing types. Again, DFA outperforms all other methods on all distance thresholds. We have two additional observations. First, DFA (stage-1) already achieves comparable results on full-body and lower-body clothes when compared with IDPR and DeepPose (stage-3). Second, upper-body clothes pose most challenges on fashion landmark detection. It is partially due to the various clothing sub-categories contained.

**Difficulty Levels.** Figure 6 shows the percentage of detection rates on different evaluation subsets, with the distance threshold fixed at 15 pixels. Two observations are made here. First, fashion landmark detection is a challenging task. Even the detection rate for normal pose set is just above 70 %. More powerful model needs to be developed. Second, DFA has the most advantages on medium pose/zoom-in subsets. Pseudo-labels provide effective shape constraints for hard cases. Please also note that DFA (stage-3) requires much less computational costs than DeepPose (stage-3).

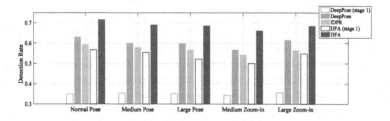

**Fig. 6.** Performance of fashion landmark detection on different evaluation subsets. The distance threshold is fixed at 15 pixels. PDL is used here.

For a $300 \times 300$ image, DFA takes around $100ms$ to detect full sets of fashion landmarks on a single GTX Titan X GPU. In contrast, DeepPose needs nearly 650 ms in the same setting. Our framework has large potential in real-life applications. Visual results of fashion landmark detection by different methods are given in Fig. 8.

### 4.3 Generalization of DFA

To test the generalization ability of the proposed framework, we further apply DFA on a related task, *i.e.* human pose estimation, as reported in Table 4. In the following, DFA is trained and evaluated on LSP dataset [40] as [11] did.

First, we compare DFA system with other state-of-the-art methods on pose estimation task. Without much adaptation, DFA achieves 74.4 mean strict PCP results, with 87, 91, 70, 56, 81, 76 for 'torso', 'head', 'u.arms', 'l.arms', 'u.legs' and 'l.legs' respectively. It shows comparable results to [11] and outperforms several recent works [10,30,32,39], showing that DFA is a general approach for structural prediction problem besides fashion landmark detection.

**Table 4.** Comparison of strict PCP results on the LSP dataset. DFA shows good generalization ability to human pose estimation.

| Method | Torso | Head | U.arms | L.arms | U.legs | L.legs | Mean |
|---|---|---|---|---|---|---|---|
| Fu *et al.* [32] | 77.7 | 85.4 | 75.0 | 71.9 | 62.1 | 48.8 | 67.7 |
| Ouyang *et al.* [39] | 85.8 | 83.1 | 63.3 | 46.6 | 76.5 | 72.2 | 68.6 |
| Pose Machines [30] | 93.1 | 83.6 | 76.8 | 68.1 | 42.2 | 85.4 | 72.0 |
| DeepPose [10] | - | - | 56 | 38 | 77 | 71 | - |
| DFA | 90.8 | **87.2** | 70.4 | 56.2 | **80.6** | 75.8 | 74.4 |
| IDPR [11] | 92.7 | 87.8 | 69.2 | 55.4 | 82.9 | 77.0 | 75.0 |
| + p.-label | 93.5 | 88.5 | 72.3 | 59.0 | 83.9 | 78.7 | 77.0 |
| + auto-routing | **94.1** | **88.9** | **74.3** | **61.5** | **85.1** | **80.4** | **78.6** |

Then, we show that pseudo-label and auto-routing scheme of DFA can be generalized to improve performance of pose estimation methods, such as IDPR [11]. [11] trained DCNN and achieved 75 mean strict PCP. We add pseudo-labels to this DCNN and include auto-routing in cascading predictions. Training and evaluation of graphical model are kept unchanged. Pseudo-labels leverage the result to 77 mean strict PCP and auto-routing leads to another 1.6 point gain. It demonstrates that pseudo-labels and auto-routing are effective and complementary techniques to current methods.

### 4.4 Applications

Finally, we show that fashion landmarks can facilitate clothing attribute prediction and clothes retrieval. We employ a subset of DeepFashion dataset [3], which contains $10K$ images, 50 clothing attributes and corresponding image pairs (*i.e.* the images containing the same clothing item). We compare fashion landmarks with different localization schemes, including the full image, the bounding box (bbox) of clothing item, and the human-body joints, where fashion landmarks are detected by DFA, human joints are obtained by the executable code of [11], and bounding boxes are manually annotated. For both tasks of attribute recognition and clothes retrieval, we use off-the-shelf CNN features as described in [35].

**Attribute Prediction.** We train a multi-layer perceptron (MLP) using the extracted CNN features as input to predict all 50 attributes. Following [41], we employ the top-$k$ recall rate as measuring criteria, which is obtained by ranking the classification scores and determine how many ground truth attributes have been found in the top-$k$ predicted attributes. Overall, the average top-5 recall rates on 50 attributes of 'full image', 'bbox', 'human joints', and 'fashion landmarks' are 27 %, 53 %, 65 % and 73 %, respectively, showing that fashion landmarks are the most effective representation for attribute prediction of fashion items. Figure 7(a) shows the top-5 recall rates of ten representative attributes,

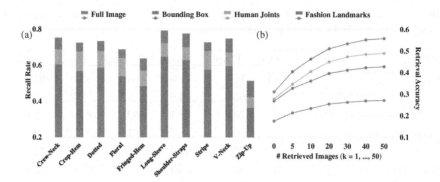

**Fig. 7.** Experimental results on clothing attribute prediction and clothes retrieval using features extracted from 'full image', 'bbox', 'human joints', and 'fashion landmarks': (a) the top-5 recall rates of clothing attributes and (b) the top-$k$ clothes retrieval accuracy.

*e.g.* 'stripe', 'long-sleeve', and 'V-neck'. We observe that fashion landmark outperforms all the other localization schemes in all the attributes, especially for part-based attributes, such as 'zip-up' and 'shoulder-straps'.

**Clothes Retrieval.** We adopt the $\ell_2$ distance between the extracted CNN features for clothes retrieval. The top-$k$ retrieval accuracy is used to measure the performance, such that given a query image, correct retrieval is considered as

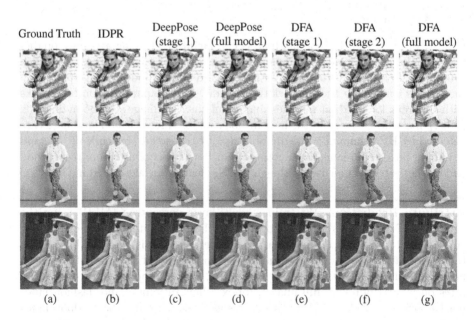

**Fig. 8.** Visual results of fashion landmark detection by different methods: (a) Ground Truth, (b) IDPR, (c) DeepPose (stage 1), (d) DeepPose (full model), (e) DFA (stage 1), (f) DFA (stage 2) and (g) DFA (full model).

the exact clothing item has been found in the top-$k$ retrieved gallery images. As shown in Fig. 7(b), the top-20 retrieval accuracies for 'full image', 'bbox', 'human joints', and 'fashion landmarks' are 25 %, 40 %, 45 %, and 51 % respectively. When $k = 1$ and $k = 5$, features extracted around fashion landmarks still perform better than the other alternatives, demonstrating that fashion landmarks provide more discriminative information beyond traditional paradigms.

## 5   Conclusions

This paper introduced fashion landmark detection, which is an important step towards robust fashion recognition. To benchmark fashion landmark detection, we introduced a large-scale fashion landmark dataset (FLD). With FLD, we proposed a deep fashion alignment network (DFA) for robust fashion landmark detection, which leverages pseudo-labels and auto-routing mechanism to reduce the large variations presented in fashion images. Extensive experiments showed the effectiveness of different components as well as the generalization ability of DFA. To demonstrate the usefulness of fashion landmark, we evaluated on two fashion applications, clothing attribute prediction and clothes retrieval. Experiments revealed that fashion landmark is a more discriminative representation than clothes bounding boxes and human joints for fashion-related tasks, which we hope could facilitate future research.

**Acknowledgements.** This work is partially supported by SenseTime Group Limited, the Hong Kong Innovation and Technology Support Programme, the General Research Fund sponsored by the Research Grants Council of the Kong Kong SAR (CUHK 416312), the External Cooperation Program of BIC, Chinese Academy of Sciences (No. 172644KYSB20150019), the Science and Technology Planning Project of Guangdong Province (2015B010129013, 2014B050505017), and the National Natural Science Foundation of China (61503366, 61472410; Corresponding author is Ping Luo).

## References

1. Huang, J., Feris, R.S., Chen, Q., Yan, S.: Cross-domain image retrieval with a dual attribute-aware ranking network. In: ICCV (2015)
2. Kiapour, M.H., Han, X., Lazebnik, S., Berg, A.C., Berg, T.L.: Where to buy it: matching street clothing photos in online shops. In: ICCV (2015)
3. Liu, Z., Luo, P., Qiu, S., Wang, X., Tang, X.: Deepfashion: powering robust clothes recognition and retrieval with rich annotations. In: CVPR, pp. 1096–1104 (2016)
4. Liu, S., Song, Z., Liu, G., Xu, C., Lu, H., Yan, S.: Street-to-shop: cross-scenario clothing retrieval via parts alignment and auxiliary set. In: CVPR, pp. 3330–3337 (2012)
5. Di, W., Wah, C., Bhardwaj, A., Piramuthu, R., Sundaresan, N.: Style finder: fine-grained clothing style detection and retrieval. In: CVPR Workshops, pp. 8–13 (2013)
6. Kiapour, M.H., Yamaguchi, K., Berg, A.C., Berg, T.L.: Hipster wars: discovering elements of fashion styles. In: Fleet, D., Pajdla, T., Schiele, B., Tuytelaars, T. (eds.) ECCV 2014. LNCS, vol. 8689, pp. 472–488. Springer, Heidelberg (2014). doi:10.1007/978-3-319-10590-1_31

7. Simo-Serra, E., Fidler, S., Moreno-Noguer, F., Urtasun, R.: Neuroaesthetics in fashion: modeling the perception of beauty. In: CVPR (2015)
8. Chen, H., Gallagher, A., Girod, B.: Describing clothing by semantic attributes. In: Fitzgibbon, A., Lazebnik, S., Perona, P., Sato, Y., Schmid, C. (eds.) ECCV 2012. LNCS, vol. 7574, pp. 609–623. Springer, Heidelberg (2012). doi:10.1007/978-3-642-33712-3_44
9. Bossard, L., Dantone, M., Leistner, C., Wengert, C., Quack, T., Gool, L.: Apparel classification with style. In: Lee, K.M., Matsushita, Y., Rehg, J.M., Hu, Z. (eds.) ACCV 2012. LNCS, vol. 7727, pp. 321–335. Springer, Heidelberg (2013). doi:10.1007/978-3-642-37447-0_25
10. Toshev, A., Szegedy, C.: Deeppose: human pose estimation via deep neural networks. In: CVPR, pp. 1653–1660 (2014)
11. Chen, X., Yuille, A.L.: Articulated pose estimation by a graphical model with image dependent pairwise relations. In: NIPS, pp. 1736–1744 (2014)
12. Tompson, J.J., Jain, A., LeCun, Y., Bregler, C.: Joint training of a convolutional network and a graphical model for human pose estimation. In: NIPS, pp. 1799–1807 (2014)
13. Carreira, J., Agrawal, P., Fragkiadaki, K., Malik, J.: Human pose estimation with iterative error feedback (2015). arXiv preprint arXiv:1507.06550
14. Pfister, T., Charles, J., Zisserman, A.: Flowing convnets for human pose estimation in videos. In: ICCV, pp. 1913–1921 (2015)
15. Fan, X., Zheng, K., Lin, Y., Wang, S.: Combining local appearance and holistic view: dual-source deep neural networks for human pose estimation. In: CVPR, pp. 1347–1355 (2015)
16. Wang, X., Zhang, T.: Clothes search in consumer photos via color matching and attribute learning. In: ACM MM, pp. 1353–1356 (2011)
17. Chen, Q., Huang, J., Feris, R., Brown, L.M., Dong, J., Yan, S.: Deep domain adaptation for describing people based on fine-grained clothing attributes. In: CVPR, pp. 5315–5324 (2015)
18. Yamaguchi, K., Kiapour, M.H., Berg, T.: Paper doll parsing: retrieving similar styles to parse clothing items. In: ICCV, pp. 3519–3526 (2013)
19. Kalantidis, Y., Kennedy, L., Li, L.J.: Getting the look: clothing recognition and segmentation for automatic product suggestions in everyday photos. In: ICMR, pp. 105–112 (2013)
20. Fu, J., Wang, J., Li, Z., Xu, M., Lu, H.: Efficient clothing retrieval with semantic-preserving visual phrases. In: Lee, K.M., Matsushita, Y., Rehg, J.M., Hu, Z. (eds.) ACCV 2012. LNCS, vol. 7725, pp. 420–431. Springer, Heidelberg (2013). doi:10.1007/978-3-642-37444-9_33
21. Yamaguchi, K., Berg, T.L., Ortiz, L.E.: Chic or social: visual popularity analysis in online fashion networks. In: ACM MM, pp. 773–776 (2014)
22. Yamaguchi, K., Kiapour, M.H., Ortiz, L.E., Berg, T.L.: Parsing clothing in fashion photographs. In: CVPR, pp. 3570–3577 (2012)
23. Yang, W., Luo, P., Lin, L.: Clothing co-parsing by joint image segmentation and labeling. In: CVPR, pp. 3182–3189 (2014)
24. Liang, X., Xu, C., Shen, X., Yang, J., Liu, S., Tang, J., Lin, L., Yan, S.: Human parsing with contextualized convolutional neural network. In: ICCV, pp. 1386–1394 (2015)
25. Ferrari, V., Marin-Jimenez, M., Zisserman, A.: Progressive search space reduction for human pose estimation. In: CVPR, pp. 1–8 (2008)
26. Yang, Y., Ramanan, D.: Articulated pose estimation with flexible mixtures-of-parts. In: CVPR, pp. 1385–1392 (2011)

27. Dantone, M., Gall, J., Leistner, C., Gool, L.: Human pose estimation using body parts dependent joint regressors. In: CVPR, pp. 3041–3048 (2013)
28. Sapp, B., Taskar, B.: Modec: Multimodal decomposable models for human pose estimation. In: CVPR, pp. 3674–3681 (2013)
29. Belagiannis, V., Rupprecht, C., Carneiro, G., Navab, N.: Robust optimization for deep regression. In: ICCV, pp. 2830–2838. IEEE (2015)
30. Ramakrishna, V., Munoz, D., Hebert, M., Andrew Bagnell, J., Sheikh, Y.: Pose machines: articulated pose estimation via inference machines. In: Fleet, D., Pajdla, T., Schiele, B., Tuytelaars, T. (eds.) ECCV 2014. LNCS, vol. 8690, pp. 33–47. Springer, Heidelberg (2014). doi:10.1007/978-3-319-10605-2_3
31. Dantone, M., Gall, J., Leistner, C., Van Gool, L.: Body parts dependent joint regressors for human pose estimation in still images. TPAMI **36**(11), 2131–2143 (2014)
32. Fu, L., Zhang, J., Huang, K.: Beyond tree structure models: a new occlusion aware graphical model for human pose estimation. In: ICCV, pp. 1976–1984 (2015)
33. Tsochantaridis, I., Hofmann, T., Joachims, T., Altun, Y.: Support vector machine learning for interdependent and structured output spaces. In: ICML, p. 104 (2004)
34. Jordan, M.I., Ghahramani, Z., Jaakkola, T.S., Saul, L.K.: An introduction to variational methods for graphical models. Mach. Learn. **37**(2), 183–233 (1999)
35. Simonyan, K., Zisserman, A.: Very deep convolutional networks for large-scale image recognition (2014). arXiv preprint arXiv:1409.1556
36. Viola, P., Jones, M.: Rapid object detection using a boosted cascade of simple features. In: CVPR, pp. 503–511 (2001)
37. Deng, J., Dong, W., Socher, R., Li, L.J., Li, K., Fei-Fei, L.: Imagenet: a large-scale hierarchical image database. In: CVPR, pp. 248–255 (2009)
38. Lee, D.H.: Pseudo-label: the simple and efficient semi-supervised learning method for deep neural networks. In: Workshop on Challenges in Representation Learning, ICML, vol. 3 (2013)
39. Ouyang, W., Chu, X., Wang, X.: Multi-source deep learning for human pose estimation. In: CVPR, pp. 2329–2336 (2014)
40. Johnson, S., Everingham, M.: Clustered pose and nonlinear appearance models for human pose estimation. In: BMVC, vol. 2, p. 5 (2010)
41. Gong, Y., Jia, Y., Leung, T., Toshev, A., Ioffe, S.: Deep convolutional ranking for multilabel image annotation (2013). arXiv preprint arXiv:1312.4894

# Human Pose Estimation Using Deep Consensus Voting

Ita Lifshitz, Ethan Fetaya[(✉)], and Shimon Ullman

Weizmann Institute of Science, Rehovot, Israel
ethan.fetaya@weizmann.ac.il

**Abstract.** In this paper we consider the problem of human pose estimation from a single still image. We propose a novel approach where each location in the image votes for the position of each keypoint using a convolutional neural net. The voting scheme allows us to utilize information from the whole image, rather than rely on a sparse set of keypoint locations. Using dense, multi-target votes, not only produces good keypoint predictions, but also enables us to compute image-dependent joint keypoint probabilities by looking at consensus voting. This differs from most previous methods where joint probabilities are learned from relative keypoint locations and are independent of the image. We finally combine the keypoints votes and joint probabilities in order to identify the optimal pose configuration. We show our competitive performance on the MPII Human Pose and Leeds Sports Pose datasets.

## 1 Introduction

In recent years, with the resurgence of deep learning techniques, the accuracy of human pose estimation from a single image has improved dramatically. Yet despite this recent progress, it is still a challenging computer vision task and state-of-the-art results are far from human performance.

The general approach in previous works, such as [22,26], is to train a deep neural net as a keypoint detector for all keypoints. Given an image $\mathcal{I}$, the net is fed a patch of the image $\mathcal{I}_y \subset \mathcal{I}$ centered around pixel $y$ and predicts if $y$ is one of the $M$ keypoints of the model. This process is repeated in a sliding window approach, using a fully convolutional implementation, to produce $M$ heat maps, one for each keypoint. Structured prediction, usually by a graphical model, is then used to combine these heat maps into a single pose prediction. This approach has several drawbacks. First, most pixels belonging to the person are not themselves any of the keypoints and therefore contribute only limited information to the pose estimation process. Information from the entire person can be used to get more reliable predictions, particularly in the face of partial

---

I. Lifshitz and E. Fetaya—Equal contribution.

**Electronic supplementary material** The online version of this chapter (doi:10. 1007/978-3-319-46475-6_16) contains supplementary material, which is available to authorized users.

© Springer International Publishing AG 2016
B. Leibe et al. (Eds.): ECCV 2016, Part II, LNCS 9906, pp. 246–260, 2016.
DOI: 10.1007/978-3-319-46475-6_16

occlusion where the keypoint itself is not visible. Another drawback is that while the individual keypoint predictors use state-of-the-art classification methods to produce high quality results, the binary terms in the graphical model, enforcing global pose consistency, are based only on relative keypoint location statistics gathered from the training data and are independent of the input image.

**Fig. 1.** Our model's predicted pose estimation on the MPII-human-pose database test-set [1]. Each pose is represented as a stick figure, inferred from predicted joints. Different limbs in the same image are colored differently, same limb across different images has the same color. (Color figure online)

To overcome these limitations, we propose a novel approach in which for every patch center $y$ we predict the location of all keypoints relative to $y$, instead of classifying $y$ as one of the keypoints. This enables us to use 'wisdom of the crowd' by aggregating many votes to produce accurate keypoint detections. In addition, by looking at agreements between votes, we infer informative image-dependent binary terms between keypoints. Our binary terms are generated by consensus voting - we look at a set of keypoints pairs, and for each possible pair of locations, we aggregate all votes for this combination. The total vote will be high if both keypoint locations get strong votes from the same voters. We show that this approach produces competitive results on the challenging MPII human-pose [21] and the Leeds sports pose [12] datasets.

## 2   Related Work

Human body pose estimation from a single image is a challenging task. The need to cope with a variety of poses in addition to a large range of appearances due to different clothing, scales and light conditions gave rise to many approaches to dealing with the various aspects of this task. One common approach is using part detectors combined with a pictorial structure for capturing relations between parts [8,28]. In addition to the standard pictorial structure [9], some methods incorporate higher-order part dependencies such as poselet-based features [21]. Alternative methods, like the chains-model [13] replace the pictorial structure with a set of voting chains, starting at the head keypoint and ending at the hand.

With the reappearance of convolutional neural nets, part detectors became more reliable, leading to a significant improvement in accuracy [3,5,22,25–27]. The works of [25,26] focus on multi-scale representation of body parts in order to infer the location of keypoints. In [22], the authors deal with simultaneous detection and pose estimation of multiple people. Recent works [3,27] use an iterative scheme to refine pose estimation. We use a neural net to generate votes on location of different keypoints. As opposed to [5], where a neural net is used to explicitly generate an image dependent binary term, in our model it arises naturally from the voting scheme. The use of voting in detecting targets of interest has been commonly used in various computer vision tasks, for example, in shape detection [2,16], object detection [10,18] and body parts detection [20].

## 3   Overview of the Method

We now describe the main parts of our algorithm, which will be explained in detail in next sections.

At test time, we first use a deep neural net, described in Sect. 4.2, to predict for each image patch $\mathcal{I}_y$ centered around pixel $y$, and for each keypoint $j$, the location of the keypoint relative to $y$. From this we can compute the probability of keypoint location $K_j$ being equal to a possible location $x$ as seen from $\mathcal{I}_y$, $P_y(K_j = x)$. We aggregate these votes over all image patches to get the probability distribution for each keypoint location $\{P(K_j = x)\}_{j=1}^{M}$. Examples of $P_y(K_j)$ and $P(K_j)$ are shown in Figs. 3(a)–(d).

Next we compute our consensus voting binary term. The voting net above was trained using a separate loss per keypoint, which is equivalent to an independence assumption, i.e. for each $y$,

$$P_y(K_i = x_i, K_j = x_j) = P_y(K_i = x_i) \cdot P_y(K_j = x_j). \tag{1}$$

If we now average over all locations $y$ we get a joint distribution

$$P(K_i = x_i, K_j = x_j) \propto \sum_y P_y(K_i = x_i) \cdot P_y(K_j = x_j) \qquad (2)$$

in which the keypoints are no longer independent. Because of the multiplication, the joint distribution is high when both locations get strong votes from the *same voters*. More details on the consensus voting can be found in Sect. 5.

Finally, we estimate the pose by minimizing an energy function over the unary and binary terms generated by the voting scheme. We do this sequentially, focusing at each step on a subset of keypoints. We start with the most reliable keypoints until making the full pose estimation. This process is presented in more details in Sect. 6.

## 4  Keypoint Voting

### 4.1  Voting Representation

The first stage in our pose-estimation method is a keypoint detector learned by a deep neural net, which we apply to the image patches in a fully convolutional fashion [17]. This is an accelerated way to run the net in a sliding window manner with the stride determined by pooling layers of the network. At each patch center $y$, the net predicts the location of each keypoint $K_1, ..., K_M$ relative to $y$. This differs from previous methods [25,26] where the net only needed to classify if the center $y$ is any of the $M$ keypoints.

The problem of predicting the relative displacement vectors $\{K_1 - y, ..., K_M - y\}$ is a regression problem which is usually solved by minimizing an $L_2$ loss function. However, for the current task the $L_2$ loss has shortcomings, as the net produces only a single prediction as output. Consequently, in cases of ambiguity, e.g. difficulty to distinguish between left and right hand, the optimal $L_2$ loss would be the mean location instead of "splitting" the vote between both locations. Indeed, when trained using this approach, we found that the net performance to be lackluster. To better address this issue, we modify the prediction task into a classification problem by discretizing the image into log-polar bins centered around $y$, as seen in Fig. 2(a). Using log-polar binning allows for more precise predictions for keypoints near $y$ and a rough estimate for far away keypoints. We classify into 50 classes, one for the central location, one for background i.e. non-person, and the rest are four log-polar rings around the center with each ring divided into 12 angular bins. Since not all people in the training set are labeled, we are unable to use background locations for training the non-person label. For this reason, we ignore image locations far from the person of interest, as seen in Fig. 2(b), and use non-person images from the PASCAL dataset [6] for non-person label training.

We augmented the 16 humanly annotated keypoints supplied in the dataset with additional 12 keypoints generated from the original ones, by taking the middle point between two neighboring skeleton keypoints, e.g. the middle point

(a) Log-polar bins         (b) Ignore mask          (c) Keypoints

**Fig. 2.** (a) Log-polar bins, used for keypoints locations voting, centered around the left upper arm; (b) Patch centers outside the person of interest, marked in blue, are not used for training; (c) Our model makes use of 30 keypoints: 16 annotated body joints, supplied in the dataset, 12 synthetically generated mid-section keypoints and estimated hands locations. Original keypoints marked in blue, synthetically generated keypoints in green (Color figure online)

between the shoulder and elbow. We also obtained estimated location of the hands by extrapolating the elbow-wrist vector by 30 %. This produces a total of 30 keypoints and allows us to have a more dense coverage of the body. All keypoints can be seen in Fig. 2(c).

### 4.2   Net Architecture

The net architecture we use is based on the VGG-16 network [24]. We use the first 13 convolutional layers parameters of the VGG-16 net (denoted by columns 1–9 in Table 1(a)), pre-trained on the imagenet dataset [23]. On top of these layers we employ a max pooling with stride 1 and use convolution with holes [4] in order to increase resolution and generate a descriptor of size 2048 every 8 pixels. To further increase resolution we learn a deconvolution layer [17] and get a probability distribution over 50 classes, indicating the relative keypoint location, every 4 pixels. The last two layers are distinct per keypoint resulting in 30 distributions on 50 bins every 4 pixels. More details about the structure of the net can be found in Table 1. Since the size of each classification bin is considerably different, we minimize a weighted softmax loss function, where each class is weighted inversely proportional to the size of its bin.

### 4.3   The Voting Scheme

At each patch center $y$ and for each keypoint $j$ the network returns a softmax probability distribution over the log-polar bins $s_y^j \in \mathbb{R}^{1 \times 1 \times C}$. At inference we use deconvolution, with a predefined fixed kernel $w \in \mathbb{R}^{H_k \times W_k \times C}$, to transform the log-polar representation $s_y^j$ back to the image space and get the probability distribution of keypoint location over pixels $P_y(K_j = x)$. The deconvolution kernel maps each channel, representing a log-polar bin, to the corresponding image

**Table 1.** Comparisons between the network architectures of $VGG_{16}$ and *deep voting* (our model), as shown in (a) and (b). Each table contains five rows, representing the 'name of layer', 'receptive field of filter - stride', 'number of output feature maps', 'activation function' and 'size of output feature maps', respectively. The terms 'conv', 'max', 'fc', 'hconv' and 'deconv' represent the convolution, max pooling, fully connection, convolution with holes [4] and deconvolution [17], respectively. The terms 'relu', 'idn', 'soft' and 'w-soft' represent the activation functions, rectified linear unit, identity, softmax and weighted-softmax, respectively. The last two layers in (b) are distinct per keypoint.

| (a) $VGG_{16}$: 244x244x3 input image; 1x1000 output labels | | | | | | | | | | | | | |
|---|---|---|---|---|---|---|---|---|---|---|---|---|---|
| | 1 | 2 | 3 | 4 | 5 | 6 | 7 | 8 | 9 | 10 | 11 | 12 | 13 |
| *layer* | 2 x conv | max | 2 x conv | max | 3 x conv | max | 3 x conv | max | 3 x conv | max | fc | fc | fc |
| *filter-stride* | 3-1 | 2-2 | 3-1 | 2-2 | 3-1 | 2-2 | 3-1 | 2-2 | 3-1 | 2-2 | - | - | - |
| *channels* | 64 | 64 | 128 | 128 | 256 | 256 | 512 | 512 | 512 | 512 | 4096 | 4096 | 1000 |
| *activation* | relu | idn | relu | idn | relu | idn | relu | idn | relu | idn | relu | relu | soft |
| *size* | 224 | 112 | 112 | 56 | 56 | 28 | 28 | 14 | 14 | 7 | 1 | 1 | 1 |

| (b) *deep voting*: 504x504x3 input image; 102x102x50x30 output label maps | | | | | | | | | | | | | | |
|---|---|---|---|---|---|---|---|---|---|---|---|---|---|---|
| | 1 | 2 | 3 | 4 | 5 | 6 | 7 | 8 | 9 | 10 | 11 | 12 | 13 | 14 |
| *layer* | 2 × conv | max | 2 × conv | max | 3 × conv | max | 3 × conv | max | 3 × hconv | max | hconv | conv | $conv_{K_i}$ | $deconv_{K_i}$ |
| *filter-stride* | 3-1 | 2-2 | 3-1 | 2-2 | 3-1 | 2-2 | 3-1 | 2-1 | 3-1 | 3-1 | 7-1 | 1-1 | 1-1 | 6-2 |
| *channels* | 64 | 64 | 128 | 128 | 256 | 256 | 512 | 512 | 512 | 512 | 2048 | 2048 | 50 | 50 |
| *activation* | relu | idn | relu | idn | relu | idn | relu | idn | relu | idn | relu | relu | idn | w-soft |
| *size* | 504 | 252 | 252 | 126 | 126 | 63 | 63 | 62 | 62 | 60 | 50 | 50 | 50 | 102 |

locations. We use a deconvolution kernel of size $(H_k \times W_k \times C) = (65 \times 65 \times 50)$ to efficiently aggregate votes from a neighborhood of $65 \times 65$ locations. Most of the kernel weights are zeros, shown as black in Fig. 3(e). At the top of the figure we show an illustration of weights for a specific bin. Since this bin corresponds to the upper left log-polar segment it is zero at all locations except for the pixels of that segment which are set to $\frac{1}{|bin|}$.

$$\hat{P}_y(K_j = x) = deconv(s_y^j, w) \tag{3}$$

Then $P_y(K_j)$ is simply $\hat{P}_y(K_j)$ translated by y. Examples for $P_y(K_j)$ are shown in Figs. 3(a) and (b). We aggregate these votes over all patch centers to get the final probability of each keypoint at each location.

$$P(K_j = x) = \sum_{y \in \mathcal{Y}} P_y(K_j = x) = deconv(s^j, w) \tag{4}$$

The term $P(K_j) \in \mathbb{R}^{(\frac{H}{4} + H_k - 1) \times (\frac{W}{4} + W_k - 1)}$ is the aggregated votes of keypoint $j$, and $s^j \in \mathbb{R}^{\frac{H}{4} \times \frac{W}{4} \times C}$ is the softmax distribution output of keypoint $j$. Examples for $P(K_j)$ are shown in Fig. 3(c) and (d). Note that the size of the aggregated distribution is larger than $\frac{H}{4} \times \frac{W}{4}$, the image size at the output resolution. This enables the algorithm to generate votes for locations outside the visible image.

During inference, we make use of the Caffe [11] implementation for deconvolution by adding an additional deconvolution layer with fixed weights $w$ on

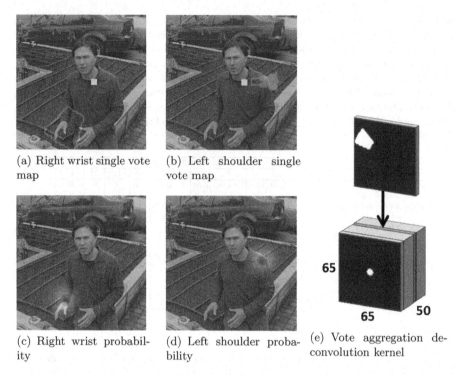

(a) Right wrist single vote map

(b) Left shoulder single vote map

(c) Right wrist probability

(d) Left shoulder probability

(e) Vote aggregation deconvolution kernel

**Fig. 3.** (a) Voting map from location y (yellow rectangle) for Right Wrist $P_y(K_{RightWrist})$; (b) Voting map from location y (yellow rectangle) for Left Shoulder $P_y(K_{LeftShoulder})$; (c) Right wrist probability $P(K_{RightWrist})$, generated by aggregating voting maps for right wrist; (d) Left shoulder probability $P(K_{LeftShoulder})$, generated by aggregating voting maps for left shoulder; (e) The vote aggregation deconvolution kernel $w$. The weights of a specific channel are illustrated at the top (Color figure online)

top of the net softmax output. This layer generates the aggregated probability distribution of each keypoint in a fast and efficient way.

## 5    Consensus Voting

The voting scheme described in Sect. 4 produces a heat map per keypoint, which represents the probability of a keypoint being at each location. The next challenge is to combine all the estimated distributions into a single pose prediction. What makes this task especially challenging is that beyond just having to handle false keypoint detections, we need to handle true detections but of other individuals in the image as well. Other challenges include self-occlusion, and confusion between left and right body parts.

The standard approach to solve this problem is to minimize an objective of the following form:

$$\sum_{i=1}^{N} \phi_i(x_i) + \sum_{(i,j)\in E} \phi_{(i,j)}(x_i, x_j) \tag{5}$$

The $\phi_i(x_i)$ unary term is the score of having keypoint $i$ at location $x_i$. The $\phi_{(i,j)}(x_i, x_j)$ binary term measures compatibility and is the score of having keypoint $i$ at location $x_i$ and keypoint $j$ at location $x_j$. The edge set $E$ is some preselected subset of pairs of keypoints.

Usually in pose estimation, the binary term is image independent and comes from a prior on relative keypoint location. For example, given the location of the shoulder, it produces a set of possible elbow displacements based on training samples pose statistics. While this can be helpful in excluding anatomically implausible configurations, an image independent binary term has limitations. For example, the location of the left shoulder relative to the head is strongly dependent on whether the person is facing forwards or backwards and this information is not incorporated into the standard binary term. One main advantage of our keypoint voting scheme is that we can compute from it an image-based "consensus voting" binary term, which has more expressive power. This is especially important for less common poses, where the image-independent prior gives a low probability to the right pose.

At each image location $y$, we compute from the net output the distribution $P_y(K_i = x)$ for each keypoint. These probabilities were trained under a (naive) independence assumption, i.e. a separate softmax loss for each keypoint. If we now average over all locations $y$, we get a joint distribution which is no longer independent (see Eq. 2). By having each center $y$ vote for a combination of keypoints, the probabilities become dependent through the voters. For $P(k_i = x_i, k_j = x_j)$ to be high, it is not enough for $x_i$ and $x_j$ to receive strong votes separately, the combination needs to get strong votes from many common voters. For this reason we call this the consensus voting term. In our algorithm, we use the unary term of the form $\phi_i(x_i) = -\log(P(K_i = x_i))$. The binary term $\phi_{(i,j)}(x_i, x_j)$ we use is a weighted combination of the joint distribution $-\log(P(k_i = x_i, k_j = x_j))$ just described and the commonly used binary term based on relative keypoint location statistics.

In Fig. 4 we show an example of the conditional probability $P(K_i = x_i | K_j = x_j)$ calculated from the previously described joint probability. As can be seen in Fig. 4(b), the left elbow of the person to the right has a weak response. In addition, there is a misleading weak response to the elbow of another individual nearby. After conditioning on the left shoulder location, we see a strong response in Fig. 4(d), but only in the correct location.

Computing the consensus voting is challenging, since calculating Eq. 2 in a naive way is computationally expensive. Each keypoint has $N^2$ possible locations, where the image is of size $N \times N$. Considering all possible combinations yields $N^4$ pairs of locations. For each pair of possible locations, we sum over all $N^2$ voters, resulting in $\mathcal{O}(N^6)$ running time. In order to reduce running time, we use the

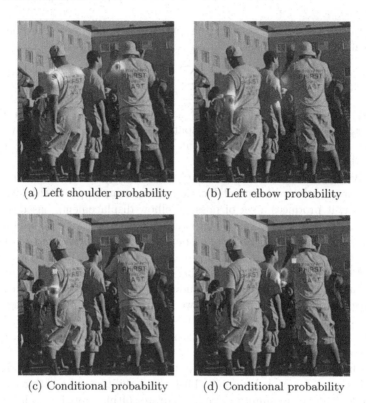

(a) Left shoulder probability          (b) Left elbow probability

(c) Conditional probability           (d) Conditional probability

**Fig. 4.** (a) Left shoulder probability $P(K_{LeftShoulder})$; (b) Left elbow probability $P(K_{LeftElbow})$; (c) Conditional probability of left elbow given left shoulder of person on the left (yellow rectangle); (d) Conditional probability of left elbow given left shoulder of person on the right (yellow rectangle) (Color figure online)

observation that Eq. 2 is in fact a convolution and use the highly optimized Caffe GPU implementation [11] to calculate the binary tables. In addition we calculate the binary term over a coarse scale of 1/12 of the image scale, using only the first two log-polar rings. This reduces the running time of a single keypoint pair to ~100 ms. The restriction to the first two rings limits the maximal distance between keypoints, which we overcome by using the augmented keypoints shown in Fig. 2(c).

## 6   Pose Prediction

In the previous sections, we described the unary and binary terms which are the basic building blocks of our algorithm. We now present additional steps that we employ to improve performance on top of these basic building blocks. First, we add geometrical constraints on our augmented keypoints. Second, we perform the inference in parts, starting from the reliable parts proceeding to the less certain ones.

## 6.1 Local Geometric Constraints

We generate additional keypoints, as seen in Fig. 2(c) by taking the mid-point between keypoints, e.g. shoulder and elbow. While we could simply minimize Eq. 5 with these added variables as well, this fails to take into account the fact that these new points are determined by other points. We can enforce these constraints by removing the new synthetic variables and rewriting our binary constraints. Assume our two original keypoints had indexes $i$ and $j$ and the middle point had index $\ell$. Focusing on the relevant terms, instead of solving

$$\min_{x_i, x_j, x_\ell} \phi_i(x_i) + \phi_j(x_j) + \phi_\ell(x_\ell) + \phi_{(i,\ell)}(x_i, x_\ell) + \phi_{(\ell,j)}(x_\ell, x_j) \qquad (6)$$

we add the geometric constraint by solving

$$\min_{x_i, x_j} \phi_i(x_i) + \phi_j(x_j) + \tilde{\phi}_{(i,j)}(x_i, x_j). \qquad (7)$$

Where we define

$$\tilde{\phi}_{(i,j)}(x_i, x_j) = \phi_\ell(f(x_i, x_j)) + \phi_{(i,\ell)}(x_i, f(x_i, x_j)) + \phi_{(\ell,j)}(f(x_i, x_j), x_j)$$

and $f(x, y) = \frac{1}{2}(x + y)$.

This is equivalent to adding the constraint that $x_\ell$ is the mid-point between $x_i$ and $x_j$, but faster to optimize. By adding this mid-point constraint, and using it as a linking feature [14], we get a more reliable binary term which also looks at the appearance of the space between the two respective keypoints.

## 6.2 Sequential Prediction

An issue that arises when optimizing Eq. 5 over all keypoint is that not all keypoints are detected with equal accuracy. Some, like the head, are detected with high accuracy while others, like the wrist, are more difficult to locate. In some cases, occluded or unclear keypoints can distort predictions of more visible keypoints. In order to have the more certain keypoints influence the prediction of less certain ones, but not vice versa, we predict the keypoints in stages. We start with the most reliable keypoints, and at each stage use the previously predicted keypoints as an "anchor" to predict the other parts. Once "anchor" points are set, we allow them only small refinement movements in subsequent stages. Optimizing Eq. 5 is performed at three stages. At the first stage we predict the location of the head, neck, thorax and pelvis. At the second stage we predict the shoulders and hips given all previously predicted keypoints. Last, we locate all remaining keypoints.

The optimization is done by the TRW-S algorithm [15] at each of the previously discussed stages. The hyper-parameters, i.e. the relative weights of the unary and binary terms, where tuned by using a grid search on a held out validation set containing 3330 annotated poses.

# 7 Results

## 7.1 MPII

We tested our method on the MPII human pose dataset [1], which consists of 19,185 training and 7,247 testing images of various activities containing over $40K$ annotated people. The dataset is highly challenging and has people in a wide array of poses. At test time we are given an image with a rough location and scale of the person of interest and need to return the location of 16 keypoints: head-top, upper-neck, thorax, pelvis, shoulders, elbows, wrist, hips, knees and ankles. The standard evaluation is made on a subset of test images, named "single person", where the person of interest is well separated from other people. We note that several images in the "single person" dataset still have another person nearby.

We trained the net described in Sect. 4 using Caffe [11] in a cascaded fashion. First, training the added layers, denoted by columns 11–14, in Table 1(b), while keeping the first 13 convolutional layers with learning rate 0. Then training layers denoted by columns 9–14 in Table 1(b), and finally fine tuning the entire network. We start with learning rate of 0.001 and no weight decay and continue with learning rate of 0.0001 and 0.0002 weight decay.

At test time, in order to restrict our algorithm to the person in question, we crop a window of size $504 \times 504$ around the person using the given position and scale, adding zero padding if needed. In addition, we multiply our mid-body keypoint heatmap (the synthetic point between thorax and pelvis) with a mask centered around the given person position, which is part of the standard input in the "single person" challenge. This zeros responses far from the given center and insures that we return the pose of the correct person. Examples of our model's predictions are shown in Fig. 1.

Performance is measured by the PCKh metric [1], where a keypoint location is considered correct if its distance to the ground truth location is no more than half the head segment length. In Table 2 we compare our results to the leading methods on the MPII human pose leaderboard. We show competitive results with mean PCKh score of 85.0 % and state-of-the-art performance on the head

Table 2. PCKh results on the MPII single person dataset.

| Method | Head | Shoulder | Elbow | Wrist | Hip | Knee | Ankle | Mean |
|---|---|---|---|---|---|---|---|---|
| Tompson et al. [26] | 95.8 | 90.3 | 80.5 | 74.3 | 77.6 | 69.7 | 62.8 | 79.6 |
| Carreira et al. [3] | 95.7 | 91.7 | 81.7 | 72.4 | 82.8 | 73.2 | 66.4 | 81.3 |
| Tompson et al. [25] | 96.1 | 91.9 | 83.9 | 77.8 | 80.9 | 72.3 | 64.8 | 82.0 |
| Pishchulin et al. [22] | 94.1 | 90.2 | 83.4 | 77.3 | 82.6 | 75.7 | 68.6 | 82.4 |
| Wei et al. [27] | **97.8** | 95.0 | 88.7 | 84.0 | 88.4 | 82.8 | 79.4 | 88.5 |
| Newell et al. [19] | 97.6 | **95.4** | **90.0** | **85.2** | **88.7** | **85.0** | **80.6** | **89.4** |
| Our model | **97.8** | 93.3 | 85.7 | 80.4 | 85.3 | 76.6 | 70.2 | 85.0 |

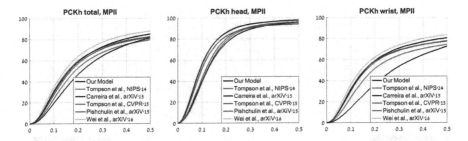

**Fig. 5.** Pose estimation results on the MPII dataset for varying PCKh thresholds.

keypoints. A detailed ablation study and further discussion of the results appear in the supplementary material.

## 7.2 Leeds Sports

The Leeds sports dataset [12] (LSP) contains 2, 000 images of people in various sport activities, 1, 000 for training and 1, 000 for testing. The task is to return 14 keypoints, the same keypoints as in the MPII dataset except for the thorax and pelvis.

The LSP dataset has two evaluation settings, person-centric (PC) and observer-centric (OC). We use the person-centric settings where right/left labels are according to body parts (same as the MPII annotation) and not according to relative image location. The standard performance measure for the LSP dataset is strict percentage of correct parts (PCP) metric. The PCP score measures limb detection: a limb is considered to be correctly detected if the distances between the detected limb endpoints and groundtruth limb endpoints are within half of the limb length.

We use the model trained on the MPII human pose dataset and fine-tune it on the LSP training set. Examples of our model's predictions are shown in Fig. 6. At test time we run our algorithm twice, once with the input image and once with it flipped up-side-down, and pick the pose with the optimal score. This is done in order to handle up-side-down people which are more common in the LSP dataset than the MPII dataset, and are therefore under-represented at training time. Additional results on the LSP dataset, without flipping images up-side-down, can be found in the supplementary material.

We compare the performance of our approach to that of other leading pose estimation methods in Table 3. Our performance is comparable to that of Pishchulin et al. [22], and superior to other methods. We note that in [22] the authors use the LSP-Extended dataset, containing additional 10,000 annotated poses, not used in our model.

**Fig. 6.** Additional results of our model's predicted joint positions on the LSP database test-set [12]

**Table 3.** PCP results on the LSP dataset (PC).

| Method | Torso | Upper leg | Lower leg | Upper arm | Forearm | Head | Mean |
|---|---|---|---|---|---|---|---|
| Tompson et al. [26] | 90.3 | 70.4 | 61.1 | 63.0 | 51.2 | 83.7 | 66.6 |
| Carreira et al. [3] | 95.3 | 81.8 | 73.3 | 66.7 | 51.0 | 84.4 | 72.5 |
| Chen and Yuille [5] | 96.0 | 77.2 | 72.2 | 69.7 | 58.1 | 85.6 | 73.6 |
| Fan et al. [7] | 95.4 | 77.7 | 69.8 | 62.8 | 49.1 | 86.6 | 70.1 |
| Pishchulin et al. [22] | 97.0 | 88.8 | 82.0 | 82.4 | 71.8 | 95.8 | 84.3 |
| Wei et al. [27] | **98.0** | 82.2 | **89.1** | **85.8** | **77.9** | **95.0** | **88.3** |
| Our model | 97.3 | **88.8** | 84.5 | 80.6 | 71.4 | 94.8 | 84.3 |

## 8  Discussion

In this work, we proposed a method for dealing with the challenging task of human pose estimation in still images. We presented a novel approach of using a deep convolutional neural net for keypoint voting rather than keypoint detection. The keypoint voting scheme has several useful properties compared to keypoint detection. First, all image regions of the evaluated person participate in the voting, utilizing the 'wisdom of the crowd' to produce reliable keypoint predictions. Second, any informative location can contribute to multiple keypoints, not just to a single one. This allows us to use consensus voting in order to compute expressive image-dependent joint keypoint probabilities. Empirical results on the diverse MPII human pose and Leeds sports pose datasets show competitive results, improving the state-of-the-art on a subset of evaluated keypoints. We showed that our model generalized well from the MPII dataset to the LSP dataset, using only 1000 samples for fine tuning. Models and code will be made publicly available. Additional contributions of the current scheme are the use of log-polar bins for location prediction rather than estimating L2 translations, and the use of convolutions for fast aggregation of votes from multiple locations.

The voting scheme is a natural tool for estimating the locations of unobserved body parts. In future work, we plan to harness this property for dealing with multiple people and occlusions, resulting from closely interacting people, which are difficult to handle by existing schemes. In addition, we plan to combine our voting scheme with iterative methods, refining predictions by feeding the output of previous iterations as input to the network.

**Acknowledgment.** This work was supported by ERC Advanced Grant 269627 Digital Baby and in part by the Center for Brains, Minds and Machines, funded by National Science Foundation Science and Technology Centers Award CCF-1231216. We thank the NVIDIA Corporation for providing GPUs through their academic program.

# References

1. Andriluka, M., Pishchulin, L., Gehler, P., Schiele, B.: 2D human pose estimation: new benchmark and state of the art analysis. In: CVPR (2014)
2. Ballard, D.H.: Generalizing the hough transform to detect arbitrary shapes. Pattern Recogn. **13**(2), 111–122 (1981)
3. Carreira, J., Agrawal, P., Fragkiadaki, K., Malik, J.: Human pose estimation with iterative error feedback (2015). arXiv preprint: arXiv:1507.06550
4. Chen, L.-C., Papandreou, G., Kokkinos, I., Murphy, K., Yuille, A.L.: Semantic image segmentation with deep convolutional nets, fully connected CRFs (2014). arXiv preprint: arXiv:1412.7062
5. Chen, X., Yuille, A.L.: Articulated pose estimation by a graphical model with image dependent pairwise relations. In: NIPS (2014)
6. Everingham, M., Van Gool, L., Williams, C.K.I., Winn, J., Zisserman, A.: The PASCAL Visual Object Classes (VOC) challenge. Int. J. Comput. Vis. **88**(2), 303–338 (2010)
7. Fan, X., Zheng, K., Lin, Y., Wang, S.: Combining local appearance and holistic view: dual-source deep neural networks for human pose estimation. In: CVPR (2015)
8. Felzenszwalb, P.F., Huttenlocher, D.P.: Pictorial structures for object recognition. Int. J. Comput. Vis. **61**, 55–79 (2005)
9. Fischler, M.A., Elschlager, R.A.: The representation and matching of pictorial structures. IEEE Trans. Comput. **22**, 67–92 (1973)
10. Gall, J., Lempitsky, V.: Class-specific hough forests for object detection. In: Criminisi, A., Shotton, J. (eds.) Decision Forests for Computer Vision and Medical Image Analysis, pp. 143–157. Springer, London (2013)
11. Jia, Y., Shelhamer, E., Donahue, J., Karayev, S., Long, J., Girshick, R., Guadarrama, S., Darrell, T.: Caffe: convolutional architecture for fast feature embedding (2014). arXiv preprint: arXiv:1408.5093
12. Johnson, S., Everingham, M.: Clustered pose and nonlinear appearance models for human pose estimation. In: BMVC (2010)
13. Karlinsky, L., Dinerstein, M., Harari, D., Ullman, S.: The chains model for detecting parts by their context. In: CVPR, pp. 25–32 (2010)

14. Karlinsky, L., Ullman, S.: Using linking features in learning non-parametric part models. In: Fitzgibbon, A., Lazebnik, S., Perona, P., Sato, Y., Schmid, C. (eds.) ECCV 2012, Part III. LNCS, vol. 7574, pp. 326–339. Springer, Heidelberg (2012)
15. Kolmogorov, V.: Convergent tree-reweighted message passing for energy minimization. IEEE Trans. Pattern Anal. Mach. Intell. **28**, 1568–1583 (2006)
16. Leibe, B., Leonardis, A., Schiele, B.: Combined object categorization and segmentation with an implicit shape model. In: Workshop on Statistical Learning in Computer Vision, ECCV, vol. 2, p. 7 (2004)
17. Long, J., Shelhamer, E., Darrell, T.: Fully convolutional networks for semantic segmentation. In: CVPR (2015)
18. Maji, S., Malik, J.: Object detection using a max-margin hough transform. In: IEEE Conference on Computer Vision and Pattern Recognition, CVPR 2009, pp. 1038–1045. IEEE (2009)
19. Newell, A., Yang, K., Deng, J.: Stacked hourglass networks for human pose estimation. Arxiv preprint (2016)
20. Okoda, R.: Discriminative generalized hough transform for object detection. In: ICCV, pp. 2000–2005 (2009)
21. Pishchulin, L., Andriluka, M., Gehler, P., Schiele, B.: Poselet conditioned pictorial structures. In: Proceedings of the IEEE Conference on Computer Vision and Pattern Recognition, pp. 588–595 (2013)
22. Pishchulin, L., Insafutdinov, E., Tang, S., Andres, B., Andriluka, M., Gehler, P., Schiele, B.: DeepCut: joint subset partition and labeling for multi person pose estimation (2015). arXiv preprint: arXiv:1511.06645
23. Russakovsky, O., Deng, J., Su, H., Krause, J., Satheesh, S., Ma, S., Huang, Z., Karpathy, A., Khosla, A., Bernstein, M.S., Berg, A.C., Li, F.-F.: ImageNet large scale visual recognition challenge. Int. J. Comput. Vis. **115**, 211–252 (2015)
24. Simonyan, K., Zisserman, A.: Very deep convolutional networks for large-scale image recognition. In: ICLR (2015)
25. Tompson, J., Goroshin, R., Jain, A., LeCun, Y., Bregler, C.: Efficient object localization using convolutional networks. In: CVPR (2015)
26. Tompson, J., Jain, A., LeCun, Y., Bregler, C.: Join training of a convolutional network and a graphical model for human pose estimation. In: NIPS (2014)
27. Wei, S.-E., Ramakrishna, V., Kanade, T., Sheikh, Y.: Convolutional pose machines. In: CVPR (2016)
28. Yang, Y., Ramanan, D.: Articulated pose estimation with flexible mixtures-of-parts. In: CVPR, pp. 1385–1392 (2011)

# Leveraging Visual Question Answering
# for Image-Caption Ranking

Xiao Lin$^{(\boxtimes)}$ and Devi Parikh

Bradley Department of Electrical and Computer Engineering,
Virginia Tech, Blacksburg, USA
{linxiao,parikh}@vt.edu

**Abstract.** Visual Question Answering (VQA) is the task of taking as input an image and a free-form natural language question about the image, and producing an accurate answer. In this work we view VQA as a "feature extraction" module to extract image and caption representations. We employ these representations for the task of image-caption ranking. Each feature dimension captures (imagines) whether a fact (question-answer pair) could plausibly be true for the image and caption. This allows the model to interpret images and captions from a wide variety of perspectives. We propose score-level and representation-level fusion models to incorporate VQA knowledge in an existing state-of-the-art VQA-agnostic image-caption ranking model. We find that incorporating and reasoning about consistency between images and captions significantly improves performance. Concretely, our model improves state-of-the-art on caption retrieval by 7.1 % and on image retrieval by 4.4 % on the MSCOCO dataset.

**Keywords:** Visual question answering · Image-caption ranking · Mid-level concepts

## 1 Introduction

Visual Question Answering (VQA) is an "AI-complete" problem that requires knowledge from multiple disciplines such as computer vision, natural language processing and knowledge base reasoning. A VQA system takes as input an image and a free-form open-ended question about the image and outputs the natural language answer to the question. A VQA system needs to not only recognize objects and scenes but also reason beyond low-level recognition about aspects such as intention, future, physics, material and commonsense knowledge. For example (*Q*: Who is the person in charge in this picture? *A*: Chef) reveals the most important person and occupation in the image. Moreover, answers to multiple questions about the same image can be correlated and may reveal

---

**Electronic supplementary material** The online version of this chapter (doi:10. 1007/978-3-319-46475-6_17) contains supplementary material, which is available to authorized users.

B. Leibe et al. (Eds.): ECCV 2016, Part II, LNCS 9906, pp. 261–277, 2016.
DOI: 10.1007/978-3-319-46475-6_17

more complex interactions. For example (*Q*: What is this person riding? *A*: Motorcycle) and (*Q*: What is the man wearing on his head? *A*: Helmet) might reveal correlations observable in the visual world due to safety regulations.

Today's VQA models, while far from perfect, may already be picking up on these semantic correlations of the world. If so, they may serve as an implicit knowledge resource to help other tasks. Just like we do not need to fully understand the theory behind an equation to use it, can we already use VQA knowledge captured by existing VQA models to improve other tasks?

In this work we study the problem of using VQA knowledge to improve image-caption ranking. Consider the image and its caption in Fig. 1. Aligning them not only requires recognizing the batter and that it is a baseball game (mentioned in the caption), but also realizing that a batter up at the plate would imply that a player is holding a bat, posing to hit the baseball and there might be another player nearby waiting to catch the ball (seen in the image). Image captions tend to be generic. As a result, image captioning corpora may not capture sufficient details for models to infer this knowledge.

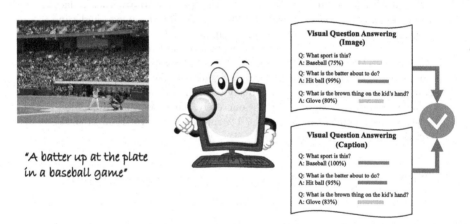

**Fig. 1.** Aligning images and captions requires high-level reasoning *e.g.* "a batter up at the plate" would imply that a player is holding a bat, posing to hit the baseball and there might be another player nearby waiting to catch the ball. There is rich knowledge in Visual Question Answering (VQA) corpora containing human-provided answers to a variety of questions one could ask about images. We propose to leverage knowledge in VQA by using VQA models learned on images and captions as "feature extraction" modules for image-caption ranking.

Fortunately VQA models try to explicitly learn such knowledge from a corpus of images, each with associated questions and answers. Questions about images tend to be much more specific and detailed than captions. The VQA dataset of [1] in particular has a collection of free-form open-ended questions and answers provided by humans. These images also have associated captions [31].

We propose to leverage VQA knowledge captured by such corpora for image-caption ranking by using VQA models learned on images and captions as "feature extraction" schemes to represent images and captions. Given an image and a caption, we choose a set of free-form open-ended questions and use VQA models learned on images and captions to assess probabilities of their answers. We use these probabilities as image and caption features respectively. In other words, we embed images and captions into the space of VQA questions and answers using VQA models. Such VQA-grounded representations interpret images and captions from a variety of different perspectives and imagine beyond low-level recognition to better understand images and captions.

We propose two approaches that incorporate these VQA-grounded representations into an existing state-of-the-art[1] VQA-agnostic image-caption ranking model [23]: fusing their predictions and fusing their representations. We show that such VQA-aware models significantly outperform the VQA-agnostic model and set state-of-the-art performance on MSCOCO image-caption ranking. Specifically, we improve caption retrieval by 7.1 % and image retrieval by 4.4 %.

This paper is organized as follows: Section 2 introduces related works. We first introduce VQA and image-caption ranking tasks as our building blocks in Sect. 3, then detail our VQA-based image-caption ranking models in Sect. 4. Experiments and results are reported in Sect. 5. We conclude in Sect. 6.

## 2    Related Work

**Visual Question Answering.** Visual Question Answering (VQA) [1] is the task of taking an image and a free-form open-ended question about the image and automatically predicting the natural language answer to the question. VQA may require fine-grained recognition, object detection, activity recognition, multi-modal and commonsense knowledge. Large datasets [1,17,35,42,57] have been made available to cover the diversity of knowledge required for VQA. Most notably the VQA dataset [1] contains 614,163 questions and ground truth answers on 204,721 images of the MSCOCO [31] dataset.

Recent VQA models [1,17,33,36,42,61] explore state-of-the-art deep learning techniques combining Convolutional Neural Networks (CNNs) and Recurrent Neural Networks (RNNs). [1] also explores a slight variant of VQA that answers a question about the image by reading a caption describing the image instead of looking at the image itself. We call this variant VQA-Caption.

VQA is a challenging task in its early stages. In this work we propose to use both VQA and VQA-Caption models as implicit knowledge resources. We show that current VQA models, while far from perfect, can already be used to improve other multi-modal AI tasks; specifically image-caption ranking.

**Semantic Mid-Level Visual Representations.** Previous works have explored the use of attributes [5,15,55], parts [3,58], poselets [4,59], objects [30], actions [43] and contextual information [9,18,50] as semantic mid-level representations for visual recognition. Benefits of using such semantic mid-level visual

---

[1] To the best of our knowledge on MSCOCO [31], [23] has the state-of-the-art caption retrieval performance. [33] has the state-of-the-art image retrieval performance.

representations include improving fine-grained visual recognition, learning models of visual concepts without example images (zero-shot learning [29,38]) and improving human-machine communication where a user can explain the target concept during image search [25,28], or give a classifier an explanation of labels [10,39]. Recent works also explore using word embeddings [46] and free-form text [12] as representations for zero-shot learning of new object categories. [21] proposes scene graphs for image retrieval. [2] proposes using abstract scenes as an intermediate representation for zero-shot action recognition. Closest to our work is the use of objects, actions, scenes [14], attributes and object interactions [27] for generating and ranking image captions. In this work we propose to use free-form open-ended questions and answers as mid-level representations and we show that they provide rich interpretations of images and captions.

**Commonsense Knowledge for Visual Reasoning.** Recently there has been a surge of interest in visual reasoning tasks that require high-level reasoning such as physical reasoning [19,60], future prediction [16,40,54], object affordance prediction [62] and textual tasks that require visual knowledge [32,44,51]. Such tasks can often benefit from reasoning with external commonsense knowledge resources. [63] uses a knowledge base learned on object categories, attributes, actions and object affordances for query-based image retrieval. [53] learns to anticipate future scenes from watching videos for action and object forecasting. [32] learns to imagine abstract scenes from text for textual tasks that need visual understanding. [44,51] evaluate the plausibility of commonsense assertions by verifying them on collections of abstract scenes and real images, respectively, to leverage the visual common sense in those collections. Our work explores the use of VQA corpora which have both visual (image) and textual (captions) commonsense knowledge for image-caption ranking.

**Images and Captions.** Recent works [6,22,23,34,37,56] have made significant progress on automatic image caption generation and ranking by applying deep learning techniques for image recognition [26,45,49] and language modeling [7, 48] on large datasets [8,31]. Algorithms can now often generate accurate, human-like natural-language captions for images. However, evaluating the quality of such automatically generated open-ended image captions is still an open research problem [13,52].

On the other hand, ranking images given captions and ranking captions given images require a similar level of image and language understanding, but are amenable to automatic evaluation metrics. Recent works on image-caption ranking mainly focus on improving model architectures. [23,37] study different architectures for projecting CNN image representations and RNN caption representations into a common multi-modal space. [34] uses multi-modal CNNs for image-caption ranking. [22] aligns image and caption fragments using CNNs and RNNs. Our work takes an orthogonal approach to previous works. We propose to leverage knowledge in VQA corpora containing questions about images and associated answers for image-caption ranking. Our proposed VQA-based image and caption representations provide complementary information to those learned using previous approaches on a large image-caption ranking dataset.

# 3    Building Blocks: Image-Caption Ranking and VQA

In this section we present image-caption ranking and VQA modules that we build on top of.

## 3.1    Image-Caption Ranking

The image-caption ranking task is to retrieve relevant images given a query caption, and relevant captions given a query image. During training we are given image-caption pairs $(I, C)$ that each corresponds to an image $I$ and its caption $C$. For each pair we sample $K - 1$ other images in addition to $I$ so the image retrieval task becomes retrieving $I$ from $K$ images $I_i, i = 1, 2 \ldots K$ given caption $C$. We also sample $K - 1$ random captions in addition to $C$ so the caption retrieval task becomes retrieving $C$ from $K$ captions $C_i, i = 1, 2 \ldots K$ given image $I$.

Our image-caption ranking models learn a ranking scoring function $S(I, C)$ such that the corresponding retrieval probabilities:

$$P_{im}(I|C) = \frac{\exp(S(I, C))}{\sum\limits_{i=1}^{K} \exp(S(I_i, C))} \qquad P_{cap}(C|I) = \frac{\exp(S(I, C))}{\sum\limits_{i=1}^{K} \exp(S(I, C_i))} \qquad (1)$$

are maximized. Let $S(I, C)$ be parameterized by $\theta$ (to be learnt). We formulate an objective function $L(\theta)$ for $S(I, C)$ as the sum of expected negative log-likelihoods of image and caption retrieval over all image-caption pairs $(I, C)$:

$$L(\theta) = \mathbb{E}_{(I,C)}[-\log P_{im}(I|C)] + \mathbb{E}_{(I,C)}[-\log P_{cap}(C|I)] \qquad (2)$$

Recent works on image-caption ranking often construct $S(I, C)$ by combining a vectorized image representation which is usually hidden layer activations in a CNN pretrained for image classification, with a vectorized caption representation which is usually a sentence encoding computed using an RNN in a multi-modal space. Such scoring functions rely on large image-caption ranking datasets to learn knowledge necessary for image-caption ranking and do not leverage knowledge in VQA corpora. We call such models VQA-agnostic models.

In this work we use the publicly available state-of-the-art image-caption ranking model of [23] as our baseline VQA-agnostic model. [23] projects a $D_{x_I}$-dimensional CNN activation $x_I$ for image $I$ and a $D_{x_C}$-dimensional RNN latent encoding $x_C$ for caption $C$ to the same $D_{x_C}$-dimensional common multi-modal embedding space as unit-norm vectors $t_I$ and $t_C$:

$$t_I = \frac{W_I x_I}{||W_I x_I||_2} \qquad t_C = \frac{x_C}{||x_C||_2} \qquad (3)$$

The multi-modal scoring function is defined as their dot product $S_t(I, C) = \langle t_I, t_C \rangle$.

The VQA-agnostic model of [23] uses the 19-layer VGGNet [45] ($D_{x_I} = 4096$) for image encoding and an RNN with 1024 Gated Recurrent Units [7] ($D_{x_C} = 1024$) for caption encoding. The RNN and parameters $W_I$ are jointly learned on the image-caption ranking training set using a margin-based objective function.

## 3.2   VQA

VQA is the task of given an image $I$ and a free-form open-ended question $Q$ about $I$, generating a natural language answer $A$ to that question. Similarly, VQA-Caption task proposed by [1] takes a caption $C$ of an image and a question $Q$ about the image, then generates an answer $A$. In [1] the generated answers are evaluated using $\min(\frac{\#\text{ humans that provided } A}{3}, 1)$. That is, $A$ is $100\%$ correct if at least 3 humans (out of 10) provide the answer $A$.

We closely follow [1] and formulate VQA as a classification task over top $M = 1000$ most frequent answers from the training set. The oracle accuracies of picking the best answer for each question within this set of answers are $89.37\%$ on training and $88.83\%$ on validation. During training, given triplets of image $I$, question $Q$ and ground truth answer $A$, we optimize the negative log-likelihood (NLL) loss to maximize the probability of the ground truth answer $P_I(A|Q, I)$ given by the VQA model. Similarly given triplets of caption $C$, question $Q$ and ground truth answer $A$, we optimize the NLL loss to maximize the VQA-Caption model probability $P_C(A|Q, C)$.

Following [1], for a VQA question $(I, Q)$ we first encode the input image $I$ using the 19-layer VGGNet [45] as a 4,096-dimensional image encoding $x_I$, and encode the question $Q$ using a 2-layer RNN with 512 Long Short-Term Memory (LSTM) units [20] per layer as a 2,048-dimensional question encoding $x_Q$. We then project $x_I$ and $x_Q$ into a common 1,024-dimensional multi-modal space as $z_I$ and $z_Q$:

$$z_I = Tanh(W_I x_I + b_I) \qquad z_Q = Tanh(W_Q x_Q + b_Q) \qquad (4)$$

As in [1] we then compute the representation $z_{I+Q}$ for the image-question pair $(I, Q)$ by element-wise multiplying $z_I$ and $z_Q$: $z_{I+Q} = z_I \odot z_Q$. The scores $s_A$ for 1,000 answers are given by:

$$s_A = W_s z_{I+Q} + b_s \qquad (5)$$

We jointly learn the question encoding RNN and parameters $\{W_I, b_I, W_Q, b_Q, W_s, b_s\}$ during training.

For the VQA-Caption task given caption $C$ and question $Q$, we use the same network architecture and learning procedure as above, but using the most frequent 1,000 words in training captions as the dictionary to construct a 1,000 dimensional bag-of-words encoding for caption $C$ as $x_C$ to replace the image feature $x_I$ and compute $z_C$, $z_{C+Q}$ respectively.

The VQA and VQA-Caption models are learned on the train split of the VQA dataset [1] using 82,783 images, 413,915 captions and 248,349 questions. These models achieve VQA validation set accuracies of $54.42\%$ (VQA) and $56.28\%$ (VQA-Caption), respectively. Next, they are used as sub-modules in our image-caption ranking approach.

# 4 Approach

To leverage knowledge in VQA for image-caption ranking, we propose to represent the images and the captions in the VQA space using VQA and VQA-Caption models. We call such representations VQA-grounded representations.

## 4.1 VQA-Grounded Representations

Let's say we have a VQA model $P_I(A|Q, I)$, a VQA-Caption model $P_C(A|Q, C)$ and a set of $N$ questions $Q_i$ and their plausible answers (one for each question) $A_i$, $i = 1, 2, \dots N$. Then given an image $I$ and a caption $C$, we first extract the $N$ dimensional VQA-grounded activation vectors $u_I$ for $I$ and $u_C$ for $C$ such that each dimension $i$ of $u_I$ and $u_C$ is the log probability of the ground truth answer $A_i$ given a question $Q_i$.

$$u_I^{(i)} = \log P_I(A_i|Q_i, I) \qquad u_C^{(i)} = \log P_C(A_i|Q_i, C), i = 1, 2, \dots, N \qquad (6)$$

For example if the $(Q_i, A_i)$ pairs are ($Q_1$: What is the person riding?, $A_1$: Motorcycle) and ($Q_2$: What is the man wearing on his head?, $A_2$: Helmet), $u_I^{(1)}$ and $u_C^{(1)}$ verify if the person in image $I$ and caption $C$ respectively is riding a motorcycle. At the same time $u_I^{(2)}$ and $u_C^{(2)}$ verify whether the man in $I$ and $C$ is wearing a helmet. Figure 1 shows another example.

In cases where there is not a man in the image or the caption, *i.e.* the assumption of $Q_i$ is not met, $P_I(A_i|Q_i, I)$ and $P_C(A_i|Q_i, C)$ may still reflect if there *were* a man or if the assumption of $Q_i$ *were* fulfilled, could he be wearing a helmet. In other words, even if there is no person present in the image or mentioned in the caption, the model may still assess the plausibility of a man wearing a helmet or a motorcycle being present. This imagination beyond what is depicted in the image or caption can be helpful in providing additional information when reasoning about the compatibility between an image and a caption. We show qualitative examples of this imagination or plausibility assessment for selected $(Q, A)$ pairs in Fig. 2 where we sort images and captions based on $P_I(A|Q, I)$ and $P_C(A|Q, C)$. Indeed, scenes where the corresponding fact $(Q, A)$ (e.g., man is wearing a helmet) is more likely to be plausible are scored higher.[2]

Based on the activation vectors $u_I$ and $u_C$, we then compute the VQA-grounded vector representations $v_I$ and $v_C$ for $I$ and $C$ by projecting $u_I$ and $u_C$ to a $D_u$-dimensional vector embedding space:

$$v_I = \sigma(W_{u_I} u_I + b_{v_I}) \qquad v_C = \sigma(W_{u_C} u_C + b_{v_C}) \qquad (7)$$

Here $\sigma$ is a non-linear activation function.

By verifying question-answer pairs on image $I$ and caption $C$ and computing vector representations on top of them, the VQA-grounded representations $v_I$ and $v_C$ explicitly project image and caption into VQA space to utilize

---

[2] Nonetheless, checking if a question applies to the target image and caption is also desirable. Contemporary work [41] has looked at modeling $P(Q|I)$, and can be incorporated in our approach as an additional feature

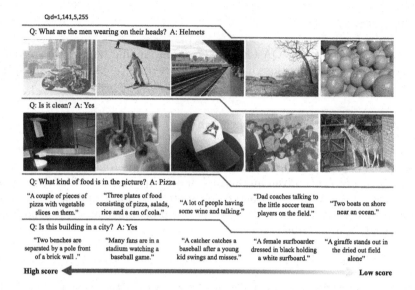

**Fig. 2.** Images and captions sorted by $P_I(A|Q, I)$ and $P_C(A|Q, C)$ assessed by our VQA (top) and VQA-Caption (bottom) models respectively. Indeed, images and captions that are more plausible for the $(Q, A)$ pairs are scored higher.

knowledge in the VQA corpora. However, that comes at a cost of losing information such as the sentence structure of the caption and image saliency. These information can also be important for image-caption ranking. As a result, we find VQA-grounded representations are most effective when they are combined with baseline VQA-agnostic models, so we propose two strategies for fusing VQA-grounded representations with baseline VQA-agnostic models: combining their prediction scores or score-level fusion (Fig. 3 left) and combining their representations or representation-level fusion (Fig. 3 right).

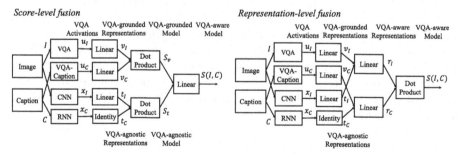

**Fig. 3.** We propose score-level fusion (left) and representation-level fusion (right) to utilize VQA for image-caption ranking. They use VQA and VQA-Caption models as "feature extraction" schemes for images and captions and use those features to construct VQA-grounded representations. The score-level fusion approach combines the scoring functions of a VQA-grounded model and a baseline VQA-agnostic model. The representation-level fusion approach combines VQA-grounded representations and VQA-agnostic representations to produce a VQA-aware scoring function.

## 4.2   Score-Level Fusion

A simple strategy to combine our VQA-grounded model with a VQA-agnostic image-ranking model is to combine them at the score level. Given image $I$ and caption $C$, we first compute the VQA-grounded score as the dot product between the VQA-grounded representations of image and caption $S_v(I, C) = \langle v_I, v_C \rangle$. We then combine it with the VQA-agnostic scoring function $S_t(I, C)$ to get the final scoring function $S(I, C)$:

$$S(I, C) = \alpha S_t(I, C) + \beta S_v(I, C) \tag{8}$$

We first learn $\{W_{u_I}, b_{u_I}, W_{u_C}, b_{u_C}\}$ on the image-caption ranking training set, and then learn $\alpha$ and $\beta$ on a held out validation set to avoid overfitting.

## 4.3   Representation-Level Fusion

An alternative to combining the VQA-agnostic and VQA-grounded representations at the score level is to inject the VQA-grounding at the representation level. Given the VQA-agnostic $D_t$-dimensional image and caption representations $t_I$ and $t_C$ used by the baseline model, we first compute the VQA-grounded representations $v_I$ for image and $v_C$ for caption introduced in Sect. 4.1. And then they are combined with VQA-agnostic representations to produce VQA-aware representations $r_I$ for image $I$ and $r_C$ for caption $C$ by projecting them to a $D_r$-dimensional multi-modal embedding space as follows:

$$r_I = \sigma(W_{t_I} t_I + W_{v_I} v_I + b_{r_I}) \qquad r_C = \sigma(W_{t_C} t_C + W_{v_C} v_C + b_{r_C}) \tag{9}$$

The final image-caption ranking score is then

$$S(I, C) = \langle r_I, r_C \rangle \tag{10}$$

In experiments, we jointly learn $\{W_{u_I}, b_{u_I}, W_{u_C}, b_{u_C}\}$ (for projecting $u_I$ and $u_C$ to the VQA-grounded representations $v_I$, $v_C$) with $\{W_{t_I}, W_{v_I}, b_{r_I}, W_{t_C}, W_{v_C}, b_{r_C}\}$ (for computing the combined VQA-aware representations $r_I$ and $r_C$) on the image-caption ranking training set by optimizing Eq. 2.

Score-level fusion and representation-level fusion models are implemented as multi-layer neural networks. All activation functions $\sigma$ are $ReLU(x) = \max(x, 0)$ (for speed) and dropout layers [47] are inserted after all $ReLU$ layers to avoid overfitting. We set the dimensions of the multi-modal embedding spaces $D_v$ and $D_r$ to 4,096 so they are large enough to capture necessary concepts for image-caption ranking. Optimization hyperparameters are selected on the validation set. We optimize both models using RMSProp with batch size 1,000 at learning rate 1e-5 for score-level fusion and 1e-4 for representation-level fusion. Optimization runs for 100,000 iterations with learning rate decay every 50,000 iterations.

Our main results in Sect. 5.1 use $N = 3000$ question-answer pairs, sampled 3 questions per image with their ground truth answers with respect to their original images from 1,000 random VQA training images. We discuss using different numbers of question-answer pairs $N$ and different strategies for selecting the question-answer pairs in Sect. 5.4.

# 5    Experiments and Results

We report results on MSCOCO [31] which is the largest available image-caption ranking dataset. Following the splits of [22,23] we use all 82,783 MSCOCO train images with 5 captions per image as our train set, 413,915 image-caption pairs in total. Note that this is the same split as the train split in the VQA dataset [1] we used to train our VQA and VQA-Caption models. The validation set consists of 1,000 images sampled from the original MSCOCO validation images. The test set consists of 5,000 images sampled from the original MSCOCO validation images that were not in the image-caption ranking validation set. Same as the train set, there are 5 captions available for each validation and test image.

We follow the evaluation metric of [22] and report caption and image retrieval performances on the first 1,000 test images following [22–24,33,37]. Given a test image, the caption retrieval task is to find any 1 out of its 5 captions from all 5,000 test captions. Given a test caption, the image retrieval task is to find its original image from all 1,000 test images. We report recall@(1, 5, 10): the fraction of times a correct item was found among the top (1, 5, 10) predictions.

## 5.1    Image-Caption Ranking Results

Table 1 shows our main results on MSCOCO. Our score-level fusion VQA-aware model using $N = 3000$ question-answer pairs ("$N = 3000$ score-level fusion VQA-aware") achieves 46.9 % caption retrieval recall@1 and 35.8 % image retrieval recall@1. This model shows an improvement of 3.5 % caption and 4.8 % image retrieval recall@1 over the state-of-the-art VQA-agnostic model of [23].

Our representation-level fusion approach adds an additional layer on top of the VQA-agnostic representations, resulting in a deeper model, so we experiment with adding an additional layer to the VQA-agnostic model for a fair comparison. That is equivalent to representation-level fusion using $N = 0$ question-answer pair ("$N = 0$ representation-level fusion", *i.e.* deeper VQA-agnostic). Comparing with the VQA-agnostic model of [23], adding this additional layer improves performance by 2.4 % caption and 2.6 % image retrieval recall@1.

By leveraging VQA knowledge our "$N = 3000$ representation-level fusion VQA-aware" model achieves 50.5 % caption retrieval recall@1 and 37.0 % image retrieval recall@1, which further improves 4.7 % and 3.4 % over the $N = 0$ VQA-agnostic representation-level fusion model. These improvements are consistent with our score-level fusion approach so this shows that the VQA corpora consistently provide complementary information to image-caption ranking.

To the best of our knowledge, the $N = 3000$ representation-level fusion VQA-aware result is the best result on MSCOCO image-caption ranking and significantly surpasses previous best results by as much as 7.1 % in caption retrieval and 4.4 % image retrieval recall@1.

Our VQA-grounded model alone ("$N = 3000$ score-level fusion VQA-grounded only") achieves 37.0 % caption and 26.2 % image retrieval recall@1. This indicates that the VQA activations $u_I$ and $u_C$ which evaluate the

**Table 1.** Caption retrieval and image retrieval performances of our models compared to baseline models on MSCOCO image-caption ranking test set. Powered by knowledge in VQA corpora, both our score-level fusion and representation-level fusion VQA-aware approaches outperform state-of-the-art VQA-agnostic models by a large margin

| MSCOCO | | | | | | |
|---|---|---|---|---|---|---|
| Approach | Caption retrieval | | | Image retrieval | | |
| | R@1 | R@5 | R@10 | R@1 | R@5 | R@10 |
| Random | 0.1 | 0.5 | 1.0 | 0.1 | 0.5 | 1.0 |
| DVSA [22] | 38.4 | 69.9 | 80.5 | 27.4 | 60.2 | 74.8 |
| FV (GMM+HGLMM) [24] | 39.4 | 67.9 | 80.9 | 25.1 | 59.8 | 76.6 |
| $m$-RNN-vgg [37] | 41.0 | 73.0 | 83.5 | 29.0 | 42.2 | 77.0 |
| $m$-$CNN_{ENS}$ [33] | 42.8 | 73.1 | 84.1 | 32.6 | 68.6 | 82.8 |
| Kiros et al. [23] (VQA-agnostic) | 43.4 | 75.7 | 85.8 | 31.0 | 66.7 | 79.9 |
| N = 3000 score-level fusion VQA-grounded only | 37.0 | 67.9 | 79.4 | 26.2 | 60.1 | 74.3 |
| N = 3000 score-level fusion VQA-aware | 46.9 | 78.6 | 88.9 | 35.8 | 70.3 | **83.6** |
| N = 0 representation-level fusion VQA-agnostic | 45.8 | 76.8 | 86.1 | 33.6 | 67.8 | 81.0 |
| N = 3000 representation-level fusion VQA-aware | **50.5** | **80.1** | **89.7** | **37.0** | **70.9** | 82.9 |

plausibility of facts (question-answer pairs) in images and captions are informative representations.

Figure 4 shows qualitative results on image retrieval comparing our approach ($N = 3000$ score-level fusion) with the VQA-agnostic model. By looking at several top retrieved images from our model for the failure case (last column), we find that our model seems to have picked up on a correlation between bats and helmets. It seems to be looking for helmets in retrieved images, while the ground truth image does not have one.

We also experiment with using the hidden activations available in the VQA and VQA-Caption models ($z_I$ and $z_C$ in Sect. 3.2) as image and caption encodings in place of the VQA activations ($u_I$ and $u_C$ in Sect. 4.1). Using these hidden activations of the VQA models is conceptually similar to using the hidden activations of CNNs pretrained on ImageNet as features [11]. These features achieve 46.8 % caption retrieval recall@1 and 35.2 % image retrieval recall@1 for score-level fusion, and 49.3 % caption retrieval recall@1 and 37.9 % image retrieval recall@1 for representation-level fusion which are as good as our semantic features $u_I$ and $u_C$. This shows that our semantically meaningful features, $u_I$ and $u_C$, performs as well as their corresponding non-sematic representations $z_I$ and $z_C$ using both score-level fusion and representation-level fusion. Note that such hidden activations may not always be available in different VQA models and the semantic features have the added benefit of being interpretable (e.g., Fig. 2).

**Fig. 4.** Qualitative image retrieval results of our score-level fusion VQA-aware model (middle) and the VQA-agnostic model (bottom). The true target image is highlighted (green if VQA-aware found it, red if VQA-agnostic found it but VQA-aware did not). (Color figure online)

## 5.2 Ablation Study

As an ablation study, we compare the following four models: (1) full representation-level fusion: our full $N = 3000$ representation-level fusion model that includes both image and caption VQA representations; (2) caption-only representation-level fusion: the same representation-level fusion model but using the VQA representation only for the caption, $v_C$, and not for the image; (3) image-only representation-level fusion: the same model but using the VQA representation only for the image, $v_I$, and not for the caption; (4) deeper VQA-agnostic: The $N = 0$ representation-level fusion model described earlier that does not use VQA representations for neither the image nor the caption.

Table 2 summarizes the results. We see that incrementally adding more VQA-knowledge improves performance. Both caption-only and image-only models outperform the $N = 0$ deeper VQA-agnostic baseline. The full representation-level fusion model which combines both representations yields the best performance.

**Table 2.** Ablation study evaluating the gain in performance as more VQA-knowledge is incorporated in the model

| MSCOCO | | | | | | |
|---|---|---|---|---|---|---|
| Approach | Caption retrieval | | | Image retrieval | | |
| | R@1 | R@5 | R@10 | R@1 | R@5 | R@10 |
| Deeper VQA-agnostic | 45.8 | 76.8 | 86.1 | 33.6 | 67.8 | 81.0 |
| Caption-only representation-level fusion | 47.3 | 77.3 | 86.6 | 35.5 | 69.3 | 81.9 |
| Image-only representation-level fusion | 47.0 | 80.0 | 89.6 | 36.4 | 70.1 | 82.3 |
| Full representation-level fusion | **50.5** | **80.1** | **89.7** | **37.0** | **70.9** | **82.9** |

## 5.3  The Role of VQA and Caption Annotations

In this work we transfer knowledge from one vision-language task (*i.e.* VQA) to another (*i.e.* image-caption ranking). However, VQA annotations and caption annotations serve different purposes.

The target language to be retrieved is caption language, and not VQA language. [1] showed qualitatively and quantitatively that the two languages are statistically quite different (in terms of information contained, and in terms of nouns, adjectives, verbs, etc. used). As a result, VQA can not be thought of as providing additional "annotations" for the captioning task. Instead, VQA provides different perspectives/views of the images (and captions). It provides an additional feature representation. To better utilize this representation for an image-caption ranking task, one would still require sufficient ground truth caption annotations for images. In fact, with varying amounts of ground truth (caption) annotations, the VQA-aware representations show improvements in performance across the board. See Fig. 5 (left).

A better analogy of our VQA representation is hidden activations (*e.g.*, fc7) from a CNN trained on ImageNet. Having additional ImageNet annotations would improve the fc7 feature. But to map this fc7 feature to captions, one would still require sufficient caption annotations. Conceptually, caption annotations and category labels in ImageNet play two different roles. The former provides ground truth for the target task at hand (image-caption ranking), and having additional annotations for the target application typically helps. The latter helps learn a better image representation (which may provide improvements in a variety of tasks).

## 5.4  Number of Question-Answer Pairs

Our VQA-grounded representations extract image and caption features based on question-answer pairs. It is important for there to be enough question-answer pairs to cover necessary aspects for image-caption ranking. We experiment with using $N = 30, 90, 300, 900, 3000$ $(Q, A)$ pairs (or facts) for both score-level and representation-level fusion. Figure 5 (right) shows caption and image retrieval performances of our approaches with varying $N$. Performance of both score-level and representation-level fusion approaches improve quickly from $N = 30$ to $N = 300$, and then starts to level off after $N = 300$.

An alternative to sampling 3 question-answer pairs per image on 1,000 images to get $N = 3000$ questions is to sample 1 question-answer pair per image from 3,000 images. Sampling multiple $(Q, A)$ pairs from the same image provides correlated $(Q, A)$ pairs. For example $(Q$: What are these animals? $A$: Giraffes) and $(Q$: Would this animal fit in a house? $A$: No). Using such correlated $(Q, A)$ pairs, the model could potentially better predict if there is a giraffe in the image by jointly reasoning if the animal looks like a giraffe and the if the animal would fit in a house, if the VQA and VQA-Caption models have not already picked up such correlations. In experiments, sampling 3 question-answer pairs per image

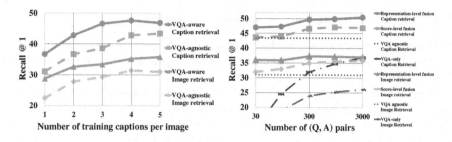

**Fig. 5. Left**: caption retrieval and image retrieval performances of the VQA-agnostic model compared with our $N = 3000$ score-level fusion VQA-aware model trained using 1 to 5 captions per image. The VQA representations in the VQA-aware model provide consistent performance gains. **Right**: caption retrieval and image retrieval performances of our score-level fusion and representation-level fusion approaches with varying number of $(Q, A)$ pairs used for feature extraction.

for correlated $(Q, A)$ pairs does not significantly outperform sampling 1 question-answer pair per image which performs $(47.7\%, 35.4\%)$ (image, caption) recall@1 using $N = 3000$ score-level fusion, so we hypothesize that our VQA and Caption-QA models have already captured such correlations.

# 6    Conclusion

VQA corpora provide rich multi-modal information that is complementary to knowledge stored in image captioning corpora. In this work we take the novel perspective of viewing VQA as a "feature extraction" module that captures VQA knowledge. We propose two approaches – score-level and representation-level fusion – to integrate this knowledge into an existing image-caption ranking model. We set new state-of-the-art by improving caption retrieval by 7.1 % and image retrieval by 4.4 % on MSCOCO.

Improved individual modules, *i.e.*, VQA models and VQA-agnostic image-caption ranking models, end-to-end training, and an attention mechanism that selects question-answer pairs (facts) in an image-specific manner may further improve the performance of our approach.

**Acknowledgment.** This work was supported in part by the Allen Distinguished Investigator awards by the Paul G. Allen Family Foundation, a Google Faculty Research Award, a Junior Faculty award by the Institute for Critical Technology and Applied Science (ICTAS) at Virginia Tech, a National Science Foundation CAREER award, an Army Research Office YIP award, and Office of Naval Research YIP award to D. P. The views and conclusions contained herein are those of the authors and should not be interpreted as necessarily representing the official policies or endorsements, either expressed or implied, of the U.S. Government or any sponsor.

# References

1. Antol, S., Agrawal, A., Lu, J., Mitchell, M., Batra, D., Zitnick, C.L., Parikh, D.: VQA: visual question answering. In: ICCV (2015)
2. Antol, S., Zitnick, C.L., Parikh, D.: Zero-shot learning via visual abstraction. In: ECCV (2014)
3. Berg, T., Belhumeur, P.N.: POOF: part-based one-vs.-one features for fine-grained categorization, face verification, and attribute estimation. In: CVPR (2013)
4. Bourdev, L., Maji, S., Brox, T., Malik, J.: Detecting people using mutually consistent poselet activations. In: Daniilidis, K., Maragos, P., Paragios, N. (eds.) ECCV 2010, Part VI. LNCS, vol. 6316, pp. 168–181. Springer, Heidelberg (2010)
5. Branson, S., Wah, C., Schroff, F., Babenko, B., Welinder, P., Perona, P., Belongie, S.: Visual recognition with humans in the loop. In: Daniilidis, K., Maragos, P., Paragios, N. (eds.) ECCV 2010, Part IV. LNCS, vol. 6314, pp. 438–451. Springer, Heidelberg (2010)
6. Chen, X., Lawrence Zitnick, C.: Mind's eye: a recurrent visual representation for image caption generation. In: CVPR (2015)
7. Cho, K., van Merriënboer, B., Bahdanau, D., Bengio, Y.: On the properties of neural machine translation: encoder-decoder approaches (2014). arXiv preprint arXiv:1409.1259
8. Deng, J., Dong, W., Socher, R., Li, L.J., Li, K., Fei-Fei, L.: ImageNet: a large-scale hierarchical image database. In: CVPR (2009)
9. Doersch, C., Gupta, A., Efros, A.A.: Unsupervised visual representation learning by context prediction. In: ICCV (2015)
10. Donahue, J., Grauman, K.: Annotator rationales for visual recognition. In: ICCV (2011)
11. Donahue, J., Jia, Y., Vinyals, O., Hoffman, J., Zhang, N., Tzeng, E., Darrell, T.: DeCAF: a deep convolutional activation feature for generic visual recognition (2013). arXiv preprint arXiv:1310.1531
12. Elhoseiny, M., Saleh, B., Elgammal, A.: Write a classifier: zero-shot learning using purely textual descriptions. In: ICCV (2013)
13. Elliott, D., Keller, F.: Comparing automatic evaluation measures for image description. In: Proceedings of 52nd Annual Meeting of the Association for Computational Linguistics, pp. 452–457 (2014)
14. Farhadi, A., Hejrati, M., Sadeghi, M.A., Young, P., Rashtchian, C., Hockenmaier, J., Forsyth, D.: Every picture tells a story: generating sentences from images. In: Daniilidis, K., Maragos, P., Paragios, N. (eds.) ECCV 2010, Part IV. LNCS, vol. 6314, pp. 15–29. Springer, Heidelberg (2010)
15. Farhadi, A., Endres, I., Hoiem, D., Forsyth, D.: Describing objects by their attributes. In: CVPR (2009)
16. Fouhey, D.F., Zitnick, C.L.: Predicting object dynamics in scenes. In: CVPR (2014)
17. Gao, H., Mao, J., Zhou, J., Huang, Z., Wang, L., Xu, W.: Are you talking to a machine? Dataset and methods for multilingual image question answering. In: NIPS (2015)
18. Gupta, A., Davis, L.S.: Beyond nouns: exploiting prepositions and comparative adjectives for learning visual classifiers. In: Forsyth, D., Torr, P., Zisserman, A. (eds.) ECCV 2008, Part I. LNCS, vol. 5302, pp. 16–29. Springer, Heidelberg (2008)
19. Hamrick, J., Battaglia, P., Tenenbaum, J.B.: Internal physics models guide probabilistic judgments about object dynamics. In: Proceedings of 33rd Annual Meeting of the Cognitive Science Society, Boston, MA (2011)

20. Hochreiter, S., Schmidhuber, J.: Long short-term memory. Neural Comput. **9**(8), 1735–1780 (1997)
21. Johnson, J., Krishna, R., Stark, M., Li, L.J., Shamma, D., Bernstein, M., Fei-Fei, L.: Image retrieval using scene graphs. In: CVPR (2015)
22. Karpathy, A., Fei-Fei, L.: Deep visual-semantic alignments for generating image descriptions. In: CVPR (2015)
23. Kiros, R., Salakhutdinov, R., Zemel, R.: Unifying visual-semantic embeddings with multimodal neural language models. In: TACL (2015)
24. Klein, B., Lev, G., Sadeh, G., Wolf, L.: Associating neural word embeddings with deep image representations using Fisher vectors. In: CVPR (2015)
25. Kovashka, A., Parikh, D., Grauman, K.: WhittleSearch: image search with relative attribute feedback. In: CVPR (2012)
26. Krizhevsky, A., Sutskever, I., Hinton, G.E.: Imagenet classification with deep convolutional neural networks. In: NIPS (2012)
27. Kulkarni, G., Premraj, V., Dhar, S., Li, S., Choi, Y., Berg, A.C., Berg, T.L.: Baby talk: understanding and generating simple image descriptions. In: CVPR (2011)
28. Kumar, N., Berg, A.C., Belhumeur, P.N., Nayar, S.K.: Describable visual attributes for face verification and image search. In: IEEE TPAMI (2011)
29. Lampert, C.H., Nickisch, H., Harmeling, S.: Learning to detect unseen object classes by between-class attribute transfer. In: CVPR (2009)
30. Li, L.J., Su, H., Fei-Fei, L., Xing, E.P.: Object bank: a high-level image representation for scene classification and semantic feature sparsification. In: NIPS (2010)
31. Lin, T.-Y., Maire, M., Belongie, S., Hays, J., Perona, P., Ramanan, D., Dollár, P., Zitnick, C.L.: Microsoft COCO: common objects in context. In: Fleet, D., Pajdla, T., Schiele, B., Tuytelaars, T. (eds.) ECCV 2014, Part V. LNCS, vol. 8693, pp. 740–755. Springer, Heidelberg (2014)
32. Lin, X., Parikh, D.: Don't just listen, use your imagination: leveraging visual common sense for non-visual tasks. In: CVPR (2015)
33. Ma, L., Lu, Z., Li, H.: Learning to answer questions from image using convolutional neural network (2015). arXiv preprint arXiv:1506.00333
34. Ma, L., Lu, Z., Shang, L., Li, H.: Multimodal convolutional neural networks for matching image and sentence. In: ICCV (2015)
35. Malinowski, M., Fritz, M.: A multi-world approach to question answering about real-world scenes based on uncertain input. In: NIPS (2014)
36. Malinowski, M., Rohrbach, M., Fritz, M.: Ask your neurons: a neural-based approach to answering questions about images. In: ICCV (2015)
37. Mao, J., Xu, W., Yang, Y., Wang, J., Huang, Z., Yuille, A.: Deep captioning with multimodal recurrent neural networks (M-RNN). In: ICLR (2015)
38. Parikh, D., Grauman, K.: Relative attributes. In: ICCV (2011)
39. Parkash, A., Parikh, D.: Attributes for Classifier Feedback. In: Fitzgibbon, A., Lazebnik, S., Perona, P., Sato, Y., Schmid, C. (eds.) ECCV 2012, Part III. LNCS, vol. 7574, pp. 354–368. Springer, Heidelberg (2012)
40. Pirsiavash, H., Vondrick, C., Torralba, A.: Inferring the why in images. CoRR abs/1406.5472 (2014). http://arXiv.org/abs/1406.5472
41. Ray, A., Christie, G., Bansal, M., Batra, D., Parikh, D.: Question relevance in VQA: identifying non-visual and false-premise questions (2016). arXiv preprint arXiv:1606.06622
42. Ren, M., Kiros, R., Zemel, R.: Exploring models and data for image question answering. In: NIPS (2015)
43. Sadanand, S., Corso, J.J.: Action bank: a high-level representation of activity in video. In: CVPR (2012)

44. Sadeghi, F., Divvala, S.K., Farhadi, A.: VisKE: visual knowledge extraction and question answering by visual verification of relation phrases. In: CVPR (2015)
45. Simonyan, K., Zisserman, A.: Very deep convolutional networks for large-scale image recognition. CoRR abs/1409.1556 (2014)
46. Socher, R., Ganjoo, M., Manning, C.D., Ng, A.: Zero-shot learning through cross-modal transfer. In: NIPS (2013)
47. Srivastava, N., Hinton, G., Krizhevsky, A., Sutskever, I., Salakhutdinov, R.: Dropout: a simple way to prevent neural networks from overfitting. JMLR **15**, 1929–1958 (2014)
48. Sutskever, I., Vinyals, O., Le, Q.V.: Sequence to sequence learning with neural networks. In: NIPS (2014)
49. Szegedy, C., Liu, W., Jia, Y., Sermanet, P., Reed, S., Anguelov, D., Erhan, D., Vanhoucke, V., Rabinovich, A.: Going deeper with convolutions. In: CVPR (2015)
50. Tang, K., Paluri, M., Fei-fei, L., Fergus, R., Bourdev, L.: Improving image classification with location context. In: ICCV (2015)
51. Vedantum, R., Lin, X., Batra, T., Zitnick, C.L., Parikh, D.: Learning common sense through visual abstraction. In: ICCV (2015)
52. Vedantum, R., Zitnick, C.L., Parikh, D.: Cider: Consensus-based image description evaluation. In: CVPR (2015)
53. Vondrick, C., Pirsiavash, H., Torralba, A.: Anticipating the future by watching unlabeled video (2015). arXiv preprint arXiv:1504.08023
54. Walker, J., Gupta, A., Hebert, M.: Patch to the future: unsupervised visual prediction. In: CVPR (2014)
55. Wang, Y., Mori, G.: A discriminative latent model of object classes and attributes. In: Daniilidis, K., Maragos, P., Paragios, N. (eds.) ECCV 2010, Part V. LNCS, vol. 6315, pp. 155–168. Springer, Heidelberg (2010)
56. Xu, K., Ba, J., Kiros, R., Cho, K., Courville, A., Salakhutdinov, R., Zemel, R., Bengio, Y.: Show, attend and tell: neural image caption generation with visual attention. In: ICML (2015)
57. Yu, L., Park, E., Berg, A.C., Berg, T.L.: Visual madlibs: fill in the blank image generation and question answering (2015). arXiv preprint arXiv:1506.00278
58. Zhang, N., Farrell, R., Iandola, F., Darrell, T.: Deformable part descriptors for fine-grained recognition and attribute prediction. In: ICCV (2013)
59. Zhang, N., Paluri, M., Ranzato, M., Darrell, T., Bourdev, L.: PANDA: pose aligned networks for deep attribute modeling. In: CVPR (2014)
60. Zheng, B., Zhao, Y., Yu, J., Ikeuchi, K., Zhu, S.C.: Beyond point clouds: scene understanding by reasoning geometry and physics. In: CVPR (2013)
61. Zhou, B., Tian, Y., Sukhbaatar, S., Szlam, A., Fergus, R.: Simple baseline for visual question answering (2015). arXiv preprint arXiv:1512.02167
62. Zhu, Y., Fathi, A., Fei-Fei, L.: Reasoning about object affordances in a knowledge base representation. In: Fleet, D., Pajdla, T., Schiele, B., Tuytelaars, T. (eds.) ECCV 2014, Part II. LNCS, vol. 8690, pp. 408–424. Springer, Heidelberg (2014)
63. Zhu, Y., Zhang, C., Re, C., Fei-Fei, L.: Building a large-scale multimodal knowledge base for visual question answering (2013). arXiv preprint arXiv:1310.1531

# DAVE: A Unified Framework for Fast Vehicle Detection and Annotation

Yi Zhou[1]($\boxtimes$), Li Liu[1], Ling Shao[1], and Matt Mellor[2]

[1] Northumbria University, Newcastle upon Tyne NE1 8ST, UK
{yi2.zhou,li2.liu,ling.shao}@northumbria.ac.uk
[2] Createc, Cockermouth, Cumbria CA13 0HT, UK
matt.mellor@createc.co.uk

**Abstract.** Vehicle detection and annotation for streaming video data with complex scenes is an interesting but challenging task for urban traffic surveillance. In this paper, we present a fast framework of Detection and Annotation for Vehicles (DAVE), which effectively combines vehicle detection and attributes annotation. DAVE consists of two convolutional neural networks (CNNs): a fast vehicle proposal network (FVPN) for vehicle-like objects extraction and an attributes learning network (ALN) aiming to verify each proposal and infer each vehicle's pose, color and type simultaneously. These two nets are jointly optimized so that abundant latent knowledge learned from the ALN can be exploited to guide FVPN training. Once the system is trained, it can achieve efficient vehicle detection and annotation for real-world traffic surveillance data. We evaluate DAVE on a new self-collected UTS dataset and the public PASCAL VOC2007 car and LISA 2010 datasets, with consistent improvements over existing algorithms.

**Keywords:** Vehicle detection · Attributes annotation · Latent knowledge guidance · Joint learning · Deep networks

## 1  Introduction and Related Work

Automatic analysis of urban traffic activities is an urgent need due to essential traffic management and increased vehicle violations. Among many traffic surveillance techniques, computer vision-based methods have attracted a great deal of attention and made great contributions to realistic applications such as vehicle counting, target vehicle retrieval and behavior analysis. In these research areas, efficient and accurate vehicle detection and attributes annotation is the most important component of traffic surveillance systems.

Vehicle detection is a fundamental objective of traffic surveillance. Traditional vehicle detection methods can be categorized into frame-based and motion-based approaches [1,2]. For motion-based approaches, frames subtraction [3], adaptive background modeling [4] and optical flow [5,6] are often utilized. However, some non-vehicle moving objects will be falsely detected with

© Springer International Publishing AG 2016
B. Leibe et al. (Eds.): ECCV 2016, Part II, LNCS 9906, pp. 278–293, 2016.
DOI: 10.1007/978-3-319-46475-6_18

motion-based approaches since less visual information is exploited. To achieve higher detection performance, recently, the deformable part-based model (DPM) [7] employs a star-structured architecture consisting of root and parts filters with associated deformation models for object detection. DPM can successfully handle deformable object detection even when the target is partially occluded. However, it leads to heavy computational costs due to the use of the sliding window procedure for appearance features extraction and classification.

With the wide success of deep networks on image classification [8–12], a Region-based CNN (RCNN) [13] combines object proposals, CNN learned features and an SVM classifier for accurate object detection. To further increase the detection speed and accuracy, Fast RCNN [14] adopts a region of interest (ROI) pooling layer and the multi-task loss to estimate object classes while predicting bounding-box positions. "Objectness" proposal methods such as Selective Search [15] and Edgeboxes [16] can be introduced in RCNN and Fast RCNN to improve the efficiency compared to the traditional sliding window fashion. Furthermore, Faster RCNN [17] employs a Region Proposal Network (RPN) with shared convolutional features to enable cost-free effective proposals. All these deep models target general object detection. In our task, we aim for real-time detection of a special object type, vehicle.

Besides, in urban traffic surveillance, another interesting and valuable task is to extract more diverse information from detected vehicles - we call it vehicle attributes annotation. Each individual vehicle on the road has its special attributes: travel direction (i.e., pose), inherent color, type and other more fine-grained information with respect to the headlight, grille and wheel. It is extremely beneficial to annotate a target vehicle's attributes accurately. Lin et al. [18] presents an auto-masking neural network for vehicle detection and pose estimation. In [19], an approach by vector matching of template is introduced for vehicle color recognition. In [20], unsupervised convolutional neural network is adopted for vehicle type classification from frontal view images. However, independent analysis of different attributes makes visual information not well explored and the process inefficient, and little work has been done for annotating these vehicle attributes simultaneously. Actually, there exist strong correlations between these vehicle attributes learning tasks. For example, vehicle type classification based on visual structures is very dependent on the viewpoint. Therefore, we believe multi-task learning [21,22] can be helpful since such joint learning schemes can implicitly learn the common features shared by these correlated tasks. Moreover, a unified multi-attributes inference model can also significantly improve the efficiency.

Inspired by the advantages and drawbacks of previous work, in this paper, we propose a fast framework DAVE based on convolutional neural networks (CNNs), as shown in Fig. 1, for vehicle detection and attributes annotation in urban traffic surveillance. In particular, DAVE consists of two CNNs: fast vehicle proposal network (FVPN) and attributes learning network (ALN). The FVPN is a shallow *fully convolutional network* which is able to predict all the bounding-boxes of vehicle-like objects in real-time. The latter ALN configured with a very

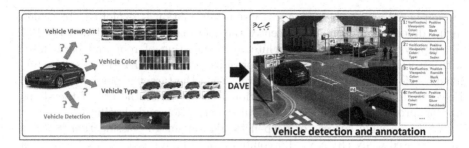

**Fig. 1. Illustration of DAVE.** Vehicle detection and corresponding pose, color and type annotation can be simultaneously achieved by DAVE as shown in the right sub-figure. (Color figure online)

deep structure can precisely verify each proposal and infer pose, color and type information for positive vehicles, simultaneously. It is noteworthy that informative features learned from the deep ALN can be regarded as latent data-driven knowledge to guide the training of the shallow FVPN, thus we bridge the ALN and FVPN with such knowledge guidance and jointly optimize these two CNNs at the same time in our architecture. In this way, more exhaustive vehicle descriptions learned from the ALN as helpful supervision benefits the FVPN with better performance. Once the joint training is finished, a two-stage inference scheme will be adopted for final vehicle annotation. The main contributions of our work are highlighted as follows:

1. We unify multiple vehicle-related tasks into one deep vehicle annotation framework DAVE which can effectively and efficiently annotate each vehicle's bounding-box, pose, color and type simultaneously.
2. Two CNNs proposed in our method, i.e., the Fast Vehicle Proposal Network (FVPN) and the vehicle Attributes Learning Network (ALN), are optimized in a joint manner by bridging two CNNs with latent data-driven knowledge guidance. In this way, the deeper ALN can benefit the performance of the shallow FVPN.
3. We introduce a new Urban Traffic Surveillance (UTS) vehicle dataset consisting of six $1920 \times 1080$ (FHD) resolution videos with varying illumination conditions and viewpoints.

## 2    Detection and Annotation for Vehicles (DAVE)

We unify vehicle detection and annotation of pose, color and type into one framework: DAVE. As illustrated in Fig. 2, DAVE consists of two convolutional neural networks called fast vehicle proposal network (FVPN) and attributes learning network (ALN), respectively. FVPN aims to predict all the positions of vehicle-like objects in real-time. Afterwards, these vehicle proposals are passed to the ALN to simultaneously verify all the positive vehicles and infer their corresponding poses, colors and types. In the training phase, FVPN and ALN are optimized jointly, while two-stage inference is used in the test phase. Specifically, training our DAVE is inspired by [23] that knowledge learned from solid deep networks can be distilled to teach shallower networks. We apply latent data-driven knowledge from the deep ALN to guide the training of the shallow FVPN. This method proves to be able to enhance the performance of the FVPN to some extent through experiments. The architecture of FVPN and ANL will be described in the following subsections.

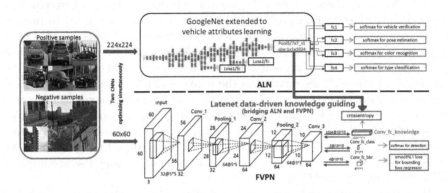

**Fig. 2. Training Architecture of DAVE.** Two CNNs: FVPN and ALN are simultaneously optimized in a joint manner by bridging them with latent data-driven knowledge guidance.

## 2.1  Fast Vehicle Proposal Network (FVPN)

Searching the whole image to locate potential vehicle positions in a sliding window fashion is prohibitive for real-time applications. Traditional object proposal methods are put forward to alleviate this problem, but thousands of proposals usually contain numerous false alarms and duplicate predictions which heavily lower the efficiency. Particularly for one specific object, we expect very fast and accurate proposal performance can be achieved.

Our proposed fast vehicle proposal network (FVPN) is a shallow *fully convolutional network*, which aims to precisely localize all the vehicle-like objects in real-time. We are interested in exploring whether or not a small scale CNN is enough to handle the single object proposal task. A schematic diagram of the FVPN is depicted in the bottom part of Fig. 2. The first convolutional layer (*conv_1*) filters the $60 \times 60$ training images with 32 kernels of size $5 \times 5$. The second convolutional layer (*conv_2*) takes as input the feature maps obtained from the previous layer and filters them with 64 kernels of size $5 \times 5$. Max pooling and Rectified Linear Units (ReLU) layers are configured after the first two convolutional layers. The third convolutional layer (*conv_3*) with 64 kernels of size $3 \times 3$ is branched into three sibling $1 \times 1$ convolutional layers transformed by traditional fully connected layers. In detail, *Conv_fc_class* outputs softmax probabilities of positive samples and the background; *Conv_fc_bbr* encodes bounding-box coordinates for each positive sample; *Conv_fc_knowledge* is configured for learning latent data-driven knowledge distilled from the ALN, which makes the FVPN be trained with more meticulous vehicle features. Inspired by [24], these $1 \times 1$ convolutional layers can successfully lead to differently purposed heatmaps in the inference phase. This property will directly achieve real-time vehicle localization from whole images/frames by our FVPN.

We employ different loss supervision layers for three corresponding tasks in the FVPN. First, discrimination between a vehicle and the background is a simple binary classification problem. A softmax loss layer is applied to predict vehicle confidence, $p^c = \{p^c_{ve}, p^c_{bg}\}$. Besides, each bounding-box is encoded by 4 predictions: $x$, $y$, $w$ and $h$. $x$ and $y$ denote the left-top coordinates of the vehicle position, while $w$ and $h$ represent the width and height of the vehicle size. We normalize all the 4 values relative to the image width and height so that they can be bounded between 0 and 1. Note that all bounding boxes' coordinates are set as *zero* for background samples. Following [14], a smooth L1 loss layer is used for bounding-box regression to output the refined coordinates vector, $loc = (\hat{x}, \hat{y}, \hat{w}, \hat{h})$. Finally, for guiding with latent data-driven knowledge of an N-dimensional vector distilled from a deeper net, the cross-entropy loss is employed for $p^{know} = \{p^{know}_0 \ldots p^{know}_{N-1}\}$.

We adopt a multi-task loss $L_{FVPN}$ on each training batch to jointly optimize binary classification of a vehicle against background, bounding-box regression and learning latent knowledge from a deeper net as the following function:

$$L_{FVPN}(loc, p^{bic}, p^{know}) = L_{bic}(p^{bic}) + \alpha L_{bbox}(loc) + \beta L_{know}(p^{know}), \qquad (1)$$

where $L_{bic}$ denotes the softmax loss for binary classification of vehicle and background. $L_{bbox}$ indicates a smooth $\ell_1$ loss defined in [14] as:

$$L_{bbox}(loc) = f_{L1}(loc - loc_t), \text{ where } f_{L1}(x) = \begin{cases} 0.5x^2, & \text{if } |x| < 1 \\ |x| - 0.5, & \text{otherwise} \end{cases} \qquad (2)$$

Furthermore, the cross entropy loss $L_{know}$ is to guide the training of the FVPN by a latent N-dimensional feature vector $t^{know}$ learned from a more solid net, which is defined as:

$$L_{know}(p^{know}) = -\frac{1}{N} \sum_i^N t^{know}_i \log p^{know}_i + (1 - t^{know}_i) \log(1 - p^{know}_i). \qquad (3)$$

It is noteworthy that a bounding-box for the background is meaningless in the FVPN back-propagation phase and will cause training to diverge early [25], *thus we set $\alpha = 0$ for background samples, otherwise $\alpha = 0.5$*. Besides, $\beta$ is fixed to 0.5.

## 2.2   Attributes Learning Network (ALN)

Modeling vehicle pose estimation, color recognition and type classification separately is less accurate and inefficient. Actually, relationships between these tasks can be explored, so that designing a multi-task network is beneficial for learning shared features which can lead to extra performance gains. The attribute learning network (ALN) is a unified network to verify vehicle candidates and annotate their poses, colors and types. The network architecture of the ALN is mainly inspired by the GoogLeNet [26] model. Specifically, we design the ALN by adding 4 fully connected layers to extend the GoogLeNet into a multi-attribute learning model. The reason to adopt such a very deep structure here is because vehicle annotation belongs to fine-grained categorization problems and a deeper net has more powerful capability to learn representative and discriminative features. Another advantage of the ALN is its high-efficiency inherited from the GoogLeNet which has lower computation and memory costs compared with other deep nets such as the VGGNet [27].

The ALN is a multi-task network optimized with four softmax loss layers for vehicle annotation tasks. Each training image has four labels in $V$, $P$, $C$ and $T$. $V$ determines whether a sample is a vehicle. If $V$ is a true vehicle, the remaining three attributes $P$, $C$ and $T$ represent its pose, color and type respectively. However, if $V$ is the background or a vehicle with a catch-all[1] type or color, $P$, $C$ and $T$ are set as *zero* denoting attributes are unavailable in the training phase. The first softmax loss layer $L_{verify}(p^V)$ for binary classification (vehicle vs. background) is the same as $L_{bic}(p^c)$ in the FVPN. The softmax loss $L_{pose}(p^P)$, $L_{color}(p^C)$ and $L_{type}(p^T)$ are optimized for pose estimation, color recognition and vehicle type classification respectively, where $p^P = \{p_1^P, \ldots, p_{np}^P\}$, $p^C = \{p_1^C, \ldots, p_{nc}^C\}$ and $p^T = \{p_1^T, \ldots, p_{nt}^T\}$. $\{np, nc, nt\}$ indicate the number of vehicle poses, colors and types respectively. The whole loss function is defined as follows:

$$L_{ALN}(p^V, p^P, p^C, p^T) = L_{verify}(p^V) + \lambda_1 L_{pose}(p^P) + \lambda_2 L_{color}(p^C) + \lambda_3 L_{type}(p^T), \quad (4)$$

where all the four sub loss functions are softmax loss for vehicle verification (*"verification" in this paper means confirming whether a proposal is vehicle*), pose estimation, color recognition and type classification. *Following the similar case of $\alpha$ in Eq. (1), parameters $\{\lambda_1, \lambda_2, \lambda_3\}$ are all fixed as 1 for the positive samples, otherwise as 0 for the background.*

### 2.3 Deep Nets Training

**Training Dataset and Data Augmentation.** We adopt the large-scale CompCars dataset [28] with more than 100,000 web-nature data as the positive training samples which are annotated with tight bounding-boxes and rich vehicle attributes such as pose, type, make and model. In detail, the web-nature part of the CompCars dataset provides five viewpoints as *front, rear, side, frontside* and *rearside*, twelve vehicle types as *MPV, SUV, sedan, hatchback, minibus, pickup, fastback, estate, hardtop-convertible, sports, crossover* and *convertible*. To achieve an even training distribution, we discard less common vehicle types

---

[1] "Catch-all" indicates other undefined types and colors which are not included in our training model.

with few training images and finally select six types with all the five viewpoints illustrated in Fig. 3(a) to train our model. Besides, since color is another important attribute of a vehicle, we additionally annotate colors on more than 10,000 images with five common vehicle colors as *black, white, silver, red* and *blue* to train our final model. Apart from positive samples, about 200,000 negative samples without any vehicles are cropped from Google Street View Images to compose our training data.

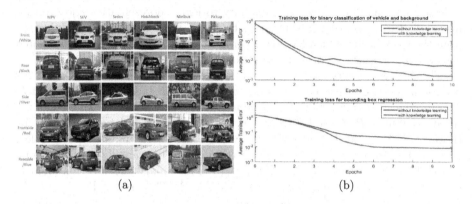

(a)                                            (b)

**Fig. 3.** (a) Examples of training data (columns indicate vehicle types, while rows indicate poses and colors), (b) training loss with/without knowledge learning. (Color figure online)

For data augmentation, we first triple the training data with increased and decreased image intensities for making our DAVE more robust under different lighting conditions. In addition, image downsampling up to 20 % of the original size and image blurring are introduced to enable that detected vehicles with small sizes can be even annotated as precisely as possible.

**Jointly Training with Latent Knowledge Guidance.** The entire training structure of DAVE is illustrated in Fig. 2. We optimize the FVPN and the ALN jointly but with different sized input training data at the same time. The input resolution of the ALN is $224 \times 224$ for fine-grained vehicle attributes learning, while it is decreased to $60 \times 60$ for the FVPN to fit smaller scales of the test image pyramid for efficiency in the inference phase. In fact, the resolution of $60 \times 60$ can well guarantee the coarse shape and texture of a vehicle is discriminative enough against the background. Besides, another significant difference between the ALN and the FVPN is that input vehicle samples for the ALN are tightly cropped, however, for the FVPN, uncropped vehicles are used for bounding-box (labeled as $loc_t$ in Eq. (2)) regressor training.

The pre-trained GoogLeNet model for 1000-class ImageNet classification is used to initialize all the convolutional layers in the ALN, while the FVPN is trained from scratch. A 1024-dimensional feature vector of the *pool5/7×7_s1* layer in the ALN, which can exhaustively describe a vehicle, is extracted as the latent data-driven knowledge guidance to supervise the same dimensional *Conv_fc_knowledge* layer in the FVPN by cross entropy loss.

We first jointly train ALN and FVPN for about 10 epochs on the selected web-nature data that only contains pose and type attributes from the CompCars. In the next 10 epochs, we fine-tune the models by a subset with our complemented color annotations. Throughout the training process, we set the batch size as 64, and the momentum and weight decay are configured as 0.9 and 0.0002, respectively. Learning rate is scheduled as $10^{-3}$ for the first 10 epochs and $10^{-4}$ for the second 10 epochs. To make our method more convincing, we train two models with and without knowledge guidance, respectively. During training, we definitely discover that knowledge guidance can indeed benefit training the shallow FVPN to obtain lower training losses. Training loss curves for the first 10 epochs are depicted in Fig. 3(b).

### 2.4 Two-Stage Deep Nets Inference

Once the joint training is finished, a two-stage scheme is implemented for inference of DAVE. First, the FVPN takes as input the 10-level test image Gaussian pyramid. For each level, the FVPN is operated over the input frame to infer *Conv_fc_class* and *Conv_fc_bbr* layers as corresponding heatmaps. All the 10 *Conv_fc_class* heatmaps are unified into one map by rescaling all the channels to the largest size among them and keeping the maximum along channels, while the index of each maximum within 10 channels is used to obtain four unified *Conv_fc_bbr* heatmaps (10 levels by similar rescaling). After unifying different levels *Conv_fc_class* heatmaps into the final vehicle proposal score map, we first filter the score map with threshold *thres* to discard low hot spots, and then local peaks on the map are detected by a circle scanner with tuneable radius $r$. In all our experiments, $r = 8$ and $thres = 0.5$ are fixed. Thus, these local maximal positions are considered as the central coordinates of proposals, $(\hat{x}_i, \hat{y}_i)$. Coarse width and height of each proposal can be simply predicted based on the bounding-box of its corresponding hot spot centered on each local peak. If one hot spot contains multiple peaks, the width and height will be shared by these peaks (i.e. proposals). For preserving the complete vehicle body, coarse width and height are multiplied by fixed parameter $m = 1.5$ to generate $(\hat{w}_i^{nobbr}, \hat{h}_i^{nobbr})$. Thus, a preliminary bounding-box can be represented as $(\hat{x}_i, \hat{y}_i, \hat{w}_i^{nobbr}, \hat{h}_i^{nobbr})$. Finally, bounding-box regression offset values (within [0,1]) are extracted from four unified heatmaps of *Conv_fc_bbr* at those coordinates $(\hat{x}_i, \hat{y}_i)$ to obtain refined bounding-box.

Vehicle proposals inferred from the FVPN are taken as inputs into the ALN. Although verifying each proposal and annotation of attributes are at the same stage, we assume that verification has a higher priority. For instance, in the inference phase, if a proposal is predicted as a positive vehicle, it will then be annotated with a bounding-box and inferred pose, color and type. However, a proposal predicted as the background will be neglected in spite of its inferred attributes. Finally, we perform non-maximum suppression as in RCNN [13] to eliminate duplicate detections. The full inference scheme is demonstrated in Fig. 4. At present, it is difficult to train a model that has the capability to annotate all the vehicles with enormously rich vehicle colors and types. During inference, a vehicle with untrained colors and types is always categorized into similar classes or a catch-all "others" class, which is a limitation of DAVE. In future work, we may expand our training data to include more abundant vehicle classes.

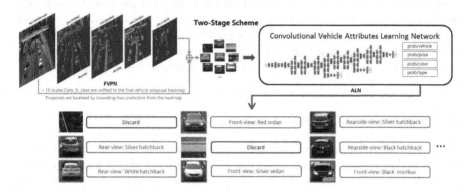

**Fig. 4. A two-stage inference phase of DAVE.** Vehicle proposals are first obtained from FVPN in real-time. Afterwards, we use ALN to verify each proposal and annotate each positive one with the vehicle pose, color and type. (Color figure online)

## 3   Experiments and Results

In this section, we evaluate our DAVE for detection and annotation of pose, color and type for each detected vehicle. Experiments are mainly divided as two parts: vehicle detection and attributes learning. DAVE is implemented based on the deep learning framework Caffe [29] and run on a workstation configured with an NVIDIA TITAN X GPU.

### 3.1   Evaluation of Vehicle Detection

To evaluate vehicle detection, we train our models using the large-scale Comp-Cars dataset as mentioned before, and test on three other vehicle datasets. We collect a full high definition (1920 × 1080) Urban Traffic Surveillance (UTS) vehicle dataset with six videos which were captured from different viewpoints and illumination conditions. Each video sequence contains 600 annotated frames. To be more convincing, we also compare our method on two other public datasets: the PASCAL VOC2007 car dataset [30] and the LISA 2010 dataset [31] with four competitive models: DPM [7], RCNN [17], Fast RCNN [14] and Faster RCNN [17]. These four methods obtain state-of-the-art performances on general object detection and the codes are publicly available. We adopt the trained car model in voc-release5 [32] for DPM, while train models (VGG-16 version) for RCNN, Fast RCNN and Faster RCNN ourselves on the CompCars dataset to implement vehicle detection as our DAVE. The vehicle detection evaluation criterion is the same as PASCAL object detection [30]. Intersection over Union (IoU) is set as 0.7 to assess correct localization.

**Testing on the UTS Dataset.** Since our FVPN can be considered as a high-accuracy proposal model for a single specific object, we test it independently. Then, results from vehicle verification by the deeper ALN (i.e., FVPN+verify in Fig. 5) are shown as our final accuracies. The detection accuracy as average precision (AP) and speed as frames-per-second (FPS) are compared in the left column of Table 1. Our model outperforms all the other methods with obvious improvements. Specifically, our method obtains an increased AP of 3.03 % compared to the best model Faster RCNN, and the shallow proposal network FVPN independently achieves 57.28 % which is only lower than Faster RCNN. The other two deep models, RCNN and Fast RCNN, do not produce satisfactory results mainly due to the low-precision proposals extracted by Selective Search [15]. Mixture-DPM with bounding-box prediction (MDPM-w-BB [7]) significantly improve the performance compared to MDPM-w/o-BB [7] by 10.77 %. For the evaluation of efficiency, our FVPN with a shallow and thin architecture can achieve real-time performance with 30 fps on FHD video frames. Although the deeper ALN slows the entire detection framework, 2 fps performance still shows competitive speed with Faster RCNN (4 fps).

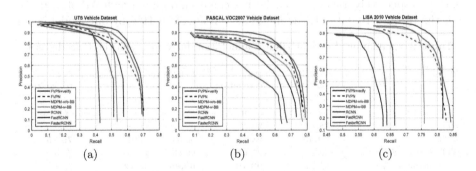

**Fig. 5.** Precision-recall curves on three vehicle datasets

We also test the FVPN trained without knowledge guidance, the AP decreases by 2.37 %, which explains the significant advancement of knowledge guidance. In addition, experiments are carried out to demonstrate that bounding-box regression can be helpful with the AP increased by 0.96 %.

**Table 1.** Vehicle detection AP (%) and speed (fps) comparison on the UTS, PASCAL VOC2007 and LISA 2010 datasets

| Methods | UTS | | PASCAL VOC2007 | | LISA 2010 | |
|---|---|---|---|---|---|---|
| | Average precision (AP) | Processing speed (fps) | Average precision (AP) | Processing speed (fps) | Average precision (AP) | Processing speed (fps) |
| MDPM-w/o-BB | 41.96 % | 0.25 | 48.44 % | 1.25 | 63.61 % | 0.7 |
| MDPM-w-BB | 52.73 % | 0.2 | 57.14 % | 1.25 | 72.89 % | 0.7 |
| RCNN | 44.87 % | 0.03 | 38.52 % | 0.08 | 55.37 % | 0.06 |
| FastRCNN | 51.58 % | 0.4 | 52.95 % | 0.5 | 53.37 % | 0.5 |
| FasterRCNN | 59.82 % | **4** | 63.47 % | **6** | 77.09 % | **6** |
| FVPN-w/o-knowledge guide | 54.91 % | 30 | 58.12 % | 46 | 72.37 % | 42 |
| FVPN-w/o-bbr | 56.32 % | 30 | 58.93 % | 46 | 71.82 % | 42 |
| **FVPN** | 57.28 % | **30** | 60.05 % | **46** | 73.46 % | **42** |
| **FVPN+Verify** | **62.85 %** | 2 | **64.44 %** | 4 | **79.41 %** | 4 |

"bbr" indicates the bounding-box regressor used in our model, while "BB" denotes bounding-box prediction used in DPM model. "w" and "w/o" are the abbreviations of "with" and "without", respectively. "Verify" denotes the vehicle verification in the ALN.

**Testing on the PASCAL VOC2007 Car Dataset and the LISA 2010 Dataset.** To make our methods more convincing, we also evaluate on two public datasets. All the images containing vehicles in the trainval and test sets (totally 1434 images) in the PASCAL VOC 2007 dataset are extracted to be evaluated. In addition, the LISA 2010 dataset contains three video sequences with low image quality captured from a on-board camera. All the results are shown in the middle and right columns of Table 2. For the PASCAL VOC2007 dataset, our model (FVPN+verify) achieves 64.44 % in AP, which outperforms MDPM-w-BB, RCNN, FastRCNN and Faster RCNN by 7.3 %, 25.92 %, 11.49 % and 0.97 %, respectively. Likewise, our FVPN can even obtain a high AP of 60.05 %. For the LISA 2010 dataset, the highest accuracy of 79.41 % by our model beats

**Table 2.** Evaluation (%) of attributes annotation for vehicles on the UTS dataset

| Tasks | Vehicle verification | Pose estimation | Vehicle type classification | | Color recognition |
|---|---|---|---|---|---|
| | | | 12 types | 6 types | |
| *Comparison of single-task learning (STL) and multi-task learning (MTL) for attributes prediction* | | | | | |
| STL | 98.73 | 96.94 | 60.37 | 88.32 | 78.33 |
| MTL | **99.45** | 98.03 | 69.64 | 94.91 | **79.25** |
| STL feature+SVM | 99.11 | 97.12 | 60.86 | 90.75 | 78.06 |
| MTL feature+SVM | 99.36 | **98.10** | **69.86** | **95.12** | 79.19 |
| *Comparison of attributes prediction with different sizes of vehicle images* | | | | | |
| 28 × 28 | 90.45 | 83.49 | 37.52 | 53.66 | 49.73 |
| 56 × 56 | 98.12 | 91.33 | 52.02 | 77.02 | 66.14 |
| 112 × 112 | 99.37 | 96.56 | 63.41 | 90.67 | **80.31** |
| 224 × 224 | **99.45** | **98.03** | **69.64** | **94.91** | 79.25 |
| *Comparison of attributes prediction with different deep models* | | | | | |
| ALN based on FVPN (depth = 4) | 95.96 | 81.21 | 27.26 | 43.12 | 65.12 |
| ALN based on AlexNet (depth = 8) | **99.51** | 95.76 | 66.01 | 89.25 | 77.90 |
| ALN based on GoogLeNet (depth = 22) | 99.45 | **98.03** | 69.04 | **94.91** | 79.25 |

all other methods as well. Therefore, it demonstrates that our method is able to stably detect vehicles with different viewpoints, occlusions and image qualities.

Figure 5 presents the precision-recall curves of all the compared methods on UTS, PASCAL VOC2007 car dataset and the LISA 2010 dataset, respectively. From all these figures, we can further discover that, for all three datasets, FVPN+Verify achieves better performance than other detection methods by comparing Area Under the Curve (AUC). Besides, some qualitative detection results including successful and failure cases are shown in Fig. 6. It can be observed that the FVPN cannot handle highly occluded cases at very small sizes, since local peaks on the FVPN heatmap for vehicles in those cases will be overlapped. The similar situation also exists in most of the deep networks based detection approaches [13,14,17,25].

**Fig. 6.** Examples of successful and failure cases for detection (a green box denotes correct localization, a red box denotes false alarm and a blue box denotes missing detection) (Color figure online)

### 3.2  Evaluation of Attributes Learning

The experiments and analysis of the ALN is mainly based on the CompCars dataset and the UTS dataset. The web-nature data in the CompCars dataset are labeled with five viewpoints and twelve types about 136000 and 97500 images, respectively. We neglect those images without type annotation and randomly split the remaining data into the training and test subsets as 7:3. In addition to pose estimation and type classification, we complement the annotation of five common vehicle colors on about 10000 images for evaluation of color recognition. Besides, for type classification, we compare the results of both the selected 6 common vehicle types and the total 12 types as mentioned in Sect. 3.2. Vehicle verification (i.e., binary classification of vehicle and background) is evaluated in all the experiments as well.

In the following subsections, we implement four different experiments to investigate the gain of the multi-task architecture, the accuracy by inputs with different image qualities, the effect of layer depths and the difficulty of fine-grained classification under different viewpoints. In addition, we also explain the superiority of our two-stage inference models compared to state-of-the-art one-net pipeline.

**Single-task Learning or Multi-task Learning?** We first compare the multi-task ALN with the case of training networks for each attribute separately (i.e., single task). In addition, results by the combination of deep learned features and an SVM classifier are compared as well. All the model architectures are based on the GoogLeNet, and 1024-dimensional features are extracted from layer $pool5/7 \times 7\_s1$ to train the corresponding SVM classifier [33]. As shown in the top part of Table 2, the multi-task model consistently achieves higher accuracies on four different tasks, which reveals the benefit of joint training. Although the combination of extracted features and SVM classifiers sometimes can lead to a small increase, we still prefer the proposed end-to-end model because of its elegance and efficiency.

**How Small a Vehicle Size Can DAVE Annotate?** Since vehicles within surveillance video frames are usually in different sizes. Visual details of those vehicles far from the camera are significantly unclear. Although they can be selected by the FVPN with coarse requirements, after rescaling to 224 × 224, these vehicle proposals with low image clarity are hard to be annotated with correct attributes by the ALN. To explore this problem, we test vehicle images with original sizes of 224, 112, 56 and 28 using the trained ALN. The middle part of Table 2 illustrates that the higher resolution the original input size is, the better accuracy it can achieve.

**Deep or Shallow?** How deep of the network is necessary for vehicle attributes learning is also worth to be explored. Since our ALN can be established on different deep models, we compare popular deep networks: AlexNet [8] and GoogLeNet with 8 layers and 22 layers, respectively. As VGGNet (16 layers version) [27] configured with numerous parameters requires heavy computation and large memory, we do not expect to employ it for our ALN. Besides, our proposed shallow FVPN with 4 layers is also used for attributes learning. From the bottom part of Table 2, we can see that a deeper network does not obtain much better performance on vehicle verification compared to a shallow one. However, for pose estimation, type classification and color recognition, the deepest GoogLeNet consistently outperforms other nets with obvious gaps. Particularly for type classification which belongs to fine-grained categorization, the shallow FVPN gives extremely poor results. It illustrates that a deeper network with powerful discriminative capability is more suitable for fine-grained vehicle classification tasks.

**Fine-Grained Categorization in Different Views.** Finally, since vehicle type classification belongs to fine-grained categorization, we are interested in investigating its difficulty in different views due to its importance for our future work such as vehicle re-identification. As demonstrated in Table 3, for both 12-type and 6-type classification, higher precision is easier to be achieved from side and rearside views, while it is difficult to discriminate vehicle types from the front view. In other words, if we aim to re-identify a target vehicle from two different viewpoints, the type annotation predicted from a side view is more credible than that from a front view.

**Table 3.** Evaluation (%) of fine-grained vehicle type classification on the UTS dataset

| Number of vehicle type | Front | Rear | Side | FrontSide | RearSide |
|---|---|---|---|---|---|
| 12 | 58.02 | 60.37 | 66.73 | 61.28 | 64.90 |
| 6 | 79.42 | 84.60 | 92.93 | 86.77 | 92.53 |

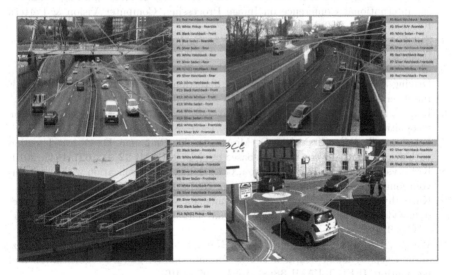

**Fig. 7.** Qualitative results of attributes annotation. Red marks denote incorrect annotation, and N/A(C) means a catch-all color. (Color figure online)

Figure 7 shows the qualitative results of our DAVE evaluated on the UTS vehicle dataset. It demonstrates that our model is robust to detect vehicles and annotate their poses, colors and types simultaneously for urban traffic surveillance. The failure cases mainly take place on incorrect colors and types.

## 4    Conclusion

In this paper, we developed a unified framework for fast vehicle detection and annotation: DAVE, which consists of two convolutional neural networks FVPN and ALN. The proposal and attributes learning networks predict bounding-boxes for vehicles and infer their attributes: pose, color and type, simultaneously. Extensive experiments show that our method outperforms state-of-the-art frameworks on vehicle detection and is also effective for vehicle attributes annotation. In our on-going work, we are integrating more vehicle attributes such as make and model into the ALN with high accuracy, and exploiting these attributes to investigate vehicle re-identification tasks.

## References

1. Sivaraman, S., Trivedi, M.M.: Looking at vehicles on the road: a survey of vision-based vehicle detection, tracking, and behavior analysis. IEEE Trans. Intell. Transp. Syst. **14**(4), 1773–1795 (2013)
2. Buch, N., Velastin, S.A., Orwell, J.: A review of computer vision techniques for the analysis of urban traffic. IEEE Trans. Intell. Transp. Syst. **12**(3), 920–939 (2011)
3. Park, K., Lee, D., Park, Y.: Video-based detection of street-parking violation. In: International Conference on Image Processing, Computer Vision & Pattern Recognition, pp. 152–156 (2007)
4. Stauffer, C., Grimson, W.E.L.: Adaptive background mixture models for real-time tracking. In: CVPR (1999)
5. Martínez, E., Díaz, M., Melenchón, J., Montero, J.A., Iriondo, I., Socoró, J.C.: Driving assistance system based on the detection of head-on collisions. In: IEEE Intelligent Vehicles Symposium, pp. 913–918 (2008)
6. Liu, L., Shao, L., Zhen, X., Li, X.: Learning discriminative key poses for action recognition. IEEE Trans. Cybern. **43**(6), 1860–1870 (2013)
7. Felzenszwalb, P.F., Girshick, R.B., McAllester, D., Ramanan, D.: Object detection with discriminatively trained part-based models. T-PAMI **32**(9), 1627–1645 (2010)
8. Krizhevsky, A., Sutskever, I., Hinton, G.E.: Imagenet classification with deep convolutional neural networks. In: NIPS, pp. 1097–1105 (2012)
9. Karpathy, A., Toderici, G., Shetty, S., Leung, T., Sukthankar, R., Fei-Fei, L.: Large-scale video classification with convolutional neural networks. In: CVPR, pp. 1725–1732 (2014)
10. Wu, D., Pigou, L., Kindermans, P.J., Nam, L., Shao, L., Dambre, J., Odobez, J.M.: Deep dynamic neural networks for multimodal gesture segmentation and recognition. IEEE T-PAMI **38**(8), 1583–1597 (2016)
11. Wu, D., Shao, L.: Leveraging hierarchical parametric networks for skeletal joints based action segmentation and recognition. In: CVPR, pp. 724–731 (2014)
12. Dong, B., Shao, L., Da Costa, M., Bandmann, O., Frangi, A.F.: Deep learning for automatic cell detection in wide-field microscopy zebrafish images. In: IEEE International Symposium on Biomedical Imaging, pp. 772–776 (2015)

13. Girshick, R., Donahue, J., Darrell, T., Malik, J.: Rich feature hierarchies for accurate object detection and semantic segmentation. In: CVPR, pp. 580–587 (2014)
14. Girshick, R.: Fast R-CNN. In: ICCV, pp. 1440–1448 (2015)
15. Uijlings, J.R., van de Sande, K.E., Gevers, T., Smeulders, A.W.: Selective search for object recognition. IJCV 104(2), 154–171 (2013)
16. Zitnick, C.L., Dollár, P.: Edge boxes: locating object proposals from edges. In: Fleet, D., Pajdla, T., Schiele, B., Tuytelaars, T. (eds.) ECCV 2014. LNCS, vol. 8693, pp. 391–405. Springer, Heidelberg (2014). doi:10.1007/978-3-319-10602-1_26
17. Ren, S., He, K., Girshick, R., Sun, J.: Faster R-CNN: towards real-time object detection with region proposal networks. In: NIPS, pp. 91–99 (2015)
18. Yang, L., Liu, J., Tang, X.: Object detection and viewpoint estimation with automasking neural network. In: Fleet, D., Pajdla, T., Schiele, B., Tuytelaars, T. (eds.) ECCV 2014. LNCS, vol. 8691, pp. 441–455. Springer, Heidelberg (2014). doi:10.1007/978-3-319-10578-9_29
19. Li, X., Zhang, G., Fang, J., Wu, J., Cui, Z.: Vehicle color recognition using vector matching of template. In: International Symposium on Electronic Commerce and Security, pp. 189–193 (2010)
20. Dong, Z., Pei, M., He, Y., Liu, T., Dong, Y., Jia, Y.: Vehicle type classification using unsupervised convolutional neural network. In: ICPR, pp. 172–177 (2014)
21. Shao, J., Kang, K., Loy, C.C., Wang, X.: Deeply learned attributes for crowded scene understanding. In: CVPR, pp. 4657–4666 (2015)
22. Liu, L., Zhou, Y., Shao, L.: DAP3D-Net: where, what and how actions occur in videos? arXiv preprint arXiv:1602.03346 (2016)
23. Hinton, G., Vinyals, O., Dean, J.: Distilling the knowledge in a neural network. arXiv preprint arXiv:1503.02531 (2015)
24. Long, J., Shelhamer, E., Darrell, T.: Fully convolutional networks for semantic segmentation. In: CVPR, pp. 3431–3440 (2015)
25. Redmon, J., Divvala, S., Girshick, R., Farhadi, A.: You only look once: unified, real-time object detection. arXiv preprint arXiv:1506.02640 (2015)
26. Szegedy, C., Liu, W., Jia, Y., Sermanet, P., Reed, S., Anguelov, D., Erhan, D., Vanhoucke, V., Rabinovich, A.: Going deeper with convolutions. In: CVPR, pp. 1–9 (2015)
27. Simonyan, K., Zisserman, A.: Very deep convolutional networks for large-scale image recognition. arXiv preprint arXiv:1409.1556 (2014)
28. Yang, L., Luo, P., Change Loy, C., Tang, X.: A large-scale car dataset for fine-grained categorization and verification. In: CVPR, pp. 3973–3981 (2015)
29. Jia, Y., Shelhamer, E., Donahue, J., Karayev, S., Long, J., Girshick, R., Guadarrama, S., Darrell, T.: Caffe: convolutional architecture for fast feature embedding. In: ACM MM, pp. 675–678 (2014)
30. Everingham, M., Van Gool, L., Williams, C.K., Winn, J., Zisserman, A.: The PASCAL visual object classes (VOC) challenge. IJCV 88(2), 303–338 (2010)
31. Sivaraman, S., Trivedi, M.M.: A general active-learning framework for on-road vehicle recognition and tracking. IEEE Trans. Intell. Transp. Syst. 11(2), 267–276 (2010)
32. Girshick, R.B., Felzenszwalb, P.F., McAllester, D.: Discriminatively trained deformable part models, release 5. http://people.cs.uchicago.edu/~rbg/latent-release5/
33. Chang, C.C., Lin, C.J.: LIBSVM: a library for support vector machines. ACM Trans. Intell. Syst. Technol. 2, 27:1–27:27 (2011). http://www.csie.ntu.edu.tw/~cjlin/libsvm

# Real-Time Joint Tracking of a Hand Manipulating an Object from RGB-D Input

Srinath Sridhar[1], Franziska Mueller[1], Michael Zollhöfer[1], Dan Casas[1], Antti Oulasvirta[2], and Christian Theobalt[1(✉)]

[1] Max Planck Institute for Informatics, Saarbrücken, Germany
{ssridhar,frmueller,mzollhoef,dcasas,theobalt}@mpi-inf.mpg.de
[2] Aalto University, Espoo, Finland
antti.oulasvirta@aalto.fi

**Abstract.** Real-time simultaneous tracking of hands manipulating and interacting with external objects has many potential applications in augmented reality, tangible computing, and wearable computing. However, due to difficult occlusions, fast motions, and uniform hand appearance, jointly tracking hand and object pose is more challenging than tracking either of the two separately. Many previous approaches resort to complex multi-camera setups to remedy the occlusion problem and often employ expensive segmentation and optimization steps which makes real-time tracking impossible. In this paper, we propose a real-time solution that uses a single commodity RGB-D camera. The core of our approach is a 3D articulated Gaussian mixture alignment strategy tailored to hand-object tracking that allows fast pose optimization. The alignment energy uses novel regularizers to address occlusions and hand-object contacts. For added robustness, we guide the optimization with discriminative part classification of the hand and segmentation of the object. We conducted extensive experiments on several existing datasets and introduce a new annotated hand-object dataset. Quantitative and qualitative results show the key advantages of our method: speed, accuracy, and robustness.

## 1 Introduction

The human hand exhibits incredible capacity for manipulating external objects via gripping, grasping, touching, pointing, caging, and throwing. We can use our hands with apparent ease, even for subtle and complex motions, and with remarkable speed and accuracy. However, this dexterity also makes it hard to track a hand in close interaction with objects. While a lot of research has explored real-time tracking of hands or objects in isolation, real-time hand-object tracking

**Electronic supplementary material** The online version of this chapter (doi:10.1007/978-3-319-46475-6_19) contains supplementary material, which is available to authorized users.

© Springer International Publishing AG 2016
B. Leibe et al. (Eds.): ECCV 2016, Part II, LNCS 9906, pp. 294–310, 2016.
DOI: 10.1007/978-3-319-46475-6_19

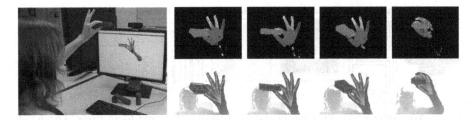

**Fig. 1.** Proposed real-time hand-object tracking approach: we use a single commodity depth camera (*left*) to classify (*top*) and track the articulation of a hand and the rigid body motion of a manipulated object (*bottom*)

remains unsolved. It is inherently more challenging due to the higher dimensionality of the problem, additional occlusions, and difficulty in disambiguating hand from object. A fast, accurate, and robust solution based on a minimal camera setup is a precondition for many new and important applications in vision-based input to computers, including virtual and augmented reality, teleoperation, tangible computing, and wearable computing. In this paper, we present a **real-time** method to **simultaneously track** a hand and the manipulated object. We support tracking objects of **different shapes, sizes**, and **colors**. Previous work has employed setups with multiple cameras [5,17] to limit the influence of occlusions which restricts use to highly controlled setups. Many methods that exploit dense depth and color measurements from commodity RGB-D cameras [8,13,14] have been proposed. However, these methods use expensive segmentation and optimization steps that make interactive performance hard to attain. At the other end of the spectrum, discriminative one-shot methods (for tracking only hands) often suffer from temporal instability [11,33,43]. Such approaches have also been applied to estimate hand pose under object occlusion [24], but the object is not tracked simultaneously. In contrast, the approach proposed here is the first to track hand and object motion simultaneously at real-time rates using only a single commodity RGB-D camera (see Fig. 1). Building on recent work in single hand tracking and 3D pointset registration, we propose a 3D articulated Gaussian mixture alignment strategy tailored to hand-object tracking. Gaussian mixture alignment aligns two Gaussian mixtures and has been successfully used in 3D pointset registration [10]. It can be interpreted as a generalization of ICP and does not require explicit, error-prone, and computationally expensive correspondence search [7]. Previous methods have used articulated 2.5D Gaussian mixture alignment formulations [27] that are discontinuous. This leads to tracking instabilities because 3D spatial proximity is not considered. We also introduce additional novel regularizers that consider occlusions and enforce contact points between fingers and objects analytically. Our combined energy has a closed form gradient and allows for fast and accurate tracking. For an overview of our approach see Fig. 2. To further increase robustness and allow for recovery of the generative tracker, we guide the optimization using a multi-layer random forest hand part classifier. We use a variational optimization strategy that optimizes

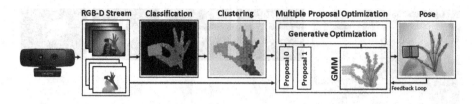

**Fig. 2.** We perform classification of the input into object and hand parts. The hand and object are tracked using 3D articulated Gaussian mixture alignment

two different hand-object tracking energies simultaneously (multiple proposals) and then selects the better solution. The main contributions are:

- A 3D articulated Gaussian mixture alignment approach for jointly tracking hand and object accurately.
- Novel contact point and occlusion objective terms that were motivated by the physics of grasps, and can handle difficult hand-object interactions.
- A multi-layered classification architecture to segment hand and object, and classify hand parts in RGB-D sequences.
- An extensive evaluation on public datasets as well as a new, fully annotated dataset consisting of diverse hand-object interactions.

## 2    Related Work

*Single Hand Tracking.* Single hand tracking has received a lot of attention in recent years with discriminative and generative methods being the two main classes of methods. Discriminative methods for monocular RGB tracking index into a large database of poses or learn a mapping from image to pose space [3,42]. However, accuracy and temporal stability of these methods are limited. Monocular generative methods optimize pose of more sophisticated 3D or 2.5D hand models by optimizing an alignment energy [6,9,15]. Occlusions and appearance ambiguities are less problematic with multi-camera setups [5]. [41] use a physics-based approach to optimize the pose of a hand using silhouette and color constraints at slow non-interactive frame rates. [28] use multiple RGB cameras and a single depth camera to track single hand poses in near real-time by combining generative tracking and finger tip detection. More lightweight setups with a single depth camera are preferred for many interactive applications. Among single camera methods, examples of discriminative methods are based on decision forests for hand part labeling [11], on a latent regression forest in combination with a coarse-to-fine search [33], fast hierarchical pose regression [31], or Hough voting [43]. Real-time performance is feasible, but temporal instability remains an issue. [19] generatively track a hand by optimizing a depth and appearance-based alignment metric with particle swarm optimization (PSO). A real-time generative tracking method with a physics-based solver was proposed in [16]. The stabilization of real-time articulated ICP based on a learned subspace prior on hand poses was used in [32]. Template-based non-rigid deformation tracking of arbitrary objects in real-time from RGB-D was shown in [45], very simple unoccluded hand poses can be tracked. Combining generative and discriminative tracking enables recovery from some tracking failures [25, 28, 39]. [27] showed real-time single hand tracking from depth using generative pose optimization under detection constraints. Similarly, reinitialization of generative estimates via finger tip detection [23], multi-layer discriminative reinitialization [25], or joints detected with convolutional networks is feasible [36]. [34] employ hierarchical sampling from partial pose distributions and a final hypothesis selection based on a generative energy. None of the above methods is able to track interacting hands and objects simultaneously and in non-trivial poses in real-time.

*Tracking Hands in Interaction.* Tracking two interacting hands, or a hand and a manipulated object, is a much harder problem. The straightforward combination of methods for object tracking, e.g. [4, 35], and hand tracking does not lead to satisfactory solutions, as only a combined formulation can methodically exploit mutual constraints between object and hand. [40] track two well-separated hands from stereo by efficient pose retrieval and IK refinement. In [18] two hands in interaction are tracked at 4 Hz with an RGB-D camera by optimizing a generative depth and image alignment measure. Tracking of interacting hands from multi-view video at slow non-interactive runtimes was shown in [5]. They use generative pose optimization supported by salient point detection. The method in [32] can track very simple two hand interactions with little occlusion. Commercial solutions, e.g. Leap Motion [1] and NimbleVR [2], fail if two hands interact closely or interact with an object. In [17], a marker-less method based on a generative pose optimization of a combined hand-object model is proposed. They explicitly model collisions, but need multiple RGB cameras. In [8] the most likely pose is found through belief propagation using part-based trackers. This method is robust under occlusions, but does not explicitly track the object. A temporally coherent nearest neighbor search tracks the hand manipulating an object in [24], but not the object, in real time. Results are prone to temporal jitter. [13] perform frame-to-frame tracking of hand and objects from RGB-D using physics-based optimization. This approach has a slow non-interactive runtime. An ensemble of Collaborative Trackers (ECT) for RGB-D based multi-object and multiple hand tracking is used in [14]. Their accuracy is high, but runtime is far from real-time. [21] infer contact forces from a tracked hand interacting with an object at slow non-interactive runtimes. [20, 38] propose methods for in-hand RGB-D object scanning. Both methods use known generative methods to track finger contact points to support ICP-like shape scanning. Recently, [37] introduced a method for tracking hand-only, hand-hand, and hand-object (we include a comparison with this method). None of the above methods can track the hand and the manipulated object in *real-time* in non-trivial poses from a *single depth camera* view, which is what our approach achieves.

*Model-Based Tracking Approaches.* A common representation for model tracking are meshes [5, 32]. Other approaches use primitives [14, 23], quadrics [29], 2.5D Gaussians [27], or Gaussian mixtures [10]. Gaussian mixture alignment has been successfully used in rigid pointset registration [10]. In contrast, we propose a 3D *articulated* Gaussian mixture alignment strategy. [44] relate template and data via a probabilistic formulation and use EM to compute the best fit. Different from our approach, they only model the template as a Gaussian mixture.

## 3   Discriminative Hand Part Classification

As a preprocessing step, we classify depth pixels as hand or object, and further into hand parts. The obtained labeling is later used to guide the generative pose optimization. Our part classification strategy is based on a two-layer random forest that takes occlusions into account. Classification is based on a three step pipeline (see Fig. 3). Input is the color $C_t$ and depth $D_t$ frames captured by the RGB-D sensor. We first perform hand-object segmentation based on color cues to remove the object from the depth map. Afterwards, we select a suitable two-layer random forest to obtain the classification. The final output per pixel is a part probability histogram that encodes the class likelihoods. Note, object pixel histograms are set to an object class probability of 1. The forests are trained based on a set of training images that consists of real hand motions re-targeted to a virtual hand model to generate synthetic data from multiple viewpoints. A virtual object is automatically inserted in the scene to simulate occlusions. To this end, we randomly sample uniform object positions between the thumb and one other finger and prune implausible poses based on intersection tests.

*Viewpoint Selection.* We trained two-layer forests for hand part classification from different viewpoints. Four cases are distinguished: observing the hand from the front, back, thumb and little finger sides. We select the forest that best matches the hand orientation computed in the last frame. The selected two-layer forest is then used for hand part classification.

*Color-Based Object Segmentation.* As a first step, we segment out the object from the captured depth map $D_t$. Similar to many previous hand-object tracking approaches [19], we use the color image $C_t$ in combination with an HSV color segmentation strategy. As we show in the results, we are able to support objects with different colors. Object pixels are removed to obtain a new depth map $\hat{D}_t$, which we then feed to the next processing stage.

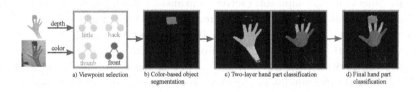

a) Viewpoint selection     b) Color-based object segmentation     c) Two-layer hand part classification     d) Final hand part classification

**Fig. 3.** Three stage hand part classification: Stage 1: Viewpoint selection, stage 2: color-based object segmentation, and stage 3: two-layer hand part classification (Color figure online)

***Two-Layer Hand Part Classification.*** We use a two-layer random forest for hand part classification. The first layer classifies hand and arm pixels while the second layer uses the hand pixels and further classifies them into one of several distinct hand parts. Both layers are per-pixel classification forests [26]. The hand-arm classification forest is trained on $N = 100k$ images with diverse hand-object poses. For each of the four viewpoints a random forest is trained on $N = 38k$ images. The random forests are based on three trees, each trained on a random distinct subset. In each image, 2000 example foreground pixels are chosen. Split decisions at nodes are based on 100 random feature offsets and 40 thresholds. Candidate features are a uniform mix of unary and binary depth difference features [26]. Nodes are split as long as the information gain is sufficient and the maximum tree depth of 19 (21 for hand-arm forest) has not been reached. On the first layer, we use 3 part labels: 1 for hand, 1 for arm and 1 to represent the background. On the second layer, classification is based on 7 part labels: 6 for the hand parts, and 1 for the background. We use one label for each finger and one for the palm, see Fig. 3c. We use a cross-validation procedure to find the best hyperparameters. On the disjoint test set, the hand-arm forest has a classification accuracy of 65.2 %. The forests for the four camera views had accuracies of 59.8 % (front), 64.7 % (back), 60.9 % (little), and 53.5 % (thumb).

# 4   Gaussian Mixture Model Representation

Joint hand-object tracking requires a representation that allows for accurate tracking, is robust to outliers, and enables fast pose optimization. Gaussian mixture alignment, initially proposed for rigid pointset alignment (e.g. [10]), satisfies all these requirements. It features the advantages of ICP-like methods, without requiring a costly, error-prone correspondence search. We extend this approach to 3D articulated Gaussian mixture alignment tailored to hand-object tracking. Compared to our 3D formulation, 2.5D [27] approaches are discontinuous. This causes instabilities, since the spatial proximity between model and data is not fully considered. We quantitatively show this for hand-only tracking (Sect. 8).

# 5   Unified Density Representation

We parameterize the articulated motion of the human hand using a kinematic skeleton with $|\mathcal{X}_h| = 26$ degrees of freedom (DOF). Non-rigid hand motion is expressed based on 20 joint angles in twist representation. The remaining 6 DOFs specify the global rigid transform of the hand with respect to the root joint. The manipulated object is assumed to be rigid and its motion is parameterized using $|\mathcal{X}_o| = 6$ DOFs. In the following, we deal with the hand and object in a unified way. To this end, we refer to the vector of all unknowns as $\mathcal{X}$. For pose optimization, both the input depth as well as the scene (hand and object) are expressed as 3D Gaussian Mixture Models (GMMs). This allows for fast and analytical pose optimization. We first define the following generic probability density distribution $\mathcal{M}(\mathbf{x}) = \sum_{i=1}^{K} w_i \mathcal{G}_i(\mathbf{x}|\boldsymbol{\mu}_i, \sigma_i)$ at each point $\mathbf{x} \in \mathbb{R}^3$ in space.

This mixture contains $K$ unnormalized, isotropic Gaussian functions $\mathcal{G}_i$ with mean $\boldsymbol{\mu}_i \in \mathbb{R}^3$ and variance $\sigma_i^2 \in \mathbb{R}$. In the case of the model distribution, the positions of the Gaussians are parameterized by the unknowns $\mathcal{X}$. For the hand, this means each Gaussian is being rigidly rigged to one bone of the hand. The probability density is defined and non-vanishing over the whole domain $\mathbb{R}^3$.

**Hand and Object Model.** The three-dimensional shape of the hand and object is represented in a similar fashion as probability density distributions $\mathcal{M}_h$ and $\mathcal{M}_o$, respectively. We manually attach $N_h = 30$ Gaussian functions to the kinematic chain of the hand to model its volumetric extent. Standard deviations are set such that they roughly correspond to the distance to the actual surface. The object is represented by automatically fitting a predefined number $N_o$ of Gaussians to its spatial extent, such that the one standard deviation spheres model the objects volumetric extent. $N_o$ is a user defined parameter which can be used to control the trade-off between tracking accuracy and runtime performance. We found that $N_o \in [12, 64]$ provides a good trade-off between speed and accuracy for the objects used in our experiments. We refer to the combined hand-object distribution as $\mathcal{M}_s$, with $N_s = N_h + N_o$ Gaussians. Each Gaussian is assigned to a class label $l_i$ based on its semantic location in the scene. Note, the input GMM is only a model of the visible surface of the hand/object. Therefore, we incorporate a visibility factor $f_i \in [0, 1]$ (0 completely occluded, 1 completely visible) per Gaussian. This factor is approximated by rendering an occlusion map with each Gaussian as a circle (radius equal to its standard deviation). The GMM is restricted to the visible surface by setting $w_i = f_i$ in the mixture. These operations are performed based on the solution of the previous frame $\mathcal{X}_{old}$.

**Input Depth Data.** We first perform bottom-up hierarchical quadtree clustering of adjacent pixels with similar depth to convert the input to the density based representation. We cluster at most $(2^{(4-1)})^2 = 64$ pixels, which corresponds to a maximum tree depth of 4. Clustering is performed as long as the depth variance in the corresponding subdomain is smaller than $\epsilon_{cluster} = 30\,\mathrm{mm}$. Each leaf node is represented as a Gaussian function $\mathcal{G}_i$ with $\boldsymbol{\mu}_i$ corresponding to the 3D center of gravity of the quad and $\sigma_i^2 = (\frac{a}{2})^2$, where $a$ is the backprojected side length of the quad. Note, the mean $\boldsymbol{\mu}_i \in \mathbb{R}^3$ is obtained by backprojecting the 2D center of gravity of the quad based on the computed average depth and displacing by $a$ in camera viewing direction to obtain a representation that matches the model of the scene. In addition, each $\mathcal{G}_i$ stores the probability $p_i$ and index $l_i$ of the best associated semantic label. We obtain the best label and its probability by summing over all corresponding per-pixel histograms obtained in the classification stage. Based on this data, we define the input depth distribution $\mathcal{M}_{d_h}(\mathbf{x})$ for the hand and $\mathcal{M}_{d_o}(\mathbf{x})$ for the object. The combined input distribution $\mathcal{M}_d(\mathbf{x})$ has $N_d = N_{d_o} + N_{d_h}$ Gaussians. We set uniform weights $w_i = 1$ based on the assumption of equal contribution. $N_d$ is much smaller than the number of pixels leading to real-time hand-object tracking.

# 6   Multiple Proposal Optimization

We optimize for the best pose $\mathcal{X}^*$ using two proposals $\mathcal{X}_i^*$, $i \in \{0,1\}$ that are computed by minimizing two distinct hand-object tracking energies:

$$\mathcal{X}_0^* = \underset{\mathcal{X}}{\operatorname{argmin}} E_{align}(\mathcal{X}), \quad \mathcal{X}_1^* = \underset{\mathcal{X}}{\operatorname{argmin}} E_{label}(\mathcal{X}). \tag{1}$$

$E_{align}$ leverages the depth observations and the second energy $E_{label}$ incorporates the discriminative hand part classification results. In contrast to the optimization of the sum of the two objectives, this avoids failure due to bad classification and ensures fast recovery. For optimization, we use analytical gradient descent (10 iterations per proposal, adaptive step length) [30]. We initialize based on the solution of the previous frame $\mathcal{X}_{old}$. Finally, $\mathcal{X}^*$ is selected as given below, where we slightly favor ($\lambda = 1.003$) the label proposal to facilitate fast pose recovery:

$$\mathcal{X}^* = \begin{cases} \mathcal{X}_1^* & \text{if } \left( E_{val}(\mathcal{X}_1^*) < \lambda E_{val}(\mathcal{X}_0^*) \right) \\ \mathcal{X}_0^* & \text{otherwise} \end{cases}. \tag{2}$$

The energy $E_{val}(\mathcal{X}) = E_a(\mathcal{X}) + w_p E_p(\mathcal{X})$ is designed to select the proposal that best explains the input, while being anatomically correct. Therefore, it considers spatial alignment to the input depth map $E_a$ and models anatomical joint angle limits $E_p$, see Sect. 7. In the following, we describe the used energies in detail.

# 7   Hand-Object Tracking Objectives

Given the input depth distribution $\mathcal{M}_d$, we want to find the 3D model $\mathcal{M}_s$ that best explains the observations by varying the corresponding parameters $\mathcal{X}$. We take inspiration from methods with slow non-interactive runtimes that used related 3D implicit shape models for full-body pose tracking [12,22], but propose a new efficient tracking objective tailored for real-time hand-object tracking. In contrast to previous methods, our objective operates in 3D (generalization of ICP), features an improved way of incorporating the discriminative classification results, and incorporates two novel regularization terms. Together, this provides for a better, yet compact, representation that allows for fast analytic pose optimization on the CPU. To this end, we define the following two objective functions. The first energy $E_{align}$ measures the alignment with the input:

$$E_{align}(\mathcal{X}) = E_a + w_p E_p + w_t E_t + w_c E_c + w_o E_o. \tag{3}$$

The second energy $E_{label}$ incorporates the classification results:

$$E_{label}(\mathcal{X}) = E_a + w_s E_s + w_p E_p. \tag{4}$$

The energy terms consider spatial alignment $E_a$, semantic alignment $E_s$, anatomical plausibility $E_p$, temporal smoothness $E_t$, contact points $E_c$, and object-hand occlusions $E_o$, respectively. The priors in the energies are chosen such that they do not hinder the respective alignment objectives. All parameters $w_p = 0.1$, $w_t = 0.1$, $w_s = 3 \cdot 10^{-7}$, $w_c = 5 \cdot 10^{-7}$ and $w_o = 1.0$ have been empirically determined and stay fixed for all experiments. We optimize both energies simultaneously using a multiple proposal based optimization strategy and employ a winner-takes-all strategy (see Sect. 6). We found empirically that using two energy functions resulted in better pose estimation and recovery from failures than using a single energy with all terms. In the following, we give more details on the individual components.

**Spatial Alignment.** We measure the alignment of the input density function $\mathcal{M}_d$ and our scene model $\mathcal{M}_s$ based on the following alignment energy:

$$E_a(\mathcal{X}) = \int_\Omega \left[ \left( \mathcal{M}_{d_h}(\mathbf{x}) - \mathcal{M}_h(\mathbf{x}) \right)^2 + \left( \mathcal{M}_{d_o}(\mathbf{x}) - \mathcal{M}_o(\mathbf{x}) \right)^2 \right] d\mathbf{x}. \qquad (5)$$

It measures the alignment between the two input and two model density distributions at every point in space $\mathbf{x} \in \Omega$. Note, this 3D formulation leads to higher accuracy results (see Sect. 8) than a 2.5D [27] formulation.

**Semantic Alignment.** In addition to the alignment of the distributions, we also incorporate semantic information in the label energy $E_{label}$. In contrast to [27], we incorporate uncertainty based on the best class probability. We use the following least-squares objective to enforce semantic alignment:

$$E_s(\mathcal{X}) = \sum_{i=1}^{N_s} \sum_{j=1}^{N_d} \alpha_{i,j} \cdot \|\boldsymbol{\mu}_i - \boldsymbol{\mu}_j\|_2^2. \qquad (6)$$

Here, $\boldsymbol{\mu}_i$ and $\boldsymbol{\mu}_j$ are the mean of the $i^{th}$ model and the $j^{th}$ image Gaussian, respectively. The weights $\alpha_{i,j}$ switch attraction forces between similar parts on and between different parts off:

$$\alpha_{i,j} = \begin{cases} 0 & \text{if } (l_i \neq l_j) \text{ or } (d_{i,j} > r_{max}) \\ (1 - \frac{d_{i,j}}{r_{max}}) \cdot p_i & \text{else} \end{cases}. \qquad (7)$$

Here, $d_{i,j} = \|\boldsymbol{\mu}_i - \boldsymbol{\mu}_j\|_2$ is the distance between the means. $l_i$ is the part label of the most likely class, $p_i$ its probability and $r_{max}$ a cutoff value. We set $r_{max}$ to 30cm. $l_i$ can be one of 8 labels: 6 for the hand parts, 1 for object and 1 for background. We consider all model Gaussians, independent of their occlusion weight, to facilitate fast pose recovery of previously occluded regions.

**Anatomical Plausibility.** The articulated motion of the hand is subject to anatomical constraints. We account for this by enforcing soft-constraints on the joint angles $\mathcal{X}_h$ of the hand:

$$E_p(\mathcal{X}) = \sum_{x_i \in \mathcal{X}_h} \begin{cases} 0 & \text{if } x_i^l \leq x_i \leq x_i^u \\ \|x_i - x_i^l\|^2 & \text{if } x_i < x_i^l \\ \|x_i^u - x_i\|^2 & \text{if } x_i > x_i^u \end{cases}. \qquad (8)$$

Here, $\mathcal{X}_h$ are the DOFs corresponding to the hand, and $x_i^l$ and $x_i^u$ are the lower and upper joint limit that corresponds to the $i^{th}$ DOF of the kinematic chain.

**Temporal Smoothness.** We further improve the smoothness of our tracking results by incorporating a temporal prior into the energy. To this end, we include a soft constraint on parameter change to enforce constant speed:

$$E_t(\mathcal{X}) = ||\nabla \mathcal{X} - \nabla \mathcal{X}^{(t-1)}||_2^2. \tag{9}$$

Here, $\nabla \mathcal{X}^{(t-1)}$ is the gradient of parameter change at the previous time step.

**Contact Points.** We propose a novel contact point objective, specific to the hand-object tracking scenario:

$$E_c(\mathcal{X}) = \sum_{(k,l,t_d)\in\mathcal{T}} \left( ||\boldsymbol{\mu}_k - \boldsymbol{\mu}_l||^2 - t_d^2 \right)^2. \tag{10}$$

Here, $(k, l, t_d) \in \mathcal{T}$ is a detected touch constraint. It encodes that the fingertip Gaussian with index $k$ should have a distance of $t_d$ to the object Gaussian with index $l$. We detect the set of all touch constraints $\mathcal{T}$ based on the last pose $\mathcal{X}_{old}$. A new touch constraint is added if a fingertip Gaussian is closer to an object Gaussian than the sum of their standard deviations. We then set $t_d$ to this sum. This couples hand pose and object tracking leading to more stable results. A contact point is active until the distance between the two Gaussians exceeds the release threshold $\delta_R$. Usually $\delta_R > t_d$ to avoid flickering.

**Occlusion Handling.** No measurements are available in occluded hand regions. We stabilize the hand movement in such regions using a novel occlusion prior:

$$E_o(\mathcal{X}) = \sum_{i=0}^{N_h} \sum_{j\in\mathcal{H}_i} (1 - \hat{f}_i) \cdot ||x_j - x_j^{old}||_2^2. \tag{11}$$

Here, $\mathcal{H}_i$ is the set of all DOFs that are influenced by the $i$-th Gaussian. The global rotation and translation is not included. The occlusion weights $\hat{f}_i \in [0, 1]$ are computed similar to $f_i$ (0 occluded, 1 visible). This prior is based on the assumption that occuded regions move consistently with the rest of the hand.

## 8     Experiments and Results

We evaluate and compare our method on more than **15 sequences** spanning 3 public datasets, which have been recorded with 3 different RBG-D cameras (see Fig. 7). Additional live sequences (see Fig. 8 and supplementary materials) show that our method handles fast object and finger motion, difficult occlusions and fares well even if two hands are present in the scene. Our method supports commodity RGB-D sensors like the *Creative Senz3D, Intel RealSense F200,* and

*Primesense Carmine.* We rescale depth and color to resolutions of $320 \times 240$ and $640 \times 480$ respectively, and capture at 30 Hz. Furthermore, we introduce a new hand-object tracking benchmark dataset with ground truth fingertip and object annotations.

***Comparison to the State-of-the-Art.*** We quantitatively and qualitatively evaluate on two publicly available hand-object datasets [37,38] (see Fig. 8 and also supplementary material). Only one dataset (IJCV [37]) contains ground truth joint annotations. We test on 5 rigid object sequences from IJCV. We track the right hand only, but our method works even when multiple hands are present. Ground truth annotations are provided for 2D joint positions, but not object pose. Our method achieves a fingertip pixel error of **8.6 px**, which is comparable (difference of only 2 px) to that reported for the slower method of [37]. This small difference is well within the uncertainty of manual annotation and sensor noise. Note, our approach runs over 60 times faster, while producing visual results that are on par (see Fig. 8). We also track the dataset of [38] (see also Fig. 8). While they solve a different problem (offline in-hand scanning), it shows that our real-time method copes well with different shaped objects (e.g. bowling pin, bottle, etc.) under occlusion.

***New Benchmark Dataset.*** With the aforementioned datasets, evaluation of object pose is impossible due to missing object annotations. We therefore introduce, to our knowledge, the first dataset[1] that contains ground truth for **both** fingertip positions and object pose. It contains 6 sequences of a hand manipulating a cuboid (2 different sizes) in different hand-object configurations and grasps. We manually annotated pixels on the depth image to mark 5 fingertip positions, and 3 cuboid corners. In total, we provide 3014 frames with ground truth annotations. As is common in the literature [23,25,27,32,33], we use the average 3D Euclidean distance $E$ between estimated and ground truth positions as the error measure (see supplementary document for details). Occluded fingertips are excluded on a per-frame basis from the error computation. If one of the annotated corners of the cuboid is occluded, we exclude it from that frame. In Fig. 4a we plot the average error over all frames of the 6 sequences. Our method has an average error (for both hand and object) of **15.7 mm**. Over all sequences, the average error is always lower than 20 mm with standard deviations under 12 mm. Average error is an indicator of overall performance, but does not indicate how consistent the tracker performs. Figure 4b shows that our method tracks almost all frames with less than 30 mm error. *Rotate* has the highest error, while *Pinch* performs best with almost all frames below 20 mm. Table 1 shows the errors for hand and object separately. Both are in the same order of magnitude.

***Ablative Analysis.*** Firstly, we show that the articulated 3D Gaussian mixture alignment formulation is superior (even for tracking only hand) to the 2.5D formulation of [27]. On the Dexter dataset [28], [27] report an average fingertip error of **19.6 mm**. In contrast, our method (**without** any hand-object specific

---

[1] http://handtracker.mpi-inf.mpg.de/projects/RealtimeHO/.

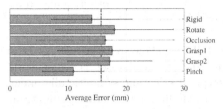 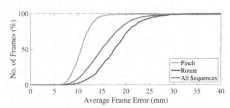

(a) We achieve low errors on each of the 6 sequences in our new benchmark dataset

(b) Tracking consistency of the best, worst and average case

**Fig. 4.** Quantitative hand-object tracking evaluation on ground truth data. The object contributes a higher error

**Table 1.** Average error (mm) for hand and object tracking in our dataset

|  | *Rigid* | *Rotate* | *Occlusion* | *Grasp1* | *Grasp2* | *Pinch* | Overall (mm) |
|---|---|---|---|---|---|---|---|
| Fingertips | 14.2 | 16.3 | 17.5 | 18.1 | 17.5 | 10.3 | **15.6** |
| Object | 13.5 | 26.8 | 11.9 | 15.3 | 15.7 | 13.9 | **16.2** |
| Combined (*E*) | 14.1 | 18.0 | 16.4 | 17.6 | 17.2 | 10.9 | **15.7** |

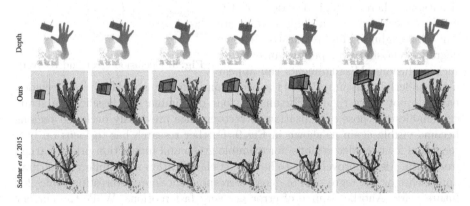

**Fig. 5.** *Top row:* Input depth, an object occludes the hand. *Middle row:* Result of our approach (different viewpoint). Our approach succesfully tracks the hand under heavy occlusion. *Bottom row:* Result of [27] shows catastrophic failure (object pixels were removed for fairness)

terms) is consistently better with an average of **17.2 mm** (maximum improvement is **5 mm** on 2 sequences). This is a result of the continuous articulated 3D Gaussian mixture alignment energy, a generalization of ICP, which considers 3D spatial proximity between Gaussians.

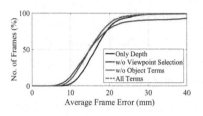

**Fig. 6.** Ablative analysis

Secondly, we show that the average error on our hand-object dataset is worse without viewpoint selection, semantic alignment, occlusion handling, and contact points term. Figure 6 shows a consistency plot with different components of the energy disabled. Using only the data term often results in large errors. The errors are even larger without viewpoint selection. The semantic alignment, occlusion handling, and contact points help improve **robustness** of tracking results and **recovery** from failures. Figure 5 shows that [27] clearly fails when fingers are occluded. Our hand-object specific terms are more robust to these difficult occlusion cases while achieving real-time performance.

***Runtime Performance.*** All experiments were performed on an Intel Xeon E5-1620 CPU with 16 GB memory and an NVIDIA GTX 980 Ti. The stages of our approach take on average: 4 ms for preprocessing, 4 ms for part classification, 2 ms for depth clustering, and 20–30 ms for pose optimization using two proposals. We achieve real-time performance of 25–30 Hz. Multi-layer random forests ran on the GPU while all other algorithm parts ran multithreaded on a CPU.

***Limitations.*** Although we demonstrated robustness against reasonable occlusions, situations where a high fraction of the hand is occluded for a long period are still challenging. This is mostly due to degraded classification performance under such occlusions. Misalignments can appear

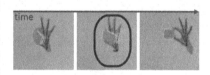

**Fig. 9.** Occlusion error and recovery

if the underlying assumption of the occlusion heuristic is violated, i. e. occluded parts do not move rigidly. Fortunately, our discriminative classification strategy enables the pose optimization to recover once previously occluded regions become visible again as shown in Fig. 9. Further research has to focus on better priors for occluded regions, for example grasp and interaction priors learned from data. Also improvements to hand part classification using different learning approaches or the regression of dense correspondences are interesting topics for future work. Another source of error are very fast motions. While the current implementation achieves 30 Hz, higher frame rate sensors in combination with a faster pose optimization will lead to higher robustness due to improved temporal coherence. We show diverse object shapes being tracked. However, increasing object complexity (shape and color) affects runtime performance. We would like to further explore how multiple complex objects and hands can be tracked.

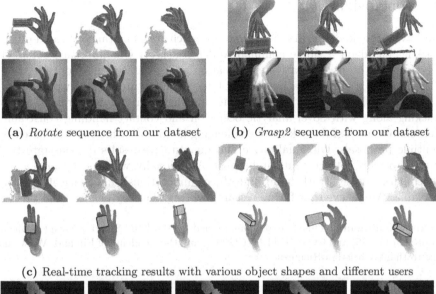

(a) *Rotate* sequence from our dataset      (b) *Grasp2* sequence from our dataset

(c) Real-time tracking results with various object shapes and different users

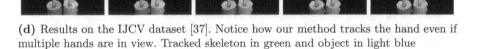

(d) Results on the IJCV dataset [37]. Notice how our method tracks the hand even if multiple hands are in view. Tracked skeleton in green and object in light blue

**Fig. 7.** (a, b) show tracking results on our dataset. (c) Shows real-time results with different object shapes and colors. (d) Shows results on a public dataset (Color figure online)

**Fig. 8.** Subset of tracked frames on the dataset of [38]. Our method can handle objects with **varying sizes, colors, and different hand dimensions.** Here we show how even a complex shape like a bowling pin can be approximated using only a few tens of Gaussians (Color figure online)

# 9  Conclusion

We have presented the first real-time approach for simultaneous hand-object tracking based on a single commodity depth sensor. Our approach combines the strengths of discriminative classification and generative pose optimization. Classification is based on a multi-layer forest architecture with viewpoint selection. We use 3D articulated Gaussian mixture alignment tailored for hand-object tracking along with novel analytic occlusion and contact handling constraints that enable successful tracking of challenging hand-object interactions based on multiple proposals. Our qualitative and quantitative results demonstrate that our approach is both accurate and robust. Additionally, we have captured a new benchmark dataset (with hand and object annotations) and make it publicly available. We believe that future research will significantly benefit from this.

**Acknowledgments.** This research was funded by the ERC Starting Grant projects CapReal (335545) and COMPUTED (637991), and the Academy of Finland. We would like to thank Christian Richardt.

# References

1. Leap Motion. https://www.leapmotion.com/
2. NimbleVR. http://nimblevr.com/
3. Athitsos, V., Sclaroff, S.: Estimating 3D hand pose from a cluttered image. In: Proceedings of IEEE CVPR, pp. 432–442 (2003)
4. Badami, I., Stckler, J., Behnke, S.: Depth-enhanced hough forests for object-class detection and continuous pose estimation. In: Workshop on Semantic Perception, Mapping and Exploration (SPME) (2013)
5. Ballan, L., Taneja, A., Gall, J., Gool, L., Pollefeys, M.: Motion capture of hands in action using discriminative salient points. In: Fitzgibbon, A., Lazebnik, S., Perona, P., Sato, Y., Schmid, C. (eds.) ECCV 2012. LNCS, vol. 7577, pp. 640–653. Springer, Heidelberg (2012). doi:10.1007/978-3-642-33783-3_46
6. Bray, M., Koller-Meier, E., Van Gool, L.: Smart particle filtering for 3D hand tracking. In: Proceedings of the International Conference on Automatic Face and Gesture Recognition, pp. 675–680 (2004)
7. Campbell, D., Petersson, L.: Gogma: globally-optimal Gaussian mixture alignment (2016). arXiv preprint arXiv:1603.00150
8. Hamer, H., Schindler, K., Koller-Meier, E., Van Gool, L.: Tracking a hand manipulating an object. In: Proceedings of IEEE ICCV, pp. 1475–1482 (2009)
9. Heap, T., Hogg, D.: Towards 3D hand tracking using a deformable model. In: Proceedings of the International Conference on Automatic Face and Gesture Recognition, pp. 140–145, October 1996
10. Jian, B., Vemuri, B.C.: Robust point set registration using Gaussian mixture models. IEEE Trans. Pattern Anal. Mach. Intell. **33**(8), 1633–1645 (2011)
11. Keskin, C., Kira, F., Kara, Y.E., Akarun, L.: Real time hand pose estimation using depth sensors. In: ICCV Workshops, pp. 1228–1234. IEEE (2011). http://dblp.uni-trier.de/db/conf/iccvw/iccvw2011.html#KeskinKKA11

12. Kurmankhojayev, D., Hasler, N., Theobalt, C.: Monocular pose capture with a depth camera using a sums-of-Gaussians body model. In: Weickert, J., Hein, M., Schiele, B. (eds.) GCPR 2013. LNCS, vol. 8142, pp. 415–424. Springer, Heidelberg (2013)

13. Kyriazis, N., Argyros, A.: Physically plausible 3D scene tracking: the single actor hypothesis. In: Proceedings of IEEE CVPR, pp. 9–16 (2013)

14. Kyriazis, N., Argyros, A.: Scalable 3D tracking of multiple interacting objects. In: Proceedings of IEEE CVPR, pp. 3430–3437, June 2014

15. de La Gorce, M., Fleet, D., Paragios, N.: Model-based 3D hand pose estimation from monocular video. IEEE TPAMI $33(9)$, 1793–1805 (2011)

16. Melax, S., Keselman, L., Orsten, S.: Dynamics based 3D skeletal hand tracking. In: Proceedings of GI, pp. 63–70 (2013)

17. Oikonomidis, I., Kyriazis, N., Argyros, A.: Full DOF tracking of a hand interacting with an object by modeling occlusions and physical constraints. In: Proceedings of IEEE ICCV, pp. 2088–2095 (2011)

18. Oikonomidis, I., Kyriazis, N., Argyros, A.: Tracking the articulated motion of two strongly interacting hands. In: Proceedings of IEEE CVPR, pp. 1862–1869 (2012)

19. Oikonomidis, I., Kyriazis, N., Argyros, A.A.: Efficient model-based 3D tracking of hand articulations using kinect. In: Proceedings of BMVC, pp. 1–11 (2011)

20. Panteleris, P., Kyriazis, N., Argyros, A.A.: 3D tracking of human hands in interaction with unknown objects. In: Proceedings of BMVC (2015). https://dx.doi.org/10.5244/C.29.123

21. Pham, T.H., Kheddar, A., Qammaz, A., Argyros, A.A.: Towards force sensing from vision: observing hand-object interactions to infer manipulation forces. In: Proceedings of IEEE CVPR (2015)

22. Plankers, R., Fua, P.: Articulated soft objects for multiview shape and motion capture. IEEE TPAMI $25(9)$, 1182–1187 (2003). http://dx.doi.org/10.1109/TPAMI.2003.1227995

23. Qian, C., Sun, X., Wei, Y., Tang, X., Sun, J.: Realtime and robust hand tracking from depth. In: Proceedings of IEEE CVPR (2014)

24. Romero, J., Kjellstrom, H., Kragic, D.: Hands in action: real-time 3D reconstruction of hands in interaction with objects. In: Proceedings of ICRA, pp. 458–463 (2010)

25. Sharp, T., Keskin, C., Robertson, D., Taylor, J., Shotton, J., Kim, D., Rhemann, C., Leichter, I., Vinnikov, A., Wei, Y., Freedman, D., Kohli, P., Krupka, E., Fitzgibbon, A., Izadi, S.: Accurate, robust, and flexible real-time hand tracking. In: Proceedings of ACM CHI (2015)

26. Shotton, J., Fitzgibbon, A., Cook, M., Sharp, T., Finocchio, M., Moore, R., Kipman, A., Blake, A.: Real-time human pose recognition in parts from single depth images. In: Proceedings of IEEE CVPR, pp. 1297–1304 (2011). http://dx.doi.org/10.1109/CVPR.2011.5995316

27. Sridhar, S., Mueller, F., Oulasvirta, A., Theobalt, C.: Fast and robust hand tracking using detection-guided optimization. In: Proceedings IEEE CVPR (2015). http://handtracker.mpi-inf.mpg.de/projects/FastHandTracker/

28. Sridhar, S., Oulasvirta, A., Theobalt, C.: Interactive markerless articulated hand motion tracking using RGB and depth data. In: Proceedings of IEEE ICCV (2013)

29. Stenger, B., Mendonça, P.R., Cipolla, R.: Model-based 3D tracking of an articulated hand. In: Proceedings of the 2001 IEEE Computer Society Conference on Computer Vision and Pattern Recognition, CVPR 2001, vol. 2, pp. II-310. IEEE (2001)

30. Stoll, C., Hasler, N., Gall, J., Seidel, H., Theobalt, C.: Fast articulated motion tracking using a sums of Gaussians body model. In: Proceedings of IEEE ICCV, pp. 951–958 (2011)
31. Sun, X., Wei, Y., Liang, S., Tang, X., Sun, J.: Cascaded hand pose regression. In: Proceedings of IEEE CVPR (2015)
32. Tagliasacchi, A., Schröder, M., Tkach, A., Bouaziz, S., Botsch, M., Pauly, M.: Robust articulated-ICP for real-time hand tracking. In: Computer Graphics Forum (Proceedings of SGP), vol. 34, no. 5 (2015)
33. Tang, D., Chang, H.J., Tejani, A., Kim, T.: Latent regression forest: structured estimation of 3D articulated hand posture. In: Proceedings of IEEE CVPR, pp. 3786–3793 (2014). http://dx.doi.org/10.1109/CVPR.2014.490
34. Tang, D., Taylor, J., Kim, T.K.: Opening the black box: hierarchical sampling optimization for estimating human hand pose. In: Proceedings of IEEE ICCV (2015)
35. Tejani, A., Tang, D., Kouskouridas, R., Kim, T.-K.: Latent-class hough forests for 3D object detection and pose estimation. In: Fleet, D., Pajdla, T., Schiele, B., Tuytelaars, T. (eds.) ECCV 2014. LNCS, vol. 8694, pp. 462–477. Springer, Heidelberg (2014). doi:10.1007/978-3-319-10599-4_30
36. Tompson, J., Stein, M., Lecun, Y., Perlin, K.: Real-time continuous pose recovery of human hands using convolutional networks. ACM TOG **33**(5), 169:1–169:10 (2014)
37. Tzionas, D., Ballan, L., Srikantha, A., Aponte, P., Pollefeys, M., Gall, J.: Capturing hands in action using discriminative salient points and physics simulation. IJCV **118**, 172–193 (2016)
38. Tzionas, D., Gall, J.: 3D object reconstruction from hand-object interactions. In: Proceedings of IEEE ICCV (2015)
39. Tzionas, D., Srikantha, A., Aponte, P., Gall, J.: Capturing hand motion with an RGB-D sensor, fusing a generative model with salient points. In: Jiang, X., Hornegger, J., Koch, R. (eds.) GCPR 2014. LNCS, vol. 8753, pp. 277–289. Springer, Heidelberg (2014). doi:10.1007/978-3-319-11752-2_22
40. Wang, R., Paris, S., Popović, J.: 6D hands: markerless hand-tracking for computer aided design. In: Proceedings of ACM UIST, pp. 549–558 (2011)
41. Wang, Y., Min, J., Zhang, J., Liu, Y., Xu, F., Dai, Q., Chai, J.: Video-based hand manipulation capture through composite motion control. ACM TOG **32**(4), 43:1–43:14 (2013)
42. Wu, Y., Huang, T.: View-independent recognition of hand postures. In: Proceedings of IEEE CVPR, pp. 88–94 (2000)
43. Xu, C., Cheng, L.: Efficient hand pose estimation from a single depth image. In: Proceedings of IEEE ICCV (2013)
44. Ye, M., Yang, R.: Real-time simultaneous pose and shape estimation for articulated objects using a single depth camera. In: 2014 IEEE Conference on Computer Vision and Pattern Recognition (CVPR), pp. 2353–2360, June 2014
45. Zollhöfer, M., Nießner, M., Izadi, S., Rehmann, C., Zach, C., Fisher, M., Wu, C., Fitzgibbon, A., Loop, C., Theobalt, C., Stamminger, M.: Real-time non-rigid reconstruction using an RGB-D camera. ACM TOG **33**(4), 156 (2014)

# DeepWarp: Photorealistic Image Resynthesis for Gaze Manipulation

Yaroslav Ganin$^{(\boxtimes)}$, Daniil Kononenko, Diana Sungatullina,
and Victor Lempitsky

Skolkovo Institute of Science and Technology, Skolkovo, Moscow Region, Russia
{ganin,daniil.kononenko,d.sungatullina,lempitsky}@skoltech.ru

**Abstract.** In this work, we consider the task of generating highly-realistic images of a given face with a redirected gaze. We treat this problem as a specific instance of conditional image generation and suggest a new deep architecture that can handle this task very well as revealed by numerical comparison with prior art and a user study. Our deep architecture performs coarse-to-fine warping with an additional intensity correction of individual pixels. All these operations are performed in a feed-forward manner, and the parameters associated with different operations are learned jointly in the end-to-end fashion. After learning, the resulting neural network can synthesize images with manipulated gaze, while the redirection angle can be selected arbitrarily from a certain range and provided as an input to the network.

**Keywords:** Gaze correction · Warping · Spatial transformers · Supervised learning · Deep learning

## 1 Introduction

In this work, we consider the task of learning deep architectures that can transform input images into new images in a certain way (deep image resynthesis). Generally, using deep architectures for image generation has become a very active topic of research. While a lot of very interesting results have been reported over recent years and even months, achieving photo-realism beyond the task of synthesizing small patches has proven to be hard.

Previously proposed methods for deep resynthesis usually tackle the resynthesis problem in a general form and strive for universality. Here, we take an opposite approach and focus on a very specific image resynthesis problem (gaze manipulation) that has a long history in the computer vision community [1,7,13,16,18,20,24,26,27] and some important real-life applications. We show that by restricting the scope of the method and exploiting the specifics of the task, we are indeed able to train deep architectures that handle gaze manipulation well and can synthesize output images of high realism (Fig. 1).

**Electronic supplementary material** The online version of this chapter (doi:10.1007/978-3-319-46475-6_20) contains supplementary material, which is available to authorized users.

© Springer International Publishing AG 2016
B. Leibe et al. (Eds.): ECCV 2016, Part II, LNCS 9906, pp. 311–326, 2016.
DOI: 10.1007/978-3-319-46475-6_20

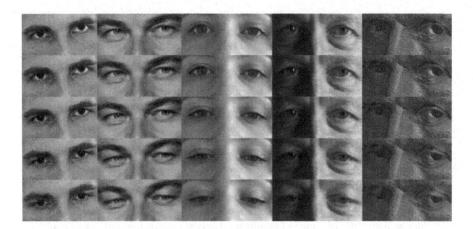

**Fig. 1.** Gaze redirection with our model trained for vertical gaze redirection. The model takes an input image (middle row) and the desired redirection angle (here varying between $-15$ and $+15°$) and re-synthesize the new image with the new gaze direction. Note the preservation of fine details including specular highlights in the resynthesized images.

Generally, few image parts can have such a dramatic effect on the perception of an image like regions depicting eyes of a person in this image. Humans (and even non-humans [23]) can infer a lot of information about of the owner of the eyes, her intent, her mood, and the world around her, from the appearance of the eyes and, in particular, from the direction of the gaze. Generally, the role of gaze in human communication is long known to be very high [15].

In some important scenarios, there is a need to digitally alter the appearance of eyes in a way that changes the apparent direction of the gaze. These scenarios include gaze correction in video-conferencing, as the intent and the attitude of a person engaged in a videochat is distorted by the displacement between the face on her screen and the webcamera (e.g. while the intent might be to gaze into the eyes of the other person, the apparent gaze direction in a transmitted frame will be downwards). Another common scenario that needs gaze redirection is "talking head"-type videos, where a speaker reads the text appearing alongside the camera but it is desirable to redirect her gaze into the camera. One more example includes editing of photos (e.g. group photos) and movies (e.g. during postproduction) in order to make gaze direction consistent with the ideas of the photographer or the movie director.

All of these scenarios put very high demands on the realism of the result of the digital alteration, and some of them also require real-time or near real-time operation. To meet these challenges, we develop a new deep feed-forward architecture that combines several principles of operation (coarse-to-fine processing, image warping, intensity correction). The architecture is trained end-to-end in a supervised way using a specially collected dataset that depicts the change of the appearance under gaze redirection in real life.

Qualitative and quantitative evaluation demonstrate that our deep architecture can synthesize very high-quality eye images, as required by the nature of the applications, and does so at several frames per second. Compared to several recent methods for deep image synthesis, the output of our method contains larger amount of fine details (comparable to the amount in the input image). The quality of the results also compares favorably with the results of a random forest-based gaze redirection method [16]. Our approach has thus both practical importance in the application scenarios outlined above, and also contributes to an actively-developing field of image generation with deep models.

## 2    Related Work

**Deep Learning and Image Synthesis.** Image synthesis using neural networks is receiving growing attention [2,3,5,8,9,19]. More related to our work are methods that learn to transform input images in certain ways [6,17,22]. These methods proceed by learning internal compact representations of images using encoder-decoder (autoencoder) architectures, and then transforming images by changing their internal representation in a certain way that can be trained from examples. We have conducted numerous experiments following this approach combining standard autoencoders with several ideas that have reported to improve the result (convolutional and up-convolutional layers [3,28], adversarial loss [8], variational autoencoders [14]). However, despite our efforts (see the supplementary material), we have found that for large enough image resolution, the outputs of the network lacked high-frequency details and were biased towards typical mean of the training data ("regression-to-mean" effect). This is consistent with the results demonstrated in [6,17,22] that also exhibit noticeable blurring.

Compared to [6,17,22], our approach can learn to perform a restricted set of image transformations. However, the perceptual quality and, in particular, the amount of high-frequency details is considerably better in the case of our method due to the fact that we deliberately avoid any input data compression within the processing pipeline. This is crucial for the class of applications that we consider.

Finally, the idea of spatial warping that lies in the core of the proposed system has been previously suggested in [12]. In relation to [12], parts of our architecture can be seen as spatial transformers with the localization network directly predicting a sampling grid instead of low-dimensional transformation parameters.

**Gaze Manipulation.** An early work on monocular gaze manipulation [24] did not use machine learning, but relied on pre-recording a number of potential eye replacements to be copy-pasted at test time. The idea of gaze redirection using supervised learning was suggested in [16], which also used warping fields that in their case were predicted by machine learning. Compared to their method, we use deep convolutional network as a predictor, which allows us to achieve

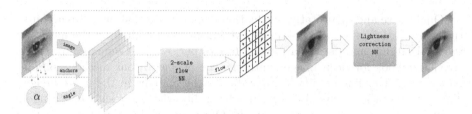

**Fig. 2.** The **proposed system** takes an input eye region, feature points (**anchors**) as well as a correction **angle** $\alpha$ and sends them to the multi-scale neural network (see Sect. 3.2) predicting a **flow** field. The flow field is then applied to the input image to produce an image of a redirected eye. Finally, the output is enhanced by processing with the lightness correction neural network (see Sect. 3.4).

better result quality. Furthermore, while random forests in [16] are trained for a specific angle of gaze redirection, our architecture allows the redirection angle to be specified as an input, and to change continuously in a certain range. Most practical applications discussed above require such flexibility. Finally, the realism of our results is boosted by the lightness adjustment module, which has no counterpart in the approach of [16].

Less related to our approach are methods that aim to solve the gaze problem in videoconferencing via synthesizing 3D rotated views of either the entire scene [1,20,26] or of the face (that is subsequently blended into the unrotated head) [7,18]. Out of this works only [7] works in a monocular setting without relying on extra imaging hardware. The general problem with the novel view synthesis is how to fill disoccluded regions. In cases when the 3D rotated face is blended into the image of the unrotated head [7,18], there is also a danger of distorting head proportions characteristic to a person.

## 3   The Model

In this section, we discuss the architecture of our deep model for re-synthesis. The model is trained on pairs of images corresponding to eye appearance before and after the redirection. The redirection angle serves as an additional input parameter that is provided both during training and at test time.

As in [16], the bulk of gaze redirection is accomplished via warping the input image (Fig. 2). The task of the network is therefore the prediction of the warping field. This field is predicted in two stages in a coarse-to-fine manner, where the decisions at the fine scale are being informed by the result of the coarse stage. Beyond coarse-to-fine warping, the photorealism of the result is improved by performing pixel-wise correction of the brightness where the amount of correction is again predicted by the network. All operations outlined above are implemented in a single feed-forward architecture and are trained jointly end-to-end.

We now provide more details on each stages of the procedure, starting with more detailed description of the data used to train the architecture.

## 3.1   Data Preparation

At training time, our dataset allows us to mine pairs of images containing eyes of the same person looking in two different directions separated by a known angle $\alpha$. The head pose, the lighting, and all other nuisance parameters are (approximately) the same between the two images in the pair. Following [16] (with some modifications), we extract the image parts around each of the eye and resize them to characteristic scale. For simplicity of explanation, let us assume that we need to handle left eyes only (the right eyes can be handled at training and at test times via mirroring).

To perform the extraction, we employ an external face alignment library [25] producing, among other things, $N = 7$ feature points $\{(x_i^{\text{anchor}}, y_i^{\text{anchor}}) \mid i = 1, \ldots, N\}$ for the eye (six points along the edge and also the pupil center). Next, we compute a tight axis-aligned bounding box $\mathcal{B}'$ of the points in the *input* image. We enlarge $\mathcal{B}'$ to the final bounding-box $\mathcal{B}$ using a characteristic radius $R$ that equals the distance between the corners of an eye. The size of $\mathcal{B}$ is set to $0.8R \times 1.0R$. We then cut out the interior of the estimated box from the input image, and also from the output image of the pair (using exactly the same bounding box coordinates). Both images are then rescaled to a fixed size ($W \times H = 51 \times 41$ in our experiments). The resulting image pair serves as a training example for the learning procedure (Fig. 4-Right).

## 3.2   Warping Modules

Each of the two warping modules takes as an input the image, the position of the feature points, and the redirection angle. All inputs are expressed as maps as discussed below, and the architecture of the warping modules is thus "fully-convolutional", including several convolutional layers interleaved with Batch Normalization layers [11] and ReLU non-linearities (the actual configuration is shown in the supplementary material). To preserve the resolution of the input image, we use 'same'-mode convolutions (with zero padding), set all strides to one, and avoid using max-pooling.

**Coarse Warping.** The last convolutional layer of the first (half-scale) warping module produces a pixel-flow field (a two-channel map), which is then upsampled $\mathbf{D}_{\text{coarse}}(I, \alpha)$ and applied to warp the input image by means of a bilinear sampler $\mathbf{S}$ [12, 21] that finds the *coarse estimate*:

$$O_{\text{coarse}} = \mathbf{S}\left(I, \mathbf{D}_{\text{coarse}}(I, \alpha)\right). \tag{1}$$

Here, the sampling procedure $S$ samples the pixels of $O_{\text{coarse}}$ at pixels determined by the flow field:

$$O_{\text{coarse}}(x, y, c) = I\{x + \mathbf{D}_{\text{coarse}}(I, \alpha)(x, y, 1), y + \mathbf{D}_{\text{coarse}}(I, \alpha)(x, y, 2), c\}, \tag{2}$$

where $c$ corresponds to a color channel (R,G, or B), and the curly brackets correspond to bilinear interpolation of $I(\cdot, \cdot, c)$ at a real-valued position. The sampling procedure (1) is piecewise differentiable [12].

**Fine Warping.** In the fine warping module, the rough image estimate $O_{\text{coarse}}$ and the upsampled low-resolution flow $\mathbf{D}_{\text{coarse}}(I, \alpha)$ are concatenated with the input data (the image, the angle encoding, and the feature point encoding) at the original scale and sent to the 1×-scale network which predicts another two-channel flow $\mathbf{D}_{\text{res}}$ that amends the half-scale pixel-flow (additively [10]):

$$\mathbf{D}(I, \alpha) = \mathbf{D}_{\text{coarse}}(I, \alpha) + \mathbf{D}_{\text{res}}(I, \alpha, O_{\text{coarse}}, \mathbf{D}_{\text{coarse}}(I, \alpha)),  \tag{3}$$

The amended flow is used to obtain the final output (again, via bilinear sampler):

$$O = \mathbf{S}(I, \mathbf{D}(I, \alpha)).  \tag{4}$$

The purpose of coarse-to-fine processing is two-fold. The half-scale (coarse) module effectively increases the receptive field of the model resulting in a flow that moves larger structures in a more coherent way. Secondly, the coarse module gives a rough estimate of how a redirected eye would look like. This is useful for locating problematic regions which can only be fixed by a neural network operating at a finer scale.

### 3.3   Input Encoding

As discussed above, alongside the raw input image, the warping modules also receive the information about the desired redirection angle and feature points also encoded as image-sized feature maps.

**Embedding the Angle.** Similarly to [6], we treat the correction angle as an attribute and embed it into a higher dimensional space using a multi-layer perceptron $\mathbf{F}_{\text{angle}}(\alpha)$ with ReLU non-linearities. The precise architecture is FC(16) → ReLU → FC(16) → ReLU. Unlike [6], we do not output separate features for each spatial location but rather opt for a single position-independent 16-dimensional vector. The vector is then expressed as 16 constant maps that are concatenated into the input map stack. During learning, the embedding of the angle parameter is also updated by backpropagation.

**Embedding the Feature Points.** Although in theory a convolutional neural network of an appropriate architecture should be able to extract necessary features from the raw input pixels, we found it beneficial to further augment 3 color channels with additional 14 feature maps containing information about the eye anchor points.

In order to get the anchor maps, for each previously obtained feature point located at $(x_i^{\text{anchor}}, y_i^{\text{anchor}})$, we compute a pair of maps:

$$\begin{aligned} \Delta_x^i[x, y] &= x - x_i^{\text{anchor}}, \\ \Delta_y^i[x, y] &= y - y_i^{\text{anchor}}, \end{aligned} \quad \forall(x, y) \in \{0, \ldots, W\} \times \{0, \ldots, H\},  \tag{5}$$

where $W, H$ are width and height of the input image respectively. The embedding give the network "local" access to similar features as used by decision trees in [16].

Ultimately, the input map stack consists of 33 maps (RGB + 16 angle embedding maps + 14 feature point embedding maps).

Input      CFW      + LCM      Mask      GT

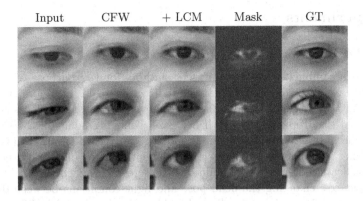

**Fig. 3.** Visualization of three challenging redirection cases where **Lightness Correction Module** helps considerably compared to the system based solely on coarse-to-fine warping (CFW) which is having difficulties with expanding the area to the left of the iris. The 'Mask' column shows the soft mask corresponding to parts where lightness is increased. Lightness correction fixes problems with inpainting disoccluded eye-white, and what is more emphasizes the specular highlight increasing the perceived realism of the result.

### 3.4  Lightness Correction Module

While the bulk of appearance changes associated with gaze redirection can be modeled using warping, some subtle but important transformations are more photometric than geometric in nature and require a more general transformation. In addition, the warping approach can struggle to fill in disoccluded areas in some cases.

To increase the generality of the transformation that can be handled by our architecture, we add the final lightness adjustment module (see Fig. 2). The module takes as input the features computed within the coarse warping and fine warping modules (specifically, the activations of the third convolutional layer), as well as the image produced by the fine warping module. The output of the module is a single map $M$ of the same size as the output image that is used to modify the brightness of the output $O$ using a simple element-wise transform:

$$O_{\text{final}}(x, y, c) = O(x, y, c) \cdot (1 - M(x, y)) + M(x, y), \qquad (6)$$

assuming that the brightness in each channel is encoded between zero and one. The resulting pixel colors can thus be regarded as blends between the colors of the warped pixels and the white color. The actual architecture for the lightness correction module in our experiments is shown in the supplementary material.

This idea can be, of course, generalized further to a larger number of colors in the *palette* for admixing, while these colors can be defined either manually or made dataset-dependent or even image-dependent. Our initial experiments along these directions, however, have not brought consistent improvement in photorealism in the case of the gaze redirection task.

# 4   Experiments

## 4.1   Dataset

There are no publicly available datasets suitable for the purpose of the gaze correction task with continuously varying redirection angle. Therefore, we collect our own dataset (Fig. 4). To minimize head movement, a person places her head on a special stand and follows with her gaze a moving point on the screen in front of the stand. While the point is moving, we record several images with eyes looking in different fixed directions (about 200 for one video sequence) using a webcam mounted in the middle of the screen. For each person we record 2–10 sequences, changing the head pose and light conditions between different sequences. Training pairs are collected, taking two images with different gaze directions from one sequence. We manually exclude bad shots, where a person is blinking or where she is not changing gaze direction monotonically as anticipated. Most of the experiments were done on the dataset of 33 persons and 98 sequences. Unless noted otherwise, we train the model for vertical gaze redirection in the range between $-30°$ and $30°$.

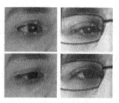

**Fig. 4.** Left – dataset collection process. Right – examples of two training pairs (input image with superimposed feature points on top, output image in the bottom).

## 4.2   Training Procedure

The model was trained end-to-end on 128-sized batches using Adam optimizer [14]. We used a regular $\ell_2$-distance between the synthesized output $O_{output}$ and the ground-truth $O_{gt}$ as the objective function. We tried to improve over this simple baseline in several ways. First, we tried to put emphasis on the actual eye region (not the rectangular bounding-box) by adding more weight to the corresponding pixels but were not able to get any significant improvements. Our earlier experiments with adversarial loss [8] were also inconclusive. As the residual flow predicted by the $1\times$-scale module tends to be quite noisy, we attempted to smooth the flow-field by imposing a total variation penalty. Unfortunately, this resulted in a slightly worse $\ell_2$-loss on the test set.

**Sampling Training Pairs.** We found that biasing the selection process for more difficult and unusual head poses and bigger redirection angles improved the results. For this reason, we used the following sampling scheme aimed at reducing the dataset imbalance. We split all possible correction angles (that is, the range between $-30°$ and $30°$) into 15 bins. A set of samples falling into a bin is further divided into "easy" and "hard" subsets depending on the input's *tilt* angle (an angle between the segment connecting two most distant eye feature points and the horizontal baseline). A sample is considered to be "hard" if its tilt is $\geqslant 8°$. This subdivision helps to identify training pairs corresponding to the rare head poses. We form a training batch by picking 4 correction angle bins uniformly at random and sampling 24 "easy" and 8 "hard" examples for each of the chosen bins.

### 4.3 Quantitative Evaluation

We evaluate our approach on our dataset. We randomly split the initial set of subjects into a development (26 persons) and a test (7 persons) sets. Several methods were compared using the mean square error (MSE) between the synthesized and the ground-truth images extracted using the procedure described in Sect. 3.1.

**Models.** We consider 6 different models:

1. A system based on Structured Random Forests (*RF*) proposed in [16]. We train it for $15°$ redirection only using the reference implementation.
2. A single-scale (*SS* ($15°$ only)) version of our method with a single warping module operating on the original image scale that is trained for $15°$ redirection only.
3. A single-scale (*SS*) version of our method with a single warping module operating on the original image scale.
4. A multi-scale (*MS*) network without coarse warping. It processes inputs on two scales and uses features from both scales to predict the final warping transformation.
5. A coarse-to-fine warping-based system described in Sect. 3 (*CFW*).
6. A coarse-to-fine warping-based system with a lightness correction module (*CFW + LCM*).

The latter four models are trained for the task of vertical gaze redirection in the range. We call such models *unified* (as opposed to single angle correction systems).

**$15°$ Correction.** In order to have the common ground with the existing systems, we first restrict ourselves to the case of $15°$ gaze correction. Following [16], we present a graph of sorted normalized errors (Fig. 5), where all errors are divided by the MSE obtained by an input image and then the errors on the test set are sorted for each model.

It can be seen that the unified multi-scale models are, in general, comparable or superior to the RF-based approach in [16]. Interestingly, the lightness

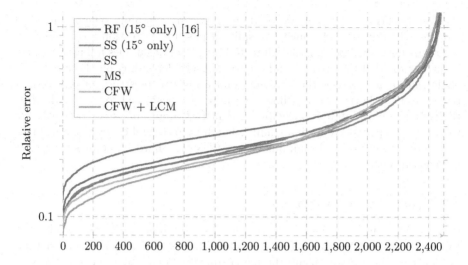

**Fig. 5.** Ordered errors for 15° redirection. Our multi-scale models (MS, CFW, CFW + LCM) show results that are comparable or superior the Random Forests (RF) [16].

adjustment extension (Sect. 3.4) is able to show quite significant improvements for the samples with low MSE. Those are are mostly cases similar to shown in Fig. 3. It is also worth noting that the single-scale model trained for this specific correction angle consistently outperforms [16], demonstrating the power of the proposed architecture. However, we note that results of the methods can be improved using additional registration procedure, one example of which is described in Sect. 4.5.

**Arbitrary Vertical Redirection.** We also compare different variants of unified networks and plot the error distribution over different redirection angles (Fig. 6). For small angles, all the methods demonstrate roughly the same performance, but as we increase the amount of correction, the task becomes much harder (which is reflected by the growing error) revealing the difference between the models. Again, the best results are achieved by the palette model, which is followed by the multi-scale networks making use of coarse warping.

### 4.4    Perceptual Quality

We demonstrate the results of redirection on 15° upwards in Fig. 7. CFW-based systems produce the results visually closer to the ground truth than RF. The effect of the lightness correction is pronounced: on the input image with the lack of white Random Forest and CFW fail to get output with sufficient eye-white and copy-paste red pixels instead, whereas CFW+LCM achieve good correspondence with the ground-truth. However, the downside effect of the LCM could be blurring/lower contrast because of the multiplication procedure (6).

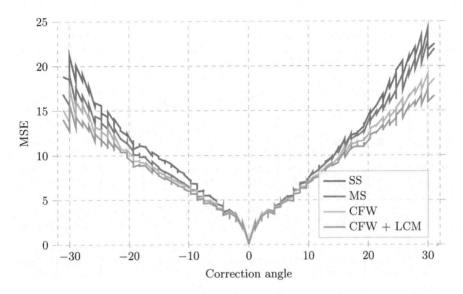

**Fig. 6.** Distribution of errors over different correction angles.

**User Study.** To confirm the improvement corresponding to different aspects of the proposed models, which may not be adequately reflected by $\ell_2$-measure, we performed an informal user study enrolling 16 subjects unrelated to computer vision and comparing four methods (RF, SS, CFW, CFW+LCM). Each user was shown 160 quadruplets of images, and in each quadruplet one of the images was obtained by re-synthesis with one of the methods, while the remaining three were unprocessed real images of eyes. 40 randomly sampled results from each of the compared methods were thus embedded. When a quadruplet was shown, the task of the subject was to click on the artificial (re-synthesized) image as quickly as possible. For each method, we then recorded the number of correct guesses out of 40 (for an ideal method the expected number would be 10, and for a very poor one it would be 40). We also recorded the time that the subject took to decide on each quadruplet (better method would take a longer time for spotting). Table 1 shows results of the experiment. Notably, here the gap between methods is much wider then it might seem from the MSE-based comparisons, with CFW+LCM method outperforming others very considerably, especially when taking into account the timings.

**Horizontal Redirection.** While most of our experiments were about vertical gaze redirection, the same models can be trained to redirect the gaze horizontally (and, with trivial generalization, by a 2D family of angles). In Fig. 8, we provide qualitative results of CFW+LCM for horizontal redirection. Some examples showing the limitations of our method are given. The limitations are concerned with cases with severe disocclusions, where large areas have to be filled by the network.

We provide more qualitative results on the project webpage [4].

| Input | RF | CFW | +LCM | GT | Input | RF | CFW | +LCM | GT |

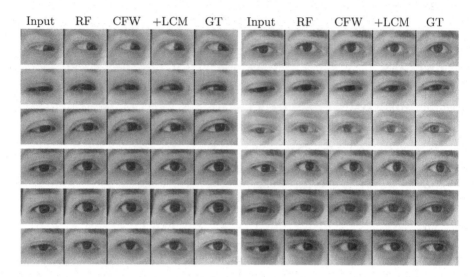

**Fig. 7.** Sample results on a hold-out. The full version of our model (CFW+LCM) outperforms other methods.

**Table 1. User assessment for the photorealism of the results for the four methods.** During the session, each of the 16 test subjects observed 40 instances of results of each method embedded within 3 real eye images. The participants were asked to click on the resynthesized image in as little time as they could. The first three parts of the table specify the number of correct guesses (the smaller the better). The last line indicates the mean time needed to make a guess (the larger the better). Our full system (coarse-to-fine warping and lightness correction) dominated the performance.

| | Random Forest | Single Scale | CFW | CFW+LCM |
|---|---|---|---|---|
| Correctly guessed (out of 40) | | | | |
| Mean | 36.1 | 33.8 | 28.8 | **25.3** |
| Median | 37 | 35 | 29 | **25** |
| Max | 40 | 39 | 38 | **34** |
| Min | 26 | 22 | 20 | **16** |
| Correctly guessed within 2 seconds (out of 40) | | | | |
| Mean | 26.4 | 21.1 | 11.7 | **8.0** |
| Median | 28.5 | 20.5 | 10 | **8** |
| Max | 35 | 33 | 23 | **17** |
| Min | 13 | 11 | 3 | **0** |
| Correctly guessed within 1 second (out of 40) | | | | |
| Mean | 8.1 | 4.4 | 1.6 | **1.1** |
| Median | 6 | 3 | 1 | **1** |
| Max | 20 | 15 | 7 | **5** |
| Min | 0 | 0 | 0 | **0** |
| Mean time to make a guess | | | | |
| Mean time, sec | 1.89 | 2.30 | 3.60 | **3.96** |

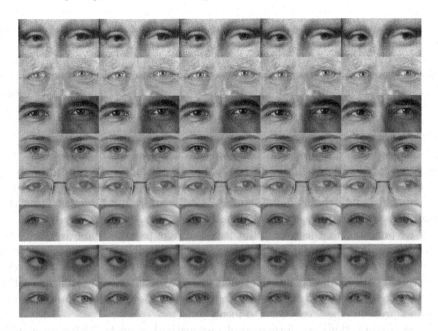

**Fig. 8. Horizontal redirection** with a model trained for both vertical and horizontal gaze redirection. For the first six rows the angle varies from $-15°$ to $15°$ relative to the central (input) image. The last two rows push the redirection to extreme angles (up to $45°$) breaking our model down.

### 4.5 Incorporating Registration

We found that results can be further perceptually improved (see [4]) if the objective is slightly modified to take into account misalignment between inputs and ground-truth images. To that end, we enlarge the bounding-box $\mathcal{B}$ that we use to extract the output image of a training pair by $k = 3$ pixels in all the directions. Given that now $O_{gt}$ has the size of $(H + 2k) \times (W + 2k)$, the new objective is defined as:

$$\mathcal{L}(O_{\text{output}}, O_{\text{gt}}) = \min_{i,j} \text{dist}\left(O_{\text{output}}, O_{\text{gt}}[i : i + H, j : j + W]\right), \qquad (7)$$

where $\text{dist}(\cdot)$ can be either $\ell_2$ or $\ell_1$-distance (the latter giving slightly sharper results), and $O_{\text{gt}}[i : i+H, j : j+W]$ corresponds to a $H \times W$ crop of $O_{\text{gt}}$ with top left corner at the position $(i, j)$. Being an alternative to the offline registration of input/ground-truth pairs [16] which is computationally prohibitive in large-scale scenarios, this small trick greatly increases robustness of the training procedure against small misalignments in a training set.

## 5 Discussion

We have suggested a method for realistic gaze redirection, allowing to change gaze continuously in a certain range. At the core of our approach is the prediction of the warping field using a deep convolutional network. We embed redirection angle and feature points as image-sized maps and suggest "fully-convolutional" coarse-to-fine architecture of warping modules. In addition to warping, photo-realism is increased using lightness correction module. Quantitative comparison of MSE-error, qualitative examples and a user study show the advantage of suggested techniques and the benefit of their combination within an end-to-end learnable framework.

Our system is reasonably robust against different head poses (e.g., see Fig. 3) and deals correctly with the situations where a person wears glasses (see [4]). Most of the failure modes (e.g., corresponding to extremely tilted head poses or large redirection angles involving disocclusion of the different parts of an eye) are not inherent to the model design and can be addressed by augmenting the training data with appropriate examples.

We concentrated on gaze redirection, although our approach might be extended for other similar tasks, e.g. re-synthesis of faces. In contrast with autoencoders-based approach, our architecture does not compress data to a representation with lower explicit or implicit dimension, but directly transforms the input image. Our method thus might be better suited for fine detail preservation, and less prone to the "regression-to-mean" effect.

The computational performance of our method is up to 20 fps on a mid-range consumer GPU (NVIDIA GeForce-750M), which is however slower than the competing method of [16], which is able to achieve similar speed on CPU. Our models are however much more compact than forests from [16] (250 Kb vs 30–60 Mb in our comparisons), while also being universal. We are currently working on the unification of the two approaches.

Speed optimization of the proposed system is another topic for future work. Finally, we plan to further investigate non-standard loss functions for our architectures (e.g. the one proposed in Sect. 4.5), as the $\ell_2$-loss is not closely enough related to perceptual quality of results (as highlighted by our user study).

**Acknowledgements.** We would like to thank Leonid Ekimov for sharing the results of his work on applying auto-encoders for gaze correction. We are also grateful to all the Skoltech students and employees who agreed to participate in the dataset collection and in the user study. This research is supported by the Skoltech Translational Research and Innovation Program.

# References

1. Criminisi, A., Shotton, J., Blake, A., Torr, P.H.: Gaze manipulation for one-to-one teleconferencing. In: ICCV (2003)
2. Denton, E.L., Chintala, S., Fergus, R., et al.: Deep generative image models using a laplacian pyramid of adversarial networks. In: NIPS (2015)
3. Dosovitskiy, A., Tobias Springenberg, J., Brox, T.: Learning to generate chairs with convolutional neural networks. In: CVPR (2015)
4. Ganin, Y., Kononenko, D., Sungatullina, D., Lempitsky, V.: Project website (2016). http://sites.skoltech.ru/compvision/projects/deepwarp/. Accessed 22 July 2016

5. Gatys, L., Ecker, A.S., Bethge, M.: Texture synthesis using convolutional neural networks. In: NIPS (2015)
6. Ghodrati, A., Jia, X., Pedersoli, M., Tuytelaars, T.: Towards automatic image editing: learning to see another you. arXiv preprint arXiv:1511.08446 (2015)
7. Giger, D., Bazin, J.C., Kuster, C., Popa, T., Gross, M.: Gaze correction with a single webcam. In: IEEE International Conference on Multimedia and Expo (2014)
8. Goodfellow, I., Pouget-Abadie, J., Mirza, M., Xu, B., Warde-Farley, D., Ozair, S., Courville, A., Bengio, Y.: Generative adversarial nets. In: NIPS (2014)
9. Gregor, K., Danihelka, I., Graves, A., Rezende, D., Wierstra, D.: Draw: a recurrent neural network for image generation. In: ICML (2015)
10. He, K., Zhang, X., Ren, S., Sun, J.: Deep residual learning for image recognition. arXiv preprint arXiv:1512.03385 (2015)
11. Ioffe, S., Szegedy, C.: Batch normalization: accelerating deep network training by reducing internal covariate shift. In: ICML (2015)
12. Jaderberg, M., Simonyan, K., Zisserman, A., et al.: Spatial transformer networks. In: NIPS (2015)
13. Jones, A., Lang, M., Fyffe, G., Yu, X., Busch, J., McDowall, I., Bolas, M.T., Debevec, P.E.: Achieving eye contact in a one-to-many 3D video teleconferencing system. ACM Trans. Graph. 28(3), 64 (2009)
14. Kingma, D., Ba, J.: Adam: a method for stochastic optimization. arXiv preprint arXiv:1412.6980 (2014)
15. Kleinke, C.L.: Gaze and eye contact: a research review. Psychol. Bull. 100(1), 78 (1986)
16. Kononenko, D., Lempitsky, V.: Learning to look up: realtime monocular gaze correction using machine learning. In: CVPR (2015)
17. Kulkarni, T.D., Whitney, W.F., Kohli, P., Tenenbaum, J.: Deep convolutional inverse graphics network. In: NIPS (2015)
18. Kuster, C., Popa, T., Bazin, J.C., Gotsman, C., Gross, M.: Gaze correction for home video conferencing. In: SIGGRAPH Asia (2012)
19. Mahendran, A., Vedaldi, A.: Understanding deep image representations by inverting them. In: CVPR (2015)
20. Okada, K.I., Maeda, F., Ichikawaa, Y., Matsushita, Y.: Multiparty videoconferencing at virtual social distance: MAJIC design. In: Proceedings of the 1994 ACM Conference on Computer Supported Cooperative Work, CSCW 1994, pp. 385–393 (1994)
21. Oquab, M.: Torch7 modules for spatial transformer networks (2015). https://github.com/qassemoquab/stnbhwd
22. Reed, S.E., Zhang, Y., Zhang, Y., Lee, H.: Deep visual analogy-making. In: NIPS (2015)
23. Wallis, L.J., Range, F., Müller, C.A., Serisier, S., Huber, L., Virányi, Z.: Training for eye contact modulates gaze following in dogs. Anim. Behav. 106, 27–35 (2015)
24. Wolf, L., Freund, Z., Avidan, S.: An eye for an eye: a single camera gaze-replacement method. In: CVPR (2010)
25. Xiong, X., Torre, F.: Supervised descent method and its applications to face alignment. In: CVPR (2013)

26. Yang, R., Zhang, Z.: Eye gaze correction with stereovision for video-teleconferencing. In: Heyden, A., Sparr, G., Nielsen, M., Johansen, P. (eds.) ECCV 2002. LNCS, vol. 2351, pp. 479–494. Springer, Heidelberg (2002). doi:10.1007/3-540-47967-8_32
27. Yip, B., Jin, J.S.: Face re-orientation using ellipsoid model in video conference. In: Proceedings of the 7th IASTED International Conference on Internet and Multimedia Systems and Applications, pp. 245–250 (2003)
28. Zeiler, M.D., Fergus, R.: Visualizing and understanding convolutional networks. In: Fleet, D., Pajdla, T., Schiele, B., Tuytelaars, T. (eds.) ECCV 2014. LNCS, vol. 8689, pp. 818–833. Springer, Heidelberg (2014). doi:10.1007/978-3-319-10590-1_53

# Non-rigid 3D Shape Retrieval via Large Margin Nearest Neighbor Embedding

Ioannis Chiotellis[1][(✉)], Rudolph Triebel[1,2], Thomas Windheuser[1],
and Daniel Cremers[1]

[1] Department of Computer Science, TU Munich, Garching, Germany
{chiotell,triebel,windheus,cremers}@in.tum.de
[2] Institute of Robotics and Mechatronics, Department of Perception and Cognition,
German Aerospace Center (DLR), Oberpfaffenhofen-Weßling, Germany
rudolph.triebel@dlr.de

**Abstract.** In this paper, we propose a highly efficient metric learning approach to non-rigid 3D shape analysis. From a training set of 3D shapes from different classes, we learn a transformation of the shapes which optimally enforces a clustering of shapes from the same class. In contrast to existing approaches, we do not perform a transformation of individual local point descriptors, but a linear embedding of the entire distribution of shape descriptors. It turns out that this embedding of the input shapes is sufficiently powerful to enable state of the art retrieval performance using a simple nearest neighbor classifier. We demonstrate experimentally that our approach substantially outperforms the state of the art non-rigid 3D shape retrieval methods on the recent benchmark data set SHREC'14 Non-Rigid 3D Human Models, both in classification accuracy and runtime.

**Keywords:** Shape retrieval · Shape representation · Supervised learning

## 1 Introduction

The analysis of 3D shapes is becoming more and more important with increasing amounts of 3D shape data becoming available through novel 3D scanning technology and 3D modeling software. Among the numerous challenges in 3D shape analysis, we will focus on the problems of non-rigid shape similarity and non-rigid 3D shape retrieval: Given a set of 3D shapes and a previously unobserved query shape, we would like to efficiently determine the similarity of the query to all shapes in the database and identify the most similar shapes in the database – see Fig. 1. The computation of shape similarity is a difficult problem, in particular if we wish to allow for non-rigid deformations of the shapes. Under such deformations the appearance of the object may change significantly. For many real-world retrieval applications on large 3D shape databases, it is of importance that the retrieval of similar shapes can be computed efficiently.

© Springer International Publishing AG 2016
B. Leibe et al. (Eds.): ECCV 2016, Part II, LNCS 9906, pp. 327–342, 2016.
DOI: 10.1007/978-3-319-46475-6_21

328    I. Chiotellis et al.

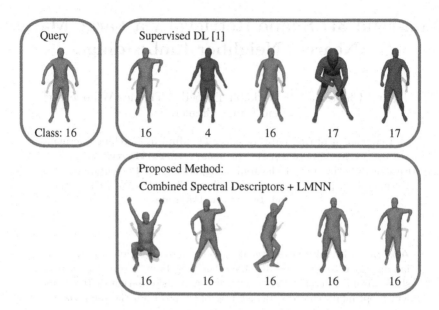

**Fig. 1.** Example of shape retrieval from SHREC'14 Humans - real (scanned) dataset. The query model (top left) belongs to class 16. The top row shows the best five matches retrieved by the Supervised Dictionary Learning method [1]. The best five matches retrieved by the proposed method (CSD+LMNN) are shown in the bottom row. The blue color indicates that the retrieved model corresponds to the correct class (i.e. 16) and the red color indicates an incorrect class. The quantitative experiments in Sect. 3 show that the proposed method outperforms the state of the art methods significantly on the SHREC'14 Humans dataset. (Color figure online)

## 1.1 Related Work

Much like in image analysis, the analysis of 3D shapes often starts with the extraction of local feature descriptors which are invariant to rigid and robust to non-rigid transformations of the shape. Popular descriptors include the Heat Kernel Signature [2], the Wave Kernel Signature [3] and the scale-invariant Heat Kernel Signature [4]. For computing a *correspondence* between 3D shapes, the shape analysis community has devised a variety of machine learning approaches to learn optimal point descriptors [5–8].

Learning approaches have also been used for shape *retrieval* as in [9] and [1]. In [1] the authors define a dictionary of point descriptors and use it to compute sparse representations of the point descriptors of each shape. Then they obtain global shape descriptors by sum pooling. The distances between them are considered to be the dis-similarity between the shapes. The authors go on to use unsupervised and supervised learning methods to optimize the classification results. In the supervised case, the authors try to minimize a loss function as in [10] using a subset of the pooled descriptors as a training set. They actually propagate the error back to the dictionary of point descriptors. This means their objective is to learn an optimal dictionary of point descriptors for the specific task of shape retrieval and similarity ranking. Although this approach yielded state of the art results, as shown in [11], the computation time needed to learn the optimal dictionary (3–4 h) prohibits it from being used for larger datasets. In [9] the main purpose of the method is to learn the invariant representation of each shape of a given dataset. The authors use a statistical framework to address classification tasks. While achieving state of the art performance, a major drawback of this method, from a learning point of view, is that it uses a large subset of the shapes (even 90 %) for training.

## 1.2   Contribution

In this work, we propose a 3D shape retrieval method which provides state of the art performance while being substantially faster than previous techniques. We achieve this using a novel combination of stacked shape descriptors and a linear embedding of their distribution by means of a metric learning approach. In contrast to the approach by Litman et al. [1], we do not employ dictionary learning to obtain shape descriptors from sparse point descriptors, but instead use weighted averaging directly on the point descriptors of a shape. We then learn a metric for the resulting shape descriptors so that samples from the same class are closer to each other than samples from different classes. Letting the learning process operate only on shape descriptors reduces our overall runtime tremendously. One of the main insights of our work is that the stacked shape descriptor alone does not lead to better performance, but in combination with the Large Margin Nearest Neighbor (LMNN) approach for metric learning, classification performance is significantly higher, reaching almost 98 % mean average precision on the challenging "SHREC' 14 Humans - scanned" data set. Furthermore, our method is much faster than previous methods, as the individual steps require comparably only a few computations: Rather than several hours, our approach only needs approximately 4 min to learn the optimal embedding of shapes using only 40 % of the shapes.

## 2   Approach

Our problem dictates to compare non-rigid shapes therefore we aim to obtain representations that capture their intrinsic properties. Our goal is to find representations such that similar shapes have proportionally similar descriptors. This becomes a particularly challenging problem when considering all possible deformations a single shape can have. In the next paragraphs we explain in detail every tool that we use. First we present an overview of our pipeline as illustrated in Fig. 2.

### 2.1   Overview

A commonly used scheme in shape analysis is to model a shape $\mathcal{S}$ as a two-dimensional manifold $\mathcal{M}$ and representing it as a triangular mesh with a set of $n$

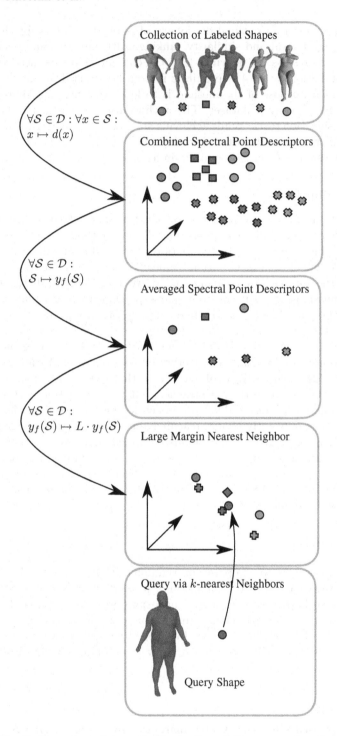

**Fig. 2. Overview:** Schematic illustration of the proposed method.

vertices $\mathcal{V} = \{v_1, v_2, \ldots, v_n\}$, a set of triangular faces $\mathcal{F} \subset \mathcal{V}^3$ and a set of edges $\mathcal{E} \subset \mathcal{V}^2$ between adjacent vertices.

At first, we compute the Laplace-Beltrami operator (LBO) for each mesh in our dataset. We then compute a point descriptor $d(x)$ - based on the LBO - for each vertex of our mesh. There are different descriptors that can be utilized. We use the Wave Kernel Signature [3] and the scale-invariant Heat Kernel Signature [4]. The reason to choose LBO-based descriptors is their inherent invariance to isometric deformations.

As a mesh can have several thousands vertices and datasets contain a large number of meshes, it becomes intractable to compare all point descriptors. Therefore we compute a weighted average of the point descriptors of each mesh and obtain a $q$-dimensional descriptor $y_f$ for each shape. The shape descriptors $y_f$ can either be the averaged siHKS, the averaged WKS or a combination of them. Our rational for the particular choice of descriptors is that siHKS captures global, while WKS focuses on local shape features. We argue that a stacked combination of them contains diverse information that can be fully exploited by a metric learning algorithm.

In the end we feed a subset of our shape descriptors $y_f$ along with their labels to a supervised metric learning algorithm (LMNN). The algorithm learns a linear mapping $L$ of the shape descriptors such that shapes with different labels are easier to distinguish from one another in the new space.

Now when we want to classify a new shape, all we need to do is to compute the same type of shape descriptor $y_f$ as the one we trained our classifier with and transform it into the new space by applying the learned mapping $L$. The labels of the $k$ closest shapes in the transformed space determine the predicted label for our query shape.

## 2.2 The Laplace-Beltrami Operator

The Laplace-Beltrami operator (LBO) is a natural generalization of the Laplace operator for Riemannian manifolds. Like the Laplacian, it is defined as the (negative) divergence of the gradient, and it is a linear operator mapping functions to functions. Therefore the LBO is often also simply referred to as the Laplacian. Formally, given a smooth scalar field $f : \mathcal{M} \to \mathbb{R}$ on the manifold $\mathcal{M}$ associated to shape $\mathcal{S}$, the Laplace-Beltrami operator $\Delta$ is defined as

$$\Delta f := -\mathrm{div}(\nabla f). \tag{1}$$

One of the most important properties of the Laplacian is that it is invariant under isometric deformations. Particularly useful are the eigenvalues $\lambda_i \in \mathbb{R}$ and the eigenfunctions $\phi_i : \mathcal{M} \to \mathbb{R}$ of the Laplacian, i.e.

$$\Delta \phi_i := \lambda_i \phi_i. \tag{2}$$

The eigenvalues $\lambda_i$ of Eq. (2) – known as the *Helmholtz equation* – are non-negative and represent a discrete set $(0 = \lambda_0 \leq \lambda_1 \leq \lambda_2 \leq \ldots \leq +\infty)$. The corresponding eigenfunctions can be chosen to form an orthonormal basis:

$$\langle \phi_i, \phi_j \rangle = \int_M \phi_i(x)\phi_j(x)dx = \begin{cases} 0, & \text{if } i \neq j \\ 1, & \text{if } i = j. \end{cases} \tag{3}$$

**Discretization.** A popular discretization of the LBO is the cotangent scheme [12,13]. It allows to compute the eigenvalues $\lambda_i$ and eigenvectors $\phi_i$ as the solutions to the generalized eigenvalue problem

$$A\phi_i = \lambda_i B\phi_i, \tag{4}$$

where $A \in \mathbb{R}^{n \times n}$ is the *stiffness matrix* and $B \in \mathbb{R}^{n \times n}$ is the *mass matrix*. Concretely, $A$ is defined as

$$A_{ij} = \begin{cases} \frac{\cot \alpha_{ij} + \cot \alpha_{ji}}{2}, & \text{if } (v_i, v_j) \in \mathcal{E} \\ -\sum_{k \in N(i)} A_{ik}, & \text{if } i = j, \end{cases} \tag{5}$$

where $\alpha_{ij}$ and $\alpha_{ji}$ are the two angles opposite of the edge $(v_i, v_j)$ and $N(i)$ is the one-ring neighborhood of vertex $v_i$. The mass matrix $B$ is defined as

$$B_{ij} = \begin{cases} \frac{a(T_1) + a(T_2)}{12}, & \text{if } (v_i, v_j) \in \mathcal{E} \\ \frac{\sum_{k \in N(i)} a(T_k)}{6}, & \text{if } i = j, \end{cases} \tag{6}$$

where $T_1, T_2$ are the triangles that share the edge $(v_i, v_j)$, and $a(T)$ is the area of triangle $T$. Often a simplified "lumped" diagonal version of the mass matrix is used:

$$B_{ii} = \frac{\sum_{k \in N(i)} a(T_k)}{3}, \tag{7}$$

i.e. $B_{ii}$ is considered as the corresponding area element of vertex $v_i$. The geometric concepts of these formulas are depicted in Fig. 3.

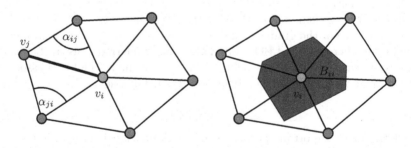

**Fig. 3. Stiffness Matrix (left):** The entries $A_{ij}$ of the stiffness matrix $A$ contain the average of the cotangents of the angles $\alpha_{ij}, \alpha_{ji}$ opposite to the edge $(v_i, v_j)$. Thus the name *cotangent scheme*. **Mass Matrix (right):** The diagonal entries $B_{ii}$ of the mass matrix $B$ correspond to the Voronoi area around vertex $v_i$.

## 2.3  Point Descriptors

Local feature descriptors have been proven particularly useful in shape analysis tasks such as shape matching (point-to-point correspondence) and shape retrieval. In the following we describe three of the most used ones.

**Heat Kernel Signature.** The HKS [2] is - as the name indicates - based on the heat diffusion process on a surface $S$ which is governed by the Heat equation:

$$\Delta u(x,t) = -\frac{\partial}{\partial t} u(x,t). \tag{8}$$

The solution $k_t(x,x)$ can be interpreted as the amount of heat that remains at point $x$ of surface $S$ after time $t$ when starting with a unit heat source $u_0$ concentrated at $x$ at $t_0 = 0$. The eigen-decomposition of the Heat Kernel is

$$k_t(x,y) = \sum_{k=0}^{\infty} e^{-\lambda_k t} \phi_k(x)\phi_k(y), \tag{9}$$

so the HKS is just

$$k_t(x,x) = \sum_{k=0}^{K-1} e^{-\lambda_k t} \phi_k(x)^2, \tag{10}$$

as we truncate the basis to the first $K$ eigenfunctions of the LBO. Concatenating the solutions for different times $\{t_1, t_2, \ldots, t_T\}$ we obtain a descriptor of the form

$$HKS(x) = (k_{t_1}(x,x), k_{t_2}(x,x), \ldots, k_{t_T}(x,x)). \tag{11}$$

**Scale Invariant Heat Kernel Signature.** Bronstein and Kokkinos [4] developed a scale-invariant version of the Heat Kernel Signature (siHKS) using the logarithm, the derivative and the Fourier transform moving from the time domain to the frequencies domain. Assuming a shape is scaled by a factor $\beta$, and rewriting time $t$ as $\alpha^\tau$, the heat kernel of the scaled shape would only be shifted in $\tau$ by $2\log_\alpha \beta$. The authors first constructed a *scale-covariant heat kernel*:

$$scHKS(x,x) = -\frac{\sum_{k=1}^{K} \lambda_k \alpha^\tau \log \alpha e^{-\lambda_k \alpha^\tau} \phi_k(x)^2}{\sum_{k=1}^{K} e^{-\lambda_k \alpha^\tau} \phi_k(x)^2}. \tag{12}$$

In the Fourier domain this shift results in a complex phase $H(\omega)e^{-i\omega 2 \log_\alpha \beta}$ where $H(\omega)$ denotes the Fourier transform of *scHKS* w.r.t. $\tau$. Finally the *scale-invariant HKS* is constructed by taking the absolute value of $H(\omega)$ (thus undoing the phase) and then sampling $|H(\omega)|$ at $q$ frequencies $\{\omega_1, \ldots, \omega_q\}$ [1]:

$$siHKS(x) = (|H(\omega_1)|, \ldots, |H(\omega_q)|)^T. \tag{13}$$

**Wave Kernel Signature.** The Wave Kernel Signature (WKS) [3] - inspired by quantum mechanics - describes the average probability over time to locate a particle with a certain energy distribution $f_E$ at point $x$. The movement of a quantum particle on a surface is governed by the wave function $\psi(x,t)$ which is a solution of the Schrödinger equation

$$\frac{\partial \psi(x,t)}{\partial t} = i\Delta\psi(x,t). \tag{14}$$

The energy distribution of a quantum particle depends on the LBO eigenvalues. Therefore the wave equation for a particle can be written as

$$\psi_E(x,t) = \sum_{k=0}^{\infty} e^{i\lambda_k t}\phi_k(x)f_E(\lambda_k). \tag{15}$$

The probability to locate the particle at point $x$ is then $|\psi_E(x,t)|^2$. Therefore the average probability over time is

$$p(x) = \lim_{T\to\infty} \frac{1}{T} \int_0^T |\psi_E(x,t)|^2 = \sum_{k=1}^{\infty} \phi_k(x)^2 f_E(\lambda_k)^2. \tag{16}$$

As we described, the LBO and its spectrum capture intrinsic properties of a shape. Therefore different choices of $f_E$ give us shape properties at different scales. Evaluating with energy distributions $\{e_1, \ldots, e_q\}$ we get the vector for the Wave Kernel Signature:

$$WKS(E,x) = (p_{e_1}(x), \ldots, p_{e_q}(x))^T. \tag{17}$$

Note that as with the HKS we must truncate the sum at the first $K$ eigenvalues. Typical values for $K$ are 50 or 100.

### 2.4  Weighted Average

Our aim is to use the shape descriptors mentioned above and the learned distance metric to classify shapes. However, for a given shape so far we only have a number of point descriptors, but for classification we would prefer to have one descriptor for the whole shape. To achieve this, we compute a weighted average over all point descriptors $d(x)$ computed from the points $x$ of a given shape $\mathcal{S}$. Thus, our shape descriptor is defined as

$$y_f(\mathcal{S}) = \sum_{x\in\mathcal{S}} w_x d(x) \quad \text{with} \quad w_x = \frac{a_x}{\sum_{y\in\mathcal{S}} a_y}, \tag{18}$$

where $a_x$ is the area element associated with vertex $x \in \mathcal{S}$. This weighted averaging is inspired by the pooling step proposed by Litman et al. [1], however with the difference that we do not use sparse coding.

In the case of WKS we normalize the point descriptors by the $L_2$-norm. Both averaged shape descriptors are also normalized by the $L_2$-norm. We compared 3 different shape descriptors, the averaged WKS, the averaged siHKS and a combination of them we refer to as Combined Spectral Descriptor (CSD):

$$y_{CSD}(\mathcal{S}) = \begin{pmatrix} y_{WKS}(\mathcal{S}) \\ y_{siHKS}(\mathcal{S}) \end{pmatrix}. \tag{19}$$

## 2.5   Large Margin Nearest Neighbor

Large Margin Nearest Neighbor (LMNN) is a machine learning algorithm that was first introduced in 2005 [14]. The authors keep updating the algorithm and their implementation is very efficient even for applications with very large datasets [15]. As of the latest version that we used, the L-BFGS algorithm is used for optimization by default.

---

**Algorithm 1.** Shape descriptors

---

**procedure** GET–AVERAGED –DESCRIPTORS
   **for** each shape $\mathcal{S} \in \mathcal{D}$ **do**
      **for** each point $x \in \mathcal{S}$ **do**
         $\tilde{d}(x) \leftarrow$ siHKS$(x)$ |WKS$(x)$
         **if** WKS **then**
            $d(x) \leftarrow \frac{\tilde{d}(x)}{||\tilde{d}(x)||_2}$
         **else**
            $d(x) \leftarrow \tilde{d}(x)$
      **end for**
      $\tilde{y}_f(\mathcal{S}) \leftarrow \sum_{x \in \mathcal{S}} w_x d(x)$ (see Eq. (18))
      $y_f(\mathcal{S}) \leftarrow \frac{\tilde{y}_f(\mathcal{S})}{||\tilde{y}_f(\mathcal{S})||_2}$
   **end for**

---

LMNN utilizes both the concept of SVMs of margin maximization and the well known $k$-$NN$ algorithm. It is specifically conceived to learn a Mahalanobis (semi-)metric $\mathcal{D}_M$ that improves the accuracy of k-NN classification. This metric is represented by the positive semi-definite matrix $M \in \mathbb{R}^{n \times n}$, such that

$$\mathcal{D}_M(\boldsymbol{x}, \boldsymbol{y}) = \langle M(\boldsymbol{x} - \boldsymbol{y}), (\boldsymbol{x} - \boldsymbol{y}) \rangle^{\frac{1}{2}}. \tag{20}$$

Equivalently $\mathcal{D}_M(\boldsymbol{x}, \boldsymbol{y})$ can be seen as the Euclidean distance between the points $\boldsymbol{x}, \boldsymbol{y}$ transformed by the linear transformation $L \in \mathbb{R}^{m \times n}$, i.e.

$$\mathcal{D}_L(\boldsymbol{x}, \boldsymbol{y}) = \|L\boldsymbol{x} - L\boldsymbol{y}\|, \tag{21}$$

as the positive semi-definiteness of $M$ allows a decomposition $M = L^{\top}L$.

The main idea of the algorithm is to find a mapping $L$ so that for each input $\boldsymbol{x}_i$ there are at least $k$ neighbors that share its label $y_i$ (see Fig. 4). This is facilitated by choosing *target neighbors* of $\boldsymbol{x}_i$, i.e. samples that are desired to be closest to $\boldsymbol{x}_i$. The target neighbors for every input are fixed during the whole learning process. Note that target neighbors are not symmetric. For instance if $\boldsymbol{x}_j$ is a target neighbor of $\boldsymbol{x}_i$ it is not necessary that $\boldsymbol{x}_i$ is also a target neighbor of $\boldsymbol{x}_j$.

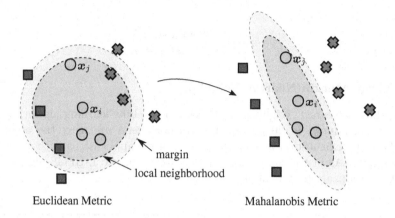

**Fig. 4. Large Margin Nearest Neighbor (LMNN)** finds the best positive semi-definite matrix $M$, such that the induced Mahalanobis (semi-)norm $\mathcal{D}_M(\boldsymbol{x}_i, \boldsymbol{x}_j) = \langle M\boldsymbol{x}_i - \boldsymbol{x}_j, \boldsymbol{x}_i - \boldsymbol{x}_j \rangle^{\frac{1}{2}}$ separates the different classes as good as possible.

Furthermore, LMNN tries to ensure that differently labeled inputs are farther away from the target neighbors so that they do not get selected by k-NN. Samples that violate this rule are called *impostors*. Ideally we would like to create a large margin between the perimeter around each input and its target neighbors, and all differently labeled inputs as illustrated in Fig. 4 on the right. This goal also explains the name of the algorithm.

**Loss Function.** The loss function consists of two competing terms. The first one pulls target neighbors together:

$$\epsilon_{\text{pull}}(L) = \sum_{i,j \rightsquigarrow i} ||L(\boldsymbol{x}_i - \boldsymbol{x}_j)||^2. \tag{22}$$

The notation in Eq. (22) implies that $\boldsymbol{x}_j$ are target neighbors of $\boldsymbol{x}_i$. The pull loss penalizes large distances between inputs and their target neighbors. This is an important difference of LMNN compared to other algorithms where large distances to *all* other similarly labeled samples are penalized. The second term pushes impostors away:

$$\epsilon_{\text{push}}(L) = \sum_{i,j \rightsquigarrow i} \sum_l (1 - y_{il})[1 + ||L(\boldsymbol{x}_i - \boldsymbol{x}_j)||^2 - ||L(\boldsymbol{x}_i - \boldsymbol{x}_l)||^2]_+, \tag{23}$$

where $[x]_+ = \max(x, 0)$ denotes the standard hinge loss and $y_{il}$ is 1 only when $y_i = y_l$ and 0 otherwise. Note that the choice of the unit margin is an arbitrary convention that sets the scale for the linear transformation $L$. If a different margin $c > 0$ was enforced, the loss function would be minimized by the same linear transformation up to an overall scale factor $\sqrt{c}$. Combining both terms we get the LMNN loss function:

$$\epsilon(L) = \mu\epsilon_{\text{pull}}(L) + (1 - \mu)\epsilon_{\text{push}}(L), \tag{24}$$

where $\mu \in [0, 1]$ is a trade-off parameter between small intra-class and large inter-class distances. Although $\mu$ can be estimated with cross validation, in practice setting $\mu = 0.5$ works well. There are several similarities with the SVM's loss function:

- One term penalizes the norm of the *parameter* vector (i.e., **w** in SVMs, **L** in LMNN)
- The hinge loss is only triggered by samples near the decision boundary
- Both loss functions can be rewritten to utilize the *kernel trick*
- Both problems can be reformulated as convex optimization problems.

**Convex Optimization.** While $\epsilon(L)$ is quadratic in $L$, Eqs. (20) and (21) allow us to restate the loss of $\epsilon$ of Eq. (24) in terms of $M$. Minimizing this loss becomes a semi-definite program (SDP) which is a convex problem that can be solved globally in polynomial time. For the SDP formulation the authors of [10] introduced slack variables $\{\xi_{ijl}\}$ for all triplets of target neighbors $\boldsymbol{x}_i, \boldsymbol{x}_j$ and impostors $\boldsymbol{x}_l$. The slack variables measure the level of margin violation. Therefore the SDP can be defined as:

$$\textbf{min. } \mu \sum_{i,j \rightsquigarrow i}(\boldsymbol{x}_i - \boldsymbol{x}_j)^T M(\boldsymbol{x}_i - \boldsymbol{x}_j) + (1 - \mu) \sum_{i,j \rightsquigarrow i,l}(1 - y_{il})\xi_{ijl}$$

$$\textbf{s.t. } (\boldsymbol{x}_i - \boldsymbol{x}_l)^T M(\boldsymbol{x}_i - \boldsymbol{x}_l) - (\boldsymbol{x}_i - \boldsymbol{x}_j)^T M(\boldsymbol{x}_i - \boldsymbol{x}_j) \geq 1 - \xi_{ijl}$$

$$\xi_{ijl} \geq 0 \qquad \forall i, j, l$$

$$M \succeq 0 \, .$$

where the last constraint implies that the matrix $M$ must be positive semi-definite. The authors created their own solver for the SDP in order to take advantage of the sparsity of the slack variables. This leads to much faster solutions.

**Optimal Training Parameters.** The LMNN optimization process requires three parameters to be specified beforehand: the dimension $m$ of the lower-dimensional space into which the samples are mapped by $L$, the number of neighbors $k$ to consider, and the number of iterations $r$ of the L-BFGS optimizer. To find good values for these parameters, a validation set is used, which is a part of the original training data. Then, the LMNN optimization is run on the remaining data with different parameter settings, that are chosen using Bayesian optimization, and evaluated on the validation set. After a given number of iterations, the parameter set that achieved the highest performance on the validation set is used to run LMNN training on the entire training set.

**Classification.** For classification, we use the $k$ nearest-neighbor classifier in the $m$-dimensional target space. Thus, for a given test shape we compute its descriptor, map it into $\mathbb{R}^m$ using the mapping $L$ found in the training step, and assign to it the most frequent label of the $k$ closest, by the Euclidean distance, mapped training samples.

## 3   Experiments

**Datasets.** We evaluated our approaches on 2 datasets from SHREC'14 - Shape Retrieval of Non-Rigid 3D Human Models [11]. Of the two main datasets, one consists of synthetic and one of real (scanned) 3D human models. Each class represents a human model and each instance of a class is a different pose of that model. This is a different setting than most classification problems where distinct classes correspond to naturally separate categories (like humans, dogs, cats, etc.). This property along with the fact that some models contain self-intersections makes these datasets particularly challenging.

We used the provided evaluation code from [11] that computes several accuracy metrics: nearest neighbor, first tier, second tier, discounted cumulative gain, e-measure, f-measure, precision and recall.

All meshes were down-sampled to 20.000 faces with *Meshlab* [16].

**Evaluation Setting.** We scaled the shapes as indicated in the available code that accompanies [1]. We truncated the bases of the LBO to the first 100 eigenfunctions. Based on them we computed 50-dimensional siHKS descriptors with the same settings as in [1] and 100-dimensional WKS descriptors, setting the variance to 6. We used 40 % of the shape descriptors to train the LMNN classifier and tested on the rest. We used 25 % of the training set as a validation set to find the optimal parameters for LMNN.[1]

**Table 1.** CSD and CSD+LMNN evaluation on the SHREC'14 real dataset.

| Metric | CSD | CSD+LMNN |
|---|---|---|
| nn | 0.5075 | 0.9792 |
| ft/fm | 0.3692 | 0.9278 |
| st | 0.5669 | 0.9868 |
| em | 0.3135 | 0.2703 |
| dcg | 0.6407 | 0.9760 |

**Table 2.** CSD and CSD+LMNN evaluation on the SHREC'14 synthetic dataset.

| Metric | CSD | CSD+LMNN |
|---|---|---|
| nn | 0.8267 | 0.9967 |
| ft/fm | 0.6789 | 0.9802 |
| st | 0.9147 | 0.9986 |
| em | 0.6358 | 0.5114 |
| dcg | 0.9066 | 0.9963 |

Our CSD approach gives remarkable results, when combined with LMNN (Tables 1 and 2). Even though the SHREC'14 datasets are considered extremely challenging, our algorithm performed better than the methods that participated in the SHREC'14 contest (see Table 3) and the most recent learning approach proposed in [9]. This is a significant result since our approach is comparatively simpler and the computation time very low.

---

[1] Our code is available at https://github.com/tum-vision/csd_lmnn.

**Table 3.** Comparison of retrieval methods in terms of mean average precision (mAP, in %) on the SHREC'14 3D Human Models datasets. In the upper part of the table, results of methods that participated in the SHREC'14 contest are documented as in [11] and the most recent learning approach proposed in [9]. In the lower part, we report the results of our approaches, averaged over 5 runs (different training/testing sets splits).

| Method | Synthetic | Real (Scanned) |
|---|---|---|
| ISPM | 90.2 | 25.8 |
| DBN | 84.2 | 30.4 |
| R-BiHDM | 64.2 | 64.0 |
| HAPT | 81.7 | 63.7 |
| ShapeGoogle(VQ) [18] | 81.3 | 51.4 |
| Unsupervised DL [1] | 84.2 | 52.3 |
| Supervised DL [1] | 95.4 | 79.1 |
| RMVM [9] | **96.3** | **79.5** |
| siHKS | 84.33 | 62.00 |
| siHKS+LMNN | 97.11 | 92.58 |
| WKS | 91.33 | 33.75 |
| WKS+LMNN | 98.11 | 76.92 |
| CSD | 82.67 | 50.75 |
| CSD+LMNN | **99.67** | **97.92** |

Figure 5 shows the result of the LMNN learning step. As one can see, LMNN is able to capture the discriminative features of the classes despite the information loss from the projection onto three dimensions, which is done to facilitate the visualization.

We noticed that using both the siHKS and the WKS performed worse than using each descriptor separately. Nevertheless, when used as input to a metric learning algorithm, the performance of the combined descriptor improved considerably. The CSD with LMNN performs better than either individual descriptor with LMNN (see Table 3). In particular, we observe that even if we add a seemingly harmful descriptor, as in the case of the WKS for the real dataset, LMNN is able to select the most useful - in terms of $k$-NN classification - dimensions of both descriptors, thereby achieving a better accuracy than the siHKS+LMNN approach. This confirms our hypothesis that metric learning can utilize the additional information contained in the combined descriptor. Adding other descriptors to the CSD such as the GPS [17] led to no improvement.

Note that in our CSD+LMNN-approach the most time-consuming part is finding the optimal parameters for LMNN. Still the total time needed for the algorithm - excluding the computation of point descriptors - is approximately

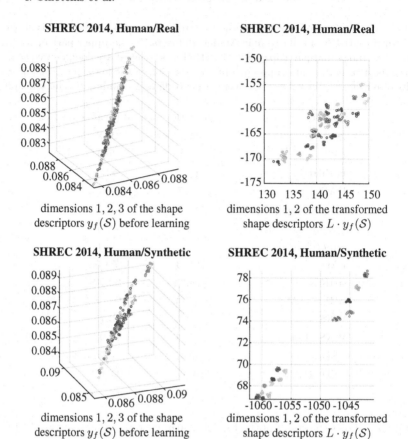

**SHREC 2014, Human/Real**

dimensions $1, 2, 3$ of the shape descriptors $y_f(\mathcal{S})$ before learning

**SHREC 2014, Human/Real**

dimensions $1, 2$ of the transformed shape descriptors $L \cdot y_f(\mathcal{S})$

**SHREC 2014, Human/Synthetic**

dimensions $1, 2, 3$ of the shape descriptors $y_f(\mathcal{S})$ before learning

**SHREC 2014, Human/Synthetic**

dimensions $1, 2$ of the transformed shape descriptors $L \cdot y_f(\mathcal{S})$

**Fig. 5. Visualization of the shape descriptors before and after learning:** Each circle corresponds to the descriptor of one shape. The colors correspond to the 40 classes of the SHREC'14 Real dataset (top row) or the 15 classes of the SHREC'14 Synthetic dataset (bottom row). It can be seen by even visualizing only two dimensions that the transformation $L$, learned by LMNN, results in a much better clustering of the shapes. This is in line with the quantitative evaluation on the datasets. (Color figure online)

2 min. In the worst case it never exceeded 4 min on a machine with a 2.0 GHz CPU. This is an extremely small amount of time compared to the supervised dictionary learning approach proposed in [1] which needs nearly 4 hours to converge on a machine with a 3.2 GHz CPU.

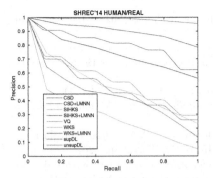
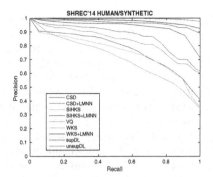

**Fig. 6.** Precision-Recall comparison on the SHREC'14 real dataset.

**Fig. 7.** Precision-Recall comparison on SHREC'14 synthetic dataset.

## 4 Conclusion

In this paper we showed that metric learning can significantly improve the classification accuracy of well known descriptors. Given a large number of features, a learning algorithm such as LMNN can select the most informative ones and weight them appropriately for the problem that we aim to solve, in this case shape retrieval. Our approach is both considerably faster and more accurate than the state of the art. The comparison in Fig. 1 demonstrates that our approach is more robust, as it is able to find the true inherent similarities between objects and does not get confused by different classes, even if they are very similar by human standards.

**Acknowledgments.** We gratefully acknowledge that this work was supported in part by the DFG Priority Programme 1527, "Autonomous Learning" and in part by the ERC Consolidator Grant "3D Reloaded".

## References

1. Litman, R., Bronstein, A., Bronstein, M., Castellani, U.: Supervised learning of bag-of-features shape descriptors using sparse coding. In: Computer Graphics Forum, vol. 33, pp. 127–136. Wiley Online Library (2014)
2. Sun, J., Ovsjanikov, M., Guibas, L.: A concise and provably informative multi-scale signature based on heat diffusion. In: Computer Graphics Forum, vol. 28, pp. 1383–1392. Wiley Online Library (2009)
3. Aubry, M., Schlickewei, U., Cremers, D.: The wave kernel signature: a quantum mechanical approach to shape analysis. In: 2011 IEEE International Conference on Computer Vision Workshops (ICCV Workshops), pp. 1626–1633. IEEE (2011)
4. Bronstein, M.M., Kokkinos, I.: Scale-invariant heat kernel signatures for non-rigid shape recognition. In: 2010 IEEE Conference on Computer Vision and Pattern Recognition (CVPR), pp. 1704–1711. IEEE (2010)

5. Bronstein, A.M.: Spectral descriptors for deformable shapes (2011). arXiv preprint arXiv:1110.5015
6. Windheuser, T., Vestner, M., Rodolà, E., Triebel, R., Cremers, D.: Optimal intrinsic descriptors for non-rigid shape analysis. In: Proceedings of the British Machine Vision Conference. BMVA Press (2014)
7. Rodola, E., Bulo, S.R., Windheuser, T., Vestner, M., Cremers, D.: Dense non-rigid shape correspondence using random forests. In: Computer Vision and Pattern Recognition (CVPR) (2014)
8. Masci, J., Boscaini, D., Bronstein, M., Vandergheynst, P.: Geodesic convolutional neural networks on Riemannian manifolds. In: ICCV Workshops (2015)
9. Gasparetto, A., Torsello, A.: A statistical model of Riemannian metric variation for deformable shape analysis. In: IEEE Conference on Computer Vision and Pattern Recognition (CVPR), June 2015
10. Weinberger, K., Saul, L.: Distance metric learning for large margin nearest neighbor classification. J. Mach. Learn. Res. 10, 207–244 (2009)
11. Pickup, D., Sun, X., Rosin, P.L., Martin, R.R., Cheng, Z., Lian, Z., Aono, M., Ben Hamza, A., Bronstein, A., Bronstein, M., Bu, S., Castellani, U., Cheng, S., Garro, V., Giachetti, A., Godil, A., Han, J., Johan, H., Lai, L., Li, B., Li, C., Li, H., Litman, R., Liu, X., Liu, Z., Lu, Y., Tatsuma, A., Ye, J.: SHREC'14 track: shape retrieval of non-rigid 3D human models. In: Proceedings of the 7th Eurographics Workshop on 3D Object Retrieval, EG 3DOR 2014, Eurographics Association (2014)
12. Pinkall, U., Polthier, K.: Computing discrete minimal surfaces and their conjugates. Exp. Math. 2(1), 15–36 (1993)
13. Reuter, M., Biasotti, S., Giorgi, D., Patan, G., Spagnuolo, M.: Discrete Laplace-Beltrami operators for shape analysis and segmentation. In: IEEE International Conference on Shape Modelling and Applications (2009)
14. Weinberger, K.Q., Blitzer, J., Saul, L.K.: Distance metric learning for large margin nearest neighbor classification. In: Advances in Neural Information Processing Systems, pp. 1473–1480 (2005)
15. Weinberger, K.: Kilian Weinberger's website, code (2015). http://www.cs.cornell.edu/kilian/code/code.html
16. CNR, V.C.L.I.: Meshlab. http://meshlab.sourceforge.net/
17. Rustamov, R.M.: Laplace-Beltrami eigenfunctions for deformation invariant shape representation. In: Proceedings of the Fifth Eurographics Symposium on Geometry Processing, Eurographics Association, pp. 225–233 (2007)
18. Bronstein, A.M., Bronstein, M.M., Guibas, L.J., Ovsjanikov, M.: Shape Google: geometric words and expressions for invariant shape retrieval. ACM Trans. Graph. (TOG) 30(1), 1 (2011)

# Multi-Task Zero-Shot Action Recognition with Prioritised Data Augmentation

Xun Xu$^{(\boxtimes)}$, Timothy M. Hospedales, and Shaogang Gong

School of Electronic Engineering and Computer Science,
Queen Mary University of London, London, UK
{xun.xu,t.hospedales,s.gong}@qmul.ac.uk

**Abstract.** Zero-Shot Learning (ZSL) promises to scale visual recognition by bypassing the conventional model training requirement of annotated examples for every category. This is achieved by establishing a mapping connecting low-level features and a semantic description of the label space, referred as visual-semantic mapping, on auxiliary data. Reusing the learned mapping to project target videos into an embedding space thus allows novel-classes to be recognised by nearest neighbour inference. However, existing ZSL methods suffer from auxiliary-target domain shift intrinsically induced by assuming the same mapping for the disjoint auxiliary and target classes. This compromises the generalisation accuracy of ZSL recognition on the target data. In this work, we improve the ability of ZSL to generalise across this domain shift in both model- and data-centric ways by formulating a visual-semantic mapping with better generalisation properties and a dynamic data re-weighting method to prioritise auxiliary data that are relevant to the target classes. Specifically: (1) We introduce a multi-task visual-semantic mapping to improve generalisation by constraining the semantic mapping parameters to lie on a low-dimensional manifold, (2) We explore prioritised data augmentation by expanding the pool of auxiliary data with additional instances weighted by relevance to the target domain. The proposed new model is applied to the challenging zero-shot action recognition problem to demonstrate its advantages over existing ZSL models.

## 1 Introduction

Action recognition has long been a central topic in computer vision [1]. A major thrust in action recognition is scaling methods to a wider and finer range of categories [2–4]. The traditional approach to dealing with a growing number of categories is to collect labeled training examples of each new category. This is not scalable, particularly in the case of actions, due to the temporally extended nature of videos compared to images, making annotation (segmentation in *both* space and time) more onerous than for images. In contrast, the Zero-Shot Learning (ZSL) [5,6] paradigm is gaining significant interest by providing an alternative to classic supervised learning which does not require an ever increasing

© Springer International Publishing AG 2016
B. Leibe et al. (Eds.): ECCV 2016, Part II, LNCS 9906, pp. 343–359, 2016.
DOI: 10.1007/978-3-319-46475-6_22

amount of annotation. Instead of collecting training data for the target categories[1] to be recognised, a classifier is constructed by re-using a visual to semantic space mapping pre-learned on a training/auxiliary set[2] of totally independent (disjoint) categories. Specifically training class labels are represented in a vector space such as attribute [5,7] or word-vectors [6,8]. Such vector representations of class-labels are referred to as *semantic label embeddings* [7]. A mapping (e.g. regression [9] or bilinear model [7]) is learned between low-level visual features and their semantic embeddings. This mapping is assumed to generalise and be re-used to project visual features of target classes into semantic embedding space and matched against target class embeddings.

A fundamental challenge for ZSL is that in the context of supervised learning of the visual-semantic mapping, the ZSL setting violates the traditional assumption of supervised learning [10] – that training and testing data are drawn from the same distribution. Thus its efficacy is reduced by *domain shift* [11–13]. For example, when a regressor is used to map visual features to semantic embedding, the disjoint training and testing classes in ZSL intrinsically require the regressor to generalise out-of-bounds. This inherently limits the accuracy of ZSL recognition. In this work, we address the issue of the generalisation capability of a ZSL mapping regressor from both the model- and data-centric perspectives: (1) by proposing a more robust regression model with better generalisation properties, and (2) improving model learning by augmenting auxiliary data with a re-weighted additional dataset according to the relevance to the target problem.

**Multi-Task Embedding.** When establishing the mapping between visual features and semantic embeddings, most ZSL methods learn each dimension of this mapping *independently* – whether semantic embedding is discrete as in the case of attributes [5,7], or continuous as in the case of word vectors [6,8]. This strategy is likely to overfit to the training classes because it treats each dimension of the label in semantic embedding independently despite the labels living on a non-uniform manifold [14] and many independent mappings result in a large number of parameters to be learned. We denote this conventional approach as Single-Task Learning (STL) due to the independent learning of mappings for each attribute/word dimension. In contrast, we advocate a Multi-Task Learning (MTL) [10,15,16] regression approach to mapping visual features and their semantic embeddings. By constraining the mapping parameters of each learning task to lie closely on a low-dimensional manifold, we gain two advantages: (1) Exploiting the relation between the response variables (dimensions of the label embedding), (2) reducing the total number of parameters to fit. The resulting visual-semantic mapping is more robust to the domain shift between ZSL training and testing classes. As a helpful byproduct, the MTL mapping, provides a lower dimensional latent space in which the nearest neighbour (NN) matching required by ZSL can be better performed [17] compared to the usual higher dimensional label semantic embedding space.

---

[1] Target and testing all refer to categories (e.g. action classes) to be recognised without labelled examples.

[2] Auxiliary and training all refer to categories (e.g. action classes) with labelled data.

**Prioritised Auxiliary Data Augmentation for Domain Adaptation.**
From a data-, rather than model-centric perspective, studies have also attempted
to improve the generalisation of ZSL methods by augmenting[3] the auxiliary
dataset with additional datasets containing a wider array of classes and instances
[9,18]. The idea is that including a broader additional set should provide better
coverage of the visual feature and label embedding spaces, therefore helping to
learn a visual-semantic mapping that better generalises to target classes, and
thus improves performance when representing and recognising target classes.
However, existing studies on exploring this idea have been rather crude, e.g.
simply expanding the training dataset by blindly concatenating auxiliary set
with additional data [9]. This is not only inefficient but also dangerous, because
it does not take into account the (dis)similarity between the extra incorporated
data and the target classes for recognition, thus risking *negative transfer* [10].
In this work, we address the issue that auxiliary and target data/categories will
have different marginal distributions (Fig. 1). We selectively re-weight those relevant instances/classes from the auxiliary data that are expected to improve
the visual-semantic mapping in the context of the specific target classes to be
recognised (target domain). We formulate this prioritised data augmentation
as a domain adaptation problem by minimizing the discrepancy between the
marginal distributions of the auxiliary and target domains. To achieve this, we
propose an importance weighting strategy to re-weight each auxiliary instance in
order to minimise the discrepancy. Specifically we generalise the classic *Kullback-
Leibler Importance Estimation Procedure* (KLIEP) [19,20] to the zero-shot learning problem.

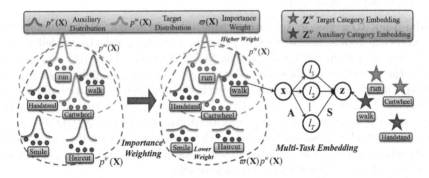

**Fig. 1.** Two strategies to improve generalisation of visual-semantic mapping in ZSL.
Left: Importance weighting to prioritise auxiliary data relevant to the target domain.
Right: Learning the mapping from visual features $\mathbf{X}$ to semantic embedding $\mathbf{Z}$ by MTL
reduces overfitting, and also provides a latent lower dimensional representation $\{l_t\}$ to
benefit nearest neighbour matching.

---

[3] In this work, data augmentation means exploiting additional data in a wider context
from multiple data sources, in contrast to synthesising more artificial variations of
one dataset as in deep learning

## 2   Related Work

**Zero-Shot Learning.** Zero-shot Learning (ZSL) [5] aims to generalize existing knowledge to recognize new categories without training examples by re-using a mapping learned from visual features to their semantic embeddings. Commonly used label embeddings are semantic attributes [5,11,21] and word-vectors [6, 9]. The latter has the advantage of being learned from data without requiring manual annotation. Commonly used visual-semantic mappings include linear [12] and non-linear regression [6,9,11], classification [5,21], and bilinear ranking [7].

Existing ZSL methods suffer from weak generalisation due to the domain-shift induced by disjoint auxiliary-target classes, an issue that has recently been highlighted explicitly in the literature [8,11–13]. Attempts to address this so far include post-processing heuristics [11–13], sparse coding regularisation [8], and simple blind enlarging of the training set with auxiliary data [9]. In contrast to [8,9], we focus on: (1) Building a visual-semantic mapping with intrinsically better generalisation properties, and (2) re-weighting the auxiliary set to prioritise auxiliary instances most relevant to the target instances and classes. Our method is complementary to [11,12] and can benefit from these heuristics.

**Zero-Shot Action Recognition.** Among many ZSL tasks in computer vision, zero-shot action recognition [9,21–24] is of particular interest because of the lesser availability of *labelled* video compared to image data and videos are more difficult to label than static images due to extended temporal duration and more complex ontology. ZSL action recognition is much less studied than still image recognition, and existing video-ZSL methods suffer from the same domain-shift drawbacks highlighted above.

**Multi-Task Regression Learning.** Multi-Task Learning (MTL) [10,25] aims to improve generalisation in a set of supervised learning tasks by modelling and exploiting shared knowledge across the tasks. An early study [15] proposed to model the weight vector for each task $t$ as a sum of a shared global task $\mathbf{w}_0$ and task specific parameter vector $\mathbf{w}_t$. However, the assumption of a globally shared underlying task is too strong, and risks inducing *negative transfer* [10]. This motivates the Grouping and Overlapping Multi-Task Learning (GOMTL) [16] framework which instead assumes that each task's weight vector is a task-specific combination of a small set of latent basis tasks. This constrains the parameters of all tasks to lie on a low dimensional manifold.

MTL methods have been studied for action recognition [26–29]. However, all of these studies focus on improving standard *supervised* action recognition with multi-task sharing. For example, considering each of multiple views [28,29], feature modalities [27], or – most obviously – action categories [26] as different tasks. Multi-view/multi-feature recognition is orthogonal to our work, while the later ones are concerned with supervised recognition, and cannot be generalised to the ZSL scenario. In contrast, we take a very different approach and treat each dimension of the visual-semantic mapping as a task, in order to leverage MTL to improve auxiliary-target generalisation across the disjoint target categories.

Finally, we note that the use of MTL to learn the visual semantic mapping provides a further benefit of a lower-dimensional space in which zero-shot recognition can be better performed due to being more meaningful for NN matching [17].

**Importance Weighting for Domain Adaptation.** Domain shift is a widely studied problem in transfer learning [10], although it is usually induced by sampling bias [30,31] or sensor change [32] rather than the disjoint categories in ZSL. Importance weighting (IW) [19,31] has been one of the main adaptation techniques to address this issue. The prior work in this area is designed for the standard domain transfer problem in a *supervised* learning setting [33], while we are the first to generalise it to the *zero-shot* learning scenario. The IW technique we generalise is related to another domain adaptation approach based on discovering a feature mapping to minimise the *Maximum Mean Discrepancy* (MMD) [34,35] between distributions. However MMD, is less appropriate for us due to focus on feature mapping rather than instance reweighing, and our expectation is that only subsets of auxiliary instances will be relevant to the target rather than the holistic auxiliary set.

**Contributions.** This paper contributes both model- and data-centric strategies to improve ZSL action recognition: (1) We formulate learning a more generalisable visual-semantic mapping in ZSL as a Multi-Task Learning problem with a lower-dimensional latent semantic embedding space for more effective matching. (2) We improve visual-semantic regression generalisation by prioritised data augmentation using importance weighting of auxiliary instances relevant to the target domain.

# 3   Visual-Semantic Mapping with Multi-Task Regression

In ZSL, we aim to recognise action categories $\mathbf{Y}$ given visual features $\mathbf{X}$ where training/auxiliary and testing/target categories do not overlap $\mathcal{Y}^{tr} \cap \mathcal{Y}^{te} = \emptyset$. The key method by which ZSL is achieved is to embed each category label in $\mathcal{Y}$ into a semantic label embedding space $\mathcal{Z}$ which provide a vector representation of any *nameable* category. Table 1 summarises the notation used in the subsequent sections.

## 3.1   Training a Visual Semantic Mapping

We first introduce briefly the conventional single task learning using regression for visual-semantic mapping [9,11,12].

**Single-Task Regression.** Given a matrix $\mathbf{V}$ describing the embedded action names[4], and per-video binary labels $\mathbf{Y}$, we firstly obtain the label embedding of any action label for a video clip as $\mathbf{z}_i = \mathbf{V}\mathbf{y}_i$. We then learn a visual-semantic

---

[4] To deal with multi-word compound action category names, e.g. "Apply Eye Makeup", we apply a simple average, summing the component word vectors [9,11].

**Table 1.** Notation summary

| Notation | Description |
|---|---|
| $n_c^{tr}; n_c^{te}$ | Number of training categories; testing categories |
| $n_x^{tr}; n_x^{te}$ | Number of all training instances; all testing instances |
| $\mathbf{X} \in \mathbb{R}^{d_x \times n_x}; \mathbf{x}_i$ | Visual feature matrix for N instances; column representing the $i$-th instance |
| $\mathbf{Y} \in \{0,1\}^{n_c \times n_x}; \mathbf{y}_i$ | Binary class labels for N instances 1-of-$n_c$ encoding; column representing the $i$-th instance |
| $\mathbf{V} \in \mathbb{R}^{d_z \times n_c};$ | Semantic label embedding for $n_c$ categories; |
| $\mathbf{Z} \in \mathbb{R}^{d_z \times n_x}; \mathbf{z}_i$ | Semantic label embedding for $n_x$ instances; column representing the $i$-th instance |
| $\mathbf{W} \in \mathbb{R}^{d_z \times d_x}; \mathbf{w}_d$ | STL regression coefficient matrix; row representing the regressor for the $d$-th dimension |
| $\mathbf{A} \in \mathbb{R}^{T \times d_x}; \mathbf{a}_t$ | MTL regression coefficient matrix; row representing the regressor for the $t$-th latent task |
| $\mathbf{S} \in \mathbb{R}^{d_z \times T}; \mathbf{s}_d$ | MTL linear combination matrix; row representing linear combination vector for the $d$-th output |
| $\mathbf{L} \in \mathbb{R}^{T \times n_x}; \mathbf{l}_i$ | Latent space embedding for visual instances; column is $i$th instance |
| $\omega \in \mathbb{R}^{n_x \times 1}$ | Weighting vector for auxiliary data |
| $f: \mathbf{X} \to \mathbf{Z}$ | Visual to semantic mapping function |

mapping function $f : \mathcal{X} \to \mathcal{Z}$ on the training categories. Given a loss function $l(\cdot,\cdot)$, we learn the mapping $f$ by optimising Eq. (1) where $\Omega(f)$ denotes regularization on the mapping:

$$\min_f \frac{1}{n_x^{tr}} \sum_{i=1}^{n_x^{tr}} l\left(f(\mathbf{x}_i), \mathbf{z}_i\right) + \Omega(f). \tag{1}$$

The most straightforward choice of mapping $f$ and loss $l$ is linear $f(\mathbf{x}) = \mathbf{W}\mathbf{x}$, and square error respectively, which results in a regularized linear (ridge) regression problem: $l(f(\mathbf{x}_i), \mathbf{z}_i) = ||\mathbf{z}_i - \mathbf{W}\mathbf{x}_i||_2^2$. A closed-form solution to $\mathbf{W}$ can then be obtained by $\mathbf{W} = \mathbf{Z}\mathbf{X}^T \left(\mathbf{X}\mathbf{X}^T + \lambda n_x^{tr}\mathbf{I}\right)^{-1}$. Each row $\mathbf{w}_d$ of regressor $\mathbf{W}$ maps visual feature $\mathbf{x}_i$ to $d$th dimension of response variable $\mathbf{z}_i$. Since regressors $\{\mathbf{w}_d\}_{d=1\cdots d_z}$ are learned independently from each other this is referred as **single-task learning (STL)** with each $\mathbf{w}_d$ defining one distinct 'task'.

**From Single to Multi-Task Regression.** In the conventional ridge-regression solution to Eq. (1), each task $\mathbf{w}_d$ is effectively learned separately, ignoring any relationship between tasks. We wish to model this relationship by discovering a latent basis of predictors such that tasks $\mathbf{w}_d$ are constructed as linear combinations of $T$ latent tasks $\{\mathbf{a}_t\}_{t=1\cdots T}$. So the $d$th regression predictor is now modelled as $\mathbf{w}_d = \sum_t s_{dt}\mathbf{a}_t = \mathbf{s}_d^T\mathbf{A}$, where $\mathbf{s}_d$ is the combination coefficient for $d$-th task. Denoting multi-task regression prediction as $f(\mathbf{x}_i, \mathbf{S}, \mathbf{A})$, we now optimise:

$$\min_{\mathbf{S},\mathbf{A}} \frac{1}{n_x^{tr}} \sum_{i=1}^{n_x^{tr}} l(f(\mathbf{x}_i, \mathbf{S}, \mathbf{A}), \mathbf{z}_i) + \lambda\Omega(S) + \gamma\Psi(\mathbf{A}). \tag{2}$$

**Grouping and Overlap Multi-Task Learning.** An effective method following the MTL design pattern above is GOMTL [16]. GOMTL uses a $\mathbf{W} = \mathbf{SA}$ task parameter matrix factorisation, where the number of latent tasks $T$ (typically $T < d_z$) is a free parameter. Requiring the combination coefficients $\mathbf{s}_t$ to be sparse, via a $\ell_1$ regulariser, the loss is written as

$$\min_{\{\mathbf{s}_t\},\mathbf{A}} \sum_{t=1}^{T} \frac{1}{n_x^{tr}} \sum_{i=1}^{n_x^{tr}} ||\mathbf{z}_{t,i} - \mathbf{s}_t\mathbf{A}\mathbf{x}_i|| + \lambda \sum_{t=1}^{T} ||\mathbf{s}_t||_1 + \gamma||\mathbf{A}||_F^2 \tag{3}$$

This can be solved by iteratively updating $\mathbf{A}$ and $\mathbf{S}$. When $\mathbf{A}$ is fixed, loss function reduces to a standard L1 regularized (LASSO) regression problem that can be efficiently solved by Alternating Direction Method of Multipliers (ADMM) [36]. When $\mathbf{S}$ is fixed, we can efficiently solve $\mathbf{A}$ by gradient descent.

**Regularized Multi-Task Learning (RMTL).** The classic RMTL method [15] models task parameters as the sum of a globally shared and task specific parameter vector: $\mathbf{w}_t = \mathbf{a}_0 + \mathbf{a}_t$. It can be seen that this corresponds to a special case of GOMTL's $\mathbf{W} = \mathbf{SA}$ predictor matrix factorisation [25]. Here there are $T = d_z + 1$ latent tasks, a fixed task combination vector $\mathbf{s}_t = [1 \quad \mathbf{1}(t = 1) \quad \mathbf{1}(t = 2) \cdots \mathbf{1}(t = d_z)]^T$ where $\mathbf{1}(\cdot)$ is the indicator function and $A = [\mathbf{a}_0^T \mathbf{a}_1^T \cdots \mathbf{a}_{d_z}^T]^T$.

**Explicit Multi-Task Embedding (MTE).** In GOMTL Eq. (3), it can be seen that the label embedding $\mathbf{z}_i$ is approximated from the data by the mapping $\mathbf{s}_t\mathbf{A}\mathbf{x}_i$, and this approximation is reached by combination via the latent representation $\mathbf{A}\mathbf{x}_i$. While GOMTL defines this space implicitly via the learned $\mathbf{A}$, we propose to model it explicitly as $\mathbf{l}_i \approx \mathbf{A}\mathbf{x}_i$. This is so the actual projections $\mathbf{l}_i$ in this latent space can be regularised explicitly, in order to learn a latent space which generalises better to test data, and hence improves ZSL matching later.

Specifically, we split the GOMTL loss $||\mathbf{z}_i - \mathbf{SA}\mathbf{x}_i||_2^2$ into two parts: $||\mathbf{l}_i - \mathbf{A}\mathbf{x}_i||_2^2$ and $||\mathbf{z}_i - \mathbf{Sl}_i||_2^2$ to learn the mapping to the latent space, and from the latent space to the label embedding respectively. This allows us to place additional regularization on $\mathbf{l}_i$ to avoid extreme values in the latent space and thus later improve neighbour matching (Sect. 3.2). Given the large and high dimensional video datasets, we apply Frobenius norm on $\mathbf{S}$ in contrast to GOMTL's $\ell_1$.

$$\min_{\{\mathbf{s}_t\},\mathbf{A},\{\mathbf{l}_i\}} \sum_{t=1}^{T} \frac{1}{n_x^{tr}} \sum_{i=1}^{n_x^{tr}} \left( ||\mathbf{z}_{t,i} - \mathbf{s}_t\mathbf{l}_i||_2^2 + ||\mathbf{l}_i - \mathbf{A}\mathbf{x}_i||_2^2 \right) +$$
$$\lambda_S \sum_{t=1}^{T} ||\mathbf{s}_t||_2^2 + \lambda_A||\mathbf{A}||_F^2 + \lambda_L \sum_{i=1}^{n_x^{tr}} ||\mathbf{l}_i||_2^2 \tag{4}$$

Our explicit multi-task embedding has similarities to [18], but our purpose is multi-task regression for ZSL, rather than embedding for video descriptions. To solve our explicit embedding model we iteratively solve $\mathbf{L}, \mathbf{A}$ and $\mathbf{S}$ while fixing the other two. With the $\ell_2$ norm on $\mathbf{S}$, this has a convenient closed-form solution to each parameter:

$$
\begin{aligned}
\mathbf{L} &= (\mathbf{S}^T\mathbf{S} + (\lambda_L n_x^{tr} + 1)\mathbf{I})^{-1}(\mathbf{S}^T\mathbf{Z} + \mathbf{A}\mathbf{X}) \\
\mathbf{S} &= \mathbf{Z}\mathbf{L}^T(\mathbf{L}\mathbf{L}^T + \lambda_S n_x^{tr}\mathbf{I})^{-1} \\
\mathbf{A} &= \mathbf{L}\mathbf{X}^T(\mathbf{X}\mathbf{X}^T + \lambda_A n_x^{tr}\mathbf{I})^{-1}
\end{aligned} \tag{5}
$$

### 3.2  Zero-Shot Action Recognition

We consider two alternative NN matching methods for zero-shot action prediction that use the MTL mappings described above.

**Distributed Space Matching.** Given a trained visual-semantic regression $f$, we project testing set visual feature $\mathbf{x}^{te}$ into the semantic label embedding space. The standard strategy [9,11,12] is then to employ NN matching in this space for zero-shot recognition. Specifically, given the matrix of label embeddings for each target category name $\mathbf{V}^{te}$, and using cosine distance norm, the testing video $\mathbf{x}^{te}$ are classified by:

$$
\mathbf{y}^* = arg \min_{\mathbf{y}^*} ||\mathbf{V}^{te}\mathbf{y}^* - f(\mathbf{x}^{te})|| \tag{6}
$$

where $f(\mathbf{x}^{te}) = \mathbf{W}\mathbf{x}^{te}$ for STL and $f(\mathbf{x}^{te}) = \mathbf{S}\mathbf{A}\mathbf{x}^{te}$ for MTL.

**Latent Space Matching.** MTL methods provide an alternative to matching in label space: Matching in the latent space. The representation of testing data in this space is the output of latent regressors $\mathbf{l}_{te} = \mathbf{A}\mathbf{x}^{te}$ (Eq. (4)). To get the representation of testing categories in the latent space we invert the combination matrix $\mathbf{S}$ to project target category names $\mathbf{V}^{te}$ into latent space. Specifically we classify by Eq. (7), where $(\mathbf{S}^T\mathbf{S})^{-1}\mathbf{S}^T$ is the Moore-Penrose pseudoinverse.

$$
\mathbf{y}^* = arg \min_{\mathbf{y}^*} ||(\mathbf{S}^T\mathbf{S})^{-1}\mathbf{S}^T\mathbf{V}^{te}\mathbf{y}^* - \mathbf{A}\mathbf{x}^{te}|| \tag{7}
$$

NN matching in the latent space is better than in semantic label space because: (i) the dimension is lower $T < d_z$, and (ii) we have explicitly regularised the latent space to be well behaved (Eq. (4)).

## 4  Importance Weighting

Augmenting auxiliary data with additional examples from other datasets has been proved to benefit learning the visual-semantic mapping [9]. However, simply aggregating auxiliary and additional datasets is not ideal as including irrelevant data risks 'negative transfer'. Therefore we are motivated to develop methodology to prioritise augmented auxiliary data that is useful for a particular ZSL recognition scenario. Specifically, we learn a per-instance weighting $\omega(\mathbf{x})$ on the auxiliary dataset $\mathbf{X}^{tr}$ to adjust each instance's contribution according to relevance to the target domain. Because Importance Weighting (IW) adapts auxiliary data to the target domain, we assume a transductive setting with access to testing data $\mathbf{X}^{te}$.

**Kullback-Leibler Importance Estimation Procedure (KLIEP).** We first introduce the way to estimate a per-instance auxiliary-data weight given the distribution of target data $\mathbf{X}^{te}$. This is based on the idea [19] of minimizing the KL-divergence $(D_{KL})$ between training $p^{tr}(\mathbf{x})$ and testing data distribution $p^{te}(\mathbf{x})$ via learning a weighting function $\omega(\mathbf{x})$. This is formalised in Eq. (8):

$$\min_{\omega} D_{KL}(p^{te}(\mathbf{x})|\omega(\mathbf{x})p^{tr}(\mathbf{x})) = \int p^{te}(\mathbf{x}) \log \frac{p^{te}(\mathbf{x})}{\omega(\mathbf{x})p^{tr}(\mathbf{x})} d\mathbf{x}$$

$$\min_{\omega} \int p^{te}(\mathbf{x}) \log \frac{p^{te}(\mathbf{x})}{p^{tr}(\mathbf{x})} d\mathbf{x} - \int p^{te}(\mathbf{x}) \log \omega(\mathbf{x}) d\mathbf{x} \tag{8}$$

The first term is fixed w.r.t. $\omega(\mathbf{x})$ so the objective to optimise is:

$$\min_{\omega} - \int p^{te}(\mathbf{x}) \log \omega(\mathbf{x}) d\mathbf{x} \approx -\frac{1}{n_x^{te}} \sum_{i=1}^{n_x^{te}} \log \omega(\mathbf{x}_i) \tag{9}$$

**Aligning Both Visual Features and Labels.** KLIEP is conventionally used for domain adaptation by reweighting instances [19,33]. In the case of transductive ZSL, we have the target data $\mathbf{X}^{te}$ and category labels $\mathbf{Z}^{te}$ respectively, although not instance-label association which is to be predicted. In this case we can further improve ZSL by extending KLIEP to align training and testing sets in both visual feature and category sense[5]. Specifically, we minimise the kullback-leibler divergence between the target and auxiliary in terms of both the visual and category distributions:

$$\min_{\omega_x, \omega_z} D_{KL}(p^{te}(X)||\omega_x(\mathbf{X})p^{tr}(\mathbf{X})) + D_{KL}(p^{te}(\mathbf{Z})||\omega_z(\mathbf{Z})p^{tr}(\mathbf{Z}))$$

$$\min_{\omega_x, \omega_z} -\frac{1}{n_x^{te}} \sum \log \omega_x(\mathbf{x}_i^{te}) - \frac{1}{n_x^{te}} \sum \log \omega_z(\mathbf{z}_i^{te}) \tag{10}$$

Given both $\mathbf{X}^{te}$ and $\mathbf{Z}^{te}$, we construct the weighting functions as a combination of Gaussian kernels centered at the testing data and categories. Specifically we define $\omega(\mathbf{x}, \mathbf{z}) = \omega_x(\mathbf{x}) + \omega_z(\mathbf{z})$ where $\omega_x(\mathbf{x})$ and $\omega_z(\mathbf{z})$ are calculated as in Eq. (11). Here $\omega(\mathbf{x}, \mathbf{z})$ extends the previous notation $\omega(\mathbf{x})$ to indicate giving a weight to each training instance given visual feature $\mathbf{x}$ and class name embedding $\mathbf{z}$. So if there are $n_x^{tr}$ instances, $\omega(\mathbf{x}, \mathbf{z})$ returns a weight vector of length $n_x^{tr}$.

---

[5] KLEIP with labels was studied by [20], but they assumed the target joint distribution of $\mathbf{X}$ and $\mathbf{Z}$ is known. So [20] is only suitable for traditional supervised learning with labeled target examples of $\mathbf{z}_i$ and $\mathbf{x}_i$ in correspondence. In our case we have the videos to classify and the zero-shot category names, but the assignment of names to videos is our task rather than prior knowledge.

$$\omega_x(\mathbf{x}) = \sum_{i=1}^{n_x^{te}} \alpha_i \phi(\mathbf{x}, \mathbf{x}_i^{te}), \quad \omega_z(\mathbf{z}) = \sum_{i=1}^{n_x^{te}} \beta_j \phi(\mathbf{z}, \mathbf{z}_i^{te}), \quad \phi(\mathbf{x}, \mathbf{x}_i^{te}) = exp\left(-\frac{||\mathbf{x} - \mathbf{x}_i^{te}||^2}{2\sigma^2}\right)$$

$$(11)$$

For ease of formulation, we denote $\mathbf{a} = [\alpha_1 \cdots \alpha_{n_x^{te}}]^T$, $\mathbf{b} = [\beta_1 \cdots \beta_{n_x^{te}}]^T$, $\Phi_\mathbf{a}(\mathbf{x}) = [\phi(\mathbf{x}, \mathbf{x}_1^{te}) \cdots \phi(\mathbf{x}, \mathbf{x}_{n_x^{te}}^{te})]^T$ and $\Phi_\mathbf{b}(\mathbf{z}) = [\phi(\mathbf{z}, \mathbf{z}_1^{te}) \cdots \phi(\mathbf{z}, \mathbf{z}_{n_x^{te}}^{te})]^T$. The optimization can be thus written as

$$\min_{\mathbf{a},\mathbf{b}} -\frac{1}{n_x^{te}} \sum_{i=1}^{n_x^{te}} \log \mathbf{a}^T \Phi_\mathbf{a}(\mathbf{x}_i^{te}) - \frac{1}{n_x^{te}} \sum_{i=1}^{n_x^{te}} \log \mathbf{b}^T \Phi_\mathbf{b}(\mathbf{z}_i^{te}), \quad s.t. \quad \frac{1}{n_x^{tr}} \sum_{i=1}^{n_x^{tr}} \omega(\mathbf{x}_i^{tr}, \mathbf{z}_i^{tr}) = 1$$

$$(12)$$

The above constrained optimization problem is convex w.r.t. both $\mathbf{a}$ and $\mathbf{b}$. It can be solved by interior point methods using the derivatives in Eq. (13):

$$\nabla \mathbf{a} = -\frac{1}{n_x^{te}} \sum_{i=1}^{n_x^{te}} \frac{1}{\mathbf{a}^T \Phi_\mathbf{a}(\mathbf{x}_i^{te})} \Phi_\mathbf{a}(\mathbf{x}_i^{te}), \quad \nabla \mathbf{b} = -\frac{1}{n_x^{te}} \sum_{i=1}^{n_x^{te}} \frac{1}{\mathbf{b}^T \Phi_\mathbf{b}(\mathbf{z}_i^{te})} \Phi_\mathbf{b}(\mathbf{z}_i^{te}) \quad (13)$$

**Weighted Visual-Semantic Regression.** Given per-instance weights $\omega$ estimated above, we can rewrite the loss function for both single-task ridge regression and multi-task regression in Sect. 3.1 as $\omega_i l(f(\mathbf{x}_i, \mathbf{A}), \mathbf{z}_i)$ and $\omega_i l(f(\mathbf{x}_i, \mathbf{S}, \mathbf{A}), \mathbf{z}_i)$ respectively. All our loss functions have quadratic form, so the weight can be expressed inside the quadratic loss e.g. $\omega_i ||\mathbf{z}_i - \mathbf{W}\mathbf{x}_i||_2^2 = ||\mathbf{z}_i\sqrt{\omega_i} - \mathbf{W}\mathbf{x}_i\sqrt{\omega_i}||_2^2$. Thus to incorporate the weight information we simply replace the original semantic embedding matrix with $\tilde{\mathbf{z}}_i = \mathbf{z}_i\sqrt{\omega_i}$ and data matrix with $\tilde{\mathbf{x}}_i = \mathbf{x}_i\sqrt{\omega_i}$.

# 5   Experiments

**Datasets and Settings.** We evaluated our contributions on three human action recognition datasets, HMDB51 [3], UCF101 [4] and Olympic Sports [37]. They contain 6766, 13320, 783 videos and 51, 101, 16 categories respectively. For all datasets we extract improved trajectory feature (ITF) [38], a state-of-the-art space-time feature representation for action recognition. We use Fisher Vectors (FV) [39] to encode three raw descriptors (HOG, HOF and MBH). Each descriptor is reduced to half of its original dimension by PCA, resulting in a 198 dim representation. Then we randomly sample 256,000 descriptors from all videos and learn a Gaussian Mixture with 128 components to obtain the FVs. The final dimension of FV encoded feature is $2 \times 128 \times 198 = 50688$ dimensions. For the label-embedding, we use 300-dimensional word2vec [40]. We use $T = n_c^{tr}$ latent tasks, and cross-validation to determine regularisation strength hyper-parameters for the models[6].

---

[6] Ridge Regression (RR) has 15M ($300 \times 50688$) parameters, whilst for HMDB51 where $T = 25$, GOMTL and MTE have 1.27M ($50688 \times 25 + 25 \times 300$) parameters.

## 5.1  Visual-Semantic Mappings for Zero-Shot Action Recognition

**Evaluation Criteria.** To evaluate zero-shot action recognition, we divide each dataset evenly into training and testing parts with 5 random splits. Using classification accuracy for HMDB51 and UCF101 and average precision for Olympic Sports as the evaluation metric, the average and standard deviation over the 5 splits are reported for each dataset.

**Compared Methods.** We study the efficacy of our contributions by evaluating the different visual-semantic mappings presented in Sect. 3.1. We compare MTL-regression methods with conventional STL Ridge Regression (denoted **RR**) for ZSL. For RR/STL, nearest neighbour matching is used to recognise target categories. Note that the RR+NN method here corresponds to the core strategy used by [9,11,12]. The multi-task models we explore include: **RMTL** [15]: assumes each task's predictor is the sum of a global latent vector and a task-specific vector. **GOMTL** [16]: Uses a predictor-matrix factorisation assumption in which tasks' predictors lie on a low-dimensional subspace. **Multi-Task Embedding (MTE):** Our model differs from GOMTL in that it explicitly models and regularises a lower dimensional latent space. For the multi-task methods, we also compare the ZSL matching strategies introduced in Sect. 3.2: **Distributed:** Standard NN matching (Eq. (6)), and **Latent:** our proposed latent-space matching (Eq. (7)).

**Results:** The comparison of single task ridge regression with our multi-task methods is presented in Table 2. From these results we make the following observations: (i) Overall our multi-task methods improve on the corresponding single-task baseline of RR. MTL regression (RMTL, GOMTL and MTE) improves single-task ridge regression by 5–10% in relative terms, with the biggest margins visible on the Olympic Sports dataset. (ii) Within multi-task models, the GOMTL with sparse $\ell_1$ regularization outperforms RMTL. This suggests learning the task combination $S$ from data is better than fixing it as in RMTL. (iii) Our MTE generally outperforms other multi-task methods supporting the

**Table 2.** Visual-semantic mappings for zero-shot action recognition: MTL ($\checkmark$) versus STL ($\times$). Latent matching ($\checkmark$) versus distributed ($\times$) matching

| ZSL model | MTL | Latent matching | HMDB51 | UCF101 | Olympic sports |
|---|---|---|---|---|---|
| RR | $\times$ | NA | $18.3 \pm 2.1$ | $14.5 \pm 0.9$ | $40.9 \pm 10.1$ |
| RMTL [15] | $\checkmark$ | $\times$ | $18.5 \pm 2.1$ | $14.6 \pm 1.1$ | $41.1 \pm 10.0$ |
| RMTL [15] | $\checkmark$ | $\checkmark$ | $18.7 \pm 1.7$ | $14.7 \pm 1.0$ | $41.1 \pm 10.0$ |
| GOMTL [16] | $\checkmark$ | $\times$ | $18.5 \pm 2.2$ | $13.1 \pm 1.5$ | $43.5 \pm 8.8$ |
| GOMTL [16] | $\checkmark$ | $\checkmark$ | $18.9 \pm 1.0$ | $14.9 \pm 1.5$ | $44.5 \pm 8.5$ |
| MTE | $\checkmark$ | $\times$ | $18.7 \pm 2.2$ | $14.2 \pm 1.3$ | $\mathbf{44.5 \pm 8.2}$ |
| MTE | $\checkmark$ | $\checkmark$ | $\mathbf{19.7 \pm 1.6}$ | $\mathbf{15.8 \pm 1.3}$ | $44.3 \pm 8.1$ |

explicit modelling and regularisation of the latent space. (iv) In most cases, NN matching in the latent space improve zero-shot performance. This is likely due to the lower dimension of the latent space compared to the dimension of the original word vector embedding, making NN matching more meaningful [17].

## 5.2 Importance Weighted Data Augmentation

We next evaluate the impact of importance weighting in data augmentation for zero-shot action recognition. We perform the same 5 random split benchmark for each dataset. For data augmentation, we augment each dataset's training split with the data from all other datasets. For instance, for ZSL on HMDB51 we augment the training data with all videos from UCF101 and Olympic Sports.

**Compared Methods:** We study the impact of the data augmentation methods: **Naive DA:** Naive Data Augmentation [9,41] simply assigns equal weight to each auxiliary training sample. **Visual KLIEP:** The auxiliary data is aligned with the testing sample distribution $\mathbf{X}^{te}$ (Eq. (8)). **Category KLIEP:** The auxiliary categories are aligned with testing category distribution $\mathbf{Z}^{te}$. This is achieved by the same procedure in Eq. (8) by replacing $\mathbf{x}$ with $\mathbf{z}$. **Full KLIEP:** The distribution of both samples $\mathbf{X}^{te}$ and categories $\mathbf{Z}^{te}$ is used to reweight the auxiliary data (Eq. (12)).

**Results:** From the results in Table 3, we draw the conclusions: (i) Both the baseline single task learning (STL) method and our Multi-Task Embedding (MTE) improve with Naive DA (compare unaugmented results in Table 2), (ii) The Visual, Category, and Full visual+category-based weightings all improve on Naive DA in the case of STL RR. (iii) We see that our MTE with Full KLIEP augmentation performs the best overall. The ability of KLIEP to improve on Naive DA suggests that the auxiliary data is indeed of variable relevance to the target data, and selectively re-weighing the auxiliary data is important. (iv) For KLIEP-based DA, either Visual or Category DA provides most of the improvement, with relatively less improvement obtained by using both together.

**Table 3.** Data augmentation and importance weighting for ZSL action recognition.

| ZSL model | Weighting model | HMDB51 | UCF101 | Olympic sports |
|-----------|-----------------|--------|--------|----------------|
| RR | Naive DA | $21.9 \pm 2.4$ | $19.4 \pm 1.7$ | $46.5 \pm 9.4$ |
| MTE | Naive DA | $\mathbf{23.4 \pm 3.4}$ | $\mathbf{20.9 \pm 1.5}$ | $\mathbf{49.4 \pm 8.8}$ |
| RR | Visual KLIEP | $23.2 \pm 2.7$ | $20.3 \pm 1.6$ | $47.2 \pm 9.3$ |
| RR | Category KLIEP | $23.0 \pm 2.1$ | $20.2 \pm 1.6$ | $51.8 \pm 8.7$ |
| RR | Full KLIEP | $23.7 \pm 2.7$ | $20.7 \pm 1.4$ | $51.3 \pm 9.0$ |
| MTE | Visual KLIEP | $23.4 \pm 2.8$ | $20.8 \pm 2.0$ | $51.4 \pm 9.2$ |
| MTE | Category KLIEP | $23.3 \pm 2.4$ | $20.9 \pm 1.7$ | $50.9 \pm 8.3$ |
| MTE | Full KLIEP | $\mathbf{23.9 \pm 3.0}$ | $\mathbf{21.9 \pm 2.7}$ | $\mathbf{52.3 \pm 8.1}$ |

**Alternative Models.** We also compare against previous state-of-the-art methods including those driven by both attributes and word-vector category embeddings. **DAP/IAP** [5]: Direct/Indirect attribute prediction are classic attribute-based zero-shot recognition models based on training SVM classifiers independently for each attribute, and using a probabilistic model to match attribute predictions with target classes. **HAA**: We implement a simplified version of the Human Actions by Attributes model [21]: We first train attribute detection SVMs, and test samples are assigned to categories based on cosine distance between their vector of attribute predictions and the target classes' attribute vectors. **SVE** [9]: Support vector regression was adopted to learn the visual to semantic mapping. **ESZSL** [42]: Embarrassingly Simple Zero-Shot Learning defines the loss function as the mean square error on label prediction in contrast to the regression loss defined in other baseline models. **SJE**: Structured Joint Embedding [7] employed a triplet hinge loss. The objective is to enforce relevant labels having higher projection values from visual features than those of non-relevant labels. **UDA**: The Unsupervised Domain Adaptation model [22] learns dictionary on auxiliary data and adapts it to the target data as a constraint on the target dictionary rather than blindly using the same dictionary. This work combines both attribute and word vector embeddings.

**Comparison Versus State of the Art:** Table 4 compares our models with various contemporary and state-of-the-art models. For clear comparison, we indicate for each method which embedding (($\mathbf{W}$)ordvector/($\mathbf{A}$)ttribute) and feature (our FV, or BoW) are used, as well as whether it has a transductive dependency on the test data ($\mathbf{TD}$) or exploits additional augmenting data ($\mathbf{Aug}$). From these results we conclude that: (i) Although data augmentation has a big impact, our non-transductive and no data augmentation method (MTE) generally outperforms prior alternatives due to learning an effective latent matching space robust to the train/test class shift; (ii) The performance of our MTE with word-vector embedding is strong when compared with DAP/IAP/HAA/ESZSL even with attribute embedding. Given the same attribute embedding, MTE outperforms all state-of-the-art models due to the discovery of latent attributes from the original attribute space; (iii) Moreover, given importance weighting on auxiliary data, our method (MTE + Full KLIEP) with word-vector embedding performs the best overall – including against [9] which also exploits data augmentation; (iv) Finally, our method is synergistic to the post processing self-training approach [11] as well as the hubness strategies [12], which further explains the advantages of our approach (MTE + Full KLIEP + PP) over other methods.

### 5.3 Qualitative Results and Further Analysis

**Importance Weighting:** To visualise the impact of our IW, we randomly select 4/16 classes as target/auxiliary sets respectively. We then estimate the weight on the 16 auxiliary video classes according to the Full KLIEP (Sect. 4). Examples of the auxiliary video weightings are presented in Fig. 2. We observe that auxiliary classes semantically related to the targets are given higher weight

**Table 4.** Comparison versus state of the art. Embed: Label embedding, Feat: Visual feature used, Aug: Data augmentation required? TD: Transductive Requirement?

| Method | Embed | Feat | TD | Aug | HMDB51 | UCF101 | Olympic sports |
|---|---|---|---|---|---|---|---|
| MTE | W | FV | X | X | $19.7 \pm 1.6$ | $15.8 \pm 1.3$ | $44.3 \pm 8.1$ |
| MTE + Full KLIEP | W | FV | ✓ | ✓ | $23.9 \pm 3.0$ | $21.9 \pm 2.7$ | $52.3 \pm 8.1$ |
| MTE + Full KLIEP + PP | W | FV | ✓ | ✓ | $\mathbf{24.8 \pm 2.2}$ | $\mathbf{22.9 \pm 3.3}$ | $\mathbf{56.6 \pm 7.7}$ |
| MTE | A | FV | X | X | N/A | $18.3 \pm 1.7$ | $55.6 \pm 11.3$ |
| DAP [5] - CVPR 2009 | A | FV | X | X | N/A | $15.9 \pm 1.2$ | $45.4 \pm 12.8$ |
| IAP [5] - CVPR 2009 | A | FV | X | X | N/A | $16.7 \pm 1.1$ | $42.3 \pm 12.5$ |
| HAA [21] - CVPR 2011 | A | FV | X | X | N/A | $14.9 \pm 0.8$ | $46.1 \pm 12.4$ |
| SVE [9] - ICIP 2015 | W | BoW | X | X | $14.9 \pm 1.8$ | $12.0 \pm 1.4$ | N/A |
| SVE [9] - ICIP 2015 | W | BoW | ✓ | X | $15.6 \pm 0.7$ | $16.5 \pm 2.4$ | N/A |
| SVE [9] - ICIP 2015 | W | BoW | X | ✓ | $19.3 \pm 4.0$ | $13.1 \pm 2.0$ | N/A |
| SVE [9] - ICIP 2015 | W | BoW | ✓ | ✓ | $22.8 \pm 2.6$ | $18.4 \pm 1.4$ | N/A |
| ESZSL [42] - ICML 2015 | W | FV | X | X | $18.5 \pm 2.0$ | $15.0 \pm 1.3$ | $39.6 \pm 9.6$ |
| ESZSL [42] - ICML 2015 | W | FV | X | ✓ | $22.7 \pm 3.5$ | $18.7 \pm 1.6$ | $51.4 \pm 8.3$ |
| ESZSL [42] - ICML 2015 | A | FV | X | X | N/A | $17.1 \pm 1.2$ | $53.9 \pm 10.8$ |
| SJE [7] - CVPR 2015 | W | FV | X | X | $13.3 \pm 2.4$ | $9.9 \pm 1.4$ | $28.6 \pm 4.9$ |
| SJE [7] - CVPR 2015 | A | FV | X | X | N/A | $12.0 \pm 1.2$ | $47.5 \pm 14.8$ |
| UDA [22] - ICCV 2015 | A | FV | ✓ | X | N/A | $13.2 \pm 1.9$ | N/A |
| UDA [22] - ICCV 2015 | A+W | FV | ✓ | X | N/A | $14.0 \pm 1.8$ | N/A |

**Fig. 2.** Visualisation of Full KLIEP auxiliary data weighting. Left: 4 target videos with category names. Right: 16 auxiliary videos with bars indicating the estimated weights.

e.g. HandstandPushups → Cartwheel in first sample, SalsaSpin → Hug and Sword Exercise → Fencing in the second sample. While the visually and semantically less relevant auxiliary videos are given much lower weights.

**Multi-Task Embedding:** We next qualitatively illustrate single versus multi-task visual-semantic mappings. Specifically we take 5 classes to be recognized and visualise their data after visual-semantic projection by tSNE [43]. A compar-

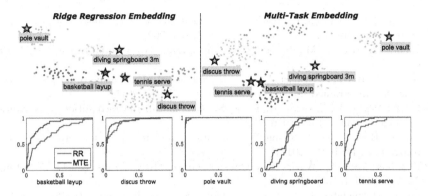

**Fig. 3.** Qualitative comparison between single-task ridge regression (RR) and multi-task embedding (MTE).

ison between the representations generated by single-task (RR) and multi-task (MTE) mappings is given in Fig. 3. The multi-task embedding discovers data in a lower dimension latent space where NN classification becomes more meaningful. The improved representation is illustrated by computing the ROC curve for each target category, as seen in Fig. 3. MTE provides improved detection over RR, demonstrating the better generalisation of this representation.

## 6 Conclusion

In this work, we focused on zero-shot action recognition from the perspective of improving generalisation of the visual-semantic mapping across the disjoint train/test class gap. We propose both model- and data-centric improvements to a traditional regression-based pipeline by respectively, multi-task embedding – to minimise overfit of the train data and to build a lower dimensional latent matching space; and prioritising data augmentation by importance weighting – to best exploit auxiliary data for the recognition of target categories. Our experiments on a set of contemporary action-recognition benchmarks demonstrate the impact of both our contributions and show state-of-the-art results overall.

## References

1. Aggarwal, J.K., Ryoo, M.S.: Human activity analysis: a review. ACM Comput. Surv. **43**(3), 16 (2011)
2. Schüldt, C., Laptev, I., Caputo, B.: Recognizing human actions: a local SVM approach. In: ICPR (2004)
3. Kuehne, H., Jhuang, H., Garrote, E., Poggio, T., Serre, T.: HMDB: a large video database for human motion recognition. In: ICCV (2011)
4. Soomro, K., Zamir, A., Shah, M.: Ucf101: a dataset of 101 human actions classes from videos in the wild (2012). arXiv preprint arXiv:1212.0402

358     X. Xu et al.

5. Lampert, C., Nickisch, H., Harmeling, S.: Learning to detect unseen object classes by between-class attribute transfer. In: CVPR (2009)
6. Socher, R., Ganjoo, M.: Zero-shot learning through cross-modal transfer. In: NIPS (2013)
7. Akata, Z., Reed, S., Walter, D., Lee, H., Schiele, B.: Evaluation of output embeddings for fine-grained image classification. In: CVPR (2015)
8. Fu, Z., Xiang, T., Kodirov, E., Gong, S.: Zero-shot object recognition by semantic manifold distance. In: CVPR (2015)
9. Xu, X., Hospedales, T., Gong, S.: Semantic embedding space for zero-shot action recognition. In: ICIP (2015)
10. Pan, S.J., Yang, Q.: A survey on transfer learning. IEEE Trans. Knowl. Data Eng. 22(10), 1345–1359 (2010)
11. Fu, Y., Hospedales, T.M., Xiang, T., Gong, S.: Transductive multi-view zero-shot learning. IEEE Trans. Pattern Anal. Mach. Intell. 37, 2332–2345 (2015)
12. Dinu, G., Lazaridou, A., Baroni, M.: Improving zero-shot learning by mitigating the hubness problem. In: ICLR (2015)
13. Lazaridou, A., Dinu, G., Baroni, M.: Hubness and pollution: delving into cross-space mapping for zero-shot learning. In: Proceedings of ACL. Association for Computational Linguistics (2015)
14. Mahadevan, S., Chandar, S.: Reasoning about linguistic regularities in word embeddings using matrix manifolds. arXiv preprint (2015)
15. Evgeniou, T., Pontil, M.: Regularized multi-task learning. In: ACM SIGKDD (2004)
16. Kumar, A., Daum, H., Iii, H.D.: Learning task grouping and overlap in multi-task learning. In: ICML (2012)
17. Beyer, K., Goldstein, J., Ramakrishnan, R., Shaft, U.: When is nearest neighbor meaningful? In: Database Theory (1999)
18. Habibian, A., Mensink, T., Snoek, C.G.M.: VideoStory: a new multimedia embedding for few-example recognition and translation of events. In: ACM Multi-media (2014)
19. Sugiyama, M., Nakajima, S., Kashima, H., Von Bünau, P., Kawanabe, M.: Direct importance estimation with model selection and its application to covariate shift adaptation. In: NIPS (2007)
20. Garcke, J., Vanck, T.: Importance weighted inductive transfer learning for regression. In: ECMLPKDD (2014)
21. Liu, J., Kuipers, B., Savarese, S.: Recognizing human actions by attributes. In: CVPR (2011)
22. Kodirov, E., Xiang, T., Fu, Z., Gong, S.: Unsupervised domain adaptation for zero-shot learning. In: ICCV (2015)
23. Gan, C., Yang, Y., Zhu, L., Zhao, D., Zhuang, Y.: Recognizing an action using its name: a knowledge-based approach. Int. J. Comput. Vis. 120, 61 (2016)
24. Chang, X., Yang, Y., Long, G., Zhang, C., Hauptmann, A.G.: Dynamic concept composition for zero-example event detection. In: AAAI (2016)
25. Yang, Y., Hospedales, T.M.: A unified perspective on multi-domain and multi-task learning. In: ICLR (2015)
26. Zhou, Q., Wang, G., Jia, K., Zhao, Q.: Learning to share latent tasks for action recognition. In: ICCV (2013)
27. Yuan, C., Hu, W., Tian, G., Yang, S., Wang, H.: Multi-task sparse learning with beta process prior for action recognition. In: CVPR (2013)

28. Liu, A.A., Xu, N., Su, Y.T., Lin, H., Hao, T., Yang, Z.X.: Single/multi-view human action recognition via regularized multi-task learning. Neurocomputing **151**, 544–553 (2015)
29. Mahasseni, B., Todorovic, S.: Latent multitask learning for view-invariant action recognition. In: ICCV (2013)
30. Torralba, A., Efros, A.A.: Unbiased look at dataset bias. In: CVPR (2011)
31. Huang, J., Gretton, A., Borgwardt, K.M., Schölkopf, B., Smola, A.J.: Correcting sample selection bias by unlabeled data. In: NIPS (2007)
32. Saenko, K., Kulis, B., Fritz, M., Darrell, T.: Adapting visual category models to new domains. In: Daniilidis, K., Maragos, P., Paragios, N. (eds.) ECCV 2010. LNCS, vol. 6314, pp. 213–226. Springer, Heidelberg (2010). doi:10.1007/978-3-642-15561-1_16
33. Pardoe, D., Stone, P.: Boosting for Regression Transfer. In: ICML (2010)
34. Gretton, A., Borgwardt, K.M., Rasch, M., Schölkopf, B., Smola, A.J.: A kernel method for the two-sample-problem. In: NIPS (2006)
35. Baktashmotlagh, M., Harandi, M., Lovell, B., Salzmann, M.: Unsupervised domain adaptation by domain invariant projection. In: ICCV (2013)
36. Boyd, S., Parikh, N., Chu, E., Peleato, B., Eckstein, J.: Distributed optimization and statistical learning via the alternating direction method of multipliers. Found. Trends Mach. Learn. **3**(1), 1–122 (2011)
37. Niebles, J.C., Chen, C.-W., Fei-Fei, L.: Modeling temporal structure of decomposable motion segments for activity classification. In: Daniilidis, K., Maragos, P., Paragios, N. (eds.) ECCV 2010. LNCS, vol. 6312, pp. 392–405. Springer, Heidelberg (2010). doi:10.1007/978-3-642-15552-9_29
38. Wang, H., Oneata, D., Verbeek, J., Schmid, C.: A robust and efficient video representation for action recognition. Int. J. Comput. Vis. **119**(3), 219–238 (2016)
39. Perronnin, F., Sánchez, J., Mensink, T.: Improving the Fisher kernel for large-scale image classification. In: Daniilidis, K., Maragos, P., Paragios, N. (eds.) ECCV 2010. LNCS, vol. 6314, pp. 143–156. Springer, Heidelberg (2010). doi:10.1007/978-3-642-15561-1_11
40. Mikolov, T., Sutskever, I., Chen, K., Corrado, G., Dean, J.: Distributed representations of words and phrases and their compositionality. In: NIPS (2013)
41. Xu, X., Hospedales, T., Gong, S.: Zero-shot action recognition by word-vector embedding. (2015). arXiv preprint arXiv:1511.04458
42. Romera-paredes, B., Torr, P.H.S.: An embarrassingly simple approach to zero-shot learning. In: ICML (2015)
43. Van Der Maaten, L.: Accelerating t-SNE using tree-based algorithms. J. Mach. Learn. Res. **15**, 3221–3245 (2014)

# Head Reconstruction from Internet Photos

Shu Liang$^{(\boxtimes)}$, Linda G. Shapiro, and Ira Kemelmacher-Shlizerman

Computer Science and Engineering Department,
University of Washington, Seattle, USA
{liangshu,shapiro,kemelmi}@cs.washington.edu

**Abstract.** 3D face reconstruction from Internet photos has recently produced exciting results. A person's face, e.g., Tom Hanks, can be modeled and animated in 3D from a completely uncalibrated photo collection. Most methods, however, focus solely on face area and mask out the rest of the head. This paper proposes that head modeling from the Internet is a problem we can solve. We target reconstruction of the rough shape of the head. Our method is to gradually "grow" the head mesh starting from the frontal face and extending to the rest of views using photometric stereo constraints. We call our method boundary-value growing algorithm. Results on photos of celebrities downloaded from the Internet are presented.

**Keywords:** Internet photo collections · Head modeling · In the wild · Unconstrained 3D reconstruction · Uncalibrated

## 1 Introduction

"If two heads are better than one, then what about double chins? On that note, I will help myself to seconds." —Jarod Kintz

Methods that reconstruct 3D models of people's heads from images need to account for varying 3D pose, lighting, non-rigid changes due to expressions, relatively smooth surfaces of faces, ears and neck, and finally, the hair. Great reconstructions can be achieved nowadays in case the input photos are captured in a calibrated lab setting or semi-calibrated setup where the person has to participate in the capturing session (see related work). Reconstructing from Internet photos, however, is an open problem due to the high degree of variability across uncalibrated photos; lighting, pose, cameras and resolution change dramatically across photos. In recent years, reconstruction of *faces* from the Internet have received a lot of attention. All face-focused methods, however, mask out the head using a fixed face mask and focus only on the face area. For real-life applications, we must be able to reconstruct a full head.

So what is it there to reconstruct except for the face? At the minimum, to create full head models we need to be able to reconstruct the ears, and at least part of the neck, chin, and overall head shape. Additionally, hair reconstruction is a difficult problem. One approach is to use morphable model methods. These,

© Springer International Publishing AG 2016
B. Leibe et al. (Eds.): ECCV 2016, Part II, LNCS 9906, pp. 360–374, 2016.
DOI: 10.1007/978-3-319-46475-6_23

however, do not fit the head explicitly but instead use fitting based on the face and provide a mostly average (non-personalized) bald model for the head.

This paper addresses the new direction of *head* reconstruction directly from Internet data. We propose an algorithm to create a rough head shape, and frame the problem as follows. Given a photo collection, obtained by searching for photos of a specific person on Google image search, we would like to reconstruct a 3D model of that person's head. Just like [1] (that focused only on the face area) we aim to reconstruct an average rigid model of the person from the whole collection. This model can be then used as a template for dynamic reconstruction, e.g., [2], and hair growing techniques, e.g., [3]. Availability of a template model is essential for those techniques.

Consider the top row photos in Fig. 1. The 3D shape of the head is clearly outlined in the different views (different 3D poses). However, if we are given only one or two photos per view, the problem is still very challenging due to lighting inconsistency across views, difficulty in segmenting the face profile from the background, and challenges in merging the images across views. Our key idea is that with many more (hundreds) of photos per 3D view, the challenges can be overcome. For celebrities, we can easily acquire such collections from the Internet; for others, we can extract such photos from Facebook or from mobile photos.

Our method works as follows: A person's photo collection is divided to clusters of approximately the same azimuth angle of the 3D pose. Given the clusters, a depth map of the frontal face is reconstructed, and the method gradually grows the reconstruction by estimating surface normals per view cluster and then

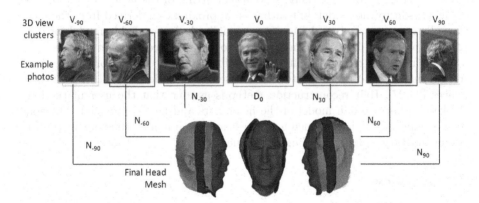

**Fig. 1.** By looking at the top row photos we can imagine how Bush's head shape looks in 3D; however, existing methods fail to do so on Internet photos, due to such facts as inconsistency of lighting, challenging segmentation, and expression variation. Given many more photos per 3D view (hundreds), however, we show that a rough full head model can be reconstructed. The head mesh is divided into 7 parts, where each part is reconstructed from a different view cluster while being constrained by the neighboring view clusters.

constraining using boundary conditions coming from neighboring views. The final result is a head mesh of the person that combines all the views.

## 2    Related Work

The related work is in calibrated and semi-calibrated setting for head reconstruction, and uncalibrated settings for face reconstruction.

Calibrated head modeling has achieved amazing results over the last decade [4–6]. Calibrated methods require a person to participate in a capturing session to achieve good results. These typically take as input a video with relatively constant lighting, and large pose variation across the video. Examples include non rigid structure from motion methods [7,8], multiview methods [9,10], dynamic kinect fusion [11], and RGB-D based methods [12,13].

Reconstruction of people from Internet photos recently achieved good results; [14] showed that it is possible to reconstruct a face from a single Internet photo using a template model of a different person. [1] later proposed a photometric stereo method to reconstruct a face from many Internet photos of the same individual. [15] showed that photometric stereo can be combined with face landmark constraints, and recent work has shown that 3D dynamic shape [2,16,17] and texture [18] can be recovered from Internet photos.

One way to approach the uncalibrated head reconstruction problem is to use the morphable model approach. With morphable models [19,20], the face is fitted to a linear space of 200 face scans, and the head is reconstructed from the linear space as well. In practice, morphable model methods work well for face tracking [21,22]. However, there is no actual fitting of the head, ears, and neck of the person to the model, but rather an approximation derived from the face; thus the reconstructed model is not personalized. A morphable model for ears [23] was proposed, but it was not applied to uncalibrated Internet photos.

Hair modeling requires a multiview calibrated setup [24,25] or can be done from a single photo by fitting to a database of synthetic hairs [3], or by fitting helices [26,27]. Hair reconstruction methods assume that the user marks hair strokes or that a rough model of the head, ears and face is provided. The goal of this paper is to provide such a rough head shape model; thus our method is complementary to hair modeling techniques.

## 3    Overview

We denote the set of photos in a view cluster as $V_i$. Photos in the same view cluster have approximately the same 3D pose and azimuth angle. Specifically, we divided the photos into 7 clusters with azimuths: $i = 0, -30, 30, -60, 60, -90, 90$. Figure 2 shows the averages of each cluster after rigid alignment using fiducial points (1st row) and after subsequent alignment using the Collection Flow method [28] (2nd row), which calculates optical flow for each cluster photo to the cluster average. A key observation is that each view cluster has one particularly well-reconstructed head area, e.g., the ears in views 90 and −90 are sharp

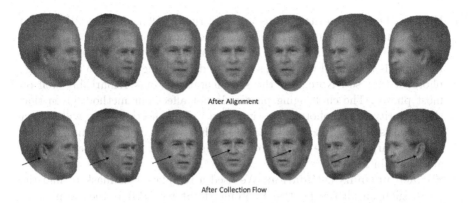

**Fig. 2.** Averages of view clusters' photos after rigid alignment (1st row) and after collection flow (2nd row). The arrows visualize head parts that are sharper in each view, e.g., the ear is sharpest in 90 and −90° (left and right). The key idea is to use the sharp (well-aligned) parts from the corresponding views to create an optimal mesh reconstruction.

while blurry in other views. Since our goal is to create a full head mesh, our algorithm will combine the optimal parts from each view into a single model. This is illustrated in Fig. 1.

It was shown in previous work that the face can be reconstructed from frontal photos using Photometric Stereo [1]. Thus, one way to implement our idea, of combining views into a single mesh, would be to reconstruct shape from each view cluster independently and then stitch them together. This turned out to be challenging as the individual shapes are reconstructed up to linear ambiguities. Although the photos are divided into pose clusters, the precise pose for each pose cluster is unknown. For example, $V_{30}$ could have a variance from 25 to 35 in the azimuth rotation angle, depending on the dominant pose of the image cluster. This misalignment will also increase the difficulty of stitching all the views. We solve those challenges by growing the shape in stages works well. We begin by describing estimation of surface normals and a depth map for view cluster $V_0$ (frontal view) in Sect. 4. This will be the initialization for our algorithm. In Sect. 5, we describe how each view cluster uses its own photos and the depth of its neighbors to contribute to the creation of a full head mesh. Data acquisition and alignment details are given in the experiments section (Sect. 6).

## 4    Head Mesh Initialization

Our goal is to reconstruct the head mesh $M$. We begin by estimating a depth map and surface normals of the frontal cluster $V_0$, and assign each reconstructed pixel to a vertex of the mesh. The depth map is estimated by extending the method of [1] to capture more of the head in the frontal face photos, i.e., we extend the reconstruction mask to a bigger area to capture the chin, part of the neck and some of the hair. The algorithm is as follows:

1. **Dense 2D alignment:** Photos are first rigidly aligned using 2D fiducial points as the pipeline of [29]. The head region including neck and shoulder in each image is segmented using semantic segmentation by [30]. Then Collection Flow [28] is run on all the photos in $V_0$ to densely align them to the average photo of that set. Note that the segementation works remarkably well on most photos. The challenging photos do not affect our method; given that the majority of the photos are segmented well, Collection Flow will correct for inconsistencies. Also, Collection Flow helps overcome differences in hair style by warping all the photos to the dominant style. See more details about alignment in Sect. 6.

2. **Surface normals estimation:** We used a template face mask to find the face region on all the photos. Photometric Stereo (PS) is then applied to the face region of the flow-aligned photos. The face region of the photos are arranged in an $n \times p_k$ matrix $Q$, where $n$ is the number of images and $p_k$ is the number of face pixels determined by the template facial mask. Rank-4 PCA is computed to factorize into lighting and normals: $Q = LN$. After we get the lighting estimation $L$ for each photo, we can compute N for all $p$ head pixels including ear, chin and hair regions.

Two key components that made PS work on uncalibrated head photos are:

(1) resolving the Generalized Bas-Relief (GBR) ambiguity using a template 3D face of a different individual, i.e., $\min_A ||N_{\text{template}} - AN_{face}||^2$,

(2) using a per-pixel surface normal estimation, where each point uses a different subset of photos to estimate the normal. We follow the per-pixel surface estimation idea as in previous work, i.e., given the initial lighting estimate $L$, the normal is computed per point by selecting a subset of $Q$'s rows that satisfy the re-projection constraint. In the full head case, we extend it to handle cases when the head is partially cropped out, by adding a constraint that a photo participates in normal estimation if it satisfies both the reprojection constraint and is inside the desired head area, i.e., part of the segmentation result from [30]. If the number of selected subset images is not enough (less than n/3), we will not use them in our depth map estimation step.

3. **Depth map estimation:** The surface normals are integrated to create a depth map $D_0$ by solving a linear system of equations that satisfy gradient constrains $dz/dx = -n_x/n_y$ and $dz/dy = -n_x/n_y$ where $(n_x, n_y, n_z)$ are components of the surface normal of each point [31]. Combining these constraints, for the $z$-value on the depth map, we have:

$$n_z(z_{x+1,y} - z_{x,y}) = n_x \qquad (1)$$

$$n_z(z_{x,y+1} - z_{x,y}) = n_y \qquad (2)$$

In the case of $n_z \approx 0$, we use a different constraint,

$$n_y(z_{x,y} - z_{x+1,y}) = n_x(z_{x,y} - z_{x,y+1}) \qquad (3)$$

This generate a sparse matrix of $2p \times 2p$ matrix M, and we can solve for:

$$\arg\min_z ||Mz - v||^2 \tag{4}$$

We do a least squares fit to solve for the $z$-value for each pixel.

Potentially, we could run the same algorithm for each view cluster. This, however, does not perform well, as we will see in the experiments section. Instead we are going to introduce two constraints, which we describe in the next section.

## 5   Boundary-Value Growing

In this section we describe our "growing" algorithm to complete the side views of the mesh. Starting from the frontal view mesh $V_0$, we gradually complete more regions of the head in the order of $V_{30}$, $V_{60}$, $V_{90}$ and $V_{-30}$, $V_{-60}$, $V_{-90}$. For each view cluster we repeat the same algorithm as in Sect. 4 with two additional key constraints:

1. **Ambiguity recovery:** Rather than recovering the ambiguity $A$ that arises from $Q = LA^{-1}AN$ using the template model, we use the already computed neighboring cluster, i.e., for $V_{\pm30}$, $N_0$ is used, for $V_{\pm60}$ we use $N_{\pm30}$, and for $V_{\pm90}$ we use $N_{\pm60}$. Specifically, we estimate the out-of-plane pose from our 3D initial mesh $V_0$ to the average image of pose cluster $V_{30}$ using the method proposed in [2]. We render the rotated mesh $V_0'$ as a reference depth map $D_0'$ to pose cluster $V_{30}$, accounting for visibility and occlusion using zbuffer. The normals on each projected pixels of $D_0'$ will serve as the reference normals to solve for the GBR ambiguity of the overlapping head region as well as the newly grown head region.
2. **Depth constraint:** In addition to the gradient constraints that are specified in Sect. 4, we modify the boundary constraints from Neumann to Dirichlet. Let $\Omega_0$ be the boundary of $D_0'$. Then we impose that the part of $\Omega_0$ that intersects the mask of $D_{30}$ will have the same depth values: $D_{30}(\Omega_0) = D_0'(\Omega_0)$. With both boundary constraints and gradient constraints, our optimization function can be written as:

$$\arg\min_z ||Mz - v||^2 + ||Wz - Wz_0||^2 \tag{5}$$

where $z_0$ is the depth constraint from $D_0'$, and $W$ is a blend mask with values decreasing from 1 to 0 on the boundary of $D_0'$. We will get the new vertex positions for grown regions and we can also update vertices on the boundary of the already computed depth map, eliminating the distortion caused by lack of photos and inaccurate $n_z$. This process is repeated for every neighboring pair of depths.

After each depth stage reconstruction $(0, 30, 60,..$ degrees$)$, the estimated depth is projected to the head mesh. By this process, the head is gradually filled in by gathering vertices from all the views.

# 6   Experiments

We describe the data collection process, alignment, evaluations and comparisons with other methods.

## 6.1   Data Collection and Processing

We collected around $1,000$ photos per person (George Bush, Vladimir Putin, Barack Obama and Hillary Clinton) by searching for photos on Google image search. The numbers of images in each pose cluster are shown in Table 1. We noticed that the numbers of side view photos are usually much smaller than frontal view photos. In order to get more photos, we searched for "Bush shakes hands", "Bush shaking hand", "Bush portrait", "Bush meets" etc. to collect more non-frontal photos. The number of photos in each cluster will affect the final result; we will demonstrate the reconstruction quality vs. number of photos later in this section.

**Table 1.** Number of photos we used in each pose cluster

| Pose | -90 | −60 | −30 | 0 | 30 | 60 | 90 |
|---|---|---|---|---|---|---|---|
| Bush | 185 | 62 | 118 | 371 | 113 | 80 | 191 |
| Putin | 131 | 58 | 151 | 413 | 121 | 61 | 151 |
| Obama | 65 | 51 | 126 | 284 | 177 | 55 | 75 |
| Clinton | 115 | 47 | 114 | 332 | 109 | 61 | 66 |

We ran face detection and fiducial detection using IntraFace [32]. For extreme side views, none of the state of the art fiducial detection algorithms was able to perform, and often times the face was not even detected. We therefore manually annotated each photo with 7 fiducials.

Once photos are aligned we run collection flow [28] on each view cluster. For completeness we review the method. The idea is to estimate a lighting subspace from all the photos in a particular cluster $V_i$ via PCA. Then each photo in the cluster $V_i^j$ is projected to the subspace to produce photo $\hat{V}_i^j$, which has a similar lighting as $V_i^j$ but an average shape. Optical flow is then estimated between $V_0^j$ and its relighted version $\hat{V}_0^j$. The process is iterated over the whole collection. In the end, all photos are warped to approximately average shape; however, they retain their lighting which makes them amenable for photometric stereo methods.

## 6.2   Results and Evaluation

Figure 3 shows the reconstruction per view that was later combined to a single mesh. For example, the ear in 90 and −90 views is reconstructed well, while the other views are not able to reconstruct the ear.

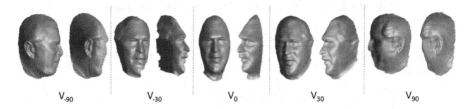

$V_{-90}$          $V_{-30}$          $V_0$          $V_{30}$          $V_{90}$

**Fig. 3.** Individual reconstructions per view cluster, with depth and ambiguity constraints. We can see that the individual views provide different shape components. For each view we show the mesh in two poses.

In Fig. 4, we shows how our two key constraints work well in the degree 90 view reconstruction result. Without the correct reference normals and depth constraint, the reconstructed shape is flat and the profile facial region is blurred, which increased the difficulty of aligning it back to the frontal view.

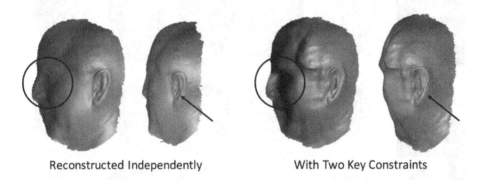

Reconstructed Independently                    With Two Key Constraints

**Fig. 4.** Comparison between without and with two key constraints. The left two shapes show the two views of 90° view shape reconstructed independently without two key constraints. The right two shapes show the two views of our result with two key constraints.

Figure 5 shows the reconstruction result for 4 subjects, each mesh is rotated to five different views. Note that the back and top part of the head are partly missing due to the lack of photos.

To evaluate how the number of photos affects the reconstruction quality, we took 600 photos for George Bush and estimated pose, lighting, texture for each image. We report the L2 intensity difference between the rendered photos and original photos. We tested our reconstruction method with 1/2, 1/4, 1/8 and 1/16 of the photos in each view cluster (see number of photos per cluster in Table 1). The method did not work in 1/16 case because some view clusters have less than 10 photos and there was not enough lighting variation within the collection for photometric stereo. Generally, we suggest using more than 100 photos for frontal view. The number of photos in side view clusters can be

**Table 2.** Reconstruction quality vs. number of photos

| Number of photos | N | N/2 | N/4 | N/8 | N/16 |
|---|---|---|---|---|---|
| Reprojection error (intensity) | $18.29 \pm 4.07$ | $18.70 \pm 4.07$ | $18.71 \pm 4.07$ | $18.80 \pm 4.04$ | N/A |

smaller (but larger than 30) because the side view of a human's head is more rigid than the frontal view (Table 2).

We also rendered a 3D model from the FaceWareHouse dataset [33] with 100 lights and 7 poses. We applied our method on these synthetic photos and got a reconstruction result as shown in Fig. 6. Since we use a template 3D model to correct GBR ambiguity, we cannot get the exact scale of the groundtruth.

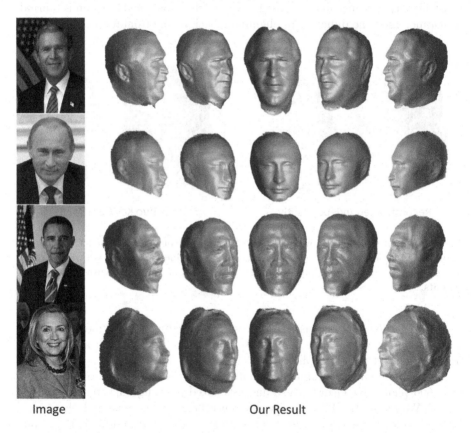

Image                                   Our Result

**Fig. 5.** Final reconstructed mesh rotated to 5 views to show the reconstruction from all sides. Each color image is an example image among our around 1,000 photo collection for each person. (Color figure online)

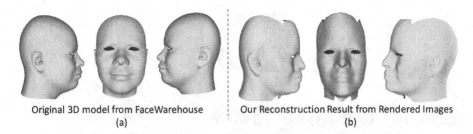

Original 3D model from FaceWarehouse          Our Reconstruction Result from Rendered Images

(a)                                                                    (b)

**Fig. 6.** Reconstruction result from the synthetic photos rendered from a 3D model in FaceWarehouse. The left three shapes are the $-90, 0, 90$ views for the groundtruth shape, and the right three shapes are our reconstruction result.

We do not claim that we have recovered the perfect shape, but the result looks reasonable with an average reprojection error of $11.1 \pm 5.72$.

### 6.3  Comparison

In Fig. 7 we show a comparison to the software FaceGen that implements a morphable model approach. For each person, we manually selected three photos (one frontal view and two side view photos) and used them as the input for FaceGen. The results of FaceGen are too averaged out and not personalized. Note that their ears look the same as each other.

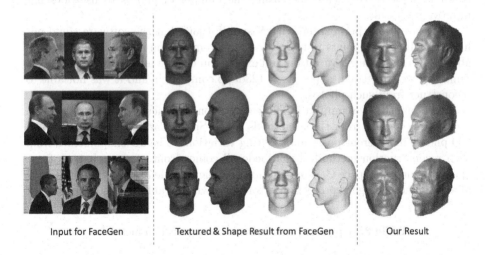

Input for FaceGen          Textured & Shape Result from FaceGen          Our Result

**Fig. 7.** Comparison to FaceGen (morphable model). We show the textured results and shape results from FaceGen in the middle and our results are on the right as comparisons. Note that the head shape reconstructed by morphable models is average like and not personalized. Additionally, texture hides shape imperfections.

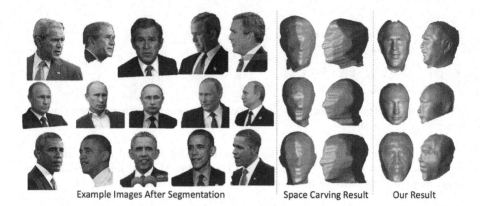

Example Images After Segmentation          Space Carving Result      Our Result

**Fig. 8.** Comparison to Space Carving method. 5 example segmented images are shown on the left for each person. The segmentations were used as silhouettes. We used around 30 photos per person.

We also tried the Space Carving method [34]. For each subject, we manually selected about 30 photos in different poses with a neutral expression. We used the segmentation result obtained from Sect. 4 as the silhouette. We assumed the camera focus length to be 100 and estimated the camera extrinisic parameters using a template 3D head model. We smoothed the carved results using [35] and showed the reconstruction in Fig. 8. The Space Carving method can produce a rough shape of the head. Increasing the number of photos to use does not improve the result.

We have also experimented with VisualSfM [36], but the software could not find enough feature points to run a structure from motion method. This is probably due to the lighting variation and expression change in the photo collection. Similarly, we have tried http://www.123dapp.com/catch, and it was not able to reconstruct from such photos.

For a quantitative comparison, for each person, we calculated the reprojection error of the shapes from three methods (ours, Space Carving and FaceGen) to 600 photos in different poses and lighting variations. The 3D shape comes from each reconstruction method. The albedo all comes from average shapes of our clusters, since the Space Carving method and the FaceGen results do not include albedos. The average reprojection error is shown in Table 3. The error map of

**Table 3.** Reprojection error from 3 reconstruction methods.

| Reprojection error | FaceGen | Visual hull | Our method |
|---|---|---|---|
| Bush | $20.1 \pm 4.84$ | $19.6 \pm 3.55$ | $18.3 \pm 4.04$ |
| Putin | $20.1 \pm 4.84$ | $17.2 \pm 4.68$ | $15.1 \pm 5.06$ |
| Obama | $21.5 \pm 4.62$ | $20.7 \pm 4.58$ | $19.7 \pm 4.40$ |

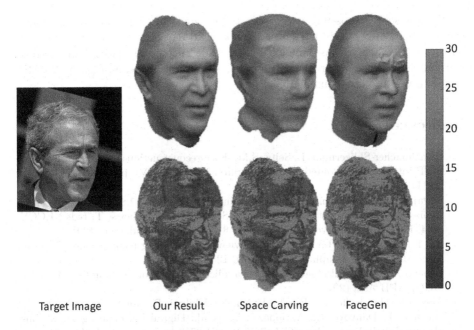

Target Image          Our Result          Space Carving          FaceGen

**Fig. 9.** Visualization of the reprojection error for 3 methods.

an example image is shown in Fig. 9. We calculated the error for the overlapping pixels of the three rendered images. Notice that the shapes from FaceGen and Space Carving might look good from the frontal view, but they are not correct when rotating to the target view. See how different the ear part is in the figure.

In future work, we will test the algorithm on more people. Collecting side view images is time consuming. Currently, there are no sets of Internet photos with their corresponding 3D models, thus it is challenging to evaluate quantitatively. We would like to help to solve that by providing our dataset. Furthermore, our GBR ambiguity is just roughly solved by a template model, so the scale might be not exactly the same as the actual mesh. We do not claim to have recovered the perfect shape, but rather show that it is possible to do so from Internet photos, and to encourage further research.

## 7  Discussion

We have shown the first results of head reconstructions from Internet photos. Our method has a number of limitations. First, we assume a Lambertian model for surface reflectance. While this works well, accounting for specularities should improve results. Second, fiducials for side views were labeled manually; we hope that this application will encourage researchers to solve the challenge of side view fiducial detection. Third, we have not reconstructed a complete model; the top of the head is missing. To solve this we would need to add photos with different elevation angles, rather than just focusing on the azimuth change.

We see several possible extensions to our method. The two we are most excited about are (1) reconstructing 3D non-rigid motion that includes the head part (not only face, as was done until now), and (2) combining with hair growing methods that can use our reconstructed shape as initialization, e.g., in [26] the template was produced manually.

# References

1. Kemelmacher-Shlizerman, I., Seitz, S.M.: Face reconstruction in the wild. In: 2011 IEEE International Conference on Computer Vision (ICCV), pp. 1746–1753. IEEE (2011)
2. Suwajanakorn, S., Kemelmacher-Shlizerman, I., Seitz, S.M.: Total moving face reconstruction. In: Fleet, D., Pajdla, T., Schiele, B., Tuytelaars, T. (eds.) ECCV 2014, Part IV. LNCS, vol. 8692, pp. 796–812. Springer, Heidelberg (2014)
3. Hu, L., Ma, C., Luo, L., Li, H.: Single-view hair modeling using a hairstyle database. ACM Trans. Graph. (TOG) **34**(4), 125 (2015)
4. Debevec, P.: The light stages and their applications to photoreal digital actors. In: SIGGRAPH Asia (2012)
5. Alexander, O., Fyffe, G., Busch, J., Yu, X., Ichikari, R., Jones, A., Debevec, P., Jimenez, J., Danvoye, E., Antionazzi, B., et al.: Digital ira: creating a real-time photoreal digital actor. In: ACM SIGGRAPH 2013 Posters, p. 1. ACM (2013)
6. Beeler, T., Bickel, B., Beardsley, P., Sumner, B., Gross, M.: High-quality single-shot capture of facial geometry. ACM Trans. Graph. (TOG) **29**(4), 40 (2010)
7. Agudo, A., Montiel, J., de Agapito, L., Calvo, B.: Online dense non-rigid 3D shape and camera motion recovery. In: BMVC (2014)
8. Garg, R., Roussos, A., Agapito, L.: Dense variational reconstruction of non-rigid surfaces from monocular video. In: Proceedings of the IEEE Conference on Computer Vision and Pattern Recognition, pp. 1272–1279 (2013)
9. Tanskanen, P., Kolev, K., Meier, L., Camposeco, F., Saurer, O., Pollefeys, M.: Live metric 3D reconstruction on mobile phones. In: Proceedings of the IEEE International Conference on Computer Vision, pp. 65–72 (2013)
10. Ichim, A.E., Bouaziz, S., Pauly, M.: Dynamic 3D avatar creation from hand-held video input. ACM Trans. Graph. (TOG) **34**(4), 45 (2015)
11. Newcombe, R.A., Fox, D., Seitz, S.M.: Dynamicfusion: reconstruction and tracking of non-rigid scenes in real-time. In: Proceedings of the IEEE Conference on Computer Vision and Pattern Recognition, pp. 343–352 (2015)
12. Thies, J., Zollhoefer, M., Niessner, M., Valgaerts, L., Stamminger, M., Theobalt, C.: Real-time expression transfer for facial reenactment. ACM Trans. Graph. (Proc. SIGGRAPH Asia) **34**(6), 183 (2015)
13. Zollhöfer, M., Nießner, M., Izadi, S., Rehmann, C., Zach, C., Fisher, M., Wu, C., Fitzgibbon, A., Loop, C., Theobalt, C., et al.: Real-time non-rigid reconstruction using an RGB-D camera. ACM Trans. Graph. (TOG) **33**(4), 156 (2014)
14. Kemelmacher-Shlizerman, I., Basri, R.: 3D face reconstruction from a single image using a single reference face shape. IEEE Trans. Pattern Anal. Mach. Intell. **33**(2), 394–405 (2011)
15. Roth, J., Tong, Y., Liu, X.: Unconstrained 3D face reconstruction. In: Proceedings of the IEEE Conference on Computer Vision and Pattern Recognition, pp. 2606–2615 (2015)

16. Garrido, P., Valgaerts, L., Wu, C., Theobalt, C.: Reconstructing detailed dynamic face geometry from monocular video. ACM Trans. Graph. **32**(6), 158–1 (2013)
17. Shi, F., Wu, H.T., Tong, X., Chai, J.: Automatic acquisition of high-fidelity facial performances using monocular videos. ACM Trans. Graph. (TOG) **33**(6), 222 (2014)
18. Suwajanakorn, S., Seitz, S.M., Kemelmacher-Shlizerman, I.: What makes tom hanks look like tom hanks. In: Proceedings of the IEEE International Conference on Computer Vision, pp. 3952–3960 (2015)
19. Blanz, V., Vetter, T.: A morphable model for the synthesis of 3D faces. In: Proceedings of the 26th Annual Conference on Computer Graphics and Interactive Techniques, pp. 187–194. ACM Press/Addison-Wesley Publishing Co. (1999)
20. Hsieh, P.L., Ma, C., Yu, J., Li, H.: Unconstrained realtime facial performance capture. In: Proceedings of the IEEE Conference on Computer Vision and Pattern Recognition, pp. 1675–1683 (2015)
21. Shapiro, A., Feng, A., Wang, R., Li, H., Bolas, M., Medioni, G., Suma, E.: Rapid avatar capture and simulation using commodity depth sensors. Comput. Anim. Virtual Worlds **25**(3–4), 201–211 (2014)
22. Li, H., Yu, J., Ye, Y., Bregler, C.: Realtime facial animation with on-the-fly correctives. ACM Trans. Graph. **32**(4), 42–1 (2013)
23. Bustard, J.D., Nixon, M.S.: 3D morphable model construction for robust ear and face recognition. In: 2010 IEEE Conference on Computer Vision and Pattern Recognition (CVPR), pp. 2582–2589. IEEE (2010)
24. Luo, L., Li, H., Rusinkiewicz, S.: Structure-aware hair capture. ACM Trans. Graph. (TOG) **32**(4), 76 (2013)
25. Hu, L., Ma, C., Luo, L., Li, H.: Robust hair capture using simulated examples. ACM Trans. Graph. (TOG) **33**(4), 126 (2014)
26. Chai, M., Luo, L., Sunkavalli, K., Carr, N., Hadap, S., Zhou, K.: High-quality hair modeling from a single portrait photo. ACM Trans. Graph. (TOG) **34**(6), 204 (2015)
27. Chai, M., Wang, L., Weng, Y., Yu, Y., Guo, B., Zhou, K.: Single-view hair modeling for portrait manipulation. ACM Trans. Graph. (TOG) **31**(4), 116 (2012)
28. Kemelmacher-Shlizerman, I., Seitz, S.M.: Collection flow. In: 2012 IEEE Conference on Computer Vision and Pattern Recognition (CVPR), pp. 1792–1799. IEEE (2012)
29. Kemelmacher-Shlizerman, I., Shechtman, E., Garg, R., Seitz, S.M.: Exploring photobios. ACM Trans. Graph. (TOG) **30**, 61 (2011). ACM
30. Zheng, S., Jayasumana, S., Romera-Paredes, B., Vineet, V., Su, Z., Du, D., Huang, C., Torr, P.H.: Conditional random fields as recurrent neural networks. In: Proceedings of the IEEE International Conference on Computer Vision, pp. 1529–1537 (2015)
31. Basri, R., Jacobs, D., Kemelmacher, I.: Photometric stereo with general, unknown lighting. Int. J. Comput. Vis. **72**(3), 239–257 (2007)
32. Xiong, X., Torre, F.: Supervised descent method and its applications to face alignment. In: Proceedings of the IEEE Conference on Computer Vision and Pattern Recognition, pp. 532–539 (2013)
33. Cao, C., Weng, Y., Zhou, S., Tong, Y., Zhou, K.: Facewarehouse: a 3D facial expression database for visual computing. IEEE Trans. Vis. Comput. Graph. **20**(3), 413–425 (2014)
34. Kutulakos, K.N., Seitz, S.M.: A theory of shape by space carving. Int. J. Comput. Vis. **38**(3), 199–218 (2000)

35. Desbrun, M., Meyer, M., Schröder, P., Barr, A.H.: Implicit fairing of irregular meshes using diffusion and curvature flow. In: Proceedings of the 26th Annual Conference on Computer Graphics and Interactive Techniques, pp. 317–324. ACM Press/Addison-Wesley Publishing Co. (1999)
36. Wu, C.: VisualSFM: a visual structure from motion system (2011)

# Support Discrimination Dictionary Learning for Image Classification

Yang Liu[1]([envelope]), Wei Chen[1,2], Qingchao Chen[3], and Ian Wassell[1]

[1] Computer Laboratory, University of Cambridge, Cambridge, UK
{yl504,wc253,ijw24}@cam.ac.uk
[2] State Key Laboratory of Rail Traffic Control and Safety,
Beijing Jiaotong University, Beijing, China
[3] Department of Electronic and Electrical Engineering,
University College London, London, UK
qingchao.chen.13@ucl.ac.uk

**Abstract.** Dictionary learning has been successfully applied in image classification. However, many dictionary learning methods that encode only a single image at a time while training, ignore correlation and other useful information contained within the entire training set. In this paper, we propose a new principle that uses the support of the coefficients to measure the similarity between the pairs of coefficients, instead of using Euclidian distance directly. More specifically, we proposed a support discrimination dictionary learning method, which finds a dictionary under which the coefficients of images from the same class have a common sparse structure while the size of the overlapped signal support of different classes is minimised. In addition, adopting a shared dictionary in a multi-task learning setting, this method can find the number and position of associated dictionary atoms for each class automatically by using structured sparsity on a group of images. The proposed model is extensively evaluated using various image datasets, and it shows superior performance to many state-of-the-art dictionary learning methods.

## 1 Introduction

Sparse representation has been successfully applied to a variety of problems in image processing and computer vision, e.g., image denoising, image restoration and image classification. In the framework of sparse representation, an image can be represented as a linear combination of a few bases selected sparsely from an over-complete dictionary. The dictionaries can be predefined by the use of some off-the-shelf basis, such as the Discrete Fourier Transform (DFT) matrix and the wavelet matrix. However, it has been shown that learning the dictionary from the training data enables a more sparse representation of the image in comparison to using a predefined one, which can lead to improved performance in the reconstruction task. Some typical reconstruction dictionary learning methods include the Method of optimal direction (MOD) [1], and K-SVD [2].

Sparse representation has also been considered in pattern recognition applications. For example, it has been used in the Sparse representation classifier

© Springer International Publishing AG 2016
B. Leibe et al. (Eds.): ECCV 2016, Part II, LNCS 9906, pp. 375–390, 2016.
DOI: 10.1007/978-3-319-46475-6_24

(SRC) [3], which achieves competitive recognition performance in face recognition. In contrast to image reconstruction which only concerns the sparse representation of an image, in pattern recognition, the main goal is to find the correct label for the query sample, consequently the discriminative capability of the learned dictionary is crucial. A variety of discriminative dictionary learning methods have recently been proposed, that involve two different strategies.

One strategy is to learn a class-specific dictionary, which discriminates different classes of images via a sparse representation residual. Instead of learning a dictionary shared by all classes, it seeks to learn a sub-dictionary for each class. Yang et al. [4] first sought to learn a dictionary for each class, and applied it to image classification. In [5], instead of considering the dictionary atoms individually at the sparse coding stage, the atoms are selected in groups according to some priors to guarantee the block sparse structure of each coding coefficient. In [6], a group-structured dirty model is used to achieve a hierarchical structure of each coding coefficient via estimating a superposition of two coding coefficients and regularising them differently. It is worth noting that the multi-task setting is adopted in [6]. However, the sub-dictionaries in all these methods are disjoint to each other, and how many and which atoms belong to each class is fixed during the entire dictionary learning process. In addition, although class-specific setting of the dictionary works well when the number of training samples in each class is sufficient, it is not scalable to the problem with a large number of classes.

Another strategy is to learn a dictionary that is shared by all classes. Commonly, a classifier based on the coding vectors is learned together with the shared dictionary by imposing some class-specific constraints on the coding vector. Rodriguez et al. [7] proposed that samples of the same class should have similar sparse coding vectors which are achieved by using linear discriminant analysis. Yang et al. [8] proposed Fisher discrimination dictionary learning (FDDL) where the Fisher discrimination criterion is imposed on the coding vectors to enhance class discrimination. Cai et al. proposed support vector guided dictionary learning methods (SVGDL) [9], which is a generalised model of FDDL, that considers the squared distances between all pairs of coding vectors. In all these methods, the similarity between two coding vectors is measured by the Euclidean distance, which allows two images of different classes to be represented by using the same set of dictionary atoms. To our knowledge so far, no multi-task setting has been used in the shared dictionary, since it is difficult to discriminate groups of coefficients between different classes owing to the lack of prior knowledge concerning subdictionary structure.

In recent years, it has been shown that adding structural constraints to the supports of coding vectors can result in improved representation robustness and better signal interpretation [10–12]. In this paper, the multi-task setting adopts a shared dictionary, however, instead of learning the dictionary with discrimination based on the Euclidean distance between the coefficients for different classes, we consider a different principle: **The support of the coding vectors from one class should be similar, while the support of the coding vectors from different classes should be dissimilar.** Here the support of a coding vector denotes the indices of the non-zero elements of the image sparse representation under some dictionary.

More specifically, we propose a support discrimination dictionary learning method (SDDL), that finds a dictionary under which the coefficients of images from the same class have a common sparse structure while the size of the overlapped signal support of different classes is minimised. Informed by the multitask learning framework [13], and the multiple measurement vector (MMV) model [14] in the signal processing field, an effective way to encourage a group of signals to share the same support is to simultaneously encode those samples. Based on this idea, we encode multiple images from the same class, requiring that their coefficient matrix is largely 'row sparse', where only a few rows have non-zero elements. In addition to the similarity of intra-class coding vectors, the main contribution of our work is that we also design a new discriminative term to guarantee the dissimilarity of inter-class coding vectors by reducing the overlapped signal support from different classes. This can be achieved by minimisation of the $\ell_0$ norm of the Hadamard product between any pair of coefficients in different classes. An iterative reweighting scheme that produces more focal estimates is adopted as the optimization progresses.

The SDDL provides the following advantages. Firstly, the previous multitask setting based dictionary learning methods all use disjoint sub-dictionaries, in which how many and which atoms belong to each class is fixed during the entire dictionary learning process. In contrast, a multi-task setting using a shared dictionary is adopted in SDDL. Our approach can automatically identify overlapped sub-dictionaries for different classes, where the size of each sub-dictionary is adjusted appropriately during the learning process to suit the training dataset. Furthermore, our approach is scalable to allow for a large number of classes, while the previous sub-dictionary based approaches cannot. Secondly, instead of using the Euclidean distance to measure the similarity and dissimilarity between different coefficients, we achieve discrimination via the support. The structural sparse constraints eases the difficulty in solving the ill-posed inverse problem in comparison to the conventional element-sparse structure [15]. The superior performance of the proposed approach in comparison to the state-of-art is demonstrated using both face and object datasets.

The paper is organised as follows. In Sect. 2, we propose the novel support discrimination dictionary learning method for classification, including the optimisation algorithm and the classification scheme. In Sect. 3, extensive experiments are performed on both face and object datasets to compare the proposed method with other state-of-art dictionary learning methods. Conclusions are drawn in Sect. 4.

## 2    Support Discrimination Dictionary Learning

### 2.1    Problem Formulation

Assume that $x \in \mathbb{R}^m$ is a $m$ dimensional image with class label $c \in \{1, 2, ..., C\}$, where $C$ denotes the number of classes. The training set with $n$ images is denoted as $X = [x_1, x_2, ..., x_n] = [X_1, X_2, ..., X_C] \in \mathbb{R}^{m \times n}$, where $X_c$ includes $n_c$ training images of class $c$. The learned dictionary is denoted by $D = [d_1, d_2, ..., d_K] \in \mathbb{R}^{m \times K} (K < n)$, where $d_k$ denotes the $k^{th}$ atom of the dictionary. $A = [A_1, A_2, ..., A_C] = [a_1, a_2, ..., a_n] \in \mathbb{R}^{K \times n}$ are the coding coefficients of $X$ over $D$. Our dictionary learning problem can be described as

$$\min_{D, A} R(X, D, A) + w_1 g(A) + w_2 f(A), \tag{1}$$

where $R(X, D, A)$ denotes the reconstruction residuals for all the images $X$ with the sparse representation matrix $A$ under the dictionary $D$, $g(A)$ is a regulariser to promote intra-class similarity, $f(A)$ is the inter-class discriminative term based on the coding vectors $A$, and $w_1 > 0$ and $w_2 > 0$ denote the weights for the final two terms in (1). In this optimisation problem, we learn a single dictionary shared among all classes while exploring the discrimination of the coding vectors.

In a common multi-task learning setting, a group of tasks share certain aspects of some underlying distribution. Here we assume the intra-class coding vectors share a similar sparse structure. In our formulation, we use the joint sparsity regularisation $\ell_p/\ell_q$ norm of a coefficient matrix corresponding to one class, rather than encoding each training image separately. More specifically, we set $p = 2, q = 0$, which means that the intra-class coefficient matrix should be 'row sparse', i.e., where each row is either all zero or mostly non-zero, and the number of non-zero rows is low. In this way, we can find the shared nonzero supports for each class automatically, rather than predefining their number and position. However, minimizing the $\ell_2/\ell_0$ norm is NP hard, so in this paper, we use $\ell_2/\ell_1$ norm instead. In this way, we can design a regulariser to promote intra-class similarity as:

$$g(A) = \sum_{i=1}^{C} \|A_i\|_{2,1} = \sum_{i=1}^{C} \sum_{k=1}^{K} \left\| a^{(ik)} \right\|_2, \tag{2}$$

where $A_i$ represents the coefficient matrix for the $i^{th}$ class and $a^{(ik)}$ denotes the $k^{th}$ row of coefficient matrix $A_i$.

In general, discrimination for different classes can be assessed by the similarity of the intra-class coding vectors and the dissimilarity of inter-class ones. As mentioned previously, the similarity of intra-class coding vectors is promoted by the $\ell_2/\ell_1$ regulariser. To encourage dissimilarity of the inter-class coding vectors, we design the following discriminative term:

$$f(A) = \sum_{i=1}^{C} \sum_{p} \sum_{q} \left\| a_{i,p} \circ a_{/i,q} \right\|_0, \tag{3}$$

where $\circ$ denotes the Hadamard (elementwise) product between two vectors $a_{i,p}$ and $a_{/i,q}$, where $a_{i,p}$ and $a_{/i,q}$ are the $p^{th}$ column of $A_i$ and the $q^{th}$ column of $A_{/i}$ respectively. $A_i \in \mathbb{R}^{K \times n_i}$ represents the coefficient matrix for the $i^{th}$

class, while $A_{/i} \in \mathbb{R}^{K \times (n-n_i)}$ denotes a sub-matrix of $A \in \mathbb{R}^{K \times n}$ without the columns in $A_i$. Alternatively, the value of $\|a_{i,p} \circ a_{/i,q}\|_0$ is the size of the overlapped support between the $p^{th}$ image of the $i^{th}$ class and the $q^{th}$ image that is not in class $i$. Therefore, $f(A)$ denotes the summation of overlapped supports between images in different classes. However, minimising $f(A)$ in Eq. (3) is an NP hard problem. Enlightened by many recent sparse approximation algorithms that rely on iterative reweighting schemes [16–18] to produce more focal estimates as optimization progresses, we use the iterative reweighted $\ell_2$ minimization to approximate the $\ell_0$ norm.

We use the vector $a^{\odot 2}$ to represent the element by element square of vector $a$, which equals to $a \circ a$. We define the weight term $w_{p,q}$ for a given pair of coefficient $(a_{i,p}, a_{/i,q})$ at each iteration as a function of those coefficients from the previous iteration as

$$w_{i,p,q} = \frac{1}{(a'_{i,p} \circ a'_{/i,q})^{\odot 2} + \epsilon} \tag{4}$$

where $a'_{i,p}$ and $a'_{/i,q}$ are the coefficients from the previous iteration and $\epsilon$ is a regularization factor that is reduced to zero as the number of iterations increases. In this case, the descrimination term $f(A)$ can be rewritten as

$$f(A) = \sum_{i=1}^{C} \sum_{p} \sum_{q} \|a_{i,p} \circ a_{/i,q}\|_0 = \sum_{i=1}^{C} \sum_{p} \sum_{q} \sum_{k} w_{i,p,q}^{(k)} \cdot (a_{i,p}^{(k)} \circ a_{/i,q}^{(k)})^2$$

$$= \sum_{i=1}^{C} \sum_{p} \sum_{q} \sum_{k} [w_{i,p,q}^{(k)} \cdot (a_{/i,q}^{(k)})^2] \circ (a_{i,p}^{(k)})^2$$

$$= \sum_{i=1}^{C} \sum_{p} \sum_{q} diag([w_{i,p,q} \circ (a_{/i,q})^{\odot 2}] \cdot (a_{i,p})^{\odot 2} = \sum_{i=1}^{C} \sum_{p} \|\Omega_{i,p} a_{i,p}\|_F^2 , \tag{5}$$

where $k$ represents the index of the corresponding vector and

$$\Omega_{i,p} = diag(\sqrt{\sum_{q} (\sqrt{w_{i,p,q}} \circ a_{/i,q})^{\odot 2}}). \tag{6}$$

However, minimising the above $f(A)$ is both time and memory consuming since we need to calculate a weight vector $w_{i,p,q}$ and thus a distinct weight matrix $\Omega_{i,p}$ for each $a_{i,p}$. Considering the effect of the $\ell_2/\ell_1$ regulariser, different coefficients in the same class should have a similar sparse pattern, hence we use the average $(\tilde{a}'_i)^{\odot 2}$ instead of $(a'_{i,p})^{\odot 2}$ in Eq. (4), where

$$\forall p, \quad (a'_{i,p})^{\odot 2} \approx (\tilde{a}'_i)^{\odot 2} = \sum_{p} (a'_{i,p})^{\odot 2} / n_i. \tag{7}$$

That is, all $p$ images of the class $i$ share the same weight vector $\boldsymbol{w}_{\tilde{i},q}$ as

$$\boldsymbol{w}_{\tilde{i},q} = \frac{1}{(\tilde{\boldsymbol{a}_i'})^{\odot 2} \circ (\boldsymbol{a}_{/i,q}')^{\odot 2} + \epsilon}. \tag{8}$$

Finally Eq. (5) can be rewritten as:

$$f(\boldsymbol{A}) = \sum_{i=1}^{C} \sum_{p} \left\| \boldsymbol{\Omega}_{i,p} \boldsymbol{a}_{i,p} \right\|_F^2 = \sum_{i=1}^{C} \left\| \tilde{\boldsymbol{\Omega}}_i \boldsymbol{A}_i \right\|_F^2, \tag{9}$$

where

$$\tilde{\boldsymbol{\Omega}}_i = diag\left( \sqrt{\sum_q (\sqrt{\boldsymbol{w}_{\tilde{i},q}} \circ \boldsymbol{a}_{/i,q})^2} \right). \tag{10}$$

By substituting the discrimination term given by Eq. (9) into (1), we can rewrite the dictionary learning problem as

$$\min_{\boldsymbol{D},\boldsymbol{A}} \sum_{i=1}^{C} \left\| \boldsymbol{X}_i - \boldsymbol{D}\boldsymbol{A}_i \right\|_F^2 + w_1 \left\| \boldsymbol{A}_i \right\|_{2,1} + w_2 \left\| \tilde{\boldsymbol{\Omega}}_i \boldsymbol{A}_i \right\|_F^2. \tag{11}$$

Although the objective function in (11) is not jointly convex to $(\boldsymbol{D}, \boldsymbol{A})$, it is convex with respect to $\boldsymbol{D}$ and $\boldsymbol{A}$ when the other is fixed. In the sequel, we provide an algorithm which alternately optimises $\boldsymbol{D}$ and $\boldsymbol{A}$.

## 2.2  Optimisation

Finding the solution of the optimisation problem in (11) involves two subproblems, i.e., to update the coding coefficients $\boldsymbol{A}$ with fixed $\boldsymbol{D}$, and to update $\boldsymbol{D}$ with fixed coefficients $\boldsymbol{A}$.

First suppose that $\boldsymbol{D}$ is fixed, and the optimisation problem can be reduced to a sparse coding problem to calculate $\boldsymbol{A} = [\boldsymbol{A}_1, \boldsymbol{A}_2, .., \boldsymbol{A}_C]$ with two constraints. Here, we compute the coefficients matrix $\boldsymbol{A}_i$ class by class. More specifically, all $\boldsymbol{A}_j (j \neq i)$ are fixed thus $\tilde{\boldsymbol{\Omega}}_i$ is fixed when computing the $\boldsymbol{A}_i$. In this way, the objective function can be further reduced to

$$\min_{\boldsymbol{A}_i} \left\| \boldsymbol{X}_i - \boldsymbol{D}\boldsymbol{A}_i \right\|_F^2 + w_1 \left\| \boldsymbol{A}_i \right\|_{2,1} + w_2 \left\| \tilde{\boldsymbol{\Omega}}_i \boldsymbol{A}_i \right\|_F^2. \tag{12}$$

We choose the alternating direction method of multipliers (ADMM) as the optimisation approach because of its simplicity, efficiency and robustness [15, 19, 20]. By introducing one auxiliary variable $\boldsymbol{Z}_i = \boldsymbol{A}_i \in \mathbb{R}^{K \times n_c}$, this problem can be reformulated as

$$\min_{\boldsymbol{A}_i, \boldsymbol{Z}_i} \left\| \boldsymbol{X}_i - \boldsymbol{D}\boldsymbol{A}_i \right\|_F^2 + w_1 \left\| \boldsymbol{Z}_i \right\|_{2,1} + w_2 \left\| \tilde{\boldsymbol{\Omega}}_i \boldsymbol{A}_i \right\|_F^2 \quad s.t.\ \boldsymbol{A}_i - \boldsymbol{Z}_i = 0. \tag{13}$$

Therefore, the augmented Lagrangian function with respect to $A_i, Z_i$ can be formed as

$$L_u(A_i, Z_i) = \|X_i - DA_i\|_F^2 + w_1 \|Z_i\|_{2,1} + w_2 \left\|\tilde{\Omega}_i A_i\right\|_F^2$$
$$- \Lambda_1^T(Z_i - A_i) + \frac{u_1}{2} \|Z_i - A_i\|_2^2, \tag{14}$$

where $\Lambda_1 \in \mathbb{R}^{K \times m}$ are the Lagrangian multipliers for equality constraints and $u_1 > 0$ is a penalty parameter. The Augmented Lagrangian function can be minimised over $A_i, Z_i$ by fixing one variable at a time and updating the other one. The entire procedure is summarised in Algorithm 1. The *Shrink* function in Eq. (17) updates $Z_i$ by using row-wise shrinkage, which can be represented as

$$z^r = max\{\|q^r\|_2 - \frac{w_1}{u_1}, 0\}\frac{q^r}{\|q^r\|_2}, r = 1, ...., K, \tag{15}$$

where $q^r = a^r + \frac{\lambda_1^r}{u_1}$ and $z^r, a^r, \lambda_1^r$ represent the $r^{th}$ row of matrix $Z_i, A_i, \Lambda_i$ respectively.

Since the above ADMM scheme computes the exact solution for each subproblem, its convergence is guaranteed by the existing ADM theory [21,22]. After we obtain the sparse coding, we secondly update dictionary $D$ column by column with fixed $A$. When updating $d_i$, all the other columns $d_j, j \neq i$ are fixed. Now the objective function in Eq. (13) is reduced to

$$\min_D \|X - DA\|_F^2, \; s.t. \|d_i\|_2 = 1. \tag{20}$$

In general, we require that each column of the dictionary $d_i$ is a unit vector. Equation (20) is a quadratic programming problem and it can be solved by using the K-SVD algorithm, which updates $d_i$ atom by atom. In practice, the exact solution by K-SVD can be computationally demanding, especially when the number of training images is large. As an alternative, in the following experiments, we use the approximate KSVD to reduce the complexity of this task [23]. The detailed derivation can be found in Algorithm 5 in [24].

## 2.3   The Classification Scheme

After obtaining the learned dictionary $D$, a test sample $y$ can be classified based on its sparse coefficients over $D$. We choose a linear classifier both for its simplicity and for the purpose of fair comparison with other dictionary learning methods, although we note that better classifier design (e.g. SRC) can potentially improve the performance further. We design the linear classifier $W \in \mathbb{R}^{C \times K}$ as [6,25]:

$$W^T = (AA^T + \eta I)^{-1} AL^T, \tag{21}$$

---

**Algorithm 1.** Sparse coding using ADMM

---

**Input**: Training Data $\boldsymbol{X} \in \mathbb{R}^{m \times n}$, learned dictionary $\boldsymbol{D} \in \mathbb{R}^{m \times K}$, Number of classes $C$, regularisation parameters $w_1, w_2$, penalty parameter $u_1$ and step length $\gamma_1$.
Initialising $\boldsymbol{A}^0 = 0, \boldsymbol{\Lambda}_1^0 = 0$, Iteration number $k = 0$ ;
**for** $i = 1 : C$ **do**

    **while** *until converge* **do**

        Set the matrix $\tilde{\boldsymbol{\Omega}}_i^k$:

$$\tilde{\boldsymbol{\Omega}}_i^k = diag\left(\sqrt{\sum_q (\sqrt{w_{i,q}^k} \circ a_{i,q}^k)^2}\right) \tag{16}$$

        Fix $\boldsymbol{A}_i$ and update $\boldsymbol{Z}_i$ by row-wise shrinkage

$$\boldsymbol{Z}_i^{k+1} = Shrink(\boldsymbol{A}_i^k + \frac{1}{u_1}\boldsymbol{\Lambda}_1^k, \frac{1}{u_1}w_1) \tag{17}$$

        Fix $\boldsymbol{Z}_i$ and update $\boldsymbol{A}_i$ by:

$$\boldsymbol{A}_i^{k+1} = arg \min_{\boldsymbol{A}_i} L_u(\boldsymbol{A}_i, \boldsymbol{Z}_i^{k+1})$$
$$= (\boldsymbol{D}^T\boldsymbol{D} + w_2\tilde{\boldsymbol{\Omega}}_i^{k}{}^T\boldsymbol{T}\tilde{\boldsymbol{\Omega}}_i^{k} + u_1\boldsymbol{I})^{-1}(\boldsymbol{D}^T\boldsymbol{X} + u_1\boldsymbol{Z}_i^{k+1} - \frac{1}{2}\boldsymbol{\Lambda}_1^k) \tag{18}$$

        Update Lagrange multipliers $\boldsymbol{\Lambda}_1$:

$$\boldsymbol{\Lambda}_1^{k+1} = \boldsymbol{\Lambda}_1^k - \gamma_1 u_1(\boldsymbol{Z}_i^{k+1} - \boldsymbol{A}_i^{k+1}) \tag{19}$$

    Increment $k$.

**Output**: Estimated sparse code $\boldsymbol{A}$

---

where $\boldsymbol{A} \in \mathbb{R}^{K \times n}$ is the final rounded coefficients of the training set. The matrix $\boldsymbol{L} \in \mathbb{R}^{C \times n}$ contains the label information of the training set. If the training data $\boldsymbol{x}_i$ belongs to the class $c$, the element $L_{c,i}$ in vector $\boldsymbol{l}_i$ is one and all the other elements in the same columns are zero. The parameter $\eta$ controls the tradeoff between the classification accuracy and the smoothness of the classifier.

Next, we can compute the sparse coefficients of the each test sample $y$ using the following objective function:

$$\min_a \|\boldsymbol{y} - \boldsymbol{D}\boldsymbol{a}\|_F^2 + w_3 \|\boldsymbol{a}\|_1, \tag{22}$$

where $w_3$ is a constant. Finally we apply the linear classifier $\boldsymbol{W}$ to the sparse coding of a test sample to get the label vector $\boldsymbol{l_y}$ and assigned it to the class $c = arg \max_c \boldsymbol{l_y}$. The overall procedure is summarised in Algorithm 2.

---

**Algorithm 2.** Overall Framework

---

**Input**: Training Data $X$, learned dictionary $D$, Number of classes $C$, test
        sample $y$ and regularisation parameters $w_1, w_2, w_3$.
Initialising $k = 0$ ;
**while** *until converge* **do**
     Fix $D^k$ and update $A^{k+1}$ by Algorithm 1;
     Fix $A^{k+1}$ and update $D^{k+1}$ by approximate K-SVD in [24];
     Increment k.
Use $A^{k+1}$ of $X$ to train a linear classifier $W$
Calculate the sparse coefficient $a_{test}$ for $y$ by Eq. (22)
Classify the test sample $y$ by $c = arg\max_c W a_{test}$.
**Output**: Classification result

---

# 3 Experimental Validation

In this section, we compare our proposed Support discrimination dictionary
learning (SDDL) method with some other existing Dictionary learning (DL)
based classification approaches. We verify the classification performance on various datasets, such as face recognition and object classification. The classification
performance is measured by the percentage of correctly classified test data. The
public datasets used are the Extended-Yale B Face Dataset [26], the AR Face
Dataset [27] and the Caltech 101 object dataset [28]. The benchmark algorithms
for comparison are the Sparse Representation Classification (SRC) [3], K-SVD
[2], Label-Consistent K-SVD (LC-KSVD) [25], Fisher Discrimination Dictionary
Learning (FDDL) [8], Support Vector Guided Dictionary Learning (SVGDL) [9]
and Group-structured Dirty Dictionary Learning method (GDDL) [6]. For all
the competing methods, we tune their parameters for the best performance.

## 3.1 Parameter Selection

**Dictionary Size:** In all experiments, the initialised dictionary is randomly
selected from the training data. As shown in [8,25], the larger the size of the
dictionary, the better is the performance it can achieve. The disadvantage of a
large dictionary is that the problem size becomes large, which is computationally demanding. Therefore, the ideal dictionary learning method should achieve
an acceptable level of performance using a relatively small size of dictionary.
Here we use the Caltech 101 object dataset as an example. For each class, we
randomly choose 30 images for training and the rest for testing. The number of
dictionary atoms per class varies from 10 to 30. As shown in Fig. 1, all the DL
methods tested improve performance when the dictionary size becomes larger.
Also, our proposed SDDL method achieves high classification accuracy and consistently outperforms all the other DL-based methods. The basic reason for good
recognition performance, even with only a small size dictionary, is that SDDL
learns a shared dictionary for all classes, while it can automatically identify

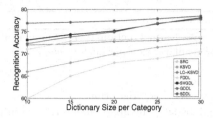

**Fig. 1.** Effect of dictionary size on the classification performance of various DL methods. For the Caltech 101 dataset, the size of training samples per class is fixed to 30. The dictionary atoms per class is varied from 10 to 30. As can be seen, our proposed method outperforms the other DL-based methods.

sub-dictionaries for different classes, where the size of each sub-dictionary is adjusted appropriately during the learning process.

**Regularisation Parameters:** There are 3 regularisation parameters $w_1, w_2, w_3$ that need to be tuned, two in the dictionary learning stage and one in the classifier. In this paper, we employ cross validation to find the regularisation parameters that give the best result.

**Stopping Criterion:** The proposed algorithm will stop either if the values of the objective function in Eq. (11) in adjacent iterations are sufficiently close in value, or if the maximum number of iterations is reached. In Fig. 2 we show empirically the value of the objective function as the number of iterations increases using the AR dataset, where we can see that the SDDL method converges rapidly.

### 3.2    Factors Affecting Performance

We will now investigate how the performance is affected by different factors in the proposed method using the face datasets, i.e., the Extended Yale B dataset and the AR dataset. We will discuss two factors as follows:

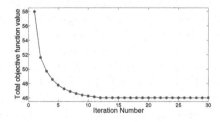

**Fig. 2.** The convergence curve of objective function on the AR database.

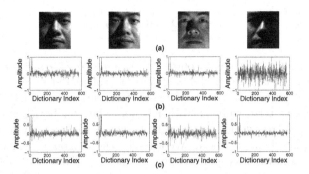

**Fig. 3.** An example for 4 test images and their corresponding coefficients. (a) Shows 4 training samples of the $2^{nd}$ subject in Extended Yale B database; (b) and (c) show the four coefficients corresponding with two dictionaries, where one is learned with $\ell_1$ regularisation while the other with $\ell_2/\ell_1$ regularisation respectively.

**Factor 1: Function of the $\ell_2/\ell_1$ Regularisation Term.** As mentioned in Sect. 2.1, the $\ell_2/\ell_1$ regularisation term is adopted to make the coefficients from the same class share a similar sparse structure. In this section, we provide a visual illustration to see if the $\ell_2/\ell_1$ regularisation term can be truly helpful in the representation of the images from the same class. We compare the sparse codings of the same test samples from two dictionaries, where one is learned with $\ell_1$ regularisation while the other with $\ell_2/\ell_1$ regularisation. Figure 3(a) shows 4 test samples of the $2^{nd}$ subject in the Extended Yale B database; Figs. 3(b) and (c) show the four coefficients corresponding with the two dictionaries respectively. Looking at the coefficients in Fig. 3(b), in which the dictionary is learned with $\ell_1$ regularisation, it can be seen that the coding vectors corresponding to the fourth image are significantly different to the other three coding vectors of the same class, which is not discriminative, owing to the poor quality of the image. However, in the Fig. 3(c), the coding vector of the fourth image now look more similar to the other coding vectors in the class, which has a high probability of being classified correctly. A benefit of such a multi-task learning framework is that 'good quality' images help constrain the coding vector of 'poor quality' ones in the training stage. In this way, even the 'poor quality' images contribute appropriately to the dictionary update.

**Factor 2: Function of the Discriminative Term $f(A)$.** As described in Sect. 2.1, the term $f(A)$ is utilised in the objective function to guarantee the discrimination of coding vectors from different classes. In this section, we illustrate both visually and numerically the influence of the discriminative term $f(A)$ with an example from the AR database, as shown in Figs. 4 and 5.

To clearly show the discrimination of coding vectors between subjects in the AR database (100 subjects in total), we calculate a symmetric scatter matrix $S \in \mathbb{R}^{100 \times 100}$, in which each element $S_{ij}$ represent the similarity between sparse codings $A_i$, $A_j$ of $i^{th}$ and $j^{th}$ subject $(i,j \in [1,100])$:

$$S_{ij} = \sum_p \sum_q \|a_{i,p} \circ a_{j,q}\|_1, \tag{23}$$

where $a_{i,p}$ and $a_{j,q}$ are the $p^{th}$ column of $A_i$ and the $q^{th}$ column of $A_j$ respectively. Following this, two scatter matrices are calculated based on the sparse codings of the same test samples from two dictionaries, where one is learned using the discriminative term while the other is not. Then for both scatter matrices, we normalise the largest element of each column or row to unity to permit comparison and plot them in Fig. 4. Accordingly, the diagonal elements represent the similarity of intra-class sparse codings while the off-diagonal elements shows the similarity of the between-subject ones. We see that, the diagonal elements of both figures are the largest, and that there is obviously more between-subject similarity in Fig. 4(a) than in 4(b). By summing the elements in the columns of the scatter matrix to quantify the similarity index for each subject, we then plot them in Fig. 5. The lower the similarity index, the less overlap there is between the pairs of coefficients between this subject and the others, i.e., the better is the discrimination of the coding coefficient. As shown in Fig. 5, the red curve learned using the discrimination term is lower than the blue one learned without the discrimination term for all the 100 subjects, which shows that learning the dictionary with the help with $f(A)$ can decrease the coefficient overlap between different subjects. These visual and numerical results both show that the dictionary learned with the $f(A)$ term can significantly enhance the discrimination performance of the coefficients. We use the Extended Yale and AR face databases to illustrate how this term can help to improve classification performance. With the help with the discrimination term $f(A)$, the recognition rate for the Extended Yale B is enhanced from 96.20 % to 98.50 %, and the recognition rate for the AR database is increased from 95.90 % to 98.00 %. The experimental setting used to obtain these result will be presented fully in Sect. 3.4.

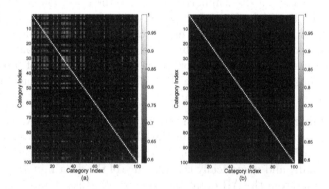

**Fig. 4.** Comparison between the scatter matrices calculated based on the sparse coding of the same test samples from two different dictionaries. In (a), the dictionary is learned without the discrimination term, and in (b), the dictionary is learned using the discrimination term.

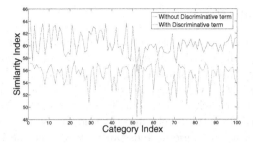

**Fig. 5.** The comparison between the similarity index calculated based on the sparse coding of the same test samples from two different dictionaries. The red line represents the similarity index calculated by the dictionary learned using the discrimination term, while the blue line represents the similarity index without. (Color figure online)

### 3.3 Object Classification

The Caltech 101 dataset is one of the benchmark datasets used in object classification. It consists of 9144 images, split between 101 distinct object classes including animals, vehicles, as well as a background class. The sample from each class has significant shape variability. In the following experiments, the spatial pyramid features are used as the input for the classifier, which is the same as used in [8,9,25]. Following [25], We vary the number of training samples per class from 10 to 30. The size of the dictionary in SDDL is $K = 510$, that is the same as the experimental setting in [9]. The experiments are carried out 10 times with differently chosen partitions. The average classification accuracy of the proposed method (SDDL) compared with other existing dictionary learning based methods is shown in Table 1. The regularisation parameters for the Caltech 101 dataset are $w_1 = 0.2, w_2 = 10, w_3 = 0.05$. The DL-based methods perform better than SRC, which shows that better performance can be achieved by learning a discriminative dictionary. Our proposed method consistently outperforms the other existing DL based methods, by at least 2.8 % points.

**Table 1.** Recognition rates (%) for object classification

| No. training | SRC | KSVD | LC-KSVD | FDDL | SVGDL | GDDL | SDDL |
|---|---|---|---|---|---|---|---|
| 10 | 58.89 | 59.80 | 62.40 | 63.10 | 63.10 | 62.30 | **66.80** |
| 15 | 63.80 | 64.20 | 66.90 | 66.60 | 68.80 | 66.20 | **71.60** |
| 20 | 67.20 | 68.70 | 69.50 | 69.80 | 70.00 | 69.80 | **73.60** |
| 25 | 68.60 | 70.20 | 71.80 | 72.30 | 73.50 | 72.30 | **76.50** |
| 30 | 70.30 | 73.40 | 73.30 | 73.10 | 74.10 | 73.40 | **76.90** |

### 3.4  Face Classification

The two benchmark face datasets are the Extended Yale B dataset and the AR dataset. With different illumination conditions and facial expressions, the Extended Yale B dataset consists of 2414 frontal images of 38 subjects (about 64 images per subject). We randomly select half as the training set and the rest as the test set for each class. As in the experimental setting in [6,25], we crop each image to $192 \times 168$ pixels, and then normalise and project it to a 504 dimension vector using a random Gaussian matrix. The dictionary size of the Extended Yale B dataset is 570, which corresponds to an average of 15 atoms per subject. As discussed previously, there is no explicit correspondence between the dictionary atoms and the labels of the individual at the training stage.

Similarly, the AR face dataset consists of over 4000 images of 126 subjects, which is more challenging owing to more variation, i.e., different illumination, expressions and facial occlusion (e.g., sunglasses, scarf). As in the experimental setting in [6,25], we use the subset of the dataset which contains 2600 images for 50 male and 50 female subjects. For each subject, we randomly select 20 and 6 images for training and testing respectively. We crop each image to $165 \times 120$ pixels, and then normalise and project it to a 540 dimension vector using a Gaussian matrix. The dictionary size of the AR dataset is 500, that corresponds to an average of 5 atoms per subject. The dictionary is shared by all subjects.

The experiments are carried out 10 times with different chosen partitions. The average classification accuracy of the proposed method compared with other existing dictionary learning based methods are shown in the Table 2. The regularisation parameters for the Extended Yale B dataset are $w_1 = 0.04, w_2 = 2, w_3 = 0.005$, and for the AR face database are $w_1 = 0.05, w_2 = 3, w_3 = 0.005$. We can see that the proposed SDDL method achieves an improvement of at least 1.7 and 2 % points over the next best scheme in terms of classification accuracy for the Extended Yale B and the AR datasets respectively.

**Table 2.** Recognition rates (%) for face classification

| Method | SRC | KSVD | LC-KSVD | FDDL | SVGDL | GDDL | SDDL |
|---|---|---|---|---|---|---|---|
| Extended Yale | 80.54 | 93.40 | 94.50 | 94.92 | 95.70 | 96.80 | **98.50** |
| AR | 66.57 | 86.30 | 93.70 | 94.10 | 96.00 | 96.00 | **98.00** |

## 4  Conclusion

We incorporate structured sparsity into the dictionary learning process and propose a support discrimination dictionary learning (SDDL) method for image classification. In contrast to other methods, we use the sparse structure, i.e., support, to measure the similarity between the pairs of coefficients, rather than the Euclidean distance which is widely adopted in many dictionary learning approaches for classification. The discrimination capability of the proposed method is enhanced in two ways. First, a row sparse regulariser is adopted so that a shared support structure for each class can be learned automatically. Second, we adopt a discriminative term to make the coefficients from different classes have minimum support overlap between each other. It can be achieved by minimisation of the $\ell_0$ norm of the Hadamard product between any pair of coefficients in different classes. It worth noting that our approach can automatically identify overlapped sub-dictionaries for different classes, where the size of each sub-dictionary is adjusted appropriately during the learning process to suit the training dataset. In this way, this proposed approach is scalable to classification tasks having a large number of classes. Extensive experimental results on object recognition and face recognition demonstrate the proposed method can generate more discriminative sparse coefficients and that it has superior classification performance to a number of state-of-the-art dictionary learning based methods.

**Acknowledgements.** This work is supported by University of Cambridge Overseas Trust, EPSRC Research Grant (EP/K033700/1) and Natural Science Foundation of China (61401018).

# References

1. Engan, K., Aase, S.O., Husøy, J.H.: Multi-frame compression: theory and design. Signal Process. **80**(10), 2121–2140 (2000)
2. Aharon, M., Elad, M., Bruckstein, A.: K-SVD: an algorithm for designing over complete dictionaries for sparse representation. IEEE Trans. Signal Process. **54**(11), 4311–4322 (2006)
3. Wright, J., Yang, A.Y., Ganesh, A., Sastry, S.S., Ma, Y.: Robust face recognition via sparse representation. IEEE Trans. Pattern Anal. Mach. Intell. **31**(2), 210–227 (2009)
4. Yang, J., Yu, K., Huang, T.: Supervised translation-invariant sparse coding. In: IEEE Conference on Computer Vision and Pattern Recognition (CVPR), pp. 3517–3524 (2010)
5. Elhamifar, E., Vidal, R.: Robust classification using structured sparse representation. In: IEEE Conference on Computer Vision and Pattern Recognition (CVPR), pp. 1873–1879 (2011)
6. Suo, Y., Dao, M., Tran, T., Mousavi, H., Srinivas, U., Monga, V.: Group structured dirty dictionary learning for classification. In: IEEE Transactions on Image Processing (ICIP), pp. 150–154 (2014)
7. Rodriguez, F., Sapiro, G.: Sparse representations for image classification: learning discriminative and reconstructive non-parametric dictionaries. Technical report, DTIC Document (2008)
8. Yang, M., Zhang, L., Feng, X., Zhang, D.: Sparse representation based Fisher discrimination dictionary learning for image classification. Int. J. Comput. Vis. **109**(3), 209–232 (2014)
9. Cai, S., Zuo, W., Zhang, L., Feng, X., Wang, P.: Support vector guided dictionary learning. In: Fleet, D., Pajdla, T., Schiele, B., Tuytelaars, T. (eds.) ECCV 2014, Part IV. LNCS, vol. 8692, pp. 624–639. Springer, Heidelberg (2014)

10. Yuan, M., Lin, Y.: Model selection and estimation in regression with grouped variables. J. R. Stat. Soc. Ser. B (Stat. Methodol.) **68**(1), 49–67 (2006)
11. Jenatton, R., Audibert, J.Y., Bach, F.: Structured variable selection with sparsity-inducing norms. J. Mach. Learn. Res. **12**, 2777–2824 (2011)
12. Eldar, Y.C., Mishali, M.: Robust recovery of signals from a structured union of subspaces. IEEE Trans. Inf. Theory **55**(11), 5302–5316 (2009)
13. Lounici, K., Pontil, M., Tsybakov, A.B., Van De Geer, S.: Taking advantage of sparsity in multi-task learning (2009). arXiv preprint: arXiv:0903.1468
14. Cotter, S.F., Rao, B.D., Engan, K., Kreutz-Delgado, K.: Sparse solutions to linear inverse problems with multiple measurement vectors. IEEE Trans. Signal Process. **53**(7), 2477–2488 (2005)
15. Deng, W., Yin, W., Zhang, Y.: Group sparse optimization by alternating direction method. In: SPIE Optical Engineering + Applications, pp. 88580R–88580R-15. International Society for Optics and Photonics (2013)
16. Chartrand, R., Yin, W.: Iteratively reweighted algorithms for compressive sensing. In: IEEE International Conference on Acoustics, Speech and Signal Processing, pp. 3869–3872 (2008)
17. Candes, E.J., Wakin, M.B., Boyd, S.P.: Enhancing sparsity by reweighted $\ell_1$ minimization. J. Fourier Anal. Appl. **14**(5–6), 877–905 (2008)
18. Wipf, D., Nagarajan, S.: Iterative reweighted and methods for finding sparse solutions. IEEE J. Sel. Top. Signal Process. **4**(2), 317–329 (2010)
19. Boyd, S., Parikh, N., Chu, E., Peleato, B., Eckstein, J.: Distributed optimization and statistical learning via the alternating direction method of multipliers. Found. Trends Mach. Learn. **3**(1), 1–122 (2011)
20. Yang, J., Zhang, Y.: Alternating direction algorithms for $\ell_1$-problems in compressive sensing. SIAM J. Sci. Comput. **33**(1), 250–278 (2011)
21. Glowinski, R., Le Tallec, P.: Augmented Lagrangian and Operator-Splitting Methods in Nonlinear Mechanics, vol. 9. SIAM, Philadelphia (1989)
22. Glowinski, R., Oden, J.: Numerical methods for nonlinear variational problems. J. Appl. Mech. **52**, 739 (1985)
23. Aharon, M., Elad, M.: Sparse and redundant modeling of image content using an image-signature-dictionary. SIAM J. Imaging Sci. **1**(3), 228–247 (2008)
24. Rubinstein, R., Zibulevsky, M., Elad, M.: Efficient implementation of the K-SVD algorithm using batch orthogonal matching pursuit. CS Tech. **40**(8), 1–15 (2008)
25. Jiang, Z., Lin, Z., Davis, L.S.: Label consistent K-SVD: learning a discriminative dictionary for recognition. IEEE Trans. Pattern Anal. Mach. Intell. **35**(11), 2651–2664 (2013)
26. Georghiades, A.S., Belhumeur, P.N., Kriegman, D.J.: From few to many: illumination cone models for face recognition under variable lighting and pose. IEEE Trans. Pattern Anal. Mach. Intell. **23**(6), 643–660 (2001)
27. Martinez, A.M.: The AR face database. CVC Technical report 24 (1998)
28. Fei-Fei, L., Fergus, R., Perona, P.: Learning generative visual models from few training examples: an incremental Bayesian approach tested on 101 object categories. Comput. Vis. Image Underst. **106**(1), 59–70 (2007)

# Accelerating the Super-Resolution Convolutional Neural Network

Chao Dong, Chen Change Loy$^{(\boxtimes)}$, and Xiaoou Tang

Department of Information Engineering, The Chinese University of Hong Kong,
Hong Kong, China
{dc012,ccloy,xtang}@ie.cuhk.edu.hk

**Abstract.** As a successful deep model applied in image super-resolution (SR), the Super-Resolution Convolutional Neural Network (SRCNN) [1,2] has demonstrated superior performance to the previous hand-crafted models either in speed and restoration quality. However, the high computational cost still hinders it from practical usage that demands real-time performance (24 fps). In this paper, we aim at accelerating the current SRCNN, and propose a compact hourglass-shape CNN structure for faster and better SR. We re-design the SRCNN structure mainly in three aspects. First, we introduce a deconvolution layer at the end of the network, then the mapping is learned directly from the original low-resolution image (without interpolation) to the high-resolution one. Second, we reformulate the mapping layer by shrinking the input feature dimension before mapping and expanding back afterwards. Third, we adopt smaller filter sizes but more mapping layers. The proposed model achieves a speed up of more than 40 times with even superior restoration quality. Further, we present the parameter settings that can achieve real-time performance on a generic CPU while still maintaining good performance. A corresponding transfer strategy is also proposed for fast training and testing across different upscaling factors.

## 1 Introduction

Single image super-resolution (SR) aims at recovering a high-resolution (HR) image from a given low-resolution (LR) one. Recent SR algorithms are mostly learning-based (or patch-based) methods [1–8] that learn a mapping between the LR and HR image spaces. Among them, the Super-Resolution Convolutional Neural Network (SRCNN) [1,2] has drawn considerable attention due to its simple network structure and excellent restoration quality. Though SRCNN is already faster than most previous learning-based methods, the processing speed on large images is still unsatisfactory. For example, to upsample an $240 \times 240$ image by a factor of 3, the speed of the original SRCNN [1] is about 1.32 fps, which is far from real-time (24 fps). To approach real-time, we should accelerate SRCNN for at least 17 times while keeping the previous performance. This

**Electronic supplementary material** The online version of this chapter (doi:10.1007/978-3-319-46475-6_25) contains supplementary material, which is available to authorized users.

© Springer International Publishing AG 2016
B. Leibe et al. (Eds.): ECCV 2016, Part II, LNCS 9906, pp. 391–407, 2016.
DOI: 10.1007/978-3-319-46475-6_25

sounds implausible at the first glance, as accelerating by simply reducing the parameters will severely impact the performance. However, when we delve into the network structure, we find *two inherent limitations* that restrict its running speed.

First, as a pre-processing step, the original LR image needs to be upsampled to the desired size using bicubic interpolation to form the input. Thus the computation complexity of SRCNN grows quadratically with the spatial size of the HR image (not the original LR image). For the upscaling factor $n$, the computational cost of convolution with the interpolated LR image will be $n^2$ times of that for the original LR one. This is also the restriction for most learning-based SR methods [3–5,7,8,10]. If the network was learned directly from the original LR image, the acceleration would be significant, *i.e.*, about $n^2$ times faster.

The second restriction lies on the costly non-linear mapping step. In SRCNN, input image patches are projected on a high-dimensional LR feature space, then followed by a complex mapping to another high-dimensional HR feature space. Dong *et al.* [2] show that the mapping accuracy can be substantially improved by adopting a wider mapping layer, but at the cost of the running time. For example, the large SRCNN (SRCNN-Ex) [2] has 57,184 parameters, which are six times larger than that for SRCNN (8,032 parameters). Then the question is how to shrink the network scale while still keeping the previous accuracy.

According to the above observations, we investigate a more concise and efficient network structure for fast and accurate image SR. *To solve the first problem*, we adopt a deconvolution layer to replace the bicubic interpolation. To further ease the computational burden, we place the deconvolution layer[1] at the end of the network, then the computational complexity is only proportional to the spatial size of the original LR image. It is worth noting that the deconvolution layer is not equal to a simple substitute of the conventional interpolation kernel like in FCN [13], or 'unpooling+convolution' like [14]. Instead, it consists of diverse automatically learned upsampling kernels (see Fig. 3) that work jointly to generate the final HR output, and replacing these deconvolution filters with uniform interpolation kernels will result in a drastic PSNR drop (*e.g.*, at least 0.9 dB on the Set5 dataset [15] for ×3).

*For the second problem*, we add a shrinking and an expanding layer at the beginning and the end of the mapping layer separately to restrict mapping in a low-dimensional feature space. Furthermore, we decompose a single wide mapping layer into several layers with a fixed filter size $3 \times 3$. The overall shape of the new structure looks like an *hourglass*, which is symmetrical on the whole, thick at the ends and thin in the middle. Experiments show that the proposed model, named as Fast Super-Resolution Convolutional Neural Networks (FSR-CNN)[2], achieves a speed-up of more than 40× with even superior performance than the SRCNN-Ex. In this work, we also present a small FSRCNN network

---

[1] We follow [11] to adopt the terminology 'deconvolution'. We note that it carries very different meaning in classic image processing, see [12].

[2] The implementation is available on the project page http://mmlab.ie.cuhk.edu.hk/projects/FSRCNN.html.

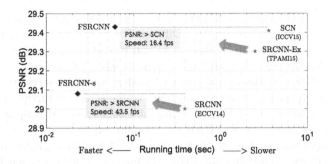

**Fig. 1.** The proposed FSRCNN networks achieve better super-resolution quality than existing methods, and are tens of times faster. Especially, the FSRCNN-s can run in real-time (>24 fps) on a generic CPU. The chart is based on the Set14 [9] results summarized in Tables 3 and 4.

(FSRCNN-s) that achieves similar restoration quality as SRCNN, but is 17.36 times faster and can run in real time (24 fps) with a generic CPU. As shown in Fig. 1, the FSRCNN networks are much faster than contemporary SR models yet achieving superior performance.

Apart from the notable improvement in speed, the FSRCNN also has another appealing property that could facilitate fast training and testing across different upscaling factors. Specifically, in FSRCNN, all convolution layers (except the deconvolution layer) can be shared by networks of different upscaling factors. During training, with a well-trained network, we only need to fine-tune the deconvolution layer for another upscaling factor with almost no loss of mapping accuracy. During testing, we only need to do convolution operations once, and upsample an image to different scales using the corresponding deconvolution layer.

Our contributions are three-fold: (1) We formulate a compact hourglass-shape CNN structure for fast image super-resolution. With the collaboration of a set of deconvolution filters, the network can learn an end-to-end mapping between the original LR and HR images with no pre-processing. (2) The proposed model achieves a speed up of at least 40× than the SRCNN-Ex [2] while still keeping its exceptional performance. One of its small-size version can run in real-time (>24 fps) on a generic CPU with better restoration quality than SRCNN [1]. (3) We transfer the convolution layers of the proposed networks for fast training and testing across different upscaling factors, with no loss of restoration quality.

## 2   Related Work

**Deep Learning for SR:** Recently, the deep learning techniques have been successfully applied on SR. The pioneer work is termed as the Super-Resolution Convolutional Neural Network (SRCNN) proposed by Dong *et al.* [1,2]. Motivated by SRCNN, some problems such as face hallucination [16] and depth map super-resolution [17] have achieved state-of-the-art results. Deeper structures have also been explored in [18,19]. Different from the conventional learning-based methods, SRCNN directly learns an end-to-end mapping between LR and HR images, leading to a fast and accurate inference. The inherent relationship between SRCNN and the sparse-coding-based methods ensures its good performance. Based on the same assumption, Wang *et al.* [8] further replace the mapping layer by a set of sparse coding sub-networks and propose a sparse coding based network (SCN). With the domain expertise of the conventional sparse-coding-based method, it outperforms SRCNN with a smaller model size. However, as it strictly mimics the sparse-coding solver, it is very hard to shrink the sparse coding sub-network with no loss of mapping accuracy. Furthermore, all these networks [8,18,19] need to process the bicubic-upscaled LR images. The proposed FSRCNN does not only perform on the original LR image, but also contains a simpler but more efficient mapping layer. Furthermore, the previous methods have to train a totally different network for a specific upscaling factor, while the FSRCNN only requires a different deconvolution layer. This also provides us a faster way to upscale an image to several different sizes.

**CNNs Acceleration:** A number of studies have investigated the acceleration of CNN. Denton *et al.* [20] first investigate the redundancy within the CNNs designed for object detection. Then Zhang *et al.* [21] make attempts to accelerate very deep CNNs for image classfication. They also take the non-linear units into account and reduce the accumulated error by asymmetric reconstruction. Our model also aims at accelerating CNNs but in a different manner. First, they focus on approximating the existing well-trained models, while we reformulate the previous model and achieves better performance. Second, the above methods are all designed for high-level vision problems (*e.g.*, image classification and object detection), while ours are for the low-level vision task. As the deep models for SR contain no fully-connected layers, the approximation of convolution filters will severely impact the performance.

## 3    Fast Super-Resolution by CNN

We first briefly describe the network structure of SRCNN [1,2], and then we detail how we reformulate the network layer by layer. The differences between FSRCNN and SRCNN are presented at the end of this section.

### 3.1    SRCNN

SRCNN aims at learning an end-to-end mapping function $F$ between the bicubic-interpolated LR image $Y$ and the HR image $X$. The network contains all convolution layers, thus the size of the output is the same as that of the input image. As depicted in Fig. 2, the overall structure consists of three parts that are analogous to the main steps of the sparse-coding-based methods [10]. The patch extraction and representation part refers to the first layer, which extracts patches from the input and represents each patch as a high-dimensional feature

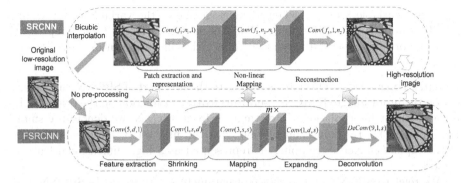

**Fig. 2.** This figure shows the network structures of the SRCNN and FSRCNN. The proposed FSRCNN is different from SRCNN mainly in three aspects. First, FSRCNN adopts the original low-resolution image as input without bicubic interpolation. A deconvolution layer is introduced at the end of the network to perform upsampling. Second, The non-linear mapping step in SRCNN is replaced by three steps in FSRCNN, namely the shrinking, mapping, and expanding step. Third, FSRCNN adopts smaller filter sizes and a deeper network structure. These improvements provide FSRCNN with better performance but lower computational cost than SRCNN.

vector. The non-linear mapping part refers to the middle layer, which maps the feature vectors non-linearly to another set of feature vectors, or namely HR features. Then the last reconstruction part aggregates these features to form the final output image.

The computation complexity of the network can be calculated as follows,

$$O\{(f_1^2 n_1 + n_1 f_2^2 n_2 + n_2 f_3^2)S_{HR}\}, \tag{1}$$

where $\{f_i\}_{i=1}^3$ and $\{n_i\}_{i=1}^3$ are the filter size and filter number of the three layers, respectively. $S_{HR}$ is the size of the HR image. We observe that the complexity is proportional to the size of the HR image, and the middle layer contributes most to the network parameters. In the next section, we present the FSRCNN by giving special attention to these two facets.

## 3.2   FSRCNN

As shown in Fig. 2, FSRCNN can be decomposed into five parts – feature extraction, shrinking, mapping, expanding and deconvolution. The first four parts are convolution layers, while the last one is a deconvolution layer. For better understanding, we denote a convolution layer as $Conv(f_i, n_i, c_i)$, and a deconvolution layer as $DeConv(f_i, n_i, c_i)$, where the variables $f_i, n_i, c_i$ represent the filter size, the number of filters and the number of channels, respectively.

As the whole network contains tens of variables (*i.e.*, $\{f_i, n_i, c_i\}_{i=1}^6$), it is impossible for us to investigate each of them. Thus we assign a reasonable value to the insensitive variables in advance, and leave the sensitive variables unset.

We call a variable sensitive when a slight change of the variable could significantly influence the performance. These sensitive variables always represent some important influential factors in SR, which will be shown in the following descriptions.

**Feature Extraction:** This part is similar to the first part of SRCNN, but different on the input image. FSRCNN performs feature extraction on the original LR image without interpolation. To distinguish from SRCNN, we denote the small LR input as $Y_s$. By doing convolution with the first set of filters, each patch of the input (1-pixel overlapping) is represented as a high-dimensional feature vector.

We refer to SRCNN on the choice of parameters – $f_1, n_1, c_1$. In SRCNN, the filter size of the first layer is set to be 9. Note that these filters are performed on the upscaled image $Y$. As most pixels in $Y$ are interpolated from $Y_s$, a $5 \times 5$ patch in $Y_s$ could cover almost all information of a $9 \times 9$ patch in $Y$. Therefore, we can adopt a smaller filter size $f_1 = 5$ with little information loss. For the number of channels, we follow SRCNN to set $c_1 = 1$. Then we only need to determine the filter number $n_1$. From another perspective, $n_1$ can be regarded as the number of LR feature dimension, denoted as $d$ – the first sensitive variable. Finally, the first layer can be represented as $Conv(5, d, 1)$.

**Shrinking:** In SRCNN, the mapping step generally follows the feature extraction step, then the high-dimensional LR features are mapped directly to the HR feature space. However, as the LR feature dimension $d$ is usually very large, the computation complexity of the mapping step is pretty high. This phenomenon is also observed in some deep models for high-level vision tasks. Authors in [22] apply $1 \times 1$ layers to save the computational cost.

With the same consideration, we add a shrinking layer after the feature extraction layer to reduce the LR feature dimension $d$. We fix the filter size to be $f_2 = 1$, then the filters perform like a linear combination within the LR features. By adopting a smaller filter number $n_2 = s << d$, the LR feature dimension is reduced from $d$ to $s$. Here $s$ is the second sensitive variable that determines the level of shrinking, and the second layer can be represented as $Conv(1, s, d)$. This strategy greatly reduces the number of parameters (detailed computation in Sect. 3.3).

**Non-linear Mapping:** The non-linear mapping step is the most important part that affects the SR performance, and the most influencing factors are the width (*i.e.,* the number of filters in a layer) and depth (*i.e.,* the number of layers) of the mapping layer. As indicated in SRCNN [2], a $5 \times 5$ layer achieves much better results than a $1 \times 1$ layer. But they are lack of experiments on very deep networks.

The above experiences help us to formulate a more efficient mapping layer for FSRCNN. First, as a trade-off between the performance and network scale, we adopt a medium filter size $f_3 = 3$. Then, to maintain the same good performance as SRCNN, we use multiple $3 \times 3$ layers to replace a single wide one. The number of mapping layers is another sensitive variable (denoted as $m$), which determines both the mapping accuracy and complexity. To be consistent, all mapping layers contain the same number of filters $n_3 = s$. Then the non-linear mapping part can be represented as $m \times Conv(3, s, s)$.

**Expanding:** The expanding layer acts like an inverse process of the shrinking layer. The shrinking operation reduces the number of LR feature dimension for the sake of the computational efficiency. However, if we generate the HR image directly from these low-dimensional features, the final restoration quality will be poor. Therefore, we add an expanding layer after the mapping part to expand the HR feature dimension. To maintain consistency with the shrinking layer, we also adopt $1 \times 1$ filters, the number of which is the same as that for the LR feature extraction layer. As opposed to the shrinking layer $Conv(1, s, d)$, the expanding layer is $Conv(1, d, s)$. Experiments show that without the expanding layer, the performance decreases up to 0.3 dB on the Set5 test set [15].

**Deconvolution:** The last part is a deconvolution layer, which upsamples and aggregates the previous features with a set of deconvolution filters. The deconvolution can be regarded as an inverse operation of the convolution. For convolution, the filter is convolved with the image with a stride $k$, and the output is $1/k$ times of the input. Contrarily, if we exchange the position of the input and output, the output will be $k$ times of the input, as depicted in Fig. 4. We take advantage of this property to set the stride $k = n$, which is the desired upscaling factor. Then the output is directly the reconstructed HR image.

When we determine the filter size of the deconvolution filters, we can look at the network from another perspective. Interestingly, the reversed network is like a downscaling operator that accepts an HR image and outputs the LR one. Then the deconvolution layer becomes a convolution layer with a stride $n$. As it extracts features from the HR image, we should adopt $9 \times 9$ filters that are consistent with the first layer of SRCNN. Similarly, if we reverse back, the deconvolution filters should also have a spatial size $f_5 = 9$. Experiments also demonstrate this assumption. Figure 3 shows the learned deconvolution filters, the patterns of which are very similar to that of the first-layer filters in SRCNN. Lastly, we can represent the deconvolution layer as $DeConv(9, 1, d)$.

Different from inserting traditional interpolation kernels (*e.g.*, bicubic or bilinear) in-network [13] or having 'unpooling+convolution' [14], the deconvolution layer learns a set of upsampling kernel for the input feature maps. As shown in Fig. 3, these kernels are diverse and meaningful. If we force these kernels to be identical, the parameters will be used inefficiently (equal to sum up the input feature maps as one), and the performance will drop at least 0.9 dB on the Set5.

**PReLU:** For the activation function after each convolution layer, we suggest the use of the Parametric Rectified Linear Unit (PReLU) [23] instead of the commonly-used Rectified Linear Unit (ReLU). They are different on the coefficient of the negative part. For ReLU and PReLU, we can define a general activation function as $f(x_i) = max(x_i, 0) + a_i min(0, x_i)$, where $x_i$ is the input signal of the activation $f$ on the $i$-th channel, and $a_i$ is the coefficient of the

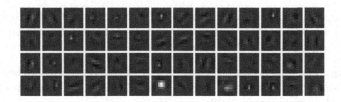

**Fig. 3.** The learned deconvolution layer (56 channels) for the upscaling factor 3.

negative part. The parameter $a_i$ is fixed to be zero for ReLU, but is learnable for PReLU. We choose PReLU mainly to avoid the "dead features" [11] caused by zero gradients in ReLU. Then we can make full use of all parameters to test the maximum capacity of different network designs. Experiments show that the performance of the PReLU-activated networks is more stable, and can be seen as the up-bound of that for the ReLU-activated networks.

**Overall Structure:** We can connect the above five parts to form a complete FSRCNN network as $Conv(5, d, 1) - PReLU - Conv(1, s, d) - PReLU - m \times Conv(3, s, s) - PReLU - Conv(1, d, s) - PReLU - DeConv(9, 1, d)$. On the whole, there are three sensitive variables (*i.e.*, the LR feature dimension $d$, the number of shrinking filters $s$, and the mapping depth $m$) governing the performance and speed. For simplicity, we represent a FSRCNN network as $FSRCNN(d, s, m)$. The computational complexity can be calculated as

$$O\{(25d + sd + 9ms^2 + ds + 81d)S_{LR}\} = O\{(9ms^2 + 2sd + 106d)S_{LR}\}. \quad (2)$$

We exclude the parameters of PReLU, which introduce negligible computational cost. Interestingly, the new structure looks like an *hourglass*, which is symmetrical on the whole, thick at the ends, and thin in the middle. The three sensitive variables are just the controlling parameters for the appearance of the hourglass. Experiments show that this hourglass design is very effective for image super-resolution.

**Cost Function:** Following SRCNN, we adopt the mean square error (MSE) as the cost function. The optimization objective is represented as

$$\min_{\theta} \frac{1}{n} \sum_{i=1}^{n} ||F(Y_s^i; \theta) - X^i||_2^2, \quad (3)$$

where $Y_s^i$ and $X^i$ are the $i$-th LR and HR sub-image pair in the training data, and $F(Y_s^i; \theta)$ is the network output for $Y_s^i$ with parameters $\theta$. All parameters are optimized using stochastic gradient descent with the standard backpropagation.

### 3.3 Differences Against SRCNN: From SRCNN to FSRCNN

To better understand how we accelerate SRCNN, we transform the SRCNN-Ex to another FSRCNN (56,12,4) within three steps, and show how much acceleration and PSNR gain are obtained by each step. We use a representative upscaling factor $n = 3$. The network configurations of SRCNN, FSRCNN and the two transition states are shown in Table 1. We also show their performance (average PSNR on Set5) trained on the 91-image dataset [10].

**Table 1.** The transitions from SRCNN to FSRCNN.

|  | SRCNN-Ex | Transition state 1 | Transition state 2 | FSRCNN (56,12,4) |
|---|---|---|---|---|
| First part | Conv(9,64,1) | Conv(9,64,1) | Conv(9,64,1) | **Conv(5,56,1)** |
| Mid part | Conv(5,32,64) | Conv(5,32,64) | **Conv(1,12,64)-** **4Conv(3,12,12)-** **Conv(1,64,12)** | **Conv(1,12,56)-** **4Conv(3,12,12)-** **Conv(1,56,12)** |
| Last part | Conv(5,1,32) | **DeConv(9,1,32)** | **DeConv(9,1,64)** | **DeConv(9,1,56)** |
| Input size | $S_{HR}$ | $S_{LR}$ | $S_{LR}$ | $S_{LR}$ |
| Parameters | 57184 | 58976 | 17088 | 12464 |
| Speedup | 1× | 8.7× | 30.1× | 41.3× |
| PSNR (Set5) | 32.83 dB | 32.95 dB | 33.01 dB | 33.06 dB |

First, we replace the last convolution layer of SRCNN-Ex with a deconvolution layer, then the whole network will perform on the original LR image and the computation complexity is proportional to $S_{LR}$ instead of $S_{HR}$. This step will enlarge the network scale but achieve a speedup of 8.7× (*i.e.*, $57184/58976 \times 3^2$). As the learned deconvolution kernels are better than a single bicubic kernel, the performance increases roughly by 0.12 dB. Second, the single mapping layer is replaced with the combination of a shrinking layer, 4 mapping layers and an expanding layer. Overall, there are 5 more layers, but the parameters are decreased from 58,976 to 17,088. Also, the acceleration after this step is the most prominent – 30.1×. It is widely observed that depth is the key factor that affects the performance. Here, we use four "narrow" layers to replace a single "wide" layer, thus achieving better results (33.01 dB) with much less parameters. Lastly, we adopt smaller filter sizes and less filters (*e.g.*, from $Conv(9, 64, 1)$ to $Conv(5, 56, 1)$), and obtain a final speedup of 41.3×. As we remove some redundant parameters, the network is trained more efficiently and achieves another 0.05 dB improvement.

It is worth noting that this acceleration is NOT at the cost of performance degradation. Contrarily, the FSRCNN (56,12,4) outperforms SRCNN-Ex by a large margin (*e.g.*, 0.23 dB on the Set5 dataset). The main reasons of high performance have been presented in the above analysis. This is the main difference between our method and other CNN acceleration works [20,21]. Nevertheless, with the guarantee of good performance, it is easier to cooperate with other acceleration methods to get a faster model.

### 3.4   SR for Different Upscaling Factors

Another advantage of FSRCNN over the previous learning-based methods is that FSRCNN could achieve fast training and testing across different upscaling factors. Specifically, we find that all convolution layers on the whole act like

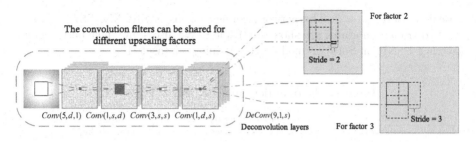

**Fig. 4.** The FSRCNN consists of convolution layers and a deconvolution layer. The convolution layers can be shared for different upscaling factors. A specific deconvolution layer is trained for different upscaling factors.

a complex feature extractor of the LR image, and only the last deconvolution layer contains the information of the upscaling factor. This is also proved by experiments, of which the convolution filters are almost the same for different upscaling factors[3]. With this property, we can transfer the convolution filters for fast training and testing.

In practice, we train a model for an upscaling factor in advance. Then during training, we only fine-tune the deconvolution layer for another upscaling factor and leave the convolution layers unchanged. The fine-tuning is fast, and the performance is as good as training from scratch (see Sect. 4.4). During testing, we perform the convolution operations once, and upsample an image to different sizes with the corresponding deconvolution layer. If we need to apply several upscaling factors simultaneously, this property can lead to much faster testing (as illustrated in Fig. 4).

# 4    Experiments

## 4.1    Implementation Details

**Training Dataset.** The 91-image dataset is widely used as the training set in learning-based SR methods [1,5,10]. As deep models generally benefit from big data, studies have found that 91 images are not enough to push a deep model to the best performance. Yang *et al.* [24] and Schulter *et al.* [7] use the BSD500 dataset [25]. However, images in the BSD500 are in JPEG format, which are not optimal for the SR task. Therefore, we contribute a new General-100 dataset that contains 100 bmp-format images (with no compression)[4]. The size of the newly introduced 100 images ranges from $710 \times 704$ (large) to $131 \times 112$ (small). They are all of good quality with clear edges but fewer smooth regions (*e.g.*, sky and ocean), thus are very suitable for the SR training. In the following

---

[3] Note that in SRCNN and SCN, the convolution filters differ a lot for different upscaling factors.

[4] We follow [26] to introduce only 100 images in a new super-resolution dataset. A larger dataset with more training images will be released on the project page.

experiments, apart from using the 91-image dataset for training, we will also evaluate the applicability of the joint set of the General-100 dataset and the 91-image dataset to train our networks. To make full use of the dataset, we also adopt data augmentation as in [8]. We augment the data in two ways. (1) Scaling: each image is downscaled with the factor 0.9, 0.8, 0.7 and 0.6. (2) Rotation: each image is rotated with the degree of 90, 180 and 270. Then we will have $5 \times 4 - 1 = 19$ times more images for training.

**Test and Validation Dataset.** Following SRCNN and SCN, we use the Set5 [15], Set14 [9] and BSD200 [25] dataset for testing. Another 20 images from the validation set of the BSD500 dataset are selected for validation.

**Training Samples.** To prepare the training data, we first downsample the original training images by the desired scaling factor $n$ to form the LR images. Then we crop the LR training images into a set of $f_{sub} \times f_{sub}$-pixel sub-images with a stride $k$. The corresponding HR sub-images (with size $(nf_{sub})^2$) are also cropped from the ground truth images. These LR/HR sub-image pairs are the primary training data.

For the issue of padding, we empirically find that padding the input or output maps does little effect on the final performance. Thus we adopt zero padding in all layers according to the filter size. In this way, there is no need to change the sub-image size for different network designs. Another issue affecting the sub-image size is the deconvolution layer. As we train our models with the *Caffe* package [27], its deconvolution filters will generate the output with size $(nf_{sub} - n + 1)^2$ instead of $(nf_{sub})^2$. So we also crop $(n - 1)$-pixel borders on the HR sub-images. Finally, for ×2, ×3 and ×4, we set the size of LR/HR sub-images to be $10^2/19^2$, $7^2/19^2$ and $6^2/21^2$, respectively.

**Training Strategy.** For fair comparison with the state-of-the-arts (Sect. 4.5), we adopt the 91-image dataset for training. In addition, we also explore a two-step training strategy. First, we train a network from scratch with the 91-image dataset. Then, when the training is saturated, we add the General-100 dataset for fine-tuning. With this strategy, the training converges much earlier than training with the two datasets from the beginning.

When training with the 91-image dataset, the learning rate of the convolution layers is set to be $10^{-3}$ and that of the deconvolution layer is $10^{-4}$. Then during fine-tuning, the learning rate of all layers is reduced by half. For initialization, the weights of the convolution filters are initialized with the method designed for PReLU in [23]. As we do not have activation functions at the end, the deconvolution filters are initialized by the same way as in SRCNN (*i.e.*, drawing randomly from a Gaussian distribution with zero mean and standard deviation 0.001).

## 4.2 Investigation of Different Settings

To test the property of the FSRCNN structure, we design a set of controlling experiments with different values of the three sensitive variables – the LR feature dimension $d$, the number of shrinking filters $s$, and the mapping depth $m$.

**Table 2.** The comparison of PSNR (Set5) and parameters of different settings.

| Settings | $m = 2$ | $m = 3$ | $m = 4$ |
|---|---|---|---|
| $d = 48, s = 12$ | 32.87 (8832) | 32.88 (10128) | 33.08 (11424) |
| $d = 56, s = 12$ | 33.00 (9872) | 32.97 (11168) | 33.16 (12464) |
| $d = 48, s = 16$ | 32.95 (11232) | 33.10 (13536) | 33.18 (15840) |
| $d = 56, s = 16$ | 33.01 (12336) | 33.12 (14640) | 33.17 (16944) |

Specifically, we choose $d = 48, 56$, $s = 12, 16$ and $m = 2, 3, 4$, thus we conduct a total of $2 \times 2 \times 3 = 12$ experiments with different combinations.

The average PSNR values on the Set5 dataset of these experiments are shown in Table 2. We analyze the results in two directions, *i.e.*, horizontally and vertically in the table. First, we fix $d, s$ and examine the influence of $m$. Obviously, $m = 4$ leads to better results than $m = 2$ and $m = 3$. This trend can also be observed from the convergence curves shown in Fig. 5(a). Second, we fix $m$ and examine the influence of $d$ and $s$. In general, a better result usually requires more parameters (*e.g.*, a larger $d$ or $s$), but more parameters do not always guarantee a better result. This trend is also reflected in Fig. 5(b), where we see the three largest networks converge together. From all the results, we find the best trade-off between performance and parameters – FSRCNN (56,12,4), which achieves one of the highest results with a moderate number of parameters.

It is worth noticing that the smallest network FSRCNN (48,12,2) achieves an average PSNR of 32.87 dB, which is already higher than that of SRCNN-Ex (32.75 dB) reported in [2]. The FSRCNN (48,12,2) contains only 8,832 parameters, then the acceleration compared with SRCNN-Ex is $57184/8832 \times 9 = 58.3$ times.

### 4.3 Towards Real-Time SR with FSRCNN

Now we want to find a more concise FSRCNN network that could realize real-time SR while still keep good performance. First, we calculate how many parameters can meet the minimum requirement of real-time implementation (24 fps). As mentioned in the introduction, the speed of SRCNN to upsample an image

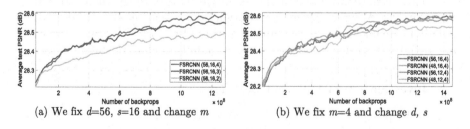

(a) We fix $d$=56, $s$=16 and change $m$      (b) We fix $m$=4 and change $d$, $s$

**Fig. 5.** Convergence curves of different network designs.

to the size $760 \times 760$ is 1.32 fps. The upscaling factor is 3, and SRCNN has 8032 parameters. Then according to Eqs. 1 and 2, the desired FSRCNN network should have at most $8032 \times 1.32/24 \times 3^2 \approx 3976$ parameters. To achieve this goal, we find an appropriate configuration – FSRCNN (32,5,1) that contains 3937 parameters. With our C++ test code, the speed of FSRCNN (32,5,1) reaches 24.7 fps, satisfying the real-time requirement. Furthermore, the FSRCNN (32,5,1) even outperforms SRCNN (9-1-5) [1] (see Tables 3 and 4).

### 4.4  Experiments for Different Upscaling Factors

Unlike existing methods [1,2] that need to train a network from scratch for a different scaling factor, the proposed FSRCNN enjoys the flexibility of learning and testing across upscaling factors through transferring the convolution filters (Sect. 3.4). We demonstrate this flexibility in this section. We choose the FSR-CNN (56,12,4) as the default network. As we have obtained a well-trained model under the upscaling factor 3 (in Sect. 4.2), we then train the network for ×2 on the basis of that for ×3. To be specific, the parameters of all convolution filters in the well-trained model are transferred to the network of ×2. During training, we only fine-tune the deconvolution layer on the 91-image and General-100 datasets of ×2. For comparison, we train another network also for ×2 but from scratch. The convergence curves of these two networks are shown in Fig. 6. Obviously, with the transferred parameters, the network converges very fast (only a few hours) with the same good performance as that training form scratch. In the following experiments, we only train the networks from scratch for ×3, and fine-tune the corresponding deconvolution layers for ×2 and ×4.

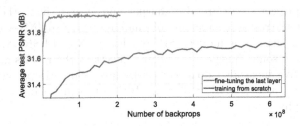

**Fig. 6.** Convergence curves for different training strategies.

### 4.5  Comparison with State-of-the-Arts

**Compare Using the Same Training Set.** First, we compare our method with four state-of-the-art learning-based SR algorithms that rely on external databases, namely the super-resolution forest (SRF) [7], SRCNN [1], SRCNN-Ex [2] and the sparse coding based network (SCN) [8]. The implementations of these methods are all based on their released source code. As they are written in different programming languages, the comparison of their test time may not be fair, but still reflects the main trend. To have a fair comparison on restoration quality, all models are trained on the augmented 91-image dataset, so the results are slightly different from that in the corresponding paper. We select two representative FSRCNN networks – FSRCNN (short for FSRCNN (56,12,4)), and FSRCNN-s (short for FSRCNN (32,5,1)). The inference time is tested with the C++ implementation on an Intel i7 CPU 4.0 GHz. The quantitative results (PSNR and test time) for different upscaling factors are listed in Table 3. We first look at the test time, which is the main focus of our work. The proposed FSRCNN is undoubtedly the fastest method that is at least 40 times faster than SRCNN-Ex, SRF and SCN (with the upscaling factor 3), while the fastest FSRCNN-s can achieve real-time performance (>24 fps) on almost all the test images. Moreover, the FSRCNN still outperforms the previous methods on the PSNR values especially for ×2 and ×3. We also notice that the FSRCNN achieves slightly lower PSNR than SCN on factor 4. This is mainly because that the SCN adopts two models of ×2 to upsample an image by ×4. We have also tried this strategy and achieved comparable results. However, as we pay more attention to speed, we still present the results of a single network.

**Compare Using Different Training Sets (Following the Literature).** To follow the literature, we also compare the best PSNR results that are reported in the corresponding paper, as shown in Table 4. We also add another two competitive methods – KK [28] and A+ [5] for comparison. Note that these results are obtained using different datasets, and our models are trained on the 91-image and General-100 datasets. From Table 4, we can see that the proposed FSR-CNN still outperforms other methods on most upscaling factors and datasets. The reconstructed images of FSRCNN (shown in Fig. 7, more examples can be found on the project page) are also sharper and clearer than other results. In another aspect, the restoration quality of small models (FSRCNN-s and SRCNN) is slightly worse than large models (SRCNN-Ex, SCN and FSRCNN). In Fig. 7, we could observe some "jaggies" or ringing effects in the results of FSRCNN-s and SRCNN. We have also done comprehensive comparisons with more SR algorithms in terms of PSNR, SSIM and IFC [29], which can be found in the supplementary file.

**Table 3.** The results of PSNR (dB) and test time (sec) on three test datasets. All models are trained on the 91-image dataset.

| Test dataset | Upscaling factor | Bicubic | | SRF [7] | | SRCNN [1] | | SRCNN-Ex [2] | | SCN [8] | | FSRCNN-s | | FSRCNN | |
|---|---|---|---|---|---|---|---|---|---|---|---|---|---|---|---|
| | | PSNR | Time | PSNR | Time | PSNR | Time | PSNR | Time | PSNR | Time | PSNR | Time | PSNR | Time |
| Set5 | 2 | 33.66 | - | 36.84 | 2.1 | 36.33 | 0.18 | 36.67 | 1.3 | 36.76 | 0.94 | 36.53 | **0.024** | **36.94** | 0.068 |
| Set14 | 2 | 30.23 | - | 32.46 | 3.9 | 32.15 | 0.39 | 32.35 | 2.8 | 32.48 | 1.7 | 32.22 | **0.061** | **32.54** | 0.16 |
| BSD200 | 2 | 29.70 | - | 31.57 | 3.1 | 31.34 | 0.23 | 31.53 | 1.7 | 31.63 | 1.1 | 31.44 | **0.033** | **31.73** | 0.098 |
| Set5 | 3 | 30.39 | - | 32.73 | 1.7 | 32.45 | 0.18 | 32.83 | 1.3 | **33.04** | 1.8 | 32.55 | **0.010** | 33.06 | 0.027 |
| Set14 | 3 | 27.54 | - | 29.21 | 2.5 | 29.01 | 0.39 | 29.26 | 2.8 | 29.37 | 3.6 | 29.08 | **0.023** | **29.37** | 0.061 |
| BSD200 | 3 | 27.26 | - | 28.40 | 2.0 | 28.27 | 0.23 | 28.47 | 1.7 | 28.54 | 2.4 | 28.32 | **0.013** | **28.55** | 0.035 |
| Set5 | 4 | 28.42 | - | 30.35 | 1.5 | 30.15 | 0.18 | 30.45 | 1.3 | **30.82** | 1.2 | 30.04 | **0.0052** | 30.55 | 0.015 |
| Set14 | 4 | 26.00 | - | 27.41 | 2.1 | 27.21 | 0.39 | 27.44 | 2.8 | **27.62** | 2.3 | 27.12 | **0.0099** | 27.50 | 0.029 |
| BSD200 | 4 | 25.97 | - | 26.85 | 1.7 | 26.72 | 0.23 | 26.88 | 1.7 | **27.02** | 1.4 | 26.73 | **0.0072** | 26.92 | 0.019 |

**Table 4.** The results of PSNR (dB) on three test datasets. We present the best results reported in the corresponding paper. The proposed FSCNN and FSRCNN-s are trained on both 91-image and General-100 dataset. More comparisons with other methods on PSNR, SSIM and IFC [29] can be found in the supplementary file.

| Test dataset | Upscaling factor | Bicubic | KK [28] | A+ [5] | SRF [7] | SRCNN [1] | SRCNN-Ex [2] | SCN [8] | FSRCNN-s | FSRCNN |
|---|---|---|---|---|---|---|---|---|---|---|
| | | PSNR | PSNR | PSNR | PSNR | PSNR | PSNR | PSNR | PSNR | PSNR |
| Set5 | 2 | 33.66 | 36.20 | 36.55 | 36.89 | 36.34 | 36.66 | 36.93 | 36.58 | **37.00** |
| Set14 | 2 | 30.23 | 32.11 | 32.28 | 32.52 | 32.18 | 32.45 | 32.56 | 32.28 | **32.63** |
| BSD200 | 2 | 29.70 | 31.30 | 31.44 | 31.66 | 31.38 | 31.63 | 31.63 | 31.48 | **31.80** |
| Set5 | 3 | 30.39 | 32.28 | 32.59 | 32.72 | 32.39 | 32.75 | 33.10 | 32.61 | **33.16** |
| Set14 | 3 | 27.54 | 28.94 | 29.13 | 29.23 | 29.00 | 29.30 | 29.41 | 29.13 | **29.43** |
| BSD200 | 3 | 27.26 | 28.19 | 28.36 | 28.45 | 28.28 | 28.48 | 28.54 | 28.32 | **28.60** |
| Set5 | 4 | 28.42 | 30.03 | 30.28 | 30.35 | 30.09 | 30.49 | **30.86** | 30.11 | 30.71 |
| Set14 | 4 | 26.00 | 27.14 | 27.32 | 27.41 | 27.20 | 27.50 | **27.64** | 27.19 | 27.59 |
| BSD200 | 4 | 25.97 | 26.68 | 26.83 | 26.89 | 26.73 | 26.92 | **27.02** | 26.75 | 26.98 |

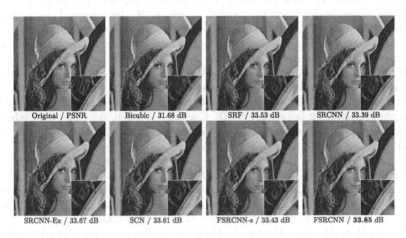

**Fig. 7.** The "lenna" image from the Set14 dataset with an upscaling factor 3.

## 5 Conclusion

While observing the limitations of current deep learning based SR models, we explore a more efficient network structure to achieve high running speed without the loss of restoration quality. We approach this goal by re-designing the SRCNN structure, and achieves a final acceleration of more than 40 times. Extensive experiments suggest that the proposed method yields satisfactory SR performance, while superior in terms of run time. The proposed model can be adapted for real-time video SR, and motivate fast deep models for other low-level vision tasks.

**Acknowledgment.** This work is partially supported by SenseTime Group Limited.

# References

1. Dong, C., Loy, C.C., He, K., Tang, X.: Learning a deep convolutional network for image super-resolution. In: Fleet, D., Pajdla, T., Schiele, B., Tuytelaars, T. (eds.) ECCV 2014, Part IV. LNCS, vol. 8692, pp. 184–199. Springer, Heidelberg (2014)
2. Dong, C., Loy, C.C., He, K., Tang, X.: Image super-resolution using deep convolutional networks. TPAMI **38**(2), 295–307 (2015)
3. Yang, C.Y., Yang, M.H.: Fast direct super-resolution by simple functions. In: ICCV, pp. 561–568 (2013)
4. Timofte, R., De Smet, V., Van Gool, L.: Anchored neighborhood regression for fast example-based super-resolution. In: ICCV, pp. 1920–1927 (2013)
5. Timofte, R., De Smet, V., Van Gool, L.: A+: adjusted anchored neighborhood regression for fast super-resolution. In: Cremers, D., Reid, I., Saito, H., Yang, M.-H. (eds.) ACCV 2014. LNCS, vol. 9006, pp. 111–126. Springer, Heidelberg (2015)
6. Cui, Z., Chang, H., Shan, S., Zhong, B., Chen, X.: Deep network cascade for image super-resolution. In: Fleet, D., Pajdla, T., Schiele, B., Tuytelaars, T. (eds.) ECCV 2014, Part V. LNCS, vol. 8693, pp. 49–64. Springer, Heidelberg (2014)
7. Schulter, S., Leistner, C., Bischof, H.: Fast and accurate image upscaling with super-resolution forests. In: CVPR, pp. 3791–3799 (2015)
8. Wang, Z., Liu, D., Yang, J., Han, W., Huang, T.: Deeply improved sparse coding for image super-resolution. In: ICCV, pp. 370–378 (2015)
9. Zeyde, R., Elad, M., Protter, M.: On single image scale-up using sparse-representations. In: Boissonnat, J.-D., Chenin, P., Cohen, A., Gout, C., Lyche, T., Mazure, M.-L., Schumaker, L. (eds.) Curves and Surfaces 2011. LNCS, vol. 6920, pp. 711–730. Springer, Heidelberg (2012)
10. Yang, J., Wright, J., Huang, T.S., Ma, Y.: Image super-resolution via sparse representation. TIP **19**(11), 2861–2873 (2010)
11. Zeiler, M.D., Fergus, R.: Visualizing and understanding convolutional networks. In: Fleet, D., Pajdla, T., Schiele, B., Tuytelaars, T. (eds.) ECCV 2014, Part I. LNCS, vol. 8689, pp. 818–833. Springer, Heidelberg (2014)
12. Xu, L., Ren, J.S., Liu, C., Jia, J.: Deep convolutional neural network for image deconvolution. In: NIPS, pp. 1790–1798 (2014)
13. Long, J., Shelhamer, E., Darrell, T.: Fully convolutional networks for semantic segmentation. In: CVPR, pp. 3431–3440 (2015)
14. Dosovitskiy, A., Tobias Springenberg, J., Brox, T.: Learning to generate chairs with convolutional neural networks. In: CVPR, pp. 1538–1546 (2015)
15. Bevilacqua, M., Roumy, A., Guillemot, C., Morel, M.L.A.: Low-complexity single-image super-resolution based on nonnegative neighbor embedding. In: BMVC (2012)
16. Zhu, S., Liu, S., Loy, C.C., Tang, X.: Deep cascaded bi-network for face hallucination. In: ECCV (2016)
17. Hui, T.W., Loy, C.C., Tang, X.: Depth map super resolution by deep multi-scale guidance. In: ECCV (2016)
18. Kim, J., Lee, J.K., Lee, K.M.: Accurate image super-resolution using very deep convolutional networks. In: CVPR (2016)
19. Kim, J., Lee, J.K., Lee, K.M.: Deeply-recursive convolutional network for image super-resolution. In: CVPR (2016)
20. Denton, E.L., Zaremba, W., Bruna, J., LeCun, Y., Fergus, R.: Exploiting linear structure within convolutional networks for efficient evaluation. In: NIPS, pp. 1269–1277 (2014)

21. Zhang, X., Zou, J., He, K., Sun, J.: Accelerating very deep convolutional networks for classification and detection. In: TPAMI (2015)
22. Lin, M., Chen, Q., Yan, S.: Network in network. arXiv:1312.4400 (2014)
23. He, K., Zhang, X., Ren, S., Sun, J.: Delving deep into rectifiers: surpassing human-level performance on imagenet classification. In: ICCV, pp. 1026–1034 (2015)
24. Yang, C.-Y., Ma, C., Yang, M.-H.: Single-Image super-resolution: a benchmark. In: Fleet, D., Pajdla, T., Schiele, B., Tuytelaars, T. (eds.) ECCV 2014, Part IV. LNCS, vol. 8692, pp. 372–386. Springer, Heidelberg (2014)
25. Martin, D., Fowlkes, C., Tal, D., Malik, J.: A database of human segmented natural images and its application to evaluating segmentation algorithms and measuring ecological statistics. In: ICCV, vol. 2, pp. 416–423 (2001)
26. Huang, J.B., Singh, A., Ahuja, N.: Single image super-resolution from transformed self-exemplars. In: CVPR, pp. 5197–5206 (2015)
27. Jia, Y., Shelhamer, E., Donahue, J., Karayev, S., Long, J., Girshick, R., Guadarrama, S., Darrell, T.: Caffe: convolutional architecture for fast feature embedding. In: ACM MM, pp. 675–678 (2014)
28. Kim, K.I., Kwon, Y.: Single-image super-resolution using sparse regression and natural image prior. TPAMI **32**(6), 1127–1133 (2010)
29. Sheikh, H.R., Bovik, A.C., De Veciana, G.: An information fidelity criterion for image quality assessment using natural scene statistics. TIP **14**(12), 2117–2128 (2005)

# Symmetric Non-rigid Structure from Motion for Category-Specific Object Structure Estimation

Yuan Gao[1](✉) and Alan L. Yuille[2,3]

[1] City University of Hong Kong, Kowloon Tong, Hong Kong
Ethan.Y.Gao@gmail.com
[2] UCLA, Los Angeles, USA
Alan.L.Yuille@gmail.com
[3] John Hopkins University, Baltimore, USA

**Abstract.** Many objects, especially these made by humans, are symmetric, *e.g.* cars and aeroplanes. This paper addresses the estimation of 3D structures of symmetric objects from multiple images of the same object category, *e.g.* different cars, seen from various viewpoints. We assume that the deformation between different instances from the same object category is non-rigid and symmetric. In this paper, we extend two leading non-rigid structure from motion (SfM) algorithms to exploit symmetry constraints. We model the both methods as energy minimization, in which we also recover the missing observations caused by occlusions. In particularly, we show that by rotating the coordinate system, the energy can be decoupled into two independent terms, which still exploit symmetry, to apply matrix factorization separately on each of them for initialization. The results on the Pascal3D+ dataset show that our methods significantly improve performance over baseline methods.

**Keywords:** Symmetry · Non-rigid structure from motion

## 1  Introduction

3D structure reconstruction is a major task in computer vision. Structure from motion (SfM) method, which aims at estimating the 3D structure by the 2D annotated keypoints from 2D image sequences, has been proposed for rigid objects [1], and was later extended to non-rigidity [2–14]. Many man-made objects have symmetric structures [15,16]. Motivated by this, symmetry has been studied extensively in the past decades [16–22]. However, this information

---

This work was been done when Yuan Gao was a visiting student in UCLA.

**Electronic supplementary material** The online version of this chapter (doi:10.1007/978-3-319-46475-6_26) contains supplementary material, which is available to authorized users.

© Springer International Publishing AG 2016
B. Leibe et al. (Eds.): ECCV 2016, Part II, LNCS 9906, pp. 408–424, 2016.
DOI: 10.1007/978-3-319-46475-6_26

has not been exploited in recent works on 3D object reconstruction [23,24], nor used in standard non-rigid structure from motion (NRSfM) algorithms [3–10,14].

The goal of this paper is to investigate how symmetry can improve NRSfM. Inspired by recent works [23,24], we are interested in estimating the 3D structure of objects, such as cars, airplanes, etc. This differs from the classic SfM problem because our input are images of several different object instances from the same category (e.g. different cars), instead of sequential images of the same object undergoing motion. In other words, our goal is to estimate the 3D structures of objects from the same class, given intra-class instances from various viewpoints. Specifically, the Pascal3D+ keypoint annotations on different objects from the same category are used as input to our method, where the symmetric keypoint pairs can also be easily inferred. In this paper, non-rigidity means the deformation between the objects from same category can be non-rigid, e.g. between sedan and SUV cars, but the objects themselves are rigid and symmetric.

By exploiting symmetry, we propose two symmetric NRSfM methods. By assuming that the 3D structure can be represented by a linear combination of basis functions (the coefficients vary for different objects): one method is an extension of [5] which is based on an EM approach with a Gaussian prior on the coefficients of the deformation bases, named Sym-EM-PPCA; the other method, i.e. Sym-PriorFree, is an extension of [9,10], which is a direct matrix factorization method without prior knowledge. For fair comparison, we use the same projection models and other assumptions used in [5] and [9,10].

More specifically, our Sym-EM-PPCA method, following [5], assumes weak perspective projection (i.e. the orthographic projection plus scale). We group the keypoints into symmetric keypoint pairs. We assume that the 3D structure is also symmetric and consists of a mean shape (of that category) and a linear combination of the symmetric deformation bases. As in [5], we put a Gaussian prior on the coefficient of the deformation bases. This is intended partly to regularize the problem and partly to deal an apparent ambiguity in non-rigid structure from motion. But recent work [25] showed that this is a "gauge freedom" which does not affect the estimation of 3D structure, so the prior is not really needed.

Our Sym-PriorFree method is based on prior free non-rigid SfM algorithms [9,10], which build on the insights in [25]. We formulate the problem of estimating 3D structure and camera parameters in terms of minimizing an energy function, which exploits symmetry, and at the same time can be re-expressed as the sum of two independent energy functions. Each of these energy functions can be minimized separately by matrix factorization, similar to the methods in [9,10], and the ambiguities are resolved using orthonormality constraints on the viewpoint parameters. This extends work in a companion paper [26], which shows how symmetry can be used to improve rigid structure from motion methods [1].

Our main contributions are: (I) Sym-EM-PPCA, which imposes symmetric constraints on both 3D structure and deformation bases. Sym-Rigid-SfM (see our companion paper [26]) is used to initialize Sym-EM-PPCA with hard symmetric constraints on the 3D structure. (II) Sym-PriorFree, which extends the matrix factorization methods of [9,10], to initialize a coordinate descent algorithm.

In this paper, we group keypoints into symmetric keypoint pairs, and use a superscript † to denote symmetry, *i.e.* $Y$ and $Y^{\dagger}$ are the 2D symmetric keypoint pairs. The paper is organized as follows: firstly, we review related works in Sect. 2. In Sect. 3, the ambiguities in non-rigid SfM are discussed. Then we present the Sym-EM-PPCA algorithm and Sym-PriorFree algorithm in Sect. 4. After that, following the experimental settings in [24], we evaluated our methods on the Pascal3D+ dataset [27] in Sect. 5. Section 5 also includes diagnostic results on the noisy 2D annotations to show that our methods are robust to imperfect symmetric annotations. Finally, we give our conclusions in Sect. 6.

## 2    Related Works

There is a long history of using symmetry as a cue for computer vision tasks. For example, symmetry has been used in depth recovery [17,18,20] as well as recognizing symmetric objects [19]. Several geometric clues, including symmetry, planarity, orthogonality and parallelism have been taken into account for 3D scene reconstruction [28,29], in which the author used pre-computed camera rotation matrix by vanishing point [30]. Recently, symmetry has been applied in more areas such as 3D mesh reconstruction with occlusion [21], and scene reconstruction [16]. For 3D keypoints reconstruction, symmetry, incorporated with planarity and compactness prior, has also been studied in [22].

SfM has also been studied extensively in the past decades, ever since the seminal work on rigid SfM [1,31]. Bregler *et al.* extended this to the non-rigid case [32]. A Column Space Fitting (CSF) method was proposed for rank-$r$ matrix factorization (MF) for SfM with smooth time-trajectories assumption [7], which was later unified in a more general MF framework [33][1]. Early analysis of NRSfM showed that there were ambiguities in 3D structure reconstruction [4]. This lead to studies which assumed priors on the NR deformations [4–7,34,35]. But it was then shown that these ambiguities did not affect the final estimate of 3D structure, *i.e.* all legitimate solutions lying in the same subspace (despite under-constrained) give the same solutions for the 3D structure [25]. This facilitated the invention of prior free matrix factorization method for NRSfM [9,10]. Recently SfM methods have also been used for category-specific object reconstruction, *e.g.* estimating the shape of different *cars* under various viewing conditions [23, 24], but the symmetry cues was not exploited. Note that repetition patterns have recently been incorporated into SfM for urban facades reconstruction [36], but this mainly focused on repetition detection and registration. Finally, in a companion paper [26], we exploited symmetry for rigid SfM.

## 3    The Ambiguities in Non-rigid SfM

This section reviews the intrinsic ambiguities in non-rigid SfM, *i.e.* (i) the ambiguities between the camera projection and the 3D structure, and (ii) the ambiguities between the deformation bases and their coefficients [25]. In the following

---

[1] However, the general framework in [33] cannot be used to SfM directly, because they did not constrain that all the keypoints have the same translation.

sections (*i.e.* in Remark 5), we will show the ambiguity between camera projection and 3D structure (*i.e.* originally the $3 \times 3$ matrix ambiguity as discussed below) can be decomposed into two types of ambiguities under the symmetric constraints, *i.e.* a scale ambiguity along the symmetry axis, and a $2 \times 2$ matrix ambiguity on the other two axes.

The key idea of non-rigid SfM is to represent the non-rigid deformations of objects in terms of a linear combination of bases:

$$\mathbf{Y} = \mathbf{RS} \quad \text{and} \quad \mathbf{S} = \mathbf{Vz}, \quad \mathbf{RR}^T = I, \tag{1}$$

where $\mathbf{Y}$ is the stacked 2D keypoints, $\mathbf{R}$ is the camera projection for the $N$ images. $\mathbf{S}$ is the 3D structure which is modeled by the linear combination of the stacked deformation bases $\mathbf{V}$, and $\mathbf{z}$ is the coefficient.

Firstly, as is well known, there are ambiguities between the projection $\mathbf{R}$ and the 3D structure $\mathbf{S}$ in the matrix factorization, *i.e.* let $\mathbf{A}_1$ be an invertible matrix, then $\mathbf{R} \leftarrow \mathbf{RA}_1$ and $\mathbf{S} \leftarrow \mathbf{A}_1^{-1}\mathbf{S}$ will not change the value of $\mathbf{RS}$. These ambiguities can be solved by imposing orthogonality constraints on the camera parameters $\mathbf{RR}^T = I$ up to a fixed rotation, which is a "gauge freedom" [37] corresponding to a choice of coordinate system.

In addition, there are other ambiguities between the coefficients $\mathbf{z}$ and the deformation bases $\mathbf{V}$ [4]. Specifically, let $\mathbf{A}_2$ be another invertible matrix, and let $\mathbf{w}$ lie in the null space of the projected deformation bases $\mathbf{RV}$, then $\mathbf{z} \leftarrow \mathbf{A}_2\mathbf{z}$ and $\mathbf{V} \leftarrow \mathbf{VA}_2^{-1}$, or $\mathbf{z} \leftarrow \mathbf{z} + \alpha\mathbf{w}$ will not change the value of $\mathbf{RVz}$. This motivated Bregler *et al.* to impose a Gaussian prior on the coefficient $\mathbf{z}$ in order to eliminate the ambiguities. Recently, it was proved in [25] that these ambiguities are also "fake", *i.e.* they do not affect the estimate of the 3D structure. This proof facilitated prior-free matrix factorization methods for non-rigid SfM [9,10].

## 4   Symmetric Non-rigid Structure from Motion

In this paper we extend non-rigid SfM methods by requiring that the 3D structure is symmetric. We assume the deformations are non-rigid and also symmetric[2]. We propose two symmetric non-rigid SfM models. One is the extension of the iterative EM-PPCA model with a prior on the deformation coefficients [5], and the other extends the prior-free matrix factorization model [9,10].

For simplicity of derivation, we focus on estimating the 3D structure and camera parameters. In practice, there are occluded keypoints in almost all images in the Pascal3D+ dataset. But we use standard ways to deal with them, such as initializing them ignoring symmetry by rank 3 recovery using the first 3 largest singular value, then treating them as missing data to be estimated by EM or coordinate descent algorithms. In our companion paper [26]), we gave details of these methods for the simpler case of rigid structure from motion.

---

[2] We assume symmetric deformations because our problem involves deformations from one symmetric object to another. But it also can be extended to non-symmetric deformations straightforwardly.

Note that we use slightly different camera models for Sym-EM-PPCA (weak perspective projection) and Sym-PriorFree (orthographic projection). This is to stay consistent with the non-symmetric methods which we compare with, namely [5] and [9,10]. Similarly, we treat translation differently by either centralizing the data or treating it as a variable to be estimated, as appropriate. We will discuss this further when presenting the Sym-PriorFree method.

### 4.1 The Symmetric EM-PPCA Model

In EM-PPCA [5], Bregler *et al.* assume that the 3D structure is represented by a mean structure $\bar{S}$ plus a non-rigid deformation. Suppose there are $P$ keypoints on the structure, the non-rigid model of EM-PPCA is:

$$\mathbb{Y}_n = G_n(\bar{\mathbb{S}} + \mathbf{V}z_n) + \mathbb{T}_n + N_n, \tag{2}$$

where $\mathbb{Y}_n \in \mathbb{R}^{2P \times 1}, \bar{\mathbb{S}} \in \mathbb{R}^{3P \times 1}$, and $\mathbb{T}_n \in \mathbb{R}^{2P \times 1}$ are the stacked vectors of 2D keypoints, 3D mean structure and translations. $G_n = I_P \otimes c_n R_n$, in which $c_n$ is the scale parameter for weak perspective projection, $\mathbf{V} = [\mathbb{V}_1, ..., \mathbb{V}_K] \in \mathbb{R}^{3P \times K}$ is the grouped $K$ deformation bases, $z_n \in \mathbb{R}^{K \times 1}$ is the coefficient of the $K$ bases, and $N_n$ is the Gaussian noise $N_n \sim \mathcal{N}(0, \sigma^2 I)$.

Extending Eq. (2) to our symmetry problem in which there are $P$ keypoint pairs $\mathbb{Y}_n$ and $\mathbb{Y}_n^\dagger$, we have:

$$\mathbb{Y}_n = G_n(\bar{\mathbb{S}} + \mathbf{V}z_n) + \mathbb{T}_n + N_n, \quad \mathbb{Y}_n^\dagger = G_n(\bar{\mathbb{S}}^\dagger + \mathbf{V}^\dagger z_n) + \mathbb{T}_n + N_n. \tag{3}$$

Assuming that the object is symmetric along the $x$-axis, the relationship between $\bar{\mathbb{S}}$ and $\bar{\mathbb{S}}^\dagger$, $\mathbf{V}$ and $\mathbf{V}^\dagger$ are:

$$\bar{\mathbb{S}}^\dagger = \mathcal{A}_P \bar{\mathbb{S}}, \quad \mathbf{V}^\dagger = \mathcal{A}_P \mathbf{V}, \tag{4}$$

where $\mathcal{A}_P = I_P \otimes \mathcal{A}$, $\mathcal{A} = \text{diag}([-1, 1, 1])$ is a matrix operator which negates the first row, and $I_P \in \mathbb{R}^{P \times P}$ is an identity matrix. Thus, we have[3]:

$$P(\mathbb{Y}_n | z_n, G_n, \bar{\mathbb{S}}, \mathbf{V}, \mathbb{T}) = \mathcal{N}(G_n(\bar{\mathbb{S}} + \mathbf{V}z_n) + \mathbb{T}_n, \sigma^2 I)$$

$$P(\mathbb{Y}_n^\dagger | z_n, G_n, \bar{\mathbb{S}}, \mathbf{V}^\dagger, \mathbb{T}) = \mathcal{N}(G_n(\mathcal{A}_P \bar{\mathbb{S}} + \mathbf{V}^\dagger z_n) + \mathbb{T}_n, \sigma^2 I) \tag{5}$$

Following Bregler *et al.* [5], we introduce a prior $P(z_n)$ on the coefficient variable $z_n$. This prior is a zero mean unit variance Gaussian. It is used for (partly) regularizing the inference task but also for dealing with the ambiguities between basis coefficients $z_n$ and bases $\mathbf{V}$, as mentioned above (when [5] was published it was not realized that these are "gauge freedom"). This enables us to treat $z_n$ as the hidden variable and use EM algorithm to estimate the structure and camera viewpoint parameters. The formulation of the problem, in terms of Gaussian distributions (or, more technically, the use of conjugate priors) means that both steps of the EM algorithm are straightforward to implement.

---

[3] We set hard constraints on $\bar{\mathbb{S}}$ and $\bar{\mathbb{S}}^\dagger$, *i.e.* replace $\bar{\mathbb{S}}^\dagger$ by $\mathcal{A}_P \bar{\mathbb{S}}$ in Eq. (5), because it can be guaranteed by the Sym-RSfM initialization in our companion paper [26]. While the initialization on $\mathbf{V}$ and $\mathbf{V}^\dagger$ by PCA cannot guarantee such a desirable property, thus a Language multiplier term is used for the constraint on $\mathbf{V}$ and $\mathbf{V}^\dagger$ in Eq. (9).

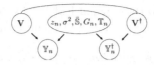

**Fig. 1.** The graphical model of the variables and parameters.

*Remark 1.* Our Sym-EM-PPCA method is a natural extension of the method in [5] to maximize the marginal probability $P(\mathbb{Y}_n, \mathbb{Y}_n^\dagger | G_n, \bar{\mathbb{S}}, \mathbf{V}, \mathbf{V}^\dagger, \mathbb{T})$ with a Gaussian prior on $z_n$ and a Language multiplier term (*i.e.* a regularization term) on $\mathbf{V}, \mathbf{V}^\dagger$. This can be solved by *general EM* algorithm [38], where both the **E** and **M** steps take simple forms because the underlying probability distributions are Gaussians (due to conjugate Gaussian prior).

**E-Step**: This step is to get the statistics of $z_n$ from its posterior. Let the prior on $z_n$ be $P(z_n) = \mathcal{N}(0, I)$ as in [5]. Then, we have $P(z_n)$, $P(\mathbb{Y}_n | z_n; \sigma^2, \bar{\mathbb{S}}, \mathbf{V}, G_n, \mathbb{T}_n)$ and $P(\mathbb{Y}_n^\dagger | z_n; \sigma^2, \bar{\mathbb{S}}, \mathbf{V}^\dagger, G_n, \mathbb{T}_n)$, which do not provide the complete posterior distribution directly. Fortunately, the conditional dependence of the variables shown in Fig. 1 (graphical model) implies that the posterior of $z_n$ can be calculated by:

$$
\begin{aligned}
&P(z_n | \mathbb{Y}_n, \mathbb{Y}_n^\dagger; \sigma^2, \bar{\mathbb{S}}, \mathbf{V}, \mathbf{V}^\dagger, G_n, \mathbb{T}_n) \\
\sim& P(z_n, \mathbb{Y}_n, \mathbb{Y}_n^\dagger | \sigma^2, \bar{\mathbb{S}}, \mathbf{V}, \mathbf{V}^\dagger, G_n, \mathbb{T}_n) \\
=& P(\mathbb{Y}_n | z_n; \sigma^2, \bar{\mathbb{S}}, \mathbf{V}, G_n, \mathbb{T}_n) P(\mathbb{Y}_n^\dagger | z_n; \sigma^2, \bar{\mathbb{S}}, \mathbf{V}^\dagger, G_n, \mathbb{T}_n) P(z_n) \\
=& \mathcal{N}(z_n | \mu_n, \Sigma_n)
\end{aligned}
\tag{6}
$$

The last equation of Eq. (6) is obtained by the fact that the prior and the conditional distributions of $z_n$ are all Gaussians (conjugate prior). Then the first and second order statistics of $z_n$ can be obtained as:

$$
\mu_n = \gamma \left\{ \mathbf{V}^T G_n^T (\mathbb{Y}_n - G_n \bar{\mathbb{S}} - \mathbb{T}_n) + \mathbf{V}^{\dagger T} G_n^T (\mathbb{Y}_n^\dagger - G_n \mathcal{A}_P \bar{\mathbb{S}} - \mathbb{T}_n) \right\}
\tag{7}
$$

$$
\phi_n = \sigma^2 \gamma^{-1} + \mu_n \mu_n^T
\tag{8}
$$

where $\gamma = (\mathbf{V}^T G_n^T G_n \mathbf{V} + \mathbf{V}^{\dagger T} G_n^T G_n \mathbf{V}^\dagger + \sigma^2 I)^{-1}$.

**M-Step**: This is to maximize the joint likelihood which is similar to the coordinate descent in Sym-RSfM (in a companion paper [26]) and that in Sym-PriorFree method in the later sections. The complete log-likelihood $Q(\theta)$ is:

$$
\begin{aligned}
\mathcal{Q}(\theta) =& -\sum_n \ln P(\mathbb{Y}_n, \mathbb{Y}_n^\dagger | z_n; G_n, \bar{\mathbb{S}}, \mathbf{V}, \mathbf{V}^\dagger, \mathbb{T}) + \lambda ||\mathbf{V}^\dagger - \mathcal{A}_P \mathbf{V}||^2 \\
=& -\sum_n \left( \ln P(\mathbb{Y}_n | z_n; G_n, \bar{\mathbb{S}}, \mathbf{V}, \mathbb{T}) + \ln P(\mathbb{Y}_n^\dagger | z_n; G_n, \bar{\mathbb{S}}, \mathbf{V}^\dagger, \mathbb{T}) \right) + \lambda ||\mathbf{V}^\dagger - \mathcal{A}_P \mathbf{V}||^2
\end{aligned}
$$

$$
\text{s. t.} \quad R_n R_n^T = I, \quad \text{where } \theta = \{G_n, \bar{\mathbb{S}}, \mathbf{V}, \mathbf{V}^\dagger, \mathbb{T}_n, \sigma^2\}.
\tag{9}
$$

The maximization of Eq. (9) is straightforward, *i.e.* taking the derivative of each unknown parameter in $\theta$ and equating it to 0. The update rule of each parameter is very similar to the original EM-PPCA [5] (except $\bar{\mathbf{S}}, \mathbf{V}, \mathbf{V}^\dagger$ should be updated jointly), which we put in supplementary material.

*Initialization.* $\mathbf{V}$ and $\mathbf{V}^\dagger$ are initialized by the PCA on the residual of the 2D keypoints minus their rigid projections iteratively. Other variables (including the rigid projections) are initialized by Sym-RSfM [26]. Specifically, $R_n$, $\bar{S}$ and the occluded points $Y_{n,p}, Y_{n,p}^\dagger$ can be initialized directly from Sym-RSfM, $c_n$ is initialized as 1, $t_n$ is initialized by $t_n = \sum_p (Y_{n,p} - R_n \bar{S}_p + Y_{n,p}^\dagger - R_n \mathcal{A} \bar{S}_p)$.

## 4.2   The Symmetric Prior-Free Matrix Factorization Model

In the Prior-Free NRSfM [9,10], Dai *et al.* also used the linear combination of several deformations bases to represent the non-rigid deformation. But, unlike EM-PPCA [5], Dai *et al.* estimated the non-rigid structure directly without using the mean structure and the prior on the coefficients. We make the same assumptions so that we can directly compare with them.

Assume that $Y_n \in \mathbb{R}^{2 \times P}$ are the $P$ keypoints for image $n$, then we have:

$$Y_n = R_n S_n = [z_{n1} R_n, ..., z_{nK} R_n][\mathbf{V}_1, ..., \mathbf{V}_K]^T = \Pi_n \mathbf{V},$$
$$Y_n^\dagger = R_n S_n^\dagger = [z_{n1} R_n, ..., z_{nK} R_n][\mathbf{V}_1^\dagger, ..., \mathbf{V}_K^\dagger]^T = \Pi_n \mathbf{V}^\dagger, \tag{10}$$

where $\mathbf{z}_n = [z_{n1}, ..., z_{nK}] \in \mathbb{R}^{1 \times K}$, $\Pi_n = R_n(\mathbf{z}_n \otimes I_3) \in \mathbb{R}^{2 \times 3K}$, and $\mathbf{V} = [\mathbf{V}_1^T, ..., \mathbf{V}_K^T]^T \in \mathbb{R}^{3K \times P}$.

Without loss of generality, we assume that the symmetry is across the $x$-axis: $S_n = \mathcal{A} S_n^\dagger$, where $\mathcal{A} = \text{diag}[-1, 1, 1]^T$ is a matrix operator negating the first row of $S_n$. Then the first two terms in Eq. (10) give us the energy function (or the likelihood) to estimate the unknown $R_n, S_n$ and recover the missing data by *coordinate descent* on:

$$\mathcal{Q}(R_n, S_n, \{Y_{n,p}, (n,p) \in IVS\}, \{Y_{n,p}^\dagger, (n,p) \in IVS^\dagger\})$$
$$= \sum_{(n,p) \in VS} ||Y_{n,p} - R_n S_{n,p}||_2^2 + \sum_{(n,p) \in VS^\dagger} ||Y_{n,p}^\dagger - R_n \mathcal{A} S_{n,p}||_2^2 +$$
$$\sum_{(n,p) \in IVS} ||Y_{n,p} - R_n S_{n,p}||_2^2 + \sum_{(n,p) \in IVS^\dagger} ||Y_{n,p}^\dagger - R_n \mathcal{A} S_{n,p}||_2^2, \tag{11}$$

where $VS$ and $IVS$ are the index sets of the *visible* and *invisible* keypoints, respectively. $Y_{n,p}$ and $S_{n,p}$ are the 2D and 3D $p$'th keypoints of the $n$'th image. We treat the $\{Y_{n,p}, (n,p) \in IVS\}, \{Y_{n,p}^\dagger, (n,p) \in IVS^\dagger\}$ as missing/hidden variables to be estimated.

*Remark 2.* It is straightforward to minimize Eq. (11) by *coordinate descent*. The missing points can be initialized simply by rank 3 recovery (*i.e.* by the reconstruction using the first 3 largest singular value) ignoring the symmetry property and non-rigidity. But it is much harder to get good initializations for the $R_n$ and $S_n$. In the following, we will describe how we get good initializations for each $R_n$ and $S_n$ exploiting symmetry after the missing points have been initialized.

Let $\mathbf{Y}$ is the stacked keypoints of $N$ images, $\mathbf{Y} = [Y_1^T, ..., Y_N^T]^T \in \mathbb{R}^{2N \times P}$, the model is represented by:

$$\mathbf{Y} = \mathbf{R}\mathbf{S} = \begin{bmatrix} R_1 S_1 \\ \vdots \\ R_N S_N \end{bmatrix} = \begin{bmatrix} z_{11}R_1, & ..., & z_{1K}R_1 \\ \vdots & \ddots & \vdots \\ z_{N1}R_N, & ..., & z_{NK}R_N \end{bmatrix} \begin{bmatrix} \mathbf{V}_1 \\ \vdots \\ \mathbf{V}_K \end{bmatrix} = \mathbf{\Pi}\mathbf{V}, \qquad (12)$$

where $\mathbf{R} = \text{blkdiag}([R_1, ..., R_N]) \in \mathbb{R}^{2N \times 3N}$ are the stacked camera projection matrices, in which blkdiag denotes block diagonal. $\mathbf{S} = [S_1^T, ..., S_N^T]^T \in \mathbb{R}^{3N \times P}$ are the stacked 3D structures. $\mathbf{\Pi} = \mathbf{R}(\mathbf{z} \otimes I_3) \in \mathbb{R}^{2N \times 3K}$, where $\mathbf{z} \in \mathbb{R}^{N \times K}$ are the stacked coefficients. Similar equations apply to $\mathbf{Y}^\dagger$.

Note that $\mathbf{R} \in \mathbb{R}^{2N \times 3N}$, $\mathbf{V} \in \mathbb{R}^{3K \times P}$ are stacked differently than how they were stacked for the Sym-EM-PPCA method (*i.e.* $\mathbf{R} \in \mathbb{R}^{2N \times 3}$, $\mathbf{V} \in \mathbb{R}^{3P \times K}$). It is because now we have $N$ different $S_n$'s (*i.e.* $\mathbf{S} \in \mathbb{R}^{3N \times P}$), while there is only one $\bar{S}$ in the Sym-EM-PPCA method.

In the following, we assume the deformation bases are symmetric, which ensures that the non-rigid structures are symmetric (*e.g.* the deformation from *sedan* to *truck* is non-rigid and symmetric since *sedan* and *truck* are both symmetric). This yields an energy function:

$$\begin{aligned} \mathcal{Q}(\mathbf{R}, \mathbf{S}) &= ||\mathbf{Y} - \mathbf{R}\mathbf{S}||_2^2 + ||\mathbf{Y}^\dagger - \mathbf{R}\mathcal{A}_N \mathbf{S}^\dagger||_2^2 \\ &= ||\mathbf{Y} - \mathbf{\Pi}\mathbf{V}||_2^2 + ||\mathbf{Y}^\dagger - \mathbf{\Pi}\mathcal{A}_K \mathbf{V}^\dagger||_2^2, \end{aligned} \qquad (13)$$

where $\mathcal{A}_N = I_N \otimes \mathcal{A}, \mathcal{A}_K = I_K \otimes \mathcal{A}$, and $\mathcal{A} = \text{diag}([-1, 1, 1])$.

*Remark 3.* Note that we cannot use the first equation of Eq. (13) to solve $\mathbf{R}, \mathbf{S}$ directly (even if not exploiting symmetry), because $\mathbf{Y}$ and $\mathbf{Y}^\dagger$ are of rank $min\{2N, 3K, P\}$ but estimating $\mathbf{R}, \mathbf{S}$ directly by SVD on $\mathbf{Y}$ and/or $\mathbf{Y}^\dagger$ requires rank $3N$ matrix factorization. Hence we focus on the last equation of Eq. (13) to get the initialization of $\mathbf{\Pi}, \mathbf{V}$ firstly. Then, $\mathbf{R}, \mathbf{S}$ can be updated by coordinate descent on the first equation of Eq. (13) under *orthogonality constraints* on $\mathbf{R}$ and *low-rank* constraint on $\mathbf{S}$.

Observe that the last equation of Eq. (13) cannot be optimized directly by SVD either, because they consist of two terms which are not independent. In other words, the matrix factorizations of $\mathbf{Y}$ and $\mathbf{Y}^\dagger$ do not give consistent estimations of $\mathbf{\Pi}$ and $\mathbf{V}$. Instead, we now discuss how to estimate $\mathbf{\Pi}$ and $\mathbf{V}$ by rotating the coordinate axes (to decouple the depended energy terms), performing matrix factorization, and using subspace intersection (to eliminate the ambiguities), which is an extension of the original prior-free method [9, 10] and our companion Sym-RSfM [26].

We first rotate coordinate systems (of $\mathbf{Y}, \mathbf{Y}^\dagger$) to obtain decoupled equations:

$$\mathbf{L} = \frac{\mathbf{Y} - \mathbf{Y}^\dagger}{2} = \hat{\mathbf{\Pi}}^1 \hat{\mathbf{V}}_x \qquad \mathbf{M} = \frac{\mathbf{Y} + \mathbf{Y}^\dagger}{2} = \hat{\mathbf{\Pi}}^2 \hat{\mathbf{V}}_{yz}, \qquad (14)$$

where the two righthand sides of the equation depend on different components of $\hat{\mathbf{\Pi}}, \hat{\mathbf{V}}$. More specifically, by discarding the all 0 rows of the bases, $\hat{\mathbf{\Pi}}^1 \in \mathbb{R}^{2N \times K}$, $\hat{\mathbf{\Pi}}^2 \in \mathbb{R}^{2N \times 2K}$, $\hat{\mathbf{V}}_x \in \mathbb{R}^{K \times P}$, $\hat{\mathbf{V}}_{yz} \in \mathbb{R}^{2K \times P}$.

This yield two independent energies to be minimized separately by SVD:

$$\mathcal{Q}(\mathbf{\Pi}, \mathbf{V}) = ||\mathbf{L} - \hat{\mathbf{\Pi}}^1 \hat{\mathbf{V}}_x||_2^2 + ||\mathbf{M} - \hat{\mathbf{\Pi}}^2 \hat{\mathbf{V}}_{yz}||_2^2 \qquad (15)$$

*Remark 4.* We have formulated Sym-PriorFree as minimizing two energy terms in Eq. (15), which consists of independent variables. This implies that we can solve them by matrix factorization on each energy term separately, which gives solutions for $\mathbf{\Pi} = \mathbf{R}(\mathbf{z} \otimes I_3)$ and for the basis vectors $\mathbf{V}$ up to an ambiguity $H$. It will be discussed more explicitly in the following and we will show how to use orthogonality of the camera parameters to partially solve for $H$.

Solving Eq. (15) by matrix factorization gives us solutions up to a matrix ambiguity $H$. More precisely, there are ambiguity matrices $H^1, H^2$ between the true solutions $\mathbf{\Pi}^1, \mathbf{V}_x, \mathbf{\Pi}^2, \mathbf{V}_{yz}$ and the initial estimation output by matrix factorization $\hat{\mathbf{\Pi}}^1, \hat{\mathbf{V}}_x, \hat{\mathbf{\Pi}}^2, \hat{\mathbf{V}}_{yz}$:

$$\mathbf{L} = \mathbf{\Pi}^1 \mathbf{V}_x = \hat{\mathbf{\Pi}}^1 H^1 (H^1)^{-1} \hat{\mathbf{V}}_x \qquad \mathbf{M} = \mathbf{\Pi}^2 \mathbf{V}_{yz} = \hat{\mathbf{\Pi}}^2 H^2 (H^2)^{-1} \hat{\mathbf{V}}_{yz} \qquad (16)$$

where $H^1 \in \mathbb{R}^{K \times K}$ and $H^2 \in \mathbb{R}^{2K \times 2K}$.

Now, the problem becomes to find $H^1, H^2$. Note that we have orthonormality constraints on each camera projection matrix $R_n$, which further impose constraints on $\Pi_n$. Thus, it can be used to partially estimate the ambiguity matrices $H^1, H^2$. Since the factorized matrix, *i.e.* $\mathbf{L}$ and $\mathbf{M}$, are the stacked 2D keypoints for all the images, thus $H^1$ and $H^2$ obtained from one image must satisfy the orthonormality constraints on other images, hence we use $\Pi_n \in \mathbb{R}^{2 \times 3K}$ (*i.e.* from image $n$) for our derivation.

Let $\hat{\Pi}_n = [\hat{\Pi}_n^1, \hat{\Pi}_n^2] = \begin{bmatrix} \hat{\pi}_n^{1,1:K}, & \hat{\pi}_n^{1,K+1:3K} \\ \hat{\pi}_n^{2,1:K}, & \hat{\pi}_n^{2,K+1:3K} \end{bmatrix}$, where $\hat{\pi}_n^{1,1:K}, \hat{\pi}_n^{2,1:K} \in$
$\mathbb{R}^{1 \times K}$ are the first $K$ columns of the first and second rows of $\hat{\Pi}_n$, and $\hat{\pi}_n^{1,K+1:3K}, \hat{\pi}_n^{2,K+1:3K} \in \mathbb{R}^{1 \times 2K}$ are the last $2K$ columns of the first and second rows of $\hat{\Pi}_n$, respectively. Thus, Eq. (16) implies:

$$L_n = \hat{\Pi}_n^1 H^1 (H^1)^{-1} \hat{\mathbf{V}}_x = \begin{bmatrix} r_n^{11} \\ r_n^{21} \end{bmatrix} \mathbf{z}_n \mathbf{V}_x, \qquad (17)$$

$$M_n = \hat{\Pi}_n^2 H^2 (H^2)^{-1} \hat{\mathbf{V}}_{yz} = \begin{bmatrix} r_n^{1,2:3} \\ r_n^{2,2:3} \end{bmatrix} (\mathbf{z}_n \otimes I_2) \mathbf{V}_{yz}, \qquad (18)$$

where $L_n, M_n \in \mathbb{R}^{2 \times P}$ are the $n$'th double-row of $\mathbf{L}, \mathbf{M}$. $[r_n^{11}, r_n^{12}]^T$ is the first column of the camera projection matrix of the $n$'th image $R_n$, and $[(r_n^{1,2:3})^T, (r_n^{2,2:3})^T]^T$ is the second and third columns of $R_n$.

Let $h_k^1 \in \mathbb{R}^{K \times 1}, h_k^2 \in \mathbb{R}^{2K \times 2}$ be the $k$th column and double-column of $H^1, H^2$, respectively. Then, from Eqs. (17) and (18), we get:

$$\hat{\Pi}_n^1 h_k^1 = \begin{bmatrix} \hat{\pi}_n^{1,1K} \\ \hat{\pi}_n^{2,1K} \end{bmatrix} h_k^1 = z_{nk} \begin{bmatrix} r_n^{11} \\ r_n^{21} \end{bmatrix} \qquad \hat{\Pi}_n^2 h_k^2 = \begin{bmatrix} \hat{\pi}_n^{1,K+1:3K} \\ \hat{\pi}_n^{2,K+1:3K} \end{bmatrix} h_k^2 = z_{nk} \begin{bmatrix} r_n^{1,2:3} \\ r_n^{2,2:3} \end{bmatrix}$$

$$\qquad (19)$$

By merging the equations of Eq. (19) together, $R_n$ can be represented by:

$$[\hat{\Pi}_n^1 h_k^1, \hat{\Pi}_n^2 h_k^2] = \begin{bmatrix} \hat{\pi}_n^{1,1:K}, & \hat{\pi}_n^{1,K+1:3K} \\ \hat{\pi}_n^{2,1:K}, & \hat{\pi}_n^{2,K+1:3K} \end{bmatrix} \begin{bmatrix} h_k^1, & \mathbf{0}_{K\times 2K} \\ \mathbf{0}_{2K\times K}, & h_k^2 \end{bmatrix} = z_{nk} R_n. \quad (20)$$

*Remark 5.* Similar to the rigid symmetry case in [26], Eq. (20) indicates that there is no rotation ambiguities on the symmetric direction. The rotation ambiguities only exist in the $yz$-plane (*i.e.* the non-symmetric plane).

The orthonormality constraints $R_n R_n^T = I$ can be imposed to estimate $h_k^1, h_k^2$:

$$[\hat{\Pi}_n^1 h_k^1, \hat{\Pi}_n^2 h_k^2][\hat{\Pi}_n^1 h_k^1, \hat{\Pi}_n^2 h_k^2]^T = z_{nk}^2 I$$

$$= \begin{bmatrix} \hat{\pi}_n^{1,1:K}, & \hat{\pi}_n^{1,K+1:3K} \\ \hat{\pi}_n^{2,1:K}, & \hat{\pi}_n^{2,K+1:3K} \end{bmatrix} \begin{bmatrix} h_k^1 h_k^{1T}, & \mathbf{0}_{K\times 2} \\ \mathbf{0}_{2K\times 1}, & h_k^2 h_k^{2T} \end{bmatrix} \begin{bmatrix} \hat{\pi}_n^{1,1:K}, & \hat{\pi}_n^{1,K+1:3K} \\ \hat{\pi}_n^{2,1:K}, & \hat{\pi}_n^{2,K+1:3K} \end{bmatrix}^T \quad (21)$$

Thus, we have:

$$\hat{\pi}_n^{1,1:K} h_k^1 h_k^{1T} (\hat{\pi}_n^{1,1:K})^T + \hat{\pi}_n^{1,K+1:3K} h_k^2 h_k^{2T} (\hat{\pi}_n^{1,K+1:3K})^T = z_{nk}^2 \quad (22)$$

$$\hat{\pi}_n^{2,1:K} h_k^1 h_k^{1T} (\hat{\pi}_n^{2,1:K})^T + \hat{\pi}_n^{2,K+1:3K} h_k^2 h_k^{2T} (\hat{\pi}_n^{2,K+1:3K})^T = z_{nk}^2 \quad (23)$$

$$\hat{\pi}_n^{1,1:K} h_k^1 h_k^{1T} (\hat{\pi}_n^{2,1:K})^T + \hat{\pi}_n^{1,K+1:3K} h_k^2 h_k^{2T} (\hat{\pi}_n^{2,K+1:3K})^T = 0 \quad (24)$$

*Remark 6.* The main difference of the derivations from the orthonormality constraints between the rigid and non-rigid cases is that, for the rigid case, the dot product of each row of $\mathbf{R}$ is equal to 1, while for non-rigid the dot product on each row of $\mathbf{\Pi}$ gives us a unknown value $z_{nk}^2$. But note that $z_{nk}^2$ is the same for the both rows, *i.e.* Eqs. (22) and (23), corresponding to the same projection.

Eliminating the unknown value $z_{nk}^2$ in Eqs. (22) and (23) (by subtraction) and rewriting in vectorized form gives:

$$\begin{bmatrix} \hat{\pi}_n^{1,1:K} \otimes \hat{\pi}_n^{1,1:K} - \hat{\pi}_n^{2,1:K} \otimes \hat{\pi}_n^{2,1:K}, & \hat{\pi}_n^{1,K+1:3K} \otimes \hat{\pi}_n^{1,K+1:3K} - \hat{\pi}_n^{2,K+1:3K} \otimes \hat{\pi}_n^{1,K+1:3K} \\ \hat{\pi}_n^{1,1:K} \otimes \hat{\pi}_n^{2,1:K}, & \hat{\pi}_n^{1,K+1:3K} \otimes \hat{\pi}_n^{2,K+1:3K} \end{bmatrix}$$

$$\cdot \begin{bmatrix} \text{vec}(h_k^1 h_k^{1T}) \\ \text{vec}(h_k^2 h_k^{2T}) \end{bmatrix} = A_n \begin{bmatrix} \text{vec}(h_k^1 h_k^{1T}) \\ \text{vec}(h_k^2 h_k^{2T}) \end{bmatrix} = 0, \quad (25)$$

Letting $\mathbf{A} = [A_1^T, ..., A_N^T]^T$, yield the constraints:

$$\mathbf{A}[\text{vec}(h_k^1 h_k^{1T})^T, \text{vec}(h_k^2 h_k^{2T})^T]^T = 0. \quad (26)$$

*Remark 7.* As shown in Xiao *et al.* [4], the orthonormality constraints, *i.e.* Eq. (26), are not sufficient to solve for the ambiguity matrix $H$. But Xiao *et al.* showed that the solution of $[\text{vec}(h_k^1 h_k^{1T})^T, \text{vec}(h_k^2 h_k^{2T})^T]^T$ lies in the null space of $\mathbf{A}$ of dimensionality $(2K^2 - K)$ [4]. Akhter *et al.* [6] proved that this was a "gauge freedom" because all legitimate solutions lying in this subspace (despite under-constrained) gave the same solutions for the 3D structure. More technically, the ambiguity of $H$ corresponds only to a linear combination of $H$'s column-triplet and a rotation on $H$ [25]. This observation was exploited by Dai *et al.* in [9,10], where they showed that, up to the ambiguities aforementioned, $h_k h_k^T$ can be solved by the intersection of 3 subspaces as we will describe in the following.

Following the strategy in [9,10], we have intersection of subspaces conditions:

$$\left\{ \mathbf{A} \begin{bmatrix} \text{vec}(h_k^1 h_k^{1T}) \\ \text{vec}(h_k^2 h_k^{2T}) \end{bmatrix} = 0 \right\} \cap \left\{ \begin{matrix} h_k^1 h_k^{1T} = 0 \\ h_k^2 h_k^{2T} \succeq 0 \end{matrix} \right\} \cap \left\{ \begin{matrix} \text{rank}(h_k^1 h_k^{1T}) = 1 \\ \text{rank}(h_k^2 h_k^{2T}) = 2 \end{matrix} \right\} \quad (27)$$

The first subspace comes from Eq. (26), $i.e.$ the solutions of the Eq. (26) lie in the null space of $\mathbf{A}$ of dimensionality $(2K^2 - K)$ [4]. The second subspace requires that $h_k^1 h_k^{1T}$ and $h_k^2 h_k^{2T}$ are positive semi-definite. The third subspace comes from the fact that $h_k^1$ is of rank 1 and $h_k^2$ is of rank 2.

Note that as stated in [9,10], Eq. (27) imposes all the necessary constraints on $[\text{vec}(h_k^1 h_k^{1T})^T, \text{vec}(h_k^2 h_k^{2T})^T]^T$. There is no difference in the recovered 3D structures using the different solutions that satisfy Eq. (27).

We can obtain a solution of $[\text{vec}(h_k^1 h_k^{1T})^T, \text{vec}(h_k^2 h_k^{2T})^T]^T$, under the condition of Eq. (27), by standard semi-definite programming (SDP):

$$\min \|h_k^1 h_k^{1T}\|_* + \|h_k^2 h_k^{2T}\|_*$$
$$\text{s. t. } h_k^1 h_k^{1T} \succeq 0, \quad h_k^2 h_k^{2T} \succeq 0 \quad \mathbf{A}[\text{vec}(h_k^1 h_k^{1T})^T, \text{vec}(h_k^2 h_k^{2T})^T]^T = 0, \quad (28)$$

where $\| \cdot \|_*$ indicates the trace norm.

*Remark 8.* After recovering $h_k^1$ and $h_k^2$, we can estimate the camera parameters $R$ as follows. Note that it does not need to the whole ambiguity matrix $H$ [9,10].

After $h_k^1, h_k^2$ has been solved, Eq. (20) ($i.e.$ $[\hat{\Pi}_n^1 h_k^1, \hat{\Pi}_n^2 h_k^2] = z_{nk} R_n$) implies that the camera projection matrix $R_n$ can be obtained by normalizing the two rows of $[\hat{\Pi}_n^1 h_k^1, \hat{\Pi}_n^2 h_k^2]$ to have unit $\ell_2$ norm. Then, $\mathbf{R}$ can be constructed by $\mathbf{R} = \text{blkdiag}([R_1, ..., R_N])$.

*Remark 9.* After estimated the camera parameters, we can solve for the 3D structure adopting the methods in [9,10], $i.e.$ by minimizing a *low-rank* constraint on rearranged ($i.e.$ more compact) $\mathbf{S}^\sharp$ under the orthographic projection model.

Similar to [9,10], the structure $\mathbf{S}$ can be estimated by:

$$\min \|\mathbf{S}^\sharp\|_*$$
$$\text{s. t. } [\mathbf{Y}, \mathbf{Y}^\dagger] = \mathbf{R}[\mathbf{S}, \mathcal{A}_N \mathbf{S}] \quad \mathbf{S}^\sharp = [\mathcal{P}_x, \mathcal{P}_y, \mathcal{P}_z](I_3 \otimes \mathbf{S}), \quad (29)$$

where $\mathcal{A}_N = I_N \otimes \text{diag}([-1,1,1])$, $\mathbf{S} = [S_1^T, ..., S_N^T]^T \in \mathbb{R}^{3N \times P}$ and $\mathbf{S}^\sharp \in \mathbb{R}^{N \times 3P}$ is rearranged and more compact $\mathbf{S}$, $i.e.$

$$\mathbf{S}^\sharp = \begin{bmatrix} x_{11}, \ ..., \ x_{1P}, \ y_{11}, \ ..., \ y_{1P}, \ z_{11}, \ ..., \ z_{1P} \\ \vdots \quad\quad \vdots \quad\quad \vdots \quad\quad \vdots \quad\quad \vdots \quad\quad \vdots \\ x_{N1}, \ ..., \ x_{NP}, \ y_{N1}, \ ..., \ y_{NP}, \ z_{N1}, \ ..., \ z_{NP} \end{bmatrix},$$

and $\mathcal{P}_x, \mathcal{P}_y, \mathcal{P}_z \in \mathbb{R}^{N \times 3N}$ are the row-permutation matrices of 0 and 1 that select $(I_3 \otimes \mathbf{S})$ to form $\mathbf{S}^\sharp$, $i.e.$ $\mathcal{P}_x(i, 3i - 2) = 1, \mathcal{P}_y(i, 3i - 1) = 1, \mathcal{P}_z(i, 3i) = 1$ for $i = 1, ..., N$.

*Remark 10.* After obtaining the initial estimates of $R_n, S_n$ (from matrix factorization as described above) and the occluded keypoints, we can minimize the full energy (likelihood) in Eq. (11) d by *coordinate descent* to obtain better estimates of $R_n, S_n$ and the occluded keypoints.

*Energy Minimization.* After obtained initial **R**, **S** and missing points, Eq. (11) can be minimized by coordinate descent. The energy about **R**, **S** is:

$$\mathcal{Q}(\mathbf{R}, \mathbf{S}) = ||\mathbf{Y} - \mathbf{R}\mathbf{S}||_2^2 + ||\mathbf{Y}^\dagger - \mathbf{R}\mathcal{A}_K\mathbf{S}||_2^2, \qquad (30)$$

Note that **S** can be updated exactly as the same as its initialization in Eq. (29) by the low-rank constraint. While each $R_n$ of **R** should be updated under the nonlinear orthonormality constraints $R_n R_n^T = I$ similar to the idea in EM-PPCA [5]: we first parameterize $R_n$ to a full $3 \times 3$ rotation matrix $Q$ and update $Q$ by its rotation increment. Please refer to the supplementary material for the details.

The occluded points $Y_{n,p}$ and $Y_{n,p}^\dagger$ with $(n, p) \in IVS$ are updated by minimizing the full energy in Eq. (11) directly:

$$Y_{n,p} = R_n S_p, \quad Y_{n,p}^\dagger = R_n \mathcal{A} S_{n,p} \qquad (31)$$

Similar to Sym-RSfM [26], after updating the occluded points, we also re-estimate the translation for each image by $t_n = \sum_p (Y_{n,p} - R_n S_p + Y_{n,p}^\dagger - R_n \mathcal{A} S_p)$, then centralize the data again by $Y_n \leftarrow Y_n - \mathbf{1}_P^T \otimes t_n$ and $Y_n^\dagger \leftarrow Y_n^\dagger - \mathbf{1}_P^T \otimes t_n$.

## 5    Experiments

### 5.1    Experimental Settings

We follow the experimental settings in [24], using the 2D annotations in [39] and 3D keypoints in Pascal3D+ [27]. Although Pascal3D+ is the best 3D dataset available, it still has some limitations for our task. Specifically, it does not have the complete 3D models for each object; instead it provides the 3D shapes of object subtypes. For example, it provides 10 subtypes for *car* category, such as *sedan, truck*, which ignores the shape variance within each subtype.

Similar to [7,9,10,35], the rotation error $e_R$ and shape error $e_S$ are used for evaluation. We normalize 3D groundtruth and our 3D estimates to eliminate different scales they may have. For each shape $S_n$ we use its standard deviations in $X, Y, Z$ coordinates $\sigma_n^x, \sigma_n^y, \sigma_n^z$ for the normalization: $S_n^{norm} = 3S_n/(\sigma_n^x + \sigma_n^y + \sigma_n^z)$. To deal with the rotation ambiguity between the 3D groundtruth and our reconstruction, we use the Procrustes method [40] to align them. Then, the rotation error $e_R$ and shape error $e_S$ can be calculated as:

$$e_R = \frac{1}{N} \sum_{n=1}^{N} ||R_n^{aligned} - R_n^*||_F, e_S = \frac{1}{2NP} \sum_{n=1}^{N} \sum_{p=1}^{2P} ||S_{n,p}^{norm\ aligned} - S_{n,p}^{norm*}||_F,$$
$$(32)$$

where $R_n^{aligned}$ and $R_n^*$ are the recovered and the groundtruth camera projection matrix for image $n$. $S_{n,p}^{norm\ aligned}$ and $S_{n,p}^{norm*}$ are the normalized estimated and the normalized groundtruth structure for the $p$'th point of image $n$. $R_n^{aligned}$ and $R_n^*$, $S_{n,p}^{norm\ aligned}$ and $S_{n,p}^{norm*}$ are aligned by Procrustes method [40].

## 5.2   Experimental Results on the Annotated Dataset

In this section, we construct the 3D keypoints for each image using the non-rigid model. Firstly, we follow the experimental setting in [24] and collect all images with more than 5 visible keypoints. Then, we do 10 iterations with rank 3 recovery to initialize the occluded/missing data. In this experiments, we use 3 deformation bases and set $\lambda$ in Sym-EM-PPCA, $i.e.$ in Eqs. (9), as 1.

We tested our algorithm on Pascal *aeroplane, bus, car, sofa, train, tv* based on the mean shape and rotation errors as in Eq. (32). For the shape error, since Pascal3D+ [27] only provides one 3D model for each subtype, we compare the reconstructed 3D keypoints for each image with their subtype groundtruth. More specifically, the reconstructed 3D keypoints for each image are grouped into subtypes, and we count the mean shape error (we also have median errors in the supplementary material) by comparing all the images within that subtype to the subtype groundtruth from Pascal3D+. While such problem does not exist for the rotation errors, $i.e.$ the groundtruth projection is available for each image in Pascal3D+ [27], thus the rotation errors are reported by each category.

The results are reported in Table 1. The results show that our method outperforms the baselines in general. But we note that our method is not as good as the baselines in some cases, especially for *tv*. The reasons might be: (i) the orthographic projection is inaccurate when the object is close to the camera. Although all the methods used the same suboptimal orthographic projection for these cases, it may deteriorate more on our model sometimes, since we model more constraints. (ii) It might be because the 3D groundtruth in Pascal3D+,

**Table 1.** The mean *shape* and *rotation* errors for *aeroplane, bus, car, sofa, train, tv*. The Roman numerals indicates the index of subtypes for the mean shape error, and mRE is short for the mean rotation error. EP, PF, Sym-EP, Sym-PF are short for EM-PPCA [5], PriorFree [9,10], Sym-EM-PPCA, Sym-PriorFree, respectively.

|  | aeroplane | | | | | | | | bus | | | | | | |
|--|--|--|--|--|--|--|--|--|--|--|--|--|--|--|--|
|  | I | II | III | IV | V | VI | VII | mRE | I | II | III | IV | V | VI | mRE |
| EP | 0.36 | 0.59 | 0.50 | 0.49 | 0.57 | 0.57 | **0.45** | 0.34 | 0.42 | 0.34 | 0.56 | 0.54 | 0.98 | 0.86 | 0.26 |
| PF | 0.99 | 1.08 | 1.13 | 1.15 | 1.22 | 1.10 | 1.11 | 0.52 | 1.62 | 1.56 | 1.75 | 1.59 | 2.09 | 1.70 | 0.47 |
| Sym-EP | **0.33** | **0.53** | **0.46** | **0.43** | **0.51** | **0.53** | 0.46 | **0.31** | **0.28** | **0.25** | **0.33** | **0.33** | **0.65** | **0.46** | **0.21** |
| Sym-PF | 0.57 | 0.76 | 0.84 | 0.76 | 0.73 | 0.61 | 0.79 | 0.46 | 1.92 | 1.95 | 1.77 | 1.54 | 1.70 | 1.42 | 1.23 |

|  | car | | | | | | | | | | | sofa | | |
|--|--|--|--|--|--|--|--|--|--|--|--|--|--|--|
|  | I | II | III | IV | V | VI | VII | VIII | IX | X | mRE | I | II | III |
| EP | 1.10 | 1.01 | 1.09 | 1.05 | 1.03 | 1.07 | 0.99 | 1.46 | 1.00 | 0.85 | 0.39 | 2.00 | 1.87 | 2.03 |
| PF | 1.76 | 1.67 | 1.76 | 1.77 | 1.65 | 1.79 | 1.67 | 1.57 | 1.70 | 1.42 | 0.86 | 1.71 | 1.41 | 1.46 |
| Sym-EP | **0.99** | **0.89** | **1.05** | **1.02** | **0.92** | **1.00** | **0.89** | **1.39** | **0.95** | **0.68** | **0.34** | **1.18** | **0.81** | **1.08** |
| Sym-PF | 1.74 | 1.41 | 1.70 | 1.48 | 1.69 | 1.58 | 1.43 | 1.69 | 1.52 | 1.30 | 0.79 | 1.33 | 1.15 | 1.36 |

|  | sofa | | | | train | | | | | tv | | | | |
|--|--|--|--|--|--|--|--|--|--|--|--|--|--|--|
|  | IV | V | VI | mRE | I | II | III | IV | mRE | I | II | III | IV | mRE |
| EP | 1.99 | 2.37 | 1.81 | 0.79 | 1.18 | 0.53 | 0.49 | 0.42 | 0.85 | **0.44** | **0.51** | **0.44** | **0.36** | **0.41** |
| PF | 2.02 | 2.66 | 1.64 | 1.36 | 1.97 | **0.27** | 0.47 | 0.34 | 0.98 | 0.56 | 1.01 | 0.97 | 0.65 | 0.80 |
| Sym-EP | 1.12 | 1.80 | **0.88** | **0.34** | **0.95** | 0.46 | **0.42** | **0.31** | **0.73** | 0.51 | 0.60 | 0.53 | 0.64 | 0.52 |
| Sym-PF | **1.02** | **1.17** | 0.95 | 0.85 | 1.52 | 0.40 | 0.49 | 0.47 | 0.99 | 0.60 | 1.01 | 1.15 | 0.51 | 0.86 |

which neglects the shape variations in the same subtype, may not be accurate enough (*e.g.* it has only one 3D model for all the *sedan* cars).

### 5.3 Experimental Results on the Noisy Annotations

We also investigate what happens if the keypoints are not perfectly annotated. This is important to check because our method depends on keypoint pairs therefore may be sensitive to errors in keypoint location, which will inevitably arise when we use features detectors, *e.g.* deep nets [41], to detect the keypoints.

To simulate this, we add Gaussian noise $\mathcal{N}(0, \sigma^2)$ to the 2D annotations and re-do the experiments. The standard deviation is set to $\sigma = sd_{max}$, where $d_{max}$ is the longest distance between all the keypoints (*e.g.* for *aeroplane*, it is the distance between the nose tip to the tail tip). We have tested for different $s$ by: 0.03, 0.05, 0.07. The other parameters are the same as the previous section.

The results for *aeroplane* with $s = 0.03, 0.05, 0.07$ are shown in Table 2. Each result value is obtained by averaging 10 repetitions. The results in Table 2 show that the performances of all the methods decrease in general with the increase in the noise level. Nonetheless, our methods still outperform our counterparts with the noisy annotations (*i.e.* the imperfectly labeled annotations).

**Table 2.** The mean *shape* and *rotation* errors for *aeroplane* with imperfect annotations. The noise is Gaussian $\mathcal{N}(0, \sigma^2)$ with $\sigma = sd_{max}$, where we choose $s = 0.03, 0.05, 0.07$ and $d_{max}$ is the longest distance between all the keypoints (*i.e.* the tip of the nose to the tip of the tail for aeroplane). Other parameters are the same as those in Table 1. Each result value is obtained by averaging 10 repetitions.

| | $\sigma = 0.03\ d_{max}$ | | | | | | | | $\sigma = 0.05\ d_{max}$ | | | |
|---|---|---|---|---|---|---|---|---|---|---|---|---|
| | I | II | III | IV | V | VI | VII | mRE | I | II | III | IV |
| EP | **0.34** | 0.59 | 0.49 | 0.45 | 0.54 | 0.55 | **0.45** | 0.33 | 0.37 | 0.58 | 0.51 | 0.47 |
| PF | 0.92 | 1.01 | 1.05 | 1.06 | 1.13 | 1.03 | 1.06 | 0.52 | 0.93 | 1.04 | 1.05 | 1.08 |
| Sym-EP | 0.34 | **0.54** | **0.47** | **0.44** | **0.52** | **0.55** | 0.46 | **0.32** | **0.35** | **0.54** | **0.47** | **0.43** |
| Sym-PF | 0.79 | 0.93 | 1.01 | 0.93 | 0.91 | 0.79 | 0.94 | 0.60 | 0.83 | 0.99 | 1.09 | 0.98 |

| | $\sigma = 0.05\ d_{max}$ | | | | $\sigma = 0.07\ d_{max}$ | | | | | | | |
|---|---|---|---|---|---|---|---|---|---|---|---|---|
| | V | VI | VII | mRE | I | II | III | IV | V | VI | VII | mRE |
| EP | 0.57 | 0.57 | 0.46 | 0.35 | 0.38 | 0.61 | 0.50 | 0.45 | 0.61 | **0.56** | **0.46** | 0.36 |
| PF | 1.15 | 1.02 | 1.07 | 0.54 | 0.94 | 1.04 | 1.08 | 1.07 | 1.15 | 1.03 | 1.08 | 0.65 |
| Sym-EP | **0.52** | **0.57** | **0.46** | **0.33** | **0.37** | **0.58** | **0.49** | **0.44** | **0.58** | 0.57 | 0.46 | **0.35** |
| Sym-PF | 0.94 | 0.84 | 1.04 | 0.63 | 0.94 | 1.06 | 1.15 | 1.04 | 1.05 | 0.89 | 1.08 | 0.70 |

## 6  Conclusion

This paper shows that non-rigid SfM can be extended to the important special case where the objects are symmetric, which is frequently possessed by man-made objects [15,16]. We derive and implement this extension to two popular non-rigid structure from motion algorithms [5,9,10], which perform well on the Pascal3D+ dataset when compared to the baseline methods.

In this paper, we have focused on constructing the non-rigid SfM model(s) that can exploit the symmetry property. In future work, we will extend to perspective projection, apply a better initialization of the occluded keypoints such as low-rank recovery, use additional object features (instead of just key-points), and detect these features from images automatically such as [41].

**Acknowledgment.** We would like to thank Ehsan Jahangiri, Cihang Xie, Weichao Qiu, Xuan Dong, Siyuan Qiao for giving feedbacks on the manuscript. This work was supported by ARO 62250-CS and ONR N00014-15-1-2356.

# References

1. Tomasi, C., Kanade, T.: Shape and motion from image streams under orthography: a factorization method. Int. J. Comput. Vis. **9**(2), 137–154 (1992)
2. Hartley, R.I., Zisserman, A.: Multiple View Geometry in Computer Vision, 2nd edn. Cambridge University Press, Cambridge (2004)
3. Torresani, L., Hertzmann, A., Bregler, C.: Learning non-rigid 3D shape from 2D motion. In: NIPS (2003)
4. Xiao, J., Chai, J., Kanade, T.: A closed-form solution to non-rigid shape and motion recovery. In: Pajdla, T., Matas, J.G. (eds.) ECCV 2004. LNCS, vol. 3024, pp. 573–587. Springer, Heidelberg (2004)
5. Torresani, L., Hertzmann, A., Bregler, C.: Nonrigid structure-from-motion: estimating shape and motion with hierarchical priors. IEEE Trans. Pattern Anal. Mach. Intell. **30**, 878–892 (2008)
6. Akhter, I., Sheikh, Y., Khan, S., Kanade, T.: Trajectory space: a dual representation for nonrigid structure from motion. IEEE Trans. Pattern Anal. Mach. Intell. **33**(7), 1442–1456 (2011)
7. Gotardo, P., Martinez, A.: Computing smooth timetrajectories for camera and deformable shape in structure from motion with occlusion. IEEE Trans. Pattern Anal. Mach. Intell. **33**, 2051–2065 (2011)
8. Hamsici, O.C., Gotardo, P.F.U., Martinez, A.M.: Learning spatially-smooth mappings in non-rigid structure from motion. In: Fitzgibbon, A., Lazebnik, S., Perona, P., Sato, Y., Schmid, C. (eds.) ECCV 2012, Part IV. LNCS, vol. 7575, pp. 260–273. Springer, Heidelberg (2012)
9. Dai, Y., Li, H., He, M.: A simple prior-free method for non-rigid structure-from-motion factorization. In: CVPR (2012)
10. Dai, Y., Li, H., He, M.: A simple prior-free method for non-rigid structure-from-motion factorization. Int. J. Comput. Vis. **107**, 101–122 (2014)
11. Ma, J., Zhao, J., Ma, Y., Tian, J.: Non-rigid visible and infrared face registration via regularized gaussian fields criterion. Pattern Recogn. **48**(3), 772–784 (2015)
12. Ma, J., Zhao, J., Tian, J., Tu, Z., Yuille, A.L.: Robust estimation of nonrigid transformation for point set registration. In: CVPR (2013)
13. Ma, J., Zhao, J., Tian, J., Bai, X., Tu, Z.: Regularized vector field learning with sparse approximation for mismatch removal. Pattern Recogn. **46**(12), 3519–3532 (2013)
14. Agudo, A., Agapito, L., Calvo, B., Montiel, J.: Good vibrations: a modal analysis approach for sequential non-rigid structure from motion. In: CVPR, pp. 1558–1565 (2014)

15. Rosen, J.: Symmetry Discovered: Concepts and Applications in Nature and Science. Dover Publications, Mineola (2011)
16. Hong, W., Yang, A.Y., Huang, K., Ma, Y.: On symmetry and multiple-view geometry: structure, pose, and calibration from a single image. Int. J. Comput. Vis. **60**, 241–265 (2004)
17. Gordon, G.G.: Shape from symmetry. In: Proceedings of SPIE (1990)
18. Kontsevich, L.L.: Pairwise comparison technique: a simple solution for depth reconstruction. JOSA A **10**(6), 1129–1135 (1993)
19. Vetter, T., Poggio, T.: Symmetric 3D objects are an easy case for 2D object recognition. Spat. Vis. **8**, 443–453 (1994)
20. Mukherjee, D.P., Zisserman, A., Brady, M.: Shape from symmetry: detecting and exploiting symmetry in affine images. Philos. Trans. Phys. Sci. Eng. **351**, 77–106 (1995)
21. Thrun, S., Wegbreit, B.: Shape from symmetry. In: ICCV (2005)
22. Li, Y., Pizlo, Z.: Reconstruction of shapes of 3D symmetric objects by using planarity and compactness constraints. In: Proceedings of SPIE-IS&T Electronic Imaging (2007)
23. Vicente, S., Carreira, J., Agapito, L., Batista, J.: Reconstructing PASCAL VOC. In: CVPR (2014)
24. Kar, A., Tulsiani, S., Carreira, J., Malik, J.: Category-specific object reconstruction from a single image. In: CVPR (2015)
25. Akhter, I., Sheikh, Y., Khan, S.: In defense of orthonormality constraints for nonrigid structure from motion. In: CVPR (2009)
26. Gao, Y., Yuille, A.L.: Exploiting symmetry and/or Manhattan properties for 3D object structure estimation from single and multiple images (2016). arXiv preprint arXiv:1607.07129
27. Xiang, Y., Mottaghi, R., Savarese, S.: Beyond PASCAL: a benchmark for 3D object detection in the wild. In: WACV (2014)
28. Grossmann, E., Santos-Victor, J.: Maximum likehood 3D reconstruction from one or more images under geometric constraints. In: BMVC (2002)
29. Grossmann, E., Santos-Victor, J.: Least-squares 3D reconstruction from one or more views and geometric clues. Comput. Vis. Image Underst. **99**(2), 151–174 (2005)
30. Grossmann, E., Ortin, D., Santos-Victor, J.: Single and multi-view reconstruction of structured scenes. In: ACCV (2002)
31. Kontsevich, L.L., Kontsevich, M.L., Shen, A.K.: Two algorithms for reconstructing shapes. Optoelectron. Instrum. Data Process. **5**, 76–81 (1987)
32. Bregler, C., Hertzmann, A., Biermann, H.: Recovering non-rigid 3D shape from image streams. In: CVPR (2000)
33. Hong, J.H., Fitzgibbon, A.: Secrets of matrix factorization: approximations, numerics, manifold optimization and random restarts. In: ICCV (2015)
34. Olsen, S.I., Bartoli, A.: Implicit non-rigid structure-from-motion with priors. J. Math. Imaging Vis. **31**(2–3), 233–244 (2008)
35. Akhter, I., Sheikh, Y., Khan, S., Kanade, T.: Nonrigid structure from motion in trajectory space. In: NIPS (2008)
36. Ceylan, D., Mitra, N.J., Zheng, Y., Pauly, M.: Coupled structure-from-motion and 3D symmetry detection for urban facades. ACM Trans. Graph. **33**, 2 (2014)
37. Morris, D.D., Kanatani, K., Kanade, T.: Gauge fixing for accurate 3D estimation. In: CVPR (2001)
38. Bishop, C.M.: Pattern Recognition and Machine Learning. Springer, New York (2006)

39. Bourdev, L., Maji, S., Brox, T., Malik, J.: Detecting people using mutually consistent poselet activations. In: Daniilidis, K., Maragos, P., Paragios, N. (eds.) ECCV 2010, Part VI. LNCS, vol. 6316, pp. 168–181. Springer, Heidelberg (2010)
40. Schönemann, P.H.: A generalized solution of the orthogonal procrustes problem. Psychometrika **31**, 1–10 (1966)
41. Chen, X., Yuille, A.L.: Articulated pose estimation by a graphical model with image dependent pairwise relations. In: NIPS, pp. 1736–1744 (2014)

# Peak-Piloted Deep Network for Facial Expression Recognition

Xiangyun Zhao[1](✉), Xiaodan Liang[2], Luoqi Liu[3,4], Teng Li[5], Yugang Han[3],
Nuno Vasconcelos[1], and Shuicheng Yan[3,4]

[1] University of California, San Diego, USA
{xiz019,nvasconcelos}@ucsd.edu
[2] Carnegie Mellon University, Pittsburgh, USA
xdliang328@gmail.com
[3] 360 AI Institute, Beijing, China
{liuluoqi,hanyugang}@360.cn
[4] National University of Singapore, Singapore, Singapore
eleyans@nus.edu.sg
[5] Institute of Automation, Chinese Academy of Sciences, Beijing, China
tenglwy@gmail.com

**Abstract.** Objective functions for training of deep networks for face-related recognition tasks, such as facial expression recognition (FER), usually consider each sample independently. In this work, we present a novel peak-piloted deep network (PPDN) that uses a sample with peak expression (easy sample) to supervise the intermediate feature responses for a sample of non-peak expression (hard sample) of the same type and from the same subject. The expression evolving process from non-peak expression to peak expression can thus be implicitly embedded in the network to achieve the invariance to expression intensities. A special-purpose back-propagation procedure, peak gradient suppression (PGS), is proposed for network training. It drives the intermediate-layer feature responses of non-peak expression samples towards those of the corresponding peak expression samples, while avoiding the inverse. This avoids degrading the recognition capability for samples of peak expression due to interference from their non-peak expression counterparts. Extensive comparisons on two popular FER datasets, Oulu-CASIA and CK+, demonstrate the superiority of the PPDN over state-of-the-art FER methods, as well as the advantages of both the network structure and the optimization strategy. Moreover, it is shown that PPDN is a general architecture, extensible to other tasks by proper definition of peak and non-peak samples. This is validated by experiments that show state-of-the-art performance on pose-invariant face recognition, using the Multi-PIE dataset.

**Keywords:** Facial expression recognition · Peak-piloted · Deep network · Peak gradient suppression

## 1 Introduction

Facial Expression Recognition (FER) aims to predict the basic facial expressions (e.g. happy, sad, surprise, angry, fear, disgust) from a human face image, as

© Springer International Publishing AG 2016
B. Leibe et al. (Eds.): ECCV 2016, Part II, LNCS 9906, pp. 425–442, 2016.
DOI: 10.1007/978-3-319-46475-6_27

426    X. Zhao et al.

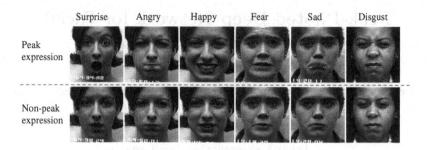

**Fig. 1.** Examples of six facial expression samples, including surprise, angry, happy, fear, sad and disgust. For each subject, the peak and non-peak expressions are shown.

illustrated in Fig. 1.[1] Recently, FER has attracted much research attention [1–7]. It can facilitate other face-related tasks, such as face recognition [8] and alignment [9]. Despite significant recent progress [4,10–12], FER is still a challenging problem, due to the following difficulties. First, as illustrated in Fig. 1, different subjects often display the same expression with diverse intensities and visual appearances. In a videostream, an expression will first appear in a subtle form and then grow into a strong display of the underlying feelings. We refer to the former as a non-peak and to the latter as a peak expression. Second, peak and non-peak expressions by the same subject can have significant variation in terms of attributes such as mouth corner radian, facial wrinkles, etc. Third, non-peak expressions are more commonly displayed than peak expressions. It is usually difficult to capture critical and subtle expression details from non-peak expression images, which can be hard to distinguish across expressions. For example, the non-peak expressions for fear and sadness are quite similar in Fig. 1.

Recently, deep neural network architectures have shown excellent performance in face-related recognition tasks [13–15]. The has led to the introduction of FER network architectures [4,16]. There are, nevertheless, some important limitations. First, most methods consider each sample independently during learning, ignoring the intrinsic correlations between each pair of samples (e.g., easy and hard samples). This limits the discriminative capabilities of the learned models. Second, they focus on recognizing the clearly separable peak expressions and ignore the most common non-peak expression samples, whose discrimination can be extremely challenging.

In this paper, we propose a novel peak-piloted deep network (PPDN) architecture, which implicitly embeds the natural evolution of expressions from non-peak to peak expression in the learning process, so as to zoom in on the subtle differences between weak expressions and achieve invariance to expression intensity. Intuitively, as illustrated in Fig. 2, peak and non-peak expressions from the same subject often exhibit very strong visual correlations (e.g., similar face parts) and can mutually help the recognition of each other. The proposed PPDN uses the feature responses to samples of peak expression (easy samples) to supervise

---

[1] This work was performed when Xiaoyun Zhao was an intern at 360 AI Institute.

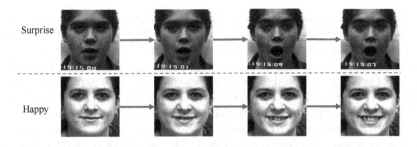

**Fig. 2.** Expression evolving process from non-peak expression to peak expression.

the responses to samples of non-peak expression (hard samples) of the same type and from the same subject. The resulting mapping of non-peak expressions into their corresponding peak expressions magnifies their critical and subtle details, facilitating their recognition.

In principle, an explicit mapping from non-peak to peak expression could significantly improve recognition. However, such a mapping is challenging to generate, since the detailed changes of face features (e.g., mouth corner radian and wrinkles) can be quite difficult to predict. We avoid this problem by focusing on the high-level feature representation of the facial expressions, which is both more abstract and directly related to facial expression recognition. In particular, the proposed PPDN optimizes the tasks of (1) feature transformation from non-peak to peak expression and (2) recognition of facial expressions in a unified manner. It is, in fact, a general approach, applicable to many other recognition tasks (e.g. face recognition) by proper definition of peak and non-peak samples (e.g. frontal and profile faces). By implicitly learning the evolution from hard poses (e.g., profile faces) to easy poses (e.g., near-frontal faces), it can improve the recognition accuracy of prior solutions to these problems, making them more robust to pose variation.

During training, the PPDN takes an image pair with a peak and a non-peak expression of the same type and from the same subject. This image pair is passed through several intermediate layers to generate feature maps for each expression image. The L2-norm of the difference between the feature maps of non-peak and peak expression images is then minimized, to embed the evolution of expressions into the PPDN framework. In this way, the PPDN incorporates the peak-piloted feature transformation and facial expression recognition into a unified architecture. The PPDN is learned with a new back-propagation algorithm, denotes peak gradient suppression (PGS), which drives the feature responses to non-peak expression instances towards those of the corresponding peak expression images, but not the contrary. This is unlike the traditional optimization of Siamese networks [13], which encourages the feature pairs to be close to each other, treating the feature maps of the two images equally. Instead, the PPDN focuses on transforming the features of non-peak expressions towards those of peak expressions. This is implemented by, during each back-propagation iteration, ignoring the gradient information due to the peak expression image in the L2-norm minimization of feature differences, while keeping that due to the non-peak expression. The gradients of the recognition loss, for both peak and non-peak expression images, are the same as in traditional back-propagation. This avoids the degradation of the recognition capability of the network for samples of peak expression due to the influence of non-peak expression samples.

Overall, this work has four main contributions. (1) The PPDN architecture is proposed, using the responses to samples of peak expression (easy samples) to supervise the responses to samples of non-peak expression (hard samples) of the same type and from the same subject. The targets of peak-piloted feature transformation and facial expression recognition, for peak and non-peak expressions, are optimized simultaneously. (2) A tailored back-propagation procedure, PGS, is proposed to drive the responses to non-peak expressions towards those of the corresponding peak expressions, while avoiding the inverse. (3) The PPDN is shown to perform intensity-invariant facial expression recognition, by effectively recognizing the most common non-peak expressions. (4) Comprehensive evaluations on several FER datasets, namely CK+ [17] and Oulu-CASIA [18], demonstrate the superiority of the PPDN over previous methods. Its generalization to other tasks is also demonstrated through state-of-the-art robust face recognition performance on the public Multi-PIE dataset [19].

## 2   Related Work

There have been several recent attempts to solve the facial expression recognition problem. These methods can be grouped into two categories: sequence-based and still image approaches. In the first category, sequence-based approaches [1, 7,18,20,21] exploit both the appearance and motion information from video sequences. In the second category, still image approaches [4,10,12] recognize expressions uniquely from image appearance patterns. Since still image methods are more generic, recognizing expressions in both still images and sequences, we focus on models for still image expression recognition. Among these, both hand-crafted pipelines and deep learning methods have been explored for FER. Hand-crafted approaches [10,11,22] perform three steps sequentially: feature extraction, feature selection and classification. This can lead to suboptimal recognition, due to the combination of different optimization targets.

Convolutional Neural Network (CNN) architectures [23–25] have recently shown excellent performance on face-related recognition tasks [26–28]. Methods that resort to the CNN architecture have also been proposed for FER. For example, Yu et al. [5] used an ensemble of multiple deep CNNs. Mollahosseini et al. [16] used three inception structures [24] in convolution for FER. All these methods treat expression instances of different intensities of the same subject independently. Hence, the correlations between peak and non-peak expressions are overlooked during learning. In contrast, the proposed PPDN learns to embed the evolution from non-peak to peak expressions, so as to facilitate image-based FER.

# 3   The Peak-Piloted Deep Network (PPDN)

In this work we introduce the PPDN framework, which implicitly learns the evolution from non-peak to peak expressions, in the FER context. As illustrated in Fig. 3, during training the PPDN takes an image pair as input. This consists of a peak and a non-peak expression of the same type and from the same subject. This image pair is passed through several convolutional and fully-connected layers, generating pairs of feature maps for each expression image. To drive the feature responses to the non-peak expression image towards those of the peak expression image, the L2-norm of the feature differences is minimized. The learning algorithm optimizes a combination of this L2-norm loss and two recognition losses, one per expression image. Due to its excellent performance on several face-related recognition tasks [29,30], the popular GoogLeNet [24] is adopted as the basic network architecture. The incarnations of the inception architecture in GoogLeNet are restricted to filters sizes $1 \times 1$, $3 \times 3$ and $5 \times 5$. In total, the GoogLeNet implements nine inception structures after two convolutional layers and two max pooling layers. After that, the first fully-connected layer produces the intermediate features with 1024 dimensions, and the second fully-connected

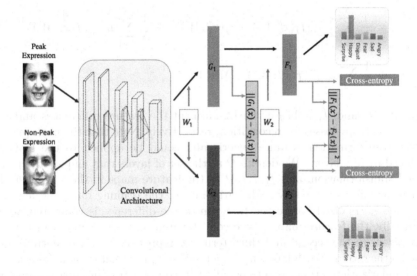

**Fig. 3.** Illustration of the training stage of PPDN. During training, PPDN takes the pair of peak and non-peak expression images as input. After passing the pair through several convolutional and fully-connected layers, the intermediate feature maps can be obtained for peak and non-peak expression images, respectively. The L2-norm loss between these feature maps is optimized for driving the features of the non-peak expression image towards those of the peak expression image. The network parameters can thus be updated by jointly optimizing the L2-norm losses and the losses of recognizing two expression images. During the back-propagation process, the Peak Gradient Suppression (PGS) is utilized.

layer generates the label predictions for six expression labels. During testing, the PPDN takes one still image as input, outputting the predicted probabilities for all six expression labels.

## 3.1 Network Optimization

The goal of the PPDN is to learn the evolution from non-peak to peak expressions, as well as recognize the basic facial expressions. We denote the training set as $S = \{x_i^p, x_i^n, y_i^p, y_i^n, i = 1, ..., N\}$, where sample $x_i^n$ denotes a face with non-peak expression, $x_i^p$ a face with the corresponding peak expression, and $y_i^n$ and $y_i^p$ are the corresponding expression labels. To supervise the feature responses to the non-peak expression instance with those of the peak expression instance, the network is learned with a loss function that includes the L2-norm of the difference between the feature responses to peak and non-peak expression instances. Cross-entropy losses are also used to optimize the recognition of the two expression images. Overall, the loss of the PPDN is

$$J = \frac{1}{N}(J_1 + J_2 + J_3 + \lambda \sum_{i=1}^{N} ||W||^2)$$

$$= \frac{1}{N} \sum_{i=1}^{N} \sum_{j \in \Omega} ||f_j(x_i^p, W) - f_j(x_i^n, W)||^2 + \frac{1}{N} \sum_{i=1}^{N} L(y_i^p, f(x_i^p; W)) \qquad (1)$$

$$+ \frac{1}{N} \sum_{i=1}^{N} L(y_i^n, f(x_i^n; W)) + \lambda ||W||^2,$$

where $J_1$, $J_2$ and $J_3$ indicate the L2-norm of the feature differences and the two cross-entropy losses for recognition, respectively. Note that the peak-piloted feature transformation is quite generic and could be applied to the features produced by any layers. We denote $\Omega$ as the set of layers that employ the peak-piloted transformation, and $f_j, j \in \Omega$ as the feature maps in the j-th layer. To reduce the effects caused by scale variability of the training data, the features $f_j$ are L2 normalized before the L2-norm of the difference is computed. More specifically, the feature maps $f_j$ are concatenated into one vector, which is L2 normalized. In the second and third terms, $L$ represents the cross-entropy loss between the ground-truth labels and the predicted probabilities of all labels. The final regularization term is used to penalize the complexity of network parameters $W$. Since the evolution from non-peak to peak expression is embedded into the network, the latter learns a more robust expression recognizer.

## 3.2 Peak Gradient Suppression (PGS)

To train the PPDN, we propose a special-purpose back-propagation algorithm for the optimization of (1). Rather than the traditional straightforward application of stochastic gradient descent [13,29], the goal is to drive the intermediate-layer responses of non-peak expression instances towards those of the corresponding peak expression instances, while avoiding the reverse. Under traditional stochastic gradient decent (SGD) [31], the network parameters would be updated with

$$
\begin{aligned}
W^+ &= W - \gamma \nabla_W J(W; x_i^p, x_i^p, y_i^n, y_i^p) \\
&= W - \frac{\gamma}{N} \frac{\partial J_1(W; x_i^n, x_i^p)}{\partial f_j(W; x_i^n)} \times \frac{\partial f_j(W; x_i^n)}{\partial W} - \frac{\gamma}{N} \frac{\partial J_1(W; x_i^n, x_i^p)}{\partial f_j(W; x_i^p)} \times \frac{\partial f_j(W; x_i^p)}{\partial W} \\
&\quad - \frac{1}{N} \gamma \nabla_W J_2(W; x_i^p, y_i^p) - \frac{1}{N} \gamma \nabla_W J_3(W; x_i^n, y_i^n) - 2\gamma W,
\end{aligned}
\tag{2}
$$

where $\gamma$ is the learning rate. The proposed peak gradient suppression (PGS) learning algorithm uses instead the updates

$$
\begin{aligned}
W^+ &= W - \frac{\gamma}{N} \frac{\partial J_1(W; x_i^n, x_i^p)}{\partial f_j(W; x_i^n)} \times \frac{\partial f_j(W; x_i^n)}{\partial W} \\
&\quad - \frac{1}{N} \gamma \nabla_W J_2(W; x_i^p, y_i^p) - \frac{1}{N} \gamma \nabla_W J_3(W; x_i^n, y_i^n) - 2\gamma W.
\end{aligned}
\tag{3}
$$

The difference between (3) and (2) is that the gradients due to the feature responses of the peak expression image, $-\frac{\gamma}{N} \frac{\partial J_1(W; x_i^n, x_i^p)}{\partial f_j(W; x_i^p)} \times \frac{\partial f_j(W; x_i^p)}{\partial W}$ are suppressed in (3). In this way, PGS drives the feature responses of non-peak expressions towards those of peak expressions, but not the contrary. In the appendix, we show that this does not prevent learning, since the weight update direction of PGS is a descent direction of the overall loss, although not a steepest descent direction.

## 4  Experiments

To evaluate the PPDN, we conduct extensive experiments on two popular FER datasets: CK+ [17] and Oulu-CASIA [18]. To further demonstrate that the PPDN generalizes to other recognition tasks, we also evaluate its performance on face recognition over the public Multi-PIE dataset [19].

### 4.1  Facial Expression Recognition

**Training.** The PPDN uses the GoogLeNet [24] as basic network structure. The peak-piloted feature transformation is only employed in the last two fully-connected layers. Other configurations, using the peak-piloted feature transformation on various convolutional layers are also reported. Since it is not feasible to train the deep network on the small FER datasets available, we pre-trained GoogLeNet [24] on a large-scale face recognition dataset, the CASIA Webface dataset [32]. This network was then fine-tuned for FER. The CASIA Webface dataset contains 494,414 training images from 10,575 subjects, which were used to pre-train the network for 60 epochs with an initial learning rate of 0.01. For fine-tuning, the face region was first aligned with the detected eyes and mouth positions. The face regions were then resized to $128 \times 128$. The PPDN takes a pair of peak and non-peak expression images as input. The convolutional layer weights were initialized with those of the pre-trained model. The weights of the fully connected layer were initialized randomly using the "xaiver" procedure [33]. The learning rate of the fully connected layers was set to 0.0001 and that of pre-trained convolutional layers to 0.000001. ALL models were trained using a batch size of 128 image pairs and a weight decay of 0.0002. The final trained model was obtained after 20,000 iterations. For fair comparison with previous methods [4,10,11], we did not use any data augmentation in our experiments.

**Testing and Evaluation Metric.** In the testing phase, the PPDN takes one testing image as the input and produces its predicted facial expression label. Following the standard setting of [10,11], 10-fold subject-independent cross-validation was adopted for evaluation in all experiments.

**Datasets.** FER datasets usually provide video sequences for training and testing the facial expression recognizers. We conducted all experiments on two popular datasets, CK+ [17] and Oulu-CASIA dataset [18]. For each sequence, the face often gradually evolves from a neutral to a peak facial expression. CK+ includes six basic facial expressions (angry, happy, surprise, sad, disgust, fear) and one non basic expression (contempt). It contains 593 sequences from 123 subjects, of which only 327 are annotated with expression labels. Oulu-CASIA contains 480 sequences of six facial expressions under normal illumination, including 80 subjects between 23 and 58 years old.

**Comparisons with Still Image-Based Approaches.** Table 1 compares the PPDN to still image-based approaches on CK+, under the standard setting in which only the last one to three frames (i.e., nearly peak expressions) per sequence are considered for training and testing. Four state-of-the-art methods are considered: common and specific patches learning (CSPL) [10], which employs multi-task learning for feature selection, AdaGabor [34] and LBPSVM [11], which are based on AdaBoost [36], and Boosted Deep Belief Network (BDBN) [4], which jointly optimizes feature extraction and feature

**Table 1.** Performance comparisons on six facial expressions with four state-of-the-art methods and the baseline using GoogLeNet in terms of average classification accuracy by the 10-fold cross-validation evaluation on CK+ database.

| Method | Average accuracy |
|---|---|
| CSPL [10] | 89.9 % |
| AdaGabor [34] | 93.3 % |
| LBPSVM [11] | 95.1 % |
| BDBN [4] | 96.7 % |
| GoogLeNet(baseline) | 95.0 % |
| PPDN | **97.3 %** |

**Table 2.** Performance comparisons on six facial expressions with UDCS method and the baseline using GoogLeNet in terms of average classification accuracy under same setting as UDCS.

| Method | Average accuracy |
|---|---|
| UDCS [35] | 49.5 % |
| GoogLeNet(baseline) | 66.6 % |
| **PPDN** | **72.4 %** |

selection. In addition, we also compare the PPDN to the baseline "GoogLeNet (baseline)," which optimizes the standard GoogLeNet with SGD. Similarly to previous methods [4,10,11], the PPDN is evaluated on the last three frames of each sequence. Table 2 compares the PPDN with UDCS [35] on Oulu-CASIA, under a similar setting where the first 9 images of each sequence are ignored, the first 40 individuals are taken as training samples and the rest as testing. In all cases, the PPDN input is the pair of one of the non-peak frames (all frames other than the last one) and the corresponding peak frame (the last frame) in a sequence. The PPDN significantly outperforms all other, achieving 97.3 % vs a previous best of 96.7 % on CK+ and 72.4 % vs 66.6 % on Oulu-CASIA. This demonstrates the superiority of embedding the expression evolution in the network learning.

**Training and Testing with More Non-peak Expressions.** The main advantage of the PPDN is its improved ability to recognize non-peak expressions. To test this, we compared how performance varies with the number of non-peak expressions. Note that for each video sequence, the face expression evolves from neutral to a peak expression. The first six frames within a sequence are usually neutral, with the peak expression appearing in the final frames. Empirically, we determined that the 7th to 9th frame often show non-peak expressions with very weak intensities, which we denote as "weak expressions." In addition to the training images used in the standard setting, we used all frames beyond the 7th for training.

Since the previous methods did not publish their codes, we only compare the PPDN to the baseline "GoogLeNet (baseline)". Table 3 reports results for CK+ and Table 4 for Oulu-CASIA. Three different test sets were considered: "weak expression" indicates that the test set only contains the non-peak expression images from the 7th to the 9th frames; "peak expression" only includes the last frame; and "combined" uses all frames from the 7th to the last. "PPDN (standard SGD)" is the version of PPDN trained with standard SGD optimization, and "GoogLeNet (baseline)" the basic GoogLeNet, taking each expression image as input and trained with SGD. The most substantial improvements are obtained on the "weak expression" test set, 83.36 % and 67.95 % of "PPDN" vs. 78.10 % and 64.64 % of "GoogLeNet (baseline)" on CK+ and Oulu-CASIA, respectively. This is evidence in support of the advantage of explicitly learning the evolution

**Table 3.** Performance comparison on CK+ database in terms of average classification accuracy of the 10-fold cross-validation when evaluating on three different test sets, including "weak expression", "peak expression" and "combined", respectively.

| Method | Weak expression | Peak expression | combined |
|---|---|---|---|
| PPDN(standard SGD) | 81.34 % | 99.12 % | 94.18 % |
| GoogLeNet (baseline) | 78.10 % | 98.96 % | 92.19 % |
| PPDN | **83.36 %** | **99.30 %** | **95.33 %** |

**Table 4.** Performance comparison on Oulu-CASIA database in terms of average classification accuracy of the 10-fold cross-validation when evaluating on three different test sets, including "weak expression", "peak expression" and "combined", respectively.

| Method | Weak expression | Peak expression | combined |
|---|---|---|---|
| PPDN(standard SGD) | 67.05 % | 82.91 % | 73.54 % |
| GoogLeNet (baseline) | 64.64 % | 79.21 % | 71.32 % |
| PPDN | **67.95 %** | **84.59 %** | **74.99 %** |

from non-peak to peak expressions. In addition, the PPDN outperforms "PPDN (standard SGD)" and "GoogLeNet (baseline)" on the combined sets, where both peak and non-peak expressions are evaluated.

**Comparisons with Sequence-Based Approaches.** Unlike the still-image recognition setting, which evaluates the predictions of frames from a sequence, the sequence-based setting requires a prediction for the whole sequence. Previous sequence-based approaches take the whole sequence as input and use motion information during inference. Instead, the PPDN regards each pair of non-peak and peak frame as input, and only outputs the label of the peak frame as prediction for the whole sequence, in the testing phase. Tables 5 and 6 compare the PPDN to several sequence-based approaches plus "GoogLeNet(baseline)" on CK+ and Oulu-CASIA. Compared with [1,7,37], which leverage motion information, the PPDN, which only relies on appearance information, achieves significantly better prediction performance. On CK+, it has gains of 5.1 % and 2 % over 'STM-ExpLet" [1] and "DTAGN(Joint)" [7]. On Oulu-CASIA it achieves 84.59 % vs. the 75.52 % of "Atlases" [20] and the 81.46 % of "DTAGN(Joint)" [7]. In addition, we evaluate this experiment without peak information, i.e. selecting image with highest classification scores for all categories as peak frame in testing. PPDN achieves 99.2 % on CK+ and 83.67 % on Oulu-CASIA.

**PGS vs. Standard SGD.** As discussed above, PGS suppresses gradients from peak expressions, so as to drive the features of non-peak expression samples towards those of peak expression samples, but not the contrary. Standard SGD uses all gradients, due to both non-peak and peak expression samples. We

**Table 5.** Performance comparisons with three sequence-based approaches and the baseline "GoogLeNet (baseline)" in terms of average classification accuracy of the 10-fold cross-validation on CK+ database.

| Method | Experimental settings | Average accuracy |
|---|---|---|
| 3DCNN-DAP [37] | sequence-based | 92.4 % |
| STM-ExpLet [1] | sequence-based | 94.2 % |
| DTAGN(Joint) [7] | sequence-based | 97.3 % |
| GoogLeNet (baseline) | image-based | 99.0 % |
| PPDN (standard SGD) | image-based | 99.1 % |
| PPDN w/o peak | image-based | **99.2 %** |
| PPDN | image-based | **99.3 %** |

**Table 6.** Performance comparisons with five sequence-based approaches and the baseline "GoogLeNet (baseline)" in terms of average classification accuracy of the 10-fold cross-validation on Oulu-CASIA.

| Method | Experimental settings | Average accuracy |
|---|---|---|
| HOG 3D [21] | sequence-based | 70.63 % |
| AdaLBP [18] | sequence-based | 73.54 % |
| Atlases [20] | sequence-based | 75.52 % |
| STM-ExpLet [1] | sequence-based | 74.59 % |
| DTAGN(Joint) [7] | sequence-based | 81.46 % |
| GoogLeNet (baseline) | image-based | 79.21 % |
| PPDN (standard SGD) | image-based | 82.91 % |
| PPDN w/o peak | image-based | **83.67 %** |
| PPDN | image-based | **84.59 %** |

hypothesized that this will degrade recognition for samples of peak expressions, due to interference from non-peak expression samples. This hypothesis is confirmed by the results of Tables 3 and 4. PGS outperforms standard SGD on all three test sets.

**Ablative Studies on Peak-Piloted Feature Transformation.** The peak-piloted feature transformation, which is the key innovation of the PPDN, can be used on all layers of the network. Employing the transformation on different convolutional and fully-connected layers can result in different levels of supervision of non-peak responses by peak responses. For example, early convolutional layers extract fine-grained details (e.g., local boundaries or illuminations) of faces, while later layers capture more semantic information, e.g., the appearance pattens of mouths and eyes. Table 7 presents an extensive comparison, by adding peak-piloted feature supervision on various layers. Note that we employ GoogLeNet [24], which includes 9 inception layers, as basic network. Four dif-

**Table 7.** Performance comparisons by adding the peak-piloted feature transformation on different convolutional layers when evaluated on Oulu-CASIA dataset.

| Method | inception layers | the last FC layer | the first FC layer | both FC layers |
|---|---|---|---|---|
| Inception-3a | ✓ | × | × | × |
| Inception-3b | ✓ | × | × | × |
| Inception-4a | ✓ | × | × | × |
| Inception-4b | ✓ | × | × | × |
| Inception-4c | ✓ | × | × | × |
| Inception-4d | ✓ | × | × | × |
| Inception-4e | ✓ | × | × | × |
| Inception-5a | ✓ | × | × | × |
| Inception-5b | ✓ | × | × | × |
| Fc1 | ✓ | × | ✓ | ✓ |
| Fc2 | ✓ | ✓ | × | ✓ |
| Average accuracy | 74.49 % | 73.33 % | 73.48 % | 74.99 % |

**Table 8.** Comparisons of the version with and without using peak information on Oulu-CASIA database in terms of average classification accuracy of the 10-fold cross-validation.

| Method | Weak expression | Peak expression | Combined |
|---|---|---|---|
| PPDN w/o peak | 67.52 % | 83.79 % | 74.01 % |
| PPDN | **67.95 %** | **84.59 %** | **74.99 %** |

**Table 9.** Face recognition rates for various poses under "setting 1".

| Method | $-45°$ | $-30°$ | $-15°$ | $+15°$ | $+30°$ | $+45°$ | Average |
|---|---|---|---|---|---|---|---|
| GoogLeNet (baseline) | 86.57 % | 99.3 % | 100 % | 100 % | 100 % | 90.06 % | 95.99 % |
| PPDN | **93.96 %** | **100 %** | **100 %** | **100 %** | **100 %** | **93.96 %** | **97.98 %** |

**Table 10.** Face recognition rates for various poses under "setting 2".

| Method | $-45°$ | $-30°$ | $-15°$ | $+15°$ | $+30°$ | $+45°$ | Average |
|---|---|---|---|---|---|---|---|
| Li et al. [38] | 56.62 % | 77.22 % | 89.12 % | 88.81 % | 79.12 % | 58.14 % | 74.84 % |
| Zhu et al. [27] | 67.10 % | 74.60 % | 86.10 % | 83.30 % | 75.30 % | 61.80 % | 74.70 % |
| CPI [28] | 66.60 % | 78.00 % | 87.30 % | 85.50 % | 75.80 % | 62.30 % | 75.90 % |
| CPF [28] | 73.00 % | 81.70 % | 89.40 % | 89.50 % | 80.50 % | 70.30 % | 80.70 % |
| GoogLeNet (baseline) | 56.62 % | 77.22 % | 89.12 % | 88.81 % | 79.12 % | 58.14 % | 74.84 % |
| PPDN | **72.06 %** | **85.41 %** | **92.44 %** | **91.38 %** | **87.07 %** | **70.97 %** | **83.22 %** |

ferent settings are tested: "inception layers" indicates that the loss of the peak-piloted feature transformation is appended for all inception layers plus the two fully-connected layers; "the first FC layer," "the last FC layer" and "both FC layers" append the loss to the first, last, and both fully-connected layers, respectively.

It can be seen that using the peak-piloted feature transformation only on the two fully connected layers achieves the best performance. Using additional losses on all inception layers has roughly the same performance. Eliminating the loss of a fully-connected layer decreases performance by more than 1%. These results show that the peak-piloted feature transformation is more useful for supervising the highly semantic feature representations (two fully-connected layers) than the early convolutional layers.

**Absence of Peak Information.** Table 8 demonstrates that the PPDN can also be used when the peak frame is not known a priori, which is usually the case for real-world videos. Given all video sequences, we trained the basic "GoogLeNet (baseline)" with 10-fold cross validation. The models were trained with 9-folds and then used to predict the ground-truth expression label in the remaining fold. The frame with the highest prediction score in each sequence was treated as the peak expression image. The PPDN was finally trained using the strategy of the previous experiments. This training procedure is more applicable to videos where the information of the peak expression is not available. The PPDN can still obtain results comparable to those of the model trained with the ground-truth peak frame information.

## 4.2 Generalization Ability of the PPDN

The learning of the evolution from a hard sample to an easy sample is applicable to other face-related recognition tasks. We demonstrate this by evaluating the PPDN on face recognition. One challenge to this task is learning robust features, invariant to pose and view. In this case, near-frontal faces can be treated easy examples, similar to peak expressions in FER, while profile faces can be viewed as hard samples, similar to non-peak expressions. The effectiveness of PPDN in learning pose-invariant features is demonstrated by comparing PPDN features to the "GoogLeNet(baseline)" features on the popular Multi-PIE dataset [19].

All the following experiments were conducted on the images of "session 1" on Multi-PIE, where the face images of 249 subjects are provided. Two experimental settings were evaluated to demonstrate the generalization ability of PPDN on face recognition. For the "setting 1" of Table 9, only images under normal illumination were used for training and testing, where seven poses of the first 100 subjects (ID from 001 to 100) were used for training and the six poses (from $-45°$ to $45°$) of the remaining individuals used for testing. One frontal face per subject was used as gallery image. Overall, 700 images were used for training and 894 images for testing. By treating the frontal face and one of the profile faces as input, the PPDN can embed the implicit transformation from profile faces to frontal faces into the network learning, for face recognition purposes. In the "setting 2" of Table 10, 100 subjects (ID 001 to 100) with seven different poses under 20 different illumination conditions were used for training and the rest with six poses and 19 illumination conditions were used for testing. This led to 14,000 training images and 16,986 testing images. Similarly to the first setting, PPDN takes the pair of a frontal face with normal illumination and one of the profile faces with 20 illuminations from the same subject as the input. The PPDN can thus learn the evolution from both the profile to the frontal face and non-normal to normal illumination. In addition to "GoogLeNet (baseline)," we compared the PPDN to four state-of-the-art methods: controlled pose feature(CPF) [28], controlled pose image(CPI) [28], Zhu et al. [27] and Li et al. [38]. The pre-trained model, prepocessing steps, and learning rate used in the FER experiments were adopted here. Under "setting 1" the network was trained with 10,000 iterations and under "setting 2" with 30,000 iterations. Face recognition performance is measured by the accuracy of the predicted subject identity.

It can be seen that the PPDN achieves considerable improvements over "GoogLeNet (baseline)" for the testing images of hard poses (i.e., $-45°$ and $45°$) in both "setting 1" and "setting 2". Significant improvements over "GoogLeNet (baseline)" are also observed for the average over all poses (97.98 % vs 95.99 % under "setting 1" and 83.22 % vs 74.84 % under "setting 2"). The PPDN also beats all baselines by 2.52 % under "setting 2". This supports the conclusion that the PPDN can be effectively generalized to face recognition tasks, which benefit from embedding the evolution from hard to easy samples into the network parameters.

## 5    Conclusions

In this paper, we propose a novel peak-piloted deep network for facial expression recognition. The main novelty is the embedding of the expression evolution from non-peak to peak into the network parameters. PPDN jointly optimizes an L2-norm loss of peak-piloted feature transformation and the cross-entropy losses of expression recognition. By using a special-purpose back-propagation procedure (PGS) for network optimization, the PPDN can drive the intermediate-layer features of the non-peak expression sample towards those of the peak expression sample, while avoiding the inverse.

**Acknowledgement.** We thank Xuecheng Nie for useful discussions. This work is partially supported by the China Postdoctoral Science Foundation (No. 2016T90148).

## Appendix

The loss

$$J_1 = \sum_{i=1}^{N} \sum_{j \in \Omega} \|f_j(x_i^p, W) - f_j(x_i^n, W)\|^2 \tag{A-1}$$

has gradient

$$\nabla_W J_1 = 2 \sum_{i=1}^{N} \sum_{j \in \Omega} (f_j(x_i^p, W) - f_j(x_i^n, W)) \nabla_W f_j(x_i^n, W)$$

$$+ 2 \sum_{i=1}^{N} \sum_{j \in \Omega} (f_j(x_i^p, W) - f_j(x_i^n, W)) \nabla_W f_j(x_i^p, W). \tag{A-2}$$

The PGS is

$$\widetilde{\nabla_W J_1} = 2 \sum_{i=1}^{N} \sum_{j \in \Omega} (f_j(x_i^p, W) - f_j(x_i^n, W)) \nabla_W f_j(x_i^n, W) \tag{A-3}$$

Defining

$$A = \sum_{i=1}^{N} \sum_{j \in \Omega} (f_j(x_i^p, W) - f_j(x_i^n, W)) \nabla_W f_j(x_i^n, W) \tag{A-4}$$

and

$$B = \sum_{i=1}^{N} \sum_{j \in \Omega} (f_j(x_i^p, W) - f_j(x_i^n, W)) \nabla_W f_j(x_i^p, W) \tag{A-5}$$

it follows that

$$< \nabla_W J_1, \widetilde{\nabla_W J_1} > = -4 < A, B > +4\|A\|^2 \tag{A-6}$$

or

$$< \nabla_W J_1, \widetilde{\nabla_W J_1} > = -4\|A\|\|B\| \cos\theta + 4\|A\|^2 \tag{A-7}$$

where $\theta$ is angle between A and B. Hence, the dot-product is greater than zero when

$$\|B\| \cos\theta < \|A\|. \tag{A-8}$$

This holds for sure as $\nabla_W f_j(x_i^n, W)$ converges to $\nabla_W f_j(x_i^p, W)$ which is the goal of optimization, but is generally true if the sizes of gradients $\nabla_W f_j(x_i^n, W)$ and $\nabla_W f_j(x_i^p, W)$ are similar on average. Since the dot-product is positive, $\widetilde{\nabla_W J_1}$ is a descent (although not a steepest descent) direction for the loss function $J_1$. Hence, the PGS is a descent direction for the total loss. Note that, because there are also the gradients of $J_2$ and $J_3$, this can hold even when (A-8) is violated, if the gradients of J2 and J3 are dominant. Hence, the PGS is likely to converge to a minimum of the loss.

## References

1. Liu, M., Shan, S., Wang, R., Chen, X.: Learning expressionlets on spatio-temporal manifold for dynamic facial expression recognition. In: Proceedings of the IEEE Conference on Computer Vision and Pattern Recognition, pp. 1749–1756 (2014)

2. Chen, H., Li, J., Zhang, F., Li, Y., Wang, H.: 3D model-based continuous emotion recognition. In: Proceedings of the IEEE Conference on Computer Vision and Pattern Recognition, pp. 1836–1845 (2015)
3. Dapogny, A., Bailly, K., Dubuisson, S.: Pairwise conditional random forests for facial expression recognition. In: Proceedings of the IEEE International Conference on Computer Vision, pp. 3783–3791 (2015)
4. Liu, P., Han, S., Meng, Z., Tong, Y.: Facial expression recognition via a boosted deep belief network. In: Proceedings of the IEEE Conference on Computer Vision and Pattern Recognition, pp. 1805–1812 (2014)
5. Yu, Z., Zhang, C.: Image based static facial expression recognition with multiple deep network learning. In: Proceedings of the 2015 ACM on International Conference on Multimodal Interaction, pp. 435–442. ACM (2015)
6. Liu, M., Li, S., Shan, S., Chen, X.: Au-aware deep networks for facial expression recognition. In: 2013 10th IEEE International Conference and Workshops on Automatic Face and Gesture Recognition (FG), pp. 1–6. IEEE (2013)
7. Jung, H., Lee, S., Yim, J., Park, S., Kim, J.: Joint fine-tuning in deep neural networks for facial expression recognition. In: Proceedings of the IEEE International Conference on Computer Vision, pp. 2983–2991 (2015)
8. Li, X., Mori, G., Zhang, H.: Expression-invariant face recognition with expression classification. In: 2006 3rd Canadian Conference on Computer and Robot Vision, p. 77. IEEE (2006)
9. Zhang, Z., Luo, P., Loy, C.C., Tang, X.: Facial landmark detection by deep multi-task learning. In: Fleet, D., Pajdla, T., Schiele, B., Tuytelaars, T. (eds.) ECCV 2014, Part VI. LNCS, vol. 8694, pp. 94–108. Springer, Heidelberg (2014)
10. Zhong, L., Liu, Q., Yang, P., Liu, B., Huang, J., Metaxas, D.N.: Learning active facial patches for expression analysis. In: Computer Vision and Pattern Recognition (CVPR), pp. 2562–2569. IEEE (2012)
11. Shan, C., Gong, S., McOwan, P.W.: Facial expression recognition based on local binary patterns: a comprehensive study. Image Vis. Comput. **27**(6), 803–816 (2009)
12. Kahou, S.E., Froumenty, P., Pal, C.: Facial expression analysis based on high dimensional binary features. In: Agapito, L., Bronstein, M.M., Rother, C. (eds.) ECCV 2014. LNCS, vol. 8926, pp. 135–147. Springer, Heidelberg (2014)
13. Chopra, S., Hadsell, R., LeCun, Y.: Learning a similarity metric discriminatively, with application to face verification. In: 2005 IEEE Computer Society Conference on Computer Vision and Pattern Recognition, CVPR 2005, vol. 1, pp. 539–546. IEEE (2005)
14. Lai, H., Xiao, S., Cui, Z., Pan, Y., Xu, C., Yan, S.: Deep cascaded regression for face alignment (2015). arXiv preprint arXiv:1510.09083
15. Li, H., Lin, Z., Shen, X., Brandt, J., Hua, G.: A convolutional neural network cascade for face detection. In: Proceedings of the IEEE Conference on Computer Vision and Pattern Recognition, pp. 5325–5334 (2015)
16. Mollahosseini, A., Chan, D., Mahoor, M.H.: Going deeper in facial expression recognition using deep neural networks (2015). arXiv preprint arXiv:1511.04110
17. Lucey, P., Cohn, J.F., Kanade, T., Saragih, J., Ambadar, Z., Matthews, I.: The extended cohn-kanade dataset (ck+): a complete dataset for action unit and emotion-specified expression. In: 2010 IEEE Computer Society Conference on Computer Vision and Pattern Recognition Workshops (CVPRW), pp. 94–101. IEEE (2010)
18. Zhao, G., Huang, X., Taini, M., Li, S.Z., Pietikäinen, M.: Facial expression recognition from near-infrared videos. Image Vis. Comput. **29**(9), 607–619 (2011)

19. Gross, R., Matthews, I., Cohn, J., Kanade, T., Baker, S.: Multi-pie. Image Vis. Comput. **28**(5), 807–813 (2010)
20. Guo, Y., Zhao, G., Pietikäinen, M.: Dynamic facial expression recognition using longitudinal facial expression atlases. In: Fitzgibbon, A., Lazebnik, S., Perona, P., Sato, Y., Schmid, C. (eds.) ECCV 2012, Part II. LNCS, vol. 7573, pp. 631–644. Springer, Heidelberg (2012)
21. Klaser, A., Marszałek, M., Schmid, C.: A spatio-temporal descriptor based on 3D-gradients. In: BMVC 2008–19th British Machine Vision Conference, British Machine Vision Association p. 275–1 (2008)
22. Sikka, K., Wu, T., Susskind, J., Bartlett, M.: Exploring bag of words architectures in the facial expression domain. In: Fusiello, A., Murino, V., Cucchiara, R. (eds.) ECCV 2012 Ws/Demos, Part II. LNCS, vol. 7584, pp. 250–259. Springer, Heidelberg (2012)
23. Krizhevsky, A., Sutskever, I., Hinton, G.E.: Imagenet classification with deep convolutional neural networks. In: Advances in neural information processing systems, pp. 1097–1105 (2012)
24. Szegedy, C., Liu, W., Jia, Y., Sermanet, P., Reed, S., Anguelov, D., Erhan, D., Vanhoucke, V., Rabinovich, A.: Going deeper with convolutions. In: Proceedings of the IEEE Conference on Computer Vision and Pattern Recognition, pp. 1–9 (2015)
25. Simonyan, K., Zisserman, A.: Very deep convolutional networks for large-scale image recognition (2014). arXiv preprint arXiv:1409.1556
26. Sun, Y., Chen, Y., Wang, X., Tang, X.: Deep learning face representation by joint identification-verification. In: Advances in Neural Information Processing Systems, pp. 1988–1996 (2014)
27. Zhu, Z., Luo, P., Wang, X., Tang, X.: Deep learning identity-preserving face space. In: Proceedings of the IEEE International Conference on Computer Vision, pp. 113–120 (2013)
28. Yim, J., Jung, H., Yoo, B., Choi, C., Park, D., Kim, J.: Rotating your face using multi-task deep neural network. In: Proceedings of the IEEE Conference on Computer Vision and Pattern Recognition, pp. 676–684 (2015)
29. Schroff, F., Kalenichenko, D., Philbin, J.: Facenet: a unified embedding for face recognition and clustering. In: IEEE CVPR, pp. 815–823 (2015)
30. Sun, Y., Liang, D., Wang, X., Tang, X.: Deepid3: face recognition with very deep neural networks (2015). arXiv preprint arXiv:1502.00873
31. Bottou, L.: Large-scale machine learning with stochastic gradient descent. In: Proceedings of COMPSTAT'2010, pp. 177–186. Springer, Heidelberg (2010)
32. Yi, D., Lei, Z., Liao, S., Li, S.Z.: Learning face representation from scratch (2014). arXiv preprint arXiv:1411.7923
33. Glorot, X., Bengio, Y.: Understanding the difficulty of training deep feedforward neural networks. In: International Conference on Artificial Intelligence and Statistics, pp. 249–256 (2010)
34. Bartlett, M.S., Littlewort, G., Frank, M., Lainscsek, C., Fasel, I., Movellan, J.: Recognizing facial expression: machine learning and application to spontaneous behavior. In: CVPR, vol. 2, pp. 568–573. IEEE (2005)
35. Xue, M., W.L., Li, L.: The uncorrelated and discriminant colour space for facial expression recognition. In: Optimization and Control Techniques and Applications, pp. 167–177 (2014)
36. Freund, Y., Schapire, R.: A decision-theoretic generalization of on-line learning and an application to boosting. In: Proceedings of the Second European Conference on Computational Learning Theory, pp. 23–27 (1995)

37. Liu, M., Li, S., Shan, S., Wang, R., Chen, X.: Deeply learning deformable facial action parts model for dynamic expression analysis. In: Cremers, D., Reid, I., Saito, H., Yang, M.-H. (eds.) ACCV 2014. LNCS, vol. 9006, pp. 143–157. Springer, Heidelberg (2015)

38. Li, A., Shan, S., Gao, W.: Coupled bias-variance tradeoff for cross-pose face recognition. IEEE Trans. Image Process. **21**(1), 305–315 (2012)

# Is Faster R-CNN Doing Well for Pedestrian Detection?

Liliang Zhang[1], Liang Lin[1(✉)], Xiaodan Liang[1], and Kaiming He[2]

[1] School of Data and Computer Science, Sun Yat-sen University, Guangzhou, China
zhangll.level0@gmail.com, linliang@ieee.org, xdliang328@gmail.com
[2] Microsoft Research, Beijing, China
kahe@microsoft.com

**Abstract.** Detecting pedestrian has been arguably addressed as a special topic beyond general object detection. Although recent deep learning object detectors such as Fast/Faster R-CNN have shown excellent performance for general object detection, they have limited success for detecting pedestrian, and previous leading pedestrian detectors were in general hybrid methods combining hand-crafted and deep convolutional features. In this paper, we investigate issues involving Faster R-CNN for pedestrian detection. We discover that the Region Proposal Network (RPN) in Faster R-CNN indeed performs well as a stand-alone pedestrian detector, but surprisingly, the downstream classifier degrades the results. We argue that two reasons account for the unsatisfactory accuracy: (i) insufficient resolution of feature maps for handling small instances, and (ii) lack of any bootstrapping strategy for mining hard negative examples. Driven by these observations, we propose a very simple but effective baseline for pedestrian detection, using an RPN followed by boosted forests on shared, high-resolution convolutional feature maps. We comprehensively evaluate this method on several benchmarks (Caltech, INRIA, ETH, and KITTI), presenting competitive accuracy and good speed. Code will be made publicly available.

**Keywords:** Pedestrian detection · Convolutional neural networks · Boosted forests · Hard-negative mining

## 1   Introduction

Pedestrian detection, as a key component of real-world applications such as automatic driving and intelligent surveillance, has attracted special attention beyond general object detection. Despite the prevalent success of deeply learned features in computer vision, current leading pedestrian detectors (*e.g.*, [1–4]) are in general *hybrid* methods that combines traditional, hand-crafted features [5,6] and deep convolutional features [7,8]. For example, in [1] a stand-alone pedestrian detector [9] (that uses Squares Channel Features) is adopted as a highly selective proposer (<3 regions per image), followed by R-CNN [10] for

© Springer International Publishing AG 2016
B. Leibe et al. (Eds.): ECCV 2016, Part II, LNCS 9906, pp. 443–457, 2016.
DOI: 10.1007/978-3-319-46475-6_28

classification. Hand-crafted features appear to be of critical importance for state-of-the-art pedestrian detection.

On the other hand, Faster R-CNN [11] is a particularly successful method for general object detection. It consists of two components: a fully convolutional Region Proposal Network (RPN) for proposing candidate regions, followed by a downstream Fast R-CNN [12] classifier. The Faster R-CNN system is thus a purely CNN-based method without using hand-crafted features (*e.g.*, Selective Search [13] that is based on low-level features). Despite its leading accuracy on several multi-category benchmarks, Faster R-CNN has not presented competitive results on popular pedestrian detection datasets (*e.g.*, the Caltech set [14]).

In this paper, we investigate the issues involving Faster R-CNN as a pedestrian detector. Interestingly, we find that an RPN specially tailored for pedestrian detection achieves competitive results as a stand-alone pedestrian detector. But surprisingly, the accuracy is degraded after feeding these proposals into the Fast R-CNN classifier. We argue that such unsatisfactory performance is attributed to two reasons as follows.

First, the convolutional feature maps of the Fast R-CNN classifier are of low solution for detecting small objects. Typical scenarios of pedestrian detection, such as automatic driving and intelligent surveillance, generally present pedestrian instances of small sizes (*e.g.*, $28 \times 70$ for Caltech [14]). On small objects (Fig. 1(a)), the Region-of-Interest (RoI) pooling layer [12,15] performed on a low-resolution feature map (usually with a stride of 16 pixels) can lead to "plain" features caused by collapsing bins. These features are not discriminative on small regions, and thus degrade the downstream classifier. We note that this is in contrast to hand-crafted features that have finer resolutions. We address this problem by pooling features from shallower but higher-resolution layers, and by the hole algorithm (namely, "à trous" [16] or filter rarefaction [17]) that increases feature map size.

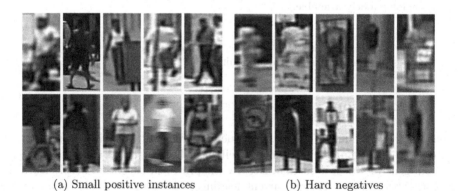

(a) Small positive instances                (b) Hard negatives

**Fig. 1.** Two challenges for Fast/Faster R-CNN in pedestrian detection. (a) Small objects that may fail RoI pooling on low-resolution feature maps. (b) Hard negative examples that receive no careful attention in Fast/Faster R-CNN.

Second, in pedestrian detection the false predictions are dominantly caused by confusions of hard *background* instances (Fig. 1(b)). This is in contrast to general object detection where a main source of confusion is from *multiple categories*. To address hard negative examples, we adopt cascaded Boosted Forest (BF) [18,19], which performs effective hard negative mining (bootstrapping) and sample re-weighting, to classify the RPN proposals. Unlike previous methods that use hand-crafted features to train the forest, in our method the BF *reuses* the deep convolutional features of RPN. This strategy not only reduces the computational cost of the classifier by sharing features, but also exploits the deeply learned features.

As such, we present a surprisingly simple but effective baseline for pedestrian detection based on RPN and BF. Our method overcomes two limitations of Faster R-CNN for pedestrian detection and gets rid of traditional hand-crafted features. We present compelling results on several benchmarks, including Caltech [14], INRIA [20], ETH [21], and KITTI [22]. Remarkably, our method has substantially better localization accuracy and shows a relative improvement of 40 % on the Caltech dataset under an Intersection-over-Union (IoU) threshold of 0.7 for evaluation. Meanwhile, our method has a test-time speed of 0.5 s per image, which is competitive with previous leading methods.

In addition, our paper reveals that traditional pedestrian detectors have been inherited in recent methods at least for two reasons. First, the higher resolution of hand-crafted features (such as [5,6]) and their pyramids is good for detecting small objects. Second, effective bootstrapping is performed for mining hard negative examples. These key factors, however, when appropriately handled in a deep learning system, lead to excellent results.

## 2  Related Work

The Integrate Channel Features (ICF) detector [5], which extends the Viola-Jones framework [23], is among the most popular pedestrian detectors without using deep learning features. The ICF detector involves channel feature pyramids and boosted classifiers. The feature representations of ICF have been improved in several ways, including ACF [6], LDCF [24], SCF [9], and many others, but the boosting algorithm remains a key building block for pedestrian detection.

Driven by the success of ("slow") R-CNN [10] for general object detection, a recent series of methods [2,3,9] adopt a two-stage pipeline for pedestrian detection. In [1], the SCF pedestrian detector [9] is used to propose regions, followed by an R-CNN for classification; TA-CNN [2] employs the ACF detector [6] to generate proposals, and trains an R-CNN-style network to jointly optimize pedestrian detection with semantic tasks; the DeepParts method [3] applies the LDCF detector [24] to generate proposals and learns a set of complementary parts by neural networks. We note that these proposers are stand-alone pedestrian detectors consisting of hand-crafted features and boosted classifiers.

Unlike the above R-CNN-based methods, the CompACT method [4] learns boosted classifiers on top of hybrid hand-crafted and deep convolutional features.

Most closely related to our work, the CCF detector [25] is boosted classifiers on pyramids of deep convolutional features, but uses no region proposals. Our method has no pyramid, and is much faster and more accurate than [25].

# 3  Approach

Our approach consists of two components (illustrated in Fig. 2): an RPN that generates candidate boxes as well as convolutional feature maps, and a Boosted Forest that classifies these proposals using these convolutional features.

## 3.1  Region Proposal Network for Pedestrian Detection

The RPN in Faster R-CNN [11] was developed as a class-agnostic detector (proposer) in the scenario of multi-category object detection. For single-category detection, RPN is naturally a detector for the only category concerned. We specially tailor the RPN for pedestrian detection, as introduced in the following.

We adopt anchors (reference boxes) [11] of a single aspect ratio of 0.41 (width to height). This is the average aspect ratio of pedestrians as indicated in [14]. This is unlike the original RPN [11] that has anchors of multiple aspect ratios. Anchors of inappropriate aspect ratios are associated with few examples, so are noisy and harmful for detection accuracy. In addition, we use anchors of 9 different scales, starting from 40 pixels height with a scaling stride of 1.3×. This spans a wider range of scales than [11]. The usage of multi-scale anchors waives the requirement of using feature pyramids to detect multi-scale objects.

Following [11], we adopt the VGG-16 net [8] pre-trained on the ImageNet dataset [26] as the backbone network. The RPN is built on top of the Conv5_3 layer, which is followed by an intermediate 3 × 3 convolutional layer and two sibling 1 × 1 convolutional layers for classification and bounding box regression (more details in [11]). In this way, RPN regresses boxes with a stride of 16 pixels (Conv5_3). The classification layer provides confidence scores of the predicted boxes, which can be used as the initial scores of the Boosted Forest cascade that follows.

It is noteworthy that although we will use the "à trous" [16] trick in the following section to increase resolution and reduce stride, we keep using the

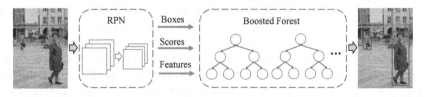

**Fig. 2.** Our pipeline. RPN is used to compute candidate bounding boxes, scores, and convolutional feature maps. The candidate boxes are fed into cascaded Boosted Forests (BF) for classification, using the features pooled from the convolutional feature maps computed by RPN.

same RPN with a stride of 16 pixels. The à trous trick is only exploited when extracting features (as introduced next), but not for fine-tuning.

## 3.2   Feature Extraction

With the proposals generated by RPN, we adopt RoI pooling [12] to extract fixed-length features from regions. These features will be used to train BF as introduced in the next section. Unlike Faster R-CNN which requires to feed these features into the *original fully-connected* (fc) layers and thus limits their dimensions, the BF classifier imposes no constraint on the dimensions of features. For example, we can extract features from RoIs on Conv3_3 (of a stride = 4 pixels) and Conv4_3 (of a stride = 8 pixels). We pool the features into a fixed resolution of $7 \times 7$. These features from different layers are simply concatenated without normalization, thanks to the flexibility of the BF classifier; on the contrast, feature normalization needs to be carefully addressed [27] for deep classifiers when concatenating features.

Remarkably, as there is no constraint imposed to feature dimensions, it is flexible for us to use features of increased resolution. In particular, given the fine-tuned layers from RPN (stride = 4 on Conv3, 8 on Conv4, and 16 on Conv5), we can use the à trous trick [16] to compute convolutional feature maps of higher resolution. For example, we can set the stride of Pool3 as 1 and dilate all Conv4 filters by 2, which reduces the stride of Conv4 from 8 to 4. Unlike previous methods [16,17] that fine-tune the dilated filters, in our method we only use them for feature extraction, without fine-tuning a new RPN.

Though we adopt the same RoI resolution ($7 \times 7$) as Faster R-CNN [11], these RoIs are on higher-resolution feature maps (*e.g.*, Conv3_3, Conv4_3, or Conv4_3 à trous) than Fast R-CNN (Conv5_3). If an RoI's input resolution is smaller than output (*i.e.*, $< 7 \times 7$), the pooling bins collapse and the features become "flat" and not discriminative. This problem is alleviated in our method, as it is not constrained to use features of Conv5_3 in our downstream classifier.

## 3.3   Boosted Forest

The RPN has generated the region proposals, confidence scores, and features, all of which are used to train a cascaded Boosted Forest classifier. We adopt the RealBoost algorithm [18], and mainly follow the hyper-parameters in [4]. Formally, we bootstrap the training by 6 times, and the forest in each stage has $\{64, 128, 256, 512, 1024, 1536\}$ trees. Initially, the training set consists of all positive examples ($\sim$50k on the Caltech set) and the same number of randomly sampled negative examples from the proposals. After each stage, additional hard negative examples (whose number is 10 % of the positives, $\sim$5k on Caltech) are mined and added into the training set. Finally, a forest of 2048 trees is trained after all bootstrapping stages. This final forest classifier is used for inference. Our implementation is based on [28].

We note that it is not necessary to handle the initial proposals equally, because our proposals have initial confidence scores computed by RPN.

In other words, the RPN can be considered as the stage-0 classifier $f_0$, and we set $f_0 = \frac{1}{2} \log \frac{s}{1-s}$ following the RealBoost form where $s$ is the score of a proposal region ($f_0$ is a constant in standard boosting). The other stages are as in standard RealBoost.

### 3.4  Implementation Details

We adopt single-scale training and testing as in [11,12,15], without using feature pyramids. An image is resized such that its shorter edge has $N$ pixels ($N = 720$ pixels on Caltech, 600 on INRIA, 810 on ETH, and 500 on KITTI). For RPN training, an anchor is considered as a positive example if it has an Intersection-over-Union (IoU) ratio greater than 0.5 with one ground truth box, and otherwise negative. We adopt the image-centric training scheme [11,12], and each mini-batch consists of 1 image and 120 randomly sampled anchors for computing the loss. The ratio of positive and negative samples is 1:5 in a mini-batch. Other hyper-parameters of RPN are as in [11], and we adopt the publicly available code of [11] to fine-tune the RPN. We note that in [11] the cross-boundary anchors are ignored during fine-tuning, whereas in our implementation we preserve the cross-boundary negative anchors during fine-tuning, which empirically improves accuracy on these datasets.

With the fine-tuned RPN, we adopt non-maximum suppression (NMS) with a threshold of 0.7 to filter the proposal regions. Then the proposal regions are ranked by their scores. For BF training, we construct the training set by selecting the top-ranked 1000 proposals (and ground truths) of each image. The tree depth is set as 5 for the Caltech and KITTI set, and 2 for the INRIA and ETH set, which are empirically determined according to the different sizes of the data sets. At test time, we only use the top-ranked 100 proposals in an image, which are classified by the BF.

## 4  Experiments and Analysis

### 4.1  Datasets

We comprehensively evaluate on 4 benchmarks: Caltech [14], INRIA [20], ETH [21] and KITTI [22]. By default an IoU threshold of 0.5 is used for determining True Positives in these datasets.

On Caltech [14], the training data is augmented by 10 folds (42782 images) following [1]. 4024 images in the standard test set are used for evaluation on the original annotations under the "reasonable" setting (pedestrians that are at least 50 pixels tall and at least 65 % visible) [14]. The evaluation metric is log-average Miss Rate on False Positive Per Image (FPPI) in $[10^{-2}, 10^0]$ (denoted as $MR_{-2}$ following [29], or in short MR). In addition, we also test our model on the new annotations provided by [29], which correct the errors in the original annotations. This set is denoted as "Caltech-New". The evaluation metrics in Caltech-New are $MR_{-2}$ and $MR_{-4}$, corresponding to the log-average Miss Rate on FPPI ranges of $[10^{-2}, 10^0]$ and $[10^{-4}, 10^0]$, following [29].

The INRIA [20] and ETH [21] datasets are often used for verifying the generalization capability of the models. Following the settings in [30], our model is trained on the 614 positive and 1218 negative images in the INRIA training set. The models are evaluated on the 288 testing images in INRIA and 1804 images in ETH, evaluated by $MR_{-2}$.

The KITTI dataset [22] consists of images with stereo data available. We perform training on the 7481 images of the left camera, and evaluate on the standard 7518 test images. KITTI evaluates the PASCAL-style mean Average Precision (mAP) under three difficulty levels: "Easy", "Moderate", and "Hard"[1].

### 4.2  Ablation Experiments

In this subsection, we conduct ablation experiments on the Caltech dataset.

### Is RPN Good for Pedestrian Detection?

In Fig. 3 we investigate RPN in terms of *proposal quality*, evaluated by the recall rates under different IoU thresholds. We evaluate on average 1, 4, or 100 proposals per image[2]. Figure 3 shows that in general RPN performs better than three leading methods that are based on traditional features: SCF [9], LDCF [24] and Checkerboards [31]. With 100 proposals per image, our RPN achieves >95 % recall at an IoU of 0.7.

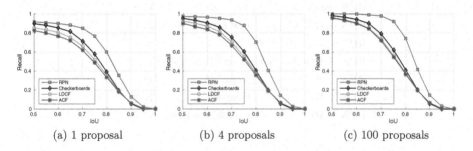

(a) 1 proposal          (b) 4 proposals          (c) 100 proposals

**Fig. 3.** Comparison of RPN and three existing methods in terms of proposal quality (recall *vs.* IoU) on the Caltech set, with on average 1, 4 or 100 proposals per image are evaluated.

More importantly, RPN as a *stand-alone pedestrian detector* achieves an MR of **14.9 %** (Table 1). *This result is competitive and is better than all but two state-of-the-art competitors on the Caltech dataset* (Fig. 4). We note that unlike RoI pooling that may suffer from small regions, RPN is essentially based on fixed-size sliding windows (in a fully convolutional fashion) and thus avoids collapsing bins. RPN predicts small objects by using small anchors.

---

[1] http://www.cvlibs.net/datasets/kitti/eval_object.php.

[2] To be precise, "on average $k$ proposals per image" means that for a dataset with $M$ images, the top-ranked $kM$ proposals are taken to evaluate the recall.

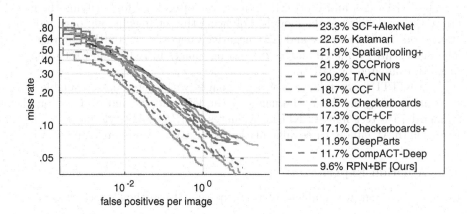

**Fig. 4.** Comparisons on the **Caltech** set (legends indicate MR).

**Table 1.** Comparisons of different classifiers and features on the Caltech set. All methods are based on VGG-16 (including R-CNN). The same set of RPN proposals are used for all entries.

| Method | RoI features | MR (%) |
|---|---|---|
| RPN stand-alone | - | 14.9 |
| RPN + R-CNN | raw pixels | 13.1 |
| RPN + Fast R-CNN | Conv5_3 | 20.2 |
| RPN + Fast R-CNN | Conv5_3, à trous | 16.2 |
| RPN + BF | Conv5_3 | 18.2 |
| RPN + BF | Conv4_3 | **12.6** |
| RPN + BF | Conv5_3, à trous | 13.7 |

**Table 2.** Comparisons of different features in our RPN + BF method on the Caltech set. All entries are based on VGG-16 and the same set of RPN proposals.

| RoI features | Time/img | MR (%) |
|---|---|---|
| Conv2_2 | 0.37 s | 15.9 |
| Conv3_3 | 0.37 s | **12.4** |
| Conv4_3 | 0.37 s | 12.6 |
| Conv5_3 | 0.37 s | 18.2 |
| Conv3_3, Conv4_3 | 0.37 s | **11.5** |
| Conv3_3, Conv4_3, Conv5_3 | 0.37 s | 11.9 |
| Conv3_3, (Conv4_3, à trous) | 0.51 s | **9.6** |

**How Important is Feature Resolution?**

We first report the accuracy of ("slow") R-CNN [10]. For fair comparisons, we fine-tune R-CNN using the VGG-16 network, and the proposals are from the same RPN as above. This method has an MR of 13.1 % (Table 1), better than its proposals (stand-alone RPN, 14.9 %). R-CNN crops raw pixels from images and warps to a fixed size (224 × 224), so suffers less from small objects. This result suggests that if reliable features (*e.g.*, from a fine resolution of 224 × 224) can be extracted, the downstream classifier is able to improve the accuracy.

Surprisingly, training a Fast R-CNN classifier on the same set of RPN proposals actually *degrades* the results: the MR is considerably increased to 20.2 % (*vs.* RPN's 14.9 %, Table 1). Even though R-CNN performs well on this task, Fast R-CNN presents a much worse result.

This problem is partially because of the low-resolution features. To show this, we train a Fast R-CNN (on the same set of RPN proposals as above) with the à trous trick adopted on Conv5, reducing the stride from 16 pixels to 8. The problem is alleviated (16.2 %, Table 1), demonstrating that higher resolution can be helpful. Yet, this result still lags far behind the stand-alone RPN or R-CNN (Table 1).

The effects of low-resolution features are also observed in our Boosted Forest classifiers. BF using Conv5_3 features has an MR of 18.2 % (Table 1), lower than the stand-alone RPN. Using the à trous trick on Conv5 when extracting features (Sec. 3.2), BF has a much better MR of 13.7 %.

But the BF classifier is more flexible and is able to take advantage of features of various resolutions. Table 2 shows the results of using different features in our method. Conv3_3 or Conv4_3 alone yields good results (12.4 % and 12.6 %), showing the effects of higher resolution features. Conv2_2 starts to show degradation (15.9 %), which can be explained by the weaker representation of the shallower layers. BF on the concatenation of Conv3_3 and Conv4_3 features reduces the MR to 11.5 %. The combination of features in this way is nearly cost-free. Moreover, unlike previous usage of skip connections [27], it is not necessary to normalize features in a decision forest classifier.

Finally, combining Conv3_3 with the à trous version of Conv4_3, we achieve the best result of **9.6 %** MR. We note that this is at the cost of extra computation (Table 2), because it requires to re-compute the Conv4 features maps with the à trous trick. Nevertheless, the speed of our method is still competitive (Table 4).

**Table 3.** Comparisons of with/without bootstrapping on the Caltech set.

| Method | RoI features | Bootstrapped? | MR (%) |
|---|---|---|---|
| RPN + Fast R-CNN | Conv5_3, à trous | | 16.2 |
| RPN + Fast R-CNN | Conv5_3, à trous | ✓ | 14.3 |
| RPN + BF | Conv5_3, à trous | ✓ | 13.7 |

**Table 4.** Comparisons of running time on the Caltech set. The time of LDCF and CCF is reported in [25], and that of CompactACT-Deep is reported in [4].

| Method | Hardware | Time/img (s) | MR (%) |
|---|---|---|---|
| LDCF [24] | CPU | 0.6 | 24.8 |
| CCF [25] | Titan Z GPU | 13 | 17.3 |
| CompACT-Deep [4] | Tesla K40 GPU | **0.5** | 11.7 |
| RPN + BF [ours] | Tesla K40 GPU | **0.5** | **9.6** |

**How Important Is Bootstrapping?**

To verify that the bootstrapping scheme in BF is of central importance (instead of the tree structure of the BF classifiers), we replace the last-stage BF classifier with a Fast R-CNN classifier. The results are in Table 3. Formally, after the 6 stages of bootstrapping, the bootstrapped training set is used to train a Fast R-CNN classifier (instead of the final BF with 2048 trees). We perform this comparison using RoI features on Conv5_3 (à trous). The bootstrapped Fast R-CNN has an MR of 14.3 %, which is closer to the BF counterpart of 13.7 %, and better than the non-bootstrapped Fast R-CNN's 16.2 %. This comparison indicates that the major improvement of BF over Fast R-CNN is because of bootstrapping, whereas the shapes of classifiers (forest *vs.* MLP) are less important.

## 4.3 Comparisons with State-of-the-Art Methods

**Caltech.** Figures 4 and 6 show the results on Caltech. In the case of using original annotations (Fig. 4), our method has an MR of **9.6 %**, which is over

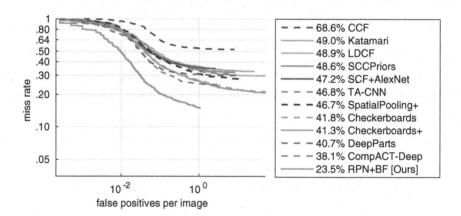

**Fig. 5.** Comparisons on the **Caltech** set using an IoU threshold of 0.7 to determine True Positives (legends indicate MR).

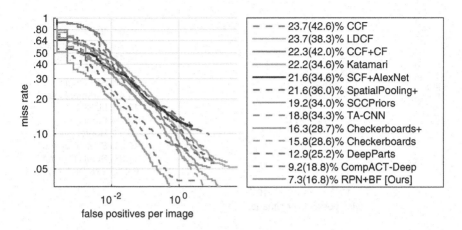

**Fig. 6.** Comparisons on the **Caltech-New** set (legends indicate $MR_{-2}$ ($MR_{-4}$)).

2 points better than the closest competitor (11.7 % of CompactACT-Deep [4]). In the case of using the corrected annotations (Fig. 6), our method has an $MR_{-2}$ of 7.3 % and $MR_{-4}$ of 16.8 %, both being 2 points better than the previous best methods.

In addition, expect for CCF (MR 18.7 %) [25], ours (MR 9.6 %) is the only method that *uses no hand-crafted features*. Our results suggest that hand-crafted features are not essential for good accuracy on the Caltech dataset; rather, high-resolution features and bootstrapping are the key to good accuracy, both of which are missing in the original Fast R-CNN detector.

Figure 5 shows the results on Caltech where an IoU threshold of 0.7 is used to determine True Positives (instead of 0.5 by default). With this more challenging metric, most methods exhibit dramatic performance drops, *e.g.*, the MR of CompactACT-Deep [4]/DeepParts [3] increase from 11.7 %/11.9 % to 38.1 %/40.7 %. Our method has an MR of 23.5 %, which is **a relative improvement of** $\sim$**40 %** over the closest competitors. This comparison demonstrates that our method has a substantially better **localization** accuracy. It also indicates that there is much room to improve localization performance on this widely evaluated dataset.

Table 4 compares the running time on Caltech. Our method is as fast as CompACT-Deep [4], and is much faster than CCF [25] that adopts feature pyramids. Our method shares feature between RPN and BF, and achieves a good balance between speed and accuracy.

**INRIA and ETH.** Figures 7 and 8 show the results on the INRIA and ETH datasets. On the INRIA set, our method achieves an MR of 6.9 %, considerably better than the best available competitor's 11.2 %. On the ETH set, our result (30.2 %) is better than the previous leading method (TA-CNN [2]) by 5 points.

**KITTI.** Table 5 shows the performance comparisons on KITTI. Our method has competitive accuracy and fast speed.

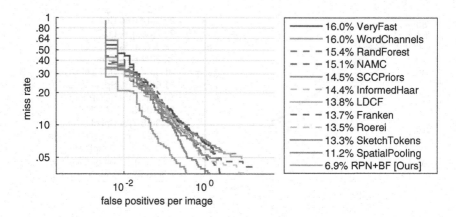

**Fig. 7.** Comparisons on the **INRIA** dataset (legends indicate MR).

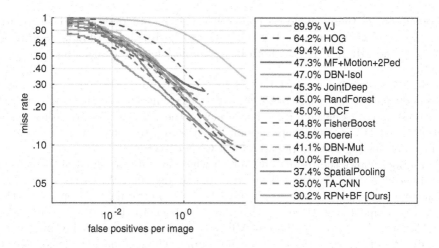

**Fig. 8.** Comparisons on the **ETH** dataset (legends indicate MR).

**Table 5.** Comparisons on the **KITTI** dataset collected at the time of submission (Feb 2016). The timing records are collected from the KITTI leaderboard. [†]: region proposal running time ignored (estimated 2 s).

| Method | mAP on Easy | mAP on Moderate | mAP on Hard | Times (s) |
|---|---|---|---|---|
| R-CNN | 61.61 | 50.13 | 44.79 | 4 |
| pAUCEnstT | 65.26 | 54.49 | 48.60 | 60 |
| FilteredICF | 67.65 | 56.75 | 51.12 | 2 |
| DeepPart | 70.49 | 58.67 | 52.78 | 1 |
| CompACT-Deep | 70.69 | 58.74 | 52.71 | 1 |
| Regionlets | 73.14 | **61.15** | **55.21** | 1[†] |
| RPN + BF [ours] | **77.12** | **61.15** | **55.12** | 0.6 |

# 5    Conclusion and Discussion

In this paper, we present a very simple but effective baseline that uses RPN and BF for pedestrian detection. On top of the RPN proposals and features, the BF classifier is flexible for (i) combining features of arbitrary resolutions from any layers, without being limited by the classifier structure of the pre-trained network; and (ii) incorporating effective bootstrapping for mining hard negatives. These nice properties overcome two limitations of the Faster R-CNN system for pedestrian detection. Our method is a self-contained solution and does not resort to hybrid features.

Interestingly, we show that *bootstrapping* is a key component, even with the advance of deep neural networks. Using the same bootstrapping strategy and the same RoI features, both the tree-structured BF classifier and the region-wise MLP classifier (Fast R-CNN) are able to achieve similar results (Table 3). Concurrent with this work, an independently developed method called Online Hard Example Mining (OHEM) [32] is developed for training Fast R-CNN for general object detection. It is interesting to investigate this end-to-end, online mining fashion *vs.* the multi-stage, cascaded bootstrapping one.

**Acknowledgement.** This work was supported in part by State Key Development Program under Grant 2016YFB1001000, in part by Guangdong Natural Science Foundation under Grant S2013050014548. This work was also supported by Special Program for Applied Research on Super Computation of the NSFC-Guangdong Joint Fund (the second phase). We thank the anonymous reviewers for their constructive comments on improving this paper.

# References

1. Hosang, J., Omran, M., Benenson, R., Schiele, B.: Taking a deeper look at pedestrians. In: IEEE Conference on Computer Vision and Pattern Recognition (CVPR) (2015)
2. Tian, Y., Luo, P., Wang, X., Tang, X.: Pedestrian detection aided by deep learning semantic tasks. In: IEEE Conference on Computer Vision and Pattern Recognition (CVPR) (2015)
3. Tian, Y., Luo, P., Wang, X., Tang, X.: Deep learning strong parts for pedestrian detection. In: IEEE International Conference on Computer Vision (ICCV) (2015)
4. Cai, Z., Saberian, M., Vasconcelos, N.: Learning complexity-aware cascades for deep pedestrian detection. In: IEEE International Conference on Computer Vision (ICCV) (2015)
5. Dollár, P., Tu, Z., Perona, P., Belongie, S.: Integral channel features. In: British Machine Vision Conference (BMVC) (2009)
6. Dollár, P., Appel, R., Belongie, S., Perona, P.: Fast feature pyramids for object detection. IEEE Trans. Pattern Anal. Mach. Intell. (TPAMI) **36**, 1532–1545 (2014)
7. Krizhevsky, A., Sutskever, I., Hinton, G.E.: Imagenet classification with deep convolutional neural networks. In: Neural Information Processing Systems (NIPS) (2012)

8. Simonyan, K., Zisserman, A.: Very deep convolutional networks for large-scale image recognition (2014). arXiv:1409.1556

9. Benenson, R., Omran, M., Hosang, J., Schiele, B.: Ten years of pedestrian detection, what have we learned? In: Agapito, L., Bronstein, M.M., Rother, C. (eds.) ECCV 2014 Workshops. LNCS, vol. 8926, pp. 613–627. Springer, Heidelberg (2015)

10. Girshick, R., Donahue, J., Darrell, T., Malik, J.: Rich feature hierarchies for accurate object detection and semantic segmentation. In: IEEE Conference on Computer Vision and Pattern Recognition (CVPR) (2014)

11. Ren, S., He, K., Girshick, R., Sun, J.: Faster R-CNN: towards real-time object detection with region proposal networks. In: Neural Information Processing Systems (NIPS) (2015)

12. Girshick, R.: Fast R-CNN. In: IEEE International Conference on Computer Vision (ICCV) (2015)

13. Uijlings, J.R.R., van de Sande, K.E.A., Gevers, T., Smeulders, A.W.M.: Selective search for object recognition. Int. J. Comput. Vis. (IJCV) **104**, 154–171 (2013)

14. Dollár, P., Wojek, C., Schiele, B., Perona, P.: Pedestrian detection: an evaluation of the state of the art. IEEE Trans. Pattern Anal. Mach. Intell. (TPAMI) **34**, 743–761 (2012)

15. He, K., Zhang, X., Ren, S., Sun, J.: Spatial pyramid pooling in deep convolutional networks for visual recognition. In: Fleet, D., Pajdla, T., Schiele, B., Tuytelaars, T. (eds.) ECCV 2014, Part III. LNCS, vol. 8691, pp. 346–361. Springer, Heidelberg (2014)

16. Chen, L.-C., Papandreou, G., Kokkinos, I., Murphy, K., Yuille, A.L.: Semantic image segmentation with deep convolutional nets, fully connected CRFs (2014). arXiv:1412.7062

17. Long, J., Shelhamer, E., Darrell, T.: Fully convolutional networks for semantic segmentation. In: IEEE Conference on Computer Vision and Pattern Recognition (CVPR) (2015)

18. Friedman, J., Hastie, T., Tibshirani, R., et al.: Additive logistic regression: a statistical view of boosting (with discussion and a rejoinder by the authors). Ann. Stat. **28**, 337–407 (2000)

19. Appel, R., Fuchs, T., Dollár, P., Perona, P.: Quickly boosting decision trees-pruning underachieving features early. In: International Conference on Machine Learning (ICML) (2013)

20. Dalal, N., Triggs, B.: Histograms of oriented gradients for human detection. In: IEEE Conference on Computer Vision and Pattern Recognition (CVPR) (2005)

21. Ess, A., Leibe, B., Gool, L.V.: Depth and appearance for mobile scene analysis. In: IEEE International Conference on Computer Vision (ICCV) (2007)

22. Geiger, A., Lenz, P., Urtasun, R.: Are we ready for autonomous driving? The kitti vision benchmark suite. In: IEEE Conference on Computer Vision and Pattern Recognition (CVPR) (2012)

23. Viola, P., Jones, M.J.: Robust real-time face detection. Int. J. Comput. Vis. (IJCV) **57**, 137–154 (2004)

24. Nam, W., Dollár, P., Han, J.H.: Local decorrelation for improved pedestrian detection. In: Neural Information Processing Systems (NIPS) (2014)

25. Yang, B., Yan, J., Lei, Z., Li, S.Z.: Convolutional channel features. In: IEEE International Conference on Computer Vision (ICCV) (2015)

26. Russakovsky, O., Deng, J., Su, H., Krause, J., Satheesh, S., Ma, S., Huang, Z., Karpathy, A., Khosla, A., Bernstein, M., Berg, A.C., Fei-Fei, L.: ImageNet large scale visual recognition challenge. Int. J. Comput. Vis. (IJCV) **115**, 211–252 (2015)

27. Liu, W., Rabinovich, A., Berg, A.C.: Parsenet: Looking wider to see better (2015). arXiv:1506.04579
28. Dollár, P.: Piotr's Computer Vision Matlab Toolbox (PMT). https://github.com/pdollar/toolbox
29. Zhang, S., Benenson, R., Omran, M., Hosang, J., Schiele, B.: How far are we from solving pedestrian detection? In: IEEE Conference on Computer Vision and Pattern Recognition (CVPR) (2016)
30. Paisitkriangkrai, S., Shen, C., van den Hengel, A.: Strengthening the effectiveness of pedestrian detection with spatially pooled features. In: Fleet, D., Pajdla, T., Schiele, B., Tuytelaars, T. (eds.) ECCV 2014, Part IV. LNCS, vol. 8692, pp. 546–561. Springer, Heidelberg (2014)
31. Zhang, S., Benenson, R., Schiele, B.: Filtered channel features for pedestrian detection. In: IEEE Conference on Computer Vision and Pattern Recognition (CVPR) (2015)
32. Shrivastava, A., Gupta, A., Girshick, R.: Training region-based object detectors with online hard example mining (2016). arXiv:1604.03540

# Coarse-to-fine Planar Regularization for Dense Monocular Depth Estimation

Stephan Liwicki[1(⊠)], Christopher Zach[1], Ondrej Miksik[2], and Philip H.S. Torr[2]

[1] Toshiba Research Europe, Cambridge, UK
stephan.liwicki@crl.toshiba.co.uk
[2] University of Oxford, Oxford, UK

**Abstract.** Simultaneous localization and mapping (SLAM) using the whole image data is an appealing framework to address shortcoming of sparse feature-based methods – in particular frequent failures in textureless environments. Hence, direct methods bypassing the need of feature extraction and matching became recently popular. Many of these methods operate by alternating between pose estimation and computing (semi-)dense depth maps, and are therefore not fully exploiting the advantages of joint optimization with respect to depth and pose. In this work, we propose a framework for monocular SLAM, and its local model in particular, which optimizes simultaneously over depth and pose. In addition to a planarity enforcing smoothness regularizer for the depth we also constrain the complexity of depth map updates, which provides a natural way to avoid poor local minima and reduces unknowns in the optimization. Starting from a holistic objective we develop a method suitable for online and real-time monocular SLAM. We evaluate our method quantitatively in pose and depth on the TUM dataset, and qualitatively on our own video sequences.

**Keywords:** SLAM · Monocular odometry · Dense tracking and mapping

## 1 Introduction

Simultaneous localization and mapping (SLAM), also known as online structure from motion, aims to produce trajectory estimations and a 3D reconstruction of the environment in real-time. In modern technology, its application ranges from autonomous driving, navigation and robotics to interactive learning, gaming and enhanced reality [1–7]. Typically, SLAM comprises two key components: (1) a local model, which generates fast initial odometry measurements (which often includes a local 3D reconstruction – *e.g.* a depth map – as byproduct), and

**Electronic supplementary material** The online version of this chapter (doi:10.1007/978-3-319-46475-6_29) contains supplementary material, which is available to authorized users.

© Springer International Publishing AG 2016
B. Leibe et al. (Eds.): ECCV 2016, Part II, LNCS 9906, pp. 458–474, 2016.
DOI: 10.1007/978-3-319-46475-6_29

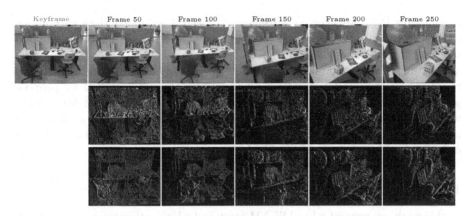

**Fig. 1.** During keyframe-to-frame comparison a dense depth map is build. Image, point cloud and depth (top to bottom) are shown as they develop, for selected frames from a *single* keyframe. (While depth is dense at the keyframe, their projections may not be.)

(2) a global model, which performs loop closures and pose refinement via large scale sub-real-time bundle adjustment. In our work, we focus on the former, and propose a new strategy for local monocular odometry and depth map estimation.

Estimating the 3D position of tracked landmarks is a key ingredient in any SLAM system, since it directly allows for the poses to be computed w.r.t. a common coordinate frame. Historically, visual landmarks are induced by sparse keypoints, but there is a recent trend to utilize a dense (or semi-dense) set of points (leading to a dense or semi-dense depth map representation) [8,9].

Another trend is the inclusion of different sensing modalities for depth estimation. Often, methods exploit (a combination of) alternative sensors, such as infrared, lidar and stereo camera setups, which natively provide fairly accurate depth data [10–13]. Such algorithms are quite advanced and are often employed even in consumer technology where hardware is controllable. Visual SLAM with only monocular camera streams is less common and still challenging in literature [8,9,14–21]. Nonetheless, the monocular setup is very suitable for (1) long range estimations, where stereo baselines are negligible, (2) light weight mobile and wearable devices aiming for a minimal amount of sensors to reduce weight and power consumption, and (3) legacy video footage recoded by a single camera.

Classical approaches for monocular visual SLAM are based on keypoint tracking and mapping [15–17], which produces a feature-based sparse depth hypothesis. A number of methods have since been proposed which essentially alternate between tracking (and pose computation) and dense depth map estimation: Most prominently, [8] presents dense tracking and mapping (DTAM) which generates a dense depth map on GPU. Similarly, [18–20] provide dense depth maps, but like [8] also rely heavily on GPU acceleration for real-time performance. In contrast to these methods large-scale direct SLAM (LSD-SLAM) [9] focusses the computation budget on a semi-dense subset of pixels and has therefore attractive running-times, even when run on CPU or mobile devices. As a direct method it computes the odometry measurements directly from image data without an intermediate representation such as feature tracks. Depth is then computed in a separate thread with small time delay. Note that all these methods employ an alternation strategy: odometry is computed with the depth map held fixed, and the depth map is updated with fixed pose estimates. In contrast, we propose joined estimation of depth and pose within a single optimization framework, which runs twice as fast as LSD-SLAM to find structure and motion. In particular, we introduce minimal additional computational cost compared to that of only the tracking thread of LSD-SLAM.

## 1.1   Contributions

In this work, we present a local SLAM front-end which estimates pose and depth truly simultaneously and in real-time (Fig. 1). We revisit traditional setups, and propose inverse depth estimation with a coarse-to-fine planar regularizer that gradually increases the complexity of the algorithm's depth perception. Note, many systems for stereo vision or depth sensors incorporate local or global planar regularization [12,13,22–24]. Similarly, we employ global planar constraints into our monocular setup, and enforce local smoothness by representing each pixel as lying on a plane that is similar to its neighbours'. Furthermore, similarly to many algorithms in stereo (*e.g.* [10,22]), we reduce depth complexity via discretization, in our case through planar splitting techniques which (in the spirit of graphical methods) create labels "on demand". In summary,

1. we formulate a global energy for planar regularized inverse depth that is optimized iteratively at each frame,
2. we revisit depth and pose optimization normally considered separately, and introduce a coarse-to-fine strategy that refines both truly simultaneously,
3. we establish our method as semi-dense, and find pose *and* depth twice as fast as LSD-SLAM, by adding minimal cost to LSD-SLAM's tracking thread,
4. we evaluate pose and depth quantitatively on the TUM dataset.

Closely related to our work is [25], where depth and pose is optimized simultaneously given the optical flow of two consecutive images. This approach is based on image pairs. Our method considers video input and incrementally improves its belief. In [26,27] planarity is proposed in conjunction with scene priors, previously learned from data, and [20] presents a hole-filling strategy for semi-dense monocular SLAM. While these methods are real-time, they rely on keypoints at image corners or gradients, which are later enriched with a planar refinement. Importantly however, such methods fail in featureless environments. Finally, we emphasis DTAM [8] performs batch operations on a set of images taken from a narrow field of view, and henceforth introduces a fixed lag before depth is perceived by the system. As this is often unacceptable for robotics setups, our method updates depth incrementally after *each* frame.

## 2    Proposed Energy for Monocular Depth Estimation

We formulate our energy function for poses and depth w.r.t. the photometric error over time. Similar to LSD-SLAM, we employ a keyframe-to-frame comparison to estimate camera displacement and each pixels' depth in the reference image. Let us denote the keyframe as $I$ and its immediately succeeding images as $(I_t)_{t=1}^T$. The tuple of valid pixel locations on the keyframe's plane is represented by $\mathcal{X} = (\mathbf{x}_i)_{i=1}^{|\mathcal{X}|}$ in *normalized* homogeneous coordinates (*i.e.* $z_i = 1$), and their corresponding *inverse* depth values are expressed by $\mathcal{D} = (d_i)_{i=1}^{|\mathcal{X}|}$. Since we aim to model planar surfaces, we use an over-parametrization given by $\mathcal{S} = (\mathbf{s}_i^{\mathrm{T}})_{i=1}^{|\mathcal{X}|} \cong \mathbb{R}^{3|\mathcal{X}|}$, where $\mathbf{s}_i = (u_i, v_i, w_i)^{\mathrm{T}}$ are planes with disparity gradients $u_i$, $v_i$, and inverse depth at 0, $w_i$. Hence, the relation $d_i = \mathbf{s}_i^{\mathrm{T}} \mathbf{x}_i$ holds.

Tuple $\varXi = (\xi_t)_{t=1}^T$ denotes the changes in camera pose, where $\xi_t \in SE(3)$ is composed of rotation $\mathbf{R}_t \in SO(3) \subset \mathbb{R}^{3 \times 3}$ and translation $\mathbf{t}_t \in \mathbb{R}^3$ between the keyframe $I$ and frame $I_t$. In principle, the complete cost function should incorporate all available images associated with the current keyframe and optimize over the depth and all poses jointly,

$$\hat{E}_{Total}(\mathcal{S}, \varXi) = \sum_{t=1}^T E_{Match}^{(t)}(\mathcal{S}, \xi_t) + E_{Smooth}(\mathcal{S}). \tag{1}$$

Here $E_{Match}^{(t)}$ and $E_{Smooth}$ are energy terms related to image-based matching costs and spatial smoothing assumptions, respectively. Before we describe these terms in more detail in subsequent sections, we modify $\hat{E}_{Total}$ to be more suitable for an incremental online approach. This is advisable since, the objective $\hat{E}_{Total}$ involves the complete history of all frames $I_t$ mapped to the current keyframe $I$. Intuitively the optimization of the poses $(\xi_t)_{t=1}^{T-1}$ is no longer relevant at time $T$, as only the current pose $\xi_T$ and $\mathcal{S}$ is required. Analytically, we introduce

$$E_{History}^{(T)}(\mathcal{S}) := \min_{(\xi_t)_{t=1}^{T-1}} \sum_{t=1}^{T-1} E_{Match}^{(t)}(\mathcal{S}, \xi_t) \tag{2}$$

where $(\xi_t)_{t=1}^{T-1}$ is the tuple of poses, minimized in previous frames. By splitting the first term in (1), the energy becomes

$$\hat{E}_{Total}(\mathcal{S}, \varXi) = E_{History}^{(T)}(\mathcal{S}) + E_{Match}^{(T)}(\mathcal{S}, \xi_T) + E_{Smooth}(\mathcal{S}). \tag{3}$$

Now we replace $E_{History}^{(T)}$ with its second order expansion around

$$(\mathcal{S}^*, \xi_1^*, \dots, \xi_{T-1}^*) = \operatorname*{argmin}_{\mathcal{S},(\xi_t)_{t=1}^{T-1}} \sum_{t=1}^{T-1} E_{Match}^{(t)}(\mathcal{S}, \xi_t), \tag{4}$$

and thus we obtain an approximation of $E_{History}^{(T)}(\mathcal{S})$, denoted $E_{Temporal}^{(T)}(\mathcal{S})$:

$$E^{(T)}_{Temporal}(\mathcal{S}):=E^{(T)}_{History}(\mathcal{S}^*) + \left(\nabla_\mathcal{S} E^{(T)}_{History}(\mathcal{S}^*)\right)^\mathrm{T}(\mathcal{S}-\mathcal{S}^*)$$

$$+\frac{1}{2}(\mathcal{S}-\mathcal{S}^*)^\mathrm{T}\left(\nabla^2_\mathcal{S} E^{(T)}_{History}(\mathcal{S}^*)\right)(\mathcal{S}-\mathcal{S}^*)$$

$$= E^{(T)}_{History}(\mathcal{S}^*) + \frac{1}{2}(\mathcal{S}-\mathcal{S}^*)^\mathrm{T}\left(\nabla^2_\mathcal{S} E^{(T)}_{History}(\mathcal{S}^*)\right)(\mathcal{S}-\mathcal{S}^*) \quad (5)$$

As $\mathcal{S}^*$ is a local minimizer of $E^{(T)}_{History}$, $\nabla_\mathcal{S} E^{(T)}_{History}(\mathcal{S}^*) = 0$. Furthermore, as our choice of terms leads to a nonlinear least-squares formulation, $\nabla^2_\mathcal{S} E^{(T)}_{History}(\mathcal{S}^*)$ is computed using the Gauss-Newton approximation. Finally, since $E^{(T)}_{History}$ jointly optimizes the inverse depths (in terms of its over-parametrization $\mathcal{S}$) and (internally) the poses, but $E^{(T)}_{Temporal}$ is solely a function of $\mathcal{S}$, we employ the Schur complement to factor out the poses $(\xi_t)_{t=1}^{T-1}$. However, as the poses link the entire depth map, the Schur complement matrix will be dense. We obtain a tractable approximation by using its block-diagonal consisting of $3 \times 3$ blocks (corresponding to $\mathbf{s}_i = (u_i, v_i, w_i)^\mathrm{T}$).[1] The resulting objective at time $T$ is therefore

$$E^{(T)}_{Total}(\mathcal{S}, \xi_T) = E^{(T)}_{Temporal}(\mathcal{S}) + E^{(T)}_{Match}(\mathcal{S}, \xi_T) + E_{Smooth}(\mathcal{S}). \quad (6)$$

There is a clear connection between $E^{(T)}_{Total}$, extended Kalman filtering and maximum likelihood estimation. If $E^{(T)}_{History}$ is interpreted as log-likelihood, then $\left(\mathcal{S}^*, (\xi_t^*)_{t=1}^{T-1}\right)$ is an asymptotically normal maximum likelihood estimate with the Hessian as (approximate) inverse covariance (i.e. precision) matrix. The Schur complement to factor out the poses (in the energy-minimization perspective) corresponds to marginalizing over the poses according to their uncertainty. $E^{(T)}_{Total}$ can be read as probabilistic fusion of past and current observation, but this correspondence is limited, since we are searching for MAP estimates and not posteriors. In the following section we discuss the remaining terms in $E^{(T)}_{Total}$.

## 2.1   Photometric Energy

The matching cost $E^{(T)}_{Match}(\mathcal{S}, \xi_T)$ is derived from an appearance (e.g. brightness) consistency assumption commonly employed in literature, e.g. [28]. Let us define the monocular warping function $W(\mathbf{x}_i, d_i, \xi_t)$ which maps point $\mathbf{x}_i$ in the keyframe to its representation $\mathbf{x}'_i$ in frame $t$ by

$$\mathbf{x}'_i = W(\mathbf{x}_i, d_i, \xi_t) = \mathrm{hom}\left(\mathbf{R}_t^\mathrm{T}(\mathbf{x}_i - \mathbf{t}_t d_i)\right), \quad (7)$$

under camera rotation $\mathbf{R}_t$ and translation $\mathbf{t}_t$, where $\mathrm{hom}(\cdot)$ normalizes the homogeneous coordinate. Now we express the matching energy as

$$E^{(T)}_{Match}(\mathcal{S}, \xi_T) = \sum_{\mathbf{x}_i \in \mathcal{X}} \|I(\mathbf{x}_i) - I_T(W(\mathbf{x}_i, d_i, \xi_T))\|_{\tau_{Match}}, \quad (8)$$

---

[1] The block-diagonal is an overconfident approximation of the precision. As compensation, we employ a forgetting factor $\lambda_{Temporal}$ in our implementation (see Sect. 3.2).

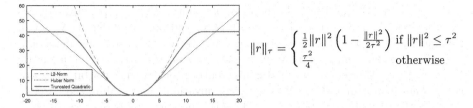

$$\|r\|_\tau = \begin{cases} \frac{1}{2}\|r\|^2 \left(1 - \frac{\|r\|^2}{2\tau^2}\right) & \text{if } \|r\|^2 \leq \tau^2 \\ \frac{\tau^2}{4} & \text{otherwise} \end{cases}$$

**Fig. 2.** The smooth truncated quadratic compared to the squared $L_2$-norm and Huber cost (left), and the smooth truncated quadratic's mathematical representation (right).

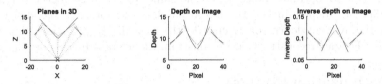

**Fig. 3.** Planes in 3D space are aligned via smoothing in the inverse depth image (black represent original planes, red represents the smoothed versions). (Color figure online)

where $I(\mathbf{x})$ and $I_T(\mathbf{x})$ are descriptors extracted around pixel $\mathbf{x}$ from keyframe and current frame respectively. We use image intensity values (*i.e.* a descriptor at pixel only), so that the disparity gradients do not need to be taken into account during warping. Robustness is achieved by employing a smooth truncated quadratic error [29] (visualized in Fig. 2) in the implementation of $\|\cdot\|_{\tau_{Match}}$.

### 2.2 Local Spatial Plane Regularizer

The smoothness constraint $E_{Smooth}(\mathcal{S})$ is based on a planar assumption often found in stereo setups [13,23,24], which we adapt in this work to support monocular video data. Surface $\mathbf{s}_i$ induces a linear extrapolation of inverse depth via $\hat{d}_i(\mathbf{x}) = \mathbf{s}_i^\mathsf{T}\mathbf{x}$. Plugging this into the homographic transformation yields

$$W(\mathbf{x}, \hat{d}_i(\mathbf{x}), \xi_t) = \mathrm{hom}\left(\mathbf{R}_t^\mathsf{T}\left(\mathbf{x} - \mathbf{t}_t \mathbf{s}_i^\mathsf{T}\mathbf{x}\right)\right) = \mathrm{hom}\left(\mathbf{R}_t^\mathsf{T}\left(\mathbf{x}_i - \mathbf{t}_t \frac{\mathbf{n}_i^\mathsf{T}}{r_i}\mathbf{x}_i\right)\right), \quad (9)$$

where $\mathbf{n}_i$ is the plane normal and $r_i$ is the point-plane distance to the camera center. Hence we can identify $\mathbf{s}_i \propto \mathbf{n}_i$ and therefore smoothing planes in inverse depth parametrization also smoothes the alignment in 3D space (Fig. 3).

With $\lambda_{Smooth}$ as balancing term, we define the spatial smoothness energy as

$$E_{Smooth}(\mathcal{S}) = \lambda_{Smooth} \sum_{\mathbf{x}_i \in \mathcal{X}} \sum_{\mathbf{x}_j \in \mathcal{N}_i} \|\mathbf{s}_i^\mathsf{T}\mathbf{x}_i - \mathbf{s}_j^\mathsf{T}\mathbf{x}_i\|_{\tau_{Smooth}}$$

$$= \lambda_{Smooth} \sum_{\mathbf{x}_i \in \mathcal{X}} \sum_{\mathbf{x}_j \in \mathcal{N}_i} \|d_i - (d_j + \mathbf{s}_j^\mathsf{T}(\mathbf{x}_i - \mathbf{x}_j))\|_{\tau_{Smooth}}, \quad (10)$$

where $\mathcal{N}_i$ denotes the 4-neighborhood of $\mathbf{x}_i$. Thus, $E_{Smooth}$ penalizes deviations between linearly extrapolated depth at $\mathbf{x}_j$ and its actual depth. Although some methods try to introduce robustness by appearance-based edge detection, *e.g.* [30], we again simply employ the smooth version of the truncated quadratic for $\| \cdot \|_{\tau_{Smooth}}$. Hence, our method is inherently robust without arbitrary color constraints. Unfortunately, (10) is not scale invariant, and scaling the baseline $\mathbf{t}_t$ scales the contribution of $E_{Smooth}$. This is a potential issue only for the first pair of frames $(I, I_1)$, since subsequent frames have their scale determined by preceding frames. It is common usage to fix the initial scale by setting $\|\mathbf{t}_1\| = 1$, but this is a suboptimal choice, since the same 3D scene geometry is regularized differently depending on the initial baseline. A more sensible choice is to fix *e.g.* the average depth (or inverse depth) to make $E_{Smooth}$ invariant w.r.t. baselines. For our reconstruction we constrain the average inverse depth to one.

# 3    Optimization Strategy

In this section we detail our optimization strategy for the energy in (6). We assume small changes between consecutive frames, as video data is used. Therefore we use a similar approach as in standard differential tracking and optical flow by locally linearizing the image intensities $I_T$ in the matching term $E_{Match}^{(T)}$. The pseudocode of the proposed method is given in Algorithm 1. The underlying idea is to optimize the energy incrementally with increased complexity using the scale-space pyramid representation and our restricted depth map update which we detail below. The aim of doing this is two-fold: Firstly it substantially reduces the number of unknowns in the main objective and therefore makes the optimization much more efficient, and secondly it provides an additional level of regularization within the algorithm and combines naturally with a scale-space framework to avoid poor local minima. We discuss this constrained depth map update in the following, and then introduce our optimization which exploits this update to allow for truly simultaneous pose and depth estimation. Finally we present a strategy for realtime performance on CPU.

## 3.1    Constrained Depth Map Updates

If we consider the current frame at time $T$ and optimize $E_{Total}$ (recall (6)) w.r.t. $\xi_T$ and $\mathcal{S}$, then our algorithmic design choice is to restrict the update $\mathcal{S} - \mathcal{S}^*$ to have low complexity in the following sense:

$$\mathbf{s}_i = \mathbf{s}_i^* + \sum_{c=1}^{C} \mathbb{I}_c(\mathbf{x}_i)\Delta_c, \tag{11}$$

where $\mathbb{I}_c : \mathcal{X} \to \{+1, -1\}$ is an indicator function, splitting the set of pixels into positive or negative parts. This means that a depth update at each pixel $\mathbf{x}_i$ is constrained to take one of $2^C$ values. With increasing cardinality $C$, the complexity of the depth map increases.

The optimization is performed greedily by adding a single component $\Delta_c$ at a time. Notice, if $\xi_T$ and $\mathcal{S}$ were to be optimized simultaneously, an equation

---

**Algorithm 1.** Dense Incremental Planar Depth Estimation

---

**Input:** Keyframe $I$ and images $(I_t)_{t=1}^{T}$.
**Output:** Final pose $\xi$ and depth hypothesis $\mathcal{S}$.
1: $\mathbf{s}_i \leftarrow [0\ 0\ 1]^{\mathrm{T}}$ and $\Lambda_i \leftarrow \mathbf{0}$ for all $\mathbf{x}_i \in \mathcal{X}$.
2: compute resolution pyramid for the keyframe $I$.
3: $\xi \leftarrow (\mathbf{I} \in \mathbb{R}^{3 \times 3}, [0\ 0\ 0]^{\mathrm{T}})$
4: **for** each frame $I_t$ **do**
5:    compute resolution pyramid for the frame $I_t$.
6:    **for** each pyramid level **do**
7:       optimize $\xi$ via lie algebra $\mathfrak{se}(3)$ through Levenberg-Marquardt.
8:       **repeat**
9:          update $\xi$ (and $\mathbf{s}_i \leftarrow \mathbf{s}_i + \mathbb{I}_c(\mathbf{x}_i)\Delta_c$ if applicable).
10:          introduce new component $\Delta_c$.
11:          estimate $\mathbb{I}_c(\mathbf{x}_i)$ via eigenvector of $\sum_{\mathbf{x}_i \in \mathcal{X}} \nabla_{\mathbf{s}_i} \nabla_{\mathbf{s}_i}^{\mathrm{T}}$.
12:          optimize $\xi$ and $\Delta_c$ through Levenberg-Marquardt.
13:       **until** improvement below $\epsilon_{Complex}$ or maximum components reached
14:    **end for**
15:    update precision $\Lambda_i$ and depth $\mathbf{s}_i^*$ for temporal constraint.
16: **end for**

---

with $6 + 3|\mathcal{X}|$ unknowns had to be solved inside a nonlinear least squares solver (*i.e.* 6 parameters for an element in the lie algebra $\mathfrak{se}(3)$ and 3 for the over-parameterized depth values at each pixel). By using the constrained shape for the updates and by using a greedy framework, we reduce the optimization to $6+3$ variables at a time (*i.e.* $\mathfrak{se}(3)$ and the 3 vector $\Delta_c$), improving the execution cost and robustness significantly.

Our methodology can be seen in analogy to multi-resolution pyramids which spatially increase the quantization of the image plane, but in addition to spatial resolution we also incrementally increase the quantization level of inverse depths. Specifically, we exploit the representation of a pixel's plane $\mathbf{s}_i$ as summed components $\Delta_c$, given in (11). These values correspond to the inverse depth resolution which increases when new components are introduced.

This coarse-to-fine depth estimation is inspired by the human vision [31], which perceives depth in relation to other areas in the scene, rather than absolute values. Specifically, we perform the introduction of new distance values in a relational setting, splitting the data points based on their desired depth value direction. The advantages of this approach are three-fold: (1) we introduce depth by enforcing a regularization across all pixels, (2) our splitting function separates the image data into multiple planes, which naturally encode the image hierarchically from coarse to fine, and (3) the incremental introduction of depth enables fast computation whilst optimizing transformation and depth simultaneously. Moreover, we emphasize while our approach is greedy, it is not final since corrections can be made through further splitting.

Our design choice to regularize the updates of $\mathcal{S}$ requires to determine the binary function $\mathbb{I}_c : \mathcal{X} \rightarrow \{+1, -1\}$. Essentially, if $\Delta_c$ is given, $\mathbb{I}_c(\mathbf{x}_i)$ corresponds to the sign of the correlation $\Delta_c^{\mathrm{T}} \nabla_{\mathbf{s}_i} E_{Total}$ between the depth update direction

$\Delta_c$ and the gradient of the objective with respect to $\mathbf{s}_i$. Since $\Delta_c$ is subject to subsequent optimization, we determine an initial estimate $\tilde{\Delta}_c$ as follows: given the current gradients $\nabla_{\mathbf{s}_i} E_{Total}$ (which we abbreviate to $\nabla_{\mathbf{s}_i}$), it is sensible to obtain $\tilde{\Delta}_c$ as principal direction of the set $\{\nabla_{\mathbf{s}_i}\}_{i=1}^{|\mathcal{X}|}$, due to the symmetric range in $\mathbb{I}_c$:

$$\tilde{\Delta}_c \leftarrow \operatorname*{argmax}_{u:\|u\|=1} \left\{ u^{\mathsf{T}} \sum_{\mathbf{x}_i \in \mathcal{X}} \nabla_{\mathbf{s}_i} \nabla_{\mathbf{s}_i}^{\mathsf{T}} u \right\}. \tag{12}$$

This can be obtained by eigenvalue or singular value decomposition of the $3 \times 3$ scatter matrix $\sum_{\mathbf{x}_i \in \mathcal{X}} \nabla_{\mathbf{s}_i} \nabla_{\mathbf{s}_i}^{\mathsf{T}}$. Finally, the indicator function is given by

$$\mathbb{I}_c(\mathbf{x}_i) = \begin{cases} 1 & \text{if } \tilde{\Delta}_c^{\mathsf{T}} \nabla_{\mathbf{s}_i} \geq 0 \\ -1 & \text{otherwise} \end{cases} = \operatorname{sgn}\left(\tilde{\Delta}_c^{\mathsf{T}} \nabla_{\mathbf{s}_i}\right). \tag{13}$$

## 3.2   Simultaneous Pose and Depth Estimation

Let us assume we have an initial estimate for $\xi_T$ and $\mathcal{S}$ available (*e.g.* $\xi_T \leftarrow \xi_{T-1}$ and $\mathcal{S} \leftarrow \mathcal{S}^*$, which is equivalent to $C = 0$ in (11)). Since our objective is an instance of nonlinear least-squares problems we utilize the Levenberg-Marquardt (LM) algorithm for robust and fast second order minimization. The robust kernels $\|\cdot\|_{\tau_{Match}}$ and $\|\cdot\|_{\tau_{Smooth}}$ are handled by an iteratively reweighed least square (IRLS) strategy. Potentially enlarging the convergence basin via a lifted representation of the robust kernel [32] is a topic for future work.

As outlined in Sect. 3.1 the complexity of depth map updates is increased greedily, which means that new components $\Delta_c$ are successively introduced. We start with $C = 0$ and iteratively increase $C$ by adding new components. After introduction of a new component $\Delta_c$ (and having an estimate for $\mathbb{I}_c$), minimizing $E_{Total}$ with respect to $\Delta_c$ and $\xi_T$ amounts to solving

$$\begin{aligned}
\operatorname*{argmin}_{\xi_T, \Delta_c} \Big\{ & \sum_{\mathbf{x}_i \in \mathcal{X}} \| I(\mathbf{x}_i) - I_T \left( W(\mathbf{x}_i, (\mathbf{s}_i + \mathbb{I}_c(\mathbf{x}_i)\Delta_c)^{\mathsf{T}} \mathbf{x}_i, \xi_T) \right) \|_{\tau_{Match}} \\
& + \lambda_{Smooth} \sum_{\mathbf{x}_i \in \mathcal{X}} \sum_{\mathbf{x}_j \in \mathcal{N}_i} \| (\mathbf{s}_i + \mathbb{I}_c(\mathbf{x}_i)\Delta_c)^{\mathsf{T}} \mathbf{x}_i - (\mathbf{s}_j + \mathbb{I}_c(\mathbf{x}_j)\Delta_c)^{\mathsf{T}} \mathbf{x}_i \|_{\tau_{Smooth}} \\
& + \sum_{\mathbf{x}_i \in \mathcal{X}} \| \mathbf{s}_i^* - (\mathbf{s}_i + \mathbb{I}_c(\mathbf{x}_i)\Delta_c) \|_{\Lambda_i} \Big\}
\end{aligned} \tag{14}$$

(via LM), followed by the update $\mathbf{s}_i \leftarrow \mathbf{s}_i + \mathbb{I}_c(\mathbf{x}_i)\Delta_c$. We emphasize, as $\Delta_c$ is shared between all pixels, this problem is unlikely to be rank deficient. Further components $\Delta_c$ are introduced as long as $E_{Total}$ is reduced sufficiently (*i.e.* an improvement larger than $\epsilon_{Complex}$). Notice, while our algorithm iteratively introduces new components $\Delta_c$, it optimizes pose and depth simultaneously. Analogous to the resolution-based scale-space pyramid, the indicator function acts as surrogate for increased resolution in depth.

For the first frame $I_1$ matched with the keyframe $I$ we need to enforce that the average inverse depth is 1 (recall Sect. 2.2), which implies that

$$\sum_{\mathbf{x}_i} (\mathbf{s}_i + \mathbb{I}_c(\mathbf{x}_i)\Delta_c)^{\mathsf{T}} \mathbf{x}_i = \sum_{\mathbf{x}_i} \left( d_i + \mathbb{I}_c(\mathbf{x}_i)\Delta_c^{\mathsf{T}} \mathbf{x}_i \right) = 1 \tag{15}$$

must hold. If $d_i$ already satisfies $\sum_{\mathbf{x}_i} d_i = 1$, then the above reduces to

$$\sum_{\mathbf{x}_i} \mathbb{I}_c(\mathbf{x}_i) \mathbf{x}_i^{\mathsf{T}} \Delta_c = 0. \tag{16}$$

We chose a projected gradient approach by projecting the gradient w.r.t. $\Delta_c$ to the feasible subspace defined by (16) inside the LM optimizer. Note that the planes are initialized to $\mathbf{s}_i = (0, 0, 1)^{\mathsf{T}}$ in the beginning of the algorithm, and by induction $\sum_{\mathbf{x}_i} \mathbf{s}_i^{\mathsf{T}} \mathbf{s}_i = \sum_{\mathbf{x}_i} d_i = 1$ is always satisfied for the first frame. In subsequent frames the constraint in (16) is not active.

Finally, to determine the precision matrices $\Lambda_i \in \mathbb{R}^{3 \times 3}$ needed for $E_{Temporal}^{(T+1)}$, we employ the approximate Hessian via the Jacobian $\mathbf{J}_{Match}$ of $E_{Match}^{(T)}$:

$$\begin{pmatrix} \tilde{H}_{\mathcal{S},\mathcal{S}} & \tilde{H}_{\mathcal{S},\xi_T}^{\mathsf{T}} \\ \tilde{H}_{\mathcal{S},\xi_T} & \tilde{H}_{\xi_T,\xi_T} \end{pmatrix} := \mathbf{J}_{Match}^{\mathsf{T}} \mathbf{J}_{Match}, \tag{17}$$

and the $3 \times 3$-diagonal block of the Schur complement $\tilde{H}_{\mathcal{S},\mathcal{S}} - \tilde{H}_{\mathcal{S},\xi_T}^{\mathsf{T}} \tilde{H}_{\xi_T,\xi_T}^{-1} \tilde{H}_{\mathcal{S},\xi_T}$ (denoted $\Lambda_{Match}$). We employ a forgetting factor $\lambda_{Temporal}$ to reduce the overconfident precision matrix, and update $\Lambda_i \leftarrow \lambda_{Temporal} \Lambda_i + \Lambda_{Match}$. Recall that $\tilde{H}_{\xi_T,\xi_T} \in \mathbb{R}^{6 \times 6}$ and $\tilde{H}_{\mathcal{S},\xi_T}$ are very sparse.

### 3.3  CPU Computation in Realtime

Thus far, we present our energy for each pixel in the input video stream. While this is generally useful for dense depth estimation, we may adopt our approach to semi-dense computation to reduce running time. Similar to LSD-SLAM, we can represent the image by its significant gradient values. By only computing on these gradients, execution is significantly reduced. In fact, in comparison to LSD-SLAM, we only need one additional LM iteration per split to introduce depth on top of pose estimation. Finally, we can limit the number of introduced depth components per resolution level to achieve constant running time.

## 4  Results

We perform our experiments on 13 video sequences in total, using 6 TUM [33] image streams and 7 sequences recoded ourselves. The TUM dataset comprises a number of video sequences with groundtruth pose, as recorded by a Vicon system, and approximate depth through depth sensors [33]. We select a subset of the handheld SLAM videos to measure system performance (*i.e.* fr1-desk, fr1-desk2, fr1-floor, fr1-room, fr2-xyz and fr3-office). As we are interested in the local aspect of SLAM (operating with single keyframe), we further divide these into smaller sequences. Notice, as we perform keyframe-to-frame comparison, the videos need to contain enough overlap with the reference image. Additionally, we record 7 videos, using a GoPro Hero 3 with a wide angle lens at 30 fps.

As a monocular approach, our method does not fix the scale. Hence, we employ a scale corrected error (SCE) for translation:

$$e(\mathbf{t}_t, \hat{\mathbf{t}}_t) = \left\| \mathbf{t}_t \frac{\|\hat{\mathbf{t}}_t\|}{\|\mathbf{t}_t\|} - \hat{\mathbf{t}} \right\|, \tag{18}$$

where $\mathbf{t}_t$ is the translational displacement of the pose $\xi_t$, and $\hat{\mathbf{t}}_t$ is the groundtruth with respect to the keyframe (or initial frame). An error in rotation is indirectly captured, as it effects the translation of future frames. We now introduce a scale invariant measure to evaluate the depth's completeness. Given true inverse depth at the keyframe $\hat{\mathcal{D}} = (\hat{d}_i)_{i=1}^{|\mathcal{X}|}$ we define the completeness as the proportion of depth values, satisfying a given accuracy $\epsilon$:

$$c\left(\hat{\mathcal{D}}, \mathcal{D}\right) = \max_\alpha \sum_i^{|\mathcal{X}|} \frac{n_\alpha(\hat{d}_i, d_i)}{|\mathcal{X}|}, \text{where } n_\alpha(\hat{d}_i, d_i) = \begin{cases} 1 \text{ if } \left\| \frac{1}{\hat{d}_i} - \frac{\alpha}{d_i} \right\| < \epsilon \\ 0 \text{ otherwise} \end{cases}. \tag{19}$$

Parameter $\alpha$ represents scale and is found via grid search and refined through gradient decent. In our work, $\epsilon = 0.05$ which corresponds to $\pm 5\,\mathrm{cm}$.

### 4.1   Quantitative Evaluation on the TUM Dataset

We compare the proposed dense and semi-dense incremental planar system (DIP and SIP respectively) to two versions of LSD-SLAM: (1) we carefully implement a LSD-SLAM version that only uses a single keyframe (LSD-Key), and (2) the original LSD-SLAM as provided by authors of [9], without loop closures or other constraints (LSD-SLAM). We further ensure that mapping is guaranteed to run after every tracking step in both LSD-SLAM systems. Finally, we include our method as disjoint optimization for pose and depth separately and sequentially. Table 1 shows the median SCE for different numbers of frames. The median is calculated over all snippets taken from the individual TUM sequences.

The sequences fr1-desk and fr1-desk2 show an office environment with high camera motion and little overlap towards keyframes. Here, the trajectories are quickly lost when a single keyframe is used. SIP performs best at early stages, while DIP is more suitable for longer tracking. The sequences fr1-floor and fr1-room also have little keyframe overlap, but with slower motion. Here LSD-SLAM performs competitively, as it benefits from keyframe generation.

Long-term tracks are achieved in fr2-xyz and fr3-office. We take a more detailed look at the results of fr3-office. Figure 4 plots the median SCE for each duration. We see that LSD-SLAM and DIP have similar performance early on, but DIP performs better at later stages. Notice, as LSD-SLAM generates new reference images, the baseline is typically small. In contrast DIP benefits from larger baselines. LSD-Key loses track quickly, while SIP performs well in early stages. The trajectory and inverse depth maps for the very first 300 frames are shown in Fig. 5. Figure 6 plots the depth completeness. Here, DIP and SIP reach a peak correctness with increasing baseline, after which they slightly degrades as points are outside the current view, and smoothing takes over their energies.

**Table 1.** Median Scale Corrected Error (in mm) for the compared methods after the listed frame number for different TUM-Dataset sequences. (Note, different characteristics of camera motion in each video lead to different length of keyframe overlaps.)

|          |           | LSD-SLAM | LSD-Key | Disjoint | SIP | DIP |
|----------|-----------|----------|---------|----------|-----|-----|
| fr1-desk | frame 5   | 34       | 34      | 33       | **25** | 27  |
|          | frame 10  | 44       | 62      | 55       | 43  | **30** |
|          | frame 30  | 106      | 130     | 119      | 135 | **46** |
| fr1-desk2| frame 5   | 68       | 68      | 53       | 23  | **18** |
|          | frame 10  | 103      | 115     | 87       | **41** | 44  |
|          | frame 20  | 207      | -       | 162      | 163 | **64** |
| fr1-floor| frame 5   | 30       | 30      | 36       | **30** | 34  |
|          | frame 10  | **55**   | 58      | 76       | 58  | 60  |
|          | frame 15  | 85       | 88      | 111      | **79** | 86  |
| fr1-room | frame 5   | 13       | 13      | 19       | **10** | 16  |
|          | frame 10  | 40       | 40      | 52       | **39** | 42  |
|          | frame 25  | **9**    | 79      | 117      | -   | 53  |
| fr2-xyz  | frame 10  | 15       | 15      | 10       | **9** | 9   |
|          | frame 30  | 54       | 68      | 28       | **18** | 23  |
|          | frame 100 | 121      | 88      | **45**   | 45  | 47  |
| fr3-office| frame 10 | **29**   | 30      | 41       | 32  | 33  |
|          | frame 50  | 90       | 121     | 182      | **53** | 100 |
|          | frame 150 | 206      | -       | 265      | -   | **123** |

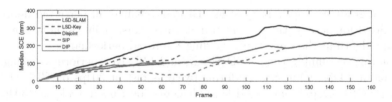

**Fig. 4.** Median SCE for videos of fr3-office. LSD-SLAM and DIP track long-term, while SIP is more accurate early on. LSD-Key loses track quickly, and the disjoint optimization (Disjoint) is consistently worse.

We remark, similar to many approaches based on gradient decent, our method converges to local minima. However our method relies on graduated optimization which aims to avoid getting trapped in bad minima by optimizing a smoother energy with gradually increased complexity [34]. In contrast to LSD-SLAM, we employ graduated optimization in depth perception as well as traditional scale-space image pyramids leading to superior results. The indicator function is a surrogate for the scale-space pyramid in depth. Finally, we note that the disjoint version is consistently worse in virtually all experiments. The difference is the

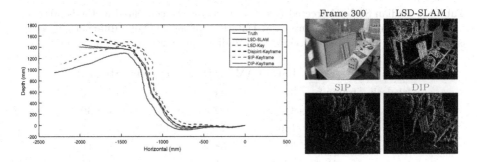

**Fig. 5.** Trajectories (left) and inverse depth maps (right) of LSD-SLAM, SIP and DIP for the initial 300 images in fr3-office. LSD-SLAM is inaccurate due to scale drift. DIP uses a single keyframe and hence does not drift as significantly. For depth, SIP and DIP benefit from larger keyframe-to-frame baseline, resulting in qualitative better depth.

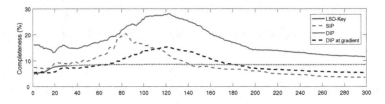

**Fig. 6.** Depth completeness of LSD-Key, SIP and DIP for initial images in fr3-office. As LSD-Key and SIP only produces depth for high gradient pixels, the results of DIP at gradient only are also shown. Note, LSD-Key remains unchanged after poor tracking.

impact of graduated optimization. For Disjoint, changes in perceived depth are not utilized for pose at the current frame. In contrast, joint optimization finds pose and depth at the same time, yielding improved performance.

In terms of running time, LSD-SLAM and LSD-Key perform tracking and mapping at 14 fps, while SIP performs twice as fast at 30 fps on CPU. DIP is slower on CPU (2 fps), but its GPU implementation runs in realtime (30 fps).

## 4.2   Qualitative Results

We conclude the experimental with example frames of our 7 additional video sequences (Fig. 7). Generally, LSD-SLAM smoothes well in the local neighborhood, while SIP and DIP perform more consistent on the global inverse depth hypothesis. We note, even with non-planar scenes our methods performs well. We argue, that the local planar surface assumption is reasonable in most environments, as was also witnessed by recent stereo systems, *e.g.* [13,23,24]. Nonetheless, in non-urban scenes, and in situations where the initial frontal plane assumption is significantly wrong (recall initialization of $\mathbf{s}_i = (0,0,1)^{\mathrm{T}}$), the results are less favorable as seen in the last row of Fig. 7.

Frame          LSD-SLAM          SIP          DIP

**Fig. 7.** Inverse depth of LSD-SLAM, SIP and DIP for 7 qualitative video sequences (far is blue, near is red). In most scenes, the local planar surface assumption holds and our method performs well. In non-urban environments and where the initialization with frontal planar surfaces does not hold, our method fails (bottom row). (Color figure online)

# 5   Conclusion

We introduced a carefully derived coarse-to-fine planar regularization strategy that optimizes for both, pose and depth simultaneously from monocular streams. Our framework is keyframe-based, and incrementally improves its depth hypothesis at each frame as new data arrives. As semi-dense approach, the proposed method runs in realtime on CPU, while realtime for the dense version can be achieved on GPU. In our evaluation, we improved upon the front-end of LSD-SLAM whilst increasing execution time by a factor of two.

**Acknowledgment.** O. Miksik is supported by Technicolor. P. Torr wishes to acknowledges the support of ERC grant ERC-2012-AdG 321162-HELIOS, EPSRC/MURI grant ref EP/N019474/1, EPSRC grant EP/M013774/1, EPSRC Programme Grant Seebibyte EP/M013774/1.

# References

1. Barfield, W.: Fundamentals of Wearable Computers and Augmented Reality, 2nd edn. CRC Press, Boca Raton (2016)
2. Engel, J., Sturm, J., Cremers, D.: Scale-aware navigation of a low-cost quadrocopter with a monocular camera. Robot. Auton. Syst. **62**(11), 1646–1656 (2014)
3. Forster, C., Pizzoli, M., Scaramuzza, D.: SVO: fast semi-direct monocular visual odometry. In: ICRA 2014, pp. 15–22 (2014)
4. Geiger, A., Lenz, P., Urtasun, R.: Are we ready for autonomous driving? The KITTI vision benchmark suite. In: CVPR 2012, pp. 3354–3361 (2012)
5. Miksik, O., Vineet, V., Lidegaard, M., Prasaath, R., Nießner, M., Golodetz, S., Hicks, S., Pérez, P., Izadi, S., Torr, P.: The semantic paintbrush: interactive 3D mapping and recognition in large outdoor spaces. In: ACM Conference Human Factors in Computing, CHI 2015, pp. 3317–3326 (2015)
6. Vineet, V., Miksik, O., Lidegaard, M., Nießner, M., Golodetz, S., Prisacariu, V., Kähler, O., Murray, D., Izadi, S., Pérez, P., Torr, P.: Incremental dense semantic stereo fusion for large-scale semantic scene reconstruction. In: ICRA 2015 (2015)
7. Schöps, T., Engel, J., Cremers, D.: Semi-dense visual odometry for AR on a smartphone. In: ISMAR 2014, pp. 145–150 (2014)
8. Newcombe, R., Lovegrove, S., Davison, A.: DTAM: dense tracking and mapping in real-time. In: IEEE International Conference on Computer Vision, ICCV 2011, pp. 2320–2327 (2011)
9. Engel, J., Schöps, T., Cremers, D.: LSD-SLAM: large-scale direct monocular SLAM. In: Fleet, D., Pajdla, T., Schiele, B., Tuytelaars, T. (eds.) ECCV 2014, Part II. LNCS, vol. 8690, pp. 834–849. Springer, Heidelberg (2014)
10. Miksik, O., Amar, Y., Vineet, V., Pérez, P., Torr, P.: Incremental dense multimodal 3D scene reconstruction. In: IROS 2015 (2015)
11. Newcombe, R., Izadi, S., Hilliges, O., Molyneaux, D., Kim, D., Davison, A., Kohli, P., Shotton, J., Hodges, S., Fitzgibbon, A.: KinectFusion: real-time dense surface mapping and tracking. In: ISMAR 2011, pp. 127–136 (2011)
12. Salas-Moreno, R., Glocker, B., Kelly, P., Davison, A.: Dense planar SLAM. In: ISMAR 2014, pp. 157–164 (2014)

13. Yamaguchi, K., McAllester, D., Urtasun, R.: Efficient joint segmentation, occlusion labeling, stereo and flow estimation. In: Fleet, D., Pajdla, T., Schiele, B., Tuytelaars, T. (eds.) ECCV 2014, Part V. LNCS, vol. 8693, pp. 756–771. Springer, Heidelberg (2014)

14. Nister, D., Naroditsky, O., Bergen, J.: Indoor positioning using multi-frequency RSS with foot-mounted INS. In: CVPR 2004, pp. 652–659 (2004)

15. Davison, A.: Real-time simultaneous localisation and mapping with a single camera. In: CVPR 2003, pp. 1403–1410 (2003)

16. Davison, A., Reid, I., Molton, N., Stasse, O.: MonoSLAM: real-time single camera SLAM. IEEE Trans. Pattern Anal. Mach. Intell. **29**(6), 1052–1067 (2007)

17. Klein, G., Murray, D.: Parallel tracking and mapping for small AR workspaces. In: ISMAR 2007 (2007)

18. Wendel, A., Maurer, M., Graber, G., Pock, T., Bischof, H.: Dense reconstruction on-the-fly. In: CVPR 2012, pp. 1450–1457 (2012)

19. Pradeep, V., Rhemann, C., Izadi, S., Zach, C., Bleyer, M., Bathiche, S.: Mono-Fusion: real-time 3D reconstruction of small scenes with a single web camera. In: IEEE on ISMAR, pp. 83–88 (2013)

20. Concha, A., Civera, J.: DPPTAM: dense piecewise planar tracking and mapping from a monocular sequence. In: IROS 2015 (2015)

21. Tarrio, J., Pedre, S.: Realtime edge-based visual odometry for a monocular camera. In: IEEE International Conference on Computer Vision, ICCV 2015, pp. 702–710 (2015)

22. Geiger, A., Roser, M., Urtasun, R.: Efficient large-scale stereo matching. In: Kimmel, R., Klette, R., Sugimoto, A. (eds.) ACCV 2010, Part I. LNCS, vol. 6492, pp. 25–38. Springer, Heidelberg (2011)

23. Sinha, S., Scharstein, D., Szeliski, S.: Efficient high-resolution stereo matching using local plane sweeps. In: CVPR 2014, pp. 1582–1589 (2014)

24. Zhang, C., Li, Z., Cheng, Y., Cai, R., Chao, H., Rui, Y.: MeshStereo: a global stereo model with mesh alignment regularization for view interpolation. In: IEEE International Conference on Computer Vision, ICCV 2015, pp. 2057–2065 (2015)

25. Becker, F., Lenzen, F., Kappes, J., Schnörr, C.: Variational recursive joint estimation of dense scene structure and camera motion from monocular high speed traffic sequences. In: IEEE International Conference on Computer Vision, ICCV 2011, pp. 1692–1699 (2011)

26. Concha, A., Hussain, W., Montano, L., Civera, J.: Incorporating scene priors to dense monocular mapping. Auton. Robots **39**(3), 279–292 (2015)

27. Salas, M., Hussain, W., Concha, A., Montano, L., Civera, J., Montiel, J.: Layout aware visual tracking and mapping. In: IROS 2015 (2015)

28. Lucas, B., Kanade, T.: An iterative image registration technique with an application to stereo vision. In: International Joint Conference on Artifical Intelligence, IJCAI 1981, pp. 674–679 (1981)

29. Li, H., Summer, R., Pauly, M.: Global correspondence optimization for non-rigid registration of depth scans. Comput. Graph. Forum **27**(5), 1421–1430 (2008)

30. Yang, J., Li, H.: Dense, accurate optical flow estimation with piecewise parametric model. In: ECCV 2015, pp. 1019–1027 (2015)

31. Westheimer, G.: Cooperative neural processes involved in stereoscopic acuity. Exp. Brain Res. **36**, 585–597 (1979)

32. Zach, C.: Robust bundle adjustment revisited. In: Fleet, D., Pajdla, T., Schiele, B., Tuytelaars, T. (eds.) ECCV 2014, Part V. LNCS, vol. 8693, pp. 772–787. Springer, Heidelberg (2014)

33. Sturm, J., Engelhard, N., Endres, F., Burgard, W., Cremers, D.: A benchmark for the evaluation of RGB-D SLAM systems. In: IROS 2012 (2012)
34. Mobahi, H., Fisher III, J.W.: On the link between Gaussian homotopy continuation and convex envelopes. In: Tai, X.-C., Bae, E., Chan, T.F., Lysaker, M. (eds.) EMMCVPR 2015. LNCS, vol. 8932, pp. 43–56. Springer, Heidelberg (2015)

# Deep Attributes Driven Multi-camera Person Re-identification

Chi Su[1], Shiliang Zhang[1(✉)], Junliang Xing[2], Wen Gao[1], and Qi Tian[3]

[1] Peking University, Beijing, China
{chisu,slzhang.jdl,wgao}@pku.edu.cn
[2] Chinese Academy of Sciences, Beijing, China
jlxing@nlpr.ia.ac.cn
[3] Department of Computer Science, University of Texas at San Antonio,
San Antonio, USA
qi.tian@utsa.edu

**Abstract.** The visual appearance of a person is easily affected by many factors like pose variations, viewpoint changes and camera parameter differences. This makes person Re-Identification (ReID) among multiple cameras a very challenging task. This work is motivated to learn mid-level human attributes which are robust to such visual appearance variations. And we propose a semi-supervised attribute learning framework which progressively boosts the accuracy of attributes only using a limited number of labeled data. Specifically, this framework involves a three-stage training. A deep Convolutional Neural Network (dCNN) is first trained on an independent dataset labeled with attributes. Then it is fine-tuned on another dataset only labeled with person IDs using our defined triplet loss. Finally, the updated dCNN predicts attribute labels for the target dataset, which is combined with the independent dataset for the final round of fine-tuning. The predicted attributes, namely *deep attributes* exhibit superior generalization ability across different datasets. By directly using the deep attributes with simple Cosine distance, we have obtained surprisingly good accuracy on four person ReID datasets. Experiments also show that a simple distance metric learning modular further boosts our method, making it significantly outperform many recent works.

**Keywords:** Deep attributes · Re-identification

## 1 Introduction

Person Re-Identification (ReID) targets to identify the same person from different cameras, datasets, or time stamps. As illustrated in Fig. 1, factors like viewpoint variations, illumination conditions, camera parameter differences, as well as body pose changes make person ReID a very challenging task. Due to its important applications in public security, *e.g.*, cross camera pedestrian searching, tracking, and event detection, person ReID has attracted lots of attention

© Springer International Publishing AG 2016
B. Leibe et al. (Eds.): ECCV 2016, Part II, LNCS 9906, pp. 475–491, 2016.
DOI: 10.1007/978-3-319-46475-6_30

from both the academic and industrial communities. Currently, research on this topic mainly focus on two aspects: (a) extracting and coding local invariant features to represent the visual appearance of a person [1–7] and (b) learning a discriminative distance metric hence the distance of features from the same person can be smaller [8–25].

Although significant progress has been made from previous studies, person ReID methods are still not mature enough for real applications. Local features mostly describe the low-level visual appearance, hence are not robust to variances of viewpoints, body poses, *etc*. On the other side, distance metric learning suffers from the poor generalization ability and the quadratic computational complexity, *e.g.*, different datasets present different visual characteristics corresponding to different metrics. Compared with low-level visual feature, human attributes like long hair, blue shirt, *etc.*, represent mid-level semantics of a person. As illustrated in Fig. 1, attributes are more consistent for the same person and are more robust to the above mentioned variances. Some recent works hence have started to use attributes for person ReID [29–34]. Because human attributes are expensive for manual annotation, it is difficult to acquire enough training data for a large set of attributes. This limits the performance of current attribute features. Consequently, low-level visual features still play a key role and attributes are mostly used as auxiliary features [31–34].

Recently, deep learning has exhibited promising performance and generalization ability in various visual tasks. For example in [35], an eight-layer deep Convolutional Neural Network (dCNN) is trained with large-scale images for visual classification. The modified versions of this network also perform impressively in object detection [36] and segmentation [37]. Motivated by the issues of low level visual features and the success of dCNN, our work targets to learn a dCNN to detect a large set of human attributes discriminative enough for person ReID. Due to the diversity and complexity of human attributes, it is a laborious

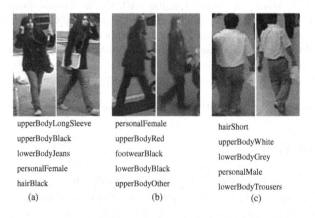

| upperBodyLongSleeve | personalFemale | hairShort |
| upperBodyBlack | upperBodyRed | upperBodyWhite |
| lowerBodyJeans | footwearBlack | lowerBodyGrey |
| personalFemale | lowerBodyBlack | personalMale |
| hairBlack | upperBodyOther | lowerBodyTrousers |
| (a) | (b) | (c) |

**Fig. 1.** Example images of the same person taken by two cameras from three datasets: (a) *VIPeR* [26], (b) *PRID* [27], and (c) *GRID* [28]. This figure also shows five of our predicted attributes shared by these two images.

task to manually label enough of attributes for dCNN training. The key issues are hence how to train this dCNN from a partially-labeled dataset and ensure its discriminative power and generalization ability in the person ReID tasks.

To address these issues, we propose a Semi-supervised Deep Attribute Learning (SSDAL) algorithm. As illustrated in Fig. 2, this algorithm involves three stages. The first stage uses an independent dataset with attribute labels to perform fully-supervised dCNN training. The resulting dCNN produces initial attribute labels for the target dataset. To improve the discriminative power of these attributes for ReID task, we start the second stage of training, *i.e.*, fine-tuning the network using the person ID labels and our defined *attributes triplet loss*. The training data for fine-tuning can be easily collected because the person ID labels are readily accessible in many person tracking datasets. The attributes triplet loss updates the network to enforce that the same person has more similar attributes and vice versa. This fine-tuned dCNN hence predicts initial attribute labels for target datasets. Finally in the third stage, the initially labeled target dataset plus the original independent dataset are combined for the final stage of fine-tuning. The attributes predicted by the final dCNN model are named as *deep attributes*. In this manner, the dCNN is firstly trained with the independent dataset, then is refined to acquire more discriminative power for person ReID task. Because this procedure involves one dataset with attribute labels and another without attribute labels, we call it a semi-supervised learning.

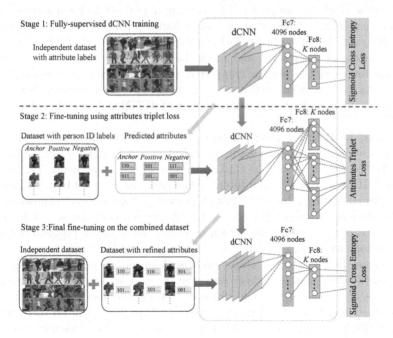

**Fig. 2.** Illustration of semi-supervised deep attribute learning (SSDAL).

To validate the performance of deep attributes, we test them on four popular person ReID datasets *without* combining with the local visual features. The experimental results show that deep attributes perform impressively, *e.g.*, they significantly outperform many recent works combining both attributes and local features [31–34]. Note that, predicting and matching deep attributes make person ReID system significantly faster, because it no longer needs to extract and code local features, compute distance metric, and fuse with other features.

Our contributions can be summarized as follows: (1) we propose a three-stage semi-supervised deep attribute learning algorithm, which makes learning a large set of human attributes from a limited number of labeled attribute data possible, (2) deep attributes achieve promising performance and generalization ability on four person ReID datasets, and (3) deep attributes release the previous dependencies on local features, thus make the person ReID system more robust and efficient. To the best of our knowledge, this is an original work predicting human attributes using dCNN for person ReID tasks. The promising results of this work guarantees further investigation in this direction.

## 2  Related Work

This work learns a dCNN for attribute prediction and person ReID. It is closely related to works using deep learning for attribute prediction and person ReID.

Currently, many studies have applied deep learning to attributes learning [38, 39]. Shankar *et al.* [38] propose a deep-carving neural net to learn attributes for natural scene images. Chen *et al.* [39] use a double-path deep domain adaptation network to get the fine-grained clothing attributes. Our work differs from them in the aspects of motivation and methodology. We are motivated by how to learn attributes of the human cropped from surveillance videos from a small set of data labeled with attributes. Our semi-supervised learning framework consistently boosts the discriminative power of dCNN and attributes for person ReID.

Inspired by the promising performance of deep learning, some researchers begin to use deep learning to learn visual features and distance metrics for person ReID [24,40–42]. In [40], Li *et al.* use a deep filter pairing neural network for person ReID, where two paired filters of two cameras are used to automatically learn optimal features. In [41], Yi *et al.* present a "siamese" convolutional network for deep distance metric learning. In [42], Ahmed *et al.* devise a deep neural network structure to transform person re-identification into a problem of binary classification, which judges whether a pair of images from two cameras is the same person. In [24], Ding *et al.* present a scalable distance learning framework based on the deep neural network with the triplet loss. Despite of their efforts to find better visual features and distance metrics, the above mentioned works are designed specifically for certain datasets and are dependent on their camera settings. Differently, we use deep learning to acquire general camera-independent mid-level representations. As a result, our algorithm shows better flexibility, *e.g.*, it could handle person ReID tasks on datasets containing different number of cameras.

Some recent works also use triplet loss for person ReID [19,43]. Our work uses attributes triplet loss for dCNN fine-tuning. This differs from the goals in these works, *i.e.*, learning distance metric among low-level features. Therefore, these works also suffer from the low flexility and the quadratic complexity.

# 3  Proposed Approach

## 3.1  Framework

Our goal is to learn a large set of human attributes for person ReID through dCNN training. We define $A = \{a_1, a_2, ..., a_K\}$ as an attribute label containing $K$ attributes, where $a_i \in \{0, 1\}$ is the binary indicator of the $i$-th attribute. Our goal is hence learning an attribute detector $\mathcal{O}$, which predicts the attribute label $A_I$ for any input image $I$, *i.e.*,

$$A_I = \mathcal{O}(I). \tag{1}$$

Because of the promising discriminative power and generalization ability, we use dCNN model as the detector $\mathcal{O}(\cdot)$. However, dCNN training requires large-scale training data labeled with human attributes. Manually collecting such data is also too expensive to conduct. To ensure effective learning of a dCNN model for person ReID from only a small amount of labeled training data, we propose the Semi-supervised Deep Attribute Learning (SSDAL) algorithm.

As illustrated in Fig. 2, the basic idea of SSDAL is firstly training an initial dCNN on an independent dataset labeled with attributes. The limited scale and label accuracy of the independent dataset motivate us to introduce the second stage of training, which utilizes the easily acquired person ID labels to refine the initial dCNN. The updated dCNN hence initially labels the target dataset by predicting attribute labels. Finally, the independent dataset plus the initially labeled target dataset are combined for the final stage of fine-tuning. In the followings, we introduce the three stages of training in detail.

## 3.2  Fully-Supervised dCNN Training

We define the independent training set with attribute labels as $T = \{t_1, t_2, ..., t_N\}$, where $N$ is the number of samples. In $T$, each sample is labeled with a binary attribute label, *e.g.*, the label of the $n$-th instance $t_n$ is $A_n$.

In the first stage of training, we use $T$ as the training set for fully-supervised learning. We refer to the AlexNet [35] to build our dCNN model for its promising performance in various vision tasks. Specifically, our dCNN is also a 8-layer network, including 5 convolutional layers and 3 fully connected layers, where the 3rd fully connected layer predicts the attribute labels. The kernel and filter sizes of each layer in our architecture are the same with the ones in [35,38]. The only difference with AlexNet is that we use a sigmoid cross-entropy loss layer instead of the softmax loss layer for its better performance in multi-label prediction. We denote the dCNN model learned in this stage as $\mathcal{O}^{S1}$. $\mathcal{O}^{S1}$ could predict attribute labels for any test sample. However, as illustrated in our experiments, the discriminative power of $\mathcal{O}^{S1}$ is weak because of the limited scale and label accuracy of the independent training set. We proceed to introduce our second stage of training.

### 3.3   dCNN Fine-Tuning with Attributes Triplet Loss

In the second stage, a larger dataset is used to fine tune the previous dCNN model $\mathcal{O}^{S1}$. The goal of our dCNN model is predicting attribute labels for person ReID tasks. The predicted attribute labels thus should be similar for the same person. Motivated by this, we use person ID labels to fine-tune $\mathcal{O}^{S1}$ and produce similar attribute labels for the same person and vice versa. We denote the dataset with person ID labels as $U = \{u_1, u_2, ..., u_M\}$, where $M$ is the number of samples and each sample has a person ID label $l$, $e.g.$, the $m$-th instance $u_m$ has person ID $l_m$.

In the second stage of training, we first use $\mathcal{O}^{S1}$ to predict the attribute label $\tilde{A}$ of each sample in $U$. For the attribute label $\tilde{A}_m$ of the $m$-th sample, we set the indicators of attributes with top $p$ highest confidence scores as 1 and set the others as 0. Note that, $p$ can be selected according to the average number of positive attributes in person ReID tasks. It is experimentally set as 10 in this paper. After this, we use the person ID labels to measure the annotation errors of $\mathcal{O}^{S1}$.

The annotation error of the $\mathcal{O}^{S1}$ is computed among three samples. The three samples are randomly selected from the $U$ through the following steps: (1) select an *anchor* sample $u_{(a)}$, (2) select another *positive* sample $u_{(p)}$ with the same person ID with $u_{(a)}$, and (3) select a *negative* sample $u_n$ with different person ID. Thus, a triplet $[u_{(a)}, u_{(p)}, u_{(n)}]$ is constructed, where the subscripts $(a)$, $(p)$, and $(n)$ denote *anchor*, *positive*, and *negative* samples, respectively. The attributes of the $e$-th triplet predicted by $\mathcal{O}^{S1}$ are $\tilde{A}^{(e)}_{(a)}$, $\tilde{A}^{(e)}_{(p)}$, and $\tilde{A}^{(e)}_{(n)}$ at the beginning of the fine-tuning, respectively.

The objectives of the fine-tuning is minimizing the triplet loss through updating the $\mathcal{O}^{S1}$, $i.e.$, minimize the distance between the attributes of $u_{(a)}$ and $u_{(p)}$, meanwhile maximize the distance between $u_{(a)}$ and $u_{(n)}$. We call this triplet loss as attributes triplet loss. We hence could formulate our objective function for fine-tuning as:

$$\mathbf{D}\left(A^{(e)}_{(a)}, A^{(e)}_{(p)}\right) + \theta < \mathbf{D}\left(A^{(e)}_{(a)}, A^{(e)}_{(n)}\right),$$
$$\forall\left(A^{(e)}_{(a)}, A^{(e)}_{(p)}, A^{(e)}_{(n)}\right) \in \mathcal{T}, \tag{2}$$

where $\mathbf{D}(.)$ represents the distance function of the two binary attribute vectors, $A^{(e)}_{(a)}$, $A^{(e)}_{(p)}$ and $A^{(e)}_{(n)}$ are predicted attributes of the $e$-th triplet during the fine-tuning. Then, the corresponding loss function can be formulated as:

$$\mathcal{L} = \sum_{e}^{E} \max\left(0, \mathbf{D}\left(A^{(e)}_{(a)}, A^{(e)}_{(p)}\right) + \theta - \mathbf{D}\left(A^{(e)}_{(a)}, A^{(e)}_{(n)}\right)\right), \tag{3}$$

where $E$ represents the number of triplets. In Eq. (3), if the $\mathbf{D}\left(A_{(a)}^{(e)}, A_{(n)}^{(e)}\right) - \mathbf{D}\left(A_{(a)}^{(e)}, A_{(p)}^{(e)}\right)$ is larger than $\theta$, the loss would be zero. Therefore, parameter $\theta$ largely controls the strictness of the loss.

The above loss function essentially enforces the dCNN to produce similar attributes for the same person. However, the person ID label is not strong enough to train the dCNN with accurate attributes. Without proper constraints, the above loss function may generate meaningless attribute labels and easily over-fit the training dataset $U$. For example, imposing a large number meaningless attributes to two samples of a person may decrease the distance between their attribute labels, but does not help to improve the discriminative power of the dCNN. Therefore, we add several regularization terms and modify the original loss function as:

$$\mathcal{L} = \sum_{e}^{E} \left\{ \max\left(0, \mathbf{D}\left(A_{(a)}^{(e)}, A_{(p)}^{(e)}\right) + \theta - \mathbf{D}\left(A_{(a)}^{(e)}, A_{(n)}^{(e)}\right)\right) + \gamma \times \mathcal{E} \right\} \quad (4)$$

$$\mathcal{E} = \mathbf{D}\left(A_{(a)}^{(e)}, \tilde{A}_{(a)}^{(e)}\right) + \mathbf{D}\left(A_{(p)}^{(e)}, \tilde{A}_{(p)}^{(e)}\right) + \mathbf{D}\left(A_{(n)}^{(e)}, \tilde{A}_{(n)}^{(e)}\right), \quad (5)$$

where $\mathcal{E}$ denotes the amount of change in attributes caused by the fine-tuning. The loss in Eq. (4) not only ensures that the same person has similar attributes, but also avoids the meaningless attributes. We hence use the above loss to update the $\mathcal{O}^{S1}$ with back propagation. We denote the resulting update dCNN as $\mathcal{O}^{S2}$.

### 3.4   Fine-Tuning on the Combined Dataset

The fine-tuning in previous stage produces more accurate attribute labels. We thus consider to combine the $T$ and $U$ for the final round of fine-tuning. As illustrated in Fig. 2, in the third stage, we first predict the attribute labels for dataset $U$ with $\mathcal{O}^{S2}$. A new dataset labeled with attribute labels can hence be generated by merging $T$ and $U$. Then, we fine-tune $\mathcal{O}^{S2}$ using sigmoid cross entropy loss on the dataset $T\&U$, which outputs the final attribute detector $\mathcal{O}$.

For any test image, we can predict its $K$-dimensional attribute label with Eq. (1). In our implementation, we only select the attributes whose confidence values predicted by $\mathcal{O}$ are larger than a specified threshold as positive, where the confidence threshold is experimentally set as 0. This essentially selects more accurate attributes. Finally, $\mathcal{O}$ produces a sparse binary $K$-dimensional attribute vector. Our person ReID system uses this binary vector as feature and measures their distance with Cosine distance to identify the same person. The validity of this three-stage training procedure and the performance of selected attributes will be tested in Sect. 4.

## 4   Experiments

### 4.1   Datasets for Training and Testing

To conduct the first stage training, we choose the *PETA* [44] dataset as the training set. Each image in *PETA* is labeled with 61 binary attributes and 4 multi-class attributes. The 4 multi-class attributes are *footwear, hair, lowerbody* and *upperbody*, each of which has 11 color labels including *Black, Blue, Brown, Green, Grey, Orange, Pink, Purple, Red, White,* and *Yellow*, respectively. We hence expand 4 multi-class attributes into 44 binary attributes, resulting in a 105-dimensional binary attribute label. For the second stage training, we choose the *MOT challenge* [45] dataset to fine-tune dCNN $\mathcal{O}^{S1}$ with attributes triplet loss. *MOT challenge* is a dataset designed for multi-target tracking and provides the trajectories of each person. We thus could get the bounding box and ID label of each person. And we use more than 20,000 images on *MOT challenge*.

To evaluate our model, we choose *VIPeR* [26], *PRID* [27], *GRID* [28], and *Market* [46] as test sets. Note that, *VIPeR, GRID* and *PRID* are included in the *PETA* dataset. When we test our algorithm on them, they will be excluded from the training set. For example, when we use the *VIPeR* for person ReID test, none of its images will be used for dCNN training. We do not use the *CUHK* for testing, because it takes nearly one third of images in *PETA*. If it is excluded, the samples for dCNN training will be insufficient.

### 4.2 Implementation Details

We select AlexNet [35] as our base dCNN architecture. We use the same kernel and filter sizes for all the hidden layers. For the loss layers of our first stage dCNN $\mathcal{O}^{S1}$ and third stage dCNN $\mathcal{O}$, we use the sigmoid cross-entropy loss layer, because each input sample has multiple positive attribute labels. We learn 105 binary attributes from *PETA*. When we fine-tune dCNN with attributes triplet loss, we follow the standard triplet loss algorithm [47] to select samples. First randomly select the *anchor* samples $u_{(a)}$. Then, we select samples with the same person ID with $u_{(a)}$ but substantially different attribute labels as *positive* samples $u_{(p)}$. Samples from other persons having similar attribute labels with $u_{(a)}$ are selected as *negative* samples $u_{(n)}$. Since each person only has 15 out of 105 positive attributes in average on training datasets, We select $p = 10$ attributes only for initialization in Stage 2, because they can be predicted with higher accuracy, i.e., $15 * 60\% (the average of classification accuracy for testing) = 9$. Moreover, we select $O = 0$ to ensure most testing images include near 15 positive attributes. Parameters for learning are empirically set via cross-validation. The $\theta$ and $\gamma$ in Eq. 4 are set as 1 and 0.01, respectively. We implement our approach with GTX TITAN X GPU, Intel i7 CPU, and 32 GB memory.

### 4.3 Accuracy of Predicted Attributes

In the first experiment, we test the accuracy of predicted attributes on three datasets, *VIPeR, PRID* and *GRID*, as well as show the effects of combining different training stages. For any input image of a person, if its GroundTruth has $n$ positive attributes, we compare the top $n$ predicted attributes against the GroundTruth to compute the classification accuracy. The results are summarized in Fig. 3. $Stage_1$ denotes the baseline dCNN $\mathcal{O}^{S1}$. $Stage_{1\&3}$ first labels $U$ with $\mathcal{O}^{S1}$, then combines $U$ and $T$ to fine-tune the $\mathcal{O}^{S1}$. $Stage_{1\&2}$ denotes the updated

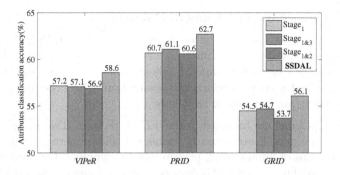

**Fig. 3.** Attributes classification accuracy(%) on three datasets.

dCNN $\mathcal{O}^{S2}$ after the second stage training. SSDAL denotes our final dCNN after the third stage training. From the experimental results, we can draw the following conclusions:

(1) Although $Stage_{1\&3}$ uses larger training set, it does not constantly outperform the baseline. This is because the expanded training data is labeled by $\mathcal{O}^{S1}$, and it does not provide new cues for fine-tuning $\mathcal{O}^{S1}$ in stage-3.
(2) $\mathcal{O}^{S2}$ produced by $Stage_{1\&2}$ does not constantly outperform baseline. This maybe because the weak person ID labels. Also, only updating the easily over-fitted fully-connected layers with triplet loss may degrade the generalization ability of $\mathcal{O}^{S2}$ on other datasets besides $U$.
(3) SSDAL is able to improve the accuracy of baseline by 1.2 % in average on three datasets. This demonstrates our three-stage training framework can learn more robust semantic attributes. To intuitively show the accuracy of predicted attributes, we use the dCNN trained by SSDAL to predict attributes on *MOT challenge* dataset. Some examples are illustrated in Fig. 4.

**Fig. 4.** Examples of predicted attributes on *MOT challenge* by the learned dCNN after three stages of training. Texts with blue color are correct attributes, while those with red color are false attributes.

## 4.4    Performance on Two-Camera Datasets

This experiment tests deep attributes on two-camera person ReID tasks. Three datasets are employed. 10 random tests are first performed for each dataset. Then, the average *Cumulative Match Characteristic* (CMC) curves of these tests are calculated and used for performance evaluation. The experimental settings on three datasets are introduced as follows:

***VIPeR***: 632 persons are included in the *VIPeR* dataset. Two images with size $48 \times 128$ of each person are taken by camera A and camera B, respectively in different scenarios of illumination, postures and viewpoints. Different from most of existing algorithms, our SSDAL does not need training on the target dataset. To make fair comparison with other algorithms, we use similar settings for performance evaluation, *i.e.*, randomly selecting 10 test sets, and each contains 316 persons.

***PRID***: This dataset is specially designed for person ReID in single shot. It contains two image sets containing 385 and 749 persons captured by camera A and camera B, respectively. These two datasets share 200 persons in common. For the purpose of fair comparison with other algorithms, we follow the protocol in [27], and create a probe set and a gallery set, where all training samples are excluded. The probe set includes images of 100 persons from camera A. The gallery set is made up of images from 649 persons capture by camera B.

***GRID***: This dataset includes images collected by 8 non-adjacent cameras fixed at a subway station. The probe set contains images of about 250 persons. The gallery set contains images of about 1025 persons, among which 775 persons do not match anyone in the probe set. For the purpose of fair comparison, images of 125 persons shared by the two sets are employed for training. The remaining 125 persons and 775 distracters are used for the testing.

***Compared Algorithms:*** We compare our approach with many recent works. Compared works that learn distance metrics for person ReID include RPML [10], PRDC [17], RSVM [52], Salmatch [48], LMF [49], PCCA [9], KISSME [13], kLFDA [14], KCCA [50],TSR [51], EPKFM [19],LOMO + XQDA [20],MRank-PRDC [28], MRank-RSVM [28], RQDA [53], MLAPG [23] and CSL [22]. Compared works based on traditional attribute learning are AIR [29], OAR [31] and LOREA [34]. Related works that leverage deep learning include DML [41], IDLA [42] and Deep-RDC [24]. The compared CMC scores at different ranks on three datasets are shown in Tables 1, 2 and 3, respectively.

The three tables clearly show that, even it is not fine-tuned with extra data, the baseline dCNN $\mathcal{O}^{S1}$ achieves fairly good results on three datasets, especially on *PRID* and *GRID*. Additionally, if we fine-tune the baseline dCNN using our attributes triplet loss, we achieve an additional 3.4 % improvement at rank 1 on *VIPeR*, 1.4 % on *PRID*, and 5.3 % on *GRID*, respectively. This indicates that our three-stage training framework improves the performance by progressively adding more information into the training procedure.

Our SSDAL algorithm has surpassed all existing algorithms on the *PRID* and *GRID* datasets. Some recent works like AIR [29], OAR [31], and LOREA [34]

**Table 1.** CMC scores, *i.e.*, percentage (%) of correct matches, of ranks 1, rank 5, rank 10, rank 20 on the *VIPeR* dataset.

| Methods | | Rank 1 | Rank 5 | Rank 10 | Rank 20 |
|---|---|---|---|---|---|
| Metric learning based ReID | RPML [10] | 27.0 | 57.0 | 69.0 | 83.0 |
| | Salmatch [48] | 30.2 | 52.4 | 65.5 | 79.1 |
| | LMF [49] | 29.1 | 52.3 | 65.9 | 80.0 |
| | KISSME [13] | 19.6 | 47.5 | 62.2 | 77.0 |
| | KCCA [50] | 37.3 | 71.4 | **84.6** | 92.3 |
| | kLFDA [14] | 32.2 | 65.8 | 79.7 | 90.9 |
| | LOMO + XQDA [20] | 40.0 | 68.9 | 81.5 | 91.1 |
| | CSL [22] | 34.8 | 68.7 | 82.3 | 91.8 |
| | MLAPG [23] | 40.7 | 69.9 | 82.3 | 92.4 |
| | TSR [51] | 31.6 | 68.6 | 82.8 | **94.6** |
| | EPKFM [19] | 36.8 | 70.4 | 83.7 | 91.7 |
| Traditional attributes learning based ReID | AIR [29] | 18.0 | 38.8 | 51.1 | 71.2 |
| | OAR [31] | 21.4 | 41.5 | 55.2 | 71.5 |
| | LORAE [34] | 42.3 | **72.2** | 81.6 | 89.6 |
| Deep learning based ReID | IDLA [42] | 34.8 | 54.3 | 76.5 | 87.6 |
| | DML [41] | 28.2 | 59.3 | 73.5 | 86.4 |
| | Deep-RDC [24] | 40.5 | 60.8 | 70.4 | 84.4 |
| Proposed | *Stage*$_1$ | 34.5 | 63.9 | 73.1 | 87.0 |
| | **SSDAL** | 37.9 | 65.5 | 75.6 | 88.4 |
| | **SSDAL + XQDA** | **43.5** | 71.8 | 81.5 | 89.0 |

**Table 2.** CMC scores, *i.e.*, percentage (%) of correct matches, of ranks 1, rank5, rank 10, rank 20 on the *PRID* dataset.

| Methods | Rank 1 | Rank 5 | Rank 10 | Rank 20 |
|---|---|---|---|---|
| RPML [10] | 4.8 | 14.3 | 21.6 | 30.2 |
| PRDC [17] | 4.5 | 12.6 | 19.7 | 29.5 |
| RSVM [52] | 6.8 | 16.5 | 22.7 | 31.5 |
| Salmatch [48] | 4.9 | 17.5 | 26.1 | 33.9 |
| LMF [49] | 12.5 | 23.9 | 30.7 | 36.5 |
| PCCA [9] | 3.5 | 10.9 | 17.9 | 27.1 |
| KISSME [13] | 4.1 | 12.8 | 21.1 | 31.8 |
| kLFDA [14] | 7.6 | 18.9 | 25.6 | 37.4 |
| KCCA [50] | 14.5 | 34.3 | 46.7 | 59.1 |
| LOREA [34] | 18.0 | 37.4 | 50.1 | 66.6 |
| LOMO + XQDA [20] | 15.3 | 35.7 | 41.2 | 53.8 |
| MLAPG [23] | 16.6 | 33.1 | 41.4 | 52.5 |
| *Stage*$_1$ | 18.7 | 46.9 | 55.0 | 65.8 |
| **SSDAL** | 20.1 | 47.4 | 55.7 | 68.6 |
| **SSDAL + XQDA** | **22.6** | **48.7** | **57.8** | **69.2** |

**Table 3.** CMC scores, *i.e.*, percentage (%) of correct matches, of ranks 1, rank5, rank 10, rank 20 on the *GRID* dataset.

| Methods | Rank 1 | Rank 5 | Rank 10 | Rank 20 |
|---|---|---|---|---|
| PRDC [17] | 9.7 | 22.0 | 33.0 | 44.3 |
| RSVM [52] | 10.2 | 24.6 | 33.3 | 43.7 |
| MRank-PRDC [28] | 11.1 | 26.1 | 35.8 | 46.6 |
| MRank-RSVM [28] | 12.2 | 27.8 | 36.3 | 49.3 |
| RQDA [53] | 15.2 | 30.1 | 39.2 | 49.3 |
| EPKFM [19] | 16.3 | 35.8 | 46.0 | 57.6 |
| LOMO + XQDA [20] | 16.6 | 35.4 | 41.8 | 52.4 |
| *Stage*$_1$ | 16.9 | 30.1 | 40.7 | 50.2 |
| **SSDAL** | 19.1 | 35.6 | 45.8 | 58.1 |
| **SSDAL + XQDA** | **22.4** | **39.2** | **48.0** | **58.4** |

also learn attributes for person ReID. The comparison in Table 1 clearly shows the advantages of our deep model in attribute prediction. Some previous works like DML [41], IDLA [42] and Deep-RDC [24] take advantages of deep learning in person ReID. Different from them, our work generates camera-independent mid-level attributes, which can be used as discriminative features for identifying persons on different datasets. The experiments results in Table 1 also show that our method outperforms these works.

Because we use the predicted binary attributes as features for person ReID, we can also learn a distance metric to further improve the ReID accuracy. We select XQDA [20] for the distance metric learning. As can be seen from three tables, our approach with XQDA [20], *i.e.*, SSDAL + XQDA, achieves the best accuracy at rank 1 on all the three datasets. It also constantly outperforms all the other algorithms at various ranks on *PRID* and *GRID*. This clearly proves that our work can easily combine with existing distance metric learning works to further boost the performance.

### 4.5    Performance on Multi-camera Dataset

We further test our approach in a more challenging multi-camera person ReID task. We employ the *Market* dataset [46], where more than 25,000 images of 1501 labeled persons are collected from 6 cameras. Each person has 17 images in average, which show substantially different appearances due to variances of viewpoints, illumination, backgrounds, *etc.* This dataset is also larger than most of existing person ReID datasets. Because *Market* has clearly provided the training set, we use images in the training set and their person ID labels to fine-tune our dCNN $\mathcal{O}^{S2}$.

In contrast to the two-camera person ReID task, the multi-camera person ReID targets to identify the query person across image sets from multiple cameras. Therefore, our task is to query and rank all images from these cameras,

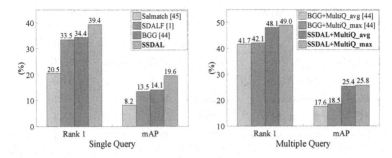

**Fig. 5.** CMC scores of rank 1 (Rank 1) and mean Average Precision (mAP) on the *Market* dataset for the scenarios of Single Query and Multiple Query.

according to the given probe image (*i.e.*, Single Query) or tracklet (*i.e.*, Multiple Query) of a person. Because this process is similar to image retrieval, we evaluate the performance by mean Average Precision (mAP) and accuracy at Rank 1, following the protocol in [46]. The results are shown in Fig. 5. MultiQ_avg and MultiQ_max denote applying average and max pooling to acquire the final feature for a person's tracklet. More details about feature pooling can be found in [46].

From Fig. 5, we can observe that our approach outperforms all the compared methods by a large margin for both single query and multi-query scenarios. For the multiple query scenario, our method successfully boosts the mAP from 18.5 % to 25.8 %, resulting in an 7.3 % absolute improvement. This indicates that our method is also superior to other methods in more challenging multi-camera person ReID tasks. This experiment also shows that our learned deep attributes are robust to significant appearance variations among multiple cameras.

## 4.6   Discussions

In this part, we further discuss some interesting aspects of our method that may have been missed in the above experimental evaluations.

By using attributes features of only 105 dimensions, our method achieves promising performance on four public datasets. It is interesting to see the ReID performance after combining the compact attribute features and classic visual features. To verify this point, we integrate the appearance-based features with attributes features for better discriminative power. Table 4 shows the performance of fusing deep attributes with appearance-based feature LOMO [20], *i.e.*, LOMO + XQDA + SSDAL. It is obvious that fusing appearance-based features further improves SSDAL, *e.g.*, CMC score achieves 45.3 at Rank-1. Therefore, combining with visual feature would further ensure the performance of attributes features in real applications.

Many image retrieval works use the output of FC-7 layer in AlexNet as image feature. Therefore, another way of learning mid-level feature for person ReID is fine-tunning the FC-7 layer with triplet loss similar to the one in SSDAL, *i.e.*,

488    C. Su et al.

**Table 4.** Additional experimental results on *VIPeR*.

| Method | Rank 1 | Rank 5 | Rank 10 | Rank 20 |
|---|---|---|---|---|
| SSDAL | 37.9 | 65.5 | 75.6 | 85.4 |
| LOMO + SSDAL + XQDA | 45.3 | 74.4 | 85.4 | 94.6 |
| FC-7 fine-tuned on $T$ | 26.5 | 48.2 | 61.1 | 72.3 |
| FC-7 fine-tuned on $U$ | 10.1 | 21.6 | 31.7 | 45.3 |
| FC-7 fine-tuned on $T + U$ | 27.4 | 49.7 | 62.3 | 74.4 |

updating the dCNN to make same person have similar FC-7 layer features and vice versa. The FC-7 features learned in this way are also not limited to the 105 dimensions, thus might be more discriminative than attributes. To test the validity of this strategy, we fine-tune the FC-7 layer of AlexNet using person ID labels on different datasets, *i.e.*, $T$, $U$, and $T + U$, respectively. Experimental results in Table 4 clearly indicates that that deep attributes outperforms such FC7 features. This clearly validates the contribution and importance of attributes.

## 5   Conclusions and Future Work

In this paper, we address the person ReID problem using deeply learned human attribute features. We propose a novel Semi-supervised Deep Attribute Learning(SSDAL) algorithm. With our attributes triplet loss, images only with person ID labels can be used for training attribute detectors in a dCNN framework. Extensive experiments on four benchmark datasets demonstrate that our method is robust in attribute detection and substantially outperforms previous person ReID methods. In addition, our algorithm does not need further training on the target datasets. This means we can train the attribute prediction dCNN model only for one time, and it would work for person ReID tasks on different datasets. The dCNN model fine-tuning only requires images with person ID labels, which can be easily obtained by Multi-target Tracking algorithms. Considering the spatial locations and correlations of attributes might further improve the accuracy of attribute detection. These would be our future work.

**Acknowledgements.** This work was supported in part to Dr. Qi Tian by ARO grants W911NF-15-1-0290 and Faculty Research Gift Awards by NEC Laboratories of America and Blippar. This work was supported in part by National Science Foundation of China (NSFC) 61429201 and 61303178. This work was supported in part to Dr. Shiliang Zhang by National Science Foundation of China (NSFC) 61572050 and 91538111.

# References

1. Farenzena, M., Bazzani, L., Perina, A., Murino, V., Cristani, M.: Person re-identification by symmetry-driven accumulation of local features. In: CVPR (2010)
2. Cheng, D.S., Cristani, M., Stoppa, M., Bazzani, L., Murino, V.: Custom pictorial structures for re-identification. In: BMVC (2011)
3. Ma, B., Su, Y., Jurie, F.: Bicov: a novel image representation for person re-identification and face verification. In: BMVC (2012)
4. Liu, C., Gong, S., Loy, C.C., Lin, X.: Person re-identification: what features are important? In: ECCV (2012)
5. Zhao, R., Ouyang, W., Wang, X.: Unsupervised salience learning for person re-identification. In: CVPR (2013)
6. Wang, X., Zhao, R.: Person re-identification: system design and evaluation overview. In: Gong, S., Cristani, M., Yan, S., Loy, C.C. (eds.) Person Re-Identification, pp. 351–370. Springer, Heidelberg (2014)
7. Zheng, L., Wang, S., Tian, L., He, F., Liu, Z., Tian, Q.: Query-adaptive late fusion for image search and person re-identification. In: CVPR (2015)
8. Ma, A.J., Yuen, P.C., Li, J.: Domain transfer support vector ranking for person re-identification without target camera label information. In: ICCV (2013)
9. Dikmen, M., Akbas, E., Huang, T.S., Ahuja, N.: Pedestrian recognition with a learned metric. In: Kimmel, R., Klette, R., Sugimoto, A. (eds.) ACCV 2010, Part IV. LNCS, vol. 6495, pp. 501–512. Springer, Heidelberg (2011)
10. Hirzer, M., Roth, P.M., Köstinger, M., Bischof, H.: Relaxed pairwise learned metric for person re-identification. In: Fitzgibbon, A., Lazebnik, S., Perona, P., Sato, Y., Schmid, C. (eds.) ECCV 2012, Part VI. LNCS, vol. 7577, pp. 780–793. Springer, Heidelberg (2012)
11. Pedagadi, S., Orwell, J., Velastin, S., Boghossian, B.: Local fisher discriminant analysis for pedestrian re-identification. In: CVPR (2013)
12. Yan, S., Xu, D., Zhang, B., Zhang, H.J., Yang, Q., Lin, S.: Graph embedding and extensions: a general framework for dimensionality reduction. PAMI 29, 40–51 (2007)
13. Köstinger, M., Hirzer, M., Wohlhart, P., Roth, P.M., Bischof, H.: Large scale metric learning from equivalence constraints. In: CVPR (2012)
14. Xiong, F., Gou, M., Camps, O., Sznaier, M.: Person re-identification using kernel-based metric learning methods. In: Fleet, D., Pajdla, T., Schiele, B., Tuytelaars, T. (eds.) ECCV 2014, Part VII. LNCS, vol. 8695, pp. 1–16. Springer, Heidelberg (2014)
15. Liu, C., Loy, C.C., Gong, S., Wang, G.: POP: person re-identification post-rank optimisation. In: ICCV (2013)
16. Li, Z., Chang, S., Liang, F., Huang, T.S., Cao, L., Smith, J.R.: Learning locally-adaptive decision functions for person verification. In: CVPR (2013)
17. Zheng, W.S., Gong, S., Xiang, T.: Re-identification by relative distance comparison. In: CVPR (2013)
18. Wang, T., Gong, S., Zhu, X., Wang, S.: Person re-identification by video ranking. In: Fleet, D., Pajdla, T., Schiele, B., Tuytelaars, T. (eds.) ECCV 2014, Part IV. LNCS, vol. 8692, pp. 688–703. Springer, Heidelberg (2014)
19. Chen, D., Yuan, Z., Hua, G., Zheng, N., Wang, J.: Similarity learning on an explicit polynomial kernel feature map for person re-identification. In: CVPR (2015)
20. Liao, S., Hu, Y., Zhu, X., Li, S.Z.: Person re-identification by local maximal occurrence representation and metric learning. In: CVPR (2015)

21. Chen, Y.C., Zheng, W.S., Lai, J.: Mirror representation for modeling view-specific transform in person re-identification. In: IJCAI (2015)
22. Shen, Y., Lin, W., Yan, J., Xu, M., Wu, J., Wang, J.: Person re-identification with correspondence structure learning. In: ICCV (2015)
23. Liao, S., Li, S.Z.: Efficient PSD constrained asymmetric metric learning for person re-identification. In: ICCV (2015)
24. Ding, S., Lin, L., Wang, G., Chao, H.: Deep feature learning with relative distance comparison for person re-identification. Pattern Recogn. **48**(10), 2993–3003 (2015)
25. Peng, P., Xiang, T., Wang, Y., Pontil, M., Gong, S., Huang, T., Tian, Y.: Unsupervised cross-dataset transfer learning for person re-identification. In: CVPR (2016)
26. Gray, D., Brennan, S., Tao, H.: Evaluating appearance models for recognition, reacquisition, and tracking. In: PETS (2007)
27. Hirzer, M., Beleznai, C., Roth, P.M., Bischof, H.: Person re-identification by descriptive and discriminative classification. In: Heyden, A., Kahl, F. (eds.) SCIA 2011. LNCS, vol. 6688, pp. 91–102. Springer, Heidelberg (2011)
28. Loy, C.C., Liu, C., Gong, S.: Person re-identification by manifold ranking (2013)
29. Layne, R., Hospedales, T.M., Gong, S., Mary, Q.: Person re-identification by attributes. In: BMVC (2012)
30. Layne, R., Hospedales, T.M., Gong, S.: Towards person identification and re-identification with attributes. In: ECCV Workshops (2012)
31. Layne, R., Hospedales, T.M., Gong, S.: Attributes-based re-identification. In: Gong, S., Cristani, M., Yan, S., Loy, C.C. (eds.) Person Re-Identification, 93–117. Springer, Heidelberg (2014)
32. Layne, R., Hospedales, T.M., Gong, S.: Re-id: Hunting attributes in the wild. In: BMVC (2014)
33. Su, C., Yang, F., Zhang, G., Tian, Q., gao, W., Davis, L.: Tracklet-to-tracklet person re-identification by attributes with discriminative latent space mapping. In: ICMS (2015)
34. Su, C., Yang, F., Zhang, S., Tian, Q., Davis, L.S., Gao, W.: Multi-task learning with low rank attribute embedding for person re-identification. In: ICCV (2015)
35. Krizhevsky, A., Sutskever, I., Hinton, G.: Imagenet classification with deep convolutional neural networks. In: NIPS (2012)
36. Girshick, R., Donahue, J., Darrell, T., Malik, J.: Region-based convolutional networks for accurate object detection and segmentation. In: PAMI (2015)
37. Long, J., Shelhamer, E., Darrell, T.: Fully convolutional networks for semantic segmentation. In: CVPR (2014)
38. Shankar, S., Garg, V.K., Cipolla, R.: Deep-carving: discovering visual attributes by carving deep neural nets. In: CVPR (2015)
39. Chen, Q., Huang, J., Feris, R., Brown, L.M., Dong, J., Yan, S.: Deep domain adaptation for describing people based on fine-grained clothing attributes. In: CVPR (2015)
40. Li, W., Zhao, R., Xiao, T., Wang, X.: Deepreid: Deep filter pairing neural network for person re-identification. In: CVPR (2014)
41. Yi, D., Lei, Z., Li, S.Z.: Deep metric learning for practical person re-identification. In: ICPR (2014)
42. Ahmed, E., Jones, M., Marks, T.K.: An improved deep learning architecture for person re-identification. In: CVPR (2015)
43. Paisitkriangkrai, S., Shen, C., Hengel, A.v.d.: Learning to rank in person re-identification with metric ensembles. In: CVPR (2015)
44. Deng, Y., Luo, P., Loy, C.C., Tang, X.: Pedestrian attribute recognition at far distance. In: ACM MM (2014)

45. Leal-Taixé, L., Milan, A., Reid, I., Roth, S., Schindler, K.: Motchallenge 2015: Towards a benchmark for multi-target tracking. arXiv preprint arXiv:1504.01942 (2015)
46. Zheng, L., Shen, L., Tian, L., Wang, S., Wang, J., Tian, Q.: Scalable person re-identification: a benchmark. In: ICCV (2015)
47. Schroff, F., Kalenichenko, D., Philbin, J.: Facenet: a unified embedding for face recognition and clustering. In: CVPR (2015)
48. Zhao, R., Ouyang, W., Wang, X.: Person re-identification by salience matching. In: ICCV (2013)
49. Zhao, R., Ouyang, W., Wang, X.: Learning midlevel filters for person reidentification. In: CVPR (2014)
50. Lisanti, G., Masi, I., Del Bimbo, A.: Matching people across camera views using kernel canonical correlation analysis. In: ICDSC (2014)
51. Shi, Z., Hospedales, T.M., Xiang, T.: Transferring a semantic representation for person re-identification and search. In: CVPR (2015)
52. Prosser, B., Zheng, W.S., Gong, S., Xiang, T., Mary, Q.: Person re-identification by support vector ranking. In: BMVC (2010)
53. Liao, S., Hu, Y., Li, S.Z.: Joint dimension reduction and metric learning for person re-identification. arXiv preprint arXiv:1406.4216 (2014)

# An Occlusion-Resistant Ellipse Detection Method by Joining Coelliptic Arcs

Halil Ibrahim Cakir[1]([✉]), Cihan Topal[2,3], and Cuneyt Akinlar[2]

[1] Dumlupinar University, Kutahya, Turkey
cakirhal@dumlupinar.edu.tr
[2] Anadolu University, Eskisehir, Turkey
{cihant,cakinlar}@anadolu.edu.tr
[3] Visea Innovative, Eskisehir, Turkey

**Abstract.** In this study, we propose an ellipse detection method which gives prospering results on occlusive cases. The method starts with detection of edge segments. Then we extract elliptical arcs by computing corners and fitting ellipse to the pixels between two consecutive corners. Once the elliptical arcs are extracted, we aim to test all possible arc subsets. However, this requires exponential complexity and runtime diverges as the number of arcs increases. To accelerate the process, arc pairing strategy is deployed by using conic properties of arcs. If any pair found to be non-coelliptic, then arc combinations including that pair are eliminated. Therefore the number of possible arcs subsets is reduced and computation time is improved. In the end, ellipse fitting is applied to remaining arc combinations to decide on final ellipses. Performance of the proposed algorithm is tested on real datasets, and better results have been obtained compare to state-of-the-art algorithms.

**Keywords:** Ellipse detection · Arc detection · Feature extraction · Hough transform

## 1 Introduction

Extracting ellipses from images is an important problem in computer vision and has a diverse area of applications from object detection to pose estimation [3,10, 11,15–17,26]. Since the projections of circular objects appear as ellipse on the camera image plane, ellipse detection is employed in many real life applications. However, ellipse detection is much more difficult than circle detection because an ellipse has 5 degrees of freedom (the center coordinates $x$ & $y$, semi-major and semi-minor axes $a$ & $b$, and rotation angle $\alpha$) whereas a circle has 3. Due to the same reason, many different shapes (i.e., a rectangular or a line) can be represented by an ellipse with a reasonable amount of accuracy.

This work is supported by The Scientific and Technological Research Council of Turkey (TUBITAK) and Anadolu University Commission of Scientific Research Projects (BAP) under the grant numbers 115E928 and 1505F319, respectively.

© Springer International Publishing AG 2016
B. Leibe et al. (Eds.): ECCV 2016, Part II, LNCS 9906, pp. 492–507, 2016.
DOI: 10.1007/978-3-319-46475-6_31

There are many studies on ellipse detection found in the literature and they are categorized in two groups, i.e. model-based and feature-based methods. Although both approaches have pros and cons, many state-of-the-art algorithms are feature-based methods and gives better results in terms of accuracy and speed. Model-based methods fits a mathematical model to plain pixel information. McLaughlin uses the famous Hough Transform (HT) for accurate ellipse detection [17]. A model-based search is a very slow operation for ellipse shape since it needs to be performed in 5-dimensional parameter space. Zhang and Liu utilize HT with convexity property of edges and obtain good results for detecting faces in images with ellipse detection [29]. Lei and Wong incorporate the symmetric property to HT to improve computation efficiency [12]. Feature-based approaches first extracts higher level geometric features, i.e. lines or arcs. In recent years, preprocessing of arc and line segments with geometrical properties are mostly investigated. Libuda et al. concatenates line and arc primitives to construct ellipses [13]. Nguyen et al. calculates ellipse parameters after getting arc pieces by using ellipse properties [18]. Nguyen and Kerautret describe an ellipse detection algorithm that works by obtaining arcs and lines from an edge map and combines these features [19]. Prasad et al. propose a heuristic ellipse detector based on convexity and edge curvature properties [21]. Fornaciari et al. choose arcs strategically and compute parameters of ellipses with HT [6]. Arcs are classified according to their convexity and then grouped to test if they compose an ellipse or not. A popular model fitting technique Random Sample Consensus (RANSAC) is also employed in both model-based and feature-based methods for ellipse detection. Watcharin and Kaewapichai makes use of the RANSAC and propose an efficient and robust ellipse detection algorithm [9]. Song and Wang use RANSAC with edge information and tangent directions to fit ellipses while eliminating useless feature points [24]. In RANSAC, fitting is applied to randomly selected points, so it is not a steady algorithm and there is no guarantee to get the equivalent results despite same inputs are given.

The reason behind the crowd literature of ellipse detection is the difficulty of the problem. In addition to the fact that different geometric shapes such as rectangle can be represented by an ellipse with a reasonable accuracy; occlusions in real life images significantly aggravates the problem. Many methods applies image specific thresholds to find the best possible result, however, this situation hinders applicability of the algorithms.

In this study, we propose a feature-based ellipse detection algorithm which gives promising results even in difficult occlusive cases. Proposed method does not perform any voting mechanism, therefore works in a parameter-free manner without applying image specific score threshold values. Unlike many other methods, the algorithm aims to evaluate all combinations of extracted elliptical arcs instead of grouping fixed number of arcs. In this way, detection of ellipses can be achieved even though arcs forming them are spread around the image. To obtain accurate results, we use analytic methods to compute ellipse fitting error instead of employing approximations. For the experimental validation, we assess our algorithm with recently published state-of-the-art methods and present quantitative results on different real image datasets.

## 2   Proposed Method

The proposed ellipse detection algorithm follows the steps of the flowchart shown in Fig. 1. Initially, the edge segments of an image are extracted as contiguous array of pixels to ease the further processing. [2]. In the second step we extract the elliptical arcs which may be part of an occluded ellipse. Next, we seek the arc combinations which form valid ellipses. For this purpose, arc pairing operation is done by utilizing the locations and orientations of detected arcs to determine whether two arcs are coelliptic or non-coelliptic in each pair. In this way, arc combinations which may not constitute a valid ellipse are eliminated without performing computationally expensive ellipse fitting and error computation operations. Finally, each of the remaining arc combinations are then tested by ellipse fitting and the final ellipses are found according to the fitting error and spanned angle ratio parameters. Steps of the proposed algorithm are explained in the following subsections in detail.

**Fig. 1.** Flowchart for ellipse detection

### 2.1   Detection of Edge Segments

The very first step of the algorithm is extracting the edge segments from the input image. For this task, we employ the EDPF method [2] which is based on the Edge Drawing algorithm [27]. It works by first determining certain anchor points in an image and joining these anchors by a smart routing procedure. By setting all ED's parameters at extremes, EDPF detects all possible edge segments in an image. The false detections are then eliminated by a validation mechanism, and thus only valid edge segments are returned. In Fig. 2 a real test image and detected edge segments are shown.

(a)                                                          (b)

**Fig. 2.** Test image and the extracted edge segments. Note that each edge segment is shown in different colors. (Color figure online)

## 2.2   Extraction of Elliptical Arcs

In this step, elliptical arcs are extracted from the edge segments in a two-stage algorithm. First, the corner locations are computed along each segment with a curvature based corner detection algorithm [4,28]. Then ellipse fit is applied to the pixels in between two consecutive corners and the pixel sets resulting low fitting error are selected as elliptical arcs.

There are two popular ellipse fitting methods in the literature [5,25]. Fitzgibbon's method guarantees that the resulted conic is an ellipse, however, it usually ends up with more eccentric ellipses and higher fitting errors. In Taubin's method, obtained ellipse contour better fits the points and gives lower error without the guarantee for an ellipse. Since we apply ellipse fitting to consecutive edge pixels rather than scattered points, we can obtain elliptical arcs with Taubin's method.

There is no straightforward way to compute ellipse fitting error. In many studies various numerical estimation methods are employed [11,16,19]. In our study we derived an iterative method based on a modified version of [20] for precise ellipse fitting error computation. Although this method constitutes a major part of our total running time, we can precisely compute Euclidean distances between pixels and ellipse contour. In Fig. 3 detected corners and arcs obtained at the end of this step are shown for the same test image shown in Fig. 2.

## 2.3   Detection of Non-Coelliptic Arc Pairs

For $n$ elliptical arcs extracted in the previous step, there are obviously $2^n - 1$ potential combinations to join and detect ellipses. In the example shown in Fig. 3(b) we have 16 arcs, hence 65535 combinations, each may yield a valid ellipse. Briefly, there is an exponential relationship between the detected elliptical arcs and ellipse hypotheses. Therefore, it becomes a troublesome procedure to test all arc combinations as the number of arcs grows.

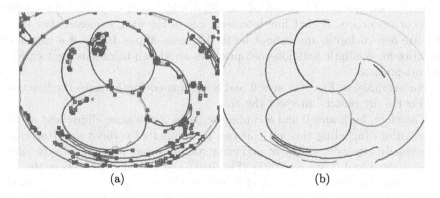

(a)                                                (b)

**Fig. 3.** Extraction of the corners and the elliptical arcs. (a) corners, (b) elliptical arcs.

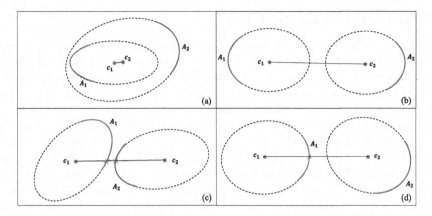

**Fig. 4.** Various scenarios on arc pairing. Successful (a, b) and unsuccessful (c, d) scenarios on arc pairing heuristic.

To reduce the number of arc combinations to test, we follow a proactive way by analyzing all arcs in pairwise to determine whether any pair can be part of the same ellipse or not. In other words, we try to find out whether any two arcs are coelliptic or non-coelliptic. Once we determine any non-coelliptic arc pair, we remove all arc subsets which includes that pair from entire $2^n - 1$ combinations to reduce the computation time. Determining whether an arc pair is non-coelliptic can be done in different ways. In this study, we derive a heuristic with a simple observation to find non-coelliptic arc pairs by utilizing conic properties of detected arcs. If two arcs' concavities are towards opposite directions, i.e. two arcs are located back-to-back, they can be considered as non-coelliptic since they cannot belong to the same ellipse. To find out whether two arcs are located back-to-back, we compute the equation of the line connecting centers of two arcs and determine that line intersects one of these arcs or not. For the arc center location, we use the center of ellipse that we obtain during the arc extraction process, i.e. center of the ellipse which is fit to pixels between two consecutive corners. If that line intersects one of the arcs, it means that those arcs are non-coelliptic and cannot be in the same ellipse. In Fig. 4 a couple of scenarios for coelliptic and non-coelliptic arcs are shown in various arc locations and orientations.

For example, in Fig. 5(a) arcs 0 and 8 are non-coelliptic, since the line connecting the arc centers intersect the arc.

Therefore, both arcs 0 and 8 cannot be parts of the same ellipse and all arc combinations including this arc pair can be eliminated without applying computationally expensive ellipse fit and error computation operations. In the same image, arcs 0 and 7 are coelliptic (Fig. 5(b)) and the line connecting the arc centers does not intersect any of the arcs. In this way, we execute arc pairing operation for all arc pairs which produces the pairing information of all detected arcs. Notice that the asymptotic complexity of arc pairing operation is polyno-

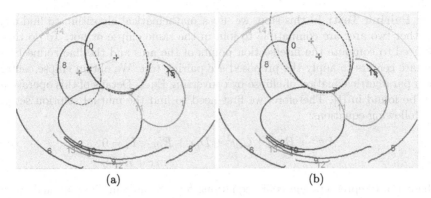

(a)                                                    (b)

**Fig. 5.** Decision making on arc pairing. (a) Line connecting the centers of arcs 0 & 8 intersects the arc 0. Thus they cannot belong to the same ellipse. (b) Line connecting the centers of arcs 0 & 7 does not intersect any of the arcs, hence they can belong to the same ellipse.

mial ($O(n^2)$) whereas testing the all combinations has exponential complexity ($O(2^n)$). In this way, each eliminated arc pair exponentially reduces the number of arc subsets in the $2^n - 1$ elements solution space.

After the arc combinations have been reduced, we finally obtain a pairing table as shown in Table 1 for the arcs shown in Fig. 3(b). This table shows whether an arc can be combined with any other arc. At the last step, we use this information to eliminate the arc combinations including at least one non-coelliptic arc pair without applying ellipse fit and error computation operations.

**Table 1.** Arc pairing table for test image in Fig. 5. "C" and "NC" stands for coelliptic and non-coelliptic, and indicates that the arc pair can be joined or not, respectively.

| Arc | 0 | 1 | 2 | 3 | 4 | 5 | 6 | 7 | 8 | ... | 15 |
|-----|---|---|---|---|---|---|---|---|---|-----|----|
| 0 | C | C | C | NC | C | C | NC | C | NC | ... | C |
| 1 | C | C | C | C | C | C | C | NC | C | ... | C |
| 2 | C | C | C | NC | C | NC | C | C | NC | ... | C |
| 3 | NC | C | NC | C | C | C | C | C | C | ... | C |
| 4 | C | C | C | C | C | C | C | C | C | ... | C |
| 5 | C | C | NC | C | C | C | C | C | C | ... | C |
| 6 | NC | C | C | C | C | C | C | C | C | ... | C |
| 7 | C | NC | C | C | C | C | C | C | C | ... | C |
| 8 | NC | C | NC | C | C | C | C | C | C | ... | C |
| ⋮ | ⋮ | ⋮ | ⋮ | ⋮ | ⋮ | ⋮ | ⋮ | ⋮ | ⋮ | ⋱ | ⋮ |
| 15 | C | C | C | C | C | C | C | C | C | ... | C |

**Arc Pairing Test:** In this step, we use a mathematical algorithm to find out whether two arcs are compatible to join in the same ellipse or not. To do this, we need to compute the intersection points of the arcs and the line connecting two arc centers to apply the proposed arc pairing test. We obtain ellipse center from parametric equation of ellipse by converting Eq. 1. Details of this operation can be found in [1]. Therefore, we first need to find the mutual solution set of the following equations:

$$A_i x^2 + B_i xy + C_i y^2 + D_i x + E_i y + F_i = 0 \tag{1}$$

$$mx + n = y \tag{2}$$

where Eq. 1 represents the conic equations for two arcs in the pair and Eq. 2 stands for the line equation which connects centers of two arcs. Using the center coordinates of the two arcs, $c_1 = (x_1, y_1)$ and $c_2 = (x_2, y_2)$, we simply find the $m$ and $n$ values in the line equation:

$$m = \frac{y_2 - y_1}{x_2 - x_1} \tag{3}$$

$$n = y_1 - mx_1 \tag{4}$$

Then we substitute $mx + n$ in place of $y$ in the conic equation:

$$\begin{aligned} x^2(A_i + mB_i + m^2 C_i) + \\ x(nB_i + 2mnC_i + D_i + mE_i) + \\ (C_i n^2 + nE_i + F_i) = 0 \end{aligned} \tag{5}$$

This quadratic equation can be solved with discriminant analysis; $\Delta = b^2 - 4ac$ where

$$a_i = A_i + mB_i + m^2 C_i \tag{6}$$

$$b_i = nB_i + 2mnC_i + D_i + mE_i \tag{7}$$

$$c_i = C_i n^2 + nE_i + F_i \tag{8}$$

They intersect always at two separate points on ellipse and we consider the point which is the closer one to the center of second arc as shown in Fig. 6. Having the $\Delta$ is computed, intersection point(s) $i_1 = (x_{i_1}, y_{i_1})$ and $i_2 = (x_{i_2}, y_{i_2})$ are computed as the following:

$$x_{i_1} = \frac{-b_i - \sqrt{\Delta_i}}{2a_i} \tag{9}$$

$$x_{i_2} = \frac{-b_i + \sqrt{\Delta_i}}{2a_i} \tag{10}$$

$$y_{i_1} = mx_{i_1} + n \tag{11}$$

$$y_{i_2} = mx_{i_2} + n \tag{12}$$

If we determine that the line and one of the arc segments intersect, we need to find whether the intersection point actually lies on the arc. Until now, we

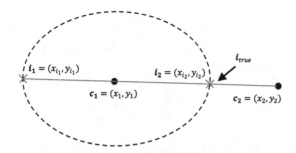

**Fig. 6.** Chosen intersection point is the closer point to the second arc.

represent arcs with the conic equation which is obtained with the ellipse fitting operation (see Eq. 1). Note that, obtained equation by ellipse fitting stands for a complete ellipse, however extracted arcs are not complete. Therefore the intersection points that we compute may be on the ellipse contour but may not be lying on the arc actually. To solve this problem, we use delimiting (start and end) angles to validate whether the point is on the arc as shown in Fig. 7(a) and 7(b).

In this way, the intersection point which is already on the ellipse contour can be used to determine whether it actually lies on the arc or not. First, we obtain the parametric equation of the ellipse ($\frac{x^2}{a} + \frac{y^2}{b} = 1$) from the conic form Eq. 1 with the steps in [1]. This operation moves the ellipse to the origin by proper translation and rotation transforms. Obviously, the same translation and rotation are applied to the computed intersection point to find the corresponding location in angular form. Once we evaluate the angular positions of starting-ending points of the arc and the intersection point (see Fig. 8), we can check whether the intersection point is in between the delimiting angles and determine the intersection is on the elliptical arc indeed.

Note that the method employed to find non-coelliptic arc pairs is a heuristic and may fail for some cases. In Fig. 9 two counter examples are presented. Although both pairs satisfy the heuristic, arcs in each pair are incompatible to lie along the same elliptic trajectory.

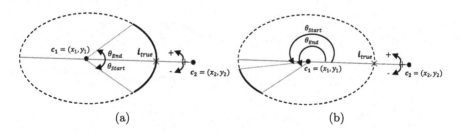

**Fig. 7.** Representation of elliptical arcs with delimiting angles. (a) Intersection is on the arc. (b) Intersection is not on the arc.

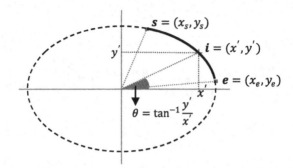

**Fig. 8.** Determining whether the intersection point $i = (x', y')$ is in between the delimiting angles.

Beside the one proposed here, there can also be different ways to determine coelliptic (or non-coelliptic) arcs that proposed algorithm can benefit in reducing number of the arc combinations.

### 2.4  Detection of Final Ellipses

In this step we reduce the number of ellipse hypotheses composed of all possible arc combinations by using non-coelliptic arc pairs. Those combinations are simply skipped and not tested with computationally expensive ellipse fitting. For combinations consisting of multiple arcs, Taubin method may result in a general conic rather that an ellipse if the arcs are not form an elliptical shape. In such cases, obtained conic equation (Eq. 1) is checked to see if $B^2 - 4AC < 0$, otherwise, combination is skipped without fitting error computation.

Eliminating arc subsets including non-coelliptic arc pairs significantly reduces the computation time. In the case of test image shown in Fig. 3(b), we have 16 arcs hence 65535 possible combinations which may yield an ellipse. If we try to check all these arc groups whether they compose an ellipse or not, we would have to execute 65535 computationally expensive ellipse fit and error computation routines. However, with the help of the Table 1 constructed by the proposed

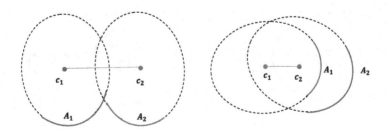

**Fig. 9.** Two counter examples of arc pairs that validate the proposed heuristic although they are incompatible to join.

heuristic, the algorithm eliminates 99.42 % of the arc subsets. Then the detection process ends up by only 382 fitting and error computation operations which 5 of them yield as a valid ellipse (see Fig. 10(b)). Eventually, we become able to check all reasonable arc subsets in the image without sacrificing computational constraints.

After elimination of arc subsets, remaining arc combinations have to pass two tests to be extracted as a valid ellipse. First, ellipse fit is applied to all arc pixels in the current arc group and fitting error is computed. If the resulted error is small, i.e. $\leq 2.0$ pixels, we test the current arc group for the spanned angle ratio (SAR) which is the ratio of the total length of arcs in the group over the perimeter of the yielded ellipse. With the computation of SAR, we can control both the allowed amount of occlusion and the number of false positive detections. For lower values of SAR, ellipses can be extracted with higher amount of occlusions, however, it also enables single and short arcs to be selected as ellipse which tends to an increase on the number of false positives. In the experiments, we set the SAR around 0.5 to make a compromise between the number of false positives and the amount of occlusion. Thus, we also prevent arc combinations consisting of only one arc to be extracted as ellipses with a small part of detected ellipse contour. In SAR computation we also need to calculate ellipse perimeter which does not have an exact formulation. Therefore we employ Ramanujan's second approximation for this task [23].

During the detection process, if an arc combination ends up in a valid ellipse, other combinations which include any arc in the current successful arc combination are eliminated from the solution space. In this manner, we both ensure that each arc can be part of only one ellipse and accelerate the algorithm as the arc combinations to test deplete more quickly. To even boost the procedure, we sort the arc combinations according to the number of arcs in descending order and start processing from crowded combinations. In this way, successful arc combinations which yield a valid ellipse cause more combinations to be removed from the list. The final detected ellipses for the input image Fig. 2(a) are shown in Fig. 10(b).

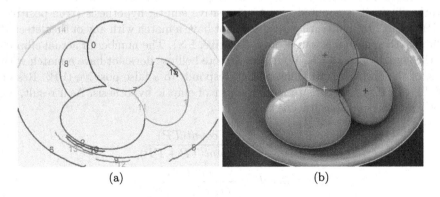

(a)                                    (b)

**Fig. 10.** Detected arcs (a) and detected ellipses (b) by arc joining.

## 3  Experimental Results

There are three publicly available datasets for ellipse detection in the literature, i.e. Prasad Dataset, Random Dataset, and Smartphone Dataset [7]. They contain $198 + 400 + 629 = 1227$ real images including tough ones with severe occlusions. We compared our algorithm with three state-of-the-art ellipse detection algorithms with the datasets mentioned above. The first algorithm is proposed by Prasad et al. and they are the owners of the Prasad Dataset [21]. The second algorithm is proposed by Fornaciari et al. who own remaining two datasets used in the experiments [6]. And the last algorithm is proposed by Libuda et al. [13]. Source codes of these algorithms are also available online [8,14,22]. All experiments are performed on a laptop computer with an Intel i7 2.40 GHz processor and 8 GB of RAM.

On the contrary to our algorithm, these three methods have a validation step which obtains the final results with an image specific score threshold value. In this procedure score value is computed using the edge pixels lying under the ellipse contour and it is assigned to each detected ellipse. As a result, this validation scheme effects the algorithm performance as the threshold value is tuned, however our proposed algorithm is purely feature based and does not employ a score thresholding or voting scheme. For a fair comparison, we run each algorithm with the same threshold value for all three datasets and pick the best results. All images in three datasets are gathered together and the best score, which gives the best average F-Measure for all images, is calculated for each algorithm. These threshold values are determined as 0.83, 0.01, and 0.78 for Prasad, Libuda, and Fornaciari, respectively.

The comparison metric is the overlap ratio calculation proposed by [21] and it is also used in [6] as:

$$Overlap\ Ratio = 1 - \frac{count(\text{XOR}(\epsilon_1, \epsilon_2))}{count(\text{OR}(\epsilon_1, \epsilon_2))} \tag{13}$$

where $\epsilon_1$ and $\epsilon_2$ are respectively the ground-truth ellipse and a valid detection. If a valid detection has at least 0.8 overlap ratio compare to any other ground-truth ellipse, it is counted as a true positive elliptic hypothesis (true positive, TP) and if a ground-truth ellipse does not have a match with any of the detected ellipses, then a miss is found (false negative, FN). The number of actual ellipses is the sum of TP and FN. When the detected ellipse does not have a match with any of the ground-truth ellipses, it corresponds to a false positive (FP). Result of TP + FP corresponds to total number of elliptic hypothesis. As a result, we get Precision and Recall values:

$$Precision = \frac{count(TP)}{count(TP + FP)} \tag{14}$$

$$Recall = \frac{count(TP)}{count(TP + FN)} \tag{15}$$

Then, F-Measure is calculated with the following formula:

$$F\text{-}Measure = \frac{2 \times Precision \times Recall}{Precision + Recall} \quad (16)$$

Average F-Measure values for each dataset is shown in Fig. 11.

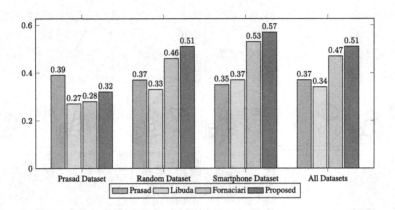

**Fig. 11.** Performances of algorithms as F-measure for each dataset.

According to results, Prasad performs best in its own dataset and the proposed method is in second place. In Random and Smartphone Datasets, proposed method outperforms all algorithms.

Eventually, proposed method performs best and it has an advantage of detecting all possible ellipses including occlusions in an image and localizing these ellipses perfectly as seen in Fig. 12.[1] For all 1227 images in 3 datasets, we found that the heuristic avoids 99.58 % of potentially unnecessary fitting operations in average. Note that there are rare situations where heuristic may fail.

In Table 2 average timing results are presented for the proposed algorithm in detail per image for each dataset.

**Table 2.** Average execution times of the proposed method with respect to the algorithm steps in milliseconds.

| Dataset | Edge detection | Corner detection | Arc extraction | Ellipse detection | TOTAL |
|---|---|---|---|---|---|
| Prasad | 3.59 ms | 0.58 ms | 0.87 ms | 7.50 ms | 12.54 ms |
| Random | 8.81 ms | 1.28 ms | 2.20 ms | 33.25 ms | 45.54 ms |
| Smartphone | 20.60 ms | 3.16 ms | 5.80 ms | 30.25 ms | 59.81 ms |

The table clearly shows that the total execution time of the proposed algorithm is strictly depends on the last step which runs with respect to the number of elliptical arcs. Timing performance of algorithms were measured in milliseconds and average timing values per image for each dataset is shown in Table 3.

---

[1] It is recommended for readers to see results in their original colorized form so as to distinguish detected ellipses.

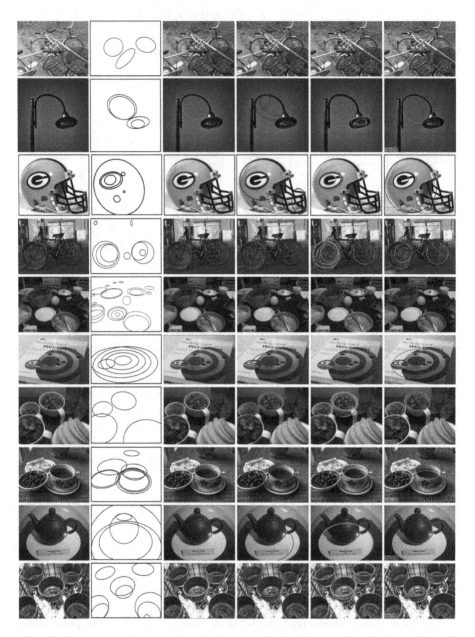

**Fig. 12.** Some results from three datasets for all algorithms. From left to right: (1) Original Image, (2) Ground Truth, (3) Prasad, (4) Libuda, (5) Fornaciari, (6) Proposed.

**Table 3.** Average execution times of algorithms per image for each dataset.

| Dataset/Algorithm | Prasad | Libuda | Fornaciari | Proposed |
|---|---|---|---|---|
| Prasad dataset | 207.1 ms | 7.35 ms | 3.46 ms | 12.54 ms |
| Random dataset | 1,842.5 ms | 16.51 ms | 10.89 ms | 45.54 ms |
| Smartphone dataset | 2,780.5 ms | 28.88 ms | 13.18 ms | 59.81 ms |

The implementations that we use are in C++ for Fornaciari, Libuda and the proposed method, and in MATLAB for Prasad. Timing results show that Fornaciari is the fastest one and its performance is very close to Libuda. In terms of computation speed, the proposed method falls behind the Fornaciari and Libuda, however, it still able to run in real-time. As a model-based method, Prasad is the slowest algorithm by far even though its timing values are divided by 50 due to the computation discrepancies between a typical application written in MATLAB and C++ with respect to the experiments held in [6].

We can list a couple of reasons that slows down our algorithm. First, our algorithm checks all possible combinations of the extracted elliptical arcs and requires exponential runtime with respect to the number of detected arcs. Second, opposite to the other methods, we employ a very precise yet computation intensive method to compute the fitting error.

## 4   Conclusions

Ellipse detection is an active research problem and there are two main strategies, i.e. model-based and feature-based. State-of-the-art methods in the literature are feature-based ones that extract primitive geometric features and aims to catch ellipses with pipelines that consist of various mathematical and geometric heuristics. This is the mainstream strategy of how recent research studies attempts to solve ellipse detection problem.

In this study an ellipse detection method is proposed, which works by extracting elliptical arcs in an image and then combines these arcs by a join strategy. For $n$ elliptical arcs, there are $2^n - 1$ different arcs combinations such that each may constitute an ellipse. In this way, any elliptical structure can be detected no matter how many arcs it is divided into due to the tough occlusions. On the contrary to the traditional model based methods, our execution time does not depend on the image size. Instead, execution time is exponentially grows as the number of arcs increases. To boost the detection process, an arc pairing operation which eliminates incompatible arc combinations including non-coelliptic arcs is executed. The remaining arc combinations are finally tested with ellipse fitting and error computation.

Experimental results show that the proposed algorithm gives the best results compare to state-of-the-art methods within a reasonable computation time. In addition to the best accuracy results, proposed method works parameter-free as a substantial contribution. In future work, we will further examine the additional ways to eliminate incompatible arc groups by using properties of conics to even accelerate the detection procedure. Moreover, we will attempt to optimize the error calculation method in terms of computation to speed up the algorithm. We also plan to decrease false detection rate by applying a validation step based on Gestalt Theory to improve the accuracy of the method.

## References

1. Adams, R.A.: Calculus: A Complete Course. Pearson Addison Wesley, Boston (2006). pp. 441–442
2. Akinlar, C., Topal, C.: EDPF: a real-time parameter-free edge segment detector with a false detection control. Int. J. Pattern Recogn. Artif. Intell. **26**(1), 1255002 (2012)
3. Carmona, E.J., Rincón, M., García-Feijoó, J., de-la Martínez Casa, J.M.: Identification of the optic nerve head with genetic algorithms. Artif. Intell. Med. **43**(3), 243–259 (2008). http://dx.doi.org/10.1016/j.artmed.2008.04.005
4. He, X.C., Yung, N.H.C.: Corner detector based on global and local curvature properties. Opt. Eng. **47**(5), 057008 (2008)
5. Fitzgibbon, A., Pilu, M., Fisher, R.B.: Direct least square fitting of ellipses. IEEE Trans. Pattern Anal. Mach. Intell. **21**(5), 476–480 (1999)
6. Fornaciari, M., Prati, A., Cucchiara, R.: A fast and effective ellipse detector for embedded vision applications. Pattern Recogn. **47**, 3693–3708 (2014)
7. Fornaciari, M.: Ellipse datasets. http://imagelab.ing.unimore.it/files/ellipse_data set.zip. Accessed 3 Apr 2015
8. Fornaciari, M.: Source Codes for Fornaciari. http://sourceforge.net/p/yaed/code/ HEAD/tree/. Accessed 3 April 2015
9. Kaewapichai, W., Kaewtrakulpong, P.: Robust ellipse detection by fitting randomly selected edge patches. World Acad. Sci. Eng. Technol. **24**, 30–33 (2008)
10. Kharma, N., Moghnieh, H., Yao, J., Guo, Y., Abu-Baker, A., Laganiere, J., Rouleau, G., Cheriet, M.: Automatic segmentation of cells from microscopic imagery using ellipse detection. IET Image Process. **1**(1), 39–47 (2007)
11. Kim, E., Haseyama, M., Kitajima, H.: Fast and robust ellipse extraction from complicated images. In: Proceedings of the IEEE International Conference on Information Technology and Applications (2002)
12. Lei, Y., Wong, K.C.: Ellipse detection based on symmetry. Pattern Recogn. Lett. **20**(1), 41–47 (1999)
13. Libuda, L., Grothues, I., Kraiss, K.F.: Ellipse detection in digital image data using geometric features. Adv. Comput. Graph. Comput. Vis. **4**, 229–239 (2007)
14. Libuda, L.: Source Codes for Libuda. http://ltilib.sourceforge.net. Accessed 3 April 2015
15. Lu, W., Tan, J.: Detection of incomplete ellipse in images with strong noise by iterative randomized hough transform (IRHT). Pattern Recogn. **41**(4), 1268–1279 (2008)
16. Martelli, S., Marzotto, R., Colombari, A., Murino, V.: FPGA-based robust ellipse estimation for circular road sign detection. In: 2010 IEEE Computer Society Conference on Computer Vision and Pattern Recognition Workshops (CVPRW), pp. 53–60, June 2010
17. McLaughlin, R.A.: Randomized hough transform: improved ellipse detection with comparison. Pattern Recogn. Lett. **19**, 299–305 (1998)

18. Nguyen, T.M., Ahuja, S., Wu, Q.M.J.: A real-time ellipse detection based on edge grouping. In: IEEE International Conference on Systems, Man and Cybernetics, pp. 3280–3286 (2009)
19. Nguyen, T.P., Kerautret, B.: Ellipse detection through decomposition of circular arcs and line segments. In: Proceedings of the 16th International Conference on Image Analysis and Processing: Part I, pp. 554–564 (2011)
20. Nurnberg, R.: Distance from a point to an ellipse. http://www2.imperial.ac.uk/rn/distance2ellipse.pdf. Accessed 3 April 2015
21. Prasad, D.K., Leung, M.K.H., Cho, S.Y.: Edge curvature and convexity based ellipse detection method. Pattern Recogn. **45**(9), 3204–3221 (2012)
22. Prasad, D.K.: Source Codes for Prasad. https://sites.google.com/site/dilipprasad/source-codes. Accessed 3 April 2015
23. Ramanujan, S.: Collected Papers of Srinivasa Ramanujan. Chelsea Publishing, New York (1962)
24. Song, G., Wang, H.: A fast and robust ellipse detection algorithm based on pseudo-random sample consensus. In: Kropatsch, W.G., Kampel, M., Hanbury, A. (eds.) CAIP 2007. LNCS, vol. 4673, pp. 669–676. Springer, Heidelberg (2007)
25. Taubin, G.: Estimation of planar curves, surfaces, and nonplanar space curves defined by implicit equations with applications to edge and range image segmentation. IEEE Trans. Pattern Anal. Mach. Intell. **13**(11), 1115–1138 (1991)
26. Teutsch, C., Berndt, D., Trostmann, E., Weber, M.: Real-time detection of elliptic shapes for automated object recognition and object tracking. Int. J. Cogn. Neurosci. **3**(1), 71–86 (2006)
27. Topal, C., Akinlar, C.: Edge drawing: a combined real-time edge and segment detector. J. Vis. Comun. Image Represent. **23**(6), 862–872 (2012). http://dx.doi.org/10.1016/j.jvcir.2012.05.004
28. Topal, C., zkan, K., Benligiray, B., Akinlar, C.: A robust CSS corner detector based on the turning angle curvature of image gradients. In: ICASSP, pp. 1444–1448. IEEE (2013). http://dblp.uni-trier.de/db/conf/icassp/icassp2013.html#TopalOBA13
29. Zhang, S.C., Liu, Z.Q.: A robust, real time ellipse detector. Pattern Recogn. **32**(2), 273–287 (2005)

# Branching Path Following for Graph Matching

Tao Wang[1,2(⊠)], Haibin Ling[1,3], Congyan Lang[2], and Jun Wu[2]

[1] Meitu HiScene Lab, HiScene Information Technologies, Shanghai, China
twang@bjtu.edu.cn
[2] School of Computer and Information Technology,
Beijing Jiaotong University, Beijing, China
{cylang,wuj}@bjtu.edu.cn
[3] Computer and Information Sciences Department,
Temple University, Philadelphia, USA
hbling@temple.edu

**Abstract.** Recently, graph matching algorithms utilizing the path following strategy have exhibited state-of-the-art performances. However, the paths computed in these algorithms often contain singular points, which usually hurt the matching performance. To deal with this issue, in this paper we propose a novel path following strategy, named *branching path following* (BPF), which consequently improves graph matching performance. In particular, we first propose a singular point detector by solving an KKT system, and then design a branch switching method to seek for better paths at singular points. Using BPF, a new graph matching algorithm named *BPF-G* is developed by applying BPF to a recently proposed path following algorithm named GNCCP (Liu &Qiao 2014). For evaluation, we compare BPF-G with several recently proposed graph matching algorithms on a synthetic dataset and four public benchmark datasets. Experimental results show that our approach achieves remarkable improvement in matching accuracy and outperforms other algorithms.

**Keywords:** Graph matching · Path following · Numerical continuation · Singular point · Branch switching

## 1 Introduction

Graph matching is a fundamental problem in computer science and closely relates to many computer vision problems including feature registration [1–3], shape matching [4–6], object recognition [7,8], visual tracking [9], activity analysis [10], etc. Despite decades of research effort devoted to graph matching, it remains a challenging problem due to the non-convexity in the objective function and the constraints over the solutions. A typical way is to utilize relaxation to harness the solution searching. Popular algorithms include, but not limited to, three categories: spectral relaxation [11–13], continuous optimization [14–18] and probabilistic modeling [19,20].

Among recently proposed graph matching algorithms, the ones utilizing the path-following strategy have exhibited state-of-the-art performances [15–18].

© Springer International Publishing AG 2016
B. Leibe et al. (Eds.): ECCV 2016, Part II, LNCS 9906, pp. 508–523, 2016.
DOI: 10.1007/978-3-319-46475-6_32

These *path following algorithms* reformulate graph matching as a *convex-concave relaxation procedure* (CCRP) problem, which is solved by interpolating between two simpler approximate formulations, and they use the *path following* strategy to recast iteratively the bistochastic matrix solution in the discrete domain. The path following algorithms can be viewed as special cases of the *numerical continuation method* (NCM) [21], which computes approximate solutions of parameterized nonlinear equation systems. These algorithms succeed at *regular points* but may fail at *singular points* (details in Sect. 4). It therefore demands research attention on how to address this issue to improve matching performance.

Motivated by above discussion, we propose a novel path following strategy, *branching path following* (BPF), to improve path following graph matching algorithms. In particular, BPF extends the traditional path following strategy by branching new paths at singular points. It first discovers singular points on the original path by determining the Jacobian of the associated KKT system, and then branches a new path at each singular point using the *pseudo-arclength continuation* method [22,23]. After searching along all branching paths, BPF chooses the best one in terms of the objective function as the final solution. Since the original path is always searched, BPF is guaranteed to achieve better or the same optimization solution, and thus the matching performance. Using the BPF strategy, we develop a new graph matching algorithm, named BPF-G, by applying BPF to the GNCCP (*graduated nonconvexity and concavity procedure*) algorithm [17]. Note that GNCCP is chosen since it is one of the latest path following algorithms, while BPF is by no means limited to working with GNCCP.

For a thorough evaluation, we test the proposed BPF-G algorithm on four popular benchmarks and a synthetic dataset. Experimental results show that, the proposed algorithm significantly improves the path following procedure and outperforms state-of-the-art graph matching algorithms in comparison.

In summary, our main contribution lies in the new path following strategy for graph matching, and the contribution is three-fold: (1) we discuss the pitfalls of path following algorithms at singular points, and propose an efficient singular point discovery method; (2) we design a novel branching path following strategy to bypass these pitfalls and thus improve matching performance; and (3) we develop a new graph matching algorithm by applying the proposed BPF strategy to the GNCCP algorithm, and demonstrate the effectiveness of the algorithm in a thorough evaluation.

## 2   Related Work

Graph matching has been investigated for decades and many algorithms have been invented, as summarized in [24,25]. In general, graph matching has a combinatorial nature that makes the global optimum solution hardly available. As a result, approximate solutions are commonly applied to graph matching. In this section we review studies that relate the most to ours, and leave general graph matching research to the surveys mentioned above. Some sampled latest studies include [26] that uses discrete methods in the linear approximation framework, and [27] that adapts discrete tabu search for graph matching.

A popular way to approximate graph matching is based on spectral relaxation with notable work by Leordeanu and Hebert [11], who model graph matching with spectral relaxation and propose an eigen-analysis solution. Later, the work is extended by Cour et al. [12] by first encoding affine constraints into the spectral decomposition and then applying bistochastic normalization. Cho et al. [13] reformulate graph matching as a vertex selection problem and introduce an affinity-preserving random walk algorithm. From a different perspective, Zass and Shashua [19] present a probabilistic framework for (hyper-)graph matching. The two lines somewhat merge in Egozi et al. [20], where a probabilistic view of the spectral relaxation scheme is presented.

Being inherently a discrete optimization problem, graph matching is often relaxed to continuous domain and many important algorithms have been designed on top of the relaxation. For example, Gold and Rangarajan [14] propose the graduated assignment algorithm to iteratively solve a series of linear approximations of the cost function using Taylor expansion. Leordeanu and Hebert [28] develop an integer projection algorithm to optimize the objective function in the integer domain. The studies that related most to ours are the so-called *path following* one. In particular, Zaslavskiy et al. [15] reformulate graph matching as a *convex-concave relaxation procedure* (CCRP) problem and then solve it by interpolating between simpler relaxed formulations. More specifically, the *path following* algorithm proposed by them iteratively searches a solution by tracing a path of local minima of a series of functions that linearly interpolate between the two relaxations. Later, Zhou and Torre [16] apply the similar strategy, and factorize an affinity matrix into a Kronecker product of smaller matrices, each of them encodes the structure of the graphs and the affinities between vertices and between edges. Liu and Qiao [17] propose the *graduated nonconvexity and concavity procedure* (GNCCP) to equivalently realize CCRP on partial permutation matrix, and GNCCP provides a much simpler way for CCRP without explicitly involving the convex or concave relaxation. Wang and Ling [29] propose a novel search strategy with adaptive path estimation to improve the computational efficiency of the path following algorithms.

Our work falls in the group using path following algorithms, but focuses on improving the path following strategy itself, which is not fully explored in previous studies. For this, we propose a novel *branching path following* (BPF) strategy, which is shown to effectively boost the graph matching performance as demonstrated in thorough evaluation (Sect. 6).

## 3    Path Following for Graph Matching

### 3.1    Problem Formulation

An undirected graph of $n$ vertices can be represented by $\mathbb{G} = (\mathbb{V}, \mathbb{E})$, where $\mathbb{V} = \{v_1, \ldots, v_n\}$ and $\mathbb{E} \subseteq \mathbb{V} \times \mathbb{V}$ denote the vertex and edge sets, respectively.

A graph is often conveniently represented by a symmetric adjacency matrix $A \in \mathbb{R}^{n \times n}$, such that $A_{ij} > 0$ if and only if there is an edge between $v_i$ and $v_j$.

For graph matching, given two graphs $\mathbb{G}^{(i)} = (\mathbb{V}^{(i)}, \mathbb{E}^{(i)})$ of size $n_i$, $i = 1, 2$, the problem is to find a vertex correspondence $X \in \{0, 1\}^{n_1 \times n_2}$ between $\mathbb{G}^{(1)}$ and $\mathbb{G}^{(2)}$ in favor of the following global consistency:

$$\mathcal{E}_1(X) = \sum_{i_1, i_2} c_{i_1 i_2} X_{i_1 i_2} + \sum_{i_1, i_2, j_1, j_2} d_{i_1 j_1 i_2 j_2} X_{i_1 i_2} X_{j_1 j_2}, \tag{1}$$

where $c_{i_1 i_2}$ measures the consistency between the $i_1$-th vertex in $\mathbb{G}^{(1)}$ and the $i_2$-th vertex in $\mathbb{G}^{(2)}$, and $d_{i_1 j_1 i_2 j_2}$ the consistency between edge $(i_1, j_1)$ in $\mathbb{G}^{(1)}$ and edge $(i_2, j_2)$ in $\mathbb{G}^{(2)}$. The correspondence matrix $X$ denotes matching result, i.e., $X_{i_1 i_2} = 1$ if and only if $v_{i_1} \in \mathbb{V}^{(1)}$ corresponds to $v_{i_2} \in \mathbb{V}^{(2)}$. In practice, the matching is often restricted to be one-to-one, which requires $X \mathbf{1}_{n_2} \leq \mathbf{1}_{n_1}$ and $X^\top \mathbf{1}_{n_1} \leq \mathbf{1}_{n_2}$, where $\mathbf{1}_n$ denotes a vector of $n$ ones.

Let $A^{(i)}$ be the adjacency matrix for $\mathbb{G}^{(i)}$, $i = 1, 2$, a more commonly used formulation for graph matching is defined as

$$\mathcal{E}_2(X) = \mathrm{tr}(C^\top X) + \alpha \|A^{(1)} - X A^{(2)} X^\top\|_F^2, \tag{2}$$

where $C = (c_{i_1 i_2}) \in \mathbb{R}^{n_1 \times n_2}$ is the vertex consistency matrix, $\alpha \geq 0$ the weight balancing between the vertex and edge comparisons, and $\|\cdot\|_F$ the Frobenius norm.

A more general formulation of Eq. (1) is formulated in a pairwise compatibility form

$$\mathcal{E}_3(\mathbf{x}) = \mathbf{x}^\top K \mathbf{x}, \tag{3}$$

where $\mathbf{x} \doteq \mathrm{vec}(X) \in \{0, 1\}^{n_1 n_2}$ is the vectorized version of matrix $X$ and $K \in \mathbb{R}^{n_1 n_2 \times n_1 n_2}$ is the corresponding affinity matrix defined as:

$$K_{\mathrm{ind}(i_1, i_2) \mathrm{ind}(j_1, j_2)} = \begin{cases} c_{i_1 i_2} & \text{if } i_1 = j_1 \text{ and } i_2 = j_2, \\ d_{i_1 j_1 i_2 j_2} & \text{if } A_{i_1 j_1}^{(1)} A_{i_2 j_2}^{(2)} > 0, \\ 0 & \text{otherwise.} \end{cases} \tag{4}$$

while $\mathrm{ind}(\cdot, \cdot)$ is a bijection mapping a vertex correspondence to an integer index.

In this paper, we mainly discuss and test graph matching algorithms for Eq. (3) since it encodes not only the difference of edge weight but also many complex graph compatibility functions.

## 3.2   The Path Following Algorithm

In [15], Zaslavskiy et al. introduce the *convex-concave relaxation procedure* (CCRP) into the graph matching problem by reformulating it as interpolation between two relaxed and simpler formulations. The first relaxation is obtained by expanding the convex quadratic function $\mathcal{E}_2(X)$ from the set of permutation matrices $\mathcal{P}$ to the set of doubly stochastic matrices $\mathcal{D}$. The second relaxation is a concave function

$$\min_{X \in \mathcal{D}} \mathcal{E}_4(X) = -\mathrm{tr}(\Delta X) - 2\mathrm{vec}(X)^\top \big((L^{(1)})^\top \otimes (L^{(2)})^\top\big) \mathrm{vec}(X), \tag{5}$$

where $\Delta$ is a matrix with element $\Delta_{ij} = \left( D_{ii}^{(1)} - D_{jj}^{(2)} \right)^2$; $D^{(i)}$ and $L^{(i)}$ represent respectively the diagonal degree matrix and the Laplacian matrix of an adjacency matrix $A^{(i)}$, $i = 1, 2$; and $\otimes$ denotes the Kronecker product. A key property is that the optimum solution of $\mathcal{E}_4(X)$ over $\mathcal{P}$ is the solution of the original graph matching problem.

The *path following* strategy proposed in [15] can be interpreted as an iterative procedure that smoothly projects an initial solution of $\mathcal{E}_2$ in the continuous space $\mathcal{D}$ to the discrete space $\mathcal{P}$ by tracking a path of local minima of a series of functionals $\mathcal{E}_\lambda$ over $\mathcal{D}$

$$\mathcal{E}_\lambda = (1 - \lambda)\mathcal{E}_2 + \lambda \mathcal{E}_4, \tag{6}$$

for $0 \leq \lambda \leq 1$. Each local minimum of $\mathcal{E}_{\lambda + d_\lambda}$ is gained by the Frank-Wolfe algorithm [30] given the local minimum of $\mathcal{E}_\lambda$ as the start point. Increasing $\lambda$ from 0 to 1, this approach searches toward a local minimum of $\mathcal{E}_4$ from the unique local minimum of $\mathcal{E}_2$, and takes it as the final solution. For more details about the path following algorithm please see the literature [15].

Recently, Liu and Qiao [17] proposed the *graduated nonconvexity and concavity procedure* (GNCCP) to equivalently realize CCRP on partial permutation matrix without explicitly involving the convex or concave relaxation. As the latest work following the path following strategy, GNCCP provides a general optimization framework for the combinatorial optimization problems defined on the set of partial permutation matrices. In Sect. 5.3, we improve GNCCP by integrating the proposed branching path following strategy.

# 4    Numerical Continuation Method Interpretation

In this section, we interpret the path following algorithms in a numerical continuation view, and then discuss their pitfalls due singular points. The discussion will guide the subsequent extension on these algorithms.

## 4.1    KKT System

According to the path following strategy described above and by converting $\mathcal{D}$ into constraints, we need to solve a series of optimization problems with equality and inequality constraints parameterized by $\lambda$:

$$\mathbf{x}^* = \arg \max_{\mathbf{x}} \mathcal{E}_\lambda(\mathbf{x}),$$
$$\text{s.t.} \quad \begin{cases} B\mathbf{x} = \mathbf{1}_{2n}, \\ \mathbf{x} \geq \mathbf{0}_{n^2}. \end{cases} \tag{7}$$

where $B\mathbf{x} = \mathbf{1}_{2n}$ encodes the one-to-one matching constraints ($B \in \mathbb{R}^{2n \times n^2}$).

Using Lagrange multipliers $\alpha_i$ and KKT multipliers $\mu_i$, the above constrained problem can be converted to the following unconstrained one

$$\mathbf{x}^* = \arg \max_{\mathbf{x}} \left( \mathcal{E}_\lambda(\mathbf{x}) + \sum_{i=1}^{2n} \alpha_i h_i(\mathbf{x}) - \sum_{i=1}^{n^2} \mu_i g_i(\mathbf{x}) \right), \tag{8}$$

$$\text{where} \quad \begin{cases} h_i(\mathbf{x}) = B(i,:)\mathbf{x} - 1, \\ g_i(\mathbf{x}) = -\mathbf{x}_i. \end{cases} \tag{9}$$

This results in the following system of Karush-Kuhn-Tucker (KKT) equations [31]:

$$\begin{cases} \nabla \mathcal{E}_\lambda(\mathbf{x}) + B^\top \alpha + \mu = \mathbf{0}_{n^2}, \\ h_i(\mathbf{x}) = 0, \quad 1 \le i \le 2n, \\ \mu_i g_i(\mathbf{x}) = 0, \quad 1 \le i \le n^2, \\ \mu_i \ge 0, \quad 1 \le i \le n^2. \end{cases} \tag{10}$$

In the next subsection we formulate the KKT system as a constrained nonlinear system $F(\lambda, \mathbf{x}, \alpha, \mu) = \mathbf{0}, \text{s.t. } \mu \ge \mathbf{0}$.

## 4.2 Numerical Continuation Method

The existing path following algorithms (PATH [15], FGM [16], GNCCP [17]) can be viewed as special cases of the *numerical continuation method* (NCM) [21]. In general, NCM computes approximate solutions of parameterized nonlinear equation systems, and it estimates curves given in the following implicit form:

$$F(\lambda, u) = \mathbf{0}_m, \text{where } F \text{ is a mapping: } \mathbb{R}^{m+1} \to \mathbb{R}^m. \tag{11}$$

This method works as well in the presence of constraints on any or all of the variables [32,33]. In particular, for graph matching, we have $u = [\mathbf{x}^\top, \alpha^\top, \mu^\top]^\top$ and $m = 2n^2 + 2n$.

Most solutions of nonlinear equation systems are iterative methods. For a particular parameter value $\lambda_0$, a mapping is repeatedly applied to an initial guess $u_0$. In fact, the existing PATH, FGM and GNCCP algorithms correspond to a particular implementation of the so-called *generic predictor corrector* (GPC) approach [21]. The solution at a specific $\lambda$ is used as the initial guess for the solution at $\lambda + \Delta\lambda$. With $\Delta\lambda$ sufficiently small the iteration applied to the initial guess converges [21].

## 4.3 Pitfalls at Singular Points

A *solution component* $\Gamma(\lambda_0, u_0)$ of the nonlinear system $F$ is a set of points $(\lambda, u)$ such that $F(\lambda, u) = 0$ and these points are connected to the initial solution $(\lambda_0, u_0)$ by a path of solutions. A *regular point* of $F$ is a point $(\lambda, u)$ at which the Jacobian of $F$ is of full rank, while a *singular point* of $F$ is a point $(\lambda, u)$ at which the Jacobian of $F$ is rank deficient. As discussed in [23], near a regular point the solution component is an isolated curve passing through the regular point. By contrast, for a singular point, there may be multiple curves passing through it. The local structure of a point in $\Gamma$ is determined by high-order derivatives of $F$.

An advantage of the GPC approach is that it uses the solution for the original problem as a black box where all that required is an initial solution. However, this approach may fail at singular points, where the branch of solutions turns around [23]. In general, solution components $\Gamma$ of a nonlinear system are branching curves where the branching points are singular [34]. Therefore, for problems with singular points, more sophisticated handling is desired.

## 5  Branching Path Following

In this section, we propose the *branching path following* (BPF) strategy that branches new curves at singular points toward potentially better matching results. BPF contains two main steps: singular point discovery and branch switching, as described in the following subsections. In the last subsection, we apply BPF to GNCCP to develop a new graph matching algorithm.

### 5.1  Singular Points Discovery

The first step in BPF is to discover singular points. Theoretically, these points can be detected by checking whether the Jacobian of $F$ is of full rank. However, it is impractical to check discrete samples by sampling $\lambda_i$, since these samples are rarely able to cover the exact singular points.

Denote $J_\lambda$ the Jacobian of $F$ parameterized by $\lambda$. A singular point $(\lambda, u)$ should have $|J_\lambda| = 0$. A reasonable assumption is that the curve formed by $(\lambda, |J_\lambda|)$ over $\lambda$ is continuous. This implies there is at least one singular point between two points $(\lambda_1, u_1)$ and $(\lambda_2, u_2)$ if $|J_{\lambda_1}|$ and $|J_{\lambda_2}|$ have different signs.

Thus inspired, we design a simple yet effective way for singular point discovery by checking the signs of determinants of Jacobian on consecutive sampled points. Specifically, denote $(\lambda_t, u_t)$ the point at iteration $t$ in the path, we mark $(\lambda_t, u_t)$ as a singular point if $|J_{\lambda_t}||J_{\lambda_{t+1}}| \leq 0$.

It is computationally expensive to decide determinants of large Jacobian matrices. Since we are only interested in the signs of these Jacobian matrices, we develop an efficient solution that first decompose the Jacobian matrices using the LU decomposition and then accumulate the signs of the diagonal elements of decomposed matrices.

### 5.2  Branch Switching

Finding the solution curves passing a singular point is called branch switching. Once a singular point $(\lambda_t, u_t)$ is discovered, we branch a new curve using the *pseudo-arclength continuation* (PAC) algorithm [22,23].

PAC is based on the observation that an ideal parameterization of a curve is through arclength $s$. With the parameterization, we extend equations in (10) to the following form

$$G(\lambda, u) = \left\{ \begin{matrix} F(\lambda, u) \\ N(\lambda, u, s) \end{matrix} \right\} = \left\{ \begin{matrix} 0 \\ 0 \end{matrix} \right\}, \tag{12}$$

where the normalization equation $N(.) = 0$ approximates the statement that $s$ represents arclength. Denote $(\dot{\lambda}, \dot{u})$ the tangent vector at point $(\lambda_t, u_t)$, we have

$$N(\lambda, u, s) = \dot{u}^\top (u - u_t) + \dot{\lambda}^\top (\lambda - \lambda_t) - s = 0. \tag{13}$$

According to the implicit function theorem [35], the tangent vector $(\dot{\lambda}, \dot{u})$ can be computed as

$$(\dot{\lambda}, \dot{u}) = \left( \Delta\lambda, \Delta\lambda \frac{\partial u}{\partial \lambda}(\lambda_t, u_t) \right) = \left( \Delta\lambda, \Delta\lambda (F_u(\lambda_t, u_t))^{-1} F_\lambda(\lambda_t, u_t) \right). \tag{14}$$

However, it is inapplicable to the bifurcation point and is computationally expensive. We therefore propose approximation of the tangent vector using previous points for computational efficiency. The tangent vector at a previous iteration $i$ ($i < t$) is approximated as $(\Delta\lambda, u_{i+1} - u_i)$, and the tangent vector $(\dot{\lambda}, \dot{u})$ at $t$ be estimated as

$$(\dot{\lambda}, \dot{u}) = \left(\Delta\lambda, \frac{\sum_{i=1}^{k}(k - i + 1)(u_{t-i+1} - u_{t-i})}{\sum_{i=1}^{k} i}\right), \tag{15}$$

where $k$ controls the size of the window used for approximation. The motivation behind this approximation is the smoothness of the path, which implies the similarity between tangent vectors of consecutive iterations.

The Jacobian of the pseudo-arclength system is the bordered matrix $\begin{bmatrix} F_u & F_\lambda \\ \dot{u} & \dot{\lambda} \end{bmatrix}$.

Appending the tangent vector as the last row can be seen as determining the coefficient of the null vector in the general solution of the Newton system [36] (particular solution plus an arbitrary multiple of the null vector).

Finally, we solve Eq. (12) using the *trust-region-reflective* algorithm [37], and then branch a new curve using the solution $(\lambda^*, u^*)$ as the initial solution.

### 5.3  Applying BPF to GNCCP

Now we apply the BPF strategy to GNCCP [17] to develop our new graph matching algorithm named BPF-G.

Note that, in both steps of singular point discovery and branch switching, we need to compute the Jacobian of $F$ in advance, which includes a parameter-dependent sub-matrix, the Jacobian of $\nabla\mathcal{E}_\lambda(\mathbf{x})$ (denoted as $J(\lambda, \mathbf{x})$). In GNCCP

$$\mathcal{E}_\lambda(\mathbf{x}) = \begin{cases} (1 - \lambda)\mathbf{x}^\top K\mathbf{x} + \lambda\mathrm{tr}(\mathbf{x}^\top\mathbf{x}), & \text{if } \lambda \geq 0, \\ (1 + \lambda)\mathbf{x}^\top K\mathbf{x} + \lambda\mathrm{tr}(\mathbf{x}^\top\mathbf{x}), & \text{if } \lambda < 0. \end{cases} \tag{16}$$

Applying BPF here, we have

$$J(\lambda, \mathbf{x}) = \begin{cases} (1 - \lambda)(K^T + K) + 2\lambda\mathbf{I}, & \text{if } \lambda \geq 0, \\ (1 + \lambda)(K^T + K) + 2\lambda\mathbf{I}, & \text{if } \lambda < 0. \end{cases} \tag{17}$$

The pseudo-code of BPF-G is shown in Algorithm 1. Note that, since the solution of the original algorithm is always in set $T$, the new algorithm is guaranteed to achieve the same or better solution in terms of objectives.

The computational complexity of GNCCP is $O(n^3)$ [17], where $n$ is the vertex number of the graph. Thus, the computational complexity of our algorithm is $O(kn^3)$, where $k$ is the number of explored additional branches. As a result, the complexity of the proposed algorithm roughly equals to $O(n^3)$ because $k$ is a small bounded integer.

---

**Algorithm 1.** Branching Path Following.

---

{$T$ is the set of candidate solutions (end points of branching paths).}
Compute path $P$ by GNCCP.
Push the end point of $P$ into set $T$.
Discover the set of singular points $S$ from $P$.
**for** each point $(\lambda, \mathbf{x})$ in $S$ **do**
    Compute the solution $(\lambda^*, u^*)$ of Eq. (12).
    Compute the new path $P^*$ using $(\lambda^*, u^*)$ as initial point.
    Push the end point of $P^*$ int set $T$.
**end for**
Select the best solution from $T$ in terms of objectives.

---

## 6    Experiments

We compare the proposed BPF-G algorithm with four state-of-the-art graph matching algorithms including GNCCP [17], IPFP [28], RRWM [13] and PSM [20], and report experimental results on a synthetic dataset and four benchmark datasets. Two indicators, matching accuracy and objective ratio, are used to evaluate algorithms. Specifically, denote $f_i$ the objective achieved by the $i$-th algorithm $g_i$, the objective ratio $r_i$ of $g_i$ is computed as $r_i = f_i / \max_k f_k$.

### 6.1    Synthetic Dataset

We first perform a comparative evaluation of the algorithms on graphs randomly synthesized following the experimental protocol in [13]. For each trial, we construct two graphs, $\mathbb{G}^{(1)}$ and $\mathbb{G}^{(2)}$, with 20 inlier nodes and later add $n_{out}$ outlier nodes to both graphs. The edges between nodes are randomly generated with respect to an edge density parameter $\rho$. Each edge $(i, j)$ in the first graph $\mathbb{G}^{(1)}$ is assigned with a random edge weight $A_{ij}^{(1)}$ distributed uniformly in [0,1], and $A_{ab}^{(2)} = A_{ij}^{(1)} + \epsilon$ the edge weight of the corresponding edge $(a, b)$ in $\mathbb{G}^{(2)}$ is perturbed by adding a random Gaussian noise $\epsilon \sim \mathcal{N}(0, \sigma^2)$. The edge affinity is computed as $K_{\mathrm{ind}(i,a)\mathrm{ind}(j,b)} = \exp\left(-(A_{ij}^{(1)} - A_{ab}^{(2)})^2/0.15\right)$ and the node affinity is set to zero.

We compare the performance of the algorithms under three different settings by varying the number of outliers $n_{out}$, edge density $\rho$ and edge noise $\sigma$, respectively. For each setting, we construct 100 different pairs of graphs and evaluate the average matching accuracy and objective ratio. In the first setting (Fig. 1(a)), we fix edge density $\rho = 0.5$ and edge noise $\sigma = 0$, and increase the number of outliers $n_{out}$ from 0 to 10. In the second setting (Fig. 1(b)), we change the edge noise parameter $\sigma$ from 0 to 0.2 while fixing $n_{out} = 0$ and $\rho = 0.5$. In the last case (Fig. 1(c)), the edge density $\rho$ ranges from 0.3 to 1, and the other two parameters are fixed as $n_{out} = 0$ and $\sigma = 0.1$.

It can be observed that in almost all of cases under varying parameters, our approach achieves the best performance in terms of both objective ratio and

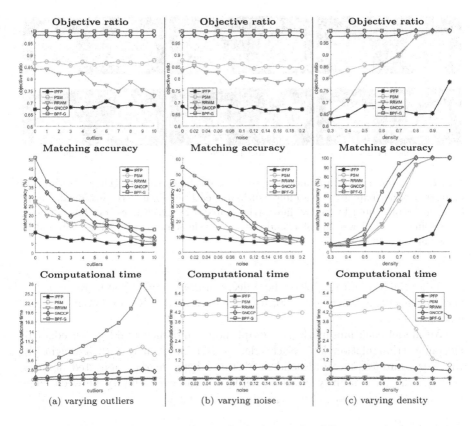

**Fig. 1.** Evaluation on the synthetic dataset by different settings.

matching accuracy. From Fig. 1(c), the PSM, RRWM and GNCCP algorithms are comparable to our approach when the graphs are close to full connections (the density parameter $\rho$ near to 1). All algorithms fail to achieve reasonable solutions when graph pairs present extreme deformation or sparsity. The comparison on the running time is also provided in Fig. 1. Our approach spends several times of running time comparing to the GNCCP algorithm of which the multiple depends on the number of explored additional branches.

## 6.2    CMU House Dataset

The CMU house dataset includes 111 frames of image sequences, where all sequences contain the same house object with transformation cross sequence gaps. In order to assess the matching accuracy, following [2,38], 30 landmarks were manually tracked and labeled across all frames. We matched all possible image pairs, in total 560 pairs gapped by 10, 20, ..., 100 frames, where increasing sampling gaps implies the increase of deformation degree. To evaluate graph matching algorithms against noise, we use two different settings of nodes

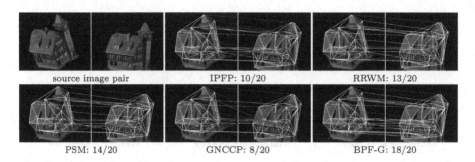

**Fig. 2.** An example of graph matching on the CMU house dataset. The algorithm, the number of true matches per ground truths for each subfigure are captioned. Graph edges are represented by yellow lines, true matches by green lines and false matches by red lines (best viewed in color, and the same style is also used for Figs. 5, 6 and 7). (Color figure online)

$(n_1, n_2) =(30,30)$ and $(20, 30)$, where decreasing $n_1$ implies the increase of outlier. In the setting where $n_1 < 30$, $n_1$ points are randomly chosen out of the 30 landmark points.

We model each landmark as a graph node, and then build graph edges by Delaunay triangulation [39]. Each edge $(i, j)$ is associated with a weight $A_{ij}$ which is computed as the Euclidean distance between the connected nodes $v_i$ and $v_j$. The node affinity is set to zero, and the edge affinity between edges $(i, j)$ in $\mathbb{G}^{(1)}$ and $(a, b)$ in $\mathbb{G}^{(2)}$ is computed as $K_{\text{ind}(i,a)\text{ind}(j,b)} = \exp(-(A_{ij}^{(1)} - A_{ab}^{(2)})^2/2500)$.

Figure 2 presents an example for graph matching with 10 outliers and significant deformation. Figure 3 shows the performance curves for $n_1 = 30$ and

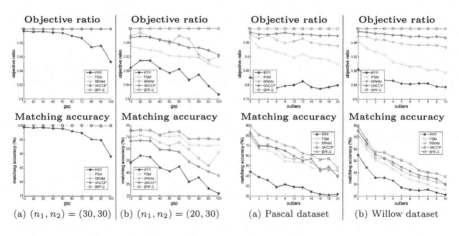

**Fig. 3.** Comparison of graph matching on the CMU house dataset.

**Fig. 4.** Evaluation on (a) the Pascal dataset, and (b) the Willow dataset.

20 with respect to variant sequence gaps. All algorithms except IPFP achieve perfect matching when no outliers existing ($n_1 = 30$). When we increase the number of outliers to 10 ($n_1 = 20$), our approach gains remarkable improvement in both accuracy and objective compared with the original GNCCP algorithm. It is interesting to see that PSM gains comparable matching accuracy to our approach with certain sequence gaps but achieves lower objectives.

### 6.3 Pascal Dataset

The Pascal dataset [40] consists of 30 pairs of car images and 20 pairs of motorbike images selected from Pascal 2007. The authors provide detected feature points and manually labeled ground-truth correspondences for each pair of images. To evaluate the performance of each algorithm against noise, we randomly select $0 \sim 20$ outlier nodes from the background.

For each node $v_i$, we associate it with a feature $p_i$ which is computed as its orientation of the normal vector at that point to the contour where the point was sampled. The node affinity between nodes $v_i$ and $v_j$ is consequently computed as $\exp(-|p_i - p_j|)$. We use Delaunay triangulation to build graph edges, and associate each edge $(i, j)$ with two features $d_{ij}$ and $\theta_{ij}$, where $d_{ij}$ is the pairwise distance between the connected nodes $v_i$ and $v_j$, and $\theta_{ij}$ is the absolute angle between the edge and the horizontal line. Consequently, the edge affinity between edges $(i, j)$ in $\mathbb{G}^{(1)}$ and $(a, b)$ in $\mathbb{G}^{(2)}$ is computed as $K_{\text{ind}(i,a)\text{ind}(j,b)} = \exp(-(|d_{ij} - d_{ab}| + |\theta_{ij} - \theta_{ab}|)/2)$.

Figure 5 presents an example for graph matching of motorbike images (with 10 outliers). The matching accuracy and objective ratio of each algorithm with respect to the outlier number was summarized in Fig. 4(a). It can be observed that our approach outperforms other algorithms remarkably in both matching accuracy and objective ratio. In the case when no outliers exist, our method achieves near 90 % matching rate which is much higher than other ones.

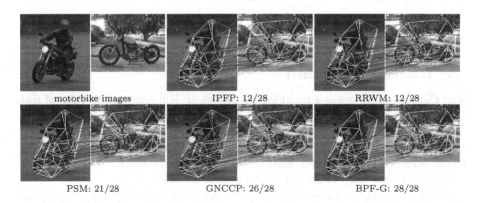

|  motorbike images   |   IPFP: 12/28   |   RRWM: 12/28   |
|  PSM: 21/28  |  GNCCP: 26/28  |  BPF-G: 28/28  |

**Fig. 5.** A matching example of motorbike images in the Pascal dataset.

## 6.4    Willow Object Dataset

In this experiment, we create 500 pairs of images using Willow object class dataset [41]. This dataset provides images of five classes, namely car, duck, face, motorbike and winebottle. Each class contains at least 40 images with different instances and 10 distinctive landmarks were manually labeled on the target object across all images in each class. We randomly select 100 pairs of images from each class respectively.

We use Hessian detector [42] to extract interesting points and SIFT descriptor [43] to represent the node attributes. To test the performance against noise, we randomly select $0 \sim 10$ outlier nodes from the background. We utilize the Delaunay triangulation to connect nodes and compute the affinity between nodes via their appearance similarity. Edge affinity is computed following the method used in Sect. 6.3.

Figure 6 shows a representative example for graph matching selected from the duck class (with 10 outliers). The comparison on matching accuracy and objective ratio of each algorithm is summarized in Fig. 4(b). Our approach achieves remarkable improvement compared with GNCCP and outperforms other algorithms.

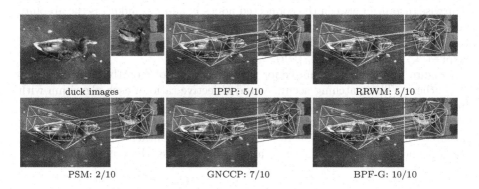

**Fig. 6.** A matching example of duck images on the Willow dataset.

## 6.5    Caltech Image Dataset

The Caltech image dataset provided by Cho et al. [13] contains 30 pairs of real images. The authors provide detected MSER keypoints [44], initial matches, affinity matrix, and manually labeled ground-truth correspondences for each image pair. In [13], the low-quality candidate matches are filtered out according to the distance between SIFT features [43]. The affinity matrix is consequently computed by the mutual projection error function [45].

Figure 7 shows a representative example for graph matching with significant deformation and plenty of repeated patterns. The matching accuracy and objective ratio of each algorithm was summarized in Table 1. Our approach gains remarkable improvement compared with the original GNCCP algorithm in both

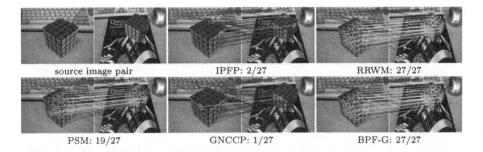

Fig. 7. A matching example on the Caltech dataset.

**Table 1.** Comparison of graph matching on the Caltech dataset (The top 1 result is indicated in red and top 2 in **blue**).

| Algorithm | IPFP [28] | RRWM [13] | PSM [20] | GNCCP [17] | BPF-G (ours) |
|---|---|---|---|---|---|
| Objective ratio | 0.91 | 0.88 | 0.75 | **0.92** | 1 |
| Accuracy(%) | 68.83 | 75.49 | 66.26 | 68.72 | **73.56** |

matching accuracy and objective ratio. It is interesting to see that RRWM performs better in terms of accuracy, whereas our approach obtains much higher objectives.

# 7    Conclusion

In this paper, we proposed a novel branching path following strategy for graph matching aiming to improve the matching performance. To avoid the pitfalls at singular points in the original path following strategy, our new strategy first discovers singular points and subsequently branches new paths from them seeking for potentially better solutions. We integrated the strategy into a state-of-the-art graph matching algorithm that utilizes the original path following strategy. Experimental results reveal that, our approach gains remarkable improvement on matching performance compared to the original algorithm, and also outperforms other state-of-the-art algorithms.

**Acknowledgments.** This work is supported by the National Nature Science Foundation of China (nos. 61300071, 61272352, 61472028, and 61301185), the National Key Research and Development Plan under Grant(No.2016YFB1001200), Beijing Natural Science Foundation (nos. 4142045 and 4162048), the Fundamental Research Funds for the Central Universities (no. 2015JBM029), and in part by the US National Science Foundation under Grants 1407156 and 1350521.

# References

1. Serradell, E., Pinheiro, M.A., Sznitman, R., Kybic, J., Moreno-Noguer, F., Fua, P.: Non-rigid graph registration using active testing search. PAMI **37**(3), 625–638 (2015)
2. Torresani, L., Kolmogorov, V., Rother, C.: Feature correspondence via graph matching: models and global optimization. In: Forsyth, D., Torr, P., Zisserman, A. (eds.) ECCV 2008, Part II. LNCS, vol. 5303, pp. 596–609. Springer, Heidelberg (2008)
3. Wang, J., Li, S.: Query-driven iterated neighborhood graph search for large scale indexing. In: ACM MM, pp. 179–188 (2012)
4. Bai, X., Yang, X., Latecki, L.J., Liu, W., Tu, Z.: Learning context-sensitive shape similarity by graph transduction. PAMI **32**(5), 861–874 (2010)
5. Michel, D., Oikonomidis, I., Argyros, A.A.: Scale invariant and deformation tolerant partial shape matching. Image Vis. Comput. **29**(7), 459–469 (2011)
6. Wang, T., Ling, H., Lang, C., Feng, S.: Symmetry-aware graph matching. Pattern Recogn. **60**, 657–668 (2016)
7. Duchenne, O., Joulin, A., Ponce, J.: A graph-matching kernel for object categorization. In: ICCV, pp. 1792–1799 (2011)
8. Wu, J., Shen, H., Li, Y., Xiao, Z., Lu, M., Wang, C.: Learning a hybrid similarity measure for image retrieval. Pattern Recogn. **46**(11), 2927–2939 (2013)
9. Cai, Z., Wen, L., Lei, Z., Vasconcelos, N., Li, S.Z.: Robust deformable and occluded object tracking with dynamic graph. TIP **23**(12), 5497–5509 (2014)
10. Chen, C.Y., Grauman, K.: Efficient activity detection with max-subgraph search. In: CVPR, pp. 1274–1281 (2012)
11. Leordeanu, M., Hebert, M.: A spectral technique for correspondence problems using pairwise constraints. In: ICCV, pp. 1482–1489 (2005)
12. Cour, T., Srinivasan, P., Shi, J.: Balanced graph matching. NIPS **19**, 313–320 (2007)
13. Cho, M., Lee, J., Lee, K.M.: Reweighted random walk for graph matching. In: ECCV, pp. 492–505 (2010)
14. Gold, S., Rangarajan, A.: A graduated assignment algorithm for graph matching. PAMI **18**(4), 377–388 (1996)
15. Zaslavskiy, M., Bach, F., Vert, J.P.: A path following algorithm for the graph matching problem. PAMI **31**(12), 2227–2242 (2009)
16. Zhou, F., De la Torre, F.: Factorized graph matching. In: CVPR, pp. 127–134 (2012)
17. Liu, Z., Qiao, H.: GNCCP - graduated nonconvexity and concavity procedure. PAMI **36**(6), 1258–1267 (2014)
18. Liu, Z., Qiao, H., Yang, X., Hoi, S.C.H.: Graph matching by simplified convex-concave relaxation procedure. IJCV **109**(3), 169–186 (2014)
19. Zass, R., Shashua, A.: Probabilistic graph and hypergraph matching. In: CVPR, pp. 1–8 (2008)
20. Egozi, A., Keller, Y., Guterman, H.: A probabilistic approach to spectral graph matching. PAMI **35**(1), 18–27 (2013)
21. Allgower, E.L., Georg, K.: Numerical Continuation Methods. Springer, Heidelberg (1990)
22. Keller, H.B.: Lectures on Numerical Methods in Bifurcation Theory. Tata Institute of Fundamental Research Lectures on Mathematics and Physics, vol. 79. Springer, Berlin (1987)

23. Dickson, K.I., Kelley, C.T., Ipsen, I.C.F., Kevrekidis, I.G.: Condition estimates for pseudo-arclength continuation. SIAM J. Numer. Anal. **45**(1), 263–276 (2007)
24. Conte, D., Foggia, P., Sansone, C., Vento, M.: Thirty years of graph matching in pattern recognition. Int. J. Pattern Recogn. Artif. Intell. **18**(3), 265–298 (2004)
25. Foggia, P., Percannella, G., Vento, M.: Graph matching and learning in pattern recognition in the last 10 years. Int. J. Pattern Recogn. Artif. Intell. **28**(1), 1–40 (2014)
26. Yan, J., Zhang, C., Zha, H., Liu, W., Yang, X., Chu, S.M.: Discrete hyper-graph matching. In: CVPR, pp. 1520–1528 (2015)
27. Adamczewski, K., Suh, Y., Lee, K.M.: Discrete tabu search for graph matching. In: ICCV, pp. 109–117 (2015)
28. Leordeanu, M., Hebert, M.: An integer projected fixed point method for graph matching and map inference. In: NIPS (2009)
29. Wang, T., Ling, H.: Path following with adaptive path estimation for graph matching. In: AAAI, pp. 3625–3631 (2016)
30. Frank, M., Wolfe, P.: An algorithm for quadratic programming. Nav. Res. Logistics Q. **3**, 95–100 (1956)
31. Kuhn, H.W., Tucker, A.W.: Nonlinear programming. In: Proceedings of 2nd Berkeley Symposium, pp. 481–492 (1951)
32. Shacham, M.: Numerical solution of constrained nonlinear algebraic equations. Int. J. Numer. Methods Eng. **23**, 1455–1481 (1986)
33. Dankowicz, H., Schilder, F.: An extended continuation problem for bifurcation analysis in the presence of constraints. J. Comput. Nonlinear Dyn. **6**(3), 1–14 (2010)
34. Crisfield, M.A.: Non-linear Finite Element Analysis Solids and Structure. Wiley, Hoboken (1996)
35. Kudryavtsev, L.: Implicit Function. Encyclopedia of Mathematics. Springer, Heidelberg (2001)
36. Deuflhard, P.: Newton Methods for Nonlinear Problems - Affine Invariance and Adaptive Algorithms. Series Computational Mathematics, vol. 35. Springer, Heidelberg (2006)
37. Branch, M.A., Coleman, T.F., Li, Y.: A subspace, interior and conjugate gradient method for large-scale bound-constrained minimization problems. SIAM J. Sci. Comput. **21**(1), 1–23 (1999)
38. Caetano, T.S., Caelli, T., Schuurmans, D., Barone, D.A.: Graphical models and point pattern matching. PAMI **28**(10), 1646–1663 (2006)
39. Lee, D.T., Schachter, B.J.: Two algorithms for constructing a delaunay triangulation. Int. J. Comput. Inf. Sci. **9**, 219–242 (1980)
40. Leordeanu, M., Sukthankar, R., Hebert, M.: Unsupervised learning for graph matching. IJCV **96**(1), 28–45 (2012)
41. Cho, M., Alahari, K., Ponce, J.: Learning graphs to match. In: ICCV, pp. 25–32 (2013)
42. Mikolajczyk, K., Schmid, C.: An affine invariant interest point detector. In: Heyden, A., Sparr, G., Nielsen, M., Johansen, P. (eds.) ECCV 2002, Part I. LNCS, vol. 2350, pp. 128–142. Springer, Heidelberg (2002)
43. Lowe, D.G.: Distinctive image features from scale-invariant keypoints. IJCV **60**(2), 91–110 (2004)
44. Donoser, M., Bischof, H.: Efficient maximally stable extremal region (MSER) tracking. In: CVPR, pp. 553–560 (2006)
45. Cho, M., Lee, J., Lee, K.M.: Feature correspondence and deformable object matching via agglomerative correspondence clustering. In: ICCV, pp. 1280–1287 (2009)

# Higher Order Conditional Random Fields in Deep Neural Networks

Anurag Arnab$^{(\boxtimes)}$, Sadeep Jayasumana, Shuai Zheng, and Philip H.S. Torr

University of Oxford, Oxford, UK
{anurag.arnab,sadeep.jayasumana,shuai.zheng,philip.torr}@eng.ox.ac.uk

**Abstract.** We address the problem of semantic segmentation using deep learning. Most segmentation systems include a Conditional Random Field (CRF) to produce a structured output that is consistent with the image's visual features. Recent deep learning approaches have incorporated CRFs into Convolutional Neural Networks (CNNs), with some even training the CRF end-to-end with the rest of the network. However, these approaches have not employed higher order potentials, which have previously been shown to significantly improve segmentation performance. In this paper, we demonstrate that two types of higher order potential, based on object detections and superpixels, can be included in a CRF embedded within a deep network. We design these higher order potentials to allow inference with the differentiable mean field algorithm. As a result, all the parameters of our richer CRF model can be learned end-to-end with our pixelwise CNN classifier. We achieve state-of-the-art segmentation performance on the PASCAL VOC benchmark with these trainable higher order potentials.

**Keywords:** Semantic segmentation · Conditional random fields · Deep learning · Convolutional Neural Networks

## 1 Introduction

Semantic segmentation involves assigning a visual object class label to every pixel in an image, resulting in a segmentation with a semantic meaning for each segment. While a strong pixel-level classifier is critical for obtaining high accuracy in this task, it is also important to enforce the consistency of the semantic segmentation output with visual features of the image. For example, segmentation boundaries should usually coincide with strong edges in the image, and regions in the image with similar appearance should have the same label.

Recent advances in deep learning have enabled researchers to create stronger classifiers, with automatically learned features, within a Convolutional Neural Network (CNN) [1–3]. This has resulted in large improvements in semantic segmentation accuracy on widely used benchmarks such as PASCAL VOC [4]. CNN

**Electronic supplementary material** The online version of this chapter (doi:10.1007/978-3-319-46475-6_33) contains supplementary material, which is available to authorized users.

© Springer International Publishing AG 2016
B. Leibe et al. (Eds.): ECCV 2016, Part II, LNCS 9906, pp. 524–540, 2016.
DOI: 10.1007/978-3-319-46475-6_33

classifiers are now considered the standard choice for pixel-level classifiers used in semantic segmentation.

On the other hand, probabilistic graphical models have long been popular for structured prediction of labels, with constraints enforcing label consistency. Conditional Random Fields (CRFs) have been the most common framework, and various rich and expressive models [5–7], based on higher order clique potentials, have been developed to improve segmentation performance.

Whilst some deep learning methods showed impressive performance in semantic segmentation without incorporating graphical models [3,8], current state-of-the-art methods [9–12] have all incorporated graphical models into the deep learning framework in some form. However, we observe that the CRFs that have been incorporated into deep learning techniques are still rather rudimentary as they consist of only unary and pairwise potentials [10]. In this paper, we show that CRFs with carefully designed higher order potentials (potentials defined over cliques consisting of more than two nodes) can also be modelled as CNN layers when using mean field inference [13]. The advantage of performing CRF inference within a CNN is that it enables joint optimisation of CNN classifier weights and CRF parameters during the end-to-end training of the complete system. Intuitively, the classifier and the graphical model learn to optimally co-operate with each other during the joint training.

We introduce two types of higher order potential into the CRF embedded in our deep network: object-detection based potentials and superpixel-based potentials. The primary idea of using object-detection potentials is to use the outputs of an off-the-shelf object detector as additional semantic cues for finding the segmentation of an image. Intuitively, an object detector with a high recall can help the semantic segmentation algorithm by finding objects appearing in an image. As shown in Fig. 1, our method is able to recover from poor segmentation unaries when we have a confident detector response. However, our method is robust to false positives identified by the object detector since CRF inference identifies and rejects false detections that do not agree with other types of energies present in the CRF.

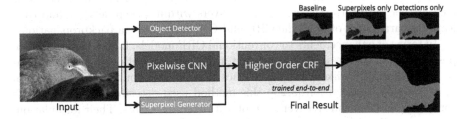

**Fig. 1. Overview of our system.** We train a Higher Order CRF end-to-end with a pixelwise CNN classifier. Our higher order detection and superpixel potentials improve significantly over our baseline containing only pairwise potentials.

526  A. Arnab et al.

Superpixel-based higher order potentials encourage label consistency over superpixels obtained by oversegmentation. This is motivated by the fact that regions defined by superpixels are likely to contain pixels from the same visual object. Once again, our formulation is robust to the violations of this assumption and errors in the initial superpixel generation step. In practice, we noted that this potential is effective for getting rid of small regions of spurious labels that are inconsistent with the correct labels of their neighbours.

We evaluate our higher order potentials on the PASCAL VOC 2012 semantic segmentation benchmark as well as the PASCAL Context dataset, to show significant improvements over our baseline and achieve state-of-the art results.

## 2 Related Work

Before deep learning became prominent, semantic segmentation was performed with dense hand-crafted features which were fed into a per-pixel or region classifier [14]. The individual predictions made by these classifiers were often noisy as they lacked global context, and were thus post-processed with a CRF, making use of prior knowledge such as the fact that nearby pixels, as well as pixels of similar appearance, are likely to share the same class label [14].

The CRF model of [14] initially contained only unary and pairwise terms in an 8-neighbourhood, which [15] showed can result in shrinkage bias. Numerous improvements to this model were subsequently proposed including: densely connected pairwise potentials facilitating interactions between all pairs of image pixels [16], formulating higher order potentials defined over cliques larger than two nodes [5,15] in order to capture more context, modelling co-occurrence of object classes [17–19], and utilising the results of object detectors [6,20,21].

Recent advances in deep learning have allowed us to replace hand-crafted features with features learned specifically for semantic segmentation. The strength of these representations was illustrated by [3] who achieved significant improvements over previous hand-crafted methods without using any CRF post-processing. Chen et al. [12] showed further improvements by post-processing the results of a CNN with a CRF. Subsequent works [9–11,22] have taken this idea further by incorporating a CRF as layers within a deep network and then learning parameters of both the CRF and CNN together via backpropagation.

In terms of enhancements to conventional CRF models, Ladicky et al. [6] proposed using an off-the-shelf object detector to provide additional cues for semantic segmentation. Unlike other approaches that refine a bounding-box detection to produce a segmentation [8,23], this method used detector outputs as a soft constraint and can thus recover from object detection errors. Their formulation, however, used graph-cut inference, which was only tractable due to the absence of dense pairwise potentials. Object detectors have also been used by [20,24], who also modelled variables that describe the degree to which an object hypothesis is accepted.

We formulate the detection potential in a different manner to [6,20,24] so that it is amenable to mean field inference. Mean field permits inference with dense pairwise connections, which results in substantial accuracy improvements [10, 12, 16]. Furthermore, mean field updates related to our potentials are differentiable and its parameters can thus be learned in our end-to-end trainable architecture.

We also note that while the semantic segmentation problem has mostly been formulated in terms of pixels [3, 10, 14], some have expressed it in terms of superpixels [25–27]. Superpixels can capture more context than a single pixel and computational costs can also be reduced if one considers pairwise interactions between superpixels rather than individual pixels [20]. However, such superpixel representations assume that the segments share boundaries with objects in an image, which is not always true. As a result, several authors [5, 7] have employed higher order potentials defined over superpixels that encourage label consistency over regions, but do not strictly enforce it. This approach also allows multiple, non-hierarchical layers of superpixels to be integrated. Our formulation uses this kind of higher order potential, but in an end-to-end trainable CNN.

Graphical models have been used with CNNs in other areas besides semantic segmentation, such as in pose-estimation [28] and group activity recognition [29]. Alternatively, Ionescu *et al.* [30] incorporated structure into a deep network with structured matrix layers and matrix backpropagation. However, the nature of models used in these works is substantially different to ours. Some early works that advocated gradient backpropagation through graphical model inference for parameter optimisation include [31–33].

Our work differentiates from the above works since, to our knowledge, we are the first to propose and conduct a thorough experimental investigation of higher order potentials that are based on detection outputs and superpixel segmentation in a CRF which is learned end-to-end in a deep network. Note that although [7] formulated mean field inference with higher order potentials, they did not consider object detection potentials at all, nor were the parameters learned.

## 3  Conditional Random Fields

We now review conditional random fields used in semantic segmentation and introduce the notation used in the paper. Take an image $\mathbf{I}$ with $N$ pixels, indexed $1, 2, \ldots, N$. In semantic segmentation, we attempt to assign every pixel a label from a predefined set of labels $\mathcal{L} = \{l_1, l_2, \ldots, l_L\}$. Define a set of random variables $X_1, X_2, \ldots, X_N$, one for each pixel, where each $X_i \in \mathcal{L}$. Let $\mathbf{X} = [X_1 \, X_2 \, \ldots \, X_N]^T$. Any particular assignment $\mathbf{x}$ to $\mathbf{X}$ is thus a solution to the semantic segmentation problem.

We use notations $\{\mathbf{V}\}$, and $\mathbf{V}^{(i)}$ to represent the set of elements of a vector $\mathbf{V}$, and the $i^{\text{th}}$ element of $\mathbf{V}$, respectively. Given a graph $G$ where the vertices are from $\{\mathbf{X}\}$ and the edges define connections among these variables, the pair $(\mathbf{I}, \mathbf{X})$ is modelled as a CRF characterised by $\Pr(\mathbf{X} = \mathbf{x}|\mathbf{I}) = (1/Z(\mathbf{I})) \exp(-E(\mathbf{x}|\mathbf{I}))$, where $E(\mathbf{x}|\mathbf{I})$ is the *energy* of the assignment $\mathbf{x}$ and $Z(\mathbf{I})$ is the normalisation factor known as the partition function. We drop the conditioning on $\mathbf{I}$ hereafter to keep the notation uncluttered. The energy $E(\mathbf{x})$ of an assignment is defined using the set of cliques $\mathcal{C}$ in the graph $G$. More specifically, $E(\mathbf{x}) = \sum_{c \in \mathcal{C}} \psi_c(\mathbf{x}_c)$, where $\mathbf{x}_c$ is a vector formed by selecting elements of $\mathbf{x}$ that correspond to random variables belonging to the clique $c$, and $\psi_c(.)$ is the cost function for the clique $c$. The function, $\psi_c(.)$, usually uses prior knowledge about a good segmentation, as well as information from the image, the observation the CRF is conditioned on.

Minimising the energy yields the maximum a posteriori (MAP) labelling of the image *i.e.* the most probable label assignment given the observation (image). When dense pairwise potentials are used in the CRF to obtain higher accuracy, exact inference is impracticable, and one has to resort to an approximate inference method such as mean field inference [16]. Mean field inference is particularly appealing in a deep learning setting since it is possible to formulate it as a Recurrent Neural Network [10].

## 4   CRF with Higher Order Potentials

Many CRF models that have been incorporated into deep learning frameworks [10,12] have so far used only unary and pairwise potentials. However, potentials defined on higher order cliques have been shown to be useful in previous works such as [7,15]. The key contribution of this paper is to show that a number of explicit higher order potentials can be added to CRFs to improve image segmentation, while staying compatible with deep learning. We formulate these higher order potentials in a manner that mean field inference can still be used to solve the CRF. Advantages of mean field inference are twofold: First, it enables efficient inference when using densely-connected pairwise potentials. Multiple works, [10,32] have shown that dense pairwise connections result in substantial accuracy improvements, particularly at image boundaries [12,16]. Secondly, we keep all our mean field updates differentiable with respect to their inputs as well as the CRF parameters introduced. This design enables us to use backpropagation to automatically learn all the parameters in the introduced potentials.

We use two types of higher order potential, one based on object detections and the other based on superpixels. These are detailed in Sects. 4.1 and 4.2 respectively. Our complete CRF model is represented by

$$E(\mathbf{x}) = \sum_i \psi_i^U(x_i) + \sum_{i<j} \psi_{ij}^P(x_i, x_j) + \sum_d \psi_d^{\text{Det}}(\mathbf{x}_d) + \sum_s \psi_s^{\text{SP}}(\mathbf{x}_s), \quad (1)$$

where the first two terms $\psi_i^U(.)$ and $\psi_{ij}^P(.,.)$ are the usual unary and densely-connected pairwise energies [16] and the last two terms are the newly introduced higher order energies. Energies from the object detection take the form $\psi_d^{\text{Det}}(\mathbf{x}_d)$, where vector $\mathbf{x}_d$ is formed by elements of $\mathbf{x}$ that correspond to the foreground pixels of the $d^{\text{th}}$ object detection. Superpixel label consistency based energies take the form $\psi_s^{\text{SP}}(\mathbf{x}_s)$, where $\mathbf{x}_s$ is formed by elements of $\mathbf{x}$ that correspond to the pixels belonging to the $s^{\text{th}}$ superpixel.

## 4.1   Object Detection Based Potentials

Semantic segmentation errors can be classified into two broad categories [34]: recognition and boundary errors. Boundary errors occur when semantic labels are incorrect at the edges of objects, and it has been shown that densely connected CRFs with appearance-consistency terms are effective at combating this problem [16]. On the other hand, recognition errors occur when object categories are recognised incorrectly or not at all. A CRF with only unary and pairwise potentials cannot effectively correct these errors since they are caused by poor unary classification. However, we propose that a state-of-the-art object detector [35,36] capable of recognising and localising objects, can provide important information in this situation and help reduce the recognition error, as shown in Fig. 2.

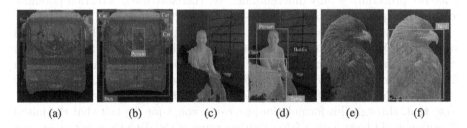

(a)          (b)          (c)          (d)          (e)          (f)

**Fig. 2. Utility of object detections as another cue for semantic segmentation.** For every pair, segmentation on the left was produced with only unary and pairwise potentials. Detection based potentials were added to produce the result on the right. Note how we are able to improve our segmentations for the bus, table and bird over their respective baselines. Furthermore, our system is able to reject erroneous detections such as the person in (b) and the bottle and chair in (d). Images were taken from the PASCAL VOC 2012 reduced validation set. Baseline results were produced using the public code and model of [10].

A key challenge in feeding-in object-detection potentials to semantic segmentation are false detections. A naïve approach of adding an object detector's output to a CRF formulated to solve the problem of semantic segmentation would confuse the CRF due to the presence of the false positives in the detector's output. Therefore, a robust formulation, which can automatically reject object detection false positives when they do not agree with other types of potentials in the CRF, is desired. Furthermore, since we are aiming for an end-to-end trainable CRF which can be incorporated into a deep neural network, the energy formulation should permit a fully differentiable inference procedure. We now propose a formulation which has both of these desired properties.

Assume that we have $D$ object detections for a given image, and that the $d^{\text{th}}$ detection is of the form $(l_d, s_d, F_d)$, where $l_d \in \mathcal{L}$ is the class label of the detected object, $s_d$ is the confidence score of the detection, and $F_d \subseteq \{1, 2, \ldots, N\}$, is the set of indices of the pixels belonging to the foreground of the detection. The foreground within a detection bounding box could be obtained using a foreground/background segmentation method (*i.e.* GrabCut [37]), and represents a crude segmentation of the detected object. Using our detection potentials, we aim to encourage the set of pixels represented by $F_d$, to take the label $l_d$. However, this should not be a hard constraint since the foreground segmentation could be inaccurate and the detection itself could be a false detection. We therefore seek a soft constraint that assigns a penalty if a pixel in $F_d$ takes a label other than $l_d$. Moreover, if other energies used in the CRF strongly suggest that many pixels in $F_d$ do not belong to the class $l_d$, the detection $d$ should be identified as invalid.

An approach to accomplish this is described in [6, 20]. However, in both cases, dense pairwise connections were absent and different inference methods were used. In contrast, we would like to use the mean field approximation to enable efficient inference with dense pairwise connections [16], and also because its inference procedure is fully differentiable. We therefore use a detection potential formulation quite different to the ones used in [6, 20].

In our formulation, as done in [6, 20], we first introduce latent binary random variables $Y_1, Y_2, \ldots Y_D$, one for each detection. The interpretation for the random variable $Y_d$ that corresponds to the $d^{\text{th}}$ detection is as follows: If the $d^{\text{th}}$ detection has been found to be valid after inference, $Y_d$ will be set to 1, it will be 0 otherwise. Mean field inference probabilistically decides the final value of $Y_d$. Note that, through this formulation, we can account for the fact that the initial detection could have been a false positive: some of the detections obtained from the object detector may be identified to be false following CRF inference.

All $Y_d$ variables are added to the CRF which previously contained only $X_i$ variables. Let each $(\mathbf{X}_d, Y_d)$, where $\{\mathbf{X}_d\} = \{X_i \in \{\mathbf{X}\} | i \in F_d\}$, form a clique $c_d$ in the CRF. We define the detection-based higher order energy associated with a particular assignment $(\mathbf{x}_d, y_d)$ to the clique $(\mathbf{X}_d, Y_d)$ as follows:

$$\psi_d^{\text{Det}}(\mathbf{X}_d = \mathbf{x}_d, Y_d = y_d) = \begin{cases} w_{\text{Det}} \frac{s_d}{n_d} \sum_{i=1}^{n_d} [x_d^{(i)} = l_d] & \text{if } y_d = 0, \\ w_{\text{Det}} \frac{s_d}{n_d} \sum_{i=1}^{n_d} [x_d^{(i)} \neq l_d] & \text{if } y_d = 1, \end{cases} \quad (2)$$

where $n_d = |F_d|$ is the number of foreground pixels in the $d^{\text{th}}$ detection, $x_d^{(i)}$ is the $i^{\text{th}}$ element of the vector $\mathbf{x}_d$, $w_{\text{Det}}$ is a learnable weight parameter, and $[.]$ is the Iverson bracket. Note that this potential encourages $X_d^{(i)}$s to take the value $l_d$ when $Y_d$ is 1, and at the same time encourages $Y_d$ to be 0 when many $X_d^{(i)}$s do not take $l_d$. In other words, it enforces the consistency among $X_d^{(i)}$s and $Y_d$.

An important property of the above definition of $\psi_d^{\text{Det}}(.)$ is that it can be simplified as a sum of pairwise potentials between $Y_d$ and each $X_d^{(i)}$ for $i = 1, 2, \ldots, n_d$. That is,

$$\psi_d^{\text{Det}}(\mathbf{X}_d = \mathbf{x}_d, Y_d = y_d) = \sum_{i=1}^{n_d} f_d(x_d^{(i)}, y_d), \text{ where,}$$

$$f_d(x_d^{(i)}, y_d) = \begin{cases} w_{\text{Det}} \frac{s_d}{n_d} [x_d^{(i)} = l_d] & \text{if } y_d = 0, \\ w_{\text{Det}} \frac{s_d}{n_d} [x_d^{(i)} \neq l_d] & \text{if } y_d = 1. \end{cases} \quad (3)$$

We make use of this simplification in Sect. 5 when deriving the mean field updates associated with this potential.

For the latent $Y$ variables, in addition to the joint potentials with $X$ variables, described in Eqs. (2) and (3), we also include unary potentials, which are initialised from the score $s_d$ of the object detection. The underlying idea is that if the object detector detects an object with high confidence, the CRF in turn starts with a high initial confidence about the validity of that detection. This confidence can, of course, change during the CRF inference depending on other information (e.g. segmentation unary potentials) available to the CRF.

Examples of input images with multiple detections and GrabCut foreground masks are shown in Fig. 3. Note how false detections are ignored and erroneous parts of the foreground mask are also largely ignored.

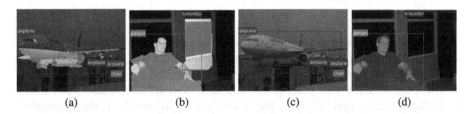

(a)              (b)              (c)              (d)

**Fig. 3. Effects of imperfect foreground segmentation.** (a, b) Detected objects, as well as the foreground masks obtained from GrabCut. (c, d) Output using detection potentials. Incorrect parts of the foreground segmentation of the main aeroplane, and entire TV detection have been ignored by CRF inference as they did not agree with the other energy terms. The person is a failure case though as the detection has caused part of the sofa to be erroneously labelled.

### 4.2  Superpixel Based Potentials

The next type of higher order potential we use is based on the idea that superpixels obtained from oversegmentation [38,39] quite often contain pixels from the same visual object. It is therefore natural to encourage pixels inside a superpixel to have the same semantic label. Once again, this should not be a hard constraint in order to keep the algorithm robust to initial superpixel segmentation errors and to violations of this key assumption.

We use two types of energies in the CRF to encourage superpixel consistency in semantic segmentation. Firstly, we use the $P^n$-Potts model type energy [40], which is described by,

$$\psi_s^{\mathrm{SP}}(\mathbf{X}_s = \mathbf{x}_s) = \begin{cases} w_{\mathrm{Low}}(l) & \text{if all } x_s^{(i)} = l, \\ w_{\mathrm{High}} & \text{otherwise,} \end{cases} \quad (4)$$

where $w_{\mathrm{Low}}(l) < w_{\mathrm{High}}$ for all $l$, and $\{\mathbf{X}_s\} \subset \{\mathbf{X}\}$ is a clique defined by a superpixel. The primary idea is that assigning different labels to pixels in the

(a)                              (b)                              (c)

**Fig. 4. Segmentation enhancement from superpixel based potentials.** (a) The output of our system without any superpixel potentials. (b) Superpixels obtained from the image using the method of [38]. Only one "layer" of superpixels is shown. In practice, we used four. (c) The output using superpixel potentials. The result has improved as we encourage consistency over superpixel regions. This removes some of the spurious noise that was present previously.

same superpixel incurs a higher cost, whereas one obtains a lower cost if the labelling is consistent throughout the superpixel. Costs $w_{\text{Low}}(l)$ and $w_{\text{High}}$ are learnable during the end-to-end training of the network.

Secondly, to make this potential stronger, we average initial unary potentials from the classifier (the CNN in our case), across all pixels in the superpixel and use the average as an additional unary potential for those pixels. During experiments, we observed that superpixel based higher order energy helps in getting rid of small spurious regions of wrong labels in the segmentation output, as shown in Fig. 4.

## 5    Mean Field Updates and Their Differentials

This section discusses the mean field updates for the higher order potentials previously introduced. These update operations are differentiable with respect to the $Q_i(X_i)$ distribution inputs at each iteration, as well as the parameters of our higher order potentials. This allows us to train our CRF end-to-end as another layer of a neural network.

Take a CRF with random variables $V_1, V_2, \ldots, V_N$ and a set of cliques $\mathcal{C}$, which includes unary, pairwise and higher order cliques. Mean field inference approximates the joint distribution $\Pr(\mathbf{V} = \mathbf{v})$ with the product of marginals $\prod_i Q(V_i = v_i)$. We use $Q(\mathbf{V}_c = \mathbf{v}_c)$ to denote the marginal probability mass for a subset $\{\mathbf{V}_c\}$ of these variables. Where there is no ambiguity, we use the short-hand notation $Q(\mathbf{v}_c)$ to represent $Q(\mathbf{V}_c = \mathbf{v}_c)$. General mean field updates of such a CRF take the form [13]

$$Q^{t+1}(V_i = v) = \frac{1}{Z_i} \exp\left(-\sum_{c \in \mathcal{C}} \sum_{\{\mathbf{v}_c | v_i = v\}} Q^t(\mathbf{v}_{c-i})\, \psi_c(\mathbf{v}_c)\right), \qquad (5)$$

where $Q^t$ is the marginal after the $t^{\text{th}}$ iteration, $\mathbf{v}_c$ an assignment to all variables in clique $c$, $\mathbf{v}_{c-i}$ an assignment to all variables in $c$ except for $V_i$, $\psi_c(\mathbf{v}_c)$ is the cost of assigning $\mathbf{v}_c$ to the clique $c$, and $Z_i$ is the normalisation constant that makes $Q(V_i = v)$ a probability mass function after the update.

**Updates from Detection Based Potentials.** Following Eq. (3) above, we now use Eq. (5) to derive the mean field updates related to $\psi_d^{\text{Det}}$. The contribution from $\psi_d^{\text{Det}}$ to the update of $Q(X_d^{(i)} = l)$ takes the form

$$\sum_{\{(\mathbf{x}_d, y_d) | x_d^{(i)} = l\}} Q(\mathbf{x}_{d-i}, y_d)\, \psi_d^{\text{Det}}(\mathbf{x}_d, y_d) = \begin{cases} w_{\text{Det}} \frac{s_d}{n_d} Q(Y_d = 0) & \text{if } l = l_d, \\ w_{\text{Det}} \frac{s_d}{n_d} Q(Y_d = 1) & \text{otherwise,} \end{cases} \tag{6}$$

where $\mathbf{x}_{d-i}$ is an assignment to $\mathbf{X}_d$ with the $i^{\text{th}}$ element deleted. Using the same equations, we derive the contribution from the energy $\psi_d^{\text{Det}}$ to the update of $Q(Y_d = b)$ to take the form

$$\sum_{\{(\mathbf{x}_d, y_d) | y_d = b\}} Q(\mathbf{x}_d)\, \psi_d^{\text{Det}}(\mathbf{x}_d, y_d) = \begin{cases} w_{\text{Det}} \frac{s_d}{n_d} \sum_{i=1}^{n_d} Q(X_d^{(i)} = l_d) & \text{if } b = 0, \\ w_{\text{Det}} \frac{s_d}{n_d} \sum_{i=1}^{n_d} (1 - Q(X_d^{(i)} = l_d)) & \text{otherwise.} \end{cases}$$
$$\tag{7}$$

It is possible to increase the number of parameters in $\psi_d^{\text{Det}}(.)$. Since we use backpropagation to learn these parameters automatically during end-to-end training, it is desirable to have a high number of parameters to increase the flexibility of the model. Following this idea, we made the weight $w_{\text{Det}}$ class specific, that is, a function $w_{\text{Det}}(l_d)$ is used instead of $w_{\text{Det}}$ in Eqs. (2), (6) and (7). The underlying assumption is that detector outputs can be very helpful for certain classes, while being not so useful for classes that the detector performs poorly on, or classes for which foreground segmentation is often inaccurate.

Note that due to the presence of detection potentials in the CRF, error differentials calculated with respect to the $X$ variable unary potentials and pairwise parameters will no longer be valid in the forms described in [10]. The error differentials with respect to the $X$ and $Y$ variables, as well as class-specific detection potential weights $w_{\text{Det}}(l)$ are included in the supplementary material.

**Updates for Superpixel Based Potentials.** The contribution from the $P^n$-Potts type potential to the mean field update of $Q(x_i = l)$, where pixel $i$ is in the superpixel clique $s$, was derived in [7] as

$$\sum_{\{\mathbf{x}_s | x_s^{(i)} = l\}} Q(\mathbf{x}_{s-i})\, \psi_s^{\text{SP}}(\mathbf{x}_s) = w_{\text{Low}}(l) \prod_{j \in c, j \neq i} Q(X_j = l) + w_{\text{High}} \left( 1 - \prod_{j \in c-i} Q(X_j = l) \right). \tag{8}$$

This update operation is differentiable with respect to the parameters $w_{\text{Low}}(l)$ and $w_{\text{High}}$, allowing us to optimise them via backpropagation, and also with respect to the $Q(X)$ values enabling us to optimise previous layers in the network.

**Convergence of Parallel Mean Field Updates.** Mean field with parallel updates, as proposed in [16] for speed, does not have any convergence guarantees in the general case. However, we usually empirically observed convergence with higher order potentials, without damping the mean field update as described in [7,41]. This may be explained by the fact that the unaries from the initial pixelwise-prediction part of our network provide a good initialisation. In cases where the mean field energy did not converge, we still empirically observed good final segmentations.

## 6   Experiments

We evaluate our new CRF formulation on two different datasets using the CRF-RNN network [10] as the main baseline, since we are essentially enriching the CRF model of [10]. We then present ablation studies on our models.

### 6.1   Experimental Set-Up and Results

Our deep network consists of two conceptually different, but jointly trained stages. The first, "unary" part of our network is formed by the FCN-8s architecture [3]. It is initialised from the Imagenet-trained VGG-16 network [2], and then fine-tuned with data from the VOC 2012 training set [4], extra VOC annotations of [42] and the MS COCO [43] dataset.

The output of the first stage is fed into our CRF inference network. This is implemented using the mean field update operations and their differentials described in Sect. 5. Five iterations of mean field inference were performed during training. Our CRF network has two additional inputs in addition to segmentation unaries obtained from the FCN-8s network: data from the object detector and superpixel oversegmentations of the image.

We used the publicly available code and model of the Faster R-CNN [36] object detector. The fully automated version of GrabCut [37] was then used to obtain foregrounds from the detection bounding boxes. These choices were made after conducting preliminary experiments with alternate detection and foreground segmentation algorithms.

Four levels of superpixel oversegmentations were used, with increasing superpixel size to define the cliques used in this potential. Four levels were used since performance on the VOC validation set stopped increasing after this number. We used the superpixel method of [38] as it was shown to adhere to object boundaries the best [39], but our method generalises to any oversegmentation algorithm.

We trained the full network end-to-end, optimising the weights of the CNN classifier (FCN-8s) and CRF parameters jointly. We initialised our network using the publicly available weights of [10], and trained with a learning rate of $10^{-10}$ and momentum of 0.99. The learning rate is low because the loss was not normalised by the number of pixels in the training image. This is to have a larger loss for images with more pixels. When training our CRF, we only used VOC 2012 data [4] as it has the most accurate labelling, particularly around boundaries.

**Table 1.** Comparison of each higher order potential with baseline on VOC 2012 reduced validation set

| Method | Reduced val set (%) |
|---|---|
| Baseline (unary + pairwise) [10] | 72.9 |
| Superpixels only | 74.0 |
| Detections only | 74.9 |
| Detections and superpixels | 75.8 |

**Table 2.** Mean IoU accuracy on VOC 2012 test set. All methods are trained with MS COCO [43] data

| Method | Test set (%) |
|---|---|
| **Ours** | **77.9** |
| DPN [9] | 77.5 |
| Centrale super boundaries [44] | 75.7 |
| Dilated convolutions [45] | 75.3 |
| BoxSup [34] | 75.2 |
| DeepLab attention [46] | 75.1 |
| CRF-RNN (baseline) [10] | 74.7 |
| DeepLab WSSL [47] | 73.9 |
| DeepLab [12] | 72.7 |

**Table 3.** Mean Intersection over Union (IoU) results on PASCAL Context validation set compared to other current methods.

| Method | Ours | BoxSup [34] | ParseNet [48] | CRF-RNN [10] | FCN-8s [3] | CFM [27] |
|---|---|---|---|---|---|---|
| Mean IoU (%) | **41.3** | 40.5 | 40.4 | 39.3 | 37.8 | 34.4 |

**PASCAL VOC 2012 Dataset.** The improvement obtained by each higher order potential was evaluated on the same reduced validation set [3] used by our baseline [10]. As Table 1 shows, each new higher order potential improves the mean IoU over the baseline. We only report test set results for our best method since the VOC guidelines discourage the use of the test set for ablation studies. On the test set (Table 2), we outperform our baseline by 3.2 % which equates to a 12.6 % reduction in the error rate. This sets a new state-of-the-art on the VOC dataset. Qualitative results highlighting success and failure cases of our algorithm, as well as more detailed results, are shown in our supplementary material.

**PASCAL Context.** Table 3 shows our state-of-the-art results on the recently released PASCAL Context dataset [49]. We trained on the provided training set of 4998 images, and evaluated on the validation set of 5105 images. This dataset augments VOC with annotations for all objects in the scene. As a result, there are 59 classes as opposed to the 20 in the VOC dataset. Many of these new labels are "stuff" classes such as "grass" and "sky". Our object detectors are therefore only trained for 20 of the 59 labels in this dataset. Nevertheless, we improve by 0.8 % over the previous state-of-the-art [34] and 2 % over our baseline [10].

## 6.2 Ablation Studies

We perform additional experiments to determine the errors made by our system, show the benefits of end-to-end training and compare our detection potentials to a simpler baseline. Unless otherwise stated, these experiments are performed on the VOC 2012 reduced validation set.

**Error Analysis.** To analyse the improvements made by our higher order potentials, we separately evaluate the performance on the "boundary" and "interior" regions in a similar manner to [34]. As shown in Fig. 5(c) and (d), we consider a narrow band (trimap [15]) around the "void" labels annotated in the VOC 2012 reduced validation set. The mean IoU of pixels lying within this band is termed the "Boundary IoU" whilst the "Interior IoU" is evaluated outside this region.

Figure 5 shows our results as the trimap width is varied. Adding the detection potentials improves the Interior IoU over our baseline (only pairwise potentials [10]) as the object detector may recognise objects in the image which the pixelwise classification stage of our network may have missed out. However, the detection potentials also improve the Boundary IoU for all tested trimap widths as well. Improving the recognition of pixels in the interior of an object also helps with delineating the boundaries since the strength of the pairwise potentials exerted by the $Q$ distributions at each of the correctly-detected pixels increase.

Our superpixel priors also increase the Interior IoU with respect to the baseline. Encouraging consistency over regions helps to get rid of spurious regions of wrong labels (as shown in Fig. 4). Figure 5 suggests that most of this improvement occurs in the interior of an object. The Boundary IoU is slightly lower than the baseline, and this may be due to the fact that superpixels do not always align correctly with the edges of an object (the "boundary recall" of various superpixel methods are evaluated in [39]).

We can see that the combination of detection and superpixel potentials results in a substantial improvement in our Interior IoU. This is the primary reason our overall IoU on the VOC benchmark increases with higher order potentials.

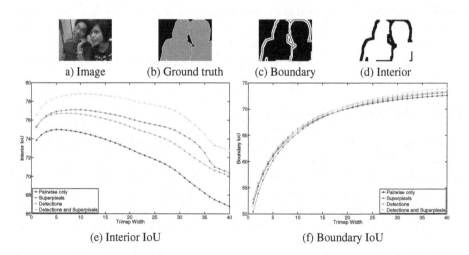

**Fig. 5. Error analysis on VOC 2012 reduced validation set.** The IoU is computed for boundary and interior regions for various trimap widths. An example of the Boundary and Interior regions for a sample image using a width of 9 pixels is shown in white in the top row. Black regions are ignored in the IoU calculation.

**Benefits of End-to-End Training.** Table 4 shows how end-to-end training outperforms piecewise training. We trained the CRF piecewise by freezing the weights of the unary part of the network, and only learning the CRF parameters.

**Table 4.** Comparison of mean IoU (%) obtained on VOC 2012 reduced validation set from end-to-end and piecewise training

| Method | FCN-8s | DCN |
|---|---|---|
| Unary only, fine-tuned on COCO | 68.3 | 68.6 |
| Pairwise CRF trained piecewise | 69.5 | 70.7 |
| Pairwise CRF trained end-to-end | 72.9 | 72.5 |
| Higher Order CRF trained piecewise | 73.6 | 73.5 |
| Higher Order CRF trained end-to-end | 75.8 | 75.0 |
| Test set performance of best model | 77.9 | 76.9 |

Our results in Table 2 used the FCN-8s [3] architecture to generate unaries. To show that our higher order potentials improve performance regardless of the underlying CNN used for producing unaries, we also perform an experiment using our reimplementation of the "front-end" module proposed in the Dilated Convolution Network (DCN) of [45] instead of FCN-8s.

Table 4 shows that end-to-end training of the CRF yields considerable improvements over piecewise training. This was the case when using either FCN-8s or DCN for obtaining the initial unaries before performing CRF inference with higher order potentials. This suggests that our CRF network module can be plugged into different architectures and achieve performance improvements.

**Baseline for Detections.** To evaluate the efficacy of our detection potentials, we formulate a simpler baseline since no other methods use detection information at inference time (BoxSup [34] derives ground truth for training using ground-truth bounding boxes).

Our baseline is similar to CRF-RNN [10], but prior to CRF inference, we take the segmentation mask from the object detection and add a unary potential proportional to the detector's confidence to the unary potentials for those pixels. We then perform mean-field inference (with only pairwise terms) on these "augmented" unaries. Using this method, the mean IoU increases from 72.9 % to 73.6 %, which is significantly less than the 74.9 % which we obtained using only our detection potentials without superpixels (Table 1).

Our detection potentials perform better since our latent $Y$ detection variables model whether the detection hypothesis is accepted or not. Our CRF inference is able to evaluate object detection inputs in light of other potentials. Inference increases the relative score of detections which agree with the segmentation, and decreases the score of detections which do not agree with other energies in the CRF. Figures 2(b) and (d) show examples of false-positive detections that have been ignored and correct detections that have been used to refine our segmentation. Our baseline, on the other hand, is far more sensitive to erroneous detections as it cannot adjust the weight given to them during inference.

## 7   Conclusion

We presented a CRF model with two different higher order potentials to tackle the semantic segmentation problem. The first potential is based on the intuitive idea that object detection can provide useful cues for semantic segmentation. Our formulation is capable of automatically rejecting false object detections that do not agree at all with the semantic segmentation. Secondly, we used a potential that encourages superpixels to have consistent labelling. These two new potentials can co-exist with the usual unary and pairwise potentials in a CRF.

Importantly, we showed that efficient mean field inference is still possible in the presence of the new higher order potentials and derived the explicit forms of the mean field updates and their differentials. This enabled us to implement the new CRF model as a stack of CNN layers and to train it end-to-end in a unified deep network with a pixelwise CNN classifier. We experimentally showed that the addition of higher order potentials results in a significant increase in semantic segmentation accuracy allowing us to reach state-of-the-art performance.

**Acknowledgment.** This work was supported by ERC grant ERC-2012-AdG 321162-HELIOS, EPSRC grant Seebibyte EP/M013774/1, EPSRC/MURI grant EP/N019474/1 and the Clarendon Fund.

## References

1. Krizhevsky, A., Sutskever, I., Hinton, G.E.: ImageNet classification with deep convolutional neural networks. In: NIPS, pp. 1097–1105 (2012)
2. Simonyan, K., Zisserman, A.: Very deep convolutional networks for large-scale image recognition. In: ICLR (2015)
3. Long, J., Shelhamer, E., Darrell, T.: Fully convolutional networks for semantic segmentation. In: CVPR (2015)
4. Everingham, M., Van Gool, L., Williams, C.K., Winn, J., Zisserman, A.: The PASCAL Visual Object Classes (VOC) challenge. IJCV **88**, 303–338 (2010)
5. Ladicky, L., Russell, C., Kohli, P., Torr, P.H.: Associative hierarchical CRFs for object class image segmentation. In: ICCV, pp. 739–746 (2009)
6. Ladický, Ľ., Sturgess, P., Alahari, K., Russell, C., Torr, P.H.S.: What, where and how many? Combining object detectors and CRFs. In: Daniilidis, K., Maragos, P., Paragios, N. (eds.) ECCV 2010, Part IV. LNCS, vol. 6314, pp. 424–437. Springer, Heidelberg (2010)
7. Vineet, V., Warrell, J., Torr, P.H.: Filter-based mean-field inference for random fields with higher-order terms and product label-spaces. IJCV **110**, 290–307 (2014)
8. Hariharan, B., Arbeláez, P., Girshick, R., Malik, J.: Simultaneous detection and segmentation. In: Fleet, D., Pajdla, T., Schiele, B., Tuytelaars, T. (eds.) ECCV 2014, Part VII. LNCS, vol. 8695, pp. 297–312. Springer, Heidelberg (2014)

9. Liu, Z., Li, X., Luo, P., Loy, C.C., Tang, X.: Semantic image segmentation via deep parsing network. In: ICCV (2015)
10. Zheng, S., Jayasumana, S., Romera-Paredes, B., Vineet, V., Su, Z., Du, D., Huang, C., Torr, P.: Conditional random fields as recurrent neural networks. In: ICCV (2015)
11. Lin, G., Shen, C., Reid, I.: Efficient piecewise training of deep structured models for semantic segmentation. In: CVPR (2016)
12. Chen, L.C., Papandreou, G., Kokkinos, I., Murphy, K., Yuille, A.L.: Semantic image segmentation with deep convolutional nets and fully connected CRFs. In: ICLR (2015)
13. Koller, D., Friedman, N.: Probabilistic Graphical Models: Principles and Techniques. MIT Press, Cambridge (2009)
14. Shotton, J., Winn, J., Rother, C., Criminisi, A.: TextonBoost for image understanding: multi-class object recognition and segmentation by jointly modeling texture, layout, and context. IJCV **81**, 2–23 (2009)
15. Kohli, P., Ladicky, L., Torr, P.: Robust higher order potentials for enforcing label consistency. IJCV **82**(3), 302–324 (2009)
16. Krähenbühl, P., Koltun, V.: Efficient inference in fully connected CRFs with Gaussian edge potentials. In: NIPS (2011)
17. Ladicky, L., Russell, C., Kohli, P., Torr, P.H.S.: Graph cut based inference with co-occurrence statistics. In: Daniilidis, K., Maragos, P., Paragios, N. (eds.) ECCV 2010, Part V. LNCS, vol. 6315, pp. 239–253. Springer, Heidelberg (2010)
18. Rabinovich, A., Vedaldi, A., Galleguillos, C., Wiewiora, E., Belongie, S.: Objects in context. In: ICCV, pp. 1–8 (2007)
19. Gonfaus, J.M., Boix, X., Van de Weijer, J., Bagdanov, A.D., Serrat, J., Gonzalez, J.: Harmony potentials for joint classification and segmentation. In: IEEE on CVPR, pp. 3280–3287 (2010)
20. Yao, J., Fidler, S., Urtasun, R.: Describing the scene as a whole: joint object detection, scene classification and semantic segmentation. In: CVPR, pp. 702–709 (2012)
21. Wojek, C., Schiele, B.: A dynamic conditional random field model for joint labeling of object and scene classes. In: Forsyth, D., Torr, P., Zisserman, A. (eds.) ECCV 2008, Part IV. LNCS, vol. 5305, pp. 733–747. Springer, Heidelberg (2008)
22. Lin, G., Shen, C., Reid, I., van den Hengel, A.: Deeply learning the messages in message passing inference. In: NIPS, pp. 361–369 (2015)
23. Yang, Y., Hallman, S., Ramanan, D., Fowlkes, C.C.: Layered object models for image segmentation. PAMI **34**, 1731–1743 (2012)
24. Sun, M., Kim, B.S., Kohli, P., Savarese, S.: Relating things and stuff via object property interactions. PAMI **36**(7), 1370–1383 (2014)
25. Carreira, J., Caseiro, R., Batista, J., Sminchisescu, C.: Semantic segmentation with second-order pooling. In: Fitzgibbon, A., Lazebnik, S., Perona, P., Sato, Y., Schmid, C. (eds.) ECCV 2012, Part VII. LNCS, vol. 7578, pp. 430–443. Springer, Heidelberg (2012)
26. Farabet, C., Couprie, C., Najman, L., LeCun, Y.: Learning hierarchical features for scene labeling. PAMI **35**, 1915–1929 (2013)
27. Dai, J., He, K., Sun, J.: Convolutional feature masking for joint object and stuff segmentation. In: CVPR (2015)
28. Tompson, J.J., Jain, A., LeCun, Y., Bregler, C.: Joint training of a convolutional network and a graphical model for human pose estimation. In: NIPS, pp. 1799–1807 (2014)

29. Deng, Z., Zhai, M., Chen, L., Liu, Y., Muralidharan, S., Roshtkhari, M.J., Mori, G.: Deep structured models for group activity recognition. In: BMVC (2015)
30. Ionescu, C., Vantzos, O., Sminchisescu, C.: Matrix backpropagation for deep networks with structured layers. In: ICCV, pp. 2965–2973 (2015)
31. Domke, J.: Learning graphical model parameters with approximate marginal inference. PAMI **35**, 2454–2467 (2013)
32. Krähenbühl, P., Koltun, V.: Parameter learning and convergent inference for dense random fields. In: ICML (2013)
33. Ross, S., Munoz, D., Hebert, M., Bagnell, J.A.: Learning message-passing inference machines for structured prediction. In: CVPR (2011)
34. Dai, J., He, K., Sun, J.: BoxSup: exploiting bounding boxes to supervise convolutional networks for semantic segmentation. In: ICCV (2015)
35. Girshick, R.: Fast R-CNN. In: ICCV (2015)
36. Ren, S., He, K., Girshick, R., Sun, J.: Faster R-CNN: towards real-time object detection with region proposal networks. In: NIPS (2015)
37. Rother, C., Kolmogorov, V., Blake, A.: GrabCut: interactive foreground extraction using iterated graph cuts. ACM TOG **23**, 309–314 (2004)
38. Felzenszwalb, P.F., Huttenlocher, D.P.: Efficient graph-based image segmentation. IJCV **59**, 167–181 (2004)
39. Achanta, R., Shaji, A., Smith, K., Lucchi, A., Fua, P., Susstrunk, S.: SLIC superpixels compared to state-of-the-art superpixel methods. PAMI **34**(11), 2274–2282 (2012)
40. Kohli, P., Kumar, M.P., Torr, P.H.: P3 & beyond: solving energies with higher order cliques. In: CVPR (2007)
41. Baqu, P., Bagautdinov, T., Fleuret, F., Fua, P.: Principled parallel mean-field inference for discrete random fields. In: CVPR (2016)
42. Hariharan, B., Arbeláez, P., Bourdev, L., Maji, S., Malik, J.: Semantic contours from inverse detectors. In: IEEE on ICCV, pp. 991–998 (2011)
43. Lin, T.-Y., Maire, M., Belongie, S., Hays, J., Perona, P., Ramanan, D., Dollár, P., Zitnick, C.L.: Microsoft COCO: common objects in context. In: Fleet, D., Pajdla, T., Schiele, B., Tuytelaars, T. (eds.) ECCV 2014, Part V. LNCS, vol. 8693, pp. 740–755. Springer, Heidelberg (2014)
44. Kokkinos, I.: Pushing the boundaries of boundary detection using deep learning. In: ICLR (2016)
45. Yu, F., Koltun, V.: Multi-scale context aggregation by dilated convolutions. In: ICLR (2016)
46. Chen, L.C., Yang, Y., Wang, J., Xu, W., Yuille, A.L.: Attention to scale: scale-aware semantic image segmentation. In: CVPR (2016)
47. Papandreou, G., Chen, L., Murphy, K., Yuille, A.L.: Weakly- and semi-supervised learning of a DCNN for semantic image segmentation. In: ICCV (2015)
48. Liu, W., Rabinovich, A., Berg, A.C.: Parsenet: looking wider to see better (2015). arXiv preprint: arXiv:1506.04579
49. Mottaghi, R., Chen, X., Liu, X., Cho, N.G., Lee, S.W., Fidler, S., Urtasun, R., et al.: The role of context for object detection and semantic segmentation in the wild. In: IEEE on CVPR, pp. 891–898 (2014)

# LSTM-CF: Unifying Context Modeling and Fusion with LSTMs for RGB-D Scene Labeling

Zhen Li[1], Yukang Gan[2], Xiaodan Liang[2], Yizhou Yu[1], Hui Cheng[2], and Liang Lin[2(⊠)]

[1] Department of Computer Science, The University of Hong Kong, Hong Kong, China
lizhen36@hku.hk, yizhouy@acm.org
[2] School of Data and Computer Science, Sun Yat-sen University, Guangzhou, China
ganyk@mail2.sysu.edu.cn, xdliang328@gmail.com, chengh9@mail.sysu.edu.cn,
linliang@ieee.org

**Abstract.** Semantic labeling of RGB-D scenes is crucial to many intelligent applications including perceptual robotics. It generates pixelwise and fine-grained label maps from simultaneously sensed photometric (RGB) and depth channels. This paper addresses this problem by (i) developing a novel Long Short-Term Memorized Context Fusion (LSTM-CF) Model that captures and fuses contextual information from multiple channels of photometric and depth data, and (ii) incorporating this model into deep convolutional neural networks (CNNs) for end-to-end training. Specifically, contexts in photometric and depth channels are, respectively, captured by stacking several convolutional layers and a long short-term memory layer; the memory layer encodes both short-range and long-range spatial dependencies in an image along the vertical direction. Another long short-term memorized fusion layer is set up to integrate the contexts along the vertical direction from different channels, and perform bi-directional propagation of the fused vertical contexts along the horizontal direction to obtain true 2D global contexts. At last, the fused contextual representation is concatenated with the convolutional features extracted from the photometric channels in order to improve the accuracy of fine-scale semantic labeling. Our proposed model has set a new state of the art, i.e., **48.1**% and **49.4**% average class accuracy over 37 categories (**2.2**% and **5.4**% improvement) on the large-scale SUNRGBD dataset and the NYUDv2 dataset, respectively.

**Keywords:** RGB-D scene labeling · Image context modeling · Long short-term memory · Depth and photometric data fusion

This work was support by Projects on Faculty/Student Exchange and Collaboration Scheme between the Higher Education in Hong Kong and the Mainland, Guangzhou Science and Technology Program under grant 1563000439, and Fundamental Research Funds for the Central Universities.

B. Leibe et al. (Eds.): ECCV 2016, Part II, LNCS 9906, pp. 541–557, 2016.
DOI: 10.1007/978-3-319-46475-6_34

# 1    Introduction

Scene labeling, also known as semantic scene segmentation, is one of the most fundamental problems in computer vision. It refers to associating every pixel in an image with a semantic label, such as table, road and wall, as illustrated in Fig. 1. High-quality scene labeling can be beneficial to many intelligent tasks, including robot task planning [1], pose estimation [2], plane segmentation [3], context-based image retrieval [4], and automatic photo adjustment [5].

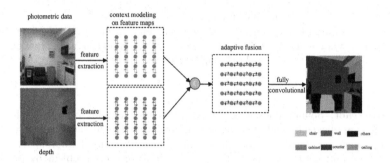

**Fig. 1.** An illustration of global context modeling and fusion for RGB-D images. Our LSTM-CF model first captures vertical contexts through a memory network layer encoding short- and long-range spatial dependencies along the vertical direction. After a concatenation operation (denoted by "C") over photometric and depth channels, our model utilizes another memory network layer to fuse vertical contexts from all channels in a data-driven way and performs bi-directional propagation along the horizontal direction to obtain true 2D global contexts. Best viewed in color. (Color figure online)

Previous work on scene labeling can be divided into two categories according to their target scenes: indoor and outdoor scenes. Compared with outdoor scene labeling [6–8], indoor scene labeling is more challenging due to a larger set of semantic labels, more severe object occlusions, and more diverse object appearances [9]. For example, indoor object classes, such as beds covered with different sheets and various appearances of curtains, are much harder to characterize than outdoor classes, e.g., roads, buildings, and sky, through photometric channels only. Recently, utilizing depth sensors to augment RGB data have effectively improved the performance of indoor scene labeling because the depth channel complements photometric channels with structural information. Nonetheless, two key issues remain open in the literature of RGB-D scene labeling.

(I) **How to effectively represent and fuse the coexisting depth and photometric (RGB) data.** For data representation, a batch of sophisticated hand-crafted features have been developed in previous methods. Such hand-crafted features are somewhat ad hoc and less discriminative than those RGB-D representations learned using convolutional neural networks (CNNs) [10–14]. However, in these CNN-related works, the fusion of depth and photometric data has often been oversimplified. For instance, in [13,14], two independent CNNs are leveraged to extract features from depth and photometric data separately, and such features are simply concatenated before used for final classification. Overlooking the strong correlation between depth and photometric channels could inevitably harm semantic labeling.

(II) **How to capture global scene contexts during feature learning.** Current CNN-based scene labeling approaches can only capture local contextual information for every pixel due to their restricted receptive fields, resulting in suboptimal labeling results. In particular, long-range dependencies sometimes play a key role in distinguishing among different objects having similar appearances, e.g., labeling "ceiling" and "floor" in Fig. 1, according to the global scene layout. To overcome this issue, graphical models, such as a conditional random field [9,11] or a mean-field approximation [15], have been applied to improve prediction results in a post-processing step. These methods, however, separate context modeling from convolutional feature learning, which may give rise to suboptimal results on complex scenes due to less discriminative feature representation [16]. An alternative class of methods adopts cascaded recurrent neural networks (RNNs) with gate structures, e.g., long short-term memory (LSTM) networks, to explicitly strengthen context modeling [16–18]. In these methods, the long- and short-range dependencies can be well memorized by sequentially running the network over individual pixels.

To address the aforementioned challenges, this paper proposes a novel Long Short-Term Memorized Context Fusion (LSTM-CF) model and demonstrates its superiority in RGB-D scene labeling. Figure 1 illustrates the brief idea of using memory networks for context modeling and fusion of different channels. Our LSTM-CF model captures 2D dependencies within an image by exploiting the cascaded bi-directional vertical and horizontal RNN models as introduced in [19].

Our method constructs HHA images [13] for the depth channel through geometric encoding, and uses several convolutional layers for extracting features. Inspired by [19], these convolutional layers are followed by a memorized context layer to model both short-range and long-range spatial dependencies along the vertical direction. For photometric channels, we generate convolutional features using the Deeplab network [12], which is also followed by a memorized context layer for context modeling along the vertical direction. Afterwards, a memorized fusion layer is set up to integrate the contexts along the vertical direction from both photometric and depth channels, and perform bi-directional propagation of the fused vertical contexts along the horizontal direction to obtain true 2D global contexts. Considering the features differences, e.g., signal frequency and other characteristics (color/geometry) [20], our fusion layer facilitates deep integration of contextual information from multiple channels in a data-driven manner rather than simply concatenating different feature vectors. Since photometric channels usually contain finer details in comparison to the depth channel [20], we further enhance the network with cross-layer connections that append convolutional features of the photometric channels to the fused global contexts before the final fully convolutional layer, which predicts pixel-wise semantic labels. Various layers in our LSTM-CF model are tightly integrated, and the entire network is amenable to end-to-end training and testing.

In summary, this paper has the following contributions to the literature of RGB-D scene labeling.

- It proposes a novel Long Short-Term Memorized Context Fusion (LSTM-CF) Model, which is capable of capturing image contexts from a global perspective and deeply fusing contextual information from multiple sources (i.e., depth and photometric channels).
- It proposes to jointly optimize LSTM layers and convolutional layers for achieving better performance in semantic scene labeling. Context modeling and fusion are incorporated into the deep network architecture to enhance the discriminative power of feature representation. This architecture can also be extended to other similar tasks such as object/part parsing.
- It is demonstrated on the large-scale SUNRGBD benchmark (including 10355 images) and canonical NYUDv2 benchmark that our method outperforms existing state-of-the-art methods. In addition, it is found that our scene labeling results can be leveraged to improve the groundtruth annotations of newly captured 3943 RGB-D images in SUNRGBD dataset.

## 2   Related Work

**Scene Labeling:** Scene labeling has caught researchers' attention frequently [6,11,12,16–18,21] in recent years. Instead of extracting features from over-segmented images, recent methods usually utilize powerful CNN layers as the feature extractor, taking advantage of fully convolutional networks (FCNs) [10] and its variants [22] to obtain pixel-wise dense features. Another main challenge for scene labeling is the fusion of local and global contexts, i.e., taking advantage of global contexts to refine local decisions. For instance, [6] exploits families of segmentations or trees to generate segment candidates. [23] utilizes an inference method based on graph cut to achieve image labeling. A pixel-wise conditional random forest is used in [11,12] to directly optimize a deep CNN-driven cost function. Most of the above models improve accuracy through carefully designed processing on the predicted confidence map instead of proposing more powerful discriminative features, which usually results in suboptimal prediction results [16]. The topological structure of recurrent neural networks (RNNs) is used to model short- and long-range dependencies in [16,18]. In [17], a multi-directional RNN is leveraged to extract local and global contexts without using a CNN, which is well suited for low-resolution and relatively simple scene labeling problems. In contrast, our model can jointly optimize LSTM layers and convolutional layers to explicitly improve discriminative feature learning for local and global context modeling and fusion.

**Scene Labeling in RGB-D Images:** With more and more convenient access to affordable depth sensors, scene labeling in RGB-D images [9,13,14,24–26] enables a rapid progress of scene understanding. Various sophisticated hand-crafted features are utilized in previous state-of-the-art methods. Specifically, kernel descriptions based on traditional multi-channel features, such as color, depth gradient, and surface normal, are used as photometric and depth features [24]. A rich feature set containing various traditional features, e.g., SIFT, HOG, LBP and plane orientation, are used as local appearance features and plane appearance features in [9]. HOG features of RGB images and HOG+HH (histogram of height) features of depth images are extracted as representations in [25] for training successive classifiers. In [27], proposed distance-from-wall features are exploited to improve scene labeling performance. In addition, an unsupervised joint feature learning and encoding model is proposed for scene labeling in [26]. However, due to the limited number of RGB-D images, deep learning for scene labeling in RGB-D images was not as appealing as that for RGB images. The release of the SUNRGBD dataset, which includes most of the previously popular datasets, may have changed this situation [13,14].

Another main challenge imposed by scene labeling in RGB-D images is the fusion of contextual representations of different sources (i.e., depth and photometric data). For instance, in [13,14], two independent CNNs are leveraged to extract features from the depth and photometric data separately, which are then simply concatenated for class prediction. Ignoring the strong correlation between depth and photometric channels usually negatively affects semantic labeling. In contrast, instead of simply concatenating features from multiple sources, the memorized fusion layer in our model facilitates the integration of contextual information from different sources in a data-driven manner,

**RNN for Image Processing:** Recurrent neural networks (RNNs) represent a type of neural networks with loop connections [28]. They are designed to capture dependencies across a distance larger than the extent of local neighborhoods. In previous work, RNN models have not been widely used partially due to the difficulty to train such models, especially for sequential data with long-range dependencies [29]. Fortunately, RNNs with gate and memory structures, e.g., long short-term memory (LSTM) [30], can artificially learn to remember and forget information by using specific gates to control the information flow. Although RNNs have an outstanding capability to capture short-range and long-range dependencies, there exist problems for applying RNNs to image processing due to the fact that, unlike data in natural language processing (NLP) tasks, images do not have a natural sequential structure. Thus, different strategies have been proposed to overcome this problem. Specifically, in [19], cascaded bi-directional vertical and horizonal RNN layers are designed for modeling 2D dependencies in images. A multi-dimensional RNN with LSTM unit has been applied to handwriting [31]. A parallel multi-dimensional LSTM for image segmentation has been proposed in [32]. In this paper, we propose an LSTM-CF model consisting of memorized context layers and a memorized fusion layer to capture image contexts from a global perspective and fuse contextual representations from different sources.

## 3   LSTM-CF Model

As illustrated in Fig. 2, our end-to-end LSTM-CF model for RGB-D scene labeling consists of four components, layers for vertical depth context extraction, layers for vertical photometric context extraction, a memorized fusion layer for incorporating vertical photometric and depth contexts as true 2D global contexts, and a final layer for pixel-wise scene labeling given concatenated convolutional features and global contexts. The inputs to our model include both photometric and depth images. The path for extracting global contexts from the photometric image consists of multiple convolutional layers and an extra memorized context layer. On the other hand, the depth image is first encoded as an HHA image, which is fed into three convolutional layers [14] and an extra memorized context layer for global depth context extraction. The other component, a memorized fusion layer, is responsible for fusing previously extracted global RGB and depth contexts in a data-driven manner. On top of the memorized fusion layer, the final convolutional feature of photometric channels and the fused global context are concatenated together and fed into the final fully convolutional layer, which performs pixel-wise scene labeling with the softmax activation function.

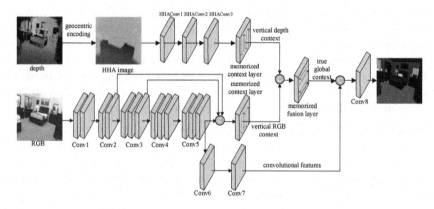

**Fig. 2.** Our LSTM-CF model for RGB-D scene labeling. The input consists of both photometric and depth channels. Vertical contexts in photometric and depth channels are computed in parallel using cascaded convolutional layers and a memorized context layer. Vertical photometric (color) and depth contexts are fused and bi-directionally propagated along the horizontal direction via another memorized fusion layer to obtain true 2D global contexts. The fused global contexts and the final convolutional features of photometric channels are then concatenated together and fed into the final convolutional layer for pixel-wise scene labeling. "C" stands for the concatenation operation. (Color figure online)

### 3.1   Memorized Vertical Depth Context

Given a depth image, we use the HHA representation proposed in [13] to encode geometric properties of the depth image in three channels, i.e., disparity, surface normal and height. Different from [13], the encoded HHA image in our pipeline is fed into three randomly initialized convolutional layers (to obtain a feature map with the same resolution as that in the RGB path) instead of layers taken from the model pre-trained on the ILSVRC2012 dataset. This is because the color distribution of HHA images is different from that of natural images (see Fig. 2) according to [20]. One top of the third convolutional layer (i.e., HHAConv3), there is an extra memorized context layer from Renet [19], which performs bi-directional propagation of local contextual features from the convolutional layers along the vertical direction. For better understanding, we denote the feature map HHAConv3 as $F = \{f_{i,j}\}$, where $F \in \mathbb{R}^{w \times h \times c}$ with $w, h$ and $c$ representing the width, height and the number of channels. Since we perform pixel-wise scene labeling, every patch in this Renet layer only contains a single pixel. Thus, vertical memorized context layer (here we choose LSTM as recurrent unit) can be formulated as

$$h_{i,j}^f = \text{LSTM}(h_{i,j-1}^f, f_{i,j}), \quad \text{for } j = 1, \ldots, h \quad (1)$$

$$h_{i,j}^b = \text{LSTM}(h_{i,j+1}^b, f_{i,j}), \quad \text{for } j = h, \ldots, 1, \quad (2)$$

where $h^f$ and $h^b$ stand for the hidden states of the forward and backward LSTM. In the forward LSTM, the unit at pixel $(i, j)$ takes $h_{i,j-1}^f \in \mathbb{R}^d$ and $f_{i,j} \in \mathbb{R}^c$ as input, and its output is calculated as follows according to [30]. The operations in the backward LSTM can be defined similarly.

$$\text{gate}_i = \delta(W_{if} f_{i,j} + W_{ih} h_{i,j-1}^f + b_i)$$

$$\text{gate}_f = \delta(W_{ff} f_{i,j} + W_{fh} h_{i,j-1}^f + b_f)$$

$$\text{gate}_o = \delta(W_{of} f_{i,j} + W_{oh} h_{i,j-1}^f + b_o)$$

$$\text{gate}_c = \tanh(W_{cf} f_{i,j} + W_{ch} h_{i,j-1}^f + b_c)$$

$$c_{i,j} = \text{gate}_f \odot c_{i,j-1} + \text{gate}_i \odot \text{gate}_c$$

$$h_{i,j}^f = \tanh(\text{gate}_o \odot c_{i,j}) \quad (3)$$

Finally, pixel-wise vertical depth contexts are collectively represented as a map, $C_{\text{depth}} \in \mathbb{R}^{w \times h \times 2d}$, where $2d$ is the total number of output channels from the vertical memorized context layer.

### 3.2 Memorized Vertical Photometric Context

In the component for extracting global RGB contexts, we adapt the Deeplab architecture proposed in [12]. Different from existing Deeplab variants, we con-catenate features at three different scales to enrich the feature representation. This is inspired by the network architecture in [33]. Specifically, since there exists hole operations in Deeplab convolutional layers, feature maps from Conv2_2, Conv3_3 and Conv5_3 have sufficient initial resolutions. They can be further elevated to the same resolution using interpolation. Corresponding pixel-wise features from these three elevated feature maps are then concatenated together before being fed into the subsequent memorized fusion layer, which again performs bi-directional propagation to produce vertical photometric contexts. Here pixel-wise vertical photometric contexts can also be represented as a map, $C_{\mathrm{RGB}} \in \mathbb{R}^{w \times h \times 2d}$, which has the same dimensionalities as the map for vertical depth contexts.

### 3.3 Memorized Context Fusion

So far vertical depth and photometric contexts are computed independently in parallel. Instead of simply concatenating these two types of contexts, the memorized fusion layer, which performs horizontal bi-directional propagation from Renet, is exploited for adaptively fusing vertical depth and RGB contexts in a data-driven manner, and the output from this layer can be regarded as the fused representation of both types of contexts. Such fusion can generate more discriminative features through end-to-end training. The input and output dimensions of the fusion layer are set to $\mathbb{R}^{w \times h \times 4d}$ and $\mathbb{R}^{w \times h \times 2d}$, respectively.

Note that there are two separate memorized context layers in the photometric and depth paths of our architecture. Since the memorized context layer and the memorized fusion layer are two symmetric components of the original Renet [19], a more natural and symmetric alternative would have a single memorized context layer preceding the memorized fusion layer in our model (i.e., whole structure of Renet including cascaded bi-directional vertical and horizonal memorized layer) and let the memorized fusion layer incorporate the features from the RGB and depth paths. Nonetheless, in our experiments, this alternative network architecture gave rise to slightly worse performance.

### 3.4 Scene Labeling

Between photometric and depth images, photometric images contain more details and semantic information that can help scene labeling in comparison with sparse and discontinuous depth images [14]. Nonetheless, depth images can provide auxiliary geometric information for improving scene labeling performance. Thus, we design a cross-layer combination that integrates pixel-wise convolutional features (i.e., Conv7 in Fig. 2) from the photometric image with fused global contexts from the memorized fusion layer as the final pixel-wise features, which are fed into the last fully convolutional layer with softmax activation to perform scene labeling at every pixel location.

## 4 Experimental Results

### 4.1 Experimental Setting

**Datasets:** We evaluate our proposed model for RGB-D scene labeling on three public benchmarks, SUNRGBD, NYUDv2 and SUN3D. SUNRGBD [20] is the largest dataset currently available, consisting of 10355 RGB-D images captured from four different depth sensors. It includes most previous datasets, such as NYUDv2 depth [34], Berkeley B3DO [35], and SUN3D [36], as well as 3943 newly captured RGB-D images [20]. 5285 of these images are predefined for training and the remaining 5050 images constitute the testing set [14].

**Implementation Details:** In our experiments, a slightly modified Deeplab pipeline [12] is adopted as the basic network in our RGB path for extracting convolutional feature maps because of its high performance. It is initialized with the publicly available VGG-16 model pre-trained on ImageNet. For the purpose of pixel-wise scene labeling, this architecture transforms the last two fully connected layers in the standard VGG-16 to convolutional layers with $1 \times 1$ kernels. For the parallel depth path, three randomly initialized CNN layers with max pooling are leveraged for depth feature extraction. In each path, on top of the aforementioned convolutional network, a vertically bi-directional LSTM layer implements the memorized context layer, and models both short-range and long-range spatial dependencies. Then, another horizontally bi-directional LSTM layer implements the memorized fusion layer, and is used to adaptively integrate the global contexts from the two paths. In addition, there is a cross-layer combination of final convolutional features (i.e., Conv7) and the integrated global representation from the horizontal LSTM layer.

Since the SUNRGBD dataset was collected by four different depth sensors, each input image is cropped to $426 \times 426$ (the smallest resolution of these four sensors) [14]. During fine-tuning, the learning rate for newly added layers, including HHAConv1, HHAConv2, HHAConv3, the memorized context layers, the memorized fusion layer and Conv8, is initialized to $10^{-2}$, and the learning rate for those pre-trained layers of VGG-16 is initialized to $10^{-4}$. All weights in the newly added convolutional layers are initialized using a Gaussian distribution with a standard deviation equal to 0.01, and the weights in the LSTM layers are randomly initialized with a uniform distribution over $[-0.01, 0.01]$. The number of hidden memory cells in a memorized context layer or a memorized fusion layer is set to 100, and the size of feature maps is $54 \times 54$. We train all the layers in our deep network simultaneously using SGD with a momentum 0.9, the batch size is set to one (due to limited GPU memory) and the weight decay is 0.0005. The entire deep network is implemented on the publicly available platform Caffe [37] and is trained on a single NVIDIA GeForce GTX TITAN X GPU with 12GB memory [1]. It takes about 1 day to train our deep network. In the testing stage, an RGB-D image takes 0.15s on average, which is significantly faster than pervious methods, i.e., the testing time in [9,24] is around 1.5 s.

## 4.2   Results and Comparisons

According to [14,22], performance is evaluated by comparing class-wise Jaccard Index, i.e., $n_{ii}/t_i$, and average Jaccard Index, i.e., $(1/n_{cl}) \sum_i n_{ii}/t_i$, where $n_{ij}$ is the number of pixels annotated as class $i$ and predicted to be class $j$, $n_{cl}$ is

---

[1] LSTM-CF model is publicly available at: https://github.com/icemansina/LSTM-CF.

the number of different classes, and $t_i = \sum_j n_{ij}$ is the total number of pixels annotated as class $i$ [10].

**SUNRGBD Dataset** [20]: The performance and comparison results on SUN-RGBD are shown in Table 1. Our proposed architecture can outperform existing techniques: 2.2 % higher than the performance reported in [22], 11.8 % higher than that in [24], 38 % higher than that in [38] and 39.1 % higher than that in [20] in terms of 37-class average Jaccard Index. Improvements can be observed in 15 class-wise Jaccard Indices. For a better understanding, we also show the confusion matrix for this dataset in Fig. 3(a).

**Table 1.** Comparison of scene labeling results on SUNRGBD using class-wise and average Jaccard Index. We compare our model with results reported in [20,24,38] and previous state-of-the-art result in [22]. Boldface numbers mean best performance.

|  | Wall | floor | cabinet | bed | chair | sofa | table | door | window | bookshelf | picture | counter | blinds | desk | shelves | curtain | dresser | pillow | mirror |
|---|---|---|---|---|---|---|---|---|---|---|---|---|---|---|---|---|---|---|---|
| [20] | 37.8 | 45.0 | 17.4 | 21.8 | 16.9 | 12.8 | 18.5 | 6.1 | 9.6 | 9.4 | 4.6 | 2.2 | 2.4 | 7.3 | 1.0 | 4.3 | 2.2 | 2.3 | 6.9 |
| [20] | 32.1 | 42.6 | 2.9 | 6.4 | 21.5 | 4.1 | 12.5 | 3.4 | 5.0 | 0.8 | 3.3 | 1.7 | 14.8 | 2.0 | 15.3 | 2.0 | 1.4 | 1.2 | 0.9 |
| [20] | 36.4 | 45.8 | 15.4 | 23.3 | 19.9 | 11.6 | 19.3 | 6.0 | 7.9 | 12.8 | 3.6 | 5.2 | 2.2 | 7.0 | 1.7 | 4.4 | 5.4 | 3.1 | 5.6 |
| [38] | 38.9 | 47.2 | 18.8 | 21.5 | 17.2 | 13.4 | 20.4 | 6.8 | 11.0 | 9.6 | 6.1 | 2.6 | 3.6 | 7.3 | 1.2 | 6.9 | 2.4 | 2.6 | 6.2 |
| [38] | 33.3 | 43.8 | 3.0 | 6.3 | 22.3 | 3.9 | 12.9 | 3.8 | 5.6 | 0.9 | 3.8 | 2.2 | 32.6 | 2.0 | 10.1 | 3.6 | 1.8 | 1.1 | 1.0 |
| [38] | 37.8 | 48.3 | 17.2 | 23.6 | 20.8 | 12.1 | 20.9 | 6.8 | 9.0 | 13.1 | 4.4 | 6.2 | 2.4 | 6.8 | 1.0 | 7.8 | 4.8 | 3.2 | 6.4 |
| [24] | 43.2 | 78.6 | 26.2 | 42.5 | 33.2 | 40.6 | 34.3 | 33.2 | 43.6 | 23.1 | 57.2 | 31.8 | 42.3 | 12.1 | **18.4** | 59.1 | 31.4 | 49.5 | 24.8 |
| [22] | **80.2** | **90.9** | **64.8** | **76.0** | **58.6** | **62.6** | **47.7** | **66.4** | 31.2 | **63.6** | 33.8 | 46.7 |  | 19.7 | 16.2 | **67.0** | **42.3** | **57.1** | 39.1 |
| Ours | 74.9 | 82.3 | 47.3 | 62.1 | 67.7 | 55.5 | 57.8 | 45.6 | 52.8 | **43.1** | 56.7 | **39.4** | **48.6** | **37.3** | 9.6 | 63.4 | 35.0 | 45.8 | **44.5** |

|  | floormat | clothes | ceiling | books | fridge | tv | paper | towel | shower | box | board | person | nightstand | toilet | sink | lamp | bathtub | bag | mean |
|---|---|---|---|---|---|---|---|---|---|---|---|---|---|---|---|---|---|---|---|
| [20] | 0.0 | 1.2 | 27.9 | 4.1 | 7.0 | 1.6 | 1.5 | 1.9 | 0.0 | 0.6 | 7.4 | 0.0 | 1.1 | 8.9 | 14.0 | 0.9 | 0.6 | 0.9 | 8.3 |
| [20] | 0.0 | 0.3 | 9.7 | 0.6 | 0.0 | 0.9 | 0.0 | 0.1 | 0.0 | 1.0 | 2.7 | 0.3 | 2.6 | 2.3 | 1.1 | 0.7 | 0.0 | 0.4 | 5.3 |
| [20] | 0.0 | 1.4 | 35.8 | 6.1 | 9.5 | 0.7 | 1.4 | 0.2 | 0.0 | 0.6 | 7.6 | 0.7 | 1.7 | 12.0 | 15.2 | 0.9 | 1.1 | 0.6 | 9.0 |
| [38] | 0.0 | 1.3 | 39.1 | 5.9 | 7.1 | 1.4 | 1.5 | 2.2 | 0.0 | 0.7 | 10.4 | 0.0 | 1.5 | 12.3 | 14.8 | 1.3 | 0.9 | 1.1 | 9.3 |
| [38] | 0.0 | 0.6 | 13.9 | 0.5 | 0.0 | 0.9 | 0.4 | 0.3 | 0.0 | 0.7 | 3.5 | 0.3 | 1.5 | 2.6 | 1.2 | 0.8 | 0.0 | 0.5 | 6.0 |
| [38] | 0.0 | 1.6 | 49.2 | 8.7 | 10.1 | 0.6 | 1.4 | 0.2 | 0.0 | 0.8 | 8.6 | 0.8 | 1.8 | 14.9 | 16.8 | 1.2 | 1.1 | 1.3 | 10.1 |
| [24] | **5.6** | 27.0 | **84.5** | 35.7 | 24.2 | 36.5 | 26.8 | 19.2 | **9.0** | 11.7 | 51.4 | 35.7 | 25.0 | 64.1 | 53.0 | 44.2 | 47.0 | 18.6 | 36.3 |
| [22] | 0.1 | 24.4 | 84.0 | **48.7** | 21.3 | 49.5 | 30.6 | 18.8 | 0.1 | 24.1 | **56.8** | 17.9 | **42.9** | **73.0** | 66.2 | 48.8 | 45.1 | **24.1** | 45.9 |
| Ours | 0.0 | **28.4** | 68.0 | 47.9 | **61.5** | **52.1** | **36.4** | **36.7** | 0 | **38.1** | 48.1 | **72.6** | 36.4 | 68.8 | **67.9** | **58.0** | **65.6** | 23.6 | **48.1** |

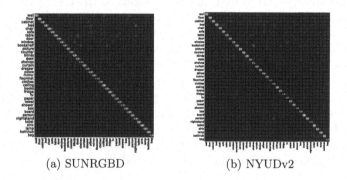

(a) SUNRGBD                    (b) NYUDv2

**Fig. 3.** Confusion matrix for SUNRGBD and NYUDv2. Class-wise Jaccard Index is shown on the diagonal. Best viewed in color. (Color figure online)

It is worth mentioning that our proposed architecture and most previous methods achieve zero accuracy on two categories, i.e., floormat and shower, which mainly results from an imbalanced data distribution instead of the capacity of our model.

**NYUDv2 Dataset:** To further verify the effectiveness of our architecture and have more comparisons with existing state-of-the-art methods, we also conduct experiments on the NYUDv2 dataset. The results are presented in Table 2, where the 13-class average Jaccard Index of our model is 20.3 % higher than that in [39]. Class frequencies and the confusion matrix are also shown in Table 2 and Fig. 3(b) respectively. According to the reported results, our proposed architecture gains 5.6 % and 5.5 % improvement in average Jaccard Index over [9] and FCN-32s [10] respectively. Considering the listed class frequencies, our proposed model significantly outperforms existing methods on high frequency categories and most low frequency categories, which primarily owes to the convolutional features of the RGB image and the fused global contexts of the complete RGB-D image. In terms of labeling categories with small and complex regions, e.g., pillows and chairs, our method also achieves a large improvement, which can be verified in the following visual comparisons.

**Table 2.** Comparison of scene labeling on NYUDv2. We compare our proposed model with existing state-of-the-art methods, i.e., [9,24–26,34]. Class-wise Jaccard Index and average Jaccard Index of 37 classes are presented. 'Freq' stands for class frequency. Boldface numbers mean best performance.

| | Wall | floor | cabinet | bed | chair | sofa | table | door | window | bookshelf | picture | counter | blinds | desk | shelves | curtain | dresser | pillow | mirror |
|---|---|---|---|---|---|---|---|---|---|---|---|---|---|---|---|---|---|---|---|
| Freq | 21.4 | 9.1 | 6.2 | 3.8 | 3.3 | 2.7 | 2.1 | 2.2 | 2.1 | 1.9 | 2.1 | 1.4 | 1.7 | 1.1 | 1.0 | 1.1 | 0.9 | 0.8 | 1.0 |
| [34] | 60.7 | 77.8 | 33.0 | 40.3 | 32.4 | 25.3 | 21.0 | 5.9 | 29.7 | 22.7 | 35.7 | 33.1 | 40.6 | 4.7 | 3.3 | 27.4 | 13.3 | 18.9 | 4.4 |
| [24] | 60.0 | 74.4 | 37.1 | 42.3 | 32.5 | 28.2 | 16.6 | 12.9 | 27.7 | 17.3 | 32.4 | 38.6 | 26.5 | 10.1 | 6.1 | 27.6 | 7.0 | 19.7 | 17.9 |
| [25] | 67.4 | 80.5 | 41.4 | 56.4 | 40.4 | 44.8 | 30.0 | 12.1 | 34.1 | 20.5 | 38.7 | 50.7 | 44.7 | 10.1 | 1.6 | 26.3 | 21.6 | 31.3 | 14.6 |
| [26] | 61.4 | 66.4 | 38.2 | 43.9 | 34.4 | 33.8 | 22.6 | 8.3 | 27.6 | 17.6 | 27.7 | 30.2 | 33.6 | 5.1 | 2.7 | 18.9 | 16.8 | 12.5 | 10.7 |
| [9] | 65.7 | 62.5 | 40.1 | 32.1 | 44.5 | 50.8 | 43.5 | **51.6** | **49.2** | 36.3 | 41.4 | 39.2 | 55.8 | **48.0** | **45.2** | 53.1 | 55.3 | **50.5** | 46.1 |
| Ours | **79.6** | **83.5** | **69.3** | **77.0** | **58.3** | **64.9** | **42.6** | 47.0 | 43.6 | **59.5** | **74.5** | **68.2** | **74.6** | 33.6 | 13.1 | **53.2** | **56.5** | 48.0 | **47.7** |

| | floormat | clothes | ceiling | books | fridge | tv | paper | towel | shower | box | board | person | nightstand | toilet | sink | lamp | bathtub | bag | mean |
|---|---|---|---|---|---|---|---|---|---|---|---|---|---|---|---|---|---|---|---|
| Freq | 0.7 | 0.7 | 1.4 | 0.6 | 0.6 | 0.5 | 0.4 | 0.4 | 0.4 | 0.3 | 0.3 | 0.3 | 0.3 | 0.3 | 0.3 | 0.3 | 0.3 | 0.2 | |
| [34] | 7.1 | 6.5 | 73.2 | 5.5 | 1.4 | 5.7 | 12.7 | 0.1 | 3.6 | 0.1 | 0.0 | 6.6 | 6.3 | 26.7 | 25.1 | 15.9 | 0.0 | 0.0 | 17.5 |
| [24] | 20.1 | 9.5 | 53.9 | 14.8 | 1.9 | 18.6 | 11.7 | 12.6 | 5.4 | 3.3 | 0.2 | 13.6 | 9.2 | 35.2 | 28.9 | 14.2 | 7.8 | 1.2 | 20.2 |
| [25] | 28.2 | 8.0 | 61.8 | 5.8 | 14.5 | 14.4 | 14.1 | 19.8 | 6.0 | 1.1 | 12.9 | 1.5 | 15.7 | 52.5 | 47.9 | 31.2 | 29.4 | 0.2 | 30.0 |
| [26] | 13.8 | 2.7 | 46.1 | 3.6 | 2.9 | 3.2 | 2.6 | 6.2 | 6.1 | 0.8 | 28.2 | 5 | 6.9 | 32 | 20.9 | 5.4 | 16.2 | 0.2 | 29.2 |
| [9] | **54.1** | **35.4** | 50.6 | 39.1 | **53.6** | **50.1** | 35.4 | 39.9 | **41.8** | **36.3** | 60.6 | 35.6 | **32.5** | 31.8 | 22.5 | 26.3 | 38.5 | **37.3** | 43.9 |
| Ours | 0.0 | 22.7 | **70.2** | **49.7** | 0.0 | 0.0 | **52.1** | **60.6** | 0 | 17.6 | **93.9** | **77.0** | 0 | **81.8** | **58.4** | **67.6** | **72.6** | 7.5 | **49.4** |

**SUN3D Dataset:** Table 3 gives comparison results on the 1539 test images in the SUN3D dataset. For fair comparison, the 12-class average Jaccard Index is used in the comparison with the state-of-the-art results recently reported in [9]. Note that the 12-class accuracy of our network is calculated through the model previously trained for 37 classes. Our model substantially outperforms the one from [9] on large planar regions such as those labeled as floors and ceilings. This also results from the incorporated convolutional features and the fused global contexts.

**Table 3.** Comparison of class-wise Jaccard Index and 12-class average Jaccard Index on SUN3D.

| | Wall | Floor | Bed | Chair | Table | Counter | Curtain | Ceiling | Tv | Toilet | Bathtub | Bag | Mean |
|---|---|---|---|---|---|---|---|---|---|---|---|---|---|
| [9] | **73** | 35 | **71** | 35 | 30 | **52** | 68 | 27 | 56 | 23 | 49 | **29** | 45.7 |
| Ours | **73** | **86** | 32 | **65** | **57** | 22 | **76** | **69** | **75** | **62** | **62** | 23 | **58.5** |

These comparison results further confirm the power and generalization capability of our LSTM-based model.

### 4.3  Ablation Study

To discover the vital elements in our proposed model, we conduct an ablation study to remove or replace individual components in our deep network when training and testing on the SUNRGBD dataset. Specifically, we have tested the performance of our model without the RGB path, the depth path, multi-scale RGB feature concatenation, the memorized context layers or the memorized fusion layer. In addition, we also conduct an experiment with a model that does not combine the final convolutional features of photometric channels (i.e., Conv7 in Fig. 2) with the global contexts of the complete RGB-D image to figure out the importance of different components. The results are presented in Table 4. From the given results, we find that the final convolutional features of the photometric channels is the most vital information, i.e., the cross-layer combination is the most effective component as the performance drops to 15.2 % without it, which is consistent with previously mentioned properties of depth and photometric data. In addition, multi-scale RGB feature concatenation before the memorized context layer also plays a vital role as it directly affects the vertical contexts in the photometric channels and the performance drops to 42.1 % without it. It is obvious that performance would be inevitably harmed without the depth path. Among the memorized layers, the memorized fusion layer is more important than the memorized context layers in our pipeline as it accomplishes the fusion of contexts in photometric and depth channels.

Table 4. Ablation study

| Model | Mean accuracy |
|---|---|
| Without RGB path, using Deeplab+Renet for depth path | 15.8 % |
| Without depth path | 43.7 % |
| Without multi-scale RGB feature concatenation | 42.1 % |
| Without cross-layer integration of RGB convolutional features | 15.2 % |
| Without memorized fusion layer | 44.7 % |
| Without memorized context layers | 45.7 % |
| Without any memorized (context or fusion) layers | 45.0 % |

### 4.4  Visual Comparisons

**SUNRGBD Dataset:** We present visual results of RGB-D scene labeling in Fig. 4. Here, we leverage super-pixel based averaging to smooth visual labeling results as being done in [9]. The algorithm in [40] is used for performing super-pixel segmentation. As can be observed in Fig. 4, our proposed deep network produces accurate and semantically meaningful labeling results, especially for large regions and high frequency labels. For instance, our model takes advantage of global contexts when labeling 'bed' in Fig. 4(a), 'wall' in Fig. 4(e) and 'mirror' in Fig. 4(i). Our proposed model can precisely label almost all 'chairs' (a high frequency label) by exploiting integrated photometric and depth information, regardless of occlusions.

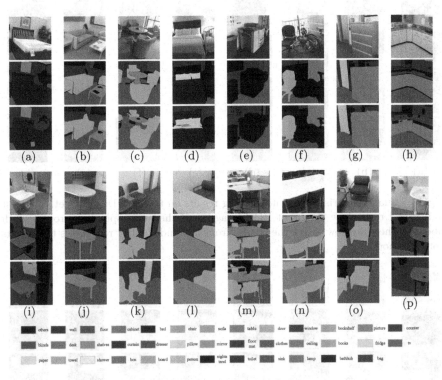

(q) legend of semantic labels

**Fig. 4.** Examples of semantic labeling results on the SUNRGBD dataset. The top row shows the input RGB images, the bottom row shows scene labeling obtained with our model and the middle row has the ground truth. Semantic labels and their corresponding colors are shown at the bottom.

**NYUDv2 Dataset:** We also perform visual comparisons on the NYUDv2 benchmark, which has complicated indoor scenes and well-labeled ground truth. We compare our scene labeling results with those publicly released labeling results from [25]. It is obvious that our results are clearly better than those from [25] both visually and numerically (under the metric of average Jaccard Index) even though scene labeling in [25] is based on sophisticated segmentation.

**Label Refinement:** Surprisingly, our model can intelligently refine certain region annotations, which might have inaccuracies due to under-segmentation, especially in the newly captured 3943 RGB-D images, as shown in Fig. 6. Specifically, the cabinets in Fig. 6(a) were annotated as 'background', the pillows in Fig. 6(g) as 'bed', and the tables in Fig. 6(n) as 'wall' by mistake. Our model can effectively deal with these difficult regions. For example, the annotation of

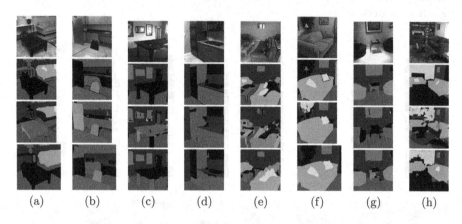

(a)        (b)        (c)        (d)        (e)        (f)        (g)        (h)

**Fig. 5.** Visual comparison of scene labeling results on the NYUDv2 dataset. The first and second rows show the input RGB images and their corresponding ground truth labeling. The third row shows the results from [25] and the last row shows the results from our model.

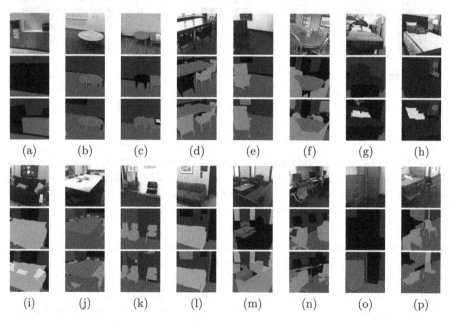

(a)        (b)        (c)        (d)        (e)        (f)        (g)        (h)

(i)        (j)        (k)        (l)        (m)        (n)        (o)        (p)

**Fig. 6.** Annotation refinement on the SUNRGBD dataset. The top row shows the input RGB images, the middle row shows the original annotations, and the bottom row shows scene labeling results from our model.

the picture in Fig. 6(e) and that of the pillows in Fig. 6(g) have been corrected. Thus, our model can be exploited to refine certain annotations in the SUNRGBD dataset, which is another contribution of our model.

## 5   Conclusions

In this paper, we have developed a novel Long Short-Term Memorized Context Fusion (LSTM-CF) model that captures image contexts from a global perspective and deeply fuses contextual representations from multiple sources (i.e., depth and photometric data) for semantic scene labeling. In future, we will explore how to extend the memorized layers with an attention mechanism, and refine the performance of our model in boundary labeling.

## References

1. Wu, C., Lenz, I., Saxena, A.: Hierarchical semantic labeling for task-relevant RGB-D perception. In: Robotics: Science and Systems (RSS) (2014)
2. Hinterstoisser, S., Lepetit, V., Ilic, S., Holzer, S., Bradski, G., Konolige, K., Navab, N.: Model based training, detection and pose estimation of texture-less 3D objects in heavily cluttered scenes. In: Lee, K.M., Matsushita, Y., Rehg, J.M., Hu, Z. (eds.) ACCV 2012, Part I. LNCS, vol. 7724, pp. 548–562. Springer, Heidelberg (2013)
3. Holz, D., Holzer, S., Rusu, R.B., Behnke, S.: Real-time plane segmentation using RGB-D cameras. In: Röfer, T., Mayer, N.M., Savage, J., Saranlı, U. (eds.) RoboCup 2011. LNCS, vol. 7416, pp. 306–317. Springer, Heidelberg (2012)
4. Schuster, S., Krishna, R., Chang, A., Fei-Fei, L., Manning, C.D.: Generating semantically precise scene graphs from textual descriptions for improved image retrieval. In: Proceedings of the Fourth Workshop on Vision and Language, pp. 70–80 (2015)
5. Yan, Z., Zhang, H., Wang, B., Paris, S., Yu, Y.: Automatic photo adjustment using deep neural networks. ACM Trans. Graph. **35**(2), 11 (2016)
6. Farabet, C., Couprie, C., Najman, L., LeCun, Y.: Learning hierarchical features for scene labeling. IEEE Trans. Pattern Anal. Mach. Intell. **35**(8), 1915–1929 (2013)
7. Gould, S., Fulton, R., Koller, D.: Decomposing a scene into geometric and semantically consistent regions. In: 2009 IEEE 12th International Conference on Computer Vision, pp. 1–8. IEEE (2009)
8. Tighe, J., Lazebnik, S.: SuperParsing: scalable nonparametric image parsing with superpixels. In: Daniilidis, K., Maragos, P., Paragios, N. (eds.) ECCV 2010, Part V. LNCS, vol. 6315, pp. 352–365. Springer, Heidelberg (2010)
9. Khan, S.H., Bennamoun, M., Sohel, F., Togneri, R., Naseem, I.: Integrating geometrical context for semantic labeling of indoor scenes using RGBD images. Int. J. Comput. Vis. **117**, 1–20 (2015)
10. Long, J., Shelhamer, E., Darrell, T.: Fully convolutional networks for semantic segmentation. In: Proceedings of the IEEE Conference on Computer Vision and Pattern Recognition, pp. 3431–3440 (2015)
11. Zheng, S., Jayasumana, S., Romera-Paredes, B., Vineet, V., Su, Z., Du, D., Huang, C., Torr, P.H.: Conditional random fields as recurrent neural networks. In: Proceedings of the IEEE International Conference on Computer Vision, pp. 1529–1537 (2015)

12. Chen, L.C., Papandreou, G., Kokkinos, I., Murphy, K., Yuille, A.L.: Semantic image segmentation with deep convolutional nets and fully connected CRFs. arXiv preprint arXiv:1412.7062 (2014)
13. Gupta, S., Girshick, R., Arbeláez, P., Malik, J.: Learning rich features from RGB-D images for object detection and segmentation. In: Fleet, D., Pajdla, T., Schiele, B., Tuytelaars, T. (eds.) ECCV 2014, Part VII. LNCS, vol. 8695, pp. 345–360. Springer, Heidelberg (2014)
14. Song, S., Xiao, J.: Deep sliding shapes for amodal 3D object detection in RGB-D images. arXiv preprint arXiv:1511.02300 (2015)
15. Liu, Z., Li, X., Luo, P., Loy, C.C., Tang, X.: Semantic image segmentation via deep parsing network. In: Proceedings of the IEEE International Conference on Computer Vision, pp. 1377–1385 (2015)
16. Liang, X., Shen, X., Xiang, D., Feng, J., Lin, L., Yan, S.: Semantic object parsing with local-global long short-term memory. In: Proceedings of the IEEE Conference on Computer Vision and Pattern Recognition (2016)
17. Byeon, W., Breuel, T.M., Raue, F., Liwicki, M.: Scene labeling with LSTM recurrent neural networks. In: Proceedings of the IEEE Conference on Computer Vision and Pattern Recognition, pp. 3547–3555 (2015)
18. Pinheiro, P., Collobert, R.: Recurrent convolutional neural networks for scene labeling. In: Proceedings of the 31st International Conference on Machine Learning (ICML 2014), pp. 82–90 (2014)
19. Visin, F., Kastner, K., Cho, K., Matteucci, M., Courville, A., Bengio, Y.: Renet: a recurrent neural network based alternative to convolutional networks. arXiv preprint arXiv:1505.00393 (2015)
20. Song, S., Lichtenberg, S.P., Xiao, J.: Sun RGB-D: a RGB-D scene understanding benchmark suite. In: Proceedings of the IEEE Conference on Computer Vision and Pattern Recognition, pp. 567–576 (2015)
21. Kumar, M.P., Koller, D.: Efficiently selecting regions for scene understanding. In: 2010 IEEE Conference on Computer Vision and Pattern Recognition (CVPR), pp. 3217–3224. IEEE (2010)
22. Kendall, A., Badrinarayanan, V., Cipolla, R.: Bayesian segnet: model uncertainty in deep convolutional encoder-decoder architectures for scene understanding. arXiv preprint arXiv:1511.02680 (2015)
23. Lempitsky, V., Vedaldi, A., Zisserman, A.: Pylon model for semantic segmentation. In: Advances in Neural Information Processing Systems, pp. 1485–1493 (2011)
24. Ren, X., Bo, L., Fox, D.: RGB-(D) scene labeling: features and algorithms. In: 2012 IEEE Conference on Computer Vision and Pattern Recognition (CVPR), pp. 2759–2766. IEEE (2012)
25. Gupta, S., Arbeláez, P., Girshick, R., Malik, J.: Indoor scene understanding with RGB-D images: bottom-up segmentation, object detection and semantic segmentation. Int. J. Comput. Vis. 112(2), 133–149 (2015)
26. Wang, A., Lu, J., Cai, J., Wang, G., Cham, T.J.: Unsupervised joint feature learning and encoding for RGB-D scene labeling. IEEE Trans. Image Process. 24(11), 4459–4473 (2015)
27. Husain, F., Schulz, H., Dellen, B., Torras, C., Behnke, S.: Combining semantic and geometric features for object class segmentation of indoor scenes. IEEE Rob. Autom. Lett. 2(1), 49–55 (2017)
28. Schmidhuber, J.: A local learning algorithm for dynamic feedforward and recurrent networks. Connection Sci. 1(4), 403–412 (1989)
29. Bengio, Y., Simard, P., Frasconi, P.: Learning long-term dependencies with gradient descent is difficult. IEEE Trans. Neural Netw. 5(2), 157–166 (1994)

30. Hochreiter, S., Schmidhuber, J.: Long short-term memory. Neural Comput. **9**(8), 1735–1780 (1997)
31. Graves, A., Schmidhuber, J.: Offline handwriting recognition with multidimensional recurrent neural networks. In: Advances in Neural Information Processing Systems, pp. 545–552 (2009)
32. Stollenga, M.F., Byeon, W., Liwicki, M., Schmidhuber, J.: Parallel multidimensional LSTM, with application to fast biomedical volumetric image segmentation. In: Advances in Neural Information Processing Systems, pp. 2980–2988 (2015)
33. Li, G., Yu, Y.: Deep contrast learning for salient object detection. In: IEEE Conference on Computer Vision and Pattern Recognition (CVPR) (2016)
34. Silberman, N., Hoiem, D., Kohli, P., Fergus, R.: Indoor segmentation and support inference from RGBD images. In: Fitzgibbon, A., Lazebnik, S., Perona, P., Sato, Y., Schmid, C. (eds.) ECCV 2012, Part V. LNCS, vol. 7576, pp. 746–760. Springer, Heidelberg (2012)
35. Janoch, A., Karayev, S., Jia, Y., Barron, J.T., Fritz, M., Saenko, K., Darrell, T.: A category-level 3D object dataset: putting the kinect to work. In: Fossati, A., Gall, J., Grabner, H., Ren, X., Konolige, K. (eds.) Consumer Depth Cameras for Computer Vision, pp. 141–165. Springer, Heidelberg (2013)
36. Xiao, J., Owens, A., Torralba, A.: SUN3D: a database of big spaces reconstructed using SfM and object labels. In: Proceedings of the IEEE International Conference on Computer Vision, pp. 1625–1632 (2013)
37. Jia, Y., Shelhamer, E., Donahue, J., Karayev, S., Long, J., Girshick, R., Guadarrama, S., Darrell, T.: Caffe: convolutional architecture for fast feature embedding. arXiv preprint arXiv:1408.5093 (2014)
38. Liu, C., Yuen, J., Torralba, A.: Sift flow: dense correspondence across scenes and its applications. IEEE Trans. Pattern Anal. Mach. Intell. **33**(5), 978–994 (2011)
39. Couprie, C., Farabet, C., Najman, L., LeCun, Y.: Toward real-time indoor semantic segmentation using depth information. J. Mach. Learn. Res. (2014)
40. Felzenszwalb, P.F., Huttenlocher, D.P.: Efficient graph-based image segmentation. Int. J. Comput. Vis. **59**(2), 167–181 (2004)

# Stereo Video Deblurring

Anita Sellent[1,2]($\boxtimes$), Carsten Rother[1], and Stefan Roth[2]

[1] Technische Universität Dresden, Dresden, Germany
anita.sellent@tu-dresden.de
[2] Technische Universität Darmstadt, Darmstadt, Germany

**Abstract.** Videos acquired in low-light conditions often exhibit motion blur, which depends on the motion of the objects relative to the camera. This is not only visually unpleasing, but can hamper further processing. With this paper we are the first to show how the availability of stereo video can aid the challenging video deblurring task. We leverage 3D scene flow, which can be estimated robustly even under adverse conditions. We go beyond simply determining the object motion in two ways: First, we show how a piecewise rigid 3D scene flow representation allows to induce accurate blur kernels via local homographies. Second, we exploit the estimated motion boundaries of the 3D scene flow to mitigate ringing artifacts using an iterative weighting scheme. Being aware of 3D object motion, our approach can deal robustly with an arbitrary number of independently moving objects. We demonstrate its benefit over state-of-the-art video deblurring using quantitative and qualitative experiments on rendered scenes and real videos.

**Keywords:** Object motion blur · Scene flow · Spatially-variant deblurring

## 1 Introduction

Stereo is one of the oldest areas of computer vision research [1]. Interestingly, the arrival of mass-produced active depth sensors [2] seems to have renewed interest also in passive stereo systems. In contrast to active depth sensors, stereo cameras are also applicable in outdoor environments. Due to their more general applicability, stereo cameras are gaining increased adoption, for example in autonomous driving [3]. Remarkably, the availability of stereo image pairs also helps in the estimation of temporal correspondences: On the KITTI optical flow benchmark [4], the best performing algorithms [5,6] are indeed scene flow algorithms that jointly estimate depth and 3D motion from stereo videos. Part of their advantage stems from an increased robustness to adverse imaging conditions [6]. One such adverse imaging condition is a shortage of light. In low-light conditions,

**Electronic supplementary material** The online version of this chapter (doi:10. 1007/978-3-319-46475-6_35) contains supplementary material, which is available to authorized users.

B. Leibe et al. (Eds.): ECCV 2016, Part II, LNCS 9906, pp. 558–575, 2016.
DOI: 10.1007/978-3-319-46475-6_35

the exposure time often needs to be increased to obtain a reasonable signal-to-noise-ratio. But when either the camera, or the objects in the scenes are moving during exposure time, this results in motion blurred images.

Motion blur is not only unsatisfactory to look at, it can also disturb further image-based processing, *e.g.* in tasks such as panorama stitching [8] or barcode recognition [9]. In stereo video setups, viewpoint-dependent motion blur hinders a post-capture adjustment of the baseline, the acquisition and visualization of 3D point clouds (see Fig. 1 for an example) or the control of tele-operated robots in the presence of rapid robot and/or object motion.

| (a) Input | (b) Blurry 3D point cloud | (c) Deblurred 3D point cloud |

**Fig. 1.** Application of stereo video deblurring: Given 2 consecutive stereo frames (a), our deblurring approach allows to estimate sharp textures from stereo video input with motion blur. Rendering scene flow geometry with the blurred input image as a colored point-cloud from a new point of view produces an unnatural motion blur (b). Our stereo video deblurring algorithm can remove the blur (c).

In this paper we address the challenge of deblurring stereo videos. In contrast to the substantial literature on removing camera shake [10–15], we aim to deal with the more general case of camera *and* object motion. In case of independent motions, mixed pixels at motion boundaries yield significant complications. Removing such spatially-variant blur is extremely challenging when attempted from single images [16,17], but video input helps to significantly increase robustness [7,18]. Unlike previous work, we leverage stereo video to obtain substantially improved and more robust deblurring results. In our approach, we exploit 3D scene flow in various ways and *make the following contributions: (i)* We show that 3D scene flow can improve video deblurring by providing more accurate motion estimates. In particular, we exploit piecewise rigid scene flow [6], which yields an over-segmentation of the image into planar patches that move with a rigid 3D motion (Figs. 2b and c). *(ii)* We demonstrate that the resulting piece-wise homographies allow to directly induce blur matrices. Thereby, we take into account that the projection of a rigid 3D motion yields non-linear motion trajectories in 2D (Fig. 3, Table 1). We find that this leads to superior deblurring results compared to inducing the blur matrices from an optical flow field [7] (Figs. 2d to f). *(iii)* We apply the homography-induced blur matrices in a robust deblurring procedure that attenuates the effects of motion discontinuities using

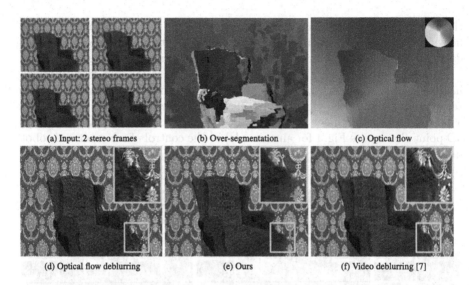

(a) Input: 2 stereo frames    (b) Over-segmentation    (c) Optical flow

(d) Optical flow deblurring    (e) Ours    (f) Video deblurring [7]

**Fig. 2.** Stereo video deblurring: For two consecutive frames of a synthetic stereo video (a) we use the scene flow approach of Vogel *et al.* [6] to compute an over-segmentation into planar patches with constant 3D rigid body motion (b). Projecting the 3D motion onto the image plane yields optical flow (c), which our baseline algorithm uses to deblur a reference frame (d). Exploiting the homographies from the 3D motion and object boundary information from the over-segmentation, our full approach obtains sharp images avoiding ringing and boundary artifacts (e). Our result is also clearly sharper than state-of-the-art video deblurring [7] (f)

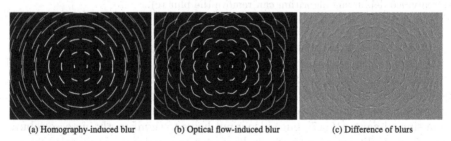

(a) Homography-induced blur    (b) Optical flow-induced blur    (c) Difference of blurs

**Fig. 3.** Descriptiveness of homography-based blur kernels: Using 3D rigid body motion to generate blur kernels, we can faithfully express, *e.g.*, yaw motion (a), while kernels constructed with spatially varying 2D displacement vectors fields [7] only yield an approximation (b). Approximation errors (c) are also present close to the rotation axis where motions are small (extremely large yaw angle and all intensities scaled for better visibility)

an iterative weighting scheme; Initial motion discontinuities are obtained from 3D scene flow. We demonstrate the superiority of the proposed stereo video deblurring over state-of-the-art monocular video deblurring using experiments on synthetic data as well as on real videos.

**Table 1.** Overview of the different sources of motion information used for video deblurring: When pure 2D correspondence is considered (top two rows), the induced blur kernels are only approximate, as motion trajectories are assumed to be linear. Exploiting homographies from scene flow allows us to capture the fact that rigid 3D object motion leads to non-linear trajectories

| Motion information | # of frames | # of views | Linear approximation of trajectories |
|---|---|---|---|
| Optical flow | 2 | 1 | Yes |
| 2D projection of scene flow | 2 | 2 | Yes |
| Homographies | 2 | 2 | No |

## 2   Related Work

The goal of this work is to obtain sharp images from stereo videos containing 3D camera and object motion. Of course, in principle blind deblurring could be applied to each frame individually. However, blind motion deblurring from a single image is a highly underconstrained problem, as blur parameters and sharp image have to be estimated from a single measurement. To cope with spatially-variant blur due to the 3D motion of the camera, single image deblurring approaches frequently use homographies [19–21]. In contrast, we apply homographies to describe spatially-variant object motion blur. Single image object motion deblurring approaches keep the number of parameters manageable by either choosing the motion of a region from a very restricted set of spatially-invariant box filters [22,23], assuming it to have a spatially-invariant, non-parametric kernel of limited size [16], or to be representable by a discrete set of basis kernels [24]. Approaches that rely on learning spatially-variant blur are also limited to a discretized set of detectable motions [17,25]. Kim et al. [26] consider continuously varying box filters for every pixel, but rely heavily on regularization.

Connecting deblurring and depth estimation, Xu and Jia [27] successfully apply stereo correspondence estimation to motion-blurred stereo frames to support blind image deblurring. Lee and Lee [28], Arun et al. [29], and Hu et al. [30] estimate sharp images and depth jointly. However, all these approaches assume the scene to be static and camera motion to be the only source of motion blur.

Cho et al. [31] deblur images of independently moving objects. The multiple input images of their algorithm are unordered, and a piecewise affine registration between the images, as well as the motion underlying the blur, has to be estimated. To restrict the parameter space, the blur kernels are assumed to be piecewise constant and linear.

Video deblurring approaches reduce the number of parameters through the assumption that the inter-frame and intra-frame motion are related by the duty cycle of the camera. He et al. [32] and Deng et al. [33] apply feature tracking of a single moving object to obtain 2D displacement-based blur kernels for deblurring. Wulff and Black [18] refine the latter approach and perform segmentation into two layers, estimation of the affine motion parameters, as well as deblurring of each layer jointly. Relaxing the assumption of two layers and affine motion, Yamaguchi et al. [34] and Kim and Lee [7] employ optical flow to approximate spatially variant blur kernels for deblurring. Yamaguchi et al. [34] propose deblurring based on the flow estimates from the blurry images. Kim and Lee [7] iteratively refine flow estimation and deblurred video frames by minimizing a joint energy. The latter method represents the state-of-the-art in video deblurring and is used for comparison in the experimental section. To the best of our knowledge, exploiting stereo video for deblurring has not been considered in the literature before.

Correspondence estimation on stereo video sequences can be improved by estimating stereo correspondences and optical flow jointly as 3D scene flow [35–37]. In our approach we build on the piecewise rigid scene flow by Vogel et al. [6] for the following reasons. First, it provides us with explicit 3D rotations and translations that we employ for accurate blur kernel construction. Second, through over-segmentation into planar patches, it also delivers occlusion information, which we use as initialization for our boundary-aware object motion deblurring. A general problem in object motion deblurring is that object boundaries with mixed foreground and background pixels can lead to severe ringing artifacts (see Fig. 2). Explicit segmentation and $\alpha$-matting [18,38] can prevent this effect, but requires restrictive assumptions on the number of moving objects. To handle general scenes with an arbitrary number of objects, we extend the robust outlier handling of Chen et al. [39] to spatially-variant deblurring based on scene flow, and apply it to the mixed pixels at object boundaries.

In contrast to the aforementioned deblurring approaches, Cho et al. [40] deblur hand-held video under the assumption that patches are sharp in some frames of the video. However, in the case of autonomous robots or objects passing the field of view with high speed, this assumption does not hold. Joshi et al. [41] attach additional inertial measurement units to the camera, but this does not account for object motion. An additional low-resolution, high frame-rate camera can provide complex motion kernels [38], but does not provide depth estimates in the way a stereo camera can.

## 3    Blurred Image Formation in Stereo Video

*Inducing Blur Matrices from 3D Rigid Object Motions.* Due to the finite exposure time $\tau$ of our stereo video camera, each frame of each camera is blurred. Our goal is to find a sharp image $I_{t_0}$ for a reference camera at time $t_0$. We base our approach on the scene flow of Vogel et al. [6], and likewise assume that the scene can be approximated with planar patches that undergo a 3D rigid body motion. If an object in the scene is non-planar, this assumption leads to an over-segmentation of the object into spatially adjacent patches (see Fig. 2b). Considering video frames where the exposure time is naturally limited by the frame rate, we additionally assume that the motion of each patch is constant during the exposure time of two consecutive frames. Note that a constant rigid motion in 3D does not necessarily imply that its 2D projection is constant; the projection may, *e.g.* in the case of a rotation, be constantly accelerated. However, our assumption excludes rapidly changing motions such as vibrations.

Constant 3D rigid body motion can be expressed as a homogeneous $4 \times 4$ matrix

$$M = \begin{pmatrix} R\ T \\ \mathbf{0}\ 1 \end{pmatrix} \tag{1}$$

with a rotation matrix $R \in \mathbb{R}^{3 \times 3}$ and a translation vector $T \in \mathbb{R}^3$. To enable our highly accurate blur kernel description, we rewrite $M = \exp(\theta \xi)$ as matrix exponential, where $\theta \in \mathbb{R}$ describes the rotation angle and $\xi$ is a $4 \times 4$ matrix that is determined by the rotation axis and the translation, see [42,43]. With $M$ describing the motion between time instants $t_0$ and $t_1$, the constant 3D motion between two arbitrary time instants $t_a$ and $t_b$ is given as

$$M_{t_b,t_a} = \exp \left( \frac{t_b - t_a}{t_1 - t_0} \theta \xi \right). \tag{2}$$

In a piecewise planar scene approximation, the 3D planes of the patches at time $t$ are defined via their scaled normals $n_t$. All points $P$ on the plane satisfy the equation $P^\mathrm{T} n_t = 1$, where $P^\mathrm{T}$ is the transposed of $P$. We can relate a moving 3D point to its corresponding pixel location on the image plane via the camera geometry. Given the calibration matrix $K$ of the reference camera and its location $T_K$, the projection from a 3D plane to the image plane at time $t$ can be written in homogeneous coordinates as $Pr_t = K - KT_K n_t^\mathrm{T}$, see *e.g.* [6].

Under the assumption of color constancy, two sharp images of the reference camera (with hypothetical infinitesimal exposure) at different times are connected via

$$I_{t_a}(x) = I_{t_b}({}^{t_b}H^{t_a}x) \quad \text{where} \quad {}^{t_b}H^{t_a} = Pr_{t_b} M_{t_b,t_a} Pr_{t_a}^{-1}. \tag{3}$$

With this notation, a blurry image pixel $x$ in the interior of a patch is formed from the reference image as

$$\hat{B}(x) = \int_{t_0 - \frac{\tau}{2}}^{t_0 + \frac{\tau}{2}} I_t(x)\, \mathrm{d}t = \int_{t_0 - \frac{\tau}{2}}^{t_0 + \frac{\tau}{2}} I_{t_0}({}^{t_0}H^t x)\, \mathrm{d}t, \tag{4}$$

where

$$ {}^{t_0}H^t = Pr_{t_0} \exp\left( -t\theta\xi \right) Pr_t^{-1} \tag{5}$$

is a homography that can be computed exactly from camera geometry, normal, and motion. To put it differently, a 3D point that is projected to $x$ on the image plane describes a certain trajectory on the image plane during the exposure time. If the 3D point follows a rigid body motion, the homography $\left({}^{t_0}H^t\right)^{-1}$ allows us to exactly describe this 2D trajectory. In contrast, optical flow based methods [7,24,44], employ 2D optical flow vectors to generate $I_t$ via forward warping. Thus the trajectory of a point on the image plane is approximated by a 2D line that is traversed with constant velocity. As optical flow is spatially variant, the trajectories may change for each pixel, hence induce blur kernels with a curved shape. However, more complex motions such as rotations can only be *approximated*, Fig. 3. In our approach, the description of trajectories due to 3D rigid body motions is *exact*. As our experiments show, this also results in more faithfully deblurred images.

By discretizing the integration over time with $\delta t = \frac{\tau}{N}$ (we fix $N = 70$) and using bilinear image interpolation, we can obtain a discretized version of Eq. (4) for vectorized reference images as $\hat{B}(x) = A_x I_{t_0}$. Here, $A_x$ denotes a sparse row vector that depends on the homography estimated at pixel $x$. Stacking the blur vectors $A_x$ for each pixel, we obtain our homography-based blur matrix $A$ leading to $\hat{B} = A I_{t_0}$.

*Motion Boundaries.* If only scene points from the same plane contribute to the color $B(x)$ of the measured blurred image at point $x$, the image formation model of Eq. (4) is exact. If at time $t$ a scene point with a different motion contributes to $B(x)$ we should also use the corresponding homography. However, within an object, the planar patches are adjacent in space and move consistently. Therefore, we approximate the blur with the row vector $A_x$ induced by the homography of $x$ at $t_0$. At motion boundaries, the homographies are very different and as pixels of foreground and background mix, transparency effects occur. While such effects can be modeled, taking them into account requires precise localization of the motion boundaries, which is very challenging. Instead, we exclude motion boundaries from the deblurring process by means of an iterative approach. In each iteration, we downweight pixels with a high difference between image formation model and measured image and try to find a sharp image that explains the remaining pixels. Under the assumption of additive Gaussian noise, we use the residual to compute a weight for each pixel as

$$w_n(x) = \exp\left(-k_\sigma \|B(x) - A_x I_{t_0}^{n-1}\|^2\right), \qquad (6)$$

where $I_{t_0}^{n-1}$ denotes the current estimate of the sharp (color) image. For normalized images we set $k_\sigma = {}^{4000}/_3$ as default value. In the first iteration we initialize $w_0$ with the binary occlusion information from the scene flow. As Fig. 4 shows, the weights converge quickly. Some pixels in the image that were initially suppressed as motion boundaries are included in deblurring at a later iteration. More importantly, other pixels where the image formation model is invalid are suppressed later on, which helps controlling ringing artifacts. Suppression may also happen due to some inaccuracies in the computed scene flow. In the experimental section, we will see how this property actually helps to improve deblurring results.

*Deblurring.* Theoretically, we could fill in the regions at motion boundaries during deblurring by using adjacent frames or information from the other camera. However, we found experimentally that correspondence estimation in these regions is too unreliable to produce visually pleasing results. Instead, we exploit that natural, sharp images follow a Laplacian distribution of their gradients [22].

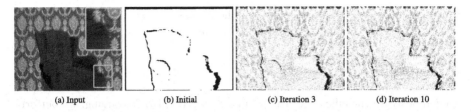

(a) Input       (b) Initial       (c) Iteration 3       (d) Iteration 10

**Fig. 4.** Downweighting of mixed pixels due to motion boundaries: Foreground and background mix at motion boundaries and violate our image formation model (a). At motion boundaries and locations of inaccurate flow estimates, the image formation model is downweighed to avoid ringing artifacts. We initialize these weights with the occlusion information provided by the scene flow (b) and refine them iteratively (c), (d)

In locations where the image formation model is unreliable, *e.g.*, at motion boundaries, we rely on this prior to provide the necessary regularization. Specifically, we obtain an estimate of the sharp reference frame by minimizing the energy

$$E(\boldsymbol{I}_{t_0}) = \sum_{x \in \Omega} \left\| w_n(x)\big(B(x) - A_x \boldsymbol{I}_{t_0}\big) \right\|^2 + \alpha \rho\big(\nabla I_{t_0}(x)\big), \qquad (7)$$

where $\Omega \subset \mathbb{N}^2$ is the image domain and the constant $\alpha$ is fixed to 0.001. Following prior work [22], we use the robust norm $\rho(c) = |c|^{0.8}$ for each color channel and gradient direction.

To solve the optimization problem in Eq. (7), we use iteratively reweighted least squares (IRLS) [45]. In each reweighting iteration, we compute the following weights

$$\rho_n(c) = \frac{1}{c}\frac{d\rho(c)}{dc} \approx \max\big(|c|, \epsilon\big)^{0.8-2} \quad \text{with} \quad \epsilon = 0.01 \qquad (8)$$

for the smoothness term using the preceding image estimate $\nabla I_{t_0}^{n-1}$. Then we minimize the least squares energy

$$E(\boldsymbol{I}_{t_0}, n) = \sum_{x \in \Omega} \left\| w_n(x)\big(B(x) - A_x \boldsymbol{I}_{t_0}^n\big) \right\|^2 + \alpha \|\rho_n \nabla I_{t_0}^n(x)\|^2 \qquad (9)$$

via conjugate gradients. We alternate between updating the occlusion weight $w_n$ and the smoothness weight $\rho_n$. In all our experiments the weights converge quickly and only a few ($\approx$10) iterations were needed in total.

To compute the 3D scene flow needed for our stereo video deblurring approach, we rely on the method of Vogel *et al.* [6]. The algorithm is originally designed for sharp images. However, its data term uses the census transform for comparing the warped images, which makes it quite robust to image blur. Of course, scene flow estimation will reach its limits for very strong motion blur. Experimentally, we find that by aggregating evidence in piecewise planar patches, the method yields a scene flow accuracy that turns out to work well in deblurring stereo videos of casual motion. As the following experiments will show, it is crucial, however, to not only rely on the robust correspondence information, but to exploit the homographies to directly induce the blur kernels.

# 4    Experiments

To demonstrate the efficacy of the proposed stereo video deblurring, we perform experiments on synthetic images with known ground truth, as well as on real images. We capture the real video footage with a *Point Grey Bumblebee2* stereo color camera, which can acquire 640 × 480 images at a frame rate of 20 Hz. We use the internal calibration and supplied software to obtain rectified and demosaiced images. The exposure time of each image can be obtained from the camera software.

In all experiments, we compute scene flow using the publicly available implementation of [6]. We take the default parameters and scale them uniformly to account for the baseline difference between our stereo camera and the KITTI dataset [4] for which they were tuned. For the 640 × 480 image in Fig. 2 our approach requires 73 s to form the discretized blur matrix $A$. Using MATLAB to optimize Eq. (7) in 25 conjugate gradient steps and 10 IRLS iterations requires 69 s on an 8-core 4 GHz CPU.

## 4.1    Comparing Flow-Based Deblurring to Homography-Based Deblurring

We begin by applying the proposed stereo video deblurring to scenes without object discontinuities. In this way we can analyze the benefit of the homography-induced motion blur model in isolation. We create synthetic sequences by simulating various 3D motions (upward and forward translation, and a combination forward translation and yaw) of a planar, roughly fronto-parallel texture, see Fig. 5a.[1] A second test set consists of rigidly moving 3D objects rendered with a raytracer at very small time steps and averaged to give motion-blurred images (see Figs. 4a, 6a and 7a for the first image of the left view). We take the central

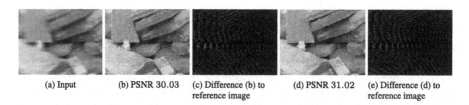

(a) Input          (b) PSNR 30.03    (c) Difference (b) to        (d) PSNR 31.02    (e) Difference (d) to
                                      reference image                             reference image

**Fig. 5.** Deblurring planar textures: For a planar texture blurred with 3D rigid body motion (a), deblurring with 2D spatially-variant ground truth displacements (b) yields ringing errors (c) that can be reduced by deblurring with our homography-based image formation model (d), (e)

---

[1] More textures and motions are evaluated in the supplemental material.

frame of each motion-blurred image as a sharp reference frame. For the rendered scenes motion discontinuities are known. In the first experiment, we disable the data term around any motion discontinuities by fixing the weights $w_n$ in these areas to zero, see Fig. 6b for an example. As the image prior stays active, the boundaries are filled in smoothly as illustrated in Fig. 6d.

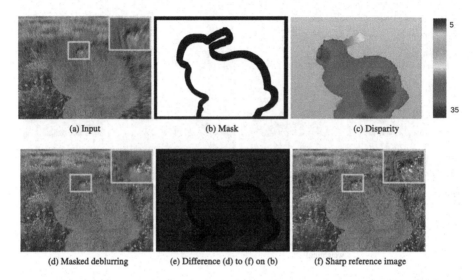

(a) Input          (b) Mask          (c) Disparity

(d) Masked deblurring     (e) Difference (d) to (f) on (b)     (f) Sharp reference image

**Fig. 6.** Deblurring with masked discontinuities: Our raytraced stereo video frames contain independent object motion of non-planar objects (a). Through the estimated disparity we can assess the shape of the objects (c). Excluding given discontinuities (b) from the computation of the data term, invalid areas are filled in smoothly (d). The masked difference image (e) to the real sharp image (f) shows that homography-based deblurring has about the same error in planar as in curved surfaces, showing the effectiveness of the over-segmentation from the scene flow

We compare our homography-induced deblurring approach against deblurring with blur matrices generated from different 2D displacement fields. We use forward and backward 2D motion as described by Kim and Lee [7] and apply them in our IRLS deblurring framework. In particular, we use the known *ground truth 2D displacement*, the *2D initial optical flow* with which the scene flow is initialized [46] (*baseline deblurring*), and the *2D projection of the scene flow* to induce blur kernels. Table 1 summarizes these settings. Table 2 shows the peak-signal-to-noise-ratio (PSNR) of the deblurred images from the different methods. We observe that the PSNR of our homography-based stereo video deblurring out-performs the results of deblurring with ground truth 2D displacement in all cases of non-fronto-parallel motion. In these cases linear motion trajectories of constant velocity are an approximation. Blur matrices induced by homographies are more expressive and improve the results. Already, deblurring with the 2D projection of scene flow achieves a consistently higher PSNR than deblurring with the

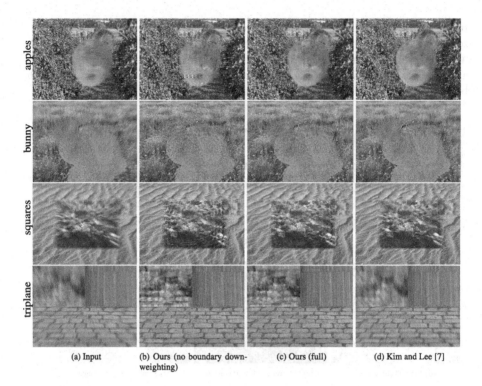

apples
bunny
squares
triplane

(a) Input          (b) Ours (no boundary down-          (c) Ours (full)          (d) Kim and Lee [7]
weighting)

**Fig. 7.** Raytraced scenes for evaluating object motion deblurring: The input images exhibit blur due to 3D object motion (a). Also when 3D homographies are used to induce blur kernels, mixed pixels at object boundaries cause some ringing artifacts (b). Iteratively downweighting the boundaries from the data term, our full stereo video deblurring (c) suppresses ringing and obtains considerably sharper images than state-of-the-art video deblurring (d). Please zoom in for detail

initial flow. Indeed, in the case of forward motion, also deblurring with the 2D projection of the scene flow outperforms deblurring with ground truth displacement. The estimated 2D displacement appears to be a better approximation to the linear, but accelerated trajectory of the 3D forward motion than the 2D ground truth displacement. Figures 5b and d show examples of deblurred images using the ground-truth 2D displacement and our homography-based approach. From the difference image between the results and the original sharp texture, Figs. 5c and e, we observe that the increase in PSNR is due to the mitigation of ringing effects throughout the image.

For the raytraced scenes the geometry of the moving objects is non-planar and the planarity assumption in our image formation model becomes an approximation. Figure 6 shows the estimated disparity of an object and the deblurred image obtained by masking out discontinuities. Looking at the difference image, Fig. 6e, we observe that the deblurring error for slightly curved surfaces is comparable to the performance on planar regions of the background, showing that the over-segmentation aids coping with curved surfaces.

**Table 2.** Deblurring without considering motion-discontinuity regions: For different motions of a planar texture (top) and moving 3D objects with masked object boundaries (bottom), we report the peak signal-to-noise ratio (PSNR) of the deblurred reference frame, the average endpoint error of the estimated motion (AEP), and the average disparity error (ADE) of the estimation. For all scenes the use of scene flow increases deblurring accuracy compared to using optical flow. For scenes with non-fronto-parallel motion (all except '*upward*' and '*apples*') homography-based object motion deblurring provides the best results (bold)

| Blur kernel source | Ground truth 2D displacement | Initial optical flow [46] | | 2D projection of scene flow | | 3D homographies | |
|---|---|---|---|---|---|---|---|
| | PSNR | AEP | PSNR | AEP | PSNR | ADE | PSNR |
| upward | **26.09** | 2.53 | 24.89 | 0.20 | 25.83 | 3.66 | 25.94 |
| forward | 34.12 | 0.09 | 34.45 | 0.10 | 34.55 | 0.19 | **34.74** |
| forward + yaw | 30.03 | 0.15 | 29.90 | 0.15 | 29.95 | 0.45 | **31.02** |
| apples | 34.36 | 0.48 | 29.39 | 0.81 | **34.74** | 4.95 | 33.33 |
| bunny | 25.01 | 0.62 | 24.87 | 0.54 | 25.09 | 0.50 | **25.19** |
| chair | 24.84 | 0.59 | 23.86 | 0.47 | 24.81 | 0.25 | **25.03** |
| squares | 25.97 | 2.32 | 22.69 | 0.97 | 25.82 | 0.65 | **27.21** |
| triplane | 27.43 | 1.16 | 27.11 | 0.49 | 27.27 | 0.12 | **28.30** |

For all rendered scenes where the disparity does not exhibit gross errors, we observe in Table 2 that 3D homography-based deblurring improves the PSNR clearly over any form of 2D deblurring. In the scene '*apples*', Fig. 7a, 1st row, depth estimation fails with a mean disparity error of 4.95 pixels. In this situation the deblurring quality of homography-based deblurring drops below that of its 2D projection. Still, both outperform the results obtained with the initial optical flow. More importantly, as we will see below, the iterative weighting scheme for treating motion discontinuities can address such disparity estimation errors as well and lead to much improved results.

## 4.2 Full Algorithm with Motion Discontinuities

We now evaluate the performance of stereo video deblurring in the presence of object motion boundaries. We use the raytraced scenes from the previous experiment, but this time without providing ground-truth information on the motion discontinuities, Fig. 7a. Additionally, we use real images captured with a stereo camera attached to a motorized rail, Fig. 8a. The camera moves forward very slowly on the rail while we capture frames with maximal exposure time and frame rate. By averaging the frames, we obtain motion-blurred images. Comparison to the central frame of the averaged frame series allows for numerical evaluation. Finally, we capture scenes with arbitrarily moving objects for which only a visual evaluation is possible, Fig. 9a. As before we compare against 2D versions of our algorithm. Additionally, we compare against the state-of-the-art video deblurring algorithm of Kim and Lee [7] that uses 3 consecutive monocular frames. We tuned their regularization parameter to obtain the most accurate results.

In Figs. 7b and c we first contrast homography-induced deblurring without and with handling of motion boundaries. When not taking into account motion boundaries explicitly, *i.e.* $w_n \equiv 1$, Fig. 7b, considerable ringing artifacts are the result, but they are successfully suppressed with our proposed iterative weighting scheme, Fig. 7c. This also becomes evident in the numerical evaluation when comparing the 3$^{rd}$ and 4$^{th}$ column of Table 3 (top)[2]. For the real sequences in Fig. 8, boundary artifacts are generally less pronounced, as all objects in the scene are static and the camera moves toward the scene. However, as shown in Fig. 4, the discontinuity weight can still compensate errors in scene flow computation. One such example is the erroneous depth estimation in the '*apples*' scene, which is disabled by the discontinuity weight. Similarly, also in the scenes with the motorized rail, our full object motion deblurring approach improves the PSNR compared to the basic homography approach, Table 3 (bottom).

When comparing to the state-of-the-art video deblurring method of Kim and Lee [7], we find that our stereo video deblurring approach yields significantly fewer ringing artifacts and considerably sharper results. This can be seen visually, comparing (d) to (c) of Figs. 7, 8 and 9, as well as quantitatively in Table 3. Interestingly, we find in Table 3 that IRLS deblurring with the 2D projection of the scene flow is already on par with video deblurring of Kim and Lee. 3D homography-based deblurring without boundary handling

**Table 3.** Deblurring with motion discontinuities: PSNR of deblurred synthetic scenes with motion discontinuities (top) and real scenes with the camera moving on a motorized rail (bottom). Our homography-based stereo video deblurring with motion boundary weighting (full) clearly outperforms monocular video deblurring with optical-flow induced blur kernels in all cases

| | Initial optical flow [46] | 2D projection of scene flow | 3D homographies | Ours (full) | Kim and Lee [7] |
|---|---|---|---|---|---|
| apples | 20.89 | 29.43 | 26.00 | **29.48** | 26.14 |
| bunny | 20.72 | 22.36 | 22.95 | **23.20** | 21.93 |
| chair | 19.03 | 21.57 | 22.19 | **23.36** | 21.78 |
| squares | 19.60 | 21.90 | 22.56 | **24.58** | 22.99 |
| triplane | 24.73 | 24.55 | 25.22 | **26.59** | 23.30 |
| bottles | 29.51 | 29.55 | 30.80 | **31.07** | 28.33 |
| office | 31.37 | 30.87 | 32.45 | **32.56** | 29.01 |
| planar | 30.71 | 31.21 | 32.33 | **32.82** | 30.01 |
| toys | 33.51 | 33.64 | 34.89 | **34.90** | 31.06 |

---

[2] In the supplemental material we also consider the Structural Similarity index [47] to compare the results.

improves on these result numerically already, highlighting the importance of our homography-induced blur kernels. Yet, our full homography-based object deblurring with motion boundary handling gives further numerical gains and a large visual improvement. Recall that the motion boundaries are initially obtained from the 3D scene flow, thus unique to our setting.

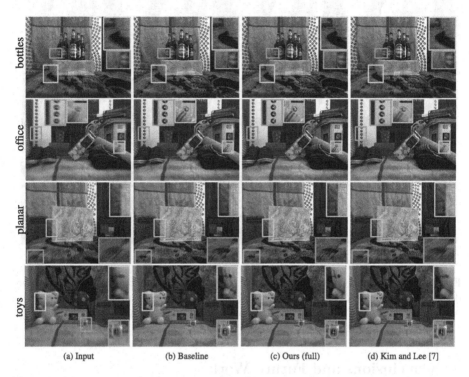

**Fig. 8.** Controlled camera motion for evaluating object motion deblurring: Our 3D deblurring (c) has less ringing artifacts than baseline deblurring with optical flow (b), and sharper results than video deblurring (d), in particular at the periphery of the images where motion is large

For the real scenes with independent object motion, Fig. 9, we observe that the optical flow-based approaches introduce ringing artifacts, particularly where strong gradients of the background coincide with the object boundary. Our stereo video deblurring algorithm can cope with this situation even in the presence of non-planar, non-rigidly moving objects such as the trousers (2nd row) are present.

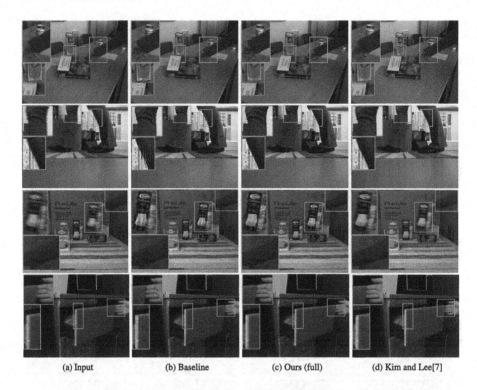

|          |              |                |                      |
|:--------:|:------------:|:--------------:|:--------------------:|
| (a) Input | (b) Baseline | (c) Ours (full) | (d) Kim and Lee[7] |

**Fig. 9.** For real scenes with independent object motion (a), our novel stereo video deblurring approach (c) generates fewer ringing artifacts due to object boundaries than baseline deblurring with optical flow (b) and sharper images than video deblurring (d)

## 5   Conclusions and Future Work

We have proposed the first stereo video deblurring approach, which is based on an image formation model that exploits 3D scene flow computed from stereo video. For scenes with an arbitrary number of moving objects, we use an over-segmentation of the scene into planar patches to establish spatially-variant blur matrices based on local homographies. Our experiments on synthetic scenes and real videos show that deblurring with these homographies is more accurate than baseline methods based on 2D linear motion approximations, as well as the current state-of-the-art in video deblurring. Combined with our robust treatment of motion boundaries through an iterative weighting scheme, our approach obtains superior results also on real stereo videos with independently moving objects. In future work we would like to improve the performance of scene flow computation at motion boundaries such that we can benefit from another view to supply information near motion boundaries.

**Acknowledgements.** The research leading to these results has received funding from the European Research Council under the European Union's Seventh Framework Programme (FP7/2007 - 2013)/ERC Grant Agreement No. 307942 and under the European Union's Horizon 2020 research and innovation programme/ERC Grant Agreement No. 647769.

# References

1. Longuet-Higgins, H.C.: A computer algorithm for reconstructing a scene from two projections. Nature **293**, 133–135 (1981)
2. Shotton, J., Girshick, R., Fitzgibbon, A., Sharp, T., Cook, M., Finocchio, M., Moore, R., Kohli, P., Criminisi, A., Kipman, A., Blake, A.: Efficient human pose estimation from single depth images. IEEE Trans. Pattern Anal. Mach. Intell. **35**(12), 2821–2840 (2013)
3. Franke, U., Joos, A.: Real-time stereo vision for urban traffic scene understanding. In: Intelligent Vehicles Symposium, pp. 273–278 (2000)
4. Geiger, A., Lenz, P., Urtasun, R.: Are we ready for autonomous driving? The KITTI vision benchmark suite. In: CVPR, pp. 3354–3361 (2012)
5. Menze, M., Geiger, A.: Object scene flow for autonomous vehicles. In: CVPR, pp. 3061–3070 (2015)
6. Vogel, C., Schindler, K., Roth, S.: 3D scene flow estimation with a piecewise rigid scene model. Int. J. Comput. Vis. **115**(1), 1–28 (2015)
7. Kim, T.H., Lee, K.M.: Generalized video deblurring for dynamic scenes. In: CVPR, pp. 5426–5434 (2015)
8. Li, Y., Kang, S.B., Joshi, N., Seitz, S.M., Huttenlocher, D.P.: Generating sharp panoramas from motion-blurred videos. In: CVPR, pp. 2424–2431 (2010)
9. Yahyanejad, S., Strom, J.: Removing motion blur from barcode images. In: CVPR, pp. 41–46 (2010)
10. Fergus, R., Singh, B., Hertzmann, A., Roweis, S.T., Freeman, W.T.: Removing camera shake from a single photograph. In: SIGGRAPH, pp. 787–794 (2006)
11. Cho, S., Lee, S.: Fast motion deblurring. ACM Trans. Graph. **28**(5), 145:1–145:8 (2009)
12. Whyte, O., Sivic, J., Zisserman, A., Ponce, J.: Non-uniform deblurring for shaken images. In: CVPR, pp. 491–498 (2010)
13. Krishnan, D., Tay, T., Fergus, R.: Blind deconvolution using a normalized sparsity measure. In: CVPR, pp. 233–240 (2011)
14. Xu, L., Zheng, S., Jia, J.: Unnatural $L_0$ sparse representation for natural image deblurring. In: CVPR, pp. 1107–1114 (2013)
15. Michaeli, T., Irani, M.: Blind deblurring using internal patch recurrence. In: Fleet, D., Pajdla, T., Schiele, B., Tuytelaars, T. (eds.) ECCV 2014, Part III. LNCS, vol. 8691, pp. 783–798. Springer, Heidelberg (2014)
16. Schelten, K., Roth, S.: Localized image blur removal through non-parametric kernel estimation. In: ICPR, pp. 702–707 (2014)
17. Couzinié-Devy, F., Sun, J., Alahari, K., Ponce, J.: Learning to estimate and remove non-uniform image blur. In: CVPR, pp. 1075–1082 (2013)
18. Wulff, J., Black, M.J.: Modeling blurred video with layers. In: Fleet, D., Pajdla, T., Schiele, B., Tuytelaars, T. (eds.) ECCV 2014, Part VI. LNCS, vol. 8694, pp. 236–252. Springer, Heidelberg (2014)

19. Tai, Y.W., Tan, P., Brown, M.S.: Richardson-lucy deblurring for scenes under a projective motion path. IEEE Trans. Pattern Anal. Mach. Intell. **33**(8), 1603–1618 (2011)
20. Gupta, A., Joshi, N., Lawrence Zitnick, C., Cohen, M., Curless, B.: Single image deblurring using motion density functions. In: Daniilidis, K., Maragos, P., Paragios, N. (eds.) ECCV 2010, Part I. LNCS, vol. 6311, pp. 171–184. Springer, Heidelberg (2010)
21. Rajagopalan, A., Chellappa, R.: Motion Deblurring: Algorithms and Systems. Cambridge University Press, Cambridge (2014)
22. Levin, A.: Blind motion deblurring using image statistics. In: NIPS, pp. 841–848 (2006)
23. Chakrabarti, A., Zickler, T., Freeman, W.T.: Analyzing spatially-varying blur. In: CVPR, pp. 2512–2519 (2010)
24. Kim, T.H., Ahn, B., Lee, K.M.: Dynamic scene deblurring. In: ICCV, pp. 3160–3167 (2013)
25. Sun, J., Cao, W., Xu, Z., Ponce, J.: Learning a convolutional neural network for non-uniform motion blur removal. In: CVPR, pp. 769–777 (2015)
26. Kim, T.H., Lee, K.M.: Segmentation-free dynamic scene deblurring. In: CVPR, pp. 2766–2773 (2014)
27. Xu, L., Jia, J.: Depth-aware motion deblurring. In: ICCP, pp. 1–8 (2012)
28. Lee, H., Lee, K.: Dense 3D reconstruction from severely blurred images using a single moving camera. In: CVPR, pp. 273–280 (2013)
29. Arun, M., Rajagopalan, A., Seetharaman, G.: Multi-shot deblurring for 3D scenes. In: CVPR, pp. 19–27 (2015)
30. Hu, Z., Xu, L., Yang, M.H.: Joint depth estimation and camera shake removal from single blurry image. In: CVPR, pp. 2893–2900 (2014)
31. Cho, S., Matsushita, Y., Lee, S.: Removing non-uniform motion blur from images. In: ICCV, pp. 1–8 (2007)
32. He, X., Luo, T., Yuk, S., Chow, K., Wong, K.Y., Chung, R.: Motion estimation method for blurred videos and application of deblurring with spatially varying blur kernels. In: ICCIT, pp. 355–359 (2010)
33. Deng, X., Shen, Y., Song, M., Tao, D., Bu, J., Chen, C.: Video-based non-uniform object motion blur estimation and deblurring. Neurocomputing **86**, 170–178 (2012)
34. Yamaguchi, T., Fukuda, H., Furukawa, R., Kawasaki, H., Sturm, P.: Video deblurring and super-resolution technique for multiple moving objects. In: Kimmel, R., Klette, R., Sugimoto, A. (eds.) ACCV 2010, Part IV. LNCS, vol. 6495, pp. 127–140. Springer, Heidelberg (2011)
35. Vedula, S., Baker, S., Rander, P., Collins, R., Kanade, T.: Three-dimensional scene flow. In: ICCV, vol. 2, pp. 722–729 (1999)
36. Quiroga, J., Devernay, F., Crowley, J.: Local/global scene flow estimation. In: ICIP, pp. 3850–3854 (2013)
37. Wedel, A., Cremers, D.: Stereo Scene Flow for 3D Motion Analysis. Springer Science & Business Media, London (2011)
38. Tai, Y.W., Du, H., Brown, M.S., Lin, S.: Correction of spatially varying image and video motion blur using a hybrid camera. IEEE Trans. Pattern Anal. Mach. Intell. **32**(6), 1012–1028 (2010)
39. Chen, J., Yuan, L., Tang, C.K., Quan, L.: Robust dual motion deblurring. In: CVPR, pp. 1–8 (2008)
40. Cho, S., Wang, J., Lee, S.: Video deblurring for hand-held cameras using patch-based synthesis. ACM Trans. Graph. **31**(4), 64:1–64:9 (2012)

41. Joshi, N., Kang, S.B., Zitnick, C.L., Szeliski, R.: Image deblurring using inertial measurement sensors. ACM Trans. Graph. **29**(4), 30:1–30:9 (2010)
42. Mei, C., Reid, I.: Modeling and generating complex motion blur for real-time tracking. In: CVPR, pp. 1–8 (2008)
43. Murray, R.M., Li, Z., Sastry, S.S.: A Mathematical Introduction to Robotic Manipulation. CRC Press, Boca Raton (1994)
44. Portz, T., Zhang, L., Jiang, H.: Optical flow in the presence of spatially-varying motion blur. In: CVPR, pp. 1752–1759 (2012)
45. Levin, A., Weiss, Y.: User assisted separation of reflections from a single image using a sparsity prior. IEEE Trans. Pattern Anal. Mach. Intell. **29**(9), 1647–1654 (2007)
46. Vogel, C., Roth, S., Schindler, K.: An evaluation of data costs for optical flow. In: Weickert, J., Hein, M., Schiele, B. (eds.) GCPR 2013. LNCS, vol. 8142, pp. 343–353. Springer, Heidelberg (2013)
47. Wang, Z., Bovik, A.C., Sheikh, H.R., Simoncelli, E.P.: Image quality assessment: from error visibility to structural similarity. IEEE Trans. Image Process. **13**(4), 600–612 (2004)

# Robust Image and Video Dehazing with Visual Artifact Suppression via Gradient Residual Minimization

Chen Chen[1(✉)], Minh N. Do[1], and Jue Wang[2]

[1] University of Illinois at Urbana-Champaign, Urbana, IL 61801, USA
{cchen156,minhdo}@illinois.edu
[2] Adobe Research, Seattle, WA 98103, USA
juewang@adobe.com

**Abstract.** Most existing image dehazing methods tend to boost local image contrast for regions with heavy haze. Without special treatment, these methods may significantly amplify existing image artifacts such as noise, color aliasing and blocking, which are mostly invisible in the input images but are visually intruding in the results. This is especially the case for low quality cellphone shots or compressed video frames. The recent work of Li *et al.* (2014) addresses blocking artifacts for dehazing, but is insufficient to handle other artifacts. In this paper, we propose a new method for reliable suppression of different types of visual artifacts in image and video dehazing. Our method makes contributions in both the haze estimation step and the image recovery step. Firstly, an image-guided, depth-edge-aware smoothing algorithm is proposed to refine the initial atmosphere transmission map generated by local priors. In the image recovery process, we propose Gradient Residual Minimization (GRM) for jointly recovering the haze-free image while explicitly minimizing possible visual artifacts in it. Our evaluation suggests that the proposed method can generate results with much less visual artifacts than previous approaches for lower quality inputs such as compressed video clips.

**Keywords:** Video dehazing · Image dehazing · Contrast enhancement · Artifact suppression

## 1 Introduction

Due to atmospheric absorption and scattering, outdoor images and videos are often degraded to have low contrast and visibility. In addition to the deterioration of visual quality, heavy haze also makes many computer vision tasks more

---

Most work was done when Chen was an intern at Adobe.

**Electronic supplementary material** The online version of this chapter (doi:10.1007/978-3-319-46475-6_36) contains supplementary material, which is available to authorized users.

© Springer International Publishing AG 2016
B. Leibe et al. (Eds.): ECCV 2016, Part II, LNCS 9906, pp. 576–591, 2016.
DOI: 10.1007/978-3-319-46475-6_36

difficult, such as stereo estimation, object tracking and detection *etc.* Therefore, removing haze from images and video becomes an important component in a post-processing pipeline. Conventional global contrast enhancement methods often do not perform well because the degradation is spatially-varying. In general, accurate haze estimation and removal from a single image is a challenging task due to its ill-posed nature.

Haze removal has been extensively studied in the literature. Early approaches focus on using multiple images or extra information [12,20,23,24] for dehazing. Recently dehazing from a single image has gained considerable attention, and they can be broadly classified into two groups: methods based on transmission estimation [7,10,19,26] and ones based on adaptive contrast enhancement [6,9, 25]. Techniques in the latter group do not rely on any physical haze model, thus often suffer from visual artifacts such as strong color shift. The state-of-the-art methods often depend on a physical haze model for more accurate haze removal. They first estimate the atmosphere transmission map along with the haze color based on local image priors such as the dark channel prior [10] and the color-line prior [7]. The latent, haze-free image is then computed by directly removing the haze component in each pixel's color. Some methods are proposed to deal with special cases. For example, planar constraints can be utilized in road images [27]. Li *et al.* proposed a method to dehaze videos when the coarse depth maps can be estimated by multi-view stereo [17].

The state-of-the-art methods usually can generate satisfactory results on high quality input images. For lower quality inputs, such as images captured and processed by mobile phones, or compressed video clips, most existing dehazing methods will significantly amplify image artifacts that are visual unnoticeable in the input, especially in heavy haze regions. An example is shown in Fig. 1, where the input image is one video frame extracted from a sequence captured by a cellphone camera. After dehazing using previous methods [10,16], strong visible artifacts appear in the sky region of the results. These artifacts cannot

**Fig. 1.** Dehaze one video frame. (a) Input image. (b) Result of He *et al.* [10]. (c) Result of Li *et al.* [16]. (d) Ours. Note the strong banding and color shifting artifacts in the sky region in (b) and (c). (Color figure online)

be easily removed using post-processing filters without hampering the image content of other regions. Similarly, removing the original artifacts completely without destroying useful image details is also non-trivial as a pre-processing step.

Li *et al.* [16] were the first to consider the problem of artifact suppression in dehazing. Their approach is designed to remove only the blocking artifacts that are usually caused by compression. In this method, the input image is first decomposed into a structure layer and a texture layer, and dehazing is performed on the structure layer and deblocking is applied on the texture layer. The final output image is produced by re-combining the two layers. This method however often does not work well for other artifacts that commonly co-exist in lower quality inputs, *e.g.*, the color banding artifact in Fig. 1 and color aliasing in later examples. In addition, their final results tend to be over-smoothed with missing fine image details, as we will show in our experimental results. This suggests that independent dehazing and deblocking on two separate layers is sub-optimal.

In this work, we propose a new method for image and video dehazing with an emphasis on preventing different types of visual artifacts in the output. Our method follows the general two-step framework and makes contributions in each step: estimating atmosphere transmission map first, then recover the latent image. In the first step, after initializing the transmission map using existing local priors such as the dark channel prior [10], we refine it using a global method based on image guided Total Generalized Variation (TGV) [3] regularization. Compared with other commonly used refinement approaches, our method tends to produce transmission maps that are physically more correct: it produces very smooth regions within the surfaces/objects, while generates strong edges at depth discontinuities. Observing that the boosted visual artifacts by existing methods are often not visible in the input image, in the second stage, we propose a novel way to recover the latent image by minimizing the gradient residual between the output and input images. It suppresses new edges which does not exist in the input image (often are artifacts), but has little effects on the edges that already exist, which are ideal properties for the dehazing task. Considering the existence of artifacts, the linear haze model may not hold on every pixel. We then explicitly introduce an "error" layer in the optimization, which could separate out the large artifacts that violate the linear haze model. Both quantitative and qualitative experimental results show that our method generates more accurate and more natural-looking results than the state-of-the-art methods on compressed inputs. In particular, our method shows significant improvement on video dehazing, which can suppress both spatial and temporal artifacts.

## 2    Overview of Transmission Map Initialization

The transmission map in our framework is required to be initialized by existing local priors, *e.g.*, the widely used dark channel prior [10]. Here we provide a quick overview of the basic image formation model and this method. Note that our main contributions, transmission map refinement and image recovery, are orthogonal to the specific method that one could choose for initializing the transmission map.

Koschmieder *et al.* [13] proposed a physical haze model as:

$$\mathbf{I}(x) = \mathbf{J}(x)t(x) + \mathbf{A}(1 - t(x)), \qquad (1)$$

where $\mathbf{I}$ is the hazy image, $\mathbf{J}$ is the scene radiance, $\mathbf{A}$ is the atmospheric light and assumed to be constant over the whole image, $t$ is the medium transmission and $x$ denotes the image coordinates. The transmission describes the portion of the light reaches to the camera without scattered. The task of dehazing is to estimate $\mathbf{J}$ (with $\mathbf{A}$ and $t$ as by-products) from the input image $\mathbf{I}$, which is a severely ill-posed problem.

The dark channel prior, proposed by He *et al.* [10], is a simple yet efficient local image prior for estimating a coarse transmission map. The dark channel is defined as:

$$J^{dark}(x) = \min_{y \in \Omega(x)} (\min_{c \in \{r,g,b\}} J^c(y)), \qquad (2)$$

where $c$ denotes the color channel and $\Omega(x)$ is a local patch around $x$. Natural image statistics show that $J^{dark}$ tends to be zero. We can rewrite Eq. (1) and take the minimum operations on both sides to get:

$$\min_{y \in \Omega(x)} (\min_c \frac{I^c(y)}{A^c}) = \min_{y \in \Omega(x)} (\min_c \frac{J(y)}{A^c} t(x)) + 1 - t(x). \qquad (3)$$

By assuming the transmission map is constant in each small local patch, we can eliminate $J^{dark}$ to obtain the coarse transmission map:

$$\tilde{t}(x) = 1 - \min_{y \in \Omega(x)} (\min_{c \in \{r,g,b\}} \frac{I^c(y)}{A^c}), \qquad (4)$$

where the atmospheric light color $\mathbf{A}$ can be estimated as the brightest pixel color in the dark channel. This coarse transmission map is computed locally, thus often need to be refined. In practice it is often refined by soft matting [14] or guided image filtering [11]. Finally, the scene radiance is recovered by:

$$\mathbf{J}(x) = (\mathbf{I}(x) - \mathbf{A})/t(x) + \mathbf{A}. \qquad (5)$$

The dark channel prior described above is an elegant solution and often achieves high quality results for high quality images. However, as observed by Li *et al.* [16], image artifacts, such as noise or blocking, can affect both dark channel computation and transmission map smoothing. The original dark channel approach often cannot generate high quality results for images with artifacts.

## 3    TGV-Based Transmission Refinement

In He *et al.*'s method, the transmission map is refined by soft matting [14] or guided image filtering [11]. Both methods are edge-aware operations. They work well with objects that have flat appearances. However, for objects/regions with strong textures, the refined transmission map using these methods tend to have false variations that are correlated with such textures. This is contradictory to the haze model, as the amount of haze in each pixel is only related to its depth, not its texture or color. Therefore, we expect the refined transmission map to be smooth inside the same object/surface, and only has discontinuities along depth edges. We thus propose a new transmission refinement method to try to achieve this goal without recovering the 3D scene.

We formulate the transmission refinement as a global optimization problem, consisting of a data fidelity term and regularization terms. Note that the transmission values of white objects are often underestimated by the dark channel method. We need a model that is robust to such outliers or errors. Instead of the commonly-used $\ell_2$ norm data term, we use the $\ell_1$ norm to somewhat tolerate outliers and errors. The second-order Total Generalized Variation (TGV) [3,8,21,28] with a guided image is adopted for regularization. Compared with conventional Total Variation (TV) regularization that encourages *piecewise constant* images and often suffers from undesired staircasing artifacts, TGV prefers *piecewise smooth* images. This is a desired property for the transmission, as we may have a slanted plane (e.g., road, brigde) whose transmission varies smoothly along with the change of depth.

Given the initial transmission $\tilde{t}$ and a guided image $I$, the optimization problem with TGV regularization is:

$$\min_{t,w}\{\alpha_1 \int |D^{1/2}(\nabla t - w)| \; \mathrm{d}x + \alpha_0 \int |\nabla w| \; \mathrm{d}x + \int |t - \tilde{t}| \; \mathrm{d}x\}, \qquad (6)$$

where $D^{1/2}$ is the anisotropic diffusion tensor [28] defined as:

$$D^{1/2} = \exp(-\gamma|\nabla I|^\beta)nn^T + n^\perp n^{\perp T}, \qquad (7)$$

where $n$ is the direction of the gradient of the guided image $n = \frac{\nabla I}{|\nabla I|}$ and $n^\perp$ is the perpendicular direction, $\gamma, \beta$ are parameters to adjust the sharpness and magnitude of the tensor, $w$ is an auxiliary variable. Our experiments show that the sharp depth edges cannot be preserved without the guided image when using the TGV regularization. Unlike the previous local refinement methods, TGV performs globally and is less sensitive to the local textures.

To solve this problem, we apply the prime-dual minimization algorithm [4] with the Legendre Fenchel transform. The transformed primal-dual problem is given by:

$$\min_{t,w} \max_{p\in P, q\in Q} \{\alpha_1 \left\langle D^{1/2}(\nabla t - w), p \right\rangle + \alpha_0 \left\langle \nabla w, q \right\rangle + \int |t - \tilde{t}| \; \mathrm{d}x\}, \qquad (8)$$

where $p, q$ are dual variables and their feasible sets are:

$$P = \{p \in R^{2MN}, \|p\|_\infty \le 1\},$$
$$Q = \{q \in R^{4MN}, \|q\|_\infty \le 1\}. \qquad (9)$$

The algorithm for transmission refinement is formally summarized in Algorithm 1.

---

**Algorithm 1.** Transmission map refinement by Guided TGV

---

**Initialization:** $t^0 = \tilde{t}, w^0, \bar{t}^0, \bar{w}^0, p^0, q^0 = 0, \sigma_p > 0, \sigma_q > 0, \tau_t > 0, \tau_w > 0$
**for** $k = 0$ **to** $Maxiteration$ **do**
$\quad p^{k+1} = \mathcal{P}[p^k + \sigma_p \alpha_1 (D^{1/2}(\nabla \bar{t}^k - \bar{w}^k))]$
$\quad q^{k+1} = \mathcal{P}[q^k + \sigma_q \alpha_0 \nabla \bar{w}^k]$
$\quad t^{k+1} = thresholding_\tau (t^k + \tau_u \alpha_1 \nabla^T D^{1/2} p^{k+1})$
$\quad w^{k+1} = w^k + \tau_w (\alpha_0 \nabla^T q^{k+1} + \alpha_1 D^{1/2} p^{k+1})$
$\quad \bar{t}^{k+1} = t^{k+1} + \theta(t^{k+1} - \bar{t}^k)$
$\quad \bar{w}^{k+1} = w^{k+1} + \theta(w^{k+1} - \bar{w}^k)$
**end for**

---

In the algorithm, $\sigma_p > 0$, $\sigma_q > 0$, $\tau_t > 0$, $\tau_w > 0$ are step sizes and $k$ is the iteration counter. The element-wise projection operators $\mathcal{P}$ is defined:

$$\mathcal{P}[x] = \frac{x}{\max\{1, |x|\}}. \tag{10}$$

The $thresholding_\tau()$ denotes the soft-thresholding operation:

$$thresholding_\tau(x) = \max(|x| - \tau, 0)\text{sign}(x). \tag{11}$$

$\theta$ is updated in every iteration as suggested by [4]. The divergence and gradient operators in the optimization are approximated using standard finite differences. Please refer to [4] for more details of this optimization method.

Figure 2 shows the transmission maps estimated by guided filter, matting followed by bilateral filter and TGV refinement. Compared with guided image

**Fig. 2.** Comparisons of transmission refinement methods. (a) Input image. (b) Result of guided image filtering [11]. (c) Result of matting followed by bilateral filtering [10]. (d) Ours. (Color figure online)

filtering or bilateral smoothing, our method is aware of the depth edges while producing smooth surface within each objects (see the buildings indicated by the yellow circles). In addition, our optimization scheme does not exactly trust the initialization and it can somewhat tolerate the errors (see the house indicated by the blue arrow).

## 4  Robust Latent Image Recovery by Gradient Residual Minimization

After the transmission map is refined, our next goal is to recovery the scene radiance $\mathbf{J}$. Many existing methods obtain it by directly solving the linear haze model (5), where the artifacts are treated equally as the true pixels. As a result, the artifacts will be also enhanced after dehazing.

Without any prior information, it is impossible to extract or suppress the artifacts from the input image. We have observed that in practice, the visual artifacts are usually invisible in the input image. After dehazing, they pop up as their gradients are amplified, introduce new image edges that are not consistent with the underlying image content, such as the color bands in Fig. 1(b,c). Based on this observation, we propose a novel way to constrain the image edges to be structurally consistent before and after dehazing. This motivates us to minimize the residual of the gradients between the input and output images under the sparse-inducing norm. We call it Gradient Residual Minimization (GRM). Combined with the linear haze model, our optimization problem becomes:

$$\min_{\mathbf{J}}\{\frac{1}{2}\int\|\mathbf{J}t-(\mathbf{I}-\mathbf{A}+\mathbf{A}t)\|_2^2\,\mathrm{d}x+\eta\int\|\nabla\mathbf{J}-\nabla\mathbf{I}\|_0\,\mathrm{d}x\}, \qquad (12)$$

where the $\ell_0$ norm counts the number of non-zero elements and $\eta$ is a weighting parameter. It is important to note that the above spares-inducing norm only encourages the non-zero gradients of $\mathbf{J}$ to be at the same positions of the gradients of $\mathbf{I}$. However, their magnitudes do not have to be the same. This good property of the edge-preserving term is very crucial in dehazing, as the contrast of the overall image will be increased after dehazing. With the proposed GRM, new edges (often caused by artifacts) that do not exist in the input image will be penalized but the original strong image edges will be kept.

Due to the existence of the artifacts, it is very possible that the linear haze model does not hold on every corrupted pixel. Unlike previous approaches, we assume there may exist some artifacts or large errors $\mathbf{E}$ in the input image, which violates the linear composition model in Eq. (1) locally. Furthermore, we assume $\mathbf{E}$ is sparse. This is reasonable as operations such as compression do not damage image content uniformly: they often cause more errors in high frequency image content than flat regions. With above assumptions, to recover the latent image, we solve the following optimization problem:

$$\min_{\mathbf{J},\mathbf{E}}\{\frac{1}{2}\int\|\mathbf{J}t-(\mathbf{I}-\mathbf{E}-\mathbf{A}+\mathbf{A}t)\|_2^2\,\mathrm{d}x+\lambda\int\|\mathbf{E}\|_0\,\mathrm{d}x+\eta\int\|\nabla\mathbf{J}-\nabla\mathbf{I}\|_0\,\mathrm{d}x\},$$
$$(13)$$

where $\lambda$ is a regularization parameter. Intuitively, the first term says that after subtracting $\mathbf{E}$ from the input image $\mathbf{I}$, the remaining component $\mathbf{I} - \mathbf{E}$, together with the latent image $\mathbf{J}$ and the transmission map $\mathbf{A}$, satisfy the haze model in Eq. (1). The second term $\mathbf{E}$ represents large artifacts while the last term encodes our observations on image edges.

However, the $\ell_0$ minimization problem is generally difficult to solve. Therefore in practice, we replace it with the closest convex relaxation – $\ell_1$ norms [5,15]:

$$\min_{\mathbf{J},\mathbf{E}}\{\frac{1}{2}\int \|\mathbf{J}t-(\mathbf{I}-\mathbf{E}-\mathbf{A}+\mathbf{A}t)\|_2^2 \, \mathrm{d}x + \lambda \int \|\mathbf{E}\|_1 \, \mathrm{d}x + \eta \int \|\nabla \mathbf{J} - \nabla \mathbf{I}\|_1 \, \mathrm{d}x\}. \tag{14}$$

We alternately solve this new problem by minimizing the energy function with respect to $\mathbf{J}$ and $\mathbf{E}$, respectively. Let $\mathbf{Z} = \mathbf{J} - \mathbf{I}$, and the $\mathbf{J}$ subproblem can be rewritten as:

$$\min_{\mathbf{Z}}\{\frac{1}{2}\int \|(\mathbf{Z}+\mathbf{I})t - (\mathbf{I}-\mathbf{E}-\mathbf{A}+\mathbf{A}t)\|_2^2 \, \mathrm{d}x + \eta \int \|\nabla \mathbf{Z}\|_1 \, \mathrm{d}x\}, \tag{15}$$

which is a TV minimization problem. We can apply an existing TV solver [1] for this subproblem. After $\mathbf{Z}$ is solved, $\mathbf{J}$ can be recovered by $\mathbf{J} = \mathbf{Z} + \mathbf{I}$. For the $\mathbf{E}$ subproblem:

$$\min_{\mathbf{E}}\{\frac{1}{2}\int \|\mathbf{J}t-(\mathbf{I}-\mathbf{E}-\mathbf{A}+\mathbf{A}t)\|_2^2 \, \mathrm{d}x + \lambda \int \|\mathbf{E}\|_1 \, \mathrm{d}x\}, \tag{16}$$

it has a closed-form solution by soft-thresholding. The overall algorithm for latent image recovery is summarized in Algorithm 2.

---

**Algorithm 2.** Robust Image Dehazing

---
**Initialization:** $E^0 = 0$, $J^0 = \frac{\mathbf{I}-\mathbf{A}}{t} + \mathbf{A}$
**for** $k = 0$ to $Maxiteration$ **do**
    $\mathbf{Z}_b = \mathbf{I} - \mathbf{E}^k - \mathbf{A} + \mathbf{A}t - \mathbf{I}t$
    $\mathbf{Z} = \arg\min_{\mathbf{Z}}\{\frac{1}{2}\int \|\mathbf{Z}t - \mathbf{Z}_b\|_2^2 \mathrm{d}x + \eta \int \|\nabla \mathbf{Z}\|_1 \mathrm{d}x\}$
    $J^{k+1} = \mathbf{I} + \mathbf{Z}$
    $\mathbf{E}^{k+1} = thresholding_\lambda(\mathbf{I} - \mathbf{J}^{k+1}t - (1-t)\mathbf{A})$
**end for**

---

The convergence of Algorithm 2 is shown in Fig. 3. We initialize $\mathbf{J}$ with the least squares solution without GRM and a zero image $\mathbf{E}$. As we could see, the oject function in Eq. (14) decreased monotonically and our method gradually converged. From the intermediate results, it can be observed that the initial $\mathbf{J}$ has visible artifacts in the sky region, which is gradually eliminated during the optimization. One may notice that $\mathbf{E}$ converged to large values on the tower and building edges. As we will show later, these are the aliasing artifacts caused by compression. And our method can successfully separate out these artifacts.

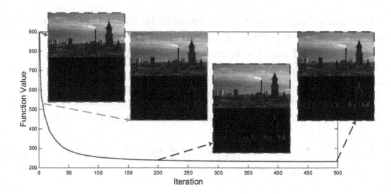

**Fig. 3.** The convergence of proposed method. The oject function in Eq. (14) is monotonically decreasing. The intermediate results of **J** and 10×**E** at iteration 1, 5, 200 and 500 are shown.

## 5   Experiments

More high resolution image and video results are in the supplementary material. For quality comparisons, all the images should be viewed on screen instead of printed version.

### 5.1   Implementation Details

In our implementation, the tensor parameters are set as $\beta = 9$, $\gamma = 0.85$. The regularization parameters are $\alpha_0 = 0.5$, $\alpha_1 = 0.05$, $\lambda = 0.01$ and $\eta = 0.1$. We found our method is not sensitive to these parameters. The same set of parameters are used for all experiments in this paper. We terminate Algorithm 1 after 300 iterations and Algorithm 2 after 200 iterations.

We use the same method in He *et al.*'s approach to estimate the atmospheric light **A**. For video inputs, we simply use the **A** computed from the first frame for all other frames. We found that fixing **A** for all frames is generally sufficient to get temporally coherent results by our model.

Using our MATLAB implementation on a laptop computer with a i7-4800 CPU and 16 GB RAM, it takes around 20 s to dehaze a $480 \times 270$ image. In comparison, 10 min per frame is reported in [17] on the same video frames. Same as many previous works [7], we apply a global gamma correction on images that become too dark after dehazing, just for better displaying.

### 5.2   Evaluation on Synthetic Data

We first quantitatively evaluate the performance of the proposed transmission estimation method using a synthetic dataset. Similar to previous practices [26], we synthesize hazy images from stereo pairs [18,22] with known disparity maps. The transmission maps are simulated in the same way as in [26]. Since our method is tailored towards suppressing artifacts, we prepare two test sets: one with high quality input images, the other with noise and compression corrupted images. To synthesize corruption, we first add 1 % of Gaussian noise to the hazy images. These images are then compressed using the JPEG codec in Photoshop, with the compression quality 8 out of 12.

In Tables 1 and 2 we show the MSE of the haze map and the recovered image by different methods, on the clean and the corrupted datasets, respectively. The results show that our method achieves more accurate haze map and latent image than previous methods in most cases. One may find that the errors for corrupted inputs sometimes are lower than those of noise-free ones. It is because the dark channel based methods underestimated the transmission on these bright indoor scenes. The transmission may be slightly preciser when noise makes the images more colorful. Comparing the results of the two tables, the improvement by our method is more significant on the second set, which demonstrates its ability to suppress artifacts.

**Table 1.** Quantitative comparisons on the clean synthetic dataset. Table reports the MSE $(10^{-3})$ of the transmission map (left) and the output image (right).

| | Aloe | Barn | Cones | Dolls | Moebius | Monopoly | Teddy | Rocks |
|---|---|---|---|---|---|---|---|---|
| He et al. [10] | 5.6/17.4 | 0.9/**7.9** | 8.6/13.7 | 8.0/14.3 | 7.5/18.6 | 11.2/30.1 | 10.3/20.1 | 4.6/11.4 |
| Li et al. [16] | 4.5/13.2 | 1.6/13.9 | 5.8/8.9 | 4.1 /7.0 | 5.7/**12.7** | 8.9/23.8 | **4.0/6.6** | 3.7/9.5 |
| Ours | **4.4/10.4** | **0.8**/9.0 | **5.6/8.0** | **3.8 /6.8** | **5.4**/12.7 | **7.9/20.7** | 6.6/10.7 | **3.2/8.0** |

**Table 2.** Quantitative comparison on the noise and compression corrupted synthetic dataset. Table reports the MSE $(10^{-3})$ of the transmission map (left) and the output image (right).

| | Aloe | Barn | Cones | Dolls | Moebius | Monopoly | Teddy | Rocks |
|---|---|---|---|---|---|---|---|---|
| He et al. [10] | 5.3/17.0 | **1.0/11.2** | 8.1/12.9 | 7.6/13.8 | 7.2/17.4 | 10.7/27.9 | 10.0/19.3 | 4.1/10.3 |
| Li et al. [16] | 4.4/13.2 | 1.5/14.2 | 5.6/8.9 | 4.0/7.1 | 5.7/12.7 | 8.8/22.6 | **4.0/6.7** | 3.6/9.3 |
| Ours | **3.9/9.9** | 1.0/12.8 | **5.2/7.1** | **3.5/6.2** | **5.1/11.4** | **7.5/18.6** | 6.5/10.1 | **2.8/6.8** |

## 5.3  Real-World Images and Videos

We compare our method with some recent works [9,16,19] on a real video frame in Fig. 4. The compression artifacts and image noise become severe after dehazing by Meng et al.'s method and the Dehaze feature in Adobe Photoshop. Galdran et al.'s result suffers from large color distortion. He et al. have pointed out the similar phenomenon of Tan et al.'s method [25], which is also based on contrast enhancement. Li et al.'s method [16] is designed for blocking artifact suppression.

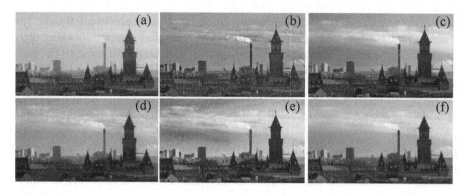

**Fig. 4.** Dehazing results of different methods. (a) Input image. (b) Meng *et al.*'s result [19]. (c) Li *et al.*'s result [16]. (d) Galdran *et al.*'s result [9]. (e) Photoshop 2015 dehazing result. (f) Our result.

Although their result does not contain such artifacts, the sky region is quite oversmoothed. Our result maintains subtle image features while at the same time successfully avoids boosting these artifacts.

Our method can especially suppress halo and color aliasing artifacts around depth edges that are common for previous methods, as shown in the zoomed-in region of the tower in Fig. 5. Except the result by our method, all other methods produce severe halo and color aliasing artifacts around the sharp tower boundary. Pay special attention to the flag on the top of the tower: the flag is dilated by all other methods except ours. Figure 5(h) visualizes the artifact map **E** in Eq. (14), it suggests that our image recovery method pays special attention to the boundary pixels to avoid introducing aliasing by dehazing. We also include our result without the proposed GRM in Fig. 5(f). The blocky artifacts and color aliasing around the tower boundary can not be reduced on this result, which demonstrates the effectiveness of the proposed model.

In Fig. 6, we compare our method with two variational methods [9,17] proposed recently on a video frame. Galdran *et al.*'s method [9] converged in a few iterations on this image, but the result still contains haze. The method in

**Fig. 5.** Zoomed-in region of Fig. 4. (a) Input image. (b) Meng *et al.*'s result [19]. (c) Li *et al.*'s result [16]. (d) Galdran *et al.*'s result [9]. (e) Photoshop 2015 result. (f) Our result without the proposed GRM. (g) Our result. (h) Our **E** × 10.

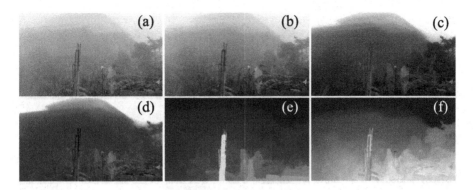

**Fig. 6.** Comparison with some recent methods. (a) Input video frame. (b) Galdran *et al.*'s result [9]. (c) Li *et al.*'s result [17]. (d) Our result. (e) Li's depth [17] (computed using the whole video). (f) Our transmission map.

[17] performs simultaneously dehazing and stereo reconstruction, thus it only works when structure-from-motion can be calculated. For general videos contain dynamic scenes or a single image, it cannot be applied. From the results, our method is comparable to that in [17], or even better. For example, our method can remove more haze on the building. This is clearer on Li's depth map, where the shape of the building can be hardly found.

We further compare our method with the deblocking based method [16] on more video sequences in Fig. 7. Li *et al.*'s method generates various artifacts in these examples, such as the over-sharpened and over-saturated sea region in the first example, the color distortion in the sky regions of the second, and the halos around the buildings and the color banding in the third example. In the bottom example, there is strong halo near the intersection of the sky and sea. Another drawback of Li *et al.*'s method is that fine image details are often lost, such as the sea region in the last example. In contrast, our results contain much less visual artifacts and appear to be more natural.

For videos, the flickering artifacts widely exist on the previous frame-by-frame dehazing methods. It is often caused by the artifacts and the change of overall color in the input video. Recently, Bonneel *et al.* proposed a new method to remove the flickering by enforcing temporal consistency using optical flow [2]. Although their method can successfully remove the temporal artifacts, it does not work for the spatial artifacts on each frame. Figure 8 shows one example frame of a video, where their result inherits all the structured artifacts from the existing method. Although we only perform frame-by-frame dehazing, the result shows that our method is able to suppress temporal artifacts as well. This is because the input frames already have good temporal consistency. Such temporal consistency is transfered into our result frame-by-frame by the proposed GRM.

We recruited 34 volunteers through the Adobe mail list for a user study of result quality, which contained researches, interns, managers, photographers *etc.* For each example, we presented three different results anonymously (always

**Fig. 7.** Comparison with Li *et al.*'s method. First column: input video frame. Second column: Li *et al.*'s result [16]. Third column: our result.

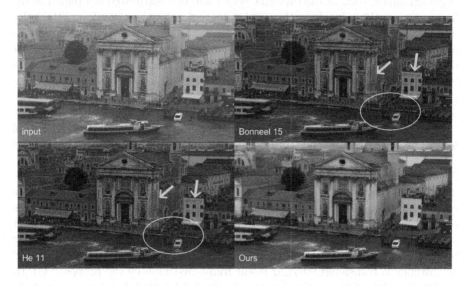

**Fig. 8.** A frame of video dehazing results. The full video is in the supplementary material. The halos around the pillars and structured artifacts are indicated by the yellow circle and arrows. (Color figure online)

including ours) in random orders, and asked them to pick the best dehazing result, based on realism, dehazing quality, artifacts *etc.* 52.9 % subjects preferred our "bali" result in Fig. 6, 47.1 % preferred the result in [17] and 0 % for He *et al.*'s [10]. We have mentioned above that [17] requires external structure-from-motion information, while ours does not and can be applied to more general dehazing. For Fig. 8, 91.2 % preffered our results over He *et al.*'s [10] and Bonneel *et al.*'s [2]. For the rest of examples in this paper, our results were the preferred ones also (by 73.5 %–91.2 % people), where overall 80.0 % picked our results over Li *et al.*'s [16] (14.7 %) and He *et al.*'s [10] (5.3 %).

## 5.4 Discussion

One may argue there are simpler alternatives to handle artifacts in the dehazing pipeline. One way is to explicitly remove the image artifacts before dehazing, such as Li *et al.*'s method. However, accurately removing all image artifacts itself is a difficult task. If not done perfectly, the quality of the final image will be compromised, as shown in various examples in this paper. Another alternative is to simply reduce the amount of haze to be removed. However, it will significantly decrease the power of dehazing, as we show in the tower example in the supplementary material. Our method is a more principle way to achieve a good balance between dehazing and minimizing visual artifacts.

Despite its effectiveness, our method still has some limitations. Firstly, our method inherits the limitations of the dark channel prior. It may over-estimate the amount of haze for white objects that are close to the camera. In addition, for very far away objects, our method can not significantly increase their contrast, which is due to the ambiguity between the artifacts and true objects covered by very thick haze. It is even difficult for human eyes to distinguish them without image context. Previous methods also have poor performance on such challenging

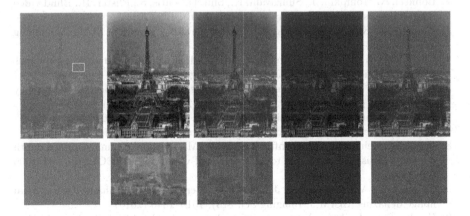

**Fig. 9.** Dehazing a low quality JPEG image. From left to right are the input image and the results by: Fattal *et al.* [7], He *et al.* [10], Li *et al.* [16] and ours. The bottom row shows the zoomed-in areas corresponding to the yellow box. (Color figure online)

tasks: they either directly amplify all the artifacts or mistakenly remove the distant objects to produce over-smoothed results.

Figure 9 shows one such example that contains some far-away buildings surrounded by JPEG artifacts. Both Fattal *et al.*' result and He *et al.*'s have serve JPEG artifacts after dehazing. On the contrary, in Li *et al.*'s result, the distant buildings are mistakenly removed by their deblocking filter, and become much less visible. Although our method cannot solve the ambiguity mentioned above to greatly enhance the far-away buildings, it can automatically take care of the artifacts and generate a more realistic result.

## 6   Conclusion

We have proposed a new method to suppress visual artifacts in image and video dehazing. By introducing a gradient residual and error layer into the image recovery process, our method is able to remove various artifacts without explicitly modeling each one. A new transmission refinement method is introduced in this work, which contributes to improving the overall accuracy of our results. We have conducted extensive evaluation on both synthetic datasets and real-world examples, and validated the superior performance of our method over the state-of-the-arts for lower quality inputs. While our method works well on the dehazing task, it can be potentially extended to other image enhancement applications, due to the similar artifacts-amplification nature of them.

## References

1. Beck, A., Teboulle, M.: Fast gradient-based algorithms for constrained total variation image denoising and deblurring problems. IEEE Trans. Image Process. **18**(11), 2419–2434 (2009)
2. Bonneel, N., Tompkin, J., Sunkavalli, K., Sun, D., Paris, S., Pfister, H.: Blind video temporal consistency. ACM Trans. Graph. **34**(6), 196 (2015)
3. Bredies, K., Kunisch, K., Pock, T.: Total generalized variation. SIAM J. Imaging Sci. **3**(3), 492–526 (2010)
4. Chambolle, A., Pock, T.: A first-order primal-dual algorithm for convex problems with applications to imaging. J. Math. Imaging Vis. **40**(1), 120–145 (2011)
5. Chen, C., Li, Y., Liu, W., Huang, J.: Image fusion with local spectral consistency and dynamic gradient sparsity. In: CVPR, pp. 2760–2765 (2014)
6. Fattal, R.: Single image dehazing. ACM Trans. Grap. **27**, 72 (2008)
7. Fattal, R.: Dehazing using color-lines. ACM Trans. Graph. **34**(1), 13 (2014)
8. Ferstl, D., Reinbacher, C., Ranftl, R., Rüther, M., Bischof, H.: Image guided depth upsampling using anisotropic total generalized variation. In: ICCV, pp. 993–1000 (2013)
9. Galdran, A., Vazquez-Corral, J., Pardo, D., Bertalmío, M.: Enhanced variational image dehazing. SIAM J. Imaging Sci. **8**(3), 1519–1546 (2015)
10. He, K., Sun, J., Tang, X.: Single image haze removal using dark channel prior. IEEE Trans. Pattern Anal. Mach. Intell. **33**(12), 2341–2353 (2011)
11. He, K., Sun, J., Tang, X.: Guided image filtering. IEEE Trans. Pattern Anal. Mach. Intell. **35**(6), 1397–1409 (2013)

12. Kopf, J., Neubert, B., Chen, B., Cohen, M., Cohen-Or, D., Deussen, O., Uytten-daele, M., Lischinski, D.: Deep photo: model-based photograph enhancement and viewing. ACM Trans. Graph. **27**, 116 (2008)
13. Koschmieder, H.: Theorie der horizontalen Sichtweite. In: Beitrge zur Physik der freien Atmosphre (1924)
14. Levin, A., Lischinski, D., Weiss, Y.: A closed-form solution to natural image mat-ting. IEEE Trans. Pattern Anal. Mach. Intell. **30**(2), 228–242 (2008)
15. Li, Y., Chen, C., Yang, F., Huang, J.: Deep sparse representation for robust image registration. In: CVPR, pp. 4894–4901 (2015)
16. Li, Y., Guo, F., Tan, R.T., Brown, M.S.: A contrast enhancement framework with JPEG artifacts suppression. In: Fleet, D., Pajdla, T., Schiele, B., Tuytelaars, T. (eds.) ECCV 2014, Part II. LNCS, vol. 8690, pp. 174–188. Springer, Heidelberg (2014)
17. Li, Z., Tan, P., Tan, R.T., Zou, D., Zhiying Zhou, S., Cheong, L.F.: Simultaneous video defogging and stereo reconstruction. In: CVPR, pp. 4988–4997 (2015)
18. Lu, S., Ren, X., Liu, F.: Depth enhancement via low-rank matrix completion. In: CVPR, pp. 3390–3397 (2014)
19. Meng, G., Wang, Y., Duan, J., Xiang, S., Pan, C.: Efficient image dehazing with boundary constraint and contextual regularization. In: ICCV, pp. 617–624 (2013)
20. Narasimhan, S.G., Nayar, S.K.: Contrast restoration of weather degraded images. IEEE Trans. Pattern Anal. Mach. Intell. **25**(6), 713–724 (2003)
21. Ranftl, R., Gehrig, S., Pock, T., Bischof, H.: Pushing the limits of stereo using variational stereo estimation. In: IEEE Intelligent Vehicles Symposium, pp. 401–407 (2012)
22. Scharstein, D., Szeliski, R.: A taxonomy and evaluation of dense two-frame stereo correspondence algorithms. Int. J. Comput. Vision **47**(1–3), 7–42 (2002)
23. Schechner, Y.Y., Narasimhan, S.G., Nayar, S.K.: Instant dehazing of images using polarization. In: CVPR, vol. 1, pp. I–325 (2001)
24. Shwartz, S., Namer, E., Schechner, Y.Y.: Blind haze separation. In: CVPR, vol. 2, pp. 1984–1991 (2006)
25. Tan, R.T.: Visibility in bad weather from a single image. In: CVPR, pp. 1–8 (2008)
26. Tang, K., Yang, J., Wang, J.: Investigating haze-relevant features in a learning framework for image dehazing. In: CVPR, pp. 2995–3002 (2014)
27. Tarel, J.P., Hautière, N., Caraffa, L., Cord, A., Halmaoui, H., Gruyer, D.: Vision enhancement in homogeneous and heterogeneous fog. IEEE Intell. Transp. Syst. Mag. **4**(2), 6–20 (2012)
28. Werlberger, M., Trobin, W., Pock, T., Wedel, A., Cremers, D., Bischof, H.: Anisotropic Huber-L1 optical flow. In: BMVC, vol. 1, p. 3 (2009)

# Smooth Neighborhood Structure Mining on Multiple Affinity Graphs with Applications to Context-Sensitive Similarity

Song Bai[1(✉)], Shaoyan Sun[2], Xiang Bai[1], Zhaoxiang Zhang[3], and Qi Tian[4]

[1] Huazhong University of Science and Technology, Wuhan, China
{songbai,xbai}@hust.edu.cn
[2] University of Science and Technology of China, Hefei, China
sunshy@mail.ustc.edu.cn
[3] CAS Center for Excellence in Brain Science and Intelligence Technology,
CASIA, Beijing, China
zhaoxiang.zhang@ia.ac.cn
[4] University of Texas at San Antonio, San Antonio, USA
qi.tian@utsa.edu

**Abstract.** Due to the ability of capturing geometry structures of the data manifold, diffusion process has demonstrated impressive performances in retrieval task by spreading the similarities on the affinity graph. In view of robustness to noise edges, diffusion process is usually *localized*, *i.e.*, only propagating similarities via neighbors. However, selecting neighbors smoothly on graph-based manifolds is more or less ignored by previous works. In this paper, we propose a new algorithm called Smooth Neighborhood (SN) that mines the neighborhood structure to satisfy the manifold assumption. By doing so, nearby points on the underlying manifold are guaranteed to yield similar neighbors as much as possible. Moreover, SN is adjusted to tackle multiple affinity graphs by imposing a weight learning paradigm, and this is the primary difference compared with related works which are only applicable with one affinity graph. Exhausted experimental results and comparisons against other algorithms manifest the effectiveness of the proposed algorithm.

**Keywords:** Diffusion process · Image/shape retrieval · Affinity graph

## 1 Introduction

In recent years, context-sensitive similarity has attracted much attention due to its superior performances in image/shape retrieval. These approaches have a very diverse nomenclature, such as contextual dissimilarity measure [1], graph transduction [2–4], affinity learning [5,6], ranking list comparison [7–9], re-ranking [10–12]. However, their inherent principle is almost the same, that is, the similarity between two images can be measured more accurately by taking the

© Springer International Publishing AG 2016
B. Leibe et al. (Eds.): ECCV 2016, Part II, LNCS 9906, pp. 592–608, 2016.
DOI: 10.1007/978-3-319-46475-6_37

underlying manifold structure into account. In order to specify the differences between them systematically, Donoser *et al.* [13] provide a generic framework called Diffusion Process and a thorough comparison of most aforementioned algorithms experimentally. Diffusion process is operated on affinity graph, with nodes representing images and edge weights denoting pairwise similarities. This affinity graph actually defines a data manifold implicitly, and the similarities are diffused along the geodesic path of the manifold.

As one of the most important conclusions quoted from [13], it is crucial to constrain the diffusion process locally, since diffusion process is susceptible to noise edges in the affinity graph. The experimental observation supports the "locality" assumption in manifold learning [14], that each data point and its neighbors lie on a linear patch of the manifold. It means that only quite short distances are reliable since they tend to associate with short geodesic distances along the manifold. As a result, the nodes that diffusion process selects to spread the similarities on the affinity graph are usually the neighbors of the query that have small dissimilarities with it. So, it is of great importance to construct robust neighborhood structures so that diffusion process is performed in a proper way.

The simplest way to establish the neighborhood structure is k-nearest neighbors (kNN) rule. Given a certain query, kNN rule selects $K$ nodes with the largest edge weights to the query as its neighborhood. Some variants of kNN are also proposed, such as $\epsilon$-neighbors, symmetric kNN, Mutual kNN [15] (also named as reciprocal kNN in [16,17]). As extensively proven in [15], kNN is prone to including noise edges and nodes, thus leading to unsatisfactory retrieval performances. To overcome its defect, Dominant Neighbors (DN) is proposed in [5] based on the analysis of dominant sets, and Consensus of kNN (CN) is proposed in [18] by exploiting the consensus information of kNN.

However, although these neighborhood analysis algorithms are embedded into some variants of diffusion process, they themselves do not capture the geometry of the data manifold. That is to say, they cannot preserve the property of *local consistency* that nearby points on the manifold are guaranteed to yield the same neighbors. For example, it usually occurs that two points belong to the same dense cluster, while they have no common neighbors if kNN rule or DN is used. In context-based retrieval, this problem is first proposed in [19], and later emphasized again in [13]. Nevertheless, they only alleviate the problem to a certain extent by localizing the diffusion process using kNN on both sides (query side and database side), and do not intend to tackle the problem seriously.

Moreover, previous works are only applicable with one affinity graph. When more affinity graphs are given, the difficulties of constructing neighborhood structures lie in two aspects, *i.e.*, the way to determine the weights of different affinity graphs and the way to aggregate the neighborhood structures produced by them. Both issues are quite difficult if no prior knowledge is available. Of course, one can use a linear combination of multiple affinity graphs with equal weights. However, as demonstrated in Sect. 4, it is a suboptimal solution since the complementary nature among them is neglected.

In this paper, we propose an algorithm called Smooth Neighborhood (SN) specifically for neighborhood structure mining. Apart from previous works, our primary contributions can be divided into three parts: (1) SN enables the neighbor selection to vary smoothly along the data manifold, thus the local similarity can be sufficiently reflected in the selection of neighbors. (2) SN is suitable to deal with more than one affinity graph. It learns the shared neighborhood structure and the importance of multiple affinity graphs in a unified framework. Therefore the neighborhood aggregation and weight learning can be done simultaneously. (3) Instead of using some heuristic rules that stem from empirical observations (*e.g.*, Mutual kNN), we give a formal formulation to SN and derive an iterative solution to the optimization problem with proven convergence.

## 2   Related Work

Tremendous developments on context-sensitive similarities advance image/shape retrieval remarkably. A family of algorithms called diffusion process is proposed in the literature, such as Graph Transduction [2], Locally Constrained Diffusion Process (LCDP) [19], Locally Constrained Mixed Diffusion (LCMD) [20], Tensor Product Graph Diffusion (TPG) [5], Shortest Path Propagation (SSP) [3], Graph-PageRank [11], *etc.* In the survey paper [13], most of these approaches are elegantly summarized in a unified framework.

As shown in [13], a proper selection of neighbors ensures the diffusion process to work well in real cases. However, most variants of diffusion process use k-nearest neighbors (kNN) rule for its simplicity. Although [13] also uses kNN rule, it points out that it is still an open issue to select a reasonable local neighborhood. Related with this task, there are two representative algorithms recently, *i.e.*, Dominant Neighbors [5] and Consensus of kNN [18].

DN borrows the idea of dominant set proposed in [21] and deems that the dominant neighbors of a given image, as a subset of its kNN, should correspond to a maximal clique in the affinity graph. Then an indicator vector is defined for each image to measure the probability of other images being its true neighbors. The indicator is subsequently learned by replicator equation [22].

Although DN achieves some improvements on retrieval performances, it still has some severe disadvantages. For example, it is prone to getting stuck at wrong local optima. In [18], a thorough analysis on DN is given and a new simple yet effective algorithm called CN is proposed. CN keeps track of the times that an image pair appears together among all rounds of kNN. The principle of CN is that if two images are similar, they tend to appear in the kNN of other images much more frequently. It is demonstrated sufficiently that CN can achieve quite stable performances than DN, especially with larger neighborhood size.

As a smooth operator to preserve the local structure of data manifold, graph Laplacian has been applied to various computer vision applications, such as feature coding [23], image annotation [24], semi-supervised learning [25]. Our approach, called Smooth Neighborhood (SN), is essentially based on the use of graph Laplacian. It interprets the procedure of neighbor selection in a probabilistic manner similar to DN.

# 3   Proposed Method

Given a collection of images $X = \{x_1, x_2, \ldots, x_N\}$, we can construct an undirect graph $\mathcal{G} = (X, W)$, where the vertices of the graph are images and $w_{ij} \in W$ measures the strength of the edge linking $x_i$ and $x_j$. The problem needed to solve now is discovering a neighborhood set with high confidences for a given vertex $x_i \in X$.

As analyzed above, neither the simplest k-nearest neighbors (kNN) rule nor some more advanced algorithms (*e.g.*, [5,18,26]) cannot satisfy the manifold assumption. To remedy this, we propose a robust algorithm to select neighbors in an unsupervised way, formally defined as

$$\min_{Y} \sum_{i<j}^{N} w_{ij} \|Y_i - Y_j\|^2 + \mu \sum_{i=1}^{N} \|Y_i - I_i\|^2, \tag{1}$$

where $Y_i = [y_{i1}, y_{i2}, \ldots, y_{iN}] \in \mathbb{R}^{1 \times N}$ is the indicator function of $x_i$ that describes the probability distribution of its neighbors, that is, $y_{ij} \in [0,1]$ measures the likelihood of $x_j$ being the true neighbor of $x_i$. $Y_i$ has exactly the same meaning as the indicator vector used in [5]. $I_i \in \mathbb{R}^{1 \times N}$ is the $i$-th row of an identity matrix $I$, indicating that $x_i$ initializes itself as its nearest neighbor.

As can be seen from Eq. (1), we hold two assumptions. The left term emphasizes that the selection of neighbors should be smooth along the underlying manifold structure, *i.e.*, nearby points (large $w_{ij}$) should yield similar neighbors (small distance between $Y_i$ and $Y_j$). The right term emphasizes that no matter how we update the indicator $Y_i$ for node $x_i$, it shall still enforce itself as its neighbor as much as possible. The trade-off between the two terms is balanced by the regularization parameter $\mu > 0$, and it should be determined empirically.

Suppose given $M \geq 2$ affinity graphs $\mathcal{G}^{(v)} = \left(X, W^{(v)}\right)_{v=1}^{M}$, we now begin to study how to select neighbors smoothly on multiple affinity graphs. To this end, we impose a weight learning paradigm into Eq. (1) to describe the importance of graphs, thus leading to our final objective function

$$\min_{\alpha, Y} \sum_{v=1}^{M} \alpha^{(v)\gamma} \sum_{i<j}^{N} w_{ij}^{(v)} \|Y_i - Y_j\|^2 + \mu \sum_{i=1}^{N} \|Y_i - I_i\|^2,$$

$$s.t. \sum_{v=1}^{M} \alpha^{(v)} = 1, 0 \leq \alpha^{(v)} \leq 1, \tag{2}$$

where $\alpha = \{\alpha^{(1)}, \alpha^{(2)}, \ldots, \alpha^{(M)}\}$ is the weight of affinity graphs, and $\gamma > 1$ controls the weight distribution across multiple affinity graphs.

Three noteworthy comments should be made here. First, weight learning procedure in Eq. (2) is implemented by adding $\alpha^{(v)\gamma}$ to the objective function, instead of using $\alpha^{(v)}$ directly. The reason behind this choice is that if $\alpha^{(v)}$ is used, the optimal solution of $\alpha$ is $\alpha^{(v)} = 1$ for the affinity graph with minimum cost and $\alpha^{(v)} = 0$ for the other graphs, in other words, only the smoothest affinity graph is actually used. It is not a good behavior since the complementary nature among different affinity graphs is neglected. By using an additional exponential variable $\gamma$, the objective function is not linear with regard to $\alpha$. Thus one can easily tune the weight distribution of these affinity graphs by varying $\gamma$.

Second, one may note that we do not set $M$ indicator functions $Y_i^{(v)}$ corresponding with different affinity graphs $\mathcal{G}^{(v)}$. Instead, only a shared indicator function $Y_i$ is utilized for node $x_i$. Such a setup has an inborn advantage that the consensus information among these affinity graphs can be exploited. Also the subsequent fusion of $M$ indicator functions is avoided. Only one indicator function can be directly attained, though more affinity graph are used. Last, Eq. (2) is equivalent to Eq. (1) when $M = 1$. Therefore, Eq. (2) can be used directly on arbitrary number of input affinity graphs without modifications.

### 3.1   Optimization

For the sake of notation convenience, the objective function in Eq. (2) can be re-written in matrix form as

$$
\mathcal{J} = \sum_{v=1}^{M} \alpha^{(v)^{\gamma}} Tr(Y^{\mathrm{T}} L^{(v)} Y) + \mu \|Y - I\|_F^2, \tag{3}
$$

where $Y = [Y_1^{\mathrm{T}}, Y_2^{\mathrm{T}}, \ldots, Y_N^{\mathrm{T}}]^{\mathrm{T}} \in \mathbb{R}^{N \times N}$, $L^{(v)}$ is the $v$-th graph Laplacian matrix defined as $L^{(v)} = D^{(v)} - W^{(v)}$, and $D^{(v)}$ is a diagonal matrix whose value $d_{ii}^{(v)} = \sum_{j=1}^{N} w_{ij}^{(v)}$. $Tr(\cdot)$ and $\|\cdot\|_F$ calculate the trace and the Frobenius norm of the input matrix respectively.

As we can see from Eq. (3), there are two variables to determine, *i.e.*, the indicator $Y$ and the weight $\alpha$. Hence, we decompose it into two sub-problems, then adopt an alternative way to solve the optimization problem iteratively.

**Fix $\alpha$, Update $Y$.** To get the optimal solution of this sub-problem, we compute the partial derivative of $\mathcal{J}$ with regard to $Y$ as

$$
\frac{\partial \mathcal{J}}{\partial F} = 2 \sum_{v=1}^{M} \alpha^{(v)^{\gamma}} L^{(v)} Y + 2\mu(Y - I). \tag{4}
$$

Setting Eq. (4) to zero, the closed-form solution of $F$ can be derived as

$$
Y = \mu \left( \sum_{v=1}^{M} \alpha^{(v)^{\gamma}} L^{(v)} + \mu I \right)^{-1}. \tag{5}
$$

Since graph Laplacian matrix is known to be positive semi-definite, we can easily derive that $\sum_{v=1}^{M} \alpha^{(v)^{\gamma}} L^{(v)}$ is also positive semi-definite. As a result, $\sum_{v=1}^{M} \alpha^{(v)^{\gamma}} L^{(v)} + \mu I$ is invertible as long as $\mu > 0$.

**Fix $Y$, Update $\alpha$.** In order to minimize Eq. (2) with regard to the graph weight $\alpha^{(v)}$, we utilize Lagrange Multiplier Method. Taking the constraint $\sum_{v=1}^{M} \alpha^{(v)} = 1$ into consideration, the Lagrange function of $\mathcal{J}$ is

$$L(\mathcal{J}, \lambda) = \sum_{v=1}^{M} \alpha^{(v)^{\gamma}} Tr(Y^{\mathrm{T}} L^{(v)} Y) + \mu \|Y - I\|_F^2 - \lambda \left( \sum_{v=1}^{M} \alpha^{(v)} - 1 \right), \quad (6)$$

whose partial derivatives with respect to $\alpha^{(v)}$ and $\lambda$ are

$$\begin{cases} \dfrac{\partial L(\mathcal{J}, \lambda)}{\partial \alpha^{(v)}} = \gamma \alpha^{(v)^{(\gamma-1)}} Tr(Y^{\mathrm{T}} L^{(v)} Y) - \lambda, \\ \dfrac{\partial L(\mathcal{J}, \lambda)}{\partial \lambda} = -\sum_{v=1}^{M} \alpha^{(v)} + 1. \end{cases} \quad (7)$$

Note that in this sub-problem, $\|Y - I\|_F^2$ is a constant, and we can omit it directly.

By setting the two derivatives in Eq. (7) to zero simultaneously, the Lagrange multiplier $\lambda$ is eliminated and the optimal solution of $\alpha^{(v)}$ is obtained finally as

$$\alpha^{(v)} = \frac{\left( Tr(Y^{\mathrm{T}} L^{(v)} Y) \right)^{\frac{1}{1-\gamma}}}{\sum_{v'=1}^{M} \left( Tr(Y^{\mathrm{T}} L^{(v')} Y) \right)^{\frac{1}{1-\gamma}}}. \quad (8)$$

For clarification, we summarize the whole procedure of optimization in Algorithm 1. After obtaining the indicator $Y_i$ for the given node $x_i$, one can take the nodes with the top-$K$ largest non-zero confidence scores to constitute k-smooth neighbor (kSN) by analogy of the standard kNN. Other variants, such as $\epsilon$-smooth neighbor, reciprocal kSN, can be also defined in a similar manner.

---

**Algorithm 1.** The pseudocode of smooth neighborhood.

---

**Input:**
$W^{(v)} \in \mathbb{R}^{N \times N}, 1 \leq v \leq M$: the affinity matrices;
Two hyperparameters: $\gamma$ and $\mu$.
**Output:**
$Y \in \mathbb{R}^{N \times N}$: the probability distribution of neighbors.
**begin**
    Initialize $\alpha^{(v)} = \frac{1}{M}$;
    **repeat**
        Update $Y$ using Eq. (5);
        Update the weight $\alpha$ using Eq (8);
    **until** *convergence*
    **return** $Y$

---

## 3.2 Remarks

**Convergence.** The convergence of the above optimization is guaranteed. For each sub-problem, we find the corresponding optimal solution. Consequently, by solving two sub-problems alteratively, the objective value of Eq. (2) keeps decreasing monotonically. Meanwhile, since the objective function is lower bounded, the convergence of the proposed algorithm can be verified.

**Affinity Initialization.** In this paper, we need to specify the similarity matrix $W$. The most common way is to use Gaussian Kernel as

$$w_{ij} = \exp\left(-\frac{\|x_i - x_j\|_2^2}{\sigma_{ij}^2}\right),\tag{9}$$

where $\sigma_{ij}$ is the bandwidth parameter that controls the speed of similarity decay. In retrieval task, it is crucial to select a good $\sigma_{ij}$ for better performances. Using a proper $\sigma_{ij}$ is expected to pull intra-class images together and push extra-class images apart. Numerous works have focused on this issue, and most affinity learning algorithms [2,19,20] use an adaptive kernel. For example, it is defined in [15] as $\sigma_{ij} = \sigma_i\sigma_j$, where $\sigma_i = \|x_i - x_{K(i)}\|_2$ and $K(i)$ is the index of the $K$-th nearest neighbor of $x_i$.

Those adaptive kernels usually require additional parameters to fix empirically, making the entire framework sophisticated. In our approach, we set $\sigma_{ij} = \sigma$, a constant for all pairs of images following the recent survey paper [13] on affinity learning. It is more helpful to figure out which part really works using a constant for affinity initialization.

**Hyperparameters.** There are two hyperparameters in our algorithm.

$\gamma$ controls the weight distribution of multiple affinity graphs. When $\gamma \to 1$, only the smoothest affinity graph is counted. When $\gamma \to \infty$, equal weights are achieved consequently. The determination of $\gamma$ depends on the degree of complementary nature among these affinity graphs. Rich complementarity prefers a larger $\gamma$.

In the naive solution where $M$ affinity graphs are weighted combined, the search space to determine the optimal value of weights grows exponentially with respect to $M$. It is trivial to determine the weights in such an exhausted way. When $M \geq 2$, the time complexity becomes unacceptable. By contrast, we only use one parameter $\gamma$ to model the graph weights, which significantly reduces the parameters of the proposed algorithm.

The other parameter $\mu$ actually reflects the degree of influence fastened by the node $x_i$ itself. For example, if $\mu \to \infty$ (imitates the extremely large influence), the indicator $Y_i$ degenerates into identity matrix $I_i$. It means that only $x_i$ itself is selected as its neighbor finally.

**Properties of $Y$.** $Y$ is a row-stochastic matrix (see Appendix for proof). This nice property satisfies the usual requirement for probabilistic algorithms (*e.g.*, dominant neighbors [5]) that for each node $x_i$, the sum of the probabilities of its neighbors is equal to 1.

# 4    Experiments

In this section, we will testify the validity of Smooth Neighborhood (SN) against other related algorithms, including Dominant Neighbors (DN) [5] and Consensus of kNN (CN) [18] on several visual retrieval tasks.

## 4.1    MPEG-7 Dataset

Following [5,13,18], the effectiveness of smooth neighborhood is first evaluated on MPEG-7 dataset [27]. It consists of $1,400$ silhouette images divided into 70 categories, where each category has 20 shapes. The retrieval performance is measured by the bull's eye score, *i.e.*, the average recall of the top-40 returned candidates.

On this dataset, we implement four different shape similarity measures that are extensively used to learn the shape manifold in related literatures. They are Inner Distance Shape Context (IDSC) [28], Shape Context (SC) [29], Aspect Shape Context (ASC) [30] and Articulation-invariant Representation (AIR) [31]. The baseline performances of the four pairwise similarities are 85.40 %, 86.79 %, 88.39 % and 93.54 % respectively.

**Qualitative Evaluation.** Inspired by contextual re-ranking algorithms that leverage neighborhood set comparison directly for re-ranking (see [9,11,17]), we first adopt a simple and basic evaluation pipeline. Let $\mathcal{N}(x_q)$ and $\mathcal{N}(x_p)$ denote the neighborhood set of the query $x_q$ and the database image $x_p$ respectively, obtained by a certain neighborhood analysis algorithm. A more faithful context-sensitive similarity can be defined using Jaccard similarity as

$$S(x_q, x_p) = \frac{|\mathcal{N}(x_q) \cap \mathcal{N}(x_p)|}{|\mathcal{N}(x_q) \cup \mathcal{N}(x_p)|}, \tag{10}$$

where $|.|$ measures the cardinality of the input set. The motivation of Eq. (10) is straightforward, *i.e.*, if two images are similar, they tend to have extensive common neighbors.

In Fig. 1, we plot the retrieval performances of Eq. (10) embedded with different neighborhood analysis algorithms as a function of neighborhood size. As analyzed above, almost all the previous works cannot deal with more than one affinity graph. In order to provide a fair comparison in this situation, the results of kNN, DN and CN are implemented using a linear combination of those graphs with equal weights. The parameter setup of the proposed SN is as follows. The weight controller $\gamma = 3$, the regularizer $\mu = 0.08$. For affinity initialization, we set $\sigma = 0.2$.

A first glance at Fig. 1 shows that SN yields much smoother neighborhood structures than the other compared algorithms. Especially at larger $K$, the advantage of SN is more dramatic. It demonstrates clearly the benefit of exploring the local consistency in the proposed method. Since there are 20 shapes per category on MPEG-7 dataset, outliers are likely to be included when the neighborhood size is larger than 20. Nevertheless, the objective function in Eq. (2)

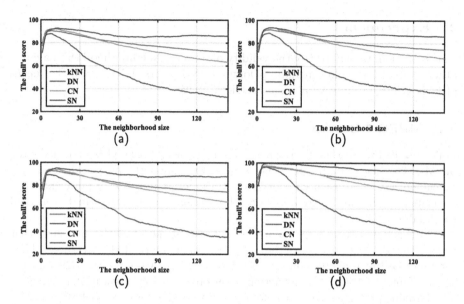

**Fig. 1.** The comparison using Eq. (10) on MPEG-7 dataset. The baseline similarities used are IDSC (a), SC (b), ASC (c) and IDSC+SC+ASC (d) respectively

regularizes that even if a relatively larger $K$ is specified, the behaviour of selecting neighbors of nearby points are forced to be as similar as possible. Thus we can find that the performance of SN is quite stable at variable neighborhood sizes. Such a nice property makes SN especially suitable to context-based re-ranking algorithms, where contextual information is described by neighborhood structures.

In [18], CN is also demonstrated to generate stable performances at larger neighborhood size. However, it is inspired by experimental observations, but lacks of theoretical analysis. In comparison, the proposed SN provides an explicit objective function based on graph Laplacian to preserve the local manifold structure, so that the neighbor selection can be as smooth as possible along the underlying manifold. It can be also found that DN yields poor performances for two reasons. First, it starts to converge into false neighbors at larger $K$ as claimed in [18]. Second, we do not give a good enough initialization for similarities using adaptive Gaussian kernels as previous works [5] do.

When integrating multiple affinity graphs, the proposed SN outperforms the other algorithms by a larger margin. The reason behind the superiority of SN is the weight learning mechanism imposed on multiple affinity graphs. On one hand, this learning paradigm can give prominence to the smoothest affinity graph and suppress the negative impacts from non-smooth affinity graphs. Moreover, it can well exploit the complementary nature and consensus information among them, which is controlled by the weight controller $\gamma$. As introduced above, rich complementary nature prefers larger $\gamma$.

**Improving Context-Sensitive Similarity.** There are many candidate context sensitive similarities to distinguish the discriminative power of neighborhood analysis algorithms (see the framework of diffusion process in [13] for a comprehensive summary). However, the convergence property of most these algorithms is not guaranteed, so the iteration has to be stopped at a "right" moment. Moreover, according to our experiments, some methods heavily rely on a proper initialization for pairwise similarities using adaptive Gaussian kernel as introduced in Sect. 3.2, *i.e.*, $\sigma_{ij}$ should be different for each pair of shapes. If $\sigma_{ij}$ is set to a constant as in this paper, these iterative algorithms, including Locally Constrained Diffusion Process (LCDP) [19], are prone to producing incorrect dense clusters. Such an experimental observation (refer to Table 2) usually occurs when the performances of the input baselines are relatively low (*e.g.*, IDSC). Finally, diffusion process usually consists of three parts: affinity initialization, the definition of transition matrix and the definition of the diffusion process. Nevertheless, the neighborhood analysis techniques only pay attention to the definition of transition matrix, since it records the neighborhood structures to constrain the diffusion process locally. In this sense, these variants of diffusion process are not proper to assess neighborhood analysis techniques.

Instead of using LCDP, we turn to a recent algorithm called Sparse Contextual Activation (SCA) [9], which is simple to implement and insensitive to parameter tuning. SCA is particularly suitable to evaluate neighborhood analysis techniques since it directly focuses on the usage of neighborhood structures by comparing two neighborhood sets in fuzzy set theory. It has two parameters to be fixed manually, *i.e.*, the parameter $k_1$ and $k_2$ determining the first-order and the second-order neighborhood size respectively. In our case, the two neighborhood sets can be obtained using kNN, DN, CN and the proposed SN.

**Table 1.** The comparison of neighborhood analysis algorithms on MPEG-7 dataset

| Methods | IDSC | SC | ASC | AIR | IDSC+SC | IDSC+SC+ASC |
|---------|------|-----|-----|-----|---------|-------------|
| SCA+kNN | 90.07 % | 93.23 % | 94.34 % | 99.97 % | 98.20 % | 97.61 % |
| SCA+DN | 90.07 % | 89.85 % | 92.49 % | 98.84 % | 96.96 % | 98.25 % |
| SCA+CN | 92.70 % | 93.97 % | 95.25 % | 99.85 % | 97.61 % | 97.86 % |
| SCA+SN | **93.52 %** | **95.25 %** | **95.98 %** | **100.00 %** | **99.25 %** | **99.81 %** |

Table 1 presents the performance comparison, and the results of kNN, DN and CN are reported at its optimal parameter setup (not necessarily the same parameter setup). Consistent with previous analysis, the proposed SN achieves the best performances. Especially when multiple similarity measures (*e.g.*, IDSC+SC or IDSC+SC+ASC) are integrated, the superiorly of SN is more distinctive. In the following experiments, we combine SCA with SN to provide the retrieval performances of our method, if not specified otherwise.

**Comparison with State-of-the-Art.** In Table 2, we give a thorough comparison with other state-of-the-art algorithms. The results in the table are carefully

**Table 2.** The bull's eye scores of different methods on MPEG-7 dataset

| Descriptors | Methods | Bull's eye score |
|---|---|---|
| IDSC | Contextual dissimilarity measure (CDM) [1] | 88.30 % |
| IDSC | Generic diffusion process (GDP)* [13] | 90.96 % |
| IDSC | Index-based re-ranking [8] | 91.56 % |
| IDSC | Graph transduction (GT) [2] | 91.61 % |
| IDSC | Locally constrained diffusion process [19] | 92.36 % |
| IDSC | RL-sim re-ranking [7] | 92.62 % |
| IDSC | Shortest path propagation (SSP) [3] | 93.35 % |
| IDSC | Mutual kNN graph (mkNN) [15] | 93.40 % |
| IDSC | Sparse contextual activation (SCA) [9] | 93.44 % |
| IDSC | **Smooth neighborhood (Ours)** | **93.52 %** |
| SC | Generic diffusion process (GDP)* [13] | 92.81 % |
| SC | Graph transduction (GT) [2] | 92.91 % |
| SC | Sparse contextual activation (SCA) [9] | 95.21 % |
| SC | **Smooth neighborhood (Ours)** | **95.25 %** |
| ASC | Generic diffusion process (GDP)* [13] | 93.95 % |
| ASC | Index-based re-ranking [8] | 94.09 % |
| ASC | RL-sim re-ranking [7] | 95.75 % |
| ASC | Locally constrained DP (LCDP) [19] | 95.96 % |
| ASC | Tensor product graph (TPG) [5] | **96.47 %** |
| ASC | **Smooth neighborhood (Ours)** | 95.98 % |
| IDSC+SC | Co-transduction [4] | 97.72 % |
| IDSC+SC | Locally constrained mixed diffusion (LCMD) [20] | 98.84 % |
| IDSC+SC | Sparse contextual activation (SCA) [9] | 99.01 % |
| IDSC+SC | **Smooth neighborhood (Ours)** | **99.25 %** |
| AIR | Tensor product graph (TPG) [5] | 99.99 % |
| AIR | Generic diffusion process (GDP) [13] | 100.00 % |
| AIR | **Smooth neighborhood (Ours)** | **100.00 %** |

classified according to the type of input baseline similarity. Since generic diffusion process [13] only reports its result with AIR as the input similarity, its performances with IDSC, SC and ASC are implemented by the authors using the public available codes in http://vh.icg.tugraz.at/index.php?content=topics/diffusion.php, thus marked with * on the upper right corner.

IDSC is the most frequently used baseline shape similarity. Combining smooth neighborhood and SCA, we report a new level performance using IDSC as the baseline, which is **93.52 %** in bull's eye score. Of course, it is not the best performance on this dataset, since some context-based re-ranking algorithms take the higher baseline AIR as the input similarity. For example, TPG [5] reports 99.99 % bull's eye score by combining adaptive Gaussian kernel, dominant neighbor and diffusion process. By contrast, we achieve the perfect score 100 % by simply using smooth neighborhood and SCA. The performance gain is especially valuable when considering the fact that we do not use a more accurate similarity initialization using adaptive Gaussian kernel as DN. Note that generic diffusion process [13] also reports 100 % accuracy by enumerating 72 variants of diffusion process (4 different affinity initializations, 6 different transition matrices and 3 different update schemes). One may note that the retrieval performances of generic diffusion are inferior with IDSC, SC or ASC. It verifies our previous claim that a proper affinity initialization using adaptive Gaussian kernel is crucial for diffusion process when lower baseline similarity is used.

Previous affinity fusion algorithms usually consider integrating only two similarity measures, *e.g.*, SC and IDSC. This is because most of them [4] are based on co-training framework that is only suitable to deal with two similarity measures. Our method potentially provides an alternative way of feature fusion at neighbor selection level. What is more important is that it does not limit to two similarity measures. Even though using more similarity measures, we can still obtain only one shared neighborhood structure, as well as the weights of different affinity graphs. It can be expected that when more complementary similarities are fused, a more robust neighborhood structure can be learned thus leading to higher retrieval performances. To support our speculation, we also report the performances of SN with a combination of similarities that is not used by previous works. For instance, by combining IDS, SC and ASC, SN can yield bull's eye score **99.81 %**. To our best knowledge now, it is the best performance on MPEG-7 dataset while AIR is not used.

### 4.2   Ukbench Dataset

We then evaluate the proposed approach on Ukbench image dataset [32]. It is comprised of $2,550$ objects and each object has 4 different view points or illuminations. All $10,200$ images are both indexed as queries and database images. The most widely-used evaluation metric is N-S score, which counts the average recall of the top-4 ranked images. Hence, the perfect N-S score on this dataset is 4.

On this dataset, we implement 4 kinds of distance measures. They are

1. Bag of Words (BoW): SIFT descriptors are extracted at interest points produced by Hessian-affine detectors, and later converted to RootSIFT [33]. A codebook with $20k$ entries is learned with K-means on independent data. We follow the pipeline of Hamming embedding [34] that uses cosine similarity for affinity initialization. The N-S score of BoW representation is 3.57.
2. Convolutional Neutral Network (CNN): Two CNN features are extracted based on the trained AlexNet model. The activations of 5-th convolutional layer and the 7-th fully-connected layer are used. For each image, the activation is first square-rooted then $L_2$ normalized. The N-S scores of the two CNN features are 3.44 and 3.65 respectively.

3. HSV: Following [11], we extract 1000 dimensional HSV color histogram (20 × 10 × 5 bins for H, S, V components respectively). The HSV histogram is first $L_1$ normalized then square-rooted. The N-S score of HSV is 3.40.

The parameter setup of SN is the same as those reported in Sect. 4.1. $\sigma = 0.5$ is used for affinity initialization.

Extensive algorithms have reported their performances on Ukbench dataset. However, in Table 3, we only collect two kinds of results for comparison, *i.e.*, post-precessing algorithms such as context-sensitive similarities, and the state-of-the-art performances ever reported. To improve the readability, the results are ordered from those using single feature to those using multiple features. Meanwhile, since the performances of baselines used by different methods are usually quite different in natural image retrieval, we also include N-S scores of those baselines in the parentheses.

**Table 3.** The N-S scores of different methods on Ukbench dataset. Note that Query Adaptive Fusion uses 5 input similarities, and the last result of our method is produced by using all the 4 similarities implemented in this paper

| Descriptors | Methods | N-S score |
|---|---|---|
| BoW (3.52) | kNN re-ranking [35] | 3.56 |
| BoW (3.22) | Tensor product graph [5] | 3.61 |
| BoW (3.26) | Co-transduction [4] | 3.66 |
| BoW (3.50) | RNN re-ranking [16] | 3.67 |
| BoW (3.54) | Graph fusion [11] | 3.67 |
| BoW (3.33) | Contextual dissimilarity measure [1] | 3.68 |
| BoW (3.56) | Sparse contextual activation [9] | 3.69 |
| BoW (3.57) | **Smooth neighborhood (Ours)** | **3.75** |
| CNN (3.44) | **Smooth neighborhood (Ours)** | **3.66** |
| CNN (3.65) | **Smooth neighborhood (Ours)** | **3.81** |
| HSV (3.17) | Graph fusion [11] | 3.28 |
| HSV (3.40) | Sparse contextual activation [9] | 3.56 |
| HSV (3.40) | **Smooth neighborhood (Ours)** | **3.56** |
| BoW (3.20,3.17,2.81) | Locally constrained mixed diffusion [20] | 3.70 |
| BoW (3.54), HSV (3.17) | Graph fusion [11] | 3.77 |
| BoW (3.54), HSV (3.17) | Graph fusion [12] | 3.83 |
| BoW (3.58), CNN (3.40), *etc.* | Query adaptive fusion [36] | 3.84 |
| BoW (3.56), HSV (3.40) | Sparse contextual activation [9] | 3.86 |
| BoW (3.13), CNN (3.87) | ONE [37] | 3.89 |
| BoW (3.57), CNN (3.44), *etc.* | **Smooth neighborhood (Ours)** | **3.98** |

Graph Fusion [11] is a representative algorithm that integrates multiple affinity graphs by averaging the strength of edges with equally weights. It reports 3.77 N-S score by fusing local SIFT feature and holistic HSV color histogram, and later reports 3.83 in [12] by iteratively constructing the graph. In some sense, our method can be also considered as a kind of graph fusion. However, the difference is that we do not consider simply averaging the edge weights. Instead, SN tries to find a robust neighborhood structure shared by different affinity graphs, so that the consensus information among them can be largely preserved. In [36], N-S score 3.84 is achieved by fusing five kinds of features. Using BoW and HSV as the input similarities, SCA [9] reports N-S score 3.86. Fusing BoW and CNN feature, ONE [37] achieves N-S score 3.89, which is the best performance to our knowledge. Besides those methods, [38] using query expansion reports NS score 3.67. [39] and [40] exploit local convolutional features, and report NS score 3.76 and 3.65 respectively. In this paper, we achieve the near perfect N-S score **3.98** by combining all the 4 similarities, including BoW, two CNN features and HSV. It outperforms the previous state-of-the-art remarkably.

## 5    Conclusions

In this paper, we propose a neighbor selection algorithm called Smooth Neighborhood (SN). Compared with related algorithms, the two key advantages of SN are the theoretical guarantee of underlying manifold structure and the capacity of dealing with multiple affinity graphs. Embedded with context-sensitive similarities, SN is evaluated on retrieval tasks and achieves much better performances than other related algorithms, including kNN, dominant neighbor and consensus of kNN. In particular, despite the perfect bull's eye score on MPEG-7 dataset, SN also achieves near perfect N-S score **3.98** on Ukbench dataset.

Since the proposed method focuses on neighborhood analysis, it can be potentially plunged into other retrieval systems (*e.g.*, RNN Re-ranking [16], kNN Reranking [35]) and other computer vision tasks (*e.g.*, image categorization [41], object detection, 3D shape recognition [42]), where a more robust neighborhood structure is required. Moreover, it should be addressed that the weight learning paradigm in our method is exerted into the entire affinity graphs. However, it is known that query specific weight is a more proper choice in retrieval task. We would like to exploit these issues in the future.

**Acknowledgments.** The authors would to thank Pedronette DCG. for providing the codes on MPEG-7 dataset. This work was supported in part by NSFC 61573160, NSFC 61429201 and China Scholarship Council. This work was supported in part to Dr. Qi Tian by ARO grants W911NF-15-1-0290 and Faculty Research Gift Awards by NEC Laboratories of America and Blippar.

# Appendix

Equation (5) can be re-written as

$$Y = \left( I + \frac{\sum_{v=1}^{M} \alpha^{(v)\gamma} L^{(v)}}{\mu} \right)^{-1}. \tag{11}$$

According to the Searle Set of Identity [43], Eq. (11) can be transformed into

$$Y = I - \frac{I}{\mu} \left( I + \frac{\sum_{v=1}^{M} \alpha^{(v)\gamma} L^{(v)}}{\mu} \right)^{-1} \left( \sum_{v=1}^{M} \alpha^{(v)\gamma} L^{(v)} \right). \tag{12}$$

Let $\mathbf{1}$ be a column vector with all elements equal to 1. We know the minimum eigenvalue of graph Laplacian matrix is 0, *i.e.*, $L^{(v)}\mathbf{1} = 0$. By postmultiplying both sides of Eq. (12) by $\mathbf{1}$, we can obtain $Y\mathbf{1} = \mathbf{1}$. The proof is complete.

# References

1. Jegou, H., Schmid, C., Harzallah, H., Verbeek, J.J.: Accurate image search using the contextual dissimilarity measure. TPAMI **32**(1), 2–11 (2010)
2. Bai, X., Yang, X., Latecki, L.J., Liu, W., Tu, Z.: Learning context-sensitive shape similarity by graph transduction. TPAMI **32**(5), 861–874 (2010)
3. Wang, J., Li, Y., Bai, X., Zhang, Y., Wang, C., Tang, N.: Learning context-sensitive similarity by shortest path propagation. Pattern Recogn. **44**(10), 2367–2374 (2011)
4. Bai, X., Wang, B., Wang, X., Liu, W., Tu, Z.: Co-transduction for shape retrieval. In: Maragos, P., Paragios, N., Daniilidis, K. (eds.) ECCV 2010, Part III. LNCS, vol. 6313, pp. 328–341. Springer, Heidelberg (2010)
5. Yang, X., Latecki, L.J.: Affinity learning on a tensor product graph with applications to shape and image retrieval. In: CVPR, pp. 2369–2376 (2011)
6. Wang, B., Tu, Z.: Affinity learning via self-diffusion for image segmentation and clustering. In: CVPR, pp. 2312–2319 (2012)
7. Pedronette, D., Torres, R.: Image re-ranking and rank aggregation based on similarity of ranked lists. Pattern Recogn. **46**(8), 2350–2360 (2013)
8. Pedronette, D., Almeida, J., Torres, R.: A scalable re-ranking method for content-based image retrieval. Inf. Sci. **265**, 91–104 (2014)
9. Bai, S., Bai, X.: Sparse contextual activation for efficient visual re-ranking. TIP **25**(3), 1056–1069 (2016)
10. Chen, Y., Li, X., Dick, A., Hill, R.: Ranking consistency for image matching and object retrieval. Pattern Recogn. **47**(3), 1349–1360 (2014)
11. Zhang, S., Yang, M., Cour, T., Yu, K., Metaxas, D.N.: Query specific fusion for image retrieval. In: Fitzgibbon, A., Lazebnik, S., Perona, P., Sato, Y., Schmid, C. (eds.) ECCV 2012, Part II. LNCS, vol. 7573, pp. 660–673. Springer, Heidelberg (2012)
12. Zhang, S., Yang, M., Cour, T., Yu, K., Metaxas, D.N.: Query specific rank fusion for image retrieval. TPAMI **37**(4), 803–815 (2015)
13. Donoser, M., Bischof, H.: Diffusion processes for retrieval revisited. In: CVPR, pp. 1320–1327 (2013)

Smooth Neighborhood Structure Mining     607

14. Roweis, S.T., Saul, L.K.: Nonlinear dimensionality reduction by locally linear embedding. Science **290**(5500), 2323–2326 (2000)
15. Kontschieder, P., Donoser, M., Bischof, H.: Beyond pairwise shape similarity analysis. In: Zha, H., Taniguchi, R., Maybank, S. (eds.) ACCV 2009, Part III. LNCS, vol. 5996, pp. 655–666. Springer, Heidelberg (2010)
16. Qin, D., Gammeter, S., Bossard, L., Quack, T., van Gool, L.: Hello neighbor: accurate object retrieval with k-reciprocal nearest neighbors. In: CVPR, pp. 777–784 (2011)
17. Pedronette, D., Penatti, O., Torres, R.: Unsupervised manifold learning using reciprocal kNN graphs in image re-ranking and rank aggregation tasks. Image Vis. Comput. **32**(2), 120–130 (2014)
18. Premachandran, V., Kakarala, R.: Consensus of k-NNs for robust neighborhood selection on graph-based manifolds. In: CVPR, pp. 1594–1601 (2013)
19. Yang, X., Koknar-Tezel, S., Latecki, L.J.: Locally constrained diffusion process on locally densified distance spaces with applications to shape retrieval. In: CVPR, pp. 357–364 (2009)
20. Luo, L., Shen, C., Zhang, C., van den Hengel, A.: Shape similarity analysis by self-tuning locally constrained mixed-diffusion. TMM **15**(5), 1174–1183 (2013)
21. Pavan, M., Pelillo, M.: Dominant sets and pairwise clustering. TPAMI **29**(1), 167–172 (2007)
22. Pelillo, M.: Matching free trees with replicator equations. NIPS **2**, 865–872 (2002)
23. Gao, S., Tsang, I.W.H., Chia, L.T., Zhao, P.: Local features are not lonely-laplacian sparse coding for image classification. In: CVPR, pp. 3555–3561 (2010)
24. Wang, J., Chang, S.F., Zhou, X., Wong, S.T.: Active microscopic cellular image annotation by superposable graph transduction with imbalanced labels. In: CVPR, pp. 1–8 (2008)
25. Zhu, X., Ghahramani, Z., Lafferty, J., et al.: Semi-supervised learning using Gaussian fields and harmonic functions. In: ICML, pp. 912–919 (2003)
26. Kuang, Z., Li, Z., Fan, J.: Discovering the latent similarities of the KNN graph by metric transformation. In: ICMR, pp. 471–474 (2015)
27. Latecki, L.J., Lakämper, R., Eckhardt, U.: Shape descriptors for non-rigid shapes with a single closed contour. In: CVPR, pp. 424–429 (2000)
28. Ling, H., Jacobs, D.W.: Shape classification using the inner-distance. TPAMI **29**(2), 286–299 (2007)
29. Belongie, S., Malik, J., Puzicha, J.: Shape matching and object recognition using shape contexts. TPAMI **24**(4), 509–522 (2002)
30. Ling, H., Yang, X., Latecki, L.J.: Balancing deformability and discriminability for shape matching. In: Maragos, P., Paragios, N., Daniilidis, K. (eds.) ECCV 2010, Part III. LNCS, vol. 6313, pp. 411–424. Springer, Heidelberg (2010)
31. Gopalan, R., Turaga, P., Chellappa, R.: Articulation-invariant representation of non-planar shapes. In: Maragos, P., Paragios, N., Daniilidis, K. (eds.) ECCV 2010, Part III. LNCS, vol. 6313, pp. 286–299. Springer, Heidelberg (2010)
32. Nistér, D., Stewénius, H.: Scalable recognition with a vocabulary tree. In: CVPR, pp. 2161–2168 (2006)
33. Arandjelović, R., Zisserman, A.: Three things everyone should know to improve object retrieval. In: CVPR, pp. 2911–2918 (2012)
34. Jegou, H., Douze, M., Schmid, C.: Hamming embedding and weak geometric consistency for large scale image search. In: Forsyth, D., Torr, P., Zisserman, A. (eds.) ECCV 2008, Part I. LNCS, vol. 5302, pp. 304–317. Springer, Heidelberg (2008)

35. Shen, X., Lin, Z., Brandt, J., Avidan, S., Wu, Y.: Object retrieval and localization with spatially-constrained similarity measure and k-NN re-ranking. In: CVPR, pp. 3013–3020 (2012)
36. Zheng, L., Wang, S., Tian, L., He, F., Liu, Z., Tian, Q.: Query-adaptive late fusion for image search and person re-identification. In: CVPR, pp. 1741–1750 (2015)
37. Xie, L., Hong, R., Zhang, B., Tian, Q.: Image classification and retrieval are one. In: ICMR, pp. 3–10 (2015)
38. Tolias, G., Jégou, H.: Visual query expansion with or without geometry: refining local descriptors by feature aggregation. Pattern Recogn. **47**(10), 3466–3476 (2014)
39. Paulin, M., Douze, M., Harchaoui, Z., Mairal, J., Perronin, F., Schmid, C.: Local convolutional features with unsupervised training for image retrieval. In: ICCV, pp. 91–99 (2015)
40. Babenko, A., Lempitsky, V.: Aggregating deep convolutional features for image retrieval. In: ICCV, pp. 1269–1277 (2015)
41. Bai, S., Bai, X., Liu, W.: Multiple stage residual model for image classification and vector compression. TMM **18**(7), 1351–1362 (2016)
42. Bai, S., Bai, X., Zhou, Z., Zhang, Z., Latecki, L.J.: Gift: a real-time and scalable 3D shape search engine. In: CVPR (2016)
43. Searle, S.R.: Matrix Algebra Useful for Statistics. Wiley-Interscience, Hoboken (1982)

# Title Generation for User Generated Videos

Kuo-Hao Zeng[1], Tseng-Hung Chen[1], Juan Carlos Niebles[2], and Min Sun[1(✉)]

[1] Departmant of Electrical Engineering, National Tsing Hua University,
Hsinchu, Taiwan
s103061614@m103.nthu.edu.tw, s104061544@m104.nthu.edu.tw,
sunmin@ee.nthu.edu.tw
[2] Department of Computer Science, Stanford University, Stanford, USA
jniebles@cs.stanford.edu

**Abstract.** A great video title describes the most salient event compactly and captures the viewer's attention. In contrast, video captioning tends to generate sentences that describe the video as a whole. Although generating a video title automatically is a very useful task, it is much less addressed than video captioning. We address video title generation for the first time by proposing two methods that extend state-of-the-art video captioners to this new task. First, we make video captioners *highlight sensitive* by priming them with a highlight detector. Our framework allows for jointly training a model for title generation and video highlight localization. Second, we induce high sentence diversity in video captioners, so that the generated titles are also diverse and catchy. This means that a large number of sentences might be required to learn the sentence structure of titles. Hence, we propose a novel *sentence augmentation* method to train a captioner with additional sentence-only examples that come without corresponding videos. We collected a large-scale *Video Titles in the Wild* (VTW) dataset of 18100 automatically crawled user-generated videos and titles. On VTW, our methods consistently improve title prediction accuracy, and achieve the best performance in both automatic and human evaluation. Finally, our sentence augmentation method also outperforms the baselines on the M-VAD dataset.

**Keywords:** Video captioning · Video and language

## 1 Introduction

Generating a natural language description of the visual contents of a video is one of the holy grails in computer vision. Recently, thanks to breakthroughs in deep learning [1] and Recurrent Neural Networks (RNN), many attempts [2–4] have been made to jointly model videos and their corresponding sentence descriptions. This task is often referred to as video captioning. Here, we focus on a much more challenging task: *video title generation*. A great video title compactly describes the most salient event as well as catches people's attention (e.g., "bmx rider gets hit by scooter at park" in Fig. 1-Top). In contrast, video captioning generates a

© Springer International Publishing AG 2016
B. Leibe et al. (Eds.): ECCV 2016, Part II, LNCS 9906, pp. 609–625, 2016.
DOI: 10.1007/978-3-319-46475-6_38

**Title (most salient event):** Bmx rider gets *hit by scooter* at park

**Captions:** A man riding on bike. A man does a stunt on a bmx bike.

**Fig. 1.** Video title (top-red) v.s. video captions (bottom-blue) of a typical user generated video. A video title describes the most salient event, which typically corresponds to a short highlight (1 sec in red box). A caption describes a video as a whole (44 secs). For a long video, there are many relevant captions, since many events have happened. In this example, "hit by scooter" is a key phrase associated to the most salient event, while captions tend to be more generic to the overall contents of the sequence. (Color figure online)

sentence to describe a video as a whole (e.g., "a man riding on bike" in Fig. 1-Bottom). Video captioning has many potential applications such as helping the visually impaired to interpret the world. We believe that video title generation can further enable Artificial Intelligence systems to communicate more naturally by describing the most salient event in a long and continuous visual observation.

Video title generation poses two main challenges for existing video captioning methods [3,4]. First of all, most video captioning methods assume that every video is trimmed into a 10–25 s short clip in both training and testing. However, the majority of videos on the web are untrimmed, such as User-Generated Videos (UGVs) which are typically 1–2 min long. The task of video title generation is to learn from untrimmed video and title pairs to generate a title for an unseen untrimmed video. In training, the first challenge is to temporally align a title to the most salient event, i.e. the video highlight (red box in Fig. 1) in the untrimmed video. Most video captioning methods, which ignore this challenge, are likely to learn an imprecise association between words and frequently observed visual evidence in the whole video. Yao et al. [3] recently propose a novel soft-attention mechanism to softly select visual observation for each word. However, we found that the learned per-word attention is prone to imprecise associations given untrimmed videos. Hence, it is important to make video title generators "highlight sensitive". As a second challenge, title sentences are extremely diverse (e.g., each word appears in only 2 sentences on average in our dataset). Note that the two latest movie description datasets [5,6] also share the same challenge of diverse sentences. On these datasets, state-of-the-art methods [3,4] have reported fairly low performance. Hence, it is important to "increase the number of sentences" for training a more reliable language model. We propose two generally applicable methods to address these challenges.

**Highlight Sensitive Captioner.** We combine a highlight detector with video captioners [3,4] to train models that can jointly generate titles and locate highlights. The highlights annotated in training can be used to further improve the highlight detector. As a result, our "highlight sensitive" captioner learns to generate title sentences specifically describing the highlight moment in a video.

**Sentence Augmentation.** To encourage the generation of more diverse titles, we augment the training set with sentence-only examples that do not come with corresponding videos. Our intuition is to learn a better language model from additional sentences. In order to allow state-of-the-art video captioners to train with additional sentence-only examples, we introduce the idea of "dummy video observation". In short, we associate all augmented sentences to the same dummy video observation in training so that the same training procedures in most state-of-the-art methods (e.g., [3,4]) can be used to train with additional augmented sentences. This method enables any video captioner to be improved by observing additional sentence-only examples, which are abundant on the web.

To facilitate the study of our task, we collected a challenging large-scale "Video Title in the Wild" (VTW) dataset[1] with the following properties:

**Highly Open-Domain.** Our dataset consists of 18100 automatically crawled UGVs as opposed to self-recorded single domain videos [7].

**Untrimmed Videos.** Each video is on an average 1.5 min (45 s median duration) and contains a highlight event which makes this video interesting. Note that our videos are almost 5–10 times longer than clips in [5]. Our highlight sensitive captioner precisely addresses the unknown highlight challenge.

**Diverse Sentences.** Each video in our dataset is associated with one title sentence. The vocabulary is very diverse, since on average each word only appears in 2 sentences in VTW, compared to 5.3 sentences in [8]. Our sentence augmentation method directly addresses the diverse sentences challenge.

**Description.** Besides titles, our dataset also provides accompanying description sentences with more detailed information about each video. These sentences differ from the multiple sentences in [8], since our description may refer to non-visual information of the video. We show in our experiments that they can be treated as augmented sentences to improve video title generation performance.

We address video title generation with the following contributions. (1) We propose a novel highlight sensitive method to adapt two state-of-the-art video captioners [3,4] to video title generation. Our method significantly outperforms [3,4] in METEOR and CIDEr. (2) Our highlight sensitive method improves highlight detection performance from 54.2 % to 58.3 % mAP. (3) We propose a novel sentence augmentation method to train state-of-the-art video captioners with additional sentence-only examples. This method significantly outperforms [3,4] in METEOR and CIDEr. (4) We show that sentence augmentation can be applied on another video captioning dataset (M-VAD [5]) to further improve the captioning performance in METEOR. (5) By combining both methods, we achieve the best video title generation performance of 6.2 % in METEOR and 25.4 % in CIDEr. (6) Finally, we collected one of the first large-scale "Video Title

---

[1] VTW dataset can be accessed at http://aliensunmin.github.io/project/video-language/.

in the Wild" (VTW) dataset to benchmark the video title generation task. The dataset will be released for research usage.

## 2   Related Work

**Video Captioning.** Early work on video captioning [7,9–14] typically perform a two-stage procedure. In the first stage, classifiers are used to detect objects, actions, and scenes. In the second stage, a model combining visual confidences with a language model is used to estimate the most likely combination of subject, verb, object, and scene. Then, a sentence is generated according to a predefined template. These methods require a few manual engineered components such as the content to be classified and the template. Hence, the generated sentences are often not as diverse as sentences used in natural human description.

Recently, image captioning methods [15,16] begin to adopt the Convolutional Neural Networks (CNN) and Recurrent Neural Networks (RNN) approaches. They learn models directly from a large number of image and sentence pairs. The CNN replaces the predefined features to generate a powerful distributed visual representation. The RNN takes the CNN features as input and learns to decode it into a sentence. These are combined into a large network that can be jointly trained to directly map an image to a sentence.

Similarly, recent video captioning methods adopt a similar approach. Venugopalan et al. [2] map a video into a fix dimension feature by average-pooling CNN features of many frames and then use a RNN to generate a sentence. However, this method discards the temporal information of the video. Rohrbach et al. [17] propose to combine different RNN architectures with multiple CNN classifiers for classifying verbs (actions), objects, and places. To capture temporal information in a video, Venugopalan et al. [4] propose to use RNN to encode a sequence of CNN features extracted from frames following the temporal order. This direct video-encoding and sentence-decoding approach outperforms [2] significantly. Concurrently, Yao et al. [3] proposes to model the temporal structure of visual features in two ways. First, it designs a 3D CNN based on dense trajectory-like features [18] to capture local temporal structure. Then, it incorporates a soft-attention mechanism to select temporal-specific video observations for generating each word. Our proposed highlight sensitive method can be considered as a hard-attention mechanism to select a video segment (i.e., a highlight) for generating the sentence. In our experiments, we find that our highlight sensitive method further improves [3]. Instead of RNN for encoding or decoding, Xu et al. [19] propose to embed both video and sentence to a joint space. Most recently, Pan et al. [20] further propose a novel framework to jointly perform visual-semantic embedding and learn a RNN model for video captioning. Pan et al. [21] propose a novel Hierarchical RNN to exploit video temporal structure in a longer range. Yu et al. [22] propose a novel hierarchical framework containing a sentence generator and a paragraph generator. Despite many new advances in video captioning, video title generation has not been well studied.

**Video Highlight Detection.** Most early highlight detection works focus on broadcasting sport videos [23–30]. Recently, a few methods have been proposed to detect highlights in generic personal videos. Sun et al. [31] automatically harvest user preference to learn a model for identifying highlights in each domain. Instead of generating a video title, Song et al. [32] utilize video titles to summarize each video. The method requires additional images to be retrieved by title search for learning visual concepts. There are also a few fully unsupervised approaches. Zhao and Xing [33] propose a quasi-real time method to generate short summaries. Yang et al. [34] propose a recurrent auto-encoder to extract video highlights. Our video title generation method is one of the first to combine explicit highlight detection (not soft-attention) with sentence generation.

**Video Captioning Datasets.** A number of video captioning datasets [5–9,35] have been introduced. Chen and Dolan [8] collect one of the first multiple-sentence video description datasets with 1967 YouTube videos. The duration of each clip is between 10 and 25 s, typically depicting a single activity or a short sequence. It requires significant human effort to build this dataset, since all 70028 sentences are labeled by crowdsourced annotators. On the other hand, we collect our dataset with a large number of video and sentence pairs fully automatically. Rohrbach et al. [6] collect a movie dataset with 54076 sentences from audio transcripts and video snippets in 72 HD movies. It also takes significant human effort to build this dataset, since each sentence is manually aligned to the movie. Torabi et al. [5] collect a movie dataset with 55904 sentences from audio transcripts and video snippets in 96 HD movies. They introduce an automatic Descriptive Video Service (DVS) segmentation and alignment method for movies. Hence, similar to our automatically collected dataset, they can scale up the collection of a DVS-derived dataset with minimal human intervention. We compare the sentences in our dataset with two movie description datasets in Sect. 3.2 and find that our vocabularies are fairly different (see [36]). In this sense, our dataset is complementary to theirs. However, both datasets are not suitable for evaluating video title generation, since they consist of short clips with 6–10 s and selecting the most salient event in the video is not critical.

## 3   Video Title Generation

Our goal is to automatically generate a title sentence for a video, where the title should compactly describe the most salient event in the video. This task is similar to video captioning, since both tasks generate a sentence given a video. However, most video captioning methods focus on generating *a relevant sentence* given a 6–10 s short clip. In contrast, video title generation aims to produce a title sentence describing the most salient event given a typical 1 min user-generated video (UGV). Hence, video title generation is an important extension of generic video captioning to understand a large number of UGVs on the web.

   To study video title generation, we have collected a new "Video Titles in the Wild" (VTW) dataset that consists of UGVs. We first introduce the dataset and discuss its unique properties and the challenges for video title generation. Then, our proposed methods will be introduced in Sect. 4.

## 3.1  Collection of Curated UGVs

Everyday, a vast amount of UGVs are uploaded to video sharing websites. To facilitate web surfers to view the interesting ones, many online communities curate a set of interesting UGVs. We program a web crawler to harvest UGVs from these communities. For this paper, we have collected 18100 open-domain videos with 1.5 min duration on average (45 s median duration). We also crawl the following curated meta information about each video (see Fig. 2): *Title:* a single and concise sentence produced by an editor, which we use as ground truth for training and testing; *Description:* 1–3 longer sentences which are different from titles, as they may not be relevant to the salient event, or may not be relevant to the visual contents; *Others:* tags, places, dates and category.

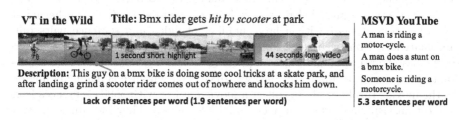

**Fig. 2.** Dataset comparison. Left-panel: VTW. Right-panel: the MSVD [8].

This data is automatically collected from well established online communities that post 10–20 new videos per day. We do not conduct any further curation of the videos or sentences so the data can be considered "in the wild".

**Unknown Highlight in UGVs.** We now describe how title generation is related to highlight in UGVs. These UGVs are on an average 1.5 min long which is 5–10 times longer than clips in video captioning datasets [5,6]. Intuitively, the title should be describing a segment of the video corresponding to the highlight (i.e., the salient event). To confirm this intuition, we manually label title-specific highlights (i.e., compact video segments well described by the titles) in a subset of videos. We found that the median highlight duration is about 3.3 s. Moreover, the non-highlight part of the video might not be precisely described by the title. In our dataset, the temporal location and extent of the highlight in most videos are unknown. This creates a challenge for a standard video captioner to learn the correct association between words in titles and video observations. In Sect. 4.2, we propose a novel highlight-sensitive method to jointly locate highlights and generate titles for addressing this challenge.

**Table 1.** Dataset Comparison. Our data is from a large-scale open-domain video repository and our total duration is 2.5 times longer than [5]. V. stands for video, and (V) denotes videos of a few minutes long, whereas clips are typically a few seconds long. Desc. stands for description. AMT stands for Amazon Mechanical Turk. DVS stands for Descriptive Video Service.

| Dataset | V. source | #Clips | Duration (H) | Desc. source | #Sentences |
|---|---|---|---|---|---|
| YouCook [9] | Cooking | 88 (V) | 2.3 | AMT | 2,668 |
| TACoS [7] | Cooking | 7,206 | 15.9 | AMT | 18,227 |
| TACoS-M [35] | Cooking | 14,105 | 27.1 | AMT | 52,593 |
| MPII-MD. [6] | Movie | 54,076 | 56.5 | Script + DVS | 54,076 |
| (DVS part) [6] | Movie | 30,680 | 34.7 | DVS | 30,680 |
| M-VAD [5] | Movie | 48,986 | 84.9 | DVS | 55,904 |
| MSVD [8] | YouTube | 1,970 | ~9.6$^2$ | AMT | 70,028 |
| VTW-title | YouTube | 18,100 (V) | 213.2 | Editor | 18,100 |
| VTW-full | YouTube | 18,100 (V) | 213.2 | Owner/editor | 44,603 |

## 3.2  Dataset Comparison

Our VTW dataset is a challenging large-scale video captioning dataset, as summarized in Table 1. The VTW dataset has the longest duration (213.2 h) and each of our videos is about 10 times longer than each clip in [5,6]. The table also shows that only movie description datasets [5,6] and VTW are: (1) at the scale of more than $10K$ open-domain videos, and (2) consisting of sophisticated sentences produced by editors instead of simple sentences produced by Turkers.

**Sentence Diversity.** Intuitively, a set of diverse sentences should have a large vocabulary. Hence, we use the ratio of the number of sentences to the size of vocabulary as a measure of sentence diversity. We found that the MSVD dataset has on an average 5.3 sentences per word, whereas both movie description datasets have less than or equal to 3 sentences per-word and VTW has about 2 sentences per word (Table 2). Therefore, sentences in VTW are twice more diverse than in the MSVD dataset and slightly more diverse than in the movie description datasets. This implies that we need more sentences for learning, even though these datasets are already the largest datasets. In Sect. 4.3, we propose a novel "sentence augmentation" method to mitigate this issue.

**Complementary Vocabulary.** Although the distribution of nouns, verbs, adjectives, and adverbs in all three datasets are similar (see Table 2), the common words are different in these two types of datasets, since VTW consists of UGVs and [5,6] consists of movie clips. We visualize the top few nouns and verbs in VTW, MPII-MD. [6], and M-VAD [5] in the technical report [36]. We believe our dataset is complementary to the movie description datasets for future study of both video captioning and title generation.

**Table 2.** Text Statistics. The first two columns are the number of sentences and non-stemmed vocabulary size, respectively. The third column is the average number of sentences per word. The last four columns are nouns, verbs, adjectives, and adverbs in order, where A;B denotes A as number and B as ratio. We compute the ratio with respect to the number of nouns. Voca. stands for vocabulary. Sent. stands for sentences. W. stands for words. Our full dataset has vocabulary with a similar size compared to two recent large-scale video description datasets.

| | #Sent | Voca | #Sent./W | #Nouns | #Verbs | #Adjective | #Adverb |
|---|---|---|---|---|---|---|---|
| MPII-MD [6] | 54076 | 20650 | 2.6 | 11397;1 | 6100;0.54 | 3952;0.35 | 1162;0.1 |
| M-VAD [5] | 55904 | 18310 | 3.0 | 10992;1 | 4945;0.45 | 3649;0.33 | 870;0.08 |
| VTW-title | 18100 | 8874 | 2.0 | 5850;1 | 2187;0.37 | 1187;0.2 | 224;0.04 |
| VTW-full | 44603 | 23059 | 1.9 | 13606;1 | 6223;0.46 | 3967;0.29 | 846;0.06 |

## 4    From Caption to Title

Both video title generation and captioning models learn from many video $V$ and sentence $S$ pairs, where $V$ contains a sequence of observations $(v_1, \ldots, v_k, \ldots, v_n)$ and $S$ a sequence of words $(s_1, \ldots, s_i, \ldots, s_m)$. In this section, we build from the video captioning task and introduce two generally applicable methods (see Fig. 3) to handle the challenges for video title generation.

### 4.1    Video Captioning

Video captioning can be formulated as the following optimization problem,

$$S^*(V; \theta) = \arg \max_S p(S|V; \theta), \tag{1}$$

where $S^*(V; \theta)$ is the predicted sentence, $\theta$ is the learned model parameters, and $p(S|V; \theta)$ is the conditional probability of sentence $S$ given a video sequence $V$. According to the probability chain rule, the full sentence conditional probability $p(S|V; \theta)$ equals to the multiplication of each word conditional probability:

$$p(S|V; \theta) = \prod_{i=1}^{m} p(s_i|S_{1:(i-1)}, V), \tag{2}$$

where $s_i$ is the $i^{th}$ word, $S_{1:(i-1)}$ is the partial sentence from the first word to the $i - 1^{th}$ word. Note that the $i^{th}$ word depends on all the previously generated words $S_{1:(i-1)}$ and the video $V$. Most state-of-the-art methods utilize Recurrent Neural Networks with Long Short Term Memory (LSTM) cells [37] to model the long-term dependency in this single word conditional probability. We use two state-of-the-art methods as examples,

– Sequence to Sequence - Video to Text (S2VT) [4]. The method proposed to use RNN to encode both the video sequence $V = (v_1, \ldots, v_k, \ldots, v_n)$ and partial sentences $S_{1:(i-1)} = (s_1, \ldots, s_{i-1})$ into a learned hidden representation $h_{n+i-1}$ so that the single word conditional probability becomes $p(s_i|h_{n+i-1}, s_{i-1})$.

- Soft-Attention (SA) [3]. The model proposed to use RNN to encode the partial sentences $S_{1:(i-1)} = (s_1, \ldots, s_{i-1})$ into a learned hidden representation $h_{i-1}$ and apply per-word soft-attention mechanism to obtain weighted average of all video observation $\varphi(V) = \sum_i^n \alpha_i v_i$, where $\sum_i^n \alpha_i = 1$. The single word conditional probability becomes $p(s_i|h_{i-1}, s_{i-1}, \varphi(V))$.

Despite their differences, they essentially model two relations:

- Word and video $(s_i|V)$. This relation is critical for associating words to video observation. However, this relation alone is only sufficient for video tagging, but not video captioning.
- Words sequence $(s_i|S_{1:(i-1)})$. Modeling this relation is the essence of language modeling. However, this relation alone is only sufficient for sentence generation (i.e., captioning), but not video captioning.

An ideal video captioning method should model both types of relations equally well. In particular, our video title generation task creates additional challenges on modeling these relations: (1) unknown highlight, (2) diverse sentences. We now present our novel and generally applicable methods for improving the modeling of these two relations for video title generation.

### 4.2 Highlight Sensitive Captioning

As we mentioned in Sect. 3.1, UGVs are on an average 1.5 min with many parts not precisely described by the title sentence. Hence, it is very challenging to learn the right $s|V$ relation given many irrelevant video observations in $V$. Intuitively, there should exist a video highlight $V^H \subset V$ which is the most relevant to the ground truth title sentence $S^{gt}$ (see Fig. 3-Top). We propose to train a highlight sensitive captioner by solving the following optimization problem,

$$\arg \min_{\theta, \{V_j^H\}_j} \sum_j \mathcal{L}(S_j^{gt}, S_j^*(V_j^H; \theta)) \; ; \; \mathcal{L}(S^{gt}, S^*(V; \theta)) = \sum_i L(s_i^{gt}, s_i^*(V; \theta)), \tag{3}$$

where $j$ is the video index (omitted for conciseness in many cases), $S^*(V; \theta)$ is the predicted sentence given the video $V$ and model parameter $\theta$, $i$ is the word index, $s_i^{gt}$ is the ground truth $i^{th}$ word, $s_i^*$ is the predicted $i^{th}$ word, and $L$ is the cross-entropy loss. This is a hard optimization problem, since jointly optimizing

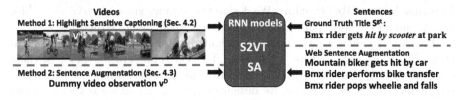

**Fig. 3.** An overview of our proposed methods: (top-row) highlight sensitive captioning (Sect. 4.2) and (bottom-row) sentence augmentation (Sect. 4.3).

the continuous variable $\theta$ and discrete variables $\{V_j^H\}_j$ is NP-hard. However, when video highlights $\{V_j^H\}_j$ are fixed, the optimization problem is the original video captioning problem.

**Training Procedure.** We propose to iteratively solve for $\theta$ and $V^H$. When $V_H$ is fixed, we use stochastic gradient descent to solve for $\theta$. Next, when $\theta$ is fixed, we use the loss $\mathcal{L}(.)$ to find the best $V^{H*}$ by solving,

$$V^{H*} = \arg \min_{V^H \in V} \mathcal{L}(S^{gt}, S^*(V; \theta)). \qquad (4)$$

The training loss typically converged within a few iterations, since $p(.)$ is a deep model with high-capacity. This implies that our iterative training procedure needs to start with a good initialization. We propose to train a highlight detector on a small set of training data with ground truth highlight labels. Then, use the detector to automatically obtain the initial video highlight $V^H$ on the whole training set to start the iterative training procedure.

At each iteration, the updated highlight $V^H$ can be used to (1) retrain the highlight detector using the full training set, and (2) update the video captioning model. As a result, our "highlight sensitive" captioner learns to generate sentences specifically describing the highlight moment in a video. We found that the refined highlight detector achieves a better performance.

## 4.3   Sentence Augmentation

As mentioned above, we are facing the lack of sentences issue due to the diverse sentence property. We argue that the ability to jointly train the captioner with sentence-only examples (with no corresponding videos) and video-sentence pairs is a critical strategy to increase the robustness of the language model. However, most state-of-the-art captioners [3,4] are strictly trained with video-sentence pairs only. This prevents video captioning to benefit from other sentence-only information on the web. Moreover, we confirm in experiment that a video-description pairs training procedure does not consistently improve performance. Hence, we propose a novel and generally applicable method to train a RNN model with both video-sentence pairs and sentence-only examples, where sentence-only examples are either the description sentences or additional sentences on the web. The idea of our technique is straight forward: let's associate a dummy video observation $v^D$ to a sentence-only example (see Fig. 3-Bottom).

**Dummy Video Observation.** We design the dummy video observation $v^D$ for SA [3] and S2VT [4], separately, by considering their model structures.

In SA, all video observations are weighted summed into a single observation $\varphi(V) = \sum_i^n \alpha_i v_i$, where $\sum_i^n \alpha_i = 1$. The video observation $\varphi(V)$ is, then, embedded to $A\varphi(V)$ in the LSTM cell. For the augmented sentences with no corresponding video observations, we design $v_i = v^D$ as an all zeros vector except a single 1 at the first entry and let it be a constant observation across time. This implies that $A\varphi(\{v^D\}) = Av^D = a^1$, where $A = [a^1, \dots]$. Intuitively, $a^1$

can be considered as a trainable bias vector to handle additional sentence-only examples. As a concrete example, the memory cell in SA is updated as below,

$$c_t = \tanh(W_c E[y_{t-1}] + U_c h_{t-1} + A_c \varphi(\{v^D\}) + b_c), \tag{5}$$

where $c_t$ is the new memory content, $E[y_{t-1}]$ is the previous word, $h_{t-1}$ is the previous hidden representation, $W_c, U_c, A_c$ are trainable embedding matrices, and $b_c$ is the original trainable bias vector. Now $A_c \varphi(\{v^D\}) = a_c^1$ can be considered as another trainable bias vector to handle the dummy video observations.

In S2VT, all video observations are sequentially encoded by RNN as well. However, if we design the $v^D$ as an all zeros vector except a single 1 at the first entry, the encoded representation $h_n$ at the end of the video sequence will be a function of all model parameters: $W_{x*}$, $W_{h*}$ and $b_*$. Hence, we simply design $v^D$ as an all zeros vector so that $h_n$ will be a function of only $W_{h*}$ and $b_*$. Intuitively, this simplifies the parameters that handle additional sentence-only examples with dummy video observations. In our experiments, we find that the all zeros vector achieves a better accuracy for S2VT (see [36] for details).

## 5    Experiments

We first describe general details of our experimental settings and implementation. Then, we define variants of our methods and compare performance on VTW and M-VAD [5].

**Benchmark Dataset.** We randomly split our dataset into 80 % training, 10 % validation, and 10 % testing as the same proportion in the M-VAD [5]. In this paper, we mainly use title sentences. This means we have 14100 video-sentence pairs for training, 2000 pairs for validation, and 2000 pairs for testing. Our dataset is extremely challenging: among 2980 unique words in testing, there are 488 words (16.4 %) which have not appeared in training, 323 words (10.8 %) which have only appeared once in training. We refer these numbers as "Testing-Word-Count-in-Training" (TWCinT) statistics and show these statistics in the technical report [36]. We also manually labeled the highlight moments in 2000 training (14.2 % of total training) and 2000 testing (100 % of total testing) videos. These labels in the training set are only used as supervision to train the initial highlight detector. These labels in the testing set are only used as ground truth for evaluating highlight detection accuracy.

**Features.** Similar to existing video captioning methods, we utilize both appearance and local motion features: we extract VGG [38] features for each frame, and C3D [39] features for 16 consecutive frames. For S2VT [4] and SA [3], we embed both features to a lower 500 and 1024 dimension space, respectively, according to their original papers. Next, we define the video observation.

**Video Observation.** We divide a video into maximum 45–50 clips due to GPU memory limit, and average-pool features within each clip.

**Highlight Detector.** We train a bidirectional RNN highlight detector (details in [36]) on 2000 training videos to predict the highlightness of each clip of 100 frames, since the median ground truth highlight duration is about 100 frames. This initial highlight detector achieves a 54.2 % mean Average Precision (mAP) on testing videos. The trained detector selects eight consecutive highlight clips (800 consecutive frames) for each training video to train a captioner. After a captioner is trained, it will select again eight consecutive clips as the highlight (see Eq. 4) to (1) retrain a highlight detector, and (2) a captioner.

**Sentence Augmentation.** Given a large corpus, we retrieve additional sentences for sentence augmentation as follows. We use each training sentence as a query and retrieve similar sentences in the corpus. We use the mean of word2vec [40] feature of non-stop words in each sentence as the sentence-based feature. Cosine similarity is used to measure sentence-wise similarity. Among sentences with similarity above 0.75, we sample a target number of sentences. On VTW, we use 14100 titles in training set to retrieve sentences from a corpus of YouTube video titles for augmentation. In detail, we use YouTube API to download video titles in a few UGVs channels. There are 3549 unique sentences with a vocabulary of 3732 words. On M-VAD, we retrieve 23635 sentences from MPII-MD [6] for augmentation.

**RNN Training.** In all experiments, we use 0.0001 learning rate, 200 maximum epochs, 10 batch size, and stochastic gradient-based solver [41] with its default parameters in TensorFlow [42] to train a model from scratch. When finetuning a model, we train for another 50 epochs. Hence, HL requires additional $50 \times N$ epochs, where N is the number of iteration, than Vanilla and HL-1. WebAug is trained with 200 epochs but with a larger number of min-batches due to sentence augmentation. All models are selected according to validation accuracy.

**Evaluation Metric.** We use the standard evaluation metric for the image captioning challenge [43] including BLEU1 to BLEU4, METEOR, and CIDEr [44]. METEOR is a metric replacing BLEU1 to BLEU4 into a single performance value, and it is designed to improve correlation with human judgments. CIDEr is a new metric recently adopted for evaluating image captioning. It considers the rareness of n-grams (computed by tf-idf), and gives higher value when a rare n-gram is predicted correctly. Since typically a few important words make a title sentence stands out (e.g., hit by scooter in Fig. 1), we also consider CIDEr as a good evaluation metric for video title generation. Other than these automatic metrics, we also ask human judges to select the better video title out of a sentence generated by a state-of-the-art video captioner [4] or a sentence generated by our best method.

### 5.1 Baseline Methods

We define variants of our methods for performance comparison.

- Vanilla represents our TensorFlow reimplementation of either S2VT [4] or SA [3] (see technical report [36] for details). Note that these are two fairly strong baseline methods.

- Vanilla-GT-HL denotes that ground truth highlight clips are used while evaluating the Vanilla model.
- HL-1 denotes the initially trained highlight-sensitive captioner. Its comparison with Vanilla shows the effectiveness of highlight detection.
- HL denotes the converged highlight-sensitive captioner. At each iteration, we finetune the model from previous iteration.
- Vanilla+Desc. treats descriptions as additional title sentences associated to their original videos in training. This is a risky assumption, since many descriptions describe the non-visual information of the videos.
- Desc. Aug. uses descriptions as augmented sentences.
- Web Aug. retrieves sentences from another corpus as augmented sentences.
- HL+Web Aug. combines highlight sensitive captioning with sentence augmentation. In detail, we take the trained Web Aug. model as the initial model. Then, we apply our HL method and finetune the model.

## 5.2   Results

**Highlight Sensitive Captioner.** When we apply our method on S2VT [4], HL-1 significantly outperforms Vanilla and HL consistently improves over HL-1 (the better B@1-4, METEOR 6.2 %, and CIDEr 24.9 % in Table 3). When we apply our method on SA [3], the similar trend appears and HL achieves the better METEOR 5.6 % and CIDEr 24.9 % than both of the Vanilla and the HL-1. Moreover, the updated highlight detector (see technical report [36] for details) achieves the best 58.3 % mAP as compared to the initial 54.2 % mAP. We also

**Table 3.** Video captioning performance of different variants of our methods (see Sect. 5.1) on VTW dataset. Our methods are applied on two state-of-the-art methods: S2VT [4] (Left-columns) and SA [3] (Right-columns). By combining highlight with sentence augmentation (HL+Web Aug.), we achieves the best accuracy consistently across all measures (highlight in bold-font). MET. stands for METEOR. B@1 denotes BLEU at 1-gram. Desc. stands for description. Aug. stands for sentence augmentation.

| VTW | S2VT [4] (%) | | | | | | SA [3] (%) | | | | | |
|---|---|---|---|---|---|---|---|---|---|---|---|---|
| Variant | B@1 | B@2 | B@3 | B@4 | MET. | CIDEr | B@1 | B@2 | B@3 | B@4 | MET. | CIDEr |
| Vanilla | 9.3 | 3.7 | 1.9 | 1.2 | 5.2 | 18.6 | 9.2 | 4.1 | 2.2 | 1.4 | 4.5 | 18.5 |
| Vanilla-GT-HL | 10.2 | 4.3 | 2.1 | 1.2 | 5.1 | 19.8 | 9.4 | 4.3 | 2.3 | 1.5 | 4.7 | 19.8 |
| HL-1 | 10.8 | 4.5 | 2.3 | 1.4 | 6.1 | 23.0 | 11.6 | **5.5** | **2.9** | 1.7 | 5.6 | 24.3 |
| HL | 11.4 | 4.9 | 2.5 | **1.6** | **6.2** | 24.9 | 11.6 | 5.3 | **2.9** | 1.8 | 5.6 | 24.9 |
| Vanilla+Desc. | 7.0 | 2.5 | 1.2 | 0.7 | 5.2 | 12.0 | 9.4 | 3.9 | 1.8 | 0.7 | 4.6 | 18.9 |
| Desc. Aug. | 10.8 | 4.6 | 2.0 | 1.1 | 6.0 | 21.6 | 10.0 | 4.3 | 2.0 | 1.1 | 4.9 | 21.3 |
| Web Aug. | 11.0 | 4.7 | 2.3 | 1.3 | 6.0 | 22.8 | 10.3 | 4.6 | 2.2 | 1.3 | 5.0 | 22.2 |
| HL+Web Aug. | **11.7** | **5.1** | **2.6** | **1.6** | **6.2** | **25.4** | **11.8** | **5.5** | **2.9** | **1.9** | **5.7** | **25.1** |

found that training considering highlight temporal location is important, since Vanilla-GT-HL does not outperform Vanilla. We further use the Vanilla model on S2VT to automatically select highlight clips. Then, we train a highlight-sensitive captioner based on these selected highlight clips as HL-0. It achieves METEOR 5.9 % and CIDEr 22.4 % which is only slightly inferior to HL on S2VT. It shows that our method trained without highlight supervision also outperforms Vanilla.

**Sentence Augmentation.** On VTW, when we apply our method on S2VT [4], Vanilla+Desc. does not consistently improve accuracy; however, both Web Aug. and Desc. Aug. improve accuracy significantly as compared to Vanilla (Table 3). When we apply our method on SA [3], the similar trend appears and Web Aug. achieves the best METEOR 5 % and CIDEr 22.2 %.

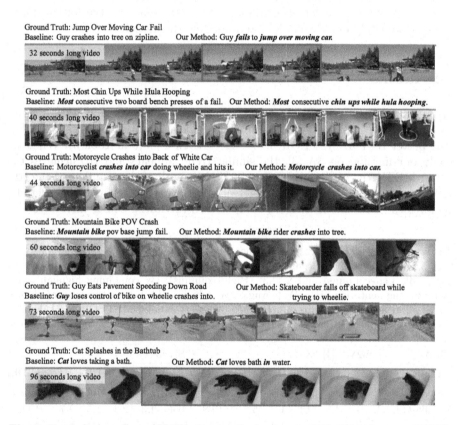

**Fig. 4.** Typical examples on VTW. Our method refers to "HL+Web Aug. on S2VT". Baseline refers to "Vanilla on S2VT". The words matched in the ground truth title are highlighted in bold and italic font. Each red box corresponds to the detected highlight with a fixed 3.3 s duration. Frames in the red box are manually selected from the detected highlight for illustration. Note that our sentence in the last row has low METEOR, but was judged by human to be better than the baseline.

**Our Full Method.** On VTW dataset, HL with Web Aug. on both S2VT and SA outperform their own variants (last row in Table 3), especially in CIDER which gives higher value when a rare n-gram is predicted correctly. Our best accuracy is achieved by combining HL with Web Aug. on S2VT. We also ask human judges to compare sentences generated by our HL+Web Aug. on S2VT method and the S2VT baseline (Vanilla) on half of the testing videos (see technical report [36] for details). Human judges decide that 59.5 % of our sentences are on par or better than the baseline sentences. We show the detected highlights and generated video titles in Fig. 4. Note that our sentence in the last row of Fig. 4 has low METEOR, but was judged by human to be better than the baseline.

**Setence Augmentation on M-VAD.** Since S2VT outperforms SA in METEOR and CIDEr on VTW, we evaluate the performance of S2VT+Web Aug. on the M-VAD dataset [5]. Our method achieves 7.1 % in METEOR as compared to 6.6 % of the S2VT baseline and 6.7 % reported in [4]. This shows its great potential to improve video captioning accuracy across different datasets.

## 6  Conclusion

We introduce video title generation, a much more challenging task than video captioning. We propose to extend state-of-the-art video captioners for generating video titles. To evaluate our methods, we harvest the large-scale "Video Title in the Wild" (VTW) dataset. On VTW, our proposed methods consistently improve title prediction accuracy, and the best performance is achieved by applying both methods. Finally, on the M-VAD [5], our sentence augmentation method (METEOR 7.1 %) outperforms the S2VT baseline (6.7 % in [4]).

**Acknowledgements.** We thank Microsoft Research Asia, MOST 103-2218-E-007-025, MOST 104-3115-E-007-005, NOVATEK Fellowship, and Panasonic for their support. We also thank Shih-Han Chou, Heng Hsu, and I-Hsin Lee for their collaboration.

## References

1. Krizhevsky, A., Sutskever, I., Hinton, G.E.: Imagenet classification with deep convolutional neural networks. In: NIPS (2012)
2. Venugopalan, S., Xu, H., Donahue, J., Rohrbach, M., Mooney, R., Saenko, K.: Translating videos to natural language using deep recurrent neural networks. In: NAACL (2015)
3. Yao, L., Torabi, A., Cho, K., Ballas, N., Pal, C., Larochelle, H., Courville., A.: Describing videos by exploiting temporal structure. In: ICCV (2015)
4. Venugopalan, S., Rohrbach, M., Donahue, J., Mooney, R., Darrell, T., Saenko, K.: Sequence to sequence - video to text. In: ICCV (2015)
5. Torabi, A., Pal, C.J., Larochelle, H., Courville, A.C.: Using descriptive video services to create a large data source for video annotation research. arXiv:1503.01070 (2015)
6. Rohrbach, A., Rohrbach, M., Tandon, N., Schiele, B.: A dataset for movie description. In: CVPR (2015)

7. Rohrbach, M., Qiu, W., Titov, I., Thater, S., Pinkal, M., Schiele, B.: Translating video content to natural language descriptions. In: ICCV (2013)
8. Chen, D.L., Dolan, W.B.: Collecting highly parallel data for paraphrase evaluation. In: Proceedings of the 49th Annual Meeting of the Association for Computational Linguistics (2011)
9. Das, P., Xu, C., Doell, R., Corso, J.: A thousand frames in just a few words: lingual description of videos through latent topics and sparse object stitching. In: CVPR (2013)
10. Guadarrama, S., Krishnamoorthy, N., Malkarnenkar, G., Venugopalan, S., Mooney, R., Darrell, T., Saenko, K.: Youtube2text: recognizing and describing arbitrary activities using semantic hierarchies and zero-shot recognition. In: ICCV (2013)
11. Krishnamoorthy, N., Malkarnenkar, G., Mooney, R.J., Saenko, K., Guadarrama, S.: Generating natural-language video descriptions using text-mined knowledge. In: AAAI (2013)
12. Thomason, J., Venugopalan, S., Guadarrama, S., Saenko, K., Mooney, R.: Integrating language and vision to generate natural language descriptions of videos in the wild. In: COLING (2014)
13. Barbu, A., Bridge, E., Burchill, Z., Coroian, D., Dickinson, S., Fidler, S., Michaux, A., Mussman, S., Narayanaswamy, S., Salvi, D., Schmidt, L., Shangguan, J., Siskind, J.M., Waggoner, J., Wang, S., Wei, J., Yin, Y., Zhang, Z.: Video in sentences out. In: UAI (2012)
14. Kojima, A., Tamura, T., Fukunaga, K.: Natural language description of human activities from video images based on concept hierarchy of actions. IJCV $50(2)$, 171–184 (2002)
15. Donahue, J., Hendricks, L.A., Guadarrama, S., Rohrbach, M., Venugopalan, S., Saenko, K., Darrell, T.: Long-term recurrent convolutional networks for visual recognition and description. In: CVPR (2015)
16. Vinyals, O., Toshev, A., Bengio, S., Erhan, D.: Show and tell: a neural image caption generator. In: CVPR (2015)
17. Rohrbach, A., Rohrbach, M., Schiele, B.: The long-short story of movie description. In: Gall, J., et al. (eds.) GCPR 2015. LNCS, vol. 9358, pp. 209–221. Springer, Heidelberg (2015). doi:10.1007/978-3-319-24947-6_17
18. Wang, H., Schmid, C.: Action recognition with improved trajectories. In: ICCV (2013)
19. Xu, R., Xiong, C., Chen, W., Corso, J.J.: Jointly modeling deep video and compositional text to bridge vision and language in a unified framework. In: AAAI, pp. 2346–2352 (2015)
20. Pan, Y., Mei, T., Yao, T., Li, H., Rui, Y.: Jointly modeling embedding and translation to bridge video and language. arXiv:1505.01861 (2015)
21. Pan, P., Xu, Z., Yang, Y., Wu, F., Zhuang, Y.: Hierarchical recurrent neural encoder for video representation with application to captioning. arXiv:1511.03476 (2015)
22. Yu, H., Wang, J., Huang, Z., Yang, Y., Xu, W.: Video paragraph captioning using hierarchical recurrent neural networks. arXiv:1510.07712 (2015)
23. Yow, D., Yeo, B., Yeung, M., Liu, B.: Analysis and presentation of soccer highlights from digital video. In: ACCV (1995)
24. Rui, Y., Gupta, A., Acero, A.: Automatically extracting highlights for TV baseball programs. In: ACM Multimedia (2000)
25. Nepal, S., Srinivasan, U., Reynolds, G.: Automatic detection of goal segments in basketball videos. In: ACM Multimedia (2001)
26. Wang, J., Xu, C., Chng, E., Tian, Q.: Sports highlight detection from keyword sequences using HMM. In: ICME (2004)

27. Xiong, Z., Radhakrishnan, R., Divakaran, A., Huang, T.: Highlights extraction from sports video based on an audio-visual marker detection framework. In: ICME (2005)
28. Kolekar, M., Sengupta, S.: Event-importance based customized and automatic cricket highlight generation. In: ICME (2006)
29. Hanjalic, A.: Adaptive extraction of highlights from a sport video based on excitement modeling. IEEE Trans. Multimedia **7**, 1114–1122 (2005)
30. Tang, H., Kwatra, V., Sargin, M., Gargi, U.: Detecting highlights in sports videos: cricket as a test case. In: ICME (2011)
31. Sun, M., Farhadi, A., Seitz, S.: Ranking domain-specific highlights by analyzing edited videos. In: Fleet, D., Pajdla, T., Schiele, B., Tuytelaars, T. (eds.) ECCV 2014, Part I. LNCS, vol. 8689, pp. 787–802. Springer, Heidelberg (2014)
32. Song, Y., Vallmitjana, J., Stent, A., Jaimes, A.: TVSum: summarizing web videos using titles. In: CVPR (2015)
33. Zhao, B., Xing, E.P.: Quasi real-time summarization for consumer videos. In: CVPR (2014)
34. Yang, H., Wang, B., Lin, S., Wipf, D., Guo, M., Guo, B.: Unsupervised extraction of video highlights via robust recurrent auto-encoders. In: ICCV (2015)
35. Rohrbach, A., Rohrbach, M., Qiu, W., Friedrich, A., Pinkal, M., Schiele, B.: Coherent multi-sentence video description with variable level of detail. In: Jiang, X., Hornegger, J., Koch, R. (eds.) GCPR 2014. LNCS, vol. 8753, pp. 184–195. Springer, Heidelberg (2014)
36. Zeng, K.H., Chen, T.H., Niebles, J.C., Sun, M.: Technical report of video title generation. http://aliensunmin.github.io/project/video-language/
37. Hochreiter, S., Schmidhuber, J.: Long short-term memory. Neural Comput. **9**, 1735–1780 (1997)
38. Simonyan, K., Zisserman, A.: Very deep convolutional networks for large-scale image recognition. In: ICLR (2015)
39. Tran, D., Bourdev, L., Fergus, R., Torresani, L., Paluri, M.: Learning spatiotemporal features with 3D convolutional networks. In: ICCV (2015)
40. Mikolov, T., Chen, K., Corrado, G., Dean, J.: Efficient estimation of word representations in vector space. arXiv:1301.3781 (2013)
41. Kingma, D.P., Ba, J.: Adam: A method for stochastic optimization. arXiv:1412.6980 (2014)
42. Abadi, M., Agarwal, A., Barham, P., Brevdo, E., Chen, Z., Citro, C., Corrado, G.S., Davis, A., Dean, J., Devin, M., Ghemawat, S., Goodfellow, I., Harp, A., Irving, G., Isard, M., Jia, Y., Jozefowicz, R., Kaiser, L., Kudlur, M., Levenberg, J., Mané, D., Monga, R., Moore, S., Murray, D., Olah, C., Schuster, M., Shlens, J., Steiner, B., Sutskever, I., Talwar, K., Tucker, P., Vanhoucke, V., Vasudevan, V., Viégas, F., Vinyals, O., Warden, P., Wattenberg, M., Wicke, M., Yu, Y., Zheng, X.: TensorFlow: large-scale machine learning on heterogeneous systems software available from tensorflow.org (2015)
43. Lin, T.-Y., Maire, M., Belongie, S., Hays, J., Perona, P., Ramanan, D., Dollár, P., Zitnick, C.L.: Microsoft COCO: common objects in context. In: Fleet, D., Pajdla, T., Schiele, B., Tuytelaars, T. (eds.) ECCV 2014, Part V. LNCS, vol. 8693, pp. 740–755. Springer, Heidelberg (2014)
44. Vedantam, R., Lawrence Zitnick, C., Parikh, D.: Cider: consensus-based image description evaluation. In: CVPR (2015)

# Natural Image Matting Using Deep Convolutional Neural Networks

Donghyeon Cho[1]($\boxtimes$), Yu-Wing Tai[2], and Inso Kweon[1]

[1] KAIST, Daejeon, South Korea
cdh12242@gmail.com, iskweon@kaist.ac.kr
[2] SenseTime Group Limited, Hong Kong, China
yuwing@gmail.com
https://sites.google.com/site/cnnmatting/

**Abstract.** We propose a deep Convolutional Neural Networks (CNN) method for natural image matting. Our method takes results of the closed form matting, results of the KNN matting and normalized RGB color images as inputs, and directly learns an end-to-end mapping between the inputs, and reconstructed alpha mattes. We analyze pros and cons of the closed form matting, and the KNN matting in terms of local and nonlocal principle, and show that they are complementary to each other. A major benefit of our method is that it can "recognize" different local image structures, and then combine results of local (closed form matting), and nonlocal (KNN matting) matting effectively to achieve higher quality alpha mattes than both of its inputs. Extensive experiments demonstrate that our proposed deep CNN matting produces visually and quantitatively high-quality alpha mattes. In addition, our method has achieved the highest ranking in the public alpha matting evaluation dataset in terms of the sum of absolute differences, mean squared errors, and gradient errors.

**Keywords:** Alpha matting · Deep CNN · Local and nonlocal matting

## 1 Introduction and Related Work

Image matting aims to extract an alpha matte of foreground given a trimap of an image. This problem can be expressed as a linear combination of foreground and background colors as follows [1]:

$$I = \alpha F + (1 - \alpha)B, \tag{1}$$

where $I, F, B$, and $\alpha$ denote the observed image (usually in RGB), foreground, background and mixing coefficients (alpha matte) respectively. Given an input $I$, finding $F, B$, and $\alpha$ simultaneously is a highly ill-posed problem.

Previous works in image matting have shown that, if we make proper assumptions, *e.g.* the color line model, about $F$ and $B$, we can solve $\alpha$ in a closed form [2]. Local affinity based methods [2,3] analyze statistical correlation among local pixels to propagate alpha values from known regions to unknown pixels. When their

© Springer International Publishing AG 2016
B. Leibe et al. (Eds.): ECCV 2016, Part II, LNCS 9906, pp. 626–643, 2016.
DOI: 10.1007/978-3-319-46475-6_39

assumptions about local color distribution were violated, unsatisfactory results can be obtained. Nonlocal affinity based approaches [4–9] and color sampling based methods [10–14] rely on the nonlocal principle. They try to relax the local color distribution assumption by searching nonlocal neighbors and color samples which provide a better description of the image matting equation (Eq. (1)). Moreover, some works utilize multiple frames such as video [9,15] and camera arrays [16,18] to get local and nonlocal information across the images for matting.

Nonlocal methods, however, do not always outperform local methods. This is because these nonlocal methods were also built on top of some assumptions, *e.g.* nonlocal matting Laplacian [6], structure and texture similarity [13], comprehensive sampling sets [14], to search for proper nonlocal neighbors. In practice, alpha mattes from local methods are spatially smoother while alpha mattes from nonlocal methods can better capture long hair structures. There are also a few works [19,20] which implicitly deal with a combination of local and nonlocal principles.

We observe that there is a synergistic effect between local and nonlocal methods. The question is how these two kinds of methods can be combined effectively without losing the advantages of both methods. The answer, however, is not straight forward. An important criterion is that the solution should be able to adapt well to different image structures without depending too much on parameter tuning. Deep learning has recently drawn a lot of attentions in object recognition [21]. It has demonstrated its strength in feature extraction, classification [22,23], object detection [24,25] and saliency detection [26,27], as well as image reconstruction tasks such as image denoising [28], dirt removal [30], super-resolution [31], and image deblurring [33]. Because of its benefits in performance, and its versatility in various tasks, we are interested in applying deep learning to the natural image matting problem to bridge the gap between local and nonlocal methods. In addition, although deep learning has a lot of parameters in its training phase, it is almost parameter-free in its testing phase. Because the testing phase requires only a single forward pass of the deep architecture, it is also very efficient in computation especially with the supports of nowadays GPU implementation [34,35].

We have designed a deep CNN whose inputs are the alpha matte from the closed form matting, the alpha matte from the KNN matting, and the normalized RGB colors of the corresponding input image. We choose the closed form matting and the KNN matting as the representative of local and nonlocal methods because both methods are simple, mathematically solid and with publicly available source codes from their original authors. Also, both methods have a few parameters, and their performance is quite stable across wide range of examples. Our deep CNN is directly learnt from more than a hundred thousand of sampled image patches whose ground truth alpha mattes were collected from various sources [36]. We adopt data augmentation to increase variations and the number of training patches. In addition, we apply clustering using the ground truth alpha mattes to balance the number of training patches of different image structures. This is necessary in order to avoid overfitting of training data to particular type of image structures, *e.g.* long hairs.

After our deep CNN model is trained, we can directly apply our trained model to alpha matte reconstruction at the original resolution of input images. This is possible because our model utilizes only convolutional layers, and the convolutional layer do not have the fixed size limitation as opposed to the fully connected layer [37]. Our proposed deep CNN method can effectively combine the benefits of local and nonlocal information to reconstruct higher quality alpha mattes than both of its inputs. Note that this reconstruction is free of parameter, and the initial alpha mattes were obtained from the default parameters of the closed form matting and KNN matting. Because of the nonlinear units across the multiple layers in our deep CNN architecture, our results cannot be reproduced by a simple linear combination of our inputs. We have also found that different image structures activate different neurons in our deep CNN, which results in the best possible alpha mattes reconstruction from our inputs. Finally, we further extend our work by combining the inputs from closed form matting, KNN matting, and comprehensive matting, and a significant performance boost has achieved.

In summary, this paper offers the following contributions:

1. We introduce a deep CNN model for natural image matting. To our knowledge, this is the first attempt to apply deep learning to the natural image matting problem.
2. Our deep CNN model can effectively combine alpha mattes of local and nonlocal methods to reconstruct higher quality alpha mattes than both of its inputs. This is because our deep CNN model can "recognize" local image structures through the activations of different neuron units, and apply appropriate reconstruction scheme to adapt different image structures. This whole process is efficient and parameter-free once our deep CNN model is trained.
3. Our deep CNN method demonstrates outstanding performance in the public alpha matting evaluation benchmark dataset [36]. Our method has achieved the highest ranking in terms of the sum of absolute differences, mean squared errors, and gradient errors.

## 2    Review of Closed Form and KNN Mattings

Our method takes results from the closed form matting [2] and the KNN matting [8] as parts of our inputs. In this section, we briefly review these two methods, and discuss their strength and weakness in the natural image matting problem.

### 2.1    Closed Form Matting

The closed form matting assumes that the local color distribution follows a color line model where colors within a local window can be expressed as a linear combination of two colors. Based on this assumption, Levin et al. derived the matting Laplacian and proved that the alpha matte of foreground can be solved in a closed form without explicit estimation of foreground and background colors. Since then, the matting Laplacian has been extensively used as a regularization term to enhance smoothness of estimated alpha mattes [5,12,13], and other applications [38,39].

**Strength:** In the closed form matting, there are only a few parameters: local window size, $\epsilon$, and $\lambda$. In practical usages, a user only needs to adjust $\lambda$ which is the regularization weight to define the strength of smoothness defined by the matting Laplacian. The value of $\lambda$ can also be fixed for wide range of applications since the performance of matting Laplacian is quite robust to the values of its parameters. Its performance is guaranteed when the color line model assumption is satisfied.

**Weakness:** Although the color line model is quite general, there are a lot of cases where the color line model assumption is violated. It happens when background contains textures or multiple colors in a local region, or when local color distributions of foreground and background are overlapped. In addition, in order to satisfy the color line model, the local window size needs to be unavoidably small (*e.g.* 3×3). A large local window also makes the sparse matting Laplacian matrix computationally intractable. Consequently, the matting Laplacian contains only local information. Since alpha mattes are estimated through the propagation by the matting Laplacian, if the initial definite foreground or definite background samples provided by a user are far away from the matting regions, the estimated alpha mattes will still be over smoothed even through the color line model is satisfied. Also, alpha mattes in isolated regions of a trimap can never be correctly estimated since alpha values are propagated to local neighborhood only. These weaknesses are illustrated in Figs. 1 and 2.

## 2.2 KNN Matting

The KNN matting was derived based on the nonlocal principle in matting originally proposed by the nonlocal matting [6]. Its goal is to resolve the limitations of matting Laplacian by allowing alpha values to be propagated across nonlocal

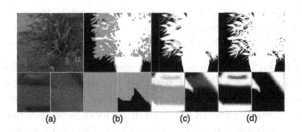

(a)          (b)          (c)          (d)

**Fig. 1.** (a) Input image. (b) Trimap. (c) Alpha matte from the closed form matting. (d) Ground truth alpha matte. Because the definite background samples are far away from object boundaries, the alpha matte in (c) is over smoothed.

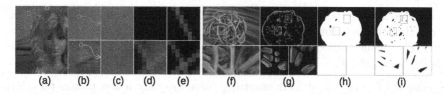

**Fig. 2.** Limitation of local principle for fine structures (a-e) and isolated regions (f-i). (a) Input image. (b) Cropped regions. (c) Double-zoom of the cropped regions. (d) Alpha mattes from the closed form matting. (e) Ground truth alpha mattes. (Red box) The alpha matte of the fine structures has disappeared because the definite foreground samples are too far away. The estimated background $(1-\alpha)$ is over smoothed. (Yellow box) The estimated foreground $\alpha$ of fine structures is over smoothed. (f) Input image. (g) Isolated regions within a trimap. (h) Alpha matte from the closed form matting. (i) Ground truth alpha matte. In this example, background pixels within the isolated trimap regions are considered as foreground because matting Laplacian cannot propagate alpha values across nonlocal neighbors. (Color figure online)

neighbors. Similar to the closed form matting, the nonlocal matting also makes an assumption about the sampled nonlocal neighbors. It assumes that the alpha value of a pixel can be described by a weighted sum of the alpha values of the nonlocal pixels that have similar appearance. In the nonlocal matting, the similar appearance is defined by colors, distance, and texture similarities. The computation of nonlocal matting, however, is very high due to the comparisons of nonlocal neighbors. The KNN matting improved the nonlocal matting by considering only the first K-nearest neighbors in a high dimensional feature space. It reduces the computation by considering only colors (in the HSV color space) and location similarity in their feature space. It also introduced a better preconditioning to further speed up computations. Interestingly, the alpha mattes by the KNN matting outperform the alpha mattes by the nonlocal matting because nonlocal neighbors at farther distance can be considered owing to the reduction of computations.

**Strength:** Similar to the closed form matting, the KNN matting also has a few parameters, and their parameters can be fixed for wide range of examples. Because the KNN matting utilizes nonlocal information, it can handle isolated regions, and better propagate alpha values across fine structures which are usually over smoothed by the closed form matting at a long distance.

**Weakness:** A major limitation of nonlocal methods is that it is difficult to define a universal feature space which can properly evaluate the nonlocal neighbors to adapt different structures of an image. Considering the KNN matting, it utilizes the HSV space instead of the RGB space in its feature vectors because the HSV feature has better quantitative performance in the alpha matting evaluation dataset [36]. However, it is controversial to conclude that the HSV feature always outperforms the RGB feature. This is illustrated in Fig. 3(a-d). Similarly, it is controversial to conclude that features that utilize more texture information can always outperform features that utilize only color information, especially for

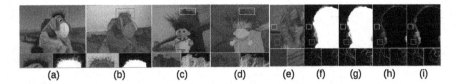

(a)          (b)          (c)          (d)          (e)     (f)     (g)     (h)     (i)

**Fig. 3.** Limitation of nonlocal principle in terms of feature space (a-d), and comparison of the closed form matting and KNN matting (e-i). (a, c) RGB images. (b, d) HSV images. The zoom-ins show the corresponding alpha mattes from the KNN matting with different color space features. The RGB feature produces better result than that of HSV feature in (a, b), but worse result in (c, d). (e) Input image. (f, g) Alpha mattes from the closed form matting and the KNN matting, respectively. (h, i) The corresponding error maps (enhanced for better visualization) of (f, g). (Color figure online)

the natural image matting problem. Because of the limitation of feature spaces, nonlocal methods can perform worse than local methods when improper nonlocal neighbors are considered.

To conclude, we compare the performance of the closed form matting and the KNN matting in Fig. 3(e-i). The closed form matting performs better in preserving local smoothness which has smaller errors in sharp, and short hair regions. In contrast, the KNN matting performs better in protecting long hair regions as shown in the zoom-in regions.

## 3   Deep CNN Matting

In this section, we first describe our deep CNN architecture. After that, we provide a deeper analysis to the activation of neurons in our deep CNN model.

### 3.1   Architecture

The architecture of our deep CNN model is illustrated in Fig. 4. Our network directly maps the input patches ($27\times27\times5$) to the output alpha matte ($15\times15\times1$) as follows:

$$\alpha = \mathcal{F}(\bar{I}, \alpha_c, \alpha_k), \tag{2}$$

where $\mathcal{F}(\cdot)$ denotes a forward pass of our network, $\bar{I} = \frac{I}{\sqrt{r^2+g^2+b^2}}$ is the input image whose intensity is normalized by the magnitude of RGB vector, $\alpha_c$ is the alpha matte from the closed form matting, and $\alpha_k$ is the alpha matte from the KNN matting. The main reason that the normalized RGB is adopted is to reduce magnitude variations of input signals since the magnitude variations are better captured in the initial alpha mattes ($\alpha_c$ and $\alpha_k$). Similarly, we do not include the trimap in our input signals because the trimap information has already implicitly encoded in $\alpha_c$ and $\alpha_k$. Also, strong edges in a trimap can

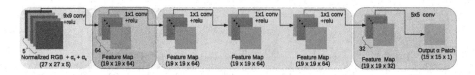

**Fig. 4.** The deep CNN architecture of our method. It consists of 6 convolutional layers. Except for the last layer, each convolutional layer is followed by a ReLU layer for the nonlinear mapping operation. The size of the convolutional kernels, and the number of channels in each layer are illustrated in the figure. In training, the input size is equal to $27 \times 27 \times 5$, and the output size is equal to $15 \times 15 \times 1$. The *Euclidean loss* cost function is used to evaluate the errors during the training. In testing, the spatial dimension of inputs and outputs are equal to the resolution of input images (with padding for input). Our deep CNN method directly outputs the resulting alpha mattes after a forward pass.

give inaccurate high activation responses which can hinder the accuracy of our reconstructed alpha mattes. The initial alpha mattes, $\alpha_c$ and $\alpha_k$, are obtained using the default parameters provided in the original source codes of [2,8].

Our deep CNN model can be roughly divided into three stages according to the size of convolution kernels. In the first stage ($\mathcal{F}_1$), the first convolutional layer is convolved with the 5-channel inputs using 64 $9 \times 9$ kernels which results in 64 response maps[1]. Mathematically, the response map after the first convolutional layer and the ReLU layer is defined as:

$$\mathcal{F}_{1,n}(\bar{I}, \alpha_c, \alpha_k) = \max(0, W_{1,n} \otimes [\bar{I}, \alpha_c, \alpha_k] + b_{1,n}), \qquad (3)$$

where $W_{1,n}$ denotes the weight of the $n$-th filter in the first layer, and $b_{1,n}$ is the bias term. We set the bias term equal to zero, and the filter weights, $W_{1,n}$, are directly learnt from training examples. The first stage serves as structure analysis which activates response of different neurons according to the weights of the filters. After this stage, the response maps capture different local image structures in different output channels.

In the second stage ($\mathcal{F}_2 \sim \mathcal{F}_5$), it stacks multiple $1 \times 1$ convolutional layers to remap the response maps to enhance or suppress the neuron responses nonlinearly according to cross channel correlation. This process is similar to the nonlinear coefficient remapping in sparse coding for image superresolution [40] as discussed in [31]. In [31], only one layer of $1 \times 1$ convolutional layer is used for the remapping. We found that stacking multiple $1 \times 1$ convolutional layers can significantly enhance the performance of our method.

In the last stage ($\mathcal{F}_6$), the alpha mattes are directly reconstructed from the response maps after the second stage:

$$\alpha = \mathcal{F}_6(\mathcal{F}_5(\bar{I}, \alpha_c, \alpha_k)) = W_6 \otimes \mathcal{F}_5(\bar{I}, \alpha_c, \alpha_k). \qquad (4)$$

---

[1] In CAFFE [34], each response map is a weighted sum of the response map of each input channel after passing through the $9 \times 9$ convolution. Thus, the number of output channels is equal to the number of filters defined in each layer, instead of the multiplication of the number of filters multiplied with the number of input channels.

We use kernels with size $5 \times 5$ for the reconstruction in order to consider spatial smoothness of the reconstructed alpha mattes.

During the training phase, the reconstructed alpha mattes are compared with the ground truth alpha mattes using the Euclidean loss cost function. The errors are back propagated to each layer to update the weights of kernels in each layer. In the testing phase, only a single forward pass is needed to reconstruct the resulting alpha mattes. We use zero padded input images, and directly apply the forward pass at the original image resolution to reconstruct a full resolution alpha matte directly from its inputs. There is no parameter tuning once the deep CNN model is learnt.

## 3.2   Analyses

**Internal Response.** We analyze the functionality of each stage by plotting the response maps $(\mathcal{F}_1 \sim \mathcal{F}_6)$ at each layer. Figure 5 shows the response maps of two local patches with different local structures. In the top example, the alpha matte from the KNN matting is more accurate, while in the bottom example, the alpha matte from the closed form matting is more accurate. As visualized in the response maps after the first stage, their filter responses are significantly different from each other. One can interpret that each of the learnt kernels in the first stage are local classifiers which detect particular type of image structures within a local window. It can also be interpreted that the learnt kernels compare the alpha mattes from the closed form matting, and the KNN matting which result in very different response maps with respect to the original image structures, and evaluate which alpha mattes are more accurate.

Compared to the response maps in the previous layers, the reconstructed alpha mattes depends only on a subset of response maps which has been activated. Because the response maps are content adaptive, the reconstruction of alpha mattes can choose the best possible weighted combinations (learnt from training examples) of response maps to reconstruct the alpha mattes which are also adaptive to local image structures. An interesting observation in this example is that the response maps in the nonlinear remapping stage are getting closer

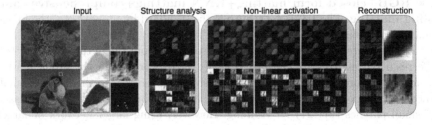

**Fig. 5.** Examples of response maps in each layer. Note that different image structures activate different neuron responses after the structure analysis stage. The non-linear activations remap the responses maps nonlinearly so that the reconstruction stage can directly reconstruct resulting alpha mattes from the response maps.

to reconstructed alpha mattes after each 1×1 convolutional and ReLU layers. This indicates that stacking multiple 1×1 convolutional and ReLU layers indeed helps to enhance the performance of our method.

**Effect of the Number of Nonlinear Activation Layers.** To further analyze the effects of nonlinear activation layers, we compare the performance of our CNN architecture by changing the number of nonlinear activation layers. We compare the performance with one, four, and eight layers of nonlinear activations. To provide a fair comparison, all architectures were trained from scratch with the same set of training examples and parameters, *e.g.* , the same initialization, learning rate, and number of iterations. Also, the number of channels of each nonlinear activation layer is fixed to 64. Table. 1 reports the average errors on a validation set and the processing time of a forward pass. As expected, more nonlinear activations can improve the results but the improvement with eight-layer architecture is marginal in compare with the results from four-layer architecture. Therefore, we choose the architecture with four-layer nonlinear activations to reduce running time and to avoid overfitting.

**Table 1.** Effect of the number of nonlinear activation layers.

| [Avg.] | Sum of absolute difference | Mean squared error | Gradient error | Time (sec.) |
|---|---|---|---|---|
| Single layer | 11.10 | 0.596 | 0.842 | 4.617 |
| Four layers | 10.30 | 0.563 | 0.804 | 5.126 |
| Eight layers | 10.17 | 0.546 | 0.792 | 6.528 |

**Effects of Initial Alpha Mattes.** We experiment the effectiveness of our network with different initial alpha mattes. In particular, without changing the network architectures, we re-train the network from scratch with different inputs: **RGB+Trimap, RGB+closed form matting, RGB+KNN matting, RGB+closed form matting+comprehensive sampling matting,** and **RGB+closed form matting+KNN matting+comprehensive sampling matting.** The **RGB+Trimap** is the standard input setting of the image matting problem.

Figure 6 shows the qualitative comparisons. Without the initial alpha mattes, the results from **RGB+Trimap** (Fig. 6(g)) are worse than the alpha mattes from conventional methods. The worse results may be deal to the usage of small network (with only one layer for structure analysis) or may be deal to the usage of small patches (27×27) for training. However, using larger network or larger patches (or entire images) for training would require significantly more training examples, and longer time to process. Also, the results from the state-of-the-art deep learning algorithm [41] for image segmentation are still imperfect which is not suitable for the image matting application. These shortcomings motivate us

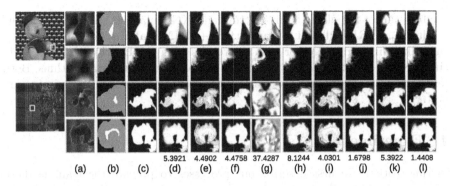

|  |  |  | 5.3921 | 4.4902 | 4.4758 | 37.4287 | 8.1244 | 4.0301 | 1.6798 | 5.3922 | 1.4408 |
| (a) | (b) | (c) | (d) | (e) | (f) | (g) | (h) | (i) | (j) | (k) | (l) |

**Fig. 6.** Effect of initial alpha mattes. (a) Input Images. (b) Trimaps. (c) Ground truth alpha mattes. (d, e, f) Alpha mattes from the closed form matting [2], KNN matting [8], comprehensive sampling matting [14], respectively. (g-l) Results from our CNN model with different inputs. (g) RGB+Trimap. (h) RGB+Closed form. (i) RGB+KNN. (j) RGB+Closed form+KNN (Our standard setting). (k) RGB+Closed form+Comprehensive. (l) RGB+Closed form+KNN+Comprehensive. Numbers in the bottom are average RMSE of this examples.

to utilize alpha mattes from conventional methods, *e.g.* closed form and KNN mattings, as an approximate solution for refinement.

Figure 6(h, i) show the results where inputs are from **RGB+closed form matting** and **RGB+KNN matting**. With the alpha mattes from closed form matting, or KNN matting, the matting results are significantly improved. However, both results depend too much on the quality of input alpha mattes. Also, the limitations of local and nonlocal methods remain in their results respectively. Our results (**RGB+closed form matting+KNN matting**) which combine the alpha mattes from closed form matting and KNN matting are presented in Fig. 6(j). The results from (**RGB+closed form matting+KNN matting**) are significantly better than both of its inputs, which favourably combines the benefits of local and nonlocal methods.

To further analyze the effects of inputs, we have also trained a network which inputs are from **RGB+closed form matting+comprehensive sampling matting**. The comprehensive matting is chosen because its algorithm combines both local and nonlocal information, and its performance is better than both closed form matting and KNN matting. However, the results (Fig. 6(k)) from **RGB+closed form matting+comprehensive sampling matting** are worse than the results (Fig. 6(j)) from **RGB+closed form matting+KNN matting**. This may be because the comprehensive sampling matting also consider local information, which introduces bias to the inputs. Consequently, this combination cannot fully utilize the nonlocal information, and their results are worse than our results from **RGB+closed form matting+KNN matting**.

Finally, on top of initial alpha mattes from the closed form matting and KNN matting, we add the alpha mattes from the comprehensive matting. As shown in Fig. 6(l), results from three initial alpha mattes are slightly better than the combination of the closed form matting and KNN matting. We submitted the results from **RGB+closed form matting+KNN matting+comprehensive sampling matting** together with the results from **RGB+closed form matting+KNN matting** to the evaluation site of alpha matting algorithms. Both results achieve the highest rank, and the results from three initial trimaps are better.

# 4  Experiment

In this section, we first describe our processes to prepare the training data. Then, we evaluate the performance of our deep CNN matting on the public alpha matting evaluation dataset [36], as well as some real world examples. Limitations and a failure case are also discussed. The trained model and testing codes are released in our website.[2]

## 4.1  Training

We collect training dataset from [36]. There are 27 examples which are composed of a RGB image, trimaps, and a ground truth alpha matte. For each example, we apply the closed form matting [2] and the KNN [8] matting to obtain their alpha mattes as part of our inputs: $\alpha_c$ and $\alpha_k$. Since our training phase processes on each $27 \times 27$ image patches, we can generate a lot of training patches from the 27 examples. We have also increased the number of training data through data augmentation. In particular, using their ground truth alpha mattes, we composite the foreground onto different background to increase variations and the number of training examples. We have also exploited different rotation, reflection and resizing to increase the number of training patches. Using data augmentation, we can generate more than a hundred thousand of training patches.

While increasing the number of training patches can enhance performance of our trained deep CNN model, we noticed that data balancing is also very important when preparing the training data. We want to avoid overfitting of the training data to a particular type of alpha mattes. To resolve this issue, we cluster the training patches according to the number of pixels with non-zero alpha values, and with non-zero alpha gradients. If a patch has many pixels with non-zero alphas, but has a few pixels with non-zero alpha gradients, the patch can be considered as a sharp boundary patch. In contrast, if a patch has a few pixels with non-zero alphas, but has many pixels with non-zero alpha gradients, the patch can be considered as a long hair patch. Based on this analysis, we cluster the training patches into 20 groups. When preparing the training data for the deep learning, we balance the number of sampled patches from each group in order to avoid the overfitting problem of training data.

After preparing the training data, we train our deep CNN model using the back propagation. It takes around 2~3 days for $10^6$ number of iterations on

---

[2] https://sites.google.com/site/cnnmatting/.

a machine with GTX 760 GPU and intel i7 3.4 GHz CPU. We use the method "xavier" (caffe parameter) to initialize the training weights. The xavier algorithm automatically determines the scale of initialization based on the number of input and output neurons. The learning rate, momentum and batch size are set to $10^{-5}, 0.9$ and $128$ respectively. In the training phase, we did not pad the image patches. Therefore, the resolution of output ($15 \times 15$) is smaller than the input ($27 \times 27$). In testing phase, we zero padded the boundary of input images with 6-pixel width ($\frac{27-15}{2} = 6$), and directly apply the forward pass at the original image resolution with zero padded boundary to reconstruct a full resolution alpha matte. Thus, the resolution of our alpha matte is the same as the resolution of input image. A forward pass takes around $4 \sim 6$ s to process an image with a resolution of $800 \times 640$ pixels.

## 4.2   Evaluation

**Quantitative Comparisons.** Table 2 shows the quantitative comparisons on the testing dataset in [36]. The ground truths of the testing dataset are unavailable to public. The quantitative results are obtained by submitting our resulting alpha mattes to the evaluation website as "anonymous_submission" and "anonymous_submission (modified version)", and the scores are directly obtained from the evaluation website. As shown in Table. 2, our results (DCNN (Closed from + KNN)) and extensions (DCNN (Closed from + KNN + Comprehensive)) have dominated the first two rank in terms of SAD, MSE, and Gradient errors. Note that all results are obtained using the same network without parameter tuning. The initial alpha mattes are obtained by using the default parameters of closed form matting, KNN matting, and comprehensive sampling matting. Also, we did not separate the training examples nor separately train the network for small/large/user trimaps. Thus, our trained network is general and is applicable to different set of inputs.

**Qualitative Comparisons.** Figure 7 shows the qualitative performance of our deep CNN matting. We compared our results with results from the state-of-the-art matting algorithms: closed form matting [2], KNN matting [8], weighted color and texture matting [13], and comprehensive matting [14]. Our results are more stable and visually pleasing for various object structures: solid boundary (*elephant*), semi transparency (*net*), overlapped color distribution (*pineapple*), and long hair (*troll*). More qualitative comparisons with other methods and the whole set of our results can be found at www.alphamatting.com.

**Additional Results.** To further evaluate the performance, we generate synthetic data using the training dataset in [36] by replacing the original backgrounds with new backgrounds. These new backgrounds are very colorful and highly textured. The color line model assumption in the closed form matting is violated, and the local color distribution of foreground and background can be overlapped in these new examples. We use the *small* trimap provided by [36] to generate the matting results. These new examples are not included in our training dataset. Figure 8 shows the qualitative comparisons on these new synthetic

**Table 2.** Quantitative Comparisons in terms of sum of absolute differences, mean squared errors, and gradient errors. Only the top 10 results are displayed. The whole set of comparisons can be found in www.alphamatting.com (While we submitted multiple results (DCNN (Closed from + KNN + Comprehensive) and DCNN (Closed from + KNN)) for the evaluation, only the first rank results, DCNN (Closed from + KNN + Comprehensive), are public. Because the second rank results are not included in the public entries, the relative ranking scores in the public entries are slightly different from the scores reported in our table). Note that our results dominate the first two rank in the evaluations. The red, green, and blue highlight the top-3 results.

| Sum of Absolute Differences | Overall | Small | Large | User | Mean Squared Error | Overall | Small | Large | User | Gradient Error | Overall | Small | Large | User |
|---|---|---|---|---|---|---|---|---|---|---|---|---|---|---|
| 1. DCNN (Closed from + KNN + Comprehensive) | 2.8 | 4.4 | 1.1 | 3 | 1. DCNN (Closed from + KNN + Comprehensive) | 4 | 5.1 | 1.8 | 5 | 1. DCNN (Closed from + KNN + Comprehensive) | 7.2 | 9.6 | 5.8 | 6.1 |
| 2. DCNN (Closed from + KNN) | 7.1 | 7.5 | 5.6 | 6.1 | 2. DCNN (Closed from + KNN) | 5.5 | 4.4 | 4.5 | 7.5 | 2. DCNN (Closed from + KNN) | 7.4 | 6.5 | 7.1 | 8.5 |
| 3. Cluster-based Sampling Matting | 7.2 | 6.5 | 8.9 | 6.1 | 3. LNSP Matting | 9.3 | 6.8 | 8.4 | 12.5 | 3. KL-Divergence Based Sparse Sampling | 10.6 | 9.3 | 8.3 | 14.3 |
| 4. LNSP Matting | 10.4 | 7.5 | 9.8 | 14.1 | 4. Cluster-based Sampling Matting | 9.9 | 9.1 | 10.3 | 10.4 | 4. Anonymous TIP submission | 10.7 | 8.9 | 8.5 | 14.6 |
| 5. Anonymous TIP submission | 11 | 11.6 | 11.1 | 10.1 | 5. Trajectory | 10.2 | 7.8 | 9.4 | 13.5 | 5. LNSP Matting | 10.9 | 8.6 | 10.1 | 14 |
| 6. Trajectory | 11.4 | 8.3 | 10.8 | 15.1 | 6. KL-Divergence Based Sparse Sampling | 12.1 | 11.8 | 10.5 | 14 | 6. Trajectory | 11.9 | 9.6 | 11.1 | 15 |
| 7. KL-Divergence Based Sparse Sampling | 11.7 | 11.3 | 10.3 | 13.6 | 7. CCM | 12.4 | 15.8 | 12.3 | 9.3 | 7. Comprehensive sampling | 12 | 12.4 | 11 | 12.6 |
| 8. Comprehensive sampling | 13.3 | 11.1 | 13 | 15.6 | 8. Anonymous TIP submission | 13 | 14.1 | 12.6 | 12.3 | 8. Cluster-based Sampling Matting | 13.5 | 13.9 | 14.1 | 12.5 |
| 9. Iterative Transductive Matting | 13.7 | 15.5 | 12.8 | 12.9 | 9. Comprehensive sampling | 13.6 | 12.6 | 13.4 | 14.8 | 9. CCM | 14.1 | 16.8 | 13.6 | 11.9 |
| 10. SVR Matting | 14 | 16.8 | 13.6 | 11.6 | 10. SVR Matting | 13.8 | 17.8 | 12.3 | 11.5 | 10. SVR Matting | 14.1 | 16.8 | 15 | 10.4 |

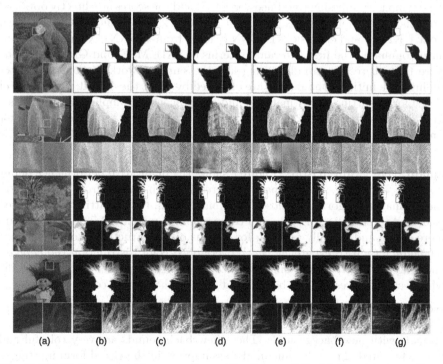

(a)       (b)       (c)       (d)       (e)       (f)       (g)

**Fig. 7.** Qualitative comparisons on the public dataset [36]. (a) Input images. (b, c, d, e) results from the closed form [2], KNN [8], weighted color and texture [13], and comprehensive [14] mattings. (f) Our results (**Closed from + KNN**). (g) Our results (**Closed from + KNN + Comprehensive**). (Color figure online)

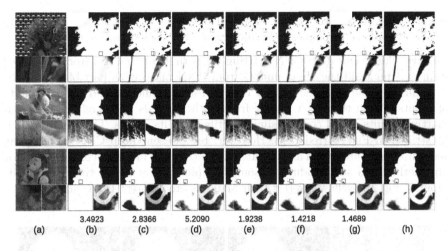

| | 3.4923 | 2.8366 | 5.2090 | 1.9238 | 1.4218 | 1.4689 | |
| (a) | (b) | (c) | (d) | (e) | (f) | (g) | (h) |

**Fig. 8.** Qualitative comparisons on synthetic dataset [36]. (a) Input images. (b, c, d, e) results from the closed form [2], KNN [8], weighted color and texture [13], comprehensive [14] matting. (f) Our results (**Closed from + KNN**). (g) Our results (**Closed from + KNN + Comprehensive**). (h) Ground truths. Numbers in the bottom are average RMSE of this examples.

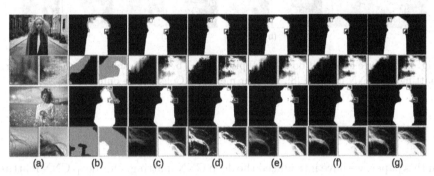

| (a) | (b) | (c) | (d) | (e) | (f) | (g) |

**Fig. 9.** Qualitative comparisons on a real world image. (a) Input images. (b) Trimaps (c, d, e) Results from the closed form [2], KNN [8], and comprehensive [14] mattings. (f) Our results (**Closed from + KNN**). (g) Our results (**Closed from + KNN + Comprehensive**).

datasets. Compared to results from the other methods, our deep CNN matting estimates more accurate alpha mattes.

Figure 9 shows qualitative comparisons on real world images. The top row example contains short curly hairs while the bottom example contains long hairs. In both examples, the closed form matting produces over smoothed alpha mattes while the KNN matting produces visually unpleasing results as shown in Fig 9(c, d), respectively. In contrast, as shown in Fig 9(f), our deep CNN matting can combine results from the closed form matting and KNN matting properly to reconstruct accurate alpha mattes automatically by recognizing local image structures. In other words, our proposed method can take advantages of both local and nonlocal principles depending on the recognized local image structures.

**Failure Case.** Our deep CNN matting takes the alpha mattes from the closed form matting, and the alpha mattes from KNN matting as part of the inputs. It is unavoidable that the quality of our results would depend on the quality of inputs. When the alpha mattes from both methods fail simultaneously, our matting results would contain similar artifacts as its inputs. This failure case is illustrated in Fig. 10 (red box). However, because our deep CNN matting can recognize structures, even alpha mattes from the both methods contain artifacts, our method can still produce reasonable alpha mattes better than both of its inputs ( Fig. 10 (yellow box)) if their artifacts are different from each other.

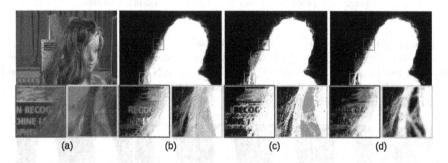

**Fig. 10.** Failure case (red box). (a) Input image. (b, c, d) Results from the closed form matting [2], KNN matting [8], and our method. (Color figure online)

## 5    Conclusion

In this paper, we have introduced the deep CNN matting. Our deep CNN matting takes the advantages of both local and nonlocal methods, and can adaptively reconstruct high quality alpha mattes from its inputs by recognizing local image structures. Our method is effective and parameter-free once the deep CNN model has been trained. Our matting results have achieved the highest rank in the benchmark dataset [36] in terms of sum of absolute differences, mean squared errors and gradient errors. To our knowledge, this is also the first attempt to apply deep learning to the natural image matting problem. We believe that our method is highly innovative and inspires follow-up works. As a future work, we are planning to study how to relax the dependency of our results with respect to the quality of the input alpha mattes.

**Acknowledgments.** This work was supported by the National Research Foundation of Korea (NRF) grant funded by the Korea government (MSIP) (No. 2010-0028680).

# References

1. Chuang, Y.Y., Curless, B., Salesin, D.H., Szeliski, R.: A Bayesian approach to digital matting. In: Proceedings of the Computer Vision and Pattern Recognition (CVPR) (2001)
2. Levin, A., Lischinski, D., Weiss, Y.: A closed-form solution to natural image matting. IEEE Trans. Pattern Anal. Mach. Intell. (TPAMI) **30**(2), 0162–8828 (2008)
3. Sun, J., Jia, J., Tang, C.K., Shum, H.Y.: Poisson matting. ACM Trans. Graph. (ToG) **23**(3), 315–321 (2004)
4. Zheng, Y., Kambhamettu, C.: Learning based digital matting. In: Proceedings of the International Conference on Computer Vision (ICCV) (2009)
5. He, K., Sun, J., Tang, X.: Fast matting using large kernel matting laplacian matrices. In: Proceedings of the Computer Vision and Pattern Recognition (CVPR) (2010)
6. Lee, P., Wu, Y.: Nonlocal matting. In: Proceedings of the Computer Vision and Pattern Recognition (CVPR) (2011)
7. Lin, H.T., Tai, Y.W., Brown, M.S.: Motion regularization for matting motion blurred objects. IEEE Trans. Pattern Anal. Mach. Intell. **33**(11), 2329–2336 (2011)
8. Chen, Q., Li, D., Tang, C.K.: KNN matting. In: Proceedings of the Computer Vision and Pattern Recognition (CVPR) (2012)
9. Choi, I., Lee, M., Tai, Y.-W.: Video matting using multi-frame nonlocal matting laplacian. In: Fitzgibbon, A., Lazebnik, S., Perona, P., Sato, Y., Schmid, C. (eds.) ECCV 2012, Part VI. LNCS, vol. 7577, pp. 540–553. Springer, Heidelberg (2012)
10. Wang, J., Cohen, M.F.: Optimized color sampling for robust matting. In: Proceedings of the Computer Vision and Pattern Recognition (CVPR) (2007)
11. Gastal, E.S.L., Oliveira, M.M.: Shared sampling for real-time alpha matting. In: EUROGRAPHICS (2010)
12. He, K., Rhemann, C., Rother, C., Tang, X., Sun, J.: A global sampling method for alpha matting. In: Proceedings of the Computer Vision and Pattern Recognition (CVPR) (2011)
13. Shahrian, E., Rajan, D.: Weighted color and texture sample selection for image matting. In: Proceedings of the Computer Vision and Pattern Recognition (CVPR) (2012)
14. Shahrian, E., Rajan, D., Price, B., Cohen, S.: Improving image matting using comprehensive sampling sets. In: Proceedings of the Computer Vision and Pattern Recognition (CVPR) (2013)
15. Li, D., Chen, Q., Tang, C.K.: Motion-aware KNN laplacian for video matting. In: ICCV (2013)
16. Joshi, N., Matusik, W., Avidan, S.: Natural video matting using camera arrays. In: ACM SIGGRAPH (2006)
17. Kim, S., Tai, Y.W., Bok, Y., Kim, H., Kweon, I.: Two-phase approach for multi-view object extraction. In: ICIP (2011)
18. Cho, D., Kim, S., Tai, Y.-W.: Consistent matting for light field images. In: Fleet, D., Pajdla, T., Schiele, B., Tuytelaars, T. (eds.) ECCV 2014, Part IV. LNCS, vol. 8692, pp. 90–104. Springer, Heidelberg (2014)
19. Rhemann, C., Rother, C., Gelautz, M.: Improving color modeling for alpha matting. In: British Machine Vision Conference (BMVC) (2008)
20. Chen, X., Zou, D., Zhou, S.Z., Zhao, Q., Tan, P.: Image matting with local and nonlocal smooth priors. In: Proceedings of the Computer Vision and Pattern Recognition (CVPR) (2013)

21. Russakovsky, O., Deng, J., Su, H., Krause, J., Satheesh, S., Ma, S., Huang, Z., Karpathy, A., Khosla, A., Bernstein, M., Berg, A.C., Fei-Fei, L.: ImageNet large scale visual recognition challenge. Int. J. Comput. Vis. (IJCV) 115(3), 211–252 (2015)

22. Simonyan, K., Zisserman, A.: Very deep convolutional networks for large-scale image recognition. CoRR abs/1409.1556 (2014)

23. Szegedy, C., Liu, W., Jia, Y., Sermanet, P., Reed, S., Anguelov, D., Erhan, D., Vanhoucke, V., Rabinovich, A.: Going deeper with convolutions. In: Proceedings of the Computer Vision and Pattern Recognition (CVPR) (2015)

24. Girshick, R.B., Donahue, J., Darrell, T., Malik, J.: Rich feature hierarchies for accurate object detection and semantic segmentation. In: Proceedings of the Computer Vision and Pattern Recognition (CVPR) (2014)

25. Girshick, R.: Fast R-CNN. In: Proceedings of the International Conference on Computer Vision (ICCV) (2015)

26. Zhao, R., Ouyang, W., Li, H., Wang, X.: Saliency detection by multi-context deep learning. In: Proceedings of the Computer Vision and Pattern Recognition (CVPR) (2015)

27. Lee, G., Tai, Y.W., Kim, J.: Deep saliency with encoded low level distance map and high level features. In: Proceedings of the Computer Vision and Pattern Recognition (CVPR) (2016)

28. Xie, J., Xu, L., Chen, E.: Image denoising and inpainting with deep neural networks. In: Proceedings of the Neural Information Processing Systems (NIPS) (2012)

29. Xu, L., Ren, J.S., Yan, Q., Liao, R., Jia, J.: Deep edge-aware filters. In: Proceedings of International Conference on Machine Learning (ICML) (2015)

30. Eigen, D., Krishnan, D., Fergus, R.: Restoring an image taken through a window covered with dirt or rain. In: Proceedings of International Conference on Computer Vision (ICCV) (2013)

31. Dong, C., Loy, C.C., He, K., Tang, X.: Learning a deep convolutional network for image super-resolution. In: Fleet, D., Pajdla, T., Schiele, B., Tuytelaars, T. (eds.) ECCV 2014, Part IV. LNCS, vol. 8692, pp. 184–199. Springer, Heidelberg (2014)

32. Ren, J.S., Xu, L., Yan, Q., Sun, W.: Shepard convolutional neural networks. In: Proceedings of Neural Information Processing Systems (NIPS) (2015)

33. Xu, L., Ren, J.S., Liu, C., Jia, J.: Deep convolutional neural network for image deconvolution. In: Proceedings of the Neural Information Processing Systems (NIPS) (2014)

34. Jia, Y., Shelhamer, E., Donahue, J., Karayev, S., Long, J., Girshick, R., Guadarrama, S., Darrell, T.: Caffe: convolutional architecture for fast feature embedding. arXiv preprint arXiv:1408.5093 (2014)

35. Chetlur, S., Woolley, C., Vandermersch, P., Cohen, J., Tran, J., Catanzaro, B., Shelhamer, E.: cuDNN: efficient primitives for deep learning. arXiv:1410.0759v3 (2014)

36. Rhemann, C., Rother, C., Wang, J., Gelautz, M., Kohli, P., Rott, P.: A perceptually motivated online benchmark for image matting. In: Proceedings of the Computer Vision and Pattern Recognition (CVPR) (2009)

37. He, K., Zhang, X., Ren, S., Sun, J.: Spatial pyramid pooling in deep convolutional networks for visual recognition. IEEE Trans. Pattern Anal. Mach. Intell. (TPAMI) 37(9), 1904–1916 (2015)

38. He, K., Sun, J., Tang, X.: Single image haze removal using dark channel prior. In: Proceedings of the Computer Vision and Pattern Recognition (CVPR) (2009)

39. He, K., Sun, J., Tang, X.: Guided image filtering. In: Daniilidis, K., Maragos, P., Paragios, N. (eds.) ECCV 2010, Part I. LNCS, vol. 6311, pp. 1–14. Springer, Heidelberg (2010)
40. Yang, J., Wright, J., Huang, T., Ma, Y.: Image super-resolution via sparse representation. IEEE Trans. Image Process. (TIP) 19(11), 2861–2873 (2010)
41. Zheng, S., Jayasumana, S., Romera-Paredes, B., Vineet, V., Su, Z., Du, D., Huang, C., Torr, P.: Conditional random fields as recurrent neural networks. In: Proceedings of the International Conference on Computer Vision (ICCV) (2015)

# Double-Opponent Vectorial Total Variation

Freddie Åström[(✉)] and Christoph Schnörr

Heidelberg Collaboratory for Image Processing, Image and Pattern Analysis Group,
Heidelberg University, Heidelberg, Germany
`freddie.astroem@iwr.uni-heidelberg.de`

**Abstract.** We present a new vectorial total variation (VTV) method
that addresses the problem of color consistent image filtering. Our approach combines insights based on the double-opponent cell representation in the visual cortex with state-of-the-art variational modelling using
VTV regularization. Existing methods of vectorial total variation regularizers have insufficient (even no) coupling between the color channels
and thus may introduce color artifacts. We address this problem by introducing a novel color channel coupling inspired from a pullback-metric
from an opponent space to the observation space. We show existence and
uniqueness of a solution in the space of vectorial functions of bounded
variation. In experiments, we demonstrate that our novel approach compares favorably to state-of-the-art methods w.r.t. to structure coherence
and color consistency.

## 1  Introduction

Color image processing poses several challenges, since the notion of
a "color edge" or a "color boundary" has no unique natural characterization. In this work we address the
problem of adaptive color image filtering exploring biological findings in the
visual cortex. We use these findings
for image enhancement and design our
new approach named *double-opponent
vectorial total variation.*

Noisy        Original        Recovered

**Fig. 1.** Example of denoising with the proposed double-opponent vectorial total variation (right) of the noisy image (left).

The connection between observed visual stimuli and color space models is
naturally described using tools from differential geometry. The model used in
this work is inspired from recent findings in color experience models and the
psychophysics of human color perception. Accordingly, we adopt a geometric
viewpoint to explore the relation between color edges and a regularizer based on
the color space geometry. Our presentation and treatment of the "geometry of
color" leads us to a perceptually plausible model for color image enhancement via
discontinuity preserving filtering. Figure 1 illustrates that our approach provides
excellent recovery of color image data, retaining sharp edges, without introducing
color artifacts.

B. Leibe et al. (Eds.): ECCV 2016, Part II, LNCS 9906, pp. 644–659, 2016.
DOI: 10.1007/978-3-319-46475-6_40

**Contributions.** We propose a VTV-based regularizer, derived from a double-opponent space. We prove that the variational problem is convex and that its solution is unique and exists in the space of vectorial functions of bounded variation. Our experiments take into account multiple noise-levels and competing state-of-the-art denoising methods. We demonstrate improved structural coherence and improved color consistency.

## 2   Related Works

**Color Space Representation.** The choice of a color space representation is application dependent, yet without reaching any general consensus, so far. At the same time, modeling psychophysical effects of color in scientific applications is a highly non-trivial problem and many spaces have been proposed, e.g., RGB, sRGB, HSV, YPbPr and the YCbCr, CIELAB to mention few. It is by now widely accepted that image processing application in the RGB (Red, Green, Blue) space is suboptimal due to the high color channel correlation. The YCbCr and the YPbPr color spaces were introduced for analog and digital television transmission, respectively [1]. The HSV (Hue, Saturation, Value) color space was developed in the 1970's for applications related to color display systems, and largely influenced by that time's computer display systems [2]. The sRGB system was proposed for consistent image rendering over a wide range of imaging devices [3]. The CIELAB color space was proposed to yield a color space which is perceptually uniform. However, as shown by [4] (and references therein) this is not the case. This motivates the use of non-Euclidean metrics, even in supposedly perceptually uniform spaces. In this work we consider the double-opponent space.

*Double-Opponent Color Representation.* The double-opponent color space is thought to describe the representation of color in the human visual cortex, see [5–8]. Therefore, and due to its geometric structure, it is of great interest to investigate this color space for image enhancement applications. Previous works using this color space include, e.g., [9,10]. Let $u = (r, g, b)^\top$ denote the red, green and blue color components of the RGB (observation) space, then the mapping from the observation space to the double-opponent space is given by the linear mapping $Ou : \mathbb{R}^3 \rightarrow \mathbb{R}^3$ where

$$O = \begin{pmatrix} 1/\sqrt{3} & 0 & 0 \\ 0 & 1/\sqrt{6} & 0 \\ 0 & 0 & 1/\sqrt{2} \end{pmatrix} \begin{pmatrix} 1 & 1 & 1 \\ 1 & 1 & -2 \\ 1 & -1 & 0 \end{pmatrix}. \tag{1}$$

The matrix $Ou = (o_1, o_2, o_3)^\top$ produces a rotation and scaling of the RGB coordinate system. The opponent component $o_1$ is nothing else than the gray-scale value, $o_2$ is the subtraction of blue from yellow (mixing red and green equals yellow), and the last component $o_3$ is the subtraction of green from red. The components $o_2$ and $o_3$ consists of the image chroma and further decomposition of $o_2, o_3$ yields the corresponding hue (the color, red, green, yellow, etc. expressed as an angle) and saturation (colorfulness).

Physiological studies have shown the existence of double-opponent cell structures which are orientation-selective w.r.t. color discrimination and color boundaries [11]. Therefore, by preserving color discontinuities in this color space, we
hypothesize that color borders trigger the activation of these double-opponent
cells and thus yields the perception of crisp color edges in the image. This motivates the use of discontinuity preserving filtering introduced next.

**Discontinuity Preserving Filtering.** Let $u : \Omega \to \mathbb{R}^M$ and $u = (u_1, ..., u_M)^\top$
where $M$ is the image dimension and $\Omega \subset \mathbb{R}^2$ is the image domain. The total
variation (TV) for scalar-valued functions ($M = 1$) [12] is defined as

$$\mathrm{TV}(u) := |\nabla u|(\Omega) = \int_\Omega |\nabla u|, \tag{2}$$

where $\nabla u$ denotes the generalized gradient which is a $\mathbb{R}^2$-valued Borel measure,
$|\nabla u|$ the total variation of this measure, and $\mathrm{TV}(u)$ the total mass. We refer
to [13, Ch. 10] for a detailed account. The function $u$ belongs to the space
of bounded variation $\mathrm{BV}(\Omega)$ if $u \in L^1(\Omega)$ and $\mathrm{TV}(u) < +\infty$. In this case, the
following representation is valid, with $\mathcal{C}_c^1(\Omega, \mathbb{R}^2)$ denoting the space of compactly
supported, continuously differentiable vector fields:

$$\mathrm{TV}(u) = \sup_{\|\varphi\|_\infty \le 1} \left\{ \int_\Omega u \, \mathrm{div}\,(\varphi) \, d\boldsymbol{x} : \varphi \in \mathcal{C}_c^1(\Omega, \mathbb{R}^2) \right\}. \tag{3}$$

Equation (3) shows that $\mathrm{TV}(u)$ is a support function in the sense of convex
analysis. In particular, it is convex and lower semicontinuous.

Extending the scalar TV to color images is a non-trivial problem. If a color
edge is insufficiently preserved in the smoothing process, artificial colors may
emerge at the smooth transition between these colors as demonstrated by Fig. 2.
The same figure also illustrates the problem of color shimmering, i.e., insufficient
filtering of homogeneous regions.

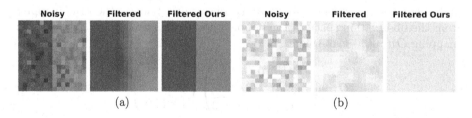

**Fig. 2.** Typical problems in color image denoising. (**a**) Introduction of artificial colors
at edges due to insufficient color channel coupling. (**b**) Color shimmering due to insufficient smoothing. Our approach (right images) exhibits neither of these drawbacks.
(Color figure online)

***Vectorial TV.*** One of the first generalizations of TV to the vector-valued case
was done by Blomgren and Chan [14]. They proposed the VTV measure

$$\mathrm{TV}_{BC}(\boldsymbol{u}) = \left( \sum_{i=1}^{M} \mathrm{TV}(u_i)^2 \right)^{1/2}, \tag{4}$$

which sums up the squared scalar TV (2) over the image channels. However, due to no handling of the RGB-space intra-channel correlation, this model produces significant color smearing artifacts and therefore does not give color consistent filtering results [15].

**Riemannian Geometry.** Sapiro and Ringach [16] observed that the first fundamental form in the given (Riemannian) metric signals the presence of color edges. They proposed a regularizer $\mathrm{TV}_{SR}$ with an integrand $\sqrt{\lambda_+ + \lambda_-}$ and $\lambda_+ > \lambda_- \geq 0$ are the eigenvalues of the metric tensor. Building on this framework, Goldluecke and Cremers [17] introduced a vectorial total variation regularizer $\mathrm{TV}_J$ based "on the largest singular value of the derivative matrix" and show the existence of a solution. In an altogether geometric setting Sochen et al. [18] introduced the Beltrami framework. In this approach, they consider images as embedding maps between Riemannian manifolds characterized by the Polyakov action [18–20]. Although there is a coupling between the color channels, these approaches produce undesired artifacts such as color shimmering in homogeneous regions.

**Dual VTV.** Bresson and Chan [21] proposed a color total variation formulation that naturally extends the dual TV formulation (3) to the vectorial case. Based on the work of Chambolle [22] and Fornasier and March [23], Bresson and Chan presented a coherent framework for vectorial total variation together with a study of well-posedness. The dual VTV is defined as follows: Let $\boldsymbol{u} \in L^1(\Omega; \mathbb{R}^M)$ and $\boldsymbol{\xi} = (\boldsymbol{\xi}_1, \dots, \boldsymbol{\xi}_M)$ with $\boldsymbol{\xi}_i \in \mathcal{C}_c^1(\Omega, \mathbb{R}^2)$, $\forall i$. Then

$$\mathrm{VTV}(\boldsymbol{u}) = \sup_{\|\boldsymbol{\xi}\|_F \leq 1} \left\{ \int_\Omega \langle \boldsymbol{u}, \mathrm{Div}(\boldsymbol{\xi}) \rangle \, d\boldsymbol{x} \right\}, \tag{5}$$

where $\| \cdot \|_F$ denotes the Frobenius norm and with the extension $\mathrm{Div}(\boldsymbol{\xi}) := (\mathrm{div}(\boldsymbol{\xi}_1), \dots, \mathrm{div}(\boldsymbol{\xi}_M))^\top \in \mathbb{R}^M$ of the divergence operator. The VTV approach, however, still exhibits some color smearing as it does not properly take into account the color channel coupling.

**Weighted VTV.** One of the most recent approaches to incorporate color into a TV formulation was presented by Ono and Yamada [9]. They define a mixed $\ell_{1,2}$-norm where the intensity and chroma, obtained via the transformation (1), are weighted independently. However, it should be noted that the subspace defined by the chroma is not decorrelated but actually consists of the components hue and saturation. As a consequence, their framework does not treat the non-uniformity of the opponent space. The implication is that direct regularizing on the chroma via an Euclidean distance metric violates the non-Euclidean structure of this opponent space. Furthermore, it is easy to construct scenarios where the image saturation changes independently, and thus further motivates that chroma should be decomposed into hue and saturation [24].

## 3 Geometry of the Double-Opponent Space

In this section we consider the double-opponent space geometry and show how to extract the color information.

**Connecting Observation and Double-Opponent Space.** Recall that we denote by the linear mapping $O: \mathbb{R}^3 \to \mathbb{R}^3$, $u = (r, g, b)^\top \mapsto Ou = o = (o_1, o_2, o_3)^\top$, with $O$ defined by (1), the transformation from the observation (RGB) color space to the double-opponent space. This linear mapping has full rank. The non-linear mapping to the hue ($h$), saturation ($s$) and lightness ($L$) representation of the opponent space is given by

$$\psi: \mathbb{R}^3 \to \mathbb{R}^3, \quad o \mapsto c = (L, h, s)^\top, \tag{6}$$

where $L = o_1, h = \arctan(o_2/o_3), s = \|(o_2, o_3)\|$. We further set $\varphi: u \to \varphi(u) := \psi(Ou) = (L, h, s)^\top$. Then, the Euclidean inner product $\langle \cdot, \cdot \rangle$ on the $Lhs$-space induces via $\varphi$ the pullback metric on the RGB-space by

$$\langle u_1, u_2 \rangle_u := \langle D\varphi(u)u_1, D\varphi(u)u_2 \rangle = \langle u_1, G(u)u_2 \rangle,$$
$$G(u) := \big(D\varphi(u)\big)^\top D\varphi(u), \tag{7}$$

where $G(u)$ is the double-opponent metric tensor and $D\varphi(u)$ is the Jacobian. Strictly speaking, we regard the RGB space as a *linear* Riemannian manifold $\mathcal{M}$ equipped with the above metric, which is an inner product on the tangent space $T_u\mathcal{M}$ that smoothly varies with $u \in \mathcal{M}$. Since every tangent space $T_u\mathcal{M}$ can be identified with $\mathcal{M}$, however, it makes sense to regard the Riemannian metric as inner product defined on the space itself. We refer, e.g., to [25] for background and further details.

**Extracting Color Information.** Next we compute the metric tensor $G(u)$ and its eigendecomposition later used to define our novel color channel coupling. Setting

$$\alpha = \alpha(u) = (b - g, r - b, g - r)^\top, \tag{8}$$
$$\beta = \beta(u) = (b + g - 2r, b + r - 2g, r + g - 2b)^\top, \tag{9}$$

one easily verifies the relations $\alpha \perp \beta$, $u \perp \alpha$, $\langle u, \beta \rangle = \|\alpha\|^2$, $\|\beta\|^2 = 3\|\alpha\|^2$. In the subsequent analysis we will return to the following decomposition

$$\|\alpha\|^2 = u^\top Pu, \quad P = \begin{pmatrix} 2 & -1 & -1 \\ -1 & 2 & -1 \\ -1 & -1 & 2 \end{pmatrix}, \tag{10}$$

where $P$ is a symmetric and positive semi-definite matrix.

The Jacobian of the mapping $\varphi$ reads

$$D\varphi(u) = \frac{1}{\sqrt{3}}\left(1, 3\frac{\alpha}{\|\alpha\|^2}, \frac{\beta}{\|\alpha\|}\right)^\top, \tag{11}$$

and the corresponding metric tensor (7) is

$$G(u) = \frac{1}{3}\left( I + \frac{9}{\|\alpha\|^4}\alpha\alpha^\top + \frac{1}{\|\alpha\|^2}\beta\beta^\top \right), \tag{12}$$

where $G(u)$ has non-normalized eigenvectors $\mathbb{1}, \alpha, \beta$ and eigenvaluematrix

$$\Lambda = \frac{1}{3}I + \text{diag}\left( 0, \frac{3}{\|\alpha\|^2}, 1 \right). \tag{13}$$

Saprio and Ringach [16] also derived the first fundamental form (i.e., $D\varphi(u)$), yet in the Euclidean space, and they concluded that the tensor's eigenvalues capture the color edge information. By contrast, we adopt the *inverse* principal directional change obtained from the eigendecomposition of the double-opponent metric tensor. Just as in the case of Saprio and Ringach, the interpretation of the decomposition is that a large eigenvalue of the tensor indicates the presence of image color change. Next we confirm this statement while investigating the information encoded in $\|\alpha\|^2$ which will constitute the basis for our filtering scheme presented in Sect. 4.

**Encoded Information.** The function $\|\alpha\|^2$, given in (10), represents the principal change of color. To illustrate this, Fig. 3 shows the corresponding response for few natural images. To further understand $\|\alpha\|^2$ we exploit the decomposition

$$\gamma(u) := \|\alpha\|^2 = (b - r)^2 + (r - g)^2 + (g - b)^2$$

$$= \|Qu\|^2, \qquad Q = \begin{pmatrix} 1 & -1 & 0 \\ 0 & 1 & -1 \\ -1 & 0 & 1 \end{pmatrix}. \tag{14}$$

Note that $P = QQ^\top$ (cmp. (10)). The coefficients of $Qu$ have previously appeared in an early work by Chambolle [26]. Chambolle defined a PDE with a

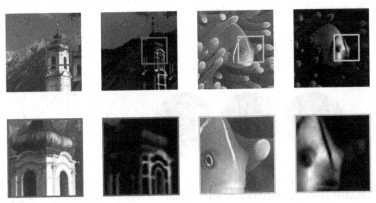

**Fig. 3.** Detected color structure in real images extracted by $\|\alpha\|^2$. In these examples, primary colors such as red, green and blue and the opponent color yellow are well characterized. (Color figure online)

directional diffusivity orthogonal to $(g-b)\nabla r + (b-r)\nabla g + (r-g)\nabla b$. However, as noted by Sapiro and Ringach [16], if two channels are equiluminant and if the third channel has an edge, this edge will remain unaffected by the filter. We remedy this drawback by considering a two component regularizer introduced in the next section.

**Proposition 1.** *The function, $\gamma$ in (14), has the properties* (P1) $\gamma(\boldsymbol{u} + c\mathbb{1}) = \gamma(\boldsymbol{u})$ *and* (P2) $\gamma(c\boldsymbol{u}) = c^2\gamma(\boldsymbol{u})$, *where c is a constant.*

*Proof.* The result follows immediately from (14).

The above result yields the following interpretation of the $\gamma$-function: *(a)* (P1) shows that $\gamma$ is invariant to intensity shifts. *(b)* (P2) shows that $\gamma$ has a quadratic dependency on intensity changes. *(c)* it follows from *(a)* that $\gamma$ depends on color changes and *(d)* it follows from *(b)* that $\gamma$ depends on color shifts. Under constant intensity, $\gamma$ captures change of color as illustrated in Fig. 4(a). In this figure we show equiluminant discs at constant intensity along with the corresponding response of $\gamma$. It is clearly visible that $\gamma$ describes the structure of the color change as there is a stronger response for highly saturated colors. In the lower half of the intensity range we predominantly detect the primary colors red, green and blue. As the intensity increases $\gamma$ shows primary responses from yellow, cyan and magenta. The intensity axis is located in the center of these discs and, as expected, we do not obtain a value of colorfulness.

The *geometric interpretation* of $\gamma$ is illustrated as an example via the $r - g$-component. The other two color difference terms follow with similar reasoning. We know that the color yellow, $y$, is composed as a sum of red and green, i.e., $y = r + g$, and written in vector form we have $r - g = (1, -1, 0)^\top$ and $y = r + g = (1, 1, 0)^\top$. We see that yellow is perpendicular to the difference $r - g$, i.e., $y \perp (r - g) = 0$. This is illustrated in Fig. 4(b). Analogous argument hold for the other terms of $\gamma$, i.e., $b - r$ is orthogonal to magenta, and $g - b$ orthogonal to cyan. In this way $\gamma$ covers the RGB space. Moreover, as $\gamma$ describes the

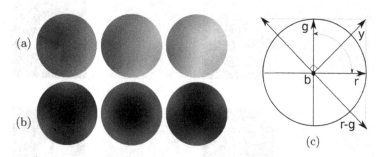

**Fig. 4.** (a) Color discs with corresponding response of $\gamma$, (14), in (b). The largest magnitude (red color) is obtained at the primary colors (red, green and blue) and the opponent colors (yellow, cyan and magenta). As expected, the response on the intensity axis (center of discs) is 0 (black). (c) Interpretation of the vector $r - g$ as an orthogonal component to yellow. (Color figure online)

color structure, preserving its edge information prevents color distortion in the filtering process. Based on this analysis, we are now prepared to introduce the double-opponent VTV regularization term.

## 4 Double-Opponent Vectorial Total Variation

**The Energy.** Channel-by-channel filtering of the RGB space is prone to introduce color artifacts [14,21]. On the other hand, purely decorrelating the color channels without considering the geometry is also sub-optimal, see e.g., [9,16]. We propose a two-component regularizer: one component performs channel-by-channel filtering penalizing *all* intra-channel content and one component which explicitly targets the color information. The color specific prior, $J_{OPP}$, defines a natural inter-channel coupling from the geometry of the double-opponent space. Let $g$ be the observed (noisy) image data. The energy we introduce is

$$\min_{u} \left\{ E(u) = \frac{\mu}{2} \|u - g\|_{L^2(\Omega)}^2 + R(u) \right\} \tag{15a}$$

$$R(u) = \alpha \sum_{i=1}^{3} \mathrm{TV}(u_i) + \beta J_{OPP}(u), \tag{15b}$$

where $\mu, \alpha, \beta > 0$.

Furthermore, let $\nabla u = (\nabla u_1, \nabla u_2, \nabla u_3) : \Omega \to \mathbb{R}^{2 \times 3}$ be the *vectorial gradient* of an color image ($M = 3$) in the generalized sense as discussed in connection with Eq. (2), and $p = (p_1, p_2, p_2) \in C_c^1(\Omega; \mathbb{R}^{2 \times 3})$ with $\mathrm{Div}\,(p) = (\mathrm{div}\,(p_1), \mathrm{div}\,(p_2), \mathrm{div}\,(p_3))^\top$.

**Definition 1 (Double-Opponent VTV).** The double opponent regularizer is defined as

$$J_{OPP}(u) := \int_\Omega \|\nabla Q u\| \tag{16a}$$

$$:= \sup_{\|p\|_\infty \leq 1} \left\{ \int_\Omega \langle Q u, \mathrm{Div}\,(p) \rangle \, dx \right\} \tag{16b}$$

where $\|p\|_\infty = \max\{|p_1|, |p_2|, |p_3|\}$.

*Remark 1.* Note that although this looks like an anisotropic TV formulation, it does incorporate a proper coupling of the channels through the matrix $Q$.

**Theorem 1 (Invariance and Convexity).** $J_{OPP}$ *is rotationally and intensity invariant, 1-homogeneous and convex.*

*Proof.* Rotational invariance follows from the isotropy of the feasible set of the dual variable $p$, that is $\|p\|_\infty = \|(p_1, p_2, p_3)\|_\infty \leq 1 \implies \|(Rp_1, Rp_2, Rp_3)\|_\infty \leq 1$, for any orthogonal matrix $R$. As a consequence of property (P1) and (P2) of Proposition 1, $J_{OPP}$ is invariant to intensity shifts, and the relation $J_{OPP}(cu) = cJ_{OPP}(u)$ is immediate, for any positive constant $c > 0$. Finally, convexity follows from the definition of $J_{OPP}$ as pointwise supremum of affine functions.

**Existence of Solution.** Next we show that the variational approach (15a) is well posed.

**Lemma 1 (Bounded Variation).** *Let* $u \in BV(\Omega; \mathbb{R}^3)$ *then* $Qu \in BV(\Omega; \mathbb{R}^3)$.

*Proof.* If $u$ is in $L^1(\Omega; \mathbb{R}^3)$, then so is $Qu$, because $Q$ is a constant matrix. Furthermore, expanding the bilinear form under the integral of (16b) results in a linear combination of terms of the form (3), which are finite by the assumption $u \in BV(\Omega; \mathbb{R}^3)$.

As a consequence, the objective function $E(u)$ (15a) is well defined. We next show that there is a unique color image $u$ minimizing $E(u)$.

**Theorem 2 (Uniqueness and Existence of Solution).** *Let* $g \in L^\infty(\Omega, \mathbb{R}^3)$ *and* $u \in BV(\Omega, \mathbb{R}^3)$. *Then there exists a unique minimizer* $u^*$ *of* $E(u)$ *in* (15a).

*Proof.* We adapt and sketch a standard proof pattern from [13]. Due to $g \in L^\infty(\Omega, \mathbb{R}^M)$, we may assume that all admissible $u$ are uniformly bounded in the sense that $|u_i(x)| \leq \|g_i\|_{L^\infty(\Omega)}$, $i = 1, 2, 3$, $\forall x \in \Omega$. Let $(u_n)_{n \in \mathbb{N}}$ be a minimizing sequence with respect to $E(u)$. Then, after passing to a subsequence $(u_{n_k})_{k \in \mathbb{N}}$, there exists a $u^* \in BV(\Omega; \mathbb{R}^3)$ with $u_{n_k} \to u^*$ strongly in $L^1_{loc}(\Omega; \mathbb{R}^3)$, $\nabla(u_i)_{n_k} \to \nabla u_i^*$ in an appropriate weak sense, and $J_{opp}(u_{n_k}) \to J_{opp}(u^*)$ in view of Lemma 1. It follows from Fatou's lemma and the lower-semicontinuity of $E(u)$ that $u^*$ minimizes $E(u)$, whereas uniqueness of $u^*$ is a consequence of the strict convexity of $E(u)$ due to the data term of (15a).

Next, we derive an efficient numerical scheme which optimize our novel energy.

**Discretization.** With slight abuse of notation, we denote again by $u, g \in \mathbb{R}^{3N}$ the discretized representations of $u$ and $g$ as column vectors where the image channels are stacked in the order $u_1, u_2, u_3$. $N$ is the number of pixels in one channel. We define the discrete image gradient for *one* channel as $D_1 = \begin{bmatrix} D_x \\ D_y \end{bmatrix} \in \mathbb{R}^{2N \times N}$, $D_x, D_y \in \mathbb{R}^{N \times N}$ and subscript denotes the forward finite difference operator in $x$ and $y$ directions, respectively. Furthermore, we let $q \in \mathbb{N}^+$ s.t. $I_q \in \mathbb{R}^{q \times q}$ denotes the identity matrix. In this notation, the three channel derivative matrix for a color image is $D = D_1 \otimes I_3 \in \mathbb{R}^{6N \times 3N}$ where $\otimes$ is the Kronecker product. Then $Du : \mathbb{R}^{3N} \to \mathbb{R}^{6N}$ is the derivative for the three channels. The discrete representation of the Laplacian is denoted $L = (D_1^\top D_1) \otimes I_3 \in \mathbb{R}^{3N \times 3N}$ such that $Lu : \mathbb{R}^{3N} \to \mathbb{R}^{3N}$. The channel coupling matrix for the discretized image is denoted as $C = Q \otimes I_N \in \mathbb{R}^{3N \times 3N}$.

**Optimization.** With the notation introduced above, we write the corresponding discretized form of (15a) as

$$\min_{u,d,e} \frac{\mu}{2} \|u - g\|_2^2 + \alpha \|d\|_1 + \beta \|e\|_1 \quad \text{s.t.} \quad d = Du, \quad e = DCu. \quad (17)$$

To minimize this objective function we may use any standard optimization technique, e.g., [27–30]. Here we adopt the Split Bregman approach [31] as it yields a simple numerical scheme. In the following, we let $\|v\|_W^2 := \langle v, Wv \rangle$ be a weighted Euclidean norm and set

$$B(u, b, d, e) := \begin{pmatrix} d \\ e \end{pmatrix} - \begin{pmatrix} D \\ DC \end{pmatrix} u - b. \qquad (18)$$

Applying the Split Bregman approach yields the iteration

$$(u^{k+1}, d^{k+1}, e^{k+1})$$
$$= \min_{u,d,e} \frac{\mu}{2}\|u - g\|_2^2 + \|d\|_1 + \|e\|_1 + \frac{1}{2}\|B(u, b, d, e)\|_W^2, \qquad (19a)$$

$$W = \begin{pmatrix} \alpha I_{6N} & 0 \\ 0 & \beta I_{6N} \end{pmatrix}, \quad \alpha, \beta > 0 \qquad (19b)$$

$$b^{k+1} = b^k + \begin{pmatrix} D \\ DC \end{pmatrix} u^{k+1} - \begin{pmatrix} d^{k+1} \\ e^{k+1} \end{pmatrix}. \qquad (19c)$$

The former problem is solved iteratively by

$$u^{k+1} = \min_u \frac{\mu}{2}\|u - g\|_2^2 + \frac{1}{2}\left\|B(u, b^k, d^k, e^k)\right\|_W^2 \qquad (20)$$

followed by two shrinkage updates for $d^{k+1}, e^{k+1}$. Regarding, subproblem (20), we set $b = [b_1^\top, b_2^\top]^\top$, $b_1, b_2 \in \mathbb{R}^{6N}$ for notational convenience and obtain the update step

$$((\mu I + \alpha I)L + \beta C^\top LC)u^{k+1}$$
$$= \mu g + \alpha D^\top(d^k - b_1^k) + \beta(DC)^\top(e^k - b_2^k). \qquad (21)$$

Our experiments confirm the observation of [31] that only computing an approximate solution accelerates the overall iterative scheme without compromising convergence. Consequently, we merely apply few conjugate gradient iterative steps to compute $u^{k+1}$. This is computationally cheap since all matrices involved are sparse.

Finally, we update $b^{k+1}$ according to (19c) and iterate all steps until $\|u^k - u^{k+1}\|_2^2 / \|u^{k+1}\|_2^2 < 0.9\sqrt{3N\sigma^2}/255^2$ and $\sigma$ is the noise level standard deviation.

## 5   Experiments

**Setup.** The experimental evaluation use all 100 images of the Berkeley validation dataset [34]. The image data is normalized to the range $[0,1]$ from an 8-bit representation. In addition to a qualitative evaluation we include the peak signal-to-noise ratio (PSNR), the structural similarity index (SSIM) [35] and the CIEDE 2000, a measure of color consistency [36]. We optimize the parameter settings in a given feasible range for each method, image and noise level with respect to the best obtained SSIM value. The following methods and parameter ranges are included in the evaluation and we refer to the respective works for further details:

654     F. Åström and C. Schnörr

- Decorrelated VTV [9] (**DVTV**): Search space for optimal parameter configuration is $\tau \in \{0.95, 1, 1.05\}$, $w \in \{0.3, 0.4, 0.5, 0.6, 0.7\}$.
- Primal-dual VTV [21] (**PDVTV**): The regularization parameter was optimized for 5 uniformly sampled values in the range $10^{-3}$ to 0.2.
- Double Opponent VTV (ours) (**OVTV**): Optimized parameter space of $\mu$ are 5 uniformly sampled values from $1/255$ to $30/255$, $\alpha = 1$ and $\beta$ was uniformly sampled from 5 values in the range $1/255$ to $5/255$.
- Total generalized variation [33] (**TGV**): Applied componentwise and only included for comparison. The regularization parameter was uniformly sampled with 5 values in the range $10^{-3}$ and 0.25.
- Color BM3D [32] (**BM3D**): Standard deviation of the additive Gaussian noise was given as input.

**Impact of Parameters.** We check the sensitivity of different parameter settings for our double-opponent regularizer in relation to the dataterm in Fig. 5. The image was corrupted with standard deviation 20 of additive Gaussian noise and in this example we consider the visual quality and the color consistency measured with the CIEDE measure (lower value is better) and SSIM value (higher is

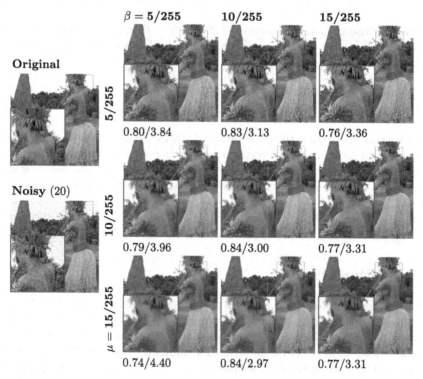

**Fig. 5.** Visual comparison of the double-opponent regularization and influence of $\mu$ and $\beta$ for fixed $\alpha = 1$. Error measures are SSIM/CIEDE. As $\mu$ increases details are oversmoothed. $\beta$ influence the double-opponent term and we see (in this example) the best performance at $\beta = 10/255$. (Color figure online)

better). The first row illustrates that the noise is not accurately removed as there is considerable amount of speckle-effect, i.e., the regularizer treats noise as structure. Increasing the influence of the data term improves the visual quality significantly and we do not observe any color shimmer. In the last row $\mu$ is clearly too large as image details are oversmoothed.

**Color Denoising.** Common artifacts in color image denoising is color shimmer in homogeneous regions and the introduction of artificial colors. Examples of these artifacts were given in Fig. 2. In this work, we introduce a challenging image recovering problem where current state of art denoising algorithms consistently show poor performance. Rather than corrupting *all* image data with additive noise, we corrupt the *color* components ($o_2$ and $o_3$) with 20, 50 or 80 standard deviations of Gaussian noise and ignore the intensity channel. Remarkably, after transforming from the (now noisy) opponent representation to the RGB space, one can show that the r, g, b components retain a Gaussian noise distribution of zero mean but with $\sqrt{2/3}$ scaled standard deviation. For this reason we also evaluate BM3D (our main competing method) which only requires an accurate estimation of the image noise, with this scaled noise variance, we denote this with

- Color BM3D with scaled noise distribution (**BM3DS**)

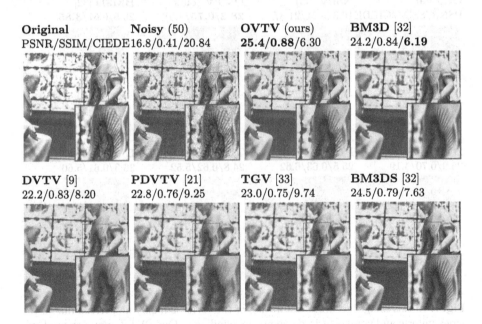

Original            **Noisy** (50)        **OVTV** (ours)     **BM3D** [32]
PSNR/SSIM/CIEDE16.8/0.41/20.84    **25.4/0.88/6.30**    24.2/0.84/**6.19**

**DVTV** [9]          **PDVTV** [21]      **TGV** [33]       **BM3DS** [32]
22.2/0.83/8.20     22.8/0.76/9.25    23.0/0.75/9.74    24.5/0.79/7.63

**Fig. 6.** Visual comparison of the compared methods and corresponding error values. The result of our OVTV produces the most accurate result, only marginally beaten by BM3D in terms of color accuracy. Yet, the visual quality of OVTV is more clear and does not suffer from desaturated colors as in DVTV. (Color figure online)

**Table 1.** Error measures for the evaluated methods. The best values are marked in bold. For lower noise levels, BM3D is the only competitor for our OVTV. As the noise level increases OVTV consistently shows the best performance. See text for details.

| $\sigma = 20$ | DVTV | PDVTV | OVTV (Ours) | TGV | BM3D | BM3DS |
|---|---|---|---|---|---|---|
| PSNR | 29.1 ± 1.94 | 27.8 ± 1.05 | 31.6 ± 2.03 | 26.4 ± 2.43 | **32.0 ± 1.93** | 31.9 ± 1.30 |
| SSIM | 0.83 ± 0.06 | 0.82 ± 0.06 | **0.89 ± 0.05** | 0.74 ± 0.07 | 0.88 ± 0.06 | 0.87 ± 0.05 |
| CIEDE | 5.40 ± 1.83 | 4.69 ± 0.73 | 2.79 ± 0.65 | 5.97 ± 3.61 | **2.77 ± 0.54** | 3.85 ± 0.64 |
| $\sigma = 50$ | | | | | | |
| PSNR | 24.6 ± 1.85 | 25.2 ± 1.91 | **27.2 ± 1.94** | 24.3 ± 2.07 | 26.1 ± 2.32 | 25.9 ± 1.71 |
| SSIM | 0.66 ± 0.06 | 0.72 ± 0.09 | **0.78 ± 0.06** | 0.66 ± 0.08 | 0.72 ± 0.10 | 0.68 ± 0.09 |
| CIEDE | 8.36 ± 1.97 | 6.10 ± 1.14 | 5.71 ± 2.17 | 8.07 ± 2.39 | **4.79 ± 0.85** | 6.26 ± 1.01 |
| $\sigma = 80$ | | | | | | |
| PSNR | 21.0 ± 0.96 | 23.7 ± 1.89 | **24.0 ± 1.73** | 22.1 ± 2.00 | 23.5 ± 2.26 | 23.4 ± 1.95 |
| SSIM | 0.44 ± 0.06 | 0.69 ± 0.09 | **0.69 ± 0.07** | 0.57 ± 0.09 | 0.63 ± 0.12 | 0.61 ± 0.10 |
| CIEDE | 13.89 ± 1.39 | 6.76 ± 1.12 | 8.07 ± 2.11 | 10.01 ± 2.74 | **6.31 ± 1.08** | 7.31 ± 1.03 |

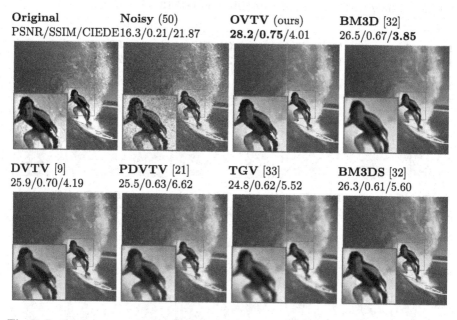

Original　　　　　Noisy (50)　　　　OVTV (ours)　　　BM3D [32]
PSNR/SSIM/CIEDE 16.3/0.21/21.87　**28.2/0.75/4.01**　26.5/0.67/**3.85**

DVTV [9]　　　　PDVTV [21]　　　TGV [33]　　　　BM3DS [32]
25.9/0.70/4.19　25.5/0.63/6.62　24.8/0.62/5.52　26.3/0.61/5.60

**Fig. 7.** In this image, accurate restoration of the surfer is highly non-trivial due to the large uniform and non-texturized regions surrounding it. Our OVTV approach produces sharp color borders which are similar to the original noise free image. Although the state of the art VTV method DVTV does restore the uniform background accurately the red color appears desaturated. PDVTV produces color shimmering. TGV and BM3D(S) both oversmooth the image. (Color figure online)

Original     Result     Corrupted    Original    Result     Blurred

**Fig. 8.** (left) Inpainting of 85 % missing data and (right) deconvolution examples. These illustrations show that the OVTV approach can accurately restore edges without introducing color artifacts also in related variational problems. (Color figure online)

Noisy        OVTV        BM3D        Noisy        OVTV        DVTV

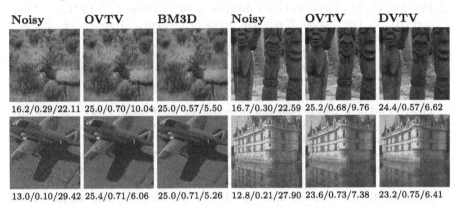

16.2/0.29/22.11 25.0/0.70/10.04 25.0/0.57/5.50   16.7/0.30/22.59 25.2/0.68/9.76 24.4/0.57/6.62

13.0/0.10/29.42 25.4/0.71/6.06   25.0/0.71/5.26   12.8/0.21/27.90 23.6/0.73/7.38 23.2/0.75/6.41

**Fig. 9.** Additional denoising results (ssim/psnr/ciede). The first and second row show recovery of data corrupted with standard deviation 50 and 80 of additive Gaussian noise. Our OVTV performs well for a wide range of images and noise levels.

*Results.* Table 1 shows the average error and standard deviation values for each method and noise level for the 100 Berkeley images. Our double-opponent approach (OVTV) compares well to DVTV and BM3D. Close-ups from few result images are given in Figs. 6 and 7. It is clearly visible that the our OVTV produces clean images, does not introduce artificial color artifacts, does not oversmooth details and does not suffer from color shimmering.

Figure 9 shows additional denoising results for standard deviation 50 (first row) and 80 (second row) of Gaussian noise. Although BM3D and DVTV show better color consistency in these examples, the structural coherence measured in PSNR is similar and SSIM is significantly improved for OVTV.

**Inpainting and Deconvolution.** We adopt our scheme to include inpainting and deconvolution in Fig. 8. As seen, homogeneous regions and edges are accurately restored without introducing color shimmering and artificial colors.

## 6    Conclusion

We have shown that the double-opponent theory can greatly improve the performance of VTV-based methods. Motivated by recent and classical results in color theory we let the mapping from the opponent-space to the observation space serve as a basis of our vectorial formulation. If the aim is consistent image filtering, then clearly the double-opponent VTV is preferable for image restoration.

**Acknowledgment.** We gratefully acknowledge support by the German Science Foundation, grant GRK 1653.

# References

1. Poynton, C.: 24 - Luma and color differences. In: Poynton, C. (ed.) Digital Video and HDTV. The Morgan Kaufmann Series in Computer Graphics, pp. 281–300. Morgan Kaufmann, San Francisco (2003)
2. Joblove, G.H., Greenberg, D.: Color spaces for computer graphics. In: Proceedings of the 5th Annual Conference on Computer Graphics and Interactive Techniques, SIGGRAPH 1978, pp. 20–25. ACM (1978)
3. sRGB: Multimedia systems and equipment - colour measurement and management - Part 2–1: colour management - default RGB colour space - sRGB. IEC 61966-2-1 (1999–10). ICS codes: 33.160.60, 37.080 - TC 100–51 pp. as amended by Amendment A1:2003 (2003)
4. Sharma, G.: Digital Color Imaging Handbook. CRC Press Inc., Boca Raton (2002)
5. Gao, S., Yang, K., Li, C., Li, Y.: A color constancy model with double-opponency mechanisms. In: ICCV, pp. 929–936, December 2013
6. Land, E.: Recent advances in retinex theory and some implications for cortical computations: color vision and the natural image. Proc. Natl. Acad. Sci. USA **80**(16), 5163–5169 (1983)
7. Land, E.: An alternative technique for the computation of the designator in the retinex theory of color vision. Proc. Natl. Acad. Sci. USA **83**(10), 3078–3080 (1986)
8. Ebner, M.: Color Constancy, 1st edn. Wiley Publishing, Hoboken (2007)
9. Ono, S., Yamada, I.: Decorrelated vectorial total variation. In: CVPR, pp. 4090–4097 (2014)
10. van de Sande, K., Gevers, T., Snoek, C.: Evaluating color descriptors for object and scene recognition. IEEE Trans. Pattern Anal. Mach. Intell. **32**(9), 1582–1596 (2010)
11. Conway, B.R., Chatterjee, S., Field, G.D., Horwitz, G.D., Johnson, E.N., Koida, K., Mancuso, K.: Advances in color science: from retina to behavior. J. Neurosci. **30**(45), 14955–14963 (2010)
12. Rudin, L.I., Osher, S., Fatemi, E.: Nonlinear total variation based noise removal algorithms. Phys. D **60**(1–4), 259–268 (1992)
13. Attouch, H., Buttazzo, G., Michaille, G.: Variational Analysis in Sovolev and BV Spaces: Aplications to PDEs and Optimization, 2nd edn. SIAM, New Delhi (2014)
14. Blomgren, P., Chan, T.: Color TV: total variation methods for restoration of vector-valued images. IEEE Trans. Image Process. **7**(3), 304–309 (1998)
15. Goldluecke, B., Strekalovskiy, E., Cremers, D.: The natural vectorial total variation which arises from geometric measure theory. SIAM J. Imaging Sci. **5**(2), 537–563 (2012)
16. Sapiro, G., Ringach, D.: Anisotropic diffusion of multivalued images with applications to color filtering. IEEE Trans Image Process. **5**(11), 1582–1586 (1996)
17. Goldluecke, B., Cremers, D.: An approach to vectorial total variation based on geometric measure theory. In: CVPR, pp. 327–333, June 2010

18. Sochen, N., Kimmel, R., Malladi, R.: A general framework for low level vision. IEEE Trans. Image Process. **7**(3), 310–318 (1998)
19. Sochen, N., Deriche, R., Lopez Perez, L.: The beltrami flow over manifolds. Research report RR-4897, INRIA (2003)
20. Kimmel, R., Sochen, N., Malladi, R.: From high energy physics to low level vision. In: ter Haar Romeny, B.M., Florack, L.M.J., Viergever, M.A. (eds.) Scale-Space 1997. LNCS, vol. 1252, pp. 236–247. Springer, Heidelberg (1997)
21. Bresson, X., Chan, T.: Fast dual minimization of the vectorial total variation norm and applications to color image processing. Inverse Prob. Imaging **2**(4), 455–484 (2008)
22. Chambolle, A.: An algorithm for total variation minimization and applications. JMIV **20**(1–2), 89–97 (2004)
23. Fornasier, M., March, R.: Restoration of color images by vector valued BV functions and variational calculus. SIAM J. Appl. Math. **68**(2), 437–460 (2007)
24. Munsell, A.: A Color Notation. G. H. Ellis Company, Indianapolis (1905)
25. Jost, J.: Riemannian Geometry and Geometric Analysis, 4th edn. Springer, Heidelberg (2005)
26. Chambolle, A.: Partial differential equations and image processing. In: Proceedings of the Image Processing, ICIP 1994, vol. 1, pp. 16–20, November 1994
27. Wahlberg, B., Boyd, S., Annergren, M., Wang, Y.: An ADMM algorithm for a class of total variation regularized estimation problems. In: Preprints of the 16th IFAC Symposium on System Identification, pp. 83–88 (2012)
28. Chambolle, A., Pock, T.: A first-order primal-dual algorithm for convex problems with applications to imaging. JMIV **40**(1), 120–145 (2011)
29. Chan, T.F., Golub, G.H., Mulet, P.: A nonlinear primal-dual method for total variation-based image restoration. SIAM J. Sci. Comput. **20**(6), 1964–1977 (1999)
30. Wu, C., Tai, X.C.: Augmented lagrangian method, dual methods, and split Bregman iteration for ROF, vectorial TV, and high order models. SIAM J. Imaging Sci. **3**(3), 300–339 (2010)
31. Goldstein, T., Osher, S.: The split Bregman method for L1-regularized problems. SIAM J. Imaging Sci. **2**(2), 323–343 (2009)
32. Dabov, K., Foi, A., Katkovnik, V., Egiazarian, K.: Color Image denoising via sparse 3D collaborative filtering with grouping constraint in luminance-chrominance space. In: IEEE International Conference on Image Processing, ICIP 2007, vol. 1, pp. I - 313-I - 316, September 2007
33. Bredies, K., Kunisch, K., Pock, T.: Total generalized variation. SIAM J. Imaging Sci. **3**(3), 492–526 (2010)
34. Arbelaez, P., Maire, M., Fowlkes, C., Malik, J.: Contour detection and hierarchical image segmentation. PAMI **33**(5), 898–916 (2011)
35. Wang, Z., Bovik, A., Sheikh, H., Simoncelli, E.: Image quality assessment: from error visibility to structural similarity. IEEE Trans. Image Process. **13**(4), 600–612 (2004)
36. Sharma, G., Wu, W., Dalal, E.N.: The CIEDE2000 color-difference formula: implementation notes, supplementary test data, and mathematical observations. Color Res. Appl. **30**(1), 21–30 (2005)

# Learning to Count with CNN Boosting

Elad Walach[(⊠)] and Lior Wolf[(⊠)]

The Blavatnik School of Computer Science, Tel Aviv University, Tel Aviv, Israel
alandor@gmail.com, wolf@cs.tau.ac.il

**Abstract.** In this paper, we address the task of object counting in images. We follow modern learning approaches in which a density map is estimated directly from the input image. We employ CNNs and incorporate two significant improvements to the state of the art methods: layered boosting and selective sampling. As a result, we manage both to increase the counting accuracy and to reduce processing time. Moreover, we show that the proposed method is effective, even in the presence of labeling errors. Extensive experiments on five different datasets demonstrate the efficacy and robustness of our approach. Mean Absolute error was reduced by 20 % to 35 %. At the same time, the training time of each CNN has been reduced by 50 %.

**Keywords:** Counting · Convolutional Neural Networks · Gradient boosting · Sample selection

## 1 Introduction

Counting objects in still images and video is a well-defined cognitive task in which humans greatly outperform machines. In addition, automatic counting has many important real-world applications, including medical microscopy, environmental surveying, automated manufacturing, and surveillance.

Traditional approaches to visual object counting were based on object detection and segmentation. This direct approach assumes the existence of adequate object localization algorithms. However, in many practical applications, object delineation is limited by significant inter-object occlusions or by cluttered background. Due to these limitations, in many cases, direct approaches can lead to gross under- or over-counting.

Starting with the seminal work of Lempitsky and Zisserman [1], a density based approach is used to translate the counting problem into a regression problem. This approach is demonstrated in Fig. 1. Each object is represented by a density kernel in a density map $F$. The goal of the algorithm is to estimate $F$ directly from the image, turning the discrete counting problem to a multivariate regression problem. Counting is then performed by integrating the density function over the entire image.

Recently, a method based on Convolutional Neural Networks (CNNs) has been proposed for the problem of crowd counting [2]. The network estimates the density map, which is then corrected by a second regression step. Like other

© Springer International Publishing AG 2016
B. Leibe et al. (Eds.): ECCV 2016, Part II, LNCS 9906, pp. 660–676, 2016.
DOI: 10.1007/978-3-319-46475-6_41

**Fig. 1.** Examples of density maps. (a) A synthetic fluorescence-light microscopy image [1] (left) and corresponding label density map (right). (b) A perspective normalized crowd image from the UCSD dataset [3] (left) and corresponding label density map (right). In both applications, machine learning techniques are used to estimate the appropriate density map values for each pixel. (c) The kernel used to create the microscopy density map. (d) The kernel used to create the crowd density map.

CNN based methods, this approach allows end-to-end training without the need to design any hand crafted image features and yields state of the art results as demonstrated on current object counting benchmarks: USCD [3] and UCF [4].

In this work, we adopt the CNN approach and introduce several novel modifications, which yield a significant improvement both in accuracy and performance. One such modification is in the boosting process. We propose a layered approach, where training is done in stages. We iteratively add CNNs, so that every new CNN is trained to estimate the residual error of the earlier prediction. After the first CNN is trained, the second CNN is trained on the difference between the estimation and the ground truth. The process then continues to the third CNN and so on.

Our second contribution is an intuitive yet powerful sample selection algorithm that yields both higher accuracy and faster training times. The idea is to streamline the training process by reducing the impact of the low quality samples, such as trivial cases or outliers. We propose to use the error of each sample as a measure of its quality. Our assumption is that very low errors indicate trivial cases. Conversely, very high errors indicate outliers. Accordingly, for a number of training epochs, we mute both low and high error samples. Reducing the impact of outliers is instrumental in increasing the overall accuracy of the method. At the same time, an effective decrease in the overall number of training samples reduces the training time of each CNN in the boosted ensemble.

It should be noted that layered boosting and selective sampling complement each other. Boosting increases the overall number of trained network layers, which drives up the training time. Boosting also leads to an over emphasis of misclassified samples such as outliers. Selective sampling mitigates both these undesirable effects.

## 2    Previous Work

The straightforward approach to counting is based on counting objects detected by an image segmentation process, see, for example, [5,6]. However, such methods are limited by the accuracy of the underlying detection methods. Accordingly, direct approaches tend to have difficulties in handling severe occlusions and cluttered backgrounds.

A direct machine learning approach was suggested in [4,7,8], which estimates the number of objects based on a predetermined set of image features such as image histograms. Naturally, the use of 1D statistics leads to a great computational efficiency. However, these global approaches tend to disregard 2D information on the object location. As a result, in some complex counting applications, accuracy may be affected.

Lempitsky et al. [1] introduced an object counting method that is based on pixel-level object density map regression. The method was shown to perform well, even in the face of a high number of objects that occlude each other. Following this work, Fiaschi et al. [9] used random forest regression in order to estimate the object density and improve training efficiency. Pham et al. [10] suggested additional improvements using modified random forests.

Deep learning is often used for tasks that are related to crowd counting such as pedestrian detection [11,12] and crowd segmentation [13]. Two recent contributions [2,14] have used deep models specifically for the application of crowd counting. In [2], a dual-loss function was suggested for the estimation of both the density function and the crowd count simultaneously. In [14], a method was proposed for counting extremely dense crowds using a CNN. In this work, the step of estimating the density function was not performed. Instead, the CNN directly estimated the number of people in the crowd. In addition, the utility of augmenting the training data with negative samples (no people) was explored.

In contrast to other methods, our approach proposes to estimate the density map directly with a single loss function. In order to mitigate the difficulty of training deep regression networks, we propose the use of relatively shallow networks augmented by the boosting framework.

*Boosting Deep Networks:* Boosting is a well-known greedy technique for ensemble learning. The basic idea is to literately train a new classifier that learns to fix the errors of the previous classifiers. In general, boosting is most powerful when used to combine weak models, and boosting stronger models is often not beneficial [15]. Specifically, only a few attempts have been made for boosting deep neural networks.

In [16], a hybrid method based on boosting is proposed. First, object candidates are determined based on low-level features extracted from the bottom layers of a trained CNN. AdaBoost [17] is then used to build a final classifier.

In this paper, we employ boosting in a straightforward manner, working iteratively with the same network. The method is general and the same network architecture is used for all the applications. Despite the simplicity of the proposed approach, it yields excellent results.

*Sample Selection:* Training deep networks is often done by utilizing very large datasets. Many methods have been proposed for data augmentation in order to increase the training set size even further. However, not all training samples are created equal. For instance, [18] proposed a sample selection scheme to choose the best samples within a sample augmentation framework. For each training sample, a continuous stream of augmented samples is created. Then, in between epochs, the network evaluates the error of each of the synthesized samples. Only high error samples are retained to form the final training set.

Sample selection is often used as a part of cascaded architectures. Cascades have been used, e.g., for face detection using either hand crafted features [19], or deep learning [20]. When constructing the next level of the cascade, the samples that did not pass the previous classifiers are filtered out.

Another commonly used method is the one of harvesting hard negative samples, which is used for face detection and for object detection in general, e.g. see [21]. Recently, in the domain of face recognition [22], it has been proposed to construct a dataset of individuals that are similar to each other and are therefore harder to identify. The face recognition network is then fine-tuned on this more challenging sample set.

## 3   Density Counting with CNNs

Following previous work, we define the density function as a real-valued function over the pixel grid, such that its integral over the image domain matches the object counts. The input to our method is a single image $I$, and, during training, a set $S$ of image locations that correspond to the centers of the objects to be counted. The density map $F$ is the image obtained by placing a 2D kernel $P$ at each location $p \in S$:

$$F(x) = \sum_{p \in S} P(x - p), \tag{1}$$

where $x$ denotes 2D image coordinates. For the microscopy dataset, we follow [1] and employ $P$ that is a normalized 2D Gaussian kernel. For the crowd-counting experiment, we follow [2] and use a specific smoothing kernel designed for this task. This filter is a human-shaped structure composed as a superposition of two Gaussians, one for the head and one for the body. In Fig. 1, examples of ground truth density maps are presented for both microscopy and crowd counting, as well as the kernels used.

Counting in the density map domain is done by spatial integration. It is important to note, however, that using the definition above, the sum of the ground truth density F over the entire image will not match the object count exactly. This effect is caused by objects that lie very close to the image boundary so that part of the associated probability mass is located outside of the image. However, for most applications, this effect can be neglected.

Any regression algorithm can be used for counting within such a framework. The objective of the regression model is to learn the mapping from the image pixels to the density map of the image. In our deep learning method, similar to [2], a CNN is used in order to map an image patch to the corresponding patch of the density image.

Patches randomly selected from the training images are treated as training samples, and the corresponding patches of the density map form the labels. As with other density based methods, counting is performed by summing the estimated density map. Note that unlike [2], we do not use the density map as a feature for a second regression model. Instead, we directly integrate over the density map. We have used two slightly different CNN architectures to address the two counting problems. In both cases, the input consists of patches of the input image $I$, and the output is an estimated density map for each patch. The CNN architecture for microscopy counting can be seen in Fig. 2(a), and the one used for crowd counting is depicted in Fig. 2(b). The differences are mainly in the size of the input patch, which, in turn, is determined by the size of the objects to be counted. In both cases, the architecture is built out of several convolutional blocks, which contain interleaving $2 \times 2$ pooling layers. After each convolutional block, we add a dropout layer [23], with a parameter 0.5. The final block is composed of a single convolutional layer (for crowd) and a series of fully connected layers without pooling. After each layer, except for the topmost hidden layer, we employ a ReLU activation function [24].

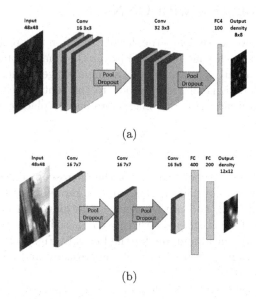

(a)

(b)

**Fig. 2.** The proposed CNN architecture. The basic network architecture is composed of 3 blocks. The first two blocks contain convolutional layers followed by max-pooling. The final block is composed of a single convolutional layer (for crowd) and a series of fully connected layers without pooling. (a) The cell counting problem. We use 2 convolutional blocks. Each block consists of $3 \times 3$ convolution layers, ending with $2 \times 2$ pooling and dropout. After the two convolutional blocks, we add a fully connected layer with 100 neurons. (b) The crowd counting problem. There are two $7 \times 7$ convolutions, each followed by $2 \times 2$ pooling. Finally, a $5 \times 5$ convolution layer followed by two fully connected layers are added.

Since we use two $2 \times 2$ pooling layers, the output density patch is $1/4$ the size of the original patch, in each dimension. We use the Euclidean (L2) distance as the loss function. This is in contrast to [2], which employs a dual regression loss function in order to overcome the relatively more challenging training of regression problems. In our case, we train using RMSProp [25] instead of Stochastic Gradient Descent and are able to train even without modifying the loss function. Weights were initialized using the Xavier-improved method [26].

At test time, patches are extracted from the test image using a sliding window approach. We adjust the stride such that there is a 50 % overlap. The density estimation of each pixel in the output image is obtained by averaging all the predictions of the overlapping patches that contain the given pixel. The final object count in the image is then obtained by summing all values of the recovered density map.

## 4   Gradient Boosting of CNNs

Gradient boosting machines belong to a family of powerful machine-learning ensemble techniques that have shown considerable success in a wide range of practical applications. Common ensemble techniques, such as random forests, rely on simple averaging of models in the ensemble. Boosting methods, including gradient boosting, are based on a different, constructive strategy for the ensemble formation. There, new models are added to the ensemble sequentially. At each iteration, a new base-learner model $f_n$ is trained to fix the errors of the previous ensemble $F_{n-1}$

$$f_n(x) = \arg \min_{f_n(x)} \underbrace{E_x[\overbrace{E_y(\Psi[y, f_n + F_{n-1}(x)])}^{\text{expected loss for one sample}} |x]}_{\text{expectation over the entire dataset}}, \tag{2}$$

where $f_n(x)$ is the n-th base-learner, $\Psi$ is the loss function and $F_{n-1} = \sum_1^{n-1} f_i$.

One can consider several different strategies for boosting, i.e. different ways to find the error-minimizing function. A well-known formulation is that of the gradient-descent method, which is called gradient boosting machines or GBMs [27,28]. The principle idea is to construct the next learner $f_n$ to be maximally correlated with the negative gradient of the loss function of the current ensemble $F_{n-1}$. Therefore, this method follows gradient descent in the function space.

For the Euclidean loss, this amounts to a simple strategy of fitting a model to the current error. In our case, in each step, we fit a new CNN model $f_n = CNN_n$ to the error of the last round $F(x) - F_{n-1}$ and update the ensemble accordingly

$$F_n \leftarrow F_{n-1} + CNN_n(\theta) \tag{3}$$

An overview of our boosting mechanism is presented in Fig. 3. The validation error can be used to obtain a stopping criterion for the boosting process. As shown in Sect. 6, the gradient boosted CNN converges after a few rounds and greatly improves the prediction accuracy.

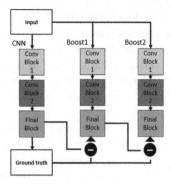

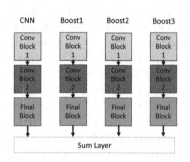

**Fig. 3.** The proposed boosting scheme. Each net has the same basic architecture with 2 convolutional blocks followed by the final block. In each iteration, we fix the trained ensemble and train a CNN to predict the current error.

**Fig. 4.** Fine-tuning a four-ensemble network. Each of the networks was trained on the error of the previous ensemble. Then, all the CNNs were joined via a sum layer and training continues jointly to all network weights.

*Fine-Tuning.* In many applications of deep neural networks, fine-tuning is used in order to improve the results. In the framework of boosted CNNs, instead of just summing the outputs of the ensemble regressors, we can fine-tune the weights of the entire network by employing backpropagation to the resulting structure. Our fine-tuning method is presented in Fig. 4. We compose all the base-networks using a sum layer. A sum layer merges several inputs by doing an element-wise sum. Then, using backpropagation, we retrain the entire ensemble simultaneously. In order to avoid overfitting, we keep early layers fixed and allow training of the last two layers of each network, only.

## 5   Sample Selection

There are several instances in which we would like to weigh down certain samples. In particular, we would like to mitigate the adverse impact of trivial samples and outliers. Trivial samples are the ones that are correctly classified early on. For example, it is easy to classify points sampled from two classes, each a multivariate Gaussian, if these points lie far away from the separating hyperplane. For the task of visual object counting, uniform background patches are easy to classify, and the trained network learns to classify such background patches fairly early in the training process. Continuing to train on such patches would consume unnecessary training resources.

**Algorithm 1.** The sample selection scheme.

$\forall s \in allSamples$:
  $Sleep[s] \leftarrow 0$
**for** each training epoch **do**
  $activeSamples \leftarrow \{s|sampleSleep[s] = 0\}$
  $\forall s \in allSamples$ , $Sleep[s] \leftarrow \max(0, Sleep[s] - 1)$
  $net \leftarrow processEpoch(net, activeSamples)$
  $\forall s \in activeSamples$ , $Err(s) \leftarrow loss$ (net, s)
  $\Theta_{low} \leftarrow percentile(Err, activeSamples, 30)$
  $\Theta_{high} \leftarrow percentile(Err, activeSamples, 97)$
  $badSamples \leftarrow \{s \in activeSamples|Err[s] < \Theta_{low} \vee Err[s] > \Theta_{high}\}$
  $\forall s \in badSamples$ , $Sleep[s] \leftarrow 4$
**end for**

Another source of training inefficiency is due to the presence of outliers. In many practical applications, outliers are caused by the mislabeled samples. Such errors in the input data are clearly detrimental to the classifier's efficacy. Indeed, it was shown that some boosting algorithms including AdaBoost are extremely sensitive to outliers [29].

Accordingly, we propose to reduce the impact of low quality training samples by decreasing their participation in the training process. This raises the question of identifying the low quality samples described above. In our method, we employ the current error of each individual training sample as a measure of the sample's quality. A very low L2 distance between the estimated and true target, indicates a trivial sample, while a high error indicates an outlier. Therefore, samples with either high or low errors are deemed to be of low quality.

After each epoch, we continue to train only on the samples with an error rate between $\Theta_{low}$ and $\Theta_{high}$, where $\Theta_{low}$ and $\Theta_{high}$ are thresholds chosen as a certain percentiles of the errors of the entire training set. Based on initial cross validation tests performed on 20 % of the training data of the UCSD dataset, we set $\Theta_{high}$ to be the 97 percentile and $\Theta_{low}$ as the 30 percentile throughout our experiments. The examples that did not meet the threshold criteria are removed from the training process for several epochs. Specifically, in our experiments, a low quality sample "sleeps" for four epochs. Algorithm 1 shows our proposed sample selection scheme.

One can think of other sample selection schemes. For instance, another scheme could be weighting each sample's gradients according to its error. However, a temporal elimination of a sample has clear advantages in terms of the training time, since irrelevant training samples are completely removed and not just weighted down.

Note that for the above mentioned parameters, at each epoch, 33 % of the active samples are removed. Viewed as a timed process in which the number of active samples converge, we obtain that at each round the same number of samples are removed. Let $N$ be the total number of training samples. At the steady state, the following equation holds: $N = x + 4 \times 0.33 \times x$, where $x$ is the number of active samples. Therefore, the number of active training samples converges to $x \approx 0.43N$. In other words, at any given epoch, after an initial number of epochs, only about 43 % of all the samples actively participate in the training process.

Our sample selection approach is simple and straightforward. Nevertheless, as demonstrated in the experiments below, it yields a significant improvement both in terms of training time and, especially for noisy labeled data, also in terms of accuracy.

# 6    Experiments

We compare our algorithm to the state of the art in two domains: Bacterial cell images and crowd counting. Overall, our experiments are more extensive than any previous counting paper. The only dataset that seems to be missing is the Expo crowd dataset [2], which is not publicly available. Additional experiments holding out 5 % of the tagging are done in order to demonstrate the method's robustness to outliers. Finally, we present surprising results for depth estimation from a single image, which are obtained using the same network we propose for the completely different task of crowd counting.

## 6.1    Bacterial Cells Microscopy Images

The dataset presented in [1] is composed out of 200 simulated fluorescence microscopy images of cell cultures, each containing $171 \pm 64$ cells on average. 100 images are reserved for training and validation, and the remaining 100 for testing. Each image has a labeled equivalent with dots marked at the center of each cell. The label density map was calculated by smoothing this point density map using a Gaussian kernel with $\sigma = 3$ pixels.

Following [9], we discard the green and red channels of the raw images and use only the blue channel. From each training image, we take 1600 random $32 \times 32$ patches. Our CNN architecture is the one presented in Fig. 2(a).

The results are summarized in Table 1. As in other counting benchmarks, the mean absolute error (MAE) is used for evaluating the accuracy of each method. As can be seen, for the given data set, without boosting, the single network does not achieve good results. However, with the increase in the number of boosting stages, MAE is reduced yielding a significant (more than 30 %) improvement over the state of the art results. While the improvement in accuracy following the booting rounds is significant, it seems that more than four rounds (five networks) are not necessary and even detrimental. This is probably due to overfitting the remaining error. On this very small dataset of 100 images, we could not improve results using fine-tuning.

The boosted classifier, which consists of multiple networks, has increased capacity. Therefore, we perform additional experiments in order to rule out the possibility that the increased performance is simply due to the increase in the capacity. For this purpose, we have added more convolutional layers creating

**Table 1.** MAE on the microscopy dataset. We present literature results as well as results for our boosted network, following 1–6 rounds of boosting. Deeper networks (without boosting) and ensemble of multiple CNNs are also shown. In our terminology, 1 boost means two networks. For completeness, we also present (rightmost column) MAE on the test set without sample selection.

| Method | MAE test | Method | MAE test | MAE validation | No selection |
|---|---|---|---|---|---|
| Detection + correction [1] | 4.9 | Our model (no boosting) | 6.82 | 8.59 | 6.93 |
| Density + MESA [1] | 3.5 | Boosted CNN (1 boost) | 3.20 | 3.46 | 3.42 |
| Regression trees [9] | 3.2 | Boosted CNN (2 boosts) | 2.81 | 3.00 | 2.71 |
| Ensemble of 2 CNNs | 6.71 | Boosted CNN (3 boosts) | 2.42 | 2.50 | 2.39 |
| Ensemble of 3 CNNs | 6.54 | Boosted CNN (4 boosts) | 2.19 | 2.16 | 2.21 |
| Ensemble of 4 CNNs | 6.42 | Boosted CNN (5 boosts) | 2.33 | 2.18 | 2.41 |
| Ensemble of 5 CNNs | 6.45 | Fine-tuned (4 boosts) | 2.19 | 2.16 | 2.22 |
| Ensemble of 6 CNNs | 6.44 | CNN twice as deep | 5.40 | 5.62 | 5.22 |
| Ensemble of 7 CNNs | 6.43 | CNN three times as deep | 16.42 | 17.39 | 14.68 |

networks twice and three times as deep. The results show that a network twice as deep is better than the shallow network we use for boosting. However, boosting significantly outperforms increase in the network depth. The network three times as deep is much worse than even the shallow network, probably due to overfitting and the difficulty of training very deep networks.

It is well known that one can improve results by creating an ensemble of CNNs trained from different random starting points. Hence, we have performed a second experiment applying this technique. The same CNN, as the one utilized for boosting, is used for the ensemble experiments. Clearly, the boosting approach outperforms that of ensemble averaging.

## 6.2 Crowd Counting Benchmarks

**The UCSD dataset** [3] is comprised of a 2000-frame video chosen from one surveillance camera on the UCSD campus. The video in this dataset was recorded at 10 fps with a frame size of $158 \times 238$. The labeled ground truth is at the center of every pedestrian. The ROI and perspective map are provided in the dataset. We follow the setup of [2], and perform perspective normalization such that a ground area of 3-m by 3-m is mapped to a 48 pixel by 48 pixel region.

The benchmark sets aside frames 601–1400 as the training data and the remaining 1200 frames as the test set. For training, we extract 800 $48 \times 48$ random patches from each training image.

Unlike some density map models that use regression on the density map [2] as a post-processing step, our estimated count is the direct integral over the density map. Comparison with other methods performing crowd counting on the UCSD dataset is presented in the Table 2. Once again, the MAE metric is employed for the accuracy evaluation. As can be seen, the proposed boosted CNN model outperforms the best state of the art method by over 30 %. In this dataset,

**Table 2.** MAE for different techniques applied on the UCSD crowd dataset. For completeness, we also present (rightmost column) MAE on the test set for a single Gaussian kernel instead of the human shaped kernel that is composed out of two guassians.

| Method | MAE test | MAE validation | MAE test Single-Gaussian |
|---|---|---|---|
| Density + MESA [1] | 1.7 | - | - |
| Crowd CNN Model with global regression [2] | 1.6 | - | - |
| COUNT forest [10] | 1.6 | - | - |
| Our CNN model (no boosting) | 1.63 | 1.42 | 1.57 |
| Boosted CNN (1 boost) | 1.15 | 1.32 | 1.19 |
| Boosted CNN (2 boosts) | 1.25 | 1.69 | 1.19 |
| Fine-tuned model (1 boost) | 1.10 | 1.28 | 1.18 |
| Twice as deep | 1.82 | 1.88 | 1.91 |
| Three times as deep | 2.42 | 2.63 | 2.88 |
| Ensemble of 2 CNNs | 1.55 | 1.55 | 1.63 |
| Ensemble of 3 CNNs | 1.53 | 1.51 | 1.56 |

one round of boosting seems optimal. The low-capacity of this benchmark is also manifested in the low performance of the twice as deep network. In this dataset, fine-tuning the boosted network, which contains two CNNs (1 boost), does improve performance. However, for this specific benchmark, the gain is relatively small (about 5 % only).

**The mall crowd counting dataset** [32] contains over 60,000 pedestrians in 2,000 video sequences taken in a city-mall. We follow the dataset setting in [32] and employ frames 1–800 for training and the remaining 1200 frames as the test set. 400 random patches of size 48 × 48 are extracted from each training image. Table 3 presents the MAE for different state-of-the-art methods and for our approach. It is interesting to note the large initial error. We hypothesize that this large error is caused by the large variability in this dataset. It is remarkable that the boosting network, as is, without any additional adaptations is able to amend this situation. Indeed, using 2-boosting stages yields 17 % decrease in the MAE (in comparison to the best literature technique). The fine-tuned network, now composed of 3 CNNs, provides additional 3 % improvement.

**The UCF 50 crowd counting dataset** [4] contains only 50 densely crowded images. Following the dataset setting in [4], we split the dataset randomly and perform 5-fold cross-validation. We ignore the perceptive effect, which varies from one image to the next and is hard to estimate. To mitigate the effect of the views, we employ a 2D gaussian kernel similar to the microscopy dataset. The results are presented in Table 4. Once again, the benefits of boosting are observed. In this case, optimum is achieved for a single boosting round, which obtains a 20 % drop in MAE compared to the best literature method.

**Table 3.** MAE for different techniques applied on the mall crowd-counting dataset.

| Method | MAE test | MAE validation |
|---|---|---|
| CA-RR [30] | 3.43 | - |
| COUNT forest [10] | 2.50 | - |
| One CNN | 9.54 | 8.51 |
| Boosted CNN (1 boost) | 2.43 | 3.19 |
| Boosted CNN (2 boosts) | 2.08 | 2.31 |
| Boosted CNN (3 boosts) | 2.13 | 2.78 |
| Fine-tuned (2 boosts) | 2.01 | 2.25 |
| Twice as deep | 10.41 | 11.24 |
| Three times as deep | 15.37 | 14.42 |
| Ensemble of 2 CNNs | 6.52 | 7.21 |
| Ensemble of 3 CNNs | 6.67 | 7.19 |

**Table 4.** MAE for different techniques applied on the UCF crowd-counting dataset.

| Method | MAE test | MAE validation |
|---|---|---|
| Density + MESA [1] | 493.4 | - |
| Idrees et al. [4] | 468.0 | - |
| Zhang et al. [2] | 467.0 | - |
| One CNN (no boost) | 434.4 | 452.4 |
| Boosted (1 boost) | 376.2 | 425.2 |
| Boosted (2 boosts) | 382.2 | 560.3 |
| Find-tuned (1 boost) | 364.4 | 341.4 |
| Twice as deep | 539.2 | 500.3 |
| Three times as deep | 914.2 | 712.8 |
| Ensemble of 2 CNNs | 414.2 | 553.2 |
| Ensemble of 3 CNNs | 474.0 | 680.5 |

## 6.3 Robustness to Outliers

The sample selection process has a dramatic effect on the training time, since, at the steady state, only 43 % of samples are used at each epoch, while the amount of epochs stays the same. However, its effect on accuracy is more limited. Table 1 shows MAE, for the cell counting dataset, with and without sample selection. As one can see, the effect on accuracy is small. For example, with four boosting steps, sample selection reduces MAE from 2.21 to 2.19.

However, as shown below, in more ambiguous tagging situations, or in cases where tagging is inaccurate, sample selection becomes crucial. In order to simulate this effect, we randomly removed 5 % of points from the set $S$ of the true object locations for the training samples.

The results are summarized in Table 5 for the cell counting benchmark and Table 6 for the mall crowd counting dataset. It is interesting to see that even a very limited 5 % corruption in the ground truth causes a very significant (up to 3-fold ) increase in the MAE. However, introduction of the selective sampling

**Table 5.** Impact of the sample selection on the MAE when 5 % of the cells are randomly untagged in the cell microscopy benchmark.

| Boost | No selection | With selection | The selection proposed in [31] |
|---|---|---|---|
| none | 18.80 | 14.55 | 15.72 |
| 1 | 10.09 | 7.88 | 8.18 |
| 2 | 8.12 | 6.25 | 6.32 |
| 3 | 8.49 | 4.94 | 5.12 |
| 4 | 9.12 | 4.96 | 5.42 |

**Table 6.** Impact of the sample selection process on the MAE when a random subset containing 5% of the people in the mall dataset are untagged.

| Boost | No selection | With selection | The selection proposed in [31] |
|---|---|---|---|
| none | 9.03 | 7.82 | 11.39 |
| 1 | 6.92 | 2.97 | 4.44 |
| 2 | 5.49 | 2.52 | 2.46 |
| 3 | 3.76 | 2.25 | 2.48 |
| 4 | 4.01 | 2.64 | 2.81 |

method allows over 40 % error rate reduction (4.94 instead of 8.49 for three boosting steps in the cell dataset).

It is interesting to note that, in the mall dataset, our method applied on the noisy ground truth data achieves better accuracy than the best literature result obtained on the uncorrupted truth set (2.25 compared to 2.50).

In addition, we evaluated the sample selection scheme proposed in [31], which employs a robust loss function based on Tukeys biweight function that weighs the training samples based on the residual magnitude. As can be seen in Tables 5 and 6, our method yields lower error than state of the art.

## 6.4 Depth Estimation

Since the proposed boosting method, at the core of our method, is general, it can be applied outside the realm of object counting. There are many image to image regression problems with a similar structure to the density estimation task. We arbitrarily select the problem of depth estimation from a single image.

The Make3D range image dataset [33,38] is used in the following depth estimation experiments. Each image in this dataset is of size 2272 × 1704 and is supplied with a 55 × 305 depth map. We adhere to the benchmark splits provided in [36], which consist of 400 training images and 134 test images.

For training, we resize the images by half and sample 800 112 × 112 patches. We use the same CNN architecture as the crowd counting(!). The only difference is the number of neurons in the final fully-connected layers. Since the last layer represents the estimated depth for a patch of size 28 × 28 pixels the final fully-connected layers contain 1000 and then 784 neurons instead of the original sizes of 400 and 200. The ground truth depth data of Make3D is inaccurate for depths greater than 80 m. Therefore, we follow the commonly applied post-processing described in [37] that classifies sky pixels and sets their depth to 80 m.

The results on the Make3D benchmark are evaluated using the RMS (root mean-squared) measure. Table 7 presents our boosting results in comparison to the literature, and Fig. 5 shows an example. The only literature methods, we are aware of, that outperform us are the Discrete-continuous CRF [37] and Deep convolutional neural fields [36]. Note that our method is local and does not use

(a)          (b)          (c)          (d)

**Fig. 5.** Examples of Make3D [33] depth maps. (a) A test image. (b) Estimation with a single CNN. (c) Estimation after 1 additional round of boosting. (d) Ground truth.

**Table 7.** Results on the depth estimation Make3D dataset [33]. We present literature results as well as results for our boosted network.

| Method | RMS(m) test | RMS(m) validation |
|---|---|---|
| Depth MRF [33] | 16.7 | - |
| Feedback cascades [34] | 15.2 | - |
| Depth transfer [35] | 15.10 | - |
| DCNF [36] | 12.89 | - |
| Discrete-continuous CRF [37] | 12.60 | - |
| Our CNN model (no boosting) | 14.36 | 13.69 |
| Boosted CNN (1 boost) | 13.69 | 13.31 |
| Boosted CNN (2 boosts) | 13.61 | 12.57 |
| Boosted CNN (3 boosts) | 13.89 | 13.12 |
| Fine-tuned model (2 boosts) | 13.28 | 12.52 |

CRF models as the other leading methods do. The application of our method is direct, and does not include the common practice of working with superpixels. Nevertheless, our simplified approach is within 5.5 % of the state of the art.

# 7 Conclusions and Future Work

In this work, we propose two contributions that improve the effectiveness of CNNs: gradient boosting and selective sampling. The efficacy of these techniques was evaluated in the domain of visual object counting. We applied the techniques on four public benchmarks and showed that our approach yields a 20 %–30 % reduction in the counting error rate. When training the CNNs, we are able to obtain more than 50 % reduction in training time of each CNN.

An additional advantage of the proposed approach is its simplicity. We are using the same basic architecture for three different counting applications (microscopy, indoor and outdoor crowd) and achieve improved results in comparison to the state-of-the-art methods tuned to each specific application. Interestingly, in all the cases we had a similar degree of accuracy improvement over the literature, even though each benchmark has its own leading method.

In this paper, we explored the basic premise of the above methods. However, there are several improvements that we would like to explore in the future. These include an adaptive parameterization for the sample selection parameters: high and low thresholds and number of muted epochs. This can be based, for example, on the relative contribution of each sample to the weight updates.

Finally, it is our intention to extend the proposed techniques to more CNN regression applications. Such problems exist in a variety of domains including tasks that differ significantly from the task of counting such as age estimation in face images and human pose estimation.

**Acknowledgments.** This research is supported by the Intel Collaborative Research Institute for Computational Intelligence (ICRI-CI).

# References

1. Lempitsky, V., Zisserman, A.: Learning to count objects in images. In: Lafferty, J.D., Williams, C.K.I., Shawe-Taylor, J., Zemel, R.S., Culotta, A. (eds.) Advances in Neural Information Processing Systems 23, pp. 1324–1332. Curran Associates Inc. (2010)
2. Zhang, C., Li, H., Wang, X., Yang, X.: Cross-scene crowd counting via deep convolutional neural networks. In: The IEEE Conference on Computer Vision and Pattern Recognition (CVPR), June 2015
3. Chan, A.B., sheng John, Z., Vasconcelos, L.N.: Privacy preserving crowd monitoring: counting people without people models or tracking. In: CVPR, pp. 1–7 (2008)
4. Idrees, H., Saleemi, I., Seibert, C., Shah, M.: Multi-source multi-scale counting in extremely dense crowd images. In: Proceedings of the 2013 IEEE Conference on Computer Vision and Pattern Recognition, CVPR 2013, pp. 2547–2554. IEEE Computer Society, Washington DC (2013)
5. Dong, L., Parameswaran, V., Ramesh, V., Zoghlami, I.: Fast crowd segmentation using shape indexing. In: IEEE 11th International Conference on Computer Vision, ICCV 2007, pp. 1–8, October 2007
6. An, S., Peursum, P., Liu, W., Venkatesh, S.: Efficient algorithms for subwindow search in object detection and localization. In: IEEE Conference on Computer Vision and Pattern Recognition, CVPR 2009, pp. 264–271, June 2009
7. Ryan, D., Denman, S., Fookes, C., Sridharan, S.: Crowd counting using multiple local features. In: Digital Image Computing: Techniques and Applications, DICTA 2009, pp. 81–88, December 2009
8. Chan, A.B., Liang, Z.S.J., Vasconcelos, N.: Privacy preserving crowd monitoring: counting people without people models or tracking. In: IEEE Conference on Computer Vision and Pattern Recognition, CVPR 2008, pp. 1–7, June 2008
9. Fiaschi, L., Koethe, U., Nair, R., Hamprecht, F.A.: Learning to count with regression forest and structured labels. In: 2012 21st International Conference on Pattern Recognition (ICPR), pp. 2685–2688, November 2012
10. Pham, V.Q., Kozakaya, T., Yamaguchi, O., Okada, R.: Count forest: co-voting uncertain number of targets using random forest for crowd density estimation. In: The IEEE International Conference on Computer Vision (ICCV), December 2015
11. Zeng, X., Ouyang, W., Wang, M., Wang, X.: Deep learning of scene-specific classifier for pedestrian detection. In: Fleet, D., Pajdla, T., Schiele, B., Tuytelaars, T. (eds.) ECCV 2014, Part III. LNCS, vol. 8691, pp. 472–487. Springer, Heidelberg (2014)
12. Zeng, X., Ouyang, W., Wang, X.: Multi-stage contextual deep learning for pedestrian detection. In: 2013 IEEE International Conference on Computer Vision (ICCV), pp. 121–128, December 2013
13. Kang, K., Wang, X.: Fully convolutional neural networks for crowd segmentation (2014). CoRR arXiv:1411.4464
14. Wang, C., Zhang, H., Yang, L., Liu, S., Cao, X.: Deep people counting in extremely dense crowds. In: Proceedings of the 23rd ACM International Conference on Multimedia, MM 2015, pp. 1299–1302. ACM, New York (2015)

15. Li, X., Wang, L., Sung, E.: A study of adaboost with SVM based weak learners. In: Proceedings of the 2005 IEEE International Joint Conference on Neural Networks, IJCNN 2005, vol. 1, pp. 196–201, July 2005
16. Karianakis, N., Fuchs, T.J., Soatto, S.: Boosting convolutional features for robust object proposals (2015). CoRR arXiv:1503.06350
17. Freund, Y., Schapire, R.E.: A decision-theoretic generalization of on-line learning and an application to boosting (1997)
18. Yamashita, T., Watasue, T., Yamauchi, Y., Fujiyoshi, H.: Improving quality of training samples through exhaustless generation and effective selection for deep convolutional neural networks. In: ICPR 2012 (2012)
19. Viola, P., Jones, M.: Rapid object detection using a boosted cascade of simple features. In: Proceedings of the 2001 IEEE Computer Society Conference on Computer Vision and Pattern Recognition, CVPR 2001, vol. 1, pp. I–511. IEEE (2001)
20. Li, H., Lin, Z., Shen, X., Brandt, J., Hua, G.: A convolutional neural network cascade for face detection. In: Proceedings of the IEEE Conference on Computer Vision and Pattern Recognition, pp. 5325–5334 (2015)
21. Sung, K.K., Poggio, T.: Example-based learning for view-based human face detection. IEEE Trans. Pattern Anal. Mach. Intell. **20**(1), 39–51 (1998)
22. Taigman, Y., Yang, M., Ranzato, M., Wolf, L.: Web-scale training for face identification (2014). CoRR arXiv:1406.5266
23. Srivastava, N., Hinton, G., Krizhevsky, A., Sutskever, I., Salakhutdinov, R.: Dropout: a simple way to prevent neural networks from overfitting. J. Mach. Learn. Res. **15**, 1929–1958 (2014)
24. Glorot, X., Bordes, A., Bengio, Y.: Deep sparse rectifier neural networks. In: Gordon, G.J., Dunson, D.B. (eds.) Proceedings of the Fourteenth International Conference on Artificial Intelligence and Statistics (AISTATS-2011), vol. 15, Journal of Machine Learning Research - Workshop and Conference Proceedings, pp. 315–323 (2011)
25. Tieleman, T., Hinton, G.: Lecture 6.5–RmsProp: divide the gradient by a running average of its recent magnitude. COURSERA: Neural Networks for Machine Learning (2012)
26. He, K., Zhang, X., Ren, S., Sun, J.: Delving deep into rectifiers: Surpassing human-level performance on imagenet classification (2015). CoRR arXiv:1502.01852
27. Friedman, J.H.: Greedy function approximation: a gradient boosting machine. Ann. Stat. **29**, 1189–1232 (2000)
28. Friedman, J.H.: Stochastic gradient boosting. Comput. Stat. Data Anal. **38**(4), 367–378 (2002)
29. Long, P.M., Servedio, R.A.: Random classification noise defeats all convex potential boosters. Mach. Learn. **78**(3), 287–304 (2009)
30. Chen, K., Gong, S., Xiang, T., Loy, C.C.: Cumulative attribute space for age and crowd density estimation. In: 2013 IEEE Conference on Computer Vision and Pattern Recognition (CVPR), pp. 2467–2474, June 2013
31. Belagiannis, V., Rupprecht, C., Carneiro, G., Navab, N.: Robust optimization for deep regression (2015). CoRR arXiv:1505.06606
32. Chen, K., Loy, C.C., Gong, S., Xiang, T.: Feature mining for localised crowd counting. In: BMVC
33. Saxena, A., Chung, S.H., Ng, A.Y.: Learning depth from single monocular images. In: NIPS 18. MIT Press (2005)

34. Li, C., Kowdle, A., Saxena, A., Chen, T.: Towards holistic scene understanding: feedback enabled cascaded classification models. In: Lafferty, J.D., Williams, C.K.I., Shawe-Taylor, J., Zemel, R.S., Culotta, A. (eds.) Advances in Neural Information Processing Systems 23, pp. 1351–1359. Curran Associates Inc. (2010)
35. Karsch, K., Liu, C., Kang, S.B.: Depth extraction from video using non-parametric sampling. In: Fitzgibbon, A., Lazebnik, S., Perona, P., Sato, Y., Schmid, C. (eds.) ECCV 2012, Part V. LNCS, vol. 7576, pp. 775–788. Springer, Heidelberg (2012)
36. Liu, F., Shen, C., Lin, G., Reid, I.D.: Learning depth from single monocular images using deep convolutional neural fields (2015). CoRR arXiv:1502.07411
37. Liu, M., Salzmann, M., He, X.: Discrete-continuous depth estimation from a single image. In: The IEEE Conference on Computer Vision and Pattern Recognition (CVPR), June 2014
38. Saxena, A., Sun, M., Ng, A.Y.: Make3D: learning 3D scene structure from a single still image. IEEE Trans. Pattern Anal. Mach. Intell. 31(5), 824–840 (2009)

# Amodal Instance Segmentation

Ke Li$^{(\boxtimes)}$ and Jitendra Malik

Department of Electrical Engineering and Computer Sciences,
University of California, Berkeley, USA
{ke.li,malik}@eecs.berkeley.edu

**Abstract.** We consider the problem of amodal instance segmentation, the objective of which is to predict the region encompassing both visible and occluded parts of each object. Thus far, the lack of publicly available amodal segmentation annotations has stymied the development of amodal segmentation methods. In this paper, we sidestep this issue by relying solely on standard modal instance segmentation annotations to train our model. The result is a new method for amodal instance segmentation, which represents the first such method to the best of our knowledge. We demonstrate the proposed method's effectiveness both qualitatively and quantitatively.

**Keywords:** Instance segmentation · Amodal completions · Occlusion reasoning

## 1 Introduction

Consider the horse shown in the left panel of Fig. 1. The task of instance segmentation requires marking the visible region of the horse, as shown in the middle panel, and has been tackled by several existing algorithms [6,7,18,19,27]. In this paper, we consider a different task, which requires marking both the visible and the occluded regions of the horse, as shown in the right panel. In keeping with terminology used in the psychology literature on visual perception [20], we refer to the former task as *modal instance segmentation* and the latter task as *amodal instance segmentation*.

A natural question to ask is if the task of amodal instance segmentation is well-posed: given only the visible portions of an object, there are many possible configurations of the hidden portions of the object, all of which appear to be plausible hypotheses to a human. This is particularly true for articulated objects under heavy occlusion. For example, if the lower body of a person is blocked from view, there is no single correct hypothesis for the configuration of the person's legs – the person could be sitting or standing, and so hypotheses consistent with either pose would be equally valid. Despite this ambiguity, humans are capable

---

**Electronic supplementary material** The online version of this chapter (doi:10.1007/978-3-319-46475-6_42) contains supplementary material, which is available to authorized users.

B. Leibe et al. (Eds.): ECCV 2016, Part II, LNCS 9906, pp. 677–693, 2016.
DOI: 10.1007/978-3-319-46475-6_42

Image          Modal Mask          Amodal Mask

**Fig. 1.** Target outputs for modal and amodal segmentation

of performing amodal completion and tend to predict the occluded regions with high degrees of consistency [40].

An amodal segmentation system would open the way to sophisticated occlusion reasoning. For instance, given an amodal segmentation mask, we can infer the presence, extent, boundary and region of occlusions by comparing it to the modal segmentation mask. We can also deduce the relative depth ordering by comparing the modal and amodal masks of the occluded and occluding objects. The information derived from the amodal segmentation mask can be further used downstream for a variety of interesting applications. For instance, we can estimate the physical dimensions of an object in the real world using its amodal bounding box, as demonstrated by Kar et al. [21].

The fact that all these occlusion reasoning problems can be reduced to amodal instance segmentation implies that amodal instance segmentation is more challenging than all these problems combined. An amodal segmentation system must not only be capable of determining if an object is occluded, but also where it is occluded. It must be able to hypothesize the shape of the occluded portion even though it has never seen the whole object before. It must be sensitive enough to detect the diminished signal from the small part of the occluded object that remains visible, but must be robust enough to avoid being misled by strong signals from occluding objects.

Furthermore, additional complicating factors arise if one were to attempt training a model for the task, the chief among them being the lack of supervised training data. While efforts are underway to collect amodal segmentation annotations [40], no amodal segmentation data is publicly available at the time of writing. In the meantime, we need to devise a clever way of using existing data to train a model for this new task.

In this paper, we present a new method for amodal instance segmentation, which to the best of our knowledge is the first such method. We train our method purely from existing modal instance segmentation data, thereby sidestepping issues arising from the lack of supervised training data. We make a key observation: while it is not possible to compute the amodal mask of an object from the modal mask by undoing occlusion, it is easy to do the reverse. Instead of undoing existing occlusion, we add synthetic occlusion and retain the original mask, which essentially becomes the true amodal mask for the composite image. We train a convolutional neural net to recover the original mask from the generated composite image. We do not assume knowledge of the amodal bounding box at test time; instead, we infer it from the amodal segmentation heatmap using a new strategy, which we dub Iterative Bounding Box Expansion. We demonstrate that despite being trained on synthetic data, the resulting model is quite effective at predicting amodal masks on images with real occlusions.

## 2  Related Work

Efforts toward understanding the semantic meaning associated with free-form regions in images started with work on figure-ground segmentation, the objective of which is to identify the foreground pixels in typically object-centric images. Early methods [4,23,25,26,38] investigated ways of combining top-down and bottom-up segmentation approaches and incorporating class-specific or object-specific templates of the foreground object's appearance. Later on, the focus shifted to the more general problem of semantic segmentation, which aims to identify the pixels that belong to each object category in more complex images. A diverse range of approaches for this problem have been developed; earlier approaches extend CRF-based formulations [3,22,24], consider combining object detections with region proposals [15], scoring groupings of over-segmented regions [35], aggregating information from multiple foreground-background hypotheses [5] and synthesizing scores from different overlapping regions to obtain a pixel-wise classification [1]. Later approaches [10,29,31,39] use feedforward or recurrent neural net models to extract features or to predict the final label of each pixel directly from images. In effort at achieving understanding of a scene at a finer level of granularity, recent work has focused on the task of instance segmentation, the goal of which is to identify the pixels that belong to each individual object instance. The predominant framework for this task is to find the bounding box of each instance using an object detector and predict the figure-ground segmentation mask inside each box. Earlier approaches rely on DPM [11] detections and predict segmentation masks using a simple appearance model [8,30,37], combine DPM detections and semantic segmentation predictions [9,12] or adopt a transductive approach [34]. More recent methods leverage the power of convolutional neural nets. SDS [18] and Dai et al. [6] use a neural net to compute features on region proposals and classifies them using an SVM, while the Hypercolumn net [19], Iterative Instance Segmentation [27] and Multi-task Network Cascades [7] predict the segmentation mask directly from the image patch. We view the task of amodal instance segmentation as the natural next step in this direction.

There has been relatively little work exploring amodal completion. Kar et al. [21] tackled the problem of predicting the amodal bounding box of an object. Gupta et al. [16] explored completing the occluded portions of planar surfaces given depth information. To the best of our knowledge, there has been no algorithmic work on general-purpose amodal segmentation. However, there has been work on collecting amodal segmentation annotations. Zhu et al. [40]

After Sampling Box          After Adding Occlusion          After Rescaling and
                                                            Sampling Modal Box

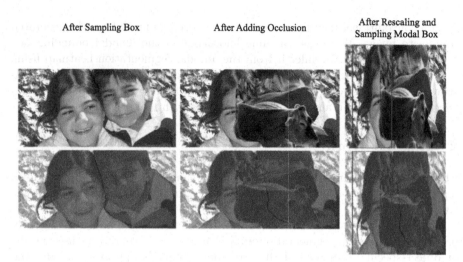

**Fig. 2.** The image patch and the target segmentation mask after each step of the sampling procedure. Red regions in the segmentation mask are assigned the positive label, white regions in the segmentation mask are assigned the negative label and blue regions in the segmentation mask are assigned the unknown label. The green box denotes the jittered modal bounding box. (Colour figure online)

collected amodal segmentation annotations on BSDS images, but has yet to make them publicly available. As far as we know, the proposed method represents the first method for amodal segmentation.

## 3    Generating Training Data

### 3.1    Overview

We generate amodal training data solely from standard modal instance segmentation annotations. In our case, we use the Semantic Boundaries (SBD) annotations [17] on the PASCAL VOC 2012 *train* set as the data source. We generate three types of data: image patches, modal bounding boxes and target segmentation masks. Image patches and modal bounding boxes are used as input to the model and target segmentation masks are used as supervisory signal on the output of the model.

The key observation we leverage is that the phenomenon of occlusion can be easily simulated by overlaying objects on top of other objects. More concretely, we first generate randomly cropped image patches that overlap with at least one foreground object instance, which we will refer to as the main object. We then extract random object instances from other images and overlay them on top of the randomly cropped patches with their modal segmentation masks serving as the alpha matte. Each overlaid object is positioned and scaled randomly in a way that ensures a moderate degree of overlap with the main object. Essentially, this procedure generates composite patches where the main object is partially occluded by other objects.

Next, for each composite patch, we find the smallest bounding box that encloses the portions of the main object that remain visible. This is essentially ground truth modal bounding box of the main object in the composite patch. To simulate noisy modal localization at test time, we jitter the bounding box randomly.

Finally, we generate the target segmentation masks corresponding to the composite patches produced above. For each patch, we take the corresponding part of its original modal segmentation mask and label the pixels belonging to the object as positive, pixels belonging to the background as negative and pixels belonging to other objects as unknown. This manner of label assignment captures what we know about the amodal mask given the modal mask – we know the visible portion of the object must be a part of the whole object and that the object cannot be occluded by the background. However, the object *may* be occluded by other objects in the image; consequently, the pixels belonging to other objects in the modal mask are labelled as unknown. Because the original modal mask is not affected by overlaid objects, this mask includes portions of the main object that were originally visible but are now occluded in the composite patch. Hence, the target mask is consistent with the true amodal mask. The data generation process is illustrated in Fig. 2 and examples of generated patches and masks are shown in Fig. 3.

## 3.2  Implementation Details

Data is generated on-the-fly during training. To generate a training example, we sample an image uniformly and then sample an object instance from the image, which will be referred to as the main object. We then randomly sample a bounding box that overlaps with the main object's bounding box along each dimension by at least 70 %. The size of the sampled box is randomly chosen and the length of each dimension is between 70 % and 200 % of the length of the corresponding dimension of the object's bounding box. Next, we choose the number of objects to overlay onto the patch inside the bounding box randomly by picking an integer from 0 to 2. To select an object to overlay, we sample an image and then sample a random object instance from the image. The object is placed at a random location that overlaps with the main object and scaled randomly so that the length of its shortest dimension is 75 % of the length of the corresponding dimension of the patch on average. After each of the above operations, we check if the proportion of the main object that remains visible falls below 30 %. If it does, we undo the most recent operation and try again. Otherwise, we proceed to find the bounding box the encloses the portion of the main object that remains visible and randomly samples a box that overlaps with the bounding box by at least 75 % along each dimension and can differ in size from the bounding box by at most 10 % in each dimension.

**Fig. 3.** Random samples from the generated training data

# 4    Predicting Amodal Mask and Bounding Box

## 4.1    Testing

We take the modal bounding box, that is, the bounding box of the visible part of the object, and the category of the object as given, which can be obtained from an object detector, like R-CNN [14], fast R-CNN [13] or faster R-CNN [32]. We then compute the modal segmentation heatmap using Iterative Instance Segmentation (IIS) [27], which is the state-of-the-art method for modal instance segmentation.

The proposed algorithm proceeds to predict the amodal segmentation mask and bounding box in an iterative fashion using a new strategy that will be referred to as Iterative Bounding Box Expansion (Fig. 4). Initially, the amodal bounding box is set to be the same as the modal bounding box. In each iteration, given the amodal bounding box, we feed the patch inside the amodal bounding box to a convolutional neural net, which predicts the amodal segmentation mask inside an expanded amodal bounding box that also includes areas immediately outside the original amodal bounding box. We compute the average heat intensity in the areas lie above, below, to the left and to the right of the original bounding box. If the average heat intensity associated with a particular direction is above a threshold, which is set to 0.1 in our experiments, we expand the bounding box in that direction and take this new bounding box to be the amodal bounding box used in the next iteration. This procedure is repeated until the average heat intensities in all directions are below the threshold. To obtain the

Image              Iteration 1              Iteration 2              Iteration 3

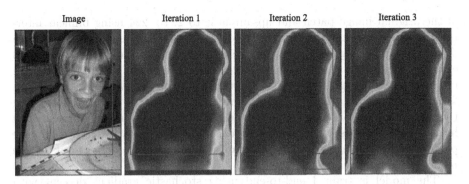

**Fig. 4.** Amodal segmentation heatmap after each iteration of Iterative Bounding Box Expansion. The green box denotes the modal bounding box and the blue box denotes the amodal bounding box. In each iteration, we use the average heat intensity *outside* the amodal bounding box to decide whether to expand the amodal bounding box in the next iteration. (Colour figure online)

final amodal segmentation mask, we colour in all pixels whose intensities in the corresponding heatmap exceed 0.7. Similarly, we obtain the modal segmentation mask by thresholding the modal heatmap at 0.8.

### 4.2 Training

The convolutional neural net we use takes in an image patch, a modal segmentation heatmap and a category and outputs the amodal segmentation heatmap. The net has the same architecture as that used by IIS, which is based on the hypercolumn architecture introduced by Hariharan et al. [19]. This architecture is designed to take advantage of both low-level image features at finer scales and high-level image features at coarser scales. It does so by making the final heatmap prediction dependent on the summation of upsampled feature maps from multiple intermediate layers, which is known as the hypercolumn representation. The version of the architecture we use is based on the VGG 16-layer net [33], which is referred to as "O-Net" in [19]. The IIS architecture is a variant of this architecture that also takes in an initial heatmap hypothesis via an additional category-dependent channel as input, which can be set to constant if no initial heatmap hypothesis is available. If an initial heatmap hypothesis is provided, the model refines the heatmap hypothesis to produce an improved heatmap prediction. Using this architecture, IIS is able to iteratively refine its own heatmap prediction by feeding in its heatmap prediction from the preceding iteration as input.

Each training example consists of an image patch, a modal bounding box and a target amodal segmentation mask. To prepare input to the net, we take the part of image patch that lies inside the modal bounding box and scale it anisotropically to 224 × 224, feed it to IIS as input. We take the modal segmentation heatmap produced by one iteration of IIS, align it to the coordinates

684 K. Li and J. Malik

of the original image patch and upsample it to $224 \times 224$ using bilinear interpolation. Because the model should predict the mask corresponding to an area larger than the image patch it sees, we remove 10 % of the image patch from each of the four sides and rescale it to $224 \times 224$. If less than 10 % of the pixels in this new patch belong to the visible portion of the object, we reject the current sample and generate a new training example. We centre the data by subtracting the mean pixel from the image patch and transforming the modal segmentation heatmap element-wise to lie between $-127$ and $128$. Finally, we feed the image patch, the modal segmentation heatmap and the target amodal mask to the model for training.

The model is trained end-to-end using stochastic gradient descent with momentum on mini-batches of 32 patches starting from weights of the model used by IIS. The loss function we use is the sum of pixel-wise negative log likelihoods over all pixels with known ground truth labels. We apply instance-specific weights that are inversely proportional to the factor by which each patch is upsampled. We train the model with a constant learning rate of $10^{-5}$, weight decay of $10^{-3}$ and momentum of 0.9 for $50,000$ iterations.

## 5 Experiments

Because there is no existing dataset with amodal instance segmentation annotations, there is no ground truth against which the predictions can be evaluated, making it difficult to perform a quantitative evaluation. We first present qualitative results and then perform an indirect quantitative evaluation against coarse-level annotations on the full PASCAL VOC 2012 *val* set. To perform a direct quantitative evaluation, we annotated 100 randomly chosen occluded objects from the same dataset with amodal segmentation masks and evaluate the proposed method on this subset.

### 5.1 Qualitative Results

We use the proposed method to generate amodal segmentation mask predictions for objects in the PASCAL VOC 2012 *val* set. Because the focus of this paper is on the segmentation system, we take the modal bounding box and the category of the object of interest as given and obtain them from the ground truth. We show the amodal heatmap and mask predictions produced by the proposed method in Figs. 5, 6 and 7, along with the modal heatmap and mask predictions generated by IIS for comparison. As shown, the proposed method is generally quite effective. In particular, even though the synthetic occlusions generated for training purposes do not appear entirely realistic, the proposed method is able to devise plausible hypotheses for hidden portions of objects caused by real occlusions.

We classify occlusions into two types: cases where the occluding object is mostly contained inside the occluded object and cases where a significant portion of the occluding object lies outside the occluded object. We will refer to the former as interior occlusions and the latter as exterior occlusions. For interior occlusions, the goal is to predict the mask between visible portions of the object, whereas for exterior occlusions, the goal is to predict the mask beyond the visible portion. There is typically a single correct way to handle interior occlusions: if it results from a true occlusion, the corresponding hole should be filled in; otherwise, it should not be. Therefore, for these cases, the task is less ambiguous and relatively easy. On the other hand, there are generally multiple equally valid ways to handle exterior occlusions: there are many possible ways to extend the visible portion that all lead to plausible amodal masks. So, for these cases, the task is more ambiguous and challenging. The method need to decide how much to extend the modal mask by in every direction. To do so, it must rely on the knowledge it learns about the general shape of objects of the particular category to produce a plausible amodal mask hypothesis.

We first examine examples of occluded objects for which the proposed method produces correct amodal segmentation masks, which are shown in Fig. 5. As shown, the proposed method is able to successfully predict the amodal mask on images with interior or exterior occlusions. Surprisingly, on some images where the modal prediction is poor, like the image with a dog on a folding chair, the proposed method is able to produce a fairly good amodal mask. Finally, the proposed method is able to produce remarkably good amodal masks on some challenging images with exterior occlusions, such as the image depicting a dog on a kayak and the images in the bottom two rows, suggesting that the proposed method is able to learn something about the general shape of objects.

Next, we take a look at examples of occluded objects for which the predicted amodal segmentation masks are incorrect, which are shown in Fig. 6. The mistakes may be caused by the rarity of unusual poses in the training set, large variation in the plausible configurations of the occluded portions of the object, similarity in appearance of adjacent objects or erroneous modal predictions.

While the preceding examples show that the model is capable of performing amodal completion, we need to make sure that the model does not hallucinate when presented with unoccluded objects. We explore some examples of unoccluded objects and the corresponding mask predictions in Fig. 7. Since the objects are unoccluded, amodal masks should be the same as modal masks. As shown, the amodal predictions are similar to or more accurate than the modal predictions. This may be explained by the robustness acquired by an amodal segmentation model: by learning to be robust to occlusion, the model also learns to be robust to variations in low-level patterns in the image that may confuse a modal segmentation model.

We include additional examples of heatmap and mask predictions in the supplementary material.

## 5.2   Indirect Evaluation

We use the proposed method combined with a modal instance segmentation method like IIS to predict the presence or absence of occlusion. We do so by

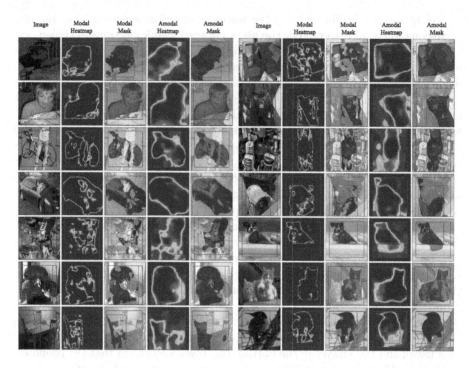

**Fig. 5.** Examples of amodal segmentation mask predictions for occluded objects which we judge to be correct. The first column shows the part of the image containing the amodal and modal bounding box, with the green box denoting the original modal bounding box that is given and the blue box denoting the expanded amodal bounding box found by Iterative Bounding Box Expansion. If a side of the amodal bounding box is adjacent to the border of the image patch, the patch abuts the corresponding border of the whole image. The next four columns show the modal segmentation heatmap and mask produced by IIS and the amodal segmentation heatmap and mask produced by the proposed method (Color figure online)

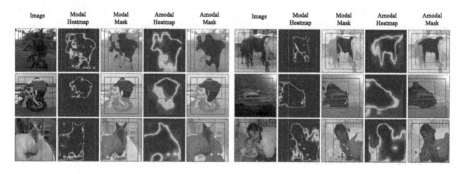

**Fig. 6.** Examples of amodal segmentation mask predictions for occluded objects which we judge to be incorrect. The visualizations follow the same format as Fig. 5

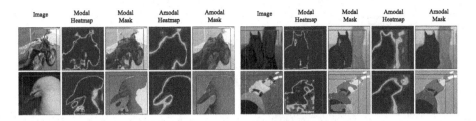

**Fig. 7.** Examples of amodal segmentation mask predictions for unoccluded objects. The visualizations follow the same format as Fig. 5

predicting the modal and amodal segmentation masks for each object in the PASCAL VOC 2012 *val* set and computing the following ratio:

$$\frac{\text{area}\,(modal\ mask \cap amodal\ mask)}{\text{area}\,(amodal\ mask)}$$

Intuitively, this ratio measures the degree by which an object is occluded. For an unoccluded object, because the amodal mask should be the same as the modal mask, this ratio should be close to 1. On the other hand, for a heavily occluded object, only a small proportion of the pixels inside the amodal mask should also be included in the modal mask; as a result, this ratio should be significantly less than 1. We will henceforth refer to this ratio as the *area ratio*.

We compare our predictions to the occlusion presence annotations in the PASCAL VOC 2012 *val* set, which are available for all object instances and specify whether they are occluded. First, we compute the modal and amodal mask predictions using IIS and the proposed method for all objects that are annotated as being occluded and plot the distribution of area ratios. We then do the same for objects that are annotated as being unoccluded. These two distributions are shown in Fig. 8a. As shown, the distribution for unoccluded objects is heavily skewed towards high area ratios, whereas the distribution for occluded objects peaks at an area ratio of around 0.75. This indicates the predicted amodal masks for occluded objects typically have more pixels outside modal masks than those for unoccluded objects, which confirms that the proposed method generally performs amodal completion only for occluded objects and not for unoccluded objects. The distribution for occluded objects is also flatter than that for unoccluded objects because the amount by which an object is occluded by can vary significantly from object to object.

This difference in the two distributions suggests that area ratio can be used to predict the presence or absence of occlusion. We can consider a simple classifier that declares an object to be unoccluded if its area ratio is greater than a threshold. For each value of the threshold, we can compute the precision and recall of this classifier. We plot the precision and recall we obtain by varying this threshold in Fig. 8b. We compute average precision and find it to be 77.17 %.

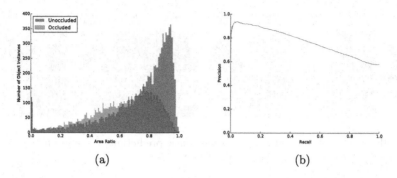

(a)                                      (b)

**Fig. 8.** (a) Distribution of area ratios of occluded and unoccluded objects in the PAS-CAL VOC 2012 *val* set. The range of possible area ratios is discretized into 100 bins of equal width and the vertical axis shows the number object instances whose area ratios lie in a particular bin. (b) The precision-recall curve for predicting the absence of occlusion by thresholding the area ratio. (Colour figure online)

## 5.3   Direct Evaluation

To evaluate the accuracy of the mask produced by the proposed method, we need ground truth amodal segmentation annotations. Because no such annotations are publicly available, we collected a set of amodal segmentation masks on 100 objects. For each category, we selected five object instances randomly from the PASCAL VOC 2012 *val* set that are labelled as occluded and annotated them with amodal segmentation masks. For this purpose, we used the annotation tool for MS COCO [28], which is based on the Open Surfaces annotation tool [2].

**Table 1.** Performance comparison of IIS and the proposed method on the task of amodal instance segmentation

| Method | Accuracy at 50 % | Accuracy at 70 % | Area under curve |
|---|---|---|---|
| IIS [27] | 68.0 | 37.0 | 57.5 |
| Proposed method | **80.0** | **48.0** | **64.3** |

We compare the overlap with ground truth achieved by the amodal mask predicted by the proposed method to that achieved by the modal mask predicted by the state-of-the-art modal segmentation method, IIS. In this setting, a modal instance segmentation system represents a fairly strong baseline since in cases where occlusion is not severe, it is possible to omit the occluded portion completely from the predicted mask without significantly lowering intersection-over-union (IoU) with the ground truth.

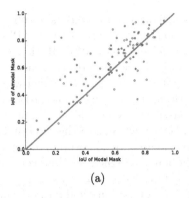
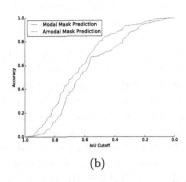

(a)                                         (b)

**Fig. 9.** (a) Comparison of overlap of the modal and amodal mask predictions with the ground truth. Overlap is measured using intersection-over-union (IoU). Each point represents an object instance and the points belonging to object instances in the same category share the same colour. Points that lie above the diagonal represent object instances whose amodal mask predictions are more accurate than their modal mask predictions. (b) Consider the setting where a predicted mask is deemed correct when it overlaps with the ground truth by at least a particular level of cutoff. This plot shows the proportion of object instances whose predicted masks are correct as a function of the cutoff. (Colour figure online)

**Segmentation Performance.** We first evaluate the segmentation system in isolation by taking the modal bounding box and the category of the object of interest from ground truth.

As shown in Fig. 9a, on most instances, the masks produced by the proposed method are significantly more accurate than the masks produced by IIS. Notably, the proposed method improves overlap compared to IIS by as much as 20–50 % in many cases. Overall, the proposed method produces better masks than IIS on 73 % of objects. Of the remaining 27 % of objects on which the proposed method performs worse than IIS, the drop in overlap is less than 5 % for the majority of objects. Hence, the masks produced by the proposed method are generally more accurate, sometimes by a sizeable margin.

In Fig. 9b, we plot the prediction accuracy if all masks with IoUs that exceed a particular cutoff are considered correct. As shown, predicting the mask using the proposed method consistently results in higher accuracy than using IIS at all levels of the cutoff. In Table 1, we report the accuracy of the proposed method and IIS at IoU cutoffs of 50 % and 70 %. Additionally, we compute the area under the accuracy curve for both methods. We find that the proposed method performs better than IIS on all metrics.

**Combined Detection and Segmentation Performance.** Next, we evaluate the performance of the combined detection and segmentation pipeline. We use faster R-CNN [32] as our detection system and compare overall performance with the proposed method as the segmentation system to IIS.

We use the amodal segmentation annotations we collected as ground truth and measure performance using mean region average precision ($mAP^r$) [18], which is a common metric used for modal instance segmentation. Region average precision is defined analogously to the standard average precision metric used for detection, except that overlap is computed by finding the pixel-wise IoU between the predicted and the ground truth masks. Because some instances are not annotated with ground truth amodal masks, we are unable to compute region overlap with some ground truth instances. Hence, we make a slight modification to the metric: we use bounding box overlap instead of region overlap to determine which ground truth instance a mask prediction is assigned to. However, we still use region overlap to decide if a mask prediction is deemed correct.

As shown in Table 2, the pipeline with the proposed method outperforms the pipeline with IIS by 11.1 points at 50% overlap and 8.6 points at 70% overlap. We also include an ablation analysis and report performance on PASCAL 3D+ [36] annotations in the supplementary material.

**Table 2.** Performance comparison of the combined detection and segmentation pipeline with faster R-CNN as the detection system and either IIS or the proposed method as the segmentation system

| Method | $mAP^r$ at 50% IoU | $mAP^r$ at 70% IoU |
| --- | --- | --- |
| Faster R-CNN [32] + IIS [27] | 34.1 | 14.0 |
| Faster R-CNN [32] + Proposed method | **45.2** | **22.6** |

# 6   Conclusion

We presented a new method for amodal instance segmentation, which represents the first such method to the best of our knowledge. We introduced a novel strategy for generating synthetic amodal instance segmentation data from modal instance segmentation annotations. This strategy enabled us to train a model for amodal instance segmentation despite the lack of publicly available amodal segmentation data. Additionally, we presented a new approach for iteratively predicting the amodal bounding box from amodal segmentations. We demonstrated the effectiveness of the proposed method in predicting amodal segmentation masks both qualitatively and quantitatively.

**Akcnowledgements.** This work was supported by ONR MURI N00014-09-1-1051 and ONR MURI N00014-14-1-0671. Ke Li thanks the Natural Sciences and Engineering Research Council of Canada (NSERC) for fellowship support. The authors also thank Saurabh Gupta and Shubham Tulsiani for helpful suggestions and NVIDIA Corporation for the donation of GPUs used for this research.

# References

1. Arbeláez, P., Hariharan, B., Gu, C., Gupta, S., Bourdev, L., Malik, J.: Semantic segmentation using regions and parts. In: 2012 IEEE Conference on Computer Vision and Pattern Recognition (CVPR), pp. 3378–3385. IEEE (2012)
2. Bell, S., Upchurch, P., Snavely, N., Bala, K.: OpenSurfaces: a richly annotated catalog of surface appearance. ACM Trans. Graph. (TOG) **32**(4), 111 (2013)
3. Boix, X., Gonfaus, J.M., Van de Weijer, J., Bagdanov, A.D., Serrat, J., Gonzàlez, J.: Harmony potentials. Int. J. Comput. Vis. **96**(1), 83–102 (2012)
4. Borenstein, E., Ullman, S.: Class-specific, top-down segmentation. In: Heyden, A., Sparr, G., Nielsen, M., Johansen, P. (eds.) ECCV 2002, Part II. LNCS, vol. 2351, pp. 109–122. Springer, Heidelberg (2002)
5. Carreira, J., Li, F., Sminchisescu, C.: Object recognition by sequential figure-ground ranking. Int. J. Comput. Vis. **98**(3), 243–262 (2012)
6. Dai, J., He, K., Sun, J.: Convolutional feature masking for joint object and stuff segmentation. In: Proceedings of the IEEE Conference on Computer Vision and Pattern Recognition, pp. 3992–4000 (2015)
7. Dai, J., He, K., Sun, J.: Instance-aware semantic segmentation via multi-task network cascades (2015). arXiv preprint: arXiv:1512.04412
8. Dai, Q., Hoiem, D.: Learning to localize detected objects. In: 2012 IEEE Conference on Computer Vision and Pattern Recognition (CVPR), pp. 3322–3329. IEEE (2012)
9. Dong, J., Chen, Q., Yan, S., Yuille, A.: Towards unified object detection and semantic segmentation. In: Fleet, D., Pajdla, T., Schiele, B., Tuytelaars, T. (eds.) ECCV 2014, Part V. LNCS, vol. 8693, pp. 299–314. Springer, Heidelberg (2014)
10. Farabet, C., Couprie, C., Najman, L., LeCun, Y.: Learning hierarchical features for scene labeling. IEEE Trans. Pattern Anal. Mach. Intell. **35**(8), 1915–1929 (2013)
11. Felzenszwalb, P.F., Girshick, R.B., McAllester, D., Ramanan, D.: Object detection with discriminatively trained part-based models. IEEE Trans. Pattern Anal. Mach. Intell. **32**(9), 1627–1645 (2010)
12. Fidler, S., Mottaghi, R., Yuille, A., Urtasun, R.: Bottom-up segmentation for top-down detection. In: Proceedings of the IEEE Conference on Computer Vision and Pattern Recognition, pp. 3294–3301 (2013)
13. Girshick, R.: Fast R-CNN. In: Proceedings of the IEEE International Conference on Computer Vision, pp. 1440–1448 (2015)
14. Girshick, R., Donahue, J., Darrell, T., Malik, J.: Rich feature hierarchies for accurate object detection and semantic segmentation. In: Proceedings of the IEEE Conference on Computer Vision and Pattern Recognition, pp. 580–587 (2014)
15. Gu, C., Lim, J.J., Arbeláez, P., Malik, J.: Recognition using regions. In: IEEE Conference on Computer Vision and Pattern Recognition, CVPR 2009, pp. 1030–1037. IEEE (2009)
16. Gupta, S., Arbelaez, P., Malik, J.: Perceptual organization and recognition of indoor scenes from RGB-D images. In: Proceedings of the IEEE Conference on Computer Vision and Pattern Recognition, pp. 564–571 (2013)
17. Hariharan, B., Arbeláez, P., Bourdev, L., Maji, S., Malik, J.: Semantic contours from inverse detectors. In: 2011 IEEE International Conference on Computer Vision (ICCV), pp. 991–998. IEEE (2011)
18. Hariharan, B., Arbeláez, P., Girshick, R., Malik, J.: Simultaneous detection and segmentation. In: Fleet, D., Pajdla, T., Schiele, B., Tuytelaars, T. (eds.) ECCV 2014, Part VII. LNCS, vol. 8695, pp. 297–312. Springer, Heidelberg (2014)

19. Hariharan, B., Arbeláez, P., Girshick, R., Malik, J.: Hypercolumns for object segmentation and fine-grained localization. In: CVPR (2015)
20. Kanizsa, G.: Organization in Vision: Essays on Gestalt Perception. Praeger Publishers, New York (1979)
21. Kar, A., Tulsiani, S., Carreira, J., Malik, J.: Amodal completion and size constancy in natural scenes. In: Proceedings of the IEEE International Conference on Computer Vision, pp. 127–135 (2015)
22. Kohli, P., Kumar, M.P.: Energy minimization for linear envelope MRFs. In: 2010 IEEE Conference on Computer Vision and Pattern Recognition (CVPR), pp. 1863–1870. IEEE (2010)
23. Kumar, M.P., Ton, P., Zisserman, A.: Obj cut. In: IEEE Computer Society Conference on Computer Vision and Pattern Recognition, CVPR 2005, vol. 1, pp. 18–25. IEEE (2005)
24. Ladicky, L., Russell, C., Kohli, P., Torr, P.H.S.: Graph cut based inference with co-occurrence statistics. In: Daniilidis, K., Maragos, P., Paragios, N. (eds.) ECCV 2010, Part V. LNCS, vol. 6315, pp. 239–253. Springer, Heidelberg (2010)
25. Leibe, B., Leonardis, A., Schiele, B.: Combined object categorization and segmentation with an implicit shape model. In: Workshop on Statistical Learning in Computer Vision, ECCV, vol. 2, p. 7 (2004)
26. Levin, A., Weiss, Y.: Learning to combine bottom-up and top-down segmentation. In: Leonardis, A., Bischof, H., Pinz, A. (eds.) ECCV 2006. LNCS, vol. 3954, pp. 581–594. Springer, Heidelberg (2006)
27. Li, K., Hariharan, B., Malik, J.: Iterative instance segmentation. In: CVPR (2016)
28. Lin, T.-Y., Maire, M., Belongie, S., Hays, J., Perona, P., Ramanan, D., Dollár, P., Zitnick, C.L.: Microsoft COCO: common objects in context. In: Fleet, D., Pajdla, T., Schiele, B., Tuytelaars, T. (eds.) ECCV 2014, Part V. LNCS, vol. 8693, pp. 740–755. Springer, Heidelberg (2014)
29. Long, J., Shelhamer, E., Darrell, T.: Fully convolutional networks for semantic segmentation. In: Proceedings of the IEEE Conference on Computer Vision and Pattern Recognition, pp. 3431–3440 (2015)
30. Parkhi, O.M., Vedaldi, A., Jawahar, C., Zisserman, A.: The truth about cats and dogs. In: 2011 IEEE International Conference on Computer Vision (ICCV), pp. 1427–1434. IEEE (2011)
31. Pinheiro, P., Collobert, R.: Recurrent convolutional neural networks for scene labeling. In: Proceedings of the 31st International Conference on Machine Learning (ICML 2014), pp. 82–90 (2014)
32. Ren, S., He, K., Girshick, R., Sun, J.: Faster R-CNN: towards real-time object detection with region proposal networks. In: Advances in Neural Information Processing Systems, pp. 91–99 (2015)
33. Simonyan, K., Zisserman, A.: Very deep convolutional networks for large-scale image recognition (2014). arXiv preprint: arXiv:1409.1556
34. Tighe, J., Niethammer, M., Lazebnik, S.: Scene parsing with object instances and occlusion ordering. In: Proceedings of the IEEE Conference on Computer Vision and Pattern Recognition, pp. 3748–3755 (2014)
35. Vijayanarasimhan, S., Grauman, K.: Efficient region search for object detection. In: 2011 IEEE Conference on Computer Vision and Pattern Recognition (CVPR), pp. 1401–1408. IEEE (2011)
36. Xiang, Y., Mottaghi, R., Savarese, S.: Beyond PASCAL: a benchmark for 3D object detection in the wild. In: IEEE Winter Conference on Applications of Computer Vision, pp. 75–82. IEEE (2014)

37. Yang, Y., Hallman, S., Ramanan, D., Fowlkes, C.C.: Layered object models for image segmentation. IEEE Trans. Pattern Anal. Mach. Intell. **34**(9), 1731–1743 (2012)
38. Yu, S.X., Shi, J.: Object-specific figure-ground segregation. In: Proceedings of 2003 IEEE Computer Society Conference on Computer Vision and Pattern Recognition, vol. 2, pp. II–39. IEEE (2003)
39. Zheng, S., Jayasumana, S., Romera-Paredes, B., Vineet, V., Su, Z., Du, D., Huang, C., Torr, P.H.: Conditional random fields as recurrent neural networks. In: Proceedings of the IEEE International Conference on Computer Vision, pp. 1529–1537 (2015)
40. Zhu, Y., Tian, Y., Mexatas, D., Dollár, P.: Semantic amodal segmentation (2015). arXiv preprint: arXiv:1509.01329

# Perceptual Losses for Real-Time Style Transfer and Super-Resolution

Justin Johnson[(✉)], Alexandre Alahi, and Li Fei-Fei

Department of Computer Science, Stanford University, Stanford, USA
{jcjohns,alahi,feifeili}@cs.stanford.edu

**Abstract.** We consider image transformation problems, where an input image is transformed into an output image. Recent methods for such problems typically train feed-forward convolutional neural networks using a *per-pixel* loss between the output and ground-truth images. Parallel work has shown that high-quality images can be generated by defining and optimizing *perceptual* loss functions based on high-level features extracted from pretrained networks. We combine the benefits of both approaches, and propose the use of perceptual loss functions for training feed-forward networks for image transformation tasks. We show results on image style transfer, where a feed-forward network is trained to solve the optimization problem proposed by Gatys *et al.* in real-time. Compared to the optimization-based method, our network gives similar qualitative results but is three orders of magnitude faster. We also experiment with single-image super-resolution, where replacing a per-pixel loss with a perceptual loss gives visually pleasing results.

**Keywords:** Style transfer · Super-resolution · Deep learning

## 1 Introduction

Many classic problems can be framed as *image transformation* tasks, where a system receives some input image and transforms it into an output image. Examples from image processing include denoising, super-resolution, and colorization, where the input is a degraded image (noisy, low-resolution, or grayscale) and the output is a high-quality color image. Examples from computer vision include semantic segmentation and depth estimation, where the input is a color image and the output image encodes semantic or geometric information about the scene.

One approach for solving image transformation tasks is to train a feed-forward convolutional neural network in a supervised manner, using a per-pixel loss function to measure the difference between output and ground-truth images.

**Electronic supplementary material** The online version of this chapter (doi:10.1007/978-3-319-46475-6_43) contains supplementary material, which is available to authorized users.

© Springer International Publishing AG 2016
B. Leibe et al. (Eds.): ECCV 2016, Part II, LNCS 9906, pp. 694–711, 2016.
DOI: 10.1007/978-3-319-46475-6_43

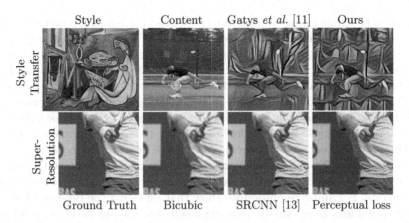

**Fig. 1.** Example results for style transfer (top) and ×4 super-resolution (bottom). For style transfer, we achieve similar results as Gatys *et al.* [11] but are three orders of magnitude faster. For super-resolution our method trained with a perceptual loss is able to better reconstruct fine details compared to methods trained with per-pixel loss.

This approach has been used for example by Dong *et al.* for super-resolution [1], by Cheng *et al.* for colorization [2,3], by Long *et al.* for segmentation [4], and by Eigen *et al.* for depth and surface normal prediction [5,6]. Such approaches are efficient at test-time, requiring only a forward pass through the trained network.

However, the per-pixel losses used by these methods do not capture *perceptual* differences between output and ground-truth images. For example, consider two identical images offset from each other by one pixel; despite their perceptual similarity they would be very different as measured by per-pixel losses (Fig. 1).

In parallel, recent work has shown that high-quality images can be generated using *perceptual loss functions* based not on differences between pixels but instead on differences between high-level image feature representations extracted from pretrained convolutional neural networks. Images are generated by minimizing a loss function. This strategy has been applied to feature inversion [7] by Mahendran *et al.*, to feature visualization by Simonyan *et al.* [8] and Yosinski *et al.* [9], and to texture synthesis and style transfer by Gatys *et al.* [10–12]. These approaches produce high-quality images, but are slow since inference requires solving an optimization problem.

In this paper we combine the benefits of these two approaches. We train feed-forward *transformation networks* for image transformation tasks, but rather than using *per-pixel* loss functions depending only on low-level pixel information, we train our networks using *perceptual loss functions* that depend on high-level features from a pretrained *loss network*. During training, perceptual losses measure image similarities more robustly than per-pixel losses, and at test-time the transformation networks run in real-time.

We experiment on two tasks: style transfer and single-image super-resolution. Both are inherently ill-posed; for style transfer there is no single correct output, and for super-resolution there are many high-resolution images that could have generated the same low-resolution input. Success in either task requires semantic reasoning about the input image. For style transfer the output must be semantically similar to the input despite drastic changes in color and texture; for super-resolution fine details must be inferred from visually ambiguous low-resolution inputs. In principle a high-capacity neural network trained for either task could implicitly learn to reason about the relevant semantics; however, in practice we need not learn from scratch: the use of perceptual loss functions allows the transfer of semantic knowledge from the loss network to the transformation network.

For style transfer our feed-forward networks are trained to solve the optimization problem from [11]; our results are similar to [11] both qualitatively and as measured by objective function value, but are three orders of magnitude faster to generate. For super-resolution we show that replacing the per-pixel loss with a perceptual loss gives visually pleasing results for ×4 and ×8 super-resolution.

## 2   Related Work

**Feed-Forward Image Transformation.** In recent years, a wide variety of image transformation tasks have been trained with per-pixel loss functions.

Semantic segmentation methods [4,6,14–17] produce dense scene labels by running networks in a fully-convolutional manner over input images, training with a per-pixel classification loss. Recent methods for depth [5,6,18] and surface normal estimation [6,19] are similar, transforming color input images into geometrically meaningful output images using a feed-forward convolutional network trained with per-pixel regression [5,6] or classification [19] losses. Some methods move beyond per-pixel losses by penalizing image gradients [6], framing CRF inference as a recurrent layer trained jointly with the rest of the network [17], or using a CRF loss layer [18] to enforce local consistency in the output.

The architecture of our transformation networks are inspired by [4] and [16], which use in-network downsampling to reduce the spatial extent of feature maps followed by in-network upsampling to produce the final output image.

**Perceptual Optimization.** A number of recent papers have used optimization to generate images where the objective is perceptual, depending on high-level features extracted from a convolutional network. Images can be generated to maximize class prediction scores [8,9] or individual features [9] in order to understand the functions encoded in trained networks. Similar optimization techniques can also be used to generate high-confidence fooling images [20,21].

Mahendran and Vedaldi [7] invert features from convolutional networks by minimizing a feature reconstruction loss in order to understand the image information retained by different network layers; similar methods had previously been used to invert local binary descriptors [22,23] and HOG features [24].

The work of Dosovitskiy and Brox [25] is particularly relevant to ours, as they train a feed-forward neural network to invert convolutional features, quickly approximating a solution to the optimization problem posed by [7]. However, their feed-forward network is trained with a per-pixel reconstruction loss, while our networks directly optimize the feature reconstruction loss of [7].

**Style Transfer.** Gatys *et al.* [11] perform artistic style transfer, combining the *content* of one image with the *style* of another by jointly minimizing the feature reconstruction loss of [7] and a *style reconstruction loss* also based on features extracted from a pretrained convolutional network; a similar method had previously been used for texture synthesis [10]. Their method produces high-quality results, but is computationally expensive since each step of the optimization problem requires a forward and backward pass through the pretrained network. To overcome this computational burden, we train a feed-forward network to quickly approximate solutions to their optimization problem. Concurrent with our work, [26,27] also propose feed-forward approaches for fast style transfer.

**Image Super-Resolution.** Image super-resolution is a classic problem for which a variety of techniques have been developed. Yang *et al.* [28] provide an exhaustive evaluation of the prevailing techniques prior to the widespread adoption of convolutional neural networks. They group super-resolution techniques into prediction-based methods (bilinear, bicubic, Lanczos, [29]), edge-based methods [30,31], statistical methods [32–34], patch-based methods [30,35–41], and sparse dictionary methods [42,43]. Recently [1] achieved excellent performance on single-image super-resolution using a three-layer convolutional neural network with a per-pixel Euclidean loss. Other recent methods include [44–46].

## 3 Method

As shown in Fig. 2, our system consists of two components: an *image transformation network* $f_W$ and a *loss network* $\phi$ that is used to define several *loss functions* $\ell_1, \ldots, \ell_k$. The image transformation network is a deep residual convolutional neural network parameterized by weights $W$; it transforms input images $x$ into output images $\hat{y}$ via the mapping $\hat{y} = f_W(x)$. Each loss function computes a scalar value $\ell_i(\hat{y}, y_i)$ measuring the difference between the output image $\hat{y}$ and

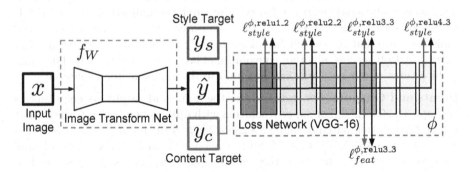

**Fig. 2.** System overview. We train an *image transformation network* to transform input images into output images. We use a *loss network* pretrained for image classification to define *perceptual loss functions* that measure perceptual differences in content and style between images. The loss network remains fixed during the training process.

a *target image* $y_i$. The image transformation network is trained using stochastic gradient descent to minimize a weighted combination of loss functions:

$$W^* = \arg\min_W \mathbf{E}_{x,\{y_i\}} \left[ \sum_{i=1} \lambda_i \ell_i(f_W(x), y_i) \right] \tag{1}$$

To address the shortcomings of per-pixel losses and allow our loss functions to better measure perceptual and semantic differences between images, we draw inspiration from recent work that generates images via optimization [7–11]. The key insight of these methods is that convolutional neural networks pretrained for image classification have already learned to encode the perceptual and semantic information we would like to measure in our loss functions. We therefore make use of a network $\phi$ pretrained for image classification as a fixed *loss network* in order to define our loss functions. Our deep convolutional transformation network is thus trained using loss functions that are also deep convolutional networks.

We use the loss network $\phi$ to define a *feature reconstruction loss* $\ell^\phi_{feat}$ and *style reconstruction loss* $\ell^\phi_{style}$ that measure differences in content and style between images. For each input image $x$ we have a *content target* $y_c$ and a *style target* $y_s$. For style transfer the content target $y_c$ is the input image $x$ and the output image $\hat{y}$ should combine the content of $x = y_c$ with the style of $y_s$; we train one network per style target. For super-resolution the input $x$ is a low-resolution input, the content target $y_c$ is the ground-truth high-resolution image, and style reconstruction loss is not used; we train one network per super-resolution factor.

### 3.1   Image Transformation Networks

Our image transformation networks roughly follow the architectural guidelines set forth by [47]. We eschew pooling layers, instead using strided and fractionally strided convolutions for in-network downsampling and upsampling. Our network body comprises five residual blocks [48] using the architecture of [49]. All non-residual convolutional layers are followed by batch normalization [50] and ReLU nonlinearities with the exception of the output layer, which instead uses a scaled tanh to ensure that the output has pixels in the range $[0, 255]$. The first and last layers use $9 \times 9$ kernels; all other convolutional layers use $3 \times 3$ kernels. The exact architectures of our networks can be found in the supplementary material[1].

**Inputs and Outputs.** For style transfer the input and output are color images of shape $3 \times 256 \times 256$. For super-resolution with upsampling factor $f$, the output is a high-resolution patch of shape $3 \times 288 \times 288$ and the input is a low-resolution patch of shape $3 \times 288/f \times 288/f$. Since the image transformation networks are fully-convolutional, at test-time they can be applied to images of any resolution.

**Downsampling and Upsampling.** For super-resolution with an upsampling factor of $f$, we use several residual blocks followed by $\log_2 f$ convolutional layers with stride $1/2$. This is different from [1] who use bicubic interpolation to

---

[1] Available at the first author's website.

upsample the low-resolution input before passing it to the network. Rather than relying on a fixed upsampling function, fractionally-strided convolution allows the upsampling function to be learned jointly with the rest of the network.

For style transfer our networks use two stride-2 convolutions to downsample the input followed by several residual blocks and then two convolutional layers with stride 1/2 to upsample. Although the input and output have the same size, there are several benefits to networks that downsample and then upsample.

The first is computational. With a naive implementation, a $3 \times 3$ convolution with $C$ filters on an input of size $C \times H \times W$ requires $9HWC^2$ multiply-adds, which is the same cost as a $3 \times 3$ convolution with $DC$ filters on an input of shape $DC \times H/D \times W/D$. After downsampling, we can therefore use a larger network for the same computational cost.

The second benefit has to do with effective receptive field sizes. High-quality style transfer requires changing large parts of the image in a coherent way; therefore it is advantageous for each pixel in the output to have a large effective receptive field in the input. Without downsampling, each additional $3 \times 3$ convolution increases the effective receptive field size by 2. After downsampling by a factor of $D$, each $3 \times 3$ convolution instead increases effective receptive field size by $2D$, giving larger effective receptive fields with the same number of layers.

**Residual Connections.** He *et al.* [48] use *residual connections* to train very deep networks for image classification. They argue that residual connections make the identity function easier to learn; this is an appealing property for image transformation networks, since in most cases the output image should share structure with the input image. The body of our network thus consists of several residual blocks, each of which contains two $3 \times 3$ convolutional layers. We use the residual block design of [49], shown in the supplementary material.

### 3.2  Perceptual Loss Functions

We define two *perceptual loss functions* that measure high-level perceptual and semantic differences between images. They make use of a *loss network* $\phi$ pretrained for image classification, meaning that these perceptual loss functions are themselves deep convolutional neural networks. In all our experiments, the *loss network* $\phi$ is the 16-layer VGG network [51] pretrained on ImageNet [52].

**Feature Reconstruction Loss.** Rather than encouraging the pixels of the output image $\hat{y} = f_W(x)$ to exactly match the pixels of the target image $y$, we instead encourage them to have similar feature representations as computed by the loss network $\phi$. Let $\phi_j(x)$ be the activations of the $j$th layer of the network $\phi$ when processing the image $x$; if $j$ is a convolutional layer then $\phi_j(x)$ will be a feature map of shape $C_j \times H_j \times W_j$. The *feature reconstruction loss* is the (squared, normalized) Euclidean distance between feature representations (Fig. 4):

$$\ell_{feat}^{\phi,j}(\hat{y}, y) = \frac{1}{C_j H_j W_j} \|\phi_j(\hat{y}) - \phi_j(y)\|_2^2 \qquad (2)$$

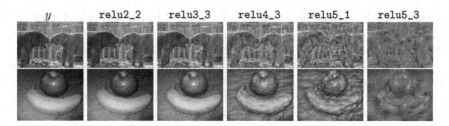

**Fig. 3.** Similar to [7], we use optimization to find an image $\hat{y}$ that minimizes the feature reconstruction loss $\ell_{feat}^{\phi,j}(\hat{y}, y)$ for several layers $j$ from the pretrained VGG-16 loss network $\phi$. As we reconstruct from higher layers, image content and overall spatial structure are preserved, but color, texture, and exact shape are not.

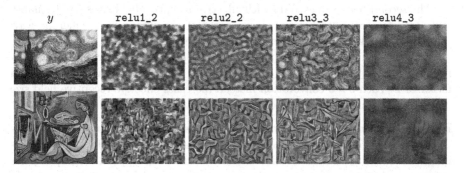

**Fig. 4.** Similar to [11], we use optimization to find an image $\hat{y}$ that minimizes the style reconstruction loss $\ell_{style}^{\phi,j}(\hat{y}, y)$ for several layers $j$ from the pretrained VGG-16 loss network $\phi$. The images $\hat{y}$ preserve stylistic features but not spatial structure.

As demonstrated in [7] and reproduced in Fig. 3, finding an image $\hat{y}$ that minimizes the feature reconstruction loss for early layers tends to produce images that are visually indistinguishable from $y$. As we reconstruct from higher layers, image content and overall spatial structure are preserved but color, texture, and exact shape are not. Using a feature reconstruction loss for training our image transformation networks encourages the output image $\hat{y}$ to be perceptually similar to the target image $y$, but does not force them to match exactly.

**Style Reconstruction Loss.** The feature reconstruction loss penalizes the output image $\hat{y}$ when it deviates in content from the target $y$. We also wish to penalize differences in style: colors, textures, common patterns, etc. To achieve this effect, Gatys *et al.* [10,11] propose the following *style reconstruction loss*.

As above, let $\phi_j(x)$ be the activations at the $j$th layer of the network $\phi$ for the input $x$, which is a feature map of shape $C_j \times H_j \times W_j$. Define the *Gram matrix* $G_j^\phi(x)$ to be the $C_j \times C_j$ matrix whose elements are given by

$$G_j^\phi(x)_{c,c'} = \frac{1}{C_j H_j W_j} \sum_{h=1}^{H_j} \sum_{w=1}^{W_j} \phi_j(x)_{h,w,c} \phi_j(x)_{h,w,c'}. \tag{3}$$

If we interpret $\phi_j(x)$ as giving $C_j$-dimensional features for each point on a $H_j \times W_j$ grid, then $G_j^\phi(x)$ is proportional to the uncentered covariance of the $C_j$-dimensional features, treating each grid location as an independent sample. It thus captures information about which features tend to activate together. The Gram matrix can be computed efficiently by reshaping $\phi_j(x)$ into a matrix $\psi$ of shape $C_j \times H_j W_j$; then $G_j^\phi(x) = \psi\psi^T/C_j H_j W_j$.

The *style reconstruction loss* is then the squared Frobenius norm of the difference between the Gram matrices of the output and target images:

$$\ell_{style}^{\phi,j}(\hat{y}, y) = \|G_j^\phi(\hat{y}) - G_j^\phi(y)\|_F^2. \tag{4}$$

The style reconstruction loss is well-defined even when $\hat{y}$ and $y$ have different sizes, since their Gram matrices will both have the same shape.

As demonstrated in [11] and reproduced in Fig. 5, generating an image $\hat{y}$ that minimizes the style reconstruction loss preserves stylistic features from the target image, but does not preserve its spatial structure. Reconstructing from higher layers transfers larger-scale structure from the target image.

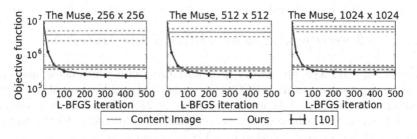

**Fig. 5.** Our style transfer networks and [11] minimize the same objective. We compare their objective values on 50 images; dashed lines and error bars show standard deviations. Our networks are trained on 256 × 256 images but generalize to larger images.

To perform style reconstruction from a set of layers $J$ rather than a single layer $j$, we define $\ell_{style}^{\phi,J}(\hat{y}, y)$ to be the sum of losses for each layer $j \in J$.

### 3.3 Simple Loss Functions

In addition to the perceptual losses defined above, we also define two simple loss functions that depend only on low-level pixel information.

**Pixel Loss.** The *pixel loss* is the (normalized) Euclidean distance between the output image $\hat{y}$ and the target $y$. If both have shape $C \times H \times W$, then the pixel loss is defined as $\ell_{pixel}(\hat{y}, y) = \|\hat{y} - y\|_2^2/CHW$. This can only be used when we have a ground-truth target $y$ that the network is expected to match.

**Total Variation Regularization.** To encourage spatial smoothness in the output image $\hat{y}$, we follow prior work on feature inversion [7,22] and super-resolution [53,54] and make use of *total variation regularizer* $\ell_{TV}(\hat{y})$.

# 4   Experiments

We perform experiments on two image transformation tasks: style transfer and single-image super-resolution. Prior work on style transfer has used optimization to generate images; our feed-forward networks give similar qualitative results but are up to three orders of magnitude faster. Prior work on single-image super-resolution with convolutional neural networks has used a per-pixel loss; we show encouraging qualitative results by using a perceptual loss instead.

## 4.1   Style Transfer

The goal of style transfer is to generate an image $\hat{y}$ that combines the content of a *target content image* $y_c$ with the *style* of a *target style image* $y_s$. We train one image transformation network per style target for several hand-picked style targets and compare our results with the baseline approach of Gatys *et al.* [11].

**Baseline.** As a baseline, we reimplement the method of Gatys *et al.* [11]. Given style and content targets $y_s$ and $y_c$ and layers $j$ and $J$ at which to perform feature and style reconstruction, an image $\hat{y}$ is generated by solving the problem

$$\hat{y} = \arg\min_{y} \lambda_c \ell_{feat}^{\phi,j}(y, y_c) + \lambda_s \ell_{style}^{\phi,J}(y, y_s) + \lambda_{TV} \ell_{TV}(y) \tag{5}$$

where $\lambda_c, \lambda_s$, and $\lambda_{TV}$ are scalars, $y$ is initialized with white noise, and optimization is performed using L-BFGS. Unconstrained optimization of Eq. 5 often results in images with pixels outside the range $[0, 255]$. For a more fair comparison with our method whose output is constrained to this range, for the baseline we minimize Eq. 5 using projected L-BFGS by clipping the image $y$ to the range $[0, 255]$ at each iteration. Optimization usually converges to satisfactory results within 500 iterations. This method is slow because each iteration requires a forward and backward pass through the VGG-16 loss network $\phi$.

**Training Details.** We train style transfer networks on the MS-COCO dataset [55]. We resize each of the 80k training images to $256 \times 256$ and train with a batch size of 4 for 40k iterations, giving roughly two epochs over the training data. We use Adam [56] with learning rate $1 \times 10^{-3}$. The output images are regularized with total variation regularization with a strength of between $1 \times 10^{-6}$ and $1 \times 10^{-4}$, chosen via cross-validation per style target. We do not use weight decay or dropout, as the model does not overfit within two epochs. For all style transfer experiments we compute feature reconstruction loss at layer relu3_3 and style reconstruction loss at layers relu1_2, relu2_2, relu3_3, and relu4_3 of the VGG-16 loss network $\phi$. Our implementation uses Torch [57] and cuDNN [58]; training takes roughly 4 hours on a single GTX Titan X GPU.

**Qualitative Results.** In Fig. 6 we show qualitative examples comparing our results with the baseline for a variety of style and content images. In all cases the hyperparameters $\lambda_c$, $\lambda_s$, and $\lambda_{TV}$ are exactly the same between the two methods; all content images come from the MS-COCO 2014 validation set.

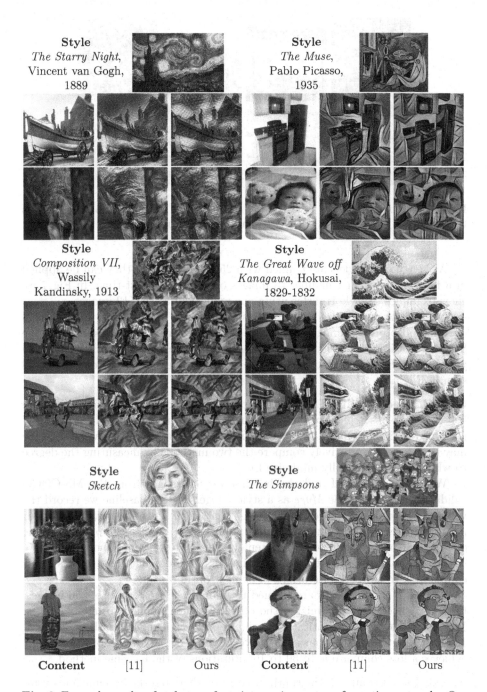

**Fig. 6.** Example results of style transfer using our image transformation networks. Our results are qualitatively similar to Gatys *et al.* [11] but are much faster to generate (see Table 1). All generated images are $256 \times 256$ pixels.

**Fig. 7.** Example results for style transfer on 512 × 512 images by applying models trained on 256 × 256 images. The style images are the same as Fig. 6.

Although our models are trained with 256 × 256 images, they can be applied in a fully-convolutional manner to images of any size at test-time. In Fig. 7 we show examples of style transfer using our models on 512 × 512 images.

Overall our results are qualitatively similar to the baseline, but in some cases our method produces images with more repetitive patterns. For example in the Starry Night images in Fig. 6, our method produces repetitive (but not identical) yellow splotches; the effect can become more obvious at higher resolutions, as seen in Fig. 7.

**Quantitative Results.** The baseline and our method both minimize Eq. 5. The baseline performs explicit optimization over the output image, while our method is trained to find a solution for any content image $y_c$ in a single forward pass. We may therefore quantitatively compare the two methods by measuring the degree to which they successfully minimize Eq. 5.

We run our method and the baseline on 50 images from the MS-COCO validation set, using *The Muse* as a style image. For the baseline we record the value of the objective function at each iteration of optimization, and for our method we record the value of Eq. 5 for each image; we also compute the value of Eq. 5 when $y$ is equal to the content image $y_c$. Results are shown in Fig. 5. The content image $y_c$ achieves a very high loss, and our method achieves a loss comparable to 50 to 100 iterations of explicit optimization.

Although our networks are trained to minimize Eq. 5 for 256 × 256 images, they also succeed at minimizing the objective when applied to larger images. We repeat the same quantitative evaluation for 50 images at 512 × 512 and 1024 × 1024; results are shown in Fig. 5. Even at higher resolutions our model achieves a loss comparable to 50 to 100 iterations of the baseline method.

**Speed.** Table 1 compares the runtime of our method and the baseline for several image sizes; for the baseline we report times for varying numbers of optimization iterations. Across all image sizes, our method takes about half the time of a single iteration of the baseline. Compared to 500 iterations of the baseline method, our

**Table 1.** Speed (in seconds) for our style transfer networks vs the baseline for various iterations and resolutions. We achieve similar qualitative results (Fig. 6) in less time than a single optimization step of the baseline. All benchmarks use a Titan X GPU.

| Image Size | Gatys et al. [11] | | | Ours | Speedup | | |
|---|---|---|---|---|---|---|---|
| | 100 | 300 | 500 | | 100 | 300 | 500 |
| $256 \times 256$ | 3.17 | 9.52s | 15.86s | **0.015s** | 212x | 636x | **1060x** |
| $512 \times 512$ | 10.97 | 32.91s | 54.85s | **0.05s** | 205x | 615x | **1026x** |
| $1024 \times 1024$ | 42.89 | 128.66s | 214.44s | **0.21s** | 208x | 625x | **1042x** |

method is three orders of magnitude faster. Our method processes $512 \times 512$ images at 20 FPS, making it feasible to run in real-time or on video.

## 4.2 Single-Image Super-Resolution

In single-image super-resolution, the task is to generate a high-resolution output image from a low-resolution input. This is an inherently ill-posed problem, since for each low-resolution image there exist multiple high-resolution images that could have generated it. The ambiguity becomes more extreme as the super-resolution factor grows; for large factors ($\times 4$, $\times 8$), fine details of the high-resolution image may have little or no evidence in its low-resolution version.

To overcome this problem, we train super-resolution networks not with the per-pixel loss typically used [1] but instead with a feature reconstruction loss (see Sect. 3) to allow transfer of semantic knowledge from the pretrained loss network to the super-resolution network. We focus on $\times 4$ and $\times 8$ super-resolution since larger factors require more semantic reasoning about the input.

The traditional metrics used to evaluate super-resolution are PSNR and SSIM [59], both of which have been found to correlate poorly with human assessment of visual quality [60–62]. PSNR and SSIM rely on low-level differences between pixels, and PSNR operates under the assumption of additive Gaussian noise. In addition, PSNR is equivalent to the per-pixel loss $\ell_{pixel}$, so as measured by PSNR a model trained to minimize per-pixel loss should always outperform a model trained to minimize feature reconstruction loss. We therefore emphasize that the goal of these experiments is not to achieve state-of-the-art PSNR or SSIM results, but instead to showcase the qualitative difference between models trained with per-pixel and feature reconstruction losses.

**Model Details.** We train models to perform $\times 4$ and $\times 8$ super-resolution by minimizing feature reconstruction loss at layer relu2_2 from the VGG-16 loss network $\phi$. We train with $288 \times 288$ patches from 10k images from the MS-COCO training set, and prepare low-resolution inputs by blurring with a Gaussian kernel of width $\sigma = 1.0$ and downsampling with bicubic interpolation. We train with a batch size of 4 for 200k iterations using Adam [56] with a learning rate of $1 \times 10^{-3}$ without weight decay or dropout. As a post-processing step, we perform histogram matching between our network output and the low-resolution input.

**Baselines.** As a baseline model we use SRCNN [1] for its state-of-the-art performance. SRCNN is a three-layer convolutional network trained to minimize per-pixel loss on 33 × 33 patches from the ILSVRC 2013 detection dataset. SRCNN is not trained for ×8 super-resolution, so we can only evaluate it on ×4.

SRCNN is trained for more than $10^9$ iterations, which is not computationally feasible for our models. To account for differences between SRCNN and our model in data, training, and architecture, we train image transformation networks for ×4 and ×8 super-resolution using $\ell_{pixel}$; these networks use identical data, architecture, and training as the networks trained to minimize $\ell_{feat}$.

**Evaluation.** We evaluate all models on the standard Set5 [65], Set14 [66], and BSD100 [46] datasets. We report PSNR and SSIM [59], computing both only on the Y channel after converting to the YCbCr colorspace, following [1,44].

**Results.** We show results for ×4 super-resolution in Fig. 8. Compared to the other methods, our model trained for feature reconstruction does a very good job at reconstructing sharp edges and fine details, such as the eyelashes in the first image and the individual elements of the hat in the second image.

In addition to the automated metrics shown in Fig. 8, we also ran a user study on Amazon Mechanical Turk to evaluate our ×4 results on the BSD100 dataset. In each trial workers were shown a nearest-neighbor upsampling of an image and results from two methods, and were asked to pick the result they preferred. All trials were randomized and five workers evaluated each image pair. Between SRCNN and $\ell_{feat}$, a majority of workers preferred $\ell_{feat}$ on 96 % of images. More details of this study can be found in the supplementary material.

Results for ×8 super-resolution are shown in Fig. 9. Again we see that our $\ell_{feat}$ model does a good job at edges and fine details compared to other models, such as the horse's legs and hooves. The $\ell_{feat}$ model does not sharpen edges indiscriminately; compared to the $\ell_{pixel}$ model, the $\ell_{feat}$ model sharpens the boundary edges of the horse and rider but the background trees remain diffuse, suggesting that the $\ell_{feat}$ model may be more aware of image semantics.

Many of the results from our $\ell_{feat}$ models have grid-like artifacts at the pixel level which harm their PSNR and SSIM compared to baseline methods. Similar artifacts are visible in Fig. 3 upon magnification, suggesting that they are a result of the feature reconstruction loss and not the architecture of the image transformation network. Figure 3 shows more pronounced distortions as images are reconstructed from higher-level features, motivating the use of the relu2_2 features used for training our $\ell_{feat}$ super-resolution models.

Since our $\ell_{pixel}$ and our $\ell_{feat}$ models share the same architecture, data, and training procedure, all differences between them are due to the difference between the $\ell_{pixel}$ and $\ell_{feat}$ losses. The $\ell_{pixel}$ loss gives fewer visual artifacts and higher PSNR values but the $\ell_{feat}$ loss does a better job at reconstructing fine details, leading to pleasing visual results.

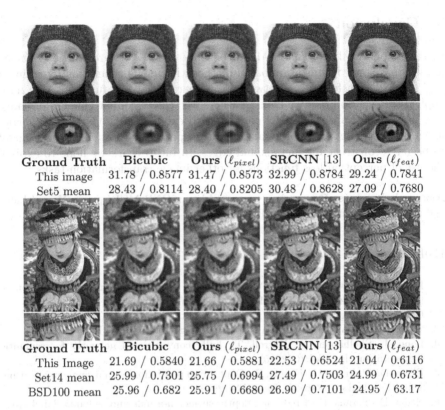

| Ground Truth | Bicubic | Ours ($\ell_{pixel}$) | SRCNN [13] | Ours ($\ell_{feat}$) |
|---|---|---|---|---|
| This image | 31.78 / 0.8577 | 31.47 / 0.8573 | 32.99 / 0.8784 | 29.24 / 0.7841 |
| Set5 mean | 28.43 / 0.8114 | 28.40 / 0.8205 | 30.48 / 0.8628 | 27.09 / 0.7680 |

| Ground Truth | Bicubic | Ours ($\ell_{pixel}$) | SRCNN [13] | Ours ($\ell_{feat}$) |
|---|---|---|---|---|
| This Image | 21.69 / 0.5840 | 21.66 / 0.5881 | 22.53 / 0.6524 | 21.04 / 0.6116 |
| Set14 mean | 25.99 / 0.7301 | 25.75 / 0.6994 | 27.49 / 0.7503 | 24.99 / 0.6731 |
| BSD100 mean | 25.96 / 0.682 | 25.91 / 0.6680 | 26.90 / 0.7101 | 24.95 / 63.17 |

**Fig. 8.** Results for ×4 super-resolution on images from Set5 (top) and Set14 (bottom). We report PSNR/SSIM for each example and the mean for each dataset. More results (including FSIM [63] and VIF [64] metrics) are shown in the supplementary material.

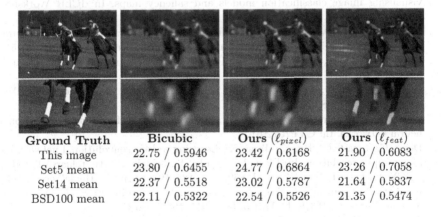

| Ground Truth | Bicubic | Ours ($\ell_{pixel}$) | Ours ($\ell_{feat}$) |
|---|---|---|---|
| This image | 22.75 / 0.5946 | 23.42 / 0.6168 | 21.90 / 0.6083 |
| Set5 mean | 23.80 / 0.6455 | 24.77 / 0.6864 | 23.26 / 0.7058 |
| Set14 mean | 22.37 / 0.5518 | 23.02 / 0.5787 | 21.64 / 0.5837 |
| BSD100 mean | 22.11 / 0.5322 | 22.54 / 0.5526 | 21.35 / 0.5474 |

**Fig. 9.** Results for ×8 super-resolution results on an image from the BSD100 dataset. We report PSNR/SSIM for the example image and the mean for each dataset. More results (including FSIM [63] and VIF [64]) are shown in the supplementary material.

# 5  Conclusion

In this paper we have combined the benefits of feed-forward image transformation tasks and optimization-based methods for image generation by training feed-forward transformation networks with perceptual loss functions. We have applied this method to style transfer where we achieve comparable performance and drastically improved speed compared to existing methods, and to single-image super-resolution where training with a perceptual loss allows the model to better reconstruct fine details and edges. In future work we hope to explore the use of perceptual loss functions for other image transformation tasks.

**Acknowledgments.** Our work is supported by an ONR MURI grant, Yahoo! Labs, and a hardware donation from NVIDIA.

# References

1. Dong, C., Loy, C.C., He, K., Tang, X.: Image super-resolution using deep convolutional networks. IEEE TPAMI **32**, 295–307 (2016)
2. Cheng, Z., Yang, Q., Sheng, B.: Deep colorization. In: ICCV (2015)
3. Zhang, R., Isola, P., Efros, A.A.: Colorful image colorization. ECCV (2016)
4. Long, J., Shelhamer, E., Darrell, T.: Fully convolutional networks for semantic segmentation. In: CVPR (2015)
5. Eigen, D., Puhrsch, C., Fergus, R.: Depth map prediction from a single image using a multi-scale deep network. In: NIPS (2014)
6. Eigen, D., Fergus, R.: Predicting depth, surface normals and semantic labels with a common multi-scale convolutional architecture. In: ICCV (2015)
7. Mahendran, A., Vedaldi, A.: Understanding deep image representations by inverting them. In: CVPR (2015)
8. Simonyan, K., Vedaldi, A., Zisserman, A.: Deep inside convolutional networks: visualising image classification models and saliency maps. In: ICLR Workshop (2014)
9. Yosinski, J., Clune, J., Nguyen, A., Fuchs, T., Lipson, H.: Understanding neural networks through deep visualization. In: ICML Deep Learning Workshop (2015)
10. Gatys, L.A., Ecker, A.S., Bethge, M.: Texture synthesis using convolutional neural networks. In: NIPS (2015)
11. Gatys, L.A., Ecker, A.S., Bethge, M.: A neural algorithm of artistic style. arXiv preprint arXiv:1508.06576 (2015)
12. Gatys, L.A., Ecker, A.S., Bethge, M.: Image style transfer using convolutional neural networks. In: CVPR (2016)
13. Dong, C., Loy, C.C., He, K., Tang, X.: Learning a deep convolutional network for image super-resolution. In: Fleet, D., Pajdla, T., Schiele, B., Tuytelaars, T. (eds.) ECCV 2014, Part IV. LNCS, vol. 8692, pp. 184–199. Springer, Heidelberg (2014)
14. Farabet, C., Couprie, C., Najman, L., LeCun, Y.: Learning hierarchical features for scene labeling. IEEE TPAMI **35**(8), 1915–1929 (2013)
15. Pinheiro, P.H., Collobert, R.: Recurrent convolutional neural networks for scene labeling. In: ICML (2014)
16. Noh, H., Hong, S., Han, B.: Learning deconvolution network for semantic segmentation. In: ICCV (2015)

17. Zheng, S., Jayasumana, S., Romera-Paredes, B., Vineet, V., Su, Z., Du, D., Huang, C., Torr, P.H.: Conditional random fields as recurrent neural networks. In: ICCV (2015)
18. Liu, F., Shen, C., Lin, G.: Deep convolutional neural fields for depth estimation from a single image. In: CVPR (2015)
19. Wang, X., Fouhey, D., Gupta, A.: Designing deep networks for surface normal estimation. In: CVPR (2015)
20. Szegedy, C., Zaremba, W., Sutskever, I., Bruna, J., Erhan, D., Goodfellow, I., Fergus, R.: Intriguing properties of neural networks. In: ICLR (2014)
21. Nguyen, A., Yosinski, J., Clune, J.: Deep neural networks are easily fooled: high confidence predictions for unrecognizable images. In: CVPR (2015)
22. d'Angelo, E., Alahi, A., Vandergheynst, P.: Beyond bits: reconstructing images from local binary descriptors. In: ICPR (2012)
23. d'Angelo, E., Jacques, L., Alahi, A., Vandergheynst, P.: From bits to images: inversion of local binary descriptors. IEEE Trans. Pattern Anal. Mach. Intell. 36(5), 874–887 (2014)
24. Vondrick, C., Khosla, A., Malisiewicz, T., Torralba, A.: Hoggles: visualizing object detection features. In: ICCV (2013)
25. Dosovitskiy, A., Brox, T.: Inverting visual representations with convolutional networks. In: CVPR (2016)
26. Ulyanov, D., Lebadev, V., Vedaldi, A., Lempitsky, V.: Texture networks: feed-forward synthesis of textures and stylized images. In: ICML (2016)
27. Li, C., Wand, M.: Precomputed real-time texture synthesis with markovian generative adversarial networks. In: ECCV (2016)
28. Yang, C.-Y., Ma, C., Yang, M.-H.: Single-image super-resolution: a benchmark. In: Fleet, D., Pajdla, T., Schiele, B., Tuytelaars, T. (eds.) ECCV 2014, Part IV. LNCS, vol. 8692, pp. 372–386. Springer, Heidelberg (2014)
29. Irani, M., Peleg, S.: Improving resolution by image registration. CVGIP: Graph. Models Image Process. 53(3), 231–239 (1991)
30. Freedman, G., Fattal, R.: Image and video upscaling from local self-examples. ACM Trans. Graph. (TOG) 30(2), 12 (2011)
31. Sun, J., Sun, J., Xu, Z., Shum, H.Y.: Image super-resolution using gradient profile prior. In: CVPR (2008)
32. Shan, Q., Li, Z., Jia, J., Tang, C.K.: Fast image/video upsampling. ACM Trans. Graph. (TOG) 27, 153 (2008). ACM
33. Kim, K.I., Kwon, Y.: Single-image super-resolution using sparse regression and natural image prior. IEEE TPAMI 32(6), 1127–1133 (2010)
34. Xiong, Z., Sun, X., Wu, F.: Robust web image/video super-resolution. IEEE Trans. Image Process. 19(8), 2017–2028 (2010)
35. Freeman, W.T., Jones, T.R., Pasztor, E.C.: Example-based super-resolution. IEEE Comput. Graph. Appl. 22(2), 56–65 (2002)
36. Chang, H., Yeung, D.Y., Xiong, Y.: Super-resolution through neighbor embedding. In: CVPR (2004)
37. Glasner, D., Bagon, S., Irani, M.: Super-resolution from a single image. In: ICCV (2009)
38. Yang, J., Lin, Z., Cohen, S.: Fast image super-resolution based on in-place example regression. In: CVPR (2013)
39. Sun, J., Zheng, N.N., Tao, H., Shum, H.Y.: Image hallucination with primal sketch priors. In: CVPR (2003)
40. Ni, K.S., Nguyen, T.Q.: Image superresolution using support vector regression. IEEE Trans. Image Process. 16(6), 1596–1610 (2007)

41. He, L., Qi, H., Zaretzki, R.: Beta process joint dictionary learning for coupled feature spaces with application to single image super-resolution. In: CVPR (2013)
42. Yang, J., Wright, J., Huang, T., Ma, Y.: Image super-resolution as sparse representation of raw image patches. In: CVPR (2008)
43. Yang, J., Wright, J., Huang, T.S., Ma, Y.: Image super-resolution via sparse representation. IEEE Trans. Image Process. **19**(11), 2861–2873 (2010)
44. Timofte, R., De Smet, V., Van Gool, L.: A+: adjusted anchored neighborhood regression for fast super-resolution. In: Cremers, D., Reid, I., Saito, H., Yang, M.-H. (eds.) ACCV 2014. LNCS, vol. 9006, pp. 111–126. Springer, Heidelberg (2015)
45. Schulter, S., Leistner, C., Bischof, H.: Fast and accurate image upscaling with super-resolution forests. In: CVPR (2015)
46. Huang, J.B., Singh, A., Ahuja, N.: Single image super-resolution from transformed self-exemplars. In: CVPR (2015)
47. Radford, A., Metz, L., Chintala, S.: Unsupervised representation learning with deep convolutional generative adversarial networks. In: ICLR (2016)
48. He, K., Zhang, X., Ren, S., Sun, J.: Deep residual learning for image recognition. In: CVPR (2016)
49. Gross, S., Wilber, M.: Training and investigating residual nets (2016). http://torch.ch/blog/2016/02/04/resnets.html
50. Ioffe, S., Szegedy, C.: Batch normalization: accelerating deep network training by reducing internal covariate shift. In: ICML (2015)
51. Simonyan, K., Zisserman, A.: Very deep convolutional networks for large-scale image recognition. In: ICLR (2015)
52. Russakovsky, O., Deng, J., Su, H., Krause, J., Satheesh, S., Ma, S., Huang, Z., Karpathy, A., Khosla, A., Bernstein, M., Berg, A.C., Fei-Fei, L.: ImageNet large scale visual recognition challenge. Int. J. Comput. Vis. (IJCV) **115**(3), 211–252 (2015)
53. Aly, H.A., Dubois, E.: Image up-sampling using total-variation regularization with a new observation model. IEEE Trans. Image Process. **14**(10), 1647–1659 (2005)
54. Zhang, H., Yang, J., Zhang, Y., Huang, T.S.: Non-local kernel regression for image and video restoration. In: Maragos, P., Paragios, N., Daniilidis, K. (eds.) ECCV 2010, Part III. LNCS, vol. 6313, pp. 566–579. Springer, Heidelberg (2010)
55. Lin, T.-Y., Maire, M., Belongie, S., Hays, J., Perona, P., Ramanan, D., Dollár, P., Zitnick, C.L.: Microsoft COCO: common objects in context. In: Fleet, D., Pajdla, T., Schiele, B., Tuytelaars, T. (eds.) ECCV 2014, Part V. LNCS, vol. 8693, pp. 740–755. Springer, Heidelberg (2014)
56. Kingma, D., Ba, J.: Adam: a method for stochastic optimization. In: ICLR (2015)
57. Collobert, R., Kavukcuoglu, K., Farabet, C.: Torch7: a Matlab-like environment for machine learning. In: NIPS BigLearn Workshop (2011)
58. Chetlur, S., Woolley, C., Vandermersch, P., Cohen, J., Tran, J., Catanzaro, B., Shelhamer, E.: cuDNN: efficient primitives for deep learning. arXiv preprint arXiv:1410.0759 (2014)
59. Wang, Z., Bovik, A.C., Sheikh, H.R., Simoncelli, E.P.: Image quality assessment: from error visibility to structural similarity. IEEE Trans. Image Process. **13**(4), 600–612 (2004)
60. Hanhart, P., Korshunov, P., Ebrahimi, T.: Benchmarking of quality metrics on ultra-high definition video sequences. In: 2013 18th International Conference on Digital Signal Processing (DSP), pp. 1–8. IEEE (2013)
61. Huynh-Thu, Q., Ghanbari, M.: Scope of validity of PSNR in image/video quality assessment. Electron. Lett. **44**(13), 800–801 (2008)

62. Kundu, D., Evans, B.L.: Full-reference visual quality assessment for synthetic images: a subjective study. In: Proceedings of the IEEE International Conference on Image Processing (2015)

63. Zhang, L., Zhang, L., Mou, X., Zhang, D.: Fsim: a feature similarity index for image quality assessment. IEEE Trans. Image Process. **20**(8), 2378–2386 (2011)

64. Sheikh, H.R., Bovik, A.C.: Image information and visual quality. IEEE Trans. Image Process. **15**(2), 430–444 (2006)

65. Bevilacqua, M., Roumy, A., Guillemot, C., Alberi-Morel, M.L.: Low-complexity single-image super-resolution based on nonnegative neighbor embedding (2012)

66. Zeyde, R., Elad, M., Protter, M.: On single image scale-up using sparse-representations. In: Boissonnat, J.-D., Chenin, P., Cohen, A., Gout, C., Lyche, T., Mazure, M.-L., Schumaker, L. (eds.) Curves and Surfaces 2011. LNCS, vol. 6920, pp. 711–730. Springer, Heidelberg (2012). Revised Selected Papers

...

# Optimization

# An Efficient Fusion Move Algorithm
# for the Minimum Cost Lifted Multicut Problem

Thorsten Beier[1]([✉]), Björn Andres[2], Ullrich Köthe[1], and Fred A. Hamprecht[1]

[1] HCI/IWR, University of Heidelberg, Heidelberg, Germany
{thorsten.beier,ullrich.koethe,fred.hamprecht}@iwr.uni-heidelberg.de
[2] Computer Vision and Multimodal Computing,
Max Planck Institute for Informatics, Saarbrücken, Germany
andres@mpi-inf.mpg.de

**Abstract.** Many computer vision problems can be cast as an optimization problem whose feasible solutions are decompositions of a graph. The minimum cost lifted multicut problem is such an optimization problem. Its objective function can penalize or reward all decompositions for which any given pair of nodes are in distinct components. While this property has many potential applications, such applications are hampered by the fact that the problem is NP-hard. We propose a fusion move algorithm for computing feasible solutions, better and more efficiently than existing algorithms. We demonstrate this and applications to image segmentation, obtaining a new state of the art for a problem in biological image analysis.

## 1 Introduction and Related Work

In 2011, Andres et al. [1], Bagon and Galun [2], Kim et al. [3,4] and Yarkony et al. [5] independently proposed formulating the image segmentation problem [6] as a minimum cost multicut problem [7,8] on a suitable graph. Given, for every pair of neighboring nodes, a cost or reward (negative cost) to be paid if these nodes are assigned to distinct components, the minimum cost multicut problem consists in finding a decomposition of the graph with minimal sum of costs. In 2015, Keuper et al. [9], using a construction from [10], proposed the minimum cost *lifted* multicut problem, a generalization with an identical feasible set whose objective function can assign a cost or reward to *every* pair of nodes, not just neighboring ones. These non-local interactions are represented in the graph by "lifted" edges which are subjected to slightly different constraints than the regular edges. The introduction of lifted edges is appealing for image segmentation, because non-local interactions can now be added without losing two key advantages of the multicut: (i) Every feasible solution of the optimization problem corresponds to a decomposition of the graph, i.e. to a consistent segmentation. (ii) No assumptions on the number or size of segments are made, making the method applicable in the typical and important scenario where such prior knowledge is not available. Since standard and lifted multicut are both NP-hard integer linear programming problems [7,8] – even for planar graphs [11,12]

© Springer International Publishing AG 2016
B. Leibe et al. (Eds.): ECCV 2016, Part II, LNCS 9906, pp. 715–730, 2016.
DOI: 10.1007/978-3-319-46475-6_44

– this paper proposes a new family of efficient heuristics inspired by [13,14] and on the basis of *fusion moves* [14,15].

So far, the computer vision community has studied three classes of algorithms addressing optimization problems of this type: (i) branch-and-cut algorithms [1,16,17] that converge to an optimal integer solution but do not admit polynomial time complexity bounds and are too slow for lifted multicuts; (ii) linear programming relaxations with subsequent rounding to an integer solution [17–19] which can yield a log-factor approximation [8] in polynomial time; (iii) constrained search algorithms [9,20,21] that find approximate integer solutions directly in polynomial time. Although no theoretical guarantees are known for the latter approximations, they tend to be better than relaxation followed by rounding.

Constrained search algorithms for the lifted multicut problem were introduced in [9]. They generalize multicut algorithms of the Kernighan/Lin [22] type from [20] and greedy additive edge contraction from [21]. We show in this paper that fusion move algorithms for the multicut as proposed in [23] can be generalized as well and actually perform better in terms of approximation quality and speed.

## 1.1 Contribution

This work makes four contributions:

1. We generalize the fusion move algorithm [23] into a new constrained search algorithm for the minimum cost lifted multicut problem defined in [9].
2. We show that our algorithm outperforms the constrained search algorithms of [9] on the same problem instances in approximation quality and speed.
3. We introduce novel non-local potentials for the segmentation problem and incorporate them into a lifted multicut formulation of the objective.
4. We apply the proposed algorithm to the biological image segmentation benchmark [24,25], achieving the highest accuracy known at the time of writing.

## 2    Optimization Problem

### 2.1    Minimum Cost Multicut Problem

The minimum cost multicut problem is an optimization problem whose feasible solutions can be identified with the decompositions of a graph. Below, we recall only the necessary basic definitions and otherwise refer to [26,27] for details.

A *decomposition* of a graph is a partition of the node set into connected subsets. More rigorously, a decomposition of a graph $G = (V, E)$ is a partition $\Pi$ of the node set $V$ such that, for every $U \in \Pi$, the subgraph of $G$ induced by $U$ is connected. Every decomposition of a graph can be identified with the set of edges that straddle distinct components. Such subsets of edges are called the multicuts of the graph.

A subset $M \subseteq E$ of edges is a *multicut* of $G$ iff there exists a decomposition $\Pi$ of $G$ such that $M$ is the set of edges straddling distinct components. Moreover, $M$ is a multicut of $G$ iff no cycle in the graph intersects with $M$ precisely once. Rigorously, for every cycle $Y \subseteq E$ of $G$: $|M \cap Y| \neq 1$. This characterization is intuitive: If one transitions from one component to another along the cycle, one needs to transition back before returning to the node from which one has started. It is used to state the minimum cost multicut problem:

For every graph $G = (V, E)$ and every $c : E \to \mathbb{R}$, the instance of the *minimum cost multicut problem* w.r.t. $G$ and $c$ is the optimization problem

$$\min_{x \in \{0,1\}^E} \sum_{e \in E} c_e x_e \tag{1}$$

$$\text{subject to} \quad \forall Y \in \text{cycles}(G) \; \forall e \in Y : \; x_e \leq \sum_{e' \in Y \setminus \{e\}} x_{e'}. \tag{2}$$

## 2.2  Minimum Cost Lifted Multicut Problem

The minimum cost multicut problem has a limitation: A multicut makes explicit only for *neighboring* nodes whether these nodes are in distinct components of the decomposition induced by the multicut. It does not make this explicit for *non-neighboring* nodes. Thus, the cost function can introduce only for pairs of neighboring nodes a cost or reward to be paid by feasibles solutions that assign these nodes to distinct components. It cannot introduce such a cost for pairs of non-neighboring nodes. As illustrated in Fig. 1, simply considering a graph with more edges does not overcome this limitation in general.

This limitation led Andres [10] to define the minimum cost lifted multicut problem w.r.t. one graph $G = (V, E)$ whose decompositions are identified with feasible solutions, and a possibly larger graph $G' = (V, E')$ with $E \subseteq E'$ for

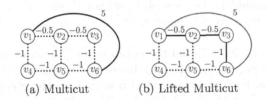

(a) Multicut           (b) Lifted Multicut

**Fig. 1.** Depicted above in (a) is an instance of the minimum cost multicut problem (1)–(2). The solution is the multicut consisting of those edges that are depicted as dotted lines. I.e. all edges except $v_1 v_6$ are cut. Depicted above in (b) is an instance of the minimum cost lifted multicut problem (3)–(6) with one edge in $E' \setminus E$ depicted in green. Here as well, the solution is the lifted multicut consisting of those edges depicted as dotted lines. Note that, unlike in (a), the lifted edge with cost 5 causes the nodes $v_1$ and $v_6$ to be connected in $G$ by a path of edges labeled 0. Thus, positive costs assigned to lifted edges are called an *attraction*.

whose every edge $vw \in E'$ it is made explicit whether the nodes $v$ and $w$ are in distinct components. By assigning a cost $c_{vw} \in \mathbb{R}$ to this edge, one can penalize or reward precisely those decompositions of $G$ (!) for which the nodes $v$ and $w$ are in distinct components. This property is used for image segmentation in [9]. We recall the minimum cost lifted multicut problem from [10, Definition 10].

For any graphs $G = (V, E)$ and $G' = (V, E')$ with $E \subseteq E'$ and every $c : E' \to \mathbb{R}$, the instance of the *minimum cost lifted multicut problem* w.r.t. $G$, $G'$ and $c$ is the optimization problem

$$\min_{x \in \{0,1\}^{E'}} \sum_{e \in E'} c_e x_e \tag{3}$$

$$\text{subject to} \quad \forall Y \in \text{cycles}(G) \ \forall e \in Y : \ x_e \le \sum_{e' \in Y \setminus \{e\}} x_{e'} \tag{4}$$

$$\forall vw \in E' \setminus E \ \forall P \in vw\text{-paths}(G) : \ x_{vw} \le \sum_{e \in P} x_e \tag{5}$$

$$\forall vw \in E' \setminus E \ \forall C \in vw\text{-cuts}(G) : \ 1 - x_{vw} \le \sum_{e \in C} (1 - x_e). \tag{6}$$

The cycle constraints (4) are identical to those in (2). Additional constraints (5) and (6) ensure, for every edge $vw \in E' \setminus E$ that $x_{vw} = 0$ if (5) and only if (6) $v$ and $w$ are connected in $G$ by a path of edges labeled 0, i.e., iff $v$ and $w$ are in the same component of $G$ defined by the multicut $M := \{e \in E | x_e = 1\}$ of $G$. Or in other words, iff a lifted edge $(vw \in E' \setminus E)$ is not cut, there must be a path of non-cut edges in the original graph connecting $v$ and $w$.

## 3    Optimization Algorithm

### 3.1    Constrained Search Algorithms

Constrained search is a class of heuristic optimization algorithms. In the computer vision community, they are also commonly referred to as move making algorithms. Examples are $\alpha$-expansion [28], $\alpha\beta$-swap [28], lazy flipping [29] and fusion [14].

Given a map $f : X \to \mathbb{R}$ and the optimization problem $\min\{f(x) \,|\, x \in X\}$, the idea of constraint search is this: Instead of optimizing $f$ over the entire feasible set $X$, which might be hard, start from an initial feasible solution $x_0 \in X$, optimize $f$ over a neighborhood $N(x_0) \subseteq X$ to obtain a new feasible solution $x_1$. Iff $f(x_1) < f(x_0)$, re-iterate, starting from $x_1$. Note that this algorithm does not require that $x_1$ be optimal.

Typically, the neighborhood function $N : X \to 2^X$ is chosen such that, for every $x \in X$, we have $x \in N(x)$. If $N$ is chosen such that, for every $x \in X$, the problem $\min\{f(x') \,|\, x' \in N(x)\}$ is of polynomial time complexity, then every iteration of the algorithm is efficient. If the optimization over the neighborhood is not known to be of polynomial complexity, it can still be less complex or smaller than the original problem and can thus be tractable in practice.

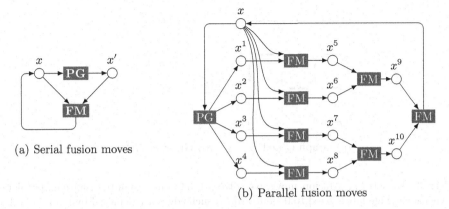

(a) Serial fusion moves

(b) Parallel fusion moves

**Fig. 2.** In a fusion move algorithm, proposal generation (PG) and fusion moves (FM) can be combined in different ways. We implement and study serial fusion moves (a) and parallel fusion moves (b).

### 3.2 Fusion Move Algorithms

Fusion move algorithms [14] are a class of constrained search algorithms. They consist of two procedures. First is *proposal generation* that computes, for every feasible solution $x \in X$ given as input, another feasible solution $\text{PG}(x) \in X$ as output, possibly in a randomized fashion. Second is *fusion*, an optimization algorithm that computes a feasible solution of an optimization problem $\min \{f(x) \mid x \in N(x)\}$ for a neighborhood $N(x)$ defined w.r.t. $x$ and $\text{PG}(x)$ such that $x \in N(x)$ and $\text{PG}(x) \in N(x)$, to obtain a feasible solution $x'$ with $f(x') \leq f(x)$ and $f(x') \leq f(\text{PG}(x))$. In a fusion move algorithm, proposal generation and fusion can be combined in different ways, as depicted in Fig. 2.

### 3.3 Fusion Moves for the Lifted Multicut Problem

Lempitsky introduced fusion moves for unconstrained quadratic programming in [14]. Beier et al. define a fusion move algorithm for the minimum cost multicut problem in [23]. Here, we generalize the idea of Beier et al. to the minimum cost lifted multicut problem. The fusion moves are defined in this section. Proposal generators are defined in the next section.

Given any feasible solutions $x^1$ and $x^2$ of the minimum cost lifted multicut problem (3)–(6), a constrained minimum cost lifted multicut problem in the variables $x \in \{0,1\}^{E'}$ is defined by (3)–(6) and the additional constraints

$$\forall e \in E: \quad x_e \leq x_e^1 + x_e^2. \tag{7}$$

That is, all edges which are labeled 0 (join) in the feasible solution $x^1$ *and* the feasible solution $x^2$ are constrained to be labeled 0 in the problem (3)–(7). By construction, $x^1$ and $x^2$ are feasible solutions of the constrained problem (3)–(7).

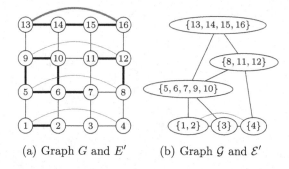

(a) Graph $G$ and $E'$          (b) Graph $\mathcal{G}$ and $\mathcal{E}'$

**Fig. 3.** To perform a fusion move, we solve a minimum cost lifted multicut problem with some edge labels fixed to 0 (join). In (a) such edges are depicted by bold lines. To solve this constrained problem, we reduce it to an unconstrained minimum cost lifted problem w.r.t. a contracted graph, depicted for this example in (b).

Next, we reduce the *constrained* minimum cost lifted multicut problem (3)–(7) to an *unconstrained* minimum cost lifted multicut problem w.r.t. a smaller graph (Lemma 1). The latter problem can be solved by existing algorithms. In practice, we solve it approximatively by means of the Kernighan-Lin-type algorithm published by Keuper et al. [9]. The construction of the smaller graph is depicted in Fig. 3 and is described below.

Let $\mathcal{G} = (\mathcal{V}, \mathcal{E})$ be the graph obtained from the graph $G$ by contracting the edges $\{e \in E \mid x_e^1 = 0 \wedge x_e^2 = 0\}^1$. Moreover, let $\mathcal{E}' \subseteq \binom{\mathcal{V}}{2}$ such that $V'W' \in \mathcal{E}'$ iff there exist $v \in V'$ and $w \in W'$ such that $vw \in E'$. Finally, let $C : \mathcal{E}' \to \mathbb{R}$ such that, for every $V'W' \in \mathcal{E}'$:

$$C_{V'W'} = \sum_{\{vw \in E' \mid v \in V' \wedge w \in W'\}} c_{vw} \qquad (8)$$

**Lemma 1.** *For every feasible solution $X : \mathcal{E}' \to \{0,1\}$ of the instance of the minimum cost lifted multicut problem w.r.t. $\mathcal{G}$, $\mathcal{G}' := (\mathcal{V}, \mathcal{E}')$ and $C$, the $x : E' \to \{0,1\}$ such that*

$$\forall vw \in E' : \quad x_e = \begin{cases} X_{V'W'} & \text{if } \exists V'W' \in \mathcal{E}' : v \in V' \wedge w \in W' \\ 0 & \text{otherwise} \end{cases} \qquad (9)$$

*is well-defined and a feasible solution of the constrained minimum cost lifted multicut problem (3)–(7). Moreover,*

$$\sum_{vw \in E'} c_{vw} x_{vw} = \sum_{V'W' \in \mathcal{E}'} C_{V'W'} X_{V'W'}. \qquad (10)$$

---

[1] I.e., $\mathcal{V}$ is a decomposition of $G$ with every $V' \in \mathcal{V}$ a maximal subset $V' \subseteq V$ of nodes of $G$ connected by edges $e \in E$ for which $x_e^1 = 0$ and $x_e^2 = 0$. In addition, for every $V'W' \in \binom{\mathcal{V}}{2}$, we have $V'W' \in \mathcal{E}$ iff there exist $v \in V'$ and $w \in W'$ such that $vw \in E$.

*Proof.* If there exist $V'W' \in \mathcal{E}'$ such that $v \in V'$ and $w \in W'$, then $V'$ and $W'$ are unique (because $\mathcal{V}$ is a partition of $V$). Thus, $x$ is well-defined.

The feasible solution $X$ defines a decomposition of $\mathcal{G}$ (because $\mathcal{M} := \{V'W' \in \mathcal{E} \mid X_{V'W'} = 1\}$ is a multicut of $\mathcal{G}$). Every decomposition of $\mathcal{G}$ induces a decomposition of $G$ (as the node set $\mathcal{V}$ of $\mathcal{G}$ is itself a decomposition of $G$). The multicut $M := \{vw \in E \mid x_{vw} = 1\}$ of this decomposition of $G$ is defined by the multicut $\mathcal{M}$ of $\mathcal{G}$ by (9) (by definition of $\mathcal{G}$). Thus, $x$ satisfies (4).

Moreover, for every $vw \in E' \setminus E$, we have $x_{vw} = 0$ iff $v$ is connected to $w$ by a path $P$ in $G$ with $x_P = 0$ (by (9) and definition of $\mathcal{G}$ and $\mathcal{E}'$). Thus, $x$ satisfies (5) and (6). Finally, (10) holds by (8) and (9). □

### 3.4 Proposal Generation for the Lifted Multicut Problem

As pointed out in [30], a proposal generator is designed with four objectives in mind. Firstly, proposed feasible solutions should be *diverse*. Otherwise, the fusion move algorithms can get trapped in local minima. Secondly, some proposed feasible solutions should be *good*. Otherwise, the fusion move algorithms cannot get close to the optimum. In the context of the minimum cost lifted multicut problem, a feasible solution is good if the recall of edges that are cut in an optimal solution is close to 1. Thirdly, the proposed feasible solutions should be *sparse*. In the context of the minimum cost lifted multicut problem, a feasible solutions is sparse if the precision of edges that are cut in an optimal solution is close to 1. Fourthly, the proposed feasible solutions should be *cheap*, i.e., proposals should be computable efficiently and in parallel. We study three proposal generators that emphasize different design objectives.

**Randomly Perturbed Proposals.** In order to obtain a proposal of high quality efficiently, we apply greedy additive edge contraction (GAEC) [9]. The key idea of this algorithm is to greedily contract edges with maximum cost until this maximum cost is equal to or smaller than zero. In order to get diverse solutions, we follow [23] and add normally distributed noise of zero mean to edge costs. In order to control the sparsity of the proposal, we replace the stopping criterion of GAEC and continue until a maximum allowed number of components is reached.

**Subgraph Proposals.** In order to obtain an objective-aware proposal for a large problem instance, we solve the minimum cost lifted multicut problem for a small subgraph. Technically, the procedure works as follows: We choose a center node $v \in V$ and the subgraph induced by the set $U$ of all nodes within a fixed path-length distance from $v$. For $E_0 := \{vw \in E \mid v \notin U \wedge w \notin U\}$ and $E_1 := \{vw \in E \mid v \in U \wedge w \notin U\}$, we solve the instance of the minimum cost lifted multicut problem w.r.t. the graph $G$ and the cost function $c$, with the additional constraints

$$\forall e \in E_0 : \quad x_e = 0 \tag{11}$$

$$\forall e \in E_1 : \quad x_e = 1. \tag{12}$$

**Watershed Proposals.** In order to obtain diverse proposals cheaply, we follow [23] in using the weighted watershed algorithm [31,32] with random seeds. From the set $\{vw \in E' \setminus E \,|\, c_{vw} < 0\}$ of lifted edges with negative cost, we draw a fixed number without replacement and assign different seeds to $v$ and $w$. Thus, a random subset of lifted edges with negative cost is cut.

## 4    Experiments

We now describe experiments in which we compare the fusion move algorithm (Algorithm 1) for the minimum cost lifted multicut problem with the Kernighan/Lin-type algorithm (KLj) and Greedy Additive Edge Contraction (GAEC) of [9] for the same problem.

In the tables below, FM-R, FM-SG and FM-WS stand for the fusion move algorithm with the randomized, subgraph and watershed proposal generators, respectively. Individual fusion problems, i.e., those problems denoted by boxes labeled "FM" in Fig. 2, are solved by KLj initialized with the output of GAEC.

In each experiment, the outer loop of fusion is terminated when no improvement is achieved for 5 consecutive iterations. Each experiment is conducted with 1, 2, 4 and 8 threads, respectively, to examine concurrency. All experiments are conducted on an Intel Core i7-4700MQ CPU operating at 2.40 GHz × 8, and equipped with 32 GB of RAM.

### 4.1    ISBI 2012 Challenge

The ISBI 2012 Challenge [24,25] offers a set of segmentation tasks where images of the Drosophila larva ventral nerve cord acquired by a serial section

---

**Data:** $\boldsymbol{G}$ : Graph $G = (V, E)$; $\boldsymbol{G'}$ : Graph $G' = (V, E')$
   $\boldsymbol{C}$ : edge weights; $\boldsymbol{x_{start}}$ : starting point solution; $\boldsymbol{GEN}$ : proposal generator
**Result:** $\boldsymbol{y}$ : improved solution

$x_{best} \leftarrow x_{start}$;
**for** $<$ *nIterations* $>$ **do**
 $P \leftarrow \emptyset$;
 **for** #*Proposals in parallel* **do**
  $x^P \leftarrow \mathrm{GEN}(x_{best})$       ▷ generate proposal;
  $x^P \leftarrow \arg\min_{x \in \{0,1\}} \sum_{e \in E'} c_e x_e$  s.t. (3)–(7), $\forall e \in E: \; x_e \leq x_e^P + x_e^{best}$.;
  $P \leftarrow P \cup \{x^P\}$;
 **end**
 **while** $|P| > 1$ **do**
           ▷ hierarchically fuse proposals ;
  $\hat{P} \leftarrow \emptyset$;
  **for** *each* $i$ *in* $|P|/2$ *in parallel* **do**
   $x^1 \leftarrow P_{2i}$;
   $x^2 \leftarrow P_{2i+1}$;
   $x^P \leftarrow \arg\min_{x \in \{0,1\}} \sum_{e \in E'} c_e x_e$  s.t. (3)–(7), $\forall e \in E: \; x_e \leq x_e^1 + x_e^2$.;
   $\hat{P} \leftarrow \hat{P} \cup \{x^P\}$;
  **end**
  $P \leftarrow \hat{P}$;
 **end**
 $x_{best} \leftarrow P_1$          ▷ update current best
**end**
**return** $x_{best}$;

**Algorithm 1.** Lifted MC - Parallel Fusion Moves (LMC-PFM)

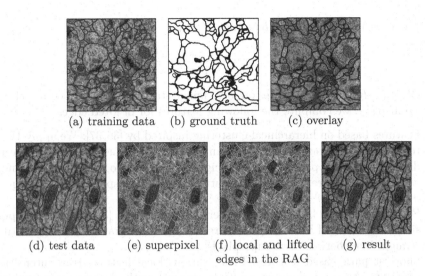

(a) training data    (b) ground truth    (c) overlay

(d) test data    (e) superpixel    (f) local and lifted    (g) result
edges in the RAG

**Fig. 4.** The ISBI 2012 Challenge [24,25] offers a set of segmentation tasks where neurons are to be delineated correctly in two-dimensional electron microscopy images, cf. (a)–(c). We start from the region adjacency graph of a superpixel segmentation (e) and train two classifiers to estimate the probability of adjacent and, respectively, non-adjacent superpixel pairs to belong to the same neuron. I.e., for edges like A-B and C-D in (f) or lifted edges E-F and G-H in (f). Solving, by fusion moves, a minimum cost multicut problem with costs defined in (13), our results on independent test images (with undisclosed ground truth) achieve the highest accuracy known at the time of writing. See (g) and Table 1.

transmission electron microscope are to be decomposed into distinct neurons, as depicted in Fig. 4c. The data set contains of 30 training images and 30 test images. Human annotations (Fig. 4b) are provided for each training image.

We propose a processing pipeline. Describing this pipeline in every technical detail is beyond the scope of this work. For the sake of reproducibility, the source code is available[2]. Overall, the pipeline consists of the following steps:

1. Start from the region adjacency graph (RAG) of an over-segmentation generated by seeded region growing [33], as shown in Fig. 4e.
2. Add lifted edges $F$ for all pairs of superpixels within a path-length distance of $r_{nl} = 4$. The difference between lifted and non-lifted edges can be seen in Fig. 4f.
3. Train two random forest classifiers: A first classifier $RF_l$ learns to predict if a pair of adjacent superpixels should be in the same neuron or not. A second classifier $RF_{nl}$ predicts the same for non-adjacent pairs of superpixels.
4. Solve an instance of the minimum cost lifted multicut problem (3)–(6) with superpixels as nodes, non-lifted and lifted edges and costs defined w.r.t. the

---

[2] https://github.com/DerThorsten/lifted_fusion_moves_eccv_2016.

probabilities estimated by $RF_l$ and $RF_{nl}$ as

$$c_{vw} := \log \frac{p(x_{vw} = 0)}{p(x_{vw} = 1)}. \tag{13}$$

To train $RF_l$ we use features on local image statistics as described in [34,35]. To train $RF_{nl}$, we compute the following features for of lifted edges:

1. Features based on hierarchical clustering inspired by [36,37]: We apply UCM to generate the complete dendrogram and use the thus defined ultrametric distance between pairs of nodes (height in the dendrogram at the moment when the nodes are merged) as a feature for the corresponding lifted edge, if it exists.
2. Features inspired by maximum intervening contours [38–40]: We compute simple statistics of local image features (e.g. average gradient) along multiple straight lines between two superpixels.
3. Shortest path based features: Using various local features (raw intensities, gradients etc.), we compute multiple shortest paths between non-adjacent superpixels and measure statistics along these paths.
4. Candidate segmentation features: We compute multiple candidate segmentations using the minimum multicut objective (with varying parameter and without lifted edges), and each edge is assigned the proportion of the segmentation where it got cut.

For all features above we use the raw data itself as input, but also a pixel wise probability map learned with a CNN [41].

A quantitative evaluation is shown in Table 1. It can be seen from this table that segmentations of the images defined by feasibles solutions of the minimum cost lifted multicut problem define a new state of the art on this highly competitive segmentation challenge. FM-R, FM-SG and KLj yield the same objective.

**Table 1.** Feasible solutions of the minimum cost lifted multicut problem define a new state of the art on the ISBI 2012 Challenge [24,25]. The performance measures VRand and VInfo are defined in [25]. A value of 1 indicates a perfect segmentation; values close to zero indicate poor segmentations. Using 8 threads, the proposed methods (FM-R, FM-SG) outperform KLj by a factor of 4. Leader board: http://brainiac2.mit.edu/isbi_challenge/leaders-board-new

| Algorithm | Objective | Time to convergence [s] (1/2/4/8 threads) | VRand | VInfo |
|---|---|---|---|---|
| | | | (Higher is better) | |
| **FM-SG** | −13560.18 | 0.62/0.37/0.28/0.21 | 0.9804 | 0.9884 |
| **FM-R** | −13560.18 | 0.77/0.42 / 0.32/0.28 | 0.9804 | 0.9884 |
| KLj | −13560.18 | 0.89 | 0.9803 | 0.9884 |
| Leader Board 2 | - | - | 0.9796 | 0.9870 |
| Leader Board 3 | - | - | 0.9768 | 0.9886 |
| Humans | - | - | 0.9978 | 0.9990 |

Even with only a single thread, FM-R and FM-SG are slightly faster than KLj. With 8 threads, the proposed methods outperform KLj by a factor of 4.

### 4.2 Image Decomposition

Keuper et al. [9] pose the image decomposition problem [6] as a minimum cost lifted multicut problem. Instances of this problem are defined w.r.t. pixel grid graphs and lifted edges connecting each pixel to the (about 300) pixels within a path-length distance of 10. Costs of non-lifted edges are derived from structured edge detection according to [42]. Costs of lifted edges are defined by probabilistic geodesic lifting [9].

These large instances of the minimum cost multicut problem pose a challenge to optimization algorithms and are thus suitable for benchmarking. Here, we compare the fusion move algorithm with watershed proposal generator (FM-WS) with GAEC and KLj initialized with the output of GAEC.

Results are shown in Table 2. It can be seen from these results that FM-WS outperforms the current state of the art (KLj) in terms of runtime and objective value. Moreover, FM-WS is about twice as fast with one thread and about six times as fast with 8 threads. The gap between FM-WS and KLj is comparatively larger than that between of KLj and GAEC. Therefore, we consider FM-WS a significant improvement over the state of the art.

**Table 2.** The proposed algorithm FM-WS outperforms KLj and GAEC on the large and hard instances of the minimum cost lifted multicut problem of [9].

| Algorithm | Objective | Time to convergence [s] (1,2,4,8 threads) |
|-----------|-----------|--------------------------------------------|
| **FM-WS** | −62748200 | 61/32/25/22 |
| GAEC | −62744700 | 10/n.a |
| KLj | −62745500 | 121/n.a |

### 4.3 Averaging Multiple Segmentations

Fusing multiple segmentations into a single one is not only important as an image analysis sub-task, but can also be used to combine multiple *manually* derived ground truth solutions into a "master" ground truth image. Multiple user-provided solutions are, for example, available for the BSDS-500 data set [6].

Recently, [43] proposed to solve this problem with an EM-algorithm based on the multicut objective. Their algorithm is defined on a complete graph derived from the region adjacency graph of an initial superpixel segmentation. In contrast to our approach, they use the plain multicut objective where all edges of the complete graph are considered local, and there are no lifted edges. Before constructioning the complete graph, every proposed segmentation $x^l$ from the given set $L$ is projected on the superpixel RAG, and all edges which are not cut in any proposal are contracted, resulting in a dramatic reduction of the graph's size. The edge costs of the remaining edges measure how often this edge is cut in $L$. Furthermore, a weight $p_l$ measuring the estimated reliability of each segmentation relative to the others is assigned to each member of $L$. The multicut objective is then optimized with $p_l$ kept fixed, and the $p_l$ are updated according to the proportion of edges in $x^l$ that agree with the current master segmentation. This is repeated in an EM manner until convergence.

We modify this approach as follows: We optimize directly on the *pixel-level*, i.e. on a 4-connected grid graph instead of a superpixel RAG, to eliminate superpixel computation as an additional source of error. Moreover, we replace the multicut objective with a *lifted multicut* objective containing only a sparse set of lifted edges up to a graph distance of 5. We do not contract any edges in pre-processing. Edge costs are defined as in [43] by

$$c_{vw} := \log \sum_{l \in |L|} (1 - x^l_{vw})p_l - \log \sum_{l \in |L|} x^l_{vw} p_l \tag{14}$$

As in [43], we use an EM-type algorithm to update $p_l$ according to the number of edges in $x^l$ that agree with the current master segmentation $\hat{x}$:

$$p_l = \frac{1}{|EF|} \sum_{x_{vw} \in EV} 1 - |x^l_{vw} - \hat{x}_{vw}| \tag{15}$$

In every iteration of EM, we solve an instance of the minimum cost lifted multicut problem using FM-SG and, for comparison, KLj. Both are initialized with the output of GAEC. We only use FM-SG results to update the $p_l$ since they were always better than the KL results. In addition to the proposals generated by the subgraph method, all $x^l$ are included into the proposal set, leading to a significant speed-up.

Results are shown in Table 3 and Fig. 5. It can be seen from Table 3 that FM-SG outperforms KLj in terms of objective value and run-time. Even with a single thread, FM-SG is twice as fast as KL. Using 8 threads, the FM-SG is six times as fast.

**Table 3.** To average multiple segmentations, we solve instances of a minimum cost lifted multicut problem as part of the EM algorithm proposed in [43]. FM-SG is an efficient algorithm to solve these instances.

| Algorithm | Objective | Time to convergence [s] (1/2/4/8 Threads) |
|---|---|---|
| **FM-SG** | **−2.29e+07** | 14.8/8.83/6.33/5.21 |
| GAEC | −1.53e+07 | 13.8 |
| GAEC + KLj | −2.27e+07 | 29.3 |

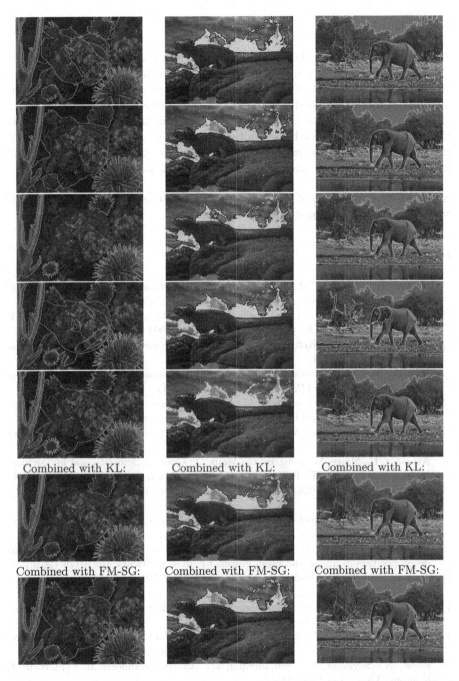

**Fig. 5.** To average multiple segmentations, we solve instances of a minimum cost lifted multicut problem as in (14)–(15). Above, Rows 1–5 show different man-made segmentations of images from the BSDS-500 benchmark [6]. Row 6 shows the combination of these segmentations by the solution using KL, row 7 shows the result with the proposed algorithm (FM-SG).

# 5    Conclusion

We have defined a fast, scalable and easy to implement fusion move algorithm for the minimum cost lifted multicut problem. Experiments with diverse instances of the problem have shown that this algorithm typically outperforms existing methods in terms of objective value and run-time. We conjecture that efficient algorithms such as the one proposed in this paper facilitate a variety of applications of the minimum cost lifted multicut problem in computer vision of which the averaging of multiple segmentations is just one example. Improved parallelization schemes of the proposed algorithm are subject of future work.

**Acknowledgments.** Partial financial support by DFG-SFB 1129, DFG-SFB 1134 and DFG-HA 4364/8-1 is gratefully acknowledged.

# References

1. Andres, B., Kappes, J.H., Beier, T., Köthe, U., Hamprecht, F.A.: Probabilistic image segmentation with closedness constraints. In: ICCV (2011)
2. Bagon, S., Galun, M.: Large scale correlation clustering optimization. CoRR abs/1112.2903 (2011). http://arxiv.org/abs/1112.2903
3. Kim, T., Nowozin, S., Kohli, P., Yoo, C.D.: Variable grouping for energy minimization. In: CVPR (2011)
4. Kim, S., Yoo, C., Nowozin, S., Kohli, P.: Image segmentation using higher-order correlation clustering. TPAMI **36**, 1761–1774 (2014)
5. Yarkony, J., Ihler, A., Fowlkes, C.C.: Fast planar correlation clustering for image segmentation. In: Fitzgibbon, A., Lazebnik, S., Perona, P., Sato, Y., Schmid, C. (eds.) ECCV 2012, Part VI. LNCS, vol. 7577, pp. 568–581. Springer, Heidelberg (2012)
6. Arbeláez, P., Maire, M., Fowlkes, C., Malik, J.: Contour detection and hierarchical image segmentation. IEEE Trans. Pattern Anal. Mach. Intell. **33**, 898–916 (2011)
7. Bansal, N., Blum, A., Chawla, S.: Correlation clustering. Mach. Learn. **56**(1–3), 89–113 (2004)
8. Demaine, E.D., Emanuel, D., Fiat, A., Immorlica, N.: Correlation clustering in general weighted graphs. Theoret. Comput. Sci. **361**(2–3), 172–187 (2006)
9. Keuper, M., Levinkov, E., Bonneel, N., Lavoué, G., Brox, T., Andres, B.: Efficient decomposition of image and mesh graphs by lifted multicuts. In: ICCV (2015)
10. Andres, B.: Lifting of multicuts. CoRR abs/1503.03791 (2015). http://arxiv.org/abs/1503.03791
11. Voice, T., Polukarov, M., Jennings, N.R.: Coalition structure generation over graphs. J. Artif. Intell. Res. **45**, 165–196 (2012)
12. Bachrach, Y., Kohli, P., Kolmogorov, V., Zadimoghaddam, M.: Optimal coalition structure generation in cooperative graph games. In: AAAI (2013)
13. Cook, W., Seymour, P.: Tour merging via branch-decomposition. INFORMS J. Comput. **15**(3), 233–248 (2003)
14. Lempitsky, V.S., Rother, C., Roth, S., Blake, A.: Fusion moves for Markov random field optimization. IEEE Trans. Pattern Anal. Mach. Intell. **32**(8), 1392–1405 (2010)

15. Kappes, J.H., Beier, T., Schnörr, C.: MAP-inference on large scale higher-order discrete graphical models by fusion moves. In: International Workshop on Graphical Models in Computer Vision (2014)
16. Andres, B., Kroeger, T., Briggman, K.L., Denk, W., Korogod, N., Knott, G., Koethe, U., Hamprecht, F.A.: Globally optimal closed-surface segmentation for connectomics. In: Fitzgibbon, A., Lazebnik, S., Perona, P., Sato, Y., Schmid, C. (eds.) ECCV 2012, Part III. LNCS, vol. 7574, pp. 778–791. Springer, Heidelberg (2012)
17. Kappes, J.H., Speth, M., Reinelt, G., Schnörr, C.: Higher-order segmentation via multicuts. Comput. Vis. Image Underst. 143, 104–119 (2016). Inference and Learning of Graphical Models Theory and Applications in Computer Vision and Image Analysis
18. Kappes, J.H., Speth, M., Andres, B., Reinelt, G., Schn, C.: Globally optimal image partitioning by multicuts. In: Boykov, Y., Kahl, F., Lempitsky, V., Schmidt, F.R. (eds.) EMMCVPR 2011. LNCS, vol. 6819, pp. 31–44. Springer, Heidelberg (2011)
19. Yarkony, J., Ihler, A., Fowlkes, C.C.: Fast planar correlation clustering for image segmentation. In: Fitzgibbon, A., Lazebnik, S., Perona, P., Sato, Y., Schmid, C. (eds.) ECCV 2012, Part VI. LNCS, vol. 7577, pp. 568–581. Springer, Heidelberg (2012)
20. Andres, B., Beier, T., Kappes, J.H.: OpenGM: a C++ library for discrete graphical models. arXiv e-prints (2012)
21. Beier, T., Kroeger, T., Kappes, J.H., Koethe, U., Hamprecht, F.: Cut, glue & cut: a fast, approximate solver for multicut partitioning. In: IEEE Conference on Computer Vision and Pattern Recognition 2014 (2014)
22. Kernighan, B.W., Lin, S.: An efficient heuristic procedure for partitioning graphs. Bell Syst. Tech. J. 49(2), 291–308 (1970)
23. Beier, T., Hamprecht, F.A., Kappes, J.H.: Fusion moves for correlation clustering. In: CVPR Proceedings (2015, in press)
24. Cardona, A., Saalfeld, S., Preibisch, S., Schmid, B., Cheng, A., Pulokas, J., Tomancak, P., Hartenstein, V.: An integrated micro- and macroarchitectural analysis of the Drosophila brain by computer-assisted serial section electron microscopy. PLoS Biol. 8(10), 1–17 (2010)
25. Arganda-Carreras, I., Turaga, S.C., Berger, D.R., Ciresan, D., Giusti, A., Gambardella, L.M., Schmidhuber, J., Laptev, D., Dwivedi, S., Buhmann, J.M., Liu, T., Seyedhosseini, M., Tasdizen, T., Kamentsky, L., Burget, R., Uher, V., Tan, X., Sun, C., Pham, T., Bas, E., Uzunbas, M.G., Cardona, A., Schindelin, J., Seung, H.S.: Crowdsourcing the creation of image segmentation algorithms for connectomics. Front. Neuroanat. 9(142), 1–13 (2015)
26. Grötschel, M., Wakabayashi, Y.: A cutting plane algorithm for a clustering problem. Math. Program. 45(1), 59–96 (1989)
27. Chopra, S., Rao, M.: The partition problem. Math. Program. 59(1–3), 87–115 (1993)
28. Kolmogorov, V., Zabih, R.: What energy functions can be minimized via graph cuts? IEEE Trans. Pattern Anal. Mach. Intell. 26(2), 147–159 (2004)
29. Andres, B., Kappes, J.H., Beier, T., Köthe, U., Hamprecht, F.A.: The lazy flipper: efficient depth-limited exhaustive search in discrete graphical models. In: Fitzgibbon, A., Lazebnik, S., Perona, P., Sato, Y., Schmid, C. (eds.) ECCV 2012, Part VII. LNCS, vol. 7578, pp. 154–166. Springer, Heidelberg (2012)
30. Lempitsky, V., Rother, C., Roth, S., Blake, A.: Fusion moves for Markov random field optimization. IEEE Trans. Pattern Anal. Mach. Intell. 32(8), 1392–1405 (2010)

31. Meyer, F.: Watersheds on edge or node weighted graphs "par l'exemple". CoRR abs/1303.1829 (2013). http://arxiv.org/abs/1303.1829
32. Meyer, F.: Stochastic watershed hierarchies. In: ICAPR 2015; 8th International Conference on Advances in Pattern Recognition. Indian Statistical Institute, Kolkata, January 2015
33. Beucher, S., Meyer, F.: The morphological approach to segmentation: the watershed transformation. Opt. Eng. **34**, 433–433 (1992)
34. Andres, B., Köthe, U., Kroeger, T., Helmstaedter, M., Briggman, K.L., Denk, W., Hamprecht, F.A.: 3D segmentation of SBFSEM images of neuropil by a graphical model over supervoxel boundaries. Med. Image Anal. **16**(4), 796–805 (2012)
35. Andres, B., Kroeger, T., Briggman, K.L., Denk, W., Korogod, N., Knott, G., Koethe, U., Hamprecht, F.A.: Globally optimal closed-surface segmentation for connectomics. In: Fitzgibbon, A., Lazebnik, S., Perona, P., Sato, Y., Schmid, C. (eds.) ECCV 2012, Part III. LNCS, vol. 7574, pp. 778–791. Springer, Heidelberg (2012)
36. Arbelaez, P.: Boundary extraction in natural images using ultrametric contour maps. In: Proceedings of 2006 Conference on Computer Vision and Pattern Recognition Workshop, CVPRW 2006, p. 182. IEEE Computer Society, Washington, DC (2006)
37. Yang, X., Prasad, L., Latecki, L.J.: Affinity learning with diffusion on tensor product graph. IEEE Trans. Pattern Anal. Mach. Intell. **35**(1), 28–38 (2013)
38. Leung, T., Malik, J.: Contour continuity in region based image segmentation. In: Burkhardt, H.-J., Neumann, B. (eds.) ECCV 1998. LNCS, vol. 1406, p. 544. Springer, Heidelberg (1998)
39. Fowlkes, C., Malik, J.: How much does globalization help segmentation? Technical report, Division of Computer Science, University of California, Berkeley, July 2004
40. Maire, M., Arbelaez, P., Fowlkes, C.C., Malik, J.: Using contours to detect and localize junctions in natural images. In: CVPR (2008)
41. Lin, M., Chen, Q., Yan, S.: Network in network. CoRR abs/1312.4400 (2013). http://arxiv.org/abs/1312.4400
42. Dollár, P., Zitnick, C.L.: Fast edge detection using structured forests. PAMI **37**, 1558–1570 (2015)
43. Alush, A., Goldberger, J.: Ensemble segmentation using efficient integer linear programming. Pattern Anal. Mach. Intell. **34**(10), 1966–1977 (2012)

# $\ell^0$-Sparse Subspace Clustering

Yingzhen Yang[1]([✉]), Jiashi Feng[2], Nebojsa Jojic[3], Jianchao Yang[4],
and Thomas S. Huang[1]

[1] Beckman Institute, University of Illinois at Urbana-Champaign, Urbana, USA
{yyang58,t-huang1}@illinois.edu
[2] Department of ECE, National University of Singapore, Singapore, Singapore
elefjia@nus.edu.sg
[3] Microsoft Research, Redmond, USA
jojic@microsoft.com
[4] Snapchat, Los Angeles, USA
jianchao.yang@snapchat.com

**Abstract.** Subspace clustering methods with sparsity prior, such as Sparse Subspace Clustering (SSC) [1], are effective in partitioning the data that lie in a union of subspaces. Most of those methods require certain assumptions, e.g. independence or disjointness, on the subspaces. These assumptions are not guaranteed to hold in practice and they limit the application of existing sparse subspace clustering methods. In this paper, we propose $\ell^0$-induced sparse subspace clustering ($\ell^0$-SSC). In contrast to the required assumptions, such as independence or disjointness, on subspaces for most existing sparse subspace clustering methods, we prove that subspace-sparse representation, a key element in subspace clustering, can be obtained by $\ell^0$-SSC for arbitrary distinct underlying subspaces almost surely under the mild i.i.d. assumption on the data generation. We also present the "no free lunch" theorem that obtaining the subspace representation under our general assumptions can not be much computationally cheaper than solving the corresponding $\ell^0$ problem of $\ell^0$-SSC. We develop a novel approximate algorithm named Approximate $\ell^0$-SSC (A$\ell^0$-SSC) that employs proximal gradient descent to obtain a sub-optimal solution to the optimization problem of $\ell^0$-SSC with theoretical guarantee, and the sub-optimal solution is used to build a sparse similarity matrix for clustering. Extensive experimental results on various data sets demonstrate the superiority of A$\ell^0$-SSC compared to other competing clustering methods.

This material is based upon work supported by the National Science Foundation under Grant No. 1318971. Any opinions, findings, and conclusions or recommendations expressed in this material are those of the author(s) and do not necessarily reflect the views of the National Science Foundation. The work of Jiashi Feng was partially supported by National University of Singapore startup grant R-263-000-C08-133 and Ministry of Education of Singapore AcRF Tier One grant R-263-000-C21-112.

**Electronic supplementary material** The online version of this chapter (doi:10.1007/978-3-319-46475-6_45) contains supplementary material, which is available to authorized users.

© Springer International Publishing AG 2016
B. Leibe et al. (Eds.): ECCV 2016, Part II, LNCS 9906, pp. 731–747, 2016.
DOI: 10.1007/978-3-319-46475-6_45

**Keywords:** Sparse subspace clustering · Proximal gradient descent

# 1   Introduction

High dimensional data often lie in a set of low-dimensional subspaces in many practical scenarios. Based on this observation, subspace clustering algorithms [2] aim to partition the data such that data belonging to the same subspace are identified as one cluster. Among various subspace clustering algorithms, the ones that employ sparsity prior, such as Sparse Subspace Clustering (SSC) [1], have been proven to be effective in separating the data in accordance with the subspaces that the data lie in under certain assumptions.

Sparse subspace clustering methods construct the sparse similarity graph by sparse representation of the data, where the vertices represent the data. Subspace-sparse representation ensures that vertices corresponding to different subspaces are disconnected in the sparse similarity graph, leading to their compelling performance with spectral clustering [3] applied on such graph. Elhamifar and Vidal [1] prove that when the subspaces are independent or disjoint, subspace-sparse representations can be obtained by solving the canonical sparse coding problem using data as the dictionary under certain conditions on the rank, or singular value of the data matrix and the principle angle between the subspaces. Under the independence assumption on the subspaces, low rank representation [4,5] is also proposed to recover the subspace structures. Relaxing the assumptions on the subspaces to allowing overlapping subspaces, the Greedy Subspace Clustering [6] and the Low-Rank Sparse Subspace Clustering [7] achieve subspace-sparse representation with high probability. However, their results rely on the semi-random model or full-random model which assumes that the data in each subspace are generated i.i.d. uniformly on the unit sphere in that subspace as well as certain additional conditions on the size and dimensionality of the data. In addition, the geometric analysis in [8] also adopts the semi-random model and it handles overlapping subspaces. Noisy SSC proposed in [9] handles noisy data that lie in disjoint or overlapping subspaces.

To avoid the non-convex optimization problem incurred by $\ell^0$-norm, most of the sparse subspace clustering or sparse graph based clustering methods use $\ell^1$-norm [1,10–14] or $\ell^2$-norm with thresholding [15] to impose sparsity on the constructed similarity graph. In addition, $\ell^1$-norm has been widely used as a convex relaxation of $\ell^0$-norm for efficient sparse coding algorithms [16–18]. On the other hand, sparse representation methods such as [19] that directly optimize objective function involving $\ell^0$-norm demonstrate compelling performance compared to its $\ell^1$-norm counterpart. It remains an interesting question whether sparse subspace clustering equipped with $\ell^0$-norm, which is the origination of the sparsity that counts the number of nonzero elements, has advantage in obtaining the subspace-sparse representation. In this paper, we propose $\ell^0$-induced sparse subspace clustering which employs $\ell^0$-norm to enforce the sparsity of representation, and present a novel A$\ell^0$-SSC for optimization. This paper offers two major contributions:

1 **We propose the $\ell^0$-induced Subspace Subspace Clustering method and prove that it almost surely renders the desired subspace-sparse representation.** We present the theory of the $\ell^0$-induced sparse subspace clustering ($\ell^0$-SSC), which shows that $\ell^0$-SSC gives subspace-sparse representation almost surely under minimum assumptions on the underlying subspaces the data lie in, i.e. subspaces are distinct. To the best of our knowledge, this is the mildest assumption on the subspaces compared to most existing sparse subspace clustering methods. Furthermore, our theory presented in Theorem 1 assumes that the data in each subspace are generated i.i.d. from arbitrary continuous distribution supported on that subspace, which is milder than the assumption of semi-random model in [6,7] that assume the data are i.i.d. uniformly distributed on the unit sphere in each subspace. Moreover, we prove that under the general conditions in Theorem 1, finding subspace representation can not be computationally cheaper than solving the corresponding $\ell^0$ problem. In fact, if there is an algorithm that obtains subspace representation for each data point, then it can be used to get the optimal solution to the $\ell^0$ problem for $\ell^0$-SSC by an additional step of polynomial complexity.

2 **We propose Approximate $\ell^0$-SSC to efficiently obtain an approximate solution to the problem of $\ell^0$-SSC with theoretical guarantee.** The optimization problem of $\ell^0$-SSC is NP-hard and it is impractical to directly pursue the global optimal solution. Instead, we develop an approximate algorithm named Approximate $\ell^0$-SSC (A$\ell^0$-SSC) which obtains a sub-optimal solution for $\ell^0$-SSC by proximal gradient descent method with theoretical guarantee. Under certain assumptions on the sparse eigenvalues of the data, the sub-optimal solution by A$\ell^0$-SSC is a critical point of the original objective, and the bound for the $\ell^2$-distance between such sub-optimal solution and the global optimal solution is given. It should be emphasized that the techniques we develop to derive such bound could be applied to more general optimization problems of sparse coding using proximal gradient descent, so as to obtain the gap between the sub-optimal solution and the global solution to the associated $\ell^0$ problem.

Similar to SSC, the sub-optimal solution by A$\ell^0$-SSC is used to build a sparse similarity matrix upon which spectral clustering is performed to obtain the data clusters. Extensive experimental results on various real data sets show the impressive performance of A$\ell^0$-SSC compared to other competing clustering methods including SSC.

The remaining parts of the paper are organized as follows. The representative subspace clustering methods, SSC [1], are introduced in the next subsection. The theoretical property of $\ell^0$-SSC, detailed formulation of A$\ell^0$-SSC and theoretical guarantee on the obtained sub-optimal solution are illustrated. We then show the clustering performance of the proposed models, and conclude the paper. We use bold letters for matrices and vectors, and regular lower letter for scalars throughout this paper. The bold letter with superscript indicates the corresponding column of a matrix, and the bold letter with subscript indicates the corresponding element of a matrix or vector. $\| \cdot \|_F$ and $\| \cdot \|_p$ denote the Frobenius norm and the $\ell^p$-norm, and diag($\cdot$) indicates the diagonal elements of a matrix.

## 1.1  Sparse Subspace Clustering and $\ell^1$-Graph

SSC [1] and $\ell^1$-graph [10,11] employ the broadly used sparse representation [13, 20–22] of the data to construct the sparse similarity graph. With the data $X = [\mathbf{x}_1,\ldots,\mathbf{x}_n] \in \mathbb{R}^{d\times n}$ where $n$ is the size of the data and $d$ is the dimensionality, SSC and $\ell^1$-graph solves the following sparse coding problem:

$$\min_{\alpha} \|\alpha\|_1 \quad s.t.\ X = X\alpha,\ \mathrm{diag}(\alpha) = 0 \tag{1}$$

Both SSC and $\ell^1$-graph construct a sparse similarity graph $G = (X, W)$ where the data $X$ are represented as vertices, $W$ of size $n \times n$ is the weighted adjacency matrix of $G$, and $W_{ij}$ indicates the edge weight, or the similarity between $\mathbf{x}_i$ and $\mathbf{x}_j$, $W$ is a sparse similarity matrix set by the sparse codes $\alpha$ as below:

$$W_{ij} = (|\alpha_{ij}| + |\alpha_{ji}|)/2 \quad 1 \le i,j \le n \tag{2}$$

There is an edge between $\mathbf{x}_i$ and $\mathbf{x}_j$ if and only if $W_{ij} \neq 0$. Furthermore, if the underlying subspaces that the data lie in are independent or disjoint, Elhamifar and Vidal [1] proves that the optimal solution to (1) is the subspace-sparse representation under several additional conditions. *The sparse representation $\alpha^i$ is called subspace-sparse representation if the nonzero elements of $\alpha^i$, namely the sparse representation of the datum $\mathbf{x}_i$, correspond to the data points in the same subspace as $\mathbf{x}_i$.* Therefore, vertices corresponding to different subspaces are disconnected in the sparse similarity graph. With the subsequent spectral clustering [3] applied on such sparse similarity graph, compelling clustering performance is achieved. Allowing some tolerance for inexact representation, robust sparse subspace clustering methods such as [9,23] turn to solve the following Lasso-type problem for SSC and $\ell^1$-graph:

$$\min_{\alpha} \|\alpha\|_1 \quad s.t.\ \|X - X\alpha\|_F \le \delta,\ \mathrm{diag}(\alpha) = 0$$

which is equivalent to the following problem

$$\min_{\alpha} \|X - X\alpha\|_F^2 + \lambda_{\ell^1} \|\alpha\|_1 \quad s.t.\ \mathrm{diag}(\alpha) = 0 \tag{3}$$

where $\lambda_{\ell^1} > 0$ is a weighting parameter for the $\ell^1$ term.

## 2  $\ell^0$-Induced Sparse Subspace Clustering

In this paper, we propose $\ell^0$-induced Sparse Subspace Clustering ($\ell^0$-SSC), which solves the following $\ell^0$ problem:

$$\min_{\alpha} \|\alpha\|_0 \quad s.t.\ X = X\alpha,\ \mathrm{diag}(\alpha) = 0 \tag{4}$$

And the solution to the above problem is used to build a sparse similarity graph for clustering. We then give the theorem about $\ell^0$-induced almost surely subspace-sparse representation, and the proof is presented in the supplementary document for this paper.

**Theorem 1.** *($\ell^0$-Induced Almost Surely Subspace-Sparse Representation) Suppose the data $\mathbf{X} = [\mathbf{x}_1, \ldots, \mathbf{x}_n] \in \mathbb{R}^{d \times n}$ lie in a union of $K$ distinct subspaces $\{\mathcal{S}_k\}_{k=1}^K$ of dimensions $\{d_k\}_{k=1}^K$, i.e. $\mathcal{S}_k \neq \mathcal{S}_{k'}$ for $k \neq k'$. Let $\mathbf{X}^{(k)} \in \mathbb{R}^{d \times n_k}$ denote the data that belong to subspace $\mathcal{S}_k$, and $\sum_{k=1}^K n_k = n$. When $n_k \geq d_k + 1$, if the data belonging to each subspace are generated i.i.d. from arbitrary unknown continuous distribution supported on that subspace,[1] then with probability 1, the optimal solution to (4), denoted by $\boldsymbol{\alpha}^*$, is a subspace-sparse representation, i.e. nonzero elements in $\boldsymbol{\alpha}^{*i}$ corresponds to the data that lie in the same subspace as $\mathbf{x}_i$.*

*Proof. (Sketch of the proof)* It can be verified that the probability measure of "inter-subspace hyperplane" is 0, and we defer the details to the supplementary.

According to Theorem 1, $\ell^0$-SSC (4) obtains the subspace-sparse representation almost surely under minimum assumption on the subspaces, i.e. it only requires that the subspaces be distinct. To the best of our knowledge, this is the mildest assumption on the subspaces for most existing sparse subspace clustering methods. Moreover, the only assumption on the data generation is that the data in each subspace are i.i.d. random samples from arbitrary continuous distributions supported on that subspace. In the light of assumed data distribution, such assumption on the data generation is much milder than the assumption of the semi-random model in [6–8] (note that the data can always be normalized to have unit norm and reside on the unit sphere). Table 1 summarizes different assumptions on the subspaces and random data generation for different subspace clustering methods including sparse subspace clustering methods. It can be seen that $\ell^0$-SSC has mildest assumption on both subspaces and the random data generation. Note that Theorem 1 is also free from the geometric assumptions such as those involving subspace incoherence in [7,8].

The $\ell^0$ sparse representation problem (4) is known to be NP-hard. One may ask if there is a shortcut to the almost surely subspace-sparse representation under the conditions in Theorem 1. We show that such shortcut is almost surely impossible. Namely, suppose there is an algorithm which, for each data point $\mathbf{x}_i$, can find the data from the same subspace as $\mathbf{x}_i$ that linearly represent $\mathbf{x}_i$, then such representation almost surely leads to the solution to the $\ell^0$ problem:

$$\min_{\boldsymbol{\alpha}^i} \|\boldsymbol{\alpha}^i\|_0 \quad s.t. \ \mathbf{x}_i = \mathbf{X}\boldsymbol{\alpha}^i, \ \alpha_{ii} = 0 \tag{5}$$

**Theorem 2.** *(There is "no free lunch" for obtaining subspace representation under the general conditions of Theorem 1) Under the assumptions of Theorem 1, if there is an algorithm which, for any data point $\mathbf{x}_i \in \mathcal{S}_k$, $1 \leq i \leq n, 1 \leq k \leq K$, can find the data from the same subspace as $\mathbf{x}_i$ that linearly represent $\mathbf{x}_i$, i.e.*

$$\mathbf{x}_i = \mathbf{X}\boldsymbol{\beta} \quad (\beta_i = 0) \tag{6}$$

---

[1] Continuous distribution here indicates that the data distribution is non-degenerate in the sense that the probability measure of any hyperplane of dimension less than that of the subspace is 0.

**Table 1.** Assumptions on the subspaces and random data generation (for randomized part of the algorithm) for different subspace clustering methods. $D_1$ means the data in each subspace are generated i.i.d. uniformly on the unit sphere in that subspace, and $D_2$ means the data in each subspace are generated i.i.d. from arbitrary continuous distribution supported on that subspace. Note that $S_1 < S_2 < S_3 < S_4$, $D_1 < D_2$, where the assumption on the right hand side of $<$ is milder than that on the left hand side. The methods that are based on these assumptions are listed as follows. $S_1$: [4,5]; $S_2$:[1]; $S_3$:[6–9]; $D_1$: [6–8,23].

| Assumption on subspaces | Explanation |
|---|---|
| $S_1$: Independent subspaces | $\mathrm{Dim}[S_1 \oplus S_2 \ldots S_K] = \sum_k \mathrm{Dim}[S_k]$ |
| $S_2$: Disjoint subspaces | $S_k \cap S_{k'} = \mathbf{0}$ for $k \neq k'$ |
| $S_3$: Overlapping subspaces | $1 \leq \mathrm{Dim}[S_k \cap S_{k'}] < \min\{\mathrm{Dim}[S_k], \mathrm{Dim}[S_{k'}]\}$ for $k \neq k'$ |
| $S_4$: Distinct subspaces ($\ell^0$-SSC) | $S_k \neq S_{k'}$ for $k \neq k'$ |
| Assumption on Random Data Generation | Explanation |
| $D_1$: Semi-random model or Full-Random model | i.i.d. uniformly on the unit sphere |
| $D_2$: IID ($\ell^0$-SSC) | i.i.d. from arbitrary continuous distribution |

*where nonzero elements of $\beta$ correspond to the data that lie in the subspace $S_k$. Then, with probability 1, solution to the $\ell^0$ problem (5) can be obtained from $\beta$ in $\mathcal{O}(\hat{n}^3)$ time, where $\hat{n}$ is the number of nonzero elements in $\beta$.*

Therefore, we have the interesting "no free lunch" conclusion: with probability 1, finding the subspace representation for each data point $\mathbf{x}_i$ can not be much computationally cheaper than solving the $\ell^0$ sparse representation (5).

It should be emphasized that our theoretical results on $\ell^0$-SSC is significantly different from that in [24]. First, our results are developed under the widely used randomized subspace clustering models, while the recovered subspaces are supposed to form a minimal union-of-subspace structure in [24]. In addition, Theorem 1 shows that any global optimal solution to $\ell^0$-SSC can almost surely recover any unknown underlying subspaces, considering that there can be multiple globally optimal solutions to $\ell^0$-SSC. In contrast, given an underlying unknown minimal union-of-subspace structure, [24] does not show which globally optimal solution to $\ell^0$-SSC can recover such minimal union-of-subspace structure.

Note that SSC-OMP [25] adopts Orthogonal Matching Pursuit (OMP) [26] to choose neighbors for each datum in the sparse similarity graph, which can be interpreted as approximately solving the $\ell^0$ problem (5) for $1 \leq i \leq n$. However, SSC-OMP does not present the nice theoretical properties of the $\ell^0$-SSC shown above. Moreover, we give the theory about the distance between the sub-optimal solution by our $A\ell^0$-SSC and the global optimal solution to the $\ell^0$-SSC problem under the assumption on the sparse eigenvalues of the data matrix. Extensive experimental results show the significant performance advantage of $A\ell^0$-SSC over the SSC-OMP.

# 3    Approximate $\ell^0$-SSC (A$\ell^0$-SSC)

Solving the $\ell^0$-SSC problem exactly is NP-hard, therefore, we introduce an approximate algorithm for $\ell^0$-SSC in this section with theoretical guarantee.

## 3.1    Optimization of A$\ell^0$-SSC

Similar to the case of SSC and $\ell^1$-graph, by allowing tolerance for inexact representation, we turn to optimize the following $\ell^0$ problem [2] for $\ell^0$-SSC.

$$\min_{\alpha \in \mathbb{R}^{n \times n}, \text{diag}(\alpha)=0} L(\alpha) = \|X - X\alpha\|_F^2 + \lambda\|\alpha\|_0 \tag{7}$$

Problem (7) is NP-hard, and it is impractical to seek for its global optimal solution. The literature extensively resorts to approximate algorithms, such as Orthogonal Matching Pursuit [26], or that use surrogate functions [27], for $\ell^0$ problems. In this paper we present A$\ell^0$-SSC that employs proximal gradient descent (PGD) method to optimize (7) and obtains a sub-optimal solution with theoretical guarantee. The sub-optimal solution is used to build a sparse similarity matrix for clustering. In the following text, the superscript with bracket indicates the iteration number of PGD. Note that problem (7) is equivalent to a set of problems

$$\min_{\alpha^i \in \mathbb{R}^n, \alpha_i^i = 0} L(\alpha^i) = \|x_i - X\alpha^i\|_2^2 + \lambda\|\alpha^i\|_0 \tag{8}$$

for $1 \leq i \leq n$. We describe PGD for optimizing $L(\alpha^i)$ with respect to the sparse code of the $i$-th data point, i.e. $\alpha^i$, for any $1 \leq i \leq n$. We initialize $\alpha$ as $\alpha^{(0)} = \alpha_{\ell^1}$ and $\alpha_{\ell^1}$ is the sparse codes generated by solving (3) with $\lambda_{\ell^1} = \lambda$. The data matrix $X$ is normalized such that each column has unit $\ell^2$-norm.

In $t$-th iteration of PGD for $t \geq 1$, gradient descent is performed on the squared loss term of $L(\alpha^i)$, i.e. $Q(\alpha^i) = \|x_i - X\alpha^i\|_2^2$, to obtain

$$\tilde{\alpha}^{i\,(t)} = \alpha^{i\,(t-1)} - \frac{2}{\tau s}(X^\top X \alpha^{i\,(t-1)} - X^\top x_i) \tag{9}$$

where $\tau$ is any constant that is greater than 1. $s$ is the Lipschitz constant for the gradient of function $Q(\cdot)$. $s$ is usually chosen as two times the largest eigenvalue of $X^\top X$. Due to the sparsity of $\alpha^i$, it is shown in Lemma 1 that $s$ can be much smaller which also ensures the shrinkage of the support of the sequence $\{\alpha^{i\,(t)}\}_t$ and the decline of the objective function. $\alpha^{i\,(t)}$ is then the solution to the following $\ell^0$ regularized problem:

$$\alpha^{i\,(t)} = \arg\min_{v \in \mathbb{R}^n, v_i = 0} \frac{\tau s}{2}\|v - \tilde{\alpha}^{i\,(t)}\|_2^2 + \lambda\|v\|_0 \tag{10}$$

It can be verified that (10) has closed-form solution, and the $j$-th element of $\alpha^{i\,(t)}$ is

$$\alpha_j^{i\,(t)} = \begin{cases} 0 & : |\tilde{\alpha}_j^{i\,(t)}| < \sqrt{\frac{2\lambda}{\tau s}} \text{ or } i = j \\ \tilde{\alpha}_j^{i\,(t)} & : \text{otherwise} \end{cases} \tag{11}$$

---

[2] Even one would stick to the very original formulation without noise tolerance, (4) is still equivalent to (7) with some Lagrangian multiplier $\lambda$.

for $1 \leq j \leq n$. The iterations start from $t = 1$ and continue until the sequence $\{L(\boldsymbol{\alpha}^{i^{(t)}})\}_t$ or $\{\boldsymbol{\alpha}^{i^{(t)}}\}_t$ converges or maximum iteration number is achieved, then a sub-optimal solution is obtained. A sparse similarity matrix is built by the sub-optimal solution upon which spectral clustering is performed to get the clustering result, as described in Algorithm 1 for A$\ell^0$-SSC. The time complexity of PGD method is $\mathcal{O}(Mn^2)$ where $M$ is the number of iterations (or maximum number of iterations) for PGD.

---

**Algorithm 1.** Data Clustering by Approximate $\ell^0$-SSC (A$\ell^0$-SSC)

---

**Input:**

The data set $\boldsymbol{X} = \{\mathbf{x}_i\}_{i=1}^n$, the number of clusters $c$, the parameter $\lambda$ for A$\ell^0$-SSC, maximum iteration number $M$, stopping threshold $\varepsilon$.

1: Initialize the coefficient matrix as $\boldsymbol{\alpha}^{(0)} = \boldsymbol{\alpha}_{\ell^1}$.

2: **for** $1 \leq i \leq n$ **do**

3:    Obtain the sub-optimal solution $\tilde{\boldsymbol{\alpha}}^i$ by PGD with (9) and (11) starting from $t = 1$. The iteration terminates either $\{\boldsymbol{\alpha}^{i^{(t)}}\}_t$ or $\{L(\boldsymbol{\alpha}^{i^{(t)}})\}_t$ converges under the threshold $\varepsilon$ or maximum iteration number is achieved (note that the optimization for $1 \leq i \leq n$ is performed in parallel).

4: **end for**

5: Obtain the resultant coefficient matrix $\tilde{\boldsymbol{\alpha}}$ where the $i$-th column is $\tilde{\boldsymbol{\alpha}}^i$.

6: Build the sparse similarity matrix by symmetrizing $\tilde{\boldsymbol{\alpha}}$: $\tilde{\mathbf{W}} = \frac{|\tilde{\boldsymbol{\alpha}}| + |\tilde{\boldsymbol{\alpha}}^\top|}{2}$, compute the corresponding normalized graph Laplacian $\tilde{\mathbf{L}} = (\tilde{\mathbf{D}})^{-\frac{1}{2}} (\tilde{\mathbf{D}} - \tilde{\mathbf{W}})(\tilde{\mathbf{D}})^{-\frac{1}{2}}$, where $\tilde{\mathbf{D}}$ is a diagonal matrix with $\tilde{\mathbf{D}}_{ii} = \sum\limits_{j=1}^n \tilde{\mathbf{W}}_{ij}$

7: Construct the matrix $\mathbf{v} = [\mathbf{v}_1, \ldots, \mathbf{v}_c] \in \mathbb{R}^{n \times c}$, where $\{\mathbf{v}_1, \ldots, \mathbf{v}_c\}$ are the $c$ eigenvectors of $\mathbf{L}^*$ corresponding to its $c$ smallest eigenvalues. Treat each row of $\mathbf{v}$ as a data point in $\mathbb{R}^c$, and run K-means clustering method to obtain the cluster labels for all the rows of $\mathbf{v}$.

**Output:** The cluster label of $\mathbf{x}_i$ is set as the cluster label of the $i$-th row of $\mathbf{v}$, $1 \leq i \leq n$.

---

### 3.2    Theoretical Analysis

In this section we present the bound for the distance between the sub-optimal solution by A$\ell^0$-SSC and the global optimal solution to the objective problem (8). We first prove that the sequence $\{\boldsymbol{\alpha}^{i^{(t)}}\}_t$ produced by PGD has shrinking support and the objective sequence $\{L(\boldsymbol{\alpha}^{i^{(t)}})\}_t$ is decreasing so that it always converges in Lemma 1. Under certain assumptions on the sparse eigenvalues of the data $\boldsymbol{X}$, we show that the sub-optimal solution by A$\ell^0$-SSC is actually a critical point, namely $\{\boldsymbol{\alpha}^{i^{(t)}}\}_t$ converges to a critical point of the objective (8), and this sub-optimal solution and the global optimal solution to (8) are local solutions of a carefully designed capped-$\ell^1$ regularized problem. Based on the established theory in [28] showing the distance between different local solutions to various sparse estimation problems including the capped-$\ell^1$ problem, the bound for $\ell^2$-distance between the sub-optimal solution and the global optimal solution is presented in Theorem 3, again under the assumption on the sparse eigenvalues of $\boldsymbol{X}$. Note that our analysis is valid for all $1 \leq i \leq n$.

In the following analysis, we let $\beta_{\mathbf{I}}$ denote the vector formed by the elements of $\beta$ with indices in $\mathbf{I}$ when $\beta$ is a vector, or matrix formed by columns of $\beta$ with indices in $\mathbf{I}$ when $\beta$ is a matrix. Also, we let $\mathbf{S}_i = \text{supp}(\boldsymbol{\alpha}^{i^{(0)}})$ and $|\mathbf{S}_i| = A_i$ for $1 \leq i \leq n$.

**Lemma 1.** *(Support shrinkage in the proximal iterations and sufficient decrease of the objective) When* $s > \max\{2A_i, \frac{2(1+\lambda A_i)}{\lambda \tau}\}$, *then the sequence* $\{\boldsymbol{\alpha}^{i^{(t)}}\}_t$ *generated by PGD with (9) and (11) satisfies*

$$\text{supp}(\boldsymbol{\alpha}^{i^{(t)}}) \subseteq \text{supp}(\boldsymbol{\alpha}^{i^{(t-1)}}), t \geq 1 \tag{12}$$

*namely the support of the sequence* $\{\boldsymbol{\alpha}^{i^{(t)}}\}_t$ *shrinks when the iteration proceeds. Moreover, the sequence of the objective* $\{L(\boldsymbol{\alpha}^{i^{(t)}})\}_t$ *decreases, and the following inequality holds for* $t \geq 1$:

$$L(\boldsymbol{\alpha}^{i^{(t)}}) \leq L(\boldsymbol{\alpha}^{i^{(t-1)}}) - \frac{(\tau - 1)s}{2}\|\boldsymbol{\alpha}^{i^{(t)}} - \boldsymbol{\alpha}^{i^{(t-1)}}\|_2^2 \tag{13}$$

*And it follows that the sequence* $\{L(\boldsymbol{\alpha}^{i^{(t)}})\}_t$ *converges. The above results hold for any* $1 \leq i \leq n$.

Before stating Lemma 2, the following definitions are introduced which are essential for our analysis.

**Definition 1.** *(Critical points) Given the non-convex function* $f \colon \mathbb{R}^n \to R \cup \{+\infty\}$ *which is a proper and lower semi-continuous function.*

- *for a given* $\mathbf{x} \in \text{dom}f$, *its Frechet subdifferential of* $f$ *at* $\mathbf{x}$, *denoted by* $\tilde{\partial}f(x)$, *is the set of all vectors* $\mathbf{u} \in \mathbb{R}^n$ *which satisfy*

$$\limsup_{\mathbf{y} \neq \mathbf{x}, \mathbf{y} \to \mathbf{x}} \frac{f(\mathbf{y}) - f(\mathbf{x}) - \langle \mathbf{u}, \mathbf{y} - \mathbf{x} \rangle}{\|\mathbf{y} - \mathbf{x}\|} \geq 0$$

- *The limiting-subdifferential of* $f$ *at* $\mathbf{x} \in \mathbb{R}^n$, *denoted by written* $\partial f(x)$, *is defined by*

$$\partial f(x) = \{\mathbf{u} \in \mathbb{R}^n : \exists \mathbf{x}^k \to \mathbf{x}, f(\mathbf{x}^k) \to f(\mathbf{x}), \tilde{\mathbf{u}}^k \in \tilde{\partial}f(\mathbf{x}_k) \to \mathbf{u}\}$$

*The point* $\mathbf{x}$ *is a critical point of* $f$ *if* $0 \in \partial f(x)$.

Also, we are considering the following capped-$\ell^1$ regularized problem, which replaces the noncontinuous $\ell^0$-norm with the continuous capped-$\ell^1$ regularization term $R$:

$$\min_{\beta \in \mathbb{R}^n, \beta_i = 0} L_{\text{capped}-\ell^1}(\beta) = \|\mathbf{x}_i - X\beta\|_2^2 + \mathbf{R}(\beta; b) \tag{14}$$

where $\mathbf{R}(\beta; b) = \sum_{j=1}^{n} R(\beta_j; b)$, $R(t; b) = \lambda \frac{\min\{|t|, b\}}{b}$ for some $b > 0$. It can be seen that $R(t; b)$ approaches the $\ell^0$-norm when $b \to 0+$.

Now we define the local solution of problem (14).

**Definition 2.** *(Local solution) A vector $\tilde{\beta}$ is a local solution to the problem (14) if*

$$\|2\mathbf{X}^{\top}(\mathbf{X}\tilde{\beta} - \mathbf{x}_i) + \dot{\mathbf{R}}(\tilde{\beta}; b)\|_2 = 0 \tag{15}$$

*where $\dot{\mathbf{R}}(\tilde{\beta}; b) = [\dot{R}(\tilde{\beta}_1; b), \dot{R}(\tilde{\beta}_2; b), \ldots, \dot{R}(\tilde{\beta}_n; b)]^{\top}$.*

Note that in the above definition and the following text, $\dot{R}(t; b)$ can be chosen as any value between the right differential $\frac{\partial R}{\partial t}(t+; b)$ (or $\dot{R}(t+; b)$) and left differential $\frac{\partial R}{\partial t}(t-; b)$ (or $\dot{R}(t-; b)$).

**Definition 3.** *(Sparse eigenvalues) The lower and upper sparse eigenvalues of a matrix $\mathbf{A}$ are defined as*

$$\kappa_-(m) := \min_{\|\mathbf{u}\|_0 \leq m; \|\mathbf{u}\|_2 = 1} \|\mathbf{A}\mathbf{u}\|_2^2 \quad \kappa_+(m) := \max_{\|\mathbf{u}\|_0 \leq m, \|\mathbf{u}\|_2 = 1} \|\mathbf{A}\mathbf{u}\|_2^2$$

It is worthwhile mentioning that the sparse eigenvalues are closely related to the Restricted Isometry Property (RIP) [29] used frequently in the compressive sensing literature. Typical RIP requires bounds such as $\delta_\tau + \delta_{2\tau} + \delta_{3\tau} < 1$ or $\delta_{2\tau} < \sqrt{2} - 1$ [30] for stably recovering the signal from measurements and $\tau$ is the sparsity of the signal, where $\delta_\tau = \max\{\kappa_+(\tau) - 1, 1 - \kappa_-(\tau)\}$. Similar to [28], we use more general conditions on the sparse eigenvalues in this paper (in the sense of not requiring bounds in terms of $\delta$) to obtain theoretical results. In the following text, sparse eigenvalues $\kappa_-$ and $\kappa_+$ are for the data matrix $\mathbf{X}$.

**Definition 4.** *(Degree of Nonconvexity of a Regularizer) For $\kappa \geq 0$ and $t \in \mathbb{R}$, define*

$$\theta(t, \kappa) := \sup_s \{-\text{sgn}(s - t)(\dot{P}(s; b) - \dot{P}(t; b)) - \kappa|s - t|\}$$

*as the degree of nonconvexity for function $P$. If $\mathbf{u} = (u_1, \ldots, u_n)^{\top} \in \mathbb{R}^n$, $\theta(\mathbf{u}, \kappa) = [\theta(u_1, \kappa), \ldots, \theta(u_n, \kappa)]$.*

Note that $\theta(t, \kappa) = 0$ for convex function $P$.

In the following lemma, we show that the sequences $\{\alpha^{i(t)}\}_t$ generated by A$\ell^0$-SSC converges to a critical point of $L(\alpha^i)$, denoted by $\hat{\alpha}^i$, under certain assumption on the sparse eigenvalues of $\mathbf{X}$. Therefore, the sub-optimal solution by A$\ell^0$-SSC is a critical point of $L(\alpha^i)$ in this case. Denote by $\alpha^{i*}$ the global optimal solution to the $\ell^0$-SSC problem(8), and let $\hat{\mathbf{S}}_i = \text{supp}(\hat{\alpha}^i)$, $\mathbf{S}_i^* = \text{supp}(\hat{\alpha}^*)$. The following lemma also shows that both $\hat{\alpha}^i$ and $\alpha^{i*}$ are local solutions to the capped-$\ell^1$ regularized problem (14).

**Lemma 2.** *For any $1 \leq i \leq n$, suppose $\kappa_-(A_i) > 0$, then the sequences $\{\alpha^{i(t)}\}_t$ generated by PGD with (9) and (11) converges to a critical point of $L(\alpha^i)$, which is denoted by $\hat{\alpha}^i$. Moreover, if*

$$0 < b < \min\{\min_{j \in \hat{\mathbf{S}}_i} |\hat{\alpha}_j^i|, \frac{\lambda}{\max_{j \notin \hat{\mathbf{S}}_i} |\frac{\partial Q}{\partial \alpha_j^i}|_{\alpha^i = \hat{\alpha}^i}|}, \min_{j \in \mathbf{S}_i^*} |\alpha_j^{i*}|, \frac{\lambda}{\max_{j \notin \mathbf{S}_i^*} |\frac{\partial Q}{\partial \alpha_j^i}|_{\alpha^i = \alpha^{i*}}|}\} \tag{16}$$

*(if the denominator is $0$, $\frac{\lambda}{0}$ is defined to be $+\infty$ in the above inequality), then both $\hat{\alpha}^i$ and $\alpha^{i*}$ are local solutions to the capped-$\ell^1$ regularized problem (14).*

Theorem 5 in [28] gives the estimation on the distance between two local solutions of the capped-$\ell^1$ regularized problem. Based on this result, we have the following theorem showing that under assumptions on the sparse eigenvalues of $\boldsymbol{X}$, the sub-optimal solution $\hat{\boldsymbol{\alpha}}^i$ obtained by A$\ell^0$-SSC has bounded $\ell^2$-distance to $\boldsymbol{\alpha}^{i^*}$, the global optimal solution to the original $\ell^0$ problem (8).

**Theorem 3.** *(Sub-optimal solution is close to the global optimal solution) For any $1 \leq i \leq n$, suppose $\kappa_-(A_i) > 0$ and $\kappa_-(|\hat{\mathbf{S}}_i \cup \mathbf{S}_i^*|) > \kappa > 0$, and $b$ is chosen according to (16) as in Lemma 2. Then*

$$\|\boldsymbol{X}(\hat{\boldsymbol{\alpha}}^i - \boldsymbol{\alpha}^{i^*})\|_2^2 \leq \frac{2\kappa_-(|\hat{\mathbf{S}}_i \cup \mathbf{S}_i^*|)}{(\kappa_-(|\hat{\mathbf{S}}_i \cup \mathbf{S}_i^*|) - \kappa)^2} \tag{17}$$

$$(\sum_{j \in \hat{\mathbf{S}}_i} (\max\{0, \frac{\lambda}{b} - \kappa|\hat{\alpha}_j^i - b|\})^2 + |\mathbf{S}_i^* \setminus \hat{\mathbf{S}}_i|(\max\{0, \frac{\lambda}{b} - \kappa b\})^2)$$

*In addition,*

$$\|(\hat{\boldsymbol{\alpha}}^i - \boldsymbol{\alpha}^{i^*})\|_2^2 \leq \frac{2}{(\kappa_-(|\hat{\mathbf{S}}_i \cup \mathbf{S}_i^*|) - \kappa)^2} \tag{18}$$

$$(\sum_{j \in \hat{\mathbf{S}}_i} (\max\{0, \frac{\lambda}{b} - \kappa|\hat{\alpha}_j^i - b|\})^2 + |\mathbf{S}_i^* \setminus \hat{\mathbf{S}}_i|(\max\{0, \frac{\lambda}{b} - \kappa b\})^2)$$

**Remark 1.** *This result follows from Lemma 2 and Theorem 5 in [28]. The property of support shrinkage in Lemma 1 guarantees that $\hat{\mathbf{S}}_i \subseteq \mathbf{S}_i$, indicating that sub-optimal solution $\hat{\boldsymbol{\alpha}}^i$ is sparse, so we can expect that $|\hat{\mathbf{S}}_i \cup \mathbf{S}_i^*|$ is reasonably small. Also note that the bound for distance between the sub-optimal solution and the global optimal solution presented in Theorem 3 does not require typical RIP conditions. Also, when $\frac{\lambda}{b} - \kappa|\hat{\alpha}_j^i - b|$ for nonzero $\hat{\alpha}_j^i$ and $\frac{\lambda}{b} - \kappa b$ are no greater than 0, or they are small positive numbers, the sub-optimal solution $\hat{\boldsymbol{\alpha}}^i$ is equal to or very close to the global optimal solution.*

The detailed proofs of the theorems and lemmas in this paper are included in the supplementary document. The theoretical results in this section are mainly derived from the optimization perspective. Due to limited space, we present an additional theorem in the supplementary which applies the bound (18) to show how accurate the sub-optimal solution $\hat{\boldsymbol{\alpha}}^i$ is from the perspective of subspace-sparse representation, connecting A$\ell^0$-SSC to the correctness of subspace clustering.

## 4    Experimental Results

The superior clustering performance of A$\ell^0$-SSC is demonstrated in this section with extensive experimental results. Two measures are used to evaluate the performance of the clustering methods, i.e. the Accuracy (AC) and the Normalized Mutual Information(NMI) [31]. We compare our A$\ell^0$-SSC to K-means (KM), Spectral Clustering (SC), SSC, Sparse Manifold Clustering and Embedding (SMCE) [12]. A$\ell^0$-SSC is also compared to SSC-OMP to show the advantage of the proposed PGD in the previous sections. By adjusting the parameters, SSC and $\ell^1$-graph solve almost the same problem and generate equivalent results, so we report their performance under the same name SSC.

## 4.1   Clustering on UCI Data

In this subsection, we conduct experiments on the Ionosphere and Heart data from UCI machine learning repository [32], revealing the performance of $A\ell^0$-SSC on general machine learning data. The Ionosphere data contains 351 points of dimensionality 34. The Heart data contains 270 points of dimensionality 13.

The clustering results on the two data sets are shown in Table 2.

**Table 2.** Clustering results on UCI ionosphere and heart.

| Data set | Measure | KM | SC | SSC | SMCE | SSC-OMP | $A\ell^0$-SSC |
|---|---|---|---|---|---|---|---|
| Ionosphere | AC | 0.7097 | 0.7350 | 0.5128 | 0.6809 | 0.6353 | **0.7692** |
| | NMI | 0.1287 | 0.2155 | 0.1165 | 0.0871 | 0.0299 | **0.2609** |
| Heart | AC | 0.5889 | 0.6037 | 0.6370 | 0.5963 | 0.5519 | **0.6444** |
| | NMI | 0.0182 | 0.0269 | 0.0529 | 0.0255 | 0.0058 | **0.0590** |

## 4.2   Clustering on COIL-20 and COIL-100 Database

COIL-20 Database has 1440 images of 20 objects in which the background has been removed, and the size of each image is $32 \times 32$, so the dimension of this data is 1024. COIL-100 Database contains 100 objects with 72 images of size $32 \times 32$ for each object. The images of each object were taken 5 degrees apart when the object was rotated on a turntable. The clustering results on these two data sets are shown in Table 3. We observe that $A\ell^0$-SSC performs consistently better than all other competing methods. On COIL-100 Database, SMCE renders slightly better results than SSC on the entire data due to its capability of modeling non-linear manifolds.

## 4.3   Clustering on Extended Yale Face Database B and More Face Data Sets

The Extended Yale Face Database B contains face images for 38 subjects with 64 frontal face images taken under different illuminations for each subject. The clustering results are shown in Table 4. We can see that $A\ell^0$-SSC achieves significantly better clustering result than SSC, which is the second best method on this data. We demonstrate more experimental results on UMIST Face, CMU PIE, AR Face, CMU Multi-PIE and Georgia Tech Face Database in Table 5, and the used data sets are introduced at http://www.face-rec.org/databases/.

**Table 3.** Clustering results on COIL-20 and COIL-100 database. $c$ in the left column is the cluster number, i.e. the first $c$ clusters of the entire data are used for clustering. $c$ has the same meaning in Table 4.

| COIL-20 # Clusters | Measure | KM | SC | SSC | SMCE | SSC-OMP | A$\ell^0$-SSC |
|---|---|---|---|---|---|---|---|
| $c = 4$ | AC | 0.6632 | 0.6701 | 1.0000 | 0.7639 | 0.9271 | **1.0000** |
|  | NMI | 0.5106 | 0.5455 | 1.0000 | 0.6741 | 0.8397 | **1.0000** |
| $c = 8$ | AC | 0.5130 | 0.4462 | 0.7986 | 0.5365 | 0.6753 | **0.9705** |
|  | NMI | 0.5354 | 0.4947 | 0.8950 | 0.6786 | 0.7656 | **0.9638** |
| $c = 12$ | AC | 0.5885 | 0.4965 | 0.7697 | 0.6806 | 0.5475 | **0.8310** |
|  | NMI | 0.6707 | 0.6096 | 0.8960 | 0.8066 | 0.6316 | **0.9149** |
| $c = 16$ | AC | 0.6579 | 0.4271 | 0.8273 | 0.7622 | 0.3481 | **0.9002** |
|  | NMI | 0.7555 | 0.6031 | 0.9301 | 0.8730 | 0.4520 | **0.9552** |
| $c = 20$ | AC | 0.6554 | 0.4278 | 0.7854 | 0.7549 | 0.3389 | **0.8472** |
|  | NMI | 0.7630 | 0.6217 | 0.9148 | 0.8754 | 0.4853 | **0.9428** |
| COIL-100 # Clusters | Measure | KM | SC | SSC | SMCE | SSC-OMP | A$\ell^0$-SSC |
| $c = 20$ | AC | 0.5850 | 0.4514 | 0.5757 | 0.6208 | 0.4243 | **0.9264** |
|  | NMI | 0.7456 | 0.6700 | 0.7980 | 0.7993 | 0.5258 | **0.9681** |
| $c = 40$ | AC | 0.5791 | 0.4139 | 0.5934 | 0.6038 | 0.2340 | **0.8472** |
|  | NMI | 0.7691 | 0.6681 | 0.7962 | 0.7918 | 0.4378 | **0.9471** |
| $c = 60$ | AC | 0.5371 | 0.3389 | 0.5657 | 0.5887 | 0.1905 | **0.8326** |
|  | NMI | 0.7622 | 0.6343 | 0.8162 | 0.7973 | 0.3690 | **0.9352** |
| $c = 80$ | AC | 0.5048 | 0.3115 | 0.5271 | 0.5835 | 0.2247 | **0.7899** |
|  | NMI | 0.7474 | 0.6088 | 0.8006 | 0.8006 | 0.4173 | **0.9218** |
| $c = 100$ | AC | 0.4996 | 0.2835 | 0.5275 | 0.5639 | 0.1667 | **0.7683** |
|  | NMI | 0.7539 | 0.5923 | 0.8041 | 0.8064 | 0.3757 | **0.9182** |

## 4.4 Parameter Setting

$\lambda$ is usually set to 0.5 for A$\ell^0$-SSC, with the maximum iteration number $M = 100$ and the stopping threshold $\varepsilon = 10^{-6}$. We observe that the average number of non-zero elements of the sparse code generated by A$\ell^0$-SSC is around 3 for most data sets. In SSC-OMP, $\|\alpha^i\|_0$ is tuned to control the sparsity of the generated sparse codes such that the aforementioned average number of non-zero elements of the sparse code matches that of A$\ell^0$-SSC. For SSC, the weighting parameter for the $\ell^1$-norm has the default value of 0.1. For all the methods that use spectral clustering to obtain the clustering results, K-meas are performed multiple times and the data partition with minimum distortion is taken as the final result.

We investigate how the clustering performance on the Extended Yale Face Database B changes by varying the weighting parameter $\lambda$ for A$\ell^0$-SSC, and illus-

**Table 4.** Clustering results on the extended Yale Face Database B.

| Yale-B # Clusters | Measure | KM | SC | SSC | SMCE | SSC-OMP | $A\ell^0$-SSC |
|---|---|---|---|---|---|---|---|
| c = 10 | AC | 0.1782 | 0.1922 | 0.7580 | 0.3672 | 0.7375 | **0.8406** |
|  | NMI | 0.0897 | 0.1310 | 0.7380 | 0.3266 | 0.7468 | **0.7695** |
| c = 15 | AC | 0.1554 | 0.1706 | 0.7620 | 0.3761 | 0.7532 | **0.7987** |
|  | NMI | 0.1083 | 0.1390 | 0.7590 | 0.3593 | 0.7943 | **0.8183** |
| c = 20 | AC | 0.1200 | 0.1466 | 0.7930 | 0.3526 | 0.7813 | **0.8273** |
|  | NMI | 0.0872 | 0.1183 | 0.7860 | 0.3771 | 0.8172 | **0.8429** |
| c = 30 | AC | 0.1096 | 0.1209 | 0.8210 | 0.3470 | 0.7156 | **0.8633** |
|  | NMI | 0.1159 | 0.1338 | 0.8030 | 0.3927 | 0.7260 | **0.8762** |
| c = 38 | AC | 0.0954 | 0.1077 | 0.7850 | 0.3293 | 0.6529 | **0.8480** |
|  | NMI | 0.1258 | 0.1485 | 0.7760 | 0.3812 | 0.7024 | **0.8612** |

**Table 5.** Clustering Results on UMIST Face, CMU PIE, AR Face, CMU Multi-PIE and Georgia Tech Face database. Note that the CMU Multi-PIE contains the facial images captured in four sessions (S1 to S4).

| Data | Measure | KM | SC | SSC | SMCE | SSC-OMP | $A\ell^0$-SSC |
|---|---|---|---|---|---|---|---|
| UMIST Face | AC | 0.4275 | 0.4052 | 0.4904 | 0.4487 | 0.4835 | **0.6730** |
|  | NMI | 0.6426 | 0.6159 | 0.6885 | 0.6696 | 0.6310 | **0.7924** |
| CMU PIE | AC | 0.0845 | 0.0729 | 0.2287 | 0.1733 | 0.0821 | **0.2591** |
|  | NMI | 0.1884 | 0.1789 | 0.3659 | 0.3343 | 0.1494 | **0.4435** |
| AR Face | AC | 0.2752 | 0.2957 | 0.5914 | 0.3543 | 0.4229 | **0.6086** |
|  | NMI | 0.5941 | 0.6248 | 0.8060 | 0.6573 | 0.6835 | **0.8117** |
| MPIE S1 | AC | 0.1164 | 0.1285 | 0.5892 | 0.1721 | 0.1695 | **0.6741** |
|  | NMI | 0.5049 | 0.5292 | 0.7653 | 0.5514 | 0.3395 | **0.8622** |
| MPIE S2 | AC | 0.1315 | 0.1410 | 0.6994 | 0.1898 | 0.2093 | **0.7527** |
|  | NMI | 0.4834 | 0.5128 | 0.8149 | 0.5293 | 0.4292 | **0.8939** |
| MPIE S3 | AC | 0.1291 | 0.1459 | 0.6316 | 0.1856 | 0.1787 | **0.7050** |
|  | NMI | 0.4811 | 0.5185 | 0.7858 | 0.5155 | 0.3415 | **0.8750** |
| MPIE S4 | AC | 0.1308 | 0.1463 | 0.6803 | 0.1823 | 0.1680 | **0.7246** |
|  | NMI | 0.4866 | 0.5280 | 0.8063 | 0.5294 | 0.3345 | **0.8837** |
| Georgia Face | AC | 0.4987 | 0.5187 | 0.5413 | 0.6053 | 0.4733 | **0.6187** |
|  | NMI | 0.6856 | 0.7014 | 0.6968 | 0.7394 | 0.6622 | **0.7400** |

trate the result in Fig. 1. The parameter sensitivity result on COIL-20 Database is presented in the supplementary document. We observe that the performance of $A\ell^0$-SSC is much better than other algorithms over a relatively large range of $\lambda$, revealing the robustness of our algorithm with respect to the weighting parameter $\lambda$.

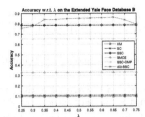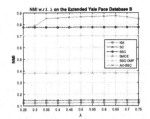

**Fig. 1.** Clustering performance with different values of $\lambda$, i.e. the weight for the $\ell^0$-norm, on the Extended Yale Face Database B. Left: Accuracy; Right: NMI. Note that the performance of SSC does not vary with $\lambda$ since its weighting parameter for the $\ell^1$-norm is chosen from $[0.1, 1]$ for the best performance.

## 5  Conclusion

We propose a novel A$\ell^0$-SSC for data clustering under the principle of $\ell^0$-induced sparse subspace clustering ($\ell^0$-SSC). Compared to the existing sparse subspace clustering methods, $\ell^0$-SSC features $\ell^0$-induced almost surely subspace-sparse representation under milder assumptions on the subspaces and random data generation. A$\ell^0$-SSC uses proximal gradient descent to solve the optimization problem of $\ell^0$-SSC and obtain a sub-optimal solution with theoretical guarantee. Extensive experimental results on various real data sets demonstrate the effectiveness and superiority of A$\ell^0$-SSC over other competing methods.

## References

1. Elhamifar, E., Vidal, R.: Sparse subspace clustering: algorithm, theory, and applications. IEEE Trans. Pattern Anal. Mach. Intell. **35**(11), 2765–2781 (2013)
2. Vidal, R.: Subspace clustering. IEEE Sig. Process. Mag. **28**(2), 52–68 (2011)
3. Ng, A.Y., Jordan, M.I., Weiss, Y.: On spectral clustering: analysis and an algorithm. In: NIPS, pp. 849–856 (2001)
4. Liu, G., Lin, Z., Yu, Y.: Robust subspace segmentation by low-rank representation. In: Proceedings of the 27th International Conference on Machine Learning (ICML-10), 21–24 June 2010, Haifa, Israel, pp. 663–670 (2010)
5. Liu, G., Lin, Z., Yan, S., Sun, J., Yu, Y., Ma, Y.: Robust recovery of subspace structures by low-rank representation. IEEE Trans. Pattern Anal. Mach. Intell. **35**(1), 171–184 (2013)
6. Park, D., Caramanis, C., Sanghavi, S.: Greedy subspace clustering. In: Advances in Neural Information Processing Systems 27: Annual Conference on Neural Information Processing Systems 8–13 December 2014, Montreal, Quebec, Canada, pp. 2753–2761 (2014)
7. Wang, Y.X., Xu, H., Leng, C.: Provable subspace clustering: when LRR meets SSC. In: Burges, C., Bottou, L., Welling, M., Ghahramani, Z., Weinberger, K. (eds.) Advances in Neural Information Processing Systems 26, pp. 64–72. Curran Associates, Inc. (2013)
8. Soltanolkotabi, M., Cands, E.J.: A geometric analysis of subspace clustering with outliers. Ann. Statist. **40**(4), 2195–2238 (2012)

9. Wang, Y., Xu, H.: Noisy sparse subspace clustering. In: Proceedings of the 30th International Conference on Machine Learning, ICML 2013, Atlanta, GA, USA, pp. 89–97, 16–21 June 2013

10. Yan, S., Wang, H.: Semi-supervised learning by sparse representation. In: SDM, pp. 792–801 (2009)

11. Cheng, B., Yang, J., Yan, S., Fu, Y., Huang, T.S.: Learning with l1-graph for image analysis. IEEE Trans. Image Process. 19(4), 858–866 (2010)

12. Elhamifar, E., Vidal, R.: Sparse manifold clustering and embedding. In: NIPS, pp. 55–63 (2011)

13. Yang, Y., Wang, Z., Yang, J., Han, J., Huang, T.: Regularized l1-graph for data clustering. In: Proceedings of the British Machine Vision Conference. BMVA Press (2014)

14. Yang, Y., Wang, Z., Yang, J., Wang, J., Chang, S., Huang, T.S.: Data clustering by Laplacian regularized l1-graph. In: Proceedings of the Twenty-Eighth AAAI Conference on Artificial Intelligence, 27–31 July 2014, Québec City, Québec, Canada, pp. 3148–3149 (2014)

15. Peng, X., Yi, Z., Tang, H.: Robust subspace clustering via thresholding ridge regression. In: AAAI Conference on Artificial Intelligence (AAAI), pp. 3827–3833 (2015)

16. Jenatton, R., Mairal, J., Bach, F.R., Obozinski, G.R.: Proximal methods for sparse hierarchical dictionary learning. In: Proceedings of the 27th International Conference on Machine Learning (ICML-10), pp. 487–494 (2010)

17. Mairal, J., Bach, F., Ponce, J., Sapiro, G.: Online learning for matrix factorization and sparse coding. J. Mach. Learn. Res. 11, 19–60 (2010)

18. Mairal, J., Bach, F.R., Ponce, J., Sapiro, G., Zisserman, A.: Supervised dictionary learning. In: Advances in Neural Information Processing Systems 21, Proceedings of the Twenty-Second Annual Conference on Neural Information Processing Systems, Vancouver, British Columbia, Canada, 8–11 December 2008, pp. 1033–1040 (2008)

19. Mancera, L., Portilla, J.: L0-norm-based sparse representation through alternate projections. In: 2006 IEEE International Conference on Image Processing, pp. 2089–2092, October 2006

20. Yang, J., Yu, K., Gong, Y., Huang, T.S.: Linear spatial pyramid matching using sparse coding for image classification. In: CVPR, pp. 1794–1801 (2009)

21. Cheng, H., Liu, Z., Yang, L., Chen, X.: Sparse representation and learning in visual recognition: theory and applications. Sig. Process. 93(6), 1408–1425 (2013)

22. Zhang, T., Ghanem, B., Liu, S., Xu, C., Ahuja, N.: Low-rank sparse coding for image classification. In: IEEE International Conference on Computer Vision, ICCV 2013, Sydney, Australia, 1–8 December 2013, pp. 281–288 (2013)

23. Soltanolkotabi, M., Elhamifar, E., Cands, E.J.: Robust subspace clustering. Ann. Statist. 2(04), 669–699

24. Wang, Y., Wang, Y.X., Singh, A.: Graph connectivity in noisy sparse subspace clustering. CoRR abs/1504.01046 (2016)

25. Dyer, E.L., Sankaranarayanan, A.C., Baraniuk, R.G.: Greedy feature selection for subspace clustering. J. Mach. Learn. Res. 14, 2487–2517 (2013)

26. Tropp, J.A.: Greed is good: algorithmic results for sparse approximation. IEEE Trans. Inf. Theor. 50(10), 2231–2242 (2004)

27. Hyder, M., Mahata, K.: An approximate l0 norm minimization algorithm for compressed sensing. In: IEEE International Conference on Acoustics, Speech and Signal Processing, ICASSP 2009, pp. 3365–3368, April 2009

28. Zhang, C.H., Zhang, T.: A general theory of concave regularization for high-dimensional sparse estimation problems. Statist. Sci. 27(4), 576–593 (2012)

29. Candes, E., Tao, T.: Decoding by linear programming. IEEE Trans. Inf. Theor. **51**(12), 4203–4215 (2005)
30. Cands, E.J.: The restricted isometry property and its implications for compressed sensing. C.R. Math. **346**(910), 589–592 (2008)
31. Zheng, X., Cai, D., He, X., Ma, W.Y., Lin, X.: Locality preserving clustering for image database. In: Proceedings of the 12th Annual ACM International Conference on Multimedia, MULTIMEDIA 2004, pp. 885–891. ACM, New York (2004)
32. Asuncion, A., D.N.: UCI machine learning repository (2007)

# Normalized Cut Meets MRF

Meng Tang[1], Dmitrii Marin[1(✉)], Ismail Ben Ayed[2], and Yuri Boykov[1]

[1] Computer Science, University of Western Ontario, London, Canada
{mtang73,yuri}@csd.uwo.ca, dmitrii.a.marin@gmail.com
[2] Ecole de Technologie Supérieure, University of Quebec, Montreal, Canada
ismail.benayed@etsmtl.ca

**Abstract.** We propose a new segmentation or clustering model that combines Markov Random Field (MRF) and Normalized Cut (NC) objectives. Both NC and MRF models are widely used in machine learning and computer vision, but they were not combined before due to significant differences in the corresponding optimization, *e.g.* spectral relaxation and combinatorial max-flow techniques. On the one hand, we show that many common applications for multi-label MRF segmentation energies can benefit from a high-order NC term, *e.g.* enforcing balanced clustering of arbitrary high-dimensional image features combining color, texture, location, depth, motion, etc. On the other hand, standard NC applications benefit from an inclusion of common pairwise or higher-order MRF constraints, *e.g.* edge alignment, bin-consistency, label cost, etc. To address NC+MRF energy, we propose two efficient multi-label combinatorial optimization techniques, *spectral cut* and *kernel cut*, using new unary bounds for different NC formulations.

## 1 Introduction

Let $\Omega$ be a collection of pixels/voxels or any other data points $p$ that may also be referred to as graph nodes. A segmentation can be equivalently represented either as a labeling $S := (S_p | p \in \Omega)$ including integer node labels $1 \le S_p \le K$ or as a partitioning $\{S^k\}$ of set $\Omega$ into $K$ segments $S^k := \{p \in \Omega | S_p = k\}$. Our general energy formulation combining Normalized Cut clustering and MRF regularization potentials is

$$E(S) = -\sum_k \frac{assoc(S^k, S^k)}{assoc(\Omega, S^k)} + \gamma \sum_{c \in \mathcal{F}} E_c(S_c) \qquad (1)$$

where the first term is the standard NC energy [1] with *association*

$$assoc(S^i, S^j) := \sum_{p \in S^i, q \in S^j} A_{pq} \equiv S^{i'} A S^j \qquad \text{for } 1 \le i, j \le K \qquad (2)$$

based on *affinity matrix* or *kernel* $\mathcal{A} := [A_{pq}]$ with $A_{pq} := A(f_p, f_q)$ defined by some similarity function $A(\cdot, \cdot)$ for node features $f_p$. The equivalent matrix expression in (2) represents segments $S^k$ as indicator vectors such that $S_p^k = 1$

© Springer International Publishing AG 2016
B. Leibe et al. (Eds.): ECCV 2016, Part II, LNCS 9906, pp. 748–765, 2016.
DOI: 10.1007/978-3-319-46475-6_46

iff $S_p = k$ and symbol $'$ means a transpose. The second term in (1) is a general formulation of arbitrary MRF *potentials* [2–4]. Constant $\gamma$ sets a relative weight of this term. Symbol $c$ represent a *factor* or subset of nodes $c \subset \Omega$ and $S_c := (S_p | p \in c)$ is a restriction of labeling $S$ to $c$. Energy terms or potentials $E_c(S_c)$ for a given set of factors $\mathcal{F}$ represent various forms of second or higher-order constraints. For example, common pair-wise factors represent smoothness and contrast/edge alignment [2,5]. Popular higher-order factors are superpixel/bin consistency [3,6], label cost [4], and many others. Section 2.2 details several standard MRF potentials used in this paper's example.

## 1.1 Motivation and Related Work

Due to significant differences in applicable optimization algorithms, Normalized Cut (NC) and Markov Random Fields (MRF) techniques are used separately in many applications of vision and learning. They have complementary strengths and weaknesses.

For example, NC can find a balanced partitioning of data points from pairwise affinities for high-dimensional features [1,7,8]. In contrast, discrete MRF as well as continuous regularization methods commonly use *model fitting* to partition image features [4,9–11]. Such *probabilistic K-means* clustering [12] is well justified when data supports low complexity models, e.g. Gaussians [9] or geometric lines/planes [4]. However, data clustering by fitting complex models like GMM or histograms [10,11] is highly sensitive to local minima and over-fitting even for low dimensional color features [6]. A similar point is made in [13] comparing [11] to a binary energy combining the Potts model and *average association*. Our multi-label energy (1) allows a general MRF framework to benefit from widely-known NC balanced clustering of high-dimensional image features. We show potent results for basic formulations of NC+MRF segmentation with features like RGBXY, RGBD, RGBM where standard MRF methods fail.

On the other hand, standard NC applications can also benefit from an inclusion of additional constraints [14–16]. We show how to add a wide class of standard MRF potentials. For example, standard NC segmentation has weak alignment to contrast edges [8]. While this can be addressed by post-processing, inclusion of the standard pair-wise Potts term [2,5] offers a principled solution. We show benefits from combining NC with lower and higher-order constraints, such as sparsity or label costs [4]. In the context of a general graph clustering, higher-order consistency terms based on a $P^n$-Potts model [3] also give significant improvements.

The synergy of the general NC+MRF segmentation energy (1) can be illustrated by juxtaposing the use of the pixel location information (XY) in standard NC and MRF techniques. The basic pairwise MRF Potts model for images typically works on the nearest-neighbor grids $\mathcal{N}_4$ or $\mathcal{N}_8$ where XY information allows accurate contrast edge alignment and enforces "smooth" segment boundaries. Wider connectivity Potts leads to denser graphs with slower optimization and poorer edge localization. In contrast, common NC methods [1] augment pixel features, *e.g.* color, with XY information using relatively wide kernels for the XY dimension. This encourages segments with spatially "compact" regions. Narrower XY kernels may improve edge alignment [8], but weaken regional color/feature consistency. On the other hand, an extremely large XY kernels ignore spatial information producing color-only clustering with incoherent segments. Combining regional color consistency with spatial coherence in a single NC energy requires a compromise XY kernel width. Our general energy (1) can separate the regional consistency (*e.g.* balanced NC clustering term) from the boundary smoothness or edge alignment (*e.g.* Potts potential). Interestingly, it may still be useful to augment colors with XY in the NC term in (1) since given width XY kernel can separate similar appearance objects at larger distances, see Sect. 3.2.1.

Our experiments (Fig. 2) also show that the standard pairwise edge-alignment MRF (Potts) term may significantly improve the energy of the NC term compared to its independent optimization via spectral relaxation. This suggests that powerful combinatorial graph cut methods may reduce sensitivity of NC to local minima.

### 1.2   Summary of Contributions

This paper proposes a new joint NC+MRF model (1) for multi-label image segmentation and general clustering, efficient move-making bound optimization algorithms, and demonstrates many useful applications. Our main contributions are outlined below:

- We propose a general multi-label segmentation or clustering energy combining Normalized Cut (NC) objective with standard second or higher-order MRF regularization potentials. NC term can enforce balanced partitioning of observed image features and MRF terms can enforce many standard regularization constraints.
- We obtain *kernel* (exact) and *spectral* (approximate) bounds for NC providing two *auxiliary functions* for our joint multi-label NC+MRF energy (1). In the context of standard MRF potentials (*e.g.* Potts, robust $P^n$-Potts, label cost) we propose move-making algorithms exploring new generalizations of $\alpha$-expansions and $\alpha\beta$-swap designed for multi-label bound optimization.[1]
- Our experiments demonstrate that typical NC applications benefit from extra MRF constraints, as well as, MRF segmentation benefit from the high-order NC term encouraging balanced partitioning of image features. In particular, NC+MRF framework works for higher-dimensional image features (*e.g.* RGBXY, RGBD, RGBM) where standard model-fitting clustering [4,10,11] fails.

---

[1] Our kernel and spectral bounds for NC can be also integrated into auxiliary functions with other standard regularization potentials (truncated, cardinality, TV) addressed by discrete (*e.g.* message passing, relaxations) or continuous (*e.g.* convex, primal-dual) algorithms.

The rest of the paper is organized as follows. Section 2 presents our spectral and kernel bounds for (1) and details combinatorial move making graph cut algorithms for its optimization. Section 3 presents many proof-of-the-concept experiments where NC benefits from the additional MRF constraints, Sect. 3.1, and common MRF formulations benefit from an additional balanced NC clustering term for high-dimensional features, Sect. 3.2.

# 2   Our Algorithms

In this section we propose *bound optimization* and *move-making* algorithms for our high-order NC+MRF functional (1). In particular, we derive bounds or *auxiliary functions* for our problem[2]. Bound optimization have recently led to competitive algorithms for different high-order binary segmentation functionals, *e.g.* distribution-matching constraints [17], entropy, or non-submodular pairwise energies [18]. These greedy procedures iteratively minimize a sequence of *auxiliary functions* for a given energy $E(S)$ assuming that they are easier to optimize. An auxiliary function $a_t(S)$ at iteration $t$ is an upper bound for $E(S)$ touching the original energy at the current solution $S_t$

$$a_t(S) \geq E(S), \qquad E(S_t) = a_t(S_t).$$

To decrease $E(S)$ one can minimize the auxiliary function $a_t$ giving the next solution

$$S_{t+1} = \arg\min_S a_t(S).$$

This iterative process guarantees the original energy decrease: $E(S_{t+1}) \leq a_t(S_{t+1}) \leq a_t(S_t) = E(S_t)$. Note that the bound does not have to be optimized globally. As long as $a_t(S_{t+1}) \leq a_t(S_t)$, the original energy is guaranteed to decrease $E(S_{t+1}) \leq E(S_t)$.

## 2.1   Unary Bounds for Normalized Cut

Below we derive two bounds for (1) and propose move-making algorithms such as *expansion* and *swap* [2] to optimize such multi-label auxiliary functions for our NC+MRF energy. To the best of our knowledge, this is the first use of move-making algorithms in the context of bound optimization. The existing high-order bound-optimization graph cut techniques apply to binary segmentation [17,18]. The computation aspects of evaluating our bounds for large-scale problems are discussed in Sec.2.1.

Our first bound, called *kernel bound*, is an exact auxiliary function for the high-order energy (1). It is expressed as a function of the pairwise affinities or kernels. Our second bound, called *spectral bound*, can be viewed as an auxiliary function for the K-means discretization step in standard spectral relaxation

---

[2] The MRF terms in (1) preclude the direct use of standard spectral methods for NC [1].

methods [1,19]. Unlike our kernel bound, this approximate bound requires eigen vector computations.

The next lemma helps to derive our kernel bound for energy (1) in Proposition 1.

**Lemma 1 (Concavity).** *Equivalently rewrite the first (NC) term in* (1) *as*

$$- \sum_k \frac{assoc(S^k, S^k)}{assoc(\Omega, S^k)} \equiv \sum_k e(S^k) \qquad for \qquad e(X) := -\frac{X'AX}{d'X} \qquad (3)$$

*using the matrix notation in* (2) *with affinity matrix* $\mathcal{A} := [A_{pq}]$ *and vector* $d := \mathcal{A}\mathbf{1}$ *of node degrees* $d_p = \sum_q A_{pq}$. *Function* $e : \mathbf{R}^{|\Omega|} \to \mathbf{R}$ *in* (3) *is concave over region* $d'X > 0$ *assuming that affinity matrix* $\mathcal{A}$ *is positive semi-definite.*

*Proof.* It follows from negative definiteness of the Hessian $\nabla\nabla e$, see [20, Lemma 1]. □

The first-order Taylor expansion $T_t(X) := e(X_t) + \nabla e(X_t)'(X - X_t)$ at a current solution $X_t$ is an obvious bound for the concave function $e(X)$ in (3). Its gradient $\nabla e(X_t) = d \frac{X_t'AX_t}{(d'X_t)^2} - AX_t \frac{2}{d'X_t}$ implies bound $T_t(X) \equiv \nabla e(X_t)'X$ and Proposition 1.

**Proposition 1 (Kernel Bound).** *For positive semi-definite affinity matrix* $\mathcal{A}$ *and any current solution* $S_t$ *the following is an auxiliary function for NC+MRF energy* (1)

$$a_t(S) = \sum_k \nabla e(S_t^k)' S^k + \gamma \sum_{c \in \mathcal{F}} E_c(S_c). \qquad (4)$$

Our kernel bound (4) for energy (1) combines a unary term and standard MRF regularization potentials. This allows to develop efficient move-making graph cut techniques for the general multi-label NC+MRF energy (1), see Sect. 2.2. Interestingly, for the degenerate case of (1) with no MRF potentials ($\gamma = 0$) iterative optimization of the first unary term in bound (4) can be shown to be equivalent to the *weighted kernel K-means* approach to NC in [21,22], see Sect. 1.3.1 and Appendix A in [20]. Note that NC with arbitrary affinity $\mathcal{A}$ can be converted to an equivalent NC objective with p.s.d. affinity $\mathcal{A} + \delta D$ where $D := diag(d)$ is a *degree matrix*, see [20, Sect. 1.3.1]. Such *diagonal shift* tricks were proposed by [23,24].

We also develop an approximate *spectral bound* for our NC+MRF energy. Note that standard spectral methods [1,19] optimize the normalized cut objective by relaxing the original integer problem to a (generalized) eigenvalue problem of the form:

$$(D - \mathcal{A})\mathbf{u} = \lambda D\mathbf{u}. \qquad (5)$$

Let $U$ denote the matrix whose rows are the (unit) eigenvectors of the eigen system (5) and $U^K$ be a matrix whose rows are the $K$ top (unit) eigenvectors in $U$. To extract integer labeling from the relaxed solutions produced by (5), spectral methods often apply the basic K-means to some *ad hoc* data embedding

$\phi_p \equiv \phi(f_p)$ based on $U^K$. For instance, [1,19] use the columns of $U^K$, *i.e.* $\phi_p = U_p^K$, while [7,25] use a weighted version $\phi_p = [\Sigma^{-\frac{1}{2}}U]_p^K$ where $\Sigma$ is a diagonal matrix of eigenvalues in (5). We did not observe much difference in practice.

Similar embeddings can also be derived in a principled fashion. Consider kernel $\mathcal{K} = D^{-1}\mathcal{A}D^{-1}$ for weighted ($w = d$) *kernel K-means* [22] equivalent to NC with affinity $\mathcal{A}$. Similarly to *multi-dimensional scaling* (MDS) [26], we obtain rank-$m$ approximate kernel $\tilde{\mathcal{K}}$ minimizing weighted Frobenius error $\sum_{pq} w_p w_q (\mathcal{K}_{pq} - \tilde{\mathcal{K}}_{pq})^2$ and deduce embedding $\tilde{\phi}_p \in \mathcal{R}^m$ satisfying isometry $\tilde{\phi}_p' \tilde{\phi}_q = \tilde{\mathcal{K}}_{pq}$, see details in [20, Sect.3]

$$\tilde{\phi}_p = \sqrt{\Lambda^m/d_p} V_p^m \qquad \text{for eigen decomposition } V'\Lambda V = D^{-\frac{1}{2}}\mathcal{A}D^{-\frac{1}{2}}. \quad (6)$$

Weighted K-means over $\{\tilde{\phi}_p\}$ corresponds to *kernel K-means* for kernel $\tilde{\mathcal{K}} \approx \mathcal{K}$ and, therefore, approximates NC. We can combine weighted K-means over $\{\tilde{\phi}_p\}$ with MRF regularization via minimizing the following *spectral approximation* of (1)

$$\tilde{E}(S) = F^w(S, \mu_S) + \gamma \sum_{c \in \mathcal{F}} E_c(S_c) \quad (7)$$

where $F^w(S, m) := \sum_k \sum_{p \in S^k} w_p \|\tilde{\phi}_p - m_k\|^2$ includes variable $m = \{m_k\}_{k=1}^K$ representing weighted segment means $m_k = \mu_{S^k}^w := \frac{\sum_{p \in S^k} w_p \tilde{\phi}_p}{w' S^k}$ in (7).

**Proposition 2 (Spectral Bound).** *The following is an auxiliary function for* (7) *at current segmentation $S_t$ with the corresponding means* $\mu_t^w := \{\mu_{S_t^k}^w\}_{k=1}^K$

$$\tilde{a}_t(S) = F^w(S, \mu_t^w) + \gamma \sum_{c \in \mathcal{F}} E_c(S_c). \quad (8)$$

*Proof.* This bound follows from a simple fact that the standard block-coordinate descent (weighted) K-means procedure is a bound optimizer, *e.g.* see [20, Theorem 1]. □

**Bound Evaluation for Large-Scale Problems.** Our kernel bound does not require eigen decomposition. The time complexity of evaluating this bound is linear with respect to the number of non-zero entries in affinity (kernel) matrix $\mathcal{A}$. Sampling heuristics [27] can be used to derive an approximate bound efficiently for large scale problems.

Obtaining the spectral bound in Proposition 2 for given $\phi_p$ has complexity $\mathcal{O}(|\Omega|Km)$. The eigen decomposition is also computationally expensive. Standard methods like [28] can substantially accelerate it allowing applications to large scale problems.

## 2.2    Move-Making NC+MRF Bound Optimization

As mentioned in the introduction, second and higher-order MRF potentials are widely used for regularization in computer vision. We demonstrate a combined

NC+MRF energy (1) in the context of several common MRF potentials outlined below and propose combinatorial bound optimization algorithms using unary bounds for NC in the previous section. We observe that many standard discrete optimization methods [2,29–31][3] can be developed to work with such unary/linear bounds for NC. For simplicity, we focus on three standard MRF potentials below allowing efficient move-making graph cut techniques for multi-label NC+MRF bound optimization.

---

**Input** : Affinity Matrix $\mathcal{A}$ of size $|\Omega| \times |\Omega|$; initial labeling $S_0^1, ..., S_0^K$
**Output**: $S^1, ..., S^K$: partition of the set $\Omega$
1  Set $t := 0$;
2  **while** *not converged* **do**
3  |  Set $a_t(S)$ to be kernel bound (4) for NC at current partition $S_t$;
4  |  **for** *each label* $\alpha \in \mathcal{L} = \{1, ..., K\}$ **do**
5  |  |  Find $S_t := \arg\min a_t(S)$ within one $\alpha$ expansion of $S_t$;
6  |  Set $t := t + 1$;

**Algorithm 1.** $\alpha$-Expansion for Kernel Cut

---

**Input** : Affinity Matrix $\mathcal{A}$ of size $|\Omega| \times |\Omega|$; initial labeling $S_0^1, ..., S_0^K$
**Output**: $S^1, ..., S^K$: partition of the set $\Omega$
1  Find top $m$ eigen values/vectors $\Lambda^m, V^m$ for matrix $D^{-\frac{1}{2}} A D^{-\frac{1}{2}}$;
2  Compute embedding $\tilde{\phi}_p$ in (6) and set $t := 0$;
3  **while** *not converged* **do**
4  |  Set $\tilde{a}_t(S)$ to be the spectral bound (8) at current partition $S_t$;
5  |  **for** *each label* $\alpha \in \mathcal{L} = \{1, ..., K\}$ **do**
6  |  |  Find $S_t := \arg\min \tilde{a}_t(S)$ within one $\alpha$ expansion of $S_t$;
7  |  Set $t := t + 1$;

**Algorithm 2.** $\alpha$-Expansion for Spectral Cut

---

Probably the most common MRF regularization potential corresponds to the second-order Potts model [2] used for **edge alignment**

$$\sum_{c \in \mathcal{F}} E_c(S_c) = \sum_{pq \in \mathcal{N}} w_{pq} \cdot [S_p \neq S_q] \qquad (9)$$

where a set of pairwise factors $\mathcal{F} = \mathcal{N}$ includes all *edges* $c = \{pq\}$ between pairs of neighboring nodes. Weight $w_{pq}$ defines a penalty for discontinuity between $p$ and $q$. It could be a constant or may be set by a decreasing function of intensity difference $I_p - I_q$ in order to attract the segmentation boundary to the contrast edges in the image [5].

A useful **bin consistency** constraint corresponds to the $P^n$-Potts model [3] defined over an arbitrary collection of high-order factors $\mathcal{F}$. Factors $c \in \mathcal{F}$ correspond to predefined subsets of nodes such as *superpixels* [3] or *bins* of pixels with the same color/feature [6,35]. The model penalizes inconsistency in segmentation of each factor

$$\sum_{c \in \mathcal{F}} E_c(S_c) = \sum_{c \in \mathcal{F}} \min\{T, |c| - |S_c|^*\} \qquad (10)$$

---

[3] As well as related continuous methods, *e.g.* [32–34].

where $T$ is some threshold and $|S_c|^* := \max_k |S^k \cap c|$ is the cardinality of the largest segment inside $c$. Clearly, potential (10) has its lowest value (zero) when all nodes in each factor are within the same segment. In this paper we use such MRF potential for NC-based image collection clustering to enforce *text-tag consistency*.

A standard label cost corresponds to an MDL **sparsity potential** [4] defined for a single high-order factor, the whole set of nodes. That is, $\mathcal{F} = \{\Omega\}$. In its simplest form this potential penalizes the number of distinct labels supported by segmentation $S$

$$\mathbf{E}_\Omega(S) = \sum_k h_k \cdot [|S^k| > 0] \tag{11}$$

where penalty $h_k$ could be a constant or a cost for each specific segment type (label).

All three MRF potentials reviewed above can be optimized by $\alpha\beta$-swap moves and $\alpha$-expansion moves. We combine these MRF terms with unary bounds for NC (Sect. 2.1). Our kernel cut and spectral cut methods are outlined in Algorithms 1 and 2.

One should decide the order of iterative move making and bound evaluation. In the case of $\alpha$-expansion, there are at least three options: updating the bound after single expansion step, or after single expansion loop, or after the convergence of $\alpha$-expansion. More frequent bound recalculation slows down the algorithm, but makes the bound tighter. The particular choice generally depends on the trade-off between the speed and solution quality. However, in our experiments more frequent update does not always improve the energy, see Fig. 1. We recommend updating the bound after a single loop of expansion, see Algorithms 1 and 2. Further by replacing expansion with swap loops in the two algorithm, we can have $\alpha\beta$-swap based version of kernel cut and spectral cut.

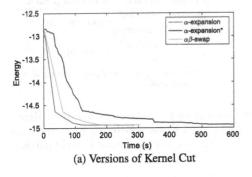

(a) Versions of Kernel Cut

| Compare | against | # of wins | p-value[†] |
|---|---|---|---|
| $\alpha$-expansion | $\alpha\beta$-swap | 135/200 | $10^{-6}$ |
| $\alpha$-expansion | $\alpha$-expansion* | 182/200[‡] | $10^{-34}$[‡] |

[†] The probability to exceed a given number of wins by random chance.

[‡] The algorithm terminated due to time limit. This may cause incorrect number of wins.

(b) BSDS500 training dataset

**Fig. 1.** Typical energy evolution wrt different moves and frequency of bound updates. *$\alpha$-expansion* updates the bound after a round of expansions, *$\alpha$-expansion** updates the bound after each expansion move. Initialization is a regular 5×5 grid of patches.

# 3   Experiments

This section is divided into two parts. The first part (Sect. 3.1) shows the benefits of extra MRF regularization for the normalized cut criterion. We consider pairwise Potts, label cost and robust bin consistency term, as discussed in Sect. 2.2. We compare to spectral clustering [1,7] and kernel K-means [22], which can be seen as degenerated versions for spectral and kernel cuts (respectively) without MRF terms. We show that MRF helps normalized cut in segmentation and image clustering. In the second part (Sect. 3.2) we replace the log-likelihoods in model-fitting methods, *e.g.* GrabCut [11], by NC term. This is particularly advantageous for high dimension features (location, depth, motion).

**Implementation Details:** The parameters of the algorithms were selected to minimize the average error over datasets. For segmentation we use affinities $A_{pq}$ defined by *KNN* (K-Nearest-Neighbours) graph due to limitations of fixed-width Gaussian kernel for multi-scale data [36]. Assuming $KNN(f_p)$ is the set of K-nearest-neighbors of feature vector $f_p$, the *KNN* affinity is $A_{pq} = A(f_p, f_q) = [f_p \in KNN(f_q)] + [f_q \in KNN(f_p)]$. The feature $f_p$ can be concatenation of RGB (color), XY (location) and M (motion or optical flow [37]). We choose 400 neighbors and randomly sample 50 neighbors for each pixel. Sampling does not degrade our segmentation but expedites bound evaluation. We also experiment with popular *mPb* contour based affinities [8] for segmentation. The window radius is set to 5 pixels. For image clustering, we extract GIST [38] feature and use Gaussian kernel to build a dense affinities matrix. For GrabCut we use histograms as models and try various bin size for spatial and depth channels.

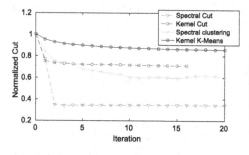

| BSDS500 training dataset | | | |
|---|---|---|---|
| Compare | against | # of wins | p-value* |
| Spectral Cut | Spectral clustering | 184/200 | $10^{-15}$ |
| Kernel Cut | Kernel K-Means | 200/200 | $10^{-60}$ |

\* The probability to exceed a given number of wins by random chance.

**Fig. 2.** Left: typical evolution of the NC term during iterative optimization. Right: adding MRF regularization helps both Spectral and Kernel clustering to escape local minima and to achieve lower value of NC. Initialization is a regular $5 \times 5$ grid of patches.

## 3.1   MRF Helps Normalized Cut

Here we add MRF regulation terms to typical normalized cut applications, such as unsupervised multi-label segmentation [8] and image clustering [39]. Our kernel and spectral cuts are used to optimize the joint energy of normalized cut and MRF (1) or (7).

### 3.1.1 Normalized Cut with Potts Regularization.

Spectral clustering [1,7] solves a (generalized) eigen problem, followed by K-means on the (weighted) eigenvectors. However, it was observed that such paradigm results in undesirable segmentation in large uniform regions [7,8], see examples in Fig. 3. Obviously such edge mis-alignment can be penalized by contrast-sensitive Potts term. Our spectral cut and kernel cut get better segmentation boundaries. As is in [22] we use spectral initialization.

**Fig. 3.** Sample results on BSDS500 with mPb affinities [8]. Top row: Spectral Clustering; Middle and bottom rows: Kernel and Spectral Cuts giving better edge alignment.

The table on the right gives quantitative results on BSDS500 dataset. Number of segments in ground truth is provided to each method. It also shows that kernel and spectral cuts give bet-

| method | Covering | PRI | VOI |
|---|---|---|---|
| Spectral relax | 0.34 | 0.76 | 2.76 |
| Our kernel cut | 0.41 | **0.78** | 2.44 |
| Our spectral cut | **0.42** | **0.78** | **2.34** |

ter covering, PRI (probabilistic rand index) and VOI (variation of information) than spectral clustering. Figure 3 gives sample results. Kernel K-means [22] gives results similar to spectral clustering and hence are not shown.

### 3.1.2 Normalized Cut with Label Cost [4].

Unlike spectral clustering, our kernel and spectral cuts do not need the number of segments beforehand. We optimize a combination of the normalized cut, Potts model and label costs terms. The label cost (11) penalizes each label by constant $h_k$. The energy is minimized by $\alpha$-expansion and $\alpha\beta$-swap moves in Sect. 2.2. We sample initial models from patches, as in [4]. Results with different label cost are shown in Fig. 4. Due to sparsity prior for normalized cut, our kernel and spectral cuts automatically prune *weak* models and determine the number of segments, yet yield regularized segmentation. We use *KNN* affinity for normalized cut and mPb [8] based Potts regularization.

### 3.1.3 Normalized Cut with High Order Consistency Term [3,6,35].

It is common that images come with multiple tags, such as those in Flickr platform or the LabelMe dataset [38]. We study how to utilize tag-based group prior for image clustering [39].

**Fig. 4.** Segmentation using our kernel cut with label cost. We experiment with increasing value of label cost $h_k$ for each label (from left to right).

We experiment on the LabelMe dataset [38] which contains 2,600 images of 8 scene categories (coast, mountain, forest, open country, street, inside city, tall buildings and highways). We use the same GIST feature, affinity matrix and group prior as used in [39]. We found the group prior to be noisy. The dominant category in each group occupies only 60 %–90 % of the group. The high-order consistency term is defined on each group. For each group, we introduce an energy term that is akin to the *robust $P^n$-Potts* [3], which can be exactly minimized within a single $\alpha\beta$-swap or $\alpha$-expansion move. Notice that here we have to use robust consistency potential instead of rigid ones.

Our kernel cut minimizes NC plus the *robust $P^n$-Potts* term. Spectral cut minimizes energy of (7). Normalized mutual information (NMI) is used as the measure of clustering quality. Perfect clustering with respect to ground truth has NMI value of 1.

Spectral clustering and kernel K-means [22] give NMI value of 0.542 and 0.572 respectively. Our kernel cut and spectral cut significantly boost the NMI to 0.683 and 0.681. Figure 5 shows the results with respect to different amount of image tags used. The left most points correspond to the case when no group prior is given. We optimize over the weight of high order consistency term, see

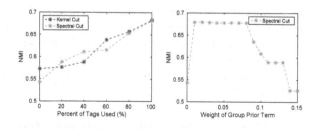

**Fig. 5.** Incorporating group prior achieves better NMI for image clustering. Here we use tags-based group prior. Our method achieved better NMI when more images are tagged. The right plot shows how the weight of bin consistency term affects our method.

Fig. 5. Note that it's not the case the larger the weight the better since the grouping prior is noisy.

## 3.2 Normalized Cut Helps MRF

In typical MRF applications we replace the log-likelihood terms by the normalized cut. We test various applications including separating similar objects, RGBD and motion segmentation.

### 3.2.1 Similar Objects Separation.
Even though objects may have similar appearances or look similar to the background (*e.g.* the top row in Fig. 6), we assume that the objects of interest are compact and have different locations. This assumption motivates using XY coordinates of pixels as extra feature for distinguishing similar or camouflaged objects[4]. Let $f_p \in \mathcal{R}^5$ be the augmented color-location feature $f_p = [L_p, a_p, b_p, \beta x_p, \beta y_p]$ at pixel $p$ where $[L_p, a_p, b_p]$ is its color, $[x_p, y_p]$ are its image coordinates, and $\beta$ is a scaling parameter.

Note that the edge-based Potts model [5] also uses the XY information. Location features in the clustering and regularization terms have complementary effect: the former solves appearance camouflage while the latter gets edge alignment. We report quantitative results on 18 images with similar objects and camouflage selected from the Berkeley database [41]. We set strokes to select one of the objects, see Fig. 6.

We test the effect of adding XY into feature space for GrabCut and Kernel Cut. We try various $\beta$ for Kernel Cut. Figure 7(a) shows the effect of different $\beta$ on *KNN*s of a pixel. For histogram-based GrabCut we change spatial bin size for the XY channel, ranging from 30 pixels to the image size. Figure 7(a) compares GrabCut and Kernel Cut.

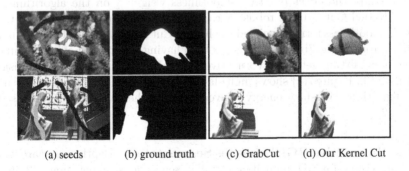

(a) seeds          (b) ground truth          (c) GrabCut          (d) Our Kernel Cut

**Fig. 6.** Sample results on Berkeley dataset.

---

[4] XY feature has also been used in [40] to build space-variant color distribution. However, such distribution used in MRF-MAP inference [40] would still overfit the data [13].

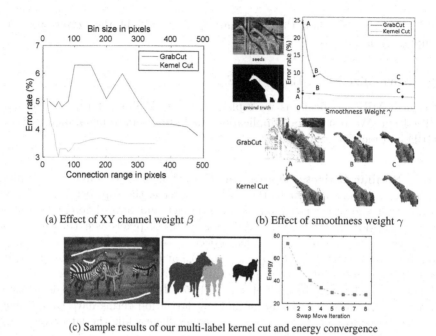

(a) Effect of XY channel weight $\beta$         (b) Effect of smoothness weight $\gamma$

(c) Sample results of our multi-label kernel cut and energy convergence

**Fig. 7.** (a) Average errors for multi-object dataset. We vary the spatial bin size for GrabCut and $\beta$ for Kernel Cut. The connection range is the average geometric distance between a pixel and its $k^{th}$ nearest neighbor. **The right-most point of the curves corresponds to the absence of XY features.** GrabCut does not benefit from XY features. Kernel Cut achieves the best error rate of 2.9 % for the connection range of 50 pixels. **(b)** Our kernel cut is robust to smoothness weight $\gamma$. **(c)** Multi-objects segmentation.

We study the effect of MRF smoothness weight $\gamma$ on the algorithms, see Fig. 7. Kernel Cut is more robust w.r.t. smoothness weight compared to Grab-Cut. If smoothness term is omitted the Kernel Cut is significantly better (4.6 % vs 24.6 % errors in Fig. 7b). MRF benefits from having NC instead of log-likelihoods since model fitting gets highly sensitive to local minima for higher dimensional features [13]. Figure 7(c) shows multi-label segmentation of similar objects using our algorithm. We show energy convergence for the swap moves discussed in Sect. 2.2.

**3.2.2 Interactive RGBD Images Segmentation.** Depth sensor are widely used in vision for 3D modelling [44,45], semantic segmentation [42,46–48], motion flow [49]. We selected 64 indoor RGBD images from semantic segmentation database NYUv2 [42] and provided bounding boxes and ground truth. In contrast to [11], the prepared dataset consists of low-quality images: there are camera motion artifacts, underexposed and overexposed regions. Such artifacts make color-based segmentation harder.

We compare GrabCut to Kernel Cut over joint features $f_p = [L_p, a_p, b_p, \beta D_p]$ as in Sect. 3.2.1. Figure 8 shows the error statistics and segmentation examples. While Kernel Cut takes advantage of the additional channel, GrabCut fails to improve.

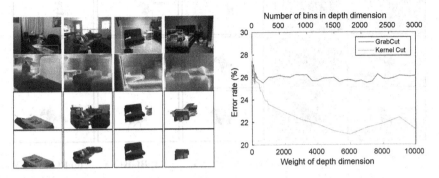

**Fig. 8.** NYUv2 database [42] **Left:** The first two rows show original images with bounding box and color-coded depth channel. The third row shows results of Grabcut, the forth row shows results of Kernel Cut. **Right:** The average errors of GrabCut and Kernel Cut methods over 64 images randomly selected and labeled.

### 3.2.3 Motion Segmentation.

Besides location and depth features, we also test segmentation with motion features. Figures 10, 11 and 9 compare motion segmentations using different feature spaces: RGB, XY, M (optical flow) and their combinations (RGBM or RGBXY or RGBXYM). Abbreviation **+XY** means Potts regularization. Here we use kernel cut (Algorithm 1) for the combination of normalized cut with the Potts term.

**Challenging Video Examples:** For videos in FBMS-59 dataset [50], our algorithm runs on individual frames instead of 3D volume. Segmentation of previous frame initializes the next frame. The strokes are provided *only* for the first frame. We use the optical flow algorithm in [37] to generate M features. Selected frames are shown in Figs. 10 and 11. Instead of tracks from all frames in [51], our segmentation of each frame uses only motion estimation between two consecutive frames. Our approach jointly optimizes normalized cut and Potts model. In contrast, [51]

| Motion Flow* | RGB+XY | MXY+XY |

**Fig. 9.** Kernel cut on image 000079_10 from *KITTI* [43]. The images show the motion flow, color-based segmentation (RGB+XY), motion based segmentation with location features (MXY+XY). * Black color shows pixels that lack motion information.

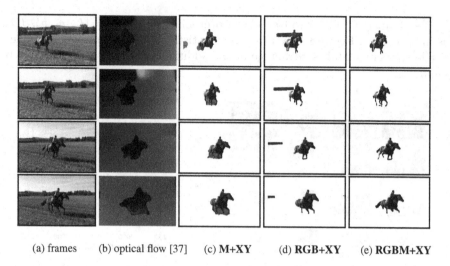

(a) frames     (b) optical flow [37]     (c) **M+XY**     (d) **RGB+XY**     (e) **RGBM+XY**

**Fig. 10.** Motion segmentation using our framework for the sequence *horses01* in FBMS-59 dataset [50]. **+XY** means with Potts model. Motion feature alone (**M+XY** in (c)) is not sufficient to obtain fine segmentation. Our framework successfully utilize motion feature to separate the horse from the barn, which have similar appearances.

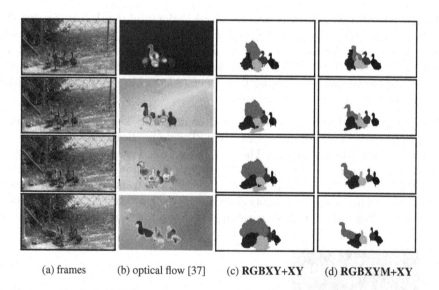

(a) frames     (b) optical flow [37]     (c) **RGBXY+XY**     (d) **RGBXYM+XY**

**Fig. 11.** Multi-label motion segmentation for the sequence *ducks01* in FBMS-59 dataset [50]. This video is challenging since the ducks here have similar appearances and even spatially overlap with each other. However, different ducks come with different motions, which helps our framework to better separate individual ducks.

first clusters semi-dense tracks via spectral clustering [50] and then obtains dense segmentation via regularization.

**Kitti Segmentation Example:** We also experiment with Kitti dataset [43]. Figure 9 shows the multi-label segmentation using either color information RGB+XY (first row) or motion MXY+XY (second row). The ground-truth motion field works as M channel. Note that the motion field is known only for approximately 20 % of the pixels. To build an affinity graph, we construct a *KNN* graph from pixels that have motion information. The regularization over 8-neighborhood on the pixel grid interpolates the segmentation labels during the optimization procedure.

# References

1. Shi, J., Malik, J.: Normalized cuts and image segmentation. IEEE Trans. Pattern Anal. Mach. Intell. **22**(8), 888–905 (2000)
2. Boykov, Y., Veksler, O., Zabih, R.: Fast approximate energy minimization via graph cuts. IEEE Trans. Pattern Anal. Mach. Intell. **23**(11), 1222–1239 (2001)
3. Kohli, P., Ladicky, L., Torr, P.H.S.: Robust higher order potentials for enforcing label consistency. Int. J. Comput. Vis. (IJCV) **82**(3), 302–324 (2009)
4. Delong, A., Osokin, A., Isack, H., Boykov, Y.: Fast approximate energy minization with label costs. Int. J. Comput. Vis. (IJCV) **96**(1), 1–27 (2012)
5. Boykov, Y., Jolly, M.P.: Interactive graph cuts for optimal boundary & region segmentation of objects in N-D images. In: ICCV, vol. I, pp. 105–112 (2001)
6. Tang, M., Gorelick, L., Veksler, O., Boykov, Y.: Grabcut in one cut. In: International Conference on Computer Vision (ICCV), Sydney, Australia, December 2013
7. Malik, J., Belongie, S., Leung, T., Shi, J.: Contour and texture analysis for image segmentation. Int. J. Comput. Vis. **43**(1), 7–27 (2001)
8. Arbelaez, P., Maire, M., Fowlkes, C., Malik, J.: Contour detection and hierarchical image segmentation. IEEE Trans. Pattern Anal. Mach. Intell. **33**(5), 898–916 (2011)
9. Chan, T., Vese, L.: Active contours without edges. IEEE Trans. Image Process. **10**(2), 266–277 (2001)
10. Zhu, S.C., Yuille, A.: Region competition: unifying snakes, region growing, and Bayes/MDL for multiband image segmentation. IEEE Trans. PAMI **18**(9), 884–900 (1996)
11. Rother, C., Kolmogorov, V., Blake, A.: Grabcut - interactive foreground extraction using iterated graph cuts. ACM Trans. Graph. (SIGGRAPH) **23**(3), 309–314 (2004)
12. Kearns, M., Mansour, Y., Ng, A.: An information-theoretic analysis of hard and soft assignment methods for clustering. In: Thirteenth Conference on Uncertainty in Artificial Intelligence (UAI), August 1997
13. Tang, M., Ayed, I.B., Marin, D., Boykov, Y.: Secrets of grabcut and kernel k-means. In: International Conference on Computer Vision (ICCV), Santiago, Chile, December 2015
14. Yu, S.X., Shi, J.: Segmentation given partial grouping constraints. IEEE Trans. Pattern Anal. Mach. Intell. **26**(2), 173–183 (2004)
15. Eriksson, A., Olsson, C., Kahl, F.: Normalized cuts revisited: a reformulation for segmentation with linear grouping constraints. J. Math. Imaging Vis. **39**(1), 45–61 (2011)

16. Chew, S.E., Cahill, N.D.: Semi-supervised normalized cuts for image segmentation. In: IEEE International Conference on Computer Vision (ICCV), December 2015
17. Ayed, I.B., Gorelick, L., Boykov, Y.: Auxiliary cuts for general classes of higher order functionals. In: CVPR, pp. 1304–1311 (2013)
18. Tang, M., Ben Ayed, I., Boykov, Y.: Pseudo-bound optimization for binary energies. In: Fleet, D., Pajdla, T., Schiele, B., Tuytelaars, T. (eds.) ECCV 2014, Part V. LNCS, vol. 8693, pp. 691–707. Springer, Heidelberg (2014)
19. Von Luxburg, U.: A tutorial on spectral clustering. Stat. Comput. **17**(4), 395–416 (2007)
20. Tang, M., Ayed, I.B., Marin, D., Boykov, Y.: Kernel Cuts: MRF meets kernel & spectral clustering. In: (July 2016, also submitted to PAMI). arXiv:1506.07439
21. Bach, F., Jordan, M.: Learning spectral clustering. Adv. Neural Inf. Process. Syst. (NIPS) **16**, 305–312 (2003)
22. Dhillon, I., Guan, Y., Kulis, B.: Kernel k-means, spectral clustering and normalized cuts. In: KDD (2004)
23. Roth, V., Laub, J., Kawanabe, M., Buhmann, J.: Optimal cluster preserving embedding of nonmetric proximity data. IEEE Trans. Pattern Anal. Mach. Intell. (PAMI) **25**(12), 1540–1551 (2003)
24. Dhillon, I., Guan, Y., Kulis, B.: Weighted graph cuts without eigenvectors: a multilevel approach. IEEE Trans. Pattern Anal. Mach. Learn. (PAMI) **29**(11), 1944–1957 (2007)
25. Belongie, S., Malik, J.: Finding boundaries in natural images: a new method using point descriptors and area completion. In: Burkhardt, H.-J., Neumann, B. (eds.) ECCV 1998. LNCS, vol. 1406, pp. 751–766. Springer, Heidelberg (1998)
26. Cox, T.F., Cox, M.A.: Multidimensional Scaling. CRC Press, Boca Raton (2000)
27. Chitta, R., Jin, R., Havens, T.C., Jain, A.K.: Approximate kernel k-means: solution to large scale kernel clustering. In: Proceedings of the 17th ACM SIGKDD International Conference on Knowledge Discovery and Data Mining, pp. 895–903. ACM (2011)
28. Fowlkes, C., Belongie, S., Chung, F., Malik, J.: Spectral grouping using the nystrom method. IEEE Trans. Pattern Anal. Mach. Intell. **26**(2), 214–225 (2004)
29. Kolmogorov, V.: Convergent tree-reweighted message passing for energy minimization. IEEE Trans. Pattern Anal. Mach. Intell. **28**(10), 1568–1583 (2006)
30. Werner, T.: A linear programming approach to max-sum problem: a review. IEEE Trans. Pattern Anal. Mach. Intell. **29**(7), 1165–1179 (2007)
31. Kappes, J.H., Andres, B., Hamprecht, F.A., Schnörr, C., Nowozin, S., Batra, D., Kim, S., Kausler, B.X., Kröger, T., Lellmann, J., et al.: A comparative study of modern inference techniques for structured discrete energy minimization problems. Int. J. Comput. Vis. **115**(2), 155–184 (2015)
32. Chambolle, A.: An algorithm for total variation minimization and applications. J. Math. Imaging Vis. **20**(1–2), 89–97 (2004)
33. Chambolle, A., Pock, T.: A first-order primal-dual algorithm for convex problems with applications to imaging. J. Math. Imaging Vis. **40**(1), 120–145 (2011)
34. Cremers, D., Rousson, M., Deriche, R.: A review of statistical approaches to level set segmentation: integrating color, texture, motion and shape. Int. J. Comput. Vis. **72**(2), 195–215 (2007)
35. Park, K., Gould, S.: On learning higher-order consistency potentials for multi-class pixel labeling. In: Fitzgibbon, A., Lazebnik, S., Perona, P., Sato, Y., Schmid, C. (eds.) ECCV 2012, Part II. LNCS, vol. 7573, pp. 202–215. Springer, Heidelberg (2012)

36. Zelnik-Manor, L., Perona, P.: Self-tuning spectral clustering. In: Advances in Neural Information Processing Systems, pp. 1601–1608 (2004)
37. Brox, T., Malik, J.: Large displacement optical flow: descriptor matching in variational motion estimation. IEEE Trans. Pattern Anal. Mach. Intell. **33**(3), 500–513 (2011)
38. Oliva, A., Torralba, A.: Modeling the shape of the scene: a holistic representation of the spatial envelope. Int. J. Comput. Vis. **42**(3), 145–175 (2001)
39. Collins, M.D., Liu, J., Xu, J., Mukherjee, L., Singh, V.: Spectral clustering with a convex regularizer on millions of images. In: Fleet, D., Pajdla, T., Schiele, B., Tuytelaars, T. (eds.) ECCV 2014, Part III. LNCS, vol. 8691, pp. 282–298. Springer, Heidelberg (2014)
40. Nieuwenhuis, C., Cremers, D.: Spatially varying color distributions for interactive multilabel segmentation. IEEE Trans. Pattern Anal. Mach. Intell. **35**(5), 1234–1247 (2013)
41. Martin, D., Fowlkes, C., Tal, D., Malik, J.: A database of human segmented natural images and its application to evaluating segmentation algorithms and measuring ecological statistics. In: Proceedings of Eighth IEEE International Conference on Computer Vision, ICCV 2001, vol. 2, pp. 416–423. IEEE (2001)
42. Silberman, N., Hoiem, D., Kohli, P., Fergus, R.: Indoor segmentation and support inference from RGBD images. In: Fitzgibbon, A., Lazebnik, S., Perona, P., Sato, Y., Schmid, C. (eds.) ECCV 2012, Part V. LNCS, vol. 7576, pp. 746–760. Springer, Heidelberg (2012)
43. Menze, M., Geiger, A.: Object scene flow for autonomous vehicles. In: Conference on Computer Vision and Pattern Recognition (CVPR) (2015)
44. Dou, M., Taylor, J., Fuchs, H., Fitzgibbon, A., Izadi, S.: 3D scanning deformable objects with a single RGBD sensor. In: Proceedings of the IEEE Conference on Computer Vision and Pattern Recognition. pp. 493–501 (2015)
45. Newcombe, R.A., Izadi, S., Hilliges, O., Molyneaux, D., Kim, D., Davison, A.J., Kohi, P., Shotton, J., Hodges, S., Fitzgibbon, A.: Kinectfusion: real-time dense surface mapping and tracking. In: 10th IEEE International Symposium on Mixed and Augmented Reality (ISMAR), pp. 127–136. IEEE (2011)
46. Deng, Z., Todorovic, S., Latecki, L.J.: Semantic segmentation of RGBD images with mutex constraints. In: International Conference on Computer Vision (ICCV), Santiago, Chile, December 2015
47. Gulshan, V., Lempitsky, V., Zisserman, A.: Humanising grabcut: learning to segment humans using the kinect. In: 2011 IEEE International Conference on Computer Vision Workshops (ICCV Workshops), pp. 1127–1133. IEEE (2011)
48. Ren, X., Bo, L., Fox, D.: Rgb-(d) scene labeling: features and algorithms. In: 2012 IEEE Conference on Computer Vision and Pattern Recognition (CVPR), pp. 2759–2766. IEEE (2012)
49. Gottfried, J.M., Fehr, J., Garbe, C.S.: Computing range flow from multi-modal kinect data. In: Bebis, G., et al. (eds.) ISVC 2011. LNCS, vol. 6938, pp. 758–767. Springer, Heidelberg (2011)
50. Brox, T., Malik, J.: Object segmentation by long term analysis of point trajectories. In: Daniilidis, K., Maragos, P., Paragios, N. (eds.) ECCV 2010, Part V. LNCS, vol. 6315, pp. 282–295. Springer, Heidelberg (2010)
51. Ochs, P., Brox, T.: Object segmentation in video: a hierarchical variational approach for turning point trajectories into dense regions. In: 2011 IEEE International Conference on Computer Vision (ICCV), pp. 1583–1590. IEEE (2011)

# Fast Global Registration

Qian-Yi Zhou, Jaesik Park, and Vladlen Koltun$^{(\boxtimes)}$

Intel Labs, Santa Clara, USA
vladlen.koltun@intel.com

**Abstract.** We present an algorithm for fast global registration of partially overlapping 3D surfaces. The algorithm operates on candidate matches that cover the surfaces. A single objective is optimized to align the surfaces and disable false matches. The objective is defined densely over the surfaces and the optimization achieves tight alignment with no initialization. No correspondence updates or closest-point queries are performed in the inner loop. An extension of the algorithm can perform joint global registration of many partially overlapping surfaces. Extensive experiments demonstrate that the presented approach matches or exceeds the accuracy of state-of-the-art global registration pipelines, while being at least an order of magnitude faster. Remarkably, the presented approach is also faster than local refinement algorithms such as ICP. It provides the accuracy achieved by well-initialized local refinement algorithms, without requiring an initialization and at lower computational cost.

## 1 Introduction

Registration of three-dimensional surfaces is a central problem in computer vision, computer graphics, and robotics. The problem is particularly challenging when the surfaces only partially overlap and no initial alignment is given. This difficult form of the problem is encountered in scene reconstruction [7,39], 3D object retrieval [15,29], camera relocalization [13], and other applications.

In order to deal with noisy data and partial overlap, practical registration pipelines employ iterative model fitting frameworks such as RANSAC [31]. Each iteration samples a set of candidate correspondences, produces an alignment based on these correspondences, and evaluates this alignment. If a satisfactory alignment is found, it is refined by a local registration algorithm such as ICP [30]. The combination of sampling-based coarse alignment and iterative local refinement is common in practice and is designed to produce a tight registration even with challenging input [7,19,39].

While such registration pipelines are common, they have significant drawbacks. Both the model fitting and the local refinement stages are iterative and perform computationally expensive nearest-neighbor queries in their inner loops. Much of the computational effort is expended on testing candidate alignments that are subsequently discarded. And the inelegant decomposition into a global alignment stage and a local refinement stage is itself a consequence of the low precision of global alignment frameworks.

© Springer International Publishing AG 2016
B. Leibe et al. (Eds.): ECCV 2016, Part II, LNCS 9906, pp. 766–782, 2016.
DOI: 10.1007/978-3-319-46475-6_47

In this paper, we present a fast global registration algorithm that does not involve iterative sampling, model fitting, or local refinement. The algorithm does not require initialization and can align noisy partially overlapping surfaces. It optimizes a robust objective defined densely over the surfaces. Due to this dense coverage, the algorithm directly produces an alignment that is as precise as that computed by well-initialized local refinement algorithms.

This direct approach has substantial benefits. It accomplishes in a single stage what is commonly done in two. This single stage optimizes a clear global objective. The optimization does not require closest-point queries in the inner loop. As a result, the presented algorithm is more than an order of magnitude faster than existing global registration pipelines, while matching or exceeding their accuracy.

Furthermore, we show that the presented algorithm can be extended to direct global alignment of multiple partially overlapping surfaces. Such joint alignment is often necessary in applications such as scene reconstruction [7,39]. Existing approaches to this problem exhaustively produce candidate alignments between pairs of surfaces and then compute a globally consistent set of poses based on these intermediate pairwise alignments. In contrast, we show that a joint alignment can be produced directly by a single optimization of a global objective.

We evaluate the presented global registration algorithm on multiple datasets. Extensive experiments demonsrate that the presented approach matches or exceeds the accuracy of state-of-the-art global registration pipelines, while being at least an order of magnitude faster. Remarkably, the presented approach is also faster than local refinement algorithms such as ICP, since it does not need to recompute correspondences. It provides the accuracy achieved by well-initialized local refinement algorithms, without requiring an initialization and at lower computational cost.

## 2  Related Work

Geometric registration has been extensively studied [15,28,36,38]. The typical workflow consists of two stages: global alignment, which computes an initial estimate of the rigid motion between two surfaces, followed by local refinement, which refines this initial estimate to obtain a tight registration [7,12,19,25,27, 37,39]. We review each of these stages in turn.

Most global alignment methods operate on candidate correspondences. Some pipelines use point-to-point matches based on local geometric descriptors [16,40], others define correspondences on pairs or tuples of points [1,8,26,29]. Once candidate correspondences are collected, alignment is estimated iteratively from sparse subsets of correspondences and then validated on the entire surface. This iterative process is typically based on variants of RANSAC [1,19,26,29,34] or pose clustering [8,26,35]. When the data is noisy and the surfaces only partially overlap, existing pipelines often require many iterations to sample a good correspondence set and find a reasonable alignment.

Another approach to global registration is based on the branch-and-bound framework [10,12,18,23,42]. These algorithms systematically explore the pose space in search of the optimal solution. The branch-and-bound framework is appealing due to its theoretical optimality guarantees. However, the systematic search can be extremely time-consuming. In practice, the sampling-based frameworks described earlier outperform the branch-and-bound approaches when large datasets are involved.

Local refinement algorithms begin with a rough initial alignment and produce a tight registration based on dense correspondences. Most such methods are based on the iterative closest point (ICP) algorithm and its variants [30,33]. In its basic form, ICP begins with an initial alignment and alternates between establishing correspondences via closest-point lookups and recomputing the alignment based on the current set of correspondences. ICP can produce an accurate result when initialized near the optimal pose, but is unreliable without such initialization. A long line of work has explored various approaches to increasing the robustness of ICP. Fitzgibbon [11] introduced nonlinear least-squares optimization to develop a robust error function that increases the radius of convergence. Bouaziz et al. [5] introduced sparsity inducing norms to deal with outliers and incomplete data. Other works explored the utility of relaxed assignments [14,24,32], distance field representations [6], and mixture models [21,41] for increasing the robustness of local registration. Nevertheless, these approaches still rely on a satisfactory initialization. Our work demonstrates that the accuracy achieved by well-initialized local refinement algorithms can be achieved reliably without an initialization, at a computational cost that is more than an order of magnitude lower than the coarse global alignment algorithms described earlier.

Joint global registration of multiple partially overlapping surfaces has also been considered [7,20,39]. However, existing approaches to joint global registration first align many pairs of surfaces and then optimize the joint global alignment based on these intermediate pairwise results. This indirect approach incurs significant computational overhead. In contrast, we show that joint global alignment of many partially overlapping surfaces can be optimized for directly.

## 3    Pairwise Global Registration

### 3.1    Objective

Consider two point sets $\mathbf{P}$ and $\mathbf{Q}$. Our task is to find a rigid transformation $\mathbf{T}$ that aligns $\mathbf{Q}$ to $\mathbf{P}$. Our approach optimizes a robust objective on correspondences between $\mathbf{P}$ and $\mathbf{Q}$. These correspondences are established by rapid feature matching that is performed before the objective is optimized. The correspondences are not recomputed during the optimization. For this reason, it is critical that the optimization be able to deal with very noisy correspondence sets. This is illustrated in Fig. 1.

Let $\mathcal{K} = \{(\mathbf{p}, \mathbf{q})\}$ be the set of correspondences collected by matching points from $\mathbf{P}$ and $\mathbf{Q}$ as described in Sect. 3.3. Our objective is to optimize the pose $\mathbf{T}$ such that distances between corresponding points are minimized, while spurious correspondences from $\mathcal{K}$ are seamlessly disabled. The objective has the following form:

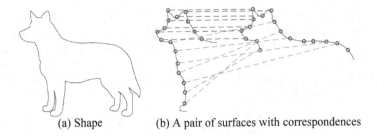

| (a) Shape | (b) A pair of surfaces with correspondences |

**Fig. 1.** An illustration with 2D point sets. (a) A latent shape. (b) Two partially over-lapping surfaces and a set of point-to-point correspondences. The blue correspondences are genuine, the red correspondences are erroneous. For fast and accurate registration, the erroneous correspondences must be disabled without sampling, validation, pruning, or correspondence recomputation. (Color figure online)

$$E(\mathbf{T}) = \sum_{(\mathbf{p},\mathbf{q})\in\mathcal{K}} \rho\left(\|\mathbf{p} - \mathbf{T}\mathbf{q}\|\right).\tag{1}$$

Here $\rho(\cdot)$ is a robust penalty. The use of an appropriate robust penalty function is critical, because many of the terms in Objective 1 are contributed by spurious constraints. To achieve high computational efficiency, we do not want to sample, validate, prune, or recompute correspondences during the optimization. A well-chosen estimator $\rho$ will perform the validation and pruning automatically without imposing additional computational costs. We use a scaled Geman-McClure estimator:

$$\rho(x) = \frac{\mu x^2}{\mu + x^2}.\tag{2}$$

Figure 2(a) shows the Geman-McClure estimator for different values of $\mu$. As can be seen in the figure, small residuals are penalized in the least-squares sense, while the sublinear growth and rapid flattening out of the estimator neutralize

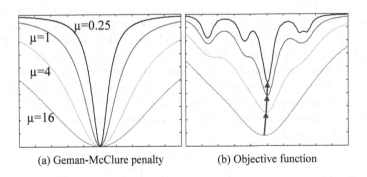

| (a) Geman-McClure penalty | (b) Objective function |

**Fig. 2.** Illustration of graduated non-convexity. As $\mu$ decreases, the objective function for the matching problem in Fig. 1 becomes sharper and the registration more precise.

outliers. The parameter $\mu$ controls the range within which residuals have a significant effect on the objective; its setting will be discussed in Sect. 3.2.

Objective 1 is difficult to optimize directly. We use the Black-Rangarajan duality between robust estimation and line processes [3]. Specifically, let $\mathbb{L} = \{l_{\mathbf{p},\mathbf{q}}\}$ be a line process over the correspondences. We optimize the following joint objective over $\mathbf{T}$ and $\mathbb{L}$:

$$E(\mathbf{T}, \mathbb{L}) = \sum_{(\mathbf{p},\mathbf{q}) \in \mathcal{K}} l_{\mathbf{p},\mathbf{q}} \|\mathbf{p} - \mathbf{Tq}\|^2 + \sum_{(\mathbf{p},\mathbf{q}) \in \mathcal{K}} \Psi(l_{\mathbf{p},\mathbf{q}}). \tag{3}$$

Here $\Psi(l_{\mathbf{p},\mathbf{q}})$ is a prior, set to

$$\Psi(l_{\mathbf{p},\mathbf{q}}) = \mu \left( \sqrt{l_{\mathbf{p},\mathbf{q}}} - 1 \right)^2. \tag{4}$$

For $E(\mathbf{T}, \mathbb{L})$ to be minimized, the partial derivative with respect to each $l_{\mathbf{p},\mathbf{q}}$ must vanish:

$$\frac{\partial E}{\partial l_{\mathbf{p},\mathbf{q}}} = \|\mathbf{p} - \mathbf{Tq}\|^2 + \mu \frac{\sqrt{l_{\mathbf{p},\mathbf{q}}} - 1}{\sqrt{l_{\mathbf{p},\mathbf{q}}}} = 0. \tag{5}$$

Solving for $l_{\mathbf{p},\mathbf{q}}$ yields

$$l_{\mathbf{p},\mathbf{q}} = \left( \frac{\mu}{\mu + \|\mathbf{p} - \mathbf{Tq}\|^2} \right)^2. \tag{6}$$

Substituting $l_{\mathbf{p},\mathbf{q}}$ into $E(\mathbf{T}, \mathbb{L})$, Objective 3 becomes Objective 1. Thus optimizing Objective 3 yields a solution $\mathbf{T}$ that is also optimal for the original Objective 1.

## 3.2   Optimization

The main benefit of the optimization objective defined in Eq. 3 is that the optimization can be performed extremely efficiently by alternating between optimizing $\mathbf{T}$ and $\mathbb{L}$. The optimization performs block coordinate descent by fixing $\mathbb{L}$ when optimizing $\mathbf{T}$ and vice versa. Both types of steps optimize the same global objective (Eq. 3). Thus the alternating algorithm is guaranteed to converge.

When $\mathbb{L}$ is fixed, Objective 3 turns into a weighted sum of $L^2$ penalties on distances between point-to-point correspondences. This objective over $\mathbf{T}$ can be solved efficiently in closed form [9]. However, such closed-form solution does not extend to joint registration of multiple surfaces, which we are interested in and will extend the presented approach to in Sect. 4. We therefore present a more flexible approach. We linearize $\mathbf{T}$ locally as a 6-vector $\xi = (\omega, \mathbf{t}) = (\alpha, \beta, \gamma, a, b, c)$ that collates a rotational component $\omega$ and a translation $\mathbf{t}$. $\mathbf{T}$ is approximated by a linear function of $\xi$:

$$\mathbf{T} \approx \begin{pmatrix} 1 & -\gamma & \beta & a \\ \gamma & 1 & -\alpha & b \\ -\beta & \alpha & 1 & c \\ 0 & 0 & 0 & 1 \end{pmatrix} \mathbf{T}^k. \tag{7}$$

Here $\mathbf{T}^k$ is the transformation estimated in the last iteration. Equation 3 becomes a least-squares objective on $\xi$. Using the Gauss-Newton method, $\xi$ is computed by solving a linear system:

$$\mathbf{J_r^\top J_r}\xi = -\mathbf{J_r^\top r}, \tag{8}$$

where $\mathbf{r}$ is the residual vector and $\mathbf{J_r}$ is its Jacobian. $\mathbf{T}$ is updated by applying $\xi$ to $\mathbf{T}^k$ using Eq. 7, then mapped back into the $SE(3)$ group.

When $\mathbf{T}$ is fixed, the objective in Eq. 3 has a closed-form solution. It is minimized when $l_{\mathbf{p},\mathbf{q}}$ satisfies Eq. 6.

**Graduated Non-convexity.** Objective 3 is non-convex and its shape is controlled by the parameter $\mu$ of the penalty function (Eq. 2). To set $\mu$ and alleviate the effect of local minima we employ graduated non-convexity [2,4]. From the standpoint of Eq. 3, $\mu$ balances the strength of the prior term and the alignment term. Large $\mu$ makes the objective function smoother and allows many correspondences to participate in the optimization even when they are not fit tightly by the transformation $\mathbf{T}$. The effect of varying $\mu$ is illustrated in Fig. 2. Our optimization begins with a very large value $\mu = D^2$, where $D$ is the diameter of the largest surface. The parameter $\mu$ is decreased during the optimization until it reaches the value $\mu = \delta^2$, where $\delta$ is a distance threshold for genuine correspondences.

## 3.3   Correspondences

To generate the initial correspondence set $\mathcal{K}$, we use the Fast Point Feature Histogram (FPFH) feature [34]. We have chosen this feature because it can be computed in a fraction of a millisecond and provides good matching accuracy across a broad range of datasets [16]. Let $\mathbf{F}(\mathbf{P}) = \{\mathbf{F}(\mathbf{p}) : \mathbf{p} \in \mathbf{P}\}$, where $\mathbf{F}(\mathbf{p})$ is the FPFH feature computed for point $\mathbf{p}$. Define $\mathbf{F}(\mathbf{Q}) = \{\mathbf{F}(\mathbf{q}) : \mathbf{q} \in \mathbf{Q}\}$ analogously.

For each $\mathbf{p} \in \mathbf{P}$, we find the nearest neighbor of $\mathbf{F}(\mathbf{p})$ among $\mathbf{F}(\mathbf{Q})$, and for each $\mathbf{q} \in \mathbf{Q}$ we find the nearest neighbor of $\mathbf{F}(\mathbf{q})$ among $\mathbf{F}(\mathbf{P})$. Let $\mathcal{K}_I$ be the set that collects all these correspondences. This set could be used directly as the input to our approach. However, in practice $\mathcal{K}_I$ has a very high fraction of outliers. We use two tests to improve the inlier ratio of the correspondence set used by the algorithm.

- **Reciprocity test.** A correspondence pair $(\mathbf{p}, \mathbf{q})$ is selected from $\mathcal{K}_I$ if and only if $\mathbf{F}(\mathbf{p})$ is the nearest neighbor of $\mathbf{F}(\mathbf{q})$ among $\mathbf{F}(\mathbf{P})$ and $\mathbf{F}(\mathbf{q})$ is the nearest neighbor of $\mathbf{F}(\mathbf{p})$ among $\mathbf{F}(\mathbf{Q})$. The resulting correspondence set is denoted by $\mathcal{K}_{II}$.
- **Tuple test.** We randomly pick 3 correspondence pairs $(\mathbf{p}_1, \mathbf{q}_1)$, $(\mathbf{p}_2, \mathbf{q}_2), (\mathbf{p}_3, \mathbf{q}_3)$ from $\mathcal{K}_{II}$ and check if the tuples $(\mathbf{p}_1, \mathbf{p}_2, \mathbf{p}_3)$ and $(\mathbf{q}_1, \mathbf{q}_2, \mathbf{q}_3)$ are compatible. Specifically, we test if the following condition is met:

$$\forall i \neq j, \quad \tau < \frac{\|\mathbf{p}_i - \mathbf{p}_j\|}{\|\mathbf{q}_i - \mathbf{q}_j\|} < 1/\tau, \tag{9}$$

where $\tau = 0.9$. Intuitively, this test verifies that the correspondences are compatible. Correspondences from tuples that pass the test are collected in a set $\mathcal{K}_{III}$. This is the set used by the algorithm: $\mathcal{K} = \mathcal{K}_{III}$.

Algorithm 1 summarizes the pairwise registration algorithm used in all subsequent experiments.

---

**Algorithm 1.** Fast pairwise registration

---

**input** : A pair of surfaces $(\mathbf{P}, \mathbf{Q})$
**output**: Transformation $\mathbf{T}$ that aligns $\mathbf{Q}$ to $\mathbf{P}$

Compute normals $\{\mathbf{n_p}\}$ and $\{\mathbf{n_q}\}$;
Compute FPFH features $\mathbf{F}(\mathbf{P})$ and $\mathbf{F}(\mathbf{Q})$;
Build $\mathcal{K}_I$ by computing nearest neighbors between $\mathbf{F}(\mathbf{P})$ and $\mathbf{F}(\mathbf{Q})$;
Apply reciprocity test on $\mathcal{K}_I$ to get $\mathcal{K}_{II}$;
Apply tuple test on $\mathcal{K}_{II}$ to get $\mathcal{K}_{III}$;
$\mathbf{T} \leftarrow \mathbf{I}, \mu \leftarrow D^2$;

**while** not converged *or* $\mu > \delta^2$ **do**
    $\mathbf{J_r} \leftarrow \mathbf{0}, \mathbf{r} \leftarrow \mathbf{0}$;
    **for** $(\mathbf{p}, \mathbf{q}) \in \mathcal{K}_{III}$ **do**
        Compute $l_{(\mathbf{p},\mathbf{q})}$ using equation 6;
        Update $\mathbf{J_r}$ and $\mathbf{r}$ of objective 3;

    Solve equation 8 and update $\mathbf{T}$;
    Every four iterations, $\mu \leftarrow \mu/2$;
Verify whether $\mathbf{T}$ aligns $\mathbf{Q}$ to $\mathbf{P}$;

---

## 4    Multi-way Registration

Many applications require aligning multiple surfaces to obtain a model of a large scene or object. To solve this multi-way registration problem, existing approaches first compute pairwise alignments between pairs of surfaces and then attempt to synchronize these alignments to obtain a global registration [7,20,39]. This has two significant disadvantages. First, the pairwise alignment stage is computationally wasteful because it is not apparent in advance which pairs will be useful. Second, pairwise registration can yield a suboptimal alignment due to local minima that could be disambiguated by a global approach that considers all surfaces jointly.

We develop an alternative approach: to directly align all surfaces based on raw dense point correspondences. Instead of optimizing separate pairwise alignments and then synchronizing the results, we can directly optimize a global registration objective over all surfaces.

## 4.1   Objective

Given a set of surfaces $\{\mathbf{P}_i\}$, our task is to estimate a set of poses $\mathbb{T} = \{\mathbf{T}_i\}$ that aligns the surfaces in a global coordinate frame. We begin by constructing a set of candidate correspondences $\mathcal{K}_{ij}$ for each pair of surfaces $(\mathbf{P}_i, \mathbf{Q}_j), i < j$. Objective 1 is extended to the multi-way setting as follows:

$$E(\mathbb{T}) = \lambda \sum_i \sum_{(\mathbf{p},\mathbf{q}) \in \mathcal{K}_i} \|\mathbf{T}_i\mathbf{p} - \mathbf{T}_{i+1}\mathbf{q}\|^2 + \sum_{i<j} \sum_{(\mathbf{p},\mathbf{q}) \in \mathcal{K}_{ij}} \rho(\|\mathbf{T}_i\mathbf{p} - \mathbf{T}_j\mathbf{q}\|). \quad (10)$$

This formulation incorporates initial odometry transformations $\{\mathbf{T}_i\}$ between consecutive surfaces, which are commonly available in surface reconstruction. The set $\mathcal{K}_i$ collects correspondences between surfaces $\mathbf{P}_i$ and $\mathbf{P}_{i+1}$ under the odometry alignment. When available, the odometry terms are penalized directly with the $L^2$ norm and serve as a backbone that stabilizes the optimization.

Define a line process $\mathbb{L} = \{l_{\mathbf{p},\mathbf{q}}\}$. The objective can now be reformulated as follows:

$$E(\mathbb{T}, \mathbb{L}) = \lambda \sum_i \sum_{(\mathbf{p},\mathbf{q}) \in \mathcal{K}_i} \|\mathbf{T}_i\mathbf{p} - \mathbf{T}_{i+1}\mathbf{q}\|^2$$
$$+ \sum_{i<j} \left( \sum_{(\mathbf{p},\mathbf{q}) \in \mathcal{K}_{ij}} l_{\mathbf{p},\mathbf{q}} \|\mathbf{T}_i\mathbf{p} - \mathbf{T}_j\mathbf{q}\|^2 + \sum_{(\mathbf{p},\mathbf{q}) \in \mathcal{K}_{ij}} \Psi(l_{\mathbf{p},\mathbf{q}}) \right). \quad (11)$$

The prior term $\Psi(l_{\mathbf{p},\mathbf{q}})$ is defined as in Eq. 4.

## 4.2   Optimization

We again use alternating optimization to solve the minimization problem. In each iteration, $E(\mathbb{T}, \mathbb{L})$ is first minimized with respect to the line process variables $\mathbb{L}$. This has a closed-form solution:

$$l_{\mathbf{p},\mathbf{q}} = \left( \frac{\mu}{\mu + \|\mathbf{T}_i\mathbf{p} - \mathbf{T}_j\mathbf{q}\|^2} \right)^2. \quad (12)$$

Next, $E(\mathbb{T}, \mathbb{L})$ is minimized with respect to all poses $\mathbb{T}$. Let $\mathbf{T}_i^k$ denote the $i$-th transformation estimated in the previous iteration. $\mathbf{T}_i$ can be locally linearized with a 6-vector $\xi_i = (\omega_i, \mathbf{t}_i) = (\alpha_i, \beta_i, \gamma_i, a_i, b_i, c_i)$:

$$\mathbf{T}_i \approx \begin{pmatrix} 1 & -\gamma_i & \beta_i & a_i \\ \gamma_i & 1 & -\alpha_i & b_i \\ -\beta_i & \alpha_i & 1 & c_i \\ 0 & 0 & 0 & 1 \end{pmatrix} \mathbf{T}_i^k. \quad (13)$$

Let $\Xi$ be a $6|\mathbb{T}|$-vector that collates $\{\xi_i\}$. $E(\mathbb{T}, \mathbb{L})$ becomes a least-squares objective on $\Xi$. It is minimized by solving the linear system

$$\mathbf{J}_\mathbf{r}^\top \mathbf{J}_\mathbf{r} \Xi = -\mathbf{J}_\mathbf{r}^\top \mathbf{r} \quad (14)$$

and updating $\mathbf{T}_i$ accordingly. Here $\mathbf{J_r}$ and $\mathbf{r}$ are the Jacobian matrix and the residual vector, respectively.

Note that the correspondences are never updated. Each iteration performs only two steps: evaluate a line process variable for each point correspondence, then build and solve a linear system with $6|\mathbb{T}|$ variables. Both steps are very efficient.

## 5    Results

### 5.1    Pairwise Registration

We evaluate the presented pairwise registration algorithm on synthetic range data, the UWA benchmark [27], and the global registration benchmark of Choi et al. [7]. We compare our algorithm with a number of prior global registration methods. GoICP is the algorithm of Yang et al. [42]. GoICP-Trimming is its trimming variant that supports partial overlap. We use a 10 % trimming percentage and use only 1,000 data points, as suggested by Yang et al. [42]. Without downsampling, GoICP and GoICP-Trimming take hours to run on our point clouds. Super4PCS is the algorithm of Mellado et al. [26]. OpenCV is a recent OpenCV implementation of the surface registration algorithm of Drost et al. [8]. PCL is a Point Cloud Library implementation of the algorithm of Rusu et al. [19,34]. CZK is the variant of Rusu's algorithm used by Choi et al. [7].

We also conduct controlled comparisons with local registration algorithms. PCL ICP is a Point Cloud Library implementation of the ICP algorithm [19]. Sparse ICP is the algorithm of Bouaziz et al. [5]. We tested these algorithms with both point-to-point and point-to-plane distance measures [33].

All execution times are measured using a single thread on an Intel Core i7-5960X CPU clocked at 3.00 GHz.

**Synthetic Range Data.** We begin by performing a series of controlled experiments on synthetic data. The availability of precise ground truth enables a detailed evaluation. To conduct controlled experiments, we used three well-known models from the AIM@SHAPE repository (Bimba, Dancing Children, and Chinese Dragon), the Berkeley Angel dataset [22], and the Stanford Bunny. For each model, we synthesized five pairs of partially overlapping range images and then corrupted these range images with 3D Gaussian noise. We used three noise levels, defined by setting the standard deviation of the Gaussian distribution to $\sigma = 0$ (no noise), $\sigma = 0.0025$, and $\sigma = 0.005$. The unit of $\sigma$ is the diameter of the surface. For each noise level, there are 25 partially overlapping global registration tests in total. The number of points in each range image varies between 8,868 and 19,749. The overlap ratio varies between 47 % and 90 %.

Figure 3 shows the accuracy achieved by the different global registration algorithms on the 25 tests at each noise level. For each algorithm and each RMSE level $\alpha$, the figure plots the $\alpha$-recall, defined as the fraction of tests for which the method achieved an RMSE $< \alpha$. (Higher is better.) The RMSE is computed on the distances between ground-truth correspondences after alignment.

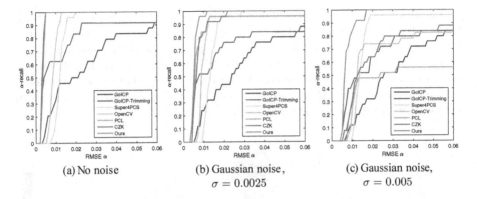

(a) No noise
(b) Gaussian noise,
$\sigma = 0.0025$
(c) Gaussian noise,
$\sigma = 0.005$

**Fig. 3.** Controlled experiments on synthetic data. $\alpha$-recall is the fraction of tests for which a given method achieves an RMSE $< \alpha$. Higher is better. The RMSE unit is the diameter of the surface. Our algorithm is more robust to noise and is more accurate than prior approaches, while being more than an order of magnitude faster.

Table 1 summarizes the average and maximal RMSE for each method. (Lower is better.) For synthetic data with no noise, our method, PCL, and CZK produce tight alignment in 100 % of the tests. (RMSE $\leq$ 0.005.) The accuracy of OpenCV and Super4PCS is worse by a multiplicative factor of at least 3, presumably due to their reliance on matching tuples of points rather than optimizing for fully dense surface registration. GoICP-Trimming produces accurate alignment in many cases but suffers from poor accuracy on others, presumably because its computational costs necessitate operation on downsampled point clouds.

**Table 1.** Average and maximal RMSE achieved by global registration algorithms on synthetic range images with noise level $\sigma$. Maximal RMSE is the maxumum among the 25 RMSE values obtained for individual pairwise registration tests. Our approach outperforms other methods by a large margin when noise is present. Specifically, for $\sigma = 0.005$, the average RMSE of our approach is more than 2 times lower than the lowest average RMSE of any prior approach, and the maximal RMSE of our approach is 5.6 times lower.

| | $\sigma = 0$ | | $\sigma = 0.0025$ | | $\sigma = 0.005$ | |
|---|---|---|---|---|---|---|
| | Average RMSE | Maximal RMSE | Average RMSE | Maximal RMSE | Average RMSE | Maximal RMSE |
| GoICP [42] | 0.029 | 0.130 | 0.032 | 0.133 | 0.037 | 0.127 |
| GoICP-Trimming [42] | 0.035 | 0.473 | 0.039 | 0.475 | 0.044 | 0.478 |
| Super 4PCS [26] | 0.012 | 0.019 | 0.014 | 0.029 | 0.017 | 0.095 |
| OpenCV [8] | 0.009 | 0.013 | 0.018 | 0.212 | 0.032 | 0.242 |
| PCL [19,34] | **0.003** | **0.005** | 0.009 | 0.061 | 0.111 | 0.414 |
| CZK [7] | **0.003** | **0.005** | 0.008 | 0.022 | 0.035 | 0.274 |
| Our approach | **0.003** | **0.005** | **0.006** | **0.011** | **0.008** | **0.017** |

On noisy data, our method is much more robust and accurate than others. For $\sigma = 0.005$, the average RMSE of our approach is more than 2 times smaller than the lowest average RMSE of any prior approach, and the maximal RMSE of our approach is *5.6 times smaller* than the lowest maximal RMSE among prior approaches. This is presumably because our approach optimizes over dense correspondences rather than matching point tuples. A qualitative comparison with GoICP-Trimming and PCL is provided in Fig. 4.

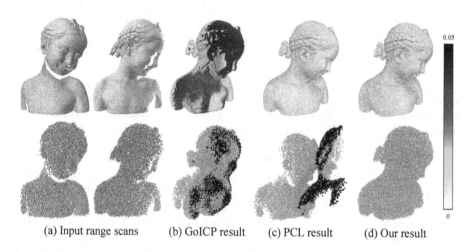

(a) Input range scans    (b) GoICP result    (c) PCL result    (d) Our result

**Fig. 4.** Visual comparison with GoICP-Trimming and PCL. Our method operates on dense point clouds and produces a tight alignment with RMSE 0.004 on clean data (top row) and RMSE 0.007 on noisy data (bottom row, $\sigma = 0.005$). In contrast, the prior approaches break down in the presence of noise: RMSE 0.129 for GoICP-Trimming and 0.326 for PCL in the bottom row. Error magnitude is coded by color, with black indicating error above 0.05. (Color figure online)

The major benefit of our approach is that it is faster by more than an order of magnitude than prior approaches. Table 2 shows the average computation time of each global registration method on each object. Our method improves registration speed by a factor of 50 relative to the fastest prior global registration algorithm (CZK). While previous methods require tens of seconds, our method takes 0.2 s on average. This is because our method avoids expensive nearest-neighbor lookups in the optimization loop.

We further analyze the computational requirements of our approach by varying the size (i.e., the point count) of the synthesized range images and measuring the execution time of individual components of our algorithm. The results are shown on the right. The majority of the time is spent on computing the FPFH features

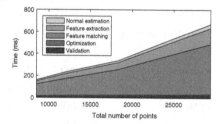

**Table 2.** Running times of global registration methods, measured in seconds. GoICP and its trimming variant operate on point clouds downsampled to 1,000. All other methods operate on full-resolution point clouds. Our algorithm is 50 times faster than the fastest prior global registration method.

| | Average # of points | GoICP [42] | GoICP-Trimming [42] | OpenCV [8] | Super 4PCS [26] | PCL [19,34] | CZK [7] | Our approach |
|---|---|---|---|---|---|---|---|---|
| Bimba | 9,416 | 19.3 | 19.4 | 41.0 | 311.4 | 18.2 | 12.8 | **0.13** |
| Children | 11,148 | 21.0 | 19.2 | 136.3 | 238.2 | 4.8 | 6.6 | **0.20** |
| Dragon | 11,232 | 94.1 | 38.4 | 57.7 | 483.7 | 8.6 | 11.9 | **0.23** |
| Angel | 12,072 | 21.0 | 20.4 | 80.9 | 171.5 | 8.7 | 11.3 | **0.26** |
| Bunny | 13,357 | 74.7 | 72.4 | 12.3 | 283.8 | 55.6 | 12.7 | **0.28** |
| Average | 11,445 | 46.0 | 34.0 | 65.6 | 297.7 | 19.2 | 11.1 | **0.22** |

and building the input correspondences. These operations are performed only once, before the optimization, and the correspondences are never updated. The optimization itself is extremely fast. Its execution time is below 30 milliseconds even for point clouds with more than 20,000 points. In addition, our method performs validation only once, after optimization has converged. This one-time validation consumes on average 3.3 % of our computation time. In contrast, sampling-based methods such as PCL perform validation thousands of times in the RANSAC loop.

We also compare our global registration algorithm with local refinement methods such as ICP and its variants. To perform a controlled evaluation, we varied the accuracy of the initial transformation provided to the local methods. The results are shown in Fig. 5. We performed two sets of experiments. In one, the local algorithms were initialized with the ground-truth translation and varying degrees of rotation. In the other, the local algorithms were initialized with the ground-truth rotation and varying degrees of translation. As shown in Fig. 5, our algorithm matches the accuracy of the local refinment methods in the idealized case when these methods are initialized with the ground-truth transformation. However, the accuracy of the local methods degrades when the initialization deviates sufficiently from the ground-truth pose: 5 degrees in rotation or 5–10 % of the point cloud diameter in translation. In contrast, our algorithm does not use an initialization and yields the same accuracy in all conditions.

We further compare the computational costs of our algorithm and the local refinement methods. The results are shown in Table 3. Remarkably, our global registration algorithm is 2.8 times faster than a state-of-the-art implementation of ICP. The key reason is that our algorithm does not need to recompute correspondences.

**UWA Benchmark.** Next, we evaluate our method on the UWA dataset [27]. This dataset has 50 scenes. Each scene has multiple objects that can be aligned to it. In total, the dataset contains 188 pairwise registration tests. Figure 6(a) shows a scene with objects aligned to it by our approach. This dataset is challenging

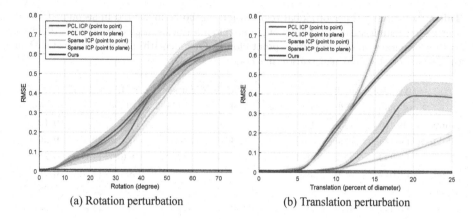

(a) Rotation perturbation          (b) Translation perturbation

**Fig. 5.** Controlled comparison with local methods. Local registration algorithms are initialized with a transformation generated by adding a perturbation in rotation (left) or translation (right) to the ground-truth alignment. The plots show the mean (bold curve) and standard deviation (shaded region) of the RMSE of each method. Lower is better. Our algorithm matches the accuracy achieved by the local algorithms when they are initialized near the ground-truth pose, but does not require an initialization.

**Table 3.** Timing comparison with local algorithms, measured in seconds. Our global algorithm is 2.8 times faster than a state-of-the-art implementation of ICP.

| | Average # of points | PCL ICP point-to-point | PCL ICP point-to-plane | Sparse point-to-point [5] | Sparse ICP point-to-plane [5] | Our approach |
|---|---|---|---|---|---|---|
| Bimba | 9,416 | 0.73 | 0.31 | 3.1 | 11.8 | **0.13** |
| Children | 11,148 | 0.75 | 0.46 | 3.9 | 15.0 | **0.20** |
| Dragon | 11,232 | 0.99 | 0.47 | 3.6 | 13.8 | **0.23** |
| Angel | 12,072 | 0.81 | 1.01 | 4.9 | 18.5 | **0.26** |
| Bunny | 13,357 | 2.10 | 1.70 | 9.2 | 10.3 | **0.28** |
| Average | 11,445 | 1.08 | 0.79 | 4.9 | 13.9 | **0.22** |

due to clutter, occlusion, and low overlap. The lowest overlap ratio in the dataset is only 21 %. As shown in Fig. 6(b), many prior global registration algorithms perform poorly on this dataset. Our algorithm achieves a 0.05-recall of 84 %, comparable with PCL and CZK (82 % and 78 %, respectively). OpenCV achieves 52 % and the other algorithms are all below 7 %.

Table 4 compares the speed of our approach with the other global registration methods on the UWA benchmark. Our approach is an order of magnitude faster than the fastest prior methods.

**Scene Benchmark.** We now evaluate on the scene benchmark provided by Choi et al. [7]. This benchmark has 4 datasets. Each dataset consists of 47 to 57 fragments of a scene. These fragments contain high-frequency noise and

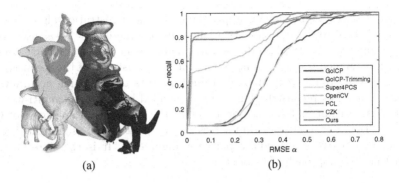

**Fig. 6.** Global registration results on the UWA benchmark [27]. (a) Our result on one of the 188 tests. The scene is colored white and objects aligned to the scene have distinct colors. (b) α-recall plot comparing our method and prior global registration algorithms. (Higher is better.) (Color figure online)

**Table 4.** Average running times of global registration methods on the 188 tests from the UWA dataset, measured in seconds.

|  | GoICP [42] | GoICP-Trimming [42] | OpenCV [8] | Super 4PCS [26] | PCL [19,34] | CZK [7] | Our approach |
|---|---|---|---|---|---|---|---|
| Average time | 18.7 | 18.6 | 17.6 | 77.4 | 8.2 | 8.7 | **0.5** |

low-frequency distortion that simulate scans created by consumer depth cameras. Global pairwise registration is performed on every pair of fragments from a given scene. Table 5 compares recall and precision (as defined by Choi et al.), and average running times.

**Table 5.** Evaluation on the scene benchmark of Choi et al. [7]. Our approach has the highest precision and the second highest recall, while being at least an order of magnitude faster.

|  | OpenCV [8] | Super 4PCS [26] | PCL [19,34] | CZK [7] | Our approach |
|---|---|---|---|---|---|
| Recall (%) | 5.3 | 17.8 | 44.9 | **59.2** | 51.1 |
| Precision (%) | 1.6 | 10.4 | 14.0 | 19.6 | **23.2** |
| Avg. time (sec) | 10 | 62 | 3 | 8 | **0.2** |

## 5.2 Multi-way Registration

We evaluate the multi-way extension of our algorithm on the Augmented ICL-NUIM dataset [7,17]. The dataset contains four sequences, each of which consists of 47 to 57 scene fragments. We apply the multi-way registration algorithm presented in Sect. 4 to these fragments. (The same parameter $\lambda = 2$ was used for all experiments.) Our method produces a global alignment of all fragments. We integrate these aligned fragments and report the mean distance of the reconstructed surface to the ground-truth model. Table 6 reports the resulting accuracy and running time. The reconstruction accuracy yielded by our direct multi-way registration algorithm matches the accuracy of the registration approach of Choi et al. [7]. However, our algorithm solves for the joint global alignment directly, without exhaustive intermediate pairwise alignments. It is therefore 60 times faster than the approach of Choi et al.

**Table 6.** Evaluation of multi-way registration on the Augmented ICL-NUIM dataset [7, 17]. Our multi-way registration algorithm matches the accuracy of the state-of-the-art multi-way registration pipeline of Choi et al., but is 60 times faster.

|  | Mean error (meters) | | Time (seconds) | |
| --- | --- | --- | --- | --- |
|  | Choi et al. [7] | Ours | Choi et al. [7] | Ours |
| Living room 1 | 0.04 | 0.05 | 8,940 | **131** |
| Living room 2 | 0.07 | 0.06 | 3,360 | **81** |
| Office 1 | 0.03 | 0.03 | 4,500 | **69** |
| Office 2 | 0.04 | 0.05 | 4,080 | **48** |
| Average | 0.05 | 0.05 | 5,220 | **82** |

## 6    Conclusion

We have presented a fast algorithm for global registration of partially overlapping 3D surfaces. Our algorithm is more than an order of magnitude faster than prior global registration algorithms and is much more robust to noise. It matches the accuracy of well-initialized local refinement algorithms such as ICP, without requiring an initialization and at lower computational cost. The algorithm may be broadly applicable in computer vision, computer graphics, and robotics.

## References

1. Aiger, D., Mitra, N.J., Cohen-Or, D.: 4-points congruent sets for robust pairwise surface registration. ACM Trans. Graph. **27**(3), 85 (2008)
2. Black, M.J., Anandan, P.: The robust estimation of multiple motions: parametric and piecewise-smooth flow fields. Comput. Vis. Image Underst. **63**(1), 75–104 (1996)
3. Black, M.J., Rangarajan, A.: On the unification of line processes, outlier rejection, and robust statistics with applications in early vision. IJCV **19**(1), 57–91 (1996)
4. Blake, A., Zisserman, A.: Visual Reconstruction. MIT Press, Cambridge (1987)

5. Bouaziz, S., Tagliasacchi, A., Pauly, M.: Sparse iterative closest point. In: Symposium on Geometry Processing (2013)
6. Bylow, E., Sturm, J., Kerl, C., Kahl, F., Cremers, D.: Real-time camera tracking and 3D reconstruction using signed distance functions. In RSS (2013)
7. Choi, S., Zhou, Q.Y., Koltun, V.: Robust reconstruction of indoor scenes. In: CVPR (2015)
8. Drost, B., Ulrich, M., Navab, N., Ilic, S.: Model globally, match locally: efficient and robust 3D object recognition. In: CVPR (2010)
9. Eggert, D.W., Lorusso, A., Fisher, R.B.: Estimating 3-D rigid body transformations: a comparison of four major algorithms. Mach. Vis. Appl. **9**(5/6), 272–290 (1997)
10. Enqvist, O., Josephson, K., Kahl, F.: Optimal correspondences from pairwise constraints. In: ICCV (2009)
11. Fitzgibbon, A.W.: Robust registration of 2D and 3D point sets. Image Vis. Comput. **21**(13–14), 1145–1153 (2003)
12. Gelfand, N., Mitra, N.J., Guibas, L.J., Pottmann, H.: Robust global registration. In: Symposium on Geometry Processing (2005)
13. Glocker, B., Izadi, S., Shotton, J., Criminisi, A.: Real-time RGB-D camera relocalization. In: ISMAR (2013)
14. Granger, S., Pennec, X.: Multi-scale EM-ICP: a fast and robust approach for surface registration. In: Heyden, A., Sparr, G., Nielsen, M., Johansen, P. (eds.) ECCV 2002, Part IV. LNCS, vol. 2353, pp. 418–432. Springer, Heidelberg (2002)
15. Guo, Y., Bennamoun, M., Sohel, F.A., Lu, M., Wan, J.: 3D object recognition in cluttered scenes with local surface features: a survey. PAMI **36**(11), 2270–2287 (2014)
16. Guo, Y., Bennamoun, M., Sohel, F.A., Lu, M., Wan, J., Kwok, N.M.: A comprehensive performance evaluation of 3D local feature descriptors. IJCV **116**(1), 66–89 (2016)
17. Handa, A., Whelan, T., McDonald, J., Davison, A.J.: A benchmark for RGB-D visual odometry, 3D reconstruction and SLAM. In: ICRA (2014)
18. Hartley, R.I., Kahl, F.: Global optimization through searching rotation space and optimal estimation of the essential matrix. In: ICCV (2007)
19. Holz, D., Ichim, A.E., Tombari, F., Rusu, R.B., Behnke, S.: Registration with the point cloud library: a modular framework for aligning in 3-D. IEEE Robot. Autom. Mag. **22**(4), 110–124 (2015)
20. Huber, D.F., Hebert, M.: Fully automatic registration of multiple 3D data sets. Image Vis. Comput. **21**(7), 637–650 (2003)
21. Jian, B., Vemuri, B.C.: Robust point set registration using Gaussian mixture models. PAMI **33**(8), 1633–1645 (2011)
22. Kolluri, R.K., Shewchuk, J.R., O'Brien, J.F.: Spectral surface reconstruction from noisy point clouds. In: Symposium on Geometry Processing (2004)
23. Li, H., Hartley, R.I.: The 3D-3D registration problem revisited. In: ICCV (2007)
24. Liu, Y.: A mean field annealing approach to accurate free form shape matching. Pattern Recogn. **40**(9), 2418–2436 (2007)
25. Makadia, A., Patterson, A., Daniilidis, K.: Fully automatic registration of 3D point clouds. In: CVPR (2006)
26. Mellado, N., Aiger, D., Mitra, N.J.: Super 4PCS: fast global pointcloud registration via smart indexing. Comput. Graph. Forum **33**(5), 205–215 (2014)
27. Mian, A.S., Bennamoun, M., Owens, R.: Three-dimensional model-based object recognition and segmentation in cluttered scenes. PAMI **28**(10), 1584–1601 (2006)

28. Mian, A.S., Bennamoun, M., Owens, R.A.: Automatic correspondence for 3D modeling: an extensive review. Int. J. Shape Model. **11**(2), 253–291 (2005)
29. Papazov, C., Haddadin, S., Parusel, S., Krieger, K., Burschka, D.: Rigid 3D geometry matching for grasping of known objects in cluttered scenes. Int. J. Robot. Res. **31**(4), 538–553 (2012)
30. Pomerleau, F., Colas, F., Siegwart, R., Magnenat, S.: Comparing ICP variants on real-world data sets - open-source library and experimental protocol. Auton. Robots **34**(3), 133–148 (2013)
31. Raguram, R., Frahm, J.-M., Pollefeys, M.: A comparative analysis of RANSAC techniques leading to adaptive real-time random sample consensus. In: Forsyth, D., Torr, P., Zisserman, A. (eds.) ECCV 2008, Part II. LNCS, vol. 5303, pp. 500–513. Springer, Heidelberg (2008)
32. Rangarajan, A., Chui, H., Mjolsness, E., Pappu, S., Davachi, L., Goldman-Rakic, P.S., Duncan, J.S.: A robust point-matching algorithm for autoradiograph alignment. Med. Image Anal. **1**(4), 379–398 (1997)
33. Rusinkiewicz, S., Levoy, M.: Efficient variants of the ICP algorithm. In: 3DIM (2001)
34. Rusu, R.B., Blodow, N., Beetz, M.: Fast point feature histograms (FPFH) for 3D registration. In: ICRA (2009)
35. Salas-Moreno, R.F., Newcombe, R.A., Strasdat, H., Kelly, P.H.J., Davison, A.J.: SLAM++: simultaneous localisation and mapping at the level of objects. In: CVPR (2013)
36. Salvi, J., Matabosch, C., Fofi, D., Forest, J.: A review of recent range image registration methods with accuracy evaluation. Image Vis. Comput. **25**(5), 578–596 (2007)
37. Shin, J., Triebel, R., Siegwart, R.: Unsupervised discovery of repetitive objects. In: ICRA (2010)
38. Tam, G.K.L., Cheng, Z., Lai, Y., Langbein, F.C., Liu, Y., Marshall, D., Martin, R.R., Sun, X., Rosin, P.L.: Registration of 3D point clouds and meshes: a survey from rigid to nonrigid. IEEE Trans. Vis. Comput. Graph. **19**(7), 1199–1217 (2013)
39. Theiler, P.W., Wegner, J.D., Schindler, K.: Globally consistent registration of terrestrial laser scans via graph optimization. J. Photogrammetry Remote Sensing **109**, 126–138 (2015)
40. Tombari, F., Salti, S., di Stefano, L.: Performance evaluation of 3D keypoint detectors. IJCV **102**(1–3), 198–220 (2013)
41. Tsin, Y., Kanade, T.: A correlation-based approach to robust point set registration. In: Pajdla, T., Matas, J.G. (eds.) ECCV 2004. LNCS, vol. 3023, pp. 558–569. Springer, Heidelberg (2004)
42. Yang, J., Li, H., Campbell, D., Jia, Y.: Go-ICP: a globally optimal solution to 3D ICP point-set registration. In: PAMI (2016, to appear)

# Poster Session 3

# Polysemous Codes

Matthijs Douze[(✉)], Hervé Jégou, and Florent Perronnin

Facebook AI Research, Paris, France
matthijs@fb.com

**Abstract.** This paper considers the problem of approximate nearest neighbor search in the compressed domain. We introduce polysemous codes, which offer both the distance estimation quality of product quantization and the efficient comparison of binary codes with Hamming distance. Their design is inspired by algorithms introduced in the 90's to construct channel-optimized vector quantizers. At search time, this dual interpretation accelerates the search. Most of the indexed vectors are filtered out with Hamming distance, letting only a fraction of the vectors to be ranked with an asymmetric distance estimator. The method is complementary with a coarse partitioning of the feature space such as the inverted multi-index. This is shown by our experiments performed on several public benchmarks such as the BIGANN dataset comprising one billion vectors, for which we report state-of-the-art results for query times below 0.3 millisecond per core. Last but not least, our approach allows the approximate computation of the k-NN graph associated with the Yahoo Flickr Creative Commons 100M, described by CNN image descriptors, in less than 8 h on a single machine.

## 1 Introduction

Nearest neighbor search, or more generally similarity search, has received a sustained attention from different research communities in the last decades. The computer vision community has been especially active on this subject, which is of utmost importance when dealing with very large visual collections.

While early approximate nearest neighbor (ANN) methods were mainly optimising the trade-off between speed and accuracy, many recent works [4,27,37,45] put memory requirements as a central criterion for several reasons. For instance, due to the memory hierarchy, using less memory means using faster memory: disks are slower than the main memory, the main memory is slower than CPU caches, etc. Accessing the memory may be the bottleneck of the search. Therefore algorithms using compact codes are likely to offer a better efficiency than those relying on full vectors. For these reasons, we focus on ANN search with compact codes, which are able to make search in vector sets comprising as much as one billion vectors on a single machine.

We distinguish two separate lines of research in ANN with compact codes. The first class of methods proposes to map the original vectors to the Hamming hypercube [33,37,49,51]. The resulting bit-vectors are efficiently compared

© Springer International Publishing AG 2016
B. Leibe et al. (Eds.): ECCV 2016, Part II, LNCS 9906, pp. 785–801, 2016.
DOI: 10.1007/978-3-319-46475-6_48

with the Hamming distance thanks to optimized low-level processor instructions such as xor and popcnt, available both on CPUs and GPUs. Another increasingly popular approach [5,18,27,39,55,56] is to adopt a quantization point of view to achieve a better distance estimation for a given code size. While these two classes of approaches are often seen as contenders, they both have their advantages and drawbacks. Binary codes offer a faster elementary distance computation and do not need external meta-data once the codes are produced. In contrast, quantization-based approaches achieve better memory/accuracy operating points.

The polysemous codes introduced in this paper offer the best of both worlds. They can be compared either with binary codes, which is especially useful in a filtering step, or with the asymmetric distance estimator of product quantization approaches. The key aspect to attain this dual interpretation is the learning procedure. Our approach is inspired by works on channel-optimized vector quantization [16]. We start by training a product quantizer [27]. We then optimize the so-called *index assignment* of the centroids to binary codes. In other terms, we re-order the numeration of the centroids such that distances between similar centroids are small in the Hamming space, as illustrated in Fig. 1.

As a result, our method is almost on par both with quantization-based methods in terms of accuracy and binary methods with respect to search efficiency. When combining this approach with a complementary approach such as the inverted multi-index [4], we outperform the state of the art by a large margin, as shown by our experiments carried out on several large public benchmarks. Interestingly, the high efficiency of our approach offers a scalable solution to

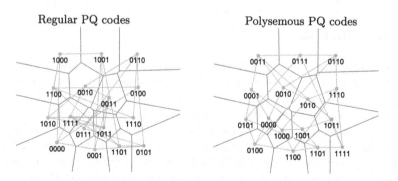

**Fig. 1.** Polysemous codes are compact representations of vectors that can be compared either with product quantization (222M distance evaluations per second per core for 8-byte codes) or as binary codes (1.19G distances per second). To obtain this property, we optimize the assignment of quantization indexes to bits such that closest centroids have a small Hamming distance. The figure shows k-means centroids (learned on points uniformly drawn in $[0,1] \times [0,1]$) and their corresponding binary representations. Observe how the codes differing by one bit (connected by red segments in the figure) generally correspond to close centroids after our optimization (*right*), which is not the case for standard PQ codes (*left*).

the all-neighbor problem, *i.e.*, to compute the k-NN graph, for the large image collection Flickr100M described by 4,096 dimensional vectors.

This paper is organized as follows. After briefly reviewing related works on ANN search with compact codes in Sect. 2, Sect. 3 describes the design of polysemous codes. The experiments analyzing our approach and comparing to the state-of-the-art are detailed in Sect. 4. Finally Sect. 5 illustrates our method on the task of constructing an image graph on a large scale.

## 2 Related Work: ANN with Compact Codes

The literature on efficient search with compact codes is vast and we refer the reader to two recent surveys [48,50] for extensive references on this subject. In this section, we present only a few popular approaches.

**Compact Binary Codes.** Locality-Sensitive hashing [11,19,24] is a pioneering binary encoding technique. Charikar [11] shows under some assumptions that the Hamming distance is statistically related to the cosine similarity (equivalently the Euclidean distance for normalized vectors). Brute-force comparison of binary hashes has been seen as a viable option for efficient image search with memory constraints [37], which was popularized by subsequent works evidencing the scalability of this approach to million-sized image collections [44]. Additionally, Norouzi and Fleet have proposed an algorithm to speed-up the search in this Hamming space [40]. Many variants have been subsequently proposed, such as spectral hashing [51] or ITQ [20] – see also [42,49,53] for representative works. Related to our work, the k-means hashing method [23] first produces a vector quantizer where the produced codes are compared with the Hamming distance.

**Quantization-Based Codes.** Several works have primarily focused on optimizing the trade-off between memory and distance estimation. In particular, it is shown that vector quantizers [27] satisfying the Lloyd conditions [22] offer statistical guarantees on the square Euclidean distance estimator, which is bounded in expectation by the quantizer squared loss. These quantization-based methods include product quantization (PQ) [27] and its optimized versions "optimized product quantization" [18] and "Cartesian k-means" [39].

These approaches are effective for approximate search within large collections of visual descriptors. Subsequent works [5,55,56] have pushed possible memory/efficiency trade-off by adopting a more general point of view, such as "Additive quantization" [5], which provides an excellent approximation and search performance, yet obtained with a much higher computational encoding cost [7]. In between PQ and this general formulation, good trade-offs are achieved by residual quantizers [10,30], which are routinely used in the non-exhaustive PQ variant [27] to reduce the quantization loss by encoding the residual error vector instead of the original vector, but also as a coding strategy on its own [1,12,38].

**Non-exhaustive Search.** The aforementioned methods for ANN search limit the memory usage per indexed vector and provide a distance estimator that is faster to compute than the exact distance. However, the search is still exhaustive in the sense that the query is compared to all database elements. For billion-sized collections, reading the codes in memory is a severe constraint leading to search times in the order of a second, typically. The limitation imposed by this memory bottleneck has led to two-stage approaches [2,26,27,31], in which the feature space is first partitioned through hashing or clustering. Practically, an inverted list storing identifiers and corresponding compact codes is stored for each region. At query time, the distance is estimated only for the codes associated with a subset of regions [4,27,36]. It is also possible to use multiple partitions as in early LSH papers, as done in joint inverted indexing [52]. These solutions however require several indexing structures and are therefore not competitive in terms of memory usage. Various partitioning methods have been proposed for the coarse level [4,41]. In particular, the inverted multi-index uses product quantization both to define the coarse level and for coding residual vectors. This strategy offers state-of-the-art performance when further combined with a re-ranking strategy based on codes [29].

**Motivation: Binary Codes Versus Quantization-Based Approaches.**
The Hamming distance is significantly faster to evaluate than the distance estimator based on table look-ups involved in quantization methods[1]. From our measurements, the acceleration factor is typically between 4× and 7×, depending on the code length. However, binary methods suffer limitations imposed by the Hamming space. First, the number of possible distances is at most $d+1$, where $d$ is the binary vector length. This problem is partially solved by asymmetric variants of LSH [15,21,25], whose estimations use compact codes for database vectors but not on the query side. Yet such asymmetric measures require look-ups, like the methods derived from product quantization, and are therefore more expensive to evaluate than the Hamming distance. On the other hand, quantization-based methods offer a better memory/accuracy compromise, which is expected since binarization is a particular case of quantization.

Binary and quantization-based codes have their own advantages and drawbacks. While the literature usually presents binary and quantized-based codes as concurrent methods, the next section introduces a method that benefits from the advantages of both classes of methods.

## 3  Polysemous Codes

We, now, introduce our strategy to take advantage of the fast computation of Hamming distances while offering the estimation accuracy of quantization-based methods. The main idea is to learn a regular product quantizer [27], and then to optimize the assignment of centroid indexes to binary codes such that the Hamming distance approximates the inter-centroid distance. In this section, we first describe the objective functions optimized to achieve this property, and then describe the optimization algorithm.

---

[1] A recent method [3] reduces the scanning by employing a lower-bounding look-up table stored in SIMD registers, however this method is efficient only on long inverted lists, which makes it sub-optimal in the usual setting.

Note that for a product quantizer, one typically optimizes separately each of the constituent sub-quantizers. Therefore, in what follows, we have one objective function (and optimization process) per sub-quantizer.

## 3.1   Objective Functions

We consider two objective functions: one that minimizes a loss based on the distance estimator and one that minimizes a ranking loss.

**Notation.** A quantizer is usually described by its set of centroids. Let $\mathcal{I}$ be the set of centroid indexes: $\mathcal{I} = \{0, 1, \ldots, 2^d - 1\}$ and $d = 8$ if each (sub-)quantizer encodes the original vectors on one byte as is standard practice. Let $c_i$ be the reproduction value associated with centroid $i$. Let $d : \mathbb{R}^D \times \mathbb{R}^D \to \mathbb{R}^+$ be a distance between centroids, for instance the Euclidean distance. Let $\pi : \mathcal{I} \to \{0, 1\}^d$ denote a bijective function that maps each centroid index to a different vertex of the unit hypercube. Finally let $h : \{0, 1\}^d \times \{0, 1\}^d \to \mathbb{R}^+$ be the Hamming distance between two $d$-dimensional binary representations.

**Distance Estimator Loss.** One possible objective if to find the bijective map $\pi$ such that the distance $d(c_i, c_j)$ between two centroids is approximated by the Hamming distance $h(\pi(i), \pi(j))$ between the two corresponding binary codes:

$$\pi^* = \arg\min_{\pi} \sum_{i \in \mathcal{I}, j \in \mathcal{I}} [h(\pi(i), \pi(j)) - f(d(c_i, c_j))]^2 \tag{1}$$

where $f : \mathbb{R} \to \mathbb{R}$ is a monotonously increasing function that maps the distance $d(c_i, c_j)$ between codewords into a range comparable to Hamming distances. In practice, we choose for $f$ a simple linear mapping. This choice is motivated by the following observations. The Hamming distance between two binary vectors randomly drawn from $\{0, 1\}^d$ follows a binomial distribution with mean $d/2$ and variance $d/4$. Assuming that the distribution of distances $d(c_i, c_j)$ can be approximated by a Gaussian distribution – which is a good approximation of the binomial – with mean $\mu$ and standard deviation sigma $\sigma$, we can force the two distributions to have the same mean and variance. This yields:

$$f(x) = \frac{\sqrt{d}}{2\sigma}(x - \mu) + \frac{d}{2} \tag{2}$$

where $\mu$ and $\sigma$ are measured empirically.

As, in the context of k-NN, it is more important to approximate small distances than large ones, we found out in practice that it is beneficial to weight the distances in the objective function (1). This leads to a weighted objective:

$$\pi^* = \arg\min_{\pi} \sum_{i \in \mathcal{I}, j \in \mathcal{I}} w(f(d(c_i, c_j))) [h(\pi(i), \pi(j)) - f(d(c_i, c_j))]^2. \tag{3}$$

We choose a function $w : \mathbb{R} \to \mathbb{R}$ of the form $w(u) = \alpha^u$ with $\alpha < 1$. In our experiments, we set $\alpha = 1/2$ but we found out that values of $\alpha$ in the range $[0.2, 0.6]$ yielded similar results.

**Ranking Loss.** In the context of k-NN search, we are interested in finding a bijective map $\pi$ that preserves the ranking of codewords. For this purpose, we adopt an Information Retrieval perspective. Let $(i, j)$ be a pair of codewords such that $i$ is assumed to be a "query" and $j$ is assumed to be "relevant" to $i$. We will later discuss the choice of (query, relevant) pairs. We take as negatives for query $i$ the codewords $k$ such that $d(c_i, c_j) < d(c_i, c_k)$. The loss for pair $(i, j)$ may be defined as:

$$r_\pi(i, j) = \sum_{k \in \mathcal{I}} \mathbb{1}\left[d(c_i, c_j) < d(c_i, c_k)\right] \mathbb{1}\left[h(\pi(i), \pi(j)) > h(\pi(i), \pi(k))\right] \quad (4)$$

where $\mathbb{1}[u] = 1$ if $u$ is true, 0 otherwise. It measures how many codewords $k$ are closer to $i$ than $j$ according to the Hamming distance while, $i$ is closer to $j$ than $k$ according to the distance between centroids. We note that the previous loss measures the number of correctly ranked pairs which is closely related to Kendall's tau coefficient.

An issue with the loss $r_\pi(i, j)$ is that it gives the same weight to the top of the list as to the bottom. However, in ranking problems it is desirable to give more weight to errors occurring in the top ranks. Therefore, we do not use directly the loss $r_\pi(i, j)$ for the pair $(i, j)$, but adopt instead a loss that increases sublinearly with $r_\pi(i, j)$. More specifically, we follow [46] and introduce a monotonously decreasing sequence $\alpha_i$ as well as the sequence $\ell_j = \sum_{i=1}^{j} \alpha_i$, which increases sublinearly with $j$. We define the weighted loss for pair $(i, j)$ as $\ell_{r_\pi(i,j)}$.

A subsequent question is how to choose pairs $(i, j)$. One possibility would be to choose $j$ among the $k$-NNs of $i$, in which case we would optimize

$$\pi^* = \arg\min_{\pi} \sum_{i \in \mathcal{I}} \sum_{j \in k-\mathrm{NN}(i)} \ell_{r_\pi(i,j)}. \quad (5)$$

An issue with this approach is that it requires choosing an arbitrary length $k$ for the NN list. An alternative is to consider all $j \neq i$ as being potentially "relevant" to $i$ but to downweight the contribution of those $j$'s which are further away from $i$. In such a case, we optimize

$$\pi^* = \arg\min_{\pi} \sum_{i \in I, j \in \mathcal{I}} \alpha_{r(i,j)} \ell_{r_\pi(i,j)}, \quad (6)$$

where we recall that $\alpha_i$ is a decreasing sequence and $r(i, j)$ is the rank of $j$ in the ordered list of neighbors to $i$:

$$r(i, j) = \sum_{k \in \mathcal{I}} \mathbb{1}\left[d(c_i, c_j) < d(c_i, c_k)\right] \quad (7)$$

In all our ranking experiments, we use Eq. (6) and choose $\alpha_i = 1/i$ (following [46]).

## 3.2   Optimization

The aforementioned objective functions aim at finding a bijective map $\pi$, or equivalently another numeration of the set of PQ centroids, that would assign similar binary codes to neighbouring centroids.

This problem is similar to that of channel optimized vector quantization [16,17,54], for which researchers have designed quantizers such that the corruption of a bit by the channel impacts the reconstruction as little as possible. This is a discrete optimisation problem that can not be relaxed, and for which we can only target a local minimum, as the set of possible bijective maps is huge. In the coding literature, such index assignment problems were first optimised in a greedy manner, for instance by using the binary switching algorithm [54]. Starting from an initial index assignment, at each iteration, this algorithm tests all possible bit swaps (*i.e.*, $d$), and keeps the one providing the best update of the objective function. As shown by Farvardin [16], this strategy rapidly gets trapped in a poor local minimum. To our knowledge, the best approach to index assignment problems is to employ simulated annealing to carry out the optimization. This choice was shown to be significantly better [16] than previous greedy approaches. The algorithm aims at optimizing a loss $L(\pi)$ that depends on the bijective mapping $\pi$ defined as a table of size $2^d$. It proceeds as follows

1. Initialize
2.      current solution $\pi := [0, ...., 2^d - 1]$
3.      temperature $t := t_0$
4. Iterate $N_{\text{iter}}$ times:
5.      draw $i, j \in \mathcal{I}, i \neq j$ at random
6.      $\pi' := \pi$, with entries $i$ and $j$ swapped
7.      compute the cost update $\Delta C := L(\pi') - L(\pi)$
8.      if $\Delta C < 0$ or at random with probability $t$:
9.         accept the new solution: $\pi := \pi'$
10.     $t := t \times t_{\text{decay}}$

The algorithm depends on the number of iterations $N_{\text{iter}} = 500,000$, the initial "temperature" $t_0 = 0.7$ and $t_{\text{decay}} = 0.9^{1/500}$, i.e. decrease by a factor 0.9 every 500 iterations. Evaluating the distance estimation loss (resp ranking loss) has a complexity in $\mathcal{O}(2^{2d})$ (resp. $\mathcal{O}(2^{3d})$). However, computing the cost update incurred by a swap can be implemented in $\mathcal{O}(2^d)$ (resp. $\mathcal{O}(2^{2d})$).

Figure 2 shows on a set of SIFT descriptors that our optimization is effective: the comparison of the codes used as binary vectors is much more correlated with the true distance after than before the optimization.

## 3.3   Discussion

Although the optimization algorithm is similar to those previously employed in channel-optimized vector quantization, our objective functions are significantly different to reflect our application scenario. In communications, it is unlikely that many bit errors occur simultaneously, in particular not on a memoryless

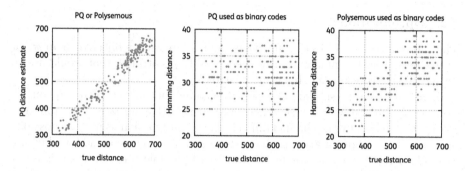

**Fig. 2.** *Left:* True distances *vs* distance estimates with PQ codes. *Middle:* True distances *vs* Hamming distances before polysemous optimization. *Right:* True distances *vs* Hamming distances after polysemous optimization. The binary comparison with Polysemous is much more discriminative, while offering the same estimation when being interpreted as PQ codes.

channel. Therefore the objective functions employed in communication focus on small Hamming distances. In contrast, for ANN the typical Hamming distances of the neighbors are relatively large.

We point out that, while the proposed binarized PQ codes offer a competitive performance, their accuracy is significantly lower than that of PQ. This suggests a two-step strategy for large-scale search. Given a query, we first filter out the majority of the database items using the fast Hamming distance on the binarized PQ codes. We then evaluate the more costly asymmetric distances for the items whose Hamming distance was below a given threshold $\tau$.

Other strategies could be contemplated for the filtering stage. One such strategy is to measure how many quantization indexes differ for the product quantizer[2]. In other terms, one can filter out vectors if more than a given number of sub-quantizers produce indexes not identical to those of the queries. As shown in the experimental Sect. 4, this method is not as efficient nor precise as the strategy proposed in this section.

Another such strategy would be to use for the filtering stage a binary encoding technique unrelated to PQ, *e.g.*, ITQ. The issue is that it would increase the memory requirements of the method as it would involve storing ITQ codes and PQ codes. In constrat, we only store one polysemous code per database item in the proposed approach – a must if the emphasis is on storage requirements.

## 4   Experiments

This section gives an analysis and evaluates our polysemous codes. After introducing the evaluation protocol, we analyze our core approach in different aspects. Then we show that our approach is compatible with the inverted multi-index (IMI) and give a comparison against the state of the art.

---

[2] Formally, this quantity is also called Hamming distance, but measured between vector of indexes and not binary vectors.

## 4.1    Evaluation Protocol

We analyze and evaluate our approach with standard benchmarks for ANN as well as a new benchmark that we introduce to evaluate the search quality.

**SIFT1M** is a benchmark [29] of 128-dimensional SIFT descriptors [35]. There are one million vectors in the database, plus 100,000 vectors for training and 10,000 query vectors. This is a relatively small set that we mainly use for parameter analysis.

**BIGANN** is a large-scale benchmark [29] widely used for ANN search, also made of SIFT descriptors. It comprises one billion database vectors, 100 million training vectors and 10,000 queries.

**FYCNN1M and FYCNN90M** are introduced to evaluate the quality of the search with more challenging features. We leverage the Yahoo Flickr Creative Commons 100M[3] image collection [43] as follows. In FYCNN90M, we split the dataset into three sets: 90M vectors are to be indexed, 10k vectors serve as queries, 5M vectors are used for training. FYCNN1M uses the same training set and queries, but the indexed set is restricted to the first million images for the purpose of analyzing our method. We extract convolutional neural networks features [34] following the guidelines of [8]: we compute the activations of the 7th layer of AlexNet [32]. This yields 4096-dimensional image descriptors. Prior to indexing we reduce these descriptors to 256D with PCA and subsequently apply a random rotation [8,28].

For all datasets, the accuracy is evaluated by recall@$R$. This metric measures the fraction of the queries for which the true nearest neighbor is returned within the top $R$ results. All reported times are on a single core of a 2.8 GHz machine.

## 4.2    Analysis of Polysemous Codes Performance

We first analyze the performance of polysemous codes. Let us introduce notations. We first consider three ways of constructing a product quantizer:

**PQ** is the baseline: we directly use the code produced by the product quantizer, without any optimization of the index assignment;

**PolyD** refers to a product quantizer whose index assignment is optimized by minimizing the distance estimator loss introduced in Sect. 3.1;

**PolyR** similarly refers to a PQ optimized with the proposed ranking loss.

Once the codebook and index assignment are learned, we consider the following methods to estimate distances based on polysemous codes:

**ADC** is the regular comparison based on an asymmetric distance estimator [27];

**binary** refers to the bitwise comparison with the Hamming distance when the codes are regarded as bitvectors, like for binary codes (*e.g.*, ITQ);

**disidx** counts how many sub-quantizers give different codes (see Sect. 3.3);

---

[3] Out of which only 95M are available for download today.

**dual** refers to the strategy employing both interpretations of polysemous codes: the Hamming codes are used to filter-out the database vectors whose distance to the query is above a threshold $\tau$. The indexed vectors satisfying this test are compared with the asymmetric distance estimator.

*Note:* Polysemous codes are primarily PQ codes. Therefore the performance of polysemous codes and regular PQ is identical when the comparison is independent from the index assignment, which is the case for ADC and disidx. For instance the combinations PolyD/ADC, PolyR/ADC and PQ/ADC are equivalent both in efficiency and accuracy.

**Table 1.** Analysis of polysemous codes (16 bytes/vector). The performance of disidx does not depend on the index assignment. We give the performance of codes when compared in binary, before (PQ/binary) and after (PolyD/binary and PolyR/binary) our optimization. Then we present the results for the proposed polysemous dual strategy, which are almost as accurate as PQ while approaching the speed of binary methods. The Hamming thresholds are adjusted on the training sets so that the Hamming comparison filters out at least 95 % of the points. The results are averaged over 5 runs, the sources of randomness being the k-means of the PQ training and the simulated annealing (the standard deviation over runs is always < 0.005). The last 3 rows are baselines provided for reference: LSH, ITQ and PQ. LSH uses a random rotation instead of random projection for better performance [9].

| | SIFT1M | | FYCNN1M | | |
| | $R@1$ | $R@100$ | $R@1$ | $R@100$ | Query (ms) |
|---|---|---|---|---|---|
| PQ/disidx | 0.071 | 0.281 | 0.031 | 0.284 | 3.66 |
| PQ/binary | 0.036 | 0.129 | 0.015 | 0.124 | 1.42 |
| PolyD/binary | 0.107 | 0.503 | 0.027 | 0.281 | 1.45 |
| PolyR/binary | 0.105 | 0.467 | 0.022 | 0.222 | 1.45 |
| PQ/dual ($\tau = 55$) | 0.312 | 0.507 | 0.116 | 0.522 | 2.59 |
| PolyD/dual ($\tau = 51$) | 0.441 | 0.987 | 0.132 | 0.804 | 2.53 |
| PolyR/dual ($\tau = 53$) | 0.439 | 0.960 | 0.130 | 0.745 | 2.47 |
| Baseline: LSH [11] | 0.114 | 0.576 | 0.089 | 0.643 | 1.45 |
| Baseline: ITQ [20] | 0.135 | 0.688 | 0.088 | 0.654 | 1.45 |
| Baseline: PQ [27] | 0.442 | 0.997 | 0.133 | 0.838 | 9.01 |

Table 1 details the performance of the aforementioned PQ constructions. First, note that the accuracy of disidx is low, and that it is also relatively slow due to the lack of a dedicated machine instruction. Second, these results show that our index assignment optimization is very effective for improving the quality of the binary comparison. Without this optimization, the binary comparison is ineffective both to rank results (PQ/binary), and to filter (PQ/dual). The ranking loss PolyR is slightly inferior to PolyD, so we adopt the latter in the following.

Figure 3 confirms the relevance of PolyD/dual. It gives the performance achieved by this method for varying Hamming thresholds $\tau$, which parametrizes the trade-off between speed and accuracy. Polysemous codes allow us to make almost no compromise: attaining the quality of PQ/ADC only requires a minor sacrifice in search time compared to binary codes. With threshold $\tau = 54$, 90–95 % of the points are filtered out; for $\tau = 42$ this raises to more than 99.5 %.

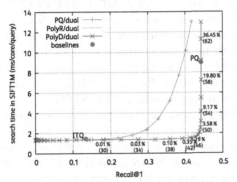

**Fig. 3.** Impact of the threshold on the dual strategy: Recall@1 vs search speed for the SIFT1M dataset, with 128 bits (16 subquantizers). The operating points for polysemous are parametrized by the Hamming threshold (in parenthesis), which influences the rate of points kept for PQ distance estimation. The tradeoffs obtained without polysemous optimization (PQ/dual) and two baselines (ITQ and PQ) are given for reference.

*Convergence:* Figure 4 shows the performance of the binary filtering as a function of the number of iterations. The algorithm typically converges in a few hundred thousand iterations (1 iteration = 1 test of possible index swaps). For a set of PQ subquantizer with 256 centroids each, this means a few seconds for the distance reconstruction loss PolyR and up to one hour for the ranking loss PolyR.

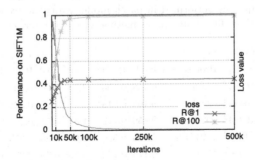

**Fig. 4.** Performance of polysemous codes (dual, $\tau = 52$, 128 bits) along the iterations for the distance-based objective function described in Sect. 3 (results with the ranking loss are similar). Note that the initial state (0 iteration) corresponds to a product quantizer not yet optimized with our method.

### 4.3   Comparison with the State of the Art

As mentioned in the related work Sect. 2, for large datasets the best trade-offs between accuracy, search time and memory are obtained by hybrid methods [4,27] that combine a preliminary space partitioning, typically implemented through clustering, with compact codes learned on residual vectors. That is why we combine our polysemous codes with IMI [4]. This method partitions the space with a product quantizer (the "coarse" partitioning level) and uses PQ to encode residual error vectors. The search proceeds by selecting a few inverted lists at the coarse level, and then use the residual PQ codes to estimate distances for the vectors associated with the selected lists. We further optimize the computation of the lookup tables involved in PQ when multiple lists are probed [6], and use an optimized rotation before encoding with PQ [18].

Building upon this method, we learn polysemous codes for the residual PQ, which allows us to introduce an intermediate stage to filter out most of the list items, hence avoiding most of the distance estimation with PQ. Table 2 gives a comparison against state-of-the-art algorithms on the BIGANN dataset. We report both the timings reported for concurrent methods and our improved re-implementation of IMI. Note already that our system obtains very competitive results compared to the original IMI. Note, in the case where a single query vector is searched at a time, as opposed to batch mode, the coarse quantization becomes 50 to 60 % more expensive. Therefore, in the following we use $K = 4096^2$ to target more aggressive operating points by reducing the fixed cost of the coarse quantizer. In this case, the results of PolyD/dual gives a clear improvement compared to IMI$\star$ and the state of the art. In particular, with 16 bytes we are able to achieve a recall@1 $= 0.217$ in less than 1 ms on one core (0.38 ms in single

**Table 2.** Comparison against the state of the art on BIGANN (1 billion vectors). We cap both the maximum number of visited lists and number of distance evaluations (column probes/cap). For the timings, using our improved implementation ($\star$), the first number is for queries performed in batch mode, while the second corresponds to a single query at a time. Our polysemous method is set to filter out 80 % of the codes.

| | Code | Sizes → | 8 bytes | | | | 16 bytes | | | |
|---|---|---|---|---|---|---|---|---|---|---|
| | K | Probes/cap | R@1 | R@100 | Time (ms) | | R@1 | R@100 | Time (ms) | |
| IMI [4] | $16384^2$ | –/10k | 0.158 | 0.706 | 6 | | 0.304 | 0.740 | 7 | |
| IMI [4] | $16384^2$ | –/30k | 0.164 | 0.813 | 13 | | 0.328 | 0.885 | 13 | |
| IMI$\star$ | $16384^2$ | 1024/10k | 0.159 | 0.719 | 1.57 | 2.58 | 0.313 | 0.753 | 1.92 | 2.89 |
| IMI$\star$ | $4096^2$ | 1024/10k | 0.125 | 0.550 | 0.99 | 1.23 | 0.255 | 0.576 | 1.16 | 1.44 |
| IMI$\star$ | $4096^2$ | 16/10k | 0.115 | 0.462 | 0.50 | 0.75 | 0.226 | 0.479 | 0.64 | 0.88 |
| IMI$\star$+PolyD+ADC | $4096^2$ | 16/10k | 0.103 | 0.332 | **0.27** | 0.51 | 0.206 | 0.397 | **0.33** | 0.58 |
| IMI$\star$ | $16384^2$ | 1024/30k | 0.162 | 0.796 | 2.20 | 3.15 | 0.330 | 0.856 | 2.77 | 3.75 |
| IMI$\star$ | $4096^2$ | 1024/30k | 0.134 | 0.696 | 1.35 | 1.61 | 0.295 | 0.755 | 1.77 | 2.07 |
| IMI$\star$ | $4096^2$ | 16/30k | 0.117 | 0.505 | 0.59 | 0.81 | 0.238 | 0.532 | 0.75 | 1.01 |
| IMI$\star$+PolyD+ADC | $4096^2$ | 16/30k | 0.106 | 0.370 | 0.33 | 0.56 | 0.217 | 0.447 | 0.38 | 0.64 |

query mode, 0.64 ms in batch mode). The binary filter divides by about 2× the search time, inducing only a small reduction of the Recall@1 score.

We now compare our method on the more challenging FYCNN90M benchmark, for which a single query amounts to searching an image in a collection containing 90 million images. Figure 5 reports the performance achieved by different methods. First observe that the non-exhaustive methods (*bottom*) are at least 2 orders of magnitude faster than the methods that compare the codes exhaustively (*top*), like ITQ. The former are able to find similar images in a few seconds. Again, our polysemous strategy IMI+PolyD/dual offers a competitive advantage over its competitor IMI. Our method is approximately 1.5× faster for a negligible loss in accuracy.

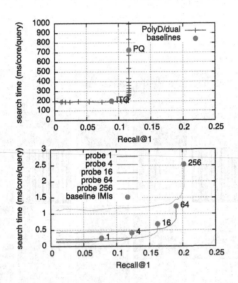

**Fig. 5.** Performance on the FYCNN90M benchmarks. We use 20 bytes per vector (128 bits for the code and 4 bytes per identifier), *i.e.*, per indexed image. *Above:* For reference we give results obtained by methods that exhaustively compare the query to all vectors indexes based on their codes. As to be expected, the non-exhaustive methods (*below*) achieve much better performance, especially when probing a large number of inverted lists (see "probe 256"). Our proposal IMI+PolyD/dual offers the best trade-off between memory, search time and accuracy by a fair margin.

## 5   Application: Large-Scale K-NN Image Graph

As an application to our fast indexing scheme, we now consider the problem of building the approximate k-NN graph of a very large image collection. For this experiment, we make use of the 95,063,295 images available in the Flickr 100M dataset. As was the case in Sect. 4, we use 4,096D AlexNet features reduced to

256D with PCA. For the graph construction, we simply compute the k-NN with $k = 100$ for each image in turn. This takes 7h44 using 20 threads of a CPU server. Note that the collection that we consider is significantly larger than the ones considered in previous works [14,47] on kNN graph. Moreover, our approach may be complementary with the method proposed by Dong *et al.* [14].

For visualization purposes, we seek the modes following a random walk technique [13]: we first iteratively compute the stationary distribution of the walk, (*i.e.* the probability of each node to be visited during the random walk) and then consider as modes each local maximum of the stationary probability in the graph. We find on the order of 3,000 such maxima. Figure 6 depicts a sample of these maxima as well as their closest neighbors. We believe that these results are representative of the typical quality of the found neighbors, except that, for

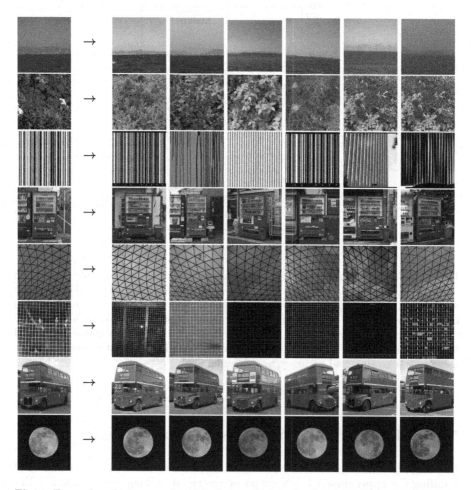

**Fig. 6.** Examples of image modes and their neighbors in the graph. For each reference image (left), we show the corresponding image neighbors in the kNN graph on its right.

privacy reasons, we do not show the numerous modes corresponding to faces, of which we found many including specialized modes of "pairs of persons", "clusters of more than two persons" or "baby faces".

# 6 Conclusion

In this work, we introduced polysemous codes, *i.e.*, codes that can be interpreted both as binary codes and as product quantization codes. These complementary views are exploited for very large-scale indexing in a simple two-stage process that first involves filtering-out the majority of irrelevant indexes using the fast Hamming distance on binary codes, and then re-ordering the short list of candidates using the more precise but also slower asymmetric distance on PQ codes. This yields a competitive indexing scheme that combines the best of both worlds: its speed is comparable to that of pure binary techniques and its accuracy matches that of PQ.

**Acknowledgements.** We are very grateful to Armand Joulin and Laurens van de Maaten for providing the Flicrk100M images and their CNN descriptors.

# References

1. Ai, L., Yu, J., Wu, Z., He, Y., Guan, T.: Optimized residual vector quantization for efficient approximate nearest neighbor search. Multimedia Syst. 1–13 (2015)
2. Andoni, A., Indyk, P., Nguyen, H.L., Razenshteyn, I.: Beyond locality-sensitive hashing. In: SODA, pp. 1018–1028 (2014)
3. André, F., Kermarrec, A.M., le Scouarnec, N.: Cache locality is not enough: high-performance nearest neighbor search with product quantization fast scan. In: Proceedings of the International Conference on Very Large DataBases (2015)
4. Babenko, A., Lempitsky, V.: The inverted multi-index. In: CVPR, June 2012
5. Babenko, A., Lempitsky, V.: Additive quantization for extreme vector compression. In: CVPR, June 2014
6. Babenko, A., Lempitsky, V.: Improving bilayer product quantization for billion-scale approximate nearest neighbors in high dimensions. arXiv preprint arXiv:1404.1831 (2014)
7. Babenko, A., Lempitsky, V.: Tree quantization for large-scale similarity search and classification. In: CVPR, June 2015
8. Babenko, A., Slesarev, A., Chigorin, A., Lempitsky, V.: Neural codes for image retrieval. In: Fleet, D., Pajdla, T., Schiele, B., Tuytelaars, T. (eds.) ECCV 2014, Part I. LNCS, vol. 8689, pp. 584–599. Springer, Heidelberg (2014)
9. Balu, R., Furon, T., Jégou, H.: Beyond project and sign for distance estimation with binary codes. In: ICASSP, April 2014
10. Barnes, C.F., Rizvi, S., Nasrabadi, N.: Advances in residual vector quantization: a review. IEEE Trans. Image Process. 5(2), 226–262 (1996)
11. Charikar, M.S.: Similarity estimation techniques from rounding algorithms. In: STOC, pp. 380–388, May 2002
12. Chen, Y., Guan, T., Wang, C.: Approximate nearest neighbor search by residual vector quantization. Sensors 10(12), 11259–11273 (2010)

13. Cho, M., Lee, K.M.: Mode-seeking on graphs via random walks. In: CVPR, June 2012
14. Dong, W., Charikar, M., Li, K.: Efficient k-nearest neighbor graph construction for generic similarity measures. In: WWW, March 2011
15. Dong, W., Charikar, M., Li, K.: Asymmetric distance estimation with sketches for similarity search in high-dimensional spaces. In: SIGIR, pp. 123–130, July 2008
16. Farvardin, N.: A study of vector quantization for noisy channels. IEEE Trans. Inform. Theor. **36**(5), 799–809 (1990)
17. Farvardin, N., Vaishampayan, V.: On the performance and complexity of channel-optimized vector quantizers. IEEE Trans. Inform. Theor. **37**(1), 155–160 (1991)
18. Ge, T., He, K., Ke, Q., Sun, J.: Optimized product quantization for approximate nearest neighbor search. In: CVPR, June 2013
19. Gionis, A., Indyk, P., Motwani, R.: Similarity search in high dimension via hashing. In: Proceedings of the International Conference on Very Large DataBases, pp. 518–529 (1999)
20. Gong, Y., Lazebnik, S.: Iterative quantization: a procrustean approach to learning binary codes. In: CVPR, June 2011
21. Gordo, A., Perronnin, F.: Asymmetric distances for binary embeddings. In: CVPR (2011)
22. Gray, R.M., Neuhoff, D.L.: Quantization. IEEE Trans. Inform. Theor. **44**, 2325–2384 (1998)
23. He, K., Wen, F., Sun, J.: K-means hashing: an affinity-preserving quantization method for learning binary compact codes. In: CVPR (2013)
24. Indyk, P., Motwani, R.: Approximate nearest neighbors: towards removing the curse of dimensionality. In: STOC, pp. 604–613 (1998)
25. Jain, M., Jégou, H., Gros, P.: Asymmetric hamming embedding. In: ACM Multimedia, October 2011
26. Jegou, H., Douze, M., Schmid, C.: Hamming embedding and weak geometric consistency for large scale image search. In: Forsyth, D., Torr, P., Zisserman, A. (eds.) ECCV 2008, Part I. LNCS, vol. 5302, pp. 304–317. Springer, Heidelberg (2008)
27. Jégou, H., Douze, M., Schmid, C.: Product quantization for nearest neighbor search. IEEE Trans. PAMI **33**(1), 117–128 (2011)
28. Jégou, H., Douze, M., Schmid, C., Pérez, P.: Aggregating local descriptors into a compact image representation. In: CVPR, June 2010
29. Jégou, H., Tavenard, R., Douze, M., Amsaleg, L.: Searching in one billion vectors: re-rank with source coding. In: ICASSP, May 2011
30. Juang, B.H., Gray, A.J.: Multiple stage vector quantization for speech coding. In: ICASSP, vol. 7, pp. 597–600. IEEE (1982)
31. Kalantidis, Y., Avrithis, Y.: Locally optimized product quantization for approximate nearest neighbor search. In: CVPR, June 2014
32. Krizhevsky, A., Sutskever, I., Hinton, G.E.: Imagenet classification with deep convolutional neural networks. In: NIPS, December 2012
33. Kulis, B., Grauman, K.: Kernelized locality-sensitive hashing for scalable image search. In: ICCV, October 2009
34. LeCun, Y., Boser, B., Denker, J., Henderson, D., Howard, R., Hubbard, W., Jackel, L.: Handwritten digit recognition with a back-propagation network. In: Advances in Neural Information Processing Systems 2, NIPS (1989)
35. Lowe, D.G.: Distinctive image features from scale-invariant keypoints. IJCV **60**(2), 91–110 (2004)

36. Lv, Q., Josephson, W., Wang, Z., Charikar, M., Li, K.: Multi-probe LSH: efficient indexing for high-dimensional similarity search. In: Proceedings of the International Conference on Very Large DataBases, pp. 950–961 (2007)
37. Lv, Q., Charikar, M., Li, K.: Image similarity search with compact data structures. In: CIKM, pp. 208–217, November 2004
38. Martinez, J., Hoos, H.H., Little, J.J.: Stacked quantizers for compositional vector compression. arXiv preprint arXiv:1411.2173 (2014)
39. Norouzi, M., Fleet, D.: Cartesian k-means. In: CVPR, June 2013
40. Norouzi, M., Punjani, A., Fleet, D.J.: Fast search in hamming space with multi-index hashing. In: CVPR (2012)
41. Paulevé, L., Jégou, H., Amsaleg, L.: Locality sensitive hashing: a comparison of hash function types and querying mechanisms. Pattern Recogn. Lett. $31$(11), 1348–1358 (2010)
42. Raginsky, M., Lazebnik, S.: Locality-sensitive binary codes from shift-invariant kernels. In: NIPS (2010)
43. Thomee, B., Shamma, D.A., Friedland, G., Elizalde, B., Ni, K., Poland, D., Borth, D., Li, L.J.: The new data and new challenges in multimedia research. arXiv preprint arXiv:1503.01817, March 2015
44. Torralba, A., Fergus, R., Freeman, W.T.: 80 million tiny images: a large database for non-parametric object and scene recognition. IEEE Trans. PAMI $30$(11), 1958–1970 (2008)
45. Torralba, A., Fergus, R., Weiss, Y.: Small codes and large databases for recognition. In: CVPR, June 2008
46. Usunier, N., Buffoni, D., Gallinari, P.: Ranking with ordered weighted pairwise classification. In: ICML, June 2009
47. Wang, J., Wang, J., Zeng, G., Tu, Z., Gan, R., Li, S.: Scalable k-NN graph construction for visual descriptors. In: CVPR, pp. 1106–1113, June 2012
48. Wang, J., Shen, H.T., Song, J., Ji, J.: Hashing for similarity search: a survey. arXiv preprint arXiv:1408.2927 (2014)
49. Wang, J., Kumar, S., Chang, S.F.: Semi-supervised hashing for large scale search. IEEE Trans. PAMI $6$(12), 1 (2012)
50. Wang, J., Liu, W., Kumar, S., Chang, S.: Learning to hash for indexing big data - a survey. CoRR abs/1509.05472 (2015). http://arxiv.org/abs/1509.05472
51. Weiss, Y., Torralba, A., Fergus, R.: Spectral hashing. In: NIPS, December 2009
52. Xia, Y., He, K., Wen, F., Sun, J.: Joint inverted indexing. In: ICCV, December 2013
53. Xu, H., Wang, J., Li, Z., Zeng, G., Li, S., Yu, N.: Complementary hashing for approximate nearest neighbor search. In: ICCV, November 2011
54. Zeger, K., Gersho, A.: Pseudo-gray coding. IEEE Trans. Commun. $38$(12), 2147–2158 (1990)
55. Zhang, T., Du, C., Wang, J.: Composite quantization for approximate nearest neighbor search. In: ICML, pp. 838–846, June 2014
56. Zhang, T., Qi, G.J., Tang, J., Wang, J.: Sparse composite quantization. In: CVPR, June 2015

# Binary Hashing with Semidefinite Relaxation and Augmented Lagrangian

Thanh-Toan Do$^{(\boxtimes)}$, Anh-Dzung Doan, Duc-Thanh Nguyen,
and Ngai-Man Cheung

Singapore University of Technology and Design, Singapore, Singapore
{thanhtoan_do,dung_doan,ducthanh_nguyen,ngaiman_cheung}@sutd.edu.sg

**Abstract.** This paper proposes two approaches for inferencing binary codes in two-step (supervised, unsupervised) hashing. We first introduce an unified formulation for both supervised and unsupervised hashing. Then, we cast the learning of one bit as a Binary Quadratic Problem (BQP). We propose two approaches to solve BQP. In the first approach, we relax BQP as a semidefinite programming problem which its global optimum can be achieved. We theoretically prove that the objective value of the binary solution achieved by this approach is well bounded. In the second approach, we propose an augmented Lagrangian based approach to solve BQP directly without relaxing the binary constraint. Experimental results on three benchmark datasets show that our proposed methods compare favorably with the state of the art.

**Keywords:** Two-step hashing · Semidefinite programming · Augmented Lagrangian

## 1 Introduction

Hashing methods construct a set of hash functions that map the original high dimensional data into low dimensional binary data. The resulted binary vectors allow efficient storage and fast searching, making hashing as an attractive approach for large scale visual search [1,2].

Existing hashing methods can be categorized as data-independent and data-dependent schemes. Data-independent hashing methods [3–6] rely on random projections for constructing hash functions. Data-dependent hashing methods use available training data for learning hash functions in unsupervised or supervised way. Unsupervised hashing methods, e.g. Spectral Hashing [7], Iterative Quantization (ITQ) [8], K-means Hashing [9], Spherical Hashing [10], Non-negative Matrix Factorization (NMF) hashing [11], try to preserve the distance similarity of samples. Supervised hashing methods, e.g. Minimal Loss Hashing [12], ITQ-CCA [8], Binary Reconstructive Embedding [13], KSH [14], Two-Step Hashing [15], FastHash [16], try to preserve the label similarity of samples.

Most aforementioned hashing methods follow two general steps for computing binary codes. The first step is to define hash functions together with a specific

© Springer International Publishing AG 2016
B. Leibe et al. (Eds.): ECCV 2016, Part II, LNCS 9906, pp. 802–817, 2016.
DOI: 10.1007/978-3-319-46475-6_49

loss function. Usually, the hash functions take the linear form [3,8,12] or non-linear (e.g. kernel) form [4,13,14]. The loss functions are typically defined by minimizing the difference between Hamming affinity (or distance) of data pairs and the ground truth [13–16]. The second step is to solve hash function parameters by minimizing the loss function under the binary constraint on the codes. The coupling of the hash function and the binary constraint often results in a highly non-convex optimization which is very challenging to solve. Furthermore, because the hash functions vary for different methods, different optimization techniques are needed for each of them.

## 1.1 Related Work

Our work is inspired by a few recent supervised hashing methods [15,16] and unsupervised hashing method [11] which rely on two-step approach to reduce the complexity of the coupled problem and to make the flexibility in using of different types of hash functions. In particular, those works decompose the learning of hash functions under binary constraint into two steps: the binary code inference step and the hash function learning step. The most difficult step is binary code inference which is NP-hard problem. After getting the binary codes, the hash function learning step becomes a classical binary classifier learning. Hence, it allows the using of various types of hash functions, i.e., linear SVM [11], kernel SVM [15], decision tree [16].

In order to infer binary codes, in [15,16], the authors form the learning of one bit of binary code as a binary quadratic problem and using non-linear optimization [15] or Graphcut [16] for solving. In [11], the authors solve the binary code inference using non-linear optimization approach or non-negative matrix factorization approach. We will brief the approaches in [11,15,16] when comparing to our methods in Sect. 2.4.

Although different methods are proposed for inferencing the binary code, the disadvantage of those methods [11,15] is that in order to overcome the hardness of the binary constraint on codes, they solve the relaxed problem, i.e., relaxing the binary constraint to continuous constraint. This may decrease the code quality and incurs some performance penalty. Furthermore, those works have not theoretically investigated the quality of the relaxed solution.

## 1.2 Contribution

Instead of considering separate formulations for supervised hashing and unsupervised hashing, we first present an unified formulation for both. Our main contributions are that we propose two approaches for inferencing binary codes. In the first approach, we cast the learning of one bit of the binary code as a Semidefinite Programming (SDP) problem which its global optimum can be achieved. After using a randomized rounding procedure for converting the solution of SDP to the binary solution, we theoretically prove that the objective value of the resulted binary solution is well bounded, i.e., it is not arbitrarily far from the global optimum objective value of the original problem. It is worth noting that although semidefinite relaxation has been applied to several computer vision problems such as image segmentation, image restoration [17,18], to the best of our knowledge, our work is the first one that applies semidefinite relaxation to the binary hashing problem. In the second approach, we propose to use Augmented Lagrangian (AL) for directly solving the binary code inference problem without relaxing the binary constraint. One important step in the AL is initialization [19]. In this work, we careful derive an initialization to achieve a good feasible starting point. For both SDP and AL approaches, their memory and computational complexity are also analyzed.

The remaining of this paper is organized as follows. Section 2 presents proposed approaches for binary code inference. Section 3 evaluates and compares proposed approaches to the state of the art. Section 4 concludes the paper.

## 2    Proposed Methods

### 2.1    Unified Formulation for Similarity Preserving Unsupervised/Supervised Hashing

Let $\mathbf{X} \in \mathbb{R}^{D \times n}$ be matrix of $n$ samples; $\mathbf{S} = \{s_{ij}\} \in \mathbb{R}^{n \times n}$ be symmetric pairwise similarity matrix, i.e., pairwise distance matrix for unsupervised hashing or pairwise label matrix for supervised hashing; $\mathbf{Z} = \{z_{ij}\} \in \{-1, 1\}^{L \times n}$ be binary code matrix of $\mathbf{X}$, where $L$ is code length; each column of $\mathbf{Z}$ is binary code of one sample; $\mathbf{D} = \{d_{ij}\} \in \mathbb{R}^{n \times n}$, where $d_{ij}$ is Hamming distance between samples $i$ and $j$, i.e., columns $i$ and $j$ of $\mathbf{Z}$; we have $0 \le d_{ij} \le L$. We target to learn the binary code $\mathbf{Z}$ such that the similarity matrix in original space is directly preserved through Hamming distance in Hamming space. In a natural means, we learn the binary code matrix $\mathbf{Z}$ by solving the following binary constrained least-squares objective function.

$$\min_{\mathbf{Z} \in \{-1,1\}^{L \times n}} \left\| \frac{1}{L} \mathbf{D} - \frac{1}{c} \mathbf{S} \right\|^2 \tag{1}$$

In (1), $c$ is a constant. The scale factors $\frac{1}{L}$ and $\frac{1}{c}$ are to make $\mathbf{D}$ and $\mathbf{S}$ same scale, i.e., belonging to the interval $[0, 1]$, when doing least-squares fitting. For unsupervised hashing, any distance function can be used for computing $\mathbf{S}$. In this work, we consider the squared Euclidean distance which is widely used in nearest neighbor search. By assuming that the samples are normalized to have unit $l_2$ norm, we have $0 \le s_{ij} \le 4$. In this case, the constant $c$ equals to 4. For supervised hashing, we define $s_{ij} = 0$ if samples $i$ and $j$ are same class. Otherwise, $s_{ij} = 1$. In this case, the constant $c$ equals to 1.

In [14], the authors show that the Hamming distance and code inner product is in one-to-one correspondence. That is

$$\mathbf{D} = \frac{\mathbf{L} - \mathbf{Z}^T \mathbf{Z}}{2} \tag{2}$$

where $\mathbf{L}$ is a matrix of all-$L$s.

---

**Algorithm 1.** Coordinate descent with Augmented Lagrangian (AL) / Semi-definite Relaxation (SDR)

---
**Input:**
    Similarity matrix $\mathbf{S}$; training data $\mathbf{X}$; code length $L$; maximum iteration number $max\_iter$.
**Output:**
    Binary code matrix $\mathbf{Z}$.

1: Initialize the binary code matrix $\mathbf{Z}$.
2: **for** $r = 1 \rightarrow max\_iter$ **do**
3:     **for** $k = 1 \rightarrow L$ **do**
4:         $\mathbf{x} \leftarrow$ solve BQP (5) for row $k$ of $\mathbf{Z}$ with SDR (Sec.2.2) or AL (Sec.2.3).
5:         Update row $k$ of $\mathbf{Z}$ with $\mathbf{x}$.
6:     **end for**
7: **end for**
8: Return $\mathbf{Z}$

---

Substituting (2) into (1), we get the unified formulation for unsupervised and supervised hashing as

$$\min_{\mathbf{Z}\in\{-1,1\}^{L\times n}} \left\|\mathbf{Z}^T\mathbf{Z} - \mathbf{Y}\right\|^2 \qquad (3)$$

where $\mathbf{Y} = \mathbf{L} - \frac{L\mathbf{S}}{2}$ and $\mathbf{Y} = \mathbf{L} - 2L\mathbf{S}$ for unsupervised and supervised hashing, respectively. Note that since $\mathbf{S}$ is symmetric, $\mathbf{Y}$ is also symmetric.

The optimization problem (3) is non-convex and difficult to solve, i.e. NP-hard, due to the binary constraint. In order to overcome this challenge, we use the coordinate descent approach which learns one bit, i.e. one row of $\mathbf{Z}$, at a time, while keeping other rows fixed. Our coordinate descent approach for learning binary codes is shown in Algorithm 1.

When solving for the bit $k$ (i.e. row $k$) of $\mathbf{Z}$, solving (3) is equivalent to solving the following problem

$$\min_{\mathbf{z}^{(k)}\in\{-1,1\}^n} \sum_{i=1}^{n}\sum_{j=1}^{n} 2z_i^{(k)} z_j^{(k)} \left(\bar{\mathbf{z}}_i^T\bar{\mathbf{z}}_j - y_{ij}\right) + const \qquad (4)$$

where $\mathbf{z}^{(k)}$ is transposing of row $k$ of $\mathbf{Z}$; $\mathbf{z}_i$ is binary code of sample $i$, i.e., column $i$ of $\mathbf{Z}$; $z_i^{(k)}$ is bit $k$ of sample $i$; $\bar{\mathbf{z}}_i$ is $\mathbf{z}_i$ excluding bit $k$.

By removing the *const* and letting $\mathbf{x} = [x_1, ..., x_n]^T = \mathbf{z}^{(k)}$ (for notational simplicity), (4) is equivalent to the following Binary Quadratic Problem (BQP)

$$\min_{\mathbf{x}} \mathbf{x}^T\mathbf{A}\mathbf{x}$$
$$s.t. \ x_i^2 = 1, \forall i = 1, ..., n. \qquad (5)$$

where $\mathbf{A} = \{a_{ij}\} \in \mathbb{R}^{n\times n}$; $a_{ij} = \bar{\mathbf{z}}_i^T\bar{\mathbf{z}}_j - y_{ij}$.

Because $\mathbf{Y}$ is symmetric, $\mathbf{A}$ is also symmetric. The constraints in (5) come from the fact that $x_i \in \{-1,1\} \Leftrightarrow x_i^2 = 1$. In Sects. 2.2 and 2.3, we present our approaches for solving (5).

## 2.2 Semidefinite Relaxation (SDR) Approach

Let us start with the following proposition

**Proposition 1.** *Let matrix* $\mathbf{B} = \mathbf{A} - \lambda_1 \mathbf{I}$, *where* $\lambda_1$ *is the largest eigenvalue of* $\mathbf{A}$, *then*

– (5) *is equivalent to*

$$\min_{\mathbf{x}} \mathbf{x}^T \mathbf{B} \mathbf{x}$$
$$s.t.\ x_i{}^2 = 1, \forall i = 1, ..., n. \tag{6}$$

– $\mathbf{B}$ *is negative semidefinite.*

*Proof.* – we have

$$\mathbf{x}^T \mathbf{B} \mathbf{x} = \mathbf{x}^T \mathbf{A} \mathbf{x} - \mathbf{x}^T (\lambda_1 \mathbf{I}) \mathbf{x}$$
$$= \mathbf{x}^T \mathbf{A} \mathbf{x} - \sum_{i=1}^{n} \lambda_1 x_i{}^2$$
$$= \mathbf{x}^T \mathbf{A} \mathbf{x} - n\lambda_1 \tag{7}$$

As $n\lambda_1$ is constant, solving (5) is equivalent to solving (6).    □
– As $\mathbf{A}$ is symmetric, $\mathbf{B}$ is also symmetric. The symmetric matrix $\mathbf{A}$ can be decomposed as $\mathbf{A} = \mathbf{U}\mathbf{E}\mathbf{U}^T$, where $\mathbf{E}$ is diagonal matrix; $diag(\mathbf{E})$ are eigenvalues of $\mathbf{A}$; columns of $\mathbf{U}$ are eigenvectors of $\mathbf{A}$ and $\mathbf{U}\mathbf{U}^T = \mathbf{I}$. We have

$$\mathbf{x}^T \mathbf{B} \mathbf{x} = \mathbf{x}^T \mathbf{U}\mathbf{E}\mathbf{U}^T \mathbf{x} - n\lambda_1$$
$$= \mathbf{v}^T \mathbf{E} \mathbf{v} - n\lambda_1$$
$$\le \lambda_1 \mathbf{v}^T \mathbf{v} - n\lambda_1$$
$$= n\lambda_1 - n\lambda_1$$
$$= 0 \tag{8}$$

where $\mathbf{v} = \mathbf{U}^T \mathbf{x}$. The second last equation comes from the fact that $\mathbf{v}^T \mathbf{v} = \mathbf{x}^T \mathbf{U}\mathbf{U}^T \mathbf{x} = \mathbf{x}^T \mathbf{x} = n$. The last equation means $\mathbf{B} \preceq 0$[1].    □

Because (5) and (6) are equivalent, we solve (6), instead of (5). The reason is that we will use the negative semidefinite property of $\mathbf{B}$ to derive the bounds on the objective value of solution of the relaxation. Note that, because $\mathbf{B} \preceq 0$, the objective function value of (6) is non-positive.

**Solving.** Solving (6) is challenge due to the binary constraint which is NP-hard. In this work, we rely on the semidefinite programming relaxation approach [20, 21]. By introducing new variable, $\mathbf{X} = \mathbf{x}\mathbf{x}^T$, (6) can be exactly rewritten as

$$\min_{\mathbf{X}} \ trace(\mathbf{B}\mathbf{X})$$
$$s.t.\ diag(\mathbf{X}) = 1; \mathbf{X} \succeq 0; rank(\mathbf{X}) = 1 \tag{9}$$

---

[1] The notations $\preceq 0$ and $\succeq 0$ mean negative semidefinite and positive semidefinite, respectively.

The objective function and the constraints in (9) are convex in $\mathbf{X}$, excepting the rank one constraint. If we drop the rank one constraint, (9) becomes a semidefinite program

$$\min_{\mathbf{X}} \; trace(\mathbf{BX})$$

$$s.t. \; diag(\mathbf{X}) = 1; \mathbf{X} \succeq 0 \tag{10}$$

We call (10) as semidefinite relaxation (SDR) of (6). The solving of SDR problem (10) has been well studied. There are several widely used convex optimization packages such as SeDuMi [22], SDPT3 [23] which use interior-point method for solving (10). Because (10) is a convex optimization, its global optimal solution can be achieved by using the mentioned packages.

After getting the global optimal solution $\mathbf{X}^*$ of (10), the only remaining problem is how to convert $\mathbf{X}^*$ to a feasible solution of (6). In this work, we follow the randomized rounding method proposed in [24]. Given $\mathbf{X}^*$, we generate vector $\xi$ by $\xi \sim \mathcal{N}(0, \mathbf{X}^*)$ and construct the feasible point $\hat{\mathbf{x}}$ of (6) as

$$\hat{\mathbf{x}} = sgn(\xi) \tag{11}$$

This process is done multiple times, and the $\hat{\mathbf{x}}$ point which provides minimum objective value (of (6)) is selected as the solution of (6).

**Bounding on the Objective Value of SDR-Rounding Solution.** Let $f_{opt}$ be global optimum objective value of (6) and $f_{SDR-round}$ be objective value at $\hat{\mathbf{x}}$ which is achieved by above rounding procedure, i.e., $f_{SDR-round} = \hat{\mathbf{x}}^T \mathbf{B} \hat{\mathbf{x}}$. We are interesting in finding how is $f_{SDR-round}$ close to $f_{opt}$. In [24,25], under some conditions on the matrix $\mathbf{B}$, the authors derived bounds on $f_{SDR-round}$ to maximization problem of the form (6). In this paper, we derive bounds for the minimization problem (6), where $\mathbf{B} \preceq 0$. The bounds on $f_{SDR-round}$ is achieved by the following theorem

**Theorem 1.** $f_{opt} \leq E[f_{SDR-round}] \leq \frac{2}{\pi} f_{opt}$

*Proof.* – Because solving SDR (10), following by rounding procedure, is relaxation approach to achieve a feasible solution for (6), we have

$$f_{opt} \leq f_{SDR-round} \tag{12}$$

– Given $\mathbf{X}^*$, i.e., the global minimum solution of (10), let the global optimum objective value of (10) at $\mathbf{X}^*$ be $f_{SDR} = trace(\mathbf{BX}^*)$; given $\hat{\mathbf{x}}$, i.e., the solution of (6), achieved from $\mathbf{X}^*$ by applying the rounding procedure, in [24], the authors show that the expected value of $f_{SDR-round}$ is

$$E[f_{SDR-round}] = E[\hat{\mathbf{x}}^T \mathbf{B} \hat{\mathbf{x}}] = \frac{2}{\pi} trace(\mathbf{B} arcsin(\mathbf{X}^*)) \tag{13}$$

where the *arcsin* function is applied componentwise. Note that since $\mathbf{X}^* \succeq 0$ and $diag(\mathbf{X}^*) = 1$, the absolute value of its elements is $\leq 1$. Hence $arcsin(\mathbf{X}^*)$ is well defined.

Because $\mathbf{X}^* \succeq 0$, we have $arcsin(\mathbf{X}^*) - \mathbf{X}^* \succeq 0$ [26]. Because $\mathbf{B} \preceq 0$, we have

$$trace\left(\mathbf{B}(arcsin(\mathbf{X}^*) - \mathbf{X}^*)\right) \leq 0$$
$$\Leftrightarrow trace(\mathbf{B}arcsin(\mathbf{X}^*)) \leq trace(\mathbf{B}\mathbf{X}^*)$$
$$\Leftrightarrow \frac{2}{\pi}trace(\mathbf{B}arcsin(\mathbf{X}^*)) \leq \frac{2}{\pi}trace(\mathbf{B}\mathbf{X}^*)$$
$$\Leftrightarrow E[f_{SDR-round}] \leq \frac{2}{\pi}trace(\mathbf{B}\mathbf{X}^*)$$
$$\Leftrightarrow E[f_{SDR-round}] \leq \frac{2}{\pi}f_{SDR} \tag{14}$$

Because (10) is a relaxation of (6) (by removing the rank-one constraint), we have

$$f_{SDR} \leq f_{opt} \tag{15}$$

By combining (14) and (15), we have

$$E[f_{SDR-round}] \leq \frac{2}{\pi}f_{opt} \tag{16}$$

The proof is done by (12) and (16). □

**The Advantages and Disadvantages of SDR Approach.** As mentioned, because (10) is a convex optimization, its global optimal solution can be achieved by using convex optimization methods. Using randomized rounding to convert SDR's solution to binary solution provides a good bound on the objective value. However, there are two main concerns, i.e., memory and computational complexity, with SDR approach. SDR approach works in the space of $n^2$ of variables, instead of $n$ as original problem. By using interior-point method which is traditional approach for solving SDP problem, (10) is solved with high complexity, i.e., $\mathcal{O}(n^{4.5})$[21]. These two disadvantages may limit the capacity of SDR approach when $n$ is large.

### 2.3  Augmented Lagrangian Approach

We propose to directly solve the equality constrained minimization (5) using Augmented Lagrangian (AL) method.

**Formulation.** In our formulation, we rewrite the binary constraints of (5) in vector form as $\Phi(\mathbf{x}) = \left[(x_1)^2 - 1, ..., (x_n)^2 - 1\right]^T$; let $\Lambda = [\lambda_1, ..., \lambda_n]^T$ be Lagrange multipliers. By using augmented Lagrangian method, we target to minimize the following unconstrained augmented Lagrangian function

$$\mathcal{L}(\mathbf{x}, \Lambda; \mu) = \mathbf{x}^T \mathbf{A}\mathbf{x} - \Lambda^T \Phi(\mathbf{x}) + \frac{\mu}{2}\|\Phi(\mathbf{x})\|^2 \tag{17}$$

where $\mu$ is penalty parameter on the constrains. The AL algorithm for solving (17) is presented in Algorithm 2.

---

**Algorithm 2.** Augmented Lagrangian Algorithm

---
**Input:**
   matrix $\mathbf{A}$; starting points $\mathbf{x}_0^s$ and $\Lambda_0$; positive numbers: $\mu_0$, $\alpha$, $\epsilon$; iteration number $T$.
**Output:**
   Solution $\mathbf{x}$

1: **for** $t = 0 \rightarrow T$ **do**
2:    Find an approximate minimizer $\mathbf{x}_t$ of (17), i.e., $\mathbf{x}_t = \arg\min\limits_{\mathbf{x}} \mathcal{L}(\mathbf{x}, \Lambda_t; \mu_t)$, using $\mathbf{x}_t^s$ as

       starting point.
3:    **if** $t > 1$ and $|\mathbf{x}_t^T \mathbf{A} \mathbf{x}_t - \mathbf{x}_t^{s\,T} \mathbf{A} \mathbf{x}_t^s| < \epsilon$ **then**
4:       break;
5:    **end if**
6:    Update Lagrange multiplier: $\Lambda_{t+1} = \Lambda_t - \mu_t \Phi(\mathbf{x}_t)$
7:    Update penalty parameter: $\mu_{t+1} = \alpha \mu_t$
8:    Set starting point for the next iteration to $\mathbf{x}_{t+1}^s = \mathbf{x}_t$
9: **end for**
10: Return $\mathbf{x}_t$

---

When $\mu$ is large, we penalize the constraint violation severely, thereby forcing the minimizer of the augmented Lagrangian function (17) closer to the feasible region of the original constrained function (5). It has been theoretically shown in [19] that because the Lagrange multiplier $\Lambda$ is improved at every step of the algorithm, it is not necessary to take $\mu \rightarrow \infty$ in order to achieve a local optimum of (5).

**Complexity Analysis of Augmented Lagrangian Approach.** The gradient of (17) is computed as follows

$$\nabla_x \mathcal{L} = 2\mathbf{A}\mathbf{x} - 2\Lambda \odot \mathbf{x} + 2\mu\Phi(\mathbf{x}) \odot \mathbf{x} \tag{18}$$

where $\odot$ denotes Hadamard product.

The complexity for computing the objective function (17) is $\mathcal{O}(n^2)$ and for computing the gradient (18) is also $\mathcal{O}(n^2)$. For finding the approximate minimizer $\mathbf{x}_t$ at line 2 of the Algorithm 2, we use LBFGS [27] belonging to the family of quasi-Newton's methods. There are two main benefits with LBFGS. Firstly, the approximated Hessian matrix does not need to be explicitly computed when computing the search direction. By using two-loop recursion [27], the complexity for computing the search direction is only $\mathcal{O}(n)$. Hence the computational complexity of LBFGS is $\mathcal{O}(t_1 n^2)$, where $t_1$ is number of iterations of LBFGS. Hence, the computational complexity of Algorithm 2 is $\mathcal{O}(t t_1 n^2)$. In our empirical experiments, $t, t_1 \ll n$, e.g., the Algorithm 2 converges for $t_1 \leq 50$ and $t \leq 10$. Secondly, because the Hessian matrix does not need to be explicitly computed, the memory complexity of LBFGS is only $\mathcal{O}(n)$. Table 1 summarizes the memory and the computational complexity of SDR and AL approaches. We can see that AL approach advances SDR approach on both memory and computational complexity. However, the performance of AL is slightly lower than SDR. We provide detail analysis on their performance in the experimental section.

**Initialization in Augmented Lagrangian.** The Algorithm 2 needs the initialization for $\mathbf{x}$ and $\Lambda$. A good initialization not only makes the algorithm robust but also leads to fast convergence. The initialization of $\mathbf{x}$ is first done by

**Table 1.** Memory and computational complexity of SDR and AL.

|       | Computational                                   | Memory             |
| ----- | ----------------------------------------------- | ------------------ |
| SDR   | $\mathcal{O}(n^{4.5})$                           | $\mathcal{O}(n^2)$ |
| AL    | $\mathcal{O}(tt_1 n^2)$; $t_1 \leq 50$; $t \leq 10$ | $\mathcal{O}(n)$   |

spectral relaxation, resulting the continuous solution. The continuous solution is then binarized, resulting binary solution. Specifically, we first solve (5) by using spectral relaxation, i.e.,

$$\min_{\|\mathbf{x}\|^2 = n} \mathbf{x}^T \mathbf{A} \mathbf{x} \tag{19}$$

The closed-form solution of (19) is $\mathbf{x} = \sqrt{n}\mathbf{u}_n$, where $\mathbf{u}_n$ is the eigenvector corresponding to the smallest eigenvalue of $\mathbf{A}$. We then optimally binarize from the first element to the last element of $\mathbf{x}$. When solving the binarizing for $i^{th}$ element of $\mathbf{x}$, we fix all remaining elements (elements 1 to $i-1$ are already binary and elements $i+1$ to $n$ are still continuous) and solve the following optimization

$$\min_{x_i \in \{-1, 1\}} \mathbf{x}^T \mathbf{A} \mathbf{x} \tag{20}$$

By expanding and removing constant terms, (20) is equivalent to

$$\min_{x_i \in \{-1, 1\}} x_i \left( \bar{\mathbf{x}}^T \bar{\mathbf{a}}_i \right) \tag{21}$$

where $\bar{\mathbf{x}}$ is vector $\mathbf{x}$ excluding $x_i$; $\bar{\mathbf{a}}_i$ is $i^{th}$ column of $\mathbf{A}$ excluding $i^{th}$ element. It is easy to see that the optimal solution of (21) is $x_i = -\mathrm{sgn}(\bar{\mathbf{x}}^T \bar{\mathbf{a}}_i)$. After solving the binarizing for all elements of $\mathbf{x}$, the resulted binary vector is used as initialization, i.e. $\mathbf{x}_0^s$, in the Algorithm 2.

After getting $\mathbf{x}_0^s$, given $\mu_0$, we compute the corresponding $\Lambda_0$ by using the optimality condition for unconstrained minimization (17), i.e., $\nabla_x \mathcal{L} = 0$. By assigning (18) to zeros and using the fact that $\Phi(\mathbf{x}_0^s)$ equals to zeros, we have

$$\Lambda_0 = (\mathbf{A}\mathbf{x}_0^s)./\mathbf{x}_0^s \tag{22}$$

where $./$ operator denotes element-wise division.

## 2.4   Relationship to Existing Methods

In [15,16], the authors use two-step hashing approach for supervised hashing while our formulations are for both supervised and unsupervised hashing. In [15], when solving for row $k$ of $\mathbf{Z}$, i.e., $\mathbf{z}^{(k)}$, the authors also form the problem as a binary quadratic problem. To handle this NP-hard problem, the authors relax the binary constraint $\mathbf{z}^{(k)} \in \{-1, 1\}^n$ to $\mathbf{z}^{(k)} \in [-1, 1]^n$. The relaxed problem is then solved by bound-constrained L-BFGS method [28]. In [16], in stead of solving for whole row $k$ of $\mathbf{Z}$ at a time as [15], the authors first split $\mathbf{z}^{(k)}$ into several blocks. The optimization is done for each block while keeping other blocks fixed. When solving one block, they consider the problem as a graph partition problem and use GraphCut algorithm [29] for finding a local optimum.

Our proposed methods differ from [15,16] in solving BQP. With Augmented Lagrangian (AL) approach, we consider the original constraint, without relaxing the variables to continuous domain. With Semidefinite Relaxation (SDR) approach, in spite of removing the rank one constraint, we theoretically show that the objective value of the binary solution achieved by applying randomized rounding on SDR solution is well bounded. Note that in [15,16], the bounding on the objective function of their binary solution is not investigated.

The very recent work [11] relies on two-step hashing for unsupervised hashing. The authors introduce two approaches for inferencing binary codes which try to preserve the original distance between samples. In their work, by considering the binary constraint on $\mathbf{Z}$ as $\mathbf{Z} \in \{0,1\}^{L \times n}$, the Hamming distance matrix $\mathbf{D}$ is computed as $\mathbf{D} = \mathbf{Z}^T \mathbf{E}^T + \mathbf{E}\mathbf{Z} - 2\mathbf{Z}^T \mathbf{Z}$, where $\mathbf{E}$ is a matrix of all $1s$. In the first approach, the authors use augmented Lagrangian for solving the following optimization

$$\min_{\mathbf{Z},\mathbf{Y}} \|\mathbf{S} - \mathbf{Y}\|^2 \ s.t. \ \mathbf{Y} = \mathbf{Z}^T \mathbf{E}^T + \mathbf{E}\mathbf{Z} - 2\mathbf{Z}^T \mathbf{Z}; \ \mathbf{Z} \in [0,1]^{L \times n} \quad (23)$$

where $\mathbf{S}$ is original distance similarity matrix; $\mathbf{Y}$ is an auxiliary variable.

In the second approach, the authors form the learning of binary code $\mathbf{Z}$ as a non-negative matrix factorization with additional constraints as follows

$$\min_{\mathbf{Z}_v,\mathbf{H}} \|\mathbf{S}_v - \mathbf{M}\mathbf{H}\mathbf{Z}_v\|^2 \ s.t. \ \mathbf{H} = \mathbf{I} \otimes (1 - \mathbf{Z}_v); \ \mathbf{Z}_v \in [0,1]^{Ln} \quad (24)$$

where $\mathbf{S}_v$ and $\mathbf{Z}_v$ are vector forms of $\mathbf{S}$ and $\mathbf{Z}$, respectively; $\mathbf{M}$ is a constant binary matrix; $\mathbf{I}$ is identity matrix; $\otimes$ is Kronecker product [11].

The differences between our AL, SDR approaches and two above approaches of [11] are quite clear. We use the coordinate descent, i.e., solving one row of $\mathbf{Z}$ at a time while the optimization in [11] is on the space of $\mathbf{Z}$. This may limit their approaches when the size of $\mathbf{Z}$ increases (i.e., when increasing the code length $L$ and the number of training samples $n$). To handle the difficulty of binary constraint, they solve the relaxed problem, i.e., relaxing the constraint $\mathbf{Z} \in \{0,1\}^{L \times n}$ to $\mathbf{Z} \in [0,1]^{L \times n}$. On the other hand, our AL approach solves the constraint strictly; with SDR approach, in spite of removing the rank one constraint, we prove that the resulted objective value is well bounded. Furthermore, in their first approach [11], the Lagrangian function only considers the first constraint of (23), i.e., the second constraint $\mathbf{Z} \in [0,1]^{L \times n}$ is not considered when finding the minimizer of the augmented Lagrangian function. After solving for the minimizer of the augmented Lagrangian function, the resulted solution is projected onto the feasible set $\mathbf{Z} \in [0,1]^{L \times n}$. Contrary to their approach, in our augmented Lagrangian function (17), the binary constraint is directly incorporated and encoded as $\Phi(\mathbf{x})$, and is solved during the optimization.

# 3  Experiments

In this section we first evaluate and compare binary inference methods. We then evaluate and compare our hashing framework to the state of the art.

## 3.1  Dataset, Implementation Note, and Evaluation Protocol

**Dataset.** CIFAR10 [30] dataset consists of 60,000 images of 10 classes. The training set (also used as database for retrieval) contains 50,000 images. The query set contains 10,000 images. Each image is represented by 320-$D$ GIST feature [31].

MNIST [32] dataset consists of 70,000 handwritten digit images of 10 classes. The training set (also used as database for retrieval) contains 60,000 images. The query set contains 10,000 images. Each image is represented by a 784-$D$ gray-scale feature vector by using its intensity.

SUN397 [33] contains about $108K$ images from 397 scene categories. We use a subset of this dataset including 42 categories with each containing more than 500 images (with total about $35K$ images). The query set contains 4,200 images (100 images per class) randomly sampled from the dataset. The rest images are used as database for retrieval. Each image is represented by a 4096-$D$ CNN feature produced by AlexNet [34].

For CIFAR10 and MNIST, we randomly select 500 training samples from each class and use them for learning, i.e., using their descriptors or their labels for computing similarity matrix in unsupervised or supervised hashing. For SUN397, we randomly select 120 training samples from each class for learning.

**Implementation Note.** After the binary code inference step with SDR/AL, the hash functions are defined by SVM with RBF kernel. The max iteration number $max\_iter$ in Algorithm 1 is empirically set to 3. For Augmented Lagrangian approach, its parameter in Algorithm 2 are empirically set by cross validation as follows: $T = 10$; $\mu_0 = 0.1$; $\alpha = 10$; $\epsilon = 10^{-6}$.

**Evaluation Protocol.** The ground truths of queries are defined by the class labels from the datasets. We use the following evaluation metrics which have been used in the state of the art [8,14,15,35] to measure the performance of methods. 1) mean Average Precision (mAP); 2) precision of Hamming radius 2 (precision@2) which measures precision on retrieved images having Hamming distance to query $\leq 2$ (if no images satisfy, we report zero precision).

## 3.2  Comparison Between Binary Inference Methods

We compare our proposed methods to other binary inference methods including nonlinear optimization (NOPT) approach (i.e. using bound-constrained L-BFGS) in [15], Graphcut approach in [16]. For compared methods, we use the implementations and the suggested parameters provided by the authors. Because the implementation of Augmented Lagrangian Method (ALM) and Nonnegative

Matrix Factorization (NMF) in [11] is not available, it is unable to compare the binary inference with those approaches.

The proposed AL, SDR, and the compared methods require an initialization for binary code matrix $\mathbf{Z}$. In our work, this is the initialization at line 1 of the Algorithm 1. To make a fair comparison, we use the same initialization, i.e. the one is proposed in [11], for all methods. We first use PCA to project the training matrix $\mathbf{X}$ from $D$ to $L$ dimensions. The projected data is then mean-thresholded, resulted binary values. After the binary code inference step, the SVM with RBF kernel is used as hash functions for all compared methods.

Figure 1 and Table 2 present the mAP and the precision of Hamming radius $r = 2$ (precision@2) of methods. In term of mAP, the proposed AL and SDR consistently outperform NOPT [15] and Graphcut [16] at all code lengths. The improvement is more clear on CIFAR10 and SUN397. In term of precision@2, the proposed AL and SDR also outperform NOPT [15] and Graphcut [16]. The improvement is more clear at low code length, i.e., $L = 8$. The improvement of AL and SDR over NOPT [15] and Graphcut [16] means that the binary codes achieved by proposed methods are better than those achieved by NOPT [15] and Graphcut [16]. In comparison AL and SDR, Fig. 1 and Table 2 show SDR approach slightly outperforms AL approach. However, as analyzed in Sects. 2.2 and 2.3, AL approach advances SDR approach in both memory and computational complexity.

**Table 2.** Precision at Hamming distance $r = 2$ of different binary inference methods on CIFAR10, MNIST, SUN397.

| $L$ | CIFAR10 | | | | MNIST | | | | SUN397 | | | |
|---|---|---|---|---|---|---|---|---|---|---|---|---|
| | 8 | 16 | 24 | 32 | 8 | 16 | 24 | 32 | 8 | 16 | 24 | 32 |
| Our-SDR | 30.57 | 46.61 | 48.22 | 48.43 | 86.33 | 93.86 | 94.26 | 94.56 | 12.11 | 59.19 | 62.98 | 61.78 |
| Our-AL | 30.07 | 46.33 | 47.95 | 48.02 | 85.96 | 93.49 | 94.09 | 94.36 | 12.03 | 57.20 | 63.14 | 61.45 |
| NOPT [15] | 29.09 | 45.69 | 47.41 | 47.66 | 81.14 | 93.41 | 93.88 | 93.84 | 10.08 | 55.70 | 60.28 | 59.30 |
| Graphcut [16] | 28.50 | 44.64 | 47.31 | 47.35 | 80.33 | 93.31 | 93.67 | 93.98 | 10.70 | 57.02 | 61.92 | 58.36 |

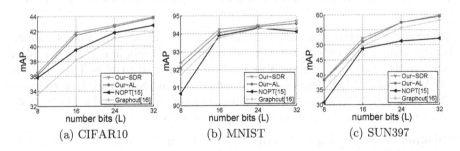

(a) CIFAR10          (b) MNIST          (c) SUN397

**Fig. 1.** mAP comparison of different binary inference methods.

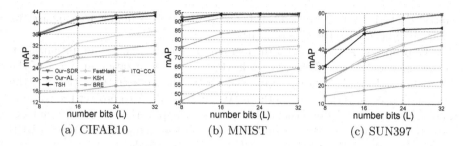

Fig. 2. mAP comparison with state-of-the-art supervised hashing methods.

**Table 3.** Precision at Hamming distance $r = 2$ comparison with state-of-the-art supervised hashing methods on CIFAR10, MNIST, and SUN397.

|  | CIFAR10 | | | | MNIST | | | | SUN397 | | | |
| --- | --- | --- | --- | --- | --- | --- | --- | --- | --- | --- | --- | --- |
| $L$ | 8 | 16 | 24 | 32 | 8 | 16 | 24 | 32 | 8 | 16 | 24 | 32 |
| Our-SDR | 30.57 | 46.61 | 48.22 | 48.43 | 86.33 | 93.86 | 94.26 | 94.56 | 12.11 | 59.19 | 62.98 | 61.78 |
| Our-AL | 30.07 | 46.33 | 47.95 | 48.02 | 85.96 | 93.49 | 94.09 | 94.36 | 12.03 | 57.20 | 63.14 | 61.45 |
| TSH [15] | 29.09 | 45.69 | 47.41 | 47.66 | 81.14 | 93.41 | 93.88 | 93.84 | 10.08 | 55.70 | 60.28 | 59.30 |
| FastHash [16] | 22.85 | 40.81 | 42.25 | 32.49 | 66.22 | 92.14 | 92.79 | 91.41 | 8.91 | 46.84 | 51.84 | 39.40 |
| KSH [14] | 24.26 | 37.26 | 40.95 | 36.52 | 54.29 | 86.94 | 89.31 | 88.33 | 11.79 | 39.41 | 51.28 | 46.48 |
| BRE [13] | 16.19 | 22.74 | 28.87 | 18.41 | 36.67 | 70.59 | 81.45 | 82.83 | 9.62 | 27.93 | 39.42 | 30.39 |
| ITQ-CCA [8] | 22.66 | 35.36 | 38.39 | 39.13 | 53.46 | 79.70 | 82.98 | 83.43 | 11.67 | 36.35 | 49.19 | 46.81 |

### 3.3 Comparison with the State of the Art

We evaluate and compare the proposed SDR and AL to state-of-the-art supervised hashing methods including Binary Reconstructive Embedding (BRE) [13], ITQ-CCA [8], KSH [14], Two-Step Hashing (TSH) [15], FashHash [16] and unsupervised hashing methods including ITQ [8], Binary Autoencoder (BA) [35], Spherical Hashing (SPH) [10], K-means Hashing (KMH) [9]. For all compared methods, we use the implementations and the suggested parameters provided by the authors.

**Supervised Hashing Results.** The mAP and precision@2 obtained by supervised hashing methods with varying code lengths are shown in Fig. 2 and Table 3, respectively. The most competitive method to AL and SDR is TSH [15]. On CIFAR10 and MNIST datasets, the proposed AL and SDR slightly outperform TSH while outperforming the remaining methods a fair margin. On SUN397 dataset, AL and SDR significantly outperform all compared methods.

**Unsupervised Hashing Results.** The mAP and precision@2 obtained by unsupervised hashing methods with varying code lengths are shown in Fig. 3 and Table 4, respectively. In term of mAP, Fig. 3 clearly shows that the proposed AL and SDR significantly outperform all compared methods. In term of precision@2, AL and SDR are comparable (e.g., $L = 16, 24$ on CIFAR10) or outperform compared methods. The improvements are more clear at high code

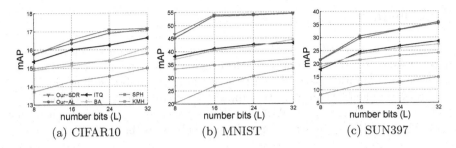

**Fig. 3.** mAP comparison with state-of-the-art unsupervised hashing methods.

**Table 4.** Precision at Hamming distance $r = 2$ comparison with state-of-the-art unsupervised hashing methods on CIFAR10, MNIST, and SUN397.

| L | CIFAR10 | | | | MNIST | | | | SUN397 | | | |
|---|---|---|---|---|---|---|---|---|---|---|---|---|
| | 8 | 16 | 24 | 32 | 8 | 16 | 24 | 32 | 8 | 16 | 24 | 32 |
| Our-SDR | 17.19 | 22.82 | 27.40 | 25.87 | 43.08 | 73.72 | 81.34 | 82.17 | 12.17 | 32.15 | 44.28 | 45.38 |
| Our-AL | 17.34 | 23.23 | 27.26 | 25.21 | 42.09 | 74.36 | 81.50 | 82.29 | 11.99 | 33.34 | 44.13 | 45.60 |
| ITQ [8] | 15.55 | 22.49 | 26.69 | 15.36 | 33.40 | 69.96 | 81.36 | 74.70 | 9.75 | 30.80 | 42.07 | 34.70 |
| BA [35] | 15.62 | 22.65 | 26.55 | 11.42 | 32.62 | 69.03 | 79.11 | 74.00 | 10.15 | 31.61 | 42.52 | 31.97 |
| SPH [10] | 14.66 | 20.32 | 24.67 | 12.32 | 20.77 | 51.74 | 72.20 | 63.38 | 6.38 | 20.66 | 30.10 | 19.97 |
| KMH [9] | 15.11 | 22.57 | 27.25 | 10.36 | 32.45 | 64.42 | 79.97 | 65.79 | 9.88 | 31.04 | 43.67 | 28.85 |

**Table 5.** Classification accuracy on CIFAR-10 and MNIST. The results of NMF and ALM are cited from the corresponding paper [11].

| L | CIFAR10 | | | MNIST | | |
|---|---|---|---|---|---|---|
| | 8 | 16 | 32 | 8 | 16 | 32 |
| Our-SDR | 21.17 | 24.90 | 29.65 | 60.68 | 73.27 | 81.24 |
| Our-AL | 21.00 | 24.75 | 28.84 | 59.96 | 72.67 | 81.13 |
| NMF[11] | 19.77 | 22.78 | 23.59 | 49.84 | 69.65 | 73.41 |
| ALM[11] | 19.41 | 22.63 | 24.27 | 54.55 | 69.46 | 73.76 |

length, i.e. $L = 32$, on all datasets. In comparison SDR and AL in unsupervised setting, two methods achieve very competitive results.

*Comparison with Augmented Lagrangian Method (ALM)* [11] *and Nonnegative Matrix Factorization (NMF)* [11]: As the implementation of ALM [11] and NMF [11] is not available, we set up the experiments on CIFAR10 and MNIST similar to [11] to make a fair comparison. For each dataset, we randomly sample 2,000 images, 200 per class, as training set. Follow [11], for CIFAR10, each image is represented by 625-$D$ HOG descriptors [36]. The hash functions are defined as linear SVM. Similar to [11], we report the classification accuracy by using $k$-NN ($k = 4$) classifier at varying code lengths. The comparative results, presented in Table 5, clearly show that the proposed AL and SDR outperform ALM [11] and NMF [11] on both datasets.

## 4    Conclusion

This paper proposes effective solutions to binary code inference step in two-step hashing where the goal is to preserve the original similarity matrix via Hamming distance in Hamming space. We cast the learning of one bit code as the binary quadratic problem. We propose two approaches: Semidefinite Relaxation (SDR) and Augmented Lagrangian (AL) for solving. Extensive experiments show that both AL and SDR approaches compare favorably with the state of the art.

## References

1. Grauman, K., Fergus, R.: Learning binary hash codes for large-scale image search. In: Cipolla, R., Battiato, S., Farinella, G.M. (eds.) Machine Learning for Computer Vision. SCI, vol. 411, pp. 55–93. Springer, Heidelberg (2013)
2. Wang, J., Shen, H.T., Song, J., Ji, J.: Hashing for similarity search: a survey. CoRR (2014)
3. Gionis, A., Indyk, P., Motwani, R.: Similarity search in high dimensions via hashing. In: VLDB (1999)
4. Kulis, B., Grauman, K.: Kernelized locality-sensitive hashing for scalable image search. In: ICCV (2009)
5. Raginsky, M., Lazebnik, S.: Locality-sensitive binary codes from shift-invariant kernels. In: NIPS (2009)
6. Kulis, B., Jain, P., Grauman, K.: Fast similarity search for learned metrics. PAMI 31, 2143–2157 (2009)
7. Weiss, Y., Torralba, A., Fergus, R.: Spectral hashing. In: NIPS (2008)
8. Gong, Y., Lazebnik, S.: Iterative quantization: a procrustean approach to learning binary codes. In: CVPR (2011)
9. He, K., Wen, F., Sun, J.: K-means hashing: an affinity-preserving quantization method for learning binary compact codes. In: CVPR (2013)
10. Heo, J.P., Lee, Y., He, J., Chang, S.F., Yoon, S.E.: Spherical hashing. In: CVPR (2012)
11. Mukherjee, L., Ravi, S.N., Ithapu, V.K., Holmes, T., Singh, V.: An NMF perspective on binary hashing. In: ICCV (2015)
12. Norouzi, M., Fleet, D.J.: Minimal loss hashing for compact binary codes. In: ICML (2011)
13. Kulis, B., Darrell, T.: Learning to hash with binary reconstructive embeddings. In: NIPS (2009)
14. Liu, W., Wang, J., Ji, R., Jiang, Y.G., Chang, S.F.: Supervised hashing with kernels. In: CVPR (2012)
15. Lin, G., Shen, C., Suter, D., van den Hengel, A.: A general two-step approach to learning-based hashing. In: ICCV (2013)
16. Lin, G., Shen, C., Shi, Q., van den Hengel, A., Suter, D.: Fast supervised hashing with decision trees for high-dimensional data. In: CVPR (2014)
17. Keuchel, J., Schnörr, C., Schellewald, C., Cremers, D.: Binary partitioning, perceptual grouping, and restoration with semidefinite programming. PAMI 25, 1364–1379 (2003)
18. Wang, P., Shen, C., van den Hengel, A.: Large-scale binary quadratic optimization using semidefinite relaxation and applications. PAMI (2015)

19. Nocedal, J., Wright, S.J.: Numerical Optimization, chap. 17, 2nd edn. World Scientific, Singapore (2006)
20. Vandenberghe, L., Boyd, S.: Semidefinite programming. SIAM Rev. **38**, 49–95 (1996)
21. Luo, Z.Q., Ma, W.K., So, A.C., Ye, Y., Zhang, S.: Semidefinite relaxation of quadratic optimization problems. IEEE Signal Process. Mag. **27**, 20–34 (2010)
22. Sturm, J.F.: Using SeDuMi 1.02, a MATLAB toolbox for optimization over symmetric cones. Optim. Methods Softw. **11**, 625–653 (1999)
23. Toh, K.C., Todd, M., Tütüncü, R.H.: SDPT3 - a MATLAB software package for semidefinite programming. Optim. Methods Softw. **11**, 545–581 (1999)
24. Goemans, M.X., Williamson, D.P.: Improved approximation algorithms for maximum cut and satisfiability problems using semidefinite programming. J. ACM **42**, 1115–1145 (1995)
25. Nesterov, Y.: Semidefinite relaxation and nonconvex quadratic optimization. Optim. Methods Softw. **9**, 141–160 (1998)
26. Ben-Tal, A., Nemirovskiaei, A.S.: Lectures on Modern Convex Optimization: Analysis, Algorithms, and Engineering Applications, chap. 3. Society for Industrial and Applied Mathematics, Philadelphia (2001)
27. Nocedal, J., Wright, S.J.: Numerical Optimization, chap. 7, 2nd edn. World Scientific, Singapore (2006)
28. Zhu, C., Byrd, R.H., Lu, P., Nocedal, J.: Algorithm 778: L-BFGS-B: fortran subroutines for large-scale bound-constrained optimization. ACM Trans. Math. Softw. **23**, 550–560 (1997)
29. Boykov, Y., Veksler, O., Zabih, R.: Fast approximate energy minimization via graph cuts. PAMI **23**, 1222–1239 (2001)
30. Krizhevsky, A.: Learning multiple layers of features from tiny images. Technical report, University of Toronto (2009)
31. Oliva, A., Torralba, A.: Modeling the shape of the scene: a holistic representation of the spatial envelope. IJCV **42**, 145–175 (2001)
32. Lecun, Y., Cortes, C.: The MNIST database of handwritten digits. http://yann.lecun.com/exdb/mnist/
33. Xiao, J., Hays, J., Ehinger, K.A., Oliva, A., Torralba, A.: SUN database: large-scale scene recognition from abbey to zoo. In: CVPR (2010)
34. Jia, Y., Shelhamer, E., Donahue, J., Karayev, S., Long, J., Girshick, R., Guadarrama, S., Darrell, T.: Caffe: convolutional architecture for fast feature embedding. arXiv preprint (2014). arXiv:1408.5093
35. Carreira-Perpinan, M.A., Raziperchikolaei, R.: Hashing with binary autoencoders. In: CVPR (2015)
36. Dalal, N., Triggs, B.: Histograms of oriented gradients for human detection. In: CVPR (2005)

# Efficient Continuous Relaxations for Dense CRF

Alban Desmaison[1](✉), Rudy Bunel[1](✉), Pushmeet Kohli[2], Philip H.S. Torr[1],
and M. Pawan Kumar[1]

[1] Department of Engineering Science, University of Oxford, Oxford, UK
{alban,rudy,pawan}@robots.ox.ac.uk, philip.torr@eng.ox.ac.uk
[2] Microsoft Research, Redmond, USA
pkohli@microsoft.com

**Abstract.** Dense conditional random fields (CRF) with Gaussian pair-wise potentials have emerged as a popular framework for several computer vision applications such as stereo correspondence and semantic segmentation. By modeling long-range interactions, dense CRFs provide a more detailed labelling compared to their sparse counterparts. Variational inference in these dense models is performed using a filtering-based mean-field algorithm in order to obtain a fully-factorized distribution minimising the Kullback-Leibler divergence to the true distribution. In contrast to the continuous relaxation-based energy minimisation algorithms used for sparse CRFs, the mean-field algorithm fails to provide strong theoretical guarantees on the quality of its solutions. To address this deficiency, we show that it is possible to use the same filtering approach to speed-up the optimisation of several continuous relaxations. Specifically, we solve a convex quadratic programming (QP) relaxation using the efficient Frank-Wolfe algorithm. This also allows us to solve difference-of-convex relaxations via the iterative concave-convex procedure where each iteration requires solving a convex QP. Finally, we develop a novel divide-and-conquer method to compute the subgradients of a linear programming relaxation that provides the best theoretical bounds for energy minimisation. We demonstrate the advantage of continuous relaxations over the widely used mean-field algorithm on publicly available datasets.

**Keywords:** Energy minimisation · Dense CRF · Inference · Linear programming · Quadratic programming

## 1 Introduction

Discrete pairwise conditional random fields (CRFs) are a popular framework for modelling several problems in computer vision. In order to use them in practice, one requires an energy minimisation algorithm that obtains the most likely

---

Joint first authors.

**Electronic supplementary material** The online version of this chapter (doi:10.1007/978-3-319-46475-6_50) contains supplementary material, which is available to authorized users.

© Springer International Publishing AG 2016
B. Leibe et al. (Eds.): ECCV 2016, Part II, LNCS 9906, pp. 818–833, 2016.
DOI: 10.1007/978-3-319-46475-6_50

output for a given input. The energy function consists of a sum of two types of terms: unary potentials that depend on the label for one random variable at a time and pairwise potentials that depend on the labels of two random variables.

Traditionally, computer vision methods have employed sparse connectivity structures, such as 4 or 8 connected grid CRFs. Their popularity lead to a considerable research effort in efficient energy minimisation algorithms. One of the biggest successes of this effort was the development of several accurate continuous relaxations of the underlying discrete optimisation problem [1,2]. An important advantage of such relaxations is that they lend themselves easily to analysis, which allows us to compare them theoretically [3], as well as establish bounds on the quality of their solutions [4].

Recently, the influential work of Krähenbühl and Koltun [5] has popularised the use of dense CRFs, where each pair of random variables is connected by an edge. Dense CRFs capture useful long-range interactions thereby providing finer details on the labelling. However, modeling long-range interactions comes at the cost of a significant increase in the complexity of energy minimisation. In order to operationalise dense CRFs, Krähenbühl and Koltun [5] made two key observations. First, the pairwise potentials used in computer vision typically encourage smooth labelling. This enabled them to restrict themselves to the special case of Gaussian pairwise potentials introduced by Tappen et al. [6]. Second, for this special case, it is possible to obtain a labelling efficiently by using the mean-field algorithm [7]. Specifically, the message computation required at each iteration of mean-field can be carried out in $O(N)$ operations where $N$ is the number of random variables (of the order of hundreds of thousands). This is in contrast to a naïve implementation that requires $O(N^2)$ operations. The significant speed-up is made possible by the fact that the messages can be computed using the filtering approach of Adams et al. [8].

While the mean-field algorithm does not provide any theoretical guarantees on the energy of the solutions, the use of a richer model, namely dense CRFs, still allows us to obtain a significant improvement in the accuracy of several computer vision applications compared to sparse CRFs [5]. However, this still leaves open the intriguing possibility that the same filtering approach that enabled the efficient mean-field algorithm can also be used to speed-up energy minimisation algorithms based on continuous relaxations. In this work, we show that this is indeed possible.

In more detail, we make three contributions to the problem of energy minimisation in dense CRFs. First, we show that the conditional gradient of a convex quadratic programming (QP) relaxation [1] can be computed in $O(N)$ complexity. Together with our observation that the optimal step-size of a descent direction can be computed analytically, this allows us to minimise the QP relaxation efficiently using the Frank-Wolfe algorithm [9]. Second, we show that difference-of-convex (DC) relaxations of the energy minimisation problem can be optimised efficiently using an iterative concave-convex procedure (CCCP). Each iteration of CCCP requires solving a convex QP, for which we can once again employ the Frank-Wolfe algorithm. Third, we show that a linear programming (LP) relaxation [2] of the energy minimisation problem can be optimised efficiently via subgradient descent. Specifically, we design a novel divide-and-conquer method to compute the subgradient of the LP. Each sub-problem of our method requires one call to the filtering approach. This results in an overall run-time of $O(N \log(N))$ per iteration as opposed to an $O(N^2)$ complexity of a naïve implementation. It is worth noting that the LP relaxation is known to provide the best theoretical bounds for energy minimisation with metric pairwise potentials [2].

Using standard publicly available datasets, we demonstrate the efficacy of our continuous relaxations by comparing them to the widely used mean-field baseline for dense CRFs.

## 2  Related Works

Krähenbühl and Koltun popularised the use of densely connected CRFs at the pixel level [5], resulting in significant improvements both in terms of the quantitative performance and in terms of the visual quality of their results. By restricting themselves to Gaussian edge potentials, they made the computation of the message in parallel mean-field feasible. This was achieved by formulating message computation as a convolution in a higher-dimensional space, which enabled the use of an efficient filter-based method [8].

While the original work [5] used a version of mean-field that is not guaranteed to converge, their follow-up paper [10] proposed a convergent mean-field algorithm for negative semi-definite label compatibility functions. Recently, Baqué et al. [11] presented a new algorithm that has convergence guarantees in the general case. Vineet et al. [12] extended the mean-field model to allow the addition of higher-order terms on top of the dense pairwise potentials, enabling the use of co-occurence potentials [13] and $P^n$-Potts models [14].

The success of the inference algorithms naturally lead to research in learning the parameters of dense CRFs. Combining them with Fully Convolutional Neural Networks [15] has resulted in high performance on semantic segmentation applications [16]. Several works [17,18] showed independently how to jointly learn the parameters of the unary and pairwise potentials of the CRF. These methods led to significant improvements on various computer vision applications, by increasing the quality of the energy function to be minimised by mean-field.

Independently from the mean-field work, Zhang and Chen [19] designed a different set of constraints that lends itself to a QP relaxation of the original problem. Their approach is similar to ours in that they use continuous relaxation to approximate the solution of the original problem but differ in the form of the pairwise potentials. The algorithm they propose to solve the QP relaxation has linearithmic complexity while ours is linear. Furthermore, it is not clear whether their approach can be easily generalised to tighter relaxations such as the LP.

Wang et al. [20] derived a semi-definite programming relaxation of the energy minimisation problem, allowing them to reach better energy than mean-field. Their approach has the advantage of not being restricted to Gaussian pairwise potentials. The inference is made feasible by performing low-rank approximation of the Gram matrix of the kernel, instead of using the filter-based method.

However, while the complexity of their algorithm is the same as our QP or DC relaxation, the runtime is significantly higher. Furthermore, while the SDP relaxation has been shown to be accurate for repulsive pairwise potentials (encouraging neighbouring variables to take different labels) [21], our LP relaxation provides the best guarantees for attractive pairwise potentials [2].

In this paper, we use the same filter-based method [8] as the one employed in mean-field. We build on it to solve continuous relaxations of the original problem that have both convergence and quality guarantees. Our work can be viewed as a complementary direction to previous research trends in dense CRFs. While [10–12] improved mean-field and [17,18] learn't the parameters, we focus on the energy minimisation problem.

## 3    Preliminaries

Before describing our methods for energy minimisation on dense CRF, we establish the necessary notation and background information.

**Dense CRF Energy Function.** We define a dense CRF on a set of $N$ random variables $\mathcal{X} = \{X_1, \ldots, X_N\}$ each of which can take one label from a set of $M$ labels $\mathcal{L} = \{l_1, \ldots l_M\}$. To describe a labelling, we use a vector $\mathbf{x}$ of size $N$ such that its element $x_a$ is the label taken by the random variable $X_a$. The energy associated with a given labelling is defined as:

$$E(\mathbf{x}) = \sum_{a=1}^{N} \phi_a(x_a) + \sum_{a=1}^{N} \sum_{\substack{b=1 \\ b \neq a}}^{N} \psi_{a,b}(x_a, x_b). \tag{1}$$

Here, $\phi_a(x_a)$ is called the *unary potential* for the random variable $X_a$ taking the label $x_a$. The term $\psi_{a,b}(x_a, x_b)$ is called the *pairwise potential* for the random variables $X_a$ and $X_b$ taking the labels $x_a$ and $x_b$ respectively. The energy minimisation problem on this CRF can be written as:

$$\mathbf{x}^\star = \operatorname*{argmin}_{\mathbf{x}} E(\mathbf{x}). \tag{2}$$

**Gaussian Pairwise Potentials.** Similar to previous work [5], we consider arbitrary unary potentials and Gaussian pairwise potentials. Specifically, the form of the pairwise potentials is given by:

$$\psi_{a,b}(i,j) = \mu(i,j) \sum_m w^{(m)} k(\mathbf{f}_a^{(m)}, \mathbf{f}_b^{(m)}), \tag{3}$$

$$k(\mathbf{f}_a, \mathbf{f}_b) = \exp\left(\frac{-\|\mathbf{f}_a - \mathbf{f}_b\|^2}{2}\right) \tag{4}$$

We refer to the term $\mu(i,j)$ as a *label compatibility* function between the labels $i$ and $j$. An example of a label compatibility function is the Potts model, where $\mu_{\text{potts}}(i,j) = [i \neq j]$, that is $\mu_{potts}(i,j) = 1$ if $i \neq j$ and 0 otherwise. Note that the label compatibility does not depend on the image. The other term, called the *pixel compatibility* function, is a mixture of gaussian kernels $k(\cdot, \cdot)$. The coefficients of the mixture are the weights $w^{(m)}$. The $\mathbf{f}_a^{(m)}$ are the features describing the random variable $X_a$. Note that the pixel compatibility does not depend on the labelling. In practice, similar to [5], we use the position and RGB values of a pixel as features.

**IP Formulation.** We now introduce a formulation of the energy minimisation problem that is more amenable to continuous relaxations. Specifically, we formulate it as an Integer Program (IP) and then relax it to obtain a continuous optimisation problem. To this end, we define the vector $\mathbf{y}$ whose components $y_a(i)$ are indicator variables specifying whether or not the random variable $X_a$ takes the label $i$. Using this notation, we can rewrite the energy minimisation problem as an IP:

$$\min \quad \sum_{a=1}^{N} \sum_{i \in \mathcal{L}} \phi_a(i) y_a(i) + \sum_{a=1}^{N} \sum_{\substack{b=1 \\ b \neq a}}^{N} \sum_{i,j \in \mathcal{L}} \psi_{a,b}(i,j) y_a(i) y_b(j),$$

$$\text{s.t.} \quad \sum_{i \in \mathcal{L}} y_a(i) = 1 \quad \forall a \in [1, N],$$

$$y_a(i) \in \{0, 1\} \quad \forall a \in [1, N] \quad \forall i \in \mathcal{L}. \tag{5}$$

The first set of constraints model the fact that each random variable has to be assigned exactly one label. The second set of constraints enforce the optimisation variables $y_a(i)$ to be binary. Note that the objective function is equal to the energy of the labelling encoded by $\mathbf{y}$.

**Filter-Based Method.** Similar to [5], a key component of our algorithms is the filter-based method of Adams et al. [8]. It computes the following operation:

$$\forall a \in [1, N], \quad v_a' = \sum_{b=1}^{N} k(\mathbf{f}_a, \mathbf{f}_b) v_b, \tag{6}$$

where $v_a', v_b \in \mathbb{R}$ and $k(\cdot, \cdot)$ is a Gaussian kernel. Performing this operation the naïve way would result in computing a sum on $N$ elements for each of the $N$ terms that we want to compute. The resulting complexity would be $\mathcal{O}(N^2)$. The filter-based method allows us to perform it approximately with $\mathcal{O}(N)$ complexity. We refer the interested reader to [8] for details. The accuracy of the approximation made by the filter-based method is explored in the supplementary material.

## 4   Quadratic Programming Relaxation

We are now ready to demonstrate how the filter-based method [8] can be used to optimise our first continuous relaxation, namely the convex quadratic programming (QP) relaxation.

**Notation.** In order to concisely specify the QP relaxation, we require some additional notation. Similar to [10], we rewrite the objective function with linear algebra operations. The vector $\phi$ contains the unary terms. The matrix $\mu$ corresponds to the label compatibility function. The Gaussian kernels associated with the $m$-th features are represented by their Gram matrix $\mathbf{K}_{a,b}^{(m)} = k(\mathbf{f}_a^{(m)}, \mathbf{f}_b^{(m)})$. The Kronecker product is denoted by $\otimes$. The matrix $\boldsymbol{\Psi}$ represents the pairwise terms and is defined as follows:

$$\boldsymbol{\Psi} = \mu \otimes \left( \sum_m \mathbf{K}^{(m)} - \mathbf{I}_N \right), \tag{7}$$

where $\mathbf{I}_N$ is the identity matrix. Under this notation, the IP (5) can be concisely written as

$$\begin{aligned} \min \quad & \phi^T \mathbf{y} + \mathbf{y}^T \boldsymbol{\Psi} \mathbf{y}, \\ \text{s.t.} \quad & \mathbf{y} \in \mathcal{I}, \end{aligned} \tag{8}$$

with $\mathcal{I}$ being the feasible set of integer solution, as defined in Eq. (5).

**Relaxation.** In general, IP such as (8) are NP-hard problems. Relaxing the integer constraint on the indicator variables to allow fractional values between 0 and 1 results in the QP formulation. Formally, the feasible set of our minimisation problem becomes:

$$\mathcal{M} = \left\{ \mathbf{y} \quad \text{such that} \quad \begin{aligned} &\sum_{i \in \mathcal{L}} y_a(i) = 1 && \forall a \in [1, N], \\ &y_a(i) \geq 0 && \forall a \in [1, N], \forall i \in \mathcal{L} \end{aligned} \right\}. \tag{9}$$

Ravikumar and Lafferty [1] showed that this relaxation is tight and that solving the QP will result in solving the IP. However, this QP is still NP-hard, as the objective function is non-convex. To alleviate this difficulty, Ravikumar and Lafferty [1] relaxed the QP minimisation to the following convex problem:

$$\begin{aligned} \min \quad & S_{cvx}(\mathbf{y}) = (\phi - \mathbf{d})^T \mathbf{y} + \mathbf{y}^T (\boldsymbol{\Psi} + \mathbf{D}) \mathbf{y}, \\ \text{s.t.} \quad & \mathbf{y} \in \mathcal{M}, \end{aligned} \tag{10}$$

where the vector $\mathbf{d}$ is defined as follows

$$d_a(i) = \sum_{\substack{b=1 \\ b \neq a}}^{N} \sum_{j \in \mathcal{L}} |\psi_{a,b}(i,j)|, \tag{11}$$

and $\mathbf{D}$ is the square diagonal matrix with $\mathbf{d}$ as its diagonal.

**Minimisation.** We now introduce a new method based on the Frank-Wolfe Algorithm [9] to minimise problem (10). The Frank-Wolfe algorithm allows to minimise a convex function $f$ over a convex feasible set $\mathcal{M}$. The key steps of the algorithm are shown in Algorithm 1. To be able to use the Frank-Wolfe

824     A. Desmaison et al.

---

**Algorithm 1.** Frank-Wolfe algorithm

1: Get $\mathbf{y}^0 \in \mathcal{M}$
2: **while** not converged **do**
3:     Compute the gradient at $\mathbf{y}^t$ as $\mathbf{g} = \nabla f(\mathbf{y}^t)$
4:     Compute the conditional gradient as $\mathbf{s} = \text{argmin}_{\mathbf{s} \in \mathcal{M}} \langle \mathbf{s}, \mathbf{g} \rangle$
5:     Compute a step-size $\alpha = \text{argmin}_{\alpha \in [0,1]} f(\alpha \mathbf{y}^t + (1-\alpha)\mathbf{s})$
6:     Move towards the negative conditional gradient $\mathbf{y}^{t+1} = \alpha \mathbf{y}^t + (1-\alpha)\mathbf{s}$
7: **end while**

---

algorithm, we need a way to compute the gradient of the objective function (Step 3), a method to compute the conditional gradient (Step 4) and a strategy to choose the step size (Step 5).

*Gradient Computation*
Since the objective function is quadratic, its gradient can be computed as

$$\nabla S_{\text{cvx}}(\mathbf{y}) = (\boldsymbol{\phi} - \mathbf{d}) + 2(\boldsymbol{\Psi} + \mathbf{D})\mathbf{y}. \tag{12}$$

What makes this equation expensive to compute in a naïve way is the matrix product with $\boldsymbol{\Psi}$. We observe that this operation can be performed using the filter-based method in linear time. Note that the other matrix-vector product, $\mathbf{D}\mathbf{y}$, is not expensive (linear in N) since $\mathbf{D}$ is a diagonal matrix.

*Conditional Gradient*
The conditional gradient is obtained by solving

$$\text{argmin}_{\mathbf{s} \in \mathcal{M}} \langle \mathbf{s}, \nabla S_{\text{cvx}}(\mathbf{y}) \rangle. \tag{13}$$

Minimising such an LP would usually be an expensive operation for problems of this dimension. However, we remark that, once the gradient has been computed, exploiting the properties of our problem allows us to solve problem (13) in a time linear in the number of random variables $(N)$ and labels $(M)$. Specifically, the following is an optimal solution to problem (13).

$$\mathbf{s}_a(i) = \begin{cases} 1 & \text{if } i = \text{argmin}_{i \in \mathcal{L}} \frac{\partial S_{\text{cvx}}}{\partial y_a(i)} \\ 0 & \text{else.} \end{cases} \tag{14}$$

*Step Size Determination*
In the original Frank-Wolfe algorithm, the step size $\alpha$ is simply chosen using line search. However we observe that, in our case, the optimal $\alpha$ can be computed by solving a second-order polynomial function of a single variable, which has a closed form solution that can be obtained efficiently. This observation has been previously exploited in the context of Structural SVM [22]. The derivations for this closed form solution can be found in supplementary material. With careful reutilisation of computations, this step can be performed without additional filter-based method calls. By choosing the optimal step size at each iteration, we reduce the number of iterations needed to reach convergence.

The above procedure converges to the global minimum of the convex relaxation and resorts to the filter-based method only once per iteration during the computation of the gradient and is therefore efficient. However, this solution has no guarantees to be even a local minimum of the original QP relaxation. To alleviate this, we will now introduce a difference-of-convex (DC) relaxation.

## 5   Difference of Convex Relaxation

### 5.1   DC Relaxation: General Case

The objective function of a general DC program can be specified as

$$S_{\mathrm{CCCP}}(\mathbf{y}) = p(\mathbf{y}) - q(\mathbf{y}). \tag{15}$$

One can obtain one of its local minima using the Concave-Convex Procedure (CCCP) [23]. The key steps of this algorithm are described in Algorithm 2. Briefly, Step 3 computes the gradient of the concave part. Step 4 minimises a convex upper bound on the DC objective, which is tight at $\mathbf{y}^t$.

In order to exploit the CCCP algorithm for DC programs, we observe that the QP (8) can be rewritten as

$$\min_{\mathbf{y}} \quad \boldsymbol{\phi}^T \mathbf{y} + \mathbf{y}^T (\boldsymbol{\Psi} + \mathbf{D})\mathbf{y} - \mathbf{y}^T \mathbf{D}\mathbf{y}, \tag{16}$$

$$\text{s.t.} \quad \mathbf{y} \in \mathcal{M}.$$

Formally, we can define $p(\mathbf{y}) = \boldsymbol{\phi}^T \mathbf{y} + \mathbf{y}^T (\boldsymbol{\Psi} + \mathbf{D})\mathbf{y}$ and $q(\mathbf{y}) = \mathbf{y}^T \mathbf{D}\mathbf{y}$, which are both convex in $\mathbf{y}$.

---

**Algorithm 2.** CCCP Algorithm

---

1: Get $\mathbf{y}^0 \in \mathcal{M}$
2: **while** not converged **do**
3:     Linearise the concave part $\mathbf{g} = \nabla q(\mathbf{y}^t)$
4:     Minimise a convex upper-bound $\mathbf{y}^{t+1} = \mathrm{argmin}_{\mathbf{y} \in \mathcal{M}} \, p(\mathbf{y}) - \mathbf{g}^T \mathbf{y}$
5: **end while**

---

We observe that, since $\mathbf{D}$ is diagonal and the matrix product with $\boldsymbol{\Psi}$ can be computed using the filter based method, the gradient $\nabla q(\mathbf{y}^t) = 2\mathbf{D}\mathbf{y}$ (Step 3) is efficient to compute. The minimisation of the convex problem (Step 4) is analogous to the convex QP formulation (10) presented above with different unary potentials. Since we do not place any restrictions on the form of the unary potentials, (Step 4) can be implemented using the method described in Sect. 4.

The CCCP algorithm provides a monotonous decrease in the objective function and will converge to a local minimum [24]. However, the above method will take several iterations to converge, each necessitating the solution of a convex QP, and thus requiring multiple calls to the filter-based method. While the filter-based method [8] allows us to compute operations on the pixel compatibility function in linear time, it still remains an expensive operation to perform. As we show next, if we introduce some additional restriction on our potentials, we can obtain a more efficient difference of convex decomposition.

## 5.2 DC Relaxation: Negative Semi-definite Compatibility

We now introduce a new DC relaxation of our objective function that takes advantage of the structure of the problem. Specifically, the convex problem to solve at each iteration does not depend on the filter-based method computations, which are the expensive steps in the previous method. Following the example of Krähenbühl and Koltun [10], we look at the specific case of negative semi-definite label compatibility function, such as the commonly used Potts model. Taking advantage of the specific form of our pairwise terms (7), we can rewrite the problem as

$$S(\mathbf{y}) = \boldsymbol{\phi}^T \mathbf{y} - \mathbf{y}^T (\boldsymbol{\mu} \otimes \mathbf{I}_N) \mathbf{y}^T + \mathbf{y}^T (\boldsymbol{\mu} \otimes \sum_m \mathbf{K}^{(m)}) \mathbf{y}. \qquad (17)$$

The first two terms can be verified as being convex. The Gaussian kernel is positive semi-definite, so the Gram matrices $\mathbf{K}^{(m)}$ are positive semi-definite. By assumption, the label compatibility function is also negative semi-definite. The results from the Kronecker product between the Gram matrix and $\mu$ is therefore negative semi-definite.

**Minimisation.** Once again we use the CCCP Algorithm. The main difference between the generic DC relaxation and this specific one is that Step 3 now requires a call to the filter-based method, while the iterations required to solve Step 4 do not. In other words, each iteration of CCCP only requires one call to the filter based method. This results in a significant improvement in speed. More details about this operation are available in the supplementary material.

## 6   LP Relaxation

This section presents an accurate LP relaxation of the energy minimisation problem and our method to optimise it efficiently using subgradient descent.

**Relaxation.** To simplify the description, we focus on the Potts model. However, our approach can easily be extended to more general pairwise potentials by approximating them using a hierarchical Potts model. Such an extension, inspired by [25], is presented in the supplementary material. We define the following notation: $K_{a,b} = \sum_m w^{(m)} k^{(m)}(\mathbf{f}_a^{(m)}, \mathbf{f}_b^{(m)})$, $\sum_a = \sum_{a=1}^N$ and $\sum_{b<a} = \sum_{b=1}^{a-1}$. With these notations, a LP relaxation of (5) is:

$$\min \; S_{LP}(\mathbf{y}) = \underbrace{\sum_a \sum_i \phi_a(i) y_a(i)}_{unary} + \underbrace{\sum_a \sum_{b \neq a} \sum_i K_{a,b} \frac{|y_a(i) - y_b(i)|}{2}}_{pairwise},$$

s.t. $\mathbf{y} \in \mathcal{M}.$ \hfill (18)

The feasible set remains the same as the one we had for the QP and DC relaxations. In the case of integer solutions, $S_{LP}(\mathbf{y})$ has the same value as the objective function of the IP described in (5). The *unary* term is the same for both formulations. The *pairwise* term ensures that for every pair of random variables $X_a, X_b$, we add the cost $K_{a,b}$ associated with this edge only if they are not associated with the same labels.

**Minimisation.** Kleinberg and Tardos [2] solve this problem by introducing extra variables for each pair of pixels to get a standard LP, with a linear objective function and linear constraints. In the case of a dense CRF, this is infeasible because it would introduce a number of variables quadratic in the number of pixels. We will instead use projected subgradient descent to solve this LP. To do so, we will reformulate the objective function, derive the subgradient, and present an algorithm to compute it efficiently.

*Reformulation*
The absolute value in the pairwise term of (5) prevents us from using the filtering approach. To address this issue, we consider that for any given label $i$, the variables $y_a(i)$ can be sorted in a descending order: $a \geq b \implies y_a(i) \leq y_b(i)$. This allows us to rewrite the pairwise term of the objective function (18) as:

$$\sum_i \sum_a \sum_{a \neq b} K_{a,b} \frac{|y_a(i) - y_b(i)|}{2} = \sum_i \sum_a \sum_{b>a} K_{a,b} y_a(i) - \sum_i \sum_a \sum_{b<a} K_{a,b} y_a(i).$$

$$(19)$$

A formal derivation of this equality can be found in supplementary material.

*Subgradient.*
From (19), we rewrite the subgradient:

$$\frac{\partial S_{LP}}{\partial y_c(k)}(\mathbf{y}) = \phi_c(k) + \sum_{a>c} K_{a,c} - \sum_{a<c} K_{a,c}. \qquad (20)$$

Note that in this expression, the dependency on the variable $\mathbf{y}$ is hidden in the bounds of the sum because we assumed that $y_a(k) \leq y_c(k)$ for all $a > c$. For a different value of $\mathbf{y}$, the elements of $\mathbf{y}$ would induce a different ordering and the terms involved in each summation would not be the same.

*Subgradient Computation*
What prevents us from evaluating (20) efficiently are the two sums, one over an upper triangular matrix ($\sum_{a>c} K_{a,c}$) and one over a lower triangular matrix ($\sum_{a<c} K_{a,c}$). As opposed to (6), which computes terms $\sum_{a,b} K_{a,b} v_b$ for all $a$ using the filter-based method, the summation bounds here depend on the random variable we are computing the partial derivative for. While it would seems that the added sparsity provided by the upper and lower triangular matrices would simplify the operation, it is this sparsity itself that prevents us from interpreting the summations as convolution operations. Thus, we cannot use the filter-based method as described by Adams et al. [8].

We alleviate this difficulty by designing a novel divide-and-conquer algorithm. We describe our algorithm for the case of the upper triangular matrix. However, it can easily be adapted to compute the summation corresponding to the lower triangular matrix. We present the intuition behind the algorithm using an example. A rigorous development can be found in the supplementary material. If we consider $N = 6$ then $a, c \in \{1, 2, 3, 4, 5, 6\}$ and the terms we need to compute for a given label are:

$$
\begin{pmatrix} \sum_{a>1} K_{a,1} \\ \sum_{a>2} K_{a,2} \\ \sum_{a>3} K_{a,3} \\ \sum_{a>4} K_{a,4} \\ \sum_{a>5} K_{a,5} \\ \sum_{a>6} K_{a,6} \end{pmatrix} = \underbrace{\left( \begin{array}{ccc|ccc} 0 & K_{2,1} & K_{3,1} & K_{4,1} & K_{5,1} & K_{6,1} \\ 0 & 0 & K_{3,2} & K_{4,2} & K_{5,2} & K_{6,2} \\ 0 & 0 & 0 & K_{4,3} & K_{5,3} & K_{6,3} \\ \hline 0 & 0 & 0 & 0 & K_{5,4} & K_{6,4} \\ 0 & 0 & 0 & 0 & 0 & K_{6,5} \\ 0 & 0 & 0 & 0 & 0 & 0 \end{array} \right)}_{\mathbf{U}} \cdot \begin{pmatrix} 1 \\ 1 \\ 1 \\ 1 \\ 1 \\ 1 \end{pmatrix} \tag{21}
$$

We propose a divide and conquer approach that solves this problem by splitting the upper triangular matrix $\mathbf{U}$. The top-left and bottom-right parts are upper triangular matrices with half the size. We solve these subproblems recursively. The top-right part can be computed with the original filter based method. Using this approach, the total complexity to compute this sum is $\mathcal{O}(N \log (N))$.

With this algorithm, we have made feasible the computation of the subgradient. We can therefore perform projected subgradient descent on the LP objective efficiently. Since we need to compute the subgradient for each label separately due to the necessity of having sorted elements, the complexity associated with taking a gradient step is $\mathcal{O}(MN \log(N))$. To ensure the convergence, we choose as learning rate $(\beta^t)_{t=1}^{\infty}$ that is a square summable but not a summable sequence such as $(\frac{1}{1+t})_{t=1}^{\infty}$. We also make use of the work by Condat [26] to perform fast projection on the feasible set. The complete procedure can be found in Algorithm 3. Step 3 to 7 present the subgradient computation for each label. Using this subgradient, Step 8 shows the update rule for $y^t$. Finally, Step 9 project this new estimate onto the feasible space.

---

**Algorithm 3.** LP subgradient descent

---

1: Get $\mathbf{y}^0 \in \mathcal{M}$
2: **while** not converged **do**
3:     **for** $i \in \mathcal{L}$ **do**
4:         Sort $y_a(i) \quad \forall a \in [1, N]$
5:         Reorder $\mathbf{K}$
6:         $\mathbf{g}(i) = \nabla S_{LP}(\mathbf{y}^t(i))$
7:     **end for**
8:     $\mathbf{y}^{t+1} = \mathbf{y}^t - \beta^t \cdot \mathbf{g}$
9:     Project $\mathbf{y}^{t+1}$ on the feasible space
10: **end while**

---

The algorithm that we introduced converges to a global minimum of the LP relaxation. By using the rounding procedure introduced by Kleinberg and Tardos [2], it has a multiplicative bound of 2 for the dense CRF labelling problem on Potts models and $\mathcal{O}(\log(M))$ for metric pairwise potentials.

# 7 Experiments

We now demonstrate the benefits of using continuous relaxations of the energy minimisation problem on two applications: stereo matching and semantic segmentation. We provide results for the following methods: the Convex QP relaxation (**QP$_{\mathbf{cvx}}$**), the generic and negative semi-definite specific DC relaxations (**DC$_{\mathbf{gen}}$** and **DC$_{\mathbf{neg}}$**) and the LP relaxation (**LP**). We compare solutions obtained by our methods with the mean-field baseline (**MF**).

## 7.1 Stereo Matching

**Data.** We compare these methods on images extracted from the Middlebury stereo matching dataset [27]. The unary terms are obtained using the absolute difference matching function of [27]. The pixel compatibility function is similar to the one used by Krähenbühl and Koltun [5] and is described in the supplementary material. The label compatibility function is a Potts model.

**Results.** We present a comparison of runtime in Fig. (1a), as well as the associated final energies for each method in Table (1b). Similar results for other problem instances can be found in the supplementary materials.

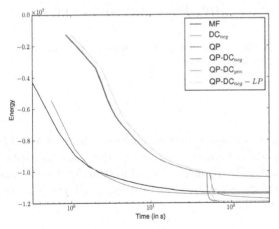

| Method | Final energy |
|---|---|
| MF | -1.137e+07 |
| DC$_{neg}$ | -1.145e+07 |
| QP | -1.037e+07 |
| QP-DC$_{neg}$ | -1.191e+07 |
| QP-DC$_{gen}$ | -1.175e+07 |
| QP-DC$_{neg}$-LP | **-1.193e+07** |

(b) Final Energy achieved

(a) Runtime comparisons

**Fig. 1.** Evolution of achieved energies as a function of time on a stereo matching problem (Teddy Image). While the **QP** method leads to the worst result, using it as an initialisation greatly improves results. In the case of negative semi-definite potentials, the specific **DC$_{neg}$** method is as fast as mean-field, while additionally providing guarantees of monotonous decrease. (Best viewed in colour) (Color figure online)

We observe that continuous relaxations obtain better energies than their mean-field counterparts. For a very limited time-budget, **MF** is the fastest method, although $\mathbf{DC}_{neg}$ is competitive and reach lower energies. When using **LP**, optimising a better objective function allows us to escape the local minima to which $\mathbf{DC_{neg}}$ converges. However, due to the higher complexity and the fact that we need to perform divide-and-conquer separately for all labels, the method is slower. This is particularly visible for problems with a high number of labels. This indicates that the LP relaxation might be better suited to fine-tune accurate solutions obtained by faster alternatives. For example, this can be achieved by restricting the LP to optimise over a subset of relevant labels, that is, labels that are present in the solutions provided by other methods. Qualitative results for the Teddy image can be found in Fig. 2 and additional outputs are present in supplementary material. We can see that lower energy translates to better visual results: note the removal of the artifacts in otherwise smooth regions (for example, in the middle of the sloped surface on the left of the image).

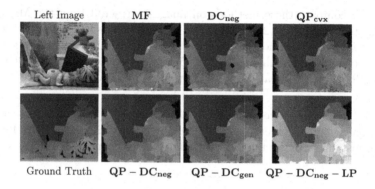

**Fig. 2.** Stereo matching results on the Teddy image. Continuous relaxation achieve smoother labeling, as expected by their lower energies

## 7.2   Image Segmentation

**Data.** We now consider an image segmentation task evaluated on the PASCAL VOC 2010 [28] dataset. For the sake of comparison, we use the same data splits and unary potentials as the one used by Krähenbühl and Koltun [5]. We perform cross-validation to select the best parameters of the pixel compatibility function for each method using Spearmint [29].

**Results.** The energy results obtained using the parameters cross validated for $\mathbf{DC_{neg}}$ are given in Table 1. **MF5** corresponds to mean-field ran for 5 iterations as it is often the case in practice [5,12].

Once again, we observe that continuous relaxations provide lower energies than mean-field based approaches. To add significance to this result, we also

**Table 1.** Percentage of images the row method outperforms the column method on final energy, average energy over the test set and Segmentation performance. Continuous relaxations dominate mean-field approaches on almost all images and improve significantly more compared to the Unary baseline. Parameters tuned for $DC_{neg}$

|                    | Unary | MF5 | MF | $QP_{cvx}$ | $DC_{gen}$ | $DC_{neg}$ | LP | Avg. E | Acc   | IoU   |
|--------------------|-------|-----|----|-----------|-----------|-----------|----|--------|-------|-------|
| Unary              | -     | 0   | 0  | 0         | 0         | 0         | 0  | 0      | 79.04 | 27.43 |
| MF5                | 99    | -   | 13 | 0         | 0         | 0         | 0  | −600   | 79.13 | 27.53 |
| MF                 | 99    | 0   | -  | 0         | 0         | 0         | 0  | −600   | 79.13 | 27.53 |
| $QP_{cvx}$         | 99    | 99  | 99 | -         | 0         | 0         | 0  | −6014  | 80.38 | 28.56 |
| $DC_{gen}$         | 99    | 99  | 99 | 85        | -         | 0         | 1  | −6429  | 80.41 | 28.59 |
| $DC_{neg}$         | 99    | 99  | 99 | 98        | 97        | -         | 4  | −6613  | 80.43 | 28.60 |
| LP                 | 99    | 99  | 99 | 98        | 97        | 87        | -  | **−6697** | **80.49** | **28.68** |

compare energies image-wise. In all but a few cases, the energies obtained by the continuous relaxations are better or equal to the mean-field ones. This provides conclusive evidence for our central hypothesis that continuous relaxations are better suited to the problem of energy minimisation in dense CRFs.

For completeness, we also provide energy and segmentation results for the parameters tuned for **MF** in the supplementary material. Even in that unfavourable setting, continuous relaxations still provide better energies. Note that, due to time constraints, we run the LP subgradient descent for only 5 iterations of subgradient descent. Moreover, to be able to run more experiments, we also restricted the number of labels by discarding labels that have a very small probability to appear given the initialisation.

Some qualitative results can be found in Fig. 3. When comparing the segmentations for **MF** and $DC_{neg}$, we can see that the best one is always the one we tune parameters for. A further interesting caveat is that although we always find a solution with better energy, it does not appear to be reflected in the quality of the segmentation. While in the previous case with stereo vision, better energy

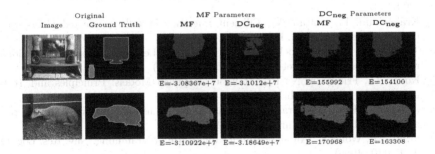

**Fig. 3.** Segmentation results on sample images. We see that $DC_{neg}$ leads to better energy in all cases compared to **MF**. Segmentation results are better for **MF** for the MF-tuned parameters and better for $DC_{neg}$ for the $DC_{neg}$-tuned parameters

implied qualitatively better reconstruction it is not so here. Similar observation was made by Wang et al [20].

# 8 Discussion

Our main contribution are four efficient algorithms for the dense CRF energy minimisation problem based on QP, DC and LP relaxations. We showed that continuous relaxations give better energies than the mean-field based approaches. Our best performing method, the LP relaxation, suffers from its high runtime. To go beyond this limit, move making algorithms such as $\alpha$-expansion [30] could be used and take advantage of the fact that this relaxation solves exactly the original IP for the two label problem. In future work, we also want to investigate the effect of learning specific parameters for these new inference methods using the framework of [18].

**Acknowledgments.** This work was supported by the EPSRC, Leverhulme Trust, Clarendon Fund and the ERC grant ERC-2012-AdG 321162-HELIOS, EPSRC/MURI grant ref EP/N019474/1, EPSRC grant EP/M013774/1, EPSRC Programme Grant Seebibyte EP/M013774/1 and Microsoft Research PhD Scolarship Program. We thank Philip Krähenbühl for making his code available and Vibhav Vineet for his help.

# References

1. Ravikumar, P., Lafferty, J.: Quadratic programming relaxations for metric labeling and Markov random field MAP estimation. In: ICML (2006)
2. Kleinberg, J., Tardos, E.: Approximation algorithms for classification problems with pairwise relationships: metric labeling and Markov random fields. JACM **49**, 616–639 (2002)
3. Kumar, P., Kolmogorov, V., Torr, P.: An analysis of convex relaxations for MAP estimation. In: NIPS (2008)
4. Chekuri, C., Khanna, S., Naor, J., Zosin, L.: Approximation algorithms for the metric labeling problem via a new linear programming formulation. In: SODA (2001)
5. Krähenbühl, P., Koltun, V.: Efficient inference in fully connected CRFs with Gaussian edge potentials. In: NIPS (2011)
6. Tappen, M., Liu, C., Adelson, E., Freeman, W.: Learning Gaussian conditional random fields for low-level vision. In: CVPR (2007)
7. Koller, D., Friedman, N.: Probabilistic Graphical Models: Principles and Techniques. MIT Press, Cambridge (2009)
8. Adams, A., Baek, J., Abraham, M.: Fast high-dimensional filtering using the permutohedral lattice. In: Eurographics (2010)
9. Frank, M., Wolfe, P.: An algorithm for quadratic programming. Nav. Res. Log. Q. **3**, 95–110 (1956)
10. Krähenbühl, P., Koltun, V.: Parameter learning and convergent inference for dense random fields. In: ICML (2013)
11. Baqué, P., Bagautdinov, T., Fleuret, F., Fua, P.: Principled parallel mean-field inference for discrete random fields. In: CVPR (2016)

12. Vineet, V., Warrell, J., Torr, P.: Filter-based mean-field inference for random fields with higher-order terms and product label-spaces. IJCV **110**, 290–307 (2014)
13. Ladicky, L., Russell, C., Kohli, P., Torr, P.H.S.: Graph cut based inference with co-occurrence statistics. In: Daniilidis, K., Maragos, P., Paragios, N. (eds.) ECCV 2010, Part V. LNCS, vol. 6315, pp. 239–253. Springer, Heidelberg (2010)
14. Kohli, P., Kumar, P., Torr, P.: P3 & beyond: solving energies with higher order cliques. In: CVPR (2007)
15. Long, J., Shelhamer, E., Darrell, T.: Fully convolutional networks for semantic segmentation. In: CVPR (2015)
16. Chen, L., Papandreou, G., Kokkinos, I., Murphy, K., Yuille, A.: Semantic image segmentation with deep convolutional nets and fully connected CRFs. In: ICLR (2015)
17. Schwing, A., Urtasun, R.: Fully connected deep structured networks. CoRR (2015)
18. Zheng, S., Jayasumana, S., Romera-Paredes, B., Vineet, V., Su, Z., Du, D., Huang, C., Torr, P.: Conditional random fields as recurrent neural networks. In: ICCV (2015)
19. Zhang, Y., Chen, T.: Efficient inference for fully-connected CRFs with stationarity. In: CVPR (2012)
20. Wang, P., Shen, C., van den Hengel, A.: Efficient SDP inference for fully-connected CRFs based on low-rank decomposition. In: CVPR (2015)
21. Goemans, M., Williamson, D.: Improved approximation algorithms for maximum cut and satisfiability problems using semidefinite programming. JACM **42**, 1115–1145 (1995)
22. Lacoste-Julien, S., Jaggi, M., Schmidt, M., Pletscher, P.: Block-coordinate Frank-Wolfe optimization for structural SVMs. In: ICML (2013)
23. Yuille, A., Rangarajan, A.: The concave-convex procedure (CCCP). In: NIPS (2002)
24. Sriperumbudur, B., Lanckriet, G.: On the convergence of the concave-convex procedure. In: NIPS (2009)
25. Kumar, P., Koller, D.: MAP estimation of semi-metric MRFs via hierarchical graph cuts. In: UAI (2009)
26. Condat, L.: Fast projection onto the simplex and the $l_1$ ball. Math. Program. **158**, 575–585 (2015)
27. Scharstein, D., Szeliski, R.: A taxonomy and evaluation of dense two-frame stereo correspondence algorithms. IJCV **47**, 7–42 (2002)
28. Everingham, M., Van Gool, L., Williams, C., Winn, J., Zisserman, A.: The PASCAL visual object classes challenge. In: VOC 2010 Results (2010)
29. Snoek, J., Larochelle, H., Adams, R.: Practical bayesian optimization of machine learning algorithms. In: NIPS (2012)
30. Boykov, Y., Veksler, O., Zabih, R.: Fast approximate energy minimization via graph cuts. PAMI **23**, 1222–1239 (2001)

# Complexity of Discrete Energy Minimization Problems

Mengtian Li[1]([✉]), Alexander Shekhovtsov[2], and Daniel Huber[1]

[1] The Robotics Institute, Carnegie Mellon University, Pittsburgh, USA
{mtli,dhuber}@cs.cmu.edu
[2] Institute for Computer Graphics and Vision, Graz University of Technology,
Graz, Austria
shekhovtsov@icg.tugraz.at

**Abstract.** Discrete energy minimization is widely-used in computer vision and machine learning for problems such as MAP inference in graphical models. The problem, in general, is notoriously intractable, and finding the global optimal solution is known to be NP-hard. However, is it possible to approximate this problem with a reasonable ratio bound on the solution quality in polynomial time? We show in this paper that the answer is no. Specifically, we show that general energy minimization, even in the 2-label pairwise case, and planar energy minimization with three or more labels are exp-APX-complete. This finding rules out the existence of any approximation algorithm with a sub-exponential approximation ratio in the input size for these two problems, including constant factor approximations. Moreover, we collect and review the computational complexity of several subclass problems and arrange them on a complexity scale consisting of three major complexity classes – PO, APX, and exp-APX, corresponding to problems that are solvable, approximable, and inapproximable in polynomial time. Problems in the first two complexity classes can serve as alternative tractable formulations to the inapproximable ones. This paper can help vision researchers to select an appropriate model for an application or guide them in designing new algorithms.

**Keywords:** Energy minimization · Complexity · NP-hard · APX · exp-APX · NPO · WCSP · Min-sum · MAP MRF · QPBO · Planar graph

## 1  Introduction

Discrete energy minimization, also known as min-sum labeling [69] or weighted constraint satisfaction (WCSP)[1] [25], is a popular model for many problems in

---

[1] WCSP is a more general problem, considering a bounded plus operation. It is itself a special case of valued CSP, where the objective takes values in a more general valuation set.

**Electronic supplementary material** The online version of this chapter (doi:10.1007/978-3-319-46475-6_51) contains supplementary material, which is available to authorized users.

© Springer International Publishing AG 2016
B. Leibe et al. (Eds.): ECCV 2016, Part II, LNCS 9906, pp. 834–852, 2016.
DOI: 10.1007/978-3-319-46475-6_51

computer vision, machine learning, bioinformatics, and natural language processing. In particular, the problem arises in maximum a posteriori (MAP) inference
for Markov (conditional) random fields (MRFs/CRFs) [43]. In the most frequently used pairwise case, the *discrete energy minimization problem* (simply
"energy minimization" hereafter) is defined as

$$\min_{x \in \mathcal{L}^{\mathcal{V}}} \sum_{u \in \mathcal{V}} f_u(x_u) + \sum_{(u,v) \in \mathcal{E}} f_{uv}(x_u, x_v), \tag{1}$$

where $x_u$ is the label for node $u$ in a graph $\mathcal{G} = (\mathcal{V}, \mathcal{E})$. When the variables $x_u$
are binary (Boolean): $\mathcal{L} = \mathbb{B} = \{0, 1\}$, the problem can be written as a quadratic
polynomial in $x$ [11] and is known as quadratic pseudo-Boolean optimization
(QPBO) [11].

In computer vision practice, energy minimization has found its place in
semantic segmentation [51], pose estimation [71], scene understanding [57], depth
estimation [44], optical flow estimation [70], image in-painting [59], and image
denoising [8]. For example, tree-structured models have been used to estimate
pictorial structures such as body skeletons or facial landmarks [71], multi-label
Potts models have been used to enforce a smoothing prior for semantic segmentation [51], and general pairwise models have been used for optimal flow estimation [70]. However, it may not be appreciated that the energy minimization
formulations used to model these vision problems have greatly varied degrees
of tractability or *computational complexity*. For the three examples above, the
first allows efficient exact inference, the second admits a constant factor approximation, and the third has no quality guarantee on the approximation of the
optimum.

The study of complexity of energy minimization is a broad field. Energy
minimization problems are often intractable in practice except for special cases.
While many researchers analyze the time complexity of their algorithms (e.g.,
using big O notation), it is beneficial to delve deeper to address the difficulty
of the underlying problem. The two most commonly known complexity classes
are P (polynomial time) and NP (nondeterministic polynomial time: all decision
problems whose solutions can be verified in polynomial time). However, these
two complexity classes are only defined for *decision* problems. The analogous
complexity classes for *optimization* problems are PO (P optimization) and NPO
(NP optimization: all optimization problems whose solution feasibility can be
verified in polynomial time). Optimization problems form a superset of decision
problems, since any decision problem can be cast as an optimization over the set
{yes, no}, i.e., P $\subset$ PO and NP $\subset$ NPO. The NP-hardness of an optimization
problem means it is at least as hard as (under Turing reduction) the hardest
decision problem in the class NP. If a problem is NP-hard, then it is not in PO
assuming P $\neq$ NP.

Although optimal solutions for problems in NPO, but not in PO, are
intractable, it is sometimes possible to guarantee that a good solution (i.e., one
that is worse than the optimal by no more than a given factor) can be found
in polynomial time. These problems can therefore be further classified into class

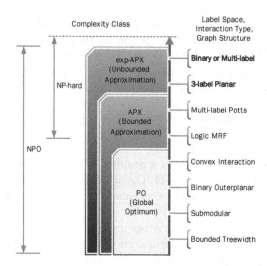

**Fig. 1.** Discrete energy minimization problems aligned on a complexity axis. Red/boldface indicates new results proven in this paper. This axis defines a partial ordering, since problems within a complexity class are not ranked. Some problems discussed in this paper are omitted for simplicity (Color figure online)

APX (constant factor approximation) and class exp-APX (inapproximable) with increasing complexity (Fig. 1). We can arrange energy minimization problems on this more detailed complexity scale, originally established in [4], to provide vision researchers a new viewpoint for complexity classification, with a focus on NP-hard optimization problems.

In this paper, we make three core contributions, as explained in the next three paragraphs. First, we prove the inapproximability result of QPBO and general energy minimization. Second, we show that the same inapproximability result holds when restricting to planar graphs with three or more labels. In the proof, we propose a novel micro-graph structure-based reduction that can be used for algorithmic design as well. Finally, we present a unified framework and an overview of vision-related special cases where the energy minimization problem can be solved in polynomial time or approximated with a constant, logarithmic, or polynomial factor.

**Binary and Multi-label Case** (Sect. 3). It is known that QPBO (2-label case) and the general energy minimization problem (multi-label case) are NP-hard [12], because they generalize such classical NP-hard optimization problems on graphs as vertex packing (maximum independent set) and the minimum and maximum cut problems [27]. In this paper, we show a stronger conclusion. *We prove that QPBO as well as general energy minimization are complete (being the hardest problems) in the class exp-APX*. Assuming P $\neq$ NP, this implies that a polynomial time method cannot have a guarantee of finding an approximation within a constant factor of the optimal, and in fact, the only possible factor in polynomial time is exponential in the input size. In practice, this means that a solution may be essentially arbitrarily bad.

**Planar Three or More Label Case** (Sect. 4). Planar graphs form the underlying graph structure for many computer vision and image processing tasks. It is known that efficient exact algorithms exist for some special cases of planar 2-label energy minimization problems [55]. In this paper, we show that for the case of three or more labels, planar energy minimization is exp-APX-complete, which means these problems are as hard as general energy minimization. It is unknown that whether a constant ratio approximation exists for planar 2-label problems in general.

**Subclass Problems** (Sect. 5). Special cases for some energy minimization algorithms relevant to computer vision are known to be tractable. However, detailed complexity analysis of these algorithms is patchy and spread across numerous papers. In Sect. 5, we classify the complexity of these subclass problems and illustrate some of their connections. Such an analysis can help computer vision researchers become acquainted with existing complexity results relevant to energy minimization and can aid in selecting an appropriate model for an application or in designing new algorithms.

## 1.1  Related Work

Much of the work on complexity in computer vision has focused on experimental or empirical comparison of inference methods, including influential studies on choosing the best optimization techniques for specific classes of energy minimization problems [26,62] and the PASCAL Probabilistic Inference Challenge, which focused on the more general context of inference in graphical models [1]. In contrast, our work focuses on theoretical computational complexity, rather than experimental analysis.

On the theoretical side, the NP-hardness of certain energy minimization problems is well studied. It has been shown that 2-label energy minimization is, in general, NP-hard, but it can be in PO if it is submodular [30] or outerplanar [55]. For multi-label problems, the NP-hardness was proven by reduction from the NP-hard multi-way cut problem [13]. These results, however, say nothing about the complexity of *approximating* the global optimum for the intractable cases. The complexity involving approximation has been studied for classical combinatorial problems, such as MAX-CUT and MAX-2SAT, which are known to be APX-complete [46]. QPBO generalizes such problems and is therefore APX-hard. This leaves a possibility that QPBO may be in APX, i.e., approximable within a constant factor.

Energy minimization is often used to solve MAP inference for undirected graphical models. In contrast to scarce results for energy minimization and undirected graphical models, researchers have more extensively studied the computational complexity of approximating the MAP solution for *Bayesian networks*, also known as *directed graphical models* [42]. Abdelbar and Hedetniemi first proved the NP-hardness for approximating the MAP assignment of directed graphical models in the value of probability, i.e., finding $x$ such that

$$\frac{p(x^*)}{p(x)} \leq r(n) \tag{2}$$

with a constant or polynomial ratio $r(n) \geq 1$ is NP-hard and showing that this problem is poly-APX-hard [2]. The probability approximation ratio is closest to the energy ratio used in our work, but other approximation measures have also been studied. Kwisthout showed the NP-hardness for approximating MAPs with the measure of additive value-, structure-, and rank-approximation [40–42]. He also investigated the hardness of expectation-approximation of MAP and found that no randomized algorithm can expectation-approximate MAP in polynomial time with a bounded margin of error unless NP $\subseteq$ BPP, an assumption that is highly unlikely to be true [42].

Unfortunately, the complexity results for directed models do not readily transfer to undirected models and vice versa. In directed and undirected models, the graphs represent different conditional independence relations, thus the underlying family of probability distributions encoded by these two models is distinct, as detailed in Appendix B. However, one can ask similar questions on the hardness of undirected models in terms of various approximation measures. In this work, we answer two questions, "How hard is it to approximate the MAP inference in the ratio of energy (log probability) and the ratio of probability?" The complexity of structure-, rank-, and expectation-approximation remain open questions for energy minimization.

## 2    Definitions and Notation

There are at least two different sets of definitions of what is considered an NP optimization problem [4,45]. Here, we follow the notation of Ausiello et al. [4] and restate the definitions needed for us to state and prove our theorems in Sects. 3 and 4 with our explanation of their relevance to our proofs.

**Definition 2.1 (Optimization Problem, [4] Definition 1.16).** An *optimization problem* $\mathcal{P}$ is characterized by a quadruple $(\mathcal{I}, \mathcal{S}, m, \text{goal})$ where

1. $\mathcal{I}$ is the set of instances of $\mathcal{P}$.
2. $\mathcal{S}$ is a function that associates to any input instance $x \in \mathcal{I}$ the set of *feasible solutions* of $x$.
3. $m$ is the *measure* function, defined for pairs $(x, y)$ such that $x \in \mathcal{I}$ and $y \in \mathcal{S}(x)$. For every such pair $(x, y)$, $m(x, y)$ provides a positive integer.
4. goal $\in \{\min, \max\}$.

Notice the assumption that the cost is positive, and, in particular, it cannot be zero.

**Definition 2.2 (Class NPO, [4] Definition 1.17).** An optimization problem $\mathcal{P} = (\mathcal{I}, \mathcal{S}, m, \text{goal})$ belongs to the class of NP optimization (NPO) problems if the following hold:

1. The set of instances $\mathcal{I}$ is recognizable in polynomial time.
2. There exists a polynomial $q$ such that given an instance $x \in \mathcal{I}$, for any $y \in \mathcal{S}(x)$, $|y| < q(x)$ and, besides, for any $y$ such that $|y| < q(x)$, it is decidable in polynomial time whether $y \in \mathcal{S}(x)$.
3. The measure function $m$ is computable in polynomial time.

**Definition 2.3 (Class PO, [4] Definition 1.18).** An optimization problem $\mathcal{P}$ belongs to the class of PO if it is in NPO and there exists a polynomial-time algorithm that, for any instance $x \in \mathcal{I}$, returns an optimal solution $y \in \mathcal{S}^*(x)$, together with its value $m^*(x)$.

For intractable problems, it may be acceptable to seek an approximate solution that is sufficiently close to optimal.

**Definition 2.4 (Approximation Algorithm [4] Definition 3.1).** Given an optimization problem $\mathcal{P} = (\mathcal{I}, \mathcal{S}, m, \text{goal})$ an algorithm $\mathcal{A}$ is an *approximation algorithm* for $\mathcal{P}$ if, for any given instance $x \in \mathcal{I}$, it returns an *approximate solution*, that is a feasible solution $\mathcal{A}(x) \in \mathcal{S}(x)$.

**Definition 2.5 (Performance Ratio, [4], Definition 3.6).** Given an optimization problem $\mathcal{P}$, for any instance $x$ of $\mathcal{P}$ and for any feasible solution $y \in \mathcal{S}(x)$, the *performance ratio*, *approximation ratio* or *approximation factor* of $y$ with respect to $x$ is defined as

$$R(x, y) = \max\left\{ \frac{m(x, y)}{m^*(x)}, \frac{m^*(x)}{m(x, y)} \right\}, \tag{3}$$

where $m^*(x)$ is the measure of the optimal solution for the instance $x$.

Since $m^*(x)$ is a positive integer, the performance ratio is well-defined. It is a rational number in $[1, \infty)$. Notice that from this definition, it follows that if finding a feasible solution, e.g. $y \in \mathcal{S}(x)$, is an NP-hard decision problem, then there exists no polynomial-time approximation algorithm for $\mathcal{P}$, irrespective of the kind of performance evaluation that one could possibly mean.

**Definition 2.6 ($r(n)$-approximation, [4], Definition 8.1).** Given an optimization problem $\mathcal{P}$ in NPO, an approximation algorithm $\mathcal{A}$ for $\mathcal{P}$, and a function $r: \mathbb{N} \to (1, \infty)$, we say that $\mathcal{A}$ is an $r(n)$-*approximate* algorithm for $\mathcal{P}$ if, for any instance $x$ of $\mathcal{P}$ such that $\mathcal{S}(x) \neq \varnothing$, the performance ratio of the feasible solution $\mathcal{A}(x)$ with respect to $x$ verifies the following inequality:

$$R(x, \mathcal{A}(x)) \leq r(|x|). \tag{4}$$

**Definition 2.7 ($F$-APX, rn [4], Definition 8.2).** Given a class of functions $F$, $F$-APX is the class of all NPO problems $\mathcal{P}$ such that, for some function $r \in F$, there exists a polynomial-time $r(n)$-approximate algorithm for $\mathcal{P}$.

The class of constant functions for $F$ yields the complexity class APX. Together with logarithmic, polynomial, and exponential functions applied in Definition 2.7, the following *complexity axis* is established:

$$\text{PO} \subseteq \text{APX} \subseteq \text{log-APX} \subseteq \text{poly-APX} \subseteq \text{exp-APX} \subseteq \text{NPO}.$$

Since the measure $m$ needs to be computable in polynomial time for NPO problems, the largest measure and thus the largest performance ratio is an exponential function. But exp-APX is not equal to NPO (assuming $P \neq NP$) because NPO contains problems whose feasible solutions cannot be found in polynomial time. For an energy minimization problem, any label assignment is a feasible solution, implying that all energy minimization problems are in exp-APX.

The standard approach for proofs in complexity theory is to perform a reduction from a known NP-complete problem. Unfortunately, the most common polynomial-time reductions ignore the quality of the solution in the approximated case. For example, it is shown that any energy minimization problem can be reduced to a factor 2 approximable Potts model [48], however the reduction is not approximation preserving and is unable to show the hardness of general energy minimization in terms of approximation. Therefore, it is necessary to use an approximation preserving (AP) reduction to classify NPO problems that are not in PO, for which only the approximation algorithms are tractable. AP-preserving reductions preserve the approximation ratio in a linear fashion, and thus preserve the membership in these complexity classes. Formally,

**Definition 2.8 (AP-reduction, [4] Definition 8.3).** Let $\mathcal{P}_1$ and $\mathcal{P}_2$ be two problems in NPO. $\mathcal{P}_1$ is said to be AP-*reducible* to $\mathcal{P}_2$, in symbols $\mathcal{P}_1 \leq_{AP} \mathcal{P}_2$, if two functions $\pi$ and $\sigma$ and a positive constant $\alpha$ exist such that[2]:

1. For any instance $x \in \mathcal{I}_1$, $\pi(x) \in \mathcal{I}_2$.
2. For any instance $x \in \mathcal{I}_1$, if $S_1(x) \neq \varnothing$ then $S_2(\pi(x)) \neq \varnothing$.
3. For any instance $x \in \mathcal{I}_1$ and for any $y \in S_2(\pi(x))$, $\sigma(x, y) \in S_1(x)$.
4. $\pi$ and $\sigma$ are computable by algorithms whose running time is polynomial.
5. For any instance $x \in \mathcal{I}_1$, for any rational $r > 1$, and for any $y \in S_2(\pi(x))$,

$$R_2(\pi(x), y) \leq r \quad \text{implies} \tag{5}$$
$$R_1(x, \sigma(x, y)) \leq 1 + \alpha(r - 1). \tag{6}$$

AP-reduction is the formal definition of the term 'as hard as' used in this paper unless otherwise specified. It defines a partial order among optimization problems. With respect to this relationship, we can formally define the subclass containing the hardest problems in a complexity class:

**Definition 2.9 ($\mathcal{C}$-hard and $\mathcal{C}$-complete, [4] Definition 8.5).** Given a class $\mathcal{C}$ of NPO problems, a problem $\mathcal{P}$ is $\mathcal{C}$-hard if, for any $\mathcal{P}' \in \mathcal{C}$, $\mathcal{P}' \leq_{AP} \mathcal{P}$. A $\mathcal{C}$-hard problem is $\mathcal{C}$-complete if it belongs to $\mathcal{C}$.

Intuitively, a complexity class $\mathcal{C}$ specifies the upper bound on the hardness of the problems within, $\mathcal{C}$-hard specifies the lower bound, and $\mathcal{C}$-complete exactly specifies the hardness.

---

[2] The complete definition contains a rational $r$ for the two mappings ($\pi$ and $\sigma$) and it is omitted here for simplicity.

# 3   Inapproximability for the General Case

In this section, we show that QPBO and general energy minimization are inapproximable by proving they are exp-APX-complete. As previously mentioned, it is already known that these problems are NP-hard [12], but it was previously unknown whether useful approximation guarantees were possible in the general case. The formal statement of QPBO as an optimization problem is as follows:

*Problem 1.* **QPBO**

> INSTANCE: A pseudo-Boolean function $f\colon \mathbb{B}^{\mathcal{V}} \to \mathbb{N}$:
>
> $$f(x) = \sum_{v \in \mathcal{V}} f_u(x_u) + \sum_{u,v \in \mathcal{V}} f_{uv}(x_u, x_v), \tag{7}$$
>
> given by the collection of unary terms $f_u$ and pairwise terms $f_{uv}$.
> SOLUTION: Assignment of variables $x \in \mathbb{B}^{\mathcal{V}}$.
> MEASURE: $\min f(x) > 0$.

**Theorem 3.1.** QPBO is exp-APX-complete.

*Proof Sketch.* (Full proof in Appendix A).

1. We observe that W3SAT-triv is known to be exp-APX-complete [4]. W3SAT-triv is a 3-SAT problem with weights on the variables and an artificial, trivial solution.
2. Each 3-clause in the conjunctive normal form can be represented as a polynomial consisting of three binary variables. Together with representing the weights with the unary terms, we arrive at a cubic Boolean minimization problem.
3. We use the method of [24] to transform the cubic Boolean problem into a quadratic one, with polynomially many additional variables, which is an instance of QPBO.
4. Together with an inverse mapping $\sigma$ that we define, the above transformation defines an AP-reduction from W3SAT-triv to QPBO, i.e. W3SAT-triv $\leq_{\text{AP}}$ QPBO. This proves that QPBO is exp-APX-hard.
5. We observe that all energy minimization problems are in exp-APX and thereby conclude that QPBO is exp-APX-complete.

This inapproximability result can be generalized to more than two labels.

**Corollary 3.2.** $k$-label energy minimization is exp-APX-complete for $k \geq 2$.

*Proof Sketch.* (Full proof in Appendix A). This theorem is proved by showing QPBO $\leq_{\text{AP}}$ $k$-label energy minimization for $k \geq 2$.

We show in Corollary B.1 the inapproximability in energy (log probability) transfer to probability in Eq. (2) as well.

Taken together, this theorem and its corollaries form a very strong inapproximability result for general energy minimization[3]. They imply not only NP-hardness, but also that there is no algorithm that can approximate general energy minimization with two or more labels with an approximation ratio better than some exponential function in the input size. In other words, any approximation algorithm of the general energy minimization problem can perform arbitrarily badly, and it would be pointless to try to prove a bound on the approximation ratio for existing approximation algorithms for the general case. While this conclusion is disappointing, these results serve as a clarification of grounds and guidance for model selection and algorithm design. Instead of counting on an oracle that solves the energy minimization problem, researchers should put efforts into selecting the proper formulation, trading off expressiveness for tractability.

## 4    Inapproximability for the Planar Case

Efficient algorithms for energy minimization have been found for special cases of 2-label planar graphs. Examples include planar 2-label problems without unary terms and outerplanar 2-label problems (i.e., the graph structure remains planar after connecting to a common node) [55]. Grid structures over image pixels naturally give rise to planar graphs in computer vision. Given their frequency of use in this domain, it is natural to consider the complexity of more general cases involving planar graphs. Figure 2 visualizes the current state of knowledge of the complexity of energy minimization problems on planar graphs. In this section, we prove that for the case of planar graphs with three or more labels, energy minimization is exp-APX-complete. This result is important because it significantly reduces the space of potentially efficient algorithms on planar graphs. The existence of constant ratio approximation for planar 2-label problems in general remains an open question[4].

**Theorem 4.1.** Planar 3-label energy minimization is exp-APX-complete.

*Proof Sketch.* (Full proof in Appendix A).

**Fig. 2.** Complexity for planar energy minimization problems. The "general case" implies no restrictions on the pairwise interaction type. This paper shows that the third category of problems is not efficiently approximable

---

[3] These results automatically generalize to higher order cases as they subsume the pairwise cases discussed here.

[4] The planar 2-label problem in general is APX-hard, since it subsumes the APX problem planar vertex cover [7].

1. We construct elementary gadgets to reduce any 3-label energy minimization problem to a planar one with polynomially many auxiliary nodes.
2. Together with an inverse mapping $\sigma$ that we define, the above construction defines an AP-reduction, i.e., 3-label energy minimization $\leq_{AP}$ planar 3-label energy minimization.
3. Since 3-label energy minimization is exp-APX-complete (Corollary 3.2) and all energy minimization problems are in exp-APX, we thereby conclude that planar 3-label energy minimization is exp-APX-complete.

**Corollary 4.2.** *Planar $k$-label energy minimization is exp-APX-complete, for $k \geq 3$.*

*Proof Sketch.* (Full proof in Appendix A). This theorem is proved by showing planar 3-label energy minimization $\leq_{AP}$ planar $k$-label energy minimization, for $k \geq 3$.

These theorems show that the restricted case of planar graphs with 3 or more labels is as hard as general case for energy minimization problems with the same inapproximable implications discussed in Sect. 3.

The most novel and useful aspect of the proof of Theorem 4.1 is the planar reduction in Step 1. The reduction creates an equivalent planar representation to any non-planar 3-label graph. That is, the graphs share the same optimal value. The reduction applies elementary constructions or "gadgets" to uncross two intersecting edges. This process is repeated until all intersecting edges are uncrossed. Similar elementary constructions were used to study the complexity of the linear programming formulation of energy minimization problems [48, 49]. Our novel gadgets have three key properties *at the same time*: (1) they are able to uncross intersecting edges, (2) they work on non-relaxed problems, i.e., all indicator variables (or pseudomarginals to be formal) are integral; and (3) they can be applied repeatedly to build an AP-reduction.

The two gadgets used in our reduction are illustrated in Fig. 3. A 3-label node can be encoded as a collection of 3 indicator variables with a one-hot constraint. In the figure, a solid colored circle denotes a 3-label node, and a solid colored rectangle denotes the equivalent node expressed with indicator variables (white circles). For example, in Fig. 3, $a = 1$ corresponds to the blue node taking the first label value. The pairwise potentials (edges on the left part of the figures) can be viewed as edge costs between the indicator variables (black lines on the right), e.g., $f_{uv}(3, 2)$ is placed onto the edge between indicator $c$ and $e$ and is counted into the overall measure if and only if $c = e = 1$. In our gadgets, drawn edges represent zero cost while omitted edges represent positive infinity[5]. While the set of feasible solutions remains the same, the gadget encourages certain labeling relationships, which, if not satisfied, cause the overall measure to be infinity. Therefore, the encouraged relationships must be satisfied by any optimal solution. The two gadgets serve different purposes:

---

[5] A very large number will also serve the same purpose, e.g., take the sum of the absolute value of all energy terms and add 1. Therefore, we are not expanding the set of allowed energy terms to include $\infty$.

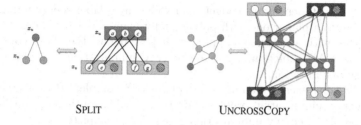

SPLIT            UNCROSSCOPY

**Fig. 3.** Gadgets to represent a 3-label variable as two 2-label variables (SPLIT) and to copy the values of two diagonal pairs of 2-label variables without edge crossing (UNCROSSCOPY) (Color figure online)

SPLIT A 3-label node (blue) is split into two 2-label nodes (green). The shaded circle represents a label with a positive infinite unary cost and thus creates a simulated 2-label node. The encouraged relationships are

- $a = 1 \Leftrightarrow d = 1$ and $f = 1$.
- $b = 1 \Leftrightarrow g = 1$.
- $c = 1 \Leftrightarrow e = 1$ and $f = 1$.

Thus $(d, f)$ encodes $a$, $(d, g)$ and $(e, g)$ both encode $b$ and $(e, f)$ encodes $c$.

UNCROSSCOPY The values of two 2-label nodes are encouraged to be the same as their diagonal counterparts respectively (red to red, green to green) without crossing with each other. The orange nodes are intermediate nodes that pass on the values. All types of lines represent the same edge cost, which is 0. The color differences visualize the verification for each of the 4 possible states of two 2-label nodes. For example, the cyan lines verify the case where the top-left (green) node takes the values $(1, 0)$ and the top-right (red) node takes the value $(0, 1)$. It is clear that the encouraged solution is for the bottom-left (red) node and the bottom-right (green) node to take the value $(0, 1)$ and $(1, 0)$ respectively.

These two gadgets can be used to uncross the intersecting edges of two pairs of 3-label nodes (Fig. 4, left). For a crossing edge $(x_u, x_v)$, first a new 3-label node $x_{v'}$ is introduced preserving the same arbitrary interaction (red line) as before (Fig. 4, middle). Then, the crossing edges (enclosed in the dotted circle) are uncrossed by applying SPLIT and UNCROSSCOPY four times (Fig. 4, right).

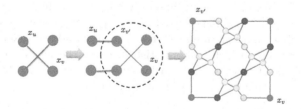

**Fig. 4.** Planar reduction for 3-label problems

Without loss of generality, we can assume that no more than two edges intersect at a common point except at their endpoints. This process can be applied repeatedly at each edge crossing until there are no edge crossings left in the graph [49].

# 5   Complexity of Subclass Problems

In this section, we classify some of the special cases of energy minimization according to our complexity axis (Fig. 1). This classification can be viewed as a reinterpretation of existing results from the literature into a unified framework.

## 5.1   Class PO (Global Optimum)

Polynomial time solvability may be achieved by considering two principal restrictions: those restricting the *structure* of the problem, i.e., the graph $G$, and those restricting the type of allowed interactions, i.e., functions $f_{uv}$.

**Structure Restrictions.** When $G$ is a chain, energy minimization reduces to finding a shortest path in the trellis graph, which can be solved using a classical dynamic programming (DP) method known as the Viterbi algorithm [20]. The same DP principle applies to graphs of bounded treewidth. Fixing all variables in a separator set decouples the problem into independent optimization problems. For treewidth 1, the separators are just individual vertices, and the problem is solved by a variant of DP [47,54]. For larger treewidths, the respective optimization procedure is known as junction tree decomposition [43]. A loop is a simple example of a treewidth 2 problem. However, for a treewidth $k$ problem, the time complexity is exponential in $k$ [43]. When $G$ is an outer-planar graph, the problem can be solved by the method of [55], which reduces it to a planar Ising model, for which efficient algorithms exist [60].

**Interaction Restrictions.** Submodularity is a restriction closely related to problems solvable by minimum cut. A quadratic pseudo-Boolean function $f$ is *submodular* iff its quadratic terms are non-positive. It is then known to be equivalent with finding a minimum cut in a corresponding network [21]. Another way to state this condition for QPBO is $\forall (u,v) \in \mathcal{E}, f_{uv}(0,1) + f_{uv}(1,0) \geq f_{uv}(0,0) + f_{uv}(1,1)$. However, submodularity is more general. It extends to higher-order and multi-label problems. Submodularity is considered a discrete analog of convexity. Just as convex functions are relatively easy to optimize, general submodular function minimization can be solved in strongly polynomial time [56]. Kolmogorov and Zabin introduced submodularity in computer vision and showed that binary $2^{nd}$ order and $3^{rd}$ order submodular problems can be always reduced to minimum cut, which is much more efficient than general submodular function minimization [34]. Živný et al. and Ramalingam et al. give more results on functions reducible to minimum cut [50,68]. For QPBO on an unrestricted graph structure, the following *dichotomy* result has been proven by Cohen et al. [16]: either the problem is submodular and thus in PO or it is

NP-hard (i.e., submodular problems are the only ones that are tractable in this case).

For multi-label problems Ishikawa proposed a reduction to minimum cut for problems with convex interactions, i.e., where $f_{uv}(x_u, x_v) = g_{uv}(x_u - x_v)$ and $g_{uv}$ is convex and symmetric [23]. It is worth noting that when the unary terms are convex as well, the problem can be solved even more efficiently [22,31]. The same reduction [23] remains correct for a more general class of submodular multi-label problems. In modern terminology, component-wise minimum $x \wedge y$ and component-wise maximum $x \vee y$ of complete labelings $x$, $y$ for all nodes are introduced $(x, y \in \mathcal{L}^{\mathcal{V}})$. These operations depend on the *order of labels* and, in turn, define a lattice on the set of labelings. The function $f$ is called *submodular on the lattice* if $f(x \vee y) + f(x \wedge y) \leq f(x) + f(y)$ for all $x$, $y$ [65]. In the pairwise case, the condition can be simplified to the form of submodularity common in computer vision [50]: $f_{uv}(i, j+1) + f_{uv}(i+1, j) \geq f_{uv}(i, j) + f_{uv}(i+1, j+1)$. In particular, it is easy to see that a convex $f_{uv}$ satisfies it [23]. Kolmogorov [32] and Arora et al. [3] proposed maxflow-like algorithms for higher order submodular energy minimization. Schlesinger proposed an algorithm to find a reordering in which the problem is submodular if one exists [53]. However, unlike in the binary case, solvable multi-label problems are more diverse. A variety of problems are generalizations of submodularity and are in PO, including symmetric tournament pair, submodularity on arbitrary trees, submodularity on arbitrary lattices, skew bisubmodularity, and bisubmodularity on arbitrary domains (see references in [64]). Thapper and Živný [63] and Kolmogorov [33] characterized these tractable classes and proved a similar dichotomy result: a problem of unrestricted structure is either solvable by LP-relaxation (and thus in PO) or it is NP-hard. It appears that LP relaxation is the most powerful and general solving technique [72].

**Mixed Restrictions.** In comparison, results with mixed structure and interaction restrictions are rare. One example is a planar Ising model without unary terms [60]. Since there is a restriction on structure (planarity) and unary terms, it does not fall into any of the classes described above. Another example is the restriction to supermodular functions on a bipartite graph, solvable by [53] or by LP relaxation, but not falling under the characterization [64] because of the graph restriction.

**Algorithmic Applications.** The aforementioned tractable formulations in PO can be used to solve or approximate harder problems. Trees, cycles and planar problems are used in dual decomposition methods [9,35,36]. Binary submodular problems are used for finding an optimized crossover of two-candidate multi-label solutions. An example of this technique, the expansion move algorithm, achieves a constant approximation ratio for the Potts model [13]. Extended dynamic programming can be used to solve restricted segmentation problems [18] and as move-making subroutine [67]. LP relaxation also provides approximation guarantees for many problems [5,15,28,37], placing them in the APX or poly-APX class.

## 5.2    Class APX and Class Log-APX (Bounded Approximation)

Problems that have bounded approximation in polynomial time usually have certain restriction on the interaction type. The Potts model may be the simplest and most common way to enforce the smoothness of the labeling. Each pairwise interaction depends on whether the neighboring labellings are the same, i.e. $f_{uv}(x_u, x_v) = c_{uv}\delta(x_u, x_v)$. Boykov et al. showed a reduction to this problem from the NP-hard multiway cut [13], also known to be APX-complete [4,17]. They also proved that their constructed alpha-expansion algorithm is a 2-approximate algorithm. These results prove that the Potts model is in APX but not in PO. However, their reduction from multiway cut is not an AP-reduction, as it violates the third condition of AP-reducibility. Therefore, it is still an open problem whether the Potts model is APX-complete. Boykov et al. also showed that their algorithm can approximate the more general problem of metric labeling [13]. The energy is called *metric* if, for an arbitrary, finite label space $\mathcal{L}$, the pairwise interaction satisfies a) $f_{uv}(\alpha, \beta) = 0$, b) $f_{uv}(\alpha, \beta) = f_{uv}(\beta, \alpha) \geq 0$, and c) $f_{uv}(\alpha, \beta) \leq f_{uv}(\beta, \gamma) + f_{uv}(\beta, \gamma)$, for any labels $\alpha$, $\beta$, $\gamma \in \mathcal{L}$ and any $uv \in \mathcal{E}$. Although their approximation algorithm has a bound on the performance ratio, the bound depends on the ratio of some pairwise terms, a number that can grow exponentially large. For metric labeling with $k$ labels, Kleinberg et al. proposed an $O(\log k \log \log k)$-approximation algorithm. This bound was further improved to $O(\log k)$ by Chekuri et al. [14], making metric labeling a problem in log-APX[6].

We have seen that a problem with convex pairwise interactions is in PO. An interesting variant is its truncated counterpart, i.e., $f_{uv}(x_u, x_v) = w_{uv} \min\{d(x_u - x_v), M\}$, where $w_{uv}$ is a non-negative weight, $d$ is a convex symmetric function to define the distance between two labels, and $M$ is the truncating constant [66]. This problem is NP-hard [66], but Kumar et al. [39] have proposed an algorithm that yields bounded approximations with a factor of $2 + \sqrt{2}$ for linear distance functions and a factor of $O(\sqrt{M})$ for quadratic distance functions[7]. This bound is analyzed for more general distance functions by Kumar [38].

Another APX problem with implicit restrictions on the interaction type is logic MRF [6]. It is a powerful higher order model able to encode arbitrary logical relations of Boolean variables. It has energy function $f(x) = \sum_i^n w_i C_i$, where each $C_i$ is a disjunctive clause involving a subset of Boolean variables $x$, and $C_i = 1$ if it is satisfied and 0 otherwise. Each clause $C_i$ is assigned a non-negative weight $w_i$. The goal is to find an assignment of $x$ to maximize $f(x)$. As disjunctive clauses can be converted into polynomials, this is essentially a pseudo-Boolean optimization problem. However, this is a special case of general 2-label energy minimization, as its polynomial basis spans a subspace of the basis of the latter. Bach et al. [6] proved that logic MRF is in APX by showing that it is a special case of MAX-SAT with non-negative weights.

---

[6] An $O(\log k)$-approximation implies an $O(\log |x|)$-approximation (see Corollary C.1).

[7] In these truncated convex problems, the ratio bound is defined for the pairwise part of the energy (1). The approximation ratio in accordance to our definition is obtained assuming the unary terms are non-negative.

# 6  Discussion

The algorithmic implications of our inapproximability have been discussed above. Here, we focus on the discussion of practical implications. The existence of an approximation guarantee indicates a practically relevant class of problems where one may expect reasonable performance. In structural learning for example, it is acceptable to have a constant factor approximation for the inference subroutine when efficient exact algorithms are not available. Finley and Joachims proved that this constant factor approximation guarantee yields a multiplicative bound on the learning objective, providing a relative guarantee for the quality of the learned parameters [19]. An optimality guarantee is important, because the inference subroutine is repeatedly called, and even a single poor approximation, which returns a not-so-bad worst violator, will lead to the early termination of the structural learning algorithm.

However, despite having no approximation ratio guarantee, algorithms such as the extended roof duality algorithm for QPBO [52] are still widely used. This gap between theory and application applies not only to our results but to all other complexity results as well. We list several key reasons for the potential lack of correspondence between theoretical complexity guarantees and practical performance.

**Complexity Results Address the Worst Case Scenario.** Our inapproximability result guarantees that for any polynomial time algorithm, there exists an input instance for which the algorithm will produce a very poor approximation. However, applications often do not encounter the worst case. Such is the case with the simplex algorithm, whose worst case complexity is exponential, yet it is widely used in practice.

**Objective Function is Not the Final Evaluation Criterion.** In many image processing tasks, the final evaluation criterion is the number of pixels correctly labeled. The relation between the energy value and the accuracy is implicit. In many cases, a local optimum is good enough to produce a high labeling accuracy and a visually appealing labeling.

**Other Forms of Optimality Guarantee or Indicator Exist.** Approximation measures in the distance of solutions or in the expectation of the objective value are likely to be prohibitive for energy minimization, as they are for Bayesian networks [40–42]. On the other hand, a family of energy minimization algorithms has the property of being *persistent* or *partial optimal*, meaning a subset of nodes have consistent labeling with the global optimal one [10,11]. Rather than being an optimality guarantee, persistency is an optimality indicator. In the worst case, the set of persistent labelings could be empty, yet the percentage of persistent labelings over the all the nodes gives us a notion of the algorithm's performance on this particular input instance. Persistency is also useful in reducing the size of the search space [29,58]. Similarly, the per-instance integrality gap of duality based methods is another form of optimality indicator and can be exponentially large for problems in general [37,61].

# 7   Conclusion

In this paper, we have shown inapproximability results for energy minimization in the general case and planar 3-label case. In addition, we present a unified overview of the complexity of existing energy minimization problems by arranging them in a fine-grained complexity scale. These altogether set up a new viewpoint for interpreting and classifying the complexity of optimization problems for the computer vision community. In the future, it will be interesting to consider the open questions of the complexity of structure-, rank-, and expectation-approximation for energy minimization.

**Acknowledgments.** This material is based upon work supported by the National Science Foundation under Grant No. IIS-1328930 and by the European Research Council under the Horizon 2020 program, ERC starting grant agreement 640156.

# References

1. The Probabilistic Inference Challenge (2011). http://www.cs.huji.ac.il/project/PASCAL/
2. Abdelbar, A., Hedetniemi, S.: Approximating MAPs for belief networks is NP-hard and other theorems. Artif. Intell. **102**(1), 21–38 (1998)
3. Arora, C., Banerjee, S., Kalra, P., Maheshwari, S.N.: Generic cuts: an efficient algorithm for optimal inference in higher order MRF-MAP. In: Fitzgibbon, A., Lazebnik, S., Perona, P., Sato, Y., Schmid, C. (eds.) ECCV 2012, Part V. LNCS, vol. 7576, pp. 17–30. Springer, Heidelberg (2012)
4. Ausiello, G., Crescenzi, P., Gambosi, G., Kann, V., Marchetti-Spaccamela, A., Protasi, M.: Complexity and Approximation: Combinatorial Optimization Problems and Their Approximability Properties. Springer, Heidelberg (1999)
5. Bach, S.H., Huang, B., Getoor, L.: Unifying local consistency and MAX SAT relaxations for scalable inference with rounding guarantees. In: AISTATS, JMLR Proceedings, vol. 38 (2015)
6. Bach, S.H., Huang, B., Getoor, L.: Unifying local consistency and MAX SAT relaxations for scalable inference with rounding guarantees. In: AISTATS, pp. 46–55 (2015)
7. Bar-Yehuda, R., Even, S.: On approximating a vertex cover for planar graphs. In: Proceedings of 14th Annual ACM Symposium on Theory of Computing, pp. 303–309 (1982)
8. Barbu, A.: Learning real-time MRF inference for image denoising. In: CVPR, pp. 1574–1581 (2009)
9. Batra, D., Gallagher, A.C., Parikh, D., Chen, T.: Beyond trees: MRF inference via outer-planar decomposition. In: CVPR, pp. 2496–2503 (2010)
10. Boros, E., Hammer, P.L., Sun, X.: Network flows and minimization of quadratic pseudo-Boolean functions. Technical report RRR 17-1991, RUTCOR, May 1991
11. Boros, E., Hammer, P.: Pseudo-Boolean optimization. Technical report, RUTCOR, October 2001
12. Boros, E., Hammer, P.: Pseudo-Boolean optimization. Discret. Appl. Math. 1–3(123), 155–225 (2002)
13. Boykov, Y., Veksler, O., Zabih, R.: Fast approximate energy minimization via graph cuts. PAMI **23**, 1222–1239 (2001)

14. Chekuri, C., Khanna, S., Naor, J., Zosin, L.: A linear programming formulation and approximation algorithms for the metric labeling problem. SIAM J. Discret. Math. 18(3), 608–625 (2005)
15. Chekuri, C., Khanna, S., Naor, J., Zosin, L.: Approximation algorithms for the metric labeling problem via a new linear programming formulation. In: Symposium on Discrete Algorithms, pp. 109–118 (2001)
16. Cohen, D., Cooper, M., Jeavons, P.G.: A complete characterization of complexity for Boolean constraint optimization problems. In: Wallace, M. (ed.) CP 2004. LNCS, vol. 3258, pp. 212–226. Springer, Heidelberg (2004)
17. Dahlhaus, E., Johnson, D.S., Papadimitriou, C.H., Seymour, P.D., Yannakakis, M.: The complexity of multiterminal cuts. SIAM J. Comput. 23(4), 864–894 (1994)
18. Felzenszwalb, P.F., Veksler, O.: Tiered scene labeling with dynamic programming. In: CVPR, pp. 3097–3104 (2010)
19. Finley, T., Joachims, T.: Training structural SVMs when exact inference is intractable. In: ICML, pp. 304–311. ACM (2008)
20. Forney Jr., G.D.: The Viterbi algorithm. Proc. IEEE 61(3), 268–278 (1973)
21. Hammer, P.L.: Some network flow problems solved with pseudo-Boolean programming. Oper. Res. 13, 388–399 (1965)
22. Hochbaum, D.S.: An efficient algorithm for image segmentation, Markov random fields and related problems. J. ACM 48(4), 686–701 (2001)
23. Ishikawa, H.: Exact optimization for Markov random fields with convex priors. PAMI 25(10), 1333–1336 (2003)
24. Ishikawa, H.: Transformation of general binary MRF minimization to the first-order case. PAMI 33(6), 1234–1249 (2011)
25. Jeavons, P., Krokhin, A., Živný, S., et al.: The complexity of valued constraint satisfaction. Bull. EATCS 2(113), 21–55 (2014)
26. Kappes, J.H., Andres, B., Hamprecht, F.A., Schnörr, C., Nowozin, S., Batra, D., Kim, S., Kausler, B.X., Kröger, T., Lellmann, J., et al.: A comparative study of modern inference techniques for structured discrete energy minimization problems. IJCV 115, 155–184 (2015)
27. Karp, R.M.: Reducibility among combinatorial problems. In: Proceedings of Symposium on the Complexity of Computer Computations, pp. 85–103 (1972)
28. Kleinberg, J., Tardos, E.: Approximation algorithms for classification problems with pairwise relationships: metric labeling and Markov random fields. J. ACM 49(5), 616–639 (2002)
29. Kohli, P., Shekhovtsov, A., Rother, C., Kolmogorov, V., Torr, P.: On partial optimality in multi-label MRFs. In: ICML, pp. 480–487 (2008)
30. Kolmogorov, V., Zabih, R.: What energy functions can be minimized via graph cuts? PAMI 26(2), 147–159 (2004)
31. Kolmogorov, V.: Primal-dual algorithm for convex Markov random fields. Technical report MSR-TR-2005-117, Microsoft Research, Cambridge (2005)
32. Kolmogorov, V.: Minimizing a sum of submodular functions. Discret. Appl. Math. 160(15), 2246–2258 (2012)
33. Kolmogorov, V.: The power of linear programming for finite-valued CSPs: a constructive characterization. In: Fomin, F.V., Freivalds, R., Kwiatkowska, M., Peleg, D. (eds.) ICALP 2013, Part I. LNCS, vol. 7965, pp. 625–636. Springer, Heidelberg (2013)
34. Kolmogorov, V., Zabin, R.: What energy functions can be minimized via graph cuts? PAMI 26(2), 147–159 (2004)
35. Komodakis, N., Paragios, N., Tziritas, G.: MRF optimization via dual decomposition: message-passing revisited. In: ICCV, pp. 1–8 (2007)

36. Komodakis, N., Paragios, N.: Beyond loose LP-relaxations: optimizing MRFs by repairing cycles. In: Forsyth, D., Torr, P., Zisserman, A. (eds.) ECCV 2008, Part III. LNCS, vol. 5304, pp. 806–820. Springer, Heidelberg (2008)
37. Komodakis, N., Tziritas, G.: Approximate labeling via graph cuts based on linear programming. PAMI **29**(8), 1436–1453 (2007)
38. Kumar, M.P.: Rounding-based moves for metric labeling. In: NIPS, pp. 109–117 (2014)
39. Kumar, M.P., Veksler, O., Torr, P.H.: Improved moves for truncated convex models. J. Mach. Learn. Res. **12**, 31–67 (2011)
40. Kwisthout, J.: Most probable explanations in Bayesian networks: complexity and tractability. Int. J. Approx. Reason. **52**(9), 1452–1469 (2011)
41. Kwisthout, J.: Structure approximation of most probable explanations in Bayesian networks. In: van der Gaag, L.C. (ed.) ECSQARU 2013. LNCS, vol. 7958, pp. 340–351. Springer, Heidelberg (2013)
42. Kwisthout, J.: Tree-width and the computational complexity of MAP approximations in Bayesian networks. J. Artif. Intell. Res. **53**, 699–720 (2015)
43. Lauritzen, S.L.: Graphical Models. No. 17 in Oxford Statistical Science Series. Oxford Science Publications, Oxford (1998)
44. Liu, B., Gould, S., Koller, D.: Single image depth estimation from predicted semantic labels. In: CVPR, pp. 1253–1260 (2010)
45. Orponen, P., Mannila, H.: On approximation preserving reductions: complete problems and robust measures. Technical report (1987)
46. Papadimitriou, C.H., Yannakakis, M.: Optimization, approximation, and complexity classes. J. Comput. Syst. Sci. **43**(3), 425–440 (1991)
47. Pearl, J.: Probabilistic Reasoning in Intelligent Systems: Networks of Plausible Inference. Morgan Kaufmann Publishers Inc., Burlington (1988)
48. Průša, D., Werner, T.: How hard is the LP relaxation of the potts min-sum labeling problem? In: Tai, X.-C., Bae, E., Chan, T.F., Lysaker, M. (eds.) EMMCVPR 2015. LNCS, vol. 8932, pp. 57–70. Springer, Heidelberg (2015)
49. Prusa, D., Werner, T.: Universality of the local marginal polytope. PAMI **37**(4), 898–904 (2015)
50. Ramalingam, S., Kohli, P., Alahari, K., Torr, P.H.: Exact inference in multi-label CRFs with higher order cliques. In: CVPR, pp. 1–8. IEEE (2008)
51. Ren, X., Bo, L., Fox, D.: RGB-(D) scene labeling: Features and algorithms. In: CVPR, pp. 2759–2766. IEEE (2012)
52. Rother, C., Kolmogorov, V., Lempitsky, V., Szummer, M.: Optimizing binary MRFs via extended roof duality. In: CVPR, pp. 1–8 (2007)
53. Schlesinger, D.: Exact solution of permuted submodular MinSum problems. In: Yuille, A.L., Zhu, S.-C., Cremers, D., Wang, Y. (eds.) EMMCVPR 2007. LNCS, vol. 4679, pp. 28–38. Springer, Heidelberg (2007)
54. Schlesinger, M.I., Hlaváč, V.: Ten Lectures on Statistical and Structural Pattern Recognition. Computational Imaging and Vision, vol. 24. Kluwer Academic Publishers, Dordrecht (2002)
55. Schraudolph, N.: Polynomial-time exact inference in NP-hard binary MRFs via reweighted perfect matching. In: AISTATS, JMLR Proceedings, vol. 9, pp. 717–724 (2010)
56. Schrijver, A.: A combinatorial algorithm minimizing submodular functions in strongly polynomial time. J. Comb. Theor. Ser. B **80**, 346–355 (2000). http://homepages.cwi.nl/ lex/files/minsubm6.ps

57. Schwing, A.G., Urtasun, R.: Efficient exact inference for 3D indoor scene understanding. In: Fitzgibbon, A., Lazebnik, S., Perona, P., Sato, Y., Schmid, C. (eds.) ECCV 2012, Part VI. LNCS, vol. 7577, pp. 299–313. Springer, Heidelberg (2012)

58. Shekhovtsov, A., Swoboda, P., Savchynskyy, B.: Maximum persistency via iterative relaxed inference with graphical models. In: CVPR (2015)

59. Shekhovtsov, A., Kohli, P., Rother, C.: Curvature prior for MRF-based segmentation and shape inpainting. In: DAGM/OAGM, pp. 41–51 (2012)

60. Shih, W.K., Wu, S., Kuo, Y.S.: Unifying maximum cut and minimum cut of a planar graph. IEEE Trans. Comput. **39**(5), 694–697 (1990)

61. Sontag, D., Choe, D.K., Li, Y.: Efficiently searching for frustrated cycles in MAP inference. In: Uncertainty in Artificial Intelligence (UAI), pp. 795–804 (2012)

62. Szeliski, R., Zabih, R., Scharstein, D., Veksler, O., Kolmogorov, V., Agarwala, A., Tappen, M., Rother, C.: A comparative study of energy minimization methods for Markov random fields with smoothness-based priors. PAMI **30**(6), 1068–1080 (2008)

63. Thapper, J., Živný, S.: The power of linear programming for valued CSPs. In: Symposium on Foundations of Computer Science (FOCS), pp. 669–678 (2012)

64. Thapper, J., Živný, S.: The complexity of finite-valued CSPs. In: Symposium on the Theory of Computing (STOC), pp. 695–704 (2013)

65. Topkis, D.M.: Minimizing a submodular function on a lattice. Oper. Res. **26**(2), 305–321 (1978)

66. Veksler, O.: Graph cut based optimization for MRFs with truncated convex priors. In: CVPR, pp. 1–8 (2007)

67. Vineet, V., Warrell, J., Torr, P.H.S.: A tiered move-making algorithm for general pairwise MRFs. In: CVPR, pp. 1632–1639 (2012)

68. Živný, S., Cohen, D.A., Jeavons, P.G.: The expressive power of binary submodular functions. Discret. Appl. Math. **157**(15), 3347–3358 (2009)

69. Werner, T.: A linear programming approach to max-sum problem: a review. PAMI **29**(7), 1165–1179 (2007)

70. Xu, L., Jia, J., Matsushita, Y.: Motion detail preserving optical flow estimation. PAMI **34**(9), 1744–1757 (2012)

71. Yang, Y., Ramanan, D.: Articulated pose estimation with flexible mixtures-of-parts. In: CVPR, pp. 1385–1392 (2011)

72. Živný, S., Werner, T., Průša, D.A.: The Power of LP Relaxation for MAP Inference. The MIT Press, Cambridge (2014)

# A Convex Solution to Spatially-Regularized Correspondence Problems

Thomas Windheuser[(✉)] and Daniel Cremers

Computer Vision Group, Technische Universität München, Munich, Germany
{thomas.windheuser,cremers}@tum.de

**Abstract.** We propose a convex formulation of the correspondence problem between two images with respect to an energy function measuring data consistency and spatial regularity. To this end, we formulate the general correspondence problem as the search for a minimal two-dimensional surface in $\mathbb{R}^4$. We then use tools from geometric measure theory and introduce 2-vector fields as a representation of two-dimensional surfaces in $\mathbb{R}^4$. We propose a discretization of this surface formulation that gives rise to a convex minimization problem and compute a globally optimal solution using an efficient primal-dual algorithm.

## 1 Introduction

The establishment of spatially dense correspondence is one of the central computational challenges in computer vision with a wide range of applications including stereo disparity estimation [1,2], optical flow estimation [3], shape matching [4] and medical image registration [5–7]. Correspondence estimation is often cast as an energy minimization problem including a (generally) non-convex data consistency term and a spatial regularizer. Although such optimization problems have been intensively studied in computer vision, to date an algorithm that finds a global optimum in polynomial time is not known.

### 1.1 Problem Statement: Diffeomorphic Matching

We consider a general correspondence estimation problem where the aim is to compute an optimal diffeomorphic image matching defined as follows. Let $\Omega \subset \mathbb{R}^2$ denote the image plane, i.e. an open simply-connected subset of $\mathbb{R}^2$. We describe the data consistency between points on both images as a map $g : \Omega \times \Omega \to \mathbb{R}_{\geq 0}$, where $g(p,q)$ measures the consistency between brightness, color, depth or some high level features at point $p \in \Omega$ in image 1 and at point $q \in \Omega$ in image 2. We define the desired correspondence between both images as the optimal solution to the constrained minimization problem

$$\min_{f \in \text{Diff}^+(\Omega,\Omega)} \int_\Omega \Big(g\big(p, f(p)\big) + \epsilon\Big) W\big(df(p)\big) dp. \tag{1}$$

Here $\text{Diff}^+(\Omega, \Omega)$ is the set of all orientation-preserving diffeomorphisms from $\Omega$ to $\Omega$ and $df(p) \in \mathbb{R}^{2\times 2}$ denotes the Jacobian (or more general the differential)

© Springer International Publishing AG 2016
B. Leibe et al. (Eds.): ECCV 2016, Part II, LNCS 9906, pp. 853–868, 2016.
DOI: 10.1007/978-3-319-46475-6_52

of $f$ at $p$. $W : \mathbb{R}^{2\times 2} \to \mathbb{R}_{\geq 0}$, $W(df) = \sqrt{\det\left(\left(\begin{smallmatrix} \mathrm{Id} \\ df \end{smallmatrix}\right)^{\top} \left(\begin{smallmatrix} \mathrm{Id} \\ df \end{smallmatrix}\right)\right)}$, measures the deviation from isometry, $\mathrm{Id} \in \mathbb{R}^{2\times 2}$ being the identity matrix. Solving (1) therefore leads to a diffeomorphic transformation of $\Omega$ favoring data consistency via the term $g(p, f(p))$ and spatial regularity (local isometry) via $W(df(p))$, with $\epsilon \in \mathbb{R}_{\geq 0}$ determining the trade-off.

## 1.2 Related Work

While the correspondence model (1) is not the only conceivable choice, most works on correspondence finding propose similar energies that include data consistency and a spatial regularizer. Moreover, we believe that the proposed solution via geometric measure theory can be generalized to other classes of cost functions. Due to the non-convexity of the data term coupled with the spatial regularizer, such problems have evaded many attempts to determine global optima.

Formally, problem (1) differs from optical flow formulations as pioneered by Horn and Schunck [3] in that we do not search for a displacement field $v : \Omega \to \mathbb{R}^2$ but rather directly for a pairing of corresponding points $f : \Omega \to \Omega$. The commonly used coarse-to-fine linearization strategies in optical flow estimation [8–10] often provide high-quality solutions in practice, yet they cannot guarantee optimal solutions.

To our knowledge, optimal solutions to such correspondence problems only exist in the one-dimensional setting (the stereo problem) as pioneered in the spatially discrete setting by Ishikawa [2] and in the spatially continuous setting by Pock et al. [11]. The latter framework has been generalized to higher dimensions [12], yet respective convex relaxations only provide approximate solutions with no (apriori) optimality guarantees.

We would like to stress that our proposed method is not related to the work of Vaillant et al. [13] that also uses currents and 2-forms: Apparently [13] solves a different problem not including a arbitrary non-convex data term. Moreover it involves optimizing a surfaces of codimension 1 while we tackle the minimal surface problem of codimension 2. It is exactly the codimension 2 which makes our problem challenging.

In this paper, we propose a convex energy for the correspondence problem in the framework of geometric measure theory to which we can find the globally optimal solution. Since this theory is not commonly used in computer vision, we will briefly review the most relevant concepts such as $m$-vectors, differential forms and currents in Sects. 3 and 4. For a more detailed presentation, we refer the reader to standard textbooks [14, 15].

## 1.3 Contribution

1. In Sect. 2, we prove that the correspondence problem (1) is equivalent to a minimal surface problem in higher dimension. Subsequently, we express this minimal surface problem as an optimization problem over 2-vector fields.

2. In Sect. 5, we propose a discretization of this minimal 2-vector field problem which gives rise to a convex optimization problem. The discrete problem can be optimized with standard convex optimization methods that converge to a globally optimal solution.
3. In Sects. 3 and 4 we select and lay out the mathematical concepts necessary for the proposed method that are normally embedded into the complex theory of geometric measure theory. We also derive Lemmas 3 and 4. They do not exist in standard textbooks, but are crucial for the numerical implementation.
4. In Sect. 6.2, we derive a solution to the mass norm's proximity operator. This proximity operator is necessary for the numerical optimization of the discrete problem detailed in Sects. 6 and 7. Additionally we derive a discrete formulation of the boundary operator for 2-vector fields.

## 2   Optimal Correspondences and Minimal Surfaces

In this section, we transform the original correspondence problem into an equivalent optimization problem, where we minimize over 2-vector fields (introduced in Sects. 3 and 4) on the product space $\Omega \times \Omega$. The transformation consists of two steps:

The first step is to turn the correspondence problem into a minimal surface problem. Instead of optimizing directly over sets of diffeomorphisms, we will optimize over subsets of the product space $\Omega \times \Omega = \Omega^2$. In the space of diffeomorphisms $f : \Omega \to \Omega$ are represented by their graphs $\{(p, f(p)) | p \in \Omega\} \subset \Omega^2$, which are 2-dimensional surfaces embedded into $\mathbb{R}^4$. Let the projections $\pi_1, \pi_2 : \Omega^2 \to \Omega$ be defined by $\pi_1(p, q) = p$, $\pi_2(p, q) = q$ for any $(p, q) \in \Omega^2$ and denote by $\pi_{1|S}, \pi_{2|S} : S \to \Omega$ the restrictions of $\pi_1, \pi_2$ to some set $S \subset \Omega^2$. Now we can reformulate (1) as the following minimal surface problem:

$$\min_{S \subset \Omega^2} \int_S w(p) dp \tag{2}$$
$$\text{s. t. } \partial S \subset \partial(\Omega^2) \text{ and } \pi_{1|S}, \pi_{2|S} \in \text{Diff}^+(S, \Omega),$$

where we define $w : \Omega^2 \to \mathbb{R}$ by $w(p) = g(\pi_1(p), \pi_2(p)) + \epsilon$ for any $p \in \Omega^2$. Note that $W(df(p))$ from (1) is now implicitly included in the surface integral $\int_S dp$ of (2). Indeed both optimization problems are equivalent:

**Proposition 1.** *Let $f^*$ be a minimizer of (1), then it's graph $\{(p, f(p)) | p \in \Omega\}$ is a minimizer of (2). If $S \subset \Omega^2$ is a minimizer of (2), then $\pi_{1|S}^{-1} \circ \pi_{2|S} : \Omega \to \Omega$ is a minimizer of (1).*

*Proof.* For any feasible $f : \Omega \to \Omega$ of (1) let $S(f) = \{(p, f(p)) | p \in \Omega\}$ be its graph. Then $h : \Omega \to \Omega^2, h(p) = (p, f(p))$ is a chart of $S(f)$. Now expand the surface integral and $w$:

$$\int_{S(f)} w(p) dp = \int_\Omega w(h(p)) \sqrt{\det(dh^\top dh)} dp$$
$$= \int_\Omega (g(p, f(p)) + \epsilon) \sqrt{\det\left(\left(\begin{smallmatrix} \text{Id} \\ df \end{smallmatrix}\right)^\top \left(\begin{smallmatrix} \text{Id} \\ df \end{smallmatrix}\right)\right)} dp. \tag{3}$$

So for any feasible $f$ of (1) there is a feasible $S(f)$ of (2), such that the energy of $f$ with respect to (1) is equalt to the energy of $S(f)$ with respect to (2).

On the other hand, for any feasible $S \subset \Omega^2$ of (2) the function $f_S = \pi_{1|S}^{-1} \circ \pi_{2|S} : \Omega \to \Omega$ is a feasible solution to (1). Note that it holds $\pi_{1|S}^{-1}(p) = \binom{p}{f_S(p)} \in \Omega^2$ and

$$\int_S w(p)dp = \int_\Omega w(\pi_{1|S}^{-1}(p)) \sqrt{\det((d\pi_{1|S}^{-1})^\top d\pi_{1|S}^{-1})} dp$$
$$= \int_\Omega (g(p, f_S(p)) + \epsilon) \sqrt{\det((\begin{smallmatrix} \mathrm{Id} \\ \frac{}{df_S} \end{smallmatrix})^\top (\begin{smallmatrix} \mathrm{Id} \\ \frac{}{df_S} \end{smallmatrix}))} dp. \tag{4}$$

$\square$

The second step of our approach is to represent the surfaces $S \subset \Omega^2$ by their tangent planes. From differential geometry we know that we can parameterize some 2-dimensional surface embedded into $\Omega^2$ by a diffeomorphic map $u : U \to \Omega^2$, where $U$ is an open subset of $\mathbb{R}^2$. [1] The directional derivatives $u_x = \frac{\partial u}{\partial x}, u_y = \frac{\partial u}{\partial y} : U \to \mathbb{R}^4$ yield tangent vectors that span the tangent planes of $S$, i.e. $u_x(u^{-1}(p)), u_y(u^{-1}(p)) \in \mathbb{R}^4$ span the tangent space $T_pS$ of $S$ at $p \in S$. The weighted area of $S$ can be evaluated by $\mathcal{A}_w(S) = \int_U w(u(p))\mathcal{A}(u_x(p), u_y(p))dp$, where $\mathcal{A}(u_x(p), u_y(p))$ is the area of the parallelogram spanned by $u_x(p), u_y(p)$. Now define the vector fields $t_x, t_y : \Omega^2 \to \mathbb{R}^4$ by

$$t_x(p) = \begin{cases} u_x(u^{-1}(p)) & \text{if } p \in S \\ 0 & \text{otherwise,} \end{cases} \quad t_y(p) = \begin{cases} u_y(u^{-1}(p)) & \text{if } p \in S \\ 0 & \text{otherwise.} \end{cases} \tag{5}$$

Using the 2-dimensional Hausdorff measure $\mathcal{H}^2$ (see Sect. 4) we can evaluate the weighted area of $S$ by $\mathcal{A}_w(S) = \int_{\Omega^2} w(p)\mathcal{A}(t_x(p), t_y(p))d\mathcal{H}^2p$. The important observation is that the integral directly depends neither on $S$ nor on the chart $u$. The key idea is that the two vector fields $t_x, t_y$ define the shape, area and boundary of $S$ and we can rewrite the minimal surface problem (2) as an optimization over two vector fields on $\Omega^2$:

$$\min_{t_x, t_y : \Omega^2 \to \mathbb{R}^4} \int_{\Omega^2} w(p)\mathcal{A}(t_x(p), t_y(p))d\mathcal{H}^2p$$

$$\text{s. t. } t_x, t_y \text{ represent a surface without boundary inside } \Omega^2 \text{ and} \tag{6}$$
$$\pi_1(t_x, t_y) = \pi_2(t_x, t_y) = \Omega.$$

Keep in mind, that this is only a loose definition of the optimization problem that we will actually solve. We will state a more refined definition in Sect. 5 that makes heavy use of the tools of geometric measure theory. Since these tools are not common in computer vision, we will introduce them in the following.

---

[1] For the sake of simplicity, we will ignore the concepts of multiple charts and changes of parameterization. They will not be necessary, as we will directly get rid of the chart $u$.

We start with the introduction $m$-vectors and alternating forms that are used to represent our two vector fields in Sect. 3. In Sect. 4 we will discuss differential forms and currents. We will glue those concepts together and propose a refined form of (6) in Sect. 5. The latter can be discretized into a convex minimization problem. This discretization will be presented in Sect. 6. Finally we will show how to optimize the convex optimization problem in Sect. 7.

## 3   $m$-Vectors and $m$-Covectors

As indicated in optimization problem (6) we want to optimize over two vector fields. At each point we need to measure the area of the parallelogram of both vectors, their boundary and orientation and make sure that both vectors are linearly independent. Especially the latter constraint will make this optimization problem hardly tractable, if we use two separate vector fields. Instead we will use more sophisticated concepts, namely simple $m$-vectors, $m$-vectors and $m$-covectors.[2]

### 3.1   $m$-Vectors

Loosely speaking, simple $m$-vectors represent an oriented $m$-dimensional subspace of $\mathbb{R}^n$ spanned by $m$ linearly independent vectors plus some positive area. The area is defined by the parallelotope of these vectors. The set of $m$-vectors is the vector space obtained by the linear extension of the set of simple $m$-vectors. $m$-covectors are the elements of the dual space to the space of $m$-vectors. We will first give a formal definition of (simple) $m$-vectors and then discuss the relevant concepts.

**Definition 1 (Simple $m$-Vectors and $m$-Vectors [15, p. 23]).** *Let $m, n \in \mathbb{N}, m \leq n$.*

1. *Define an equivalence relation $\sim$ on $(\mathbb{R}^n)^m$, such that for any $(v_1, \ldots, v_m) \in (\mathbb{R}^n)^m$ and any $\alpha \in \mathbb{R}$ it is*

$$(v_1, \ldots, \alpha v_i, \ldots, v_j, \ldots, v_m) \sim (v_1, \ldots, v_i, \ldots, \alpha v_j, \ldots, v_m), \tag{7}$$

$$(v_1, \ldots, v_i, \ldots, v_j, \ldots, v_m) \sim (v_1, \ldots, v_i + \alpha v_j, \ldots, v_j, \ldots, v_m) \text{ and} \tag{8}$$

$$(v_1, \ldots, v_i, \ldots, v_j, \ldots, v_m) \sim (v_1, \ldots, v_j, \ldots, -v_i, \ldots, v_m). \tag{9}$$

   *Denote the equivalence class of any $(v_1, \ldots, v_m) \in (\mathbb{R}^n)^m$ with respect to $\sim$ by $v_1 \wedge \ldots \wedge v_m$ and call it a* simple $m$-vector.

2. *Consider the vector space of all linear combinations of simple $m$-vectors and define the equivalence relation $\approx$ on this vector space by*

$$\alpha(v_1 \wedge v_2 \wedge \ldots \wedge v_m) \approx (\alpha v_1) \wedge v_2 \wedge \ldots \wedge v_m \text{ and} \tag{10}$$

$$(v_1 \wedge v_2 \wedge \ldots \wedge v_m) + (v_1' \wedge v_2 \wedge \ldots \wedge v_m) \approx (v_1 + v_1') \wedge v_2 \wedge \ldots \wedge v_m \tag{11}$$

---

[2] We will not proof most of the statements in Sects. 3 and 4 but refer to the textbooks [14–16].

*for any* $v_1', v_1, \ldots, v_m \in \mathbb{R}^n, \alpha \in \mathbb{R}$. *Denote this vector space modulo* $\approx$ *by* $\Lambda_m \mathbb{R}^n$ *and call any element of* $\Lambda_m \mathbb{R}^n$ *an* $m$-*vector. Additionally define* $\Lambda_0 \mathbb{R}^n = \mathbb{R}$.

$\cdot \wedge \cdot$ is called the *wedge product*. It will be generalized later in Definition 5. For the time being, let us take a closer look at simple $m$-vectors and make a first observation:

**Observation.** The $m$-vector $\omega \in \Lambda_m \mathbb{R}^n$ is simple if and only if there exist $v_1, \ldots, v_m \in \mathbb{R}^n$ such that $\omega = v_1 \wedge \ldots \wedge v_m$.

Let $e_1, \ldots, e_n \in \mathbb{R}^n$ be the oriented orthonormal basis of $\mathbb{R}^n$ pointing in the standard direction. We call this basis the *standard basis* of $\mathbb{R}^n$. This basis induces an orthonormal basis $\{e_{i_1} \wedge \ldots \wedge e_{i_m}\}_{i_1 < \ldots < i_m} \subset \Lambda_m \mathbb{R}^n$ of $\Lambda_m \mathbb{R}^n$. Let us call this basis the *standard basis* of $\Lambda_m \mathbb{R}^n$. It directly follows that $\dim \Lambda_m \mathbb{R}^n = \binom{n}{m}$. We can write any $m$-vector $\omega$ as a weighted sum of basis $m$-vectors: $\omega = \sum_{i_1 < \ldots < i_m} \omega_{i_1 \cdots i_m} e_{i_1 \cdots i_m}$, where $\{\omega_{i_1 \cdots i_m} \in \mathbb{R}\}_{i_1 < \ldots < i_m}$ are the *coefficients* or *coordinates* (with respect to the standard basis).

**Notation.** For some indexed set of vectors $\{v_i\}_i$ we abbreviate the wedge product by $v_{i_1 \cdots i_m} = v_{i_1} \wedge \ldots \wedge v_{i_m}$. For example $e_{132} = e_1 \wedge e_3 \wedge e_2$. Additionally we will abbreviate the decomposition of some $m$-vector $\omega$ into basis vectors by $\omega = \sum_\sigma \omega_\sigma e_\sigma$.

**Definition 2.** *For any two vectors* $\omega = \sum_\sigma \omega_\sigma e_\sigma, \xi = \sum_\sigma \xi_\sigma e_\sigma \in \Lambda_m \mathbb{R}^n$ *we define the* standard inner product $\langle \cdot, \cdot \rangle : \Lambda_m \mathbb{R}^n \times \Lambda_m \mathbb{R}^n \to \mathbb{R}$ *of* $\Lambda_m \mathbb{R}^n$ *by* $\langle \omega, \xi \rangle = \sum_\sigma \omega_\sigma \xi_\sigma$ *and define the* Euclidean norm $\|\cdot\|_2 : \Lambda_m \mathbb{R}^n \to \mathbb{R}$ *on* $\Lambda_m \mathbb{R}^n$ *by* $\|\omega\|_2 = \sqrt{\langle \omega, \omega \rangle}$ *for any* $\omega \in \Lambda_m \mathbb{R}^n$.

**Observation.** Whenever the $m$-vector $\omega$ is simple, then for every decomposition $\omega = v_1 \wedge \ldots \wedge v_m, v_1, \ldots, v_m \in \mathbb{R}^n$, it holds that the $m$-dimensional volume of the parallelotope spanned by $v_1, \ldots, v_m$ is exactly $\|\omega\|_2$. It directly follows the important property that $\omega = 0$ if and only if $v_1, \ldots, v_m$ are not linearly independent.

If the simple $m$-vector $\omega = v_1 \wedge \ldots \wedge v_m \neq 0$, then $v_1, \ldots, v_m$ is an oriented basis of the $m$-dimensional subspace $V \subset \mathbb{R}^n$. For any orthonormal basis $w_1, \ldots, w_m$ of $V$ with the same orientation it holds:

$$v_1 \wedge \ldots \wedge v_m = \|\omega\|_2 (w_1 \wedge \ldots \wedge w_m). \tag{12}$$

In other words, there is a one-to-one correspondence between simple $m$-vectors and oriented $m$-dimensional subspaces (also called *oriented* $m$-*planes* through 0) of $\mathbb{R}^n$ with an associated positive volume. Furthermore we can set all simple $m$-vectors of unit-length and all oriented $m$-dimensional subspaces of $\mathbb{R}^n$ into a one-to-one correspondence. These concepts are illustrated in Fig. 1.

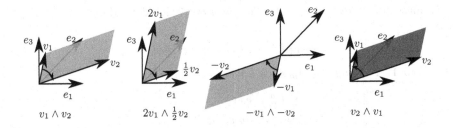

$$v_1 \wedge v_2 \qquad\qquad 2v_1 \wedge \tfrac{1}{2}v_2 \qquad\qquad -v_1 \wedge -v_2 \qquad\qquad v_2 \wedge v_1$$

**Fig. 1. Examples of simple 2-vectors in $\mathbb{R}^3$:** From Definition 1 it follows that the 2-vectors $v_1 \wedge v_2 = 2v_1 \wedge \tfrac{1}{2}v_2 = -v_1 \wedge -v_2 \in \Lambda_2\mathbb{R}^3$ are identical. This is in line with the geometric interpretation of the corresponding vector pairs $(v_1, v_2), (2v_1, \tfrac{1}{2}v_2), (-v_1, -v_2)$: All three span the same 2-dimensional subspace of $\mathbb{R}^2$, induce the same orientation on this subspace and their parallelogram has the same area. On the other hand $v_1 \wedge v_2 \neq v_2 \wedge v_1 = -(v_1 \wedge v_2)$, since the orientations of the corresponding subspaces are inverted.

### 3.2 The Mass Norm

What is the difference between $m$-vectors and simple $m$-vectors? Indeed up to $\mathbb{R}^3$ all $m$-vectors are simple. The most basic example of a non-simple $m$-vector is $e_{12} + e_{34} \in \Lambda_2\mathbb{R}^4$ (i.e. $= (e_1 \wedge e_2) + (e_3 \wedge e_4)$). This 2-vector cannot be decomposend into a single wedge product $(v_1 \wedge v_2)$ between two vectors in $\mathbb{R}^4$. Interestingly the two subspaces spanned by $e_{12}$ and $e_{34}$ intersect only at the origin and therefore $e_{12} + e_{34}$ does not represent a "simple subspace". Now the important observation is that while the areas of the two parallelograms spanned by $e_{12}$ and $e_{34}$ add up to 2 the Euclidean norm $\|e_{12} + e_{34}\|_2 = \sqrt{2}$ is strictly smaller. This is a problem because an optimization of 2-vectors in $\mathbb{R}^4$ with respect to the Euclidean norm would naturally prefer non-simple 2-vectors while the minimal surfaces we are looking for are represented by simple 2-vectors. The solution is the so-called mass norm. Its definition is based on duality, so we will introduce it along the definition of $m$-covectors. Recall that the dual of some real vector space $V$ is the set of all real linear functions $f : V \to \mathbb{R}$ on that space.

**Definition 3 ($m$-Covectors).** *The dual space $(\Lambda_m\mathbb{R}^n)^*$ of $\Lambda_m\mathbb{R}^n$ is called the space of $m$-covectors and is denoted by $\Lambda^m\mathbb{R}^n$. We write $\langle \phi, \omega \rangle = \phi(\omega) \in \mathbb{R}$ for any $\omega \in \Lambda_m\mathbb{R}^n, \phi \in \Lambda^m\mathbb{R}^n$.*

**Observation.** $\Lambda^m\mathbb{R}^n = (\Lambda_m\mathbb{R}^n)^* = \Lambda_m(\mathbb{R}^{n*})$ holds, such that the dual basis $e_1^*, \dots, e_n^* \in \mathbb{R}^{n*}$ induces the dual inner product $\langle \cdot, \cdot \rangle$ and the dual Euclidean norm $\|\cdot\|_{2*}$ on $\Lambda^m\mathbb{R}^n$.

**Definition 4 (Mass Norm and Comass Norm).** *The comass norm denoted by $\|\cdot\|_*$ is the norm on $\Lambda^m\mathbb{R}^n$ defined for any $\phi \in \Lambda^m\mathbb{R}^n$ by*

$$\|\phi\|_* = \sup\{\langle \phi, \omega \rangle \mid \omega \in \Lambda_m\mathbb{R}^n \text{ is simple}, \|\omega\|_2 \leq 1\}. \tag{13}$$

*The* mass norm *denoted by* $\|\cdot\|$ *is the norm on* $\Lambda^m\mathbb{R}^n$ *defined for any* $\omega \in \Lambda_m\mathbb{R}^n$
*by*

$$\|\omega\| = \sup\{\langle \phi, \omega \rangle \mid \phi \in \Lambda_m\mathbb{R}^n, \|\phi\|_* \leq 1\}. \tag{14}$$

**Lemma 1.** *For any* $\omega \in \Lambda_m\mathbb{R}^n$ *it holds*

$$\|\omega\|_2 \leq \|\omega\| \leq \left(\tfrac{n}{m}\right)^{\frac{1}{2}} \|\omega\|_2,$$
$$\|\omega\|_2 = \|\omega\| \Leftrightarrow \omega \text{ is simple and}$$
$$\|\omega\| = \inf\left\{ \sum_{i=1}^N \|\omega_i\|_2 \mid \omega = \sum_{i=1}^N \omega_i, \omega_i \text{ is simple} \right\}. \tag{15}$$

Continuing the discussion from above, Lemma 1 gives us the intuition why the mass norm is the right choice: If some $m$-vector is not simple, its mass norm will be strictly larger than its Euclidean norm and from the decomposition identity of Eq. (15) we can deduce that the mass norm $\|e_{12} + e_{34}\| = 2$ has the "correct" value.

### 3.3  Grassmann Algebra

Recall that the gradient of a scalar field is a vector field and the divergence of a vector field is a scalar field. In the next section we will apply integration and differentiation to $m$-vector fields, which will require us to change the "order" of the $m$-vector field in a similar fashion. Therefor we will now introduce the Grassmann algebra, the wedge product and the interior product.

**Definition 5 (Grassmann Algebra).** *The* Grassmann algebra *(or* exterior algebra) *of* $\mathbb{R}^n$, *denoted by the* $\Lambda_*\mathbb{R}^n$, *is the union of* $\Lambda_m\mathbb{R}^n$, *i.e.* $\Lambda_*\mathbb{R}^n = \bigcup_m \Lambda_m\mathbb{R}^n$, *together with the* exterior multiplication *(or* wedge product) $\wedge$ : $\Lambda_*\mathbb{R}^n \times \Lambda_*\mathbb{R}^n \to \Lambda_*\mathbb{R}^n$. *The exterior product of two simple vectors* $(v_1 \wedge \ldots \wedge v_m) \in \Lambda_m\mathbb{R}^n$ *and* $(u_1 \wedge \ldots \wedge u_k) \in \Lambda_k\mathbb{R}^n$ *is defined by*

$$(v_1 \wedge \ldots \wedge v_m) \wedge (u_1 \wedge \ldots \wedge u_k) = v_1 \wedge \ldots \wedge v_m \wedge u_1 \wedge \ldots \wedge u_k \in \Lambda_{m+k}\mathbb{R}^n \tag{16}$$

*and is linearly extended to all* $m$-vectors in $\Lambda_*\mathbb{R}^n$. *Define the Grassmann algebra* $\Lambda^*\mathbb{R}^n$ *with respect to covectors analoguously.*

**Definition 6 (Interior Product).** *Let* $\phi \in \Lambda^m\mathbb{R}^n$ *and* $\omega \in \Lambda_p\mathbb{R}^n$, *if* $p \leq m$, *the* interior product $\omega \rfloor \phi \in \Lambda^{m-p}\mathbb{R}^n$ *is an alternating* $m - p$ *form defined by* $\langle \omega \rfloor \phi, \xi \rangle = \langle \phi, \xi \wedge \omega \rangle$ *for any* $\xi \in \Lambda_{m-p}\mathbb{R}^n$. *If* $p \geq m$, *the interior product* $\omega \rfloor \phi \in \Lambda_{p-m}\mathbb{R}^n$ *is an* $p - m$ *vector defined by* $\langle \theta, \omega \rfloor \phi \rangle = \langle \phi \wedge \theta, \omega \rangle$ *for any* $\theta \in \Lambda^{p-m}\mathbb{R}^n$.

## 4  Differential Forms and Currents

Denote the tangent space of $\mathbb{R}^n$ at point $p \in \mathbb{R}^n$ by $T_p\mathbb{R}^n$ and its dual space by $T_p\mathbb{R}^{n*}$. We can construct Grassman algebras from both spaces because they can be identified with $\mathbb{R}^n$. Denote the standard basis of $T_p\mathbb{R}^n$ by $\partial_1, \ldots, \partial_n \in T_p\mathbb{R}^n$ and the standard basis of $T_p\mathbb{R}^{n*}$ by $dx_1, \ldots, dx_n \in T_p\mathbb{R}^{n*}$.

## 4.1 Differential Forms

**Definition 7 ($m$-Vector Fields and Differential $m$-Forms).** *An $m$-vector field on $\mathbb{R}^n$ is a function $\omega : \mathbb{R}^n \to \Lambda_m T_p \mathbb{R}^n$. Any $m$-vector field $\omega$ on $\mathbb{R}^n$ can be uniquely decomposed into $\omega(p) = \sum_\sigma \omega_\sigma(p) \partial_\sigma$, where $\omega_\sigma : \mathbb{R}^n \to \mathbb{R}$ are $\omega$'s coefficient functions.*

*A differential $m$-form $\phi$ on $\mathbb{R}^n$ is a field of $m$-covectors of $T_p \mathbb{R}^n$, i.e. $\phi : \mathbb{R}^n \to \Lambda^m T_p \mathbb{R}^n$, such that each coefficient function $\phi_\sigma : \mathbb{R}^n \to \mathbb{R}$ of $\phi(p) = \sum_\sigma \phi_\sigma(p) dx_\sigma$ is differentiable. For simplicity we will call differential $m$-forms just $m$-forms. We denote the set of all $m$-forms on $\mathbb{R}^n$ by $\mathcal{D}^m \mathbb{R}^n = \{\phi : \mathbb{R}^n \to \Lambda^m T_p \mathbb{R}^n\}$.*

*The support of $\phi$ is the closure of $\{p \in \mathcal{M} | \phi(p) \neq 0\}$ and is denoted by spt $\phi$.*

**Definition 8 (Exterior Derivative).** *Let $\phi(p) = \sum_\sigma \phi_\sigma(p) dx_\sigma \in \mathcal{D}^m \mathbb{R}^n$. The exterior derivative $d\phi \in \mathcal{D}^{m+1} \mathbb{R}^n$ of $\phi$ is defined by*

$$d\phi = \sum_\sigma d\phi_\sigma \wedge dx_\sigma, \ where \ d\phi_\sigma = \frac{\partial \phi_\sigma}{\partial x_1} dx_1 + \cdots + \frac{\partial \phi_\sigma}{\partial x_n} dx_n. \qquad (17)$$

**Lemma 2 ([15] Lemma 6.1.8).** *Let $\phi \in \mathcal{D}^m \mathbb{R}^n, \theta \in \mathcal{D}^p \mathbb{R}^n$, it holds $d(\phi \wedge \theta) = (d\phi) \wedge \theta + (-1)^m \phi \wedge (d\theta)$.*

## 4.2 Currents

**Definition 9 (Currents).** *We denote the dual space of $\mathcal{D}^m \mathbb{R}^n$ by $\mathcal{D}_m \mathbb{R}^n = (\mathcal{D}^m \mathbb{R}^n)^*$. The elements of $\mathcal{D}_m \mathbb{R}^n$ are called $m$-currents.*

We will mostly use currents that are constructed from measures and $m$-vector fields. We start by defining 0-currents induced by measures:

**Definition 10 (Measure Induced Currents).** *Let $\mu$ be a measure on $\mathbb{R}^n$, we define the associated current $\mu \in \mathcal{D}_0 \mathbb{R}^n$ induced by measure $\mu$ by*

$$\mu(\phi) = \int_{\mathbb{R}}^n \langle \phi(p), 1 \rangle d\mu p \qquad (18)$$

*for any $\phi \in \mathcal{D}^0 \mathbb{R}^n$. (The meaning of $\mu$ will be directly clear from the context.)*

The only measure we will use is the Hausdorff measure (see [16, p. 9]):

**Definition 11 (Hausdorff Measure).** *The $m$-dimensional Hausdorff measure $\mathcal{H}^m$ of some set $A \subset \mathbb{R}^n$ is defined by*

$$\mathcal{H}^m(A) = \lim_{\delta \to 0} \inf \left\{ \sum_j \alpha_m \left( \frac{\mathrm{diam}(S_j)}{2} \right)^m | A \subset \bigcup_j S_j, \mathrm{diam}(S_j) < \delta \right\}, \qquad (19)$$

*where $S_j$ are $n$-dimensional balls and $\alpha_m$ is the volume of the $m$-dimensional unit ball.*

*Define the Hausdorff measure restricted to some $B \subset \mathbb{R}^n$ by $\mathcal{H}^m_B(\cdot) = \mathcal{H}^m(\cdot \cap B)$.*

We combine currents with vector fields and differential forms by:

**Definition 12.** *Let* $T \in \mathcal{D}_k \mathbb{R}^n$, $\xi \in \mathcal{D}^l \mathbb{R}^n$ *and* $\omega$ *an* $l$-*vector field on* $\mathbb{R}^n$, *we define* $(T \lfloor \xi) \in \mathcal{D}_{k-l} \mathbb{R}^n$ *and* $(T \wedge \omega) \in \mathcal{D}_{k+l} \mathbb{R}^n$ *by*

$$\begin{aligned} (T \lfloor \xi)(\phi) &= T(\xi \wedge \phi) \quad for any \phi \in \mathcal{D}^{k-l}\mathbb{R}^n and \\ (T \wedge \omega)(\phi) &= T(\omega \rfloor \phi) \qquad for any \phi \in \mathcal{D}^{k+l}\mathbb{R}^n. \end{aligned} \tag{20}$$

It directly follows from Definition 12 that we can combine some measure $\mu$ and an $m$-vector $\omega$ on $\mathbb{R}^n$ to an $m$-current $\mu \wedge \omega \in \mathcal{D}_m \mathbb{R}^n$ that evaluates on any $m$-form $\phi$ to

$$(\mu \wedge \omega)(\phi) = \mu(\omega \rfloor \phi) = \int_{\mathbb{R}^n} \langle \omega \rfloor \phi, 1 \rangle d\mu = \int_{\mathbb{R}^n} \langle \phi, 1 \wedge \omega \rangle d\mu = \int_{\mathbb{R}^n} \langle \phi, \omega \rangle d\mu. \tag{21}$$

**Definition 13 (Partial Derivative).** *Let* $T \in \mathcal{D}_k \mathbb{R}^n$, *its* partial derivative $D_{x_i} T \in \mathcal{D}_k \mathbb{R}^n$ *is again a* $k$-*current defined, sucht that for any* $\phi \in \mathcal{D}^k \mathbb{R}^n$ *it holds:* $(D_{x_i} T)(\phi) = -T(\frac{\partial \phi}{\partial x_i})$.

**Definition 14 (Boundary).** *The* boundary $\partial T$ *of some* $k$-*current* $T \in \mathcal{D}_k \mathbb{R}^n$ *is again a current in* $\mathcal{D}_{k-1} \mathbb{R}^n$ *of dimension* $k - 1$ *defined, such that for any* $\phi \in \mathcal{D}^{k-1} \mathbb{R}^n$ *it holds* $\partial T(\phi) = T(d\phi)$.

**Definition 15 (Mass).** *The* mass $\mathbf{M}(T) \in \mathbb{R}_{\geq 0}$ *of some* $T \in \mathcal{D}_m \mathbb{R}^n$ *is defined by* $\mathbf{M}(T) = \sup\{T(\phi) | \phi \in \mathcal{D}^m \mathbb{R}^n, \sup_{p \in \mathbb{R}^n} \|\phi(p)\|^* \leq 1\}$.

**Observation.** If $S$ is an (oriented) $m$-dimensional surface and $\omega$ is an $m$-vector field induced by the tangent planes of $S$, we can associate with $S$ a current $T_S = \mathcal{H}^m \wedge \omega$. The important insight from geometric measure theory is that the notion of mass and boundary of a current coincides exactly with the area and boundary definition from differential geometry. I.e. $\mathbf{M}(T_S) = \mathcal{A}(S)$, $\partial T_S = T_{\partial S}$ and $\mathbf{M}(\partial T_S) = \mathcal{A}(\partial S)$.

In the next section, we will cast our optimization problem as an optimization over the set of currents induced by 2-vectors and we need to numerically compute their boundary. We will now introduce a general notion of divergence that will eventually lead to the crucial Lemma 4, which enables us to discretize the boundary operator as a matrix-vector multiplication.

**Definition 16 (Divergence).** *The* divergence div $\omega$ *of some differentiable* $m$-*vector field* $\omega$ *on* $\mathbb{R}^n$ *is an* $m - 1$ *vector field defined by* div $\omega = \sum_{i=1}^n \frac{\partial \omega}{\partial x_i} \lfloor dx_i$.

Indeed this is a generalization of the known divergence of (differentiable) 1-vector fields $\omega = \sum_j \omega_j \partial_j$ since div $\omega = \sum_{i,j} \frac{\partial \omega_j}{\partial x_i} \partial_j \lfloor dx_i = \sum_i \frac{\partial \omega_i}{\partial x_i}$.

**Lemma 3.** *Let* $\omega$ *be a differentiable* $m$-*vector field on* $\mathbb{R}^n$ *and let* $T \in \mathcal{D}_0 \mathbb{R}^n$, *then* $\partial(T \wedge \omega) = -T \wedge \text{div } \omega - \sum_i (D_{x_i} T) \wedge (\omega \lfloor dx_i)$.

**Lemma 4.** *Let* $U \subset \mathbb{R}^n$ *be open,* $\mathbf{n}_{\partial U}$ *the* 1-*form associated to the outward-pointing unit vector orthogonal to* $\partial U$ *and* $\omega$ *an differentiable* $m$-*vector field, it holds that* $\partial(\mathcal{H}_U^n \wedge \omega) = -\mathcal{H}_U^n \wedge \text{div } \omega + (-1)^m \mathcal{H}_{\partial U}^{n-1} \wedge (\omega \lfloor \mathbf{n}_{\partial U})$.

## 5    Minimal 2-Vector Problem

Using the tools introduced in previous sections, we will now propose a formulation of the minimal surface problem (2) that is based on 2-vector fields of minimal mass. Let $S \subset \Omega^2$ be a surface satisfiying the constraints of (2). Obviously $\pi_{1|S}^{-1} : \Omega \to \Omega^2$ is a chart of $S$. Define the two vector fields $t_x^S, t_y^S : \Omega^2 \to T_p\mathbb{R}^4$ by

$$t_x^S(p) = \begin{cases} \frac{\partial \pi_{1|S}^{-1}}{\partial x_1}(\pi_1(p)) & \text{if } p \in S \\ 0 & \text{otherwise,} \end{cases} \quad t_y^S(p) = \begin{cases} \frac{\partial \pi_{1|S}^{-1}}{\partial x_2}(\pi_1(p)) & \text{if } p \in S \\ 0 & \text{otherwise.} \end{cases}$$
$$(22)$$

The wedge product of $t_x^S, t_y^S$ is a 2-vector field we will denote by $\omega_S = t_x^S \wedge t_y^S : \Omega^2 \to \Lambda_2 T_p\mathbb{R}^4$. Now the important observation is that we can write the area of $S$ weighted by the data term $w$ as the mass of the current $\mathcal{H}_S^2 \wedge w \wedge \frac{\omega_S}{\|\omega_S\|} \in \mathcal{D}_2\mathbb{R}^4$:

$$\int_S w(p)dp = \int_{\Omega^2} w(p)\frac{\|\omega_S(p)\|}{\|\omega_S(p)\|}d\mathcal{H}_S^2 p = \mathbf{M}(\mathcal{H}_S^2 \wedge w \wedge \frac{\omega_S}{\|\omega_S\|}). \quad (23)$$

This allows us to modify (2) into

$$\min_{S \subset \Omega^2} \mathbf{M}(\mathcal{H}_S^2 \wedge w \wedge \frac{\omega_S}{\|\omega_S\|})$$
$$\text{s. t. } \partial S \subset \partial(\Omega^2) \text{ and } \pi_{1|S}, \pi_{2|S} \in \text{Diff}^+(S, \Omega). \quad (24)$$

While we now have an objective based on the integration of some 2-vector field we still have several problems: we still optimze over $S \subset \Omega^2$, the measure $\mathcal{H}_S^2$ depends on $S$ and $\omega_S$ jumps when entering $S$ from $\Omega^2 \backslash S$. We will overcome these problems by the observation that we can approximate any $\omega_S$ by a differentiable 2-vector field $\omega : \Omega^2 \to \Lambda_2 T_p\mathbb{R}^4$ (i.e. a 2-vector field whose coefficient functions are differentiable). We are thus able to state our final optimization problem:

$$\inf_{\omega:\Omega^2 \to \Lambda_2 T_p\mathbb{R}^4} \mathbf{M}(\mathcal{H}^4 \wedge w \wedge \omega) = \int_{\Omega^2} w(p)\|\omega(p)\|d\mathcal{H}^4 p$$
$$\text{s. t. } \omega\text{'s coefficient functions are differentiable,} \quad (25)$$
$$\text{div}\,\omega = 0 \text{ and}$$
$$\pi_1(\omega) = \pi_2(\omega) = \Omega.$$

The constraint on the divergence of $\omega$ directly comes from Lemma 4. Although the infimum is not attained in the continuous setting, this formulation has several key benefits. If we discretize Problem (25) as described in Sect. 6, it has the following properties:

1. The search space of differentiable 2-vector fields is convex.
2. The objective is convex.
3. The divergence div is a linear operator leading to a convex constraint.
4. The projections $\pi_1, \pi_2$ are linear operators leading to convex constraints.

In summary, the discrete version of (25) is a convex optimization problem, which can be optimized with standard methods that converge to a globally optimal solution. On the downside we cannot prove that the optimal 2-vector field of (25) is simple. While our intuition and experiments suggest that this holds, it is still an open question and a formal proof would be a major challenge and is well beyond the scope of this paper.

# 6    Discretization

We would like to discretize all normal 2-currents in $\mathbb{R}^n$ that have the form $\mathcal{H}^n \wedge \omega$, where $\omega$ is a differentiable 2-vector field with support on the open set $P \subset \mathbb{R}^n$. We will do this by sampling $\omega$ on the integer grid.

Let $w_1, \ldots, w_n \in \mathbb{N}$, define $P = \{1, \ldots, w_1\} \times \cdots \times \{1, \ldots, w_n\} \subset \mathbb{N}^n \subset \mathbb{R}^n$, then a 2-vector field sampled at points $P$ is a function $\omega : P \to \Lambda_2 T_p \mathbb{R}^n$ and we have a discrete representation of any such $\omega$ via the coefficient functions $\alpha_{ij} : P \to \mathbb{R}, i < j$, such that $\omega(p) = \sum_{i<j} \alpha_{ij}(p) \partial_{ij}$, for any $p \in P$. For the relevant case of $n = 4$, the space of all 2-vectors is represented by the six scalar functions $\alpha_{12}, \alpha_{13}, \alpha_{14}, \alpha_{23}, \alpha_{24}, \alpha_{34} : P \to \mathbb{R}$ or just by $\alpha : P \to \mathbb{R}^6$.

## 6.1    Divergence

We define the partial derivatives of $\omega$ using finite differences by $\frac{\partial \omega}{\partial x_i} = \omega(p + \partial_i) - \omega(p)$. Now fix some point $p_0 \in P$, denote $\alpha^0 = \alpha(p_0)$ and $\alpha^k = \alpha(p_0 + \partial_k)$ and let $\delta^k = \alpha^k - \alpha^0$. It is $\frac{\partial \omega(p_0)}{\partial x_k} = \sum_{i<j} \delta_{ij}^k \partial_{ij}$. Expanding Definition 16 and some calculations yield

$$\operatorname{div} \omega(p_0) = \sum_i \left( \partial_i \left( \sum_{j:j<i} \left( \alpha_{ji}^j - \alpha_{ji}^0 \right) + \sum_{j:i<j} \left( \alpha_{ij}^0 - \alpha_{ij}^j \right) \right) \right). \quad (26)$$

For $n = 4$, the discrete divergence operator expands to

$$
\begin{aligned}
\operatorname{div} \omega(p_0) =& (\alpha_{12}^0 + \alpha_{13}^0 + \alpha_{14}^0 - \alpha_{12}^2 - \alpha_{13}^3 - \alpha_{14}^4) \partial_1 + \\
& (-\alpha_{12}^0 + \alpha_{23}^0 + \alpha_{24}^0 + \alpha_{12}^1 - \alpha_{23}^3 - \alpha_{24}^4) \partial_2 + \\
& (-\alpha_{13}^0 - \alpha_{23}^0 + \alpha_{34}^0 + \alpha_{13}^1 + \alpha_{23}^2 - \alpha_{34}^4) \partial_3 + \\
& (-\alpha_{14}^0 - \alpha_{24}^0 - \alpha_{34}^0 + \alpha_{14}^1 + \alpha_{24}^2 + \alpha_{34}^3) \partial_4.
\end{aligned}
\quad (27)
$$

## 6.2    Mass Norm

The primal-dual algorithm for convex optimization used in Sect. 7 solves in each step a minimization problem that depends on the current point in the search space. This minimization problem is described by the so-called *proximity operator* $\operatorname{prox}_f : V \to V$ defined by

$$\operatorname{prox}_f(x) = \arg\min_{y \in V} {}^1/_2 \|x - y\|_2^2 + f(y), \quad (28)$$

where $f : V \to \mathbb{R} \cup \{\infty\}$ is a convex function on the normed vector space $V$. In this section we will derive a solution of the proximity operator $\mathrm{prox}_{\frac{c}{L}\|\cdot\|}$ : $\Lambda_2 \mathcal{T}_p \mathbb{R}^4 \to \Lambda_2 \mathcal{T}_p \mathbb{R}^4$, where $c, L \in \mathbb{R}_{>0}$ are positive constants. Each 2-vector $\phi = \sum_{i<j} \phi_{ij} \partial_{ij} \in \Lambda_2 \mathbb{R}^4$ can be represented by a skew-symmetric matrix $S(\phi) \in \mathbb{R}^{4\times4}$, defined as

$$S(\phi) = \begin{pmatrix} 0 & \phi_{12} & \phi_{13} & \phi_{14} \\ -\phi_{12} & 0 & \phi_{23} & \phi_{24} \\ -\phi_{13} & -\phi_{23} & 0 & \phi_{34} \\ -\phi_{14} & -\phi_{24} & -\phi_{34} & 0 \end{pmatrix}. \tag{29}$$

Clearly $\|\phi\|_2 = \frac{1}{\sqrt{2}}\|S(\phi)\|_F$, where $\|\cdot\|_F$ is the Frobenius norm.

Let $U(\phi), T(\phi) \in \mathbb{R}^{4\times4}$ be two matrices where $U(\phi)$ is orthogonal and $T(\phi)$ has the form

$$T(\phi) = \begin{pmatrix} 0 & T_{12} & 0 & 0 \\ -T_{12} & 0 & 0 & 0 \\ 0 & 0 & 0 & T_{34} \\ 0 & 0 & -T_{34} & 0 \end{pmatrix}, \tag{30}$$

such that $S(\phi) = U(\phi)T(\phi)U(\phi)^\top$. Such a decomposition of $S(\phi)$ is called a *(real) Schur decomposition*. From linear algebra we know, that such a decomposition always exists and $T_{12}i, -T_{12}i, T_{34}i, -T_{34}i$ are the purely imaginary eigenvalues of $S(\phi)$.

Interestingly, $\|\phi\| = \frac{1}{2}\|T(\phi)\|_1$. This allows us to express the proximity operator as

$$\begin{aligned} \mathrm{prox}_{\frac{c}{L}\|\cdot\|}(\phi) &= \arg\min_{\psi \in \Lambda_2\mathbb{R}^4} \frac{1}{4}\|S(\phi - \psi)\|_F^2 + \frac{c}{2L}\|T(\psi)\|_1 \\ &= \arg\min_{\psi \in \Lambda_2\mathbb{R}^4} \frac{1}{2}\|U(\phi)^\top S(\phi - \psi)U(\phi)\|_F^2 + \frac{c}{L}\|T(\psi)\|_1 \\ &= \arg\min_{\psi \in \Lambda_2\mathbb{R}^4} \frac{1}{2}\|T(\phi) - U(\phi)^\top S(\psi)U(\phi)\|_F^2 + \frac{c}{L}\|T(\psi)\|_1 \\ &= \arg\min_{\psi \in \Lambda_2\mathbb{R}^4} \frac{1}{2}\|T(\phi) - T(\psi)\|_F^2 + \frac{c}{L}\|T(\psi)\|_1, \text{ s.t. } U(\phi) = U(\psi). \end{aligned} \tag{31}$$

The objective in the last line is identical to the well known $\|\cdot\|_1$-prox operator thus

$$\mathrm{prox}_{\frac{c}{L}\|\cdot\|}(\phi) = U(\phi)\tilde{T}(\phi)U(\phi)^\top, \text{ s.t. } \tilde{T}(\phi)_{ij} = \mathrm{sign}(T(\phi)_{ij})\max\{0, |T(\phi)_{ij}| - \frac{c}{L}\}. \tag{32}$$

## 7  Optimization

Let $c \in \mathbb{R}^n, b \in \mathbb{R}^m$ and $A \in \mathbb{R}^{m\times6n}$ where $m, n \in \mathbb{N}$. After discretization we can find the optimum of (25) by solving an optimization problem of the following form:

$$\min_{x \in \mathbb{R}^{6n}} \sum_{i=1}^{n} c_i\|X_i\| \text{ s. t. } Ax = b, \tag{33}$$

where $X_i \in \mathbb{R}^6$ is the $i$-th column of matrix $X \in \mathbb{R}^{6 \times n}$ that is the reshaped vector $x$. These $X_i$ represent the 2-vector at point $p$ by its six coefficients. $A, b$ represent the discrete divergence and projection operators and constraints. The system can be transformed into the primal-dual framework by defining the functions $F : \mathbb{R}^m \to \overline{\mathbb{R}}, G : \mathbb{R}^N \to \mathbb{R}$ by

$$F(y) = \begin{cases} 0 & \text{if } y = b, \\ \infty & \text{otherwise,} \end{cases} \quad \text{and } G(x) = \sum_{i=1}^{n} c_i \|X_i\|. \tag{34}$$

Clearly the primal problem

$$\min_{x \in \mathbb{R}^N} \mathcal{P}(x) = \min_{x \in \mathbb{R}^N} F(Ax) + G(x) \tag{35}$$

has the same optimimum and optimizer as Problem (33), but is now a convex unconstrained problem, that can be directly solved by the primal-dual algorithm [17–19]. It is also possible to use ADMM for the optimization.

## 8   Experiments

In this Section we will present typical correspondence maps that we computed with the discretization of our proposed optimization problem. Since the minimal surface is represented by a discrete 2-vector field on the discrete product space $\Omega^2$ corresponding points might not be unique. We will take the center of gravity to construct the map $f : \Omega \to \Omega$: Let $x : \Omega^2 \to \Lambda_2 \mathcal{T}_p \mathbb{R}^4$ be the optimal 2-vector

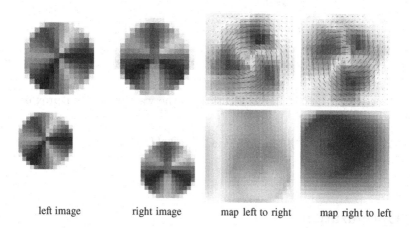

left image          right image          map left to right          map right to left

**Fig. 2. Examples of optimal solutions computed by the proposed method:** we computed correspondences between two pais of images. In the first row we see that the energy function prefers isometric transformations. The rotation between the two images is correctly recovered. In the second row we add a quite large translation. In both cases we see that the proposed method generates solutions that are dense and continuous in both directions.

field, $p \in \Omega$, then define $f$ by $f(p) = \sum_{q \in \Omega} \|x(p,q)\| q$. We define the map in the other direction analoguously.

In Fig. 2 we depict two examples of optimal correspondences computed by the proposed approach. We used the distance in color space for the data term. Boundary conditions ensure that the boundary of one image is mapped to the boundary of the other image. The correspondence map $f$ is visualized by the transformation vectors $t : \Omega \to \mathbb{R}^2$, such that $f = \mathrm{Id} + t$. These vectors are then color coded using the HSV color space.

# 9  Conclusion

We proposed a method for computing regularized dense correspondences between two images. The key idea is to rephrase the correspondence estimation in the framework of geometric measure theory. To this end, we first introduce a fairly general correspondence cost function on the space of diffeomorphisms which combines a generally non-convex data term with a smoothness regularizer that favors isometries. Secondly, we turn this problem into a minimal surface problem in higher dimension which can be written as an optimization over 2-vector fields. The latter problem can be discretized as a convex optimization problem for which we can efficiently compute an optimal solution using (for example) a primal-dual algorithm.

# References

1. Veksler, O.: Stereo matching by compact windows via minimum ratio cycle. IEEE Int. Conf. Comput. Vis. (ICCV). **1**, 540–547 (2001)
2. Ishikawa, H.: Exact optimization for Markov random fields with convex priors. IEEE Trans. Pattern Anal. Mach. Intell. **25**(10), 1333–1336 (2003)
3. Horn, B.K., Schunck, B.G.: Determining optical flow. In: 1981 Technical Symposium East, International Society for Optics and Photonics, pp. 319–331 (1981)
4. Bronstein, A.M., Bronstein, M.M., Kimmel, R.: Generalized multidimensional scaling: a framework for isometry-invariant partial surface matching. Proc. Nat. Acad. Sci. **103**(5), 1168–1172 (2006)
5. Modersitzki, J.: Numerical Methods for Image Registration. Oxford University Press, Oxford (2003)
6. Ashburner, J.: A fast diffeomorphic image registration algorithm. Neuroimage **38**(1), 95–113 (2007)
7. Vercauteren, T., Pennec, X., Perchant, A., Ayache, N.: Diffeomorphic demons: efficient non-parametric image registration. NeuroImage **45**(1), S61–S72 (2009)
8. Alvarez, L., Weickert, J., Sánchez, J.: Reliable estimation of dense optical flow fields with large displacements. Int. J. Comput. Vision **39**(1), 41–56 (2000)
9. Memin, E., Perez, P.: Hierarchical estimation and segmentation of dense motion fields. Int. J. Comput. Vision **46**(2), 129–155 (2002)
10. Brox, T., Bruhn, A., Papenberg, N., Weickert, J.: High accuracy optical flow estimation based on a theory for warping. In: Pajdla, T., Matas, J.G. (eds.) ECCV 2004. LNCS, vol. 3024, pp. 25–36. Springer, Heidelberg (2004)

11. Pock, T., Cremers, D., Bischof, H., Chambolle, A.: Global solutions of variational models with convex regularization. SIAM J. Imaging Sci. **3**(4), 1122–1145 (2010)
12. Lellmann, J., Strekalovskiy, E., Koetter, S., Cremers, D.: Total variation regularization for functions with values in a manifold. In: IEEE International Conference on Computer Vision (ICCV), Sydney, Australia, December 2013
13. Vaillant, M., Glaunès, J.: Surface matching via currents. In: Christensen, G.E., Sonka, M. (eds.) IPMI 2005. LNCS, vol. 3565, pp. 381–392. Springer, Heidelberg (2005)
14. Federer, H.: Geometric Measure Theory. Springer, Heidelberg (1969)
15. Krantz, S.G., Parks, H.R.: Geometric Integration Theory. Springer, Heidelberg (2008)
16. Morgan, F.: Geometric Measure Theory: A Beginner's Guide. Academic Press, Cambridge (2000)
17. Pock, T., Cremers, D., Bischof, H., Chambolle, A.: An algorithm for minimizing the piecewise smooth Mumford-Shah functional. In: IEEE International Conference on Computer Vision (ICCV), Kyoto, Japan (2009)
18. Chambolle, A., Pock, T.: A first-order primal-dual algorithm for convex problems with applications to imaging. J. Math. Imaging Vis. **40**(1), 120–145 (2011)
19. Pock, T., Chambolle, A.: Diagonal preconditioning for first order primal-dual algorithms in convex optimization. In: 2011 IEEE International Conference on Computer Vision (ICCV), pp. 1762–1769. IEEE (2011)

# A Deep Learning-Based Approach to Progressive Vehicle Re-identification for Urban Surveillance

Xinchen Liu[1], Wu Liu[1(✉)], Tao Mei[2], and Huadong Ma[1]

[1] Beijing Key Lab of Intelligent Telecommunication Software and Multimedia,
Beijing University of Posts and Telecommunications, Beijing 100876, China
liuwu@bupt.edu.cn
[2] Microsoft Research, Beijing 100080, China

**Abstract.** While re-identification (Re-Id) of persons has attracted intensive attention, vehicle, which is a significant object class in urban video surveillance, is often overlooked by vision community. Most existing methods for vehicle Re-Id only achieve limited performance, as they predominantly focus on the generic appearance of vehicle while neglecting some unique identities of vehicle (e.g., license plate). In this paper, we propose a novel deep learning-based approach to PROgressive Vehicle re-ID, called "PROVID". Our approach treats vehicle Re-Id as two specific progressive search processes: coarse-to-fine search in the feature space, and near-to-distant search in the real world surveillance environment. The first search process employs the appearance attributes of vehicle for a coarse filtering, and then exploits the Siamese Neural Network for license plate verification to accurately identify vehicles. The near-to-distant search process retrieves vehicles in a manner like human beings, by searching from near to faraway cameras and from close to distant time. Moreover, to facilitate progressive vehicle Re-Id research, we collect to-date the largest dataset named VeRi-776 from large-scale urban surveillance videos, which contains not only massive vehicles with diverse attributes and high recurrence rate, but also sufficient license plates and spatiotemporal labels. A comprehensive evaluation on the VeRi-776 shows that our approach outperforms the state-of-the-art methods by 9.28 % improvements in term of mAP.

**Keywords:** Vehicle re-identification · Progressive search · Deep learning · License plate verification · Spatiotemporal relation

## 1 Introduction

Vehicle, as a significant object class in urban video surveillance, attracts massive focuses in computer vision research field, such as detection [1], classification [2], and pose estimation [3]. However, **vehicle re-identification** (Re-Id) is still a frontier but important topic which is often neglected by researchers. The task of vehicle Re-Id is, given a probe vehicle image, to search in a database for images that contain the same vehicles captured by multiple cameras. Vehicle Re-Id has

B. Leibe et al. (Eds.): ECCV 2016, Part II, LNCS 9906, pp. 869–884, 2016.
DOI: 10.1007/978-3-319-46475-6_53

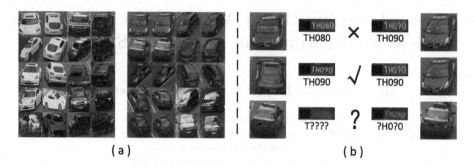

**Fig. 1.** (a) Large intra-instance differences of the same vehicles from different views (left) and subtle inter-instance differences of similar vehicles (right). (b) The license plates for vehicle Re-Id. (Part of the plate is covered due to privacy.)

pervasive applications in video surveillance [4], intelligent transportation [5], and urban computing [6], which can quickly discover, locate, and track the target vehicles in large-scale surveillance videos.

Different from vehicle detection, tracking or classification, vehicle Re-Id can be found as an instance-level object search problem. In the real-world vehicle Re-Id, this problem can be handled by a progressive process. For example, if the monitoring staves want to find a suspect vehicle in huge amount of surveillance videos, they will firstly filter out large numbers of vehicles by appearance features, such as colors, shapes and types, to narrow down the search space. Then, for the remaining vehicles, the license plate is utilized to accurately identify the suspects as shown in Fig. 1(b). Furthermore, the search scope is expanded from near cameras to faraway, and search period is extended from close time to distant. Therefore, the spatiotemporal information can also provide great assistance as shown in Fig. 2. The real-world practice inspires us for constructing a progressive vehicle Re-Id method, which includes two progressive search processes: (1) from-coarse-to-fine search in feature space; (2) from-near-to-distant search in the real-world spatiotemporal environment.

However, the implementation of progressive vehicle Re-Id method in real-world urban traffic surveillance still faces several significant challenges: first of all, the appearance-based approaches can hardly give optimal results due to the large intra-instance differences of the same vehicle in different cameras, and subtle inter-instance differences between different vehicles in the same views as shown in Fig. 1(a). Furthermore, traditional license plate recognition techniques may fail in unconstrained surveillance scenes due to the various illuminations, viewpoints, and resolutions as shown in Fig. 1(b). Besides, the license plate recognition is a complex multi-step process including plate detection, segmentation, shape adjustment, and character recognition as in [7,8]. How to effectively and efficiently utilize the license plate information in unconstrained traffic scenes remains great challenging. Finally, in the urban surveillance scene, it is difficult to model the patterns of vehicle's behaviors in unconstrained conditions. The

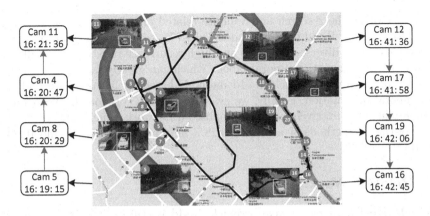

**Fig. 2.** The spatiotemporal information of a vehicle in the surveillance network.

traffic conditions, road maps, and weather can affect the routes of vehicles. The utilization of the spatiotemporal cues also remains challenging.

Existing methods for vehicle Re-Id mainly focus on appearance-based models [1,9]. However, these methods cannot distinguish the vehicles with similar appearance and neglect the license plate to uniquely identify a vehicle. Different from these methods, we consider both the appearance features and the license plate in a coarse-to-fine fashion. The appearance-based model firstly filters out the dissimilar vehicles, then the license plates are utilized for accurate vehicle search. Besides, most methods didn't consider the spatiotemporal information for assistance. Spatiotemporal relations have been employed in many areas such as multi-camera surveillance [10], cross-camera tracking [11], and object retrieval [12]. With spatiotemporal information in the surveillance network, we handle the search process with a from-near-to-distant principle in both the time scale and space scale.

In this paper, we propose the PROVID, a deep learning-based progressive vehicle Re-Id approach for urban surveillance, which is featured by following properties: (1) adopting the progressive approach to search for vehicles as in real-world practice; (2) an appearance attribute model learned from deep convolutional neural networks (CNNs) is exploited as a coarse vehicle filter; (3) the Siamese neural network-based license plate verification is proposed to match the license plate images; and (4) the spatiotemporal relations are explored to assist the search process. In particular, for the appearance-based coarse filtering, we adopt the fusion model of low-level and high-level features to find the similar vehicles. For license number plate, instead of accurate recognizing the characters of the license plate, we just need to verify whether two plate images belong to the same vehicle. Therefore, a Siamese neural network is trained with large numbers of plate images for license plate verification. At last, a spatiotemporal relation model is utilized to re-rank vehicles to further improve the final results of vehicle Re-Id.

To facilitate the research and validate related algorithms, we build a comprehensive vehicle Re-Id dataset named VeRi-776, which contains not only massive vehicles with diverse attributes and high recurrence rate, but also sufficient license plates and spatiotemporal labels, which can greatly facilitate the investigation of progressive vehicle Re-Id methods based on license plate and spatiotemporal information. Finally, we evaluate the PROVID on the VeRi-776 to demonstrate the effectiveness of the proposed framework, which outperforms the state-of-the-art methods by achieving 9.28 % improvements in mAP and 10.94 % in HIT@1.

## 2   Related Work

**Vehicle Re-Id.** In recent years, vehicle Re-Id is still on its early stage with a handful of related works. Feris *et al.* [1] proposed a vehicle detection and retrieval system, in which vehicles are classified into different types and colors by appearance, then indexed and searched by these attributes in the database. Recently, Liu *et al.* [9] firstly evaluated and analyzed several appearance-based models, including the texture, color, and semantic attribute, then proposed a fusion model of low-level features and high-level semantic attributes for vehicle Re-Id. However, the appearance-based approaches cannot uniquely identify a vehicle due to the similarity of vehicles and various environment factors such as illuminations, viewpoints, and occlusion. More importantly, as the unique ID of each vehicle, the license plate should be considered for accurate vehicle Re-Id.

**License Plate Verification.** In industry, license plate recognition has been widely used in identifying vehicles [7,8]. However, due to the high demand on the quality of plate images, existing methods can only be used in constrained conditions such as park entrances and toll gates. The license plate recognition may fail in unconstrained surveillance scenes due to the various environmental factors [1,9]. Therefore, we use the license plate verification instead of the recognition for vehicle Re-Id. In recent years, deep neural networks have achieved great success in computer vision such as object classification [13], detection [14], image understanding [15], video analysis [16], and multimedia search [17]. Among them, the Siamese Neural Network (SNN) was proposed to verify hand-write signatures by Bromley *et al.* [18]. SNN takes two weight-shared convolutional neural networks and a contrastive loss function. During training, it can simultaneously minimize the distances of similar object pairs and maximize the distances of dissimilar pairs. Chopra *et al.* [19] adopted the SNN for face verification and obtained excellent results. Zhang *et al.* [20] achieved the optimal performance in gait recognition for person identification with SNN. Therefore, we utilize SNN in license plate verification for accurate vehicle Re-Id.

**Spatiotemporal Relation.** Spatiotemporal relations have been widely used in multi-camera systems [10–12]. Among them, Kettnaker *et al.* [10] proposed to assemble likely paths of objects using Bayesian estimates over cameras. Javed *et al.* [11] utilized spatiotemporal information to estimate the inter-camera correspondence for object tracking. Xu *et al.* [12] proposed a graph-based object retrieval system in distributed camera network. However, these methods mainly focused on slow-moving objects such as persons in constrained environments like campuses. In the large-scale unconstrained traffic scene, it is difficult to model the patterns of vehicles due to the complicated traffic conditions, road maps, and weather.

# 3  The Proposed Method

## 3.1  Overview

Figure 3 shows the architecture of the proposed progressive vehicle Re-Id approach. The query contains an image of the vehicle with the camera ID and timestamp which record where and when it is captured. Given the query, the proposed method considers the task of vehicle Re-Id as progressive processes: (1) appearance-based coarse filtering: the appearance-based model is utilized to filter out most vehicles with different colors, textures, shapes, and types in the vehicle database; (2) license plate-based fine search: for remaining filtered vehicles, the license plate similarities between query and source vehicles are calculated by the Siamese neural network to find the most similar vehicles; (3) Based on the proposed from-near-to-distant principle, the spatiotemporal properties are exploited to re-rank the vehicles, which further improve the vehicle search process.

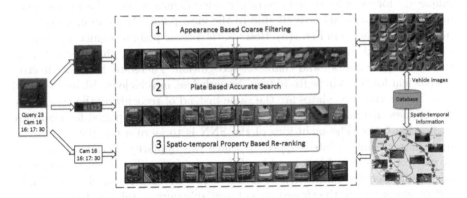

**Fig. 3.** The architecture of the PROVID method.

## 3.2  Appearance Attributes Extracted by CNN

In real-world practice, appearance features such as colors, shapes, and types are very effective to filter out the dissimilar vehicles. In addition, they are efficient to be extracted and searched in large-scale dataset. Consequently, we adopt the fusion model of texture, color and semantic attribute which have been evaluated by Liu *et al.* [9] as the coarse filter to find the vehicles with similar appearance to the query.

The **texture feature** is represented by the conventional descriptors such as Scale-Invariant Feature Transform (SIFT) [21]. Then the descriptors are encoded by the bag-of-words (BOW) model due to its accuracy and efficiency in image retrieval [22]. The **color feature** is extracted by Color Name (CN) model [23] which is quantized by the BOW model for its excellent performance in person Re-Id [24]. The **high-level attribute** is learned by a deep convolutional neural network (CNN), i.e., the GoogLeNet [25]. This model is fine-tuned on the Comp-Cars dataset [2] to detect the detailed attributes of vehicles, such as the number of doors, the shape of lights, the number of seats, and the model of vehicles. At last, the three types of features are integrated by the distance-level fusion.

By fusion of texture, color, and semantic attribute, the appearance-based approach can filter out most of the vehicles that have different colors, shapes, and types to the query. Therefore, the search space narrows down from the whole vehicle database to a relatively small amount of vehicles. However, appearance-based model cannot uniquely identify a vehicle due to the similarity of the vehicles and the environment factors. So we utilize the license plate, which is the unique ID of vehicles, for accurate vehicle Re-Id.

### 3.3   Siamese Neural Network-Based License Plate Verification

For accurate vehicle search, license plate is a significant cue because it is the unique ID for vehicle. In unconstrained surveillance scenes, the license plate may not be recognized correctly due to the view points, low illuminations, and image blurs as shown in Fig. 1(b). Besides, the license plate recognition technique is a complicated process which includes plate localization, shape adjustment, character segmentation, and character recognition. Therefore, it is not effective and efficient for the vehicle Re-Id task. Nonetheless, in vehicle Re-Id, we just need to verify whether two plates are the same instead of recognizing the characters. The Siamese neural network (SNN) introduced in [18] is applied for signature verification tasks. The main idea of the SNN is to learn a function that maps input patterns into a latent space, in which the similarity metric will be large for pairs of the same objects, and small for pairs from different ones. Therefore, it is best suited for verification scenarios where the number of classes is large, and/or samples of all the classes are not available during training. Definitely, the license plate verification is one of such scenarios.

The SNN designed for plate verification contains two parallel CNNs as illustrated in Fig. 4. Each CNN is stacked with two parts: (1) two convolution layers and max-pooling layers, and (2) three full connection layers. The contrastive loss layer is connected on the top of the output layers. The network parameters are set as shown in Fig. 4. Before training, two license plate images are paired as a training sample and labeled with 1 if they belong to the same vehicle and 0 otherwise. During training, the pairwise plate images are fed into the two CNNs separately. After the forward propagation, the outputs of CNNs are combined into the contrastive loss layer to compute the loss of the model. Then through

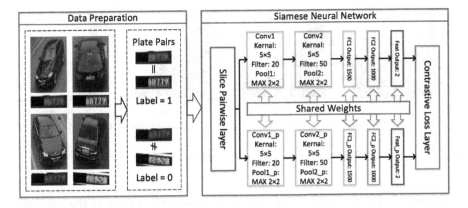

**Fig. 4.** The structure of the Siamese neural network for license plate verification.

the back propagation with the contrastive loss, the shared weights of the two CNNs are optimized simultaneously.

Specifically, let $W$ be the weights of the SNN, given a pair of license plate images $x_1$ and $x_2$, we can map the data into the latent metric space as $S_W(x_1)$ and $S_W(x_2)$. Then, the energy function, $E_W(x_1, x_2)$, which measures the compatibility between $x_1$ and $x_2$, is defined as

$$E_W(x_1, x_2) = ||S_W(x_1) - S_W(x_2)||. \tag{1}$$

With the energy function, the contrastive loss can be formulated as

$$L(W, (x_1, x_2, y)) = (1 - y) \cdot max(m - E_W(x_1, x_2), 0) + y \cdot E_W(x_1, x_2), \tag{2}$$

where $(x_1, x_2, y)$ is a pair of samples with the label, $m$ is a positive margin. In the implementation, we adopt the Caffe framework [26] with the default margin value, $m = 1$. During test, we use the learned SNN to extract the 1000-D feature of the FC2 layer from the plate images. The Euclidean distance is adopted to estimate the similarity scores of two plate images.

### 3.4   Vehicle Re-ranking Based on Spatiotemporal Relation

As discussed in Sect. 1, in real-world practice, it is reasonable to perform vehicle search with a from-near-to-distant fashion in spatiotemporal domain. Based on this principle, we exploit the spatiotemporal relation to further improve the vehicle Re-Id.

However, in the unconstrained traffic scenarios, it is difficult to model the travel patters of vehicles and predict the spatiotemporal relations of two arbitrary vehicles. To investigate whether the spatiotemporal relation is effective for vehicle Re-Id, we analyze the space and time distances of 20,000 image pairs from the same vehicles and 20,000 pairs from randomly selected vehicles. The statistics are illustrated in Fig. 5. We obviously find that the space and time

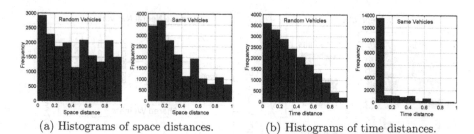

(a) Histograms of space distances.     (b) Histograms of time distances.

**Fig. 5.** Statistics of spatiotemporal information.

distances of the same vehicles are relatively smaller than those of the randomly selected vehicles. From this observation, we make a general assumption that: two images have higher possibility to be the same vehicle if they have small space or time distance, and lower possibility to be the same vehicle if they have large space or time distance. With this assumption, for each query image $i$ and test image $j$, the spatiotemporal similarity $ST(i,j)$ is defined as:

$$ST(i,j) = \frac{|T_i - T_j|}{T_{max}} \times \frac{\delta(C_i, C_j)}{D_{max}} \qquad (3)$$

where $T_i$ and $T_j$ are the timestamps of query image $i$ and test image $j$, $T_{max}$ is the maximal time difference between all query images and test tracks. $\delta(C_i, C_j)$ is the length of the shortest path between camera $C_i$ and $C_j$, $D_{max}$ is the maximal length between all cameras. The shortest path between two cameras is obtained from the Google Map and stored in a matrix as shown in Fig. 6. At last, either a post-fusion strategy or a re-ranking strategy can be adopt for the combination of the spatiotemporal information with the appearance and plate features.

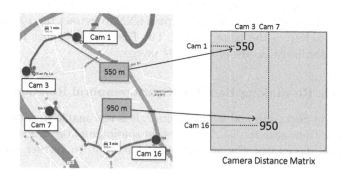

**Fig. 6.** The real-world camera distance matrix obtained from the Google map.

# 4    Experiments

## 4.1    Dataset

To well investigate the spatiotemporal relation and evaluate the proposed progressive vehicle Re-Id approach, we build the VeRi-776 dataset from the VeRi dataset in [9]. The VeRi dataset has three featured properties. First, it contains about 40,000 images of 619 vehicles captured by 20 surveillance cameras. In addition, the images are captured in a real-world unconstrained traffic scene and labeled with varied attributes, e.g. BBoxes, types, colors, and brands. Furthermore, each vehicle is captured by $2 \sim 18$ cameras in different viewpoints, illuminations, and occlusions, which provides high recurrence rate for vehicle Re-Id. Finally, we extend the VeRi dataset with (1) data volume expansion, (2) license plate labels, and (3) spatiotemporal information.[1]

**Data Volume Expansion.** With the video frames provided by Liu *et al.* [9], we add over 20 % new vehicles into the VeRi dataset. The new vehicles are also labeled with BBoxes, types, colors, brands, and cross-camera relations as in [9]. This makes the dataset contain over 50,000 vehicle images, about 9000 tracks, and 776 vehicles, which further improves the scalability for vehicle Re-Id.

**License Plate Annotation.** The most important contribution of the new VeRi-776 dataset is the annotation of license plates. Before annotating, we divide the dataset into the testing set of 200 vehicles and 11,579 images, and the training set of 576 vehicles and 37,781 images. For the testing set, we pick out one image from each track as the query and obtain 1,678 queries. Then, for each query image and test image, we annotate the BBox of license plate if the plate can be detected by the annotators. For the quality of annotation, each image is annotated by at least three human annotators with the majority vote. At last, we obtain 999 plate images from the query images, 4,825 plate images from the test images, and 7,647 plate images from the train images. About 50 % of the query and test images can utilize the license plate to improve the vehicle Re-Id.

**Spatiotemporal Relation Annotation.** We annotate the spatiotemporal relation for tracks of all vehicles. The track is the trajectory of a vehicle captured by one camera at the same time, the images belonging to one track are clustered together. For each track, we firstly label the ID (from 1 to 20) of the camera which captures the track. Then we use the timestamp of the first captured image in the track as its timestamp. Furthermore, to facilitate the computation of the space distances used in the spatiotemporal relation-based re-ranking, we obtain the length of the shortest path between each pair of the 20 cameras in the surveillance network via Google Map as shown in Fig. 6.

## 4.2    Experimental Settings

The VeRi-776 dataset is divided into two subsets for training and testing as in Sect. 4.1. The training set has 576 vehicles with 37,781 images and the testing set

---

[1] The latest dataset can be obtained at https://github.com/VehicleReId/VeRidataset.

has 200 vehicles with 11,579 images. In the evaluation, the cross-camera search is performed, which means we use one image of a vehicle from one camera to search for tracks of the same vehicle in other cameras. Moreover, in [9], the vehicle Re-Id is in an image-to-image manner, which means using a query image to search for the target images as in person Re-Id [24]. Different from [9], we conduct the vehicle Re-Id in an image-to-track fashion, in which the query is an image, while the target units are tracks of vehicles. The similarity between a query image and a test track is denoted by the maximum of the similarities between the query image and all images of the track. In real-world practice, we just need to find the track in one camera to capture the target vehicle. Therefore, the image-to-track search is more reasonable in the practical scenario. For the image-to-track search, we have 1,678 query images and 2,021 testing tracks.

For the VeRi-776 dataset, there are multiple ground truths for each query. Therefore, we adopt mean average precision (mAP) which considers both precision and recall to evaluate the overall performance for vehicle Re-Id. For each query image, we calculate the average precision (AP) as

$$AP = \frac{\sum_{k=1}^{n} P(k) \times gt(k)}{N_{gt}} \qquad (4)$$

where $n$ is the number of test tracks, $N_{gt}$ is the number of ground truths, $P(k)$ is the precision at cut-off $k$ in the result lists, and $gt(k)$ is an indicator function equaling 1 if the $k$th result is correct. The mAP is computed over all queries as

$$mAP = \frac{\sum_{q=1}^{Q} AP(q)}{Q} \qquad (5)$$

where $Q$ is the number of queries. Besides, we also adopt the Cumulative Matching Characteristic (CMC) curve, HIT@1, and HIT@5 which are widely used in person Re-Id [24].

## 4.3    Evaluation of Plate Verification

To evaluate the Siamese neural network-based plate verification, we compare it with the conventional handcraft features, SIFT [21]. We combine the plate features with the FACT model by post-fusion to test their performance for the appearance-based model. The settings of the two models are as follows:

(1) **FACT + Plate-SIFT**. This method adopts the conventional SIFT as the local descriptor. Then the descriptors of the plate is quantized with the bag-of-words (BOW) model. Before testing, we train a codebook of the BOW model with the training plates of VeRi-776, the size of codebook is 1000. In the test stage, each plate is represented as an 1000-D BOW feature.
(2) **FACT + Plate-SNN**. Before performing the search, we firstly train the Siamese neural network for license plate verification. With the 7,647 training plate images, we randomly pick out about 50,000 pairs of plates belonging

to the same vehicles as the positive samples and 50,000 pairs of plates of different vehicles as the negative samples. We adopt the Caffe [9] to implement the SNN as in Sect. 3.3 and train the SNN with the Stochastic Gradient Descent solver. We use the model of 60,000 iterations to extract the 1000-D FC2-layer output as the representation of license plates.

For both of the two models, the image-to-track search is performed, the similarity is calculated by the Euclidean distance. The weights for post-fusion is 0.4 for the FACT and 0.6 for the Plate-SNN. The mAP, HIT@1, and HIT@5 are used to evaluate the performance. Table 1 shows the search results which demonstrate that the deep learned model is much better than the SIFT feature. The results demonstrate that traditional handcraft features are not robust to the various illuminations, viewpoints, and resolutions in unconstrained surveillance scenes. While the SNN model which is trained on large amount of plate pairs can map input patterns into a latent space, in which the similarity metric is larger for pairs of the same objects, and lower for pairs from different ones. The abundant training license plate samples guarantee the robustness of the learned model.

**Table 1.** Comparison of different models for plate verification.

| Methods | mAP | HIT@1 | HIT@5 |
|---------|-----|-------|-------|
| FACT [9] + Plate-SIFT | 18.49 | 50.95 | 73.48 |
| FACT [9] + Plate-SNN | **25.88** | **61.08** | **77.41** |

### 4.4  Evaluation of Vehicle Re-Id Methods

To validate the effectiveness of progressive vehicle Re-Id, we compare eight methods on the built VeRi-776 dataset:

(1) **BOW-CN** [24]. This is the Bag-of-Words with Color Name descriptor which is one of the state-of-the-art appearance features for person Re-Id. It is also adopted as the color feature for vehicle re-id as in [9].
(2) **LOMO** [27]. This is the state-of-the-art texture features for person Re-Id which can effectively overcome the various illumination in real-world surveillance environment.
(3) **GoogLeNet** [2]. This method utilizes the GoogLeNet model [25] which is fine-turned on the CompCars [2]. We adopt it as a feature extractor to obtain the high-level semantic attributes of the appearance.
(4) **FACT** [9]. We adopt the FACT [9] to estimate the appearance similarities between the query images and the test tracks. The FACT considers all of the colors, textures, shapes, and semantic attributes for appearance-based filtering.

(5) **Plate-SNN**. This scheme only uses the license plate similarities between the query and tracks to search for the nearest target in test tracks. The features are calculated by the SNN model trained as the **Plate-SNN** in Sect. 4.3.

(6) **FACT + Plate-SNN**. We firstly use the FACT as the coarse vehicle filter. Then we adopt the post-fusion strategy which combines the similarities of FACT model and Plate-SNN model as fine search. The weights used in summation are 0.4 and 0.6 respectively for the FACT and the Plate-SNN due to their individual performances in vehicle Re-Id.

(7) **FACT + Plate-REC**. In this scheme, we adopt a commercial plate recognition system (Plate-REC) to replace the Place-SNN as the fine search.

(8) **FACT + Plate-SNN + STR**. This scheme integrates the similarities of the FACT, Plate-SNN, and spatiotemporal relations (STR). The spatiotemporal similarity between the query and test is calculated by Eq. 3. Then, the similarity matrixes of the FACT + Plate-SNN and STR are both normalized to $(0,1)$. At last, the two matrixes are summed with different weights. The weights are 0.8 and 0.2 respectively due to their individual performances. By this means, the appearance, license plate, and spatiotemporal relations are combined together for the progressive vehicle search.

Table 2 illustrates the mAP, HIT@1, and HIT@ of the above models. The CMC curves are plotted in Fig. 7. From the results, we can find that:

**(1)** For the appearances based models, the BOW-CN, LOMO, GoogLeNet, and FACT have competitive performances which are all not very good for vehicle Re-Id. The FACT is better than GoogLeNet, because the GoogLeNet model only considers the semantic attributes, while the FACT also combines color and texture features. This demonstrates that the low-level features as well as high level features are both effective for appearance-based filtering. In addition, the appearance-based model can only find the vehicles that have similar appearance to the query but cannot accurately identify the vehicles.

**(2)** The progressive combination of the appearance-based model and Plate-SNN model achieves 7.39 % improvement in mAP and 10.13 % in HIT@1 for

**Table 2.** Comparison of different methods on VeRi-776 dataset.

| Methods | mAP | HIT@1 | HIT@5 |
|---|---|---|---|
| BOW-CN [24] | 12.20 | 33.91 | 53.69 |
| LOMO [27] | 9.64 | 25.33 | 46.48 |
| GoogLeNet [2] | 17.04 | 49.82 | 71.16 |
| FACT [9] | 18.49 | 50.95 | 73.48 |
| Plate-SNN | 15.74 | 36.29 | 46.60 |
| FACT + Plate-REC | 18.62 | 51.19 | 73.60 |
| FACT + Plate-SNN | 25.88 | 61.08 | 77.41 |
| FACT + Plate-SNN + STR | **27.77** | **61.44** | **78.78** |

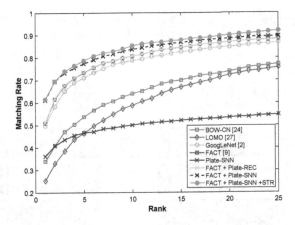

**Fig. 7.** The CMC curves of different methods.

vehicle Re-Id compared with the FACT model. The results validate the effectiveness of our progressive search with appearance-based coarse filtering and plate-based accurate search. The appearance-based filter can filter out most of the dissimilar vehicles, especially the vehicles have similar license plates to the query. Then, for the remaining vehicles with similar appearance to the query, the plate-based method can search for the vehicles of which the license plates are also similar to avoid the mistaken matching. The plate recognition methods could fail due to the various illuminations, occlusions, and resolutions. So the Plate-REC method only achieve marginal improvement.

(3) The FACT + Plate-SNN + STR model obtains further improvements compared with the former methods. This demonstrates that with the from-near-to-distant principle, the progressive search in the spatial and temporal domains also improves the vehicle Re-Id. In total, the proposed PROVID method achieves 9.28 % improvements in mAP, 10.94 % in HIT@1, and 5.3 % in HIT@5 compared with the state-of-the-art appearance-based model. The results validate the effectiveness of our progressive vehicle search framework and the indispensability of each feature for accurate vehicle Re-Id. More importantly, we also evaluate the speed of progressive method (157 ms/query), which reduces 87.84 % time cost than the strategy without progressive fusion (1,292 ms/query). This demonstrates that the progressive search can dramatically improve the instant-level search accuracy and speed in real-world space.

Figure 8 shows several examples of the PROVID method on VeRi-776 dataset. Sample (a) and (b) illustrate the significant effect of the license plate-based Re-Id. The appearance-based filter find the similar vehicles, but the targets are not ranked in the front of the results. Then, with the license plate-based method, the vehicles are correctly searched. Sample (c) and (d) show that the license plate-based search fails due to the severe blur and distortion of the plates. However, in these samples, the target vehicles are searched with the assistance of the spatiotemporal relations. Sample (e) perfectly shows the effectiveness of the

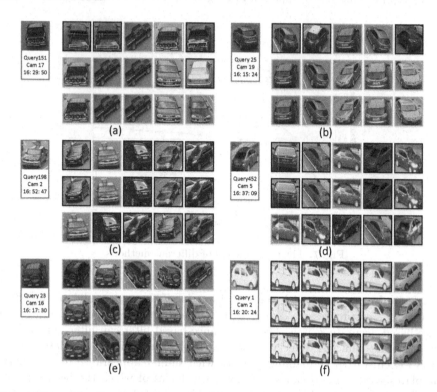

**Fig. 8.** Examples of the PROVID on VeRi-776 dataset with the top-5 results. The true positive is in green box, otherwise red. In each example, the three rows are the results of the FACT, FACT + Plate-SNN, and FACT + Plate-SNN + STR. (Best seen in color.) (Color figure online)

PROVID method. In this sample, the vehicles have similar appearance are firstly found, then the license plate-based model achieves accurate search. At last, the spatiotemporal relations guarantee the target vehicles are ranked in the top position. Sample (f) is a failure case of the proposed method. The vehicles that have different colors to the query are not filtered out due to the illuminations, so the proposed method do not distinguish the yellow cars and white cars. Besides, without the license plate in the query, the unique ID cannot be utilized to accurately search the vehicles. Therefore, the spatiotemporal relation also fails in such an uncertain situation. To overcome these problems, we need to exploit an appearance-based model which is more robust to the environment factors such as illuminations and occlusions. Furthermore, we will further utilize the license plate such as integrating the plate recognition and verification in an end-to-end multi-task deep neural network.

# 5    Conclusions

In this paper, we propose a deep learning-based progressive vehicle Re-Id approach, which employs the deep CNN to extract the appearance attributes as the coarse filter, and Siamese neural network-based license plate verification as the fine search. Furthermore, the spatiotemporal relations of vehicle in real-world urban surveillance is investigated and combined into the proposed method. To facilitate the research, we build one of the largest vehicle Re-Id dataset from urban surveillance videos with diverse vehicle attributes, sufficient license plates, and accurate spatiotemporal information.

**Acknowledgements.** This work is supported by the National High Technology Research and Development Program of China (No. 2014AA015101), the National Natural Science Foundation of China under Grant No. 61332005, the Funds for Creative Research Groups of China under Grant No. 61421061, the Cosponsored Project of Beijing Committee of Education, the Beijing Training Project for the Leading Talents in S&T (ljrc 201502), and the Fundamental Research Funds for the Central Universities (No. 2016RC43).

# References

1. Feris, R.S., Siddiquie, B., Petterson, J., Zhai, Y., Datta, A., Brown, L.M., Pankanti, S.: Large-scale vehicle detection, indexing, and search in urban surveillance videos. IEEE Trans. Multimedia 14(1), 28–42 (2012)
2. Yang, L., Luo, P., Loy, C.C., Tang, X.: A large-scale car dataset for fine-grained categorization and verification. In: IEEE Conference on Computer Vision and Pattern Recognition, pp. 3973–3981 (2015)
3. Matei, B.C., Sawhney, H.S., Samarasekera, S.: Vehicle tracking across nonoverlapping cameras using joint kinematic and appearance features. In: IEEE Conference on Computer Vision and Pattern Recognition, pp. 3465–3472 (2011)
4. Valera, M., Velastin, S.A.: Intelligent distributed surveillance systems: a review. IEE Proc. - Vis. Image Sign. Process. 152(2), 192–204 (2005)
5. Zhang, J., Wang, F.Y., Wang, K., Lin, W.H., Xu, X., Chen, C.: Data-driven intelligent transportation systems: a survey. IEEE Trans. Intell. Transp. Syst. 12(4), 1624–1639 (2011)
6. Zheng, Y., Capra, L., Wolfson, O., Yang, H.: Urban computing: concepts, methodologies, and applications. ACM Trans. Intell. Syst. Technol. 5(38), 1–55 (2014)
7. Du, S., Ibrahim, M., Shehata, M., Badawy, W.: Automatic license plate recognition (ALPR): a state-of-the-art review. IEEE Trans. Circuits Syst. Video Technol. 23(2), 311–325 (2013)
8. Wen, Y., Lu, Y., Yan, J., Zhou, Z., Von Deneen, K.M., Shi, P.: An algorithm for license plate recognition applied to intelligent transportation system. IEEE Trans. Intell. Transp. Syst. 12(3), 830–845 (2011)
9. Liu, X.C., Liu, W., Ma, H.D., Fu, H.Y.: Large-scale vehicle re-identification in urban surveillance videos. In: IEEE International Conference on Multimedia and Expo (2016, Accepted and to appear)
10. Kettnaker, V., Zabih, R.: Bayesian multi-camera surveillance. In: IEEE Conference on Computer Vision and Pattern Recognition, pp. 253–259 (1999)

11. Javed, O., Shafique, K., Rasheed, Z., Shah, M.: Modeling inter-camera space-time and appearance relationships for tracking across non-overlapping views. Comput. Vis. Image Underst. **109**(2), 146–162 (2008)
12. Xu, J., Jagadeesh, V., Ni, Z., Sunderrajan, S., Manjunath, B.: Graph-based topic-focused retrieval in distributed camera network. IEEE Trans. Multimedia **15**(8), 2046–2057 (2013)
13. Krizhevsky, A., Sutskever, I., Hinton, G.E.: Imagenet classification with deep convolutional neural networks. In: Advances in Neural Information Processing Systems, pp. 1097–1105 (2012)
14. Girshick, R.: Fast R-CNN. In: IEEE International Conference on Computer Vision, pp. 1440–1448 (2015)
15. Frome, A., Corrado, G.S., Shlens, J., Bengio, S., Dean, J., Mikolov, T., et al.: Devise: a deep visual-semantic embedding model. In: Advances in Neural Information Processing Systems, pp. 2121–2129 (2013)
16. Liu, W., Mei, T., Zhang, Y., Che, C., Luo, J.: Multi-task deep visual-semantic embedding for video thumbnail selection. In: IEEE Conference on Computer Vision and Pattern Recognition, pp. 3707–3715 (2015)
17. Mei, T., Rui, Y., Li, S., Tian, Q.: Multimedia search reranking: a literature survey. ACM Comput. Surv. **46**(3), 38 (2014)
18. Bromley, J., Bentz, J.W., Bottou, L., Guyon, I., LeCun, Y., Moore, C., Säckinger, E., Shah, R.: Signature verification using a siamese time delay neural network. Int. J. Pattern Recogn. Artif. Intell. **7**(04), 669–688 (1993)
19. Chopra, S., Hadsell, R., LeCun, Y.: Learning a similarity metric discriminatively, with application to face verification. In: IEEE Conference on Computer Vision and Pattern Recognition, pp. 539–546 (2005)
20. Zhang, C., Liu, W., Ma, H.D., Fu, H.Y.: Siamese neural network based gait recognition for human identification. In: IEEE International Conference on Acoustics, Speech and Signal Processing, pp. 2832–2836 (2016)
21. Lowe, D.G.: Distinctive image features from scale-invariant keypoints. Int. J. Comput. Vis. **60**(2), 91–110 (2004)
22. Sivic, J., Zisserman, A.: Video Google: a text retrieval approach to object matching in videos. In: IEEE International Conference on Computer Vision, pp. 1470–1477 (2003)
23. Van De Weijer, J., Schmid, C., Verbeek, J., Larlus, D.: Learning color names for real-world applications. IEEE Trans. Image Process. **18**(7), 1512–1523 (2009)
24. Zheng, L., Shen, L., Tian, L., Wang, S., Wang, J., Tian, Q.: Scalable person re-identification: a benchmark. In: IEEE International Conference on Computer Vision, pp. 1116–1124 (2015)
25. Szegedy, C., Liu, W., Jia, Y., Sermanet, P., Reed, S., Anguelov, D., Erhan, D., Vanhoucke, V., Rabinovich, A.: Going deeper with convolutions. In: IEEE Conference on Computer Vision and Pattern Recognition, pp. 1–9 (2015)
26. Jia, Y., Shelhamer, E., Donahue, J., Karayev, S., Long, J., Girshick, R., Guadarrama, S., Darrell, T.: Caffe: convolutional architecture for fast feature embedding. In: ACM International Conference on Multimedia, pp. 675–678 (2014)
27. Liao, S., Hu, Y., Zhu, X., Li, S.Z.: Person re-identification by local maximal occurrence representation and metric learning. In: IEEE Conference on Computer Vision and Pattern Recognition Proceedings, pp. 2197–2206 (2015)

# Author Index